Copyright 2014 Robert G. Yorks

ISBN-13: 978-0692324998
ISBN-10: 0692324992

Volume I

South Oxford Press
2139 County Road 3
Oxford, New York 13830
Email: southoxfordpress@live.com
Website: www.southoxfordpress.com

FOREWORD

This book Is dedicated to my paternal grandmother, **Lottie Zella Milks**, without whom, this book would not have been made. Lottie was the matriarch of our family for many years and was both a strong personality and at the same time, a gentle woman, and an outstanding grandmother. She was a great-granddaughter of Freeborn Garrettson Milks. Freeborn was born in New York, moved to Quebec, Canada as a young man, where he lived most of his adult life, and where he raised his extensive family. Freeborn and his wife, Sarah "Sally" Moore, are credited with parenting most of the Milks family in Canada. Freeborn returned to the USA in his later life and settled in Grand Traverse County, Michigan, along with some of his sons. Lottie was born in Michigan and raised two families in Grand Traverse County. As a result of this heritage, I have ancestral ties to many Canadian cousins as well as to my many U.S. cousins.

As many of you already know, the basis for this book is Grace Croft's book, *"The History and Genealogy of the Milk-Milks Family"*, published in 1952 and in 1956. I became interested in extending her work because the book was over 40 years old when I stumbled across it and I knew that there had been a lot of growth in the family since its publication. What I didn't know, at the time was that, working with several other researchers, we would find some early branches in the family tree that Grace had not located. So not only have we extended the family into the 21st century, but we have added some names and families from the earlier years.

Having said this, I can also tell you that there are a few other families, especially in New York, who carry the Milk(s) name, but for whom we have not been able to establish definite links to one of our branches. So the job is not yet complete.

Not only is our history, here and in Canada, composed of families with the spelling of the surname as Milk and Milks, but you will also find in this book, families who are recorded with the surnames of Milcks, Mylks, and Mylkes. The predominant spelling, however, is Milks.

Like most families, we have no U. S. Presidents in our family, nor do we have any great military officers. We do have many men who proudly served with a military service in all of the recorded wars starting with the Revolutionary War in the U.S. And that includes not just men from the United States, but also many men from Canada. Where those service records are known they are included in the family data.

We do have men who have served in the political arena as mayors, state senators, and representatives. We have men who have built great reputations and great wealth as cattle barons and land owners. You will also find one particular woman in the family, Lydia Zeruie 'Ada' Bothwell

Milks who not only raised her family under harsh frontier conditions, but managed, without her husband, a ranch of one thousand, one hundred and twenty acres. We also have, I am sorry to say, our share of miscreants, from murderers (whom you will read about) to sex offenders (none of whom are identified as such here).

We do have a few notables of our own, among them DICK CLARK, of *American Bandstand* fame. HIBBERT HENRY "HIB" MILKS, a professional hockey player from Canada. JUDSON FABIAN 'JAY' KIRKE, a professional baseball player born in Delaware County, New York. DAVID CALEB COOK, the "Godfather of the Sunday School". The Case brothers of Cattaraugus County, New York, who developed the popular Case pocket knife, and built a flourishing knife manufacturing business, now owned by Zippo Lighters. FLORENCE ANN (MILKS) WARREN, written about in 1923 as Southern California's only woman engineer. And, no, HARVEY MILK, of San Francisco, was not a member of our family. His parents were from another European country.

I also want to mention that you, probably, will find errors of various kinds in this work. Hopefully nothing catastrophic. If you do find significant errors, and would like to see them corrected, feel free to send them to me either by email or by regular mail. I will keep addresses on every buyer of the book, and at an appropriate time, I will send everyone an addendum with all corrections.

Finally, you will notice, in the later sections of the book, that some personal names and dates have been omitted, and mention is made only of a certain number of children. In most cases this is because the families or the individuals have requested that their data not be included. I have tried to respect those requests. If I inadvertently erred, I apologize. It was not intentional. As I have told many people, personal data is rampant on the internet. For 95% of people over the age of 21, in the U.S., I can easily locate ages, addresses, phone numbers, spouse, and children's names, and birth dates, all at no cost. It would be much more difficult, costly and time consuming for some miscreant to purchase a copy of this book to gather personal information, than it would for him to go on-line and find it.

If you, or members of your family, do not appear in the book, I apologize. I have tried through various means, using direct mail, email, and social media such as Facebook to solicit input from family members. Many have responded, some have not. If you would like your family to be included in any new addition, please contact me.

It is my hope that this book will be of value to our children's children and to their grandchildren.

Bob Yorks

CONTRIBUTORS

A work of this magnitude is never the work of one person. I have many researchers, current family members and contributors from Croft's book to thank for their unselfish contributions, suggestions, and time that they have spent on this project. It's time for all of us to breathe a sigh of relief, kick back, and relax. I have mentioned many of the contributors in various sections of the book, and I thank them again for their contributions. I want to highlight a few individuals here who have been particularly helpful.

GRACE CROFT: without her groundbreaking work on the family, this would have been an even more daunting task. I still can't fully comprehend how she accomplished so much in the 1940s and 1950s, without most of the technical advances we have today. I have sat down, across kitchen tables in New York, with families that she interviewed in the 1950s and some of them still remembered her visit.

DONALD GORDON McEDWARD: Without ever having met me, Donald graciously loaned me his personal copy of Grace Croft's 1956, 2nd Edition, because I couldn't find one to purchase. I have since returned it to him and we continue to correspond. Donald is part of the Milks family. At the time of this publication, Donald is 94 years young and has the appearance of a man who may endure another 94 years. I encourage you to read his contributions to this book.

DOLLIE CREGGER MORGAN: Dolly and I, independently discovered some siblings of Freeborn Garrettson Milks, one in particular of interest was FREEMAN MILKS, from whom Dolly was descended. We discovered that we were both working on this family and we got together on one of Dolly's trips to New York and shared notes and thoughts. Dolly did all of the work in putting together her family going back to FREEMAN. Before she departed this life, too early, she shared with me her results and they have been included in this book.

GRACE CROFT'S assistant Editors: LEE MILK (Walton, NY), GRACE IRENE BARNHART (El Monte, CA), MABEL WARNER (Orlando, FL), NELSON C. MILKS (Sebring, FL), MABEL G. MILKS (Lowville, NY), AND LEMUEL MILK (Kankakee, IL).

In addition to the above major contributors, there have been many more who have unselfishly shared their research and their family data. There is not room to list them all here, but you will find their names scattered throughout the book in close proximity to their families. Hopefully, I have not left anyone out. If you believe that I have overlooked someone, please let me know and I will make sure that they get in the next edition.

Lastly, I want to thank the many members of my close family who have been considerate enough to take the time to update their own personal family data for inclusion in the book. Their contribution was considerable and very much appreciated.

CONTENTS

Section		Page No.
Generation	1	1
Generation	2	3
Generation	3	5
Generation	4	9
Generation	5	15
Generation	6	25
Generation	7	53
Generation	8	125
Generation	9	267
Generation	10	465
Generation	11	713
Generation	12	853
Generation	13	905

A FEW FAMILY STATISTICS

TOTAL NUMBER OF INDIVIDUALS: 22912

TOTAL NUMBER OF MARRIAGES: 8495

TOTAL NUMBER OF GENERATIONS: 16

TOTAL NUMBER OF DIFFERENT SURNAMES: 4473

AVERAGE LIFESPAN: 61 YEARS, 9 MONTHS

TOTAL NUMBER OF WORDS IN MAIN TEXT: 526,698

ILLUSTRATIONS

ITEM	PAGE
Lottie Zella Milks	Frontispiece
John Milk's house	2
Map of Boston	4
House built by Benjamin Milk – 1780	35
Clarence Bridge, Brodhead, Wisconsin	37
Replica of Clarence Bridge, Brodhead, Wisconsin	38
Lemuel Milk – 1820	55
Carriage House (Lemuel Milk)	56
Six sons of Richard Milks – 1820	73
Joseph Milks (1848) family	155
Hibbert Henry "Hib" Milks	159
Anthony Milks House, Cantley, Quebec	163
David Cook, "Godfather of the Sunday School"	181
Classic Case Pocket Knife	237
Harold Milks, Foreign Correspondent	535
Judson Fabian "Jay" Kirke	556
Richard Wagstaff "Dick" Clark	721
Dollie "Dolly" Mae (Cregger) Morgan	726

DESCENDANTS of JOHN MILK

Generation No. 1

1. JOHN[1] MILK was born Abt. 1630, probably in Norfolk County, England, and died in 1689 in Massachusetts. He married SARAH WESTON 03 Apr 1665 in Salem, Massachusetts[1]. She was born Abt. 1630.

On 7 April 1662, John Milk was appointed cowherd for the town of Salem, Mass.

"The cows were sent to the common pasture, and a herdsman by the appropriate name of John Milk conducted the herd back and forth . . . " The cattle were to be kept all summer for £ 20, one quarter of this to be paid in butter, one quarter in wheat, and the other half in Indian corn.

During this same year, John Milk was chosen for the duty of chimney sweep, and his compensation was fixed at 4d. a chimney where cash was paid, or 6d. where payment was made in barter.

On 1 Apr. 1677 John Milk was warned by Harry West to appear before worshipful Mayor Hawthorne to take the oath of allegiance.

"Mr. Hale conveyed the lot to John Milk of Salem, Mass., Oct. 6, 1666. It is now nearly all included in Federal St. {Opposite the tabernacle meeting house.} Mr. Milk built a house upon the lot, lived in it, and died possessed of the same in 1689. By his Will he devised the northern half of the lot and house to his son John, and the southern half of the lot and barn to his daughter Mary Milk, to be equally divided lengthwise. His widow Sarah lived in the house. John Wesson of Reading and his wife Sarah, granddaughter of John Milk Sr., deceased, and probably daughter and heir of Mr. Milk's daughter Mary, conveyed the southern half to Joshua Hicks of Salem, shopkeeper, April 11, 1726. The northern half of the lot was conveyed by John Milk of Boston and James Milk of Falmouth, Me., shipwrights, sons and heirs of John Milk Jr., to Joshua Hicks, May 13, 1734. The old house apparently was then gone."
(Reference: Essex Antiquarian 2:174.)

The Will of John Milk, dated 16 Mar. 1687/8, mentions wife Sarah, son John, and dau. Mary Milk; it appoints his wife and son executors. Witnesses were William Dounten, Rebecca Dounten, and William Smith. The Will was proved by the witnesses 26 Nov. 1689; inventory 1 July 1691 amounted to £71: 2s: 1d. (Reference: Essex Inst. Hist. Collections 5:45.)

Children of JOHN MILK and SARAH WESTON are:

2. i. JOHN[2] MILK, JR., b. 08 Jan 1668/69, Salem, Massachusetts; d. Bef. 1720, Boston, Massachusetts?.
    ii. MARY MILK, b. 22 Nov 1670, Salem, Massachusetts[2]; m. JOHN WESTON; b. Abt. 1670.
    [from: "Massachusetts, Births and Christenings, 1639-1915"
    Name: Mary Milk.; Gender: Female; Birth Date: 22 Nov 1670; Birthplace: Salem, Essex, Massachusetts
    Father's Name: John Milk; Mother's Name: Sara Weston]

1 November 2014

A sketch of what the house of John Milk Jr. (1668/69) may have looked like.
John lived in Boston, on the corner of Sun Court, just across
the square from where Paul Revere lived.
A Catholic Church now stands on the site.

Generation No. 2

2. JOHN² MILK, JR. *(JOHN¹)* was born 08 Jan 1668/69 in Salem, Massachusetts[2], and died Bef. 1720 in Boston, Massachusetts. He married (1) ELIZABETH HEMPFIELD 20 Aug 1689 in Marblehead, Massachusetts[3,4], daughter of EDMUND HEMPFIELD. She was born in Of Salem (Mass.). He married (2) MARY SCOLLY[5] 23 Oct 1707 in Boston, Mass, by Rev. Thomas Cheever[6,7]. She was born Abt. 1670. John was a shipwright in Boston.

Children of JOHN MILK and ELIZABETH HEMPFIELD are:
      i.   JOHN³ MILK, b. Abt. 1690; d. Died young.
3.   ii. JOB MILK, b. Abt. 1694, Boston, Massachusetts; d. Abt. 1775.

Children of JOHN MILK and MARY SCOLLY are:
4.   iii. JOHN³ MILK III, b. 23 Jun 1708, Boston, Massachusetts; d. 19 May 1756, Boston, Massachusetts.
5.   iv. DEACON JAMES MILK, b. 31 Jan 1710/11, Boston, Massachusetts; d. 19 Nov 1772, Falmouth (Portland), Maine.
      v.   MARY JANE MILK, b. Abt. 1713[8].

"On the corner of Sun Court stood, until within a few years, one of the most primitive looking houses in Boston, with a prodigious chimney and an overhanging second story, diamond-shaped window lights, and a quaint outside staircase. In the annexed cut we have a peep through a gateway leading to the old house of the Milk family, once a fine residence. . . ." (*Ramble in Old Boston,* by Rev. Edward G. Porter, 1887, p.288)

The facing picture is adapted from the drawing and description in *Rambles in Old Boston*.. Although some fifty years older, the Milk home apparently was very much like the Paul Revere home which stands no more than 300 feet away, across a little square from the corner of Sun County and Moon Street. Located on the crest of a long, gradually sloping hill, the Milk home at one time must have commanded an excellent view of the ocean.

About two blocks north of the Milk home site, overlooking the bay formed by the Charles River and the Atlantic Ocean, is Copp's Hill Burying Ground, where several of John Milk's descendants are interred.

A short distance south, leading into Atlantic Avenue which borders the harbor, is "Milk Street", named after this early Bostonian – perhaps the street led to the site of his shipbuilding business. (ref. : Croft 1956)

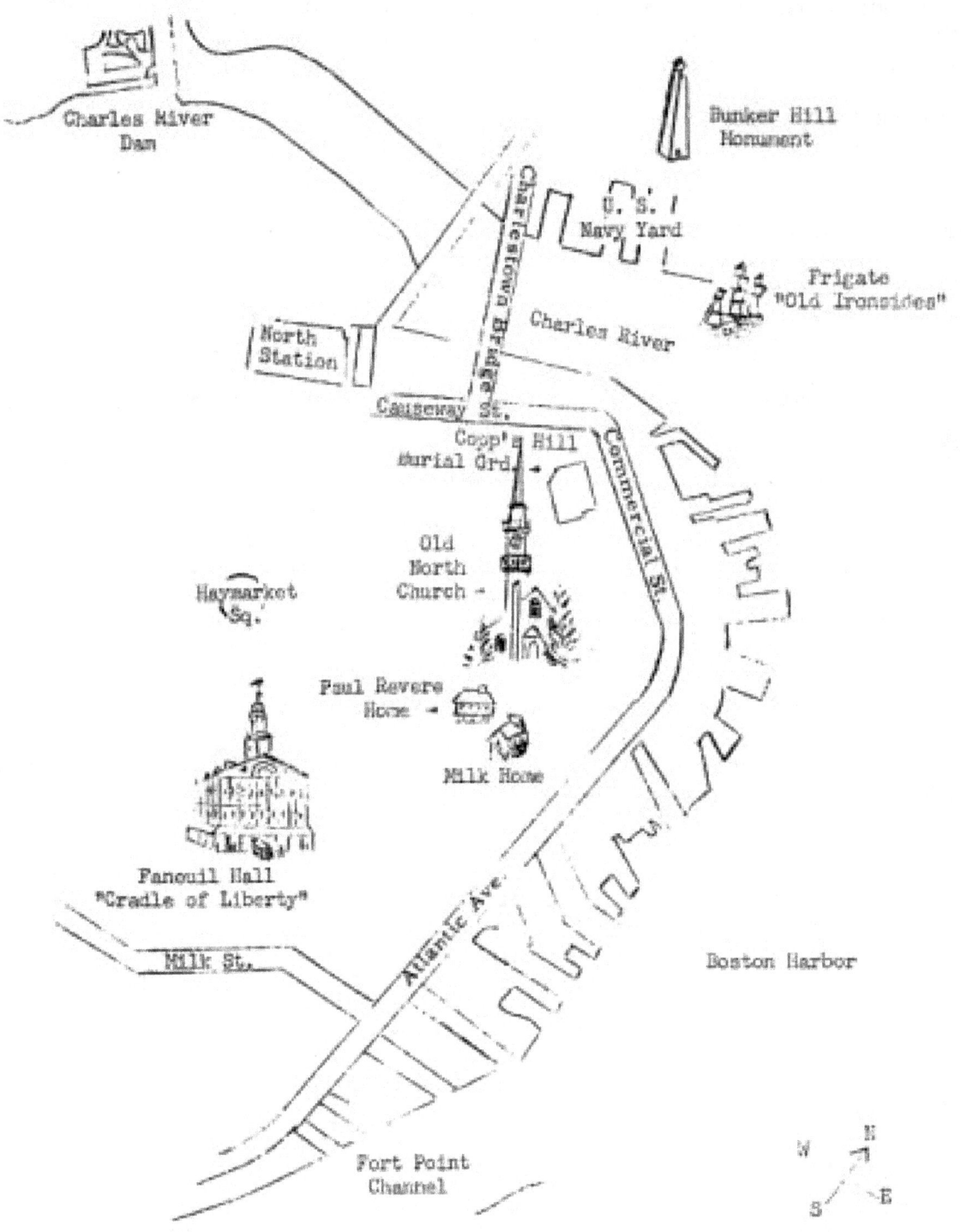

MAP OF NORTHEASTERN BOSTON

Generation No. 3

3. JOB^3 MILK *(JOHN^2, JOHN^1)* was born Abt. 1694 in Boston, Massachusetts, and died Abt. 1775. He was married to ABIGAIL DAVOL 12 Jul 1719 in Little Compton, Rhode Island, by Richard Billings, Justice^9, daughter of JONATHAN DAVOL and HANNAH AUDLEY. She was born Abt. 1694.

Little Compton, R.I., chosen by Job Milk for his home, is rolling land. To those who came from Boston and its environs, as the first Quakers in America did, it was a Promised Land -- a mild climate, fertile soil, and a refuge from the persecutions of Plymouth. " 'Aquidneck, Isle of Peace', so the red men called Rhode Island; and a place of peace it proved to be for the persecuted settlers who found sanctuary upon it." (Maude Howe Elliott) From the hills one gains a fine view of the pretty farms and pastures. Eastward are the lowlands, necks, and "salt rivers". In summer the early settlers cut hay on the farthest points of land and brought it up the salt rivers to their farms by boats and barges. So much hay was transported that it caused controversy among local authorities.

Land holdings of Job Milk in Dartmouth indicate he may have been a "proprietor" there. He probably bought Rights before embarking at Boston for the then frontier. Although a Will of his father's has not been found, it is probably that he was given a sum of money for that purpose.

Dartmouth was an extension of Plymouth Colony to the Narragansett Bay. The settlers of the "Acoaxet" section of Old Dartmouth (referring to Westport, Little Compton, and Tiverton) were of two classes: the administrators for the Rights of the land and their followers and the settlers from Plymouth; and the Quakers from the Island of Rhode Island (including Portsmouth and Newport) who were the earliest settlers, having bought their land from the Indians, who had the country well occupied. (Among these early comers were the following families: Davol, Fish, Brownell, Gifford, Sisson, Mosher, Tripp, Lawton, etc. Reference: Austin's Gen. Dict. of R.I.)

It is probable that Job Milk came with the Plymouth group. He was not among those who came from the Island of Rhode Island. His marriage with Abigail Davol in 1719 is evidence that he soon chose the early Island Quakers as friends and neighbors. Likewise, his descendants intermarried with descendants of these early comers, as the following pages will reveal.

"The history of Old Dartmouth is the history of Quakers . . . The conflict between the Pilgrims and Quakers in ancient Dartmouth, where the latter were largely in the majority, was not paralleled in any other locality in New England." (From Old Dartmouth: Historical Sketches, issued by the New Bedford Hist. Soc.) Although a record has never been found specifying that Job Milk and his family were Quakers, their association with and acceptance by Quakers would imply their membership.

The following accounts of land transfers are given to show the extent of Job Milk's holdings in Dartmouth, the nature of the land, and who were some of his neighbors. (Reference: Land Records, Taunton, Bristol Co., Mass. 1)

1732. Job Milk of Dartmouth, yeoman, £ 28, sells to Zacheus Toby, 29 acres in Dartmouth. Wit's Wm. Allen, Stephen West. (Vol. 23, p.149)

1740. Benjamin Wait of Dartmouth to Job Milk of Dartmouth and Thos. Pell of Rochester, £ 25, 13s, 2-1/3 acres, Cedar Swamp in Dartmouth in Paschachast Cedar Swamp, bounded on N. by sd. Job Milk, E. on sd. Job Milk upland, S. on Jos. Tripp's Cedar Swamp, W. on Chase's land. (Vol. 28, p.339)

4 May 1750. Job Milk of Dartmouth to William Read, merchant of Newport, 100 acres in Dartmouth, it being Job Milk's homestead adjoining Enos Gifford and other lands of sd. Job Milk, £ 400. (Vol. 37, p.468)

1752. Job Milk of Dartmouth and Abigail Milk his wife, to Ezekial Chase of Dartmouth, 6 acre Lot of Cedar Swamp in Dartmouth, "northerly part of Leander's Swamp conveyed to me by John Tripp, to me and Richard Sisson equal shares." Wits. Judah Chase, Abigail Milk. (Vol. 46, p.314)

20 Oct. 1752. Job Milk of Dartmouth to Samuel Borden of Tiverton, "Homestead farm in Dartmouth where I and my son Jonathan Milk now liveth . . . £ 200 . . . North boundary, the Line between Dartmouth and that part of Tiverton which hath of late been annexed to Freetown. West boundary, Paschachast Cedar Swamp. South, middle of Hemlock Gutter. East, Undivided land. Another tract of land bought of John Earl. Another tract of Cedar Swamp bough of Benj. Wait and Thos. Pell . . . and Sixty-three acres I bought of Daniel Davol and he bought it of Enos Gifford." (Vol. 70, p.533)

Job Milk may have had lumber interests in the hemlock and cedar tracts of land mentioned in his Deeds. (Much of the land is now abandoned and growing up into woods again.)

The year 1742 marks the beginning of the Quaker migration from Old Dartmouth to Quaker Hill, Dutchess Co., NY. It is recorded that Phineas Chase (neighbor of Job Milk in Dartmouth and later in Dutchess Co.) was a Quaker and that he was a member of the "Oblong Monthly Meeting" (Quaker Hill Mt.) in 1742. (New England Hist. & Gen. Reg.,

87:133).

The farmers who lived on the salt waters of southwestern Massachusetts were experienced seamen and water was their preferred route of travel. The voyage through Long Island Sound from Newport to the Hudson River was beautiful, and, no doubt, Job Milk and his Quaker friends early discovered that business might be combined with pleasure.

It took a period of years to establish themselves in their new home in Dutchess Co., NY. Job Milk did not close out his holdings in Dartmouth until 1752,1 although we find his name on the Tax List in Dutchess Co., NY, as early as 1746, when it appears at Beekman His daughter Sarah, wife of Seth Chase, was living there at that time. Likewise, several of Job's former neighbors preceded him to Beekman.2 In 1756, Job Milk appears at Crom Elbow township and later he is listed at Amenia (Amenia, from Latin signifying "pleasant", was a township divided from Beekman).

At the first town meeting of Amenia in 1762, when the township was organized, Job Milk was chosen one of the overseers of highways. In 1772, Job Milk was chosen one of the overseers of the poor who were "to serve for nothing".

Daniel Merritt kept a store at Quaker Hill and in 1771 Job Milk's name is among those having accounts. It was the custom in those days of barter to straighten out accounts by suits in the courts -- to make equitable adjustment. These suits did not imply an unwillingness to pay a debt. In a suit against Thomas Beadle, later founder of Beadle Hill or Easton, one of the jurors (1765) was Job Milk.

The title of the farm owned by Job Milk, when an early settler in Beekman, probably was transferred to his grandson in 1774 or 1775 and was the farm sold by the latter in 1796. The name of Job Milk's widow listed on the tax list in 1778 enables us to calculate the date of his decease. He lived to a good age and may have remarried.

Children of JOB MILK and ABIGAIL DAVOL are:
6.   i. DAVID^4 MILK, b. 03 May 1720, Dartmouth, Massachusetts; d. 1770, Dartmouth, Massachusetts.
    ii. DESIRE MILK, b. 21 Jul 1721, Dartmouth, Massachusetts[10]; d. 11 May 1725, Dartmouth, Massachusetts[11].
7.   iii. SARAH MILK, b. 17 Apr 1723, Dartmouth, Massachusetts.
8.   iv. JOB MILK, JR., b. 17 Apr 1725, Dartmouth, Massachusetts; d. Abt. 30 Apr 1804, Alford, Berkshire County, Massachusetts.
    v. KEZIAH MILK, b. 08 Dec 1726, Dartmouth, Massachusetts[12]; d. 13 May 1727, Dartmouth, Massachusetts[13].
9.   vi. JONATHAN MILK, b. 09 Mar 1727/28, Dartmouth, Massachusetts; d. 17 Feb 1800, Valley Falls (Pittstown), Washington County, New York.
10.   vii. ABIGAIL MILK, b. Abt. 1730, Dartmouth, Massachusetts.
    viii. ELIZABETH MILK, b. Abt. 1732, Dartmouth, Massachusetts.
    ix. MARY MILK, b. Abt. 1734, Dartmouth, Massachusetts.

4. JOHN^3 MILK III *(JOHN^2, JOHN^1)* was born 23 Jun 1708 in Boston, Massachusetts[14], and was baptised 11 Mar 1710/11, Second Church in Boston. He died 19 May 1756 in Boston, Massachusetts[15,16]. He married JANE MARVIN 03 Feb 1730/31 in Boston, Massachusetts, by Mr. John Webb, Presn.[17], daughter of CHRISTOPHER MARVIN and JANE BUDD. She was born 18 Mar 1710/11 in Boston, Massachusetts.

John Milk III, shipwright, b. 23 June 1708/9, in Boston (son of John 1668/9), m. 3 Feb. 1731, Jane Marvin (Marvel) of Boston. He d. 19 May 1756 and is buried in old Copp's Hill Burying Ground, Boston. "On the highest point of the hill is a stone bearing the name John Milk, for whom Milk Street is named".

The inscription on his tombstone reads:
"Here Lies Ye Body of Mr. John Milk, died May 19th 1756, Aged 47 yrs., 10 mos., 27 days"

Copp's Hill Burying Ground, named after its original owner, William Copp, is at the summit of a long hill that slopes toward the ocean. It is surrounded by an iron fence placed on top of a low stone wall, and is fairly well cared for. Many tombstones have been taken from their rightful places and are now leaning against the stone wall outlining the cemetery. Other stones are placed in borders along the main path. Such is the case of two Milk stones, one placed on each side of the main path, opposite each other. To keep them from falling, as have so many other monuments, the Milk stones have been imbedded deeper in the ground, so that one now cannot read the full inscriptions. In Copp's Hill are the graves of many men whose names are linked with Boston's history.

Children of JOHN MILK and JANE MARVIN are:
11. i. JOHN[4] MILK, b. 04 Dec 1732, Boston, Massachusetts.
     ii. JAMES MILK, b. 07 Mar 1733/34, Boston, Massachusetts[18]; d. 23 Jan 1735/36, Boston, Massachusetts[19]. Baptism: 09 Mar 1734/35, New North Church, Boston, Massachusetts[20]
12. iii. MARY MILK, b. 25 Mar 1737, Boston, Massachusetts.
13. iv. JANE MILK, b. 16 Sep 1739, Boston, Massachusetts.

5. DEACON JAMES[3] MILK *(JOHN[2], JOHN[1])*, a boat builder by trade, was born 31 Jan 1710/11 in Boston, Massachusetts[21], and died 19 Nov 1772 in Falmouth (Portland), Maine[22]. He married (1) SARAH BROWN 08 Sep 1735 in Falmouth (Portland), Maine[23]. She was born Jun 1720 in Falmouth (Portland), Maine?[24], and died 29 Apr 1761 in Falmouth (Portland), Maine. He married (2) ANNIE 'MOLLIE' DUNN 29 Dec 1763[25]. She was born Abt. 1711 in Of Kittery, Maine, and died 07 Sep 1769 in Falmouth (Portland), Maine.

The following inscription appears on the tombstone of James Milk, in the Old Burying Ground at Portland, Me.:

"Here lies interred the body of Deac. James Milk, who was born in Boston, January, A.D. 1710/11. He removed to Falmouth as soon as he arrived at manhood, and lived there in good reputation, being honored with several offices of trust and importance, which he executed with fidelity. He fell asleep after two days' illness, November 19, A.D. 1772. His bereaved children have erected this Monument as a Testimony of their Remembrance of his parental affection, strict virtues, and exemplary piety." (Reference: New Eng. Gen. & Hist. Reg., 8:77)

From Journal of Smith and Dean, 1849: "James Milk was born in Boston in 1711 and was here {Falmouth, Me.} previous to 1735, when he married Sarah Brown. He was by trade a boat builder, and of such industrious habits and provident management as to have accumulated a large estate for that day, and at the same time acquired a more sterling capital in the character of an upright man. He commanded a company of scouts in pursuit of Indians in 1756. He was a selectman of the town 16 years and Deacon of the First Church more than 21 years, from 1751 to his death. He owned the two Hog Islands in the harbour and the large tract on the east side of Exchange Street from near Middle Street to low water mark, including the flats on which Long Wharf stands. He lived on this lot fronting the present passage on to Long Wharf in a two-story house afterward acquired by his son-in-law, Mr. Ingraham, which was burnt in the destruction of the town in 1775. The children who survived him were James, who died the year after his father, aged 29; Mary, married Moses Little, then of Compton, NH, after-wards of Newburyport; Eunice to John Deering; Abigail to Joseph H. Ingraham; and Lucy to John Nichols, all of Portland. His wife died Sept. 7, 1769, aged 58. All his children are dead and the name is now extinct here, having expired with his son James, but his posterity is numerous through his several daughters. Mr. Milks married for his second wife Mrs. Deering of Kittery, Me., the mother of Nathaniel Deering and thirteen other children by her first husband. Two of her sons by the first marriage, viz: Nathaniel and John, married two of Deacon Milk's daughters, Dorcas and Eunice; and her daughter Mary married Deacon Milk's only son James. By his purchases of tracts of land in different parts of the city and his innate business sagacity, he {Deacon Milk} laid the foundation of the present Deering estate. Among these purchases was the beautiful Grove of Oaks, later given to the city of Portland by the Deering heirs and immortalized by Longfellow's poem, 'My Lost Youth'. Mr. Smith preached a funeral sermon on the occasion of the death of Deacon Milk from the text -- 'Behold, an Israelite indeed, in whom there is no guile.' This alone is a sufficient commentary upon his character.

From Portland Times, Sunday, Oct 28, 1900: "John Deering Jr., sea captain, died at sea 1758. Three of his 14 children died young. Nathaniel became the support of his mother and the 11 children. All came to Portland. In 1762 James Milk married Mrs. Deering. James Milk had 11 children by his first wife. In 1763 James Milk Jr. married Mary Deering."

According to *Babson, Colonial Families of America, 6:118*, James Milk and Sarah Brown had 7 children. Present research discloses the names of 9 children, b. in Falmouth:
James and both of his wives are buried in Eastern Cemetery, Portland, Cumberland County, Maine.

Children of JAMES MILK and SARAH BROWN are:
  i. MARTHA[4] MILK, b. Abt. 1742, Falmouth (Portland), Maine[27]; d. 25 Nov 1764, Portland, Cumberland County, Maine[27]; m. ALEXANDER TODD, 01 Jan 1757[28]; b. Abt. 1735. Martha is buried in Eastern Cemetery in Portland. Her gravestone inscription is:
     "Here lies buried ye mortal part of Martha Todd, wife to Alexander Todd & Dautr of Deacon James & Mrs. Sarah Milk, who departed this Life . . ." [rest is unclear]
  ii. SARAH MILK, b. 28 Jan 1737/38, Falmouth (Portland), Maine; d. 18 Nov 1760, Falmouth (Portland), Maine. Burial: Eastern Cemetery, Portland, Cumberland County, Maine

	iii.	LUCY MILK, b. Abt. 1740, Falmouth (Portland), Maine; m. JOHN NICHOLS, Abt. 1760; b. Abt. 1740.
14.	iv.	DORCAS MILK, b. 1741, Falmouth (Portland), Maine; d. 1826, Portland, Maine?.
	v.	MARY MILK, b. 10 Jun 1742, Falmouth (Portland), Maine.
15.	vi.	JAMES MILK, b. 1744, Falmouth (Portland), Maine; d. 12 Apr 1773, Portland, Cumberland County, Maine.
	vii.	ELIZABETH MILK, b. 1748, Falmouth (Portland), Maine.
	viii.	EUNICE MILK, b. 1749, Falmouth (Portland), Maine.
	ix.	ABIGAIL MILK, b. Abt. 1751, Falmouth (Portland), Maine.

Generation No. 4

6. DAVID[4] MILK *(JOB[3], JOHN[2], JOHN[1])* was born 03 May 1720 in Dartmouth, Massachusetts[29], and died 1770 in Dartmouth, Massachusetts. He married REBECCAH LAWTON 09 Jan 1745/46 in Dartmouth, Mass.[30], daughter of JOHN LAWTON and PATIENCE CARBY. She was born 15 Dec 1726 in Dartmouth, Massachusetts, and died 09 Oct 1805 in Dartmouth, Massachusetts[31].

Children of DAVID MILK and REBECCAH LAWTON are:

16.	i.	LEMUEL[5] MILK, b. 1747, Dartmouth, Massachusetts; d. 18 Jan 1820, Westport, Bristol County, Massachusetts.
17.	ii.	RHODA MILK, b. Abt. 1750, Dartmouth, Massachusetts.
18.	iii.	ISABEL MILK, b. 1753, Dartmouth, Massachusetts; d. 06 Aug 1846, Westport, Massachusetts.
19.	iv.	PATIENCE MILK, b. 14 May 1753, Dartmouth, Massachusetts; d. Dec 1823, Washington County, NY
	v.	ELIZABETH MILK, b. Abt. 1758, Dartmouth, Massachusetts; m. WILLIAM POTTER, 03 Feb 1785, Dartmouth, Mass.[32]; b. Abt. 1758, Dartmouth, Massachusetts.
20.	vi.	JOB MILK, b. 22 Feb 1763, Dartmouth, Massachusetts; d. 18 Feb 1849, Hawleyton, Broome County, NY.
21.	vii.	ABIGAIL MILK, b. 28 Sep 1765, Dartmouth, Massachusetts; d. 29 Aug 1837, Westport, Mass.?.
	viii.	LYDIA MILK, b. Abt. 1767, Dartmouth, Massachusetts; m. ABNER DAVOL, 30 Jul 1786, Dartmouth, Mass.[32]; b. Abt. 1767, Dartmouth, Massachusetts.

7. SARAH[4] MILK *(JOB[3], JOHN[2], JOHN[1])* was born 17 Apr 1723 in Dartmouth, Massachusetts[33]. She married SETH CHASE 13 Jan 1745/46 in New Bedford, Bristol County, Massachusetts[34], son of PHINEAS CHASE and DESIRE WING. He was born 1722 in Dartmouth, Massachusetts[35], and died 1811 in Clinton County, New York[35].

Children of SARAH MILK and SETH CHASE are:

22.	i.	AMY[5] CHASE, b. 19 Aug 1747, Quaker Hill, Dutchess County, New York; d. 08 Jan 1835, Hoosic Falls, NY.
	ii.	ABIGAIL CHASE, b. 12 Mar 1749/50, Dutchess County, New York; m. ISAAC LANGDON; b. Abt. 1750.
23.	iii.	DAVID CHASE, b. 01 Feb 1752, Dutchess County, New York; d. 26 Oct 1835, White Creek, New York.
	iv.	EUNICE CHASE, b. 1753, Dutchess County, New York; m. ISAAC WILCOX; b. Abt. 1750.
	v.	DANIEL CHASE, b. 18 Mar 1755, Dutchess County, New York; d. 30 Jul 1841; m. (1) ELIZABETH BAKER; b. Abt. 1755; m. (2) CHARLOTTE/CHARITY HYDE; b. Abt. 1755.

8. JOB[4] MILK, JR. *(JOB[3], JOHN[2], JOHN[1])* was born 17 Apr 1725 in Dartmouth, Massachusetts[36], and died Abt. 30 Apr 1804 in Alford, Berkshire County, Massachusetts[37,38]. He married AMY FISH[39] 02 Nov 1746 in Portsmouth, Newport, RI, by William Sanford, Justice[39]. She was born 29 Oct 1729 in Portsmouth, Massachusetts?[40].

The name of Job Milk Jr., together with that of his father Job, appears on the tax list of Crom Elbow, Dutchess Co., NY, Feb 1756. In June 1762 the name of Job Jr. appears at Amenia (divided from Beekman Township). He migrated 1762-63 to Alford, Berkshire Co., Mass. Living across the New York state line from his brother Jonathan Milk and his sisters, Sarah and Abigail, who had married Chase brothers.

In 1776, Job Milk "was a selectman; in 1787 he had a gristmill on his farm where Toby Brook flows in the Seekonk River." (Hist. Of Berkshire Co., Mass., I:587). Chn., 2:

Children of JOB MILK and AMY FISH are:

	i.	BENJAMIN[5] MILK, b. 1747.
24.	ii.	SARAH MILK, b. 1749, Amenia, Dutchess County, New York; d. 1830, Hull, Quebec, Canada.
	iii.	JOB MILK, b. 1751, Dartmouth, Massachusetts.
25.	iv.	JONATHAN MILK, b. 1751.
	v.	MARY MILK, b. Abt. 1752[41]; m. HEINRICH "HENRY" CABEL[41,42]; b. Abt. 1750. They moved to Maryland, Otsego County, New York.
	vi.	JOHN MILK, b. 1753.
	vii.	DAVID MILK, b. 1757.
	viii.	CABEL MILK, b. 1759.
	ix.	THOMAS AMBROSE MILK, b. 1761.
	x.	AMY MILK, b. 1763.

9. JONATHAN⁴ MILK *(JOB³, JOHN², JOHN¹)* was born 09 Mar 1727/28 in Dartmouth, Massachusetts[43,44,45], and died 17 Feb 1800 in Valley Falls (Pittstown), Washington County, New York[46]. He married MERCY TROWBRIDGE 08 Sep 1747 in Dartmouth, Mass.[47], daughter of JOHN TROWBRIDGE and RUTH LAWTON. She was born 30 Nov 1726 in Newport, Rhode Island[48], and died in Easton, Washington County, New York. JONATHAN is buried in Old Presbyterian Cemetery in Schaghticoke, Rensselaer County, New York

GENEALOGY OF MERCY TROWBRIDGE

For the interest of the myriad known descendants, genealogy is here included on the wife of Jonathan Milk, who was Mercy Trowbridge (Strowbridge). (See Pedigree Chart, p. 65.) According to Dartmouth, Mass., marriage records: Jonathan Milk of Dartmouth, son of Job, and Mercy Strowbridge of Dartmouth, dau of Ruth1, were married 8 Sep. 1747. Trowbridge Genealogy, by Francis Bacon Trowbridge, states that the names of Strowbridge and Trowbridge are the same; it further mentions "John Trowbridge of Sandwich married Feb 3, 1725-6 in Portsmouth, RI , Ruth Lawton of Dartmouth, Mass. Chn. b. in Newport, RI, Mercy b. Nov 30, 1726; George b. May 25, 1732."

R.I. Vital Records, Portsmouth Marriages: Ruth Lawton and John Trowbridge 3 Feb. 1725-6. Since later records mention only the name of his wife, Ruth, it is assumed that John Trowbridge either died within a few years or he lived elsewhere. There is no verification of such, but he may have been the John Trowbridge of Newport, RI, mariner, who, having been imprisoned for indebtedness, signed a petition which came before the general assembly of R.I. In October 1735. (Petitions to the R. I. General Assembly 1728-1733, Vol. II). Evidence that he was a "mariner" with an "indebtedness unto divers persons as well out of this colony as in", would seem to indicate that this John Trowbridge had been shipping cargo on a large scale and that he had met with a disaster at sea of sufficient magnitude to place him in financial straits.

Ruth Lawton was the dau. of George and Mary (Dennis) Lawton. Mary Dennis was b. 20 Sept 1673, Portsmouth, RI, dau. of Robert Dennis and Sarah Howland. Sarah was a dau. of Henry, a brother of John Howland who came on the Mayflower (both sons of Henry Howland Sr. of Fen Stanton, Huntingdonshire, England). Henry Jr. also lived in Plymouth where he was, 1624 "owner of the black cow". "He apparently joined (1657) the Friends sect which was just beginning to spread in America and as a result endured for the remainder of his life the various persecutions to which this sect was subjected. . . . Toward the end of his life he became a large possessor of real estate". He d. 17 Jan 1671. His wife was Mary Newlands, dau. Of Henry and sister of William, the noted Quaker. (New England Gen., Cutter, Vol. IV)

Robert Dennis was b. 1647, son of Robert and Mary Dennis of Yarmouth, Barnstable Co., Mass. Robert Dennis Jr., who d. 5 June 1691, left in his Will, twelve shillings to his grandchild Ruth Lawton to buy a bible. He deeded land for a Quaker burying place "for the love I bear to the truth and the people of God which are in scorn called Quakers." (Genealogical Dict. Of R.I., Austin). On the 19 Nov. 1672 he m. Sarah, dau. Of Henry And Mary (Newlands) Howland of Duxbury, Mass., "at the house of Joshua Coggeshall of Portsmouth before the people of God." (Quakers) (New Eng. Hist. & Gen. Reg., Vol. 49).

Mercy Trowbridge's mother, Ruth Lawton, descended from Thomas Laughton, b. abt. 1550, of Cranfield, Bedfordshire, Eng. His son George Laughton (Lawton) was b. 1581 at Cranfield; m. 13 Nov 1606, Isbell Smith, who became the parents of the emigrant George Lawton, christened 23 Sept 1607 at Cranfield, founder of an important R. I. Family. (New Eng. Gen. Dict., III:64). He came to Portsmouth 1638, was a Deputy 1662-1680 and Assistant 1680-1690. He m. Elizabeth Hazard, dau. of Thomas and Martha Hazard. George and Elizabeth Lawton's son John m. Mary, dau. of Matthew and Eleanor Boomer1. They became the parents of George Lawton who m. Mary Dennis.

Thomas Hazard was b. abt. 1610 and came to Boston not later than 1635 from Wales or England. In 1639 he was one of a group that founded the Colony of Newport on Rhode Island. About 1655 he lived for a time at Newton, Long Island. "This family occupies a prominent position in the civil, commercial, judicial, and military history of R.I." (Gen. of New Eng., Cutter) The Hazard family has grown in importance and numbers. At one time thirty-three Tom Hazards were living in So. Kingston, all at the same time, a situation that drives Hazard genealogists to desperation.

THE MILK FAMILY IN NEW YORK STATE

Although Jonathan Milk (1728) was living in Dartmouth, Mass. In 1752, as evidenced by the following deed:

20 Oct 1752. Job Milk of Dartmouth to Samuel Borden of Tiverton . . . homestead farm in   Dartmouth where I and my son Jonathan now liveth. . . ,

The Milk family had property interests in Dutchess Co., NY, as early as 1746, when Job Milk's name appears on the Tax

List for Beekman. After leaving Dartmouth, Jonathan and his father Job lived in Dutchess Co. (see p. 6); later Jonathan moved to Rensselaer, Saratoga, and Washington Cos., NY. In order to help understand the motives for his meanderings, pertinent history of those locales is given.

We gratefully acknowledge information derived from the Quaker Hill Series – Quaker Hill in the Eighteenth Century, by Rev. Warren H. Wilson, of Brooklyn, NY. Quotations are from this pamphlet which is published by the Quaker Hill Conference Association, Quaker Hill, NY.

Quaker Hill, Dutchess Co., was the first settlement made by Friends in "The Oblong". The boundary line between the states of New York and Conn. was not agreed upon until the year 1731. Then a valley in Amenia, a strip of land two miles wide and six to seven miles in extent, was added to New York state. This oblong strip, now Amenia Union and South Amenia, was originally in the area that separated the Dutch of the Hudson from the English-Scotch-Irish Presbyterians of Connecticut. "The feeling between them was far from friendly." When the peace-loving Quakers came as settlers in "The Oblong" their neighbors on both sides willingly accepted them. Mostly they came from "Old Dartmouth", the southernmost part of Mass., including a small part of R.I. There is a "Briggs family tradition of the first pair of boots owned on Quaker Hill borrowed in turn by every man who made a visit to Dartmouth."

The Friends of Quaker Hill, or "The Oblong Meeting as it has always been called, did not isolate themselves from the issues of their day. They inaugurated the struggle for freedom of the slave one hundred years before Abraham Lincoln. "The fugitive slave was fed and lodged . . . and there must never be any distinction made in the family on account of his color; he sat at the same table."

The Revolutionary War they could not escape. George Washington made his headquarters on the climbing road to Quaker Hill and one First Day, as meeting closed, soldiers marched in and took possession of the Quaker Hill Meeting House which was used for a hospital as long as needed.

The struggle for freedom from feudalistic-landlordism had been most severe and prolonged in eastern New York. In Dutchess Co. in 1740 "not more than one man in twenty in the county was an owner of land." Legal title to large areas was granted by both New York State and the King of England to a privileged few who refused to sell the land and exacted rentals. The frustration and resentment of the settlers culminated in the Prendergast Insurrection of 1766.

Job Milk (1694) and his sons Job and Jonathan had property interests at Quaker Hill as early as 1746. It may have been the pioneer spirit that impelled them to seek homes in a new country. Job Jr. (brother of Jonathan), who lived in Crom Elbow 1756-1761, left Quaker Hill in the spring of 1763 and found a home in Berkshire Co., Mass. From 1766 until 1773 "Jonathan Milk's Farm" was carried on the Amenia (Quaker Hill) Tax List.

About 1765 Jonathan left all behind and went into a wilderness. He even discarded his long name and thereafter was known only as "John". He found a location in Rensselaer Co. which apparently was very desirable; it was at the headwaters of the Little Hoosick River which flows north and the Kinderhook Creek that flows south. Only a few rods separate these waters and there John Milk and two or three other men made a settlement, far from roads and neighbors. One of them "came as far as Douglas with a cart and went on with horses and on foot. It was 12 years before he went for his cart." (History of Rensselaer Co., Sylvester, from which the adjacent map is also taken.

Rensselaer Manor was surveyed (1767) for the Patroon by John R. Bleecher, and the location of John Milk is on this map, but his name is not among the thirty-three who received leases.

Two years later he was in Mass., perhaps near his brother, Job. In 1773, Ebenezer Cook and his five sons settled in a new plat, in "Saratoga" -- Subdivision of Lot No. 40 (Old Saratoga, now known as Washington Co.). John Milk owned "Farm No. I." First it was called "Cooks' Hollow", later "South Easton" and now Beadle Hill has crowded out the historic name of Easton.

The Saratoga Patent which was granted in 1684 extended seventeen miles along the Hudson River and six miles on each side. Easton was the East Town and was known as Saratoga until after the Revolutionary War. Settlement in Easton began as early as 1713 near Fort Saratoga, which was destroyed in 1745. "Friends who were in Easton, when the French War broke out, did not leave their homes as did other settlers." (Hist. of Washington Co., Stone.) At the close of the French and Indian War, in 1760, many settlers came; but again they left at the outbreak of the Revolutionary War. "While Burgoyne was on the banks of the Hudson . . . the farmers had mostly deserted their homes. Now and then, during this time, one or more men ventured back to them for the purpose of observation and intelligence." (Hist. of Rensselaer Co., Weise.)

Washington Co. has been called the "war path of America." Indians used this route for their raids and wars on the early Colonists. When General Burgoyne sent his Hessians and Indians from their camp on the Hudson to Bennington, Vt., their first night was spent at Easton. They raided the farms as they crossed the county and the Battle of Bennington was fought not in Vermont, but in Washington Co.

John Milk was not one of those who fled from their homes. He took part in the local warfare; but no Revolutionary War record can now be found. His son Jonathan (b. 1769) could remember that his father fought, while the women and children sought safety in the woods. During one engagement this "small boy" (Jonathan 1769, see p. 212) climbed to a hilltop and watched the fighting. He said that after the smoke of battle cleared away he could pick out his father because he was so tall. Perhaps the "small boy" watched the Battle of Saratoga which was fought on the banks of the Hudson River. This battlefield is plainly seen from any one of Easton's high hills including "Willard's Mt., where the American spies watched Burgoyne while he was camped on the Hudson."

After the Battle of Saratoga, one British soldier who had surrendered there espoused the American Cause and the same year enlisted in the Colonial Army. He was James Sidway (see p. 68). Rebecca Milk, daughter of John, was then eighteen years of age. At the close of the War, James and Rebecca were married.

While living in Saratoga (Easton) John Milk left few traces of his life. He attended the Quaker marriage of Nicholas Barker and Clarinda Folger on the 23rd day of the 10th month in 1783, and signed his name as one of 29 witnesses. He carried an account at the store of Benjamin Starbuck, where there was a balancing of accounts among Friends and customers.

Before 1790, John Milk, with his sons David and Benjamin, had settled in Rensselaer Co. near the Washington Co. line. His sons Lemuel and George had located west of the Hudson River in Saratoga Co. In 1793, John Milk signed a deed without a wife's signature. In 1795, "John Milk and Sarah Crandle his wife" signed; but in 1799 "John Milk and Sarah his wife" deeded land and the signatures were John Milk and Sarah Milk. In 1795 Benjamin Milk witnessed their signatures.

Someone has written that Dutchess Co. is the graveyard of genealogy; that has been expanded to read "All New York State is the graveyard of genealogy."

There are no records to prove that all the following were children of Jonathan and Mercy Trowbridge (Strowbridge). Undoubtedly there were more children and further research may disclose daughters who married into Crandall, Benson, and other Easton families.:

Children of JONATHAN MILK and MERCY TROWBRIDGE are:
26. i. JOB[5] MILK, b. 1748, Dartmouth, Massachusetts.
27. ii. BENJAMIN MILK, b. 1750, Dartmouth, Mass.; d. 06 Mar 1813, Shandaken, Ulster County, New York.
28. iii. DAVID MILK, b. 1752; d. 15 Jun 1806, Milk Grove Farm, Valley Falls (Pittstown), NY.
29. iv. LEMUEL MILK, b. 1753, Beekman, Dutchess County, New York; d. 1853.
30. v. REBECCA MILK, b. 18 Mar 1759; d. 24 Mar 1843, Buffalo, New York.
31. vi. GEORGE MILK, b. Abt. 1762.
32. vii. JONATHAN MILK, b. 1769, Massachusetts; d. Abt. 1849, Dayton, Cattaraugus County, New York.

10. ABIGAIL[4] MILK *(JOB[3], JOHN[2], JOHN[1])* was born Abt. 1730 in Dartmouth, Massachusetts. She married NATHAN CHASE Abt. 1756 in Dutchess County, New York[49], son of PHINEAS CHASE and DESIRE WING. He was born 1723 in Hoosick, NY, and died Abt. 1806.

The name of Nathan Chase first appears on the tax list of Beekman, Dutchess Co., NY in 1757 and remains there until 1769. Abigail and Nathan left about 1769 for the Hoosick Patent, Rensselaer Co., NY, and lived at Hoosick Falls, their home lying a distance south of their sister and brother, Sarah (Milk) and Seth Chase.

Abigail and Nathan Chase undoubtedly were married in Dutchess Co., but the fact that Nathan was not taxed until 1757 suggests that they were not married until after 1755-56.

Even though the Chase family was of Quaker faith, Nathan Chase served in the Army during the American Revolution. He was enlisted in the 14th Regt. of Albany Co., NY, militia. Chn., 13:

Children of ABIGAIL MILK and NATHAN CHASE are:
33. i. LEMUEL[5] CHASE, b. 1765, Beekman, Dutchess Co., NY; d. 1830, Orangeville, Wyoming County, New York.
    ii. ABRAHAM CHASE, b. Abt. 1760, Beekman, Dutchess Co., NY; m. CATHERINE ROGERS; b. Abt. 1760. He Lived in: Bay County, Canada
34. iii. JUSTUS CHASE, b. 1762, Beekman, Dutchess Co., NY; d. 1829.
    iv. ISABEL CHASE, b. 16 Aug 1764, Beekman, Dutchess Co., NY; m. MIAL PERSE; b. Abt. 1764. They lived in: Cooperstown, Otsego County, New York
    v. MARY CHASE, b. Abt. 1765, Beekman, Dutchess Co., NY; m. DAVID/JOHN BUCK; b. Abt. 1765. They lived in Queensbury, Vermont
35. vi. RHODA CHASE, b. 10 Oct 1767, Beekman, Dutchess Co., NY; d. 18 Sep 1848, Adams, Jefferson County, New York.
36. vii. NATHAN CHASE, JR., b. 04 Jul 1768, Beekman, Dutchess Co., NY; d. 06 Jun 1844.

      viii. REBECCA CHASE, b. 11 Oct 1769, Hoosick Falls, Rensselaer Co., NY; m. NATHAN PERSE, 1784; b. Abt. 1769.
They lived in Germantown, New York
      ix. LOVICE CHASE, b. 1770, Hoosick Falls, Rensselaer Co., NY; m. DANIEL WALLACE. Lived in: Mapleton, New York
      x. PATIENCE CHASE, b. Hoosick Falls, Rensselaer Co., NY; m. JONATHAN PAGE.. Lived in: Pittstown, New York
      xi. ESTHER CHASE, b. Hoosick Falls, Rensselaer Co., NY.
37.   xii. JOHN CHASE, b. Jun 1774, Hoosick Falls, Rensselaer Co., NY; d. 1865, Fenner, New York.
38.   xiii. DESIRE CHASE, b. Abt. 1760, Hoosick Falls, Rensselaer Co., NY; d. 20 Nov 1843, Providence, Saratoga County, New York ?.

11. JOHN[4] MILK *(JOHN[3], JOHN[2], JOHN[1])* was born 04 Dec 1732 in Boston, Massachusetts[50]. He married SUSANNAH BROWNE 03 Feb 1763 in New North Church, Boston, Massachusetts[51]. She was born Abt. 1735.

    John was baptized: 17 Dec 1732, New North Church, Boston, Massachusetts[52]. His occupation was a boat builder, ship building[53]. Lived on Moon Street, Boston, Massachusetts[53]

Children of JOHN MILK and SUSANNAH BROWNE are:
      i. SUSANNAH[5] MILK, b. Sep 1763, Boston, Massachusetts. Baptism: 18 Sep 1763, New North Church, Boston, Massachusetts[54]
39.   ii. JOHN MILK, b. 1765, Boston, Massachusetts; d. 11 Jul 1808, Boston, Massachusetts.
      iii. WILLIAM MILK, b. Nov 1766, Boston, Massachusetts. Baptism: 07 Dec 1766, New North Church, Boston, Massachusetts[54]
40.   iv. ELIZABETH 'BETSEY' MILK, b. Abt. 1767, Boston, Massachusetts?.
      v. JAMES MILK, b. Aug 1768, Boston, Massachusetts. Baptism: 28 Aug 1768, New North Church, Boston, Massachusetts[54]

12. MARY[4] MILK *(JOHN[3], JOHN[2], JOHN[1])* was born 25 Mar 1737 in Boston, Massachusetts[55,56]. She married LEVI DREW 01 Dec 1756 in Boston, Mass[57], son of JOSHUA DREW and JOANNA KEMPTON. He was born 21 May 1734 in Plymouth, Mass, and died 15 May 1787. Mary was baptized: 03 Apr 1737, New North Church, Boston, Massachusetts[58]. LEVI DREW is listed in *Massachusetts Soldiers and Sailors in the War of the Revolution, Volume 4 page 972* "Drew, Levi. Seaman, brigantine Independence, " commanded by Capt. Simeon Samson; engaged June 8, 1776; service to Feb. 14, 1777, 8 mos. 6 days. Roll dated Plymouth."

Children of MARY MILK and LEVI DREW are:
      i. MARY[5] DREW, b. 09 Nov 1756, Plymouth, Plymouth, Mass.[59]; m. JAMES FIELD; b. Abt. 1756.
      ii. JOANNA DREW, b. 11 Jun 1759, Plymouth, Plymouth, Mass.; d. 09 Nov 1760.
      iii. LEVI DREW, b. 29 Jul 1761, Plymouth, Plymouth, Mass.; d. 09 Sep 1762[60].
      iv. CHILD DREW[61], b. 29 May 1763, Plymouth, Mass (Birth?? or Death??)[61]; d. 1763, Plymouth, Massachusetts.
      v. LYDIA DREW, b. 03 Aug 1764, Plymouth, Plymouth, Mass..
      vi. LEVI DREW, b. 10 Dec 1766, Plymouth, Plymouth, Mass..
      vii. JOHN MILK DREW, b. 21 Mar 1769, Plymouth, Plymouth, Mass.[62].

13. JANE[4] MILK *(JOHN[3], JOHN[2], JOHN[1])* was born 16 Sep 1739 in Boston, Massachusetts[63]. She married EDWARD BURBECK 27 Mar 1761 in New North Church, Boston, Massachusetts[64], son of WILLIAM BURBECK. He was born 1741, and died 23 Jun 1782 in Newburyport, Mass.. Jane was baptized: 23 Sep 1739, New North Church, Boston, Massachusetts[65]

    Edward Burbeck, b. 1738-40, son of Edward and Martha (Shute) Burbeck, was a member of the Boston Tea Party, a Capt. in Col. Richard Gridley's Artillery Reg. On his return he located in Newburyport, Mass., where he was killed by lightning 23 June 1782. He was a Captain in the Massachusetts Line and commanded a company of artillery.

Children of JANE MILK and EDWARD BURBECK are:
      i. JANE[5] BURBECK, b. Abt. 1762, Massachusetts; d. 29 Apr 1845; m. EBENEZER LITTLE, 05 Aug 1783; b. 25 Jan 1762; d. 15 Jan 1833.

      ii. JAMES BURBECK, b. 15 Jan 1763, Boston, Mass..
      iii. WILLIAM BURBECK, b. 03 Aug 1771, Boston, Mass..

14. DORCAS[4] MILK *(JAMES[3], JOHN[2], JOHN[1])* was born 1741 in Falmouth (Portland), Maine, and died 1826 in Portland, Maine?. She married NATHANIEL DEERING, son of JOHN DEERING and ANNIE DUNN. He was born 17 Jan 1738/39 in Kittery, Maine, and died 1795 in Portland, Maine.

Children of DORCAS MILK and NATHANIEL DEERING are:
41.   i. JAMES[5] DEERING, b. 23 Aug 1766, Portland, Maine.
      ii. MARY DEERING, b. 1770, Portland, Maine.

15. JAMES[4] MILK *(JAMES[3], JOHN[2], JOHN[1])* was born 1744 in Falmouth (Portland), Maine, and died 12 Apr 1773 in Portland, Cumberland County, Maine. He married (1) MARY DEERING 29 Sep 1763[66], daughter of JOHN DEERING and ANNIE DUNN. She was born 30 Jun 1742. He married (2) SARAH HALL Abt. 28 Feb 1769[66]. She was born Abt. 1745. James is buried in Eastern Cemetery, Portland, Cumberland County, Maine

Child of JAMES MILK and SARAH HALL is:
      i. LYDIA HALL[5] MILK, b. Feb 1770, Portland, Cumberland County, Maine; d. 20 Apr 1771, Portland, Cumberland County, Maine. Burial: Eastern Cemetery, Portland, Cumberland County, Maine

Generation No. 5

16. LEMUEL[5] MILK *(DAVID[4], JOB[3], JOHN[2], JOHN[1])* was born 1747 in Dartmouth, Massachusetts, and died 18 Jan 1820 in Westport, Bristol County, Massachusetts[66]. He married MARY SISSON 17 Dec 1767 in Dartmouth, Mass.[66,67], daughter of WILLIAM SISSON and LYDIA POTTER. She was born Abt. 1747, and died 18 May 1821 in Scipio, Cayuga Co., NY. Lemuel as an Innkeeper at the head of the Westport River[68]

Children of LEMUEL MILK and MARY SISSON are:

42.	i.	CYNTHIA[6] MILK, b. 1768, Westport, Bristol County, Massachusetts; d. 14 Jan 1814, Scituate, Massachusetts.
	ii.	PHOEBE MILK, b. 22 Jun 1773, Westport, Bristol County, Massachusetts; d. 19 Feb 1852, Dartmouth, Massachusetts[69]; m. OTHNIEL TRIPP, 20 Feb 1791, Dartmouth, Mass. (int.)[70]; b. 06 Nov 1769, Dartmouth, Massachusetts; d. 13 Aug 1852, Dartmouth, Massachusetts[71].
43.	iii.	WILLIAM MILK, b. 18 Oct 1783, Westport, Bristol County, Massachusetts; d. Abt. 23 Aug 1866, Fleming, Cayuga County, New York.
44.	iv.	JOHN MILKS, b. Abt. 1790, Westport, Bristol County, Massachusetts; d. Will County, Illinois.

17. RHODA[5] MILK *(DAVID[4], JOB[3], JOHN[2], JOHN[1])* was born Abt. 1750 in Dartmouth, Massachusetts. She married GEORGE BROWNELL 12 Jul 1770 in Dartmouth, Mass.[72], son of THOMAS BROWNELL and HANNAH _____. He was born 09 Dec 1746 in Dartmouth, Massachusetts.

Children of RHODA MILK and GEORGE BROWNELL are:

	i.	HANNAH[6] BROWNELL, b. 10 Aug 1771, Dartmouth, Massachusetts.
	ii.	REBECCA BROWNELL, b. 28 Sep 1772, Dartmouth, Massachusetts.
	iii.	DOROTHY BROWNELL, b. 22 May 1774, Dartmouth, Massachusetts.
	iv.	DANIEL BROWNELL, b. 02 Apr 1776, Dartmouth, Massachusetts.
	v.	AMY BROWNELL, b. 1777, Dartmouth, Massachusetts.
	vi.	ELIZABETH BROWNELL, b. 28 Jul 1779, Dartmouth, Massachusetts.
	vii.	POLLY BROWNELL, b. 04 Oct 1781, Dartmouth, Massachusetts.
	viii.	SARAH 'SALLY' BROWNELL, b. 25 Nov 1783, Dartmouth, Massachusetts.
	ix.	PATIENCE BROWNELL, b. 02 Mar 1786, Dartmouth, Massachusetts.
45.	x.	DAVID MILK BROWNELL, b. 08 Oct 1789, Dartmouth, Massachusetts; d. 30 Dec 1864.
46.	xi.	GEORGE MILK BROWNELL, b. 15 Nov 1787, Dartmouth, Massachusetts; d. Bet. 20 - 30 Sep 1830, Westport, Massachusetts ?.

18. ISABEL[5] MILK *(DAVID[4], JOB[3], JOHN[2], JOHN[1])* was born 1753 in Dartmouth, Massachusetts[73], and died 06 Aug 1846 in Westport, Massachusetts[73]. She married JOHN GIFFORD 18 Sep 1777 in Dartmouth, Mass.[74], son of RECOMPENSE GIFFORD and SUSAN TABER. He was born 1747 in Newport, Tiverton, RI[75,76], and died 1851[76]. John was a Sergeant in Col. Robert Elliott's Regiment - Pay 25 pounds, 17 shillings 7 pence

Children of ISABEL MILK and JOHN GIFFORD are:

	i.	AMY[6] GIFFORD, b. Abt. 1778.
	ii.	PATIENCE GIFFORD.
	iii.	PEACE GIFFORD.
	iv.	REBECCA GIFFORD.
	v.	SYLVIA GIFFORD.
	vi.	NANCY GIFFORD, b. Abt. 1788; m. (1) JOHN SNELL; b. Abt. 1788; m. (2) JOB GIFFORD; b. Abt. 1788.
	vii.	ALDEN GIFFORD.
	viii.	ZACHEUS GIFFORD.
	ix.	DAVID GIFFORD.
47.	x.	SQUIRE GIFFORD, b. 14 Oct 1795; d. 06 Mar 1878, New Bedford, Bristol County, Massachusetts.
	xi.	NICHOLAS GIFFORD.
48.	xii.	JOHN GIFFORD, b. 09 Mar 1800, Massachusetts; d. 10 Sep 1880, Watertown, Jefferson County, New York.

19. PATIENCE[5] MILK *(DAVID[4], JOB[3], JOHN[2], JOHN[1])* was born 14 May 1753 in Dartmouth, Massachusetts, and died Dec 1823 in Washington County, New York (Date ??). She married JONATHAN DEUEL 09 Jun 1775 in Dartmouth, Mass. (int.)[77], son of WILLIAM DAVOL and MEHITABLE TRIPP. He was born Abt. 1753 in Dartmouth, Massachusetts, and died Abt. 1802 in Salem, Washington County, New York ?. Patience and Jonathan moved to The Oblong, Dutchess Co., NY, later to Hebron, near White Creek, NY.

It is interesting to note the circumstances leading to the change in the spelling of the name Davol or Devol to Deuel, Duel, or Dewell. History tells us that the founder of that family in New York became annoyed at being called "Devil" and changed his name to Deuel, Duel, or Dewell. The following entries on tax lists in Dutchess Co. show such changes in spelling: Beekman, June 1746 (first entry), "Ben Divil"; Beekman, June 1756, "Benjamin Dewell."

The Will of Jonathan Deuel was probated 1802 (Probate Court Records, Salem, Washington Co., NY). Patience Deuel and William Deuel (the latter probably a brother of Jonathan) were appointed administrators, and children Abner and Rebecca Deuel were mentioned.

Children of PATIENCE MILK and JONATHAN DEUEL are:
49.   i. LEWIS[6] DEUEL, b. Abt. 1782, Hebron, New York.
      ii. ABNER DEUEL, b. 22 Sep 1787, Hebron, New York; m. SARAH ELY; b. Abt. 1790, Hebron, New York.
      iii. REBECCA DEUEL, m. SAMUEL ELY.
50.   iv. LILLYS DEUEL, b. Aug 1785; d. 02 Oct 1832.

20. JOB[5] MILK *(DAVID[4], JOB[3], JOHN[2], JOHN[1])* was born 22 Feb 1763 in Dartmouth, Massachusetts[78,79], and died 18 Feb 1849 in Hawleyton, Broome County, New York[80]. He married PHEBE BROWNELL 08 Nov 1781 in Dartmouth, Bristol County, Massachusetts[81,82], daughter of BENJAMIN BROWNELL and PHOEBE POTTER. She was born 06 Nov 1758 in Dartmouth, Massachusetts[83], and died 29 Dec 1840 in Westport, Bristol County, Massachusetts[84].

Job Milk was initiated into the Masons, New Bedford, Massachusetts, on 17 Jan 1804. He is shown as "passed" on 1 May, 1804, and was "Raised" on 2 October 1804. (Reference: Mason membership card for Job Milk)

Phoebe's Will was probated Aug. 1841. She is buried in the Brownell Plot, Central Village near Westport, Massachusetts

Children of JOB MILK and PHEBE BROWNELL are:
51.   i. ALICE[6] MILK, b. 09 Jul 1783, Westport, Bristol County, Massachusetts; d. 07 Apr 1866, Westport, Bristol County, Massachusetts.
52.   ii. JOHN MILK, b. 30 Aug 1786, Westport, Bristol County, Massachusetts; d. 14 Jul 1876, Westport, Bristol County, Massachusetts.
53.   iii. ELI S. MILK, b. 12 Jan 1797, Westport, Bristol County, Massachusetts; d. Dec 1852, Hawleyton, Broome Co., NY.

21. ABIGAIL[5] MILK *(DAVID[4], JOB[3], JOHN[2], JOHN[1])* was born 28 Sep 1765 in Dartmouth, Massachusetts[85,86], and died 29 Aug 1837 in Westport, Mass.?[87]. She married BENJAMIN BROWNELL, JR. 18 Mar 1784[87,88], son of BENJAMIN BROWNELL and PHEBE POTTER. He was born 02 Feb 1760 in Dartmouth, Massachusetts[89], and died 14 Apr 1830 in Westport, Mass.?[89].

Children of ABIGAIL MILK and BENJAMIN BROWNELL are:
      i. PHOEBE[6] BROWNELL, b. 07 Jan 1785, Westport, Mass.[89]; m. PELEG GIFFORD; b. Abt. 1785.
54.   ii. JIRAH BROWNELL, b. 17 Jun 1786, Westport, Mass.; d. 13 Jan 1864.
      iii. PRUDENCE BROWNELL, b. 24 Feb 1788, Westport, Mass.; d. 1854; m. LEVI GIFFORD; b. Abt. 1788.
      iv. LEMUEL BROWNELL, b. 13 Feb 1790, Westport, Mass.; d. 24 May 1885; m. ELIZABETH BRIGHTMAN; b. Abt. 1790.
      v. DAVID BROWNELL, b. 09 May 1793, Westport, Mass.; m. PATIENCE BRIGGS; b. Abt. 1793.
      vi. LYDIA BROWNELL, b. 03 Dec 1794, Westport, Mass.; m. AMOS BAKER; b. Abt. 1794.
      vii. CYNTHIA M. BROWNELL, b. 17 Sep 1795, Westport, Mass.; d. 08 Jun 1817.
      viii. RUBY BROWNELL, b. 06 May 1799, Westport, Mass.; m. THADDEUS MANCHESTER.
55.   ix. HOLDER WHITE BROWNELL, b. 16 Oct 1800, Westport, Mass.; d. 1861.
      x. WILLIAM THOMAS BROWNELL, b. 02 May 1802, Westport, Mass.; m. MARY DAVOL; b. Abt. 1802.
      xi. ALMEDIA BROWNELL, b. 20 Jan 1806, Westport, Mass.; m. ASA POTTER.

22. AMY[5] CHASE *(SARAH[4] MILK, JOB[3], JOHN[2], JOHN[1])* was born 19 Aug 1747 in Quaker Hill, Dutchess County, New York, and died 08 Jan 1835 in Hoosic Falls, New York[90]. She married ISAAC BULL III 1766[90], son of ISAAC BULL and REBECCA BROWNING. He was born 23 Mar 1745/46[90], and died 1837 in Hoosic Falls, New York. Both are buried in the Baptist Church Yard, Hoosick Falls, Rensselaer County, New York

Children of AMY CHASE and ISAAC BULL are:
- i. PEACE[6] BULL, b. 02 Nov 1767, Hoosic Falls, New York; d. 04 Nov 1841, Shinnston, Virginia (West Virginia)[91]; m. JOHN J. WALDO, 15 Jan 1786, Hoosick Falls, New York[92]; b. 16 Feb 1762, Windham, Connecticut[93]; d. 10 Dec 1840, Harrison County, Virginia (West Virginia)[93]. Had 10 children John J Waldo burial: Bridgeport Cemetery, Bridgeport, Harrison County, West Virginia, USA   John was a Baptist Minister.
- ii. SARAH BULL, b. 29 Jan 1769, Hoosic Falls, New York; m. JOSEPH DORR; b. Abt. 1769. Lived in Hoosick Falls and had 4 children.
- 56. iii. ESTHER BULL, b. 27 Oct 1770, Hoosic Falls, New York; d. 04 Nov 1866, Hoosic Falls, New York.
- iv. MORDECAI BULL, b. 1776, Hoosic Falls, New York; d. 1852; m. POLLY NORTHRUP; b. 19 Dec 1779.
- v. ARCHIBALD BULL, b. Abt. 1780, Hoosic Falls, New York; m. POLLY PIERCE; b. 1785; d. 1820. Lived in: Troy, NY.
- vi. REBECCA BULL, b. Hoosic Falls, New York; m. NATHANIEL BISHOP.
- vii. ABIGAIL BULL, b. 19 Jun 1781, Hoosic Falls, New York; m. BERNARDUS BRATT LOTTRIDGE, 04 Jun 1799; b. 1779.
- viii. PALSIPIANA BULL, b. 25 Feb 1783, Hoosic Falls, New York; m. DR. RUSSELL DORR; b. Abt. 1780.
- ix. MEHITABLE BULL, b. Hoosic Falls, New York; m. JOSEPH PARKER.
- x. HENRY BULL, b. Hoosic Falls, New York.

23. DAVID[5] CHASE *(SARAH[4] MILK, JOB[3], JOHN[2], JOHN[1])* was born 01 Feb 1752 in Dutchess County, New York, and died 26 Oct 1835 in White Creek, New York. He married (1) ABIGAIL SNYDAM. She was born 1757, and died 12 Dec 1813. He married (2) SALOMA ELDRIDGE. She was born Abt. 1760.

Child of DAVID CHASE and ABIGAIL SNYDAM is:
- i. MEHITABLE[6] CHASE, b. 1777, Hoosic Falls, New York; d. 27 Aug 1858; m. DAVID GOODING; b. 1769; d. 28 May 1846.

24. SARAH[5] MILK *(JOB[4], JOB[3], JOHN[2], JOHN[1])* was born 1749 in Amenia, Dutchess County, New York, and died 1830 in Hull, Quebec, Canada. She married DUDLEY MOORE 1768 in Amenia, Dutchess County, New York, son of JEDEDIAH MOORE and DOROTHY BEGNELL. He was born 1747 in Nine Partners, Dutchess County, New York, and died 1815 in Eardley, Quebec, Canada.

Children of SARAH MILK and DUDLEY MOORE are:
- i. GEORGE[6] MOORE.
- ii. SARAH MOORE, b. 1769, Saratoga Springs, Saratoga County, New York; d. 27 Aug 1834, Hull, Quebec, Canada.
- iii. JEDEDIAH DYER MOORE, b. 1771, Saratoga Springs, Saratoga County, New York; d. 1854, Hull, Quebec, Canada.
- 57. iv. DUDLEY MOORE, b. 08 Aug 1773, Saratoga Springs, Saratoga County, New York; d. 17 Mar 1852, Hull, Quebec, Canada.
- v. BENJAMIN MOORE, b. 1774, Saratoga Springs, Saratoga County, New York; d. 1815, Hull, Quebec, Canada.
- vi. ROGER MOORE, b. 1775, Rutland, Rutland County, Vermont; d. 1831, Nepean, Ontario, Canada.
- vii. MARTIN MOORE, b. 1776, Saratoga Springs, Saratoga County, New York; d. 18 Sep 1860, Eardley, Quebec, Canada.
- viii. REBECCA MOORE, b. 1785, Saratoga Springs, Saratoga County, New York; d. Ottawa, Kansas
- ix. JOB MOORE, b. 24 May 1791, Dorset, Bennington, Vermont; d. 03 Aug 1831, Hull, Quebec, Canada.
- x. DAVID MOORE, b. 04 Apr 1793, Saratoga Springs, Saratoga County, New York; d. 17 Mar 1852, Quebec, Quebec, Canada.
- xi. BENJAMIN MOORE, b. 1790, New York\Vermont; d. 1815, Falls, Texas.

25. JONATHAN[5] MILK *(JOB[4], JOB[3], JOHN[2], JOHN[1])* was born 1751[94]. He married PHEBE _____. She was born 1753[94]. Jonathan Milk is credited with the following services in the Revolutionary War: "Private, Capt. George King's Co., Col. Hopkins' (Berkshire Co.) regt.; entered service July 15, 1776; discharged Aug. 2, 1776; service, 18 days; company made up of detachments from four companies and marched to the Highlands, New York; also Corporal, Capt. Sylvanus Willcox's Co., Col. John Ashley's (Berkshire Co.) regt.; entered service Sep. 19, 1777; discharged Oct. 17, 1777, service 28 days, with Northern Army; also same Co. and Regt.; enlisted Oct. 15, 1780; service 2 days, on an alarm; company allowed horse rations". (Reference: *Mass. Soldiers and Sailors of the War of the American Revolution.*

Children of JONATHAN MILK and PHEBE _____ are:
58.   i.   ELKANAH[6] MILKS, b. 1776, Alford, Berkshire County, Massachusetts.
59.   ii. AMY MILKS, b. 05 Nov 1778, Alford, Berkshire County, Massachusetts; d. 21 Jul 1850, Stockbridge, Berkshire County, Massachusetts.
60.   iii. JOB MILKS, b. 1781, Alford, Berkshire County, Massachusetts; d. 11 May 1875, White Store, Chenango County, NY.
61.   iv. JOHN MILKS, b. 1786, Alford, Berkshire County, Massachusetts; d. Bet. 1860 - 1870, Canaan, Columbia County, New York.
62.   v.   JONATHAN MILKS, JR., b. Bet. 1789 - 1790, Alford, Berkshire County, Massachusetts; d. 03 Mar 1874, Maryland, Otsego County, NY.
      vi. MARY MILKS, b. Abt. 1779, Alford, Berkshire County, Massachusetts.

26. JOB[5] MILK *(JONATHAN[4], JOB[3], JOHN[2], JOHN[1])*[94,95,96,97] was born 1748 in Dartmouth, Massachusetts[98]. He married ELIZABETH _____[99] Abt. 1773. She was born 1753 in Connecticut[99,100], and died 25 Mar 1843 in Lee, Oneida County, NY[101,102] where she is buried in the Lee Valley Cemetery.
where Job Milk, b. between 1748-1755, Dartmouth, Mass. (son of Jonathan 1728), is shown on the Tax Lists of Amenia, Dutchess Co., NY, in 1775 and later.

He is not to be confused with his Uncle Job Milk Jr. (b. 1725, son of Job Sr. 1694) whose name appears on the Tax List of Crom Elbow, Dutchess Co., Feb 1756, and on the Tax List of Amenia (divided from Beekman Township) in June 1762. This Uncle Job Milk migrated to Alford, Berkshire Co., Mass., 1762-63 (see p. 49).

Job Milk Sr. (1694), his grandfather, lived in Pawling, the southern division of Beekman. The village of Pawling was the post office and business center for Quaker Hill. Grandfather Job, who had property interests at Quaker Hill as early as 1746, remained on the Dutchess Co. Tax Lists until 1778, when his name was replaced with "Job Milck's Widow."

In the Justice Court, Job Milk Jr. was involved in several suits after 1775. In the early years he was the debtor, but never for sums of more than one pound. In later years he was the collector of debts of nine and ten pounds. These suits may suggest he was in some business and his finances improved during these years.

Job Milk Jr. served in the Revolutionary War -- 6th Regt., Dutchess Co. Militia (New York in the Revolution, Roberts, p. 249).

In 1794, Job Milk of Amenia mortgaged his farm for £ 350, and two years later, "I, Job Milk of Pittstown, Rensselaer Co., NY, yeoman," deeded the same land "upwards of 100 acres" to Joseph Cook of Amenia. Job may have bought property from his brother Benjamin in Rensselaer Co., as a local historian has stated.

Later, Job may have followed some of his children to Canada, in line with a general movement from Rensselaer Co. at that time. The waterways pointing to the north, the Hudson River, Lake George, Lake Champlain, the St. Lawrence River, Lake Ontario, and the other Great Lakes, permitted easy access to lands in the North in early times. The great possibilities in lumbering, construction, farming, and fur trading intrigued many to take up homes in Canada.

According to the 1790 census of Amenia, Dutchess Co., NY, Job Milk had a family of four males under 16 years of age and five females, including his wife. He is shown in the 1800 census of Schaghticoke, Rensselaer Co., NY, as over 45 years of age, with two male children under 10 years of age, one male 10-16, one male 16-25, and one female 16-26 in addition to his wife over 45 years of age. The following are probably his descendants.:

Children of JOB MILK and ELIZABETH _____ are:
      i.   DAUGHTER-A[6] MILKS, b. Bet. 1774 - 1784. [Possibly the Mary Milks b1782-1783, died May 1, 1838, aged 55 years, buried in Lafayette, Onondaga Co., NY; married Russell Greene]
63.   ii. LEMUEL MILKS, b. Bef. 1775.
64.   iii. RUTH MILKS, b. 1775; d. 17 Feb 1853, Rome, Oneida Co, NY.

	iv.	SON-B MILKS, b. Bet. 1775 - 1784[104].
65.	v.	JOHN MILKS, b. Abt. 1781, United States.
66.	vi.	FREEMAN MILKS, b. Bet. 1785 - 1786.
	vii.	DAUGHTER-C MILKS, b. Bef. 1790.
	viii.	DAUGHTER-D MILKS, b. Bef. 1790.
	ix.	SON-D MILKS, b. Bef. 1790.
67.	x.	DAVID MILKS, b. Bet. 1793 - 1794, New York.
68.	xi.	FREEBORN GARRETTSON MILKS, b. 10 Aug 1797, New York; d. 06 Jul 1878, Kingsley, Michigan.
69.	xii.	SAMUEL MILK, b. 1799, New York; d. 23 May 1880, Wilson, Kalkaska County, Michigan.

27. BENJAMIN[5] MILK *(JONATHAN[4], JOB[3], JOHN[2], JOHN[1])* was born 1750 in Dartmouth, Mass., and died 06 Mar 1813 in Shandaken, Ulster County, New York[105]. He married LYDIA _____, daughter of BENJAMIN? _____ and ABIGAIL? _____. She was born Abt. 1750. Benjamin lived in Washington County, New York and served in the 14th Albany County Militia.

Children of BENJAMIN MILK and LYDIA _____ are:

	i.	ABIGAIL[6] MILK, b. Abt. 1770; m. MISTRE PALMER. Lived in: Ithaca, Tompkins County, New York
70.	ii.	MARIA MILK, b. Abt. 1770.
71.	iii.	JONATHAN MILK, b. Bet. 1774 - 1775, Albany County, New York; d. Bet. 1860 - 1870, Toledo, Lucas County, Ohio.
72.	iv.	BENJAMIN MILK, JR., b. 10 Oct 1780, Washington County, New York; d. 05 Jun 1856, Town of Jefferson, Schoharie County, New York.
	v.	BETSEY MILK, b. 1784. Lived in Summit, New York. (never married)
73.	vi.	TROWBRIDGE MILK, b. 22 Mar 1785, Milk Grove Farm, Valley Falls, New York; d. 11 Feb 1857, Greene County, New York.

28. DAVID[5] MILK *(JONATHAN[4], JOB[3], JOHN[2], JOHN[1])* was born 1752, and died 15 Jun 1806 in Milk Grove Farm, Valley Falls (Pittstown), NY[106]. He married PATIENCE _____. She was born 1757 in New York[106], and died 22 Apr 1845 in Valley Falls (Pittstown), NY[106].
   Both are buried in the Old Presbyterian, Schaghticoke, Rensselaer County, New York
Gravestone Inscriptions:
"David Milk   Died June 15, 1806 in the 55 year of his age."

O! Cease to drop the pensive tear,
Tho' dust to dust lies moulding here.
My better part has winged its way,
To regions of Immortal day.
I've gone the way that you must go,
I've paid the debt that you still owe.
I've try'd the world that's still untry'd,
By you who's lived and never died."

"PATIENCE   wife of DAVID MILK. Died April 22, 1845. in the 89, year of her age."

Children of DAVID MILK and PATIENCE _____ are:

74.	i.	EZRA[6] MILKS, b. 1781, Valley Falls, Renss. Co, NY; d. 19 Mar 1847, Green County, Wis..
75.	ii.	DAVID MILKS, b. Abt. 1785, Pittstown, Rensselaer County, New York.
76.	iii.	SILAS W. MILKS, b. 09 Jul 1786, Pittstown, Rensselaer County, New York; d. 02 May 1857, Valley Falls (Pittstown), NY.
	iv.	SARAH MILKS, b. Abt. 1787.
77.	v.	BENJAMIN MILKS, b. 20 Jul 1799; d. 1879, Allegany County, New York.

29. LEMUEL[5] MILK *(JONATHAN[4], JOB[3], JOHN[2], JOHN[1])* was born 1753 in Beekman, Dutchess County, New York[108], and died 1853[108]. He married MARY THURSTON Abt. 1773. She was born 12 Feb 1753 in New Port, Newport, Rhode Island to Thomas Thurston. Lemuel is buried in the Milks Burying Ground, West Seneca, New York. They lived on the west side of Lake George, near Bolton, New York

Children of LEMUEL MILK and MARY THURSTON are:
- i. CHILD[6] MILK, b. Bet. 1773 - 1785.
- 78. ii. PATIENCE MILK, b. Bet. 1773 - 1785; d. Abt. 1825, New York.
- 79. iii. MARY MILK, b. Abt. 1785; d. Abt Dec 1829, Sandy Hill/Hudson Falls, Washington County, New York.
- 80. iv. ELIZABETH 'BETSEY' MILK, b. 16 Jul 1787.
- 81. v. ABIGAIL MILK, b. Abt. 1790, New York; d. Aft. 1860.
- 82. vi. SARAH 'SALLY' MILK, b. 05 Jul 1787, Washington Co./Warren Co., NY; d. 16 Oct 1856, Otto, Cattaraugus Co., NY.
- 83. vii. BENJAMIN MILKS, b. 18 May 1794, Bolton Landing, Washington County, New York; d. 04 Jun 1874, Otto, Cattaraugus County, New York.
- 84. viii. JOB MILK, b. 18 Mar 1798, Bolton, Warren County, New York; d. 03 Feb 1864, Waukon, Allamakee County, Iowa.

30. REBECCA[5] MILK *(JONATHAN[4], JOB[3], JOHN[2], JOHN[1])* was born 18 Mar 1759, and died 24 Mar 1843 in Buffalo, New York. She married JAMES SIDWAY 14 Aug 1781 in Goshen, Orange County, New York. He was born 08 May 1759 in Dudley, Woodside, England, and died 18 Mar 1836 in Buffalo, New York. James was a drummer in the British Army at Saratoga (captured by American army). Both are buried in Forest Lawn Cemetery in Buffalo, New York.

Children of REBECCA MILK and JAMES SIDWAY are:
- 85. i. WILLIAM[6] SIDWAY, b. Abt. 1782, Goshen, Orange County, New York.
- 86. ii. JONATHAN SIDWAY, b. 01 Apr 1784, Goshen, Orange County, New York; d. 21 Jan 1847, Buffalo, Erie County, New York.

31. GEORGE[5] MILK *(JONATHAN[4], JOB[3], JOHN[2], JOHN[1])* was born Abt. 1762. He married UNKNOWN. She was born Abt. 1762.

The 1800 census of Providence, Saratoga County, New York shows a George Milk(s) between the ages of 26 and 45, with a wife in the same age range, one male under 10, two males 10-15, one male 16-25, two females under 10, and one female 10-15, a total of 7 children and nine people. Also shown, nearby in this census is another George and his family, that Croft mistook for George Milks. The name on the census page, though, is clearly George Mills, with the second "l" accentuated as though correcting a mistake. This second George (Mills) is also shown in the 1810 and 1820 census records with some of the same neighbors in the 1810 and 1820 censuses.

George Milk has not been found in the 1790 census, so it is likely that he was living with another family at that time, perhaps with his parents or with a sibling. Since he was married c1785, or before, and had at least two children in 1790 it might be possible to find him.

We have been unable to find any record for George Milk(s) - 1762 after the 1800 census. It is possible that he died before 1810 or that he was living with someone else who was listed as the head-of-household, and that could have been a son or a married daughter.

Children of GEORGE MILK and UNKNOWN are:
- i. SONONE[6] MILK, b. Bet. 1774 - 1784, New York.
- ii. DAUONE MILK, b. Bet. 1784 - 1790, New York.
- iii. SONTWOA MILK, b. Bet. 1784 - 1790, New York.
- iv. SONTWOB MILK, b. Bet. 1784 - 1790, New York.
- v. DAUTHREE MILK, b. Bet. 1790 - 1800, New York.
- vi. DAUTWO MILK, b. Bet. 1790 - 1800, New York.
- 87. vii. DAVID MILK, b. 1795, Washington County, New York; d. 17 Sep 1860, Leon, Cattaraugus County, New York.

32. JONATHAN[5] MILK *(JONATHAN[4], JOB[3], JOHN[2], JOHN[1])* was born 1769 in Massachusetts[108], and died Abt. 1849 in Dayton, Cattaraugus County, New York. He married (1) SOPHRONIA BENSON Abt. 1790. She was born Abt. 1770. He married (2) MARGARET ENGLISH Abt. 1795, daughter of LUKE ENGLISH and MARY PRINCE. She was born 1777 in Easton, Washington Co., New York[109], and died 1837 in Dayton, Cattaraugus Co., New York[109].

Jonathan Milk, b. 1769, in Mass. (son of Jonathan 1728), lived the early part of his married life near Easton,

Washington County, NY, where he is shown in the 1810 census.

In 1827 he was living near Perrysburg, Cattaraugus Co., NY, as evidenced in a deed recorded at Hudson Falls, Washington Co., NY, in which deed Jonathan Milk and his wife Margaret conveyed a "piece of land" near Easton to John Bragg and Jacob Hoag for $1,800; Isaac Waite, son-in-law of Jonathan, was witness. Part of the family moved to Cattaraugus Co., probably via the Erie Canal, opened in 1825, which means of transportation was used by other Milks families originating in Eastern, NY. History of Cattaraugus Co., pub. 1879, p. 482 states: "A class of Methodists were formed at Milk's schoolhouse about 1826 . . . . "

Also in the year 1827, in June, Jonathan Milk "of Washington Co." purchased a parcel of land near Dayton, Cattaraugus Co., from the Holland Land Co. "Jonathan Milk was first settler in the southern part of Town of Dayton." (See History of Cattaraugus Co., pub. 1893) Thereafter there are recorded in Little Valley, the county seat of Cattaraugus Co., numerous deeds showing land transfers to and from the children and nephews of Jonathan.

It is interesting to note that the lands purchased by the Holland Land Co. embraced an area of about 3,600,000 acres and were conveyed by the State of Massachusetts to Robert Morris in four deeds dated in 1791. Since originally aliens were legally incompetent to hold and convey real estate, the lands of the Dutch proprietors within the state of New York were purchased for their account from Robert Morris, and conveyed, for their benefit, to trustees. Cattaraugus Co. derived its name from the Seneca (Indian) word meaning "bad smelling banks", which probably referred to the odor of natural gas leaking from the seams of certain rocks lining the Cattaraugus River.

The Milk family proved prolific in Cattaraugus Co. and it may be safely stated that there are now more individuals bearing the name of Milk-Milks in Cattaraugus Co. than in any other section of the United States.

There were frequent Reunions of the Milks Family of Cattaraugus Co. held at the Fair Grounds, in Little Valley, until World War II. Upon some occasions there were as many as 600 members of the family in attendance.

The children of Jonathan Milk were probably all born near Easton, Washington Co., NY, where he is shown in the 1810 census as having a wife under 26 years of age and 6 children, 3 boys and 3 girls. History of Cattaraugus Co., pub. 1893, lists his children as: "John, Benjamin, Jonathan, Prince W., Luke, Mary, Bathsheba, Sarah, and Deborah."

Jonathan Milk m. (1) Sophronia Benson and probably only his two eldest children, Mary and John, were born of this union. (Mrs. Lucy Waite Watson, who lives near Cattaraugus, NY, has some silver teaspoons that belonged to Sophronia Benson.) Jonathan m. (2) Margaret English. The names of the parents of Margaret are not known, but she had brothers named George and Luke English and probably a married sister named Mary Green, as evidenced by a letter in possession of editor Grace Croft. Chn. b. in Washington Co., NY, of 1st m., 2:

The 1850 census for Napoli, Cattaraugus Co., shows that Jonathan was born in Mass.; and at the time of the census he was 81 years of age and was living with his son John. A letter written by his daughter Deborah in 1855 states: "Father is living with John and is well for a man his age." The home in which he passed his latter years is located on one of the highest hills near Napoli, where the Clyde Benson family now resides. Jonathan lived a long and useful life, and as an affectionate grandfather was frequently called upon to recount early pioneer and war stories. Dade Milks (Harvey R.) remembered climbing upon his grandfather Jonathan's lap and begging for the story of the "small boy" in the Revolution

Children of JONATHAN MILK and SOPHRONIA BENSON are:
88. i.   MARY[6] MILKS, b. 08 Jul 1791, Easton, Washington County, New York; d. 1870, Cattaraugus County, New York.
89. ii. JOHN MILK, b. 08 Oct 1793, Washington County, New York; d. 27 Aug 1859, Napoli, Cattaraugus County, New York.

Children of JONATHAN MILK and MARGARET ENGLISH are:
90. iii. DEBORAH[6] MILKS, b. 1798, Easton, Washington County, New York; d. Feb 1870, Easton, Washington County, NY.
91. iv. BENJAMIN MILKS, b. 01 Jun 1800, Washington County, New York; d. 13 May 1843, Persia, Cattaraugus County, NY.
92. v.   PRINCE WILLIAM MILKS, b. 1802, Washington County, New York; d. 12 Aug 1880, New Albion, Cattaraugus County, New York.
93. vi. BATHSHEBA MILKS, b. Abt. 1804, Washington County, New York; d. 05 Sep 1866, Olin, Jones County, Iowa.
94. vii. JONATHAN MILKS, JR., b. 1809, Washington County, New York; d. 26 Feb 1893, Sherman, Chautauqua County, NY.
95. viii. SARAH MILKS, b. 1812, Washington County, New York; d. 17 Mar 1884, Wauponsee Township, Grundy

County, Illinois.
- 96. ix. LUKE MILK, b. Jun 1812, Washington County, New York; d. 21 Nov 1890, Fairbank, Black Hawk County, Iowa.

33. LEMUEL[5] CHASE *(ABIGAIL[4] MILK, JOB[3], JOHN[2], JOHN[1])* was born 1765 in Beekman, Dutchess Co., NY, and died 1830 in Orangeville, Wyoming County, New York. He married AMY HORTON Abt. 1786. She was born Abt. 1765.

Children of LEMUEL CHASE and AMY HORTON are:
- i. WILLIAM[6] CHASE, b. 30 Apr 1787.
- ii. JOHN CHASE.
- iii. DAVID CHASE.
- iv. NATHAN CHASE.
- v. LEMUEL CHASE.
- vi. SQUIRE CHASE. [was a Missionary to Liberia]
- vii. BETHANA CHASE, m. ISAAC WARDWELL.
- viii. DELILA CHASE, m. TRALL WARDWELL.

34. JUSTUS[5] CHASE *(ABIGAIL[4] MILK, JOB[3], JOHN[2], JOHN[1])* was born 1762 in Beekman, Dutchess Co., NY, and died 1829. He married RUTH MOSIER. She was born Abt. 1765. Lived in: Providence, Saratoga County, New York

Children of JUSTUS CHASE and RUTH MOSIER are:
- i. ESTHER[6] CHASE, m. WILLIAM RHODES.
- ii. ROSANNA CHASE, m. WILLIAM CLOTHANT.
- iii. ABIGAIL CHASE, m. ISAAC PITCHER.
- iv. ELIZABETH CHASE, m. ISHMAEL COLE.
- v. ANNIS CHASE, m. MR. MAYER.
- vi. GEORGE CHASE.
- vii. JUSTUS CHASE.
- viii. DANIEL CHASE.
- ix. WALTER CHASE.
- x. STEPHEN CHASE, m. SARAH _____.

35. RHODA[5] CHASE *(ABIGAIL[4] MILK, JOB[3], JOHN[2], JOHN[1])* was born 10 Oct 1767 in Beekman, Dutchess Co., NY[110,111], and died 18 Sep 1848 in Adams, Jefferson County, New York[111]. She married ISAAC ROGERS, son of ISAAC ROGERS and SARAH ROSE. He was born 1759 in Westerly, Washington County, Rhode Island[111], and died 26 Jan 1846 in Adams, Jefferson County, New York[111]. Both are buried in Union Cemetery, Adams Center, Jefferson County, New York.

From the Follett Tree on ancestry.com: *Rhoda was the daughter of Nathan Chase, 1723-1806, and Abigail Milk, 1730-1774. According to the Sons of the America Revolution application for membership 63752, Nathan Chase was a patriot who joined the 14th regiment of the New York state militia.*

Children of RHODA CHASE and ISAAC ROGERS are:
- 97. i. ISAAC[6] ROGERS, JR., b. 1783, Rensselaer County, New York; d. 21 Feb 1869, Brownville, Jefferson County, New York.
- ii. NATHAN ROGERS, b. 1786, Rensselaer County, New York.
- iii. SARAH H. ROGERS, b. Rensselaer County, New York.
- iv. HANNAH ROGERS, b. Rensselaer County, New York.
- v. JOHN ROGERS, b. Rensselaer County, New York.
- vi. JONATHAN ROGERS, b. Rensselaer County, New York.
- vii. ABIGAIL ROGERS, b. Rensselaer County, New York.
- viii. STEPHEN JOHN ROGERS, b. Rensselaer County, New York.
- ix. ELISHA ROGERS, b. Rensselaer County, New York.
- x. OLIVE ROGERS, b. Rensselaer County, New York.

36. NATHAN[5] CHASE, JR. *(ABIGAIL[4] MILK, JOB[3], JOHN[2], JOHN[1])* was born 04 Jul 1768 in Beekman, Dutchess Co., NY, and died 06 Jun 1844. He married BETSEY SMITH 04 Jul 1786. She was born 21 May 1768, and died 12 Aug 1845.

They lived in Grafton and Hoosick, New York

Children of NATHAN CHASE and BETSEY SMITH are:
- i. OLLIVER[6] CHASE, b. 04 Oct 1788.
- ii. HANNAH CHASE, b. 18 Jan 1790; m. NATHANIEL WILDER; b. Abt. 1790.
- iii. LUCY CHASE, b. 17 Jan 1792; m. FRANCIS MITTLEBERG; b. Abt. 1790.
- iv. SIBYL CHASE, b. 1794; m. DANIEL JENKS; b. Abt. 1794.
- v. JOB CHASE, b. 1796.
- vi. SARAH CHASE, b. 1798; m. THOMS SMITH; b. Abt. 1798.
- vii. ASENATH CHASE, b. 1802; m. SETH WITHERELL; b. Abt. 1800.
- viii. ARCHIBALD CHASE, b. 1804, twin; m. ABIGAIL STURTEVANT; b. Abt. 1805.
- ix. LYDIA CHASE, b. 1804, twin; m. MARTIN WALDON; b. Abt. 1804.
- x. MARY CHASE, b. 1807; m. HIRAM STURTEVANT, 15 Jan 1829; b. Abt. 1805.
- xi. JOHN S. CHASE, b. 09 Aug 1809.

37. JOHN[5] CHASE *(ABIGAIL[4] MILK, JOB[3], JOHN[2], JOHN[1])* was born Jun 1774 in Hoosick Falls, Rensselaer Co., NY, and died 1865 in Fenner, New York. He married (1) DORCAS CHASE Abt. 1792, daughter of JOHN CHASE and DEBORAH WING. She was born Abt. 1775. He married (2) NOT KNOWN Aft. 1810. She was born Abt. 1775.

Children of JOHN CHASE and DORCAS CHASE are:
- i. ARCHIBALD[6] CHASE, b. 03 Oct 1794; d. 02 Oct 1795.
- ii. DEBORAH CHASE, b. 09 Oct 1795; m. BENAJAH MAYO; b. Abt. 1795.
- iii. DELIGHT CHASE, b. 25 Apr 1797; d. (unmarried).
- iv. HARRISON CHASE, b. 19 Jul 1798; m. ANNA WEBB; b. Abt. 1800.
- v. MELINDA CHASE, b. 22 Jun 1795; d. 1800.
- vi. THIRMA CHASE, b. 22 Jun 1800; m. (1) NELSON GROVER, Abt. 1818; b. Abt. 1800; m. (2) HALLETT HOLMES, Aft. 1818; b. Abt. 1800.
- 98. vii. ORRIN CHASE, b. 14 Jul 1802; d. 20 May 1875, Eaton, Madison County, New York.
- viii. JIRAH CHASE, b. 29 Jun 1806; m. PHOEBE RICE; b. Abt. 1806.
- ix. SIDNEY CHASE, b. 22 Aug 1807; m. EUNICE HUTTON; b. Abt. 1807.
- x. SYLVIA CHASE, b. 05 Sep 1809; m. (1) JOHN CROSEMAN, Nov 1827; b. Abt. 1809; m. (2) DENNIS/DANIEL HORTON, 01 Apr 1861; b. Abt. 1809.

Children of JOHN CHASE and NOT KNOWN are:
- xi. JOHN[6] CHASE.
- xii. EMILY CHASE.

38. DESIRE[5] CHASE *(ABIGAIL[4] MILK, JOB[3], JOHN[2], JOHN[1])* was born Abt. 1760 in Hoosick Falls, Rensselaer Co., NY[112], and died 20 Nov 1843 in Providence, Saratoga County, New York ?. She married (1) WILLIAM JOLLY 20 Jan 1776 in New Fairfield, Connecticut, by Rev. Elijah Sill[113]. He was born Abt. 1760, and died 20 Jan 1778 in Montgomery County, New York[113]. She married (2) IDIEL MAPES Bet. 1839 - 1843 in Saratoga County, New York. Both are buried in Woodard Cemetery, Saratoga County, New York.

William Jolly served Bet. 08 Jun 1777 - 20 Jan 1778, Pvt, NY Line, 1st Regt, Capt Hicks Company[114]

The widow, Desire Jolly's pension application states that Sally was an only child.

Child of DESIRE CHASE and WILLIAM JOLLY is:
- i. SALLY[6] JOLLY, b. 1777[115]; d. 25 Mar 1855, Saratoga County, New York[116]; m. SAMUEL MOSHER[116]; b. 10 Aug 1774[116,117]; d. 16 Apr 1854, Saratoga County, New York[118,119]. Both are buried in Woodard Cemetery, Saratoga County, New York

39. JOHN[5] MILK *(JOHN[4], JOHN[3], JOHN[2], JOHN[1])* was born Mar. 1765 in Boston, Massachusetts, and died 11 Jul 1808 in Boston, Massachusetts[120]. He married ELEANOR BODEN 06 Jun 1790 in New North Church, Boston, Massachusetts[121]. She was born Abt. 1765. John Milk was buried in Copp's Hill Burial Ground, Boston. Tombstone inscription: "*In memory of John Milk who died July 11, 1808, aged 43 years. He was valued in life and died lamented.*"

John Milk (1765) was born in Boston in 1765. He was baptized on 17 March 1765 at the New North Church. On 06

June 1790 he was married to Eleanor Boden/Bowden at the New North Church in Boston by the Rev. Mr. Clark. John and Eleanor had 5 children, at least 3 of whom died young before their father (see James Milk, Eleanor Milk & Susanna "Sukey" Milk. John Milk was probably a shipwright like his grandfather & father (both John Milk also).

John Milk (1765) died on 11 July 1808 at the age of 43 years. His death notice ran in The Democrat newspaper in Boston, MA for 13 July 1808. His funeral was held on 13 July 1808 at 4:30 PM at the Meeting House of Mr. Murray in Boston (probably Rev. John Murray founder of the Universalist denomination in Boston). Interestingly, the funeral notice invited all members of the Engine Companies of Boston & Charlestown to come to his funeral, as John Milk had been a Member of Engine Company Number 8 in Boston.

His Grandfather, John Milk (1708-1756) is at Memorial #40663796 (Copp's Hill Plot #F-289).

Children of JOHN MILK and ELEANOR BODEN are:

99.   i.   JOHN[6] MILK, b. 31 Mar 1791, Boston, Massachusetts; d. 26 Jan 1865, Boston, Massachusetts.
        ii.   JAMES MILK, b. 02 Jul 1792, Boston, Massachusetts[123]; d. 16 Jul 1792, Boston, Massachusetts[124].
        iii.   ELEANOR MILK, b. 21 Aug 1793, Boston, Massachusetts; d. 07 Nov 1794, Boston, Massachusetts[125].
        iv.   SUSANNA 'SUKEY' MILK, b. 31 May 1795, Boston, Massachusetts; d. 04 Aug 1802, Boston, Massachusetts[125].
100.   v.   ELEANOR MILK, b. Mar 1797, Boston, Massachusetts; d. 19 Feb 1867, Boston, Massachusetts.

40. ELIZABETH 'BETSEY'[5] MILK *(JOHN[4], JOHN[3], JOHN[2], JOHN[1])*[126] was born Abt. 1767 in Boston, Massachusetts?. She married THOMAS CHRISTY 09 Mar 1794 in New North Church, Boston, Massachusetts[127]. He was born Abt. 1765.

Child of ELIZABETH MILK and THOMAS CHRISTY is:
        i.   JOHN M.[6] CHRISTY, b. Abt. 1807, Boston, Suffolk, Mass.; d. 11 Nov 1877, Boston, Suffolk, Mass.. John was a marble worker, and never married.

41. JAMES[5] DEERING *(DORCAS[4] MILK, JAMES[3], JOHN[2], JOHN[1])* was born 23 Aug 1766 in Portland, Maine. He married ALMIRA ILSLEY.

Child of JAMES DEERING and ALMIRA ILSLEY is:
        i.   ELLEN MARIA[6] DEERING, d. 23 Jul 1857.

Generation No. 6

42. CYNTHIA[6] MILK (*LEMUEL[5], DAVID[4], JOB[3], JOHN[2], JOHN[1]*) was born 1768 in Westport, Bristol County, Massachusetts, and died 14 Jan 1814 in Scituate, Massachusetts. She married HOLDER WHITE, SR. 30 Aug 1788 in Dartmouth, Mass.[128], son of JONATHAN WHITE and ABIGAIL WING. He was born 1768 in Dartmouth, Massachusetts, and died 12 Jan 1853 in Westport, Massachusetts.

Children of CYNTHIA MILK and HOLDER WHITE are:
- i. AMY[7] WHITE, b. 1789, Westport, Massachusetts.
- ii. ALDEN WHITE, b. 1794, Westport, Massachusetts.
- iii. STEPHEN WHITE, b. 1794, Westport, Massachusetts.
- iv. LEMUEL WHITE, b. 1799, Westport, Massachusetts.
- v. TILLINGHAST WHITE, b. 1801, Westport, Massachusetts.
- vi. PHEBE WHITE, b. 1803, Westport, Massachusetts.
- vii. MARY WHITE, b. 1805, Westport, Massachusetts.
- viii. ABIGAIL WHITE, b. 1807, Westport, Massachusetts.
- 101. ix. DEBORAH WHITE, b. 1808, Westport, Massachusetts.
- x. WILLIAM G. WHITE, b. Westport, Massachusetts.
- xi. DAVID M. WHITE, b. Westport, Massachusetts.
- 102. xii. HOLDER WHITE, JR., b. 1812, Westport, Massachusetts.

43. WILLIAM[6] MILK (*LEMUEL[5], DAVID[4], JOB[3], JOHN[2], JOHN[1]*) was born 18 Oct 1783 in Westport, Bristol County, Massachusetts, and died Abt. 23 Aug 1866 in Fleming, Cayuga County, New York. He married (1) MARY HATHAWAY 10 Mar 1802 in Dartmouth, Mass.[128], daughter of PAUL HATHAWAY and SARAH WINSLOW. She was born 16 Oct 1779 in Dartmouth, Massachusetts, and died 14 Aug 1838 in Auburn, Cayuga County, New York. He married (2) ROWENA SHAW Abt. 1840 in Cayuga County, NY. She was born Mar 1798 in New Bedford, Massachusetts, and died Apr 1887 in Auburn, Cayuga County, New York. William was a blacksmith and also raised beef cattle.

The 1840 census for Fleming, Cayuga County, New York shows William Milk, aged 50-60 with a female aged 40-50 and two males, one aged 15-20 (b.1820-1835) and one aged 20-30 (b.1810-1820).

William and his wives are buried in: Ft. Hill Cemetery, Auburn, Cayuga County, New York
- William: Burial: Plot: Council Ground Lot 26 Grave 2,
- Mary: Burial: Plot: Council Ground Lot 26 Grave 3,
- Rowena: Burial: Plot: Council Ground Lot 26 Grave 1,

Children of WILLIAM MILK and MARY HATHAWAY are:
- i. OTHNEIL TRIPP[7] MILK, b. 1801, Massachusetts (Date??); d. 01 Sep 1825.
- 103. ii. DAVID MILK, b. Abt. 1806, Massachusetts; d. 20 Jul 1873, Cayuga County, New York.
- 104. iii. WILLIAM W. MILK, b. 1807, Massachusetts; d. 01 Dec 1871, Auburn, Cayuga County, New York.
- iv. GEORGE MILKS[129], b. Bet. 1808 - 1809, Seneca/Cayuga County, New York; d. May 1880, Wilson, Kalkaska County, Michigan; m. CHLOE COMSTOCK[129]; b. 1804, Adams, Massachusetts[130]; d. 20 May 1840, Fleming, Cayuga County, New York[131]. Chloe is buried in Arnold - Comstock Cemetery, (Old burying ground), Fleming North Hill, Cayuga County, NY

The "*History and Genealogy of the Comstock Family*" mentions a George Milks who was born in Cayuga County, New York and married Chloe Comstock from Adams, Massachusetts. Chloe is shown as dying in May 1840 in Fleming, Cayuga County, New York. No further mention of George is given.

The 1880 census of Wilson, Kalkaska County, New York shows a George Milks, widower, aged 71 born in New York living with a Keach family. The 1880 census of Persons who Died during the census year ending May 31, 1880, also shows that George, aged 71, died during the month of May 1880. No further information is available

- 105. v. CYNTHIA MILK, b. 10 Jun 1810, Cayuga County, New York; d. 28 Nov 1841, Fleming, Cayuga County, New York.
- 106. vi. CHARLES G. MILK, b. 02 Oct 1815, Cayuga County, New York; d. 27 Apr 1870, Auburn, Cayuga County, New York.
- vii. OBED H. MILK, b. 1818, Cayuga County, New York; d. 25 Jan 1838, Auburn, Cayuga County, New York.

Burial: Plot: Council Ground Lot 26 Grave 4, Ft. Hill Cemetery, Auburn, Cayuga County, NY
107. viii. LEMUEL MILK, b. 18 Oct 1820, Ledyard, Cayuga County, New York; d. 19 Jul 1893, Kankakee, Illinois.

44. JOHN[6] MILKS *(LEMUEL[5] MILK, DAVID[4], JOB[3], JOHN[2], JOHN[1])* was born Abt. 1790 in Westport, Bristol County, Massachusetts, and died in Will County, Illinois. He married (1) DIANTHA MAXWELL Abt. 1810. She was born Jun 1792 in Rutledge, VT, and died 02 Nov 1861 in Will County, Illinois[132]. He married (2) MELVINA LOVINA LAVALLA? 28 Aug 1865 in Will County, Illinois[133]. She was born Abt. 1814 in New York.

In 1853 John Milks was elected Street Commissioner for the newly incorporated village of Lockport, Will County, Illinois.

From: "*The History of Will County, Illinois*", : "Lockport is a grain market of considerable importance. Trade in grain began here on the opening of the Canal in 1848. ... John Milks .... was among the first who entered the business."

John Milks owned a sawmill at Lockport, Illinois. He was a Drummer Boy in the War of 1812, and is buried in the Lockport Cemetery. Lovina received a pension for John's service.

Children of JOHN MILKS and DIANTHA MAXWELL are:
108. i. ALANSON[7] MILKS, b. Abt. 1810; d. 10 Apr 1875, Morris, Illinois.
109. ii. VINCENT S. MILKS, b. Abt. 1814; d. Port Burwell, Elgin, Ontario, Canada.
       iii. ELIZA MILKS, b. Abt. 1815; m. MR. TYLER.
110. iv. LAURA ANN MILKS, b. 1817, New York; d. 23 Jan 1871, Wilmington, Illinois.
111. v. HARRIET MARIAH MILKS, b. Feb 1823, New York; d. 13 Aug 1902, Chicago, Cook County, Illinois.
112. vi. MARIAH E. MILKS, b. Abt. 1828, New York; d. Bet. 1880 - 1900, Lockport, Will County, Illinois.
113. vii. JANE OPHELIA MILKS, b. Aug 1833, New York; d. 1901, Waterloo, Black Hawk County, Iowa.

45. DAVID MILK[6] BROWNELL *(RHODA[5] MILK, DAVID[4], JOB[3], JOHN[2], JOHN[1])* was born 08 Oct 1789 in Dartmouth, Massachusetts, and died 30 Dec 1864. He married ZILPHA DAVOL Abt. 1815 in Dartmouth, Massachusetts ?. She was born 21 Oct 1797, and died 30 May 1864.

List of persons whose names have been changed in Massachusetts, 1780-1892
June 20, 1816. ...*David Brownell, of Westport, in the county of Bristol, son of George Brownell, late of said Westport, shall be allowed to take the name of David Milk Brownell;* ...

Children of DAVID BROWNELL and ZILPHA DAVOL are:
   i. HARRIET[7] BROWNELL, b. Abt. 1820; m. FREDERICK WHEELER BROWNELL; b. Abt. 1820.
   ii. RHODA M. BROWNELL, b. 26 Aug 1825; d. 22 Oct 1852; m. NATHANIEL W. WINCHESTER; b. Abt. 1825.
   iii. ADELAIDE BROWNELL, b. Abt. 1820; m. JAMES HARVEY SHERMAN; b. Abt. 1820.
   iv. GEORGE FRANK BROWNELL, b. Abt. 1820; m. NANCY JANE MACOMBER; b. Abt. 1820.
   v. RUTH LOUISE BROWNELL, b. Abt. 1820; d. 1858; m. WILLIAM HENRY GIFFORD; b. Abt. 1820.
   vi. EDMOND BROWNELL.
   vii. JULIA BROWNELL, b. 07 Oct 1833; m. JOHN WADY; b. Abt. 1830.
   viii. AMELIA S. BROWNELL, b. 07 Oct 1833; d. 27 May 1869.
   ix. EMILY S. BROWNELL, b. 05 Nov 1836; d. 12 Jul 1868; m. CHARLES H. FREELOVE; b. Abt. 1835.
   x. MARIA BROWNELL, b. 09 Aug 1842; d. 18 Sep 1875; m. GEORGE HANDY; b. Abt. 1840.

46. GEORGE MILK[6] BROWNELL *(RHODA[5] MILK, DAVID[4], JOB[3], JOHN[2], JOHN[1])* was born 15 Nov 1787 in Dartmouth, Massachusetts, and died Bet. 20 - 30 Sep 1830 in Westport, Massachusetts ?. He married (1) MARY DAVIS 19 Jul 1809[133], daughter of WILLIAM DAVIS and ELIZABETH _____. She was born Abt. 1790 in Of Maine. He married (2) FALLIE (DAVOL) TRIPP Abt. 1820. She was born 10 Oct 1797 in Of Tiverton, R.I., and died 08 Feb 1879.

Children of GEORGE BROWNELL and MARY DAVIS are:
114. i. AMY SHEPHERD[7] BROWNELL, b. 30 Oct 1814, Westport, Massachusetts; d. 25 Sep 1865, Westport, Massachusetts.
      ii. PHILIP BROWNELL, b. 1810, Westport, Massachusetts; d. d.y..
      iii. JOHN DAVIS BROWNELL, b. 05 Jun 1812, Westport, Massachusetts; d. 21 Apr 1894; m. (1) RHODA ALLEN HOWLAND; b. Abt. 1815; m. (2) ELIZABETH W. LITTLE; b. Abt. 1812; m. (3) ALMIRA RATHBONE; b. Abt. 1815.

Children of GEORGE BROWNELL and FALLIE TRIPP are:
- iv. MARY DAVIS[7] BROWNELL, b. 25 May 1824; d. 16 Jan 1860; m. FRANCIS W. TILTON; b. Abt. 1824.
- v. GEORGE A. BROWNELL, b. 15 Sep 1826; d. At Sea.
- vi. PHILIP H. BROWNELL, b. 04 Jun 1828; d. 29 Dec 1891; m. EMILY SOULE; b. Abt. 1830.
- vii. ANN ELIZA BROWNELL, b. 04 Aug 1830; m. LUTHER M. DAYTON; b. Abt. 1830.

47. SQUIRE[6] GIFFORD *(ISABEL[5] MILK, DAVID[4], JOB[3], JOHN[2], JOHN[1])* was born 14 Oct 1795, and died 06 Mar 1878 in New Bedford, Bristol County, Massachusetts. He married SOPHIA MACOMBER Abt. 1811. She was born 26 Jul 1795, and died 1889.

Children of SQUIRE GIFFORD and SOPHIA MACOMBER are:
- 115. i. ALFRED M.[7] GIFFORD, b. 06 Oct 1812.
- 116. ii. ALDEN M. GIFFORD, b. 06 Jul 1814; d. 1864.
- iii. HARRIET S. GIFFORD, b. 16 Sep 1816.
- 117. iv. MARY EARLE GIFFORD, b. 21 Oct 1818; d. 10 Sep 1895.
- 118. v. DAVID M. GIFFORD, b. 12 Jan 1820; d. 1884.
- vi. REBECCA M. GIFFORD, b. 25 May 1822.
- 119. vii. HARRIET S. GIFFORD, b. 19 Mar 1824.
- 120. viii. JOHN A. GIFFORD, b. 09 Mar 1826; d. 1864, New Bedford, Bristol County, Massachusetts.
- ix. CHRISTOPHER C. GIFFORD, b. 03 Dec 1829; m. MISS CHASE; b. Abt. 1830.
- x. JAMES H. GIFFORD, b. 01 Feb 1831.
- xi. WILLIAM A. GIFFORD, b. 12 Dec 1832; d. 1890.
- xii. CHARLES L. GIFFORD, b. 30 Apr 1836; m. SUSAN REED; b. Abt. 1836.
- xiii. HENRY H. GIFFORD, b. 21 Apr 1841.

48. JOHN[6] GIFFORD *(ISABEL[5] MILK, DAVID[4], JOB[3], JOHN[2], JOHN[1])* was born 09 Mar 1800 in Massachusetts[133,134], and died 10 Sep 1880 in Watertown, Jefferson County, New York[134]. He married DEBORAH FREEMAN GOTHAM 26 Jul 1827 in Watertown, Jefferson County, New York[135], daughter of JOHN GOTHAM and NANCY PENNIMAN. She was born Bet. 1810 - 1811 in New York[136,137], and died 09 Mar 1876 in Watertown, Jefferson County, New York[138].

John moved to the Watertown area in 1822 and married Deborah Freeman Gotham on July 26,1827. They had 13 children.

John and Deborah are buried in Brookside Cemetery, Watertown, Jefferson County, New York

Children of JOHN GIFFORD and DEBORAH GOTHAM are:
- i. FREDERICK HENRY[7] GIFFORD, b. 05 Apr 1828.
- ii. MARY ROWELL GIFFORD, b. 07 Mar 1829; m. MR. SHIPMAN. Lived in: Pitcairn, New York
- 121. iii. GEORGE WASHINGTON GIFFORD, b. 28 Aug 1830; d. 1905, Watertown, Jefferson County, New York.
- 122. iv. ALDEN GIFFORD, b. 21 Nov 1831.
- v. SUSAN C. GIFFORD, b. 12 Jul 1833; m. MR. GRANT; b. Abt. 1833. Lived in: E. Wrightstown, Wisconsin
- vi. CHARLES W. GIFFORD, b. 23 Dec 1834.
- vii. CORNELIA GIFFORD, b. 02 Jul 1836; m. MR. SHIPMAN; b. Abt. 1835. Lived in: Osseo, Wisconsin
- viii. NANCY D. GIFFORD, b. 28 Apr 1838.
- ix. JOHN GIFFORD, JR., b. 11 Jul 1840. Lived in: Watertown, Jefferson County, New York
- x. ISABEL M. GIFFORD, b. 13 Apr 1842; m. MR. ROSBROOK; b. Abt. 1840. Lived in: Pamelia, New York
- 123. xi. GUSTAVUS A. GIFFORD, b. 18 Jul 1844.
- xii. MARTHA ADELAIDE GIFFORD, b. 16 Jan 1847.
- xiii. BYRON GIFFORD, b. 07 Oct 1852; d. d.y..

49. LEWIS[6] DEUEL *(PATIENCE[5] MILK, DAVID[4], JOB[3], JOHN[2], JOHN[1])* was born Abt. 1782 in Hebron, New York. He married MARY 'NANCY' BARTON Abt. 1901. She was born Abt. 1785. Lived in: Saratoga, New York

Children of LEWIS DEUEL and MARY BARTON are:
- i. OSMYN MERRIT[7] DEUEL, b. 01 Jan 1802, Galway, Saratoga County, New York.
- ii. ALONZO DEUEL.
- iii. SALLEY DEUEL.

	iv.	MARY ANN DEUEL.
124.	v.	WILLIAM HENRY DEUEL, b. 31 Dec 1811, Greenfield, Saratoga County, New York; d. 01 May 1891, Escalante, Utah.

50. LILLYS[6] DEUEL *(PATIENCE[5] MILK, DAVID[4], JOB[3], JOHN[2], JOHN[1])* was born Aug 1785, and died 02 Oct 1832. She married ISAAC HOAG, son of JONATHAN HOAG and SARAH HALL. He was born 09 Dec 1784, and died 02 Oct 1859.

Children of LILLYS DEUEL and ISAAC HOAG are:

	i.	PHEBE[7] HOAG, b. 1812; d. 1825.
125.	ii.	JULIA E. HOAG, b. 24 Aug 1813.
126.	iii.	JANE HOAG, b. 25 Feb 1815, Saratoga County, New York; d. 30 May 1888, Easton, New York.
	iv.	ESTHER HOAG, b. 1816; d. 1838.
	v.	ELIAS HOAG, b. 1818; d. 1839.
	vi.	ABRAHAM HOAG, b. 1820; d. 1843.
	vii.	SARAH HOAG, b. 1823; d. 1832.
127.	viii.	JACOB HOAG, b. 20 Jan 1825; d. 06 Nov 1855.
	ix.	ISAAC HOAG, JR., b. 1827; d. 1838.
	x.	ANNA HOAG, b. 27 May 1829; d. 28 Mar 1881; m. ELISHA GIFFORD.
	xi.	MARY HOAG, b. 1831; d. 1856, Died in childbirth.; m. JOSHUA RICH.

51. ALICE[6] MILK *(JOB[5], DAVID[4], JOB[3], JOHN[2], JOHN[1])* was born 09 Jul 1783 in Westport, Bristol County, Massachusetts[139], and died 07 Apr 1866 in Westport, Bristol County, Massachusetts. She married ELIJAH BLOSSOM, JR. 23 Sep 1803 in Westport, Massachusetts, by Abner Brownell, Justice of Peace.. He was born 04 Aug 1779 in Freetown, Massachusetts, and died 18 Mar 1840 in Westport, Massachusetts.

Children of ALICE MILK and ELIJAH BLOSSOM are:

	i.	ELI[7] BLOSSOM, b. Mar 1805, Westport, Massachusetts; d. 16 Jun 1873, Westport, Massachusetts (Unm.). Eli was a blacksmith and a farmer.
	ii.	BENJAMIN B. BLOSSOM, b. 13 Sep 1807, Westport, Massachusetts; d. 12 Feb 1909, Westport, Massachusetts.
128.	iii.	BENJAMIN B. BLOSSOM, b. 17 Sep 1811, Westport, Massachusetts; d. 14 May 1880, Dartmouth, Mass..
	iv.	MARY HANDY BLOSSOM, b. 16 Apr 1813, Westport, Massachusetts; d. 09 Aug 1868, Westport, Massachusetts (Unm.).
129.	v.	CLARISSA BLOSSOM, b. 03 Jul 1815, Westport, Massachusetts (Twin); d. 1903, Westport, Massachusetts (Unm.).
	vi.	CLARINDA BLOSSOM, b. 03 Jul 1815, Westport, Massachusetts (Twin); d. 11 Dec 1838, Westport, Massachusetts.
130.	vii.	ESTHER B. BLOSSOM, b. 03 Sep 1821, Westport, Massachusetts; d. 23 Jul 1895, New Bedford, Massachusetts.
131.	viii.	BARNABAS BLOSSOM, b. 03 Oct 1825, Westport, Massachusetts; d. Bet. 1880 - 1900, Bristol County, Massachusetts.

52. JOHN[6] MILK *(JOB[5], DAVID[4], JOB[3], JOHN[2], JOHN[1])* was born 30 Aug 1786 in Westport, Bristol County, Massachusetts[140], and died 14 Jul 1876 in Westport, Bristol County, Massachusetts[141]. He married (1) BETSEY _____ Abt. 1809 in Massachusetts. She was born Abt. 1790, and died Abt. 1831 in Westport, Bristol County, Massachusetts. He married (2) EUNICE ALLEN 31 Dec 1832 in Orange, Grafton, NH ?[142]. She was born Abt. 1786. John lived in Orange, Grafton County, NH.

Child of JOHN MILK and BETSEY _____ is:

132.	i.	MARY M.[7] MILK, b. 10 Jan 1810, New Bedford, Massachusetts (adopted); d. 16 Aug 1886, Westport, Bristol County, Massachusetts.

53. ELI S.[6] MILK *(JOB[5], DAVID[4], JOB[3], JOHN[2], JOHN[1])* was born 12 Jan 1797 in Westport, Bristol County, Massachusetts[143], and died Dec 1852 in Hawleyton, Broome Co., NY[144]. He married MARGARET _____. She was born Abt. 1795 in New York, and died Apr 1875 in Hawleyton, Broome Co., NY[145].

There is some uncertainty about the birth year of Eli. His gravestone inscription says: "*Died Dec 1852, aged 65*", which would imply a birth in 1787. However there are two other records which put that "age 65" in doubt. There is a town clerk's record, for Westport, Bristol County, Massachusetts, which has his birth recorded as "January 12th AD 1797". Then the 1790 census for Job Milk and his family in Westport, shows only one male child "under the age of 16", and that should be John Milk, who was born August 30, 1786.

Eli is buried in Milk Cemetery, Hawleyton, Broome Co., NY. He lived in: 1850, Town of Chenango, Broome County, New York where he was a farmer. Margaret also is buried in the Milk Cemetery.

Military service: 1819, Lieutenant, in Major John McClave's Battalion, NY State Militia, Duanesburg, Schenectady County, New York

Children of ELI MILK and MARGARET _____ are:
- 133. i. JOHN[7] MILKS, b. 03 Jul 1813, Duanesburg, NY; d. 01 Jun 1890, Binghamton, Broome County, NY.
- ii. MARY MILKS, b. 1823, Duanesburg, NY[146,147]; d. 1861, Hawleyton, Broome Co., NY.
- 134. iii. DAVID MILKS, b. 1825, New York.
- 135. iv. PHEBE MILKS, b. 1826, Duanesburg, NY.
- 136. v. BENJAMIN B. MILKS, b. Jul 1828, Massachusetts; d. Abt. 1912, Binghamton, NY.
- vi. ABNER MILKS, b. Bet. 1828 - 1829, New York[148]; d. 1852, Hawleyton, Broome Co., NY.
- vii. MORTIMER MILK, b. 1834[149,150]; d. 1852, Hawleyton, Broome Co., NY[150].

54. JIRAH[6] BROWNELL *(ABIGAIL[5] MILK, DAVID[4], JOB[3], JOHN[2], JOHN[1])* was born 17 Jun 1786 in Westport, Mass., and died 13 Jan 1864. He married SARAH KIRBY. She was born Abt. 1786 in Massachusetts.

Child of JIRAH BROWNELL and SARAH KIRBY is:
- 137. i. EZRA PLUMMER[7] BROWNELL, b. 10 Aug 1819, Westport, Massachusetts; d. Bet. 1870 - 1880.

55. HOLDER WHITE[6] BROWNELL *(ABIGAIL[5] MILK, DAVID[4], JOB[3], JOHN[2], JOHN[1])* was born 16 Oct 1800 in Westport, Mass., and died 1861. He married LOVE G. BAKER. She was born 1806[151,152], and died 1899.

Child of HOLDER BROWNELL and LOVE BAKER is:
- i. MARY J.[7] BROWNELL, b. 1840; d. 1934; m. GEORGE SHERMAN, 1861.

56. ESTHER[6] BULL *(AMY[5] CHASE, SARAH[4] MILK, JOB[3], JOHN[2], JOHN[1])* was born 27 Oct 1770 in Hoosic Falls, New York, and died 04 Nov 1866 in Hoosic Falls, New York. She married ROBERT LOTTRIDGE 05 May 1792 in Albany, New York[153], son of THOMAS LOTTRIDGE and MARIA BRATT. He was born 23 Jul 1773, and died 14 Aug 1853 in Hoosic Falls, New York[154].

Both are buried in the Baptist Church Yard, Hoosick Falls, Rensselaer County, New York

Children of ESTHER BULL and ROBERT LOTTRIDGE are:
- 138. i. AMY[7] LOTTRIDGE, b. 15 Nov 1793, Hoosic Falls, New York; d. 15 Dec 1856, Troy, New York.
- 139. ii. THOMAS LOTTRIDGE, b. 18 May 1795, Hoosic Falls, New York; d. 09 Mar 1853, Hoosic Falls, New York ?.
- 140. iii. ISAAC BULL LOTTRIDGE, b. 08 Nov 1798, Hoosic, New York; d. 05 Jul 1855, Gilbert, New York.
- 141. iv. JOHN B. LOTTRIDGE, b. 31 Dec 1800, Hoosic Falls, New York; d. 24 Dec 1874, Hoosic Falls, New York.
- 142. v. MORDECAI LOTTRIDGE, b. 25 Oct 1802, Hoosic Falls, New York; d. 16 Jan 1884, Schenectady, New York.
- 143. vi. MARIA LOTTRIDGE, b. 25 Feb 1806, Hoosic Falls, New York; d. 02 Jan 1881, McArthur, Ohio.
- 144. vii. ROBERT LOTTRIDGE, JR., b. 10 May 1808, Hoosic Falls, New York.
- 145. viii. ELIZA LOTTRIDGE, b. 03 Jun 1810, Hoosic Falls, New York; d. 03 Sep 1858, McArthur, Ohio.
- 146. ix. DELIA LOTTRIDGE, b. 16 Jan 1812, Hoosic Falls, New York; d. 03 May 1894, Columbus, Mississippi.
- x. SARAH LOTTRIDGE, b. 24 Oct 1814, Hoosic Falls, New York; m. HIRAM K. DENNY/DENNING; b. Abt. 1814. No children.

57. DUDLEY[6] MOORE *(SARAH[5] MILK, JOB[4], JOB[3], JOHN[2], JOHN[1])* was born 08 Aug 1773 in Saratoga Springs, Saratoga County, New York, and died 17 Mar 1852 in Hull, Quebec, Canada. He married MARY MOULTON Abt. 1794. She was born 30 Jun 1774 in Newburyport, Essex, Massachusetts, and died 10 Oct 1845 in Hull, Quebec, Canada.

Children of DUDLEY MOORE and MARY MOULTON are:
- i. ABIGAIL[7] MOORE, b. 10 Feb 1795, Hull, Quebec, Canada; d. 06 Aug 1865, Hull, Quebec, Canada.
- ii. ELI MOORE, b. 08 Jun 1796, Rutland, Rutland County, Vermont; d. Mar 1870, Rutland, Rutland County, Vermont.
- iii. ELIAS MOORE, b. 08 Jun 1796, Rutland, Rutland County, Vermont; d. Mar 1870, Hull, Quebec, Canada.
- 147. iv. SARAH "SALLY" E. MOORE, b. 14 Oct 1799, Rutland, Rutland County, Vermont; d. 06 Jul 1880, Kingsley, Michigan.
- v. LEVI MOORE, b. 04 Jul 1802, Rutland, Rutland County, Vermont; d. 02 Jun 1877, Hull, Quebec, Canada.
- vi. ELIAS MOORE, b. 08 Dec 1804, Hull, Quebec, Canada; d. 23 Aug 1885, Renfrew, Ontario, Canada.
- vii. LEONARD MOORE, b. 27 Aug 1807, Rutland, Rutland County, Vermont; d. 1831, Hull, Quebec, Canada.
- viii. HANNAH MOORE, b. 30 Nov 1809, Hull, Quebec, Canada; d. 1825, Hull, Quebec, Canada.
- ix. OLIVE MOORE, b. 05 Sep 1813, Ottawa, Ontario, Canada; d. 06 Mar 1814, Ottawa, Ontario, Canada.
- x. MAHITABLE MOORE, b. 05 Feb 1815, Hull, Quebec, Canada; d. 1818, Hull, Quebec, Canada.
- 148. xi. DAVID MOORE, b. 20 Jan 1819, Hull, Quebec, Canada; d. 26 Jan 1901, North Ogden, Weber, Utah.
- xii. JAMES MOORE, b. 1830, ?.

58. ELKANAH[6] MILKS (*JONATHAN[5] MILK, JOB[4], JOB[3], JOHN[2], JOHN[1]*) was born 1776 in Alford, Berkshire County, Massachusetts. He married MARY WATERMAN Abt. 1800 in Berkshire County, Massachusetts?. She was born 1778 in Connecticut. In 1800 they lived in Alford, Berkshire County, Massachusetts

Child of ELKANAH MILKS and MARY WATERMAN is:
- i. SONONE[7] MILKS[155], b. Bet. 1800 - 1819.

59. AMY[6] MILKS (*JONATHAN[5] MILK, JOB[4], JOB[3], JOHN[2], JOHN[1]*) was born 05 Nov 1778 in Alford, Berkshire County, Massachusetts[156], and died 21 Jul 1850 in Stockbridge, Berkshire County, Massachusetts. She married EPHRAIM I. ANDREWS Abt. 1800. He was born 1772, and died 16 Apr 1824 in Austerlitz, New York.

At this time (2012) there is no direct evidence that Amy was a daughter of Jonathan and Phebe, however, circumstantial evidence points to it, so we will go with it until we can prove otherwise. She is buried in South Cemetery, West Stockbridge, Berkshire County, Massachusetts. along with Ephraim.

Some of the data and much of the personal comments are courtesy of Dennis Lamoureux. denlamour@yahoo.com

Children of AMY MILKS and EPHRAIM ANDREWS are:
- 149. i. SALLY[7] ANDREWS, b. 29 Aug 1801, Austerlitz, Columbia County, New York; d. 13 Feb 1874, West Stockbridge, Berkshire County, Massachusetts.
- ii. PHEBE ANDREWS, b. Austerlitz, New York.
- iii. AMY ANDREWS, b. Austerlitz, New York; m. CHESTER WILCOX; b. Of Johnstown, New York.

60. JOB[6] MILKS (*JONATHAN[5] MILK, JOB[4], JOB[3], JOHN[2], JOHN[1]*) was born 1781 in Alford, Berkshire County, Massachusetts, and died 11 May 1875 in White Store, Chenango County, NY. He married SALLY FIELDS Abt. 1808. She was born 1788, and died 08 Sep 1848 in White Store, Chenango County, NY.

Job was a miller in the Town of Guilford, Chenango County, NY. He and Sally are buried in Greenwood Cemetery, White Store, Chenango County, NY

Children of JOB MILKS and SALLY FIELDS are:
- 150. i. PHOEBE[7] MILKS, b. Bet. 1809 - 1810, New York; d. Fayette, Iowa.
- 151. ii. ICHABOD MILKS, b. Abt. 1810, New York; d. Bet. 1843 - 1849, Lewis County, New York.
- 152. iii. DAVID MILKS, b. Abt. 1812, Massachusetts; d. Jan 1884, Gilbertsville, Otsego County, New York.
- 153. iv. MARIA MILKS, b. 1818, New York; d. 12 Mar 1889, White Store, Chenango County, New York.
- 154. v. JOHN/JONATHAN L. MILKS, b. 1821, New York; d. 21 Jun 1905, Scott Depot, Putnam County, West Virginia.
- 155. vi. EBENEZER MILKS, b. 17 Apr 1827, New York; d. 19 Nov 1902, Sidney, Delaware County, New York.
- vii. EMILY MILKS, b. 17 Jun 1830, New York[157]; d. 18 Jul 1853[157]. Burial: Pope Cemetery, Otego, Otsego County, New York

61. JOHN[6] MILKS *(JONATHAN[5] MILK, JOB[4], JOB[3], JOHN[2], JOHN[1])* was born 1786 in Alford, Berkshire County, Massachusetts, and died Bet. 1860 - 1870 in Canaan, Columbia County, New York. He married SYLVIA GRAVES 08 Apr 1812[158]. She was born 1792 in of Albany, NY, and died Bet. 1880 - 1900 in Canaan, Columbia County, New York.

Children of JOHN MILKS and SYLVIA GRAVES are:
156.   i.   HARRIETT EMELINE[7] MILKS, b. 1813, New York.
157.   ii.   CHARLES ROLLAND MILKS, b. 24 Jun 1815, New York.
          iii.   RICHARD G. MILKS, b. 1825.

62. JONATHAN[6] MILKS, JR. *(JONATHAN[5] MILK, JOB[4], JOB[3], JOHN[2], JOHN[1])* was born Bet. 1789 - 1790 in Alford, Berkshire County, Massachusetts[159], and died 03 Mar 1874 in Maryland, Otsego County, NY[160]. He married LAURA A. EVENCE/EVEREST Abt. 1815. She was born 15 Jun 1792 in Connecticut[161], and died 01 Apr 1882 in Maryland, Otsego County, NY[162]. Jonathan and Laura are buried in Elk Creek Cemetery, Maryland, Otsego Co., NY

John's gravestone inscription:
*"Let me go for the morning is breaking,
Let me go I no longer can wait,
I'll away to the land of the living,
Where I'll wait for you all at the gate."*

Children of JONATHAN MILKS and LAURA EVENCE/EVEREST are:
158.   i.   ELKANAH B.[7] MILKS, b. 13 Aug 1816, Otsego County, New York; d. 29 Jul 1897, Maryland, Otsego County, New York.
159.   ii.   MARY ANN MILKS, b. 21 Dec 1820, Otsego County, New York; d. 23 Apr 1872, Otsego County, New York.
160.   iii.   CHRISTINE MILKS, b. 08 Oct 1821, Otsego County, New York; d. 06 Jun 1896, Otsego County, New York.
161.   iv.   LAURA JANE MILKS, b. 1824, Otsego County, New York; d. 07 Apr 1882, Otsego County, New York.
          v.   HARRIET MILKS, b. 1828, Otsego County, New York; d. Abt. 1868, Westford, Otsego County, New York; m. WILLIAM KINGSLEY[163]; b. 1818, of Westford, Otsego County, New York; d. Bet. 1892 - 1900, Westford, Otsego County, New York. No children. Burial: Westford, Otsego County, New York

          vi.   JULIA MILKS, b. 14 Apr 1830, Otsego County, New York[164]; d. 23 Feb 1905, Maryland, Otsego County, NY[164]; m. CLAY BECKER[165], Abt. 1869, Otsego County, New York; b. Abt. 1843, New York.
             March 3, 1905, The Otsego Farmer, page 6
             The funeral of Mrs. Julia Milks, who died at Schenevus was held at the house of C.W. Patrick on Saturday with interment in Elk Creek cemetery. Rev. A. Clarke officiating. Burial: Elk Creek Cemetery, Maryland, Otsego County, New York, USA
             Grace Croft had Julia as marrying a Mr. Clapper, however there is no evidence of that. Julia is shown living with her parents in the 1850 and 1860 census records. In the 1870 census she is shown married to Clay Becker, living in Westford, Otsego County, New York. Her parents, Jonathan, 83 and Laura 79 are also living with them. In the 1880 census, Julia and Laura are shown living together and both are recorded as "Widowed". In the 1900 census, Julia is living with the German Wright family in Maryland, Otsego County and is listed as "widowed" and as a "nurse" There is no census record showing Julia with any children.

          vii.   JOHN MILKS, b. 24 Feb 1834, Otsego County, New York[166]; d. 09 Mar 1878, Maryland, Otsego County, NY[167]; m. ANGELA _____, Bet. 1863 - 1870, Otsego County, New York; b. Jan 1836, New York[168]; d. 31 Mar 1881, Maryland, Otsego County, NY[169]. Registered for the draft (Civil War) in June 1863. Listed as 'single'. He and Angela are buried in
Elk Creek Cemetery, Maryland, Otsego Co., NY. In the 1865 NY state census, John was listed as a "Constable".

63. LEMUEL[6] MILKS *(JOB[5] MILK, JONATHAN[4], JOB[3], JOHN[2], JOHN[1])* was born Bef. 1775. He married UNKNOWN WIFE. She was born Bef. 1775.
     In the 1810 census Lemuel is shown in Washington County, New York. He is shown with 2 male children, 2 female children and a wife. None of their names have been discovered.

Children of LEMUEL MILKS and UNKNOWN WIFE are:
- i. DAUGHTERA[7] MILKS, b. Bet. 1784 - 1790.
- ii. SONA MILKS, b. Bet. 1784 - 1790.
- iii. DAUGHTERB MILKS, b. Bet. 1791 - 1800.
- iv. SONB MILKS, b. Bet. 1791 - 1800.

64. RUTH[6] MILKS *(JOB[5] MILK, JONATHAN[4], JOB[3], JOHN[2], JOHN[1])*[170] was born 1775[170], and died 17 Feb 1853 in Rome, Oneida Co, NY[171]. She married ADONIJAH BARNARD[172]. He was born Bet. 1769 - 1770[173], and died 25 Jul 1843 in Lee, Oneida County, NY[174]. Both are buried in Lee Valley Cemetery.

As noted in Dolly Creggar Morgan's genealogy research notes: Ruth Milks is the ggg grandmother of Dick Clark (American Bandstand).

Children of RUTH MILKS and ADONIJAH BARNARD are:
- i. ELIZABETH 'BETSEY'[7] BARNARD, b. 11 Mar 1794, Rome, Oneida County, New York; d. 28 Jul 1864; m. MARTIN MILLER.
- 162. ii. POLLY BARNARD, b. 13 Mar 1796, Rome, Oneida County, New York; d. 29 Jan 1864, Lee, Oneida County, New York.
- iii. JOHN BARNARD, b. 02 Mar 1798, Rome, Oneida County, New York; d. 06 Oct 1864, Lee Center, Oneida County, New York.
- iv. SAMUEL BARNARD, b. 1800, Rome, Oneida County, New York; d. 1801, New York.
- v. BENJAMIN BARNARD, b. 26 Feb 1802, Rome, Oneida County, New York; d. 01 Feb 1864, New York; m. SARAH ANN DINGMAN. They had 3 sons and 3 daughters.
- vi. JOBE BARNARD, b. 17 Dec 1803, Rome, Oneida County, New York; d. 01 Feb 1870, Rome, Oneida County, New York.
- 163. vii. GEORGE BARNARD, b. 12 Oct 1805, Rome, Oneida County, New York; d. 06 May 1868, Rome, Oneida County, New York.
- viii. ANNE MARIE BARNARD, b. 08 Jul 1808, Rome, Oneida County, New York; d. 01 Dec 1810, New York.
- 164. ix. ADONIJAH BARNARD, JR., b. 05 Mar 1811, Rome, Oneida County, New York; d. 03 Feb 1891, Oneida County, New York.
- x. HANNAH BARNARD, b. 21 Mar 1813, Rome, Oneida County, New York; d. 1880.
- 165. xi. HARRIET BARNARD, b. 11 Apr 1815, Rome, Oneida County, New York; d. 19 Mar 1875, New York.

65. JOHN[6] MILKS *(JOB[5] MILK, JONATHAN[4], JOB[3], JOHN[2], JOHN[1])* was born Abt. 1781 in United States[175]. He married ELEANOR _____. She was born Abt. 1801 in Ireland[175]. In 1842 in Eardley, Quebec, John lived next door to F. G. Milk (Freeborn Garrettson). John is shown in a family of 4 at that time. JOHN MILKS and ELEANOR had three childrenn[176].

66. FREEMAN[6] MILKS *(JOB[5] MILK, JONATHAN[4], JOB[3], JOHN[2], JOHN[1])* was born Bet. 1785 - 1786[177]. He married EXPERIENCE _____. She was born 31 Mar 1787[177,178], and died 25 May 1852 in Lee, Oneida County, NY[178].

In 1850 George lived in: 1850 in Lee, Oneida County, NY next door to George & Melissa Milks.

Experience is buried in Lee Valley Cemetery. Freeman and Experience had at least 5 children, but the names of three of them, born between 1804 and 1820 are unknown.

Freeman and his second wife, Afinity, were living in the Poor House in Onondaga County, New York on 13 Apr 1868 [Book PH, #3, Page 197]. Afinity could have been a sister of Freeman, instead of his wife. I have no data either way, other than the facts that they were living together in 1860 and both were in the Poor House in Onondaga County in 1868

Children of FREEMAN MILKS and EXPERIENCE _____ are:
- i. CORNELIA[7] MILKS, b. 30 Sep 1824[179]; d. 08 May 1842, Lee, Oneida County, NY[180]. Burial: Lee Valley Cemetery, Oneida Co., NY[181]
- 166. ii. GEORGE MILKS, b. Bet. 1822 - 1823; d. Bef. Apr 1880, New York.

67. DAVID[6] MILKS *(JOB[5] MILK, JONATHAN[4], JOB[3], JOHN[2], JOHN[1])* was born Bet. 1793 - 1794 in New York. He married SARAH INMAN[182,183]. She was born Abt. 1803 in New York.

From Croft: *David Milks, b. abt. 1793, migrated to Canada and there married a French girl named Julia LaVern.*

He later lived in New York, where some of his children were born.

David and his wife are shown in the 1840 census of Peru Tp. Huron Co., Ohio, as of 40-50 years of age, with a family consisting of two males under 5 years, one male between 15-20 years, one female 5-10, one female 10-15, and one female 20-30 years. Before the 1850 census, David moved prob. to Michigan. However, in Peru Tp.. in the 1850 census were Moses Milk, aged 30, and Robert Milk, aged 21, undoubtedly sons of David; the revelation of their birthplace as New York is of significance.

David was said to have had double teeth all around. He hoed ten acres of corn at the age of 93 when he visited his son Robert. He reportedly had 13 children, including probably all of the following (Marriage Records, Huron Co., Ohio):

Children of DAVID MILKS and SARAH INMAN are:

      i. J.[7] MILKS[184], b. ????.
167.   ii. MOSES MILKS, b. Abt. 1820, New York.
     iii. SAMANTHA MILKS, b. Abt. 1820; m. OLIVER SMITH, 01 Nov 1840, Huron County, Ohio , By Levi R. Sutton, JP[184,185]; b. Abt. 1820.
168.   iv. SARAH S. MILKS, b. 21 Oct 1824, Pennsylvania; d. 13 Oct 1909, Townsend Twp., Huron County, Ohio.
169.   v. ROBERT DUDLEY MILKS, b. Bet. 1828 - 1829, New York\Pennsylvania; d. 19 Feb 1907, Coldwater, Branch County, Michigan.
     vi. ARHTABERLER? MILKS, b. Abt. 1831, New York.
     vii. MARLA? MILKS, b. Abt. 1833, Pennsylvania?.
     viii. MARY A. MILKS, b. Abt. 1835, Pennsylvania?.
     ix. MARTHA JANE MILKS, b. Bet. 1837 - 1838, Ohio[186]; m. (1) MARION MCKISSON, 08 Apr 1861, Cuyahoga County, Ohio[187]; b. Abt. 1835; m. (2) CHARLES W. CURTIS, 01 Jan 1882, Grand Rapids, Kent County, Michigan[188]; b. 1847, New York City; m. (3) ANDREW J. ROGERS, 14 Mar 1888, Grand Rapids, Kent County, Michigan[189]; b. 1834, New York[190].
170.   x. GEORGE JEROME MILKS, b. 15 Nov 1841, Huron County, Ohio (See Croft, p72); d. 08 Apr 1915, State Hospital, Traverse City, Michigan.
171.   xi. CATHERINE LUCRETIA 'KATE' MILKS, b. Bet. 1842 - 1843, Ohio.
     xii. LUCINDA MILKS, b. Bet. 1844 - 1845, Ohio[191].

68. FREEBORN GARRETTSON[6] MILKS *(JOB[5] MILK, JONATHAN[4], JOB[3], JOHN[2], JOHN[1])* was born 10 Aug 1797 in New York, and died 06 Jul 1878 in Kingsley, Michigan. He married SARAH "SALLY" E. MOORE[192] Abt. 1819, daughter of DUDLEY MOORE and MARY MOULTON. She was born 14 Oct 1799 in Rutland, Rutland County, Vermont, and died 06 Jul 1880 in Kingsley, Michigan.

Freeborn was undoubtedly named after the Reverend Freeborn Garrettson, prominent Methodist evangelist for some fifty years, who owned property in Dutchess, Delaware, and Ulster Counties, NY, and who lived in Rhinebeck, Dutchess Co. The Reverend lived only fifteen miles from Job Milk in Amenia. The Reverend is also of record in deeds for the sale of property to Benjamin Milk (see p. 96). Of interest, also, is the similarity in the names of the descendants of Freeborn Garrettson Milks and David Milk (born 1752) who lived in Rensselaer Co., NY.

As a young man 17 years of age, Freeborn Garrettson Milks moved to Eardley, Quebec, Canada, where he followed the trade of carpenter and millwright, which occupations were practiced by many of his progeny. He is listed in the 1842 census of Eardley as possessing a family of 8. He is also shown in the 1861 census as living in a "blockhouse", with his wife Sarah and children: Mary, Charles, Almira, and Peter and his family.

Later in life, Freeborn returned to the United States, as evidenced by a Land Patent dated 25 Apr 1877 issued by Rutherford B. Hayes, then President of the United States, to Freeborn Garrettson Milk, for a tract of land in Grand Traverse Co., Mich. (Liber 15 of Deeds, p. 326, Grand Traverse Co.). He homesteaded 40 acres of land four miles east of Kingsley, Mich. On 15 June 1878 this parcel of land was deeded by Freeborn and his wife Sarah M. to their son Peter Milks. The log house Freeborn built still stands, although some years ago it was bought, taken down and reassembled on the Main Road on the 40 acres north of his homestead. Chn. b. in Eardley, Que., Can., 13:

Freeborn and Sarah were second cousins. Their grandfathers Job and Jonathan Milk were brothers, the sons of Job Milk and Abigail Devol (Davol). Both are buried in Evergreen Cemetery, Kingsley, Mich., on the 5th lot inside the north main gate of the original cemetery on the east side of the main driveway, a tombstone marking the place.

Children of FREEBORN MILKS and SARAH MOORE are:
172.   i. RICHARD[7] MILKS, b. 16 Apr 1820, Eardley, Quebec; d. 18 Jul 1903, Paradise, Michigan (Bright's disease).
173.   ii. BENJAMIN MILKS, b. 05 Jun 1821, Eardley, Quebec, Canada; d. 09 Apr 1905, Eardley, Quebec, Canada.

174.	iii.	AMBROSE MILKS, b. Apr 1823, Quebec, Canada; d. 1856, Quyon, Quebec, Canada.
175.	iv.	JOHN MILKS, b. 25 Apr 1824, Eardley, Quebec, Canada; d. 20 Jan 1895, Cantley, Quebec.
	v.	CATHERINE "KATE" MILKS, b. Abt. 1825, Eardley, Quebec, Canada.
	vi.	NELSON MILKS, b. Abt. 1827.
176.	vii.	DAVID MILKS, b. 10 May 1829, Eardley, Quebec, Canada; d. 01 Mar 1904, Eardley, Quebec, Canada.
	viii.	HECTOR MILKS, b. 10 May 1830, Cantley, Quebec[193]. Cause of Death: Tuberculosis
177.	ix.	MELISSA MILKS, b. 29 Mar 1832, Eardley, Quebec, Canada; d. 23 Oct 1907, Paradise Twnp, Grand Traverse Co., Michigan.
	x.	MARY MILKS, b. 04 Mar 1833, Quebec, Canada[194,195]; d. 26 May 1907, Paradise, Grand Traverse County, Michigan[196]; m. JEREMIAH PRICE[197], 20 Aug 1874, Paradise, Grand Traverse County, Michigan[197]; b. Bet. 1824 - 1825, Fife Lake, Michigan[197]; d. 09 Mar 1898, Paradise, Grand Traverse County, Michigan. No children.
178.	xi.	CHARLES MILKS, b. Apr 1835, Eardley, Quebec, Canada; d. 19 Dec 1926, Coleman, Temiskaming, Ontario, Canada.
179.	xii.	PETER MILKS, b. 25 Dec 1837, Eardley Twp., Quebec, Canada; d. 14 Jun 1918, Kingsley, Paradise Township, Mich.
180.	xiii.	ALMIRA MILKS, b. Bet. 1842 - 1843, Eardley, Quebec, Canada; d. Aft. 15 Apr 1910, Snohomish, WA.

69. SAMUEL⁶ MILK (JOB⁵, JONATHAN⁴, JOB³, JOHN², JOHN¹) was born 1799 in New York[198,199], and died 23 May 1880 in Wilson, Kalkaska County, Michigan[200]. He married PHEBE GILES[201]. She was born 1807 in New York[202,203], and died Bet. 1870 - 1880 in Chautauqua County, New York?. Samuel is buried in Evergreen Cemetery, Village of Kalkaska ??

Children of SAMUEL MILK and PHEBE GILES are:

181.	i.	GILES⁷ MILKS, b. 1827, New York; d. 25 Oct 1893, Kalkaska County, Michigan.
182.	ii.	HELEN L. MILKS, b. 1834, New York.
	iii.	ELIZABETH MILKS[205], b. Bet. 1835 - 1836, New York[205].
183.	iv.	ESTHER ANN (HESTER) MILKS, b. Aug 1838, New York; d. 31 Jan 1917, Fremont, Isabella County, Michigan.
	v.	MARY MILKS[205], b. 1841, New York[205].

70. MARIA⁶ MILK (BENJAMIN⁵, JONATHAN⁴, JOB³, JOHN², JOHN¹)[206] was born Abt. 1770. She married PIETER GOEWY[206] 23 May 1792 in Schaghticoke Dutch Reformed Church, Schaghticoke, Saratoga, NY[207,208], son of JOHN GOEWAY and MARY _____. He was born 16 Aug 1763[209], and died Jun 1806 in Brunswick, Rensselaer County, New York[209]. Maria and Pieter are buried in Goeway Cemetery, Brunswick, Rensselaer County, NY

Children of MARIA MILK and PIETER GOEWY are:
- i. DANIEL⁷ GOEWY, b. 17 Feb 1795, Albany, NY[210].
- ii. JOHN GOEWY, b. 15 Sep 1798[211]. Baptism: 18 Mar 1799, Gilead Lutheran Church, Brunswick, NY
- iii. BENJAMIN GOEWY, m. PHEBE _____.
- iv. JACOB GOEWY, m. MARY ANN _____.. Lived in: 1860, Richfield, Otsego County, New York
- v. SOLOMON GOEWY.

71. JONATHAN⁶ MILK (BENJAMIN⁵, JONATHAN⁴, JOB³, JOHN², JOHN¹) was born Bet. 1774 - 1775 in Albany County, New York[212], and died Bet. 1860 - 1870 in Toledo, Lucas County, Ohio. He married MARY _____ Abt. 1795 in Ulster County, NY ?. She was born Bet. 1776 - 1777 in Long Island City, Queens, NY?, and died Bet. 1850 - 1860 in Dryden, Tompkins County, New York ?.

The area of Albany County where Jonathan and his parents lived, in 1790, became Rensselaer County in 1791. Jonathan lived in Dryden, Tompkins County, New York between 1830 and 1850.

Children of JONATHAN MILK and MARY _____ are:
- i. DAUA⁷ MILK[213], b. Bet. 1795 - 1800, Town of Middletown, Ulster County, New York.
- ii. SONA MILK[214], b. Abt. 1800, Shandaken, Ulster County, New York.
- iii. DAUB MILK[215], b. Bet. 1800 - 1810, Town of Middletown, Ulster County, New York.
- iv. DAUC MILK[216], b. Bet. 1800 - 1810, Town of Middletown, Ulster County, New York[217].
- v. DAUD MILK[218], b. Bet. 1800 - 1810, Shandaken, Ulster County, New York.

184.	vi.	CYNTHIA MILK, b. Abt. 1812, Shandaken, Ulster County, New York.
185.	vii.	WILLIAM JEWETT MILK, b. 23 Apr 1813, Delaware County, New York; d. 31 Dec 1885, Danby, New York.
186.	viii.	CHARLES MILK, b. Abt. 1814, New York.
187.	ix.	ISAAC MILK, b. Dec 1815, of Newfield, Tompkins County, New York; d. 27 Mar 1907, Galena, Ohio.
188.	x.	HENRY MILK, b. Bet. 1817 - 1819, New York; d. 21 Dec 1897, South Milford, Indiana.
	xi.	ELIZA A. MILK, b. Abt. 1821, New York; m. UNKNOWN CONLEY; b. Abt. 1820.

72. BENJAMIN^6 MILK, JR. *(BENJAMIN^5, JONATHAN^4, JOB^3, JOHN^2, JOHN^1)* was born 10 Oct 1780 in Washington County, New York, and died 05 Jun 1856 in Town of Jefferson, Schoharie County, New York[219]. He married MARY BAKER Abt. 1801, daughter of DANIEL BAKER. She was born 28 Nov 1780, and died 13 Jul 1844 in Town of Jefferson, Schoharie County, New York[219] and baptized 12 May 1811, First Summit Baptist church, Jefferson, Schoharie County, New York

With appreciation to Lee Milk, Belle Hollenbeck, Viola Burnett, Alfred Dyer, Dr. Jonathan B. Cook, and others for their extensive work on this family.

Benjamin Milk, b. 10 Oct. 1780, in Washington Co., NY (son of Benjamin 1750); m. Mary Baker, b. 28 Nov. 1780, dau. of Daniel Baker. Benjamin served in the War of 1812 under Lt. Col. McComb of 3d Regt. of Artillery. He bought a farm of 108 acres in the Town of Jefferson, Schoharie Co., NY, known as the Bruyn Tract, Lot 31, map of 1793. This was sold by Severyn Bruyn, of Kingston, NY, who was also interested in selling the Reverend Freeborn Garrettson property to Benjamin (1750).

In 1825 Benjamin built, from stones on the farm, a house which, in 1956 was still occupied as the farm home. He was an expert stone mason and built a gristmill, now abandoned although some of the walls are still in good condition. He owned and operated sawmills, as did his father. In his household, according to the census of 1825, there were woven during the year previous, 171 yards of cloth from the wool and flax produced on the 40 acres of cleared farm land.

Benjamin d. 6 June 1856, and Mary d. 13 June 1844. Both are buried in the field near the stone house. The children of Benjamin and Mary were all born at Jefferson and all but Permelia and David lived most of their lives in this area, as have many of their descendants.

Children of BENJAMIN MILK and MARY BAKER are:
189.	i.	DEBORAH^7 MILK, b. 24 Mar 1802, Town of Jefferson, Schoharie County, New York; d. 17 Sep 1893, Sacramento, California.
190.	ii.	STEPHEN MILK, b. 07 Feb 1804, Town of Jefferson, Schoharie County, New York; d. Aft. 01 Jun 1860.
191.	iii.	BETSEY MILK, b. 20 Oct 1805, Town of Jefferson, Schoharie County, New York; d. 25 Apr 1889, Schoharie County, New York.

192.	iv.	PERLINA MILK, b. 10 Jan 1808, Town of Jefferson, Schoharie County, New York; d. 03 Jun 1887, Town of Jefferson, Schoharie County, New York.
193.	v.	PERMELIA MILK, b. 07 May 1810, Town of Jefferson, Schoharie County, New York; d. 27 Jul 1901, Chicago, Illinois.
	vi.	AMANDA MILK, b. 14 Apr 1812, Town of Jefferson, Schoharie County, New York; d. 30 May 1814, Town of Jefferson, Schoharie County, New York.
194.	vii.	JANET MILK, b. 1815, Town of Jefferson, Schoharie County, New York; d. 1884.
	viii.	MARY MILK, b. 11 Feb 1818, Town of Jefferson, Schoharie County, New York. In the 1855 New York state census, Mary Milk is listed as "Insane".
195.	ix.	DAVID MILK, b. 25 May 1820, Town of Jefferson, Schoharie County, New York; d. 13 Oct 1907, Hancock, Delaware Co., NY.
	x.	JOHN MILK, b. 12 Jul 1822, Town of Jefferson, Schoharie County, New York; d. 20 Nov 1830, Town of Jefferson, Schoharie County, New York.
196.	xi.	LEVI 'STEPHEN' MILKS, b. 14 Apr 1825, Town of Jefferson, Schoharie County, New York; d. 13 Oct 1907, Delaware County, New York.

73. TROWBRIDGE^6 MILK (*BENJAMIN^5, JONATHAN^4, JOB^3, JOHN^2, JOHN^1*) was born 22 Mar 1785 in Milk Grove Farm, Valley Falls, New York[220], and died 11 Feb 1857 in Greene County, New York[220]. He married (1) MISS SMITH Abt. 1811. She was born Abt. 1785 in of Pine Hill, New York, and died Abt. 1821. He married (2) JANE BLISH 1823 in Pine Hill, Ulster County, New York, daughter of SILAS BLISH and HANNA PHELPS. She was born 14 Jun 1800 in Colchester, Connecticut, and died 13 Sep 1888.

Trowbridge was a millwright and he erected several saw mills in the Catskills.

In 1820 he was living in Shandaken, Ulster County, New York, and in 1930 he had moved to Griffin's Corners, Delaware County, New York. Trowbridge is buried in Van Valkenburgh Cemetery, Spruceton, Green County, New York.

Notes for TROWBRIDGE MILK: by Lee Milk, with the valuable assistance of Mrs. Olive Bailey, Mrs. Charles Coughtry, Mrs Dema Howe, and several others.

Children of TROWBRIDGE MILK and MISS SMITH are:

197.	i.	LYDIA JANE^7 MILK, b. 07 Jul 1812; d. 13 Jan 1856.
198.	ii.	CATHERINE MILK, b. 1820.

Children of TROWBRIDGE MILK and JANE BLISH are:

199.	iii.	ANN ELIZA^7 MILK, b. 1824.
200.	iv.	BENJAMIN MILK, b. 04 Dec 1824; d. 18 Mar 1888, Greene County, New York.
201.	v.	JULIA ANN MILK, b. 10 Jan 1829; d. 17 Dec 1898.
	vi.	JEHIAL MILK, b. 1830[221]; d. 1857, Nyack, New York (drowned in Hudson River).
	vii.	ALFRED MILK, b. 1833[221]; d. 1844.
	viii.	WESLEY MILK, b. 1837[221]; d. 1857, Nyack, New York (drowned in Hudson River near Nyack, New York).
202.	ix.	CYNTHIA JANE MILK, b. Feb 1840, New York.

74. EZRA^6 MILKS (*DAVID^5 MILK, JONATHAN^4, JOB^3, JOHN^2, JOHN^1*) was born 1781 in Valley Falls, Renss. Co, NY[222], and died 19 Mar 1847 in Green County, Wis.[222]. He married (1) RUTH MARSH[223] Abt. 1801 in Rensselaer Co, NY?. She was born Bet. 1781 - 1783, and died 27 Aug 1833 in Erie County, PA[224]. He married (2) HARRIET (UNKNOWN) EVANS[225] Bet. 1833 - 1840 in Erie County, PA. She was born 06 Feb 1793 in Maryland[225], and died 21 Sep 1884 in East Ripley, Chautauqua County, New York[226].

About 1843 Ezra, with his 2nd wife and some of his children moved by covered wagon tot Green County, Wisconsin. It took them six weeks to make the trip. Ezra died there. His wife, Harriet, eventually moved back to East Ripley, New York where she lived with a daughter, from her first marriage, Elizabeth B. (Evans) Hall and her husband, Hervey Hall. Harriet died in East Ripley and is buried in a local cemetery.

From: ***A twentieth century history of Erie County, Pennsylvania** : a narrative account of its historical progress, its people and its principal interests*, Vol. 1 - 1909

CHAPTER VI. — FRANKLIN.

The township of Franklin was established in 1844 out of portions of McKean, Washington and Elkcreek, and given the name of the printer, philosopher and patriot of the Revolution on the suggestion of Hon. John H. Walker. J. P. Silverthorn was the principal person in circulating petitions and working for its creation. The viewers were Robert Porter and Elijah Drury of Girard and Thomas R. Miller of Springfield. Franklin township is exactly five miles square and contains 16,896 acres.

Franklin is so remote from the main lines of travel that settlement was delayed until a much later period than any other section of the county. The State road, which was opened by the Commonwealth in 1802 from the head waters of the Delaware to the Ohio line, passes through the centre of the township, and on this road immediately afterwards a few settlers located, but it was so remote that they left soon afterwards, and from that time until 1829, it cannot be learned that anyone chose this section for a home. It remained the whole of that quarter of a century an unbroken wilderness, save for the thread through it made by the State road, a section of the great forest in its virgin condition. In 1829 L. D. Rouse went in from Connecticut, but so far as is now known, was without a neighbor, far or near, until 1832, when William and Levi Francis from New York, James P. Silverthorn from Girard township, Henry Floward from Vermont, and .Messrs. Goodban and Longley from England took up land and became permanent residents. In 1833 there were added Thomas Spence and Thomas McLaughlin from Ireland, William Vorse from Chautauqua county, N. Y.; Allen Mead from Saratoga county, N. Y.; Ezra Milks and his son Amos from Rensselaer county, N. Y.; Curtis Cole and father from Unadilla, N. Y., and Andrew Proudfit from York county, Pennsylvania. Isaac Fry from Vermont and John Tuckey, an Englishman, took up land in 1834; John Lover from Eastern Pennsylvania in 1835; Levi Howard from Vermont in 1840, and James B. Robinson from Pompey, N. Y., in 1844. Levi Silverthorn also went in during 1844, the year the township was organized. John Gilbert was born in Somerset county, Pa.

Ezra is buried in Juda, Green County, Wisconsin. Ruth is buried in Miller Cemetery, Girard, Erie County, Pennsylvania.

Harriet moved back to New York after Ezra's death and lived with her daughter, Elizabeth, in East Ripley, Chautauqua County, where she is buried in the East Ripley Cemetery.

Children of EZRA MILKS and RUTH MARSH are:
- 203. i. AMOS MARSH^7 MILKS, b. 05 Mar 1802, Rensselaer County, New York; d. 08 Nov 1878, Erie County, Pennsylvania.
- 204. ii. SARAH "SALLY" ANN MILKS, b. 21 Jun 1803, Valley Falls, Rensselaer County, New York; d. 04 Jun 1892, Green County, Wisconsin.
- 205. iii. DANIEL MILKS, b. Abt. 1805, Rensselaer County, New York; d. Bef. 1843, Erie County, Pennsylvania.
- 206. iv. PRUDENCE MILKS, b. 1807, Rensselaer County, New York; d. Green County, Wisconsin?.
- 207. v. PATIENCE MILKS, b. Abt. 1809, New York.
- 208. vi. PARTHENIA MILKS, b. 30 Nov 1812, Tioga County, New York?; d. 12 Jan 1894, Juda, Green County, Wisconsin.
- 209. vii. DAVID B. MILKS, b. 1817, Tompkins County, New York?; d. 1897, Ithaca, Tompkins County, New York.
- 210. viii. EZRA MILKS, b. Jan 1820, Tompkins County, New York; d. 14 Mar 1907, Soldiers' Home, Leavenworth, Kansas.
- 211. ix. PHOEBE ANN MILKS, b. 11 Nov 1822, Tompkins County, New York; d. 03 Apr 1899, Warren, Jo Daviess County, Illinois.
- x. POLLY MILKS, b. Abt. 1825, Tompkins County, New York.

**Clarence Bridge built by David Milks east of Brodhead, Wisconsin
(torn down in 1931)**

75. DAVID[6] MILKS *(DAVID[5] MILK, JONATHAN[4], JOB[3], JOHN[2], JOHN[1])* was born 1786 in Pittstown, Rensselaer County, New York. He married (1) MARTHA IRELAND Abt. 1811 in Schaghticoke, Rensselaer County, New York. She was born Abt. 1785 in New York. He married (2) ANNAH _____ Abt. 1817. She was born Abt. 1798[226], and died 29 May 1862 in Erie County, Pennsylvania.   ANNAH is buried in Crane Cemetery, Albion, Erie County, Pennsylvania

David began his married life in Canada, then moved to Erie County, Pennsylvania.. In the early 1840s he was living in Green County, Wisconsin, where he built houses and built the covered bridge (Clarence Bridge), shown above, which spanned the Sugar River on highway 11-81. The bridge was torn down in 1931, but there still is a park in the area called Clarence Bridge Park. A replica of the bridge has been built over a tributary of the Sugar River a couple of miles north of the original location. David moved back to Erie County, Pennsylvania where his wife and some of his children died and are buried. David's burial site has not been located.

Replica of the Clarence Bridge

Rod MacDonald's PAF File Sept 2008 (unsourced)

David Milks: Birth: 9 Jan 1793 in Valley Falls (formerly Pittstown) Rensselaer Co/New York; Death: 3 Feb 1879 in Napa County, California; Burial: Tulocay Cemetery, Napa Cty, California

David Milks (b. 9 Jan 1793, not in 1786 as stated in the Croft book) went from Rensselaer to Jefferson Cty N.Y. He is in the 1820 census there with a wife, 1 male child and 3 female children. Then he came to Kitley Twp and appears in the 1824 census. In Kitley, they had one more son and one daughter before 1824.

His wife Martha Ireland died in Kitley or Elizabethtown in 1825/6. He remarried to Anna Wade in 1827 and had two more children. He purchased property in Kitley in 1831. Then he mortgaged it and sold it to his eldest son, Ezra Milks. David took the two youngest children and left Canada for Wayne, N.Y.

In 1832, Ezra sold the land and there is a quitclaim deed from David to the new owner. In the quitclaim deed it says David is formerly of Elizabethtown and now of the State of New York.

In the 1840 census in Erie Co., PA, David and Ezra appear next to each other in the census and Ezra is between 20 & 30 with 1 child.

David is listed as a carpenter and Ezra as a ship's carpenter

In 1826 and 1827, he farmed/lived on Con 10 - Lot 16

In 1829 he farmed/lived on Con 11 - Lot 17 Kitley Twp., Leeds Cty., Upper Canada.

In 1831 he purchased land in Elizabethtown

In 1833 he sold his land to son Ezra and moved to Wayne N.Y.

Later in 1833 Ezra sold the land to David Whaley with David providing a quitclaim.

David and Ezra and their families moved to Erie Pa.

1840 Elk Creek Twp., Erie Cty., Pa. 3 males, 4 females - I can't read the ages on the document

1850 Elk Creek Twp - David Milks, Anna Milks, Albert Milks, Eliza Milks and Claudius Ducolon in the household. In this census he lists his age as 64 which would place his birth at 1786 but we know from his father's estate file that he was actually born in 1793.

Ezra moved to California and David followed after 1850.

David MILKS died in Napa, Napa County, California on 3 FEB 1879. He is interred at Tulocay Cemetery in Napa, California. His 3rd wife was Eunice A. BROWN, widow of James BROWN. David and Eunice were married in Napa County California on 12 NOV 1876. The marriage record (Book 2; Page 125) lists his first wife as Martha IRELAND and his second wife as Anna WADE. David was living in Napa, Napa County, California in the 1879 census.

Child of DAVID MILKS and MARTHA IRELAND is:

212   i.   DAVID[7] MILKS, b. 05 Sep 1813, Augusta, Grenville, Ontario, Canada; d. 03 Apr 1866, Augusta, Grenville, Ontario, Canada.

Children of DAVID MILKS and ANNAH _____ are:

213.   ii.   EZRA[7] MILKS, b. Abt. 1818, Canada; d. Bet. 1874 - 1880, Vallejo, Solano, California?.
        iii.   DAVID MILKS[226], b. Abt. 1821, Canada[227]; d. 28 Feb 1845, Erie County, Pennsylvania[228].
214.   iv.   ALBERT MILKS, b. 01 Oct 1828, Canada; d. 27 Feb 1920, Erie, Pennsylvania.
        v.   ELIZA MILKS, b. 1829[229]; d. 25 Dec 1851, Erie County, Pennsylvania[230]. Gravestone inscription: "age 22 yrs, daughter of David & Anna Milks" Burial: Crane Cemetery, Albion, Erie County, Pennsylvania

76. SILAS W.[6] MILKS (*DAVID[5] MILK, JONATHAN[4], JOB[3], JOHN[2], JOHN[1]*) was born 09 Jul 1786 in Pittstown, Rensselaer County, New York[230], and died 02 May 1857 in Valley Falls (Pittstown), NY[230]. He married SARAH 'SALLY' W. _____. She was born Bet. 1787 - 1788[231], and died 19 Feb 1872 in Schaghticoke, New York[232]. Silas and Sarah are buried in Old Presbyterian, Schaghticoke, Rensselaer County, New York

Children of SILAS MILKS and SARAH _____ are:
        i.   LEMUEL[7] MILKS.
215.   ii.   HARRIS MILKS, b. 09 Jul 1809, Pittstown, Rensselaer County, New York; d. 15 Dec 1871, Hope, Barry County, Michigan.
216.   iii.   JULIA ANN MILKS, b. 1814, Pittstown, Rensselaer County, New York; d. 28 Aug 1903, Lansingburgh, New York.
217.   iv.   DAVID MILK, b. 1815; d. 16 Jun 1864, Near Petersburg.
218.   v.   MATTHEW G. MILKS, b. 07 Feb 1816, Valley Falls (Pittstown), Rensselaer County, New York; d. 29 Oct 1875, Valley Falls (Pittstown), Rensselaer County, New York.
219.   vi.   CATHERINE I. MILKS, b. 1822, Pittstown, Rensselaer County, New York; d. Aft. 1900, Lansingburgh, Rensselaer County, New York.
220.   vii.   LUCETTA MILK, b. Abt. 1823, New York; d. 29 Nov 1882, Bangor, Van Buren County, Michigan.
        viii.   SILAS W. MILKS, JR., b. 30 May 1823, Pittstown, Rensselaer County, New York[232]; d. 16 Oct 1829, Valley Falls (Pittstown), New York[232]. Burial: Old Presbyterian, Schaghticoke, Rensselaer County, New York
        ix.   SALLY M. MILKS, b. 10 Feb 1825, Valley Falls (Pittstown), NY[233]; d. 26 Oct 1829, Valley Falls (Pittstown), NY[233].
Burial: Old Presbyterian, Schaghticoke, Rensselaer County, New York

Notes for SALLY M. MILKS:
Tombstone inscription:

Happy Infants early bless'd
And, in peaceful slumber rest;
Early ___ened from the cares,
____ rich _____ with growning years.

        x.   JEROME MILKS, b. Abt. 1829, Pittstown, Rensselaer County, New York; d. Prob d.y..

77. BENJAMIN[6] MILKS (*DAVID[5] MILK, JONATHAN[4], JOB[3], JOHN[2], JOHN[1]*) was born 20 Jul 1799[234], and died 1879 in Allegany County, New York[235]. He married DORCAS C. GRINNELL. She was born Bet. 1803 - 1804 in New York[236], and died 1879 in Allegany County, New York[237]. Benjamin's occupation was as a Hotel Keeper in Whitesville, Allegany County, New York. He and Dorcas are buried in Fairlawn Cemetery, Scio, Allegany County, NY

Children of BENJAMIN MILKS and DORCAS GRINNELL are:
- 221. i. PERRY M.[7] MILKS, b. 25 Jul 1830, Pennsylvania; d. 19 Mar 1864, Scio, Allegany County, New York.
- ii. MARIAH MILKS, b. 1832, Pennsylvania. Lived in: Kansas City, Missouri
- 222. iii. BENJAMIN FRANKLIN MILKS, b. 03 Dec 1833, Pennsylvania; d. Dec 1919, Town of Amity, Allegany County, New York.

78. PATIENCE[6] MILK *(LEMUEL[5], JONATHAN[4], JOB[3], JOHN[2], JOHN[1])* was born Bet. 1773 - 1785, and died Abt. 1825 in New York. She married HEMAN WOOLMAN Abt. 1805 in New York. He was born Abt. 1784.

Children of PATIENCE MILK and HEMAN WOOLMAN are:
- 223. i. GEORGE W.[7] WOOLMAN, b. 28 Mar 1810, Lake George, Warren County, New York ?; d. 18 Dec 1883, Lakefield, Saginaw County, Michigan ?.
- ii. RALPH WOOLMAN, b. Abt. 1807, New York; d. Aft. 1880, Prob. Cattaraugus County, New York. Never married.
- 224. iii. LEMUEL WOOLMAN, b. Abt. 1808, New York; d. Aft. 1880, Prob. Cattaraugus County, New York.
- iv. DAU WOOLMAN, b. Abt. 1809, New York.

79. MARY[6] MILK *(LEMUEL[5], JONATHAN[4], JOB[3], JOHN[2], JOHN[1])* was born Abt. 1785, and died Abt. Dec 1829 in Sandy Hill/Hudson Falls, Washington County, New York[238]. She married JOSHUA PROSSER Abt. 1802, son of ELIAS PROSSER and RACHEL BURDICK. He was born 30 May 1782[238], and died 09 Jan 1815 in Washington County, New York.

Mary Milk, called "Mercy" and "Polly", b. abt. 1785 (dau. of Lemuel 1753), "died in the late winter," 1829, at the home of her married dau. in Hudson Falls or Sandy Hill, NY; m. abt. 1802, Joshua Prosser, b. 30 May 1782. Tombstone inscription reads: "Joshua Prosser was drowned Jan. 9th, 1815. Aged 32 yrs, 7 mos.

Joshua and Barney Prosser (who m. Betsey Milk, sister of Mary Milk) were brothers. Their birth records are entered in "A Brief Concordance of the Holy Scriptures" by John Brown, New York, "The property of Rachel Prosser." Joshua and Barney were sons of Elias Prosser, b. 20 Sep. 1750, d. 10 Nov. 1839, and Rachel (Burdick) Prosser, b. 29 Apr. 1760, d. 22 Nov. 1839.

Elias Prosser had an Indian ancestress who, he said, was the daughter of a Mohawk Chief; and some of Elias' children bore Indian resemblance. Mrs. Allen M. Thatcher, Lake George NY, 2d great granddaughter of Elias Prosser, states: "My grandmother told me her grandfather Elias Prosser said that he was descended from a powerful Mohawk Indian Chief named 'Hiawatha' who formed the confederation of the Iroquois known as the Five Nations. It is a family tradition that we are direct descendants of this Mohawk Indian Chief." Dr. Jonathan Prosser, a brother of Elias, was called an "Indian doctor and was said to be of part Indian blood" (Hist. of Dutchess Co., NY, by F. H. Smith).

During the Revolutionary War, Dr. Jonathan and his brothers Elias, Joshua and Benjamin, of Beekman, Dutchess Co., were apprehended by the N. Y. "Commission for Detecting Conspiracies."

The brothers, "being of the people called Quakers" and declaring their loyalty, were released. "Elias helped to care for the sick and wounded during the war" (Mrs. Thatcher). After the War, "Elias Prosser and Nathan Burdick" were two of the first settlers on Lake George (Lake George and Lake Champlain, by W. Max Reid).

Joshua Prosser was a school teacher. He was teaching at Pilot Knob on the east shore of Lake George in the winter of 1814-15. After school the 9th of January, he skated across the lake to Caldwell, the home of his parents, to get school books that had been delivered there. Returning at night along the side of the lake, he skated into open water where a brook flows into the lake. Mary said she heard him scream for help. These cries never left her and during the remainder of her life she wandered, unable to care for her children. Chn., 5 known of a probable 7:

Children of MARY MILK and JOSHUA PROSSER are:
- i. MARY[7] PROSSER, b. Bet. 1802 - 1803; d. 07 Mar 1819.
- ii. DAVID PROSSER, b. Dec 1805; d. 14 Jul 1828.
- iii. SOPHIA MATILDA PROSSER, b. Abt. 1808; m. DAVID WHIPPLE; b. Abt. 1808.
- 225. iv. ADELIA PROSSER, b. 24 Jun 1812, New York; d. 18 Feb 1873, Lanark, Portage County, Wisconsin.
- 226. v. JANE PROSSER, b. 10 Jan 1815, Washington County, New York.

80. ELIZABETH 'BETSEY'[6] MILK *(LEMUEL[5], JONATHAN[4], JOB[3], JOHN[2], JOHN[1])* was born 16 Jul 1787. She married (1) BARNEY PROSSER Abt. 1806 in Warren County, New York ?, son of ELIAS PROSSER and RACHEL BURDICK. He was born

03 Dec 1785, and died 23 May 1814. She married (2) ELIJAH COLE Abt. 1915. He was born Abt. 1787.

The children, Maria, James, Emily, and Lucy were recorded in the family bible of Betsey Moore Truesdale.

Children of ELIZABETH MILK and BARNEY PROSSER are:
227.   i.   MARIA LYNDIA[7] PROSSER, b. 26 May 1807, Bolton, Warren County, New York; d. 24 Feb 1884.
228.   ii.   JAMES LEMUEL 'NELSON' PROSSER, b. 28 Feb 1809, Bolton, Warren County, New York; d. 07 May 1889, Warren County, New York.
         iii.   EMILY PROSSER, b. 26 Apr 1811.
         iv.   LUCY PROSSER, b. 31 Jan 1813.

81. ABIGAIL[6] MILK *(LEMUEL[5], JONATHAN[4], JOB[3], JOHN[2], JOHN[1])* was born Abt. 1790 in New York, christened: 24 Jun 1830, in the Reformed Dutch Church, Greenwich, Washington County, New York, and died Aft. 1860. She married PETER CRAPO. He was born Abt. 1788 in New York, christened: 01 Apr 1832, in the Reformed Dutch Church, Greenwich, Washington County, New York, and died Abt. 1855 in Cattaraugus County, New York. They lived in Persia, Cattaraugus County, New York.

    From **New York Gen. & Biog. Soc.**, edited by Vosburgh, Reformed Protestant Church, Tiashoke and Easton: "1830, Members received by certificate, Mrs. Abigail Crapo. 1832, Adults baptized: Lemuel, Sarah and Peter Crapo. 1834, Baptism of children: Job, Benjamin, Moses Cowan, Abigail, Jacob Fonda, children of Abigail and Peter Crapo." (Moses Cowan and Jacob Fonda were the names of past and present pastors of the church.)
    From the 1830 Census for Easton, Washington County, New York, it appears that Peter and Abigail Crapo had at least 11 children, 7 males and 4 females, OR one of the older children was married and living with Peter and Abigail.

Children of ABIGAIL MILK and PETER CRAPO are:
       i.   LEMUEL[7] CRAPO, b. Bet. 1808 - 1816, New York. Christening: 01 Apr 1832, Reformed Dutch Church, Greenwich, Washington County, New York
       ii.   SARAH CRAPO, b. Bet. 1808 - 1816, New York. Christening: 01 Apr 1832, Reformed Dutch Church, Greenwich, Washington County, New York
       iii.   JOB CRAPO, b. Bef. 1834, New York. Christening: 19 Jul 1834, Reformed Dutch Church, Greenwich, Washington County, New York
       iv.   BENJAMIN CRAPO, b. Bef. 1834, New York. Christening: 19 Jul 1834, Reformed Dutch Church, Greenwich, Washington County, New York
       v.   ABIGAIL CRAPO, b. Bef. 1834, New York. Christening: 19 Jul 1834, Reformed Dutch Church, Greenwich, Washington County, New York
       vi.   MOSES COWAN CRAPO, b. Abt. 1833, New York. Christening: 19 Jul 1834, Reformed Dutch Church, Greenwich, Washington County, New York
       vii.   JACOB FONDA CRAPO, b. Abt. 1832, Greenwich, Washington County, New York. Christening: 15 Nov 1834, Reformed Dutch Church, Greenwich, Washington County, New York[239]
       viii.   WILLIAM CRAPO, b. Abt. 1840, New York.
       ix.   PETER? CRAPO, b. Abt. 1815, New York. Lived in: 1860, East Hanover, Chautauqua County, New York (2 houses away from Abigail and son Moses .)

82. SARAH 'SALLY'[6] MILK *(LEMUEL[5], JONATHAN[4], JOB[3], JOHN[2], JOHN[1])* was born 05 Jul 1787 in Washington Co./Warren Co., NY[240], and died 16 Oct 1856 in Otto, Cattaraugus Co., New York[240]. She married ASA BATES Abt. 1814 in Washington/Warren County, New York. He was born 07 Jul 1793 in Massachusetts[241], and died 16 Apr 1852 in Otto, Cattaraugus County, New York[242]. Sally and Asa are buried in North Otto Cemetery, Cattaraugus County, New York

BIBLE RECORDS OF PHILEMA MARIAH BATES
    (Handwritten notes in Bible, signed by Mrs P.M. Sewall. Dated 10 April 1864)
    original in possession of Joy Freundschuh, a great granddaughter of Philema Bates
My father Asa Bates was born July the 7th 1793
Sarah Milks born July the 11th 1791 (could be 1793)

Their Children
- *Roxcena Bates born April 5th 1815*
- *John A. Bates born June 28th 1819*
- *Rosanna Bates born Oct 14 1821*
- *Job L Bates born March 15th 1825*
- *Mary Ann Bates born June 1st 1826*
- *Nelson L Bates born May 27th 1827*
- *Charles W Bates born July 25th 1830*
- *Alexander J (or S) Bates born April 30th 1832*
- *Daniel (?) Bates born Oct 12th 1833*
- *Philema M Bates born Oct 23rd 1836*
- *George F Bates born March 18th 1839*

Marriages
- *Derias Babcock and Roxcena Bates married Jan 29 1838*
- *John A Bates and Martha Hutton married March 6 1842*
- *Benjamin Sanders and Rosanna Bates married Dec 28 1842*
- *Job L Bates and Jane Porter married March 7 1847*
- *____ Satterly and Mary Ann Bates married Dec 16 1845*
- *Nelson L Bates and Margrett Satterly married march 4 1850*
- *Charles W Bates and Juliett Satterly married Feb 27 1851*

Children of SARAH MILK and ASA BATES are:

229.   I.   ROXCENA[7] BATES, b. 05 Apr 1815, WashIngton Co./Warren Co., NY; d. 1894, Otto, Cattaraugus Co., New York.

230.   ii.   JOHN A. BATES, b. 28 Jun 1819, New York; d. 06 Jun 1900.

        iii.   ROSANNA BATES, b. 14 Oct 1821, New York; m. BENJAMIN SANDERS, 28 Dec 1842; b. Abt. 1820.

        iv.   JOB L. BATES, b. 15 Mar 1825, New York[243]; d. 22 Oct 1865, Otto, Cattaraugus County, New York[243]; m. JANE PORTER, 07 Mar 1847; b. Abt. 1825.

231.   v.   MARY ANN BATES, b. 01 Jun 1826, Otto, Cattaraugus County, New York; d. 06 Nov 1892, Cattaraugus County, NY.

232.   vi.   NELSON L. BATES, b. 27 May 1827, New York; d. 16 Feb 1866, Cattaraugus County, New York.

233.   vii.   CHARLES W. BATES, b. 25 Jul 1830, New York.

        viii.   ALEXANDER J S BATES, b. 30 Apr 1832, New York.

        ix.   DANIEL BATES[244], b. 12 Oct 1833, New York.

        x.   PHILEMA M. BATES[244], b. 23 Oct 1836, New York; m. MISTRE SEWALL; b. Abt. 1835.

        xi.   GEORGE FRANKLIN BATES[244], b. 18 Mar 1839, New York. Military service: 02 Sep 1864, Private, Co. D, 9th Cavalry; Civil War

83. BENJAMIN[6] MILKS *(LEMUEL[5] MILK, JONATHAN[4], JOB[3], JOHN[2], JOHN[1])* was born 18 May 1794 in Bolton Landing, Washington County, New York, and died 04 Jun 1874 in Otto, Cattaraugus County, New York. He married (1) ____ RUSSELL Abt. 1812. She was born Abt. 1795, and died Abt. 1819 in Bolton Landing, Washington County, New York. He married (2) POLLY MOORE Abt. 1823 in Bolton Landing, Washington County, New York. She was born 25 Jun 1806 in Bolton Landing, Washington County, New York, and died 26 Jun 1873 in West Seneca, Erie County, New York. Benjamin and Polly are buried in Hillcrest Cemetery, Hamburg, Erie County, New York

Child of BENJAMIN MILKS and ____ RUSSELL is:

        i.   MARY[7] MILK, b. 1813, Bolton Landing, Warren County, New York[245]; d. 1819, Bolton Landing, Warren County, New York.

Children of BENJAMIN MILKS and POLLY MOORE are:

234.   ii.   MARY JANE[7] MILKS, b. 28 Sep 1824, Bolton, Warren County, New York; d. 30 Apr 1873.

235.   iii.   HENRY BENJAMIN MILKS, b. 24 Jul 1826, Bolton, Warren County, New York; d. 1920, Kansas City, Jackson County, Missouri.

236.   iv.   CHARLES JONATHAN MILKS, b. 24 Mar 1828, Bolton, Warren County, New York; d. 1898, Magnolia, Rock

		County, Wisconsin.
237.	v.	DAVID WESLEY MILKS, b. 13 Jun 1830, Otto, Cattaraugus County, New York; d. 13 Nov 1901, Chesaning, Saginaw, Michigan.
	vi.	MARTIN LEMUEL MILKS, b. 13 Apr 1832, Otto, Cattaraugus County, New York; d. 20 May 1835, Otto, Cattaraugus County, New York.
238.	vii.	CALISTA ELIZABETH MILKS, b. 18 Jun 1834, Otto, Cattaraugus County, New York; d. 12 Sep 1922, Cattaraugus County, New York ?.
239.	viii.	PHEBE EMELIA MILKS, b. 13 Mar 1836, Otto, Cattaraugus County, New York; d. 1910, Chesaning, Saginaw County, Michigan.
	ix.	BUREN LEMUEL MILKS, b. 21 Jan 1838, Otto, Cattaraugus County, New York.
240.	x.	MERRITT SIDWAY MILKS, b. 21 Jan 1840, Otto, Cattaraugus County, New York; d. 01 Mar 1891, Spring Valley, Rock County, Wisconsin; Stepchild.
241.	xi.	SOPHIA BETSEY MILKS, b. 10 Apr 1843, Otto, Cattaraugus County, New York.
242.	xii.	JAMES FRANKLIN MILKS, b. 18 Mar 1845, West Seneca, Erie County, New York; d. Bet. 1920 - 1930, New York; Stepchild.
243.	xiii.	IRA NELSON MILKS, b. 04 Feb 1847, West Seneca, Erie County, New York; d. 1896, West Seneca, NY.

84. JOB[6] MILK *(LEMUEL[5], JONATHAN[4], JOB[3], JOHN[2], JOHN[1])* was born 18 Mar 1798 in Bolton, Warren County, New York[246], and died 03 Feb 1864 in Waukon, Allamakee County, Iowa[246]. He married ANNA INGRAM Abt. 1824 in Warren County, New York?. She was born 11 Aug 1805 in Bolton, Warren County, New York?[246], and died 04 Oct 1881 in Hurley, Turner County, S. Dak.[246]. Anna is buried in Hurley Cemetery, Turner County, South Dakota [Plot: Lot 1 Grave 9] Job is buried in Sand Cove Cemetery, Waukon, Allamakee County, Iowa

They commenced their married life in Warren Co. and their first children were born there. By 1830 Job and family were living in Otto Township, Cattaraugus Co.,, NY, and in 1840 they were living in Mansfield Township, same county.

In 1855 they moved by way of the Great Lakes to Waukegan, Ill. In a letter dated Aug. 5, 1855, J. Milks (son of Job) tells of their journey: "... we paid $18 on the boat. We had a first rate time. They had music and dancing on the boat all but one night and then it rained. The lake was rather rougher than I liked . . . "

Within a week the family moved from Waukegan to McHenry, Ill., and J. Milks describes their home in the following words: *"Mother and Betsey, James and Dallas, and Alfredine and Arthur live together in a little cement house in a very pleasant place. The house stands on a little hill. We can see for miles around and we can see the cows from the house. There is wood around the house but they do not look like woods. The woods here look like orchards."* The other members of the family found employment immediately on other farms and in other homes.

Some time later the family moved to Iowa, from which state Job wrote to his brother Benjamin, March 17, 1861, *"Tomorrow if I live to see it, I shall be 62 years old . . . "* He died 3 Feb. 1864 and is buried at Waukon, Iowa. Some of his children subsequently moved to near Hurley, So. Dakota, where Ann, his wife, is buried, she having died 4 Oct. 1881. All six of their sons served in the Civil War.

Children of JOB MILK and ANNA INGRAM are:

	i.	EMILY M.[7] MILKS, b. 05 Jan 1825, Warren County, New York; d. 15 May 1835, Cattaraugus County, NY.
	ii.	MARY S. MILKS, b. 16 Nov 1826, Warren County, New York; d. 28 May 1835, Cattaraugus County, NY.
244.	iii.	ELIZABETH A. "BETSEY" MILKS, b. 23 May 1828, Warren County, New York; d. 12 Jun 1900, Parsons, Labette County, Kansas.
245.	iv.	JONATHAN B. MILKS, b. 04 Jun 1830, Cattaraugus County, New York; d. 07 Jul 1914, Machias, Cattaraugus County, New York.
246.	v.	CAROLINE "PHEBE" E. MILKS, b. 04 Sep 1832, Cattaraugus County, New York; d. 20 Apr 1925.
	vi.	NELSON P. MILKS, b. 09 May 1834, Cattaraugus County, New York[246,247,248]; d. 15 Feb 1864, Waukon, Allamakee County, Iowa[249]. He is buried in Sand Cove Cemetery, Alamakee, Iowa

It is possible that Nelson married Louisa Bennett, dau. of Darius & Phebe Bennett, between 1856 and 1860. She is shown next to him in the 1860 Federal Census for Alamakee County, Iowa, with the surname of Milks. However, her brother Gidean Bennett is also shown with the surname of Milks, so her marital status is unknown. She doesn't show up in any later census with either or the Milks or Bennett surnames.

Nelson enlisted on 13 August 1862 and was assigned on 1 Sept. 1862 to Company B, Iowa 27th Infantry Regiment. He mustered out on 15 Feb 1864 at Memphis, TN.

247.	vii.	JEMIMA DIANTHA MILKS, b. 22 Mar 1836, Cattaraugus County, New York; d. 29 Mar 1915, Mt. Ida, Grant

248.	viii.	DAVID FRANKLIN MILKS, b. 26 Jan 1838, Cattaraugus County, New York; d. 02 Jul 1892, Parsons, Labette County, Kansas.
249.	ix.	HUMPHREY W. MILKS, b. 18 Feb 1840, Cattaraugus County, New York; d. 12 Dec 1882, Hurley, Turner County, S. Dak..
250.	x.	ANNA ADELIA MILKS, b. 17 May 1842, Cattaraugus County, New York; d. 30 Jun 1910, Waukegan, Lake County, Illinois.
	xi.	JOB DALLAS MILKS[250], b. 01 Sep 1844, Cattaraugus County, New York[251,252]; d. 05 Dec 1916, Hurley, Turner County, S. Dakota[252]; m. MARY JANE 'BELLE' HALLECK[253], 20 Oct 1867, De Soto, Vernon County, Wisconsin[254,255,256]; b. 30 Oct 1847, Ohio[257]; d. 09 Apr 1918, Hurley, Turner County, S. Dakota[258,259], daughter of H. W. & Christine Hallock. Both are buried in Hurley Cemetery, Hurley, Turner County, S. Dak. No children. Military service: Company F, 6th Iowa Cavalry (Civil War). Occupation: 1900, Landlord
251.	xii.	JAMES HARTMAN MILKS, b. 17 Nov 1846, Cattaraugus County, New York; d. 1917, Bowman County, North Dakota.

85. WILLIAM[6] SIDWAY *(REBECCA[5] MILK, JONATHAN[4], JOB[3], JOHN[2], JOHN[1])* was born Abt. 1782 in Goshen, Orange County, New York. He married ELIZABETH DANES. She was born Abt. 1782.

Child of WILLIAM SIDWAY and ELIZABETH DANES is:

252.	i.	GEORGE[7] SIDWAY, b. Abt. 1805.

86. JONATHAN[6] SIDWAY *(REBECCA[5] MILK, JONATHAN[4], JOB[3], JOHN[2], JOHN[1])* was born 01 Apr 1784 in Goshen, Orange County, New York[260], and died 21 Jan 1847 in Buffalo, Erie County, New York[260]. He married PARNELL ST. JOHN 01 Jan 1826. She was born 12 Jun 1801 in Aurelius, Cayuga County, New York[260], and died 22 Apr 1879 in Buffalo, Erie County, New York[260]. Jonathan was the Landlord of a hotel in Buffalo, New York. He and Parnell are buried in Forest Lawn Cemetery, Buffalo, Erie County, New York

Children of JONATHAN SIDWAY and PARNELL ST. JOHN are:

253.	i.	KATHERINE R.[7] SIDWAY, b. 15 Jan 1827, Buffalo, Erie County, New York; d. 15 Mar 1890, Buffalo, Erie County, NY.
	ii.	DEWITT SIDWAY, b. 27 Feb 1829, Buffalo, Erie County, New York; d. 11 Jul 1833, Buffalo, Erie County, New York. Burial: Forest Lawn Cemetery, Buffalo, Erie County, New York
	iii.	MARIA SIDWAY, b. 26 Aug 1830, Buffalo, Erie County, New York; d. 01 Sep 1831, Buffalo, Erie County, New York. Burial: Forest Lawn Cemetery, Buffalo, Erie County, New York
254.	iv.	JONATHAN SIDWAY, b. Mar 1832, Buffalo, Erie County, New York; d. Bet. 1900 1910, Manhattan, New York City, New York ?.
255.	v.	FRANKLIN SIDWAY, b. 23 Jul 1834, Buffalo, Erie County, New York; d. 07 Mar 1920, St Augustine, St Johns, Florida.
	vi.	PARNELL SIDWAY, b. 29 Apr 1836, Buffalo, Erie County, New York; d. 09 Dec 1849, Buffalo, Erie County, New York. Burial: Forest Lawn Cemetery, Buffalo, Erie County, New York
	vii.	JAMES HENRY SIDWAY, b. 09 Aug 1839, Buffalo, Erie County, New York; d. 25 Jan 1865, Buffalo, Erie County, New York. Draft Registration: 01 Jul 1863, At Buffalo, NY, Civil War Draft Registrations, Occ.: Gentleman
	viii.	H. CORNELIA SIDWAY, b. 03 Mar 1842, Buffalo, Erie County, New York; d. 17 Feb 1845, Buffalo, Erie County, New York. Burial: Forest Lawn Cemetery, Buffalo, Erie County, New York

87. DAVID[6] MILK *(GEORGE[5], JONATHAN[4], JOB[3], JOHN[2], JOHN[1])*[261] was born 1795 in Washington County, New York[262], and died 17 Sep 1860 in Leon, Cattaraugus County, New York. He married (1) SAMANTHA PRINCE, daughter of JOB PRINCE and RHODA KIBBE. She was born 29 May 1798 in New York[263], and died 10 Jun 1844 in Dayton, Cattaraugus County, New York[263]. He married (2) PRUDENCE _____ Abt. 1845 in Cattaraugus County, New York. She was born Bet. 1798 - 1804 in Schoharie County, New York[264]. David and Samantha are buried in Koningisor Farm Cemetery, East Leon, Cattaraugus County, New York. Samantha's father, Job PRINCE, was born 31 January 1750 and died 31 January 1827. He served in the Revolutionary War from 1775 to 1782. He was in the 16th militia in Albany Co., Cambridge town, New York.

Children of DAVID MILK and SAMANTHA PRINCE are:
- 256. i. CHARLES[7] MILKS, b. 10 Dec 1819, Chenango Co., NY ???; d. 29 Sep 1885, Cattaraugus County, New York.
- 257. ii. ALEXANDER B. MILK, b. 08 Jun 1824, Saratoga County, New York; d. 20 Sep 1901, Mansfield, Cattaraugus County, New York.
- iii. HARRIET MILKS, b. Abt. 1825, Cattaraugus County, New York; m. WOLCOTT MARSH. Lived in: Iowa[265]
- 258. iv. DAVID W. MILKS, b. 1830, Cattaraugus County, New York; d. 06 Nov 1911, Coldspring, Cattaraugus County, New York.
- 259. v. MONTERVILLE MILKS, b. 03 Jun 1833, Cattaraugus County, New York; d. 19 Sep 1912, Cattaraugus County, NY.
- 260. vi. WASHINGTON G. MILKS, b. 1836, Cattaraugus County, New York.
- vii. PERRY MILKS, b. 1838, Cattaraugus County, New York; d. Aft. 1863. Lived in: Ohio
- viii. JONATHAN MILKS, b. 1840, Cattaraugus County, New York; d. Bet. 1850 - 1860, Cattaraugus County, New York.

88. MARY[6] MILKS *(JONATHAN[5] MILK, JONATHAN[4], JOB[3], JOHN[2], JOHN[1])* was born 08 Jul 1791 in Easton, Washington County, New York, and died 1870 in Cattaraugus County, New York. She married ISAAC WAITE 1808 in Easton, Washington County, New York. He was born 08 Feb 1786, and died 1837 in Easton, Washington County, New York.

Mary Milks, b. 8 July 1791, Easton, Washington Co., NY (dau of Jonathan 1769); m. Isaac Waite, b. 8 Feb. 1787, near Cambridge, Washington Co., NY, son of Stephen & Jemima (Babcock) Waite. In 1830 Isaac came to East Leon, Cattaraugus Co., NY. In 1831 Mary and her children left Washington Co. and traveled over the Erie Canal route to Buffalo, where Isaac met them with an ox-team and sleigh. The children had contracted measles en route, but, wrapped in blankets, they made the sleigh trip to East Leon without suffering any complications. History of Cattaraugus Co., by Everts, p. 230, states that Isaac Waite was in possession of Lot 1, Dayton. According to Cattaraugus Co. records at the courthouse in Little Valley, Isaac bought 78½ acres in East Leon on 24 Oct 1831, for $187.75.

Isaac Waite was a farmer and carpenter by trade. He frequently returned to Washington Co. to do carpentry. During one of his business ventures back East, he fell from an apple tree he was trimming, and sustained injuries that caused a paralysis and his eventual death in 1835, at Easton. He was buried in Washington Co. and his Will filed there. Mary, however, returned to East Leon and reared her children there. Part of the data in this section (history and descendants of Mary Milk and Isaac Waite was taken from the unpublished manuscript, "Descendants of Stephen Waite6 of Washington Co. and Cattaraugus Co., NY" compiled by Clara Waite Burroughs10 of Pottersville, NY, 1932-1934, 1949, pp 12-15.

Mary is buried in Kendall Flats Cemetery, Cattaraugus County, New York

Children of MARY MILKS and ISAAC WAITE are:
- 261. i. MARTIN[7] WAITE, b. 18 Jul 1809, Washington County, New York; d. 1897.
- 262. ii. BATHSHEBA WAITE, b. 08 May 1811, Washington County, New York; d. 1876, Cattaraugus County, NY.
- 263. iii. DAVID WAITE, b. 13 Apr 1814, Washington County, New York; d. 17 Sep 1891, Coldwater, Branch County, Michigan.
- 264. iv. MARY ANN WAITE, b. 26 Feb 1816, Washington County, New York; d. 06 Feb 1892, Machias, Cattaraugus County, New York.
- 265. v. JONATHAN WAITE, b. 28 Jul 1819, Washington County, New York; d. 1858, Cattaraugus County, NY.
- 266. vi. ISAAC WAITE, JR., b. 09 May 1821, New York; d. 09 Sep 1875, Battle Creek, Calhoun County, Michigan.
- 267. vii. GEORGE C. WAITE, b. 13 Jan 1825, Washington County, New York.
- 268. viii. JANE WAITE, b. 23 Apr 1827, Washington County, New York; d. 1891.
- 269. ix. BENJAMIN WAITE, b. 05 Mar 1829, Washington County, New York; d. 31 Jul 1891.
- 270. x. BUTLER R. WAITE, b. 29 Dec 1830, Washington County, New York.

89. JOHN[6] MILK *(JONATHAN[5], JONATHAN[4], JOB[3], JOHN[2], JOHN[1])* was born 08 Oct 1793 in Washington County, New York[266], and died 27 Aug 1859 in Napoli, Cattaraugus County, New York[266]. He married ANNA WAITE Abt. 1811 in Washington County, New York. She was born 07 Apr 1792 in Washington Co., New York, and died 07 Apr 1861 in Napoli, Cattaraugus County, New York[267].

John Milks, b. 8 Oct 1793, Washington Co., NY (son of Jonathan 1769); m. Anna Waite, b. 7 Apr 1792, Washington Co., dau of Stephen & Jemima (Babcock) Waite. In 1824 John and Anna moved from Washington Co. to Napoli, Cattaraugus Co., NY, living the first year in the central part of the town near Anna's father, Stephen Waite. A short while later, to be away from frosts, they moved to the hill in western Napoli (Stanley Haas farm). Title for this land was secured from the Holland Land Co.

"Buffalo was the nearest trading center and when John Milks built their home, he drove by the old Chautauqua Road (two days each way) to bring back glass for the windows. John Milks was a farmer and tried small cases in court as a lawyer." (Reference: "Descendants of Stephen Waite of Washington and Cattaraugus Cos.," unpublished manuscript by Clara Waite Burroughs, and as told by Mary Milks Haas, granddaughter of John Milks.) It was in this home on the hill that his father, Jonathan, spent his declining years.

"John Milk was supervisor of the town of Napoli in 1840. He came from Cambridge, NY, when this country was a wilderness." (History of Cattaraugus Co., 1893.)

John d. 27 Aug. 1859, in Napoli; his Will was probated 19 Sep 1859. His wife Anna d. 7 Apr 1861, in Napoli. Both are bur. in the family plot, in South Napoli Cemetery, Cattaraugus County, New York.

Children of JOHN MILK and ANNA WAITE are:

271.	i.	JEMIMA[7] MILKS, b. 1812, Washington County, New York; d. Bef. 1859, Cattaraugus County, New York.	
272.	ii.	JOHN MILKS, b. 1815; d. 08 Nov 1884, Napoli, Cattaraugus County, New York.	
273.	iii.	BENJAMIN B. MILKS, b. 14 Apr 1816, Washington County, New York; d. 16 May 1884, East Randolph, Cattaraugus County, New York.	
274.	iv.	DAVID MILK, b. 02 May 1818, Easton, Washington County, New York; d. 16 Aug 1855, Little Valley, Cattaraugus County, New York.	
275.	v.	DEBORAH MILKS, b. 1819, Washington County, New York; d. 1869, Little Valley, Cattaraugus County, New York.	
276.	vi.	GEORGE MILKS, b. 12 Feb 1823, Washington County, New York; d. 1867, Cattaraugus County, New York.	
277.	vii.	MARY MILKS, b. 1825; d. 05 Apr 1861, New Albion, Cattaraugus County, New York.	
	viii.	SUSAN MILKS, b. Abt. 1827.	
278.	ix.	GILES MILKS, b. 22 Jan 1830, Napoli, Cattaraugus County, New York; d. 09 Jan 1906.	
279.	x.	HIRAM MILKS, b. 09 Jun 1832, Napoli, Cattaraugus Co, NY; d. 23 Jan 1883, Napoli, Cattaraugus Co, NY (measles epidemic).	
280.	xi.	MARTIN MILKS, b. 1836, Cattaraugus County, New York; d. 19 Apr 1896, Napoli, Cattaraugus County, New York.	

90. DEBORAH[6] MILKS *(JONATHAN[5] MILK, JONATHAN[4], JOB[3], JOHN[2], JOHN[1])* was born 1798 in Easton, Washington County, New York, and died Feb 1870 in Easton, Washington County, New York[268]. She married RICHARD HARRINGTON, JR. Abt. 1820, son of RICHARD HARRINGTON and MARY ALLEN. He was born 1796, and died 12 Feb 1875 in Easton, Washington Co., NY. Deborah died of Typhoid Fever

Children of DEBORAH MILKS and RICHARD HARRINGTON are:

281.	i.	JOB[7] HARRINGTON, b. 1821, Easton, Washington County, New York; d. 30 Jun 1883.
282.	ii.	RUTH HARRINGTON, b. 1824, Easton, Washington County, New York; d. 22 Feb 1892, Easton, Washington County, New York.
	iii.	SIMON HARRINGTON, b. 03 Jun 1828, Easton, Washington County, New York; d. 23 Mar 1887, Easton, Washington County, New York; m. (1) LOUISA PITTS; b. Abt. 1828; m. (2) LOVICA HARRINGTON; b. Abt. 1928. No children.
283.	iv.	BENJAMIN HARRINGTON, b. 1833, Easton, Washington County, New York; d. 21 Jan 1890, Easton, Washington County, New York.
284.	v.	DAVID W. HARRINGTON, b. 17 Oct 1834, Easton, Washington County, New York; d. 24 Jun 1906, Easton, Washington County, New York.
285.	vi.	ALLEN HARRINGTON, b. Feb 1843, Easton, Washington County, New York; d. 31 Dec 1882, Greenwich, New York.
286.	vii.	JOHN J. HARRINGTON, b. Abt. 1849, Blossburg, Pennsylvania; d. 26 Aug 1930.

91. BENJAMIN[6] MILKS *(JONATHAN[5] MILK, JONATHAN[4], JOB[3], JOHN[2], JOHN[1])* was born 01 Jun 1800 in Washington County, New York[269], and died 13 May 1843 in Persia, Cattaraugus County, New York[269]. He married ALIDA MILLER.

She was born 10 Nov 1800 in Easton, Washington County, New York[269], and died 23 Jun 1877 in Persia, Cattaraugus Co, NY[269].

Benjamin and Alida are buried in the Milks Cemetery, Town of Persia, Cattaraugus Co, NY

Children of BENJAMIN MILKS and ALIDA MILLER are:

287.   i.   LEONARD[7] MILKS, b. Bet. 1820 - 1821, Easton, Washington County, New York; d. Aft. 29 Oct 1898.
            ii.   CHARLES H. MILKS, b. 22 Sep 1822, Persia, Cattaraugus County, New York[269]; d. 03 Aug 1856, Persia, Cattaraugus County, New York[269]. Burial: Milks Cemetery, Town of Persia, Cattaraugus Co, NY unmarried.
288.   iii.   CORDELIA MILKS, b. 12 Dec 1823, Washington County, New York; d. 15 Sep 1882, Persia, Cattaraugus Co, NY
            iv.   BETSEY MILKS, b. Abt. 1825; m. RUFUS MCKENZIE.
289.   v.   GARRETT T. MILKS, b. 27 Jul 1828, Cattaraugus County, New York; d. 23 Nov 1907, Persia, Cattaraugus County, NY.
            vi.   FREEMAN MILKS, b. 22 Jul 1831, Dayton, Cattaraugus Co., NY[270,271]; d. 09 Dec 1900, Cattaraugus, New Albion, Cattaraugus Co, NY[272,273]; m. JOANNA FRANKLIN[274], 1856[274]; b. 24 Jul 1836, New York[275,276]; d. Bet. 1910 - 1920, Dayton, Cattaraugus County, New York (No children). Freeman owned real estate in Buffalo as well as in Dayton, Cattaraugus County. Owned a 500 acre farm and a sawmill. Freeman is buried in Liberty Park Cemetery, Village of Cattaraugus, Cattaraugus Co, NY No children.
290.   vii.   JOANNA IRENE MILKS, b. Abt. 1834, Cattaraugus County, New York.
291.   viii.   DEBORAH MILKS, b. Aug 1836, Cattaraugus County, New York; d. Bet. 1920 - 1930, Cattaraugus County, New York.
292.   ix.   GILBERT MILKS, b. Mar 1838, Cattaraugus County, New York; d. 23 Feb 1911, New Albion, Cattaraugus County, NY.

92. PRINCE WILLIAM[6] MILKS *(JONATHAN[5] MILK, JONATHAN[4], JOB[3], JOHN[2], JOHN[1])* was born 1802 in Washington County, New York, and died 12 Aug 1880 in New Albion, Cattaraugus County, New York[277]. He married ELIZABETH PHILBRICK[278,279]. She was born 26 Jul 1811 in Cardiff, NY[279,280], and died 04 Feb 1885 in New Albion, Cattaraugus Co, NY[281].

Prince William Milks, b. 1802, Washington Co., NY (son of Jonathan 1769), d. 1880; m. Elizabeth Philbrick, b. 1812, of Cardiff, NY. Although Prince became blind in later life, he maintained meticulous care of his person. His grandchildren tell of watching Prince stand in front of the mirror to shave his face, although he had no vision. On one occasion these youngsters tried to play a prank on him by placing a flat pan over the mirror. Prince seemed readily aware of their cause for joviality and joked at the gesture. At one time he lived in Cardiff, Onondaga Co., NY, where his wife and some of his chn. were b. Res. later, Napoli, Cattaraugus Co., NY. Chn., 5: Prince and Elizabeth are buried in Tug Hill Cemetery, New Albion, Cattaraugus Co, NY

Children of PRINCE MILKS and ELIZABETH PHILBRICK are:

293.   i.   JONATHAN B. "TIP"[7] MILKS, b. 17 Nov 1829; d. 17 Apr 1891, New Albion, Cattaraugus County, New York.
294.   ii.   LUTHER P. MILKS, b. 16 Oct 1831, Cardiff, Onondaga Co, New York; d. 26 Feb 1893, Napoli, Cattaraugus County, NY.
295.   iii.   MARY ELIZABETH MILKS, b. Nov 1839, Cardiff, Onondaga Co., New York; d. 07 Jan 1902, New Albion, NY.
296.   iv.   MINA FRANCES MILKS, b. 22 Feb 1842; d. 01 Jan 1921, New Albion, Cattaraugus Co, NY.
            v.   RUTH MILKS[281,282], b. 04 Mar 1852[283]; d. 14 Mar 1933, New Albion, Cattaraugus Co, NY[283]. Burial: Tug Hill Cemetery, New Albion, Cattaraugus Co, NY

93. BATHSHEBA[6] MILKS *(JONATHAN[5] MILK, JONATHAN[4], JOB[3], JOHN[2], JOHN[1])* was born Abt. 1804 in Washington County, New York, and died 05 Sep 1866 in Olin, Jones County, Iowa. She married HORACE GIBBS SEELEY, son of JEDUTHA SEELEY and SALLY GIBBS. He was born 30 Oct 1804 in Onondaga Co., NY, and died Mar 1898 in Jones Co., Iowa.

The Seeley family "were large people, many were well over six-foot-two and of sturdy build, "according to Clarence Luke Milks of Willett, NY, himself a descendant of the Milks family two ways, through Bathsheba Milks Seeley and through her brother Luke Milks (see p. 266). *History of Cattaraugus Co., NY,* by Everts, p. 477, gives accounts of daring adventures and prowess of Horace Seeley and his brothers.

Horace Seeley moved to Whitesides Co., Ill. where his parents and brothers lived at that time. There, before

October 1848, he remarried Mary Chatterton. Before 1855 he moved to Rome Tp., Jones Co., Iowa. (See also *History of Whitesides Co., Ill.*)

Bathsheba probably moved west during the California Gold Rush in 1849, in company with her married daughters, Caroline Seeley Bothwell and Mary Seeley Graft, and their families. In 1855 Bathsheba was living with her sister, Deborah Milks Harrington, in Easton, Washington Co., NY. An excerpt from a letter Bathsheba sent from Easton to her sister Sarah Milks Benson, in Illinois, dated 25 Mar 1855, gives insight as to her thoughts. Bathsheba wrote: *"My prospects for another world are brightening. Sarah, although I am far from you, my heart is with you. I warn you to bear up with trials and tribulations with patience, hoping there is a coming day when we shall all be free from sin and sorrow. . . . I expect you received the letter I sent to you concerning the death of my George. . . . "* This George undoubtedly was her son.

About 1862 Bathsheba remarried (to name unknown), according to information in a letter written by her sister-in-law Saloma Milks.

Children of BATHSHEBA MILKS and HORACE SEELEY are:
297.   i.   CAROLINE P.[7] SEELEY, b. 20 Sep 1829, Cattaraugus Co., New York [date ?? 1835-1837]; d. 08 Oct 1913, Ainsworth, Brown County, Nebraska.
        ii.   MARY SEELEY, b. Abt. 1834, Cattaraugus Co., New York.
        iii.   MILO F. SEELEY, b. 11 Apr 1837, Cattaraugus Co., New York. Lived in: 1960, Leon, Cattaraugus County, New York
        iv.   GEORGE W. SEELEY, b. 10 Apr 1839, Cattaraugus Co., New York; d. Abt. 1855.

94.   JONATHAN[6] MILKS, JR. *(JONATHAN[5] MILK, JONATHAN[4], JOB[3], JOHN[2], JOHN[1])* was born 1806 in Washington County, New York[284], and died 26 Feb 1893 in Sherman, Chautauqua County, New York[284]. He married (1) CHARLOTTE _____. She was born Abt. 1809, and died Abt. 1847. He married (2) SOPHIA ANN _____ Abt. 1848 in Cattaraugus County, New York. She was born Abt. 1822[285], and died 07 Dec 1867 in Sherman, Chautauqua County, New York. He married (3) ANNA JOHNSON[286] 1874. She was born Abt. 1838 in Ohio, and died 24 Jul 1926 in Sherman, Chautauqua County, New York.

Jonathan, Sophia, and Anna are buried in Sherman Cemetery, Sherman, Chautauqua County, New York

Children of JONATHAN MILKS and CHARLOTTE _____ are:
298.   i.   ZERUAH[7] MILKS, b. 1831, Dayton, Cattaraugus County, New York.
299.   ii.   LYDIA A. MILKS, b. Abt. 1832, Dayton, Cattaraugus County, New York.
        iii.   FRANCES MILKS, b. 1839, Dayton, Cattaraugus County, New York.
        iv.   J. WILLIAM MILKS, b. 1841, Dayton, Cattaraugus County, New York; d. 21 Feb 1914, Chautauqua County, New York.
        v.   EMOGENE MILKS, b. 1846, Dayton, Cattaraugus County, New York.
300.   vi.   ESTHER J. MILKS, b. 1847, Dayton, Cattaraugus County, New York.

Child of JONATHAN MILKS and ANNA JOHNSON is:
301.   vii.   ZELLA L.[7] MILKS, b. 06 Mar 1875, Chautauqua County, New York; d. 22 Nov 1944, San Diego, California.

95.   SARAH[6] MILKS *(JONATHAN[5] MILK, JONATHAN[4], JOB[3], JOHN[2], JOHN[1])* was born 1812 in Washington County, New York, and died 17 Mar 1884 in Wauponsee Township, Grundy County, Illinois. She married (1) SENECA BENSON. He was born 21 Apr 1810 in Cincinnatus, Cortland County, New York, and died 29 May 1869 in Wauponsee Township, Grundy Co., Illinois. She married (2) RICHARD HARRINGTON, JR. Abt. 1880[287], son of RICHARD HARRINGTON and MARY ALLEN. He was born 1796, and died 12 Feb 1875 in Easton, Washington Co., NY.

Sarah Milks, b. 15 Dec 1812, Washington Co., NY (dau of Jonathan 1769); m. (1) Seneca Benson, b. 21 Apr 1810, Cincinnatus, NY, son of Bildad & Lydia (Hutchinson) Benson and a descendant of John & Mary Benson who came to America in 1638. Sarah moved with her parents to Cattaraugus Co., NY, about the time of the opening of the Erie Canal in 1825. Seneca prob. left Cincinnatus at the time some other Bensons of his age migrated from Cortland Co. to Cattaraugus Co. The 1840 census shows Sarah and Seneca living near Persia, Cattaraugus Co., with 6 children.

In 1848 they moved to Illinois. Seneca and his future son-in-law, Orrin Satterlee, journeyed West each driving a team of horses and wagon. Sarah and the children traveled via boat over the Great Lakes to Chicago, where they were met by Seneca and Orrin. Near Joliet, the men hired out in the harvest fields, but their horses were overworked and one team died. Seneca and family first settled in Wauponsee Township, near Morris, Grundy Co., on the "Sparr" place; they put in a crop here, but the "call of the West" urged them to abandon the harvest and move on to Iowa. It was but a short while before they realized that Illinois was the land of their choice and they returned to Wauponsee Township to settle on the "Sample" place. Later they purchased 160 acres of very productive land in Oxbow Bottoms, title to which farm is still held in the Benson name. It is interesting to note that Orrin Satterlee's father and brothers and sisters soon settled nearby and the following fall Orrin married Mary Jane Benson, eldest dau. of Sarah and Seneca.

Seneca died here on 29 May 1869. Sarah subsequently m. (2) Richard Harrington, widower of her sister Deborah Milks (see p. 219). Since Richard had a family and lived in Easton, NY, and Sarah's children and her home were in Illinois, her time was divided between the two states. Richard d. 12 Feb 1875, clasping in his hand a letter from Sarah, who at that time was visiting in Illinois. Thus the ties between the families of the two sisters, Sarah and Deborah, were very close at one time, although they were widely separated. As Richard Harrington was a veteran of the War of 1812, Sarah received a government pension during the remainder of her life; she d. 17 Mar 1884, near Morris, and is bur. beside Seneca and 3 of her chn. in White Cemetery. Sarah and Seneca are buried in White Cemetery, Grundy County, Illinois

Children of SARAH MILKS and SENECA BENSON are:

302.	i.	MARY JANE[7] BENSON, b. 24 Dec 1831, Cattaraugus County, New York; d. 17 Dec 1856, Morris, Grundy County, Illinois.
303.	ii.	LYDIA BENSON, b. 07 May 1833, Cattaraugus County, New York; d. 04 Sep 1915, Grundy County, Illinois.
304.	iii.	RUTH BENSON, b. 05 Jun 1839, Cattaraugus County, New York; d. 21 Jun 1888, Felix Twp, Grundy County, Illinois.
	iv.	RIAL RYAN BENSON, b. 28 Feb 1842, Cattaraugus County, New York; d. 19 Aug 1856, Grundy County, Illinois. Burial: White Cemetery, Grundy County, Illinois
305.	v.	CAROLINE SARAH BENSON, b. 05 Sep 1843, Cattaraugus County, New York; d. 09 Jan 1903, Grundy County, Illinois.
	vi.	CHARLES BENSON, b. 1845, Cattaraugus County, New York; d. 11 Jan 1905, Grundy County, Illinois (unmarried). Burial: Sample Cemetery, Morris, Grundy County, Illinois (unmarked)
306.	vii.	ARVILLA BENSON, b. 1847, Cattaraugus County, New York; d. 1913.
307.	viii.	JOHN MILKS BENSON, b. 13 Jul 1849, Grundy County, Illinois; d. 11 Jun 1918, Grundy County, Illinois.

96. LUKE[6] MILK (*JONATHAN[5], JONATHAN[4], JOB[3], JOHN[2], JOHN[1]*) was born Jun 1812 in Washington County, New York[288,289,290,291], and died 21 Nov 1890 in Fairbank, Black Hawk County, Iowa[292]. He married SALOMA ADAMS Abt. 1830 in Cattaraugus County, New York. She was born 15 Jun 1813 in Cattaraugus County, New York[293], and died 01 Jun 1894 in Fairbank, Black Hawk County, Iowa[293]. Both are buried in Fairbank Cemetery, Fairbank, Buchanan Co., Iowa

Luke Milk(s) is shown as 40 yrs old in the 1850 census (being born c1810), but in the 1860, 1870, and 1880 censuses he is shown as 48, 58, and 68 respectively (being born c1812 as his tombstone records).

With their son Benjamin and family, and several of Saloma's people, the Adams, moved to near Fairbank, Iowa, between 1858 and 1861. A letter written by Saloma and Benjamin to Sarah Milks Benson, in 1862, tells of their pioneering in the West and their family ties. Saloma wrote:

"We are trying to get a living in Iowa. We have had very good luck since we came here. We bought 40 acres of land and paid for it, and 8 cows. They did very well and made aplenty of butter and cheese for our family and some to sell. Keeping stock is our chief business. We have 14 cows. We have 40 head of cattle in all, and a very nice horse and aplenty of hogs and poultry. . . . We have a place that suits me very well for this country. It has a nice little grove around the house, aplenty of wild plums and grapes close to the house. We have raised aplenty of grain to sell every year. . . . I feel very lonesome . . . . when I left Nancy Maria I left all the girl I had. It makes me unhappy and I cannot help it. I have her second boy with me. He seems very near to me, as he was born to our house and used to live with me a great deal before we left there. I think they will come here sometime, but I cannot tell when. She has four more boys to home with her . . . ."

Benjamin wrote in the same letter: *"I like this country first rate . . . I want to know if you let your mind travel back to York State. It is fresh in my memory. When Mary Jane [dau. of Sarah Milks Benson] and Nancy Maria were with us, when I think back, to tell the truth, the west is a lone place to me but the rest likes it first rate and I go with the crowd "*

Children of LUKE MILK and SALOMA ADAMS are:

308.   i.   NANCY MARIA[7] MILKS, b. 18 Feb 1833, Dayton, Cattaraugus County, New York; d. 1912, Maynard, Fayette County, Iowa.

309.   ii.   BENJAMIN FRANKLIN MILKS, b. 25 Jan 1835, Dayton, Cattaraugus County, New York; d. 17 Apr 1904, Black Hawk County, Iowa.

97. ISAAC[6] ROGERS, JR. *(RHODA[5] CHASE, ABIGAIL[4] MILK, JOB[3], JOHN[2], JOHN[1])* was born 1783 in Rensselaer County, New York, and died 21 Feb 1869 in Brownville, Jefferson County, New York. He married RACHEL _____. She was born Abt. 1785.

Children of ISAAC ROGERS and RACHEL _____ are:

310.   i.   URSULA[7] ROGERS, b. 1810, Rensselaer County, New York; d. 1899, Palermo, Oswego County, New York.

    ii.   CHANCY ROGERS, b. 1821, New York.

    iii.   TENERA ROGERS, b. 1823, New York.

    iv.   ANN ROGERS, b. 1826, New York.

    v.   ELI ROGERS, b. 1831, New York (twin).

    vi.   EMILINE ROGERS, b. 1831, New York (twin).

98. ORRIN[6] CHASE *(JOHN[5], ABIGAIL[4] MILK, JOB[3], JOHN[2], JOHN[1])* was born 14 Jul 1802, and died 20 May 1875 in Eaton, Madison County, New York. He married DEIADAMIA BUTTON 23 Apr 1822 in Winfield, New York, by Rev. William Hunt, daughter of JOHN BUTTON and POLLY WELCH. She was born 27 Jul 1802[294], and died 12 Mar 1869 in Eaton, Madison County, New York[294]. Both are buried in Eaton Village Cemetery, Eaton, Madison County, New York

Deiadamia practiced medicine, phrenology, and clairvoyance. Interesting accounts of Orrin Chase, Deiadamia, her forebears, and her descendants are given in: Trials and Triumphs of an Orphan Girl; or The Biography of Mrs. Deiadamia Chase, Physician and Phrenologist, by Hammond, 1859. Res. Georgetown and Nelson, NY.

Children of ORRIN CHASE and DEIADAMIA BUTTON are:

    i.   LUCIEN R.[7] CHASE, b. 14 Apr 1824; d. 14 Apr 1824.

    ii.   ALONZO AVERY CHASE, b. 23 Mar 1826; m. SARAH ROGERS, Jun 1847; b. Abt. 1826, Of Pharsalia, Chenango County, New York.

    iii.   CHARLES H. CHASE, b. 29 Oct 1827; d. 29 Oct 1827.

    iv.   MARYANNETTE CHASE, b. 17 Jan 1829; m. LYMAN H. WARREN, May 1844; b. Abt. 1829, Of Augusta, Oneida County, New York.

311.   v.   ALZINA BIANCA CHASE, b. 14 Aug 1830, Nelson, Madison County, New York; d. 31 Dec 1913, Georgetown, Madison County, New York.

    vi.   JAMES B. CHASE, b. 29 Oct 1832; d. 29 Oct 1832.

    vii.   LUNA M. CHASE, b. 17 Feb 1835; d. 18 Jun 1914, Augusta, Oneida County, New York, m. (1) AMOS HAMMOND; b. Abt. 1835; m. (2) MR. WHITNEY; b. Abt. 1835.

    viii.   SARAH A. CHASE, b. 31 Oct 1836; d. 25 Nov 1897; m. THOMAS P. MORSE; b. Abt. 1835, Of Cortland County, NY.

    ix.   SULLIVAN G. CHASE, b. 26 Jul 1838; d. 29 Apr 1861; m. MISS RICHARDSON; b. Abt. 1838.

    x.   JULIUS M. CHASE, b. 28 Jun 1841; d. 09 May 1925.

    xi.   DIOGENES D. CHASE, b. 27 Oct 1842; d. 07 Jan 1914; m. HARRIET BABCOCK; b. Abt. 1842.

    xii.   DEIADAMIA CHASE, b. 03 Apr 1844; d. 03 Apr 1844.

    xiii.   POLLY MARIA VERNETTE CHASE, b. 27 Mar 1845; d. 25 May 1929; m. FRANK SPERRY; b. Abt. 1845.

99. JOHN[6] MILK *(JOHN[5], JOHN[4], JOHN[3], JOHN[2], JOHN[1])* was born 31 Mar 1791 in Boston, Massachusetts[295], and died 26 Jan 1865 in Boston, Massachusetts[296,297]. He married ELIZABETH WATERS[298] 26 Nov 1820 in Boston, Massachusetts[299], daughter of EBENEZER WATERS and ELIZABETH _____. She was born 09 Nov 1801 in Boston, Massachusetts[300], and died 27 Mar 1875 in Boston, Massachusetts[301,302].

They lived at 4 Moon St. Court, Boston, Massachusetts (which was just across the square from the home of Paul Revere. Benjamin Franklin was born at 1 Milk Street in Boston, which was just a few blocks away, and was the street that John Milk took to get down to the wharfs where he was a boat builder.

Children of JOHN MILK and ELIZABETH WATERS are:
- 312. i. JOHN[7] MILK, JR., b. 14 Mar 1822, Boston, Massachusetts; d. 18 Dec 1872, Boston, Suffolk, Mass..
- ii. ELIZABETH MILK, b. 12 Sep 1824, Boston, Massachusetts[303]; d. 14 Nov 1911, Boston, Mass. (Never married).
  Baptism: 18 Apr 1852, Baldwin Place Baptist Church in Boston Dismissed: 26 Oct 1875, Baldwin Place Baptist Church in Boston
- 313. iii. HARRIET MILK, b. 17 Jul 1827, Boston, Massachusetts; d. 28 Apr 1907, Boston, Mass..
- 314. iv. JAMES MADISON MILK, b. 14 Feb 1831, Boston, Massachusetts; d. 03 Aug 1906, Hamilton, Massachusetts.
- v. EDWIN MILK, b. 13 May 1840, Boston, Massachusetts[303]; d. 14 Sep 1843, Boston, Suffolk, Mass. (death date?)[304].

100. ELEANOR[6] MILK *(JOHN[5], JOHN[4], JOHN[3], JOHN[2], JOHN[1])* was born Mar 1797 in Boston, Massachusetts, and died 19 Feb 1867 in Boston, Massachusetts[305]. She married JOSIAH NOTTAGE LONGLEY 12 Sep 1819 in Boston, Massachusetts[306,307], son of GEORGE LONGLEY and MARY _____. He was born 01 Sep 1796 in Boston, Massachusetts[308], and died 12 Mar 1834 in Boston, Massachusetts?. Josiah is buried in Granary Burial Ground, Boston.

Eleanor Long is shown living with her brother John Milk and his family in the 1850 census. Eleanor Longley is shown living with her brother Henry & Harriet Hemenway in the 1860 Boston census, along with James M. & Rosa A. Milk (ages: 31/28). This family lived next door to Eleanor's brother, John Milk.

Child of ELEANOR MILK and JOSIAH LONGLEY is:
- 315. i. ELEANOR[7] LONGLEY, b. 1827, Boston, Mass.; d. 16 Jul 1897, Somerville, Massachusetts.

Generation No. 7

101. DEBORAH[7] WHITE *(CYNTHIA[6] MILK, LEMUEL[5], DAVID[4], JOB[3], JOHN[2], JOHN[1])* was born May 1804 in Westport, Massachusetts and died 19 November 1887 in Bristol County, Massachusetts. She married JOSHUA POTTER son of GARDNER POTTER and ELIZABETH TRIPP. He was born 13 November 1799 in New Bedford, Massachusetts and died 29 June 1882 in Bristol County, Massachusetts.. All children were born in Dartmouth, Bristol County, Massachusetts.

Children of DEBORAH WHITE and JOSHUA POTTER are:
- i. CHARLES WILLIAM POTTER, b. 1827 Dartmouth, d. 9 Jan. 1894 Dartmouth.
- ii. LEMUEL M. POTTER, b. 1830 Dartmouth
- iii. ALDEN T. POTTER, b. 1833 Dartmouth
- iv. JAMES E. POTTER, b. 1838 Dartmouth
- 316. v. HOLDER WHITE POTTER, b. 1841 Dartmouth, d. 1922 Dartmouth
- vi. EDWARD E. POTTER, b. 1845 Dartmouth.

102. HOLDER[7] WHITE, JR. *(CYNTHIA[6] MILK, LEMUEL[5], DAVID[4], JOB[3], JOHN[2], JOHN[1])* was born 1812 in Westport, Massachusetts. He married AMY SHEPHERD BROWNELL Abt. 1836 in Westport, Massachusetts ?, daughter of GEORGE BROWNELL and MARY DAVIS. She was born 30 Oct 1814 in Westport, Massachusetts, and died 25 Sep 1865 in Westport, Massachusetts.

Children of HOLDER WHITE and AMY BROWNELL are:
- 317. i. GEORGE MILK[8] WHITE, b. 17 Sep 1837; d. 13 Jan 1915.
- ii. CYNTHIA WHITE, b. 16 Jul 1840.
- iii. ELLEN CORNELIA WHITE, b. 04 Apr 1843.
- iv. MARY ELIZA WHITE, b. 06 Apr 1845.
- v. WILLIAM JAMES WHITE, b. 18 Jan 1848; d. 25 May 1849.
- vi. ABBIE ADELIA WHITE, b. 13 Feb 1853; d. 13 Jan 1915.

103. DAVID[7] MILK *(WILLIAM[6], LEMUEL[5], DAVID[4], JOB[3], JOHN[2], JOHN[1])* was born Abt. 1806 in Massachusetts[309,310,311,312], and died 20 Jul 1873 in Cayuga County, New York. He married (1) CHLOE COMSTOCK?[314] Abt. 1823, daughter of SETH COMSTOCK and MARY ARNOLD. She was born Abt. 1805 in Adams, Berkshire County, Massachusetts, and died 20 May 1840 in Cayuga County, New York. He married (2) LYDIA _____, daughter of _____ and _____. She was born Abt. 1820 in New York, and died 24 Apr 1901 in Chicago, Cook County, Illinois[313]. Chloe is buried in Arnold-Comstock Cemetery, Fleming, Cayuga County, New York

In 1850 David and Lydia ran a boarding house in Seneca Falls and had a four year old orphan girl staying there, Hattie Deremer. They raised Hattie in their home, where she was still living in 1870 at the age of 23. Bet. 1862 - 1863, they ran a hotel and "eating house" at 5 Ovid St, Seneca Falls (also his residence). In 1870 they were living in Auburn, Cayuga County, and he is buried there in Ft. Hill Cemetery. Lydia is buried in Oakwood Cemetery, Chicago, Cook County, Illinois

Child of DAVID MILK and CHLOE COMSTOCK? is:
- i. GEORGE O.[8] MILK, b. Oct 1824, Seneca County, New York[315,316]; d. 14 Feb 1902, Seneca Falls, Seneca County, New York[316]; m. (1) LAVINIA C. _____[317,318], Bef. 1850, Seneca County, New York[319]; b. Abt. 1830, New York[320]; d. 30 Mar 1851, Seneca Falls, Seneca County, New York; m. (2) CAROLINE B. GOULD, Bet. 1857 - 1858, Seneca County, New York[321]; b. 1827, Seneca County, New York[322]; d. 1915, Seneca Falls, Seneca County, New York[322]. No children.
  George, Lavinia, and Caroline are buried in Restvale Cemetery, Seneca Falls, Seneca County, New York
  Between 1862 and 1863, George ran a saloon at 81 Fall St, Seneca Falls, NY

104. WILLIAM W.[7] MILK *(WILLIAM[6], LEMUEL[5], DAVID[4], JOB[3], JOHN[2], JOHN[1])* was born 1807 in Massachusetts[323], and died 01 Dec 1871 in Auburn, Cayuga County, New York. He married (1) HARRIET MOORE Abt. 1836 in Cayuga County, New York. She was born Abt. 1810, and died Abt. 1843 in Cayuga County, New York. He married (2) ELIZABETH CHRIST[324] 12 May 1844, daughter of BARNET CHRIST and ELIZABETH COOL. She was born 26 Aug 1822, and died 1907 in Auburn, Cayuga County, New York[325]. William and Elizabeth are buried in Arnold-Comstock Cemetery, Fleming,

Cayuga County, New York in Plots: Council Ground Lot 26, Grave 9 and Grave 10.

Children of WILLIAM MILK and HARRIET MOORE are:
- 318. i. OBED H.[8] MILK, b. 1837, Cayuga County, New York.
- 319. ii. HARRIET MILK, b. 1839, Port Byron, Cayuga County, New York.
- iii. OSCAR W. MILK, b. 16 Jan 1841, Cayuga County, New York[326]; d. 29 May 1851, Auburn, Cayuga County, New York[327].
  Burial: Mt. Pleasant Cemetery, Port Byron, Cayuga County, New York

Children of WILLIAM MILK and ELIZABETH CHRIST are:
- 320. iv. SILAS WRIGHT[8] MILK, b. 26 Oct 1847, Cayuga County, New York; d. 17 Sep 1931, Auburn, Cayuga County, New York.
- 321. v. GEORGE WASHINGTON MILK, b. 30 Nov 1850, Port Byron, Cayuga County, New York; d. 31 Mar 1926, Kankakee, IL.
- vi. WILLIAM LEMUEL MILK, b. 12 Feb 1853, Cayuga County, New York; d. 27 Jul 1855, Cayuga County, New York.
  Burial: Mount Pleasant Cemetery, Port Byron, Cayuga County, New York
- vii. MARY MILK[328], b. Abt. 1855, Cayuga County, New York; d. Bet. 1855 - 1860.
- viii. EMMA ELIZABETH MILK, b. 18 Apr 1857, Cayuga County, New York; d. 1910, Cayuga County, New York (unm.).

105. CYNTHIA[7] MILK *(WILLIAM[6], LEMUEL[5], DAVID[4], JOB[3], JOHN[2], JOHN[1])* was born 10 Jun 1810 in Cayuga County, New York, and died 28 Nov 1841 in Fleming, Cayuga County, New York. She married SAMUEL WILBUR COOLEY Abt. 1829 in Cayuga County, New York, son of ASAHEL COOLEY and SALLY WILBUR. He was born 26 Nov 1807 in Fleming, Cayuga County, New York, and died 05 Apr 1847 in Fleming, Cayuga County, New York. They are buried in Fort Hill Cemetery, Auburn, Cayuga County, New York

Children of CYNTHIA MILK and SAMUEL COOLEY are:
- i. FRANKLIN[8] COOLEY, b. 05 Jul 1830, Fleming, Cayuga County, New York; d. 1853, Fleming, Cayuga County, New York.
  Burial: Fort Hill Cemetery, Auburn, Cayuga County, New York
- ii. HENRY H. COOLEY, b. 12 Jul 1832, Fleming, Cayuga County, New York. Lived in: Chicago, Illinois
- iii. CHARLES G. COOLEY, b. 12 Nov 1834, Fleming, Cayuga County, New York.
- 322. iv. MARY ELIZA COOLEY, b. 15 Apr 1836, Fleming, Cayuga County, New York.
- 323. v. HELEN M. COOLEY, b. 03 Mar 1838, Fleming, Cayuga County, New York; d. 06 Apr 1920, Auburn, Cayuga County, New York.
- vi. WILLIAM COOLEY, b. 05 Apr 1840, Fleming, Cayuga County, New York. Lived in: Chicago, Illinois

106. CHARLES G.[7] MILK *(WILLIAM[6], LEMUEL[5], DAVID[4], JOB[3], JOHN[2], JOHN[1])* was born 02 Oct 1815 in Cayuga County, New York[329], and died 27 Apr 1870 in Auburn, Cayuga County, New York[330,331]. He married MARIA WHEATON[332] Abt. 1836, daughter of WILBER WHEATON and MARY CLAY. She was born 1809, and died 29 Dec 1864 in Seneca County, New York[333].
They lived in Seneca Falls, Seneca County, New York. where Charles ran a Blind and Sash Factory in partnership with his son.
Both are buried in Restvale Cemetery, Seneca Falls, Seneca County, NY

Children of CHARLES MILK and MARIA WHEATON are:
- i. PHEBE TRIPP[8] MILK, b. 05 Apr 1837, Seneca Falls, Seneca County, New York; d. 06 Feb 1858, Seneca Falls, Seneca County, New York. Burial: Restvale Cemetery, Seneca Falls, Seneca County, New York
- ii. LODESKA ASENTH MILK, b. 04 Oct 1839, Seneca Falls, Seneca County, New York[334]; d. 01 Mar 1841, Seneca Falls, Seneca County, New York. Burial: Restvale Cemetery, Seneca Falls, Seneca County, New York
- 324. iii. LOUISE CAROLINE MILK, b. 08 Jul 1842, Seneca Falls, Seneca County, New York; d. 04 Aug 1880, Cayuga County, New York.
- 325. iv. AUGUSTA FRANCES MILK, b. 1844, Seneca Falls, Seneca County, New York; d. Oct 1916, Cayuga County,

New York.
- v. JAMES BENTON MILK, b. 04 Feb 1847, Seneca Falls, Seneca County, New York; d. 27 Jan 1881, Chicago, Cook County, Illinois[335]; m. LILLIAN WICKES[336]; b. Abt. 1850, New York. Military service: Bet. 08 Apr - 27 Jul 1865, Private, C Co., 8th Cavalry, New York, Union Army. James is buried in Restvale Cemetery, Seneca Falls, Seneca County, NY

326.
- vi. ELLA MILK, b. 1849, Seneca Falls, Seneca County, New York; d. 1872, Auburn, Cayuga County, New York.
- vii. EMMA MILK, b. Abt. 1853, Seneca Falls, Seneca County, New York.

107. LEMUEL[7] MILK *(WILLIAM[6], LEMUEL[5], DAVID[4], JOB[3], JOHN[2], JOHN[1])* was born 18 Oct 1820 in Ledyard, Cayuga County, New York[336], and died 19 Jul 1893 in Kankakee, Illinois[336]. He married (1) JANE A. PLATT 01 Jun 1854 in Kankakee, Illinois[336], daughter of SLOSSON PLATT and MINERVA SHERWOOD. She was born 20 May 1831 in Butternuts, Otsego County, New York, and died 07 Dec 1881 in El Paso, Texas[337]. He married (2) MAY ELIZABETH SHERWOOD[338] 30 Nov 1886 in Saint Barnabas Episcopal Church,Tullahoma,Coffee,Tennessee[338,339], daughter of CHARLES SHERWOOD and CHARLOTTE FERRIS. She was born 01 Sep 1866 in Rushford, Fillmore County, Minnesota[340], and died 26 Dec 1944 in Alexandria, Virginia[340].
Lemuel, Jane, and May Elizabeth are buried in Mound Grove Cemetery, Kankakee, Illinois

LEMUEL MILK 1820 - 1893

In an article "Prairie Kings of Yesterday", appearing in *The Saturday Evening Post*, 4 July 1931, the author, George Ade, writes: "Something must be said of Lemuel Milk, a man of heroic proportions from Cayuga Co., NY, of Quaker parents, hailing from New Bedford, Mass., once more the business fundamentals of New England operating at high pressure and performing miracles in the Middle West. In 1852 he acquired 25,000 acres in Iroquois Co., IL, which he subdivided into fifty-six improved farms. He was a friend of Abraham Lincoln and during the Civil War he equipped a whole company at his own expense. He and his partners came over into our county and bought about 40,000 acres in the Beaver Lake region. They drained 9,000 acres of wet spots. He had on the lake range at one time 10,000 sheep, 2,500 cattle, and 300 horses. One field of corn covered 2,000 acres. Mr. Milk and his partners gathered up immense herds of cattle in Illinois and drove them over to our state {Indiana} to graze in a tidy pasture of 30,000 acres until they were ready to be taken back to Illinois in the autumn and be corn-fed for the Chicago market. Mrs. Jennie Conrad, a capable and highly intelligent woman, daughter of Lemuel Milk, still manages several thousand acres of the Indiana estate from her attractive country place at Conrad, Indiana. Her father lived to be seventy-three and was up and doing, on a magnificent scale, to the last of his days. He departed thirty-seven years ago, but they still talk about him up north, with wonderment and admiration, as a Goliath of unbounded ambition and generosity."

In the July 19, 1930 issue of *Kankakee Daily Republican*, newspaper, Burt E. Burroughs wrote:

"Perhaps no man who has ever lived in Kankakee was better known by the populace generally. Perhaps no individual memory was ever more generally revered by the populace as a whole in the wide realm in which he so long operated than that of Lemuel Milk, pioneer citizen, farmer, stock-man, and merchant.

LEMUEL MILK's carriage house – Kankakee, Illinois
Built in the 1860s, now a Historic Landmark.

"Who was Lemuel Milk? In our youthful imagination he was a giant -- a superman. The wealth of Croesus was but pin-money compared with that what he possessed. He was a big man physically who radiated energy to that extent that often an idle, aimless atom of a man by mere association would be galvanized into action, at least for a time. A man just naturally could not hang around where Lemuel Milk was without feeling the impulse to grab an axe, a hoe or a spade and get busy on something. Perhaps the most compelling feature of this composite nature was the indomitable quality,, the yearning for some worth-while task to concentrate upon . . . according to his gospel there was no short cut . . . no royal road to riches, no worth-while method short of work. And that which he set forth as axioms for the rank and file to follow he exemplified throughout his life . . . the outstanding quality of this remarkable man was his ceaseless, tireless, unremitting zeal for work.

"Lemuel Milk was primarily a man of the soil. Next to that he was a stock-man and next to that a merchandiser He was a staunch Republican throughout his life and so was his popularity an influence that, had he chosen to enter politics, he could have achieved considerable prominence with but little difficulty. The only political honor he ever accepted was the appointment of trustee at the Eastern Illinois Hospital for the Insane. On the other hand, he liked to do things in a big way for the candidates of his party and the barbecues given at the famous Milk's Grove farm, in the grove, on the occasion of his birthday, October 18, during the campaign years of 1883 and 1887, lived for years in the memories of thousands as an evidence of the bigness of his hospitality. Those were great days in politics and the glory and glamour and excitement of torchlight processions, brass bands, drum corps, and impassioned oratory all tended to add to the bigness of the stature of a man of the type of Lemuel Milk who sought nothing of political glory or emolument for himself.

". . . Lemuel Milk was credited as being the owner of 150 farms . . . located mainly in the neighborhood of Chebanse and Clifton and operated by tenants with whom he settled yearly or after the marketing of the crops . . . The farms of Mr. Milk, with alternate fields of grain and meadow . . . could be viewed from the 'Hurricane Hill', so named because when Mr. Milk was attempting to erect the farm mansion which now crowns its summit, the frame was blown down three times and as often put up by its undaunted proprietor . . . As a stock-man Mr. Milk had few equals . . . For years his men at the Grove farm gathered together hundreds of head of cattle in the spring and drove them across country to his ranch in the Bogus Island country of Indiana, there to be pastured during the summer months. The going and coming back of these herds became, in time, the harbingers of spring and fall, as unfailing in their significance as the migrations of the birds . . . In the spring of 1868, Mr. Milk built a notable mercantile establishment at Chebanse, known for years as 'Milks Combination Store.' . . . The building, which was called 'Milks Block' . . . housed a very complete dry goods department, grocery stock, boots and shoes, a tailor shop, a hardware stock, a complete drug stock, and a thoroughly equipped tin-working department, for, in that day, the tinware on the shelves of the hardware store originated in the local shop . . . To the west of the main part were four rooms which contained a millinery shop, a harness shop, Thomas S. Sawyer's bank and the Chebanse Herald, and a five-chair barber shop."

There is also an account of Lemuel Milk in *Biographical Dictionary and Portrait Gallery of Representative Men of United States*, Illinois Ed. II:427.

MAY ELIZABETH SHERWOOD, widow of Lemuel Milk, died at the home of her daughter, Mrs. H.C. Barton in Alexandria, Va. Mrs. Barton brought the ashes of her mother to Kankakee and following Christian Science funeral services at the home of Mrs. B.E. Burroughs, interment was made in the Mound Grove Cemetery. The deceased is survived by her daughter Mrs. Barton; a sister, Mrs. R.E. Curry of Index, Washington.

Children of LEMUEL MILK and JANE PLATT are:
327. i. JENNIE MINERVA[8] MILK, b. 05 Jun 1855, Kankakee, Illinois; d. 09 Sep 1939, Prob. at Conrad, Indiana.
      ii. SHERWOOD PLATT MILK, b. 08 Feb 1858, Kankakee, Illinois; d. 20 Jun 1883, Chicago, Cook County, Illinois (n.m.)[341].
          Never married.

Child of LEMUEL MILK and MAY SHERWOOD is:
328. iii. MARY SHERWOOD[8] MILK, b. 17 Jul 1888, Kankakee, Illinois; d. Apr 1978, Silver Spring, Montgomery, Maryland.

108. ALANSON[7] MILKS *(JOHN[6], LEMUEL[5] MILK, DAVID[4], JOB[3], JOHN[2], JOHN[1])* was born Abt. 1810, and died 10 Apr 1875 in Morris, Illinois[342]. He married (1) ELIZABETH SIDEBOTHAM Bef. 1850. She was born Abt. 1810 in New York[343]. He married (2) MARGARET 'NELLIE' KELLOGG Abt. 1868 in Illinois. She was born Abt. 1844 in Illinois[344].

from : ***The History of Kendall County, Illinois***: "... there followed, in the same year, Alanson Milks, who afterward bought and sold a number of prominent tavern stands .."
"Mr. Sidebotham took up a large tract of land, but died the following year. He was a brother-in-law of Alanson Milks, who had just bought out Mr. Davis, and opened a tavern, well known afterwards as the Patrick stand, and there Mr. Sidebotham was buried." In May 1865, Alanson had a Federal Tax assessment of $59.10 on an income of $1182.

Child of ALANSON MILKS and MARGARET KELLOGG is:
      i. JOHN J. ALONSON[8] MILKS, b. Oct 1869, Illinois[344].

109. VINCENT S.[7] MILKS *(JOHN[6], LEMUEL[5] MILK, DAVID[4], JOB[3], JOHN[2], JOHN[1])* was born Abt. 1814, and died in Port Burwell, Elgin, Ontario, Canada. He married (1) MARY ANN KIPP[345] Abt. 1835 in New York. She was born Abt. 1815 in New York ?. He married (2) LOUISA _____[346] Bet. 1841 - 1850 in Rochester, Monroe County, New York ?. She was born Abt. 1815 in New York. He married (3) BRIDGET SHAY[347] 20 Nov 1879 in Port Burwell, Elgin, Ontario, Canada[347,348], daughter of JOHN SHAY and MARY _____. She was born Abt. 1834. In 1850, Vincent lived in Rochester, Monroe County, NY

Children of VINCENT MILKS and MARY KIPP are:
329. i. SARAH JANE[8] MILKS, b. Bet. 1837 - 1838, New York; d. 20 Mar 1924, Bayham, Elgin, Ontario, Canada.
      ii. GEORGE O. MILKS, b. Bet. 1840 - 1841, New York; d. 20 Aug 1931, Elgin, St. Thomas, Ontario, Canada[349].
          Employed by: Binks Express, Chicago, Illinois

110. LAURA ANN[7] MILKS *(JOHN[6], LEMUEL[5] MILK, DAVID[4], JOB[3], JOHN[2], JOHN[1])* was born 1817 in New York, and died 23 Jan 1871 in Wilmington, Illinois[350]. She married ABRAHAM WILKINS Abt. 1835. He was born 12 Nov 1810 in Leicestershire, England, and died 17 Oct 1894 in Will County, Illinois. Laura and Abraham are buried in Oakwood Cemetery, Wilmington, Will County, Illinois

Children of LAURA MILKS and ABRAHAM WILKINS are:
      i. CHARLES W.[8] WILKINS, b. Abt. 1838, Will County, Illinois.

      ii. RUTH A. WILKINS, b. Abt. 1840, Will County, Illinois.

      iii. ALBERT B. WILKINS, b. Abt. 1843, Will County, Illinois; d. 05 Aug 1868, Will County, Illinois[351]. Military service: PVT, Co A, 100th IL Inf, Union Army, Civil War[351] Burial: Oakwood Cemetery, Wilmington, Will County, Illinois

330.   iv. FRANCES ALMEDA WILKINS, b. 14 Feb 1845, Will County, Illinois; d. 03 Oct 1935, Joliet, Will County, Illinois.

      v. SARAH B. WILKINS, b. Abt. 1846, Will County, Illinois; d. 17 Mar 1876, Will County, Illinois. Burial: Oakwood Cemetery, Wilmington, Will County, Illinois

331.   vi. HARRIET M. 'HATTIE' WILKINS, b. Feb 1850, Will County, Illinois; d. Bef. 1900.

      vii. ALICE WILKINS, b. Abt. 1851, Will County, Illinois.

      viii. JESSE WILKINS, b. Abt. 1853, Will County, Illinois. Shown as MALE in the 1860 census and as FEMALE in the 1870 census.

      ix. ALANSING J. WILKINS, b. 11 Sep 1856, Will County, Illinois; d. 11 Apr 1874, Will County, Illinois. Burial: Oakwood Cemetery, Wilmington, Will County, Illinois

      x. LAURA WILKINS, b. Abt. 1860, Will County, Illinois.

111. HARRIET MARIAH[7] MILKS *(JOHN[6], LEMUEL[5] MILK, DAVID[4], JOB[3], JOHN[2], JOHN[1])* was born Feb 1823 in New York[352], and died 13 Aug 1902 in Chicago, Cook County, Illinois[353]. She married ORVILLE DEAN CAGWIN 29 Oct 1840, son of THOMAS CAGWIN and EUNICE JOSLIN. He was born 20 Aug 1811 in New York[354], and died Bet. 1880 - 1900. HARRIET is buried in Oakwood Cemetery, Joliet, Will County, Illinois[355]

    Orville is recorded as being in Lockport, Illinois during the 1850 census (taken in Lockport on 17 Aug 1850), but he then shows up in Weaverville, El Dorado County, California (along with his brother Hamden A. Cagwin) in the same 1850 census, but taken on 3 Oct, 1850 in Weaverville. It is likely that Orville went to California in the 1849 gold rush.

    In the 1870 census, Orville is in Gold Hill, Boise County, Idaho Territory, while Harriet is living with her parents in Lockport, Illinois.

    Orville is recorded at home, in Joliet, in both the 1860 and 1880 census records, but Harriet is shown as a widow in the 1900 census.

Children of HARRIET MILKS and ORVILLE CAGWIN are:

      i. ORVILLE D.[8] CAGWIN, JR., b. 20 Aug 1841, Joliet, Will County, Illinois[356]; d. 07 Aug 1852, Joliet, Will County, Illinois[356]. Burial: Oakwood Cemetery, Joliet, Will County, Illinois.

332.   ii. EUNICE ADELAIDE CAGWIN, b. 21 Jan 1843, Joliet, Will County, Illinois; d. 22 Apr 1922, Peoria, Peoria County, Illinois.

333.   iii. ALICE V. CAGWIN, b. Feb 1846, Joliet, Will County, Illinois; d. 1924, Coldwater, Branch County, Michigan.

      iv. CHILDA CAGWIN[357], b. Abt. 1848, Joliet, Will County, Illinois; d. d.y..

      v. CHILDB CAGWIN, b. Abt. 1850, Joliet, Will County, Illinois; d. d.y.[357].

112. MARIAH E.[7] MILKS *(JOHN[6], LEMUEL[5] MILK, DAVID[4], JOB[3], JOHN[2], JOHN[1])* was born Abt. 1828 in New York, and died Bet. 1880 - 1900 in Lockport, Will County, Illinois. She married JOHN H. WEEKS, son of NATHANIEL WEEKS and ABIAH HASELTINE. He was born Feb 1830 in New York, and died Bet. 1900 - 1910 in Lockport, Will County, Illinois. John was a harness maker by trade.

Children of MARIAH MILKS and JOHN WEEKS are:

334.   i. EDWIN L.[8] WEEKS, b. May 1856, Lockport, Will County, Illinois.

      ii. FRANK J. WEEKS, b. Apr 1859, Lockport, Will County, Illinois; d. Bet. 1860 - 1865.

113. JANE OPHELIA[7] MILKS *(JOHN[6], LEMUEL[5] MILK, DAVID[4], JOB[3], JOHN[2], JOHN[1])* was born Aug 1833 in New York, and died 1901 in Waterloo, Black Hawk County, Iowa. She married SOLOMON S. KNAPP, JR.[358] 26 Jan 1852, son of SOLOMON KNAPP and MARIA LANFEAR. He was born Jan 1829 in New York, and died Aft. 1900 in Waterloo, Black Hawk County, Iowa. Number of Children (Facts: 1900, 7 children, 4 living.)

Children of JANE MILKS and SOLOMON KNAPP are:

335.   i. HARRIET E.[8] KNAPP, b. Apr 1853, Will County, Illinois; d. Abt. 1927, Black Hawk County, Iowa.

      ii. HANNAH OPHELIA KNAPP[358], b. 1854, Illinois; d. Bef. 1900, Black Hawk County, Iowa.

336.   iii. JOHN FREMONT KNAPP, b. May 1856, Black Hawk County, Iowa; d. 27 Oct 1904, Chicago, Cook County,

337. iv. FRANK F. KNAPP, b. Jul 1859, Black Hawk County, Iowa; d. Bet. 1920 - 1925, Black Hawk County, Iowa.
v. MARY KNAPP, b. Abt. 1860, Black Hawk County, Iowa.
vi. PRUDENCE JANE KNAPP, b. Abt. 1863, Black Hawk County, Iowa; d. Bef. 1900, Black Hawk County, Iowa; m. CHARLES EDGAR BAILEY, 22 Dec 1890, Buffalo Gap, Custer County, South Dakota; b. 02 Jul 1863; d. 1907, Brule, Brule County, South Dakota.

114. AMY SHEPHERD[7] BROWNELL *(GEORGE MILK[6], RHODA[5] MILK, DAVID[4], JOB[3], JOHN[2], JOHN[1])* was born 30 Oct 1814 in Westport, Massachusetts, and died 25 Sep 1865 in Westport, Massachusetts. She married HOLDER WHITE, JR. Abt. 1836 in Westport, Massachusetts ?, son of HOLDER WHITE and CYNTHIA MILK. He was born 1812 in Westport, Massachusetts.

Children are listed above under (**102**) Holder White, Jr..

115. ALFRED M.[7] GIFFORD *(SQUIRE[6], ISABEL[5] MILK, DAVID[4], JOB[3], JOHN[2], JOHN[1])* was born 06 Oct 1812.

Child of ALFRED M. GIFFORD is:
i. LYSANDER[8] GIFFORD.

116. ALDEN M.[7] GIFFORD *(SQUIRE[6], ISABEL[5] MILK, DAVID[4], JOB[3], JOHN[2], JOHN[1])* was born 06 Jul 1814, and died 1864. He married PRISCILLA HAMMOND. She was born Abt. 1815.

Children of ALDEN GIFFORD and PRISCILLA HAMMOND are:
338. i. STEPHEN C.[8] GIFFORD, b. Dec 1836, New Bedford, Bristol County, Massachusetts.
ii. WILLIAM F. GIFFORD, b. Abt. 1839, New Bedford, Bristol County, Massachusetts.
iii. GEORGE P. GIFFORD, b. Abt. 1842, New Bedford, Bristol County, Massachusetts; m. EMILY MOWRY.
iv. ISABELLA GIFFORD, b. Abt. 1846, New Bedford, Bristol County, Massachusetts; m. WILLIAM METCALF.
v. JOHN H. GIFFORD, b. Abt. 1848, New Bedford, Bristol County, Massachusetts; m. ELIZABETH CHASE.
vi. ROBERT GIFFORD, b. Abt. 1849, New Bedford, Bristol County, Massachusetts; d. Bet. 1850 - 1860, New Bedford, Bristol County, Massachusetts.
vii. EDWARD A. GIFFORD, b. Abt. 1858, New Bedford, Bristol County, Massachusetts.

117. MARY EARLE[7] GIFFORD *(SQUIRE[6], ISABEL[5] MILK, DAVID[4], JOB[3], JOHN[2], JOHN[1])* was born 21 Oct 1818, and died 10 Sep 1895. She married CORLAN B. LUCAS Abt. 1836. He was born Abt. 1818.

Children of MARY GIFFORD and CORLAN LUCAS are:
i. GEORGE F.[8] LUCAS.
339. ii. LYDIA B. LUCAS.

118. DAVID M.[7] GIFFORD *(SQUIRE[6], ISABEL[5] MILK, DAVID[4], JOB[3], JOHN[2], JOHN[1])* was born 12 Jan 1820, and died 1884. He married ELIZABETH HOWLAND.

Child of DAVID GIFFORD and ELIZABETH HOWLAND is:
340. i. CLARA F.[8] GIFFORD.

119. HARRIET S.[7] GIFFORD *(SQUIRE[6], ISABEL[5] MILK, DAVID[4], JOB[3], JOHN[2], JOHN[1])* was born 19 Mar 1824. She married PALMER BROWN. He was born Abt. 1824.

Children of HARRIET GIFFORD and PALMER BROWN are:
341. i. HARRIET P.[8] BROWN.
ii. SARAH BROWN.
iii. CRANSTON BROWN.

120. JOHN A.[7] GIFFORD *(SQUIRE[6], ISABEL[5] MILK, DAVID[4], JOB[3], JOHN[2], JOHN[1])* was born 09 Mar 1826, and died 1864 in New Bedford, Bristol County, Massachusetts[359]. He married ELIZABETH LUCAS Abt. 1845 in Bristol County,

Massachusetts ?. She was born Abt. 1826, and died 1908 in New Bedford, Bristol County, Massachusetts[359].

Children of JOHN GIFFORD and ELIZABETH LUCAS are:
- 342. i. DEBORAH M.[8] GIFFORD, b. Mar 1847, New Bedford, Bristol County, Massachusetts.
- ii. ELIZABETH A. GIFFORD, b. Bet. 1848 - 1849, New Bedford, Bristol County, Massachusetts; m. CHARLES DEXTER.
  Lived in: Acushnet, Massachusetts
- iii. CHARLES A. GIFFORD, b. Bet. 1850 - 1851, New Bedford, Bristol County, Massachusetts (twin); m. ANNIE BORDEN.
- iv. DANIEL HENRY GIFFORD, b. Bet. 1850 - 1851, New Bedford, Bristol County, Massachusetts (twin); m. PRISCILLA FAUNCE.
- v. JOHN A. GIFFORD, b. Bet. 1854 - 1855, New Bedford, Bristol County, Massachusetts; m. HANNAH CRAPO.
- vi. SQUIRE A. GIFFORD, b. Bet. 1855 - 1856, New Bedford, Bristol County, Massachusetts; m. AZUBAH A. ALLEN.
- vii. WILLIAM W. GIFFORD, b. Bet. 1857 - 1858, New Bedford, Bristol County, Massachusetts.
- viii. CHARLOTTE C. GIFFORD, b. Bet. 1861 - 1862, New Bedford, Bristol County, Massachusetts; m. ALBERT LEWIS.
  Lived in: Davenport, North Dakota
- ix. ALFRED M. GIFFORD, b. Bet. 1862 - 1863, New Bedford, Bristol County, Massachusetts; m. HARRIET SMITH.

121. GEORGE WASHINGTON[7] GIFFORD *(JOHN[6], ISABEL[5] MILK, DAVID[4], JOB[3], JOHN[2], JOHN[1])* was born 28 Aug 1830, and died 1905 in Watertown, Jefferson County, New York. He married PAMELIA SMITH? Abt. 1854 in Jefferson County, New York ?. She was born Abt. 1830, and died Bet. 1880 - 1900 in Watertown, Jefferson County, New York. George had 3 other children that we have no data on.

Children of GEORGE GIFFORD and PAMELIA SMITH? are:
- 343. i. LADETTE GEORGE[8] GIFFORD, b. 1857, Jefferson County, New York; d. 08 Apr 1895, Watertown, Jefferson County, NY.
- ii. PAMELIA GIFFORD[360], b. Abt. 1859, Jefferson County, New York.

122. ALDEN[7] GIFFORD *(JOHN[6], ISABEL[5] MILK, DAVID[4], JOB[3], JOHN[2], JOHN[1])* was born 21 Nov 1831. He married SARAH J. KEYES 21 Nov 1861. She was born 27 Dec 1839. They lived in Rome, New York where Alden was an M. D.

Children of ALDEN GIFFORD and SARAH KEYES are:
- 344. i. IDA EMME[8] GIFFORD, b. 26 Mar 1864.
- 345. ii. MINNE ELECTRA GIFFORD, b. 11 Oct 1865.

123. GUSTAVUS A.[7] GIFFORD *(JOHN[6], ISABEL[5] MILK, DAVID[4], JOB[3], JOHN[2], JOHN[1])* was born 18 Jul 1844. He married MARY M. MCHALE 20 Oct 1867. She was born 25 Dec 1840. GUSTAVUS was an M. D.

Children of GUSTAVUS GIFFORD and MARY MCHALE are:
- i. IDA MAUD[8] GIFFORD, b. 08 Aug 1869.
- ii. SUSIE EVA GIFFORD, b. 31 Dec 1871.
- iii. BYRON ADOLPHUS GIFFORD, b. 14 Apr 1873.
- iv. CORREL H. GIFFORD, b. 20 Jun 1876.

124. WILLIAM HENRY[7] DEUEL *(LEWIS[6], PATIENCE[5] MILK, DAVID[4], JOB[3], JOHN[2], JOHN[1])* was born 31 Dec 1811 in Greenfield, Saratoga County, New York, and died 01 May 1891 in Escalante, Utah. He married ELIZA AVERY WHITING 01 Jan 1837 in Freedom, Cattaraugus County, New York[361]. She was born 14 Oct 1819 in Gifford, Vermont, and died 19 Jan 1878 in Utah of black smallpox, which she contracted while nursing the sick.

William joined the Church of Jesus Christ of Latter-day Saints at Freedom, NY, moved to Nauvoo, IL, and made the trek across the plains to Utah in 1847. He and his brother, Osmyn M. Deuel, built the first house in Utah, which now stands in a pergola in Temple Square, Salt Lake City, He was instrumental in founding the cities of Centerville and

Kanarraville, Utah. His granddaughter, Polly Ann (Deuel) Spencer, describes him as a blacksmith, an honest, strong, and hard-working man, typical of Longfellow's Village Blacksmith, "with large and sinewy hands . . . He could look the whole world in the face for he owed not any man."

Children of WILLIAM DEUEL and ELIZA WHITING are:
- i. JOSEPH MERIT[8] DEUEL.
- ii. ALONZO MERIT DEUEL.
- 346. iii. MINERVA ADELINE DEUEL, b. 03 Mar 1843, Montrose, Iowa; d. 10 Feb 1873, Porterville, Utah.
- iv. MERCY ANN DEUEL, b. 30 Jul 1845, Montrose, Iowa; m. MYRON ROUNDY; b. Abt. 1845.
- v. WILLIAM HENRY DEUEL, b. 03 Aug 1848; d. 1912; m. MARCY JANE BARNEY.
- 347. vi. LEWIS DEUEL, b. 16 Jul 1851, Centerville, Utah; d. 05 May 1929, Escalante, Utah.
- vii. ELIZA FRANCES DEUEL, b. 23 Jun 1854, Centerville, Utah; m. MR. GOODRICH; b. Abt. 1854.
- viii. GEORGE AMOS DEUEL, b. 23 Nov 1857; d. 11 Sep 1918; m. MELISSA SHIRTS; b. Abt. 1857.
- ix. NATHANIEL DEUEL.

125. JULIA E.[7] HOAG (*LILLYS[6] DEUEL, PATIENCE[5] MILK, DAVID[4], JOB[3], JOHN[2], JOHN[1]*) was born 24 Aug 1813. She married LOUIS FORT.

Children of JULIA HOAG and LOUIS FORT are:
- 348. i. J. WARREN[8] FORT, b. 1834; d. 1905.
- ii. GEORGE FORT, m. SARAH B. THOMAS.
- iii. ROBERT FORT, d. dy.

126. JANE[7] HOAG (*LILLYS[6] DEUEL, PATIENCE[5] MILK, DAVID[4], JOB[3], JOHN[2], JOHN[1]*) was born 25 Feb 1815 in Saratoga County, New York, and died 30 May 1888 in Easton, New York. She married RUSSELL SMITH BORDEN, son of SMITH BORDEN and LUSINAH SHAW. He was born 12 Mar 1812 in Portsmouth, Rhode Island, and died 13 Apr 1883 in Easton, New York.

Children of JANE HOAG and RUSSELL BORDEN are:
- i. LILLIS LUCY[8] BORDEN.
- ii. ELIZABETH URUSLA BORDEN, b. 04 Jan 1831; d. 1831.
- iii. RUSSELL SMITH BORDEN, JR., b. 15 Jun 1839; d. dy.
- iv. ISAAC S. BORDEN.
- v. ELIAS H. BORDEN.

127. JACOB[7] HOAG (*LILLYS[6] DEUEL, PATIENCE[5] MILK, DAVID[4], JOB[3], JOHN[2], JOHN[1]*) was born 20 Jan 1825, and died 06 Nov 1855. He married JANE GREEN.

Child of JACOB HOAG and JANE GREEN is:
- i. LILLYS[8] HOAG, m. EDWARD ATKIN.

128. BENJAMIN B.[7] BLOSSOM (*ALICE[6] MILK, JOB[5], DAVID[4], JOB[3], JOHN[2], JOHN[1]*) was born 17 Sep 1811 in Westport, Massachusetts[362], and died 14 May 1880 in Dartmouth, Mass.[363]. He married SARAH M. REED 07 Dec 1833 in Dartmouth, Mass.[364]. She was born Abt. 1812. Benjamin was a farmer.

Children of BENJAMIN BLOSSOM and SARAH REED are:
- i. BENJAMIN C.[8] BLOSSOM, b. 1839; m. SARAH A. POOLE, 01 Dec 1873, Dartmouth, Mass.[365]; b. 1851[366].
- ii. CLARINDA D. BLOSSOM, b. 1841, Dartmouth, Mass.; d. 06 Apr 1900, Dartmouth, Mass.; m. JOHN L. REED, 02 Apr 1867, Dartmouth, Mass.[367]; b. 1837; d. Bef. 1900, Dartmouth, Mass.. Burial: Dartmouth, Mass.
- iii. ALICE ANN BLOSSOM, b. 31 May 1834, Dartmouth, Mass.[368]; d. 20 May 1912, Dartmouth, Mass.[368]; m. CAPT. JOHN C. HASKINS; b. Abt. 1834; d. Bef. 1912.

129. CLARISSA[7] BLOSSOM (*ALICE[6] MILK, JOB[5], DAVID[4], JOB[3], JOHN[2], JOHN[1]*) was born 03 Jul 1815 in Westport, Massachusetts (Twin), and died 1903 in Westport, Massachusetts (Unm.).

Child of CLARISSA BLOSSOM is:
346.   i.   ELI WALTER[8] BLOSSOM, b. 22 Jan 1850, Westport, Massachusetts; d. 23 Mar 1941.

130. ESTHER B.[7] BLOSSOM *(ALICE[6] MILK, JOB[5], DAVID[4], JOB[3], JOHN[2], JOHN[1])* was born 03 Sep 1821 in Westport, Massachusetts, and died 23 Jul 1895 in New Bedford, Massachusetts. She married JOSEPH B. BOWMAN 04 Sep 1842 in New Bedford, Massachusetts[369], son of NATHAN BOWMAN and HANNAH BRALEY. He was born 20 Apr 1820 in Falmouth, Massachusetts[370,371], and died 24 Nov 1897 in Chelsea, Massachusetts[372]. Joseph was a ship joiner. They lived in New Bedford, Mass. where they are buried.

Children of ESTHER BLOSSOM and JOSEPH BOWMAN are:
    i.   MARY ANN[8] BOWMAN, b. Bet. 1843 - 1844, New Bedford, Massachusetts.
    ii.   WILLIAM C. BOWMAN[373], b. Bet. 1847 - 1848, New Bedford, Massachusetts; d. Bef. 1850, New Bedford, Massachusetts.
    iii.   HANNAH ALICE BOWMAN, b. 18 Sep 1850, New Bedford, Massachusetts; d. 17 Jun 1897, Medford, Massachusetts[374]; m. EDWIN C. BURBANK; b. Abt. 1850. Burial: Oak Grove Cemetery, Medford, Massachusetts
    iv.   NATHAN BOWMAN, b. Bet. 1852 - 1853, New Bedford, Massachusetts.
    v.   THOMAS BOWMAN, b. 16 Jun 1855, New Bedford, Massachusetts[375].

131. BARNABAS[7] BLOSSOM *(ALICE[6] MILK, JOB[5], DAVID[4], JOB[3], JOHN[2], JOHN[1])* was born 03 Oct 1825 in Westport, Massachusetts, and died Bet. 1880 - 1900 in Bristol County, Massachusetts. He married NANCY MARIE DAVIS. She was born Bet. 1830 - 1831 in Massachusetts, and died Aft. 1900 in Bristol County, Massachusetts. Lived in: Fall River, Massachusetts

Children of BARNABAS BLOSSOM and NANCY DAVIS are:
    i.   JEREMIAH DAVIS[8] BLOSSOM, b. Abt. 1852, Fall River, Bristol County, Mass.; m. MARY E. TOMPKINS, 1877; b. Aug 1852, Rhode Island.
350.   ii.   WILLIAM ELIJAH BLOSSOM, b. Mar 1860, Fall River, Bristol County, Mass.; d. Fall River, Massachusetts.
351.   iii.   FRANCES MARIA BLOSSOM, b. Sep 1850, Fall River, Bristol County, Mass..

132. MARY M.[7] MILK *(JOHN[6], JOB[5], DAVID[4], JOB[3], JOHN[2], JOHN[1])* was born 10 Jan 1810 in New Bedford, Massachusetts (adopted)[376], and died 16 Aug 1886 in Westport, Bristol County, Massachusetts[377]. She married HUMPHREY B. ALLEN 22 Jun 1829 in Westport, Massachusetts, son of GREEN ALLEN and PHEBE SANFORD. He was born 30 Apr 1809 in Westport, Massachusetts[378], and died 05 Apr 1848 in Westport, Massachusetts[379,380]. Humphrey was a carpenter. They are buried in Green Allen Cemetery, Westport, Bristol County, Mass.

Children of MARY MILK and HUMPHREY ALLEN are:
    i.   BETSEY J.[8] ALLEN, b. Abt. 1831, Westport, Massachusetts[381]; d. 23 Nov 1902, New Bedford, Massachusetts[381]; m. ELLERY LINCOLN; b. Abt. 1830. Burial: Westport, Massachusetts
    ii.   JOHN M. ALLEN[382], b. 1837, Westport, Massachusetts.
    iii.   BENJAMIN W. ALLEN[383], b. 15 Jan 1839, Westport, Massachusetts[383]; d. 1923, Westport, Massachusetts[383]; m. HARRIET N. SPOONER[383], 28 Feb 1861, Westport, Massachusetts ?[383]; b. 1839[383]; d. 1919, Westport, Massachusetts[383]. They are buried in Green Allen Cemetery, Westport, Bristol County, Mass.
    iv.   CHARLES H. ALLEN[384], b. 29 Dec 1840, Westport, Massachusetts[384]; d. 31 Dec 1910, Westport, Massachusetts[384].
    v.   ALBERT M. ALLEN[385], b. Aug 1842, Westport, Massachusetts[385]; d. 27 Oct 1899, Westport, Massachusetts[385]; m. (1) EMMA J. BRADLEY[385]; b. 13 Oct 1846[385]; d. 24 Oct 1874, Westport, Massachusetts[385]; m. (2) ELIZA J. _____[385]; b. 1858; d. 1934, Westport, Massachusetts. Albert was a blacksmith. He served in the Civil War as a Private, E Company, 3rd Mass. Infantry, GAR He is buried in Beach Grove Cemetery, Westport, Bristol County, Mass.
    vi.   ELLEN A. ALLEN[385], b. 09 Sep 1844, Westport, Massachusetts[385]; d. 20 Oct 1864, Westport, Massachusetts[385,386].
Burial: Green Allen Cemetery, Westport, Bristol County, Mass.
    vii.   GREEN B. ALLEN[387], b. Nov 1846, Westport, Massachusetts[388]; m. EMMA C. _____; b. 1847.

viii. ANN W. ALLEN, b. Abt. 1833, Westport, Bristol County, Massachusetts[389]; d. 07 May 1895, Westport, Bristol County, Massachusetts[389]; m. WILLIAM D. SHERMAN[389].

ix. SUSAN ALLEN, b. Abt. 1835, Westport, Bristol County, Massachusetts[389]; d. 08 May 1908, New Bedford, Bristol County, Massachusetts[389]; m. JOSEPH PERRY[390].

133. JOHN[7] MILKS (*ELI S.[6] MILK, JOB[5], DAVID[4], JOB[3], JOHN[2], JOHN[1]*) was born 03 Jul 1813 in Duanesburg, NY[391,392], and died 01 Jun 1890 in Binghamton, Broome County, NY[393,394,395]. He married EVALINE LUCINDA BRIMMER Abt. 1853 in Broome County, New York[396], daughter of MR. BRIMMER and EPHA _____. She was born 06 Feb 1825 in Petersburg, Renss. Co, NY[397,398], and died 12 May 1893 in Binghamton, Broome County, NY[398].

Evaline Lucinda Brimmer, b. 6 Feb. 1825, Petersburg, Renss. Co., NY descendant of Anneka Jan Weber, early Dutch settler of New Amsterdam. John Milks moved with his parents to Hawleyton; when he grew to maturity he moved to Binghamton, NY, where he went into business. He owned a carding mill, and a cigar box and wagon factory. John and Evaline are buried in Glenwood Cemetery, Binghamton, NY

Children of JOHN MILKS and EVALINE BRIMMER are:

    i. HENRIETTA[8] MILKS, b. Nov 1854, Binghamton, Broome County, NY[399,400]; d. 31 Oct 1939, Binghamton, NY?[401,402,403].
Unmarried. Occupation: Milliner. Burial: Glenwood Cemetery, Binghamton, NY

    ii. WILLIAM ELI MILKS, b. Oct 1855, Binghamton, Broome County, NY[404,405,406]; d. 1926, Binghamton, NY (unmarried)[406].
Burial: Glenwood Cemetery, Binghamton, NY

    iii. ALICE EVA MILKS, b. 02 Jun 1859, Binghamton, Broome County, NY[407]; d. 11 Sep 1941, Binghamton, Broome County, NY[408,409]; m. JAMES B. DOUGHAN[410], Abt. 1896, Broome County, New York[411]; b. 1859, New York[412]; d. 1908, Binghamton, Broome County, NY[413,414]. Alice and James are buried in Glenwood Cemetery, Binghamton, Broome County, New York

352.   iv. MARGARET MILKS, b. 07 Apr 1864, Binghamton, Broome County, NY; d. 14 Feb 1919, Binghamton, NY?.

    v. CHARLES MILKS, b. 27 Oct 1865, Binghamton, Broome County, NY[415,416,417]; d. 18 Mar 1949, Binghamton, NY (unmarried)[418,419].

134. DAVID[7] MILKS (*ELI S.[6] MILK, JOB[5], DAVID[4], JOB[3], JOHN[2], JOHN[1]*) was born 1825 in New York[420]. He married ELIZABETH _____ Abt. 1860. She was born Bet. 1835 - 1841 in New York. David was a farmer.

Children of DAVID MILKS and ELIZABETH _____ are:

    i. EDGAR[8] MILKS, b. 1861; d. (unmarried).

353.   ii. GEORGE MILKS, b. 20 Jun 1862, Brackney, Pennsylvania; d. 30 Oct 1928.

    iii. ANNA MILKS, b. 1868, adopted; m. BERT WEBSTER; b. Abt. 1868.

354.   iv. DEWITT WILLIAM MILKS, b. 04 Jul 1878, Hawleyton, Broome County, New York; d. 12 Oct 1947, Broome County, New York.

135. PHEBE[7] MILKS (*ELI S.[6] MILK, JOB[5], DAVID[4], JOB[3], JOHN[2], JOHN[1]*) was born 1826 in Duanesburg, NY[421]. She married UNKNOWN BRADLEY.

Child of PHEBE MILKS and UNKNOWN BRADLEY is:

355.   i. MARY[8] BRADLEY, b. 1854; d. 1897, Broome County, New York.

136. BENJAMIN B.[7] MILKS (*ELI S.[6] MILK, JOB[5], DAVID[4], JOB[3], JOHN[2], JOHN[1]*)[422] was born Jul 1828 in Massachusetts[422], and died Abt. 1912 in Binghamton, NY[422]. He married EMILY L. MOSHER[422] 12 Dec 1860[422], daughter of BENJAMIN MOSHER and SARAH STEVENS. She was born 07 Sep 1842[423,424], and died 08 Dec 1869 in Binghamton, NY[424]. BENJAMIN was a farmer in Hawleyton, Broome County, New York

Children of BENJAMIN MILKS and EMILY MOSHER are:

    i. JOHN J.[8] MILKS[424], b. Dec 1861, Hawleyton, Broome Co., NY[425,426]; d. 30 Nov 1912, Binghamton, NY (unmarried)[427,428].

    ii. SARAH AMANDA MILKS[428], b. Oct 1865, Hawleyton, Broome Co., NY[429,430]; d. 11 May 1952, Binghamton, NY[431,432].

Unmarried. Sarah was an Artist[433,434]

356. iii. FRANCIS "FRANK" ELI MILKS, b. Sep 1868, Hawleyton, Broome Co., NY; d. 03 May 1926, Hawleyton, Broome Co., NY.

137. EZRA PLUMMER[7] BROWNELL *(JIRAH[6], ABIGAIL[5] MILK, DAVID[4], JOB[3], JOHN[2], JOHN[1])* was born 10 Aug 1819 in Westport, Massachusetts[435], and died Bet. 1870 - 1880. He married ANN MARIE ALLEN, daughter of STEPHEN ALLEN and HANNAH BAKER. She was born 1820 in New Bedford, Massachusetts, and died 12 Oct 1899 in Westport, Massachusetts[436]. EZRA was a Member of the Massachusetts State Legislature, House and Senate. His occupation was as a Cattle Dealer.

Children of EZRA BROWNELL and ANN ALLEN are:

  i. STEPHEN A.[8] BROWNELL, b. 1842, Westport, Massachusetts[436]; d. 20 Sep 1843, Westport, Massachusetts[436].

357. ii. STEPHEN A. BROWNELL, b. 05 Jan 1844, Chilmark, Massachusetts; d. 13 Dec 1898, New Bedford, Massachusetts.

  iii. HANNAH A. BROWNELL, b. 12 Apr 1846, Westport, Massachusetts[437]; m. SYLVESTER C. MANLEY, 26 Oct 1869, Westport, Massachusetts[438]; b. 1846.

  iv. WILLIAM HENRY BROWNELL, b. 28 Jan 1848, Westport, Massachusetts[439]; d. d.y. - Westport, Massachusetts.

  v. SUSAN A. BROWNELL, b. 26 Oct 1850, Westport, Massachusetts[439]; d. 27 Apr 1887, Westport, Massachusetts[440]. Never married

  vi. ALMY ANN BROWNELL, b. 08 Apr 1853, Westport, Massachusetts[441]; d. 26 Mar 1905, Westport, Massachusetts[442]; m. ZEBEDEU EDWIN DAVIS, 06 Apr 1880, Tiverton, Newport County, Rhode Island[443]; b. 1843. Burial: Linden Grove Cemetery, Westport, Massachusetts

  vii. WILLIAM H. BROWNELL, b. 19 Apr 1856, Westport, Massachusetts[444]; d. 18 Apr 1858, Westport, Massachusetts[445].

  viii. ELIZABETH M. 'LIZZIE' BROWNELL, b. 06 Mar 1859, Westport, Massachusetts[446]; m. SIMEON W. LUTHER, 29 Mar 1891, Westport, Massachusetts[447]; b. Bet. 1850 - 1851, Massachusetts.

  ix. WILLIAM R. BROWNELL, b. 06 May 1862, Westport, Massachusetts[448].

138. AMY[7] LOTTRIDGE *(ESTHER[6] BULL, AMY[5] CHASE, SARAH[4] MILK, JOB[3], JOHN[2], JOHN[1])* was born 15 Nov 1793 in Hoosic Falls, New York, and died 15 Dec 1856 in Troy, New York. She married GEORGE REX DAVIS Abt. 1810. He was born 1788 in Johnston, New York, and died 24 Jun 1867 in Troy, New York.

Child of AMY LOTTRIDGE and GEORGE DAVIS is:

  i. CHARLOTTE M.[8] DAVIS, b. Abt. 1815, Troy, New York; m. THADDEUS W. PATCHEN, 07 Mar 1837, Troy, New York[449]; b. Abt. 1810, New York. Thaddeus was a Railroad Clerk.

  1860 United States Federal Census for Thaddeus W. Patchen:
  Name: Thaddeus W Patchen
  Home in 1860:   Buffalo Ward 9, Erie, New York
  Name   Age
  Thaddeus W Patchen 50
  Charlotte M Patchen   45
  Caroline D Patchen   17
  Adelaide D Patchen   15
  Mary H Patchen   12
  John M Patchen   6
  Mary Ryan   24

139. THOMAS[7] LOTTRIDGE *(ESTHER[6] BULL, AMY[5] CHASE, SARAH[4] MILK, JOB[3], JOHN[2], JOHN[1])* was born 18 May 1795 in Hoosic Falls, New York, and died 09 Mar 1853 in Hoosic Falls, New York ?. He married MARY CAPLES/KEPPLE 27 Feb 1821[449]. She was born 22 Feb 1798, and died 23 Jul 1892 in Hoosic Falls, New York ?.

Children of THOMAS LOTTRIDGE and MARY CAPLES/KEPPLE are:
- i. ROBERT T.[8] LOTTRIDGE, b. 31 Dec 1821, Hoosic Falls, New York; d. 30 Dec 1850, Hoosic Falls, New York.
- ii. ESTHER MARIA LOTTRIDGE, b. 04 Nov 1825, Hoosic Falls, New York; m. HORACE FONDA, 1848; b. Abt. 1825.
- iii. MORDECAI JAMES LOTTRIDGE, b. 25 May 1827, Hoosic Falls, New York; d. 17 May 1892; m. MARY SHARPE, 25 May 1869; b. Abt. 1830.
- iv. JOHN HENRY LOTTRIDGE, b. 30 Oct 1829, Hoosic Falls, New York; m. JERMINA A. JONES, 1852; b. Abt. 1830.
- v. STEPHEN SMITH LOTTRIDGE, b. 10 May 1831, Hoosic Falls, New York; d. 29 Sep 1903.
- vi. DORR LOTTRIDGE, b. 12 Dec 1833, Hoosic Falls, New York; d. 22 Dec 1833, Hoosic Falls, New York.
- 358. vii. ALVIN DURHAM LOTTRIDGE, b. 27 Feb 1835, Hoosic Falls, New York; d. 12 Mar 1898, Hoosic Falls, New York.
- viii. FITCH LOTTRIDGE, b. 18 Jul 1839, Hoosic Falls, New York; d. 1917; m. (1) ADELAIDE BATTERSHALL, 1861; b. Abt. 1840; m. (2) HELEN HAINES, 1886; b. Abt. 1840.

140. ISAAC BULL[7] LOTTRIDGE *(ESTHER[6] BULL, AMY[5] CHASE, SARAH[4] MILK, JOB[3], JOHN[2], JOHN[1])* was born 08 Nov 1798 in Hoosic, New York, and died 05 Jul 1855 in Gilbert, New York. He married MELISSA COMSTOCK 19 Nov 1820 in Hoosick Falls, New York[449], daughter of JOHN COMSTOCK and HANNAH GRAVES. She was born 15 Jan 1799 in Hoosic Falls, New York, and died 07 Sep 1840 in Comstock, New York.

Children of ISAAC LOTTRIDGE and MELISSA COMSTOCK are:
- 359. i. FRANCES CAROLINE[8] LOTTRIDGE, b. 22 Dec 1821, Hoosic Falls, New York; d. 02 Oct 1903, Troy, New York.
- 360. ii. MARY ELLEN LOTTRIDGE, b. 12 Dec 1825, Hoosic Falls, New York; d. 19 Nov 1916, Buffalo, New York.
- 361. iii. CHARLES LOTTRIDGE, b. 08 Nov 1829, Hoosic Falls, New York; d. 18 Oct 1908, Hudson, New York ?.
- iv. AMY DAVIS LOTTRIDGE, b. 20 May 1837, Hoosic Falls, New York; d. 13 Feb 1915, Bedford City, Virginia; m. ROBERT COFFIN; b. 24 May 1833, Middlebrook, New York; d. 30 Jan 1914, Bedford City, Virginia. They are buried in Longwood Cemetery, Bedford City, Virginia

141. JOHN B.[7] LOTTRIDGE *(ESTHER[6] BULL, AMY[5] CHASE, SARAH[4] MILK, JOB[3], JOHN[2], JOHN[1])* was born 31 Dec 1800 in Hoosic Falls, New York, and died 24 Dec 1874 in Hoosic Falls, New York. He married (1) JULIA ANN HASWELL 19 Mar 1835 in Hoosick, Rensselaer County, New York[450]. She was born 1808, and died 13 Apr 1860 in Hoosic Falls, New York. He married (2) HARRIETT H. BRECKENRIDGE 28 Feb 1861 in Cleveland, Ohio. She was born Abt. 1820.

Child of JOHN LOTTRIDGE and JULIA HASWELL is:
- i. JOSEPH HASWELL[8] LOTTRIDGE, b. 1847; d. 19 Jan 1890, Hoosic Falls, New York; m. SARAH WELCH. Burial: Hoosic Falls, New York

142. MORDECAI[7] LOTTRIDGE *(ESTHER[6] BULL, AMY[5] CHASE, SARAH[4] MILK, JOB[3], JOHN[2], JOHN[1])* was born 25 Oct 1802 in Hoosic Falls, New York, and died 16 Jan 1884 in Schenectady, New York. He married CAROLINA FRANCETTA YATES 23 Jul 1828 in Pittstown, New York[451]. She was born 07 Oct 1806 in Pittstown, New York, and died 14 Apr 1885 in Schenectady, New York.

Child of MORDECAI LOTTRIDGE and CAROLINA YATES is:
- 362. i. JANIE ESTHER[8] LOTTRIDGE, b. 1833, Schenectady, New York.

143. MARIA[7] LOTTRIDGE *(ESTHER[6] BULL, AMY[5] CHASE, SARAH[4] MILK, JOB[3], JOHN[2], JOHN[1])* was born 25 Feb 1806 in Hoosic Falls, New York, and died 02 Jan 1881 in McArthur, Ohio. She married GEORGE WILLIAM BENEDICT 20 Apr 1835[451]. He was born 1803, and died 14 Oct 1884 in McArthur, Ohio.

Child of MARIA LOTTRIDGE and GEORGE BENEDICT is:
- 363. i. ALICE HANNING[8] BENEDICT, b. 31 Oct 1851, Ohio ?; d. 27 Mar 1919.

144. ROBERT[7] LOTTRIDGE, JR. *(ESTHER[6] BULL, AMY[5] CHASE, SARAH[4] MILK, JOB[3], JOHN[2], JOHN[1])* was born 10 May 1808 in Hoosic Falls, New York. He married SARAH 'SALLY' WHALLEY Abt. 1830. She was born Abt. 1810.

Children of ROBERT LOTTRIDGE and SARAH WHALLEY are:
364.   i.   ESTHER^8 LOTTRIDGE, b. 1831, Hoosick, New York; d. 1901.
          ii.   CHAUNCEY 'BURRELL' LOTTRIDGE, b. 1833, Hoosic, New York.
          iii.   JOSEPHUS LOTTRIDGE, b. 1837, Hoosic, New York.
          iv.   HARRY D. LOTTRIDGE, b. 1841, Hoosic, New York.
          v.   FRANCES J. LOTTRIDGE, b. 1843, Hoosic, New York.
          vi.   MARY LORING LOTTRIDGE, b. 1847, Hoosic, New York.

145.   ELIZA^7 LOTTRIDGE *(ESTHER^6 BULL, AMY^5 CHASE, SARAH^4 MILK, JOB^3, JOHN^2, JOHN^1)* was born 03 Jun 1810 in Hoosic Falls, New York, and died 03 Sep 1858 in McArthur, Ohio. She married DR. ANDREW WOLF 11 Nov 1834 in Hoosick, Rensselaer County, New York. He was born 1810, and died 1896 in McArthur, Ohio.

Children of ELIZA LOTTRIDGE and ANDREW WOLF are:
365.   i.   SARAH MARIA^8 WOLF, b. 25 May 1836; d. 28 Aug 1859.
          ii.   AMY D. WOLF, b. 28 Jun 1839.
366.   iii.   LYDIA M. WOLF, b. 19 Nov 1840; d. 1915.
          iv.   CHARLES B. WOLF, b. 19 Nov 1842.

146.   DELIA^7 LOTTRIDGE *(ESTHER^6 BULL, AMY^5 CHASE, SARAH^4 MILK, JOB^3, JOHN^2, JOHN^1)* was born 16 Jan 1812 in Hoosic Falls, New York, and died 03 May 1894 in Columbus, Mississippi. She married REV. THOMAS C. TEASDALE 16 Nov 1831, son of THOMAS TEASDALE and HANNAH COX. He was born 02 Dec 1808, and died 04 Apr 1891 in Columbus, Mississippi.

Children of DELIA LOTTRIDGE and THOMAS TEASDALE are:
          i.   GEORGE R.^{8} TEASDALE, b. 16 Sep 1832.
          ii.   EMMA H. TEASDALE, b. 17 Oct 1834.
          iii.   ROBERT L. TEASDALE, b. 24 Sep 1836.
          iv.   THOMAS A. TEASDALE, b. 10 Dec 1838.
          v.   HOWARD H. TEASDALE, b. 30 Mar 1841.
          vi.   JOHN E. TEASDALE, b. 15 Apr 1845.
          vii.   CHARLES H. TEASDALE, b. 24 Dec 1847.
367.   viii.   CATHRYNE 'KATIE' TEASDALE, b. 23 Jun 1851, Springfield, Illinois; d. 11 Dec 1901.

147.   SARAH "SALLY" E.^{7} MOORE *(DUDLEY^6, SARAH^5 MILK, JOB^4, JOB^3, JOHN^2, JOHN^1)*[451] was born 14 Oct 1799 in Rutland, Rutland County, Vermont, and died 06 Jul 1880 in Kingsley, Michigan. She married FREEBORN GARRETTSON MILKS Abt. 1819, son of JOB MILK and ELIZABETH _____. He was born 10 Aug 1797 in New York, and died 06 Jul 1878 in Kingsley, Michigan. Freeborn and Sarah are buried in Evergreen Cemetery, Kingsley, Grand Traverse County, Michigan, on the 5th lot inside the north main gate of the original cemetery on the east side of the main driveway, a tombstone marking the place.

Children are listed above under (**68**) Freeborn Garrettson Milks.

148.   DAVID^7 MOORE *(DUDLEY^6, SARAH^5 MILK, JOB^4, JOB^3, JOHN^2, JOHN^1)* was born 20 Jan 1819 in Hull, Quebec, Canada, and died 26 Jan 1901 in North Ogden, Weber, Utah[452]. He married (1) SUSAN ____ Bef. 1850 in Canada ?. She was born Abt. 1810 in Vermont, and died Bet. 1880 - 1900 in Weber County, Utah. He married (2) SARAH BARKER 1850 in Weber County, Utah[453]. She was born Aug 1829 in England, and died 12 Jul 1908 in Weber County, Utah[454]. He married (3) DIANA HERRICK 1854 in Weber County, Utah[455], daughter of LEMUEL HERRICK and SALLY JUDD. She was born 29 Sep 1832 in Missouri[456], and died 07 Aug 1905 in Weber County, Utah[457]. David was a Bishop in the Mormon Church in Utah. He corresponded regularly with his sister, Sarah Moore Milks in Michigan.

Children of DAVID MOORE and SARAH BARKER are:
          i.   DAVID M.^{8} MOORE, b. Abt. 1851, Ogden, Weber County, Utah.
          ii.   MARYANN MOORE, b. Abt. 1853, Ogden, Weber County, Utah.
          iii.   JOSEPH MOORE, b. Abt. 1855, Ogden, Weber County, Utah.
          iv.   ELLEN MOORE, b. Abt. 1858, Ogden, Weber County, Utah.

	v.	FRANKLIN MOORE, b. Nov 1861, Ogden, Weber County, Utah; d. 22 Jan 1942, Weber County, Utah.

368.

Children of DAVID MOORE and DIANA HERRICK are:
369. vi. LESTER J.[8] MOORE, b. Oct 1855, Weber County, Utah; d. 05 Jan 1926, Weber County, Utah.
 vii. GEORGE ALBERT MOORE, b. Abt. 1859, Weber County, Utah.
 viii. HENRY D. MOORE, b. Abt. 1862, Weber County, Utah.
370. ix. CLARA DIANA MOORE, b. Apr 1863, Weber County, Utah; d. 01 Oct 1948, Ogden, Weber County, Utah.
371. x. PARLEY PARKER MOORE, b. Nov 1865, Weber County, Utah; d. 05 Jul 1931, Salt Lake County, Utah.
 xi. BELLE MOORE, b. Abt. 1869, Weber County, Utah.

149. SALLY[7] ANDREWS *(AMY[6] MILKS, JONATHAN[5] MILK, JOB[4], JOB[3], JOHN[2], JOHN[1])* was born 29 Aug 1801 in Austerlitz, Columbia County, New York, and died 13 Feb 1874 in West Stockbridge, Berkshire County, Massachusetts. She married FRANCIS BAINWAY. He was born 23 Aug 1801 in Canada, and died 05 Feb 1875 in West Stockbridge, Berkshire County, Massachusetts. They are buried in South Cemetery, West Stockbridge, Berkshire County, Massachusetts

Child of SALLY ANDREWS and FRANCIS BAINWAY is:
372. i. MARY IDA[8] BAINWAY, b. 04 Oct 1844, Alford, Berkshire County, Massachusetts; d. 20 Dec 1899, Pittsfield, Berkshire County, Massachusetts.

150. PHOEBE[7] MILKS *(JOB[6], JONATHAN[5] MILK, JOB[4], JOB[3], JOHN[2], JOHN[1])* was born Bet. 1809 - 1810 in New York[458], and died in Fayette, Iowa[459]. She married JONATHAN PERRY. He was born Abt. 1804 in New York[460], and died in Fayette, Iowa[461]. Lived in: 1850, Ashford, Fond du Lac, Wisconsin

Children of PHOEBE MILKS and JONATHAN PERRY are:
373. i. GEORGE[8] PERRY, b. Abt. 1830, New York.
 ii. BENEDICT A. PERRY, b. Abt. 1838, New York.

151. ICHABOD[7] MILKS *(JOB[6], JONATHAN[5] MILK, JOB[4], JOB[3], JOHN[2], JOHN[1])* was born Abt. 1810 in New York, and died Bet. 1843 - 1849 in Lewis County, New York. He married SAVINA SMITH Abt. 1835, daughter of ELIJAH SMITH and LOIS SPENCER. She was born 23 Jun 1811 in Maryland, Otsego County, New York, and died in Kankakee County, Illinois? After Ichabod died, Savina married Nathan Underwood. .

Ichabod lived first at Schenevus, NY; lived in Harrisburg, NY in 1835; on 25 Nov 1843 he purchased 45 acres in Watson, NY from Vincent LeRay De Chaumet. He came from Schenevus on horseback "when this country was still a wilderness and bears and wolves and panthers were frequently encountered – my mother often told me this." (Mabel G. Milks)

Sally and Herman (the children of Ichabod and Savina) were living with Savina and Nathan Underwood in Jefferson County, New York in 1850. In 1855, Savina was living with her daughter, Sally Higby and Sally's husband, Sherill, in Watson, Lewis County, New York, along with her son, Herman.

In 1853, Nathan Underwood, bought land in Kankakee County, Illinois, and in 1860 he was living (without Savina) with his son John Underwood in Kankakee. I have not found any record for Savina after 1855, nor any record for Herman in 1860. Although we know from Civil War records that Herman enlisted, from Wilmington in Will County, Illinois, and rose from private to Corporal while serving with Company E, 39th Regiment, Illinois infantry. He was mustered out on Dec. 6, 1865.

Children of ICHABOD MILKS and SAVINA SMITH are:
374. i. SALLY A.[8] MILKS, b. 29 Jun 1836, Harrisburg, Lewis County, New York; d. 24 Sep 1887, Watson, Lewis County, New York.
375. ii. HERMAN MILKS, b. 23 Apr 1842, Watson, Lewis County, New York; d. 18 Oct 1899, Lowville, Lewis County, New York.

152. DAVID[7] MILKS *(JOB[6], JONATHAN[5] MILK, JOB[4], JOB[3], JOHN[2], JOHN[1])* was born Abt. 1812 in Massachusetts, and died Jan 1884 in Gilbertsville, Otsego County, New York[461]. He married (1) ELIZABETH _____. She was born Abt. 1815 in Massachusetts. He married (2) HANNAH _____. She was born Abt. 1822, and died in White Store, Chenango County, New York. David lived in Butternuts, Otsego County, New York.

Child of DAVID MILKS and HANNAH _____ is:
      i. EMMA[8] MILKS, b. Abt. 1870, New York (adopted).

153. MARIA[7] MILKS *(JOB[6], JONATHAN[5] MILK, JOB[4], JOB[3], JOHN[2], JOHN[1])* was born 1818 in New York, and died 12 Mar 1889 in White Store, Chenango County, New York. She married JOHN REDINGTON. He was born Abt. 1818, and died Bef. 1880. lived in: Butternuts, Otsego County, New York

Child of MARIA MILKS and JOHN REDINGTON is:
376.   i. WILLARD DENNIS[8] REDINGTON, b. 15 Jun 1856, Otsego County, New York; d. 26 Sep 1940, Binghamton, Broome County, New York.

154. JOHN/JONATHAN L.[7] MILKS *(JOB[6], JONATHAN[5] MILK, JOB[4], JOB[3], JOHN[2], JOHN[1])* was born 1821 in New York, and died 21 Jun 1905 in Scott Depot, Putnam County, West Virginia[462,463]. He married (1) ELIZABETH (SPERRY) BARNES Abt. 1847 in New York. She was born Abt. 1825. He married (2) SARAH L. MCKIE Abt. 1870 in Green Lake County, Wisconsin[464,465]. She was born Abt. 1829 in Pennsylvania, and died Aft. 1905.

    John was a miller by trade, owned and operated a gristmill first in Cooperstown, NY, then in Oneonta, NY and later in Markesan, Wis. After the death of his dau. Mary, he went to WV to live with his daughter Sarah and her husband, William Losee.

Children of JOHN/JONATHAN MILKS and ELIZABETH BARNES are:
377.   i. SARAH ERSULA[8] MILKS, b. 30 Sep 1849, Cooperstown, Otsego County, New York; d. 29 Apr 1922, Huntington, Cabell County, West Virginia.
      ii. MARY F. MILKS, b. Abt. 1850, Oneonta, Otsego County, New York; d. 1894, Markesan, Wisconsin; m. HIRAM COOLEY, 02 Feb 1869, Methodist Episcopal Parsonage, Oneonta, NY, by Rev. J. W. Mevis[466]; b. 1846, of Oneonta; d. 1897. No children.

Children of JOHN/JONATHAN MILKS and SARAH MCKIE are:
      iii. BELL[8] MCKIE, b. Abt. 1860, Wisconsin.
      iv. NELLIE DODGE, b. Abt. 1855, Wisconsin; m. JOHN W. LAUGHLIN, 19 Feb 1874, Green Lake County, Wisconsin[467]; b. Abt. 1855, Michigan.

155. EBENEZER[7] MILKS *(JOB[6], JONATHAN[5] MILK, JOB[4], JOB[3], JOHN[2], JOHN[1])* was born 17 Apr 1827 in New York[468], and died 19 Nov 1902 in Sidney, Delaware County, New York[468]. He married SARAH N. MILLIER Abt. 1882 in Garretsville, Otsego County, New York[468]. She was born 02 Jun 1837[468], and died 16 Aug 1904 in Sidney, Delaware County, New York[468]. Ebenezer raised thoroughbred race horses in Walton, Delaware County, New York. Both Ebenezer and Sarah are buried in
Fly Creek Valley Cemetery, Otsego County, New York

Children of EBENEZER MILKS and SARAH MILLIER are:
378.   i. EMMA[8] MILKS, b. 13 Feb 1863, Delaware County, New York; d. 07 Aug 1886, Delaware County, New York.
379.   ii. CLARA MILKS, b. 11 May 1871, Delaware County, New York; d. 20 Dec 1925.

156. HARRIETT EMELINE[7] MILKS *(JOHN[6], JONATHAN[5] MILK, JOB[4], JOB[3], JOHN[2], JOHN[1])* was born 1813 in New York. She married JOSEPH RUSSELL HEMINGWAY 31 Oct 1832[470], son of MR. HEMINGWAY and MERCY _____. He was born Abt. 1813 in Connecticut.

Children of HARRIETT MILKS and JOSEPH HEMINGWAY are:
      i. JOHN[8] HEMINGWAY, b. 23 Apr 1833, New York[471]; d. 23 Apr 1889, Connecticut[471]; m. LOUISE MARSH[472], 15 Jun 1859, Litchfield County, Connecticut[472]; b. Abt. 1845, Connecticut.
380.   ii. JOSEPH R. HEMINGWAY, b. Abt. 1842, New York; d. Bet. 1880 - 1900, Canaan, Columbia County, New York.
      iii. ELIZABETH ADELINE HEMINGWAY, b. Abt. 1847, New York.

	iv.	MARY HEMINGWAY, b. 1849, Canaan, Columbia County, New York.
381.	v.	WILLIAM HEMINGWAY, b. Abt. 1852, Canaan, Columbia County, New York.
	vi.	HARRIET HEMINGWAY, b. Abt. 1855, Canaan, Columbia County, New York.

157. CHARLES ROLLAND[7] MILKS *(JOHN[6], JONATHAN[5] MILK, JOB[4], JOB[3], JOHN[2], JOHN[1])* was born 24 Jun 1815 in New York[473]. He married ELIZABETH G. OMAN Abt. 1836. She was born 1819 in Watson, New York[473], and died 1874 in Elsmere, Albany Co., New York[473]. The entire family, parents and 4 children, are shown in the 1851 census of Hastings County, Canada.

In 1851 they were living in Thurlow, Hastings County, Ontario (Canada West). In 1870 Charles was living, by himself, in a hotel in Glen, Montgomery County, New York, where he was recorded as being an "inventor".

Children of CHARLES MILKS and ELIZABETH OMAN are:

382.	i.	RICHARD GRAVES[8] MILKS, b. Aug 1838, Lowville, Lewis County, New York; d. Aft. 1910, Columbia County, New York
383.	ii.	CHARLOTTE H. 'LOTTIE' MILKS, b. Sep 1841, New York; d. 18 Sep 1922, King, Waupaca County, Wisconsin.
384.	iii.	HELEN MILKS, b. Abt. 1845, New York; d. 1914, Washington County, New York.
	iv.	WILLARD B. MILKS[474], b. Abt. 1849, Thurlow, Hastings County, Ontario, Canada[474]; d. Aft. 1900. In 1880, Willard was single and living with his sister, Charlotte, and her husband George Chase in Portage, Columbia County, Wisconsin. He is listed as a painter with left side paralysis. b. Canada. In 1900 he was living in Berlin, Green Lake County, Wisconsin and he was single.
	v.	MATTIE MILKS, b. 20 Mar 1861, Greenbush, Albany County, New York[475]; d. 20 May 1921, Volusia County, Florida[475]; m. JOHN FRANCIS VAN DEUSEN, 04 Jun 1896, Pittsfield, Berkshire County, Massachusetts; b. Oct 1847, Hudson, Columbia, New York, son of JOHN VANDEUSEN and HARRIET S. DUXBURY. Lived in New Smyrna, Volusia County, Florida in 1910. Mattie is buried in Hawk Park Cemetery, Edgewater, Volusia County, Florida No children. Lived in: 1910, New Smyrna, Volusia County, Florida

158. ELKANAH B.[7] MILKS *(JONATHAN[6], JONATHAN[5] MILK, JOB[4], JOB[3], JOHN[2], JOHN[1])* was born 13 Aug 1816 in Otsego County, New York, and died 29 Jul 1897 in Maryland, Otsego County, New York. He married MARY GRISWOLD 15 Nov 1838, daughter of WICKHAM GRISWOLD and LUCY WATERMAN. She was born 05 Jul 1818 in Connecticut[476], and died 24 Oct 1902 in Westford, Otsego County, NY[476,477]. They are buried in Elk Creek Cemetery, Otsego County, New York

Children of ELKANAH MILKS and MARY GRISWOLD are:

385.	i.	HORACE B.[8] MILKS, b. Nov 1838, Otsego County, New York; d. 06 May 1904, Westford, Otsego County, NY; Stepchild.
386.	ii.	SARAH ANN MILKS, b. 22 Nov 1844, Westford, Otsego County, NY; d. 08 Feb 1917, Des Moines, Iowa; Stepchild.
387.	iii.	CHARLES B. MILKS, b. 17 Jan 1847, Westford, Otsego County, NY; d. 30 Jan 1931, Otsego Co., NY; Stepchild.
	iv.	MARY ELLEN MILKS, b. 29 May 1851, Westford, Otsego County, NY[478]; d. 19 Dec 1856, Westford, Otsego County, NY[478]; Stepchild. Burial: Elk Creek Cemetery, Maryland, Otsego Co., NY
	v.	ELDORA MILKS, b. 21 Oct 1860, Otsego County, New York; d. 08 Feb 1953, Ainsworth, Brown County, Nebraska[479]; Stepchild; m. THOMAS JAMES LAWSON[480], 09 Nov 1896, Perry, Dallas County, Iowa[480]; b. 12 Jun 1862, Brant, South Bruce, Ontario, Canada; d. 24 Jan 1938, Ainsworth, Brown County, Nebraska[481]. Thomas was a member of the Masonic Order.

159. MARY ANN[7] MILKS *(JONATHAN[6], JONATHAN[5] MILK, JOB[4], JOB[3], JOHN[2], JOHN[1])* was born 21 Dec 1820 in Otsego County, New York[482], and died 23 Apr 1872 in Otsego County, New York[483]. She married LYMAN GRISWOLD, son of WICKHAM GRISWOLD and LUCY WATERMAN. He was born 20 Mar 1816 in Of Westford, Otsego Co., NY[484], and died 22 Mar 1864 in Otsego County, New York[484]. Mary is buried in Schenevus Cemetery, Schenevus, Otsego County, New York. Lyman is buried in Maple Grove Cemetery, Worcester, Otsego County, New York

Children of MARY MILKS and LYMAN GRISWOLD are:

388.	i.	ROSAMOND[8] GRISWOLD, b. Dec 1842.

388.	ii.	JOHN J. GRISWOLD, b. 1846, Westford, Otsego County, New York; d. 29 Jan 1923, Otsego County, New York.
390.	iii.	LAURA A. GRISWOLD, b. Jan 1850, Otsego County, New York.

160. CHRISTINE[7] MILKS *(JONATHAN[6], JONATHAN[5] MILK, JOB[4], JOB[3], JOHN[2], JOHN[1])* was born 08 Oct 1821 in Otsego County, New York[485], and died 06 Jun 1896 in Otsego County, New York[485]. She married WELLINGTON ELIJAH CRIPPEN Abt. 1841, son of PHILLIP CRIPPEN and SALLY GRISWOLD. He was born 22 Jul 1818 in Worcester, Otsego County, New York[485], and died 10 May 1900 in Worcester, Otsego County, New York[485]. They are buried in Elk Creek Cemetery, Maryland, Otsego County., New York.

Children of CHRISTINE MILKS and WELLINGTON CRIPPEN are:

	i.	EVELYN[8] CRIPPEN, b. 30 Nov 1842, Worcester, Otsego County, New York; d. 27 Mar 1848, Worcester, Otsego County, New York.
391.	ii.	EUGENE CRIPPEN, b. 12 Aug 1844, Worcester, Otsego County, New York; d. 30 Jan 1930, Worcester, Otsego County, New York.
392.	iii.	JOHN A. CRIPPEN, b. 20 May 1849, Worcester, Otsego County, New York; d. 09 Aug 1905, Texarkana, Texas.
	iv.	HERBERT CRIPPEN, b. 06 Apr 1855, Worcester, Otsego County, New York[486]; d. 1934, Otsego County, New York[487]; m. ABBIE PIXLEY, 18 Feb 1877, Otsego County, New York[488]; b. 11 Apr 1853, Hartwick, New York[489]; d. 06 Jun 1940, Cleveland Heights, Cuyahoga County, Ohio[490]. Herbert is buried in Elk Creek Cemetery, Maryland, Otsego Co., NY
		Although Herbert and Abbie were married, it appears that they never lived together. Herbert is shown in all subsequent census records as living in Unadilla, Otsego County, New York, listed as a boarder, married but no wife shown with him.
		It would appear that Abbie was handicapped, in some way, because she remained with her mother after her marriage, and then was placed in the Northern Ohio Baptist Home after her father died and probably at the time her mother died. She apparently lived there from before 1910 until her death in 1940. No Children Abbie is buried in Highland Cemetery, Cleveland Heights, Cuyahoga County, Ohio
	v.	JULIAN CRIPPEN, b. 16 Oct 1856, Worcester, Otsego County, New York; d. 1930, Otsego County, New York[491]; m. FLORA E. HOUGHTON, 29 Aug 1882, Otsego County, New York; b. Jan 1861, Davenport, Delaware County, New York; d. 1936, Otsego County, New York[491]. Julian and Flora are buried in Laurens Village Cemetery, Otsego County, New York. No children

161. LAURA JANE[7] MILKS *(JONATHAN[6], JONATHAN[5] MILK, JOB[4], JOB[3], JOHN[2], JOHN[1])*[492,493] was born 1824 in Otsego County, New York[494], and died 07 Apr 1882 in Otsego County, New York[494]. She married JAMES E. TYLER Abt. 1844 in Otsego County, New York ?[495]. He was born Jun 1822 in Otsego County, New York[496], and died 08 Feb 1904 in Otsego County, New York[497]. They are buried in Schenevus Cemetery, Schenevus, Otsego County, New York

Children of LAURA MILKS and JAMES TYLER are:

	i.	HELEN C.[8] TYLER, b. Bet. 1848 - 1849, Westford, Otsego County, New York; d. Bef. 1860, d.y..
	ii.	CARIE TYLER, b. Bet. 1855 - 1856, Westford, Otsego County, New York; d. Bef. 1870, d.y..
	iii.	JAMES E. TYLER, JR., b. Bet. 1867 - 1868, Maryland, Otsego County, New York; d. Bef. 1880, d.y..

162. POLLY[7] BARNARD *(RUTH[6] MILKS, JOB[5] MILK, JONATHAN[4], JOB[3], JOHN[2], JOHN[1])* was born 13 Mar 1796 in Rome, Oneida County, New York, and died 29 Jan 1864 in Lee, Oneida County, New York. She married ALPHEUS SPINNING, son of DANIEL SPINNING and JERUSHA STANDISH. He was born 15 Mar 1795 in Vermont, and died 05 Apr 1869 in Lee, Oneida County, New York.

Child of POLLY BARNARD and ALPHEUS SPINNING is:

	i.	MERRITT[8] SPINNING.

163. GEORGE[7] BARNARD *(RUTH[6] MILKS, JOB[5] MILK, JONATHAN[4], JOB[3], JOHN[2], JOHN[1])* was born 12 Oct 1805 in Rome, Oneida County, New York, and died 06 May 1868 in Rome, Oneida County, New York. He married JULIA ANN MUDGE 22 Feb 1832 in Rome, Oneida County, New York. She was born 07 Nov 1803 in Broadalbin, Fulton County, New York, and died 01 Jul 1869 in Rome, Oneida County, New York.

Children of GEORGE BARNARD and JULIA MUDGE are:
393. i.   GEORGE^8 BARNARD, b. 27 Oct 1833, Rome, Oneida County, New York; d. 29 Jan 1896.
      ii. JULIA H. BARNARD, b. Abt. 1835, Rome, Oneida County, New York.

164. ADONIJAH^7 BARNARD, JR. *(RUTH^6 MILKS, JOB^5 MILK, JONATHAN^4, JOB^3, JOHN^2, JOHN^1)* was born 05 Mar 1811 in Rome, Oneida County, New York, and died 03 Feb 1891 in Oneida County, New York. He married PHEBE BAILEY. She was born 1815 in New York, and died Aft. 1880 in New York.

Children of ADONIJAH BARNARD and PHEBE BAILEY are:
       i.   CLARK^8 BARNARD, b. Oct 1835; d. 28 Jul 1836, Lee, Oneida County, NY.
394.   ii. MARTIN MILLER BARNARD, b. 18 Jan 1834, Lee, Oneida County, New York; d. 06 Jul 1908, Fernwood, Oswego County, New York.
       iii. RUTH A. BARNARD, b. 23 Mar 1842, Lee, Oneida County, New York; d. 13 Aug 1882; m. MR. WETHERBEE.

165. HARRIET^7 BARNARD *(RUTH^6 MILKS, JOB^5 MILK, JONATHAN^4, JOB^3, JOHN^2, JOHN^1)* was born 11 Apr 1815 in Rome, Oneida County, New York, and died 19 Mar 1875 in New York. She married SILAS TUTTLE. He was born 1814 in Vermont, and died 02 Oct 1885 in New York.

Children of HARRIET BARNARD and SILAS TUTTLE are:
       i.   BETSEY^8 TUTTLE, b. Bet. 1849 - 1850, Lee, Oneida County, New York.
       ii. CHARLES H. TUTTLE, b. 18 Nov 1851, Oneida County, New York; d. 09 Feb 1888, Lee, Oneida County, New York; m. ELLA BROWN; b. 26 Jul 1858, New York; d. 28 Oct 1944, Oneida County, New York.

166. GEORGE^7 MILKS *(FREEMAN^6, JOB^5 MILK, JONATHAN^4, JOB^3, JOHN^2, JOHN^1)* was born Bet. 1822 - 1823^{499}, and died Bef. Apr 1880 in New York. He married MALISSA DUNBAR Abt. 1844 in Oneida County, New York. She was born Bet. 1823 - 1824^{499}, and died Aft. Apr 1880.

It is speculation on my part that George is a son of Freeman and Experience. He fits in the same age bracket as Cornelia, b:1824, who was a daughter of Freeman and Experience, and I have no other logical family in which to place him.

George and Malissa lived in Lee, Oneida County, New York^{500,501}

After George died, Malissa went to live with her daughter Ora Amelia, in Rich Valley, Smyth County, Virginia.

Children of GEORGE MILKS and MALISSA DUNBAR are:
       i.   LORENZO D.^{8} TANNER, b. 02 Jul 1840, Oneida County, New York (step-child of George); d. 22 Nov 1913, Washington County, Virginia.
395.   ii. ELIZABETH ANN 'BETSY' MILKS, b. 28 Nov 1845, Lee, Oneida County, New York; d. 25 Aug 1905, Bon Homme County, South Dakota.
       iii. JAMES H. MILKS, b. Bet. 1847 - 1848, Lee, Oneida County, New York.
396.   iv. BENJAMIN L. MILKS, b. 26 Dec 1851, Lee, Oneida County, New York; d. 26 Oct 1919, Essex, Essex County, Vermont.
397.   v.   ORA AMELIA 'AMY' MILKS, b. 09 Jul 1856, Lee, Oneida County, New York; d. 04 Apr 1939, Saltville, Smyth County, Virginia.

167. MOSES^7 MILKS *(DAVID^6, JOB^5 MILK, JONATHAN^4, JOB^3, JOHN^2, JOHN^1)* was born Abt. 1820 in New York^{503}. He married HARRIET G. BOAM 01 Jan 1846 in Huron County, Ohio, by Benjamin E. Parker^{504}. She was born Abt. 1826 in New York^{505,506}. In 1860 they lived in Fairview, Jones County, Iowa. By 1870 they had moved to Benton, Nemaha County, Neb.

Children of MOSES MILKS and HARRIET BOAM are:
       i.   SARAH^8 MILKS, b. Abt. 1849, Peru Township, Huron County, Ohio^{507}; d. Prob. d.y. (not in 1860 census).
       ii. JOHN H. MILKS, b. 1852, Aurora, Ohio^{508}; m. MARY E. ARMSTRONG^{509}, 16 Nov 1871, Pawnee City, Pawnee County, Nebraska^{509}; b. 1853, Butler County, Pennsylvania.

168. SARAH S.[7] MILKS *(DAVID[6], JOB[5] MILK, JONATHAN[4], JOB[3], JOHN[2], JOHN[1])* was born 21 Oct 1824 in Pennsylvania[510], and died 13 Oct 1909 in Townsend Twp., Huron County, Ohio[510]. She married ADAM KILE 15 Feb 1844 in Huron County, Ohio , By Edward Baker, JP[511,512]. He was born Abt. 1820 in Ohio[513], and died 14 Jan. 1892 in Townsend Twp, Huron County, Ohio. They are buried in Townsend Twp., Huron County, Ohio

Children of SARAH MILKS and ADAM KYLE are:
- i. MARY ELLEN[8] KILE, b. 15 Jan 1846, Cuyahoga County, Ohio, and d. 2 March 1918 in Townsend Twp., Huron County, Ohio. She married a Mr. Tougle.
- 398. ii. CHESTER PIERCE KILE, b. 19 Nov 1853, Ohio; d. 05 Dec 1912, Lorain, Lorain County, Ohio.

169. ROBERT DUDLEY[7] MILKS *(DAVID[6], JOB[5] MILK, JONATHAN[4], JOB[3], JOHN[2], JOHN[1])* was born Bet. 1828 - 1829 in New York\Pennsylvania[515,516], and died 19 Feb 1907 in Coldwater, Branch County, Michigan[517]. He married (1) LAURA ANN TURNER[518] 06 May 1851 in Huron County, Ohio[519]. She was born Abt. 1833 in Ohio[520,521]. He married (2) MARY E. BENNETT[522] 14 Jan 1893 in Branch County, Michigan[522]. She was born 1846 in Ohio. In 1860 they lived in Woodstock Township, Lenawee County, Michigan

Children of ROBERT MILKS and LAURA TURNER are:
- 399. i. FRANCES LAVERN[8] MILKS, b. Abt. 1852, Huron County, Ohio; d. 11 Dec 1931, Branch County, Michigan.
- 400. ii. EDWIN H. MILKS, b. May 1854, Huron County, Ohio.

170. GEORGE JEROME[7] MILKS *(DAVID[6], JOB[5] MILK, JONATHAN[4], JOB[3], JOHN[2], JOHN[1])* was born 15 Nov 1841 in Huron County, Ohio (See Croft, p72)[523,524], and died 08 Apr 1915 in State Hospital, Traverse City, Michigan[525,526]. He married (1) MARY HILL 23 April 1860 in Wood County, Ohio. She was born Bet. 1842 - 1843 in Ohio[527]. He married (2) MARY ANN TANNER 13 Oct 1866 in Somerset, Hillsdale Co., Michigan. She was born 12 Nov 1846 in Rollin, Lenawee County, Michigan, and died 17 May 1916 in Empire, Michigan[528]. They are buried in Maple Grove Cemetery, Kaleva, Manistee County, Michigan[529]

George Jerome enlisted at Cleveland, Ohio in Aug 1861 and served in Co. A., 103d Infantry Regt., 2nd Brig., 3d Div., 23d Army Corp. for 3 years during the Civil War. His death was attributed to Organic Brain Disease.

George's first wife, Mary Hill Milks, married (2) Langdon C. Hubbard 10 Aug 1865 in Wood County, Ohio.

Children of GEORGE MILKS and MARY TANNER are:
- 401. i. SARAH ELIZABETH[8] MILKS, b. 21 Jan 1868, Michigan; d. 01 Mar 1928, Bear Creek, Manistee Co., Michigan.
- 402. ii. EVA ARABELLA MILKS, b. 10 Apr 1870, Rollin, Lenawee County, Michigan; d. 06 Mar 1940, Aberdeen, Washington.
- 403. iii. DAVID TILDEN MILKS, b. 07 Jun 1872, Hillsdale, Michigan; d. 03 Nov 1949, Muskegon, Michigan.
- 404. iv. MILLIE MAY MILKS, b. 23 Aug 1876, Hudson, Lenawee County, Michigan; d. 08 May 1941, Aberdeen, Washington.
- 405. v. GEORGE JEROME MILKS, JR., b. 03 May 1878, Hudson, Lenawee County, Michigan; d. 09 Nov 1959, Aberdeen, Grays Harbor County, Washington.
- 406. vi. BERT LEROY MILKS, b. 08 Mar 1880, Manistee, Michigan; d. Aug 1968, Kaleva, Manistee Co., Michigan.
- 407. vii. EDWIN ELMER MILKS, b. 06 May 1882, Maple Grove Twsp., Manistee County, Michigan; d. 02 Jan 1952, Maple Grove Twp., Manistee County, Michigan.
- 408. viii. WILLIAM HENRY MILKS, b. 21 Mar 1885, Manistee County, Michigan; d. 1957, Manistee County, Michigan.

171. CATHERINE LUCRETIA 'KATE'[7] MILKS *(DAVID[6], JOB[5] MILK, JONATHAN[4], JOB[3], JOHN[2], JOHN[1])* was born Bet. 1842 - 1843 in Ohio[530]. She married (1) JEROME HICE. He was born Abt. 1845 in Maryland, and died Abt. 1897 in Grand Rapids, Kent County, Michigan ?. She married (2) JOHN A. ANDERSON 27 Apr 1899 in Grandville, Kent County, Michigan[531], son of JEBB ANDERSON. He was born 1840 in Sweden.

Child of CATHERINE MILKS and JEROME HICE is:
- i. ROY[8] HICE, b. 06 Oct 1882, Grand Rapids, Kent County, Michigan[532]; m. JENNY KILSTROM, 21 Sep 1904, Grand Rapids, Kent County, Michigan[533]; b. 1881, Michigan.

172. RICHARD[7] MILKS (*FREEBORN GARRETTSON*[6], *JOB*[5] *MILK*, *JONATHAN*[4], *JOB*[3], *JOHN*[2], *JOHN*[1]) was born 16 Apr 1820 in Eardley, Quebec, and died 18 Jul 1903 in Paradise, Michigan (Bright's disease)[534]. He married MARGARET MALINDA CORBITT[535] Abt. 1843 in Eardley, Quebec, daughter of NATHAN CORBITT and LORINDA WALLER. She was born 20 Sep 1823 in Canada (Eastern)[535], and died 06 Oct 1912 in Kingsley, Michigan[535].

In 1864 Richard and his family moved to Michigan. They came from Canada on a steamer, landed at Port Huron, Mich., then traveled again by steamer to what was known then as "East Head" or the south end of the east arm of Grand Traverse Bay. A few years later the family moved 20-25 miles south of there and took up a homestead in the wilderness, east of Kingsley. There were no roads at that time, just Indian trails, and supplies had to be carried from Traverse City. All of the children of Richard were b. in Canada, where he is shown in the 1861 census; the first children were b. in Quebec but the last child was b. in Ottawa. Richard was a carpenter and worked in a sawmill. He and Margaret are buried in Evergreen Cemetery, Kingsley, Michigan?[537]

Children of RICHARD MILKS and MARGARET CORBITT are:

409.	i.	LEONARD[8] MILKS, b. 27 Sep 1844, Eardley, Quebec; d. 02 Jan 1916, Kingsley, Michigan.
	ii.	NELSON MILKS, b. Aug 1846, Canada (Eastern)[538]; d. Bef. Oct 1945. Never married. Nelson was a Woodsman and tended to move around a lot. His mother remarked in a letter that she never knew where he was or if he was alive. In 1910 he lived in Moran, Mackinac County, Michigan, but by 1911 had moved to Deroche, Algoma West, Ontario, Canada
410.	iii.	MELINDA A. MILKS, b. Jul 1848, Canada; d. 01 Apr 1921, Grand Traverse County, Michigan.
411.	iv.	EMALINE MILKS, b. Aug 1850, Quebec, Canada; d. 02 Apr 1921, Grand Traverse County, Michigan.
412.	v.	LYDIA ANN MILKS, b. 1853, Quebec, Canada; d. 19 Jul 1878, Paradise Twp., Grand Traverse County, MI.
413.	vi.	EZRA MILKS, b. 05 May 1854, Quebec, Canada; d. Apr 1924, Traverse City, Michigan.
414.	vii.	RICHARD AMBROSE MILKS, b. 25 Feb 1857, Quebec, Canada; d. 07 Jul 1944, Traverse City, Michigan.
	viii.	EDGAR BUTLER MILKS, b. 11 Jun 1860, Quebec, Canada[539,540,541]; d. 05 Dec 1917, Traverse City, Michigan Cause of Death: Tuberculosis
415.	ix.	ZADIA ELLA MILKS, b. 03 Aug 1863, Canada; d. 08 Jun 1915, Paradise Township, Grand Traverse County, Michigan (Cerebral Hemorrhage).
416.	x.	LEWIS ETHIL MILKS, b. Apr 1865, Canada (Eastern); d. Abt. 01 Oct 1947, Cornwell, Delta County, MI.

The six sons of Richard Milks (1820-1903) [photo courtesy of Michael Walter Milks]

173. BENJAMIN⁷ MILKS *(FREEBORN GARRETTSON⁶, JOB⁵ MILK, JONATHAN⁴, JOB³, JOHN², JOHN¹)* was born 05 Jun 1821 in Eardley, Quebec, Canada, and died 09 Apr 1905 in Eardley, Quebec, Canada[543]. He married DEBORAH LUSK 20 Jul 1844 in Onslow, Canada East (Quebec). She was born 26 Jul 1827 in Eardley, Quebec, Canada, and died 17 Feb 1911 in Eardley, Quebec, Canada[543]. Benjamin's farm was situated at the town line between S. Onslow and Eardley in 1861. They are buried in St. Luke's Anglican Cemetery, Eardley, Quebec, Canada

Children of BENJAMIN MILKS and DEBORAH LUSK are:
- 417. i. JOSEPH⁸ MILKS, b. 01 Apr 1848, Eardley, Quebec; d. 26 Oct 1932, Ottawa, Carleton, Ontario.
- ii. DAVID MILKS, b. 30 Jan 1851, Eardley, Quebec; d. 25 Feb 1875, Eardley, Quebec, Canada.
- 418. iii. BENJAMIN J. MILKS, b. 27 Jan 1853, Eardley, Quebec; d. 18 Apr 1924, Eardley, Quebec.
- 419. iv. ISAAC MILKS, b. 06 Sep 1855, Eardley, Quebec; d. 18 Mar 1929, Montreal, Quebec, Canada.
- 420. v. HECTOR MAYNE MILKS, b. 17 Nov 1857, Eardley, Quebec; d. 25 Dec 1906, Aylmer, Quebec, Canada.
- 421. vi. ALMIRA MILKS, b. 19 Feb 1860, Eardley, Quebec; d. 15 Sep 1944, Eardley, Quebec.
- 422. vii. WILLIAM THOMAS MILKS, b. 26 Apr 1862, Eardley, Quebec; d. 06 Oct 1943, Eardley, Quebec.
- 423. viii. ROBERT KENNETH MILKS, b. 20 Aug 1864, Eardley, Quebec; d. 20 Oct 1945, Ottawa, Carleton, Ontario, Canada.
- 424. ix. IDA MATILDA MILKS, b. 03 Mar 1867, Eardley, Quebec; d. 24 Jul 1945, Fitzroy Harbour, Ontario, Canada.

174. AMBROSE⁷ MILKS *(FREEBORN GARRETTSON⁶, JOB⁵ MILK, JONATHAN⁴, JOB³, JOHN², JOHN¹)* was born Apr 1823 in Quebec, Canada, and died 1856 in Quyon, Quebec, Canada. He married JERUSHA CORBETT Abt. 1845 in Quebec, Canada?. She was born Abt. 1825 in Canada?. Jerusha is buried on the Ambrose Milks property in South Onslow, Canada

A boat, in which Ambrose was transporting bricks across the Ottawa River, capsized and his body was never found.

Children of AMBROSE MILKS and JERUSHA CORBETT are:
- 425. i. CATHERINE "KATE"⁸ MILKS, b. Abt. 1846, Quebec, Canada.
- ii. SARAH "SALLY" MILKS, b. Abt. 1848, Quebec, Canada; m. UNKN BULLIS; b. Abt. 1846. Lived in: Gracefield, Quebec, Canada
- iii. MARY JERUSHA MILKS, b. Abt. 1850, Quebec, Canada; d. Abt. 1857, Quebec, Canada.
- 426. iv. GARRISON MILKS, b. 20 Feb 1852, Onslow, Quebec, Canada; d. 24 Aug 1916, Bristol Mines, Quebec, Canada.

175. JOHN⁷ MILKS *(FREEBORN GARRETTSON⁶, JOB⁵ MILK, JONATHAN⁴, JOB³, JOHN², JOHN¹)* was born 25 Apr 1824 in Eardley, Quebec, Canada[544], and died 20 Jan 1895 in Cantley, Quebec[544]. He married MARY ANN MCALINDEN[545] 25 Jun 1849 in Cantley, Quebec, daughter of ANTHONY MCALINDEN and MARGARET BYRNE. She was born 1826 in Limerick, Ireland[546], and died 11 Jan 1887 in Cantley, Quebec[547].

For some time John resided with his sister Kate Bullis at Wakefield, Que. He met Mary, an Irish immigrant, in Cantley, where she resided with her parents, and after they were married they lived in Cantley. John was a carpenter and farmer; all his sons became carpenters and some of them also took up farming. He and his family are shown in the 1871 census of Hull, West Ottawa. John and Mary Ann are buried in Ste. Elizabeth Cemetery, Cantley, Hull Township, Gatineau County, Quebec, Canada

Children of JOHN MILKS and MARY MCALINDEN are:
- 427. i. PATRICK 'PATT' ALBERT THOMAS⁸ MILKS, b. 16 Mar 1848, Cantley, Quebec, Canada; d. 04 Dec 1927, Ottawa, Carleton, Ontario, Canada.
- ii. JOHN H. MILKS, b. Bet. 1852 - 1853, Hull, Ottawa, Quebec[548,549].
- 428. iii. PETER MILKS, b. 1854, Hull, Ottawa, Quebec; d. Bef. 1911, Hull, Ottawa, Quebec, Canada.
- iv. JAMES MILKS, b. 1854, Hull, Ottawa, Quebec[550]; d. 26 Dec 1876, Cantley, Quebec[551]. Burial: Ste Elizabeth's Cemetery, Cantley, Quebec, Canada
- 429. v. MARY ANN MILKS, b. 15 Feb 1858, Cantley, Quebec; d. 1914, Cantley, Quebec.
- 430. vi. ANTHONY MILKS, b. 17 May 1859, Cantley, Quebec; d. 09 Apr 1937, Cantley, Quebec.
- 431. vii. DAVID MILKS, b. 31 Mar 1861, Cantley, Quebec, Canada; d. 13 Sep 1918, Ottawa, Ontario.
- 432. viii. PETER FELIX MILKS, b. Bet. 1863 - 1864, Hull, Ottawa, Quebec; d. Abt. 1910, Lac des Iles, Quebec.
- ix. EDWARD MILKS, b. 21 May 1866, Cantley, Quebec[552]; d. 15 Jan 1936, Seattle, King County,

        Washington[552].
        Baptism: 02 Aug 1871, Cantley, Quebec[553]
433.   x.   DANIEL MILKS, b. 11 Aug 1871.
      xi.   CHILDELEVEN MILKS.
      xii.   CHILDTWELVE MILKS.

176. DAVID[7] MILKS *(FREEBORN GARRETTSON[6], JOB[5] MILK, JONATHAN[4], JOB[3], JOHN[2], JOHN[1])* was born 10 May 1829 in Eardley, Quebec, Canada[554], and died 01 Mar 1904 in Eardley, Quebec, Canada. He married SARAH JANE MCALLISTER 25 Dec 1856 in Eardley, Quebec, Canada[555]. She was born Abt. 1837 in Quebec, Canada[556], and died 04 Nov 1896 in Eardley, Quebec, Canada.

Children of DAVID MILKS and SARAH MCALLISTER are:
434.   i.   SARAH JANE[8] MILKS, b. 05 Feb 1858, Quebec, Canada; d. 1937, Eardley, Quebec.
435.   ii.   JOSEPH FINLEY MILKS, b. 24 Jul 1859, Eardley, Quebec, Canada; d. 13 Jul 1930, Rochester, Minnesota.
436.   iii.   DUNCAN WILLIAM HECTOR MILKS, b. 06 Mar 1862, Onslow, Quebec, Canada; d. 10 Jan 1927, Carleton, Ontario, Canada.
      iv.   GEORGE ALFRED MILKS, b. 18 Jan 1865, Eardley, Quebec, Canada; d. 1883, Eardley, Canada.

177. MELISSA[7] MILKS *(FREEBORN GARRETTSON[6], JOB[5] MILK, JONATHAN[4], JOB[3], JOHN[2], JOHN[1])* was born 29 Mar 1832 in Eardley, Quebec, Canada[557], and died 23 Oct 1907 in Paradise Twp, Grand Traverse Co., Michigan[558]. She married JAMES NEWMARCH[559] 1852 in Quebec, Canada?[560], son of JOHN NEWMARCH and LUCY PARKER. He was born 28 Dec 1822 in Croxton, Lincoln, England[561], and died 08 Mar 1906 in Paradise, Grand Traverse Co., Michigan[561]. James Newmarch's death certificate says they had 10 children/6 living
    JAMES NEWMARCH was baptized on 02 Jan 1823, in CROXTON, LINCOLNSHIRE, ENGLAND[562]
Melissa and James are buried in Evergreen Cemetery, Kingsley, Grand Traverse County, Michigan

Children of MELISSA MILKS and JAMES NEWMARCH are:
437.   i.   ISAAC JAMES[8] NEWMARCH, b. 10 Apr 1854, Quebec, Canada; d. 1937, Grand Traverse County, Michigan.
438.   ii.   ANDREW THOMPSON NEWMARCH, b. 27 Jul 1855, Grand Traverse County, Michigan; d. 11 Jun 1921, Grand Traverse County, Michigan.
439.   iii.   DAVID NEWMARCH, b. Oct 1857, Quebec, Canada.
440.   iv.   WILLIAM C. NEWMARCH, b. Apr 1859, Quebec, Canada.
441.   v.   HOWARD B. NEWMARCH, b. 1862; d. 1931.
      vi.   SARAH E. NEWMARCH, b. Abt. 1866, Quebec, Canada; m. CHARLES J. SLEIGHT, 14 Jun 1888, Paradise Twp., Grand Traverse County, Michigan[563]; b. 1850, England.

178. CHARLES[7] MILKS *(FREEBORN GARRETTSON[6], JOB[5] MILK, JONATHAN[4], JOB[3], JOHN[2], JOHN[1])* was born Apr 1835 in Eardley, Quebec, Canada[564], and died 19 Dec 1926 in Coleman, Temiskaming, Ontario, Canada[565,566]. He married SARAH DAVIS. She was born Jun 1841 in Ottawa, Canada[566], and died 1915 in Ottawa, Canada[566]. Charles is buried in Ottawa, Canada. Sarah is buried in Beachwood Cemetery - Section 39, Ottawa East of the Rideau, Ottawa, Canada[567]

Children of CHARLES MILKS and SARAH DAVIS are:
      i.   SUSAN R.[8] MILKS, b. 1862, Ottawa, Canada[568]; d. Unknown, Kirkland Lake, Ontario, Canada; m. SAMUEL O'ROURKE[568]; b. 1860[568]; d. 1950, Kirkland Lake, Ontario, Canada (?Date?)[568]. They are buried in Kirkland Lake Cemetery - Block F, Teck Township, Timiskaming District, Ontario, Canada
      ii.   ELLEN JANE MILKS, b. 17 Jan 1867, Ottawa, Canada[568]; d. 1956, Ottawa, Ontario, Canada[568]; m. THOMAS EDWIN RANDALL, 17 Jan 1889, Ottawa, Ontario, Canada[569]; b. 1863[570]; d. 1928, Ottawa, Ontario, Canada[570]. They are buried in Beachwood Cemetery - Section 39, Ottawa East of the Rideau, Ottawa, Canada
442.   iii.   ANNA ADA MILKS, b. 17 Jan 1869, Ottawa, Canada; d. 11 Nov 1918, Ottawa, Carleton, Ontario, Canada.
      iv.   MARTHA ALICE MILKS, b. Abt. 1874, Ottawa, Canada.
      v.   ANNIE MILKS, b. Abt. 1879, Ottawa, Ontario, Canada; d. 16 Oct 1902, Ottawa, Ontario, Canada. Annie is buried in
Beachwood Cemetery - Section 39,Ottawa East of the Rideau, Ottawa, Canada Her gravestone inscription:

A dear one from our midst is gone
A voice we loved is stilled
A place is vacant in our home
Which never can be filled.

    vi.   HATTIE MILKS, b. Ottawa, Canada.
    vii.   MINNIE MILKS, b. Ottawa, Canada.
    viii.   JOHN WESLEY MILKS, b. Ottawa, Canada; d. d.y..
    ix.   JOHN WESLEY MILKS, 2ND, b. Ottawa, Canada; d. d.y..
    x.   VICTORIA ADELINE MILKS[571], b. 21 Jan 1883, Renfrew, Ontario, Canada.

179. PETER[7] MILKS *(FREEBORN GARRETTSON[6], JOB[5] MILK, JONATHAN[4], JOB[3], JOHN[2], JOHN[1])* was born 25 Dec 1837 in Eardley Twp., Quebec, Canada[572], and died 14 Jun 1918 in Kingsley, Paradise Township, Mich[573]. He married ELIZABETH SMITH 1859. She was born Mar 1838 in New York, and died 16 Jun 1924 in Kingsley, Mich. He immigrated to Michigan from Canada in 1870. Peter and Elizabeth are buried in Evergreen Cemetery, Kingsley, Grand Traverse County, Michigan.

Children of PETER MILKS and ELIZABETH SMITH are:
443.   i.   JOHN SMITH[8] MILKS, b. 07 Sep 1859, Canada; d. 11 Jun 1922, Trenton, Wayne County, Michigan.
444.   ii.   MARTHA MILKS, b. 22 Nov 1860, Eardley, Quebec, Canada; d. 07 May 1948, East Jordan, Michigan.
445.   iii.   HENRY MILKS, b. 27 Dec 1862, Quebec, Canada; d. 18 Oct 1942, Cadillac, Wexford County, Michigan.
    iv.   AMBROSE MILKS, b. 21 Sep 1866, Quebec, Canada[575]; d. 11 May 1951, Muskegon, Muskegon County, Michigan[576]; m. (1) VIETTA ADEL RYAN[577], 26 Aug 1889, Traverse City, Grand Traverse County, Michigan[578]; b. Bet. 1862 - 1863, Kalamazoo, Michigan[579]; m. (2) EVELYN RUSHLOW, 24 Dec 1906, Traverse City, Grand Traverse County, Michigan[580]; b. 25 Aug 1869, Wayne County, Michigan[581]; d. 17 Jun 1944, Dalton, Muskegon County, Michigan[582]. Ambrose immigrated to Michigan from Canada in 1870. He had no children.
446.   v.   SARAH EMMA MILKS, b. 21 Aug 1868, Quebec, Canada; d. 07 Feb 1946.
    vi.   AURELIA "MELIA" MILKS, b. 12 Apr 1872, Michigan; d. 26 Jan 1948; m. MILON RYAN[584], 1891, Grand Traverse County, Michigan[585]; b. Bet. 1865 - 1866, Michigan[586]. No children.
    vii.   PETER GARFIELD MILKS[587,588], b. 14 Jan 1880, Michigan[589]; m. ANNA MAY SWEET, 08 Jun 1903, Kingsley, Grand Traverse Co, Mich[590]; b. 08 Jun 1888, Inland, Benzie County, Michigan[591]; d. Oct 1965[591], daughter of Charles W. & Addie (Fish) Sweet. Peter was a shipbuilder with the Detroit Ship Building Company.

180. ALMIRA[7] MILKS *(FREEBORN GARRETTSON[6], JOB[5] MILK, JONATHAN[4], JOB[3], JOHN[2], JOHN[1])* was born Bet. 1842 - 1843 in Eardley, Quebec, Canada[592], and died Aft. 15 Apr 1910 in Snohomish, Washington. She married WILLIAM HODGINS Abt. 1860 in Quebec, Canada. He was born 25 Dec 1839 in Canada[593], and died 18 Jul 1915 in Everett, Snohomish County, Washington[593]. William ran a saw mill in Snohomish County, Washington.

Some data on this family is from Carolyn La Porte, claporte@shaw.ca.

Children of ALMIRA MILKS and WILLIAM HODGINS are:
    i.   JOSEPHINE[8] HODGINS, b. Bet. 1862 - 1863, Canada; d. Aft. 1910.
    ii.   SALOMA HODGINS, b. Bet. 1864 - 1865, Canada; d. Aft. 1910.
    iii.   ARTHUR G. HODGINS, b. May 1866, Canada; d. 02 Nov 1909, Seattle, King County, Washington[594].
447.   iv.   WILLIAM RUGLESS HODGINS, b. Bet. 1868 - 1869, Canada; d. 27 Apr 1951, Everett, Snohomish County, Washington.
448.   v.   ETHEL MAUDE HODGINS, b. Apr 1874, Canada; d. 22 May 1946, Sedro Woolley Rural, Skagit, Washington.
    vi.   MINIA HODGINS, b. Bet. 1876 - 1877, Canada; d. Aft. 1910.
449.   vii.   ASA F. HODGINS, b. 04 Apr 1878, Canada; d. 15 Sep 1912, Snohomish, Washington.

181. GILES[7] MILKS *(SAMUEL[6] MILK, JOB[5], JONATHAN[4], JOB[3], JOHN[2], JOHN[1])*[595] was born 1827 in New York[595,596], and died 25 Oct 1893 in Kalkaska County, Michigan[597]. He married (1) FANNIE _____ Abt. 1855. She was born Abt. 1830 in Vermont[598], and died 08 Jun 1890 in Kalkaska County, Michigan[599,600]. He married (2) SARAH M PALMER 23 Mar

1892 in Kalkaska, Kalkaska County, Michigan[601], daughter of AL PALMER. She was born 1828 in Pennsylvania[602]. Giles and Fannie are buried in Evergreen Cemetery, Kalkaska, Kalkaska County, Michigan.

Kalkaska Co., MI -- General Land Office Records - 1807-1907
MILKS, GILES   22 27 N   8 W   80.00 (acres)   11   4991   1883/03/10

G. Milks' young son was taken some three weeks ago with inflammatory rheumatism, and on Friday last his left side was paralyzed. At this writing (Wednesday) he is not expected to live, though somewhat recovered from the shock. Dr. Boyd is attending him. - *Kalkaska Leader*, June 2, 1881

DEATH NOTICE
- MILKS: Sunday morning, June 5, 1881, Willie, son of G. W. and Fanny Milks, age 12 years, 5 months, and 17 days. - *Kalkaska Leader*, June 9, 1881

G. W. Milks advertises his farm of 80 acres for sale. Since the sad death of his son, which leaves the home circle without any children, Mrs. Milks cannot reconcile herself to longer remain on the place, but desires to remove to Traverse City, where a son is located. The figure for which the farm is afforded is very low, but since it is to them home no longer, they are willing to make the sacrifice. There are several advantages that a purchaser would have, which are not mentioned in the notice, and everything will be found as good or better than represented; crops may be seen on the ground, and a personal inspection invited. We will give full particulars on application. - *Kalkaska Leader*, June 9, 1881

Children of GILES MILKS and FANNIE _____ are:
- i. JOSIAH CYRUS[8] MILKS[603,604], b. 30 May 1856, New Albion, Cattaraugus County, New York[604,605]; d. 25 Jul 1878, Kalkaska County, Michigan (not married)[606,607,608]. Burial: Evergreen Cemetery, Village of Kalkaska
- ii. CORA CARRIE MILKS[609], b. 1858, Cattaraugus County, New York[610].
- 450. iii. MARK C. MILKS, b. Abt. 1862, New York; d. 24 Mar 1928, San Diego, California.
- iv. WILLIAM GILES "WILLIE" MILKS[611], b. 21 Sep 1868, New York[612,613]; d. 05 Jun 1881, Wilson Township, Kalkaska County, Michigan[614]. Burial: Evergreen Cemetery, Village of Kalkaska. Cause of Death: Spinal Meningitis

182. HELEN L.[7] MILKS (*SAMUEL[6] MILK, JOB[5], JONATHAN[4], JOB[3], JOHN[2], JOHN[1]*)[615] was born 1834 in New York[615]. She married ERASTUS J. BEMUS in New York. He was born Abt. 1824 in Greece, New York, and died Bef. Apr 1900. Military service for Erastus: 01 Sep 1859, New York, for a 3 yr term, 9 yrs prior naval service.

Children of HELEN MILKS and ERASTUS BEMUS are:
- 451. i. OSCAR E.[8] BEMUS, b. Oct 1863, Buffalo, New York.
- ii. PHEBE BEMUS, b. 10 Feb 1867, Buffalo, Erie County, New York. Christening: 26 Feb 1867, Grace Episcopal Church, Buffalo, Erie County, New York
- 452. iii. ELIZABETH 'LIBBIE' BEMUS, b. Jul 1868, New York; d. 1949, Osceola County, Michigan.
- iv. MINNIE E. BEMUS, b. 11 Oct 1871, Kennedy, New York[616]; d. 20 Jul 1941, Highland Park, Wayne County, Michigan[616]; m. Mr. ALWARD.

183. ESTHER ANN (HESTER)[7] MILKS (*SAMUEL[6] MILK, JOB[5], JONATHAN[4], JOB[3], JOHN[2], JOHN[1]*)[617] was born Aug 1838 in New York[617], and died 31 Jan 1917 in Fremont, Isabella County, Michigan[618]. She married FRANCIS 'FRANK' WILLIAMS 1866 in New York, son of FATHER and MOTHER. He was born Nov 1838 in New York, and died 1919 in Isabella County, Michigan.
Esther and Francis are buried in Burial: Union Cemetery, Blanchard, Isabella County, Michigan. Number of Children (Facts: 1900, 7 children, 6 living

FRANCIS 'FRANK' WILLIAMS: Military service: Bet. 07 Sep 1862 - 25 Sep 1863, Corporal, Co. B., 164 Regt, NY Inf. - Civil War

Children of ESTHER MILKS and FRANCIS WILLIAMS are:
- 453. i. HARRY J.[8] WILLIAMS, b. 02 May 1872, Cattaraugus County, New York; d. 10 Aug 1934, Fremont, Isabella County, Michigan.
- 451. ii. HELEN E. WILLIAMS, b. 02 May 1872, New York; d. 17 Dec 1917, Coe Township, Isabella County, Michigan (married).

| | iii. | CATHERINE WILLIAMS, b. Jan 1874, New York; d. 1961, Riverdale, Gratiot County, Michigan.
455. | iv. | JOHN C. WILLIAMS, b. Aug 1876, Michigan; d. 1956, Isabella County, Michigan (no children); m. MATHILDE R _____; b. 25 Jun 1888, Michigan[619]; d. Feb 1978, Shepherd, Isabella County, Michigan[619]. They are buried in Union Cemetery, Blanchard, Isabella County, Michigan
| | v. | ESTHER A. 'NETTIE' WILLIAMS, b. 1878, Michigan; d. 1938, Isabella County, Michigan (never married). Burial: Union Cemetery, Blanchard, Isabella County, Michigan
| | vi. | MARY F. WILLIAMS, b. 28 Apr 1881, Berlin, Isabella County, Michigan[620].

184. CYNTHIA[7] MILK *(JONATHAN[6], BENJAMIN[5], JONATHAN[4], JOB[3], JOHN[2], JOHN[1])*[621] was born Abt. 1812 in Shandaken, Ulster County, New York. She married HENRY MOOERS. He was born 1807 in Lansing, Tompkins County, New York[622], and died 10 Dec 1892 in Toledo, Lucas County, Ohio[622]. Henry was a "moulder" in Ithaca. Value- Personal Property: 1870, $10,000. Value of Real Estate: 1870, $50,000

Children of CYNTHIA MILK and HENRY MOOERS are:

456. i. MARY[8] MOOERS, b. Bet. 1835 - 1836, Ithaca, Tompkins County, New York; d. 20 Mar 1891, Toledo, Lucas County, Ohio.
 ii. ADELINE C. 'DELIA' MOOERS, b. Bet. 1837 - 1838, Ithaca, Tompkins County, New York; d. 14 Mar 1896, Toledo, Lucas County, Ohio[623]. Never married
 iii. ANN ELIZA 'LYDA' MOOERS, b. 27 Sep 1840, Ithaca, Tompkins County, New York[624]; d. 23 Nov 1914, Toledo, Lucas County, Ohio[625,626]. Never married. In 1900, Elizabeth lived in Toledo, Ohio and had 4 nephews living with her: Edward & Wilmot Blake, George H. Cooke, and Frank C. Mooers. In 1910, only Frank C. Mooers and his wife Irene were living with her. Burial: Forest Cemetery, Toledo, Lucas County, Ohio
457. iv. CYNTHIA MOOERS, b. Bet. 1842 - 1843, Ithaca, Tompkins County, New York.
458. v. ESTHER MOOERS, b. Bet. 1844 - 1845, Ithaca, Tompkins County, New York; d. 11 May 1875, Toledo, Lucas County, Ohio.
459. vi. HENRY CLAY MOOERS, b. 16 Nov 1849, Ithaca, Tompkins County, New York; d. 30 Jul 1920, Flint, Genesee County, Michigan.
 vii. SAMUEL MOOERS?.

185. WILLIAM JEWETT[7] MILK *(JONATHAN[6], BENJAMIN[5], JONATHAN[4], JOB[3], JOHN[2], JOHN[1])* was born 23 Apr 1813 in Delaware County, New York, and died 31 Dec 1885 in Danby, New York. He married MARY THOMAS 25 Apr 1839. She was born 21 Dec 1817 in New Jersey, and died 28 Sep 1908. William is buried in Ellis Hollow Cemetery, Ellis Hollow Road, Dryden, Tompkins County, New York He was a Wagon Maker & Farmer, 97 acres After William died, Mary went to live with her daughter, Genny (Ann Jane), and her family, in Auburn, Cayuga County, New York. They lived at 94 Washington St.

Children of WILLIAM MILK and MARY THOMAS are:

460. i. WILLIAM JEWETT[8] MILK, b. 05 Nov 1842, Varna, Tompkins County, New York; d. 1943, Candor, Tioga County, New York.
461. ii. BENJAMIN F. MILK, b. 1842; d. 04 Jan 1897, Dryden, Tompkins County, New York.
462. iii. ANN JANE MILK, b. 1845, Dryden, Tompkins County, New York; d. 20 May 1916.
463. iv. GEORGE HENRY MILK, b. 14 Mar 1847, Dryden, Tompkins County, New York; d. 04 Apr 1926, Town of Kirkwood, Broome County, New York.
 v. MARSHALL MILK, b. 1849, Dryden, Tompkins County, New York[627]; d. 28 Nov 1867, Dryden, Tompkins County, New York.

186. CHARLES[7] MILK *(JONATHAN[6], BENJAMIN[5], JONATHAN[4], JOB[3], JOHN[2], JOHN[1])* was born Abt. 1814 in New York. He married UNKNOWN WIFE. She was born Abt. 1810. Lived in 1840 in Lansing, Tompkins County, New York

Children of CHARLES MILK and UNKNOWN WIFE are:
 i. FIRST DAUGHTER[8] MILK, b. Bet. 1834 - 1840.
 ii. SECOND DAUGHTER MILK, b. Bet. 1834 - 1840.

187. ISAAC[7] MILK *(JONATHAN[6], BENJAMIN[5], JONATHAN[4], JOB[3], JOHN[2], JOHN[1])* was born Dec 1815 in of Newfield, Tompkins County, New York[628], and died 27 Mar 1907 in Galena, Ohio. He married (1) ELIZABETH "BETSEY" SUMMERS Abt. 1845. She was born 1827 in New York, and died 18 Aug 1866 in Lagrange County, Indiana[629]. He married (2) LUCINDA SWAIN 14 Oct 1867 in LaGrange Co., Indiana, daughter of HORACE SWAIN and KIZIAH MILLER. She was born Abt. 1828 in New York, and died 1899[630]. Isaac was a carpenter and a lumberman. He is buried in Galena Cemetery, Galena, Delaware County, Ohio

Elizabeth is buried in Tamarack Cemetery, Lagrange County, Indiana

Children of ISAAC MILK and ELIZABETH SUMMERS are:
- 464. i. LYDIA[8] MILK, b. 1845.
- 465. ii. EDGAR ROMAIN MILK, b. 12 Jun 1850, Tompkins County, New York; d. 15 Sep 1931, Galena, Delaware County, Ohio.
-      iii. IDA MILK, b. 1854, Indiana[630].
-      iv. ELIZABETH MILK, b. 1857, Indiana[630].

Child of ISAAC MILK and LUCINDA SWAIN is:
- 466. v. MARY KIZIAH[8] MILK, b. Jul 1869, South Milford, Ind.; d. 07 Apr 1936, Columbus, Ohio.

188. HENRY[7] MILK *(JONATHAN[6], BENJAMIN[5], JONATHAN[4], JOB[3], JOHN[2], JOHN[1])* was born Bet. 1817 - 1819 in New York[631], and died 21 Dec 1897 in South Milford, Indiana[632]. He married ALMIRA C. SUMMERS Abt. 1842. She was born 22 Mar 1821 in Pennsylvania?[633], and died in Lagrange County, Indiana[634]. Name spelling changed between 1860 and 1880 from Milk to Milks. Same for son John. Lived in: 1850, Newfield, Tompkins Co., NY and moved in Sept. 1854 to Ontario, LaGrange County, Indiana. Henry was a lumberman and a Master Carpenter.

Almira Summers was said to have been a daughter of Capt. Summers, who served in the Revolutionary War. The date of death on her gravestone is unreadable. Burial: South Milford Cemetery, South Milford, Lagrange County, Indiana

Children of HENRY MILK and ALMIRA SUMMERS are:
- 467. i. JOHN WESLEY[8] MILKS, b. 19 Mar 1843, Tompkins County, NY; d. 26 Jan 1929, South Milford, Indiana.
- 468. ii. CHARLES H. MILK, b. 25 Mar 1845, Tompkins Co., NY; d. 26 Sep 1917, South Milford, Ind..
-      iii. ELIZA J. MILK, b. 1846, Tompkins County, New York; d. Aft. 1860. Living in 1860, age 13. (see Croft who says she prob. d.y. Maybe not!
- 469. iv. ELIZABETH 'BETSEY' A. MILK, b. 25 Jul 1849, Tompkins Co., New York; d. 30 Jun 1918, Adrian, Hillsdale, Michigan.
- 470. v. CYNTHIA MILK, b. Jul 1853, South Milford, LaGrange County, Indiana; d. Bet. 1900 - 1910, Portland, Multnomah County, Oregon.
-      vi. STELLA MILK, b. 1862, Indiana.

189. DEBORAH[7] MILK *(BENJAMIN[6], BENJAMIN[5], JONATHAN[4], JOB[3], JOHN[2], JOHN[1])* was born 24 Mar 1802 in Town of Jefferson, Schoharie County, New York, and died 17 Sep 1893 in Sacramento, California[634]. She married (1) JOHN CULVER RODMAN 15 Feb 1824 in Schoharie County, New York?, son of ASA RODMAN and OLIVE CULVER. He was born 16 Dec 1802 in Fulton, Schoharie County, New York[635], and died 1854 in Clinton County, Iowa[635]. She married (2) CHRISTOPHER KERL 1879 in Sacramento, California. He was born Abt. 1820 in Germany[636]. In 1870, Deborah lived in Putah, Yolo County, California. She is buried in Kilgore Cemetery, Rancho Cordova, Sacramento County, California

John Rodman moved to Waterford, Clinton County, Iowa before 1856, where he, his wife Deborah and their two youngest children, David and Elizabeth were counted in the 1856 Iowa State census. John was a Junk Dealer

Children of DEBORAH MILK and JOHN RODMAN are:
- 471. i. ASA BENJAMIN[8] RODMAN, b. 31 Jan 1832, Fulton, Schoharie County, New York; d. 05 Apr 1902, Clinton County, Iowa.
- 472. ii. MARY RODMAN, b. 1827, Fulton, Schoharie County, New York.
- 473. iii. WILLIAM HENRY RODMAN, b. 04 May 1830, Fulton, Schoharie County, New York (date ???); d. 28 Nov 1915, Sutter, Sacramento, California.
- 4674. iv. LEVI GALLOP RODMAN, b. 29 Apr 1832, Fulton, Schoharie County, New York; d. 30 Sep 1898, San Francisco, California.

475.	v.	EZRA COOK RODMAN, b. Jul 1836, Fulton, Schoharie County, New York; d. 02 Aug 1908, Hawleyton, Broome County, New York.
476.	vi.	DAVID E. RODMAN, b. 05 Jun 1841, Fulton, Schoharie County, New York; d. 24 Aug 1914, Adams County, Iowa.
477.	vii.	PERMELIA ELIZABETH RODMAN, b. 06 Jun 1844, Fulton, Schoharie County, New York; d. 26 Jan 1921, Shasta County, California.
	viii.	EMELINE RODMAN, b. Abt. 1853, Fulton, Schoharie County, New York; d. Bef. 1856.

190. STEPHEN^7 MILK (*BENJAMIN^6, BENJAMIN^5, JONATHAN^4, JOB^3, JOHN^2, JOHN^1*) was born 07 Feb 1804 in Town of Jefferson, Schoharie County, New York, and died Aft. 01 Jun 1860. He married ANN ELIZA DIBBLE 03 Jun 1829 in ??? Date???, daughter of PATRICK DIBBLE and MARGARET HOGOBOAN. She was born Abt. 1808 in New York^{638}, and died 18 May 1887 in Cazenovia, Madison County, New York^{638}. Ann is buried in Evergreen Cemetery, Cazenovia, Madison County, New York

It appears that Stephen and Ann Eliza were separated or divorced before 1850, as Ann lived in Cazenovia in 1850 when Stephen lived in Hancock, NY, then Ann lived in Fulton, NY in 1860 while Stephen lived in Cazenovia. It is not known where Stephen is buried.

Children of STEPHEN MILK and ANN DIBBLE are:

	i.	MARGARET M.^{8} MILK, b. 1826, Schoharie County, New York.
	ii.	DAU MILK, b. Abt. 1828, Schoharie County, New York.
478.	iii.	MARY E. 'POLLY' MILK, b. 28 Nov 1829, Schoharie County, New York; d. 29 Oct 1901, Cazenovia, Madison County, New York.
479.	iv.	JOHN B. MILK, b. 04 Mar 1831, New York; d. 12 Jan 1866, Cazenovia, Madison County, New York.

191. BETSEY^7 MILK (*BENJAMIN^6, BENJAMIN^5, JONATHAN^4, JOB^3, JOHN^2, JOHN^1*) was born 20 Oct 1805 in Town of Jefferson, Schoharie County, New York, and died 25 Apr 1889 in Schoharie County, New York. She married CALEB DIBBLE 30 Jan 1824 in Schoharie County, New York?, son of PATRICK DIBBLE and MARGARET HOGOBOAN. He was born 16 Dec 1801 in New York, and died Abt. 23 Jan 1892 in Schoharie County, New York. Betsey is buried in Eminence Walled Cemetery, Schoharie County, New York

Children of BETSEY MILK and CALEB DIBBLE are:

480.	i.	PERLINA^8 DIBBLE, b. 16 Dec 1825, Fulton, Schoharie County, New York; d. 12 Sep 1874, Schoharie County, New York.
481.	ii.	POLLY MARGARET DIBBLE, b. 23 Oct 1827, Fulton, Schoharie County, New York; d. 11 Oct 1915, Schoharie County, New York.
492.	iii.	JAMES PATRICK DIBBLE, b. 09 Apr 1830, Fulton, Schoharie County, New York; d. 31 Dec 1874, Putnam County, Illinois.
483.	iv.	ADELINE DIBBLE, b. 21 Mar 1833, West Fulton, Schoharie County, New York; d. 08 Jun 1910, Schenectady, New York.
484.	v.	ISAAC DIBBLE, b. 21 May 1836, Fulton, Schoharie County, New York; d. 25 Dec 1918, Schoharie County, New York.
485.	vi.	BENJAMIN DIBBLE, b. 04 Jul 1838, Fulton, Schoharie County, New York; d. 12 Apr 1918, Dibble Hollow, Schoharie County, New York.
486.	vii.	SARAH EMELINE DIBBLE, b. 10 Sep 1844, Fulton, Schoharie County, New York; d. 06 Sep 1912, Eminence, New York.
487.	viii.	MARION G. DIBBLE, b. 30 Oct 1847, West Fulton, Schoharie County, New York; d. 12 Jul 1928, Schoharie County, New York.

192. PERLINA^7 MILK (*BENJAMIN^6, BENJAMIN^5, JONATHAN^4, JOB^3, JOHN^2, JOHN^1*) was born 10 Jan 1808 in Town of Jefferson, Schoharie County, New York, and died 03 Jun 1887 in Town of Jefferson, Schoharie County, New York^{639}. She married WINTHROP DYER 23 Jul 1830 in Schoharie County, New York, son of WINTHROP DYER and POLLY VINTON. He was born 20 Aug 1808 in Town of Jefferson, Schoharie County, New York^{640}, and died 09 Mar 1885 in Town of Jefferson, Schoharie County, New York^{641}.

Children of PERLINA MILK and WINTHROP DYER are:
- i. PERMILLA[8] DYER, b. 27 Jun 1831, Jefferson, Schoharie County, New York; d. 09 Apr 1895, Jefferson, Schoharie County, New York; m. (1) DERIUS JACKSON; b. Abt. 1830; m. (2) DR. ALFRED A. WOOD, 12 Aug 1849; b. Abt. 1826, New York[642]; d. Bet. 1870 - 1880, Schoharie County, New York. No children. They lived in Blenheim, Schoharie County, New York where Alfred was a Physician and Surgeon
- ii. CALVIN DYER, b. 15 Apr 1833, Jefferson, Schoharie County, New York; d. 16 Jan 1893.
- iii. POLLY DYER, b. 1835, Jefferson, Schoharie County, New York; d. Sep 1908, Jefferson, Schoharie County, New York; m. DAVID STEVENS, 1873; b. Abt. 1835.
- 488. iv. PHEBE DYER, b. 27 Mar 1837, Jefferson, Schoharie County, New York; d. 17 Jul 1873, Jefferson, Schoharie County, New York.
- v. RALPH V. DYER, b. 29 Jun 1839, Jefferson, Schoharie County, New York; d. 12 Oct 1862, Jefferson, Schoharie County, New York. Burial: Old School Baptist Cemetery in Jefferson, NY
- vi. BETSEY DYER, b. 22 Sep 1841, Jefferson, Schoharie County, New York; d. 10 Sep 1864, Jefferson, Schoharie County, New York. Burial: Old School Baptist Cemetery in Jefferson, NY
- 489. vii. LEWIS DYER, b. 09 Feb 1848, Jefferson, Schoharie County, New York; d. 27 Dec 1926.

193. PERMELIA[7] MILK *(BENJAMIN[6], BENJAMIN[5], JONATHAN[4], JOB[3], JOHN[2], JOHN[1])* was born 07 May 1810 in Town of Jefferson, Schoharie County, New York, and died 27 Jul 1901 in Chicago, Illinois[643]. She married REV. EZRA SPRAGUE COOK 16 Jan 1834 in West Fulton, Schoharie County, New York, son of NATHANIEL COOK and HULDAH SPRAGUE. He was born 01 May 1811 in West Fulton, Schoharie County, New York, and died 25 Jan 1881 in Chicago, Illinois.

Children of PERMELIA MILK and EZRA COOK are:
- 490. i. NATHANIEL EZRA[8] COOK, b. 26 Mar 1836, West Fulton, Schoharie County, New York; d. 14 Dec 1901, Winters, California.
- 491. ii. LOUISE DESIRE COOK, b. 03 Feb 1839, Coxsackie, New York.
- 492. iii. EZRA ASHER COOK, b. 05 Nov 1841, Windsor, Connecticut; d. 1911.
- 493. iv. MARY AMELIA COOK, b. 11 Mar 1844, Great Barrington, Massachusetts.
- v. RUTH HELENA COOK, b. 10 Jul 1846, Windham Center, Greene County, New York; d. 25 May 1847, Windham Center, Greene County, New York.
- 494. vi. DAVID CALEB COOK, b. 28 Aug 1850, East Worcester, New York; d. 30 Jul 1927, Elgin, Illinois.
- vii. EMMA R. COOK, b. 11 Jan 1851, East Worcester, New York; d. 15 Sep 1858, Proviso, Illinois.

194. JANET[7] MILK *(BENJAMIN[6], BENJAMIN[5], JONATHAN[4], JOB[3], JOHN[2], JOHN[1])* was born 1815 in Town of Jefferson, Schoharie County, New York, and died 1884. She married REDMOND JUDD 25 Mar 1841. He was born Abt. 1815 in Of Jefferson, Schoharie County, New York.

Children of JANET MILK and REDMOND JUDD are:
- 495. i. RACHAEL[8] JUDD, b. 18 Sep 1844, Schoharie County, New York.
- ii. HARVEY JUDD, b. 01 Nov 1849, Schoharie County, New York; d. Mar 1921; m. MARY CRASPER; b. Abt. 1849; d. 20 Feb 1943. No children.

195. DAVID[7] MILK *(BENJAMIN[6], BENJAMIN[5], JONATHAN[4], JOB[3], JOHN[2], JOHN[1])* was born 25 May 1820 in Town of Jefferson, Schoharie County, New York[644], and died 13 Oct 1907 in Hancock, Delaware Co., NY[644]. He married (1) SALLY ANN NEER, daughter of PHILIP NEER and CORNELIA SPITZER. She was born 09 Jul 1826, and died 28 Jun 1845 in Hancock, Delaware Co., NY. He married (2) LUCINDA NEER 18 Mar 1846 in Hancock, NY, daughter of PHILIP NEER and CORNELIA SPITZER. She was born 01 Apr 1830 in Schoharie County, New York[644], and died 26 Apr 1921 in Hancock, Delaware Co., NY[644]. David had a stone quarry on his property, and worked it.

The Neer sisters were daughters of Philip and Cornelia (Spitzer) Neer, of Summit, NY. The first Neer, Karl Nehr, came from the lower Rhine valley to Rhinebeck, NY, in 1710. His grand-son, Charles, grandfather of Lucinda, served in the Revolutionary War as a scout and was noted as a sharpshooter. Perhaps this may explain why so many of his descendants loved to hunt and were noted as marksmen.

The refusal of many of the patroons and recipients of large land grants to sell their lands forced many of these Palatine workers of the Hudson valley to move to an area where land could be purchased. Among those who moved to the Schoharie area was the Neer family. A common joke in that region was that there were three kinds of Dutch: the "Amsterdam Dutch," the "Rotterdam Dutch," and the "Schoharie damn Dutch."

This period of pressure for farm lands caused the Anti-rent War. Many of the young men went to western New York and some farther west. David Milk became one of the leaders in a migration from Schoharie Co. to the town of Hancock, Delaware Co., NY, known as South Woods. This was a forest area occupied by only one family, that of John Gould, for whom the post office was later named. David selected his land in 1847. These pioneers, with axe and saw, carved farms from the forest. The timber was drawn to the river banks, fastened onto a raft and floated down the Delaware River to Philadelphia, and sold there. Hard work and thrift eventually produced debt-free farms.

David Milk was well informed by the Bible and the New York Tribune. His industry was evidenced by the many erect stone walls that still bound the fields of the farm. His independence and integrity were characteristic of his New England ancestry.

All of David Milk's children, grandchildren, and most of the later generations were born in this area. Nearly all of them have kept closely related to rural life as farmers, as were their ancestors, and have enjoyed the independence of owning their own homes. The introduction of growing cauliflower for the New York City market by Milton Smith, a great grandson of David, has been fortunate for this community. The high altitude, pure air, and stony soil produce the finest cauliflower sold in the city.

In 1930 a David and Lucinda Milk reunion group was formed on the original farm of David, later owned by his grandson Arlyn Milk and occupied by Edward Milk. This farm has been owned by a member of the Milk family since 1847. This Reunion group holds its annual reunion at the Goulds Church, the Sunday before Labor Day; about one hundred attend each year.

David was a farmer, primarily raising sugar beets. "*Apr 27, 1891, David MILK has made over 700 lbs of sugar this spring.*"

David and Lucinda are buried in Marysville Cemetery, Goulds, Delaware County, New York

OBITUARY - Sullivan County Democrat in an issue printed May 8 2001
"DOWN THE DECADES - 1921 Mrs. Lucinda Milk, 91 died April 26 1921 at the home of her daughter, Mrs. Melvin Brazie of East Branch.

She was born in Schoharie County and in 1843.

She was united in marriage with David Milk and came to Goulds to reside.

She was one of the first settlers here and when she and her husband came into this community she helped drive the cattle along the blazed trails and carried a rifle on her shoulder. She loved to relate stories of those early days especially those about fighting off the wolves at night while her husband was carrying grain to the mill to be ground, and those about her brothers who fought in the Civil War." (per Helen (Holly) Bossley)

Children of DAVID MILK and LUCINDA NEER are:

    i. JOHN^8 MILK, b. 06 Jan 1849, Hancock, Delaware County, New York; d. 04 Oct 1898, Davisville, California (no children)[645]; m. MARGARET B. GIBSON[646]; b. May 1847, Iowa[647]. Lived in Putah, Yolo County, California.

    WILL

    Woodland Daily Democrat, Woodland, California, October 14, 1898

    The will of the late John Milks, who died in Davisville in October, 1898, was filed for probate in the Superior Court today by Attorney C. W. Thomas, who represents the surviving widow, Mrs. Margaret B. Milks. The estate consists of a mortgage held against W. S. Montgomery and wife valued at $1,700 and personal property worth $343. By the terms of the will the widow is named as Executor and made the sole legatee. The only other relatives of deceased are Mr. and Mrs. David Milks of Gould, New York.

496. ii. GEORGE H. MILK, b. 11 Oct 1850, Delaware County, New York; d. 11 Mar 1917, Hancock, Delaware Co., NY.
497. iii. ANNA SARAH MILK, b. 16 May 1854, Delaware County, New York; d. 19 Sep 1935, Boonville, NY.
498. iv. ABRAM LINCOLN MILK, b. 14 Oct 1860, Delaware County, New York; d. 26 Mar 1925, Goulds, Delaware County, New York.
499. v. WILLIAM MILK, b. 16 Aug 1865, Delaware County, New York; d. 03 Jan 1952, Hancock, Delaware County, New York.

196. LEVI 'STEPHEN'^{7} MILKS *(BENJAMIN^6 MILK, JR., BENJAMIN^5, JONATHAN^4, JOB^3, JOHN^2, JOHN^1)* was born 14 Apr 1825 in Town of Jefferson, Schoharie County, New York[647], and died 13 Oct 1907 in Delaware County, New York[648]. He married LEMIRA A. FULLER. She was born May 1847 in New York[649,650], and died Aft. Jan 1920.

In 1881, the Stamford Daily Mirror newspaper reported: "Levi Milks, of Jefferson, who is troubled with insanity, at times, has been sent to the County Poor House."

In 1892, Levi was incarcerated in the New York State Asylum for Insane Criminals, at Auburn, New York.

In 1900, Levi was again living with his family in Jefferson, Schoharie County, but using the name of Stephen.

Children of LEVI MILKS and LEMIRA FULLER are:
- i. CARRIE E.[8] MILKS, b. Bet. 1878 - 1879, Town of Jefferson, Schoharie County, New York. Carrie may have gotten married before the 1900 census. She was 14 yrs in the 1892 NY census, living in the Town of Jefferson, but does not appear after that.
- 500. ii. PEARL MILKS, b. Abt. 1881, Town of Jefferson, Schoharie County, New York.
- iii. RALPH L. MILKS, b. 06 Sep 1886, Town of Jefferson, Schoharie County, New York[650,651]; d. 15 Jan 1919, Otsego County, New York????? (never married). Lived in: 1917, Oneonta, Otsego County, New York

197. LYDIA JANE[7] MILK *(TROWBRIDGE[6], BENJAMIN[5], JONATHAN[4], JOB[3], JOHN[2], JOHN[1])* was born 07 Jul 1812, and died 13 Jan 1856. She married JAMES GILBERT VAN VALKENBURGH[652] Abt. 1835. He was born 13 Nov 1813, and died Jun 1875.

Children of LYDIA MILK and JAMES VAN VALKENBURGH are:
- 501. i. CHRISTCHANA[8] VAN VALKENBURGH, b. 24 May 1836; d. 18 Apr 1921.
- 502. ii. GEORGE ANGELO VAN VALKENBURGH, b. 24 Feb 1838; d. 01 Jan 1903, New York.
- 503. iii. BENJAMIN VAN VALKENBURGH, b. 24 Aug 1845.
- 504. iv. LODEMA VAN VALKENBURGH, b. 16 Feb 1847; d. Dec 1905.
- 505. v. WESLEY VAN VALKENBURGH, b. 21 Jun 1848; d. 09 Jan 1906.
- vi. ALFRED J. VAN VALKENBURGH, b. 01 Jan 1856; d. 1867.

198. CATHERINE[7] MILK *(TROWBRIDGE[6], BENJAMIN[5], JONATHAN[4], JOB[3], JOHN[2], JOHN[1])* was born 1820. She married LEWIS SMITH Abt. 1838. He was born 1812 in Of Lexington, New York.

Children of CATHERINE MILK and LEWIS SMITH are:
- i. EZRA[8] SMITH, b. 1839.
- 506. ii. LYDIA JANE SMITH, b. 25 Apr 1841, Lexington, Greene County, New York; d. 22 May 1881, Westkill, Greene County, New York.
- iii. JAMES SMITH, b. 1843.
- iv. HARRIETT SMITH, b. 1845.
- v. TROWBRIDGE SMITH, b. 1847.
- vi. WILBUR SMITH, b. 1852.
- vii. MARY A. SMITH, b. 1855.

199. ANN ELIZA[7] MILK *(TROWBRIDGE[6], BENJAMIN[5], JONATHAN[4], JOB[3], JOHN[2], JOHN[1])* was born 1824. She married REVILLO SHARPE. He was born 1823. Revillo was a tanner and a trader in Halcott, New York.

Children of ANN MILK and REVILLO SHARPE are:
- i. HORATIO[8] SHARPE, b. 1844.
- ii. JANE SHARPE, b. 1847; m. UNKNOWN DRYER; b. Abt. 1845.
- iii. JOHN SHARPE, b. 1848.
- iv. JEHIAL SHARPE, b. 1850.
- v. JULIA SHARPE, b. 1852.
- vi. STANLEY SHARPE, b. Abt. 1854.
- 507. vii. VIOLA SHARPE, b. 10 Apr 1856; d. 27 Apr 1901, Griffin Corners/Fleischmanns, Delaware County, N Y.
- viii. LYDIA SHARPE, b. 1859.

200. BENJAMIN[7] MILK *(TROWBRIDGE[6], BENJAMIN[5], JONATHAN[4], JOB[3], JOHN[2], JOHN[1])* was born 04 Dec 1824[653], and died 18 Mar 1888 in Greene County, New York[653]. He married ELIZABETH C. RUNDELL, daughter of ELLIOTT RUNDELL. She was born 04 Nov 1836[653], and died 09 Nov 1886 in Greene County, New York[653]. They are buried in Hunter Village

Cemetery, Hunter, Greene County, New York

Children of BENJAMIN MILK and ELIZABETH RUNDELL are:
- 508. i. LENA A.[8] MILK, b. 28 Nov 1862; d. 12 Apr 1899.
- ii. MINNIE J. MILK[654], b. 01 May 1863, Hunter, Greene County, New York; d. 01 Jan 1871, Hunter, Greene County, New York.
- iii. WESLEY E. MILK[654], b. 1866, Hunter, Greene County, New York; d. 08 Jan 1871, Hunter, Greene County, New York.
- 509. iv. MARIAN ALICE MILK, b. 23 Apr 1870, Lexington, New York; d. 12 Sep 1944, Los Angeles, California.
- v. ERNEST R. MILK, b. 1873; d. 1898. Unmarried. Ernest was a River Pilot on the Hudson River.

201. JULIA ANN[7] MILK (*TROWBRIDGE[6], BENJAMIN[5], JONATHAN[4], JOB[3], JOHN[2], JOHN[1]*) was born 10 Jan 1829[655], and died 17 Dec 1898. She married JAMES GILBERT VAN VALKENBURGH[656] 11 May 1856. He was born 13 Nov 1813, and died Jun 1875.

Children of JULIA MILK and JAMES VAN VALKENBURGH are:
- 510. i. SAMANTHA[8] VAN VALKENBURGH, b. 17 Feb 1859; d. 1906.
- 511. ii. JANE VAN VALKENBURGH, b. 04 Jun 1861; d. 22 Dec 1915.
- 512. iii. CARRIE VAN VALKENBURGH, b. 15 Mar 1863; d. 21 Jun 1940.
- 513. iv. JAMES VAN VALKENBURGH, b. 11 Jan 1867; d. 23 Dec 1939, Lexington, Greene County, New York.
- 514. v. ELLA VAN VALKENBURGH, b. 15 Jul 1871; d. 12 Dec 1947.

202. CYNTHIA JANE[7] MILK (*TROWBRIDGE[6], BENJAMIN[5], JONATHAN[4], JOB[3], JOHN[2], JOHN[1]*) was born Feb 1840 in New York[657]. She married AUGUSTUS MARTIN Abt. 1865[657]. He was born 02 Nov 1839 in Williamsport, Pennsylvania, and died Abt. 1904 in Parsons, Labette County, Kansas. Augustus was a Civil War Veteran.

Children of CYNTHIA MILK and AUGUSTUS MARTIN are:
- 515. i. JENNIE[8] MARTIN, b. 1867, Spruceton, New York; d. Abt. 1938, San Diego, California.
- 516. ii. CHARLES BRIGGS MARTIN, b. 23 Dec 1872, Spruceton, New York; d. Aft. 1940, Parsons, Labette County, Kansas ?.

203. AMOS MARSH[7] MILKS (*EZRA[6], DAVID[5] MILK, JONATHAN[4], JOB[3], JOHN[2], JOHN[1]*) was born 05 Mar 1802 in Rensselaer County, New York, and died 08 Nov 1878 in Erie County, Pennsylvania. He married POLLY STEPHENS 29 Jun 1824 in Ithaca, NY, daughter of LEANDER STEPHENS and SUSANNAH PALMER. She was born 09 Mar 1804 in Norway, NY, and died 27 May 1874 in Erie County, Pennsylvania.

Amos's obituary states that he moved from Rensselaer Co., NY; doubtless, he was b. near Pittstown, NY. He m. Polly Stephens, b. 9 Mar. 1804, of Herkimer Co., NY, d. 27 May 1874, Erie Co., Pa. Amos and Polly were m. in Ithaca, NY, and are shown in the 1830 census there. About 1833 they moved to Elk Creek, Erie Co., Pa., where they endured the privations of early pioneers.

Both were members of the Free Baptist Church at Wellsburg, in Elk Creek Tp., where Amos was a deacon and a subscriber to his denominational paper, "The Morning Star", for over 40 yrs. During the Civil War, Amos and Polly received considerable publicity for their activities in caring for runaway slaves. Polly often pointed out to her grandchildren, with pride, the place where she secreted slaves until they could make their way to Lake Erie, approximately ten miles from the Milks farm, and secure freedom in Canada. Chn., 9: Amos served with the Union Forces during the Civil War as a Private in Co. I, 40th Infantry, Wisconsn[658]

Children of AMOS MILKS and POLLY STEPHENS are:
- 517. i. CALVIN HARVY[8] MILKS, b. 28 Aug 1825, Ithaca, Tompkins County, New York; d. 1864, Libby Prison (Civil War).
- ii. WILLIAM R. MILKS, b. 1828, Ithaca, Tompkins County, New York; d. 1850, Erie County, Pennsylvania (unmarried).
- iii. IRA WINCHEL MILKS, b. 1830, Ithaca, Tompkins County, New York; d. 1860, Erie County, Pennsylvania (unmarried).
- 518. iv. CAROLINE C. MILKS, b. 04 Jul 1832, Ithaca, Tompkins County, New York; d. 04 Feb 1917, Erie County, Pennsylvania.

519.	v.	DAVID BENJAMIN MILKS, b. 15 Feb 1835, Erie County, Pennsylvania; d. 01 Oct 1902, Erie County, Pennsylvania.
	vi.	SUSAN L. MILKS, b. Apr 1837, Erie County, Pennsylvania; d. 1904, Erie County, Pennsylvania, m. GEORGE H. WARNER, Abt. 1858, Erie County, Pennsylvania[659]; b. Apr 1833. No children. Susan was a Dress Maker, George was an Oak Finisher.
	vii.	REUBEN ROSIAS MILKS, b. 1839, Erie County, Pennsylvania; d. 1839, Erie County, Pennsylvania (8 mos.).
520.	viii.	PARTHENIA ANN MILKS, b. Dec 1844, Elk Creek, Erie County, Pennsylvania; d. 1929, Cranesville, Erie County, Pennsylvania.
	ix.	HARRIET MILKS, b. 1845, Erie County, Pennsylvania; d. No children; m. UNKNOWN LLOYD; b. Abt. 1845.

204. SARAH "SALLY" ANN[7] MILKS (*EZRA*[6], *DAVID*[5] *MILK, JONATHAN*[4], *JOB*[3], *JOHN*[2], *JOHN*[1])[660] was born 21 Jun 1803 in Valley Falls, Rensselaer County, New York[661], and died 04 Jun 1892 in Green County, Wisconsin[662]. She married REUBEN DOTY STEPHENS[663] Abt. 1820 in Ithaca, Tompkins County, New York[663], son of LEANDER STEPHENS and SUSANNAH PALMER. He was born 08 Aug 1799 in Herkimer Co, NY[663], and died 22 Apr 1858 in Green County, Wisconsin[663].

Reuben bought 40 acres in Green County, Wis., Feb 10, 1848, and another 40 acres on April 1, 1848, plus another 80 acres on April 1, 1848. Sarah and Reuben are buried in Mount Vernon Cemetery, Juda, Green County, Wisconsin
OBITUARY - Journal-Gazette (Monroe, Wisconsin), June 14, 1892, p. 8, col. 1
IN MEMORIAM.

Mrs. Sarah Milks Stephens passed to her reward from the home of her son, Sylvester Stephens, June 4th, 1892. She began her earthly journey in the state of New York, June 21st, 1803. In her pilgrimage she journeyed to Erie county, Pennsylvania, in 1835, and in 1842 to Wisconsin.

On 1823 [probably 1821 or 1822] she gave her heart and hand to Reuben Stephens. God blessed this union with the following children: Sylvester, Clarisa, Prudence, Patience, Ezra, Betsy Ann, John, James and Arabut.

The husband and five children preceded the wife and mother to the better land. Thus closed painlessly and in peace, a busy, toiling life, full of industry and full of years. She lived the life and died the faith of a Christian, - That Faith which alone can bring the lost one back to the Shepherd. Grief tells us that we have lost a loved one, faith gives us consolation that all is for the best, and hope whispers that she is better off in a happier, sunnier clime.

The funeral was held from the Baptist church, June 10th. Services were conducted by Rev. H.H. Brenaman, assisted by Rev. Peterson, of Oshkosh. "For we are strangers before Thee, and sojourners as were all our fathers." As we beheld "mother" sleeping beneath a mound of flowers gathered by loving hands, we could not help but think, truly charity is abroad in our land and "while winged angels hover dimly in our air."

Children of SARAH MILKS and REUBEN STEPHENS are:

521.	i.	SYLVESTER REESE[8] STEPHENS, b. 22 Sep 1822, Enfield, Tompkins County, New York; d. 03 May 1909, Juda, Green County, Wisconsin.
522.	ii.	CLARISSA STEPHENS, b. 1824, Enfield, Tompkins County, New York; d. 14 Oct 1885, David City, Butler County, Nebraska.
	iii.	PRUDENCE STEPHENS[663], b. 15 Oct 1826, Enfield, Tompkins County, New York[663]; d. 29 Sep 1844, Juda, Green County, Wisconsin Territory[663]. Burial: Mt. Vernon Cemetery, Judah, Green Co, Wisconsin
	iv.	PATIENCE STEPHENS[663], b. 16 Nov 1828, Enfield, Tompkins County, New York[663].
523.	v.	EZRA MILKS STEPHENS, b. 08 Jan 1831, Enfield, Tompkins County, New York; d. 16 Jun 1917, David City, Butler County, Nebraska.
524.	vi.	JAMES PARKER STEPHENS, b. 27 Apr 1833, Enfield, Tompkins County, New York; d. 21 Oct 1921, David City, Butler County, Nebraska.
	vii.	JOHN PALMER STEPHENS[663], b. Abt. 1835, Erie County, Pennsylvania?[663]; d. 02 Oct 1840, Erie County, Pennsylvania[663].
	viii.	BETSEY ANN STEPHENS[663], b. 31 Aug 1837, Erie County, Pennsylvania[663].
	ix.	ARABUT LUDLOW STEPHENS[663], b. 13 Dec 1844, Juda, Green County, Wisconsin Territory[663]; d. 29 Oct 1851, Juda, Green County, Wisconsin Territory. Burial: Mt. Vernon Cemetery, Judah, Green Co, Wisconsin

205. DANIEL[7] MILKS (*EZRA*[6], *DAVID*[5] *MILK, JONATHAN*[4], *JOB*[3], *JOHN*[2], *JOHN*[1]) was born Abt. 1805 in Rensselaer County, New York, and died Bef. 1843 in Erie County, Pennsylvania. He married ANGELINE _____. She was born Abt. 1813 in Pennsylvania.

Child of DANIEL MILKS and ANGELINE _____ is:
525. i. RUTH ANN[8] MILKS, b. 1840, Erie County, Pennsylvania.

206. PRUDENCE[7] MILKS *(EZRA[6], DAVID[5] MILK, JONATHAN[4], JOB[3], JOHN[2], JOHN[1])* was born 1807 in Rensselaer County, New York, and died in Green County, Wisconsin?. She married JEREMIAH 'JERRY' LOVELACE Abt. 1931. He was born 1807 in New York, and died in Green County, Wisconsin?.

Children of PRUDENCE MILKS and JEREMIAH LOVELACE are:
526. i. CALVIN S.[8] LOVELACE, b. 1832, New York; d. Bet. 1880 - 1900.
      ii. ANSON W. LOVELACE, b. 1834, Erie County, Pennsylvania. Lived in Sylvester, Green County, Wisconsin (with parents)
          Military service: 3rd Regiment, Wisconsin Infantry, Co. C (Civil War)
527. iii. JEFFERSON LOVELACE, b. 1837, Erie County, Pennsylvania; d. 07 Oct 1869, Jefferson, Green County, Wisconsin.
528. iv. HARRISON 'HANK' LOVELACE, b. Feb 1839, Erie County, Pennsylvania.
529. v. ELIZABETH RUTH LOVELACE, b. 04 Oct 1843, Erie County, Pennsylvania.
530. vi. NELSON R. LOVELACE, b. Feb 1846, Green County, Wisconsin.
      vii. ANN LOVELACE, b. 1849, Green County, Wisconsin; d. Juda, Green County, Wisconsin (d.y.).

207. PATIENCE[7] MILKS *(EZRA[6], DAVID[5] MILK, JONATHAN[4], JOB[3], JOHN[2], JOHN[1])* was born Abt. 1809 in New York. She married GEORGE W. STEPHENS[664] Abt. 1823, son of LEANDER STEPHENS and SUSANNAH PALMER. He was born 1792[664], and died 09 Feb 1880 in Black Earth, Wisconsin[664]. George is buried in Oak Hill Cemetery, Black Earth, Wisconsin[664]

Some of the information on this family is from Lois Wolff White.

Children of PATIENCE MILKS and GEORGE STEPHENS are:
531. i. LEANDER MILKS[8] STEPHENS, b. 08 Feb 1824, Tompkins County, New York; d. 09 May 1902, Jennings, Louisiana.
      ii. DAU STEPHENS, b. Bet. 1825 - 1830, Tompkins County, New York[665].

208. PARTHENIA[7] MILKS *(EZRA[6], DAVID[5] MILK, JONATHAN[4], JOB[3], JOHN[2], JOHN[1])* was born 30 Nov 1812 in Tioga County, New York?[666], and died 12 Jan 1894 in Juda, Green County, Wisconsin[667]. She married DAVID B. GILLETTE 1853 in Green County, Wisconsin[668]. He was born 15 Aug 1799[669], and died 28 Dec 1859 in Mount Pleasant, Green County, Wisconsin[669].

OBITUARY - Brodhead Independent (Brodhead, Wisconsin), January 18, 1894, p. 6, col. 1
  MRS. DAVID GILLETT
Parthenia Milks was born in the state of New York, Nov. 30, 1812, and died at her home in Juda, Jan. 12, 1894. She resided in New York until she was eighteen years of age, when she removed with her parents to Pennsylvania. She remained there until 1852, when she removed to Wisconsin and in the following year was married to Mr. David Gillett and with him located in the town of Mt. Pleasant, in this county. She resided there until 1867, when she removed to the village of Juda, where she made her home until her death. She became a Christian in early life and when she came to Wisconsin, she united with the M.E. Church.
  One marked characteristic of Mrs. Gillett was her unfailing cheerfulness during her long and intense suffering. And while passing through the valley of the shadow of death, she feared no evil, for death to her was but going home. The funeral services were conducted by Rev. R. Peeples. The remains were interred in the Juda Cemetery. (Mount Vernon Cemetery, Juda, Green County, Wisconsin)

Child of PARTHENIA MILKS and DAVID GILLETTE is:
      i. ALBURTIS AMOS 'BURT'[8] GILLETTE, b. 10 Nov 1854, Mount Pleasant, Green County, Wisconsin[670]; d. Jun 1936, Madison, Dane County, Wisconsin[670]. Burial: Mount Vernon Cemetery , Juda, Green County, Wisconsin, USA

Commemorative Biographical Record of the Counties of Rock, Green, Grant, Iowa and Lafayette, Wisconsin, Containing Biographical Sketches of Prominent and Representative Citizens, and of Many

of the Early Settled Families (Chicago: J.H. Beers, 1901), pp. 807-808.

ALBURTIS A. GILLETT, one of the representative citizens of Juda, Green county, is of English descent. David B. Gillett, his father, was born in 1801, and died Dec. 28, 1859. He was twice married. To him and his first wife were born the following named children: Marcus, William, Edwin, John, Mary and Amelia; to Mr. Gillett and his second wife, Parthenia Milks, whom he married in 1853, came only one child, Alburtis A., born in the township of Mt. Pleasant, Green county, Nov. 10, 1854.

When he was but five years of age Alburtis A. Gillett suffered the loss of his father. In November, 1867, he removed with his widowed mother to Juda, where he has since resided. His mother was stricken with an incurable disease, and died Jan. 10, 1894, at the age of eighty-two years. Our subject cared for her tenderly and faithfully through her long and painful illness, cheerfully granting her wish to have him ever near her. Mr. Gillett began life as a poor boy, but is now the owner of considerable property in the village of Juda, and a small farm with good buildings adjoining the village. He is devoted to mechanical pursuits, and is a manufacturer of woven wire fencing, gates, etc. He is a public spirited citizen, and ever ready to lend a helping hand to any measure that will be beneficial to the community. Politically he is an accredited Prohibitionist, but those who know him best say he is entirely independent, both in his politics and in his religion.

Mr. Gillett has remained single up to this writing. As a strictly self-made man he deserves honorable mention in this volume, as he has made his way against great obstacles. He has a genial disposition, and has a host of friends, who have been quick to detect and properly appreciate his modest but genuine manhood, and sincere moral purpose.

209. DAVID B.[7] MILKS (*EZRA*[6], *DAVID*[5] *MILK, JONATHAN*[4], *JOB*[3], *JOHN*[2], *JOHN*[1]) was born 1817 in Tompkins County, New York?, and died 1897 in Ithaca, Tompkins County, New York. He married MARGARET WELLEN Abt. 1856. She was born 1834, and died 1909 in Ithaca, Tompkins County, New York.

David and Margaret moved to Green County, Wisconsin, with other members of his father's family, but they returned to Tompkins County, New York. David was a boat builder and carpenter by trade.

Children of DAVID MILKS and MARGARET WELLEN are:
532.   i.   BENJAMIN FRANKLIN[8] MILKS, b. 14 Jan 1857, Ithaca, Tompkins County, New York; d. 06 Jul 1929, Ithaca, Tompkins County, New York.
           ii.   STELLA MILKS, b. 03 Dec 1859, Ithaca, Tompkins County, New York; d. 28 Nov 1935; m. GEORGE HAMMOND; b. Abt. 1859. No children.
533.   iii.   LEGRANDE MILKS, b. 20 Dec 1865, Ithaca, Tompkins County, New York; d. 26 Aug 1934.
           iv.   HARRIET MILKS[671], b. Abt. 1866, Ithaca, Tompkins County, New York; d. Bet. 1872 - 1875, Ithaca, Tompkins County, New York[672]. Burial: Ithaca City Cemetery, Ithaca, Tompkins County, New York[673]
           v.   LOUISE HARRIET MILKS, b. 1870, Ithaca, Tompkins County, New York; d. 1931; m. WILLIAM HORNER; b. Abt. 1870.
No children.

210. EZRA[7] MILKS (*EZRA*[6], *DAVID*[5] *MILK, JONATHAN*[4], *JOB*[3], *JOHN*[2], *JOHN*[1])[674] was born Jan 1820 in Tompkins County, New York[675,676], and died 14 Mar 1907 in Soldiers' Home, Leavenworth, Kansas[677]. He married (1) POLLY PHILLIPS 05 May 1847 in Green County, Wisconsin[678], daughter of JACOB PHILLIPS and REBECCA _____. She was born 11 Aug 1825 in Tompkins County, New York[679], and died 20 Sep 1854 in Green County, Wisconsin[679]. He married (2) SARAH "SALLY" ROUND 04 Jan 1855 in Springhill, Green County, Wisconsin[680,681], daughter of LINA ROUND and PATIENCE _____. She was born 15 Nov 1827 in Trenton, Massachusetts[682], and died 06 Jun 1909 in Albany, Wisconsin[683,684]. He married (3) RACHEL (UNKNOWN) RUSSELL Abt. 1864. She was born Abt. 1842 in Ohio, and died in Arkansas City, Kansas?. Ezra enlisted as a private in Company I, 5th Infantry Regiment Wisconsin on 29 August 1864. Mustered out Company I, 5th Infantry Regiment Wisconsin on 20 June 1865   Polly and Sarah are buried in Gap Cemetery, Brodhead, Green County, Wisconsin

from Croft (1956)

Ezra Milks Jr., b. abt. 1820, Rensselaer Co., NY (son of Ezra 1781); m. (1) a girl from Janesville, Wis., prob. named Jane Whitecotton, and lived in Erie Co., Pa. Later Ezra went West, possibly to Calif.; his wife sold the Erie Co. home and moved to Iowa. Ezra subsequently returned East, as far as Green Co., Wis., where four of his sisters and their families were living. There he m. (2) Polly Phillips, b. 1824, dau. of Jacob & Rebecca Phillips. Polly d. and Ezra m. (3) Mrs. Sarah "Sally" (Round) Mosher, who was b. 15 Nov. 1827 at Taunton, Mass., moved with her parents to Ohio and later to Iowa, where she m. (1) in 1843, James Mosher, and had a son and a dau. When Mr. Mosher d. she moved to Juda, Wis., to be with her father, and there met and m. Ezra Milks. When they separated, Ezra moved West to near Agra, Kans.; he d. abt 1906 and is bur. at Soldiers' Home in Leavenworth, Kans. Sarah d. June 1909 in Albany, Wis., and is bur. in Gap Cem., near Juda, Wis. Ezra had 10 chn.:

Ezra probably was born in Hector, New York in 1820 or 1821. Hector is where Ezra's family lived at the time of the 1820 census (officially August 7, 1820). The 1820 census data records 3 males under the age of 10, one of which may have been Ezra. At that time Hector was a part of Tompkins County. In the 1830 census (June 1, 1930) Ezra's family lived in Ithaca, Tompkins county where Ezra, the youngest son, is recorded as betwee the ages of 5 and 9 years old. Ezra's family moved to Franklin Township, Erie County, Pennsylvania in 1833 and stayed until 1843. Ezra is again recorded in the 1840 census (June 1, 1840) as between the ages of 15 and 19. If we believe the age ranges given for Ezra in these three censuses, then the conclusion would be that Ezra was born between June 1, 1920 and Aug 6, 1920. Regardless of the month of Ezra's birth, it is safe to say that he was born in 1820.

It also is possible, from the 1820 and 1830 census data, that there was another male child, that we do not have data on, born between the years 1810 and 1815. He probably would have been out of the family house by the time of the 1840 census, and thus probably would have been living either in Tompkins County, New York or in Erie County, Pennsylvania. Another thought is that this could be a child from another family staying with the Milks family. This was fairly common in those days. I have been unable to locate another un-connected Milks family that would fit the 'missing' child birth period.

Ezra moved to Green County, Wisconsin with his father about 1843, where he married for the first time, in 1847, Polly Phillips. Ezra and Polly had 3 children, Amos, Thomas, and Hattie. Polly died in 1854, and Ezra married, in 1855, Sarah Round, who had a 2 year old daughter, Martha, by her first husband, James? Mosher. Ezra and Sarah had four children, Frank, Ruth, David, and Ella. Ezra and Sarah parted ways, with Ezra marrying, about 1865, Rachel   , who had a daughter Frances, b: Wis., by her first husband, Mister Russell. In 1870 they lived in Benton County, Iowa, where their first child, Charles, was born. During the 1870s they moved to Missouri, where their second child, Hetty, was born, and in 1880 they settled in Arkansas City, Cowley County, Kansas, where their third and last child, Carl, was born.

Ezra and Rachel divorced in Kansas in the early 1880s and were living separately in 1885, both living in Arkansas City and Frances (Russell), Hetty, and Carl living with Rachel.

Ezra was listed as deaf in the 1880 census. In 1891 he entered U.S. National Home for Disabled Volunteer Soldiers, in Leavenworth, Kansas. He remained there until his death in 1907. His daughter, Hetty Shaffer paid to have his body shipped to Shawnee, Pottawatomie County, Oklahoma, where she lived, and where Ezra is buried in Fairview Cemetery.

OBITUARY - *Albany Vindicator* (Albany, Wisconsin), June 10, 1909, p. 8, col. 2

Sally Round Milks was born Nov. 15, 1827, near Trenton, Mass. While still a child she moved with her parents to Ohio, and later to Iowa. On August 29, 1843, she was married to James Mosher. The only child of this union that survived is Mrs. Martha E. Dodge of this village.

In the fall of 1853 she came to live with her father in Monroe, Wis., where she was married December 5, 1854, to Ezra Milks, two sons, Frank of Rock City, Ill., and David of Ashley, Ind., and one daughter, Mrs. Luther Estes of Albany from this marriage surviving her.

Since breaking up her own home about seven years ago Mrs. Milks has lived with her children. On Sunday, June 6, 1909, she died peacefully at the home of her daughter, Mrs. Dodge. Death was due to after effects of a serious siege of grip.

In accordance with her expressed wishes, simple funeral services were held at the home, Rev. R. Pengilly of the M.E. Church conducting them, and interment was in the cemetery.

Mrs. Milks, though quiet and reserved, will long be remembered by many as a great lover of her home, a great worker for her loved ones and as one who was thoughtful and kind to all.

In addition to her two daughters and two sons, the following friends from a distance were present at the funeral: Messrs. and Mesdames Ed. Stephens, Z. Davis and Mr. Bert Gillett of Juda.

Burial: Gap Cemetery , Brodhead, Green County, Wisconsin, USA

Children of EZRA MILKS and POLLY PHILLIPS are:
534.   i. AMOS E.[8] MILKS, b. Bet. 1847 - 1848, Sylvester Township, Green Co., Wisconsin; d. 10 Jul 1926, Pueblo, Pueblo County, Colorado.

535.	ii.	THOMAS W. MILKS, b. 28 Oct 1850, Green County, Wisconsin; d. Mar 1928, Burchard, Pawnee County, Nebraska.
536.	iii.	HARRIET "HATTIE" MILKS, b. 1853, Sylvester, Green County, Wisconsin; d. 1888, Kansas.

Children of EZRA MILKS and SARAH ROUND are:

537.	iv.	FRANK WHEELER[8] MILKS, b. 12 Mar 1857, Green County, Wisconsin; d. Apr 1934, Juda, Green County, Wisconsin.
538.	v.	RUTH MILKS, b. 1859, Green County, Wisconsin; d. Abt. 1889, Green County, Wisconsin.
539.	vi.	DAVID MILKS, b. 03 Apr 1861, Albany, Green County, Wisconsin; d. 06 Dec 1923.
540.	vii.	ELLA MILKS, b. Abt. 1863, Green County, Wisconsin; d. Abt. 1937, No children.

Children of EZRA MILKS and RACHEL RUSSELL are:

	viii.	FRANCES[8] RUSSELL, b. Abt. 1865, Wisconsin (step-daughter)[686].
	ix.	CHARLES MILKS, b. Abt. 1868, Iowa; d. Bet. 1880 - 1885, Arkansas City, Cowley County, Kansas. Burial: Riverview Cemetery , Arkansas City, Cowley County, Kansas, USA Plot: OLD addn, blk E, lot 21, spc 5
541.	x.	HETTY MILKS, b. Jun 1872, Missouri; d. Aft. 14 Mar 1907.
	xi.	CARL MILKS, b. Abt. 1877, Arkansas City, Cowley County, Kansas.
	xii.	EDWARD MILKS, b. Abt. 1880, Arkansas City, Cowley County, Kansas; d. Bet. 1880 - 1885, Arkansas City, Cowley County, Kansas. Burial: Riverview Cemetery, Arkansas City, Cowley County, Kansas

211. PHOEBE ANN[7] MILKS *(EZRA[6], DAVID[5] MILK, JONATHAN[4], JOB[3], JOHN[2], JOHN[1])* was born 11 Nov 1822 in Tompkins County, New York, and died 03 Apr 1899 in Warren, Jo Daviess County, Illinois. She married EBENEZER B. HILLIARD 04 May 1845 in Green County, Wisconsin[687]. He was born 27 Oct 1817 in Schuyler Falls, New York, and died 13 Oct 1891 in Warren, Jo Daviess County, Illinois. Phoebe was a member of the Adventist Church. They are buried in Elmwood Cemetery, Warren, Jo Davies County, Illinois

Children of PHOEBE MILKS and EBENEZER HILLIARD are:

542.	i.	DANIEL MARENOS[8] HILLIARD, b. 01 Feb 1846, Illinois; d. California.
543.	ii.	EZRA MILKS HILLIARD, b. 22 Mar 1849, Green County, Wisconsin; d. 09 Jun 1929, Warren, Jo Daviess County, Illinois.
544.	iii.	LONSON DARIUS HILLIARD, b. 22 Mar 1849, Green County, Wisconsin; d. 23 Nov 1903, Albany, Green County, Wisconsin.
	iv.	HARRIETT AMELIA HILLIARD, b. 16 Mar 1851, Green County, Wisconsin; d. 29 Oct 1859, Green County, Wisconsin.
545.	v.	CLARA CLARINDA HILLIARD, b. 19 Apr 1855, Green County, Wisconsin.
546.	vi.	DR. SUMNER HALE HILLIARD, b. 05 May 1858, Green County, Wisconsin; d. 29 Mar 1917, Miami, Florida?.
	vii.	LAURA JOSEPHINE HILLIARD, b. 15 Dec 1864, Green County, Wisconsin; d. 18 Aug 1948, Warren, Jo Daviess County, Illinois. Never married. Occupation: Registered Nurse. Burial: Elmwood Cemetery, Warren, Jo Davies County, Illinois

212. DAVID[7] MILKS *(DAVID[6], DAVID[5] MILK, JONATHAN[4], JOB[3], JOHN[2], JOHN[1])*[688] was born 05 Sep 1813 in Augusta, Grenville, Ontario, Canada[689], and died 03 Apr 1866 in Augusta, Grenville, Ontario, Canada[690,691]. He married AMELIA WHITE[692] 22 Mar 1831 in Ontario, Canada[693]. She was born Bet. 14 Mar 1811 - 1812 in Augusta, Grenville, Ontario, Canada[694,695], and died 04 Mar 1878 in Augusta, Grenville, Ontario, Canada[696]. David and Amelia are buried in Read's Cemetery, Augusta, Ontario, Canada

David and Martha (IRELAND) MILKS came to Leeds & Grenville in the early 1800`s from Rensselaer County , New York. Their child David Milks listed below was born in Augusta Twp., Some members of the family changed the spelling of their surname to MYLKS.

Leeds & Grenville OGS listing for Read's Cemetery lists his grave. They write: " David Milks, died Apr. 3, 1866, aged 52 yrs 6 ms 28 dys"

Land records for Grenville County: Book E Mem # 66 David Milks purchased land from Guy Carlton Read on 5 JUN 1832 in Augusta Twp at age 23.

Augusta By-Law #47 - 12 Feb 1852 - To remove John Wright from the Office of Overseer of Highways in and for the 6th Division of the 3rd Range and to appoint David Milks in his place.

Tombstone Inscription:
MYLKS
Amelia White, wife of David Mylks
born Mar 14, 1___ - died March __, ____
Mary McLean Mylks, wife of H. Watson
born June 12, 1840 - died June 18, 1913

Children of DAVID MILKS and AMELIA WHITE are:

547.	i.	JOHN W.[8] MYLKS, b. 1833, Augusta, Leeds, Ontario, Canada.
548.	ii.	HARMON WILLIAM MYLKS, b. 23 Mar 1836, Augusta, Grenville, Ontario, Canada; d. 19 May 1917, Wellington County, Ontario, Canada.
549.	iii.	DAVID SHEPHERD MYLKS, b. 1838, Augusta, Grenville, Ontario, Canada; d. 17 May 1909, Elizabethtown, Leeds, Ontario, Canada.
	iv.	MARY MCLEAN MYLKS[697], b. 12 Jun 1840, Augusta, Grenville, Ontario, Canada[697]; d. 18 Jun 1913, Brockville, Leeds, Ontario[697]; m. H. WATSON; b. Abt. 1840. Burial: Read Cemetery, Augusta, Ontario, Canada
550.	v.	MANUEL MYLKS, b. Abt. 1843, Augusta, Grenville, Ontario, Canada; d. 26 Feb 1933, Kingston, Ontario.
	vi.	CATHERINE JANE MILKS, b. 23 Oct 1846, Augusta, Grenville, Ontario, Canada; d. 24 Jan 1855, Augusta, Grenville, Ontario, Canada[697]. Burial: Read's Cemetery, Augusta, Ontario, Canada[697]

213. EZRA[7] MILKS (*DAVID[6], DAVID[5] MILK, JONATHAN[4], JOB[3], JOHN[2], JOHN[1]*) was born Abt. 1818 in Canada, and died Bet. 1874 - 1880 in Vallejo, Solano, California?[698]. He married (1) ARELIA A. WHIPPLE. She was born Abt. 1819 in Ohio. He married (2) THERESA M. DRUMMOND 08 Sep 1859 in Sacramento, California[699]. She was born Abt. 1827 in Maine, and died Aft. 1880 in Vallejo, Solano, California?.

In the 1840 Census, Elk Creek, Erie County, Pennsylvania Ezra lived next door to his father David Milks - 1785, who was a brother to Ezra Milks - 1781 Ezra was a ship carpenter.

Sometime around 1858, Ezra left his family in Erie, Pennsylvania and relocated to California. He first shows up in the marriage records of Sacramento where he married Teresa M. Drummond on 8 September 1859. In the 1860 Census Ezra and Teresa are living in Placer County, California. From 1862 through 1868 Ezra shows up in the City Directory for San Francisco where he worked at the North Shipyard and was registered to vote. On September 24, 1868 he was removed from the registered voter records in San Francisco, and then appears on the Voter Registers for Solano County on September 29, 1868. Shortly afterwards, on October 29, 1868 his voter registration is transferred from Solano County to Napa County, although on 5 July 1870, during the 1870 Federal Census, Ezra, Teresa and their son George are still enumerated in Vallejo, Solano County. In 1874 George is shown in the Sacramento, California City Directory, residing at 70 Pennsylvania (St.) and still shown as a 'ship carpenter'. In the 1880 Census, Teresa is shown as a widow, living in Vallejo, Solano County.

Children of EZRA MILKS and ARELIA WHIPPLE are:

551.	i.	CHARLES BARNEY[8] MILKS, b. Dec 1839, Erie County, Pennsylvania.
552.	ii.	SILAS E. MILKS, b. Abt. 1841, Erie County, Pennsylvania; d. 1920, Conneaut, Ohio.
553.	iii.	ADELAIDE "ADDIE" MILKS, b. 22 Aug 1843, Erie County, Pennsylvania; d. 20 Nov 1928, Manchester, Delaware County, Iowa.

Child of EZRA MILKS and THERESA DRUMMOND is:

	iv.	GEORGE[8] MILKS, b. Abt. 1859, California.

214. ALBERT[7] MILKS (*DAVID[6], DAVID[5] MILK, JONATHAN[4], JOB[3], JOHN[2], JOHN[1]*) was born 01 Oct 1828 in Canada[700], and died 27 Feb 1920 in Erie, Pennsylvania[700]. He married DEBORAH FOGG 27 Sep 1855 in Erie Co., Pennsylvania?. She was born 12 Apr 1834 in Springfield, Pennsylvania?[700], and died 04 Oct 1907 in Erie, Pennsylvania[700]. Albert owned the American Hotel on 9th & Peach Streets, Erie, Pennsylvania. He and Deborah are buried in Section MM--Lot 107, Erie Cemetery, Erie, Pennsylvania

Children of ALBERT MILKS and DEBORAH FOGG are:

	i.	CHARLES[8] MILKS, b. Abt. 1855, Cranesville, Erie County, Pennsylvania.
554.	ii.	SARAH ANNA MILKS, b. 14 Aug 1858, Cranesville, Erie County, Pennsylvania; d. 09 Jan 1929, Erie, Erie

555. iii. MARY E. MILKS, b. 13 Nov 1861, Cranesville, Erie County, Pennsylvania; d. 30 Apr 1928, Erie, Erie County, Pennsylvania.

215. HARRIS[7] MILKS *(SILAS W.[6], DAVID[5] MILK, JONATHAN[4], JOB[3], JOHN[2], JOHN[1])* was born 09 Jul 1809 in Pittstown, Rensselaer County, New York[701], and died 15 Dec 1871 in Hope, Barry County, Michigan[702]. He married BARTHENA HOYT[703] Abt. 1850 in New York, daughter of JESSE HOYT and CHRISTINA QUACKENBUSH. She was born 01 Mar 1831 in New York[704], and died 1916 in Hope, Barry County, Michigan[704]. They are buried in Cedar Creek Cemetery, Barry County, Michigan

Children of HARRIS MILKS and BARTHENA HOYT are:
- 556. i. WARREN "JACK"[8] MILKS, b. 09 Nov 1850, Pittstown, NY (See Croft, p155); d. 21 Feb 1915, Farrel, Clare County, Michigan.
- ii. GEORGE W. MILKS, b. 03 Feb 1851; d. 03 Jun 1899, Deerfield, Mecosta, Michigan[705]; m. HANNAH EWINGS[706], 08 Dec 1894, Morley, Mecosta, Michigan[707]; b. Oct 1851 Canada[708], d. 1924 Morley, Mecosta County, Michigan. No children
  George and Hannah are buried in Boyd Cemetery, Deerfield, Mecosta, Michigan
- 557. iii. CHRISTINA MILKS, b. Bet. 1852 - 1853, Pittstown, NY; d. 07 Oct 1886, Morley, Mecosta County, Michigan.
- 558. iv. ERNEST L. MILKS, b. 01 Jan 1856, Pittstown, NY; d. 24 May 1941, Barry County, Michigan.
- 559. v. JESSE MILKS, b. Sep 1858, Pittstown, Rensselaer County, New York; d. 1941.
- vi. FREMONT MILKS, b. 1863, Pittstown, NY[709]; d. 05 Mar 1905, Northern Michigan Asylum, Traverse City, Michigan (unmarried)[710]. Never married. Burial: Morley, Mecosta Co., Michigan[711]
- 560. vii. FRANKLIN GRANT MILKS, b. 30 Dec 1863, Pittstown, New York; d. Bef. 1930, Michigan.
- viii. HARRY MILKS, b. 14 Jul 1868, Michigan[712,713]; d. 1872, Hope, Barry County, Michigan. Burial: Cedar Creek Cemetery, Barry County, Michigan
- 561. ix. JULIA ANN MILKS, b. 26 May 1872, Hope, Barry County, Michigan.

216. JULIA ANN[7] MILKS *(SILAS W.[6], DAVID[5] MILK, JONATHAN[4], JOB[3], JOHN[2], JOHN[1])* was born 1814 in Pittstown, Rensselaer County, New York, and died 28 Aug 1903 in Lansingburgh, New York. She married HENRY ROWLEY. He died Bef. 1877.
Julia and Henry are buried in Lansingburgh Cemetery, Rensselaer County, New York

Children of JULIA MILKS and HENRY ROWLEY are:
- i. SARAH M.[8] ROWLEY, b. 1835, Lansingburgh, New York; d. 15 Nov 1855, Lansingburgh, New York.
- ii. SILAS H. ROWLEY, b. Bet. 1837 - 1838, Lansingburgh, New York; d. 15 Feb 1865, Fort Fisher, North Carolina.:
  Military service: 169th Regt, Co. K, N.Y.S.V. - Civil War (killed in action). Burial: Lansingburgh Cemetery, Lansingburgh, New York

217. DAVID[7] MILK *(SILAS W.[6] MILKS, DAVID[5] MILK, JONATHAN[4], JOB[3], JOHN[2], JOHN[1])* was born 1815, and died 16 Jun 1864 in Near Petersburg. He married CAROLINE L. FINCH Abt. 1855. She was born 1835, and died 1907.
David enlisted Aug 27, 1862 into the 125th Inf., Co. K; Civil War; Corporal; died in the army.

Children of DAVID MILK and CAROLINE FINCH are:
- i. CHARLES[8] MILK, b. 25 Oct 1859, Valley Falls (Pittstown), New York[714]; d. 20 Oct 1861, Valley Falls (Pittstown), New York[715]. Burial: Old Presbyterian, Schaghticoke, Rensselaer County, New York
- 562. ii. ANNA MILK, b. 1861, Valley Falls (Pittstown), New York; d. 1942.

218. MATTHEW G.[7] MILKS *(SILAS W.[6], DAVID[5] MILK, JONATHAN[4], JOB[3], JOHN[2], JOHN[1])* was born 07 Feb 1816 in Valley Falls (Pittstown), Rensselaer County, New York[716], and died 29 Oct 1875 in Valley Falls (Pittstown), Rensselaer County, New York[716]. He married MARGARET H. ALLEN, daughter of TIMOTHY ALLEN and HARRIET GROFF. She was born 28 Sep 1824 in New York[716], and died 05 Aug 1896 in Schaghticoke, Saratoga Co., New York[716]. They are buried in Elmwood Cemetery, Schaghticoke, NY

Matthew retained ownership of Milk Grove Farm, originally occupied by his grandfather David Milk (1752). In

1879, his wife Margaret deeded Milk Grove Farm to Julia A. Norton and Arthur G. Atwood. Mr. Cheney was the owner in 1956.

Children of MATTHEW MILKS and MARGARET ALLEN are:

563.   i. EMMA A.[8] MILKS, b. 1849, Valley Falls (Pittstown), Rensselaer County, New York; d. 1909, Troy, New York.
       ii. HARRIET M. MILKS, b. 1851, Valley Falls (Pittstown), Rensselaer County, New York; m. MONTGOMERY DUNNETT; b. Of Troy, NY; d. 1910.
564.   iii. ELLIS DAVID MILKS, b. 1855, Valley Falls (Pittstown), Rensselaer County, New York; d. 1914, Valley Falls (Pittstown), Rensselaer County, New York.
565.   iv. ALLEN EDGAR MILKS, b. 13 Jul 1856, Valley Falls (Pittstown), New York; d. 23 Apr 1924, Valley Falls (Pittstown), New York.
566.   v. JULIA FRANCES MILKS, b. 1857, Valley Falls (Pittstown), Rensselaer County, New York.

219. CATHERINE I.[7] MILKS (SILAS W.[6], DAVID[5] MILK, JONATHAN[4], JOB[3], JOHN[2], JOHN[1]) was born 1822 in Pittstown, Rensselaer County, New York, and died Aft. 1900 in Lansingburgh, Rensselaer County, New York. She married LORENZO ROBBINS Abt. 1860 in Pittstown, Rensselaer County, New York, son of MAXON ROBBINS and HARRIET _____. He was born Abt. 1836 in Rensselaer County, New York, and died Aft. 1900 in Lansingburgh, Rensselaer County, New York.

Child of CATHERINE MILKS and LORENZO ROBBINS is:
    i. SARAH H.[8] ROBBINS[717,718], b. Abt. 1862, Pittstown, Rensselaer County, New York; d. Bet. 1870 - 1880, Rensselaer County, New York.

220. LUCETTA[7] MILK (SILAS W.[6] MILKS, DAVID[5] MILK, JONATHAN[4], JOB[3], JOHN[2], JOHN[1])[719,720,721,722] was born Abt. 1823 in New York[723], and died 29 Nov 1882 in Bangor, Van Buren County, Michigan[724]. She married ISAAC WAITE, JR. Abt. 1847 in Rensselaer County, New York, son of ISAAC WAITE and MARY MILKS. He was born 09 May 1821 in New York[725], and died 09 Sep 1875 in Battle Creek, Calhoun County, Michigan[726]. Residence: Bet. 1870 - 1882, Bangor, Van Buren County, Michigan

Child of LUCETTA MILK and ISAAC WAITE is:
567.   i. ANGELINA[8] WAITE, b. Nov 1849, Rensselaer County, New York; d. 1931, Bangor, Van Buren County, Michigan.

221. PERRY M.[7] MILKS (BENJAMIN[6], DAVID[5] MILK, JONATHAN[4], JOB[3], JOHN[2], JOHN[1]) was born 25 Jul 1830 in Pennsylvania[727,728], and died 19 Mar 1864 in Scio, Allegany County, New York[729]. He married ELIZA HAMILTON, daughter of GLOUDY HAMILTON. She was born Abt. 1830 in Scio, Allegany County, New York. Perry is buried in Fairlawn Cemetery, Scio, Allegany County, NY

Child of PERRY MILKS and ELIZA HAMILTON is:
568.   i. FRANK[8] MILKS, b. Dec 1857, Scio, Allegany County, New York; d. Bet. 1900 - 1910, Train Wreck.

222. BENJAMIN FRANKLIN[7] MILKS (BENJAMIN[6], DAVID[5] MILK, JONATHAN[4], JOB[3], JOHN[2], JOHN[1]) was born 03 Dec 1833 in Pennsylvania[730], and died Dec 1919 in Town of Amity, Allegany County, New York[731]. He married (1) SARAH JANE ROSENBARK 1858, daughter of CHARLES ROSENBARK. She was born 1838[731], and died 1888 in Amity, Allegany County, New York[731]. He married (2) LAURA LEONORA GILLETT[732] Apr 1890 in New York, daughter of ISAAC GILLETT and SARAH WHITNEY. She was born 08 May 1847 in Perry, Wyoming County, NY, and died May 1921 in Town of Amity, Allegany County, New York. Benjamin was a millwright. Benjamin and Sarah are buried in Fairlawn Cemetery, Scio, Allegany County, NY

DEATH NOTICE - *(Perry, NY, Herald, May 18, 1921)*
Mrs. Laura Milks
The funeral of Mrs. Laura Milks of Scio will be held this afternoon at 3 o'clock from the home of her brother, W. A. Gillett, 32 South Center street. Mrs. Milks is survived by three sons, one brother and one sister. Burial: Hope Cemetery, Perry, Wyoming County, New York, USA

Child of BENJAMIN MILKS and LAURA GILLETT is:
  i. EARL PERRY[8] MILKS, b. 30 Dec 1890[733,734]; d. Sep 1989, Scio, Allegany County, New York[735]; m. DOROTHEA CARPENTER, 24 Nov 1916, Scio, Allegany County, New York?[736]; b. 1884, North Harmony, Chautauqua County, New York[737]; d. 1968, Allegany County[737]. Earl and Dorothea are buried in Fairlawn Cemetery, Scio, Allegany County, NY No children.

  Dorothea graduated from Alfred University, Ph.D. and was a School Teacher & Librarian

  From: **The Historic Annal of Southwestern New York;** Vol 3, p275-6
  Earl P. Milks

  In his varied activities as a farmer, business man, oil producer, public official and civic leader, E. P. Milks ranks as one of the most prominent figures in the community of Scio, New York, where he owns and operates a large hardware business and is associated with the Exchange Oil Company.

  Mr. Milks was born at Scio, town of Amity, December 30, 1890, the son of Benjamin Franklin and Laura (Gillette) Milks, both natives of this State, the former from West Union, Steuben County, and the latter from Perry, Wyoming County. His father, who like his mother is now deceased, was a millwright by trade and is said to have superintended the erection of some of the first circular sawmills in the northwestern part of the State of Wisconsin. He returned to New York State in 1870 and settled on a farm in Amity, which he conducted for the remainder of his life and which is now owned by Mr. Milks. After a general education in the public schools, Mr. Milks continued to assist in the management of the family homestead and remained here until 1930 when he was appointed postmaster of Scio, an office he occupied with distinction and success until 1933. At that time he returned to the family farm, continued here for three years and then bought the hardware business of W. M. Moore, in Scio, which he has conducted since. Throughout much of his life Mr. Milks has been an active and prominent figure in the oil industry of this region, both as a producer and owner of oil land. Recently he disposed of much of this property and today retains his interest in the business as an associate of the Exchange Oil Company.

  Aside from his business achievements Mr. Milks is widely known for the active and prominent part he has taken in community affairs. He has been a member of the Scio School Board for a number of years, served as clerk for the body and recently was appointed in the same capacity for the new centralized school board. For a number of years he has also been secretary and treasurer of the Scio Free Library, and in his religious convictions holds membership in the Universalist Church of Friendship. He was Postmaster of Scio, Chmn of School Board, and owned a hardware store in Scio

  On November 24, 1916, Mr. Milks married Dorothea Carpenter, of North Harmony, Chautauqua County. Mrs. Milks, who is now librarian for the Scio Free Library, is a graduate of Alfred University.

223. GEORGE W.[7] WOOLMAN (*PATIENCE[6] MILK, LEMUEL[5], JONATHAN[4], JOB[3], JOHN[2], JOHN[1]*) was born 28 Mar 1810 in Lake George, Warren County, New York ?, and died 18 Dec 1883 in Lakefield, Saginaw County, Michigan ?. He married ELIZABETH SUSAN SANDERS Abt. 1837 in New York. She was born 18 Mar 1820 in Rupert, Bennington, Vermont, and died 12 May 1900 in Richland, Saginaw County, Michigan[738]. They are buried in Hemlock Cemetery, Hemlock, Saginaw County, Michigan

Children of GEORGE WOOLMAN and ELIZABETH SANDERS are:
  i. POLLY[8] WOOLMAN, b. Abt. 1838, New York.
  ii. SAMUEL WOOLMAN, b. Abt. 1839, New York.
  iii. MARY A. WOOLMAN, b. Abt. 1843, New York.
  iv. ELIZABETH A. WOOLMAN, b. Abt. 1845, Michigan.
569. v. GEORGE MARTIN WOOLMAN, b. Abt. 1847, Michigan; d. 1920, Arenac County, Michigan.
  vi. MARTHA WOOLMAN, b. Abt. 1857, Michigan.
570. vii. NELSON JOSEPH WOOLMAN, b. Aug 1859, Michigan.

224. LEMUEL[7] WOOLMAN (*PATIENCE[6] MILK, LEMUEL[5], JONATHAN[4], JOB[3], JOHN[2], JOHN[1]*) was born Abt. 1808 in New York, and died Aft. 1880 in Prob. Cattaraugus County, New York. He married SALLY _____ Abt. 1848 in Cattaraugus County, New York. She was born Abt. 1821 in New York.

Child of LEMUEL WOOLMAN and SALLY _____ is:
      i. BETSEY A.[8] WOOLMAN, b. Abt. Aug 1849, Otto, Cattaraugus County, New York.

225. ADELIA[7] PROSSER *(MARY[6] MILK, LEMUEL[5], JONATHAN[4], JOB[3], JOHN[2], JOHN[1])* was born 24 Jun 1812 in New York, and died 18 Feb 1873 in Lanark, Portage County, Wisconsin[739]. She married IRA WHIPPLE 1842 in Erie County, New York, son of JOB WHIPPLE and SARAH SMITH. He was born 07 Sep 1819 in East Hamburg, Erie County, New York, and died 14 May 1888 in Portage County, Wisconsin[739].

The summer they were married, 1842, they made a wedding journey from Erie Co., NY, to Chicago, Ill. Relatives and friends helped to fill their covered wagon and the journey was remembered as a very happy one. In 1848 after a few years at Bloomingdale, Ill., they resumed their travels in the covered wagon, now followed by a hired man and a drove of cattle. Their destination was Clayton, Winnebago Co., Wis., where they arrived May 5. Ira served in the Civil War bet. 17 Mar 1864 - 26 Jul 1865, Civil War, Company B, Wisconsin 38th Infantry Regiment

Children of ADELIA PROSSER and IRA WHIPPLE are:
- 571.   i. ANNETTE ADELIA[8] WHIPPLE, b. 26 Feb 1846, Bloomingdale, Illinois; d. 19 Jun 1938, Seattle, Washington.
- 572.   ii. IRA FRANK WHIPPLE, b. 26 Feb 1849, Clayton, Winnebago County, Wisconsin; d. 15 Jun 1905, Waupaca, Wisconsin?.
-      iii. JANE EMERETTE WHIPPLE, b. 18 Apr 1853, Clayton, Winnebago County, Wisconsin; d. 11 Aug 1877, South Dakota ?.
She was a missionary to the Sioux Indians in South Dakota

226. JANE[7] PROSSER *(MARY[6] MILK, LEMUEL[5], JONATHAN[4], JOB[3], JOHN[2], JOHN[1])* was born 10 Jan 1815 in Washington County, New York[740]. She married WILLIAM FERRILL. He was born Abt. 1811 in Ireland[741]. Lived in: 1850, New Albion, Cattaraugus County, New York

Children of JANE PROSSER and WILLIAM FERRILL are:
     i. ADELIA[8] FERRILL, b. Abt. 1833, New York[741].
     ii. NEWELL FERRILL, b. Abt. 1839, New York[741].

227. MARIA LYNDIA[7] PROSSER *(ELIZABETH 'BETSEY'[6] MILK, LEMUEL[5], JONATHAN[4], JOB[3], JOHN[2], JOHN[1])* was born 26 May 1807 in Bolton, Warren County, New York, and died 24 Feb 1884. She married DANIEL L. MOORE Abt. 1830 in Warren County, New York ?. He was born 1801, and died 25 Aug 1868 in Bolton, Warren County, New York.

Children of MARIA PROSSER and DANIEL MOORE are:
- 573.   i. ADDISON[8] MOORE, b. Abt. 1831, Bolton, Warren County, New York; d. 1900.
- 574.   ii. MASSENA MOORE, b. 1833, Bolton, Warren County, New York.
-      iii. SON MOORE, b. Bolton, Warren County, New York; d. d.y..
-      iv. SONTWO MOORE, b. Bolton, Warren County, New York; d. d.y..
-      v. MARETTE MOORE, b. 10 Mar 1839, Bolton, Warren County, New York; m. EDWARD SMITH; b. Abt. 1839. No children.
- 575.   vi. BETSEY MOORE, b. 11 Mar 1842, Bolton, Warren County, New York; d. 04 Jan 1911, Diamond Point (Hill View), New York.
- 576.   vii. EMILY MOORE, b. 27 Oct 1844, Bolton, Warren County, New York; d. 08 Oct 1924, Little River, Rice County, Kansas.
-      viii. MINERVA MOORE, b. 26 Feb 1847, Bolton, Warren County, New York; d. 1870, Bolton, Warren County, New York. Never married.
- 577.   ix. MARIA FRANCES MOORE, b. 26 Feb 1847, Bolton, Warren County, New York; d. 1927.

228. JAMES LEMUEL 'NELSON'[7] PROSSER *(ELIZABETH 'BETSEY'[6] MILK, LEMUEL[5], JONATHAN[4], JOB[3], JOHN[2], JOHN[1])* was born 28 Feb 1809 in Bolton, Warren County, New York, and died 07 May 1889 in Warren County, New York. He married MARY ANN BROWN Abt. 1845 in New York. She was born 09 Mar 1827, and died 1895 in Warren County, New York. They are buried in Old Cemetery, Lake George Village, Warren County, New York

Children of JAMES PROSSER and MARY BROWN are:
     i. HELEN[8] PROSSER, b. Abt. 1850, New York; m. FRANK GRIFFIN; b. Abt. 1850.

578. ii. ELMINA M. PROSSER, b. 21 Oct 1851, New York.

229. ROXCENA[7] BATES *(SARAH 'SALLY'[6] MILK, LEMUEL[5], JONATHAN[4], JOB[3], JOHN[2], JOHN[1])*[742] was born 05 Apr 1815 in Washington Co./Warren Co., NY[742], and died 1894 in Otto, Cattaraugus Co., New York[743]. She married DARIUS BABCOCK 29 Jan 1838. He was born 1820 in Vermont[744], and died 1895 in Otto, Cattaraugus Co., New York[745]. They are buried in North Otto Cemetery, Cattaraugus County, New York

Children of ROXCENA BATES and DARIUS BABCOCK are:
579. i. ELLEN A.[8] BABCOCK, b. 1840, Otto, Cattaraugus Co., New York; d. 09 Nov 1879, East Otto, Cattaraugus County, New York.
      ii. EMILY ADELIA BABCOCK, b. 1842, Otto, Cattaraugus Co., New York; d. 1937, Otto, Cattaraugus Co., New York; m. ALLAN A. BATES; b. Oct 1836, Otto, Cattaraugus Co., New York; d. 1925, Otto, Cattaraugus Co., New York. They are buried in North Otto Cemetery, Cattaraugus County, New York
580. iii. JULIA CATHERINE BABCOCK, b. 1846, Otto, Cattaraugus Co., New York; d. 1934, Otto, Cattaraugus Co., New York.

230. JOHN A.[7] BATES *(SARAH 'SALLY'[6] MILK, LEMUEL[5], JONATHAN[4], JOB[3], JOHN[2], JOHN[1])* was born 28 Jun 1819 in New York[746], and died 06 Jun 1900[746]. He married (1) MARTHA ANN BUTTON HUTTON 06 Mar 1842. She was born 05 Jul 1826 in Madison County, New York[746], and died 10 Nov 1881 in Otto, Cattaraugus Co., New York[746]. He married (2) LURINDA F. _____[747] Abt. 1884 in Cattaraugus County, New York[747]. She was born Apr 1821 in New York. John and Martha are buried in North Otto Cemetery, Otto, Cattaraugus County, New York

Children of JOHN BATES and MARTHA HUTTON are:
  i.   CHARLES O.[8] BATES, b. Abt. 1843, Otto, Cattaraugus Co., New York.
  ii.   ORRIN BATES, b. Abt. 1845, Otto, Cattaraugus Co., New York.
  iii. TRIPHENA BATES, b. Abt. 1847, Otto, Cattaraugus Co., New York; d. 1859, Otto, Cattaraugus Co., NY.
  iv.   ANSON BATES, b. 1849, Otto, Cattaraugus Co., New York.
  v.   ROSANNA BATES, b. Abt. 1851, New Albion, Cattaraugus County, New York.
  vi.   LUCENA BATES, b. Abt. 1854, New Albion, Cattaraugus County, New York.
  vii. JULIETT BATES, b. Abt. 1856, New Albion, Cattaraugus County, New York.
  viii. FANNY A. BATES, b. Abt. Jan 1860, New Albion, Cattaraugus County, New York.
  ix.   MARTHA A. BATES, b. Abt. 1864, New Albion, Cattaraugus County, New York.
  x.   JOHN L. BATES, b. Abt. 1867, New Albion, Cattaraugus County, New York.

231. MARY ANN[7] BATES *(SARAH 'SALLY'[6] MILK, LEMUEL[5], JONATHAN[4], JOB[3], JOHN[2], JOHN[1])* was born 01 Jun 1826 in Otto, Cattaraugus County, New York, and died 06 Nov 1892 in Cattaraugus County, New York. She married ZINA SATTERLEE 16 Dec 1845, son of JOSEPH SATTERLEE and DORCAS BABCOCK. He was born 05 Jan 1824 in Pike, Wyoming County, New York, and died 26 Feb 1865 in Lovettsville, Loudoun County, Virginia. Zina and Mary Ann are buried in North Otto Cemetery, Cattaraugus County, New York

The book, **History of the Ninth Regiment, New York Volunteer Cavalry, War of 1861 to 1865** described some of the regiment's activities during Zina's final days: "Feb. 6 (1865). The 9th N.Y. moved into the camp vacated by the 20th Pa. While in camp near Lovettsville a number of men were sick and several died. Feb. 22. A national salute was fired at noon at Harper's Ferry for the capture of Charleston and Wilmington and the retaking of Fort Sumter as well as for the celebration of Washington's birthday ... Feb. 24. The 2d brigade, now under command of Col. Fitzhugh left camp at Lovettsville and marched through Hillsboro (Virginia) to the Potomac opposite Sandy Hook. Feb. 25. Reveille at 3 a.m., moved at 5 a.m. Marched to near Berryville (VA.) and went into camp in a cold storm of sleet. The men make beds of pine brush from which they had thawed the frozen sleet over their camp fires. The wagon train moved with the regiment as far as Bolivar Heights from which place a number of unserviceable horses were sent back. Feb. 26. Marched to Winchester (Va.) and camped a little way south east of the town and joined the division. Drew rations, forage and ammunition for a long march including 15 days of coffee, sugar, and salt."

Zina had probably become ill at the camp near Lovettsville toward the beginning of the month. It was the closest point mentioned to Harpers Ferry. He died less than 2 months before the war's end. From the recorded settlement of his estate, some other facts were learned. Mary Ann Satterlee filed the petition for Zina's estate on 7 Mar. 1866. Mary Ann was noted as the administratrix of his estate. A receipt is present which was made out to "Miss Maryann

Satturlee" for $47. and 50 cents, received by C.W. Bates in March 1865 "for traveling fees and incidental Expenses for the Burial of her Husband." Another receipt was made out for a payment of $20. to a Dr. Henry H. Elcthison of Harper's Ferry, Va. for embalming "the Body of Zena Saterlee." It is dated March 8, 1865 and was given to Mr. Charles W. Bates. Another receipt was made out to "Chas. W. Bates (of) Cattaraugus Sta. N.Y." for $30. for the transportation of the corpse of Zina Satterlee. It was made out by the Adams Express Company, Great Eastern, Western, and Southern Express Forwarders, (of) Harper's Ferry, Va. Mary Ann's brother, Charles, obviously travelled to Harpers Ferry for Mary Ann to bring Zina's body back to Cattaraugus Co. Zina was buried in the North Otto Cemetery, within a stone's throw of his father's grave.

Mary Ann remained in the family home until her death. Her oldest son, David, stayed in the house with his mother, as did his wife and children, and he continued to farm the land and provide for Mary Ann. Mary Ann was listed in the Cattaraugus Co. 1883 Pension List for Civil War Veterans and their families. It lists her No. of Certificate as 111,109; the cause of her being the pensioner as "widow"; and the amount received as $8.00/month. Mary Ann (Bates) Satterlee's will was dated 9 Nov. 1886 and in part read:

To my daughter Sarah L. Hawkins one rocking chair, my set of cane seated chairs, and one hundred and fifty dollars. Said rocking chair is cane seated. Second I give and bequeath to my son, Emer D. Satterlee, one Feather Bed and one hundred and fifty dollars. Third I give and bequeath to my daughter Alice J. Brooks my Bureau, my best bed and what belongs with it and one hundred and fifty dollars. Fourth I give and bequeath to my daughter Sarah L. Hawkins and Alice J. Brooks all my wearing apparel to be divided equally between them. Fifth I give and bequeath to my son, David B. Satterlee the balance residue and remainder of all my property of whatever name and kind to have hold and enjoy forever...

Witnesses: John A. Bates Cattaraugus N.Y.; Lurinda F. Bates Cattaraugus N.Y.

Appraisal of the Estate of Zina Satterlee
Zina Satterlee's personal property was appraised on 18 Apr. 1866 by Delotus O. Babcock and Robert S. Moore.
Money: $400.00
Notes: $ 34.00
Lumber: $ 43.00

Inventory of the Estate of Zina Satterlee
1 Wheel Cooking utensil
1 Loom 1 Table
2 Stoves for the family use 6 chairs
10 Sheep 6 Knives + forks
1 cow 6 Plates
1 Hog 6 teacups + saucers
3 Beds + Beding for the family use 1 Sugar dish
1 milk pot
1 tea pot
6 spoons

In addition to the above enumerated articles exempt from appraisal We the said aprisors do inventory apprise and set apart for the use of the Widdow and Minor Children the following articles not to exced $150.
2 cows $60 1 Ax $ .50
10 Sheep 30 1 Hoe .25
1 horse 25 1 Shovel .50
1 Waggon 10 1 Fork .25
1 Cutter 2 1 Sled 1.
1 Drag 4 16 Chickens 1.25
1 Chain 1.50 Dishes 4.50
1 Harnes 4

                                                April 19th 1866
                                                Delotus C. Babcock: Apprisors
                                                Robert L. Moore

Children of MARY BATES and ZINA SATTERLEE are:
581.   i.   DAVID B.[8] SATTERLEE, b. 17 Feb 1847, Otto, Cattaraugus Co., New York; d. Bet. 1910 - 1920, East Otto,

582. ii.   SARAH L. SATTERLEE, b. 12 Jul 1850, Otto, Cattaraugus County, New York.
583. iii. EMER DARIUS SATTERLEE, b. 11 Nov 1855, East Otto, Cattaraugus County, New York; d. 1939, East Otto, Cattaraugus County, New York.
584. iv.   ALICE J. SATTERLEE, b. 30 Jun 1861, East Otto, Cattaraugus County, New York; d. 19 Oct 1919, Cattaraugus County, New York.

232. NELSON L.[7] BATES *(SARAH 'SALLY'[6] MILK, LEMUEL[5], JONATHAN[4], JOB[3], JOHN[2], JOHN[1])* was born 27 May 1827 in New York[748], and died 16 Feb 1866 in Cattaraugus County, New York. He married MARYETTE SATTERLEE 04 Mar 1850, daughter of JOSEPH SATTERLEE and DORCAS BABCOCK. She was born Abt. 1830 in Pike, Wyoming County, New York,. Nelson was a farmer and a drover. He is buried in North Otto Cemetery, Cattaraugus County, New York

Child of NELSON BATES and MARYETTE SATTERLEE is:
  i. DORCAS VIOLA[8] BATES, b. 1852, Otto, Cattaraugus County, New York.

233. CHARLES W.[7] BATES *(SARAH 'SALLY'[6] MILK, LEMUEL[5], JONATHAN[4], JOB[3], JOHN[2], JOHN[1])*[749] was born 25 Jul 1830 in New York. He married (1) JULIETTE SATTERLEE 27 Feb 1851, daughter of JOSEPH SATTERLEE and DORCAS BABCOCK. She was born Abt. 1830 in Pike, Wyoming County, New York, and died in (twin). He married (2) CLARINDA ROBERTS Abt. 1875 in Chautauqua County, New York. She was born Abt. 1845 in New York.

Child of CHARLES BATES and JULIETTE SATTERLEE is:
  i. EMMA F.[8] BATES, b. Abt. 1854, Otto, Cattaraugus County, New York.

Children of CHARLES BATES and CLARINDA ROBERTS are:
585. ii.   CHARLES FRANKLIN[8] BATES, b. 08 Mar 1878, Forestville\Hanover, Chautauqua County, New York; d. 16 Feb 1977, Brocton, Plymouth County, Massachusetts.
586. iii. FLORA M. BATES, b. Mar 1880, Forestville\Hanover, Chautauqua County, New York.

234. MARY JANE[7] MILKS *(BENJAMIN[6], LEMUEL[5] MILK, JONATHAN[4], JOB[3], JOHN[2], JOHN[1])* was born 28 Sep 1824 in Bolton, Warren County, New York, and died 30 Apr 1873. She married ARNOLD D. PIERCE 10 May 1848, son of OLIVER PIERCE. He was born 01 Jan 1816 in Clarendon, Rutland County, Vermont, and died 30 Dec 1903 in Water Valley, New York. They lived in West Seneca, Erie County, NY, and are buried in Hillcrest Cemetery, Armor, Erie County, New York

Children of MARY MILKS and ARNOLD PIERCE are:
587. i.   SUSAN MARIA[8] PIERCE, b. 27 Feb 1849, West Seneca, Erie County, New York; d. 08 Jun 1874.
588. ii.   LAURA A. PIERCE, b. 27 Sep 1850, West Seneca, Erie County, New York; d. 22 Oct 1931.
589. iii. HERBERT DOUGLAS PIERCE, b. 02 May 1863, West Seneca, Erie County, New York; d. 12 Dec 1928, Water Valley, Erie County, New York.

235. HENRY BENJAMIN[7] MILKS *(BENJAMIN[6], LEMUEL[5] MILK, JONATHAN[4], JOB[3], JOHN[2], JOHN[1])* was born 24 Jul 1826 in Bolton, Warren County, New York, and died 1920 in Kansas City, Jackson County, Missouri. He married (1) ROSE _____ Abt. 1854. She was born Abt. 1830. He married (2) ANNA HOAG Abt. 1860. She was born Jul 1832 in Pennsylvania[750].

UNION MISSOURI VOLUNTEERS
Regiment Name: 14th Regiment, Missouri Cavalry - Union Army - Company: ? - Rank In: Major - Rank Out: Major
   Organized at St. Louis and Springfield, Mo., November 30, 1864, to May 13, 1865. Attached to District of St. Louis, Mo., to June, 1865. District of the Plains, Dept. of Missouri, to November, 1865.
   Duty at St. Louis, Mo., till June, 1865. Scout from Waynesville to Coal Camp Creek May 23-26. Moved to Nebraska, and frontier duty on the Plains till November. Mustered out November 17, 1865.
   Lost during service 2 killed and 34 by disease. Total 36.
CIVIL WAR SOLDIERS AND SAILORS SYSTEM, National Park Service, Washington, D. C., researched by Richard Parker, May 2010
   Henry Benjamin Milks, b. 24 July 1826, Bolton Landing, NY (son of Benjamin 1794), made the long journey over the Erie Canal to Western NY when he was but 4 years old. He m. (1) Rose, and a son Jerome, was born to them.

Henry Benjamin and Rose were very dear friends of another young couple, Mr. and Mrs. Anna (Hoag) Lewis. In fact, they were so attracted to one another that in a course of time both couples divorced and exchanged marriage partners, the husbands keeping the children born to them. Thus, Anna (Hoag) Lewis became the stepmother of Jerome Milks. At which date this took place we have no record, but to Anna and Henry Benjamin were born two sons, Lewis in 1861 and Harry J. in 1870.

The Civil War found Henry Benjamin ready and willing to give service to his country; he enlisted in Mo., 3 M.S.M. Cav., Co. H. In 1863 he wrote to his sister Calista: "Ann is boarding about 3 mile from camp. I get to see her seldom and when I do little Lewis cries to ride with pa. . . Ann must write to you about him."

A letter dated 20 Mar. 1863, from Patterson, Mo. addressed to his parents in West Seneca, NY, is of considerable interest:

". . . The peculiar circumstances in which I am placed and the unsettled condition of our once happy country makes the receipt of a letter such as I have just read which is from your pen the source of more joy than on ordinary occasions.

"When I wrote you last I was at Pilot Knob. Now I am 35 miles south of that place . . . . On the 3d inst. I was promoted to captain. Our captain resigned and I was elected by the members of the company (not a dissenting vote). The capacity in which I now have to act is one of great responsibility - - - but from its duties I never shall shrink . . . . We are the advance guard of the Army

. . . . and are daily expecting an attack from the enemy who are seven or eight thousand strong. We are all ready to meet them. Of course, we don't expect to fight such unequal numbers but will hold

them in check till reinforced or have orders to fall back.

"As for arming the Negro I am in favour of it, but as to making him an equal to the white man I think it impossible. Though I have come to this conclusion, that the blackest and most degraded slave of the south is far superior to any man in arms against our Government.

"Dear Mother, you are nearer to my heart than any other person. I heed your counsels with great respect and duly consider your advice, but I must beg to differ with you on the political question of the day. I have engaged in this contest with patriotic motives and do not intend to lay down my arms till this Union is restored, for I am fighting for the enforcement of the laws and maintenance of the Government, not the Negro."

A letter to his sister Calista, dated 13 Sep. 1863, shows further Henry Benjamin's character and his ability to express himself:

. . . . "I am no politician nor have I been since the first gun was fired at Sumter and it grieves me much when I consider that this great struggle is prolonged by political demagogues. I try to take a fair and matter-of-fact view of our national troubles. Never was there a more Christian or holy body of people than our pilgraim fathers. They left their homes with all the associations that cluster around them and their churches of moss grown architecture of a thousand years where their fathers had worshipped for generations before them, that they might form a free government. And our Revolutionary fathers with their blood reared a beautiful monument to self and free government and on the 4th day of July 1776 the Goddess of Liberty descended with thirteen bright and shining stars

from the blue vault of Heaven and placed them on our national banner, where they have waved beautiful and triumphant on that monument. And shall I stand an idle spectator when those who have grown powerful and strong under its protection attempt to raze that monument to the ground and trail our flag in the dust? No, never. As long as I have a voice I shall shout 'Rally round the Flag, Boys, rally once again, shouting the battle cry of Freedom.' And when upon close inspection we find that that monument has in it a few rotten rocks, we will pick them out with our bayonets and sabers and replace them with pure white marble that it may stand as long as time shall last."

Henry Benjamin was promoted to the rank of Major, and after his discharge he lived in Missouri and Kansas. The roar of cannons caused him permanently to lose his hearing, but he lived to be in his 90's. A late address was Eldorado, Kansas. At one time he manufactured sewing machines. Burial: Elmwood Cemetery, Kansas City, Missouri
Lived in: 1900, Leon, Butler County, Kansas

Child of HENRY MILKS and ROSE _____ is:
590.   i. JEROME[8] MILKS, b. 17 Nov 1854, Erie County, New York; d. Bef. 30 Apr 1910, Lone Star, Wagoner County, Oklahoma.

Children of HENRY MILKS and ANNA HOAG are:
591. ii. LEWIS LYONS[8] MILKS, b. 15 Jul 1861, Jonesburg, St. Louis, Missouri; d. 10 Sep 1928, Cincinnati, Ohio.
592. iii. HARRY J. MILKS, b. Jun 1869, Meramec, St. Louis County, Missouri.

236. CHARLES JONATHAN[7] MILKS *(BENJAMIN[6], LEMUEL[5] MILK, JONATHAN[4], JOB[3], JOHN[2], JOHN[1])* was born 24 Mar 1828 in Bolton, Warren County, New York[751], and died 1898 in Magnolia, Rock County, Wisconsin[751]. He married MARY E. HILL. She was born Feb 1833 in Vermont, and died 1907 in Magnolia, Rock County, Wisconsin. Charles was a carpenter.

Children of CHARLES MILKS and MARY HILL are:
593. i. IDA A.[8] MILKS, b. 09 Mar 1855, West Seneca, Erie County, New York.
594. ii. FREEMAN B. MILKS, b. 09 Jul 1864, Magnolia, Rock County, Wisconsin; d. 18 Oct 1893, Magnolia, Rock County, Wisconsin.
595. iii. JESSIE EDNA MILKS, b. 07 Dec 1865, Magnolia, Rock County, Wisconsin; d. 27 Nov 1935, Brodhead, WI.

237. DAVID WESLEY[7] MILKS *(BENJAMIN[6], LEMUEL[5] MILK, JONATHAN[4], JOB[3], JOHN[2], JOHN[1])* was born 13 Jun 1830 in Otto, Cattaraugus County, New York[752], and died 13 Nov 1901 in Chesaning, Saginaw, Michigan[752]. He married HARRIET 'HATTIE' E. TURNER[753] 20 Oct 1850, daughter of JOSEPH TURNER and ELIZABETH KELCH. She was born 21 Feb 1830 in Herkimer County, New York[754], and died 16 Aug 1906 in Chesaning, Saginaw, Michigan[755,756]. They are buried in Wildwood Cemetery, Chesaning, Saginaw, Michigan

David W. Milks, farmer, sec. 13, was born in Cattaraugus Co., N. V., June 30, 1830; parents were Benjamin and Polly (Moore) Milks; former was born near Lake George, N. Y., and served in war of 1812; subject was raised on a farm; received common-school education; was married Oct. 20, 1850, to Harriet Turner, daughter of Joseph and Elizabeth (Kelch) Turner; wife was born in Herkimer Co., N. Y.. Feb. 21, 1830; they have 3 children—Joseph E., born Aug. 1, 1851; Polly A., born April 13, 1854, and Barney R., born March 30, 1864; subject settled in Chesaning tp. in June, 1856; owns 40 acres of land; is neutral in politics; himself and wife are Seventh-Day Adventists, assisting in organizing said society in Saginaw county.

More About HARRIET 'HATTIE' E. TURNER:
Burial: Wildwood Cemetery, Chesaning, Saginaw, Michigan[757]
Cause of Death: Senile dementia

Children of DAVID MILKS and HARRIET TURNER are:
596. i. JOSEPH EDWIN[8] MILKS, b. 01 Aug 1851, Buffalo, New York; d. 22 Jan 1932, Albee Township, Saginaw County, MI
597. ii. POLLIE ALPHA MILKS, b. 18 Apr 1854, Hamburg, Erie County, New York; d. 20 Nov 1940, Chesaning, Saginaw County, Michigan.
598. iii. PARNA ROZELIA MILKS, b. 30 Mar 1864, Saginaw County, Michigan; d. 16 May 1954, Chesaning, Saginaw County, Michigan.

238. CALISTA ELIZABETH[7] MILKS *(BENJAMIN[6], LEMUEL[5] MILK, JONATHAN[4], JOB[3], JOHN[2], JOHN[1])* was born 18 Jun 1834 in Otto, Cattaraugus County, New York, and died 12 Sep 1922 in Cattaraugus County, New York ?. She married JOSEPH CLARK BURCHARD 08 May 1859 in Cattaraugus County, New York, son of JOSEPH BURCHARD and MARTHA BIRCHARD. He was born 08 Jan 1833 in Otto, Cattaraugus County, New York, and died 25 Dec 1909 in Cattaraugus County, NY.

Part of Calista's girlhood was spent with her grandmother, Elizabeth (Livingston) Moore, at North Otto, where she is shown in the 1850 census. She and at least one of her brothers attended the Academy at Black Rock, where, among other subjects, she became proficient in algebra. When in her 80's, she helped the writer {Grace Irene Barnhart} do problems, seemingly remembering clearly the principles of the subject. She taught school for a number of years, one district being the Bowen District in East Otto, where she boarded around, as was the custom in those days. She seldom had a bed to herself, usually sleeping with one or two young children of the family whose turn it was to have the teacher for a week. The pay for teachers in those days was 75 cents or a little more per week.

While teaching in East Otto a young farmer, tall and blue-eyed, made her acquaintance. Little is known of their courtship, but Calista told of watching Clark Burchard coming for her, driving a beautiful team of horses to take them to Squire Johnston's at West Seneca on that day, 8 May 1859, for the marriage ceremony.

Their first home was the old Burchard homestead, at East Otto. It is thought Clark's mother was then a widow, and, as Clark was the youngest of her 17 children, it was expected that Calista should stay with her. After 2 years, this home was sold and Calista and Clark bought the original Horace Wells farm at East Otto "Corners". The house and other buildings were only a few rods from the center of the village, while the level farm and the sugar bush on the knoll spread north and west as a fan encompassing 108 acres, bordered on the east and south by roads. Here they reared their family of four daughters.

The people of the village depended much on Calista in times of trouble. They confided in her, which confidence she never betrayed. For 25 years not a child was born in the village that Calista was not called upon. Her family used to note her absence at breakfast and always were ready to ask, "Boy or girl?" when she arrived home. Clark's mother grew feeble and became Calista's great care; but her pride in Calista was always apparent, for when asked about what she would or would not like, she'd reply, "Whatever Calista says." Calista kept her neat, with her hair curled and her aprons white; she died in her 80's after being confined as a bed-patient for 3 years.

The generosity of Calista and her husband became known to many. They always seemed to know whose woodshed was becoming empty or who needed help; many hams, sacks of corn or oats, and other food, as well as loads of wood, were delivered after dark or when the recipients were away. It was said they gave away enough to have paid for another farm.

Their married life, which was broken seven months after their golden wedding, has stood as a beautiful, harmonious pattern. Grandma Calista once said they always slept hand in hand; and after he passed away, she kept his best suit hanging beside her best dress, feeling, as she said, he was still with her.

An unusual thing happened on Christmas Day, 1909. At 3:00 o'clock in the morning both Calista and Clark were awake and both saw and talked about the writing in gold letters across the wall of the room. They wondered what it represented; they could not read it as it seemed to be in some foreign letters. However, Clark thought it must be a warning of some kind. Two hours later he was taken ill and died within an hour.

Calista later sold her home and lived with her married daughters the rest of her life. She died also of a heart ailment, 88 years of age, 12 Sep. 1922. She and Clark are buried in the family plot in East Otto cemetery, where one can look north over the fertile valley and homes that now occupy their once treasured homestead.

One time, the writer realizing that her grandmother had many, many friends, asked her the reason for it. Her reply has always been remembered: "I made up my mind when I was seventeen that if I couldn't speak well of a person, I'd keep still, and when malicious gossip came to my ears I'd ask in return, "Isn't there something good to be said of him, or her?"

CALISTA ELIZABETH MILKS: and JOSEPH CLARK BURCHARD are buried in East Otto Cemetery, Cattaraugus County, NY

Children of CALISTA MILKS and JOSEPH BURCHARD are:
- i. CHARLES ELMER[8] BURCHARD, b. 29 Dec 1860, East Otto, Cattaraugus County, New York; d. 01 May 1863, East Otto, Cattaraugus County, New York. Burial: East Otto Cemetery, Cattaraugus County, New York. Cause of Death: Scarlet Fever
- 599. ii. MARA ELEANOR BURCHARD, b. 07 Apr 1862, East Otto, Cattaraugus County, New York; d. 03 Nov 1941, Alhambra, Los Angeles County, California.
- 600. iii. GRACE ANNA BURCHARD, b. 07 May 1869, East Otto, Cattaraugus County, New York.
- iv. IDA JEAN BURCHARD, b. 05 May 1874, East Otto, Cattaraugus County, New York; d. 15 Nov 1886, East Otto, Cattaraugus County, New York. Cause of Death: Typhoid Fever
- 601. v. BEATRICE A. E. BURCHARD, b. 14 Jan 1877, East Otto, Cattaraugus County, New York.
- 602. vi. EDITH SOPHIA BURCHARD, b. 27 Dec 1864, East Otto, Cattaraugus County, New York.

239. PHEBE EMELIA[7] MILKS (*BENJAMIN[6], LEMUEL[5] MILK, JONATHAN[4], JOB[3], JOHN[2], JOHN[1]*) was born 13 Mar 1836 in Otto, Cattaraugus County, New York[758], and died 1910 in Chesaning, Saginaw County, Michigan[758]. She married CHARLES S. MASTERS, son of GEORGE MASTERS and DOROTHY HATFIELD. He was born 1841 in New York[759], and died 15 Jan 1917 in Chesaning, Saginaw County, Michigan[759]. They are buried in Wildwood Cemetery, Chesaning, Saginaw County, Michigan. Charles' military service: Civil War, CO D 5 Mich. Cav.

Children of PHEBE MILKS and CHARLES MASTERS are:
- i. WILLIAM IRA[8] MASTERS, b. 1866[760]; d. Aft. 1880.
- ii. GEORGE BENJAMIN MASTERS, b. 1868; d. d.y..

240. MERRITT SIDWAY[7] MILKS *(BENJAMIN[6], LEMUEL[5] MILK, JONATHAN[4], JOB[3], JOHN[2], JOHN[1])* was born 21 Jan 1840 in Otto, Cattaraugus County, New York, and died 01 Mar 1891 in Spring Valley, Rock County, Wisconsin[761]. He married HANNAH MAHALA BREWER, daughter of JEREMIAH BREWER and MAHALA CROY. She was born May 1842 in Rensselaer County, New York[762,763]. Merritt lived in: 1860, Otto, Cattaraugus Co., NY, and moved to Green County, Wisconsin, probably right after the end of the Civil War.

Children of MERRITT MILKS and HANNAH BREWER are:
- i. JOHN[8] MILKS[764], b. Nov 1869, Green County, Wisconsin[765]; d. Bet. 1870 - 1880, Prob. d.y. (not in 1880 census).
- 603. ii. ELBERT B. MILKS, b. 14 Oct 1870, Green County, Wisconsin.
- iii. NETTIE M. MILKS, b. 16 Jan 1873, Otto, Cattaraugus Co., NY[766,767]; d. 15 Aug 1948, Decatur, Green County, Wisconsin (never married).

241. SOPHIA BETSEY[7] MILKS *(BENJAMIN[6], LEMUEL[5] MILK, JONATHAN[4], JOB[3], JOHN[2], JOHN[1])* was born 10 Apr 1843 in Otto, Cattaraugus County, New York. She married (1) CHARLES WOODRUFF Abt. 1860. He was born Abt. 1820. She married (2) HARRY THOMAS. He was born Abt. 1840.

Child of SOPHIA MILKS and MISTTER WOODRUFF is:
- i. ALICE[8] WOODRUFF, d. aged 5 yrs.

242. JAMES FRANKLIN[7] MILKS *(BENJAMIN[6], LEMUEL[5] MILK, JONATHAN[4], JOB[3], JOHN[2], JOHN[1])* was born 18 Mar 1845 in West Seneca, Erie County, New York, and died Bet. 1920 - 1930 in New York. He married MATILDA LITTLE Abt. 1870, daughter of DANIEL LITTLE and ISABELLA _____. She was born Abt. 1846 in Crawford County, Pennsylvania[768], and died Bet. 1905 - 1910 in Buffalo, New York[769]. They lived in Buffalo, New York where James was a Policeman.

Children of JAMES MILKS and MATILDA LITTLE are:
- i. ELIZABETH[8] MILKS, b. 27 Jan 1872, Buffalo, New York; d. Bet. 1953 - 1954, Eden, Erie County, New York (No children); m. WILLIAM B. FISCHER, Abt. 1896, New York[770]; b. Abt. 1871; d. 1950, Eden, Erie County, New York[771].
  They lived in: Eden, New York, where William was a truck gardener.
- 604. ii. ELMER F. MILKS, b. 19 May 1873, Buffalo, New York; d. May 1963, Buffalo, New York.
- 605. iii. DANIEL BENJAMIN MILKS, b. 18 Mar 1875, Buffalo, New York; d. 08 May 1953, Erie County, New York.
- 606. iv. WILLIAM H. MILKS, b. 21 Feb 1878, Buffalo, New York; d. Sep 1965, Buffalo, New York.
- 607. v. MERRILL V. MILKS, b. 07 Mar 1880, Buffalo, New York; d. Bef. Apr 1930.

243. IRA NELSON[7] MILKS *(BENJAMIN[6], LEMUEL[5] MILK, JONATHAN[4], JOB[3], JOHN[2], JOHN[1])* was born 04 Feb 1847 in West Seneca, Erie County, New York, and died 1896 in West Seneca, New York. He married SARAH A. CALDWELL. She was born Abt. 1850.

Children of IRA MILKS and SARAH CALDWELL are:
- 608. i. GEORGE RICHARD[8] MILKS, b. 23 Oct 1871, West Seneca, New York; d. 1935.
- 608. ii. CLARA MAHALA MILKS, b. 19 Sep 1875, West Seneca, New York.
- 610. iii. NELSON CLARENCE MILKS, b. 03 Sep 1879, West Seneca, NY; d. 30 Aug 1953.

244. ELIZABETH A. "BETSEY"[7] MILKS *(JOB[6] MILK, LEMUEL[5], JONATHAN[4], JOB[3], JOHN[2], JOHN[1])* was born 23 May 1828 in Warren County, New York, and died 12 Jun 1900 in Parsons, Labette County, Kansas. She married CYRUS MORRIS 25 Dec 1850 in Cattaraugus County, New York, son of JOHN MORRIS and RUTH MOON. He was born Feb 1824 in Hartford, Washington County, New York[772], and died 31 Oct 1875 in Hurley, Turner County, South Dakota[772].
Cyrus' Service Record: Enlisted as a Private on 22 August 1862 at the age of 27. Enlisted in Company B, 32nd Infantry Regiment Iowa on 11 Sep 1862. Discharged for wounds Company B, 32nd Infantry Regiment Iowa on 14 Jun 1865 at New Orleans, LA. He is buried in Hurley Cemetery, Hurley, Turner County, South Dakota

Children of ELIZABETH MILKS and CYRUS MORRIS are:
- 611. i. ANNA ALFREDINE[8] MORRIS, b. 26 Dec 1851, Cattaraugus County, New York; d. 15 Aug 1909, Stutsman, North Dakota.

      ii. JOHN ARTHUR MORRIS, b. 1854, Cattaraugus County, New York.
      iii. IDA MORRIS, b. 1857, Illinois.
612.   iv. MARY ETTA MORRIS, b. Apr 1860, Iowa; d. Missouri.
613.   v. WEBSTER CYRUS MORRIS, b. Sep 1873, South Dakota; d. 18 Jan 1944, Deschutes, Oregon.

245. JONATHAN B.[7] MILKS *(JOB[6] MILK, LEMUEL[5], JONATHAN[4], JOB[3], JOHN[2], JOHN[1])* was born 04 Jun 1830 in Cattaraugus County, New York, and died 07 Jul 1914 in Machias, Cattaraugus County, New York[773]. He married RUTH ANN _____ Abt. 1858. She was born 1836[773], and died 1901 in Machias, Cattaraugus County, New York[773]. They are buried in Maple Grove Cemetery, Machias, Cattaraugus County, New York.

Military service for Jonathan: Pvt., Co. A, 188th NY Infantry, Civil War

Children of JONATHAN MILKS and RUTH _____ are:
      i. HARLIN A.[8] MILKS, b. 1860, Ellicottville, Cattaraugus County, New York[774]; d. 1883, Cattaraugus County, New York[775].
        Burial: Maple Grove Cemetery, Machias, Cattaraugus County, New York.
      ii. EVA J. MILKS, b. 1865, Cattaraugus County, New York[776]; d. 1917, Machias, Cattaraugus County, New York (unmarried):
        Burial: Maple Grove Cemetery, Machias, Cattaraugus County, New York.
      iii. ELBERT DANIEL MILKS, b. Mar 1875, Cattaraugus County, New York. Lived in: 1920, Mansfield, Cattaraugus County, New York (single). In the 1940 census, Elbert was still single.

246. CAROLINE "PHEBE" E.[7] MILKS *(JOB[6] MILK, LEMUEL[5], JONATHAN[4], JOB[3], JOHN[2], JOHN[1])* was born 04 Sep 1832 in Cattaraugus County, New York, and died 20 Apr 1925. She married EBENEZER CULLINGS, JR. 04 Mar 1856 in McHenry County, Illinois. He was born 22 May 1832, and died 10 Apr 1909.

Children of CAROLINE MILKS and EBENEZER CULLINGS are:
614.   i. JAMES EBENEZER[8] CULLINGS, b. 24 Jun 1858, Fredericksburg, Iowa; d. 25 Feb 1944, Wahoo, Nebraska.
      ii. ELIZABETH 'TIBBY' CULLINGS, b. 1859, Fredericksburg, Iowa; d. Sep 1894, (unmarried).
      iii. MARGARET ADELL CULLINGS, b. 24 Mar 1866, Fredericksburg, Iowa; d. 07 Jan 1934, (unmarried).
615.   iv. CLARA F. CULLINGS, b. 1868, Fredericksburg, Iowa; d. 23 Feb 1945, Riceville, Iowa.
      v. FITZ J. CULLINGS, b. 03 Dec 1873, Fredericksburg, Iowa; d. 21 Mar 1941, (unmarried).

247. JEMIMA DIANTHA[7] MILKS *(JOB[6] MILK, LEMUEL[5], JONATHAN[4], JOB[3], JOHN[2], JOHN[1])* was born 22 Mar 1836 in Cattaraugus County, New York, and died 29 Mar 1915 in Mt. Ida, Grant County, Wisconsin. She married SILAS BURR PETTIT Apr 1856[778]. He was born 13 Oct 1835 in Albany, New York, and died 29 Sep 1914 in Mt. Ida, Grant County, Wisconsin. Silas founded the Methodist Church in Mt. Ida, Wisconsin[778]

Children of JEMIMA MILKS and SILAS PETTIT are:
616.   i. MARY ETTOLA[8] PETTIT, b. 01 Jun 1859, Mt. Ida, Grant County, Wisconsin; d. 05 Nov 1930, Joliet, Will County, Illinois.
617.   ii. FRANK BURR PETTIT, b. 16 Jul 1862, Mt. Ida, Grant County, Wisconsin; d. 01 Mar 1929, Walnut Grove, Minnesota.
618.   iii. FRED SILAS PETTIT, b. 13 Jul 1865, Mt. Ida, Grant County, Wisconsin; d. 29 Apr 1954, Kalispell, Montana.
619.   iv. WILL D. PETTIT, b. Abt. 1867, Mt. Ida, Grant County, Wisconsin.

248. DAVID FRANKLIN[7] MILKS *(JOB[6] MILK, LEMUEL[5], JONATHAN[4], JOB[3], JOHN[2], JOHN[1])* was born 26 Jan 1838 in Cattaraugus County, New York, and died 02 Jul 1892 in Parsons, Labette County, Kansas[779]. He married (1) MELISSA 'MARTHA' BEAVER BEEVER Abt. 1865. She was born Bet. 1847 - 1848 in New York[780], and died 22 Mar 1869 in Allamakee County, Iowa?[781]. He married (2) MARY MELVINA STREATOR 04 Oct 1869 in Waukon, Iowa, daughter of HARRY STREATOR and RHODA HORTON. She was born 17 Apr 1848 in Cuba, NY. Melissa is buried in Sand Cove Cemetery, Allamakee County, Iowa

    David's Service Record: Enlisted in Company F, Illinois 15th Infantry Regiment on 22 Sep 1861. Mustered out on 20 Jul 1864. Transferred to Company E, Illinois Vet Battn Infantry Battalion on 20 Jul 1864. Mustered out on 24 Mar 1865. Transferred to Company E, Illinois 15th Infantry Regiment on 24 Mar 1865. Mustered out on 30 May 1865.

Sources: Illinois: Roster of Officers and Enlisted Men Research provided by HDS subscriber

Children of DAVID MILKS and MELISSA BEEVER are:
- 620. i. CHARLES NELSON[8] MILKS, b. 10 Apr 1866, New Albin, Iowa; d. 27 Jul 1940, Lennox, South Dakota.
- ii. EDWIN JAMES MILKS, b. 03 Sep 1867, New Albin, Iowa; d. 08 Oct 1944, Hurley, Turner County, South Dakota. (unmarried). Burial: Hurley Cemetery, Turner County, South Dakota

Children of DAVID MILKS and MARY STREATOR are:
- 621. iii. PEARL MELISSA[8] MILKS, b. 06 Feb 1871, New Albin, Allamakee, Iowa; d. 28 Apr 1972, Hurley, Turner, South Dakota
- iv. WILLIE C. MILKS[782], b. 19 Aug 1872, New Albin, Iowa; d. 27 Sep 1872, New Albin, Iowa. Buried: Sand Cove Cemetery
- v. INEZ M. MILKS, b. 05 Nov 1873, New Albin, Iowa; d. 31 May 1884, New Albin, Iowa. Burial: Sand Cove Cemetery, Allamakee County, Iowa
- vi. SON MILKS, b. 05 Nov 1875, New Albin, Iowa; d. 05 Nov 1875, New Albin, Iowa. Buried: Sand Cove Cemetery
- 622. vii. HARRY STREATOR MILKS, b. 10 Apr 1878, New Albin, Iowa; d. Aft. 1956.
- viii. FRANKLIN J. MILKS, b. 19 Mar 1880, New Albin, Iowa[783]; d. 30 May 1884, New Albin, Iowa[783]. Burial: Sand Cove Cemetery, Allamakee County, Iowa
- 623. ix. DAVID HARTMAN MILKS, b. 05 Oct 1883, New Albin, Iowa; d. Oct 1967, Parsons, Labette County, Kansas.
- 624. x. SHERMAN GEORGE MILKS, b. 14 Apr 1886, New Albin, Iowa.
- 625. xi. GLADYS ANNA MILKS, b. 25 Apr 1889, New Albin, Iowa.
- 626. xii. ALVIN LUCIUS MILKS, b. 16 Jan 1892, New Albin, Iowa; d. 25 Jul 1927, Parsons, Labette County, Kansas.

249. HUMPHREY W.[7] MILKS *(JOB[6] MILK, LEMUEL[5], JONATHAN[4], JOB[3], JOHN[2], JOHN[1])* was born 18 Feb 1840 in Cattaraugus County, New York[784,785], and died 12 Dec 1882 in Hurley, Turner County, S. Dak.[786]. He married (1) GEORGIANNA POOLE Abt. 1865, daughter of CHARLES POOLE and CAROLINE _____. She was born 10 Jun 1843 in New Bristol, England, and died 17 Feb 1934 in Boise, Idaho. He married (2) MARY ELLA BRIGGS Abt. 1874 in Iowa. She was born Mar 1853 in New York.
Humphrey's Military service: Co. F., 15 Illinois Infantry - Civil War. He is buried in Hurley Cemetery, Turner County, South Dakota [Plot: Lot 18 Grave 10] Mary Ella lived in 1893 in Nevada, Story County, Iowa

Children of HUMPHREY MILKS and GEORGIANNA POOLE are:
- i. WILLIAM B.[8] MILKS, b. 05 Apr 1866, Chickasaw, Iowa[787]; d. 08 Aug 1930, Boise, Idaho (unm.).
- 627. ii. CORA ANNABELLE MILKS, b. 08 Dec 1873, Chickasaw, Iowa; d. 29 Sep 1945, Boise, Idaho.
- iii. LEROY CHARLES MILKS, b. 23 Jul 1876, Chickasaw, Iowa[787,788]; d. Abt. 20 Apr 1956, Idaho Falls, Idaho (no children)[789]; m. ALMA DAHLBERG, 25 Jul 1926, Ustick, Ada County, Idaho[790]; b. 31 May 1888, Minnesota[791]; d. 01 Sep 1969, Boise, Idaho[791,792]. They are buried in Morris Hill Cemetery, Boise, Ada County, Idaho [Plot: MHILL_MAUSA_2_11]

Children of HUMPHREY MILKS and MARY BRIGGS are:
- 628. iv. ELENORE 'ELLA' MARY[8] MILKS, b. May 1876, Atlantic, Cass County, Iowa.
- 629. v. HUMPHREY MILKS, b. 13 Aug 1879, Cass County, Iowa.
- 630. vi. GEORGE THEODORE MILCKS, b. 24 Dec 1882, Pottawattamie County, Iowa.

250. ANNA ADELIA[7] MILKS *(JOB[6] MILK, LEMUEL[5], JONATHAN[4], JOB[3], JOHN[2], JOHN[1])* was born 17 May 1842 in Cattaraugus County, New York[793,794], and died 30 Jun 1910 in Waukegan, Lake County, Illinois[794]. She married ALFONSO SEWELL, son of SENECA SEWELL and SALLY _____. He was born 07 May 1834 in New York[795,796], and died 29 Jan 1909 in Waukegan, Lake County, Illinois[796]. They are buried in Oakwood Cemetery, Waukegan, Lake County, IL.

Children of ANNA MILKS and ALFONSO SEWELL are:
- i. GEORGE D.[8] SEWELL, b. 01 Sep 1863, Allamakee, Iowa[796]; d. 02 Apr 1928, Waukegan, Lake County, Illinois (unmarried)[796]. Burial: Oakwood Cemetery, Waukegan, Lake County, Illinois
- ii. SARAH SEWELL, b. 07 Sep 1869, Allamakee, Iowa[796]; d. 14 Jan 1912, Waukegan, Lake County, Illinois (unmarried)[796].

Burial: Oakwood Cemetery, Waukegan, Lake County, Illinois

251. JAMES HARTMAN[7] MILKS *(JOB[6] MILK, LEMUEL[5], JONATHAN[4], JOB[3], JOHN[2], JOHN[1])* was born 17 Nov 1846 in Cattaraugus County, New York, and died 1917 in Bowman County, North Dakota. He married (1) EMALINE _____. She was born 05 Sep 1850, and died 30 Aug 1870 in Allamakee County, Iowa?. He married (2) ADELINE 'ADDIE' FERRIS[797] Abt. 1873 in Alamakee County, Iowa[797], daughter of LEANDER FERRIS and CAROLINE MCDONALD. She was born Abt. 1856 in New York[798]. He married (3) CATHERINE HEALEY 26 Feb 1884 in Alamakee County, Iowa[799], daughter of MICHAEL HALEY and HANNAH _____. She was born Bet. 1860 - 1861 in Ohio[800], and died 1909 in Manchester, South Dakota. Emaline is buried in Sand Cove Cemetery, Allamakee County, Iowa. Catherine is buried in Saint Thomas Catholic Cemetery, De Smet, Kingsbury County, South Dakota

James H Milks Military Service Record: Enlisted as a Private on 22 October 1864 at the age of 18
Enlisted in Company F, 6th Cavalry Regiment Iowa on 31 October 1864.
Mustered out Company F, 6th Cavalry Regiment Iowa on 17 October 1865 in Sioux City, IA

Child of JAMES MILKS and ADELINE FERRIS is:
      i.   EMERY WILLIAM[8] MILKS, b. Abt. 1874, Iowa[801].   Lived in: Waukon, Iowa

Children of JAMES MILKS and CATHERINE HEALEY are:
      ii.   RICHARD N.[8] MILKS[802], b. Abt. Aug 1879, Allamakee County, Iowa; d. Dec 1879, Allamakee County, Iowa[803].
      iii.   JOHN DALLAS MILKS, b. 05 Jan 1881, Allamakee County, Iowa[804]; d. 1907, Allamakee County, Iowa[805].
          Burial: Saint Thomas Catholic Cemetery, De Smet, Kingsbury County, South Dakota[805]
          Cause of Death: RR accident
      iv.   ELLEN E. MILKS, b. 15 Jan 1883, Allamakee County, Iowa; m. (1) MISTTER CARLSON; b. Abt. 1880; m. (2) BOB CHRISTENSEN; b. Abt. 1880.

631.   v.   ANNA H. MILKS, b. 28 Jul 1884, New Albin, Allamakee County, Iowa; d. 1946, Huron, South Dakota.
632.   vi.   FRANK MILKS, b. 07 Mar 1887, New Albin, Iowa.
633.   vii.   ALEX MILKS-COX, b. 16 Sep 1888, New Albin, Allamakee County, Iowa.
634.   viii.   ANDREW HARTMAN MILKS, b. 16 Dec 1889, De Smet, South Dakota; d. 1966, Dubuque County, Iowa.
635.   ix.   WILLIAM JOB MILKS, b. 04 Oct 1892, Manchester, Kingsbury County, So. Dakota; d. 07 Jan 1968, Los Angeles, California.
      x.   NELSON LORENZO MILKS, b. 31 Jul 1895, Manchester, S. Dakota; d. 1905, Manchester, S. Dakota (killed by a baseball).

252. GEORGE[7] SIDWAY *(WILLIAM[6], REBECCA[5] MILK, JONATHAN[4], JOB[3], JOHN[2], JOHN[1])* was born Abt. 1805. He married EMELINE DOUGLAS. She was born Abt. 1805.

Child of GEORGE SIDWAY and EMELINE DOUGLAS is:
636.   i.   GILBERT DOUGLAS[8] SIDWAY.

253. KATHERINE R.[7] SIDWAY *(JONATHAN[6], REBECCA[5] MILK, JONATHAN[4], JOB[3], JOHN[2], JOHN[1])* was born 15 Jan 1827 in Buffalo, Erie County, New York[806], and died 15 Mar 1890 in Buffalo, Erie County, New York[807]. She married ASAPH S. BEMIS. He was born 21 Apr 1817 in Erie County, New York[808], and died 07 May 1888 in Buffalo, Erie County, New York[809]. They are buried in Forest Lawn Cemetery, Buffalo, Erie County, New York

Children of KATHERINE SIDWAY and ASAPH BEMIS are:
      i.   JOHNNY SIDWAY[8] BEMIS, b. 16 Sep 1845, Buffalo, Erie County, New York; d. 18 Jul 1846, Buffalo, Erie County, New York. Burial: Forest Lawn Cemetery, Buffalo, Erie County, New York
      ii.   ANNA TRACY BEMIS, b. 21 Feb 1848, Buffalo, Erie County, New York; d. 16 Sep 1849, Buffalo, Erie County, New York.
          Burial: Forest Lawn Cemetery, Buffalo, Erie County, New York
      iii.   FRANK SIDWAY BEMIS, b. 21 Feb 1848, Buffalo, Erie County, New York; d. 28 Aug 1849, Buffalo, Erie County, New York. Burial: Forest Lawn Cemetery, Buffalo, Erie County, New York
      iv.   PARNELL CORNELIA BEMIS, b. 14 Jan 1852, Buffalo, Erie County, New York; d. 20 Feb 1854, Buffalo, Erie

County, New York. Burial: Forest Lawn Cemetery, Buffalo, Erie County, New York

254. JONATHAN[7] SIDWAY *(JONATHAN[6], REBECCA[5] MILK, JONATHAN[4], JOB[3], JOHN[2], JOHN[1])* was born Mar 1832 in Buffalo, Erie County, New York, and died Bet. 1900 - 1910 in Manhattan, New York City, New York ?. He married CAROLINE BALDWIN TAUNT Abt. 1855, daughter of EMORY TAUNT and MARTHA _____. She was born Jan 1835 in Rhode Island[810], and died Aft. 1910 in Manhattan, New York City, New York. Jonathan was the landlord of a hotel in Buffalo, New York.

Children of JONATHAN SIDWAY and CAROLINE TAUNT are:
- i. CAROLINE GERTRUDE[8] SIDWAY, b. 26 Apr 1856, Buffalo, Erie County, New York. Christening: 16 Jun 1867, Grace Episcopal Church, Buffalo, Erie, New York
- ii. JONATHAN EDWARD SIDWAY, b. 09 Apr 1858, Buffalo, Erie County, New York; m. ROSE A. _____, 28 Jan 1902; b. 16 Feb 1862, New York City. Christening: 16 Jun 1867, Grace Episcopal Church, Buffalo, Erie, New York
- 637. iii. WILLIAM HENRY SIDWAY, b. 07 Mar 1860, Buffalo, Erie County, New York.
- 638. iv. KATE BALDWIN SIDWAY, b. 24 Apr 1861, Buffalo, Erie County, New York; d. Aft. 26 Apr 1929.

255. FRANKLIN[7] SIDWAY *(JONATHAN[6], REBECCA[5] MILK, JONATHAN[4], JOB[3], JOHN[2], JOHN[1])* was born 23 Jul 1834 in Buffalo, Erie County, New York[811], and died 07 Mar 1920 in St Augustine, St Johns, Florida[811]. He married CHARLOTTE SPAULDING 17 Feb 1866[812], daughter of ELBRIDGE SPAULDING and NANCY STRONG. She was born 17 Jul 1843[813], and died 20 Jan 1934 in Erie County, New York[813]. They are buried in Forest Lawn Cemetery, Buffalo, Erie County, New York

Draft Registration for Franklin: 01 Jul 1863, At Buffalo, NY, Civil War Draft Registrations, Occ.: Gentleman
Occupation: 1880, Banker.
Value of Franklin's Personal Estate: 1870, $3,000; Value of his Real Estate: 1870, $100,000
Value of Charlotte's Personal Estate: 1870, $8,000; Value of her Real Estate: 1870, $15,000

Children of FRANKLIN SIDWAY and CHARLOTTE SPAULDING are:
- 639. i. HAROLD SPAULDING[8] SIDWAY, b. 26 Apr 1868, Buffalo, Erie County, New York.
- 640. ii. FRANK ST. JOHN SIDWAY, b. 05 Dec 1869, Buffalo, Erie County, New York; d. 17 Jan 1938, Buffalo, Erie County, New York.
- 641. iii. EDITH SIDWAY, b. 12 Jan 1872, Buffalo, Erie County, New York.
- 642. iv. CLARENCE SPAULDING SIDWAY, b. 12 Feb 1877, Buffalo, Erie County, New York; d. Bet. 1941 - 1956.
- 643. v. RALPH HUNTINGTON SIDWAY, b. 15 Dec 1884, Buffalo, Erie County, New York; d. 12 Dec 1936, Buffalo, Erie County, New York.

256. CHARLES[7] MILKS *(DAVID[6] MILK, GEORGE[5], JONATHAN[4], JOB[3], JOHN[2], JOHN[1])* was born 10 Dec 1819 in Chenango Co., NY ???[813], and died 29 Sep 1885 in Cattaraugus County, New York[813]. He married MARGARET MARIA HASKINS. She was born 19 Jun 1820 in Cortland County, New York[813], and died 09 Apr 1891 in Cattaraugus County, New York[813]. They are buried in Parklawn Cemetery, Wesley, Cattaraugus County, New York

Children of CHARLES MILKS and MARGARET HASKINS are:
- 644. i. WILLIAM ALONZO[8] MILKS, b. Feb 1845, New York; d. 1905, Hamburg, NY??.
- ii. LYDIA MELISSA MILKS, b. 21 Mar 1847.
- 645. iii. HARRIET LOUISE MILKS, b. 1848, New York (Mar 1851).
- 646. iv. TERESSA L. MILKS, b. 1852; d. Abt. Jul 1880.
- 647. v. DENCY M. MILKS, b. 06 May 1854.
- 648. vi. CHARLES "NEWMAN" MILKS, b. May 1856, Cattaraugus County, New York.
- 649. vii. SARAH SOPHRONIA MILKS, b. 1858.
- 650. viii. MARY J. MILKS, b. 1860, New York.
- ix. THEODORA M. MILKS, b. 07 May 1863; d. 05 Sep 1951, Gowanda, Cattaraugus County, New York (no children); m. FREDERICK JOHNSON; b. Abt. 1860.

257. ALEXANDER B.[7] MILK *(DAVID[6], GEORGE[5], JONATHAN[4], JOB[3], JOHN[2], JOHN[1])* was born 08 Jun 1824 in Saratoga County, New York[814], and died 20 Sep 1901 in Mansfield, Cattaraugus County, New York[814]. He married (1) MARY

FARRINGTON. She was born 27 Feb 1818 in Saratoga County, New York[814], and died 15 Apr 1886 in Mansfield, Cattaraugus County, New York[814]. He married (2) ROSE M. SIMONS. Alexander and Mary are buried in Maples Cemetery, Mansfield, Cattaraugus County, New York

Children of ALEXANDER MILK and MARY FARRINGTON are:

651. i.   DAVID W.[8] MILKS, b. Mar 1848, Persia, Cattaraugus County, New York; d. 27 Oct 1931, Salamanca, Cattaraugus County, New York.
652. ii.   GEORGE PRINCE MILKS, b. 15 Jul 1850, Mansfield, Cattaraugus County, New York; d. 27 Jun 1917, Cattaraugus County, New York.
653. iii. ROBERT S. MILK, b. 07 Apr 1852, Mansfield, NY; d. 07 Jan 1937, Great Valley, Cattaraugus County, NY.
654. iv.   ELIZABETH MILK, b. 16 Aug 1853, Mansfield, Cattaraugus County, NY; d. 24 Apr 1896, Cattaraugus County, New York?.
655. v.   JOHN OSCAR MILKS, b. Aug 1858, Mansfield, NY; d. 1922, Pike, Wyoming County, New York.
      vi.   FRANKLIN PIERCE MILK, b. 1859, Mansfield, NY; d. 11 Feb 1936, (never married). Burial: Maples Cemetery, Cattaraugus Co., NY[814]
656. vii. EDGAR MILKS, b. 19 Feb 1861, Mansfield, NY; d. 04 May 1939, New York.

Child of ALEXANDER MILK and ROSE SIMONS is:
657. viii. DAISEY[8] MILKS, b. Sep 1887, Mansfield, Cattaraugus County, New York.

258. DAVID W.[7] MILKS (DAVID[6] MILK, GEORGE[5], JONATHAN[4], JOB[3], JOHN[2], JOHN[1]) was born 1830 in Cattaraugus County, New York, and died 06 Nov 1911 in Coldspring, Cattaraugus County, New York[815,816]. He married (1) LOIS _____ Abt. 1855. She was born 1836 in Warren County, New York, and died 1903[816]. He married (2) LUCETTA J. SEMPLE Aft. 1903. She was born Abt. 1830. David and Lois are buried in Allegany Protestant Cemetery, Cattaraugus County, New York[817]

Children of DAVID MILKS and LOIS _____ are:
658. i.   MANLEY H.[8] MILKS, b. Abt. 1857, Cattaraugus County, New York; d. Bef. 17 Sep 1913.
659. ii.   EVA MILKS, b. Oct 1859, Cattaraugus County, New York.
      iii. BLANCHE B. MILKS, b. Jun 1869, Cattaraugus County, New York[818,819]; d. 1957, Cattaraugus County, New York[819]; m. SYLVENOUS B. BARGY, 1886, Cattaraugus County, New York; b. Jan 1865, Salamanca, Cattaraugus County, New York[819]; d. 1947, Cattaraugus County, New York[819]. They lived in Killbuck, New York, and both are buried in Crawford Cemetery, Salamanca, Cattaraugus County, New York. No children
660. iv.   FRED A. MILKS, b. Abt. 1873, Cattaraugus County, New York; d. 1898.

259. MONTERVILLE[7] MILKS (DAVID[6] MILK, GEORGE[5], JONATHAN[4], JOB[3], JOHN[2], JOHN[1])[819] was born 03 Jun 1833 in Cattaraugus County, New York[820], and died 19 Sep 1912 in Cattaraugus County, New York[820]. He married (1) CAROLINE A. DREW[821,822] 1855. She was born 23 May 1837 in Huron County, Ohio[823,824], and died 26 Feb 1896 in Cattaraugus County, New York[824]. He married (2) SARAH BAKER Abt. 1898. She was born Abt. 1835. Monterville and Caroline are buried in : Maples Cemetery, Mansfield, Cattaraugus County, New York

Children of MONTERVILLE MILKS and CAROLINE DREW are:
661. i.   JEROME BONAPARTE[8] MILKS, b. 1857, Mansfield, Cattaraugus Co., NY.
662. ii.   FRANK EDWIN MILKS, b. 17 Mar 1859, Napoli, Cattaraugus Co, NY; d. 09 Oct 1938, Tuna, McKean County, Pennsylvania.
      iii. ELIZABETH "LIBBIE" MILKS, b. 1861, Cattaraugus Co, NY; d. 05 Sep 1877, Cattaraugus Co, NY (unmarried)[824,825]. Burial: Maples Cemetery[826]
663. iv.   HENRY JOSEPH MILKS, b. 1862, Mansfield, Cattaraugus Co., NY; d. Feb 1949, Ellicottville, Cattaraugus Co, NY.
      v.   MARY "MATE" MILKS, b. 21 Jan 1865, Cattaraugus Co, NY[826,827]; d. 17 Apr 1901, Cattaraugus Co, NY (unmarried)[828,829].
664. vi.   ORSON LEROY MILKS, b. 16 Jan 1871, Mansfield, Cattaraugus Co., NY; d. 24 Jun 1960, Yamhill County, Oregon.

vii. ADA C. MILKS[830,831], b. 21 May 1877, Cattaraugus Co, NY[832]; d. 11 May 1900, Cattaraugus County, New York (unmarried).

260. WASHINGTON G.[7] MILKS *(DAVID[6] MILK, GEORGE[5], JONATHAN[4], JOB[3], JOHN[2], JOHN[1])* was born 1836 in Cattaraugus County, New York. He married AMANDA SNYDER, daughter of JOHN SNYDER and ESTHER. She was born 1840.

Children of WASHINGTON MILKS and AMANDA SNYDER are:
- i. SON[8] MILKS, b. Abt. 1861; d. d.y..
- 665. ii. FRANK ALBERT MILKS, b. 13 Oct 1863, Persia, Cattaraugus County, New York.
- 666. iii. ESTHER MILKS, b. 11 Jul 1871, Little Valley, Cattaraugus County, New York; d. 25 Feb 1933, South Dayton, Cattaraugus County, New York ?.

261. MARTIN[7] WAITE *(MARY[6] MILKS, JONATHAN[5] MILK, JONATHAN[4], JOB[3], JOHN[2], JOHN[1])* was born 18 Jul 1809 in Washington County, New York, and died 1897[833]. He married (1) LOVINA ADAMS Abt. 1835. She was born Abt. 1810. He married (2) MARIAH _____[834,835,836] Abt. 1855. She was born Abt. 1836 in New York. Martin is buried in Union Cemetery, Hortonville, Outagamie County, Wisconsin

Children of MARTIN WAITE and LOVINA ADAMS are:
- i. MARY[8] WAITE, b. 1836, Dayton, Cattaraugus County, New York.
- 667. ii. MARTIN B. WAITE, b. 1841, Dayton, Cattaraugus County, New York; d. 1923, Winnebago County, Wisconsin.
- iii. ESTHER WAITE, b. 1844, Dayton, Cattaraugus County, New York.
- 668. iv. JONATHAN WAITE, b. 10 Oct 1845, Dayton, Cattaraugus County, New York; d. Abt. 15 Mar 1932, Hortonville, Outagamie County, Wisconsin.
- v. LUKE WAITE, b. 29 Oct 1847, Dayton, Cattaraugus County, New York; d. 03 Dec 1874, Hortonville, Outagamie County, Wisconsin[837]. Burial: Union Cemetery, Hortonville, Outagamie County, Wisconsin
- 669. vi. HORACE WAITE, b. 22 Jul 1850, Dayton, Cattaraugus County, New York; d. 17 Oct 1913.

Children of MARTIN WAITE and MARIAH _____ are:
- 670. vii. FRANKLIN[8] WAITE, b. Abt. 1856, Ellington, Outagamie County, Wisconsin.
- viii. JANE E. WAITE, b. Abt. 1858, Ellington, Outagamie County, Wisconsin.
- 671. ix. CLARA WAITE, b. Mar 1867, Ellington, Outagamie County, Wisconsin.

262. BATHSHEBA[7] WAITE *(MARY[6] MILKS, JONATHAN[5] MILK, JONATHAN[4], JOB[3], JOHN[2], JOHN[1])* was born 08 May 1811 in Washington County, New York, and died 1876 in Cattaraugus County, New York. She married WILLIAM POTTER. He was born Abt. 1810 in Of Hoosick, New York[838], and died Bet. 1892 - 1900 in Cattaraugus County, New York.

Children of BATHSHEBA WAITE and WILLIAM POTTER are:
- i. BUTLER[8] POTTER, b. Abt. 1835, Leon, Cattaraugus County, New York.
- ii. MARY J. POTTER, b. Abt. 1837, Leon, Cattaraugus County, New York.
- iii. ALLEN POTTER, b. Abt. 1839, Leon, Cattaraugus County, New York.
- iv. MELISSA T. POTTER, b. Abt. 1842, Leon, Cattaraugus County, New York; m. MISTTER COOK.
- v. MERCY POTTER, b. Abt. 1844, Leon, Cattaraugus County, New York.
- vi. GEORGE POTTER, b. Abt. 1846, Leon, Cattaraugus County, New York; m. ALLIDA _____; b. Abt. 1843.
- vii. SILAS POTTER, b. Abt. 1848, Leon, Cattaraugus County, New York.
- viii. PETER POTTER, b. Abt. 1852, Leon, Cattaraugus County, New York.

263. DAVID[7] WAITE *(MARY[6] MILKS, JONATHAN[5] MILK, JONATHAN[4], JOB[3], JOHN[2], JOHN[1])* was born 13 Apr 1814 in Washington County, New York, and died 17 Sep 1891 in Coldwater, Branch County, Michigan[839]. He married MERCY ROBINSON. She was born Abt. 1819.

Grandchildren of David Waite were Mrs. Mercy Herrington, 115 11th St., Troy, NY, and Mrs. Edith Allen, 16 Blakely Ct., Troy, NY.

Children of DAVID WAITE and MERCY ROBINSON are:
- i. JOHN R.[8] WAITE, b. Abt. 1840, Easton, Washington County, New York.
- ii. ANNETTE H. 'NETTIE' WAITE, b. Abt. 1843, Easton, Washington County, New York.
- iii. HANNAH G. WAITE, b. Abt. 1845, Easton, Washington County, New York.
- iv. ADELIA WAITE, b. Abt. 1848, Easton, Washington County, New York.
- v. ALFRED WAITE, b. Abt. Apr 1850, Easton, Washington County, New York.
- vi. SUSAN B. WAITE, b. Abt. 1854, Easton, Washington County, New York; m. MISTTER CRANDALL.
- vii. JESSIE WAITE, b. Abt. 1856, Easton, Washington County, New York; m. MISTTER BURCH.
- viii. MARY WAITE, b. Abt. 1860, Easton, Washington County, New York.
- ix. ELMER WAITE, b. Abt. 1863, Easton, Washington County, New York.
- x. MILLY WAITE, b. Abt. 1865, Easton, Washington County, New York; d. Bef. 1880, Easton, Washington County, New York.

264. MARY ANN[7] WAITE *(MARY[6] MILKS, JONATHAN[5] MILK, JONATHAN[4], JOB[3], JOHN[2], JOHN[1])* was born 26 Feb 1816 in Washington County, New York, and died 06 Feb 1892 in Machias, Cattaraugus County, New York. She married SILAS POTTER, son of DANIEL POTTER and LYDIA _____. He was born 21 Jun 1818 in Genesee County, New York, and died 03 Mar 1879 in Machias, Cattaraugus County, New York.

Children of MARY WAITE and SILAS POTTER are:
- i. MARYETTE[8] POTTER, b. Abt. 1842, Machias, Cattaraugus County, New York.
- ii. ISAAC POTTER, b. Abt. 1844, Machias, Cattaraugus County, New York.
- iii. MERRITT POTTER, b. Aug 1846, Machias, Cattaraugus County, New York.
- iv. WILBER POTTER, b. Mar 1848, Machias, Cattaraugus County, New York.
- v. SARAH M. POTTER, b. Abt. 1851, Machias, Cattaraugus County, New York.
- vi. LUCETTA POTTER, b. Abt. 1854, Machias, Cattaraugus County, New York.
- 672. vii. WILLIAM POTTER, b. May 1857, Machias, Cattaraugus County, New York.

265. JONATHAN[7] WAITE *(MARY[6] MILKS, JONATHAN[5] MILK, JONATHAN[4], JOB[3], JOHN[2], JOHN[1])* was born 28 Jul 1819 in Washington County, New York, and died 1858 in Cattaraugus County, New York. He married JANE WILLIAMS. She was born 1826, and died 1894 in Cattaraugus County, New York. They are buried in Kendall Flats Cemetery, Cattaraugus County, New York

Children of JONATHAN WAITE and JANE WILLIAMS are:
- i. HELEN[8] WAITE, b. 1849, Dayton, Cattaraugus County, New York.
- ii. WARREN D. WAITE, b. Sep 1850, Cattaraugus County, New York; d. 1932, Cattaraugus County, New York; m. BLANCHE HUNT, 1894, Cattaraugus County, New York; b. Feb 1869; d. 1919, Cattaraugus County, New York. They are buried in Kendall Flats Cemetery, Cattaraugus County, New York. No children.
- iii. ADELAIDE 'ADDIE' WAITE, b. 1853, Cattaraugus County, New York.
- iv. BUTLER G. WAITE, b. 1857, Cattaraugus County, New York.

266. ISAAC[7] WAITE, JR. *(MARY[6] MILKS, JONATHAN[5] MILK, JONATHAN[4], JOB[3], JOHN[2], JOHN[1])* was born 09 May 1821 in New York[840], and died 09 Sep 1875 in Battle Creek, Calhoun County, Michigan[841]. He married LUCETTA MILK[842,843,844,845] Abt. 1847 in Rensselaer County, New York, daughter of SILAS & SARAH MILKS. She was born Abt. 1823 in New York[846], and died 29 Nov 1882 in Bangor, Van Buren County, Michigan[847].

Child is listed above under (217) Lucetta Milk.

267. GEORGE C.[7] WAITE *(MARY[6] MILKS, JONATHAN[5] MILK, JONATHAN[4], JOB[3], JOHN[2], JOHN[1])* was born 13 Jan 1825 in Washington County, New York. He married (1) ELIZABETH S. POTTER Abt. 1860, daughter of PETER & RACHEL POTTER. She was born Abt. 1825. He married (2) MARY LOCKWOOD Abt. 1875, daughter of PHILO & MARY LOCKWOOD. She was born Abt. 1830.

Child of GEORGE WAITE and ELIZABETH POTTER is:
- i. HENRY[8] WAITE, b. 04 Apr 1861, Collins, Erie County, New York.

Children of GEORGE WAITE and MARY LOCKWOOD are:
- ii. JENNIE[8] WAITE, b. 19 Jul 1877, Eden, Erie County, New York.
- iii. RAYMOND WAITE, b. 16 Aug 1879, Eden, Erie County, New York.

268. JANE[7] WAITE *(MARY[6] MILKS, JONATHAN[5] MILK, JONATHAN[4], JOB[3], JOHN[2], JOHN[1])* was born 23 Apr 1827 in Washington County, New York, and died 1891. She married CHARLES BARKER. He was born Abt. 1827 in Of Leon, New York.

Children of JANE WAITE and CHARLES BARKER are:
- i. ANNETTE[8] BARKER, d. Scarlet fever.
- ii. ALICE BARKER, d. Scarlet fever.
- iii. AARON BARKER, d. Scarlet fever.
- 673. iv. EMMA JANELLA 'NELLIE' BARKER, b. 1868, Leon, Cattaraugus County, New York; d. 1923.

269. BENJAMIN[7] WAITE *(MARY[6] MILKS, JONATHAN[5] MILK, JONATHAN[4], JOB[3], JOHN[2], JOHN[1])* was born 05 Mar 1829 in Washington County, New York, and died 31 Jul 1891. He married MARTHA BARSE. She was born Abt. 1830.

Benjamin purchased land from the Holland Land Company, which was later occupied by his son Albert and subsequently his granddaughter Nettie Waite Gill.

Children of BENJAMIN WAITE and MARTHA BARSE are:
- i. VERNELIA[8] WAITE, b. 20 Nov 1855, East Leon, Cattaraugus County, New York; d. 31 Aug 1930, Cherry Creek, Chautauqua County, New York; m. (1) MISTTER ROBERTS; b. Abt. 1855; m. (2) MISTTER WELLS; b. Abt. 1855; m. (3) MISTTER RHOADES; b. Abt. 1855.
- 674. ii. ALBERT WAITE, b. 07 Mar 1857, Concord, Erie County, New York; d. 04 Dec 1936, Leon, Cattaraugus County, New York.
- 675. iii. FRED WAITE, b. 13 May 1863, East Leon, Cattaraugus County, New York.
- 676. iv. LUCY J. WAITE, b. 19 May 1868, East Leon, Cattaraugus County, New York.

270. BUTLER R.[7] WAITE *(MARY[6] MILKS, JONATHAN[5] MILK, JONATHAN[4], JOB[3], JOHN[2], JOHN[1])* was born 29 Dec 1830 in Washington County, New York. He married (1) OLIVE FULLER. She was born Abt. 1835, and died 10 Jan 1858. He married (2) MISS WEST. She was born Abt. 1830. He married (3) EMILY CASTEN Abt. 1859. She was born Abt. 1830.

Butler was a farmer and a cattle dealer and later lived in Iowa.

Children of BUTLER WAITE and EMILY CASTEN are:
- 677. i. GEORGE B.[8] WAITE, b. 29 Oct 1859, Leon, Cattaraugus County, New York.
- 678. ii. WILLIAM A. WAITE, b. 02 Feb 1861, Leon, Cattaraugus County, New York.

271. JEMIMA[7] MILKS *(JOHN[6] MILK, JONATHAN[5], JONATHAN[4], JOB[3], JOHN[2], JOHN[1])* was born 1812 in Washington County, New York, and died Bef. 1859 in Cattaraugus County, New York. She married MANLEY M. HUBBARD. He was born 1810, and died 1882 in Leon, New York. Manley is buried in Leon, Cattaraugus County, New York

Children of JEMIMA MILKS and MANLEY HUBBARD are:
- 679. i. EMILY[8] HUBBARD, b. 1834, Napoli, Cattaraugus County, New York; d. 05 Aug 1857.
- ii. MARY HUBBARD, b. 1837, Napoli, Cattaraugus County, New York; d. Jun 1885, Fredonia, Chautauqua County, New York; m. (1) JESSE WORDEN CASE; b. 23 Jul 1823; d. 09 Aug 1870, Fredonia, Chautauqua County, New York; m. (2) ALBERT H. WHEELOCK; b. Abt. 1837.
- iii. SUSAN HUBBARD, b. 1839, Napoli, Cattaraugus County, New York; m. JOHN HUNTON; b. Abt. 1839.
- iv. ALMINA HUBBARD, b. 1842, Napoli, Cattaraugus County, New York; m. ALFRED EARLE, Abt. 1859, Cattaraugus County, New York; b. Abt. 1842. Number of Children (Facts: 1900, 2 children, 2 living
- v. MARVIN HUBBARD, b. 1848, Napoli, Cattaraugus County, New York.
- vi. WILLIAM HUBBARD, b. 1854, Napoli, Cattaraugus County, New York.

272. JOHN[7] MILKS *(JOHN[6] MILK, JONATHAN[5], JONATHAN[4], JOB[3], JOHN[2], JOHN[1])* was born 1815, and died 08 Nov 1884 in Napoli, Cattaraugus County, New York. He married ANNA PHILLIPS Abt. 1840. She was born 1816 in Washington Co., NY, and died 07 Aug 1912 in Napoli, New York. Number of Children (Facts: 1900, 11 children, 4 living.

Children of JOHN MILKS and ANNA PHILLIPS are:
- 680. i. NEWTON[8] MILKS, b. 09 Jan 1842, Napoli, Cattaraugus County, New York; d. 16 May 1917, New Albion, Cattaraugus Co, NY.
- ii. HIRAM MILKS, b. 1843, Napoli, Cattaraugus County, New York; d. Bef. 1900, Napoli, Cattaraugus County, New York.
- 681. iii. WILLARD MILKS, b. Jun 1844, Napoli, Cattaraugus County, New York; d. 17 May 1911, Napoli, Cattaraugus County, New York.
- iv. ELIZABETH ANN MILKS, b. 31 Jan 1847, Napoli, Cattaraugus County, New York; d. 09 Mar 1861, Napoli, Cattaraugus County, New York. Burial: Snyders Corners Cemetery, Cattaraugus County, New York
- 682. v. JOHN D. MILKS, b. 14 Jan 1849, Napoli, Cattaraugus County, New York; d. Bef. 1900, Napoli, Cattaraugus County, New York.
- vi. HORACE 'BLAKE' MILKS, b. 07 Apr 1852, Napoli, Cattaraugus County, New York; d. 16 Feb 1928, Napoli, Cattaraugus County, New York; m. ELIZABETH FOX; b. 09 Apr 1860; d. 08 Feb 1932, Napoli, Cattaraugus County, New York.
  No children.
- vii. JANETTE MILKS, b. 1854, Napoli, Cattaraugus County, New York; d. Bef. 1900, Napoli, Cattaraugus County, New York.
- 683. viii. NANCY S. MILKS, b. 12 Mar 1858, Napoli, Cattaraugus County, New York; d. 24 Jul 1928, East Randolph, Cattaraugus Co., NY.

273. BENJAMIN B.[7] MILKS *(JOHN[6] MILK, JONATHAN[5], JONATHAN[4], JOB[3], JOHN[2], JOHN[1])*[848] was born 14 Apr 1816 in Washington County, New York[848,849], and died 16 May 1884 in East Randolph, Cattaraugus County, New York[850,851]. He married POLLY ANN ARNOLD[851]. She was born 30 Apr 1824[852,853], and died May 1910 in East Randolph, Cattaraugus Co, NY[854,855]. They are buried in East Randolph Cemetery, Cattaraugus Co, NY[856,857]

Children of BENJAMIN MILKS and POLLY ARNOLD are:
- 684. i. HENRY BENSON[8] MILKS, b. 22 Oct 1844, Napoli, Cattaraugus Co, NY; d. 09 Nov 1910, Bainbridge Twp., Geauga County, Ohio.
- ii. WILLIAM L. MILKS[858,859], b. 1846, Napoli, Cattaraugus Co, NY[860,861,861]; d. 16 Feb 1917, East Randolph, Cattaraugus Co, NY (unmarried)[862,863,864]. Burial: East Randolph Cemetery, Cattaraugus Co, NY
- 685. iii. ELEANOR R. MILKS, b. Dec 1847, Napoli, New York; d. 1925, Geauga County, Ohio.
- 686. iv. ALVIN L. MILKS, b. 14 Jul 1849, Napoli, Cattaraugus County, New York; d. 10 Dec 1924, Springfield, Sarpy County, Nebraska.
- 687. v. EUGENE BENJAMIN MILKS, b. 1851, Napoli, New York; d. Bet. 1930 - 1940, Cattaraugus County, New York.
- vi. SUSAN E. MILKS, b. 1853, Napoli, New York; d. Jun 1918, Lusk, Wyoming; m. JAMES HAMMOND DEVOE; b. 23 Nov 1826, New York; d. 13 Mar 1913, Dewittville, Chautauqua County, New York. On Jan 9, 1911, James entered the Chautauqua County Almshouse, aged 83, married, self-supporting. James is buried in Chautauqua County Poor House Cemetery, Dewittville, Chautauqua County, New York Military service: Bet. 1862 - 23 Apr 1864, Civil War, enlisted at Ellington. Co. B, 112th Infantry
- 688. vii. EMILY H. MILKS, b. 1855, Napoli, New York.
- viii. ANDREW P. MILKS, b. 1860, Napoli, Cattaraugus Co, NY[865]; d. 15 Sep 1865, Napoli, Cattaraugus Co, NY[865]. Burial: Maple Hill Cemetery, Cattaraugus County, NY
- ix. MARYETTA MILKS, b. Apr 1863, Napoli, New York; d. East Randolph, Cattaraugus Co., NY; m. (1) JAMES JOSEPH HANCOCK, 02 Dec 1886; b. Nov 1866, Wales\England[866,867]; d. Abt. 1923, Lusk, Niobrara County, Wyoming; m. (2) WILLIAM BOSWELL, 01 Sep 1925, Cattaraugus County, New York[868]; b. Abt. 1858, Ohio; d. Bet. 1930 - 1940, Cattaraugus County, New York. No children.

274. DAVID[7] MILK *(JOHN[6], JONATHAN[5], JONATHAN[4], JOB[3], JOHN[2], JOHN[1])* was born 02 May 1818 in Easton, Washington County, New York[869], and died 16 Aug 1855 in Little Valley, Cattaraugus County, New York[870]. He married (1) JOANNA FREEMAN Abt. 1842, daughter of HIRAM FREEMAN and ELIZABETH _____. She was born 1825, and died 20 Jul 1844 in Napoli, Cattaraugus Co., NY[871]. He married (2) EMELINE L. KINNICUTT Abt. 1845, daughter of JOHN KINNICUTT and SOPHRONIA CHAPEL. She was born 15 Jan 1826 in New Albion, NY[872], and died 09 Sep 1855 in Little Valley, Cattaraugus Co., NY[873]. All three are buried in South Napoli Cemetery, Cattaraugus County, New York

Child of DAVID MILK and JOANNA FREEMAN is:

689.   i.   ELMER F.[8] MILKS, b. Jul 1843, Napoli, Cattaraugus Co., NY.

Children of DAVID MILK and EMELINE KINNICUTT are:

690.   ii.   EDWARD R.[8] MILKS, b. Apr 1846, Napoli, Cattaraugus Co, NY; d. Bet. 1920 - 1930, Olean, Cattaraugus County, New York ??.
691.   iii.   EVELINE LOUISE MILKS, b. 10 Jan 1849, Napoli, Cattaraugus Co., NY; d. 13 Jan 1928, Valmont, Boulder County, Colorado.
692.   iv.   MANLEY DAVID MILKS, b. Nov 1852, Napoli, Cattaraugus Co., NY; d. 1937, Reynoldsville, Jefferson County, Pennsylvania.

275. DEBORAH[7] MILKS *(JOHN[6] MILK, JONATHAN[5], JONATHAN[4], JOB[3], JOHN[2], JOHN[1])* was born 1819 in Washington County, New York, and died 1869 in Little Valley, Cattaraugus County, New York. She married JOB RUSSELL CASE Abt. 1844 in Cattaraugus County, New York, son of WILLIAM CASE and SOPHIA ARNOLD. He was born 05 Jul 1821 in Spafford, Washington County, New York, and died 1915 in Little Valley, Cattaraugus County, New York.

Job Case was a farmer who bought tracts of land and lumbered, a strict prohibitionist, and in favor of woman suffrage.

Children of DEBORAH MILKS and JOB CASE are:

693.   i.   ANNA VIRGINIA[8] CASE, b. 17 May 1844, Napoli, Cattaraugus County, New York; d. 06 May 1914, Little Valley, Cattaraugus County, New York.
694.   ii.   THERESA MARY CASE, b. 16 Jul 1845, Napoli, Cattaraugus County, New York; d. 10 Jan 1893, Buffalo, New York.
695.   iii.   WILLIAM R. CASE, b. Aug 1847, Napoli, Cattaraugus County, New York.
        iv.   EUGENE CASE, b. 1850, Napoli, Cattaraugus County, New York; d. 1851, Napoli, Cattaraugus County, New York.
696.   v.   JEAN J. CASE, b. 10 Aug 1853, Napoli, Cattaraugus County, New York; d. 19 Aug 1935, Napoli, Cattaraugus County, New York.
697.   vi.   EMMA E. CASE, b. 1855, Napoli, Cattaraugus County, New York; d. 1901, Little Valley, Cattaraugus County, New York.
698.   vii.   JESSIE CASE, b. 1856, Napoli, Cattaraugus County, New York.
698.   viii.   JOHN DEBORAH CASE, b. 12 Jul 1858, Napoli, Cattaraugus County, New York; d. 15 Jul 1929, Little Valley, Cattaraugus County, New York.
700.   ix.   ANDREW J. CASE, b. 04 Mar 1862, Napoli, Cattaraugus County, New York; d. 15 Jan 1940, Little Valley, Cattaraugus County, New York.

276. GEORGE[7] MILKS *(JOHN[6] MILK, JONATHAN[5], JONATHAN[4], JOB[3], JOHN[2], JOHN[1])* was born 12 Feb 1823 in Washington County, New York, and died 1867 in Cattaraugus County, New York. He married MAHALA ARNOLD, daughter of ADOLPHUS ARNOLD and LYDIA BURROUGHS. She was born 25 Jun 1827, and died 27 Jun 1920 in Cattaraugus County, New York. They are buried in Pigeon Valley Cemetery, Cattaraugus Co., NY The cause of death for George was Pneumonia brought on by boating accident on the Allegheny River

After the death of her mother, Mahala was reared by her grandfather, Porter Burroughs, at Vesper, Onondaga Co., NY, until she was married to George at the age of 14. George Milks was injured on a raft taking a large load of lumber down the Allegheny River to Pittsburgh. He managed to return home, but d. within a few days of pneumonia, in 1867. Mahala was left with the care of 8 Children, ranging in ages from 16 to 3 years.

Children of GEORGE MILKS and MAHALA ARNOLD are:

701.   i.   SUSAN J.[8] MILKS, b. 26 Jan 1844, Napoli, Cattaraugus County, New York; d. 11 Sep 1913, New Albion, Cattaraugus County, New York.
702.   ii.   SARAH JANE MILKS, b. 25 Nov 1846, Napoli, Cattaraugus Co., NY; d. 16 Nov 1929, Great Valley, Cattaraugus County, New York.
703.   iii.   GEORGE WILSON MILKS, b. 06 Nov 1848, Napoli, Cattaraugus County, New York; d. 29 Aug 1931, New Albion, Cattaraugus County, New York.
704.   iv.   HARVEY R. 'DADE' MILKS, b. 16 Oct 1850, Napoli, Cattaraugus County, New York; d. 08 Aug 1932, Napoli,

Cattaraugus County, New York.
705.   v.   LYDIA MILKS, b. 06 Jun 1853, Napoli, Cattaraugus Co., NY; d. 1940, Cattaraugus County, New York.
706.   vi.   FRANK W. MILKS, b. 07 Nov 1856, Napoli, Cattaraugus Co, NY; d. 06 Sep 1927.
       vii.   EMMET EUGENE MILKS, b. 1858, Napoli, Cattaraugus Co., NY; d. 1858, Cattaraugus County, New York.
707.   viii.   FRED MILKS, b. 27 Jul 1860, Napoli, Cattaraugus Co., NY; d. 13 Jan 1931, Cattaraugus County, New York.
708.   ix.   NETTIE MILKS, b. 14 Oct 1865, Napoli, Cattaraugus County, New York; d. 30 Nov 1942, Buffalo, Erie County, New York.

277. MARY^7 MILKS *(JOHN^6 MILK, JONATHAN^5, JONATHAN^4, JOB^3, JOHN^2, JOHN^1)* was born 1825, and died 05 Apr 1861 in New Albion, Cattaraugus County, New York. She married LEANDER W. KINNICUTT, son of JOHN KINNICUTT and SOPHRONIA CHAPEL. He was born 25 Mar 1822 in New Albion, NY^{874}, and died 03 Apr 1861 in New Albion, NY^{874}.

Children of MARY MILKS and LEANDER KINNICUTT are:
      i.   ELVINA E.^{8} KINNICUTT, b. 1848, New Albion, New York. 8 children.
      ii.   ANNA A. KINNICUTT, b. 1850, New Albion, New York. 2 children.

278. GILES^7 MILKS *(JOHN^6 MILK, JONATHAN^5, JONATHAN^4, JOB^3, JOHN^2, JOHN^1)* was born 22 Jan 1830 in Napoli, Cattaraugus County, New York, and died 09 Jan 1906. He married SOPHIA EARLE Abt. 1850. She was born 1837, and died Abt. 27 Jan 1893.

Children of GILES MILKS and SOPHIA EARLE are:
      i.   LEROY^8 MILKS, b. 05 Mar 1853, Napoli, Cattaraugus County, New York; d. 10 Feb 1905, Napoli, Cattaraugus County, New York; m. CORA EARLE, Abt. 1880; b. 1864, New York; d. No children.
709.   ii.   FRANCES ELLEN MILKS, b. Feb 1854, Napoli, Cattaraugus County, New York.
710.   iii.   JAMES MILKS, b. Dec 1863, Napoli, Cattaraugus County, New York.
711.   iv.   BERT MILKS, b. 22 Oct 1874, Napoli, Cattaraugus County, New York.

279. HIRAM^7 MILKS *(JOHN^6 MILK, JONATHAN^5, JONATHAN^4, JOB^3, JOHN^2, JOHN^1)* was born 09 Jun 1832 in Napoli, Cattaraugus Co, NY^{875}, and died 23 Jan 1883 in Napoli, Cattaraugus Co, NY (measles epidemic)^{875}. He married MARTHA CASE. She was born 10 Jun 1836^{876,877}, and died 21 Aug 1909 in Little Valley, Cattaraugus Co., NY^{878}. They are buried in South Napoli Cemetery, Cattaraugus County, New York.
DEATH NOTICE - From the *Randolph Register* 25 Jan 1883:
"Hiram Milks of that apparently ill-fated family at Napoli, died on Tuesday night of measles. This is the fourth victim to the disease in this family within a month." In later editions the Register reported that Mrs. Milks and other daughters also suffered from the disease but had recovered.

Children of HIRAM MILKS and MARTHA CASE are:
712.   i.   ADELBERT^8 MILKS, b. Sep 1854, Napoli, Cattaraugus County, New York; d. Bet. 1920 - 1930, Cattaraugus County, New York.
      ii.   EFFIE E. MILKS, b. 02 Nov 1856, Napoli, Cattaraugus Co, NY; d. 25 Dec 1880, Napoli, Cattaraugus Co, NY^{881}; m. EMMETT BEERS WAITE; b. Abt. 1859, Cattaraugus County, New York. Burial: South Napoli Cemetery, Cattaraugus County, New York
713.   iii.   SIDNEY DAVID MILKS, b. 05 Mar 1858, Cattaraugus County, New York; d. 04 Dec 1931, Mt. Pleasant, Iowa.
      iv.   ELMER F. MILKS, b. 05 Sep 1860, Napoli, Cattaraugus Co, NY; d. 12 Jan 1883, Napoli, Cattaraugus Co, NY (measles epidemic)^{882}. Apparently never married. Burial: South Napoli Cemetery, Cattaraugus County, New York^{883}
Cause of Death: Measles
714.   v.   WALLACE H. MILKS, b. 12 Jan 1863; d. 19 Sep 1932, East Randolph, Cattaraugus County, New York.
      vi.   CLIFFORD PAUL MILKS, b. 07 Jul 1865, Napoli, Cattaraugus Co, NY^{884}; d. 05 Jan 1883, Napoli, Cattaraugus Co., NY^{885}.
Prob. Never married. Burial: South Napoli Cemetery, Cattaraugus County, New York^{886} Cause of Death: Measles
      vii.   ROSA M. MILKS, b. 25 Nov 1867, Napoli, Cattaraugus Co, NY^{887}; d. 15 Jan 1883, Napoli, Cattaraugus Co, NY (measles epidemic)^{887}. Never married. Burial: South Napoli Cemetery, Cattaraugus Co., NY. Cause

		of Death: Measles
715.	viii.	MARY B. MILKS, b. 20 Jun 1870, Napoli, Cattaraugus County, New York.
	ix.	JOHN HERBERT MILKS, b. 07 Jun 1872, Napoli, Cattaraugus Co, NY; d. 07 Jul 1876, Napoli, Cattaraugus Co, NY[888].
		Burial: South Napoli Cemetery, Cattaraugus County, New York[889]
716.	x.	SIBYL MILKS, b. 07 Dec 1876, Napoli, Cattaraugus County, New York; d. Aft. Jan 1930, Cattaraugus County, New York.
717.	xi.	MANLEY KENNETH MILKS, b. 26 May 1880, Napoli, Cattaraugus Co., NY; d. 14 Mar 1941.

280. MARTIN[7] MILKS (JOHN[6] MILK, JONATHAN[5], JONATHAN[4], JOB[3], JOHN[2], JOHN[1]) was born 1836 in Cattaraugus County, New York[890], and died 19 Apr 1896 in Napoli, Cattaraugus County, New York. He married MARY ELIZABETH EARLE Abt. 1859, daughter of LEWIS EARLE and ANNA WOODWORTH. She was born 1842 in New York[890], and died 19 Apr 1903 in Napoli, Cattaraugus County, New York.

Children of MARTIN MILKS and MARY EARLE are:

718.	i.	ANNIE J.[8] MILKS, b. 28 Jan 1860, Napoli, Cattaraugus County, New York; d. 1915, Cattaraugus County, New York.
719.	ii.	MARY A. MILKS, b. 11 Jul 1861, Napoli, Cattaraugus County, New York.
720.	iii.	HARVEY C. MILKS, b. 19 Dec 1863, Napoli, Cattaraugus County, New York; d. 22 Feb 1942.
721.	iv.	CLAUDIA E. MILKS, b. 1865, Napoli, Cattaraugus County, New York; d. In Childbirth.
722.	v.	GEORGE B. MILKS, b. 17 Nov 1867, Napoli, Cattaraugus County, New York; d. 02 Jul 1949, Jamestown, New York.
	vi.	ZELLA MILKS, b. 1868, Napoli, Cattaraugus County, New York; d. 1870, Napoli, Cattaraugus County, New York (drowned).
723.	vii.	ELIZABETH "LIZZIE" MILKS, b. Apr 1870, Napoli, Cattaraugus County, New York.
724.	viii.	ALMYRA "MYRA" MILKS, b. 01 Apr 1872, Napoli, Cattaraugus County, New York; d. 1954, Salamanca, Cattaraugus County, New York.
725.	ix.	MARTIN "VAN" MILKS, b. 1875, Napoli, Cattaraugus County, New York; d. 01 Jul 1953, Little Valley, Cattaraugus County, New York.
726.	x.	EMMET EARL MILKS, b. 23 Oct 1876, Napoli, Cattaraugus County, New York; d. 18 Mar 1946, Cattaraugus County, New York.
727.	xi.	HORACE 'LEE' MILKS, b. 10 Oct 1878, Little Valley, Cattaraugus County, New York; d. 10 Nov 1936, Salamanca, Cattaraugus County, New York.
	xii.	BEN MILKS, b. 1880, Napoli, Cattaraugus County, New York; d. Abt. 1882, Napoli, Cattaraugus County, New York (Scarlet fever).
728.	xiii.	RUBY C. MILKS, b. 1883, Napoli, Cattaraugus Co, NY.
	xiv.	LEWIS MILKS, b. 1884, Napoli, Cattaraugus County, New York; d. 1898, Napoli, Cattaraugus County, New York.
		Burial: Little Valley, Cattaraugus County, New York
	xv.	JOHN MILKS, b. 1888, Napoli, Cattaraugus County, New York; d. 25 Jan 1905, Napoli, Cattaraugus County, New York.

281. JOB[7] HARRINGTON (DEBORAH[6] MILKS, JONATHAN[5] MILK, JONATHAN[4], JOB[3], JOHN[2], JOHN[1]) was born 1821 in Easton, Washington County, New York, and died 30 Jun 1883. He married (1) ELLEN _____. She was born 1830, and died 10 Oct 1927. He married (2) ESTHER ELIZABETH OBERN Abt. 1858 in New York. She was born 05 Jul 1835, and died 30 Jul 1870.

Children of JOB HARRINGTON and ESTHER OBERN are:

	i.	DEBORAH[8] HARRINGTON, b. 1859, Easton, Washington County, New York; d. 14 Jul 1878, Easton, Washington County, New York.
729.	ii.	CYNTHIA HARRINGTON, b. 16 Oct 1862, Easton, Washington County, New York; d. Greenwich, Washington County, New York.
730.	iii.	LUCY HARRINGTON, b. 15 Jul 1865, Easton, Washington County, New York; d. 20 Jan 1932, Greenwich, Washington County, New York.

282. RUTH[7] HARRINGTON *(DEBORAH[6] MILKS, JONATHAN[5] MILK, JONATHAN[4], JOB[3], JOHN[2], JOHN[1])* was born 1824 in Easton, Washington County, New York, and died 22 Feb 1892 in Easton, Washington County, New York. She married HARVEY TUBBS Abt. 1845. He was born 04 Apr 1820, and died 22 Jan 1897 in Easton, Washington County, New York.

Children of RUTH HARRINGTON and HARVEY TUBBS are:
- i. DEBORAH[8] TUBBS, b. 1846; d. 16 Oct 1908.
- ii. JOSEPH R. TUBBS, b. 1848.
- iii. ANNA MARY TUBBS, b. 1850.
- iv. NELSON TUBBS, b. 1854; d. Sep 1923, Greenwich, Washington County, New York.
- v. PERRY TUBBS, b. 1860.

283. BENJAMIN[7] HARRINGTON *(DEBORAH[6] MILKS, JONATHAN[5] MILK, JONATHAN[4], JOB[3], JOHN[2], JOHN[1])* was born 1833 in Easton, Washington County, New York, and died 21 Jan 1890 in Easton, Washington County, New York. He married HANNAH HARRINGTON Abt. 1855, daughter of WILLIAM HARRINGTON and SALLY NARCROSS. She was born 1837, and died 1866 in Easton, Washington County, New York. They are buried in Methodist Stump Church Cemetery, Cambridge, Washington County, New York

Children of BENJAMIN HARRINGTON and HANNAH HARRINGTON are:
- i. ELIZABETH[8] HARRINGTON, b. 14 Jun 1856, Easton, Washington County, New York; d. 28 Dec 1932; m. WILLIAM KENNETH RATHBURN; b. 29 Aug 1847, Easton, Washington County, New York; d. 26 Jul 1921.
- 731. ii. HOWARD HARRINGTON, b. 24 Feb 1860, Easton, Washington County, New York; d. 18 Feb 1903.
- 732. iii. DORA HARRINGTON, b. 11 Mar 1862, Cambridge, Washington County, New York; d. 04 Mar 1930, Easton, Washington County, New York.

284. DAVID W.[7] HARRINGTON *(DEBORAH[6] MILKS, JONATHAN[5] MILK, JONATHAN[4], JOB[3], JOHN[2], JOHN[1])* was born 17 Oct 1834 in Easton, Washington County, New York, and died 24 Jun 1906 in Easton, Washington County, New York. He married ALICE B. SNELL Abt. 1857. She was born 23 Feb 1835, and died 14 Mar 1913.

Children of DAVID HARRINGTON and ALICE SNELL are:
- 733. i. THOMAS A.[8] HARRINGTON, b. 04 Oct 1858, Greenwich, Washington County, New York; d. 30 Oct 1935, Flagler Beach, Florida.
- 734. ii. MERRITT R. HARRINGTON, b. 13 Dec 1863, Greenwich, Washington County, New York; d. 13 May 1927, Greenwich, Washington County, New York.

285. ALLEN[7] HARRINGTON *(DEBORAH[6] MILKS, JONATHAN[5] MILK, JONATHAN[4], JOB[3], JOHN[2], JOHN[1])* was born Feb 1843 in Easton, Washington County, New York, and died 31 Dec 1882 in Greenwich, New York. He married (1) MARY MATILDA HARRINGTON, daughter of HARVEY HARRINGTON and MYRA CLARK. She was born 1848, and died 1868 in Washington County, New York. He married (2) LUCY HILLMAN, daughter of HENRY HILLMAN and MARGARET WARNER. She was born May 1852[891], and died 1924.

Children of ALLEN HARRINGTON and MARY HARRINGTON are:
- 735. i. GEORGE[8] HARRINGTON, b. 30 Oct 1865, Greenwich, Washington County, New York; d. 09 Jun 1902.
- ii. JOHN M. HARRINGTON, b. 1867, Greenwich, Washington County, New York; d. 1868, Greenwich, Washington County, New York.

Children of ALLEN HARRINGTON and LUCY HILLMAN are:
- 736. iii. LEWIS[8] HARRINGTON, b. 1871, Easton, Washington County, New York; d. 13 Feb 1951, Dorset, Bennington County, Vermont.
- 737. iv. WILLIAM HARRINGTON, b. 1872, Easton, Washington County, New York.
- 738. v. EDWARD HARRINGTON, b. 1874, Jackson, New York.
- vi. LEA HARRINGTON, b. Sep 1875, Greenwich, Washington County, New York; d. 15 Aug 1876, Greenwich, Washington County, New York.
- vii. ALLEN HARRINGTON, b. 15 Mar 1877, Greenwich, Washington County, New York; d. 02 Jun 1915, Unmarried.
- viii. HARVEY HARRINGTON, b. 1880, Jackson, New York; d. 1960, Unmarried.

286. JOHN J.[7] HARRINGTON *(DEBORAH[6] MILKS, JONATHAN[5] MILK, JONATHAN[4], JOB[3], JOHN[2], JOHN[1])* was born Abt. 1849 in Blossburg, Pennsylvania, and died 26 Aug 1930. He married MARY BROTH. She was born Abt. 1850.

Child of JOHN HARRINGTON and MARY BROTH is:
    i. JOHN J.[8] HARRINGTON, JR., b. Of Syracuse, New York.

287. LEONARD[7] MILKS *(BENJAMIN[6], JONATHAN[5] MILK, JONATHAN[4], JOB[3], JOHN[2], JOHN[1])* was born Bet. 1820 - 1821 in Easton, Washington County, New York[892], and died Aft. 29 Oct 1898. He married (1) AMANDA HOWARD Abt. 1840, daughter of HARRY HOWARD and DELILA BACON. She was born Abt. 1821 in Dayton, Cattaraugus County, New York, and died 1844 in Dayton, Cattaraugus County, New York. He married (2) SARAH ANN FARRINGTON Abt. 1849. She was born 1824.

Record Number 170
Date of Admission: Oct 29, 1898
Records of Inmates Cattaraugus County Poor House, under Act Chap. 140, Laws of 1875
Leonard Milks, male, age:76, widower, birth: NY
County: Washington, town: Easton
Occupation: Farmer
Self-supporting
Five living children
Existing cause of Dependence: Rheumatism & old age.

Child of LEONARD MILKS and AMANDA HOWARD is:
739.   i. HENRY[8] MILKS-HOWARD, b. Apr 1844, Cattaraugus County, New York; d. 1914, Cattaraugus County, New York.

Children of LEONARD MILKS and SARAH FARRINGTON are:
740.   ii. EDGAR[8] MILKS, b. 05 Dec 1849, Mansfield, Cattaraugus County, New York; d. 12 Oct 1917, Gowanda, Cattaraugus County, New York.
       iii. EDWIN MILKS, b. 1849, Persia, Cattaraugus County, New York; d. 1849, Persia, Cattaraugus County, New York.
       iv. GILBERT MILKS, b. Abt. 1850, Persia, Cattaraugus County, New York.
742.   v. FRANCIS JAMES 'FRANK' MILKS, b. 13 Jul 1851, Persia, Cattaraugus County, New York; d. Nov 1929, Cattaraugus County, New York.
       vi. ELIZABETH A. MILKS[893], b. 1854, Persia, Cattaraugus County, New York; d. d.y..
       vii. LEONARD E. MILKS, b. 1858, Persia, Cattaraugus County, New York[894]; d. 27 May 1861, Persia, Cattaraugus Co, NY[895].
         Burial: Milks Cemetery, Town of Persia, Cattaraugus Co, NY
       viii. TWIN CHILD MILKS, b. 1858, Persia, Cattaraugus County, New York; d. d.y..
       ix. JOSEPHINE A. MILKS, b. 1861, Persia, Cattaraugus County, New York; d. 1890, Persia, Cattaraugus County, New York; m. WILLIAM B. EASTERLY; b. 1859, Cattaraugus County, New York; d. 1931, Cattaraugus County, New York.
         Josephine died in 1890 when twin children were born. The twins must have died also because I have been unable to find any record of their further existence. William is buried in Snyders Corners Cemetery, Cattaraugus County, New York
       x. MARY E. MILKS, b. 1863, Persia, Cattaraugus County, New York[896]; d. 1922, Persia, Cattaraugus Co, NY[896]; m. DANIEL I. FIEDLER, Abt. 1904[897]; b. Abt. 1856, Pennsylvania. In the 1910 census, Mary states that her marriage to Daniel Fiedler is her first marriage, and his second marriage. No children.
         Milks Cemetery Record, Town of Persia, Cattaraugus County, New York (Rootsweb)
         MILKS, Mary E., wife of D.I. FIEDLER 1863 - 1922

288. CORDELIA[7] MILKS *(BENJAMIN[6], JONATHAN[5] MILK, JONATHAN[4], JOB[3], JOHN[2], JOHN[1])* was born 12 Dec 1823 in Washington County, New York[898,899], and died 15 Sep 1882 in Persia, Cattaraugus Co, NY (Year ??)[900]. She married (1) ASAHEL 'ASA' LOOP Abt. 1845. He was born Abt. 1822 in New York. She married (2) ALFRED PURDY Bet. 1860 - 1870 in Cattaraugus County, New York. He was born Abt. 1810 in Vermont[901], and died Bet. 1875 - 1880 in Leon,

Cattaraugus County, New York.

In 1850 Cordelia was married to Asahel Loop and living in Dodge County, Wisconsin with Asahel and Eliza Jane Loop, 1 yr old daughter..

In 1860 Cordelia was back in Leon, Cattaraugus County, NY using her maiden name, with daughter, Leda J. Milks, age 11 yrs, living with the Alfred Purdy family.

In 1870 Cordelia was married to Alfred Purdy and living in Leon, along with her dau. Alida.

She is buried in Milks Cemetery, Town of Persia, Cattaraugus Co, NY

Child of CORDELIA MILKS and ASAHEL LOOP is:
- 742. i. ELIZA JANE 'ALIDA'[8] LOOP, b. 1848, Hubbard, Dodge County, Wisconsin; d. 1924, Carrollton, Cattaraugus County, New York.

289. GARRETT T.[7] MILKS *(BENJAMIN[6], JONATHAN[5] MILK, JONATHAN[4], JOB[3], JOHN[2], JOHN[1])* was born 27 Jul 1828 in Cattaraugus County, New York[902], and died 23 Nov 1907 in Persia, Cattaraugus County, New York[902]. He married (1) MARY ANN HOWARD[903] Abt. 1853. She was born 16 Mar 1836[904,905], and died 07 Aug 1865 in Persia, Cattaraugus Co, NY[905]. He married (2) MARIA KENYON[906] 1870 in Cattaraugus County, New York[907], daughter of MERRITT KENYON and LOUISA FULLER. She was born 20 Jun 1842 in Washington County, New York[908], and died 22 Dec 1922 in Persia, Cattaraugus County, New York[908]. Garrett and Mary Ann are buried in Milks Cemetery, Town of Persia, Cattaraugus Co, NY. In 1920, Maria was living with Freeman and Emogene Milks, and listed as Mother-in-law.

Children of GARRETT MILKS and MARY HOWARD are:
- 743. i. GEORGE HENRY[8] MILKS, b. 1854, Persia, Cattaraugus Co., NY; d. Bef. 05 May 1913.
  - ii. EDSON MILKS[909,910], b. 1856, Persia, Cattaraugus County, New York[911]; d. 07 Jan 1950, Cattaraugus Co, NY; m. (1) MARY HURD, Abt. 1904, Cattaraugus County, New York[912]; b. 16 May 1856, Napoli, Cattaraugus Co, NY; d. 26 Dec 1920, S. Dayton, NY; m. (2) GERTRUDE LANEY (SHELDON) JOHNSTON[913], 18 Oct 1925, Buffalo, New York[914]; b. 27 Sep 1874, Napoli, Cattaraugus Co, NY; d. 26 Sep 1961, Cattaraugus County, New York. Edson had no children.
    Edson is buried in Snyders Corner Cemetery (Milks Cemetery) Persia, Catt. Co, NY Gertrude is buried in Treat Memorial Cemetery, Leon, Cattaraugus County, New York
  - iii. FREEMAN R. MILKS[915], b. Sep 1858, Cattaraugus County, New York[916,917,918]; d. 1946, Persia, Cattaraugus Co, NY[919]; m. EMOGENE HILLEBERT[920], Abt. 1904, Cattaraugus County, New York; b. Nov 1867, New York[921,922]; d. 1946, Persia, Cattaraugus Co, NY[923]. No children. They are buried in Milks Cemetery, Town of Persia, Cattaraugus Co, NY
- 744. iv. ALEDA MILKS, b. 11 Jul 1860, Persia, Cattaraugus County, New York; d. 13 Oct 1955, Los Angeles, Calif.
  - v. JOHN LAVERN MILKS[923], b. 19 Jul 1865[923,924]; d. 02 Feb 1890, Persia, Cattaraugus Co, NY[925,926].
    from **"Death Notices 1819-1899"** *Fredonia Censor*, vol II, p370 by Lois Barris 1994.
    "Milks, John Lavern d: 1 Feb 1890, murdered by his brother, George Henry, during a quarrel in the Southern part of the town of Persia. George was arrested and taken to Gowanda. "John was shot by his brother George H. Milks. (at the home of their father in Gowanda) He is buried in Milks Cemetery, Town of Persia, Cattaraugus Co, NY

Children of GARRETT MILKS and MARIA KENYON are:
- 745. vi. DELPHINE[8] MILKS, b. 18 Oct 1871, Persia, Cattaraugus County, New York; d. 1920, Randolph, Cattaraugus County, New York.
- 746. vii. JOANNAH DAISY MILKS, b. 22 Jul 1879, Persia, Cattaraugus County, New York.

290. JOANNA IRENE[7] MILKS *(BENJAMIN[6], JONATHAN[5] MILK, JONATHAN[4], JOB[3], JOHN[2], JOHN[1])* was born Abt. 1834 in Cattaraugus County, New York[927]. She married AARON ALLEN Abt. 1850. He was born Abt. 1835 in Ohio, and died 26 Jun 1865. Military service: Bet. 24 Aug 1864 - 26 Jun 1865, Private, Co. 2, 29th Wisconsin Infantry (died in service)

After her husband, Aaron Allen, died from disease while serving in the Civil War, Joanna returned to Cattaraugus County, New York and was forced to split up her children. Her oldest son, Gilbert Wallace apparently chose to stay in Wisconsin, where he is shown in Clark County in the 1870 census. In 1870, Joanna was living with the Reuben Ross family in Dayton, Cattaraugus County. Her oldest daughter, Harriet (Hattie) was living with the Cyrus Fuller family, also in Dayton. In 1870 Rose also lived in Dayton, Cattaraugus County with her uncle Freeman Milks and her grandmother, Alida. However she returned to Wisconsin and married Arthur Miles there in 1874.

Children of JOANNA MILKS and AARON ALLEN are:
747.   i.   GILBERT WALLACE[8] ALLEN, b. Abt. 1851, Wisconsin.
        ii.   HARRIETT ALLEN, b. Abt. 1853, Wisconsin.
748.   iii. ROSALIE 'ROSE' ALLEN, b. Feb 1858, Wisconsin; d. 1928, Loyal, Clark County, Wisconsin.
        iv.   CHARLES ALLEN, b. Abt. 1859, Wisconsin.

291. DEBORAH[7] MILKS (BENJAMIN[6], JONATHAN[5] MILK, JONATHAN[4], JOB[3], JOHN[2], JOHN[1]) was born Aug 1836 in Cattaraugus County, New York, and died Bet. 1920 - 1930 in Cattaraugus County, New York. She married (1) CYRUS HEWITT FULLER Abt. 1855, son of HENRY FULLER and BETSEY ELY. He was born 07 May 1833 in Shelburne, Chittenden County, Vermont[928], and died 15 Nov 1881 in Dayton, Cattaraugus County, New York[928]. She married (2) MITCHEL SMITH 1891 in Cattaraugus County, New York[929]. He was born Abt. 1839 in New York[930], and died Bet. 1900 - 1910 in Cattaraugus County, New York. Cyrus is buried in Park Lawn Cemetery, Village of Wesley, Cattaraugus County, New York.

Children of DEBORAH MILKS and CYRUS FULLER are:
        i.   WILSON D.[8] FULLER, b. 1856, Dayton, Cattaraugus County, New York.
              Burial: Liberty Park Cemetery, Cattaraugus, Cattaraugus County, New York
749.   ii.   S. JACKSON FULLER, b. Oct 1861, Dayton, Cattaraugus County, New York; d. 1925, Cattaraugus County, New York.
        iii. CHARLES F. FULLER, b. 1862, Dayton, Cattaraugus County, New York.

292. GILBERT[7] MILKS (BENJAMIN[6], JONATHAN[5] MILK, JONATHAN[4], JOB[3], JOHN[2], JOHN[1]) was born Mar 1838 in Cattaraugus County, New York, and died 23 Feb 1911 in New Albion, Cattaraugus County, New York. He married CLARISSA PAYNE, daughter of DOROUS PAYNE and CATHERINE SMITH. She was born 1848, and died 1909.
    Gilbert was Supervisor of the Town of New Albion, Cattaraugus County, New York in 1877.

Children of GILBERT MILKS and CLARISSA PAYNE are:
750.   i.   HERBERT[8] ROLFE, b. 06 Sep 1867, Perrysburg, Cattaraugus County, New York (adopted son); d. 10 Jun 1944, Randolph, Cattaraugus County, New York.
        ii.   BLANCHE ROLFE, b. 1872, New York (adopted dau.).

293. JONATHAN B. "TIP"[7] MILKS (PRINCE WILLIAM[6], JONATHAN[5] MILK, JONATHAN[4], JOB[3], JOHN[2], JOHN[1])[932] was born 17 Nov 1829[933], and died 17 Apr 1891 in New Albion, Cattaraugus County, New York[933]. He married (1) MARY CARTER[934] Abt. 1850. She was born Abt. 1830. He married (2) JENNIE BAKER/BECKER[934,935] Abt. 1879. She was born 27 Sep 1851[935], and died 23 Feb 1937 in New Albion, Cattaraugus County, New York[935]. Jonathan and Jennie are buried in Tug Hill Cemetery, New Albion, Cattaraugus Co, NY   Jonathan was a Money Lender.

Child of JONATHAN MILKS and MARY CARTER is:
        i.   MARY MARIA[8] MILKS[938].

Child of JONATHAN MILKS and JENNIE BAKER/BECKER is:
        ii.   HORTON CHESTER[8] MILKS[939,940], b. 10 Dec 1880, Cattaraugus County, New York[941]; d. 07 Mar 1954, Warsaw, Wyoming County, New York[941]; m. JOHANNA C. _____[942], Bet. 1904 - 1905, New York[942]; b. Bet. 1878 - 1879, New York[942].
              Burial: Liberty Park Cemetery, Village of Cattaraugus, Cattaraugus Co, NY. Lived in: 1920, Town of Geneseo, Livingston Co., NY. Military service: Served in WWI Occupation: 1930, President - State Bank, Avon, Livingston County, NY.

294. LUTHER P.[7] MILKS (PRINCE WILLIAM[6], JONATHAN[5] MILK, JONATHAN[4], JOB[3], JOHN[2], JOHN[1]) was born 16 Oct 1831 in Cardiff, Onondaga Co, New York[943], and died 26 Feb 1893 in Napoli, Cattaraugus County, New York[943]. He married MARY ANN WILLIAMS 22 Nov 1859, daughter of DAVIS WILLIAMS and JUNE _____. She was born 23 Jul 1839 in Leon, Cattaraugus County, New York, and died 03 Dec 1893 in Napoli, Cattaraugus Co, New York. They are buried in Hoxie Farm 'Cemetery', Napoli, Cattaraugus County, New York

Children of LUTHER MILKS and MARY WILLIAMS are:
- 751. i. ABBIE J.[8] MILKS, b. 20 May 1861, Napoli, Cattaraugus County, New York; d. 1945, Erie, Pennsylvania.
- 752. ii. ARCHIE B. MILKS, b. 17 Feb 1867, Napoli, Cattaraugus County, New York; d. 20 May 1930, East Randolph, Cattaraugus County, New York.
- 753. iii. WILLIAM A. MILKS, b. 10 Jun 1872, New York; d. 04 Feb 1920, East Randolph, Cattaraugus County, New York.
- iv. OLIN R. MILKS, b. 21 Apr 1881[944]; d. 15 Apr 1966, E. Randolph, Cattaraugus Co., NY (unmarried)[945]. Olin contributed many records of his family. Burial: East Randolph Cemetery (NW Section), Cattaraugus County, New York

295. MARY ELIZABETH[7] MILKS *(PRINCE WILLIAM[6], JONATHAN[5] MILK, JONATHAN[4], JOB[3], JOHN[2], JOHN[1])* was born Nov 1839 in Cardiff, Onondaga Co., New York, and died 07 Jan 1902 in New Albion, New York. She married JAMES M. LYON Abt. 1855 in Cattaraugus County, New York?. He was born 1834 in Cattaraugus Co., NY, and died 1907 in Fairbank, Iowa. They are buried in Tug Hill Cemetery, New Albion, Cattaraugus County, New York

Children of MARY MILKS and JAMES LYON are:
- 754. i. MARY ELIZABETH[8] LYON, b. 1856, Cattaraugus Co., NY; d. 1918.
- 755. ii. JAMES B. LYON, b. 04 Jun 1858, Cattaraugus Co., NY; d. Apr 1924, Fairbank, Iowa.
- 756. iii. CHARLES H. LYON, b. 02 Aug 1860, Cattaraugus Co., NY; d. Jun 1912.
- 757. iv. JESSE LYON, b. 11 Nov 1862, Cattaraugus Co., NY; d. 29 Nov 1914, Fairbank, Iowa.
- 758. v. NORA R. LYON, b. 03 Aug 1867, Cattaraugus Co., NY; d. 24 Apr 1917.
- 759. vi. PRINCE ARTHUR "TIMOTHY" LYON, b. Jun 1874, Fairbank, Iowa; d. 1926, Steamburg, Cattaraugus County, New York.

296. MINA FRANCES[7] MILKS *(PRINCE WILLIAM[6], JONATHAN[5] MILK, JONATHAN[4], JOB[3], JOHN[2], JOHN[1])*[946,947] was born 22 Feb 1842[948], and died 01 Jan 1921 in New Albion, Cattaraugus Co, NY[948]. She married (1) MISTTER KENYON. He was born Abt. 1842. She married (2) MISTTER WHITCAER?. He was born Abt. 1842. She married (3) CLARENDON DAY 13 Mar 1899 in McKean County, Pennsylvania. He was born Abt. 1842. Mina is buried in Tug Hill Cemetery, New Albion, Cattaraugus Co, NY

Child of MINA MILKS and MISTTER KENYON is:
- i. ALBERT G.[8] KENYON.

297. CAROLINE P.[7] SEELEY *(BATHSHEBA[6] MILKS, JONATHAN[5] MILK, JONATHAN[4], JOB[3], JOHN[2], JOHN[1])* was born 20 Sep 1829 in Cattaraugus Co., New York [date ?? 1835-1837][949,950], and died 08 Oct 1913 in Ainsworth, Brown County, Nebraska[950]. She married (1) JOHN BRADY BOTHWELL 17 Jan 1849 in Dubuque, Dubuque County, Iowa[951]. He was born 12 Jun 1805 in Scotland/Pennsylvania [date: 1809-1814][952], and died 04 Jan 1892[953]. She married (2) ALLEN B. CAPWELL 1895[954] son of John G. Capwell. He was born Feb 1835 in Rhode Island or New York, and died Bet. 1900 - 1910 in Nebraska. Caroline is buried in Ainsworth Cemetery, Brown County, Nebraska. Number of Children (Facts: 1900, 10 children, 5 living. John Brady Bothwell was a Mexican War Veteran. He is buried in Lincoln Township Cemetery, Harlan, Shelby County, IA.

Children of CAROLINE SEELEY and JOHN BOTHWELL are:
- i. CORA[8] BOTHWELL, d. d.y..
- ii. HORACE BOTHWELL, d. d.y..
- 760. iii. MARY E. BOTHWELL, b. 1849, Jones County, Iowa; d. Abt. 1939, Harlan, Iowa.
- 761. iv. CAROLINE A. BOTHWELL, b. 1851, Jones County, Iowa.
- 762. v. FLORA J. BOTHWELL, b. 1857, Jones County, Iowa.
- 763. vi. JOHN J. BOTHWELL, b. 1859, Jones County, Iowa.
- 764. vii. LYDIA ZERUIE 'ADA' BOTHWELL, b. 15 Dec 1865, Olin, Jones County, Iowa; d. 14 Mar 1935, McGraw, Cortland County, New York.
- 762. viii. GEORGE GRANT BOTHWELL, b. 1867, Jones County, Iowa.
- ix. JOSEPHINE 'JOSIE' BOTHWELL, b. Dec 1869, Rome, Jones County, Iowa; d. D. aged 10 yrs.

298. ZERUAH[7] MILKS *(JONATHAN[6], JONATHAN[5] MILK, JONATHAN[4], JOB[3], JOHN[2], JOHN[1])* was born 1831 in Dayton, Cattaraugus County, New York. She married PETER BACON. He was born Abt. 1830.

Children of ZERUAH MILKS and PETER BACON are:
766. i. LUCIUS[8] BACON, b. 1855, Chautauqua County, New York; d. 14 Apr 1888, Napoli, Cattaraugus County, New York.
  ii. ALBERT BACON, d. d.y..
  iii. FRANCIS BACON, d. d.y..

299. LYDIA A.[7] MILKS *(JONATHAN[6], JONATHAN[5] MILK, JONATHAN[4], JOB[3], JOHN[2], JOHN[1])* was born Abt. 1832 in Dayton, Cattaraugus County, New York. She married HIRAM BENTLEY. He was born Abt. 1828 in Ellington, Chautauqua County, New York. Hiram served during the Civil War between 1864 - 06 Jun 1865, Albany, New York.

Children of LYDIA MILKS and HIRAM BENTLEY are:
767. i. DEFOREST[8] BENTLEY, b. 26 Feb 1854, Ellington, Chautauqua County, New York; d. 31 Dec 1922, Wichita Falls, Wichita County, Texas.
  ii. NELLIE BENTLEY, b. Abt. 1856, Ellington, Chautauqua County, New York.
  iii. WILLIAM 'WILLIE' BENTLEY, b. 1859, Ellington, Chautauqua County, New York.

300. ESTHER J.[7] MILKS *(JONATHAN[6], JONATHAN[5] MILK, JONATHAN[4], JOB[3], JOHN[2], JOHN[1])* was born 1847 in Dayton, Cattaraugus County, New York. She married MISTTER BARNES. He was born Abt. 1847.

Child of ESTHER MILKS and MISTTER BARNES is:
  i. IONE[8] BARNES, m. MISTTER MAY.

301. ZELLA L.[7] MILKS *(JONATHAN[6], JONATHAN[5] MILK, JONATHAN[4], JOB[3], JOHN[2], JOHN[1])* was born 06 Mar 1875 in Chautauqua County, New York[955], and died 22 Nov 1944 in San Diego, California[955]. She married CHARLES H. WOOD 1894 in Chautauqua County, New York[956]. He was born Mar 1872 in New York.

Child of ZELLA MILKS and CHARLES WOOD is:
  i. ESTHER[8] WOOD, b. 27 Jun 1894, Chautauqua County, New York; d. 27 Apr 1984, San Diego, California; m. MISTTER PEARSON[957].

302. MARY JANE[7] BENSON *(SARAH[6] MILKS, JONATHAN[5] MILK, JONATHAN[4], JOB[3], JOHN[2], JOHN[1])* was born 24 Dec 1831 in Cattaraugus County, New York, and died 17 Dec 1856 in Morris, Grundy County, Illinois. She married ORRIN SATTERLEE Abt. 1850, son of AARON SATTERLEE. He was born 1827 in New York. Mary Jane is buried in White Cemetery, Grundy County, Illinois

Children of MARY BENSON and ORRIN SATTERLEE are:
768. i. GEORGE W.[8] SATTERLEE, b. 16 Feb 1852, Grundy County, Illinois; d. 16 Sep 1911, Elk County, Kansas.
  ii. BENJAMIN SATTERLEE, b. 01 Dec 1854, Grundy County, Illinois; d. 11 Nov 1856, Grundy County, Illinois.

303. LYDIA[7] BENSON *(SARAH[6] MILKS, JONATHAN[5] MILK, JONATHAN[4], JOB[3], JOHN[2], JOHN[1])* was born 07 May 1833 in Cattaraugus County, New York, and died 04 Sep 1915 in Grundy County, Illinois. She married WILLIAM WHITE 23 Jun 1850 in Morris, Grundy County, Illinois[958], son of WILLIAM WHITE and MARY _____. He was born 27 Jan 1822 in Marietta, Ohio, and died 18 Feb 1909 in Grundy County, Illinois. Lydia is buried in Evergreen Cemetery, Morris, Grundy County, Illinois
William White is buried in White Cemetery, Grundy County, Illinois

Children of LYDIA BENSON and WILLIAM WHITE are:
769. i. MARY[8] WHITE, b. Jul 1852, Grundy County, Illinois.
770. ii. SARAH WHITE, b. 25 Jun 1854, Grundy County, Illinois; d. 01 Mar 1934, Kansas.
771. iii. CHARLES WHITE, b. 1856, Grundy County, Illinois; d. Kansas.
  iv. JANE ELIZABETH WHITE, b. 1858, Grundy County, Illinois; m. CHARLES PERRY. No children.
  v. GEORGE WHITE, b. 07 Oct 1860, Grundy County, Illinois; d. 14 Oct 1861, Grundy County, Illinois.

	vi.	WILLIAM H. WHITE, b. 12 Nov 1864, Grundy County, Illinois (Date??); d. 23 Dec 1916, Unmarried.
	vii.	ANGIE WHITE, b. 16 Apr 1865, Grundy County, Illinois; d. 04 Dec 1865, Grundy County, Illinois.
772.	viii.	LYDIA WHITE, b. 18 Dec 1867, Grundy County, Illinois; d. 1945, Morris, Illinois.
	ix.	MARGARET I. WHITE, b. 11 Feb 1871, Grundy County, Illinois; m. (1) LOUIS CHITTICK; b. Abt. 1870; m. (2) ORVIL O. PETERS; b. 1880; d. 1940. They lived in Chicago. No children.
	x.	JOHN FRANKLIN WHITE, b. 11 Feb 1871, Grundy County, Illinois; d. 12 Mar 1927, Unmarried.

304. RUTH^7 BENSON *(SARAH^6 MILKS, JONATHAN^5 MILK, JONATHAN^4, JOB^3, JOHN^2, JOHN^1)* was born 05 Jun 1839 in Cattaraugus County, New York, and died 21 Jun 1888 in Felix Twp, Grundy County, Illinois. She married LAWRENCE JAMES WHITE, son of WILLIAM WHITE and MARY _____. He was born 07 Jun 1814 in Marietta, Ohio, and died 27 May 1906 in Grundy County, Illinois.

Children of RUTH BENSON and LAWRENCE WHITE are:

773.	i.	WILLIAM J.^{8} WHITE, b. 23 Feb 1855, Grundy County, Illinois; d. 27 May 1937, Morris, Grundy County, Illinois.
774.	ii.	CAROLINE WHITE, b. 25 Feb 1858, Grundy County, Illinois; d. 04 Nov 1930.
775.	iii.	ALMIRA D. WHITE, b. 12 Feb 1861, Grundy County, Illinois; d. 28 Dec 1931, Morris, Grundy County, Illinois.
776.	iv.	SUSAN LINDSEY WHITE, b. 07 Sep 1864, Grundy County, Illinois; d. 01 Mar 1944, Morris, Grundy County, Illinois.
777.	v.	SAMUEL HOLDERMAN WHITE, b. 07 Apr 1866, Grundy County, Illinois; d. 12 Dec 1945, Morris, Grundy County, Illinois.
	vi.	MARY ISABELLE WHITE, b. 09 Apr 1870, Grundy County, Illinois; d. 13 Apr 1950, Morris, Grundy County, Illinois; m. MIKE REDMOND, 08 Apr 1896; b. 25 Dec 1868; d. 21 Sep 1942, Morris, Grundy County, Illinois. No children.
	vii.	LUCY WHITE, b. 01 Mar 1873, Grundy County, Illinois; d. 05 Apr 1873, Grundy County, Illinois.
778.	viii.	GEORGE PERRY WHITE, b. 05 Jul 1874, Grundy County, Illinois; d. 14 Mar 1940.
	ix.	MINERVA RUTH WHITE, b. 14 Oct 1877, Grundy County, Illinois; d. no children.; m. FRANK HOWE, 17 Nov 1911; b. 17 Nov 1873, Ithaca, Wisconsin.

305. CAROLINE SARAH^7 BENSON *(SARAH^6 MILKS, JONATHAN^5 MILK, JONATHAN^4, JOB^3, JOHN^2, JOHN^1)* was born 05 Sep 1843 in Cattaraugus County, New York, and died 09 Jan 1903 in Grundy County, Illinois. She married WILLIAM MARSHALL Abt. 1863, son of NOYES MARSHALL and ZILPHA RICHARDSON. He was born 25 Oct 1836 in Toledo, Ohio, and died 1902 in Grundy County, Illinois. Caroline is buried in Sample Cemetery, Grundy County, Illinois

Children of CAROLINE BENSON and WILLIAM MARSHALL are:

779.	i.	SARAH^8 MARSHALL, b. 24 Aug 1864, Grundy County, Illinois; d. 09 Aug 1941, Morris, Grundy County, Illinois.
780.	ii.	HESTER MARSHALL, b. 21 Apr 1867, Grundy County, Illinois; d. 15 Jul 1908, Morris, Grundy County, Illinois.
781.	iii.	GEORGE W. MARSHALL, b. 01 Feb 1869, Grundy County, Illinois; d. Sep 1931.
	iv.	JOHN MARSHALL, b. 08 Jan 1871, Grundy County, Illinois; d. 25 Nov 1932; m. LYDIA LYONS; b. 18 Jun 1870, Morris, Grundy County, Illinois; d. 02 Apr 1937, no children..

306. ARVILLA^7 BENSON *(SARAH^6 MILKS, JONATHAN^5 MILK, JONATHAN^4, JOB^3, JOHN^2, JOHN^1)* was born 1847 in Cattaraugus County, New York, and died 1913. She married (1) UNKNOWN.   She married (2) ANANIAS SMITH 18 Dec 1877 in Ottawa, La Salle County, Illinois[958], son of BARTIMEUS SMITH and BARBARA E. REESE. She married (3) WILLIAM COBBLER 1888[959], son of BYARD COBBLER and C. SUTTON. He was born Feb 1853 in Indiana\Illinois, and died 04 Sep 1916. In the 1910 Census, Arvilla says she was married 3 times.

Benjamin, apparently, was not a son of William Cobbler. Arvilla and William were married in 1888, according to the 1900 Federal Census. (1890 according to the 1910 census).

In the 1880 census, Benjamin is shown as 9 yrs old and a grandson of Sarah Milks Benson, but without any notation on who his parents are. Also in the 1880 census, Arvilla says she was married within the census year, but there is no information on the name of her spouse.

Child of ARVILLA BENSON and UNKNOWN is:
782.   i.   BENJAMIN J.[8] BENSON, b. 31 Aug 1870, Grundy County, Illinois.

307. JOHN MILKS[7] BENSON *(SARAH[6] MILKS, JONATHAN[5] MILK, JONATHAN[4], JOB[3], JOHN[2], JOHN[1])* was born 13 Jul 1849 in Grundy County, Illinois, and died 11 Jun 1918 in Grundy County, Illinois. He married RACHAEL OLIVIA SHAFFER 17 Nov 1881 in Oakdale, Nebraska, daughter of SAMUEL SHAFFER and MARGARET WISE. She was born 07 Aug 1863 in Mason, Illinois, and died 26 Jan 1933 in Morris, Grundy County, Illinois.

All but two years of John Milks Benson's life were spent on the homestead he inherited from his parents. These two years he lived in Antelope, Neb., near his father-in-law. John was a successful farmer, of high character, and was respected by all. His picture appears on p. 241

Hist. Encyclopedia of Ill. & Hist. of Grundy Co., p. 764, gives this account:
"John Milks Benson, one of Grundy County's substantial and representative men, is owner and proprietor of a somewhat famous tract of land in Wauponsee Township, known as the Fossil Bed Farm, this name being applied on account of a fossil bed found there that has interested scientists for years."

These fossils contain the imprints of tree- and shrub-like ferns (frond, tongue, coned, and calamite type), the bark of scale trees, jointed rush, and worms, and are found in a confined area along the banks and on the floor of the Mazon Creek which divides the Benson farm. They represent some of the early historical documents of life's beginnings in ancient Illinois, some 100 million years ago. And as one might expect, other remnants of the Carboniferous Age are to be found on the Benson property; coal lies under the surface of much of the ground. At one time a coal mine was opened on the farm, but John Milks Benson, visualizing the resultant debris, railroads, and strangers desecrating his "good earth", had the mine closed.

Children of JOHN BENSON and RACHAEL SHAFFER are:
783.   i.   JOHN RIAL[8] BENSON, b. 04 Jan 1883, Grundy County, Illinois; d. 29 Dec 1954, Morris, Grundy County, Illinois.
784.   ii. GRACE MAE BENSON, b. 30 Dec 1885, Grundy County, Illinois; d. 17 Feb 1952, Pasadena, California.
       iii. MAUDIE BELLE BENSON, b. 1887, Antelope, Nebraska; d. 1887, Antelope, Nebraska.
       iv. MABEL MARY BENSON, b. 1889, Morris, Grundy County, Illinois; d. 1889, Morris, Grundy County, Illinois.
785.   v.   ROY EDWARD BENSON, b. 22 Mar 1891, Grundy County, Illinois; d. 06 Apr 1955, Morris, Grundy County, Illinois.
786.   vi. MYRTLE OLIVIA BENSON, b. 27 Feb 1894, Pine Grove, Grundy County, Illinois; d. 30 Apr 1966, Morris, Grundy County, Illinois.
       vii. EVELYN ELSIE BENSON, b. 02 Oct 1896, Grundy County, Illinois; d. 08 Feb 1957, Morris, Grundy County, Illinois (no children); m. (1) HERBERT E. CLAYTON; b. 1895, Coal City, Illinois; d. 14 Jul 1934, Morris, Grundy County, Illinois; m. (2) LEO ALOYSIUS A'HERN; b. 11 Oct 1892, Morris, Grundy County, Illinois; d. Oct 1965, Morris, Grundy County, Illinois. Evelyn, Herbert, and Leo are buried in Evergreen Cemetery, Morris, Grundy County, Illinois
       Evelyn was a Beautician. Leo was a Sheet Metal Contractor
787.   viii. CLARENCE EUGENE BENSON, b. 08 Jan 1900, Grundy County, Illinois.
788.   ix. EFFIE ADELLA BENSON, b. 24 Nov 1904, Grundy County, Illinois.
789.   x.   FRED ERNEST BENSON, b. 14 Feb 1907, Grundy County, Illinois.
790.   xi. ADELBERT THEODORE BENSON, b. 27 Mar 1910, Grundy County, Illinois.

308. NANCY MARIA[7] MILKS *(LUKE[6] MILK, JONATHAN[5], JONATHAN[4], JOB[3], JOHN[2], JOHN[1])* was born 18 Feb 1833 in Dayton, Cattaraugus County, New York[960], and died 1912 in Maynard, Fayette County, Iowa[960]. She married JULIUS CAESAR RANNEY 29 Aug 1849 in Cattaraugus County, New York, son of ELI RANNEY and EVALINE PARMALEE. He was born 20 Feb 1829 in Augusta, Oneida County, New York[960], and died 09 May 1906 in Maynard, Fayette County, Iowa[960,961]. They are buried in Long Grove Cemetery, Maynard, Fayette County, Iowa

Children of NANCY MILKS and JULIUS RANNEY are:
791.   i.   LUKE WINFIELD[8] RANNEY, b. 30 Jul 1850, Perrysburg, Cattaraugus County, New York; d. 01 Oct 1916, Humbolt, Iowa.
792.   ii. NATHAN AMES RANNEY, b. 27 Aug 1853, Perrysburg, Cattaraugus County, New York; d. 03 May 1925, Glasgow, Montana.

	iii.	BENJAMIN FRANKLIN RANNEY, b. 07 Apr 1856, Cattaraugus County, New York[962]; d. 07 Mar 1884, Maynard, Fayette County, Iowa[962]. Benjamin is buried with his parents and is shown on the same gravestone, which probably means he was not married.
793.	iv.	ALFRED HERRICK RANNEY, b. 03 Oct 1858, Perrysburg, Cattaraugus County, New York; d. 30 Sep 1934, Cerro Gordo County, Iowa.
	v.	HENRY B. RANNEY, b. 21 Apr 1861, Cattaraugus County, New York; d. 1865, Cattaraugus County, New York.
794.	vi.	HERMAN RANNEY, b. 08 Jul 1863, Cattaraugus County, New York; d. 12 Jun 1919, Maynard, Fayette County, Iowa.
795.	vii.	EVALINE SALOME RANNEY, b. 22 Nov 1867, Pennsylvania; d. Bet. 1910 - 1918, South Dakota.
796.	viii.	JUSTIN WARREN RANNEY, b. 08 Dec 1870, Fairbank, Black Hawk County, Iowa; d. 28 Apr 1941, Maynard, Fayette County, Iowa.

309. BENJAMIN FRANKLIN[7] MILKS *(LUKE[6] MILK, JONATHAN[5], JONATHAN[4], JOB[3], JOHN[2], JOHN[1])* was born 25 Jan 1835 in Dayton, Cattaraugus County, New York[962], and died 17 Apr 1904 in Black Hawk County, Iowa[962]. He married ORINDA LAWRENCE in New York, daughter of HIRAM LAWRENCE. She was born 03 Sep 1839 in Michigan, and died 04 Jul 1928 in Black Hawk County, Iowa. Benjamin is buried in Fairbank Cemetery, Buchanan County, Iowa.

Land Owners 1887: LESTER TOWNSHIP, BLACK HAWK, IOWA; 1887 Land Owners Twp. 90 Range 11

		Acres	Section
MILKS	B. F.	80	2
MILKS	Luke	40	2

Children of BENJAMIN MILKS and ORINDA LAWRENCE are:

797.	i.	JENNIE[8] MILKS, b. 1857, Cattaraugus County, New York; d. 06 Jan 1946, Oelwein, Fayette County, Iowa.
798.	ii.	IDA LOUISE MILKS, b. 27 Mar 1858, Cattaraugus County, New York; d. 12 Aug 1947, Lynch, Nebraska.
799.	iii.	BUTLER WEBSTER MILKS, b. 12 Sep 1862, Black Hawk County, Iowa; d. 27 Mar 1943, Peace River, Alberta, Canada.
800.	iv.	NANCY MARIA MILKS, b. 10 May 1865, Black Hawk County, Iowa; d. 15 Aug 1913, Fairbank, Iowa.
801.	v.	RUTH ANN MILKS, b. 15 Jul 1869; d. 07 Dec 1959.
802.	vi.	THOMAS BENJAMIN MILKS, b. 26 Apr 1876, Lester Township, Black Hawk Co., Iowa; d. 07 Feb 1936, Waterloo, Iowa.

310. URSULA[7] ROGERS *(ISAAC[6], RHODA[5] CHASE, ABIGAIL[4] MILK, JOB[3], JOHN[2], JOHN[1])* was born 1810 in Rensselaer County, New York, and died 1899 in Palermo, Oswego County, New York. She married DANIEL GILMAN 1837. He was born Abt. 1810, and died 01 Oct 1864 in Jeffersonville, Indiana. Daniel served during the Civil War in Co. D., 16th Reg., U.S. Infantry, and died of Typhoid Fever while in service.

Children of URSULA ROGERS and DANIEL GILMAN are:

	i.	GEORGE[8] GILMAN, b. 1838. George also served in the same regiment as his father, during the Civil War, and also died of Typhoid Fever.
803.	ii.	MARY GILMAN, b. 14 Dec 1840, Brownville, Jefferson County, New York; d. 19 May 1929, Palermo, Oswego County, New York.
	iii.	JANE GILMAN, b. 1842; m. WILLIAM COOK; b. Abt. 1840.

311. ALZINA BIANCA[7] CHASE *(ORRIN[6], JOHN[5], ABIGAIL[4] MILK, JOB[3], JOHN[2], JOHN[1])* was born 14 Aug 1830 in Nelson, Madison County, New York[963], and died 31 Dec 1913 in Georgetown, Madison County, New York[963]. She married ABEL S. HOLMES 27 Apr 1847 in Madison County, New York. He was born 11 Jul 1818 in Hamilton, Madison County, New York[963], and died 07 Apr 1891 in Georgetown, Madison County, New York[963]. They are buried in Erieville Cemetery, Nelson, Madison County, New York

Children of ALZINA CHASE and ABEL HOLMES are:

	i.	ELLEN[8] HOLMES, b. 1847, Madison County, New York.
	ii.	CHARLES HOLMES, b. 1849, Madison County, New York.
	iii.	LOUISA/LOVINA HOLMES, b. 1851, Madison County, New York.

- iv. DANIEL HOLMES, b. 1853, Madison County, New York.
- v. GEORGE W. HOLMES, b. 15 Mar 1855, Madison County, New York[963]; d. 07 Mar 1914, Madison County, New York[963].
- vi. ANNETTE 'NETTIE' HOLMES, b. 1857, Georgetown, Madison County, New York; d. 1887, Cazenovia, Madison County, New York; m. ADOLPHUS KELLOGG; b. Abt. 1857.
- vii. SIDNEY HOLMES, b. 1859, Madison County, New York; d. 1925, Madison County, New York.
- viii. IDA R. L. HOLMES, b. 11 Oct 1859, Madison County, New York[963]; d. 05 Apr 1874, Madison County, New York[963].
- 804. ix. SULLIVAN G. HOLMES, b. 10 May 1862, Georgetown, Madison County, New York; d. Dec 1938, Newport, Herkimer County, New York.
- x. FRANK L. HOLMES, b. 1865, Madison County, New York; d. 1890, Madison County, New York.
- xi. DIOGENES D. HOLMES[963], b. 07 Nov 1868, Madison County, New York[963]; d. 10 Feb 1869, Madison County, New York[963]. Burial: Erieville Cemetery, Nelson, Madison County, New York.

312. JOHN[7] MILK, JR. *(JOHN[6], JOHN[5], JOHN[4], JOHN[3], JOHN[2], JOHN[1])* was born 14 Mar 1822 in Boston, Massachusetts[964], and died 18 Dec 1872 in Boston, Suffolk, Mass.[965]. He married MARGARET DOYLE 23 Jun 1844 in Boston, Massachusetts[966]. She was born Bet. 1826 - 1827 in Boston, Massachusetts[967], and died 24 Feb 1879 in Boston, Suffolk, Mass.[968]. Margaret was baptized, 21 April 1842, in the Baldwin Place Baptist Church of Boston, but was excluded from membership in the church.

John registered for service in the Civil War June 27, 1863, but no record that he actually served. He died of Brights Disease. He was a Copper Smith and lived at 3/4 Moon Court, Boston   Obviously, the Milk family lived in Moon Court for quite a few years, since before the Revolutionary War.

Children of JOHN MILK and MARGARET DOYLE are:
- i. MARGARET F.[8] MILK, b. 04 Aug 1848, Boston, Massachusetts[969]; d. 07 Aug 1848, Boston, Massachusetts[969].
- 805. ii. WILLIAM EDWIN MILK, b. 22 Nov 1849, Boston, Massachusetts; d. 12 Apr 1905, Boston, Suffolk, Mass..

313. HARRIET[7] MILK *(JOHN[6], JOHN[5], JOHN[4], JOHN[3], JOHN[2], JOHN[1])* was born 17 Jul 1827 in Boston, Massachusetts[970], and died 28 Apr 1907 in Boston, Mass.[971]. She married (1) JACOB F. BELL Abt. 1847 in Boston, Massachusetts. He was born Abt. 1825, and died 01 Jan 1852 in Boston, Mass.. She married (2) HENRY C. HEMMENWAY 23 Dec 1855 in Boston, Massachusetts[972], son of PETER HEMMENWAY. He was born Abt. 1830 in Boston, Massachusetts[973], and died Bef. 1907 in Boston, Mass.. Jacob was a Druggist in Boston.

Child of HARRIET MILK and JACOB BELL is:
- i. HARRIET ELIZABETH[8] BELL, b. 25 Jun 1849, Boston, Massachusetts[974]; m. RICHARD A. ATWOOD; b. 1846.

Child of HARRIET MILK and HENRY HEMMENWAY is:
- ii. HENRY CLAY[8] HEMMENWAY, b. 23 May 1859, Boston, Massachusetts[974].

314. JAMES MADISON[7] MILK *(JOHN[6], JOHN[5], JOHN[4], JOHN[3], JOHN[2], JOHN[1])* was born 14 Feb 1831 in Boston, Massachusetts[975], and died 03 Aug 1906 in Hamilton, Massachusetts[976]. He married ROSANNA DOYLE[977] 23 May 1853 in Boston, Massachusetts, daughter of ENOCH DOYLE and CATHERINE _____. She was born 1834 in Boston, Massachusetts[978], and died 21 Jan 1886 in Boston, Massachusetts[979].

James registered for service during the Civil War on June 27, 1863, and served in E. Co., 60th Massachusetts Mil., Infantry, Pvt. He was a Tinsmith in Boston, living at 3 Moon Court. He is buried in Forest Hills, Suffolk Co., Massachusetts

Children of JAMES MILK and ROSANNA DOYLE are:
- i. JAMES M.[8] MILK, b. 22 Mar 1854, Boston, Massachusetts; d. 12 Jun 1854, Boston, Massachusetts.
- 806. ii. JAMES MADISON MILK, JR., b. 03 Jun 1855, Boston, Massachusetts; d. 09 Nov 1882, Boston, Massachusetts.
- iii. SUSAN FRANCES MILK, b. 07 Jan 1859, Boston, Massachusetts[980]; d. 18 Nov 1859, Boston, Massachusetts[981].
- iv. LUCY MATILDA MILK, b. 07 Sep 1860, Boston, Massachusetts[982]; d. 20 Oct 1860, Boston, Massachusetts.

       v.   HENRY FRANKLIN MILK, b. 29 Dec 1861, Boston, Suffolk, Mass.[983]; d. 14 Sep 1862, Boston, Suffolk, Mass.[983].

807.   vi. JOHN HENRY MILK, b. 19 Jul 1864, Boston, Massachusetts.

315. ELEANOR[7] LONGLEY *(ELEANOR[6] MILK, JOHN[5], JOHN[4], JOHN[3], JOHN[2], JOHN[1])* was born 1827 in Boston, Mass.[984], and died 16 Jul 1897 in Somerville, Massachusetts[985]. She married BENJAMIN B. HARTFORD 11 Jan 1851 in Boston, Massachusetts[986], son of JOHN HARTFORD and ELIZA COWDON. He was born 1829 in Moultonboro, New Hampshire[987], and died 04 Nov 1892 in Boston, Mass.[987]. B B Hartford and Eleanor Milk were living in the same boarding house in Boston Ward 4, in the 1850 census, but were not yet married. Both ages shown as 23. Benjamin was a Produce Dealer. Eleanor is buried in Forest Hills Cemetery, Jamaica Plain, Massachusetts

Child of ELEANOR LONGLEY and BENJAMIN HARTFORD is:
       i.   CHARLES B.[8] HARTFORD, b. 1853, Boston, Suffolk County, Mass.[988]; d. 30 May 1860, Boston, Suffolk County, Mass.[989].

Generation No. 8

316. HOLDER WHITE POTTER (*DEBORAH^7 WHITE, CYNTHIA^6 MILK, LEMUEL^5, DAVID^4, JOB^3, JOHN^2, JOHN^1*) was born 1841 in Dartmouth, Bristol County, Massachusetts, and died 1922 in Dartmouth. He married SARAH A. CODDING abt. 1865. She was born 1843 in Bristol County, Massachusetts and died 24 February 1900 in Dartmouth.

Children of HOLDER WHITE POTTER and SARAH A. CODDING are::
- i. ABBIE M. POTTER, b. 1867, d. 1949
- ii. LEON C. POTTER, b. 1871

317. GEORGE MILK^8 WHITE (*HOLDER^7, CYNTHIA^6 MILK, LEMUEL^5, DAVID^4, JOB^3, JOHN^2, JOHN^1*) was born 17 Sep 1837, and died 13 Jan 1915. He married LOUISA VON BONBECQUE SMITH 06 Oct 1861 in Westport, Massachusetts. She was born 29 Dec 1841, and died 30 Apr 1937. George was a Merchant.

Child of GEORGE WHITE and LOUISA SMITH is:
- 808. i. ELIZABETH BROWNELL^9 WHITE, b. 10 Oct 1871, Westport, Massachusetts.

318. OBED H.^{8} MILK (*WILLIAM W.^{7}, WILLIAM^6, LEMUEL^5, DAVID^4, JOB^3, JOHN^2, JOHN^1*) was born 1837 in Cayuga County, New York. He married MARY _____ Abt. 1857 in Cayuga County, New York. She was born Abt. 1838 in Ireland^{990}. Obed was a Butcher.

Children of OBED MILK and MARY _____ are:
- i. MATA^9 MILK, b. 29 Nov 1857, Cayuga County, New York; d. 17 Mar 1860, Cayuga County, New York^{991}. Burial: Mount Pleasant Cemetery, Port Byron, Cayuga County, New York
- ii. HARRIET B. 'HATTIE' MILK^{992}, b. Feb 1860, Mentz, Cayuga County, New York.
- iii. IDA E. MILK, b. Mar 1868, Mentz/Port Byron, Cayuga County, New York; d. 1904, Cayuga County, NY. Never married. Burial: 09 Jun 1904, Fort Hill Cemetery, Auburn, Cayuga County, New York
- 809. iv. MARY V. MILK, b. Feb 1873, Auburn, Cayuga County, New York; d. Apr 1958, Auburn, Cayuga County, New York.

319. HARRIET^8 MILK (*WILLIAM W.^{7}, WILLIAM^6, LEMUEL^5, DAVID^4, JOB^3, JOHN^2, JOHN^1*) was born 1839 in Port Byron, Cayuga County, New York. She married AUGUSTUS KELLY Abt. 1860. He was born Abt. 1839 in Trumansburg, New York, and died 16 Jan 1906.

Augustus was nominated by the President as Postmaster at Port Byron (from the *Clyde Times*, April 26, 1888, He also was a Surveyor on the Erie Canal.

Children of HARRIET MILK and AUGUSTUS KELLY are:
- i. WILLIAM WOLFORD^9 KELLY, b. Abt. 1860, Cayuga County, New York. Residence: Detroit, Wayne County, Michigan^{993}
- 810. ii. KATHERINE ELIZABETH KELLY, b. 25 Aug 1863, Port Byron, Cayuga County, New York; d. 19 Nov 1942, Syracuse, Onondaga County, New York.

320. SILAS WRIGHT^8 MILK (*WILLIAM W.^{7}, WILLIAM^6, LEMUEL^5, DAVID^4, JOB^3, JOHN^2, JOHN^1*) was born 26 Oct 1847 in Cayuga County, New York, and died 17 Sep 1931 in Auburn, Cayuga County, New York. He married ELIZABETH 'LIBBY' HALL Abt. 1884. She was born 28 May 1858, and died 05 Jul 1895 in Auburn, Cayuga County, New York. They lived in Waldron, Kankakee County, Illinois, but they both are buried in Fort Hill Cemetery, Auburn, Cayuga County, New York, Silas in Plot: Council Ground Lot 26 Grave 13, and Elizabeth in Plot: Ridgeland Lot 40 Grave

Children of SILAS MILK and ELIZABETH HALL are:
- i. MARY ELIZABETH 'BESSIE'^{9} MILK, b. 10 Dec 1885, Waldron, Kankakee County, Illinois; d. Jan 1963^{994}. She lived in Auburn, Cayuga County, New York. Never married. Burial: Plot: Council Ground Lot 26 Grave 14, Ft. Hill Cemetery, Auburn, Cayuga County, NY
- 811. ii. CYNTHIA BLANCHE MILK, b. 10 Jan 1887, Waldron, Kankakee County, Illinois.
- iii. EMMA FRANCES MILK, b. 21 Apr 1894, Waldron, Kankakee County, Illinois; m. FREDERICK T. MURNAN;

b. Abt. 1890. Lived in: Auburn, Cayuga County, New York

321. GEORGE WASHINGTON[8] MILK *(WILLIAM W.[7], WILLIAM[6], LEMUEL[5], DAVID[4], JOB[3], JOHN[2], JOHN[1])* was born 30 Nov 1850 in Port Byron, Cayuga County, New York[995], and died 31 Mar 1926 in Kankakee, Illinois[995]. He married MARY ANN GODDARD[996] 24 Dec 1882 in Newton, Indiana[996], daughter of WILLIAM GODDARD and ELIZABETH GRAVES. She was born 07 Oct 1851 in Battleground, Tippecanoe County, Illinois[996,997], and died 16 Aug 1925 in Morocco, Indiana[997].

Children of GEORGE MILK and MARY GODDARD are:

812.	i.	LEMUEL[9] MILK, b. 29 May 1884, Clifton, Iroquois County, Illinois; d. 26 Sep 1968, Kankakee, Illinois.
813.	ii.	FAYE ELIZABETH MILK, b. 13 Aug 1888, Clifton, Illinois.
8014.	iii.	ELLA MAE MILK, b. 21 Sep 1892, Clifton, Illinois.
	iv.	GEORGIANA 'GEORGIA' WARNER MILK, b. 14 Sep 1894, Beaver Lake, Indiana; d. 1981, Morocco, Newton County, Indiana[998]; m. LLOYD EVANS PERRY, 01 Nov 1926, Chicago, Illinois; b. 07 Jul 1888, Kankakee, Illinois; d. 16 Jun 1950, Veterans' Hospital, Indianapolis, Indiana. No children. Georgiana is buried in Oakland Cemetery, Morocco, Newton County, Indiana

   LLOYD EVANS PERRY was employed by: Indiana State Highway Commission. Military service: Ill. Sgt 108 Engineers 33 Div * W W I

322. MARY ELIZA[8] COOLEY *(CYNTHIA[7] MILK, WILLIAM[6], LEMUEL[5], DAVID[4], JOB[3], JOHN[2], JOHN[1])* was born 15 Apr 1836 in Fleming, Cayuga County, New York. She married GEORGE WARREN ELLIOTT Abt. 1864. He was born 1830 in Aurelius, New York, and died 1916.

Children of MARY COOLEY and GEORGE ELLIOTT are:
   i.   MARY COOLEY[9] ELLIOTT, b. 1865; d. 1871.
   ii. HELEN ELLIOTT, b. 1072; d. 1904; m. MR. SMITH; b Abt. 1870.

323. HELEN M.[8] COOLEY *(CYNTHIA[7] MILK, WILLIAM[6], LEMUEL[5], DAVID[4], JOB[3], JOHN[2], JOHN[1])* was born 03 Mar 1838 in Fleming, Cayuga County, New York, and died 06 Apr 1920 in Auburn, Cayuga County, New York. She married JONATHAN SQUIRE MANRO 1857 in Cayuga County, New York, son of PHILIP MANRO and SIBEL ROBERTS. He was born 10 Aug 1821 in Throop, Cayuga County, New York, and died 19 Jun 1890 in Auburn, Cayuga County, New York.
OBITUARY: Auburn, New York, *The Weekly Bulletin newspaper*, Thursday, June 19, 1890, Page 5, Column 1
   DEATH OF JONATHAN S. MANRO
   Passing Away Quietly At an Early Hour This Morning.
   Jonathan S. Manro died at his home, No. 6 McMaster street, an en early hour this morning. Mr. Manro had been sick for about a month, but the announcement of his death will be a surprise to many friends. The deceased was born about one mile west of Throopsville on the old Manro homestead, August 10th, 1821, and the whole of his life has been spent on the farm. He afterwards became engaged in the manufacture of woolen yarns and conducted that business in this city and in Seneca Falls. During the past seven years he has resided in McMaster street and for that time has been the senior member of the firm of Manro & Hugg, coal dealers. Besides his wife, who survives him, the immediate members of his family now living are Thomas J. Manro of this city, his brother, and Mary M. Harlow, Betsey L. Atwater and Cynthia H. Benham of his city, his sisters, Fred J. and Charles H. Manro of this city, sons, Mrs. Asa R. Barnes of this city and Mrs. Jennie M. Eldredge of North Fair Haven, daughters. Mr. Manro was a highly respected citizen and his bereaved family will have the sympathy of the community in their sorrow.
 Burial: Fort Hill Cemetery, Auburn, Cayuga County, New York, Plot: Linden View Lot 25-26 Grave 4

Children of HELEN COOLEY and JONATHAN MANRO are:

	i.	HELEN[9] MANRO, b. 03 Nov 1858, Throop, Cayuga County, New York[998]; d. 05 Mar 1859, Throup, Cayuga County, New York[998].
815.	ii.	ELIZABETH COOLEY MANRO, b. 30 Sep 1860, Auburn, Cayuga County, New York; d. 18 Jun 1927, Auburn, Cayuga County, New York.
816.	iii.	FRED JONATHAN MANRO, b. 10 Oct 1863, Aurelius, Cayuga County, New York; d. 03 Jun 1942, Auburn, Cayuga County, New York.
817.	iv.	JENNIE BELL MANRO, b. 17 Sep 1866, Throop, Cayuga County, New York; d. 18 Feb 1962, Auburn, Cayuga County, New York.
818.	v.	CHARLES HENRY MANRO, b. 1871, Throop, Cayuga County, New York; d. 1934.

324. LOUISE CAROLINE[8] MILK *(CHARLES G.[7], WILLIAM[6], LEMUEL[5], DAVID[4], JOB[3], JOHN[2], JOHN[1])* was born 08 Jul 1842 in Seneca Falls, Seneca County, New York[998], and died 04 Aug 1880 in Cayuga County, New York[998]. She married JOHN DIXON ROBINSON[999] Abt. 1868 in New York, son of JAMES ROBINSON and EVALINA DIXON. He was born 03 Jan 1841 in Sennett, Cayuga County, New York[1000,1001], and died 10 May 1908 in Auburn, Cayuga County, New York[1002]. They are buried in Soule Cemetery, Sennett, Cayuga County,NY[1002]

John was a farmer and enlisted at Sennett, New York on 6 August 1862 as a Corporal, in Co. I, New York 9th Heavy Artillery Regiment. He was promoted to 2nd Lieutenant on March 1, 1865 and mustered out on July 6, 1865 as a 1st Lieutenant; Co.D 143rd Regiment 9th New York.

Children of LOUISE MILK and JOHN ROBINSON are:
- i. LENA M.[9] ROBINSON, b. 1870, Virginia.
- ii. GUY CHARLES ROBINSON, b. 1873, Cayuga County, New York; d. 1892, Cayuga County, New York.
- 819. iii. ADELLE 'DELLA' ROBINSON, b. 1874, Cayuga County, New York; d. 1934.

325. AUGUSTA FRANCES[8] MILK *(CHARLES G.[7], WILLIAM[6], LEMUEL[5], DAVID[4], JOB[3], JOHN[2], JOHN[1])*[1004] was born 1844 in Seneca Falls, Seneca County, New York[1005], and died Oct 1916 in Cayuga County, New York[1006]. She married CHARLES F. GUION[1007] 03 Dec 1862 in Cayuga County, New York[1008,1009]. He was born Dec 1837 in Connecticut[1010], and died Feb 1920 in Cayuga County, New York[1011]. They were members of the St. Peters Episcopal Church. They are buried in Fort Hill Cemetery, Auburn, Cayuga County, New York   Charles was a Sash and Blind Manufacturer.

Augusta's sisters, Ella and Emma were living with Augusta and Charles Guion in 1870. Their mother had died in 1864 and their father had just died in Apr 1870.

Children of AUGUSTA MILK and CHARLES GUION are:
- 820. i. FRANCES A.[9] GUION, b. Feb 1866, Auburn, Cayuga County, New York.
- ii. ELLA GERTRUDE GUION, b. May 1870, Auburn, Cayuga County, New York.
- 821. iii. ELIZABETH IVES GUION, b. 29 Sep 1875, Auburn, Cayuga County, New York; d. Dec 1969, Auburn, Cayuga County, New York.

326. ELLA[8] MILK *(CHARLES G.[7], WILLIAM[6], LEMUEL[5], DAVID[4], JOB[3], JOHN[2], JOHN[1])* was born 1849 in Seneca Falls, Seneca County, New York, and died 1872 in Auburn, Cayuga County, New York. She married CHARLES SHULINGBARGER[1012]. He was born in Of Chicago, Illinois. Ella is buried in Fort Hill Cemetery, Auburn, Cayuga County, New York [Plot: Glen Alpine Lot 17 Grave 3]

Child of ELLA MILK and CHARLES SHULINGBARGER is:
- i. GERTRUDE AUGUSTA[9] SHULINGBARGER, b. 1872, Auburn, Cayuga County, New York; d. 1872, Auburn, Cayuga County, New York. Burial: Fort Hill Cemetery, Auburn, Cayuga County, New York [Plot: Glen Alpine Lot 17 Grave 3]

327. JENNIE MINERVA[8] MILK *(LEMUEL[7], WILLIAM[6], LEMUEL[5], DAVID[4], JOB[3], JOHN[2], JOHN[1])* was born 05 Jun 1855 in Kankakee, Illinois, and died 09 Sep 1939 in Prob. at Conrad, Indiana. She married GEORGE EDWARD CONRAD[1013], son of ANSOR CONRAD and MARY _____. He was born Abt. 1838 in Ithaca, New York[1013]. Jennie is buried in Mound Grove Cemetery, Kankakee, Illinois

Child of JENNIE MILK and GEORGE CONRAD is:
- i. PLATT MILK[9] CONRAD[1013], b. 22 Mar 1880, Chicago, Cook County, Illinois[1013]. Never married.

325. MARY SHERWOOD[8] MILK *(LEMUEL[7], WILLIAM[6], LEMUEL[5], DAVID[4], JOB[3], JOHN[2], JOHN[1])*[1014] was born 17 Jul 1888 in Kankakee, Illinois[1015], and died Apr 1978 in Silver Spring, Montgomery, Maryland[1015]. She married HUBERT CRAMPTON BARTON 10 Mar 1909 in Amherst, Massachusetts[1016], son of GEORGE BARTON and LUCY NICHOLS. He was born 04 Feb 1887 in Chicago, Illinois, and died 18 May 1957 in Alexandria, Virginia[1017]. They lived in Alexandria, Virginia. Hubert was a Federal Consultant in Washington, D. C.

Children of MARY MILK and HUBERT BARTON are:
- 822. i. HUBERT CRAMPTON[9] BARTON, b. 12 Jan 1910, Chicago, Illinois; d. Jul 1985, San Juan, Puerto Rico.
- ii. SHERWOOD MILK BARTON, b. 02 Apr 1911[1018]; d. 23 Apr 1914, Amherst, Massachusetts[1018].

823.	iii.	DR. PRESTON NICHOLS BARTON, b. 14 Jun 1913, Amherst, Massachusetts; d. Sep 1978, Mountain Side, Union County, New Jersey.
824.	iv.	ELIZABETH SHERWOOD BARTON, b. 15 Jul 1916, Amherst, Massachusetts; d. 17 May 1999, Amherst, Hampshire County, Massachusetts.
	v.	WILLIAM IRVING BARTON, b. 09 May 1919, Amherst, Massachusetts; m. KATHERINE DORAN, 10 Jul 1943; b. 30 Aug 1918[1019]; d. 31 Jan 2005, Concord, Middlesex County, Massachusetts[1019]. Lived in: Concord, Massachusetts
825.	vi.	THYRZA STEVENS BARTON, b. 23 Jul 1921, Amherst, Massachusetts.
826.	vii.	MARY HATHAWAY BARTON, b. 24 May 1923, Amherst, Massachusetts; d. 24 Nov 2002, Silver Spring, Montgomery County, Maryland.

329. SARAH JANE[8] MILKS *(VINCENT S.[7], JOHN[6], LEMUEL[5] MILK, DAVID[4], JOB[3], JOHN[2], JOHN[1])* was born Bet. 1837 - 1838 in New York, and died 20 Mar 1924 in Bayham, Elgin, Ontario, Canada[1020]. She married JOHN TEDFORD 23 Feb 1861 in Elgin, Ontario, Canada[1021]. Lived in: Malahide, Elgin, Ontario, Canada[1022]

Children of SARAH MILKS and JOHN TEDFORD are:
    i. ERWIN[9] TEDFORD, b. 10 Apr 1870, Malahide, Elgin, Ontario, Canada[1023].
    ii. EDWIN TEDFORD, b. 27 Dec 1878, Malahide, Elgin, Ontario, Canada[1024].
    iii. GEORGE TEDFORD, b. 27 Dec 1878, Malahide, Elgin, Ontario, Canada[1024].

330. FRANCES ALMEDA[8] WILKINS *(LAURA ANN[7] MILKS, JOHN[6], LEMUEL[5] MILK, DAVID[4], JOB[3], JOHN[2], JOHN[1])* was born 14 Feb 1845 in Will County, Illinois[1025], and died 03 Oct 1935 in Joliet, Will County, Illinois[1026]. She married ARCHIBALD M. STEPHENSON. He was born Jun 1844 in Indiana[1027], and died 1913 in Joliet, Will County, Illinois[1028]. They are buried in Oakwood Cemetery, Joliet, Will County, Illinois

Children of FRANCES WILKINS and ARCHIBALD STEPHENSON are:
827.	i.	URA MAE/MAY[9] STEPHENSON, b. Abt. 1872, Joliet, Will County, Illinois; d. 27 May 1950, Joliet, Illinois.
828.	ii.	ALTA MAE STEPHENSON, b. 15 Nov 1876, Joliet, Will County, Illinois; d. 04 Jan 1929, Evanston, Cook County, Illinois.
	iii.	FRANCIS 'FRANK' STEPHENSON, b. Jul 1884, Joliet, Will County, Illinois; d. 1906, Joliet, Illinois. Burial: Oakwood Cemetery, Joliet, Will County, Illinois

331. HARRIET M. 'HATTIE'[8] WILKINS *(LAURA ANN[7] MILKS, JOHN[6], LEMUEL[5] MILK, DAVID[4], JOB[3], JOHN[2], JOHN[1])* was born Feb 1850 in Will County, Illinois, and died Bef. 1900. She married JOHN BERNARD DESELMA 1874, son of JACOB DESELMA and HARRIET _____. He was born 20 May 1844 in Fremont, Ohio[1029], and died 15 Aug 1920 in River Forest, Cook County, Illinois[1029]. John was a Railway Mail Clerk. They lived in Rockville, Kankakee County, Illinois and are buried in Kankakee County.

Children of HARRIET WILKINS and JOHN DESELMA are:
	i.	ARTHUR W.[9] DESELMA, b. Abt. 1875, Kankakee County, Illinois.
	ii.	JOHN ELMER DESELMA, b. Abt. 1878, Kankakee County, Illinois.
829.	iii.	ALTA MAE DESELMA, b. 07 Oct 1879, Kankakee County, Illinois; d. 01 Dec 1958, Santa Barbara, CA.
	iv.	HARRY DESELMA, b. Abt. 1881, Kankakee County, Illinois.
	v.	ETHEL H. DESELMA, b. Abt. 1883, Kankakee County, Illinois.
	vi.	JENNIE DESELMA, b. Abt. 1885, Kankakee County, Illinois.
	vii.	LESTER DESELMA, b. Abt. 1888, Kankakee County, Illinois.

332. EUNICE ADELAIDE[8] CAGWIN *(HARRIET MARIAH[7] MILKS, JOHN[6], LEMUEL[5] MILK, DAVID[4], JOB[3], JOHN[2], JOHN[1])* was born 21 Jan 1843 in Joliet, Will County, Illinois, and died 22 Apr 1922 in Peoria, Peoria County, Illinois[1030]. She married HENRY FRANKLIN ELLIOTT 15 Oct 1861. He was born 27 Nov 1831 in Manchester, Vermont, and died 22 Mar 1898. Eunice is buried in Springdale Cemetery and Mausoleum, Peoria, Peoria County, Illinois. Henry is buried in Elliott Cemetery, Matteson, Cook County, Illinois

    From 1853 to 1858 Henry was engaged in the lumber business in Bloomington, Illinois. In 1859 he moved to Joliet, remaining there until 1862 when he moved to Lincoln, Logan County, where he served three 2-year terms as an Alderman.

Children of EUNICE CAGWIN and HENRY ELLIOTT are:
- i. JENNIE MARIAM[9] ELLIOTT, b. 1862; d. 1919; m. LESTER A. ROSE; b. of Streator, Illinois.
- ii. LILLIAN EUGENIA ELLIOTT, b. 14 Jun 1864, Lincoln, Illinois[1031]; d. 16 Aug 1937, Oak Park, Cook County, Illinois[1031]; m. LYNN J. ELDREDGE[1032]; b. Abt. 1864. Burial: Arlington Cemetery, Addison, DuPage County, Illinois
  Lived in: Oak Park, Cook County, Illinois
- iii. ADELE MAY ELLIOTT, b. 19 Apr 1866, Lincoln, Illinois[1033]; d. 04 May 1928, Peoria, Peoria County, Illinois[1033]; m. ROBERT N. MCCORMICK[1034]; b. Abt. 1865. Burial: Springdale Cemetery, Peoria, Peoria County, Illinois. Lived in: Peoria, Peoria County, Illinois

333. ALICE V.[8] CAGWIN *(HARRIET MARIAH[7] MILKS, JOHN[6], LEMUEL[5] MILK, DAVID[4], JOB[3], JOHN[2], JOHN[1])* was born Feb 1846 in Joliet, Will County, Illinois, and died 1924 in Coldwater, Branch County, Michigan. She married (1) JOHN FREMONT KNAPP 1884 in Illinois[1035], son of SOLOMON KNAPP and JANE MILKS. He was born May 1856 in Black Hawk County, Iowa, and died 27 Oct 1904 in Chicago, Cook County, Illinois. She married (2) CHARLES E. BLOOD 15 Apr 1908 in Coldwater, Branch County, Michigan[1036], son of CHARLES BLOOD and MARIA AVERY. He was born Abt. 1847 in New York. Alice is buried in Oak Grove Cemetery, Coldwater, Branch County, Michigan

Child of ALICE CAGWIN and JOHN KNAPP is:
- i. MAUD EMILY ANTHONY[9] KNAPP, b. Jan 1887, Illinois; m. UNNAMED, 21 Feb 1903, Racine, Wisconsin[1037].

334. EDWIN L.[8] WEEKS *(MARIAH E.[7] MILKS, JOHN[6], LEMUEL[5] MILK, DAVID[4], JOB[3], JOHN[2], JOHN[1])* was born May 1856 in Lockport, Will County, Illinois. He married FLORENCE E. WILLS. She was born Feb 1863 in Illinois.

Children of EDWIN WEEKS and FLORENCE WILLS are:
- i. RENA M.[9] WEEKS, b. Jan 1883, Will County, Illinois.
- 830. ii. HOWARD W. WEEKS, b. 29 Feb 1888, Will County, Illinois; d. 18 Aug 1947, Cameron County, Texas.

335. HARRIET E.[8] KNAPP *(JANE OPHELIA[7] MILKS, JOHN[6], LEMUEL[5] MILK, DAVID[4], JOB[3], JOHN[2], JOHN[1])* was born Apr 1853 in Will County, Illinois, and died Abt. 1927 in Black Hawk County, Iowa[1038]. She married ANDERSON BRUCE COX 20 Mar 1893 in Black Hawk County, Iowa[1039], son of SYLVENUS COX and SALLY BOMENT. He was born 1861 in Waterloo, Iowa[1040], and died Bet. 1920 - 1925. Harriet is buried in Hillcrest Cemetery, East Waterloo, Black Hawk County, Iowa[1041]

Child of HARRIET KNAPP and ANDERSON COX is:
- i. FRANK FREMONT[9] COX[1042], b. Jun 1894, Cedar Falls, Black Hawk County, Iowa[1043].
  Frank's birth record in Iowa shows his name as Frank Fremont Cox, but for some reason his mother listed his name as Bruce in the 1895 Iowa state census and in the 1900 Federal census. For 1910 and later he is shown as Frank or Frank F. Cox.

336. JOHN FREMONT[8] KNAPP *(JANE OPHELIA[7] MILKS, JOHN[6], LEMUEL[5] MILK, DAVID[4], JOB[3], JOHN[2], JOHN[1])* was born May 1856 in Black Hawk County, Iowa, and died 27 Oct 1904 in Chicago, Cook County, Illinois. He married ALICE V. CAGWIN 1884 in Illinois[1043], daughter of ORVILLE CAGWIN and HARRIET MILKS. She was born Feb 1846 in Joliet, Will County, Illinois, and died 1924 in Coldwater, Branch County, Michigan. Alice is buried in Oak Grove Cemetery, Coldwater, Branch County, Michigan

Child is listed above under (330) Alice V. Cagwin.

334. FRANK F.[8] KNAPP *(JANE OPHELIA[7] MILKS, JOHN[6], LEMUEL[5] MILK, DAVID[4], JOB[3], JOHN[2], JOHN[1])* was born Jul 1859 in Black Hawk County, Iowa, and died Bet. 1920 - 1925 in Black Hawk County, Iowa. He married ALICE M. JAMES 1883, daughter of ELROY JAMES and LUCY BOVER. She was born Feb 1860 in Iowa, and died Aft. 1930. Frank was a Justice of the Peace in Waterloo, Black Hawk County, Iowa.

Children of FRANK KNAPP and ALICE JAMES are:
- i. FRANK E.[9] KNAPP, b. Dec 1884, Black Hawk County, Iowa.
- ii. MYRTIE G. KNAPP, b. Aug 1887, Black Hawk County, Iowa.

iii. PEARL F. KNAPP, b. Jul 1889, Black Hawk County, Iowa.
iv. MINNIE B. KNAPP, b. Feb 1891, Black Hawk County, Iowa.
v. BESSIE M. KNAPP, b. Feb 1893, Black Hawk County, Iowa.
vi. CHILD KNAPP, b. Abt. 1896, Black Hawk County, Iowa; d. Bef. 1900, Black Hawk County, Iowa.
vii. FOREST GRANT KNAPP, b. Jul 1899, Black Hawk County, Iowa.
viii. MAUDE KNAPP, b. Abt. 1902, Black Hawk County, Iowa.
ix. CLAIR W. KNAPP, b. Abt. 1905, Black Hawk County, Iowa.

338. STEPHEN C.[8] GIFFORD (ALDEN M.[7], SQUIRE[6], ISABEL[5] MILK, DAVID[4], JOB[3], JOHN[2], JOHN[1]) was born Dec 1836 in New Bedford, Bristol County, Massachusetts. He married ELIZABETH B. JENNEY 31 Mar 1866. She was born Abt. 1846.

Children of STEPHEN GIFFORD and ELIZABETH JENNEY are:
i. JAMES A.[9] GIFFORD, b. 04 Oct 1866.
ii. JENNEY B. GIFFORD.
iii. ISABEL GIFFORD.

339. LYDIA B.[8] LUCAS (MARY EARLE[7] GIFFORD, SQUIRE[6], ISABEL[5] MILK, DAVID[4], JOB[3], JOHN[2], JOHN[1]) She married GIDEON D. GIFFORD.

Children of LYDIA LUCAS and GIDEON GIFFORD are:
i. GIDEON D.[9] GIFFORD, JR..
ii. CARRIE K. GIFFORD.

340. CLARA F.[8] GIFFORD (DAVID M.[7], SQUIRE[6], ISABEL[5] MILK, DAVID[4], JOB[3], JOHN[2], JOHN[1]) She married (1) MR. SMITH. She married (2) J. B. HALL.

Child of CLARA GIFFORD and MR. SMITH is:
i. ALTA B.[9] SMITH.

341. HARRIET P.[8] BROWN (HARRIET S.[7] GIFFORD, SQUIRE[6], ISABEL[5] MILK, DAVID[4], JOB[3], JOHN[2], JOHN[1]) She married GEORGE W. EDWARDS. He was born in Of Detroit, Michigan.

Children of HARRIET BROWN and GEORGE EDWARDS are:
i. ANNIE M.[9] EDWARDS.
ii. EMMA S. EDWARDS.
iii. HARRIET B. EDWARDS.

342. DEBORAH M.[8] GIFFORD (JOHN A.[7], SQUIRE[6], ISABEL[5] MILK, DAVID[4], JOB[3], JOHN[2], JOHN[1]) was born Mar 1847 in New Bedford, Bristol County, Massachusetts. She married EDWARD C. NEAGUS. He was born May 1845 in Massachusetts.

Children of DEBORAH GIFFORD and EDWARD NEAGUS are:
i. ADA K.[9] NEAGUS[1044], b. Feb 1870, New Bedford, Bristol County, Massachusetts; d. Bet. 1870 - 1880, New Bedford, Bristol County, Massachusetts.
ii. EDWARD C. NEAGUS, b. Jan 1873, New Bedford, Bristol County, Massachusetts.
iii. ADDIE K. NEAGUS, b. Feb 1880, New Bedford, Bristol County, Massachusetts.
iv. ALBERT C. NEAGUS, b. Nov 1884, New Bedford, Bristol County, Massachusetts.

343. LADETTE GEORGE[8] GIFFORD (GEORGE WASHINGTON[7], JOHN[6], ISABEL[5] MILK, DAVID[4], JOB[3], JOHN[2], JOHN[1])[1045] was born 1857 in Jefferson County, New York[1045], and died 08 Apr 1895 in Watertown, Jefferson County, New York[1045]. He married HATTIE E. _____[1046] Bef. Nov 1882 in Jefferson County, New York ?. She died 25 Mar 1895 in Watertown, Jefferson County, New York[1046].
From the *Directory of Deceased American Physicians, 1804-1929* about **LaDette George Gifford**:
Birth Date: 1857 Death Date: 8 Apr 1895, Death Place: Watertown, NY
Type Practice: Allopath

Medical School: New York University Medical College, New York: Univ. of City of New York Med. Dept., 1884, (G)
JAMA Citation: 24:609

Child of LADETTE GIFFORD and HATTIE _____ is:
    i. IVAN[9] GIFFORD, b. Jun 1884, New York.

344. IDA EMME[8] GIFFORD *(ALDEN[7], JOHN[6], ISABEL[5] MILK, DAVID[4], JOB[3], JOHN[2], JOHN[1])* was born 26 Mar 1864. She married EMORY I. STONE 02 Nov 1884. He was born Abt. 1864.

Child of IDA GIFFORD and EMORY STONE is:
    i. SARAH LUCILLE[9] STONE, b. 22 Aug 1885.

345. MINNE ELECTRA[8] GIFFORD *(ALDEN[7], JOHN[6], ISABEL[5] MILK, DAVID[4], JOB[3], JOHN[2], JOHN[1])* was born 11 Oct 1865. She married FRANK K. JONES 06 Dec 1883. He was born Abt. 1865.

Children of MINNE GIFFORD and FRANK JONES are:
    i. IRVINE CLIFFORD[9] JONES, b. 24 Aug 1886; d. 04 Sep 1886.
    ii. IDA MAY JONES, b. 27 Mar 1891.
    iii. FRANCESS CORNELIA JONES, b. 10 Apr 1893.

346. MINERVA ADELINE[8] DEUEL *(WILLIAM HENRY[7], LEWIS[6], PATIENCE[5] MILK, DAVID[4], JOB[3], JOHN[2], JOHN[1])* was born 03 Mar 1843 in Montrose, Iowa, and died 10 Feb 1873 in Porterville, Utah. She married ALMA PORTER 15 Nov 1858[1047], son of CHANCEY PORTER and AMY SUMNER. He was born 15 Dec 1834 in Missouri, and died 1903.

Children of MINERVA DEUEL and ALMA PORTER are:
    i. MARY[9] PORTER, b. 19 Sep 1860, Centerville, Utah; m. SAMUEL URIAH PORTER; b. Abt. 1860.
831.   ii. ANN ELIZA PORTER, b. 22 Oct 1862, Porterville, Utah; d. 12 Jun 1927, Farmington, Davis County, Utah.
    iii. CHARLES PORTER, b. 17 Dec 1867, Porterville, Utah; m. RHEUEMMA WALTON; b. Abt. 1867.
832.   iv. ORSON MERRITT PORTER, b. 26 Jul 1869, Porterville, Utah; d. 08 May 1935, Otto, Wyoming.
    v. GEORGE MYRON PORTER, b. 17 Mar 1871, Porterville, Utah; m. LORETTA CHAPMAN; b. Abt. 1871.
    vi. VILATE PORTER, b. 28 Jan 1872, Porterville, Utah; m. THOMAS WASHINGTON WHITE; b. Abt. 1870.

347. LEWIS[8] DEUEL *(WILLIAM HENRY[7], LEWIS[6], PATIENCE[5] MILK, DAVID[4], JOB[3], JOHN[2], JOHN[1])* was born 16 Jul 1851 in Centerville, Utah, and died 05 May 1929 in Escalante, Utah. He married (1) SARAH ANDERSON Abt. 1908 in Hatch, Utah. She was born 01 Jan 1837. He married (2) CATHERINE KELSEY 10 Jun 1871 in Kanarah, Utah[1047]. She was born 20 Feb 1851 in Union Fort, Salt Lake County, Utah, and died 28 Apr 1906 in Union, Oregon.

    Lewis Deuel was a farmer, cattle raiser, and a fine musician; he helped found the town of Escalante, Utah, and maintained a hotel there. His wife Catherine was a nurse who not only cared for the sick in other homes, but brought them into her own. She was adept in hat-making from straw she gleaned from the fields, bleached, and braided attractively.

Child of LEWIS DEUEL and SARAH ANDERSON is:
    i. AMOS[9] DEUEL, d. Salt Lake City, Salt Lake County, Utah.

Children of LEWIS DEUEL and CATHERINE KELSEY are:
    ii. MINERVA ELIZABETH[9] DEUEL, b. 26 Nov 1873, Panguitch, Utah; m. DAVID W. CAMPBELL; b. Abt. 1870.
    iii. AVERY JEANNETTE DEUEL, b. 10 Jan 1875, Kanarah, Utah; m. JOHN R. CAMPBELL; b. Abt. 1875.
    iv. ZEPHER LOIS DEUEL, b. 14 Nov 1877, Escalante, Utah; m. JOHN STEELE; b. Abt. 1877.
    v. POLLY ANN DEUEL, b. 23 Aug 1880, Escalante, Utah; m. THOMAS SPENCER; b. Abt. 1880.
    vi. LEWIS EASTON DEUEL, b. 24 Oct 1881, Escalante, Utah; m. CLEMA BARNEY; b. Abt. 1881.
    vii. FRANCES MAHALIA DEUEL, b. 21 Dec 1882, Escalante, Utah.
833.   viii. KATIE ROSILLA DEUEL, b. 05 Mar 1884, Escalante, Utah.

348. J. WARREN[8] FORT *(JULIA E.[7] HOAG, LILLYS[6] DEUEL, PATIENCE[5] MILK, DAVID[4], JOB[3], JOHN[2], JOHN[1])* was born 1834, and died 1905. He married (1) ELIZA GIFFORD, daughter of NATHAN GIFFORD and BETSEY KENYON. He married (2) ALICE C. BROWNELL, daughter of ELIJAH BROWNELL and DEBORAH GIFFORD. She was born 1847, and died 1922.

Child of J. FORT and ELIZA GIFFORD is:
- i. EDWIN JAMES[9] FORT.

Children of J. FORT and ALICE BROWNELL are:
- ii. LOUIS[9] FORT.
- iii. SOPHIA FORT.
- iv. JOHN GIFFORD FORT.
- v. J. WARREN FORT, b. 1878; d. 1959.
- vi. JULIA FORT.

349. ELI WALTER[8] BLOSSOM *(CLARISSA[7], ALICE[6] MILK, JOB[5], DAVID[4], JOB[3], JOHN[2], JOHN[1])* was born 22 Jan 1850 in Westport, Massachusetts, and died 23 Mar 1941. He married ELLA J. YOUNG.

Children of ELI BLOSSOM and ELLA YOUNG are:
- 834. i. MARY ELLA[9] BLOSSOM, b. 06 Jul 1879.
- ii. ALICE MILK BLOSSOM, b. 21 Apr 1882. Unmarried, Lived in: North Westport, Massachusetts
- iii. CLARISSA LINWOOD BLOSSOM, b. 01 May 1884; m. SAMUEL A. LOCKHART; b. Abt. 1884. No children
- 835. iv. SUSAN MILLER BLOSSOM, b. 20 Jul 1887.

350. WILLIAM ELIJAH[8] BLOSSOM *(BARNABAS[7], ALICE[6] MILK, JOB[5], DAVID[4], JOB[3], JOHN[2], JOHN[1])* was born Mar 1860 in Fall River, Bristol County, Mass., and died in Fall River, Massachusetts. He married MABEL RIPLEY Bet. 1882 - 1883 in Massachusetts[1048]. She was born Feb 1864 in Massachusetts, and died 1941. William was a Bookkeeper.

Children of WILLIAM BLOSSOM and MABEL RIPLEY are:
- i. ROMAINE F.[9] BLOSSOM, b. Sep 1883, Bristol County, Massachusetts; m. MR. HARRIS.
- ii. WILLIAM WESLEY BLOSSOM, b. Sep 1886, Bristol County, Massachusetts; d. 1950
- iii. LUTHER R. BLOSSOM, b. Mar 1888, Bristol County, Massachusetts; d. 1950.

351. FRANCES MARIA[8] BLOSSOM *(BARNABAS[7], ALICE[6] MILK, JOB[5], DAVID[4], JOB[3], JOHN[2], JOHN[1])* was born Sep 1850 in Fall River, Bristol County, Mass.[1048]. She married EDWIN L. WEST[1049]. He was born Abt. 1847 in Massachusetts, and died Bet. 1880 - 1900 in Bristol County, Massachusetts.

Child of FRANCES BLOSSOM and EDWIN WEST is:
- i. LUCILLE[9] WEST, b. Aug 1879, Fall River, Massachusetts[1050]; d. Aft. 1900.

352. MARGARET[8] MILKS *(JOHN[7], ELI S.[6] MILK, JOB[5], DAVID[4], JOB[3], JOHN[2], JOHN[1])* was born 07 Apr 1864 in Binghamton, Broome County, NY[1051], and died 14 Feb 1919 in Binghamton, NY?[1052]. She married LUCIAN JOHN WOODRUFF 05 Sep 1883 in Binghamton, NY[1052]. He was born 15 Aug 1859 in Montrose, PA[1052,1053], and died 29 Mar 1933 in Binghamton, NY[1054,1055]. They were buried in Glenwood Cemetery, Binghamton, Broome County, New York

Children of MARGARET MILKS and LUCIAN WOODRUFF are:
- 836. i. JULIA EVALYN[9] WOODRUFF, b. 17 Jul 1884, Binghamton, Broome County, NY.
- ii. CHARLES SELDON WOODRUFF, b. 18 Sep 1886, Binghamton, Broome County, New York[1056]; d. Sep 1970, Binghamton, Broome County, New York[1056].

353. GEORGE[8] MILKS *(DAVID[7], ELI S.[6] MILK, JOB[5], DAVID[4], JOB[3], JOHN[2], JOHN[1])* was born 20 Jun 1862 in Brackney, Pennsylvania, and died 30 Oct 1928. He married (1) EVA B. GERMOND. She was born 1861, and died 1897 in Broome County, New York. He married (2) JANE E. BROWN[1057] Bet. 1897 - 1898[1057]. She was born Nov 1866 in Pennsylvania, and died Aft. 1930. George and Eva are buried in Floral Park Cemetery, Johnson City, Broome County, New York. George was an Electrician.

Child of GEORGE MILKS and EVA GERMOND is:
- i. ELIZABETH[9] MILKS, b. Jul 1883, Broome County, New York[1057,1058]; d. 1957, Broome County, New York (unmarried)[1058]. Burial: Floral Park Cemetery, Johnson City, Broome County, New York
Occupation: Manager, Milks Electric Company, Binghamton, New York

354. DEWITT WILLIAM⁸ MILKS *(DAVID⁷, ELI S.⁶ MILK, JOB⁵, DAVID⁴, JOB³, JOHN², JOHN¹)* was born 04 Jul 1878 in Hawleyton, Broome County, New York, and died 12 Oct 1947 in Broome County, New York. He married EMMA MAY MANN Abt. 1903 in Broome County, New York, daughter of STEPHEN MANN and ELIZA _____. She was born 10 Jan 1878 in New York, and died 21 Dec 1966 in Broome County, New York. They are buried in Vestal Hills Memorial Park, Vestal, Broome County, New York

Children of DEWITT MILKS and EMMA MANN are:

837.   i. ELIZABETH⁹ MILKS, b. 29 Jul 1905, Broome County, New York; d. 17 May 1938, Broome County, New York.
     ii. ELIZA MILKS[1059], b. Abt. 1906, Broome County, New York[1059]; m. (1) H. PIKE; b. Abt. 1906; m. (2) MR. PRINTZ; b. Of Endicott, NY.
838.   iii. ESTHER J. MILKS, b. Abt. 1908, Broome County, New York.

355. MARY⁸ BRADLEY *(PHEBE⁷ MILKS, ELI S.⁶ MILK, JOB⁵, DAVID⁴, JOB³, JOHN², JOHN¹)* was born 1854, and died 1897 in Broome County, New York[1060]. She married THOMAS C. BAKER[1061,1062]. He was born May 1841 in Connecticut, and died 1922 in Broome County, New York[1063]. They are buried in Floral Park Cemetery, Johnson City, Broome County, New York. Mary, age 15, was living with her uncle, David Milks and his wife Elizabeth, in 1870.

Child of MARY BRADLEY and THOMAS BAKER is:

     i. LYNN BRADLEY⁹ BAKER[1064,1065], b. 11 Jan 1882, Broome County, New York; m. ALICE M. _____, Bet. 1906 - 1907[1066]; b. Abt. 1884, Pennsylvania. No children.

356. FRANCIS "FRANK" ELI⁸ MILKS *(BENJAMIN B.⁷, ELI S.⁶ MILK, JOB⁵, DAVID⁴, JOB³, JOHN², JOHN¹)*[1067] was born Sep 1868 in Hawleyton, Broome Co., NY[1068], and died 03 May 1926 in Hawleyton, Broome Co., NY[1069,1070]. He married GRACE MARIA DEAN[1071] Abt. 1905[1071], daughter of ALMON DEAN and ANTOINETTE SANFORD. She was born 22 Apr 1889 in Hawleyton, Broome Co., NY[1072], and died 03 Mar 1941 in Binghamton, NY[1073]. They are buried in Milks Hill Cemetery, Hawleyton, Broome Co., NY. Frank was a Potato Farmer and Trapper

    Much of the data on this family has been contributed by JOHN C. KOBUSKIE (of Vestal, New York), spouse of Miriam Harlene Milks. John has researched this family and has also contributed a lot of interesting narrative on the family and on the property in Hawleyton.

    History of the Milks Road Property

    During the time the land was employed for farming it was used for growing potatoes and grain, and raising chickens and milk cows.

    The farm was purchased by Eli S. Milk in March 1851 for $700 from a William Averill of Cooperstown New York. The land was originally Lot No 44 in the Manor of Fredonia, or Coopers Patent so called, and consisted of 100 acres which included a hilltop.

    Deeds are not available to cover all transfers of the property. It would seem that upon Eli's death in 1852 the entire 100 acres went to his sons John and David, and his daughter Phebe. In 1862 these three sold the northern 50 acres to another of Eli's sons, Benjamin, for $800. In 1876 Benjamin assigned this portion to his children John, Sarah (Amanda), and Francis (Frank). In 1894 David's son Edgar sold the 50 acre south portion to James Cadden for $1000. James and Ellen Cadden sold 25 acres of the south portion to John and Frank in 1907 and the remaining 25 acres in 1908. Upon John's death in 1912 he left half of his holdings to his brother Frank and the other half to his sister Amanda. At this point, therefore, Frank and Amanda each owned half of the north portion, and Frank three fourths and Amanda one fourth of the south portion. Frank died in 1925 and his portion likely went to his wife Grace.

    From 1936 to 1941 the land was bought by the Broome County Board of Supervisors in various tax sales as property taxes were not being paid by Grace Milks. Grace died on March 3, 1941. On May 15, 1941 Harley E. Milks, Grace's son, bought the land for back taxes for something around $500. In 1963 Harley's brother Everett and sister Betty attempted to claim an interest in the property (Harley's brother Charles was also a named party in the case but was not personally interested in perusing the claim). On March 28, 1963 the Broome County Supreme Court declared that Harley had absolute, unencumbered title to the property. On April 16, 1963 the property was deeded from Harley to Harley and Kathryn as tenants by the entirety. In 1982 a six acre (approximately) portion was sold to William and Katherine Affeldt. In 1995 Kathryn transferred the remaining property (approximately 94 acres) to her children Harley G., Miriam and Carol as tenants in common. Following Kathryn's death in 2002, the subdivided land was assigned to each of the children. A portion of Carol's allotment was transferred to her son Christopher Utyro where he built a house.

Consequently, the north portion of the property has been continuously owned by six generations of the Milks family for 160 years, with the south portion being in the family for all but 14 of those 160 years. The .44 acre cemetery contains about 27 graves and includes the plot of Job (1763-1849), Eli's father, other Milks family members, as well as some other individuals from surrounding homes.

The First House

At the time of his death in 1852, Eli was living in a house at the top of the hill. The house was located about 1000 feet to the south of the cemetery on the road that runs through the property which was then called the Montrose Turnpike (so called because it was the main route from Binghamton to Montrose

Pennsylvania), now Milks Road, on the easterly side of the road . It has been said that in 1852 the water supply serving the home became infected with typhoid. Eli and his sons Abner and Mortimer all died from typhoid fever within a short time of each other. Even today the foundation of this 1850's home and the well heads are visible, as are the lilac bushes that lined the south side of the house and the foundation blocks of the barn that sat across the road.

The Second House

Another house occupied the northern portion of the property throughout the 1900's until 2002. It was located lower on the hill and closer to Pennsylvania Avenue. The origin of this structure is unclear. Some accounts have the house as being the same one where Eli and his sons died, having been physically moved from the hilltop to this new location in the 1800's. There is no record of any Milks occupying the house in the 1910 census. The 1920 census shows the house being occupied by Frank, Grace, Harley and Charles (Elwood).

Harley Milks recollected that the foundation for the house had been hand dug, and a second story added in 1909. This house was furnished with a tin bath tub in 1909, being perhaps the first permanently installed indoor tub in the Town of Binghamton. An indoor toilet was not added until 1941, an outhouse serving the purpose until that time. Electrical fixtures were installed in the house in 1945. The day the Foley Company crew was to construct the new power line coincided with the end of World War II. The work crew took to spirited celebration and many of the men became inebriated. Harley, very anxious to have electric light, used his own horses to assist in pulling the poles to their proper locations. The house stood until 2002, when it was removed to make way for the building of a new home by Christopher Utyro, a grandson of Harley.

The Hill

At an elevation of 1760 feet, Milks Hill is one of the highest in Broome County, higher even than the Broome County Airport at 1636 ft. Because of its elevation it became the site of some of the first television viewing in Broome County. When WNBF transmitted a test pattern for a number of months before it began full operation in 1949, Harley became impatient and decided to test reception on the hilltop. He had available some small gauge wire and ran 1000 feet of it from the house to the hilltop.

With all this wire, voltage was only about 108 volts, but enough to power the 10 inch TV he would lug up the hill every night. He and the family were able to view broadcasts from Syracuse and Philadelphia. TV night became popular in the neighborhood and more and more people would attend. A tent was added, and then an old school bus donated by neighbor Stan Progy. Eventually WNBF began full operation and that era ended.

The site then became a haven for the Binghamton Amateur Radio Association (BARA) and Harley constructed a 15 foot by 25 foot building made out of wood and flooring that he and his friend Carl Pancoast salvaged from the Water Street Bowling Alleys which were being decommissioned. The "shack" still remains, and is still used by BARA. Also on the hilltop a repeater transmitter tower was installed in 1976 to improve reception of educational broadcasting at the Brookside school.

Today

Much of the farmland has reverted to woodland. Only a few acres are still open field. In 1986 Harley G. Milks and his brother-in-law John Kobuskie planted 1000 white spruce trees in one of the remaining open fields with the notion of starting a Christmas tree farm. Most of these trees remain, left to grow as nature sees fit.

Children of FRANCIS MILKS and GRACE DEAN are:
839.   i. HARLEY EDWARD[9] MILKS, b. 14 Apr 1908, Hawleyton, Broome Co., NY; d. 09 Mar 1995, Hawleyton, Broome Co., NY.
        ii. CHARLES ELWOOD MILKS, b. 07 Jul 1913, Hawleyton, Broome Co., NY[1074]; d. 24 Oct 1982, Johnson City, Broome, NY[1074]; m. RETHA EVA ELDRED[1075,1076], 05 Dec 1936, Conklin Ave. Baptist Church, Binghamton,

Broome Co., NY[1077]; b. 24 May 1905, Town of Binghamton, Binghamton Co., NY[1078,1079]; d. 02 Feb 1986, Binghamton, NY[1080].

While in the South Pacific during WWII, Charles contracted a skin disease known as "Jungle Rot", and came back to the states on a hospital ship. This affected his skin for the rest of his life and he had to use ointments to alleviate the problem, but he refused to seek any service-related disability benefits. Burial: Hawleton Cemetery, Saddlemire Rd, Hawleyton, Broome Co., NY. Military service: 21 Apr 1943, Enlisted in Binghamton, served in Air Corps Maintenance in the South Pacific

EULOGY by Thomas C. Haines 10/27/82

Grandfather, Charles E. Milks, was many good things to all of us here. He was a loving husband to Retha, a close brother to Harley, a compassionate father to Eleanor, and an inspiring uncle, grandfather and in-law to all who were related to him. His idea of family went beyond blood, embracing his friends and neighbors in Hawleyton, the Vulcan, Morris Distributing, and all the others he met during his life. Whether you called him Charlie, Elwood, Elmer, Al, Pa, Pappy, Gramps, Uncle C., or Brub, he was our friend. Everyone was family to Charlie.

We all knew him as a hard worker who would do whatever he could for us. Everyone he touch was helped somewhere along the road by him. He was a patient, smiling man willing to listen. His generosity was a beautiful thing to behold.

He was a man of the earth bringing forth bountiful garden, building his home, and fixing anything that could possibly move. He possessed many skills. He knew what to do and how to do it.

As an able woodsman he worked serenely in the forest on Ingraham Hill, cutting the forest with a sense of who would come after him. His generosity and love included other creatures and the environment. His values were timeless: respect for life.

In his own way he was a spiritual man. By this I mean he had a firm sense of the spirit of the earth. Through his gardening, wood chopping, and love of life, he glorified that spirit. He respected his body and looked much younger than his sixty-nine years. I was always amazed at how strong he could be. He realized he had been given a great gift and he made the most of it by sharing his alive, strong body and spirit with us. He passed this spirit on to us, one of his many gifts. It was difficult to return his gifts because it seemed he had everything. He was a complete man.

He found happiness in simple things. He was very content and happy with the life he led whether he was working in his garden, petting his giant cat Muffy, cutting wood, enjoying the fresh air, or eating Retha's meals. His joy came through the things he did.

The old saying "You reap what you sow," is very true when I think of Gramps. He loved his wife Retha, and over their many years together, he cultivated this love through honest feelings and respect for her. He was a great provider. Their love is simply beautiful.

He also cultivated our respect by his honest hard work, his physical strength and his easy, intelligent common sense. We are all very fortunate to have him touch our lives.

Over the years I have grown to appreciate and love Gramps. For most of you here, that love and appreciation has been even longer. We will all miss his strength and smiling good nature.

He leaves me with a good example of how to be sensitive yet strong. The kind of man he was is rare. A rare combination of many good qualities.

We are all left with warm memories of Charlie. I think of riding in his pickup truck with my brother and sisters, fishing on Black Lake with him and Gram, or just sitting in a chair and talking with him. He died in the autumn with his garden done and harvested. Like a true farmer he felt in tune with the cycle of the seasons. The sun was shining peacefully like today, the cool autumn breeze passed through the forests and under the sky he appreciated and loved.

He died as he had live, peacefully and easily with Retha beside him.

His body with rest next to the garden, trees, water, and the woman he loved and nurtured. His spirit lives in everyone he touched.

• He worked as a factory worker. • He served in the military Enlisted as a Private, 21 Apr 1943 in Binghamton, Broome, New York. Education: Grammar School, unskilled occupations in manufacture of boots and shoes,

OBITUARY

Retha E. Milks, 80, of Box 188 Saddlemire Rd., Hawleyton, N.Y., died suddenly Sunday morning February 2, at Binghamton General Hospital.

She is survived by one daughter and son-in-law, Eleanor and William Haines, Sunrise Terrace,

Binghamton; a granddaughter, Patricia Haines Possemato and her husband, Gregory, Voorheesville, N.Y.; a granddaughter, Lisa Mary Haines, Grapevine, Tex.; grandsons William Haines, Irving, Tex., Thomas Haines, Ingram Hill Rd., Town of Binghamton; also one great-grand-daughter, Sonya Posemato; also a dear friend Louise Henning, Binghamton.

She will be greatly missed by her loving Family and many friends. She was a member of the Hawleyton United Methodist Church; a retired employee of Endicott Johnson. Also, during World War II, she was employed by Remington Rand and Link Aviation. She was predeceased in October 1982 by her husband Charles E. Milks. Burial will be in Hawleyton Cemetery.

840.	iii.	EVERETT W. MILKS, SR., b. 18 Dec 1921, Hawleyton, Broome Co., NY; d. 12 Apr 1998, Chenango Co., NY.
841.	iv.	BETTY E. MILKS, b. Bet. 1924 - 1925, Hawleyton, Broome Co., NY; d. Abt. 1985, Tennessee.

357. STEPHEN A.[8] BROWNELL *(EZRA PLUMMER[7], JIRAH[6], ABIGAIL[5] MILK, DAVID[4], JOB[3], JOHN[2], JOHN[1])* was born 05 Jan 1844 in Chilmark, Massachusetts[1081], and died 13 Dec 1898 in New Bedford, Massachusetts[1082]. He married MARY L. SISSON. She was born Abt. 1845 in Massachusetts. In the 1910 census, Mary says she had 6 children, but only 2 living.

Stephen was a merchant, bank director, President Dartmouth & Westport R.R., Board of Trade of New Bedford, Mayor of New Bedford, member of Massachusetts State Legislature. (Reference: *Biographical & Historical History of Berkshire, Mass.*). He is buried in New Bedford, Massachusetts

Children of STEPHEN BROWNELL and MARY SISSON are:

842.	i.	ALBERT R.[9] BROWNELL, b. Jun 1865, New Bedford, Massachusetts.
	ii.	MABEL W. BROWNELL, m. ALBERT C. BRALEY, Abt. 1893, Massachusetts. No children.

358. ALVIN DURHAM[8] LOTTRIDGE *(THOMAS[7], ESTHER[6] BULL, AMY[5] CHASE, SARAH[4] MILK, JOB[3], JOHN[2], JOHN[1])* was born 27 Feb 1835 in Hoosic Falls, New York, and died 12 Mar 1898 in Hoosic Falls, New York. He married ELLEN JANE SEARS 04 Feb 1860 in Pittsfield, Massachusetts[1083], daughter of ENOS SEARS and MARY RUSSELL. She was born 19 Mar 1838 in White Creek, New York, and died 05 Nov 1915 in Hoosic Falls, New York.

Children of ALVIN LOTTRIDGE and ELLEN SEARS are:

843.	i.	EMMA LODUSKA[9] LOTTRIDGE, b. 08 Oct 1860, Hoosick Falls, Rensselaer County, New York; d. 29 Jul 1929, Englewood, New Jersey.
844.	ii.	ARTHUR CLIFFORD LOTTRIDGE, b. 01 Jun 1862, Hoosic Falls, New York.
	iii.	BENN LEROY LOTTRIDGE, b. 07 Feb 1864, Hoosic Falls, New York; d. 01 Sep 1867, Hoosic Falls, New York.
	iv.	SON LOTTRIDGE, b. 1865, Hoosic Falls, New York; d. 1865, Hoosic Falls, New York.
845.	v.	ETTA LOTTRIDGE, b. 18 Aug 1867, Hoosic Falls, New York; d. 26 Aug 1949, Shaftsbury, Vermont.
	vi.	ALVIN DURHAM LOTTRIDGE, JR., b. 18 Mar 1870, Hoosic Falls, New York; d. 04 Jan 1950, Florida.
846.	vii.	STEPHEN SMITH LOTTRIDGE, b. 26 Apr 1873, Hoosic Falls, New York; d. 08 Feb 1950, Stillwater, New York.

359. FRANCES CAROLINE[8] LOTTRIDGE *(ISAAC BULL[7], ESTHER[6] BULL, AMY[5] CHASE, SARAH[4] MILK, JOB[3], JOHN[2], JOHN[1])* was born 22 Dec 1821 in Hoosic Falls, New York, and died 02 Oct 1903 in Troy, New York. She married CHARLES LYMAN PRESCOTT 11 Nov 1844. He was born 25 Nov 1821 in Troy, New York, and died 24 Mar 1869 in Monroe, Michigan. Frances is buried in Troy, New York

Children of FRANCES LOTTRIDGE and CHARLES PRESCOTT are:

	i.	CHARLES[9] PRESCOTT.
	ii.	WILLIAM PRESCOTT.
847.	iii.	HARRY LAUSON PRESCOTT, b. 29 Jul 1852, Stillwater, New York; d. 28 Feb 1887.

360. MARY ELLEN[8] LOTTRIDGE *(ISAAC BULL[7], ESTHER[6] BULL, AMY[5] CHASE, SARAH[4] MILK, JOB[3], JOHN[2], JOHN[1])* was born 12 Dec 1825 in Hoosic Falls, New York, and died 19 Nov 1916 in Buffalo, New York. She married (1) THOMAS JAMES 04 Apr 1844 in Troy, New York. He was born 14 Nov 1810 in New York City, and died 05 Mar 1852 in Alexander, New York, where he is buried. She married (2) JOSEPH B. GATCHEL 25 Dec 1854 in Lockport, New York. He was born 02 Jul 1818 in Canada, and died 28 May 1895 in Median, New York. Joseph is buried in Buffalo, New York.

Children of MARY LOTTRIDGE and THOMAS JAMES are:
- i. ELIZA FRANCES[9] JAMES, b. 18 Feb 1845; d. 20 May 1846.
- 848. ii. GERTRUDE C. JAMES, b. 19 Dec 1846; d. 03 Nov 1873, Kansas City, Missouri.

Child of MARY LOTTRIDGE and JOSEPH GATCHEL is:
- iii. ALICE L.[9] GATCHEL, b. 10 Aug 1857.

361. CHARLES[8] LOTTRIDGE *(ISAAC BULL[7], ESTHER[6] BULL, AMY[5] CHASE, SARAH[4] MILK, JOB[3], JOHN[2], JOHN[1])* was born 08 Nov 1829 in Hoosic Falls, New York, and died 18 Oct 1908 in Hudson, New York ?. He married MARY E. YORKER 29 Apr 1856. She was born 16 May 1839, and died 23 Feb 1907 in Hudson, New York, where she is buried.

Children of CHARLES LOTTRIDGE and MARY YORKER are:
- i. MARY CAROLINE[9] LOTTRIDGE, b. 09 Dec 1864.
- ii. HARRIET PARK LOTTRIDGE, b. 04 Feb 1857; d. 01 Jul 1922, Hudson, New York ?. Burial: Hudson, NY.

362. JANIE ESTHER[8] LOTTRIDGE *(MORDECAI[7], ESTHER[6] BULL, AMY[5] CHASE, SARAH[4] MILK, JOB[3], JOHN[2], JOHN[1])* was born 1833 in Schenectady, New York. She married RICHARD ROSA 06 Oct 1857 in Burnthills, New York. He was born 1819, and died 1894.

Children of JANIE LOTTRIDGE and RICHARD ROSA are:
- i. FRANCES CAROLINE[9] ROSA, b. 11 Jun 1859, Schenectady, New York; d. 22 Dec 1936.
- ii. MORDECAI JAMES ROSA, b. 26 Sep 1861, Schenectady, New York; d. 18 Oct 1925; m. MARGARET WALSH; b. 1859; d. 1927.
- 849. iii. RICHARD ROSA, JR., b. 06 Dec 1863, Schenectady, New York; d. 27 Jun 1918.
- 850. iv. GERTRUDE BANKER ROSA, b. 01 Jul 1869, Schenectady, New York; d. 02 Jun 1889.

363. ALICE HANNING[8] BENEDICT *(MARIA[7] LOTTRIDGE, ESTHER[6] BULL, AMY[5] CHASE, SARAH[4] MILK, JOB[3], JOHN[2], JOHN[1])* was born 31 Oct 1851 in Ohio ?, and died 27 Mar 1919. She married JOHN C. PUGH 1881[1083]. He was born 1848, and died 1907.

Children of ALICE BENEDICT and JOHN PUGH are:
- i. GEORGIA BENEDICT[9] PUGH, b. 19 Aug 1882.
- ii. ELLIS MARIA PUGH, b. 21 Jan 1884.
- iii. MABEL HANNING PUGH, b. 21 Sep 1885.
- iv. ADA GRACE PUGH, b. 20 Dec 1886; d. 1887.
- v. FLORENCE LORRAINE PUGH, b. 25 Jun 1888.

364. ESTHER[8] LOTTRIDGE *(ROBERT[7], ESTHER[6] BULL, AMY[5] CHASE, SARAH[4] MILK, JOB[3], JOHN[2], JOHN[1])* was born 1831 in Hoosick, New York, and died 1901. She married JAMES IRWIN. He was born Abt. 1830.

Children of ESTHER LOTTRIDGE and JAMES IRWIN are:
- 851. i. LIBBIE[9] IRWIN, b. 1851; d. 23 Mar 1926.
- 852. ii. WILLIS IRWIN, b. 1857.
- 853. iii. ALICE IRWIN, b. 1860.

365. SARAH MARIA[8] WOLF *(ELIZA[7] LOTTRIDGE, ESTHER[6] BULL, AMY[5] CHASE, SARAH[4] MILK, JOB[3], JOHN[2], JOHN[1])* was born 25 May 1836, and died 28 Aug 1859. She married GEORGE B. BOTHWELL 23 Jan 1855. He was born 1824, and died 1907.

Children of SARAH WOLF and GEORGE BOTHWELL are:
- i. CHARLES[9] BOTHWELL, b. Abt. 1856, McArthur, Ohio.
- 854. ii. CHARLOTTE ELIZA BOTHWELL, b. 01 May 1858, McArthur, Ohio; d. 09 Aug 1927, Wilmington, NJ.

366. LYDIA M.[8] WOLF *(ELIZA[7] LOTTRIDGE, ESTHER[6] BULL, AMY[5] CHASE, SARAH[4] MILK, JOB[3], JOHN[2], JOHN[1])* was born 19 Nov 1840, and died 1915. She married DAVID V. RANNELLS 1858. He was born Abt. 1840, and died 1898 in

McArthur, Ohio.

Children of LYDIA WOLF and DAVID RANNELLS are:
- i. ELIZA HUGHES[9] RANNELLS, b. 19 Sep 1859.
- 855. ii. HELENA DORR RANNELLS, b. 11 Aug 1861.
- iii. ANDREW V. RANNELLS, b. 1863.
- iv. DAVID ARCH RANNELLS, b. 10 Jan 1866; m. ALICE COX; b. Abt. 1866.
- 856. v. ANNA KING RANNELLS, b. 02 Apr 1867; d. 14 Feb 1904, Oakland, California.
- 857. vi. PAULINE WOLF RANNELLS, b. 28 Oct 1868; d. 01 Feb 1930.
- vii. GERTRUDE BELL RANNELLS, b. 19 Sep 1877.

367. CATHRYNE 'KATIE'[8] TEASDALE *(DELIA[7] LOTTRIDGE, ESTHER[6] BULL, AMY[5] CHASE, SARAH[4] MILK, JOB[3], JOHN[2], JOHN[1])* was born 23 Jun 1851 in Springfield, Illinois, and died 11 Dec 1901. She married THOMAS LANIER MOSES 28 Dec 1871 in Columbus, Mississippi[1083]. He was born 13 Dec 1849, and died 03 Dec 1916.

Child of CATHRYNE TEASDALE and THOMAS MOSES is:
- 858. i. DELIA LOTTRIDGE[9] MOSES, b. 28 Sep 1872; d. 31 Jan 1942.

368. FRANKLIN[8] MOORE *(DAVID[7], DUDLEY[6], SARAH[5] MILK, JOB[4], JOB[3], JOHN[2], JOHN[1])* was born Nov 1861 in Ogden, Weber County, Utah, and died 22 Jan 1942 in Weber County, Utah[1084]. He married JULIA G. TAYLOR. She was born Sep 1865 in Ogden, Weber County, Utah, and died 25 May 1948 in Weber County, Utah[1084].

Children of FRANKLIN MOORE and JULIA TAYLOR are:
- i. SARAH E.[9] MOORE, b. Dec 1884, North Ogden, Weber County, Utah.
- ii. JULIA E. MOORE, b. Aug 1886, North Ogden, Weber County, Utah.
- iii. JANE V. MOORE, b. Sep 1888, North Ogden, Weber County, Utah.
- iv. MARY G. MOORE, b. Apr 1890, North Ogden, Weber County, Utah.
- v. MABEL A. MOORE, b. Jan 1893, North Ogden, Weber County, Utah.
- vi. HARRIET MOORE, b. Nov 1895, North Ogden, Weber County, Utah.
- vii. LILLIAN R. MOORE, b. Jan 1897, North Ogden, Weber County, Utah.
- viii. MOSETTE L MOORE, b. Aug 1898, North Ogden, Weber County, Utah.

369. LESTER J.[8] MOORE *(DAVID[7], DUDLEY[6], SARAH[5] MILK, JOB[4], JOB[3], JOHN[2], JOHN[1])* was born Oct 1855 in Weber County, Utah[1085], and died 05 Jan 1926 in Weber County, Utah[1086]. He married SERAPH ____ Abt. 1893 in Weber County, Utah. She was born Mar 1876 in Weber County, Utah. Lester was a farmer.

Children of LESTER MOORE and SERAPH ____ are:
- i. GEORGE LESTER[9] MOORE, b. 08 Feb 1894, Weber County, Utah[1087]; m. VIOLET M. SEAMONS, Abt. 1929; b. Abt. 1906, Utah. Military service: 145th U.S. Field Artillery. Residence: 1930, Los Angeles, California
- ii. MAYBELLE MOORE, b. May 1897, Weber County, Utah.
- iii. ELLSWORTH J. MOORE, b. 31 Dec 1899, Weber County, Utah[1088]; d. 31 Mar 1972, Los Angeles, Calif[1088]. Military service: Bet. 08 May 1818 - 16 Jul 1819, Served in France in WWI
- iv. ESTELLE J. MOORE, b. Abt. 1902, Weber County, Utah.
- v. LEILA MOORE, b. Abt. 1905, Weber County, Utah.
- 859. vi. EDITH MOORE, b. Abt. 1911, Weber County, Utah.
- vii. DERRELL MOORE, b. Abt. 1914, Weber County, Utah.

370. CLARA DIANA[8] MOORE *(DAVID[7], DUDLEY[6], SARAH[5] MILK, JOB[4], JOB[3], JOHN[2], JOHN[1])* was born Apr 1863 in Weber County, Utah, and died 01 Oct 1948 in Ogden, Weber County, Utak[1089]. She married (1) LARENCE WALLACE MARTIN. She married (2) ANTONY FRONK 1882 in Utah[1090]. He was born Mar 1862 in Holland, and died 30 Nov 1906 in Ogden, Weber County, Utak[1091].

Children of CLARA MOORE and ANTONY FRONK are:
- i. JENNIE[9] FRONK, b. Jan 1886, Utah.
- ii. BELLE FRONK, b. May 1888, Utah.

860. iii. ANTONIA WILLIAM FRONK, b. Sep 1890, Utah.
      iv. PEARL FRONK, b. Oct 1893, Utah.
      v. LESTER HENRY FRONK, b. 26 Feb 1897, Utah[1092,1093]; d. Jan 1969, Pleasant Grove, Utah[1093].
861. vi. DAVID FRONK, b. 30 Apr 1899, Utah; d. Apr 1973, Ogden, Weber County, Utah.

371. PARLEY PARKER[8] MOORE (*DAVID[7], DUDLEY[6], SARAH[5] MILK, JOB[4], JOB[3], JOHN[2], JOHN[1]*) was born Nov 1865 in Weber County, Utah[1094], and died 05 Jul 1931 in Salt Lake County, Utah[1095]. He married ELIZABETH HORROCKS[1096] 1890 in Utah. She was born Mar 1871 in Utah[1097], and died 27 Jan 1912 in Salt Lake County, Utah[1098].

Children of PARLEY MOORE and ELIZABETH HORROCKS are:
862. i. HAROLD RAYMOND[9] MOORE, b. 01 Apr 1891, Salt Lake County, Utah; d. 12 Nov 1946, Los Angeles County, California.
      ii. LILLIAN R. MOORE, b. Aug 1893, Salt Lake County, Utah. Residence: 1930, Spokane, Washington (single)
863. iii. DOROTHY E. MOORE, b. May 1895, Salt Lake County, Utah.
864. iv. PARLEY EUGENE MOORE, b. 30 Jan 1897, Ogden, Weber County, Utah; d. 03 Apr 1987, Orange County, California.
865. v. EVA ELIZABETH MOORE, b. 25 Jan 1899, Salt Lake County, Utah; d. 26 Oct 1990, Los Angeles, California.
      vi. GLENN H. MOORE, b. Abt. 1901, Salt Lake County, Utah.
      vii. CLARA MOORE, b. 27 Feb 1903, Salt Lake County, Utah[1099].
      viii. IDA BELLE MOORE, b. Abt. 1905, Salt Lake County, Utah.
      ix. VERA LAVINIA MOORE, b. 26 Sep 1908, Salt Lake County, Utah[1100]; d. 13 Jun 1992, Ventura, California[1100]; m. Mr. MARTIN[1100]; b. Abt. 1908.

372. MARY IDA[8] BAINWAY (*SALLY[7] ANDREWS, AMY[6] MILKS, JONATHAN[5] MILK, JOB[4], JOB[3], JOHN[2], JOHN[1]*) was born 04 Oct 1844 in Alford, Berkshire County, Massachusetts, and died 20 Dec 1899 in Pittsfield, Berkshire County, Massachusetts. She married CHARLES S. HARVEY 24 Dec 1863. He was born 24 Jan 1843 in Austerlitz, Columbia County, New York, and died 23 Dec 1906 in Springfield, Hampden County, Massachusetts.

Mary married her husband Charles on December 24, 1863. Shortly after, in February of 1864, Charles went off to war. Charles unfortunately was captured and became a POW. I'm sure this was a very difficult time for Mary. Charles was released nearly eight months later during a prisoner exchange. Mary was once again reunited with her husband. Mary died at the age of 55 at the home of her Daughter in Pittsfield, Massachusetts five days after surgery to remove a tumor. She is buried in South Cemetery, West Stockbridge, Berkshire County, Massachusetts

The monument for Charles indicates his birth as being in 1842 but a hand written Bible record indicates he was born January 24, 1843. Charles led a very tough life. In his youth he fought in the Civil War and was captured during the Battle of the Wilderness. He was in Company "D" 57th Massachusetts Regiment. He was taken to one of the most inhumane prison camps, Andersonville Prison then on to Florence Prison. After a prisoner of war exchange, he went on living his life with medical problems. He survived many of his children and his wife until he died 1906 in Springfield, Massachusetts. Burial: South Cemetery, West Stockbridge, Berkshire County, Massachusetts

Children of MARY BAINWAY and CHARLES HARVEY are:
      i. ARTHUR C.[9] HARVEY, b. 05 Sep 1873, West Stockbridge Cemetery, Berkshire County, Massachusetts; d. 08 Oct 1879, Lenox, Berkshire County, Massachusetts. Burial: South Cemetery, West Stockbridge, Berkshire County, Massachusetts
866. ii. HATTIE E. HARVEY, b. 27 Sep 1875, Pittsfield, Berkshire County, Massachusetts; d. 07 Feb 1906, Meriden, New Haven County, Connecticut.

373. GEORGE[8] PERRY (*PHOEBE[7] MILKS, JOB[6], JONATHAN[5] MILK, JOB[4], JOB[3], JOHN[2], JOHN[1]*) was born Abt. 1830 in New York. He married MARY J. _____ Abt. 1860 in Wisconsin. She was born Sep 1843 in Wisconsin. Military service: Pvt., Company H, 8th Regt., Wisconsin Infantry, Civil War.

In 1880 they lived in Stapleton, Chickasaw, Iowa. In 1900 Mary lived in Fayette, Fayette County, Iowa (widow).

Children of GEORGE PERRY and MARY _____ are:
      i. MALCOM[9] PERRY, b. Abt. 1861, Wisconsin.
      ii. MILTON W. PERRY, b. Aug 1866, Wisconsin (twin); m. MARY F. _____, 1898; b. Aug 1872, Iowa.
      iii. VINCENT PERRY, b. Abt. 1866, Wisconsin (twin).

iv. JESSEY PERRY, b. Abt. 1870, Iowa.
v. LESLIE/LEMONT S. PERRY, b. May 1879, Iowa.

374. SALLY A.[8] MILKS *(ICHABOD[7], JOB[6], JONATHAN[5] MILK, JOB[4], JOB[3], JOHN[2], JOHN[1])* was born 29 Jun 1836 in Harrisburg, Lewis County, New York, and died 24 Sep 1887 in Watson, Lewis County, New York. She married SHERILL HIGBY 03 Mar 1855 in Lewis County, New York[1101], son of WILLIAM HIGBY and FANNY DEAN. He was born 20 Sep 1831 in Turin, Lewis County, New York[1101], and died 25 Jun 1904 in Watson, Lewis County, New York. They are buried in Beaches Bridge Cemetery, Watson, Lewis County, New York

Sherill Higby had 100 acres in the Town of Watson, Lewis County, New York. where he was a Justice of the Peace.

Children of SALLY MILKS and SHERILL HIGBY are:
i. CHARLES B.[9] HIGBY, b. 26 Dec 1855, Watson, Lewis County, New York; d. 09 Aug 1877, Lyons Falls. Lewis County, New York. He was burned to death on the Steamer "Lyman R. Lyon" at Lyons Falls, New York. Unmarried
Burial: Beaches Bridge Cemetery, Watson, Lewis County, New York
ii. MARY S. HIGBY, b. 31 Dec 1859, Watson, Lewis County, New York; d. 17 Oct 1888, Watson, Lewis County, New York.
Burial: Beaches Bridge Cemetery, Watson, Lewis County, New York

375. HERMAN[8] MILKS *(ICHABOD[7], JOB[6], JONATHAN[5] MILK, JOB[4], JOB[3], JOHN[2], JOHN[1])* was born 23 Apr 1842 in Watson, Lewis County, New York, and died 18 Oct 1899 in Lowville, Lewis County, New York. He married (1) LOUISA PUFFER 1869. She was born 19 Apr 1836, and died 22 May 1871. He married (2) LOUISA SASENBURY 16 May 1872 in Boonville, NY, daughter of CHRISTIAN SASENBURY and MARGARET WAUFUL. She was born 15 Aug 1855 in Ava, Oneida County, NY, and died 02 Jun 1927 in Lowville, NY.

Herman Milks, b. 23 Apr 1842, Watson, NY (son of Ichabod). After the death of his father and his mother's remarriage, he moved with his mother to Illinois, probably around Gardner or Wilmington. On 12 Sept 1861 Herman enlisted at Wilmington, Ill. For service in the Civil War, was mustered in 11 Oct 1861 at Chicago, Ill. And received an honorable discharge 6 Dec 1865 at Norfolk, VA. He served in Co. E., 39th Ill. Vol. Regt. Under Major Minor Milliman of Oak Park–Chicago Regt., called Yates Phalanx, after Gov. Richard Yates of Ill., and engaged in many battles in Maryland, Virginia, and So. Carolina. A letter written by Herman Milks to his cousin Smith Lewis, prob. In 1864, gives light on Civil War experiences and an insight as to his character and attitudes:

"Well, Smith, I have seen some pretty hard old times since I last saw you. I was in Illinois two years before I came into the Army. I was one winter of that time in Wisconsin, that was one hard old place for me. I have been in the army three years and five days. My time should have been out on the 12th of this month if I had not reenlisted, but as I have, I have got two years and three months to stay yet. I think if I live until that time expires I will have enough of soldiering to do me for a spell. They are trying to get volunteers to go into the regular army. There are several in my company that talk of going – they say that they will go if I will – I can't see the going. . . .

I was home to Illinois on a furlow last winter and had a fine old time too. We are within one mile and a half of Petersburg. Our fellows throw a shell into the city every day – it is a large place. I should judge it is as large as Lowville. We can see it quite plain from here. There was a large fire there last night. I think they were buildings that our fellows set on fire by those shells. Our picket line and the rebs are close together. We have heavy breast works. We dare not show our heads above the works, if we do the Jonneys will ? away at us. There was one man killed today, the ball hit him in the head, killed him inst.

You must excuse this poor writing as I said before I do not feel much like it. If there be any girls there who would like to correspond with a soldier, tell them that I am the chap, tell them that I am a regular rebellion smasher and one of the homeliest chaps that ever lived and would like to correspond with some good looking young girl just for the fun . . . They are drumming a fellow out of camp for cowardice. He has got his head shaved and a board nailed on his back with company and ward marked on it . . . I am very much obliged to you for your well wishes toward me. Goodbye."
(signed) Herman Milks ; Co. E., 39th Reg. Ill. Vol., 10th Army Corps, Ft. Monroe, VA.

In 1866 Herman returned to Lowville, Lewis Co., NY to be with his sister, Mrs. Sherill (Sally Milks) Higby. In 1869 he m. (1) Louisa Puffer, b. 19 Apr 1836, d. 22 May 1871; he was m. (2) on 16 May 1872, by Rev. C. Phillips, at the home of the bride's father on Schuyler St., Boonville, NY, to Louisa Sasenbury, b. 15 Aug 1855, at Ava, Oneida Co., NY, dau of

Christian & Margaret (Wauful) Sasenbury, d. 2 June 1927 at Lowville. Herman was a stationary engineer and practiced his trade until illness prevented; he d. suddenly on 18 Oct 1899 at the family home in Lowville. He is buried in Lowville Rural Cemetery, Lewis County, New York

Children of HERMAN MILKS and LOUISA SASENBURY are:
- i. CHARLES^9 MILKS, b. 01 May 1873, Boonville, Oneida County, NY; d. 02 Feb 1885, Dannetburg, Lewis County, New York.
    Charles died from an injury received while playing in a mill at Dannetburg, New York. He was caught in the unguarded shaft of a wheel and his right arm was torn from his body. He lived 3 days.
- 867. ii. HOMER P. MILKS, b. 15 May 1877, Watson, Lewis County, New York; d. 29 Nov 1957, Lewis County, New York.
- iii. RAY MILKS, b. 17 Sep 1880, Watson, Lewis County, New York; d. 25 Oct 1898, Lowville, Lewis County, New York.
    Burial: Lowville Rural Cemetery, Lowville, Lewis County, New York
- iv. MABEL G. MILKS, b. 23 Mar 1890, Dannetburg, Lewis County, New York. Never married
    Mabel graduated from Lowville Academy, 1911; grad. Frederick Ferris Thomson Hospital, Canandaigua, NY with R.N., 1915; served in U.S. Nave Nurse Corps in Navy hospitals in NY, VA, Washington D.C., RI, and Ill. Until retired, 1933. Mabel is assistant author of History and Genealogy of Milk-Milks Family.

376. WILLARD DENNIS^8 REDINGTON *(MARIA^7 MILKS, JOB^6, JONATHAN^5 MILK, JOB^4, JOB^3, JOHN^2, JOHN^1)* was born 15 Jun 1856 in Otsego County, New York, and died 26 Sep 1940 in Binghamton, Broome County, New York. He married ETHEL MAE ABELL^{1102} 1878 in New York^{1103}. She was born 25 Nov 1860 in New York^{1103}, and died 31 Mar 1924 in Binghamton, Broome County, New York. Residence: 1880, Unadilla, Otsego County, New York

Children of WILLARD REDINGTON and ETHEL ABELL are:
- i. INEZ B.^{9} REDINGTON, b. 27 Sep 1880, Binghamton, Broome County, New York; d. Aft. 16 Apr 1930; m. WILLIAM H. COLEMAN, Bet. 1901 - 1902, New York; b. Abt. 1870, Pennsylvania^{1104}; d. Aft. 16 Apr 1930. No children. Lived in: 1930, Towanda, Bradford County, Pennsylvania. In 1920, William was General Foreman, Powder works
- ii. BESSIE LYLE REDINGTON, b. 18 Nov 1887, Binghamton, Broome County, New York; d. 26 Feb 1893, Binghamton, Broome County, New York.

377. SARAH ERSULA^8 MILKS *(JOHN/JONATHAN L.^{7}, JOB^6, JONATHAN^5 MILK, JOB^4, JOB^3, JOHN^2, JOHN^1)* was born 30 Sep 1849 in Cooperstown, Otsego County, New York^{1105}, and died 29 Apr 1922 in Huntington, Cabell County, West Virginia^{1106}. She married WILLIAM L. LOSEE Bet. 1872 - 1873 in Oneonta, Otsego County, New York, son of JOEL LOSEE and ELIZABETH _____. He was born Sep 1842 in New York, and died Bef. 29 Apr 1922. William was a telegraph operator on Chesapeake & Ohio R.R.
   Sarah died of a cerebral Hemorrhage and is buried in Hurricane, W. Va. On the death certificate for Sarah, it is stated that her mother's maiden name was Sperry. (as attested to by her son Albert Losee)

Children of SARAH MILKS and WILLIAM LOSEE are:
- i. FANNIE AGNES^9 LOSEE, b. 25 Jun 1877, Hurricane, W. Va.^{1107}; d. 14 Mar 1878, Hurricane, W. Va.^{1107}.
- ii. SPERRY BARNES LOSEE, b. 13 May 1878, Hurricane, W. Va.; d. 13 May 1878, Hurricane, W. Va..
- 868. iii. ALBERT ROBERT LOSEE, b. 16 Jul 1880, Hurricane, W. Va..
- 869. iv. WILLIAM GUY LOSEE, b. 28 Aug 1884, Hurricane, W. Va.; d. 06 May 1950, Boyd, Kentucky.

378. EMMA^8 MILKS *(EBENEZER^7, JOB^6, JONATHAN^5 MILK, JOB^4, JOB^3, JOHN^2, JOHN^1)* was born 13 Feb 1863 in Delaware County, New York^{1108}, and died 07 Aug 1886 in Delaware County, New York^{1108}. She married ELIAS POLLOCK HOWLAND 07 May 1878 in Walton, Delaware County, New York. He was born 11 Feb 1847 in Hamden, Delaware County, New York^{1108}, and died 08 Sep 1906 in Delaware County, New York^{1108}. Elias ran a grist mill at Walton, Delaware County, New York. Emma and Elias are buried in Walton Cemetery, Delaware County, New York

Children of EMMA MILKS and ELIAS HOWLAND are:
- 870. i. LIZZIE^9 HOWLAND, b. 10 Apr 1883, Delaware County, New York.

871. ii. SETH ADAN HOWLAND, b. 29 Aug 1885, Delaware County, New York; d. Nov 1964, Oxford, Chenango County, New York.

379. CLARA[8] MILKS *(EBENEZER[7], JOB[6], JONATHAN[5] MILK, JOB[4], JOB[3], JOHN[2], JOHN[1])* was born 11 May 1871 in Delaware County, New York, and died 20 Dec 1925. She married GEORGE CURTIS 13 Jan 1887. He was born 19 Aug 1867, and died 17 Dec 1949.

Children of CLARA MILKS and GEORGE CURTIS are:
872. i. MINNIE M.[9] CURTIS, b. 19 Aug 1888, New York; d. Dec 1983, Sidney, Delaware County, New York.
     ii. EMMA CURTIS, b. 10 Oct 1893, Gilbertsville, Otsego County, New York[1109]; d. Sep 1982, Unadilla, Otsego Count, New York[1109]. Lived in: Unadilla, Chenango Count, New York. Occupation: Beauty Parlor owner
873. iii. RAYMOND CURTIS, b. 21 Oct 1898, West Exeter, Otsego County, New York.
874. iv. REXFORD CURTIS, b. 20 Dec 1902, Richfield, Otsego County, New York.

380. JOSEPH R.[8] HEMINGWAY *(HARRIETT EMELINE[7] MILKS, JOHN[6], JONATHAN[5] MILK, JOB[4], JOB[3], JOHN[2], JOHN[1])* was born Abt. 1842 in New York, and died Bet. 1880 - 1900 in Canaan, Columbia County, New York. He married (1) CLARA _____ Abt. 1864 in Canaan, Columbia County, New York ?. She was born Abt. 1845 in New York, and died Bet. 1874 - 1875 in Canaan, Columbia County, New York. He married (2) MARY A. _____ Abt. 1870. She was born Abt. 1853 in Ohio.

Children of JOSEPH HEMINGWAY and CLARA _____ are:
   i. JANE 'JENNIE'[9] HEMINGWAY, b. Abt. 1865, Canaan, Columbia County, New York.
   ii. JOHN HEMINGWAY, b. Abt. 1867, Canaan, Columbia County, New York.
   iii ELIZABETH 'LIBBIE' HEMINGWAY, b. Abt. 1871, Columbia County, New York
   iv. FRANK HEMINGWAY, b. Abt. 1874, Columbia County, New York.

381. WILLIAM[8] HEMINGWAY *(HARRIETT EMELINE[7] MILKS, JOHN[6], JONATHAN[5] MILK, JOB[4], JOB[3], JOHN[2], JOHN[1])* was born Abt. 1852 in Canaan, Columbia County, New York. He married ARAMINTA _____[1110] Bet. 1875 - 1876 in Canaan, Columbia County, New York ?[1110]. She was born Abt. 1855 in New York.

Child of WILLIAM HEMINGWAY and ARAMINTA _____ is:
   i. HARRIET 'HATTIE'[9] HEMINGWAY, b. Bet. 1876 - 1877, Canaan, Columbia County, New York.

382. RICHARD GRAVES[8] MILKS *(CHARLES ROLLAND[7], JOHN[6], JONATHAN[5] MILK, JOB[4], JOB[3], JOHN[2], JOHN[1])*[1111,1112] was born Aug 1838 in Lowville, Lewis County, New York[1113,1114], and died Aft. 1910 in Columbia County, New York ?. He married CATHERINE J. 'KATE' BENTLEY. She was born Dec 1839 in New York[1114], and died Aft. 1910 in Columbia County, New York. Richard was a Clerk in the Capitol State House. Granted deed to land along New Scotland Road, Bethlehem, and Delaware Turnpike

Children of RICHARD MILKS and CATHERINE BENTLEY are:
875. i. ARTHUR ROLLAND[9] MILKS, b. 29 Oct 1863, New York; d. Jul 1947, Denver, Colorado.
     ii. KATE BENTLEY MILKS, b. 1867, New York[1115,1116]; d. 1952; m. JACOB S. CONGDON[1117,1118,1119,1120], 1893; b. Jan 1868, Bethlehem, Albany County, New York. No children. Lived at 15 N. Main Ave., Albany, NY Jacob was a Cashier at a RR Company.
     iii. WENDALL MILLER MILKS, b. Bet. 1874 - 1875, New York[1121,1122,1123]; d. 21 May 1949[1124]; m. IDAY MAE MACBAIN[1125], Bet. 1903 - 1904[1126]; b. Bet. 1884 - 1885, New York[1127,1128]. No children.

   The following is an excerpt from **"A Good Albanian Dies,"** by E. S. Van Olenda, in an Albany, NY newspaper:
   "The death of Wendall Miller Milks was a great shock to his host of friends in Albany, where he had lived most of his life. He was the son of the late Mr. Richard G. Milks of Elsmere. His father for many years was in the office of the State Treasurer. Wendall Milks spent most of his active life in the banking business, beginning as a bookkeeper, later a teller, and lastly in the mortgage department. While in this he was stricken with blindness.
   Wendall Milks was an excellent musician and played the piano like a professional. He had a fine

baritone voice and sang in the Mendelssohn Club for many years. His most noteworthy contribution to the city's civic life was his service to St. Peter's Episcopal Church, where he was chimer for many years. The office of chimer of St. Peter's was a test of fortitude, courage and good health. The chimes are situated in the Tweedle Memorial Tower, necessitating the climb of several hundred steps to reach the keyboard of the set of bells. It was very hot in summer and extremely cold in winter, but these climatic changes did not deter Mr. Milks and he performed his duties with devotional fidelity to the church and to the city of Albany on the occasions when St. Peter's chimes antedated the present municipal set of carillons. Mr. Milks played hymns and patriotic anthems to augment the parodies taking place in the street, hundreds of feet below. The New Year is always rung in from the tower of St. Peter's Church on the famous Queen Ann bell and Mr. Milks had an enviable record of devotion to his tasks.

Mr. Milks was a gentleman, whose friendship was valued by all who had the privilege of knowing him. He was modest, self-effacing, always cheerful in spite of his handicap of blindness. In his quiet, unassuming way he made a considerable imprint on the sands of time in the city he loved and in which he was loved. He was a "Good Albanian' in every sense of the term."

876.   iv.   RICHARD GRAVES MILKS, b. Bet. 1876 - 1877, New York; d. 19 Jul 1947, Penfield, NY.

383. CHARLOTTE H. 'LOTTIE'^{8} MILKS *(CHARLES ROLLAND^7, JOHN^6, JONATHAN^5 MILK, JOB^4, JOB^3, JOHN^2, JOHN^1)*^{1129} was born Sep 1841 in New York^{1129,1130}, and died 18 Sep 1922 in King, Waupaca County, Wisconsin. She married GEORGE HIRAM CHASE, son of GILBERT CHASE and LUCEY RUBIN. He was born 21 May 1843 in New York or Vermont (1850 census), and died 30 Jul 1918 in Clifton, Greenlee County, Arizona^{1131}. Charlotte is buried in Wisconsin Veterans Memorial Cemetery, King, Waupaca County, Wisconsin [Plot: SECTION 10 ROW 5OS SITE 46]. Charlotte lived in Appleton, Outagamie County, Wisconsin. In 1905 she stated that her occupation was "Capitalist".

George is buried in Clifton Cemetery, Clifton, Greenlee County, Arizona, USA

George was a Sergeant Major in Companies A & L; 2nd New York Cavalry; Union Army, CIVIL WAR. He enlisted at the age of 19, on 23 Sep 1861 at Fort Edward, NY. Mustered in as Private, Company L, 2nd New York Cavalry for a period of 3 years. Re-enlisted on 29 Dec 1863. Was missing in action (date unknown) and returned to the unit on 7 Aug 1864.

Transferred to Company A on 29 Aug 1864 with the rank of Sergeant. Promoted to Sergeant Major on 1 Jan 1865. Mustered out with the unit on 23 Jun 1865 at Alexandria, VA. He was commissioned as a 2nd Lieutenant on 31 May 1865, with an effective date of 28 Apr 1865; however, the unit mustered out before he could be "mustered in" as an officer.

It appears from Veteran's payment cards, that George was receiving Veteran benefits as an 'invalid' beginning in Sept. 1884. In addition, his first wife, Charlotte Milks Chase, also received part of his benefits because of "desertion" by George.

GEORGE H. CHASE, Senator from Greenlee County, is a veteran of the Civil War, an absolutely reliable business man, an all around booster, and one of the most gentlemanly and substantial citizens of Arizona.

He was born in New York in 1843, and has been a resident of this State since 1898.

While Senator Chase can hardly be classified as a pioneer, he comes of a line of pioneers and statesmen. His father, Samuel P. Chase, was a well known pioneer of that section of New York in which the Senator was born, and like his distinguished relative Salmon P. Chase, of national reputation, was known as a progressive, wide awake citizen whose word was as good as his bond.

Since coming to Arizona, Senator Chase has been actively engaged in its up-building, and when Arizona was ready for admission to the Union, the people of his county united in choosing him their first representative in the State Senate, regardless of their political belief, for, although they knew him to be a progressive Democrat, they also knew what manner of man he is. George H. Chase is a fighter and builder, and he has aided in many of the important building enterprises of the Senate, especially mining buildings of Clifton-Morenci district, which bear the stamp of approval of competent judges. Senator Chase is a Blue Lodge Mason of more than forty years standing, and is a member of Winnebago Lodge No. 33, of Portage, Wisconsin.

During the Civil War he served three years as cavalryman and was wounded three times, and left the service a Sergeant-Major with two commissions in his pocket, neither of which he accepted. Like his military record, his record since has been without blemish, the credit for which he is perfectly willing to share with Mrs. Chase, who is known throughout Gila Valley as "Aunt Maggie", where she numbers her friends by her acquaintants, and her delight is in doing good. Mr. and Mrs. Chase are a splendid and interesting old couple, though George H. denies being old. They have two daughters and one son. At the first session of the Legislature Senator Chase was Chairman of the Committee on Mines and Mining and member of five other committees, and at the special session was Chairman of the Committee on Education and Public Institutions and member of the Enrolling and Engrossing, Labor, Mines and Mining, Constitutional Amendments and Referendum, and Corporations Committees. When the First Legislature of Arizona has completed its work, there is no man whose record as a member will more readily prove up under the searchlight than the "Gentleman from Greenlee", one of the staunch sort, of whom the State may well be proud.

Children of CHARLOTTE MILKS and GEORGE CHASE are:
       i. CARRIE E.^{9} CHASE, b. 14 Oct 1866, Lowville, Columbia County, Wisconsin[1132].
877. ii. WILLIAM G. CHASE, b. 02 Aug 1869, Waterford, Saratoga County, New York.
878. iii. MARTHA 'MATTIE' SCOVIL CHASE, b. 21 Oct 1878, Lowville, Columbia County, Wisconsin.
       iv. MALE CHASE, b. 01 Mar 1881, Portage, Columbia County, Wisconsin[1133].

384. HELEN^8 MILKS *(CHARLES ROLLAND^7, JOHN^6, JONATHAN^5 MILK, JOB^4, JOB^3, JOHN^2, JOHN^1)*[1134] was born Abt. 1845 in New York[1135,1136], and died 1914 in Washington County, New York. She married FRANCIS JAMES 'FRANK' BIGGART. He was born Abt. 1843 in Vermont[1137,1138], and died 1923 in Washington County, New York. They are buried in Union Cemetery, Fort Edward, Washington County, New York, Francis was a farmer.

Child of HELEN MILKS and FRANCIS BIGGART is:
       i. GERTRUDE M.^{9} BIGGART, b. Abt. 1870, Washington County, New York. Occupation: School Teacher

385. HORACE B.^{8} MILKS *(ELKANAH B.^{7}, JONATHAN^6, JONATHAN^5 MILK, JOB^4, JOB^3, JOHN^2, JOHN^1)* was born Nov 1838 in Otsego County, New York[1139], and died 06 May 1904 in Westford, Otsego County, NY. He married LANEY C. NELLIS Abt. 1861 in Otsego County, New York ?[1139]. She was born Aug 1842 in New York[1139], and died 1917 in Westford, Otsego County, NY. They are buried in Elk Creek Cemetery, Maryland, Otsego Co., NY

Children of HORACE MILKS and LANEY NELLIS are:
       i. CARRIE H.^{9} MILKS, b. 1863, Otsego County, New York[1140]; d. 1864, Otsego County, New York[1140]. Burial: 1864, Elk Creek Cemetery, Maryland, Otsego Co., NY
879. ii. CLARA MILKS, b. 06 Dec 1864, Westford, Otsego County, New York; d. 27 Sep 1950, Milford, New York.
       iii. LEROY MILKS, b. 29 Jun 1867, Otsego County, New York?[1141,1142]; d. 11 Jul 1937, Maryland, Otsego County, NY (Never married)[1142]. Burial: Elk Creek Cemetery, Maryland, Otsego Co., NY. Never married.
          "**SCHENEVUS MAN IN ILL HEALTH TAKES OWN LIFE** ... An investigation revealed a chain unhooked on the rear right basement door of a barn leading into an old chicken coop.
          Mr. Finigan found the door braced inside with a stick, pushed it open and discovered the body hanging from a rafter. The victim had placed the knot of the noose under the point of his chin and died from a broken neck and strangulation. Two small boxes near the body he had apparently kicked from under him.
          The troopers said he left three notes, one addressed to his sister, Mrs. Jacob Baldwin of Milford. Mr. Milks retired from farming ten years ago on account of ill health. Born in the town of Westford June 29, 1867, the son of Horace and Laney (Nellis) Milks, he formerly operated a farm at Elk Creek. He suffered poor eyesight and hearing.
          In addition to his sister, he is survived by one niece, Mrs. M. D. Dewey of Milford; one nephew, Jesse Nellis of Schenevus, R. D.; and several cousins ..." [The Otsego Farmer & Republican" (Cooperstown, NY), Jul. 16, 1937, Vol. LI, No. 37]

386. SARAH ANN^8 MILKS *(ELKANAH B.^{7}, JONATHAN^6, JONATHAN^5 MILK, JOB^4, JOB^3, JOHN^2, JOHN^1)* was born 22 Nov 1844 in Westford, Otsego County, NY, and died 08 Feb 1917 in Des Moines, Iowa[1143]. She married JOHN SIDNEY CRIPPIN 05 Apr 1864 in Ballard's Hotel, Oneonta, Otsego County, New York, by Rev. G. O. Phelps[1144]. He was born 26 Jan 1842 in Worcester, NY, and died 26 Feb 1915 in Des Moines, Iowa[1145].

Children of SARAH MILKS and JOHN CRIPPIN are:
880. i. MARGARET^9 CRIPPIN, b. 10 Feb 1865, Worcester, Otsego County, New York; d. 1947.
881. ii. MARY L. CRIPPIN, b. 29 May 1866, Worcester, Otsego County, New York; d. Sep 1943.
       iii. FRANCES 'FRANKIE' CRIPPIN, b. 04 Nov 1867, Worcester, Otsego County, New York; d. 06 Jul 1953, Amatlan de Canas, Nay Mexico; m. JOSEPH B. MULHALL, 18 Dec 1888, Kansas[1145]; b. 26 Jan 1856; d. St.

        Louis, Missouri. Lived bet. 1900 - 1953, in Amatlan de Canas, Nay Mexico
- iv. CORA C. CRIPPIN, b. 09 Feb 1871, Worcester, Otsego County, New York; d. 25 Mar 1954, Carlisle, Iowa; m. (1) A. C. PRUM[1146], 03 Jan 1891, La Marlle, Polk County, Iowa[1146]; b. 1862, Maquoketa; d. Bef. Nov 1899, Iowa; m. (2) EDWARD SANDERS[1146], 19 Nov 1899, Warren, Warren County, Iowa[1146]; b. Oct 1870, Carlisle, Iowa. No children. Residence: Des Moines, Iowa
- v. PHILO CRIPPIN, b. 20 Sep 1872, Worcester, Otsego County, New York; d. 08 May 1924; m. FLORENCE _____, Bet. 1910 - 1920; b. 1876, Iowa. Occupation: 1920, Painter in Paint shop. Residence: 1920, Kansas City, Jackson County, Missouri
- vi. JAMES CRIPPIN, b. 04 Feb 1874, Worcester, Otsego County, New York; m. (1) NELLIE C. KELLEY[1146], 14 Aug 1897, Des Moines, Polk County, Iowa[1146]; b. Abt. 1880, Iowa; m. (2) IDA WILLITS, 03 Jul 1917, Des Moines, Iowa; b. Abt. 1868, Indiana. Residence: Carlisle, Iowa
- vii. CHARLES CRIPPIN, b. 25 Apr 1876, Worcester, Otsego County, New York; d. 16 Feb 1880, Worcester, Otsego County, New York.
- 882. viii. JOHN R. CRIPPIN, b. 06 Nov 1880, Brighton, Washington County, Iowa; d. Feb 1925.
- ix. MARCUS A. CRIPPIN, b. 14 Jun 1886, Des Moines, Iowa[1147]; d. 13 Dec 1934, Iowa[1148]. Military service: WWI

387. CHARLES B.[8] MILKS *(ELKANAH B.[7], JONATHAN[6], JONATHAN[5] MILK, JOB[4], JOB[3], JOHN[2], JOHN[1])* was born 17 Jan 1847 in Westford, Otsego County, NY[1149], and died 30 Jan 1931 in Otsego Co., NY[1149]. He married JULIA AGNES CHASE Abt. 1876, daughter of HORACE CHASE and JULIA GROFF. She was born 11 Dec 1847 in Westford, Otsego County, New York[1149], and died 29 Jan 1931 in Otsego Co., NY[1149]. They are buried in Elk Creek Cemetery, Maryland, Otsego Co., NY

DEATH NOTICE

"Death last week claimed two aged residents of the town of Maryland within twenty-four hours of each other, both victims of pneumonia ... Charles B. Milks was born in the town of Westford, January 17, 1847, the son of Elkanah and Mary Griswold Milks. He was a farmer and for many years the family resided on the Elk Creek-Westford road. Mr. Milks is also survived by a sister, Mrs. Eldora Lawson, who resides in the west. A double funeral service was conducted at the home at 1 o'clock Sunday afternoon, the Rev. Robert E. Fletcher, pastor of the Schenevus Methodist church, officiating. Burial was made in the Elk Creek Cemetery." ["The Otsego Farmer & Republican" (Cooperstown, N.Y.), Feb 6 1931, p. 6]

Children of CHARLES MILKS and JULIA CHASE are:
- 883. i. OSCAR[9] MILKS, b. 24 May 1877, Otsego Co., NY; d. 10 Jun 1911, Worcester, Otsego County, New York.
- 884. ii. LUELLA B. MILKS, b. 08 Sep 1880, Otsego County, New York; d. 1970, Otsego County, New York.

388. ROSAMOND[8] GRISWOLD *(MARY ANN[7] MILKS, JONATHAN[6], JONATHAN[5] MILK, JOB[4], JOB[3], JOHN[2], JOHN[1])* was born Dec 1842[1150]. She married MORDECAI KNAPP 1867 in Otsego County, New York. He was born Sep 1841 in New York[1150].

Children of ROSAMOND GRISWOLD and MORDECAI KNAPP are:
- i. WILLIE L.[9] KNAPP, b. Bet. 1866 - 1867, Otsego County, New York.
- ii. EVALINE KNAPP, b. Bet. 1868 - 1869, Otsego County, New York.
- iii. LYMAN KNAPP, b. Bet. 1870 - 1871, Otsego County, New York; m. CLAUDINE _____, Bet. 1902 - 1903, Otsego County, New York; b. Bet. 1872 - 1873, New York. Residence: 1910, Oneonta, Otsego County, New York
- iv. HARRY KNAPP, b. Oct 1883, Otsego County, New York.

389. JOHN J.[8] GRISWOLD *(MARY ANN[7] MILKS, JONATHAN[6], JONATHAN[5] MILK, JOB[4], JOB[3], JOHN[2], JOHN[1])* was born 1846 in Westford, Otsego County, New York[1151], and died 29 Jan 1923 in Otsego County, New York[1151]. He married (1) ELIZABETH 'LIBBIE' VAN WIE Abt. 1867. She was born 1841[1152,1153], and died 1891 in Schenevus, Otsego Co., NY[1154,1155]. He married (2) HATTIE L. (TRUAX) CHAMPION[1156] 1893 in Otsego County, New York[1156]. She was born Feb 1860 in Otsego County, New York, and died 1925 in Otsego County, New York. Hattie is buried in Maple Grove Cemetery, Worcester, Otsego County, New York

DEATH NOTICE

"John Griswold, a life-long resident of Maryland township, died at his home on East street in Schenevus Monday evening, after an illness of three weeks of bronchial pneumonia, aged 76 years. Mr. Griswold was twice married, two

sons survive him, Wickham, and Charles Griswold, both of Schenevus, and the present wife who was Miss Truax. The funeral services will be held from his late home Thursday at 2 o'clock. The Rev. George Scobey of the Baptist Church will officiate and the remains will be placed in the vault to be interred later in the family plot in Schenevus cemetery." ["The Otsego Farmer & Republican" (Cooperstown, NY), Feb. 2, 1923, Page 7]   Burial: Schenevus Cemetery, Schenevus, Otsego County, New York

Children of JOHN GRISWOLD and ELIZABETH VAN WIE are:
- i. MATIE[9] GRISWOLD[1157], b. 1868, Otsego County, New York[1157]; d. 1876, Otsego County, New York[1157]. Burial: Schenevus Cemetery, Schenevus, Otsego County, New York
- 885. ii. WICKHAM H. GRISWOLD, b. 27 Mar 1876, Otsego County, New York; d. 10 Mar 1950, Schenevus, Otsego County, New York.
- iii. CHARLES GRISWOLD, b. 1884, Otsego County, New York; d. 18 May 1953, Cooperstown, Otsego County, New York.

OBITUARY

"The death of Charles Griswold, aged 68, occurred suddenly Monday morning at his room in the Knox school dormitory following a heart attack. Mr. Griswold, who had been a resident of Cooperstown for about six years, had finished his morning duties in the kitchen at the school where he was employed and had returned to his room about 9:30 a. m. He was found about an hour later by a fellow worker.

He was born in Schenevus on August 14, 1884, a son of John and Elizabeth (Van Wie) Griswold, and had always lived in that community until he moved to Cooperstown where he was employed at Knox. He never married.

Surviving is a sister-in-law, Mrs. Nettie Griswold of Schenevus; two nieces; and several cousins.

Funeral services were held Thursday afternoon at 2 o'clock at the Tillapaugh Funeral Home here with the Rev. Kenneth E. Hardy, pastor of the First Baptist church, officiating. Burial was in Schenevus cemetery." ["The Otsego Farmer & Republican" (Cooperstown, NY), Friday, May 22, 1953, Page Three]
   Burial: Schenevus Cemetery, Otsego County, New York

390. LAURA A.[8] GRISWOLD *(MARY ANN[7] MILKS, JONATHAN[6], JONATHAN[5] MILK, JOB[4], JOB[3], JOHN[2], JOHN[1])* was born Jan 1850 in Otsego County, New York. She married THOMAS BARNES Abt. 1869. He was born Abt. 1849, and died Bef. 1900 in Otsego County, New York.

Children of LAURA GRISWOLD and THOMAS BARNES are:
- i. FRED[9] BARNES, b. Abt. 1878, Otsego County, New York; d. Bef. 1900, Otsego County, New York.
- ii. STEWART BARNES, b. Jan 1885, Otsego County, New York.
- iii. EMMA E. BARNES, b. Aug 1870, Otsego County, New York; m. WILLIAM D. HANFORD, Bet. 1896 - 1897, Otsego County, New York; b. Sep 1874, New York. Residence: Unadilla, New York

391. EUGENE[8] CRIPPEN *(CHRISTINE[7] MILKS, JONATHAN[6], JONATHAN[5] MILK, JOB[4], JOB[3], JOHN[2], JOHN[1])* was born 12 Aug 1844 in Worcester, Otsego County, New York, and died 30 Jan 1930 in Worcester, Otsego County, New York. He married (1) SOPHRONIA SMITH 26 Jun 1865 in Otsego County, New York, daughter of JOHN SMITH and ANNA _____. She was born 24 Nov 1841 in Otsego County, New York, and died 26 Sep 1905 in Worcester, Otsego County, New York. He married (2) AUGUSTA WARNER 30 Mar 1907 in Otsego County, New York.

OBITUARY

"Eugene Crippen, eighty-six-year-old retired farmer of Worcester, died at the home of his cousin, Harrison Crippen, early Thursday night of last week. Mr. Crippen had been in ill health for the last three years.

Mr. Crippen was born in Worcester on August 12, 1844, the son of Wellington E., and Christine Milks Crippen.

In 1865 he was married to Sophronia Smith, who died in 1905. Two sons were born to this marriage, both of whom are dead.

In 1907 Mr. Crippen married Mrs. Augusta Mabie, who survives him and who has been most devoted in her care of him.

Crippen was a farmer as long as health permitted and always lived in Worcester. There are no surviving relatives besides the wife, and several cousins." ["The Otsego Farmer & Republican" (Cooperstown, NY), Fri., Feb. 7, 1930, Page Eight]
   Burial: Maple Grove Cemetery, Worcester, Otsego County, New York

Children of EUGENE CRIPPEN and SOPHRONIA SMITH are:
- i. WELLINGTON[9] CRIPPEN, b. 12 Aug 1866, Otsego County, New York; d. 26 Jan 1922, Otsego County, New York; m. BELLE TABOR; b. 14 Mar 1863, Otsego County, New York; d. 10 Dec 1919, Otsego County, New York. Burial: Maple Grove Cemetery, Worcester, Otsego County, New York
- ii. HARRISON CRIPPEN, b. 22 Oct 1868, Otsego County, New York; d. 16 Mar 1880, Otsego County, New York. Burial: Maple Grove Cemetery, Worcester, Otsego County, New York

392. JOHN A.[8] CRIPPEN (*CHRISTINE[7] MILKS, JONATHAN[6], JONATHAN[5] MILK, JOB[4], JOB[3], JOHN[2], JOHN[1]*) was born 20 May 1849 in Worcester, Otsego County, New York, and died 09 Aug 1905 in Texarkana, Texas. He married KATE HALLOCK, daughter of DAVID HALLOCK. Residence: 1880, Joliet, Will County, Illinois. Listed as 'single' in 1880 Will County, Illinois census. Killed in RR accident. Occupation: 1880, RR Employee

Children of JOHN CRIPPEN and KATE HALLOCK are:
886. i. CORA[9] CRIPPEN, b. 27 Oct 1869, Otsego County, New York; d. 07 Oct 1955, Oneonta, Otsego County, NY.
887. ii. GRACE CRIPPEN, b. 18 May 1876, Otsego County, New York; d. 14 Jul 1900, Otsego County, New York.

393. GEORGE[8] BARNARD (*GEORGE[7], RUTH[6] MILKS, JOB[5] MILK, JONATHAN[4], JOB[3], JOHN[2], JOHN[1]*) was born 27 Oct 1833 in Rome, Oneida County, New York, and died 29 Jan 1896. He married JANE SOPHIA FULLER 24 Aug 1858 in Rome, Oneida County, New York, daughter of CHARLES FULLER and ALIVIA COLE. She was born 11 Jul 1835, and died 18 Jun 1924 in Rome, Oneida County, New York.

Children of GEORGE BARNARD and JANE FULLER are:
888. i. CHARLES FULLER[9] BARNARD, b. 11 Dec 1859, Rome, Oneida County, New York; d. 27 Oct 1905, Rome, Oneida County, New York.
- ii. JAMES ELWELL BARNARD, b. 26 Feb 1862, Rome, Oneida County, New York; d. 15 Apr 1939, Rome, Oneida County, New York; m. EMMA WHITE.
- iii. FRED M. BARNARD, b. 1864, Rome, Oneida County, New York.
- iv. HARRY COLE BARNARD, b. 17 Aug 1866, Rome, Oneida County, New York; d. 29 Apr 1871, Rome, Oneida County, New York.

394. MARTIN MILLER[8] BARNARD (*ADONIJAH[7], RUTH[6] MILKS, JOB[5] MILK, JONATHAN[4], JOB[3], JOHN[2], JOHN[1]*) was born 18 Jan 1834 in Lee, Oneida County, New York, and died 06 Jul 1908 in Fernwood, Oswego County, New York. He married LAURA HICKS. She was born 16 Aug 1846, and died 10 Feb 1938.

Child of MARTIN BARNARD and LAURA HICKS is:
- i. GEORGE[9] BARNARD, b. 12 Sep 1872, Fernwood, Oswego County, New York; d. 02 Jul 1943, Syracuse, Onondaga County, New York; m. EFFA A. BERRY; b. 17 Jun 1871, Fernwood, Oswego County, New York; d. 28 Nov 1938, Pulaski, Oswego County, New York.

395. ELIZABETH ANN 'BETSY'[8] MILKS (*GEORGE[7], FREEMAN[6], JOB[5] MILK, JONATHAN[4], JOB[3], JOHN[2], JOHN[1]*) was born 28 Nov 1845 in Lee, Oneida County, New York, and died 25 Aug 1905 in Bon Homme County, South Dakota. She married IRA KELLOGG 02 Nov 1859 in Port Hope, Haldimand Township, Ontario, Canada, son of IRA KELLOGG and REBECCA _____. He was born 22 Aug 1835 in Haldimand Township, Ontario, Canada, and died 12 Jun 1907 in Bon Homme County, South Dakota.

Children of ELIZABETH MILKS and IRA KELLOGG are:
889. i. GEORGE HENRY[9] KELLOGG, b. 1861, Trenton, Ontario, Canada; d. 25 Dec 1925, Bon Homme County, SD.
890. ii. JAMES MONROE KELLOGG, b. 1863, Ontario, Canada; d. Aft. 1930, Missouri.
891. iii. EVA LOUISE KELLOGG, b. 1869, Putnam, Fayette County, Iowa; d. 11 Nov 1945, Wapato, Yakima Co., WA.
892. iv. MATILDA MELISSA KELLOGG, b. Dec 1870, Iowa; d. 1935, Fayetteville, Washington County, Arkansas.
893. v. BENJAMIN F. KELLOGG, b. 1873, Iowa; d. 05 May 1949, Yakima County, Washington.
894. vi. BERTHA MAY KELLOGG, b. 31 Jul 1879, Iowa; d. 24 Sep 1934, Prob. Sioux County, Nebraska.
- vii. STELLA A. KELLOGG, b. 1883, Bon Homme County, South Dakota.
- viii. LEONARD A. KELLOGG, b. 03 Sep 1885, Bon Homme County, South Dakota; d. 10 Jun 1959, Bon Homme County, South Dakota; m. NETTA ASHDOWN, 21 May 1908, Bon Homme County, South Dakota; b. 17

Feb 1886, Sioux City, Iowa; d. Nov 1983, Bon Homme County, South Dakota.
- ix. HARRISON CLEMONT KELLOGG, b. 07 Nov 1888, Bon Homme County, South Dakota; d. 31 Dec 1944, Prob. Greybull, Big Horn County, Wyoming; m. EVA BISHOP, 04 Aug 1924, Minnehaha, South Dakota; b. Abt. 1889, Kansas City, Missouri; d. Bef. 1930.

396. BENJAMIN L.[8] MILKS *(GEORGE[7], FREEMAN[6], JOB[5] MILK, JONATHAN[4], JOB[3], JOHN[2], JOHN[1])* was born 26 Dec 1851 in Lee, Oneida County, New York, and died 26 Oct 1919 in Essex, Essex County, Vermont. He married SARAH SMITH, daughter of PETER SMITH and HARRIET. She was born 08 Apr 1855 in Ontario, Canada, and died Aft. 1920 in Vermont.

Children of BENJAMIN MILKS and SARAH SMITH are:
- 895. i. GEORGE HENRY[9] MYLKES, b. 25 Nov 1875, Rome, New York; d. 01 Feb 1936, Burlington, Chittenden Co., VT.
- 896. ii. HARRIETT 'HATTIE' MELISSA MYLKES, b. 27 Jun 1878, Belleville, Hastings, Ontario, Canada.
- 897. iii. CHARLES FREDERICK 'FRED' MYLKES, b. 11 Sep 1882, Hastings, Ontario, Canada; d. Apr 1964, New York.

397. ORA AMELIA 'AMY'[8] MILKS *(GEORGE[7], FREEMAN[6], JOB[5] MILK, JONATHAN[4], JOB[3], JOHN[2], JOHN[1])* was born 09 Jul 1856 in Lee, Oneida County, New York, and died 04 Apr 1939 in Saltville, Smyth County, Virginia. She married (1) WILLIAM ROBINSON Abt. 1870 in Lee, Oneida County, NY?. He was born Bet. 1836 - 1837, and died Abt. 1876 in New York. She married (2) HENRY T. GILBERT Abt. 1878, son of JOHN GILBERT and JANE FULCHER. He was born 07 Sep 1847 in Patrick County, Virginia, and died 23 May 1901 in Smyth County, Virginia.

Children of ORA MILKS and WILLIAM ROBINSON are:
- 898. i. MELISSA VIRGINIA 'JENNIE'[9] ROBINSON, b. 1871, New York; d. Abt. 1930, Saltville, Smyth County, Virginia
- 899. ii. WILLIAM ROBINSON, JR., b. 1873, New York; d. Aft. 1930, Virginia.

Children of ORA MILKS and HENRY GILBERT are:
- 900. iii. EMMETT RAY[9] GILBERT, b. 28 Apr 1879, Saltville, Smyth County, Virginia; d. 10 Feb 1940, Mt. Hope, Fayette County, West Virginia.
- 901. iv. EMORY HENRY GILBERT, b. 28 Apr 1879, Saltville, Smyth County, Virginia; d. 21 Apr 1951, Palatka, Putnam County, Florida.
- 902. v. MAUDE GILBERT, b. 04 Nov 1882, Saltville, Smyth County, Virginia; d. 1945, Tennessee.
- 903. vi. CARRIE MYRTLE GILBERT, b. 30 Oct 1884, Saltville, Smyth County, Virginia; d. Nov 1974, Indiana.
- 904. vii. REBECCA GILBERT, b. Oct 1886, Saltville, Smyth County, Virginia; d. Abt. 1954, Saltville, Smyth County, Virginia.
- 905. viii. MARY GILBERT, b. 20 Mar 1889, Saltville, Smyth County, Virginia; d. May 1968, Tennessee.
- ix. GEORGE GILBERT, b. Abt. 1890, Saltville, Smyth County, Virginia; d. Abt. 1917, Virginia. George had convulsions, and he froze to death walking through the mountains. His remains were found later.
- 906. x. FRED GILBERT, b. 30 Nov 1891, Saltville, Smyth County, Virginia; d. 17 Jul 1959, Saltville, Smyth County, VA.
- xi. LOU E. GILBERT, b. 1892, Saltville, Smyth County, Virginia; d. 21 Oct 1892, Saltville, Smyth County, Virginia.
- xii. UNNAMED GILBERT, b. 15 Dec 1895, Saltville, Smyth County, Virginia; d. 21 Dec 1895, Saltville, Smyth County, Virginia.
- xiii. UNNAMED2 GILBERT, b. 15 Dec 1895, Saltville, Smyth County, Virginia; d. 25 Dec 1895, Saltville, Smyth County, Virginia.
- 907. xiv. ALBERT GILBERT, b. 05 Sep 1896, Saltville, Smyth County, Virginia; d. May 1973, Abingdon, Virginia.
- 908. xv. HATTIE GILBERT, b. 24 Jul 1897, Saltville, Smyth County, Virginia; d. 09 Mar 1918, Virginia.

398. CHESTER PIERCE[8] KILE *(SARAH S.[7] MILKS, DAVID[6], JOB[5] MILK, JONATHAN[4], JOB[3], JOHN[2], JOHN[1])* was born 19 Nov 1853 in Ohio, and died 05 Dec 1912 in Lorain, Lorain County, Ohio. He married JEANETTE PETEMAN 07 Apr 1885 in Florence, Erie County, Ohio. She was born Aug 1867 in Pennsylvania.

Child of CHESTER KILE and JEANETTE PETEMAN is:

909. i. HAZEL VIOLET[9] KILE, b. 18 Oct 1887, Greenwich, Huron County, Ohio; d. 24 Oct 1946, Rocky River, Cuyahoga County, Ohio.

399. FRANCES LAVERN[8] MILKS *(ROBERT DUDLEY[7], DAVID[6], JOB[5] MILK, JONATHAN[4], JOB[3], JOHN[2], JOHN[1])* was born Abt. 1852 in Huron County, Ohio[1165], and died 11 Dec 1931 in Branch County, Michigan[1166]. She married DIGHTON WILLIAM KIMBALL[1167] 14 Jul 1870 in Rollin, Lenawee County, Michigan, by Levi Jennings, J.P.[1168], son of ROBERT KIMBALL and SARAH COOPER. He was born 29 Mar 1846 in Allegany County, New York[1169,1170], and died 25 Mar 1920 in Branch County, Michigan[1171,1172]. They are buried in Oak Grove Cemetery, Coldwater, Branch County, Michigan

Dighton's Occupation: 1870, Farm laborer. Prisoner: 15 Jun 1878, Jackson State Prison, 5 yrs for burglary[1173]

Children of FRANCES MILKS and DIGHTON KIMBALL are:

910. i. CORA E.[9] KIMBALL, b. Bet. 1870 - 1871, Rollin, Lenawee County, Michigan.
911. ii. MINNIE M. KIMBALL, b. Mar 1873, Rollin, Lenawee County, Michigan.
      iii. LAVERNE E. KIMBALL[1174], b. 15 Jan 1875, Rollin, Lenawee County, Michigan[1174,1175]; d. 09 May 1905, Toledo, Lucas County, Ohio[1175]. Reported as 'Single' in death index
912. iv. ROBERT HOMER KIMBALL, b. Bet. 1876 - 1877, Rollin, Lenawee County, Michigan; d. Bet. 1896 - 1900, Michigan.
      v. LEONA SILVANIA KIMBALL[1176], b. 16 Jul 1885, Greenville, Montcalm County, Michigan[1177]; LEROY COPLIN, 31 Dec 1914, Albion, Calhoun County, Michigan[1178]; b. 25 Jun 1883, Butler, Michigan[1179,1180,1181]; d. 05 May 1955, Quincy, Branch County, Michigan[1182]. Leroy was a jeweler. Prob divorced 1920-1930; He is buried in Lake View Cemetery, Quincy, Branch County, Michigan

400. EDWIN H.[8] MILKS *(ROBERT DUDLEY[7], DAVID[6], JOB[5] MILK, JONATHAN[4], JOB[3], JOHN[2], JOHN[1])* was born May 1854 in Huron County, Ohio[1183,1184]. Possibly adopted. He married ALICE J. SAGE[1185], daughter of FATHER and MOTHER. She was born May 1859 in New York[1186,1187]. Edwin was a Freight Agent - Railroad Company.

Children of EDWIN MILKS and ALICE SAGE are:

913. i. ADA A.[9] MILKS, b. Apr 1876, Coldwater, Branch County, Michigan.
      ii. MIRTA MILKS[1188], b. Bet. 1877 - 1878, Coldwater, Branch County, Michigan[1188]; d. 1880-1900.
      iii. PEARL F. MILKS[1189], b. 28 May 1882, Hudson, Lenawee County, Michigan[1190]; m. HENRIETTA S. ADAMS, 08 Nov 1904, Coldwater, Branch County, Michigan[1191]; b. 1877, Ohio; d. 07 Apr 1944, Branch County, Michigan[1192]. Occupation: 1930, Salesman. No children.
914. iv. HARRIET B. MILKS, b. 29 Feb 1884, Indiana; d. 14 Apr 1951, Berkley, Oakland County, Michigan.
915. v. HAZEL TURNER MILKS, b. 30 Dec 1888, Hudson, Lenawee County, Michigan; d. Oct 1974, Aberdeen, Brown County, South Dakota.

401. SARAH ELIZABETH[8] MILKS *(GEORGE JEROME[7], DAVID[6], JOB[5] MILK, JONATHAN[4], JOB[3], JOHN[2], JOHN[1])* was born 21 Jan 1868 in Michigan, and died 01 Mar 1928 in Bear Creek, Manistee Co., Michigan. She married SAMUEL DAVID HILLIARD 1884 in Michigan[1193], son of PHILLIP HILLIAD and ESTHER SANDERSON. He was born 08 Jan 1860 in Butler County, Pennsylvania[1193], and died 18 Mar 1939 in Flint, Genesee County, Michigan. They are buried in Maple Grove Township Cemetery, Kaleva, Manistee County, Michigan

Children of SARAH MILKS and SAMUEL HILLIARD are:

916. i. WILLIAM EZRA[9] HILLIARD, b. 26 May 1885, Manistee County, Michigan; d. 06 Sep 1954, Kaleva, Manistee County, Michigan.
      ii. MARY HILLIARD, b. Abt. 1887, Michigan; d. Bef. 1900, Michigan.
      iii. CHILD HILLIARD, b. Abt. 1890, Michigan; d. Bef. 1900.
      iv. CHILDTWO HILLIARD, b. Abt. 1893, Michigan; d. Bef. 1900.
      v. ROSE MAY HILLIARD, b. Aug 1895, Michigan; d. 1974, Michigan; m. A OSCAR HARJU; b. 1893, North Dakota; d. 1980, Michigan. Burial: Maple Grove Township Cemetery, Kaleva, Manistee County, Michigan
917. vi. HAZEN I. HILLIARD, b. May 1898, Michigan.
      vii. PEARL HILLIARD, b. Abt. 1903, Michigan.

402. EVA ARABELLA[8] MILKS *(GEORGE JEROME[7], DAVID[6], JOB[5] MILK, JONATHAN[4], JOB[3], JOHN[2], JOHN[1])*[1194] was born 10 Apr 1870 in Rollin, Lenawee County, Michigan[1194], and died 06 Mar 1940 in Aberdeen, Washington. She married (1) ISAAC N. HILLIARD 1887 in Michigan. He was born Jun 1865 in Pennsylvania. She married (2) JOHN E. EPTON Bet. 1910 - 1920. He was born Abt. 1867 in England, and died Bet. 1920 - 1930 in Grays Harbor County, Washington. Lived in: 1910, Grand Rapids, Kent County, Michigan. Isaac was a farmer.

Children of EVA MILKS and ISAAC HILLIARD are:
- i. LEWIS[9] HILLIARD, b. Jul 1889, Michigan.
- ii. CHARLES HILLIARD, b. May 1892, Michigan.
- iii. ANDREW HILLIARD, b. Jun 1894, Michigan.
- iv. CLARENCE HILLIARD, b. Apr 1896, Michigan.
- v. ALMA HILLIARD, b. Abt. 1903, Michigan.

403. DAVID TILDEN[8] MILKS *(GEORGE JEROME[7], DAVID[6], JOB[5] MILK, JONATHAN[4], JOB[3], JOHN[2], JOHN[1])* was born 07 Jun 1872 in Hillsdale, Michigan[1195,1196], and died 03 Nov 1949 in Muskegon, Michigan[1196]. He married (1) ADELLA 'DELLA' LORETTA SANDERS 22 Jul 1893 in Manistee County, Michigan[1197,1198], daughter of ALBERT SANDERS and ALICE AYERS. She was born 24 Feb 1875 in Manistee County, Michigan, and died 1960 in Manistee County, Michigan[1199,1200]. He married (2) JOSIE PETE 14 Nov 1919 in Ludington, Mason County, Michigan[1201], daughter of CHARLES PETE and ROSIE ROBISON. She was born 1896 in Custer, Michigan, and died 21 Nov 1939 in Muskegon, Michigan. David and Adella are buried in Maple Grove Cemetery, Kaleva, Manistee County, Michigan. Josie is buried in Mona View Cemetery, Muskegon Heights, Muskegon County, Michigan [Plot: 116-A-12]. Josie's race was recorded as Indian[1202]

Della contributed many records of descendants of George Jerome Milks.

Children of DAVID MILKS and ADELLA SANDERS are:
- i. MABEL ALICE[9] MILKS, b. 23 Jul 1894, Maple Grove Twp., Manistee County, Michigan[1203]; d. 25 Dec 1898, Kaleva, Michigan (when home burned)[1204]. Mabel burned to death in house fire
- ii. BRUCE T. MILKS, b. 07 Jul 1896, Kaleva, Michigan[1205]; d. 25 Dec 1898, Kaleva, Michigan (when home burned)[1206,1207].
  Burial: Maple Grove Cemetery, Manistee, Michigan[1208] Cause of Death: Burned to death in house fire
- 918. iii. HERBERT JAMES MILKS, b. 10 Apr 1901, Kaleva, Manistee County, Michigan; d. 17 Sep 1974, Kaleva, Manistee Co., Michigan.
- 919. iv. HUBERT EMANUEL 'JACK' MILKS, b. 16 Jun 1912, Kaleva, Michigan; d. 04 Feb 1994, Garfield, Grand Traverse Co., Mich.
- 920. v. HOWARD 'ESTLE' MILKS, b. 13 Jul 1914, Kaleva, Michigan; d. 29 Mar 1995, Traverse City, Michigan.

404. MILLIE MAY[8] MILKS *(GEORGE JEROME[7], DAVID[6], JOB[5] MILK, JONATHAN[4], JOB[3], JOHN[2], JOHN[1])* was born 23 Aug 1876 in Hudson, Lenawee County, Michigan[1209], and died 08 May 1941 in Aberdeen, Washington[1210]. She married JOHN 'JACK' MCCLELLAND 08 Sep 1892 in Manistee County, Michigan[1211,1212], son of ROBERT MCCLELLAND and SARAH JOHNSON. He was born 1866[1212].

Children of MILLIE MILKS and JOHN MCCLELLAND are:
- 921. i. HATTIE[9] MCCLELLAND, b. Jul 1893, Michigan; d. White Cloud, Newaygo County, Michigan.
- ii. ALICE J. MCCLELLAND[1213], b. May 1895, Michigan.
- iii. BLANCH MCCLELLAND[1214], b. 1898, Manistee County, Michigan; d. 20 Jul 1899, Springdale, Manistee County, MI.
- iv. EDWARD MCCLELLAND[1215], b. Aft. 1900.
- v. ERNEST MCCLELLAND[1215], b. Aft. 1900.

405. GEORGE JEROME[8] MILKS, JR. *(GEORGE JEROME[7], DAVID[6], JOB[5] MILK, JONATHAN[4], JOB[3], JOHN[2], JOHN[1])*[1216] was born 03 May 1878 in Hudson, Lenawee County, Michigan[1217,1218], and died 09 Nov 1959 in Aberdeen, Grays Harbor County, Washington[1219]. He married (1) NELLIE ELSIE LARUE 29 Jan 1902 in Maple Grove Twp., Manistee County, Michigan[1220], daughter of OLMSTEAD LARUE and ANNA BRIGGS. She was born 20 Aug 1881 in Bear Lake, Manistee County, Michigan[1221], and died 20 May 1966 in Manistee County, Michigan[1221]. He married (2) FRANCES 'NILLA' CASE 02 May 1911 in Grand Rapids, Kent County, Michigan[1222], daughter of FRANK CASE and ANGIE SHERMAN. She was born Nov 1888 in Bethel, Branch County, Michigan[1223], and died 28 Oct 1921 in Coldwater, Branch County, Michigan[1223]. Frances is buried in Oak Grove Cemetery, Coldwater, Branch County, Michigan

Nellie Elsie Larue was the youngest of four daughters of Anna Jane (Briggs) and Olmstead A. Larue. She grew up on the family farm in Bear Lake Township and attended Bear Lake High School.

She lived most of her adult life in Manistee, Michigan and in her family home on Maple Street in Bear Lake.

She was the mother of Bertha Milks (Mrs. Elmer Matthews), Emma Jane Milks (Mrs. Harold P. Snyder), Jack Hansen(Elaine Iverson), and Larue Hansen. Several other children died in infancy.

Nellie loved to keep scrapbooks of local newspaper articles about Bear Lake. As a result much of the family history was preserved for future generations to enjoy. She is buried in: Bear Lake Township Cemetery, Bear Lake, Manistee County, MI,

Children of GEORGE MILKS and NELLIE LARUE are:
922. i. BERTHA GLADYS[9] MILKS, b. 19 Nov 1902, Bear Lake, Manistee County, Michigan; d. 12 Apr 1989, Frankfort, Benzie County, Michigan.
      ii. EMMA JANE MILKS[1224], b. 26 May 1908, Bear Lake, Manistee County, Michigan[1224,1225]; d. 14 Mar 1965, Traverse City, Grand Traverse County, Michigan[1225]; m. HAROLD PETER SNYDER, 15 Jun 1933, Michigan; b. 29 May 1907, Pleasanton, Manistee County, Michigan[1225]; d. 02 Jan 1987, East Grand Rapids, Kent County, Michigan[1225]. Lived in Bear Lake, Manistee County, Michigan. They are buried in Pleasanton Township Cemetery, Manistee County, Michigan

Child of GEORGE MILKS and FRANCES CASE is:
      iii. LELAND D.[9] MILKS, b. 11 Sep 1915, Tillamook County, Oregon[1226]; d. 06 Mar 1932, Aberdeen, Grays Harbor County, Washington[1226]. It appears that Leland was 'adopted' by another family in Aberdeen, Washington, because his Death Certificate lists Everett Lean and Lyda Berry as his father and mother.

406. BERT LEROY[8] MILKS *(GEORGE JEROME[7], DAVID[6], JOB[5] MILK, JONATHAN[4], JOB[3], JOHN[2], JOHN[1])*[1227] was born 08 Mar 1880 in Manistee, Michigan[1227], and died Aug 1968 in Kaleva, Manistee Co., Michigan[1228]. He married (1) MYRTLE HILLIARD 09 Dec 1901 in Manistee, Manistee County, Michigan[1229], daughter of ISAAC HILLIARD and MARGARET ____. She was born 1887 in Browntown, Michigan[1230]. He married (2) LOUISA L. WOLFE Bet. 1920 - 1930 in Michigan, daughter of ERNEST WOLFE and ANNA GRAF. She was born Aug 1887 in Kankakee, Illinois[1231,1232], and died 1945 in Kaleva, Manistee County, Michigan. Bert and Louisa are buried in Maple Grove Twp. Cemetery, Kaleva, Manistee County, Michigan

Children of BERT MILKS and MYRTLE HILLIARD are:
923. i.   EVA[9] MILKS, b. 20 Dec 1903, Michigan.
924. ii. ROBERT BART MILKS, b. 13 Mar 1907, Michigan; d. 04 Dec 1992, Beverly Hills, Oakland Co., Michigan.
925. iii. WILLIAM WILLARD W. MILKS, b. 07 Sep 1909, Kaleva, Michigan; d. 17 Mar 1988, Garden City, Wayne Co., Michigan.

407. EDWIN ELMER[8] MILKS *(GEORGE JEROME[7], DAVID[6], JOB[5] MILK, JONATHAN[4], JOB[3], JOHN[2], JOHN[1])* was born 06 May 1882 in Maple Grove Twp., Manistee County, Michigan[1233,1234], and died 02 Jan 1952 in Maple Grove Twp., Manistee County, Michigan. He married MYRTA MAY BAHR 22 Mar 1910 in by Rev. F.H. Clapp[1236], daughter of CHARLES BAHR and ELLEN SIVERLY. She was born 23 May 1882 in Michigan[1237], and died 1950. Edwin was a farmer and a trucker in Kaleva, Michigan. Edwin and Nellie are buried in Maple Grove Township Cemetery, Kaleva, Manistee County, Michigan.

Child of EDWIN MILKS and MYRTA BAHR is:
926. i. LORIN CHARLES[9] MILKS, b. 31 Jul 1913, Michigan; d. Oct 1978, Lebanon, New London, CT.

408. WILLIAM HENRY[8] MILKS *(GEORGE JEROME[7], DAVID[6], JOB[5] MILK, JONATHAN[4], JOB[3], JOHN[2], JOHN[1])* was born 21 Mar 1885 in Manistee County, Michigan[1238], and died 1957 in Manistee County, Michigan[1239]. He married EMMA B. SCHULTZ SCHMIDT 18 Nov 1912, daughter of FATHER SCHULTZ and MOTHER. She was born 1892 in Michigan[1239,1240], and died 1950 in Manistee County, Michigan[1241,1242]. William was a truck driver. He and Emma are buried in Maple Grove Twp. Cemetery, Kaleva, Manistee County, Michigan

Children of WILLIAM MILKS and EMMA SCHMIDT are:
927. i. ARLENE E.[9] MILKS, b. 26 Jul 1915, Brethren, Manistee County, Michigan; d. 25 Feb 2003, Flint, Genesee County, Michigan.
ii. CHARLOTTE E. MILKS[1243], b. Bet. 1916 - 1917, Brethren, Manistee County, Michigan[1243]. Lived in: Montrose, Michigan
928. iii. WARREN W. MILKS, b. 28 Nov 1922, Brethren, Manistee County, Michigan; d. 06 Jul 2012, Winter Haven, Florida.
iv. RHENETTA J. MILKS[1243], b. Bet. 1928 - 1929, Brethren, Manistee County, Michigan[1243]; d. Bef. 06 Jul 2012.

409. LEONARD[8] MILKS *(RICHARD[7], FREEBORN GARRETTSON[6], JOB[5] MILK, JONATHAN[4], JOB[3], JOHN[2], JOHN[1])* was born 27 Sep 1844 in Eardley, Quebec[1244], and died 02 Jan 1916 in Kingsley, Michigan[1244]. He married (1) MARY JANE RILEY 1866[1244], daughter of JOHN RILEY and UNKNOWN. She was born 30 Jan 1845 in Eardley, Canada[1244], and died 05 Mar 1904 in Kingsley, Michigan[1244]. He married (2) MARTHA STOREY 15 Nov 1906 in South Boardman, Grand Traverse County, Michigan[1245,1246], daughter of STEPHEN STOREY and LUCY BEALE. She was born 01 Feb 1840 in New York[1247,1248,1249], and died 03 Jan 1916 in Traverse City, Grand Traverse County, Michigan[1250,1251]. Leonard worked in a Saw Mill. Leonard died from an acute attack of dysentery. He is buried in Evergreen Cemetery, Kingsley, Michigan[1252]

Mary Jane died from Gangrene followed by Septic Infection. Her death certificate says she had 8 children with only 2 living in 1904 She is buried in Burial: Evergreen Cemetery, Kingsley, Michigan?[1252]

Children of LEONARD MILKS and MARY RILEY are:
i. LUCY ANN[9] MILKS[1253], b. 23 Feb 1870, East Bay, Grand Traverse County, Michigan[1254]; d. 23 Mar 1871, East Bay, Grand Traverse County, Michigan (lung fever)[1255].
ii. DAVID MILKS[1255], b. 30 Sep 1875, Fife Lake, Grand Traverse County, Michiga[1256]; d. 13 May 1876, Fife Lake, Grand Traverse County, Michigan[1257].
929. iii. SILAS EDGAR MILKS, b. 02 Jun 1878, Fife Lake, Michigan; d. 30 Jun 1959, Grand Traverse County, Michigan.
930. iv. DONALD HENRY MILKS, b. 22 May 1881, Fife Lake, Grand Traverse County, Michigan; d. 19 Dec 1946, Grand Traverse County, Michigan.

410. MELINDA A.[8] MILKS *(RICHARD[7], FREEBORN GARRETTSON[6], JOB[5] MILK, JONATHAN[4], JOB[3], JOHN[2], JOHN[1])* was born Jul 1848 in Canada[1258], and died 01 Apr 1921 in Grand Traverse County, Michigan[1259]. She married (1) WILLIAM HARDING CASE 21 Aug 1871 in Traverse City, Grand Traverse County, Michigan, by Reuben Hutch, Minister[1260,1261]. He was born Bet. 1844 - 1845 in Michigan[1262]. She married (2) MISTER SILVERS Bet. 1873 - 1884 in Michigan. He was born Abt. 1848. She married (3) GILBERT ADAMS Bet. 1884 - 1885 in Michigan[1263]. He was born 1838 in New York, and died 13 Oct 1905 in Blair Twp., Grand Traverse County, Michigan[1264]. She married (4) WILLIAM DICKENS 22 Sep 1910 in Middleville, Barry County, Michigan[1265,1266], son of JONATHAN DICKENS and MARY HURST. He was born 1840 in Virginia[1267], and died 13 Sep 1912 in Traverse City, Grand Traverse County, Michigan[1267]. She married (5) JOSIAH SNYDER 09 Sep 1916 in Traverse City, Grand Traverse County, Michigan[1268], son of JOSIAH SNYDER and AMANDA MILLER. He was born 1840 in New York.

Child of MELINDA MILKS and WILLIAM CASE is:
931. i. MAGGIE OLIVIA[9] CASE, b. 12 Aug 1873, Grand Traverse County, Michigan; d. 13 May 1936, Traverse City, Grand Traverse County, Michigan.

411. EMALINE[8] MILKS *(RICHARD[7], FREEBORN GARRETTSON[6], JOB[5] MILK, JONATHAN[4], JOB[3], JOHN[2], JOHN[1])* was born Aug 1850 in Quebec, Canada[1269], and died 02 Apr 1921 in Grand Traverse County, Michigan[1270]. She married JAMES RILEY Abt. 1867 in Quebec, Canada. He was born Jun 1846 in Quebec, Canada[1271], and died 02 Feb 1921 in Grand Traverse County, Michigan[1272]. Lived in: 1870, East Bay, Grand Traverse County, Michigan

Children of EMALINE MILKS and JAMES RILEY are:
932. i. FLORENCE[9] RILEY.
933. ii. WILLIAM J. RILEY, b. Bet. 1868 - 1869, Quebec, Canada; d. 28 Aug 1941, Grand Traverse County, Michigan.
iii. SARAH JANE RILEY, b. 13 Mar 1876, Paradise Twp., Grand Traverse County, Michigan[1273]; d. 28 Apr 1912, Traverse City, Grand Traverse County, Michigan[1274]; m. (1) MISTER SNYDER, Abt. 1895; m. (2) ERNEST

COLTON, 30 Aug 1902, Traverse City, Grand Traverse County, Michigan[1275]; b. 1879, Ludington, Mason County, Michigan.
    iv. CORA NELL RILEY, b. 13 Jan 1880, Paradise Twp., Grand Traverse County, Michigan; m. (1) THOMAS SMITH; m. (2) ALVIN L. CHASE, 19 Jan 1895, Traverse City, Grand Traverse County, Michigan[1275]; b. 1874, Grand Traverse County, Michigan.

934.   v. EDITH REBECCA RILEY, b. 09 Oct 1883, Paradise Twp., Grand Traverse County, Michigan; d. Bet. 1913 - 12 Sep 1918, Traverse City, Grand Traverse County, Michigan.

412. LYDIA ANN[8] MILKS *(RICHARD[7], FREEBORN GARRETTSON[6], JOB[5] MILK, JONATHAN[4], JOB[3], JOHN[2], JOHN[1])* was born 1853 in Quebec, Canada, and died 19 Jul 1878 in Paradise Twp., Grand Traverse County, Michigan[1276]. She married WESLEY ILIFF Abt. 1874 in Michigan, son of WILLIAM ILIFF and ELIZABETH ____. He was born Bet. 1836 - 1837 in NJ.

Children of LYDIA MILKS and WESLEY ILIFF are:
935.   i. CHAUNCY EMORY[9] ILIFF, b. 01 Mar 1875, Kingsley, Grand Traverse County, Michigan; d. 19 May 1950.
    ii. LYDIA IRENE ILIFF, b. 09 Sep 1878, Kingsley, Grand Traverse County, Michigan; d. 04 Oct 1895, Traverse City, Grand Traverse County, Michigan[1277].

413. EZRA[8] MILKS *(RICHARD[7], FREEBORN GARRETTSON[6], JOB[5] MILK, JONATHAN[4], JOB[3], JOHN[2], JOHN[1])* was born 05 May 1854 in Quebec, Canada[1278], and died Apr 1924 in Traverse City, Michigan. He married MINERVA A. SWAINSTON 26 Mar 1879 in Paradise, Grand Traverse County, Michigan, by James Montieth, Justice of the Peace[1279,1280], daughter of JOSEPH SWAINSTON and JANE IRONS. She was born 11 Jul 1858 in Canada, West[1281,1282], and died 13 Jan 1919 in Traverse City, Grand Traverse Co., Michigan[1282]. They are buried in Evergreen Cemetery, Kingsley, Mich
    EZRA MILKS::Immigration: 1869, From Canada[1283]   Naturalization: 1892, Michigan[1284]
    Occupation: 1870, Works in Saw Mill. MINERVA A. SWAINSTON: Immigration: 1854, From Canada[1285]   Cause of Death: Pneumonia following influenza

Children of EZRA MILKS and MINERVA SWAINSTON are:
936.   i. DAISY ELLEN[9] MILKS, b. 27 Jan 1880, Kingsley, Grand Traverse County, Michigan; d. Mar 1941, Kingsley, Grand Traverse County, Michigan.
937.   ii. OSCAR WYAN MILKS, b. 12 Oct 1883, Kingsley, Michigan.
    iii. ADA MILKS[1286], b. 10 Jun 1885, Paradise Township, Grand Traverse County, Michigan[1286,1287]; d. 14 Jun 1885, Paradise Township, Grand Traverse County, Michigan (Consumption)[1288,1289].
938.   iv. LOTTIE ZELLA MILKS, b. 24 Aug 1886, Kingsley, Michigan; d. 10 May 1969, Hamilton, Butler County, Ohio.
939.   v. WESLEY JONATHON 'DOAD' MILKS, b. 08 Jul 1892, Kingsley, Mich; d. 27 May 1972, Grand Traverse County, Mich.

414. RICHARD AMBROSE[8] MILKS *(RICHARD[7], FREEBORN GARRETTSON[6], JOB[5] MILK, JONATHAN[4], JOB[3], JOHN[2], JOHN[1])* was born 25 Feb 1857 in Quebec, Canada, and died 07 Jul 1944 in Traverse City, Michigan. He married (1) OLIVE E. DIPLEY[1290] 06 Nov 1879 in Fife Lake, Grand Traverse County, Michigan, by Wm. M. Hickey, Justice of the Peace[1291,1292], daughter of CHARLES GIPLEY and NETTA? SMITH. She was born 30 Dec 1862 in New York[1293], and died 10 Sep 1919 in Traverse City, Grand Traverse Co., Michigan[1294]. He married (2) MARGARET E. 'MAGGIE' HALSTEAD 1928 in Grand Traverse County, Michigan[1295]. She was born Mar 1863 in New Jersey[1296]. Richard and Olive are buried in Oakwood Cemetery, Traverse City, Grand Traverse County, Michigan.

Children of RICHARD MILKS and OLIVE DIPLEY are:
940.   i. MABEL ROSE[9] MILKS, b. 16 Apr 1881, Michigan; d. 31 Mar 1942, Grand Traverse County, Michigan.
941.   ii. NELSON LESLIE MILKS, b. 04 Mar 1884, Traverse City, Michigan; d. 30 Dec 1963, Grand Traverse County, Michigan.
942.   iii. MARGARET EURETTA "RETTA" MILKS, b. 28 Jun 1886, Traverse City, Michigan; d. 27 Dec 1969, Grand Traverse County, Michigan.
    iv. CHARLES E. MILKS, b. 31 Dec 1890[1297]; d. 1898. Burial: East Jordan, Michigan (Croft)
    v. RICHARD R. MILKS[1298], b. 31 Dec 1889, Michigan; d. 09 Apr 1898, East Jordan, Charlevoix County, Michigan[1299]. Cause of Death: Pneumonia
943.   vi. BLANCHE LUELLA MILKS, b. 10 Apr 1892, Traverse City, Michigan; d. 09 Aug 1974, Plainwell, Allegan County, Michigan,.

944.	vii.	AGNES IDA MILKS, b. 22 Jun 1895, Traverse City, Michigan; d. 15 Nov 1962, Niles, Berrien County, Michigan.
945.	viii.	ERNEST AMBROSE MILKS, b. 30 Apr 1898, Traverse City, Michigan; d. 09 Sep 1974, Traverse City, Michigan.
946	ix.	IRA ELDIE MILKS, b. 08 Aug 1900, Traverse City, Grand Traverse County, Michigan; d. 24 May 1964, Saginaw County, Michigan.
	x.	BESSIE IONA MILKS[1300], b. 08 Nov 1904, Grand Traverse Co., Michigan[1301]; d. 29 Mar 1905, Paradise Twp, Grand Traverse Co., Michigan[1301]. Burial: Evergreen Cemetery, Kingsley, Grand Traverse Co., Michigan[1301] Cause of Death: Pneumonia

415. ZADIA ELLA[8] MILKS (*RICHARD[7], FREEBORN GARRETTSON[6], JOB[5] MILK, JONATHAN[4], JOB[3], JOHN[2], JOHN[1]*) was born 03 Aug 1863 in Canada[1302,1303], and died 08 Jun 1915 in Paradise Township, Grand Traverse County, Michigan (Cerebral Hemorrhage)[1304,1305]. She married ALEXANDER SAYERS 25 Dec 1879 in Fife Lake, Grand Traverse County, Michigan, by Wm. M. Hickey, Justice of the Peace[1306], son of PAUL SAYERS and ELIZABETH EMLOU. He was born 24 Jan 1852 in New York[1307], and died Jan 1932 in Metamora, Michigan. Zadia died from a cerebral hemorrhage and is buried in Evergreen Cemetery, Kingsley, Grand Traverse Co., Michigan

Children of ZADIA MILKS and ALEXANDER SAYERS are:

947.	i.	MYRTLE ORINDA[9] SAYERS, b. 02 Mar 1883, Kingsley, Michigan; d. 15 Dec 1940, Grand Traverse County, Michigan.
	ii.	EDGAR LEE SAYERS[1308], b. 28 May 1885, Grand Traverse County, Michigan[1308,1309]; d. 09 Nov 1949; m. (1) HANNAH MAE CAMPBELL, 12 Apr 1905, Grand Traverse County, Michigan[1310,1311]; b. Nov 1883, Fife Lake, Grand Traverse County, Michigan[1312]; m. (2) MARY STOLL, 14 Nov 1918; b. Abt. 1885. In 1918, Edgar was a grinder at Ford Motor Company and lived in Detroit, Wayne County, Michigan
	iii.	LYLE E. SAYERS[1313], b. 04 May 1888, Grand Traverse County, Michigan[1313]; d. 31 May 1908, Green Lake, Grand Traverse County, Michigan[1314]. Cause of Death: Drowned while fishing on Green Lake
948.	iv.	BRUCE ALVIN SAYERS, b. 04 Apr 1890, Grand Traverse County, Michigan; d. 21 Jul 1973, Grand Traverse County, Michigan.
949.	v.	BERNICE ISABELLE SAYERS, b. 21 May 1893, Grand Traverse County, Michigan.
950.	vi.	WALTER PAUL SAYERS, b. 27 Jul 1895, Kingsley, Grand Traverse County, Michigan; d. Dec 1970, Shelby, Oceana County, Michigan.
	vii.	ALBERT WILLIAM SAYERS, b. 21 Jul 1899, Grand Traverse County, Michigan; d. 08 Apr 1900, Grand Traverse County, Michigan. Cause of Death: Pneumonia
	viii.	KENNETH CLAYTON SAYERS, b. 15 May 1902, Grand Traverse County, Michigan; d. 10 Mar 1904, Grand Traverse County, Michigan. Cause of Death: Anemia
	ix.	ZELLA DELPHENA SAYRES[1314], b. 22 Aug 1906, Paradise, Grand Traverse County, Michigan[1314]; d. 07 Sep 1907, Paradise, Grand Traverse County, Michigan[1314]. Cause of Death: Anemia

416. LEWIS ETHIL[8] MILKS (*RICHARD[7], FREEBORN GARRETTSON[6], JOB[5] MILK, JONATHAN[4], JOB[3], JOHN[2], JOHN[1]*)[1315] was born Apr 1865 in Canada (Eastern)[1316,1317,1318], and died Abt. 01 Oct 1947 in Cornwell, Delta County, Michigan[1319]. He married (1) THERESA L. HASKINS 1887 in Grand Traverse County, Michigan[1320]. He married (2) OLIVE 'OLLIE' L. LARABY 1898, daughter of JOHN LARABY and SARAH _____. She was born Oct 1867 in Michigan[1321], and died Bef. Oct 1947.

DEATH NOTICE - Traverse City Record Eagle, FRIDAY, OCTOBER 3, 1947
Former Resident Dies -
Word has been received by Wesley Milks, Randolph Road of the death of his uncle, Lewis Milks, 86, a former resident of this city, which occurred at the home of his daughter, Mrs. Mildred Dahl of Cornwell. He was here in August for a visit at the Milks home. Mr. Milks resided in this city until the age of 25, when he located at Rapid River and lived there until six years ago, moving at that time to Cornwell. He was the last of his generation, six brothers having passed away. His wife and a step-daughter also preceded him in death. Funeral services were held today at Cornwell, with burial there.

Child of LEWIS MILKS and OLIVE LARABY is:

951.	i.	MILDRED M.[9] MILKS, b. 06 Sep 1899, Michigan; d. 22 Apr 1994, Menominee, Menominee Co., Michigan.

417. JOSEPH[8] MILKS *(BENJAMIN[7], FREEBORN GARRETTSON[6], JOB[5] MILK, JONATHAN[4], JOB[3], JOHN[2], JOHN[1])* was born 01 Apr 1848 in Eardley, Quebec[1322], and died 26 Oct 1932 in Ottawa, Carleton, Ontario[1323,1324]. He married (1) ANNIE LOUISA WRIGHT 18 Jun 1879 in Eardley, Quebec, daughter of CHARLES WRIGHT and MARY WHITCOMB. She was born 21 Jun 1856[1325], and died 08 Aug 1891 in Eardley, Quebec[1325]. He married (2) MARY HELEN WRIGHT 21 Sep 1892 in Eardley, Quebec, daughter of JOHN WRIGHT and MARY TUCKER. She was born 26 May 1859 in Westmeath, Ontario, and died 07 Jul 1924 in Ottawa, Ontario, Canada[1326].

JOSEPH MILKS FAMILY

OBITUARY - Ottawa Citizen - 1932 - Joseph Milks

Joseph Milks, former well-known businessman of Upper Eardley, Quebec and father of W.A. Milks, boys' work secretary of the Ottawa YMCA, died suddenly at his home, 15 Fourth Avenue, yesterday. Mr. Milks, who was in his 85th year, had been in fairly good health up until yesterday, and the news of his death will come as a shock to his many friends in both Ottawa and Eardley.

A son of the late Mr. and Mrs. Benjamin Milks, he was born in Upper Eardley and received his education there. He was at first connected with the lumber business, but later branched out for himself in the dry-goods business. He came to Ottawa about 30 years ago and here he joined the old firm of T. Lindsay dry-goods merchants.

Although in retirement for the past 12 years, he had been in excellent health and had taken a keen interest in public affairs and in the affairs of St. James United church, of which congregation he was a highly respected member. He had also formerly been a member of the LOL of Lower Eardley.

His wife, the former Helen Wright predeceased him eight years ago, and left to mourn his passing are three sons; W.A. Milks, J.O. Milks connected with the CPR at Schreiber, Ontario and Charles H. Milks of the American Bank Note Company, New York City. Another son, Jack W. Milks was killed while serving with the Canadian forces overseas, two daughters; Mrs. F.A. Mulligan, Ottawa and Miss Eva Milks of the E.B. Eddy Company, two brothers; W.T. Milks of Ottawa, father of 'Hib' Milks, well-known Ottawa hockey player, and R.K. Milks also of Ottawa and two sisters; Mrs. A. Craig, Fitzroy Harbour and Mrs. William Dowe, Upper Eardley, Quebec.

The funeral will be held from his late residence on Friday at 2 pm and the service will be conducted by Rev. Norman Rawson. Interment will be in the Upper Eardley cemetery, Quebec, Canada

OBITUARYY - Ottawa Citizen - 1924 -

Late Mrs. Jos. Milks

The funeral will take place to Eardley, by motor, on Wednesday morning at 11:30 o'clock, from the family residence, 15-1/2 Fourth Avenue, of the late Mrs. Mary Helen Milks, wife of Mr. Joseph Milks, whose death occurred on Monday. The late Mrs. Milks, who was in her sixty-sixth year, was born at Westmeath, Ontario where she spent her early life, and had been a resident of the Capital for nearly a quarter of a century.

A prominent member and active supporter of St. Paul's Methodist Church, the late Mrs. Milks was well known and esteemed throughout the Glebe district, and was a member of Lorraine Chapter, Order of the Eastern Star.

She is survived, in addition to her husband, by three sons, William A. Milks of this city, Joseph O. Milks, Schrieber, Ontario and Charles H. Milks, New York, two daughters; Mrs. F.A. Mulligan and Miss Eva Milks at home. Three brothers, Messrs. John Wright, Westmeath, Silas Wright, Los Angeles, Dr. J.A. Wright, Montana and three sisters; Mrs. F. Grylie, Mrs. M. Russell and Mrs. I. Ferris.

Burial: St. Lukes Upper Eardley Anglican Church Cemetery, Quebec, Canada

Children of JOSEPH MILKS and ANNIE WRIGHT are:

      i.   IDA CLARISSA^9 MILKS, b. 24 Mar 1882, Eardley, Quebec^{1327}; d. 11 May 1910, Ottawa, Carleton, Ontario^{1328}.

952.   ii.   LENA ALMIRA MILKS, b. 27 Apr 1884, Eardley, Quebec; d. 1975, Ottawa, Carleton, Ontario, Canada.

953.   iii.   JOSEPH OSBORNE MILKS, b. 25 Jul 1886, Eardley, Quebec; d. 1965.

954.   iv.   WILLIAM ASAHEL "ACE" MILKS, b. 27 Nov 1888, Eardley, Quebec; d. 05 Jul 1955, Ottawa, Carleton, Ontario.

Children of JOSEPH MILKS and MARY WRIGHT are:

      v.   EVA LOUISE^9 MILKS, b. 02 Dec 1893, Eardley, Quebec. Unmarried. Residence: Ottawa, Canada

955.   vi.   CHARLES HECTOR MILKS, b. 16 Feb 1895, Eardley, Quebec, Canada; d. 28 Jul 1972, Lakeland, Polk County, Florida.

      vii.   JOHN WRIGHT MILKS^{1329}, b. 19 Jan 1897, Ottawa, Ontario, Canada; d. 28 Aug 1918, France (WW I).

          OBITUARY

          In memory of JOHN WRIGHT MILKS, WWI Gunner who died on August 28, 1918.

          Service Number: 320035

          Age: 21   Force: Army   Regiment: Canadian Field Artillery   Unit: 51st Bty. .

          Burial Information: Cemetery: ACHICOURT ROAD CEMETERY (ACHICOURT), Pas de Calais, France

          Grave Reference: D. 17.

          Location: Achicourt is a village and commune in the Department of the Pas-de-Calais, immediately South of Arras. The Achicourt Road Cemetery lies between the villages of Achicourt and Beaurains, a little East of the main road from Arras to Amiens, about two kilometers from Arras railway station. The cemetery covers an area of 700 square yards and is surrounded by a low brick wall. It is planted with Siberian crab trees and flowering shrubs.

          Information courtesy of the Commonwealth War Graves Commission.

418. BENJAMIN J.^{8} MILKS *(BENJAMIN^7, FREEBORN GARRETTSON^6, JOB^5 MILK, JONATHAN^4, JOB^3, JOHN^2, JOHN^1)* was born 27 Jan 1853 in Eardley, Quebec, and died 18 Apr 1924 in Eardley, Quebec^{1330}. He married ELIZABETH MARGARET SALLY. She was born 20 Aug 1864 in Quebec, Canada^{1330}, and died 1947 in Eardley, Quebec^{1330}. They are buried in St. Luke's Anglican Cemetery, Eardley, Quebec, Canada

Child of BENJAMIN MILKS and ELIZABETH SALLY is:

      i.   LYLA ELLEN^9 MILKS^{1330}, b. 07 Mar 1885, Quebec, Canada; d. 21 Jun 1920, Eardley, Quebec^{1331}; m. ALFRED COCHRANE, Aft. 1911; b. 1882, Quebec, Canada^{1332}; d. 1956, Eardley, Quebec^{1332}. They are buried in St. Luke's Anglican Cemetery, Eardley, Quebec, Canada

419. ISAAC^8 MILKS *(BENJAMIN^7, FREEBORN GARRETTSON^6, JOB^5 MILK, JONATHAN^4, JOB^3, JOHN^2, JOHN^1)* was born 06 Sep 1855 in Eardley, Quebec, and died 18 Mar 1929 in Montreal, Quebec, Canada^{1332}. He married FLORENCE PALMER.

She was born May 1862, and died 09 Dec 1927 in Montreal, Quebec, Canada[1332]. They are buried in Mount Royal Cemetery, Montreal, Quebec, Canada

Children of ISAAC MILKS and FLORENCE PALMER are:
- i. GEORGE DANE[9] MILKS, b. 06 Jun 1886[1333]; d. 17 May 1952, Vancouver, British Columbia, Canada[1333]; m. EMMA BLANCHE HEWITT[1334]; d. Bef. 17 May 1952. Burial: Mountain View Cemetery, Vancouver, British Columbia, Canada
- ii. HAROLD MILKS, b. 10 Dec 1890.
- iii. REUBEN CLIFFORD MILKS, b. 15 Nov 1893, Renfrew, Renfrew, Ontario[1335].
- iv. ELIZABETH DEBRA MILKS, b. 04 May 1895, Renfrew, Renfrew, Ontario (twin).
- v. HERBERT BENJAMIN MILKS, b. 04 May 1895, Renfrew, Renfrew, Ontario (twin)[1336]; d. 01 Jun 1967, Quebec, Canada.
  Burial: Section L-2010-GH, Mount Royal Cemetery, Montreal, Quebec, Canada
- vi. LILLIAN MINERVA MILKS, b. Aug 1896, Montreal, Quebec, Canada; d. 28 May 1928, Montreal, Quebec, Canada[1337].
  Burial: Mount Royal Cemetery, Montreal, Quebec, Canada
- vii. FLORENCE MILKS, b. 20 Apr 1898, Montreal, Quebec, Canada.
- viii. GORDON MILKS, b. Mar 1905, Montreal, Quebec, Canada.

420. HECTOR MAYNE[8] MILKS *(BENJAMIN[7], FREEBORN GARRETTSON[6], JOB[5] MILK, JONATHAN[4], JOB[3], JOHN[2], JOHN[1])* was born 17 Nov 1857 in Eardley, Quebec[1338,1339], and died 25 Dec 1906 in Aylmer, Quebec, Canada[1339]. He married MARY ALICE SMITH 08 Jun 1898 in Aylmer, Quebec, Canada, daughter of JOHN SMITH and AGNES LAUGHREN. She was born 12 Feb 1874 in Quebec, Canada[1339], and died 11 Nov 1971 in Ontario, Canada[1339]. They are buried in Bellevue Cemetery, Center Section, Aylmer, Gatineau County, Quebec, Canada

Children of HECTOR MILKS and MARY SMITH are:
- i. HELEN MAYNE[9] MILKS, b. 17 Mar 1899, Wright, Quebec, Canada[1340,1341]; d. 1983, Quebec, Canada[1341]. Helen immigrated to Providence, Rhode Island in 1923, where she was a nurse Butler Hospital. She is buried in Bellevue Cemetery, Center Section, Aylmer, Gatineau County, Quebec, Canada
- ii. GERTRUDE MILDRED MILKS, b. 07 Aug 1900, Wright, Quebec, Canada[1342,1343,1344]; d. 1991, Ottawa, Ontario, Canada[1344]; m. JAMES E. LOGAN, 27 Aug 1945; b. 1894[1344]; d. 1980, Ottawa, Ontario, Canada[1344]. No children. They are buried in
  Pinecrest Cemetery - Section E, Nepean Township, Ottawa West of the Rideau, Ontario, Canada
- iii. AGNES 'DOROTHY' ALICE MILKS, b. 04 May 1902, Wright, Quebec, Canada[1345,1346]; d. 08 Jun 1988, Ottawa, Ontario, Canada; m. RODERICK MALCOLM MCCOLL, 1936, New Glasgow, Pictou, Nova Scotia, Canada; b. 08 Jun 1901, New Glasgow, Pictou County, Nova Scotia, Canada; d. 15 Jan 1999, St. Isidore, Ontario, Canada.
  OBITUARY
  Dorothy A. McColl, of 1285 Richmond Road, Ottawa, died Wednesday, June 8, in Elisabeth Bruyere Health Centre, Ottawa.
  Born in Aylmer, Quebec, she was a daughter of the late Hecotr and Alice (Smith) Milks.
  Educated in Ottawa schools, she continued her training in Butler Hospital, Providence, R.I. Returning to Ottawa, she joined the Victorian Order of Nurses (VON). After working in several Ontario cities, she attended Western University, London, Ont., graduating with a degree in public health. She returned to the VON and, in 1933, moved to New Glasgow, where she was put in charge of the local VON branch.
  In 1936, she married R. Malcolm McColl and in 1937 they moved to Sydney where, during the Second World War, she served with the St. John Ambulance Brigade. In 1943, she and her husband returned to New Glasgow where she was active in the IODE and St. Andrew's Presbyterian Church Ladies Guild. Moving to Halifax in 1954, she was elected to the board of management of Victoria Hall, a retirement home for aged ladies. In 1976, they moved to Ottawa and joined St. Andrew's Presbyterian Church. Besides her husband, Malcolm, she is survived by two sisters, a nephew, and three nieces.
  She was predeceased by a brother. The body was cremated. Committal services will be held in Aylmer at a later date.

  OBITUARY - RODERICK MALCOLM McCOLL, HERALD - JANUARY 30, 1999

Roderick Malcolm (Mack) Peacefully on Friday, January 15, 1999, at the Centre d'Accueil Lise Manard, St. Isidore, Ont., at the age of 97. Predeceased by his beloved wife, Dorothy.

Survived by his nephews, Donald MacPherson (Margaret), Kanata, Ont. and Hugh Macpherson (heanne), Bedford; grandvieces, Catherine Macpherson, Barb ara Nowers and Janet Ressor; grandnephew, Gordon Macpherson and seven great-grandnieces and nephews.

Born June 8, 1901, in New Glasgow, Mack spent his working life in Pictou County and Halifax, where he retired as a director of the Nova Scotia Accident Prevention Association and moved to Ottawa in 1976.

A member of the Scottish Rite, 32nd degree, a Serving Brother of the Order of St. John of Jerusalem and the congregation of Calvin Presbyterian Church.

Private cremation. A memorial service will take place at St. Andrew's Church, Wellington, and Kent Streets, Ottawa, on February 15 at 3.p.m. Internment in Aylmer, Que. Flowers gratefully declined.

    iv. HECTOR KENNETH MILKS, b. 25 Feb 1904, Wright, Quebec, Canada[1347,1348]; d. 1987, Ontario, Canada; m. GRACE EMMA FAIRBAIRN, 04 Sep 1937; b. 30 Sep 1905, Ottawa, Canada; d. 1993, Ontario, Canada. They are buried in Saint Andrews Presbyterian Cemetery, Spencerville, Ontario, Canada. No children.

421. ALMIRA[8] MILKS (*BENJAMIN[7], FREEBORN GARRETTSON[6], JOB[5] MILK, JONATHAN[4], JOB[3], JOHN[2], JOHN[1]*) was born 19 Feb 1860 in Eardley, Quebec[1349], and died 15 Sep 1944 in Eardley, Quebec[1350]. She married WILLIAM DOWE ROWE. He was born 16 Dec 1843[1351], and died 16 Sep 1912 in Eardley, Quebec[1352]. They are buried in St. Luke's Anglican Cemetery, Eardley, Quebec, Canada

Child of ALMIRA MILKS and WILLIAM ROWE is:

956.   i. HECTOR H.[9] DOWE, b. 24 May 1891, Eardley, Quebec.

422. WILLIAM THOMAS[8] MILKS (*BENJAMIN[7], FREEBORN GARRETTSON[6], JOB[5] MILK, JONATHAN[4], JOB[3], JOHN[2], JOHN[1]*)[1353] was born 26 Apr 1862 in Eardley, Quebec, and died 06 Oct 1943 in Eardley, Quebec. He married FRANCES LAURA "FANNY" BOUCHER 25 Apr 1888 in South March, Carleton, Ontario, daughter of HENRY BOUCHER and ANNE _____. She was born 20 Dec 1860 in Dunrobin, Ontario[1354], and died 29 May 1935 in Ottawa, Ontario, Canada. They are buried in St. Luke's Anglican Cemetery, Upper Eardley, Eardley Twp, Pontiac County, Quebec

OBITUARY

Ottawa Citizen - October 6, 1943 - Father of Hib Milks Dies at Beechgrove

A resident of Ottawa for the past 25 years, and father of Hib Milks, a hockey player with the former Ottawa Senators, William T. Milks, died this morning at the residence of his daughter, Mrs. Ira Merrifield, Beechgrove, Quebec. He was 81.

Born at Eardley, Quebec, the son of the late Deborah Lusk and Benjamin Milks, he came to Ottawa 25 years ago where he was a carpenter. He married the former Frances Boucher in 1887. She predeceased him by nine years. He was a member of St. Luke's Anglican Church, Eardley.

Other survivors are two daughters, Mrs. E.H. Hall of Ottawa and Mrs. Ira Merrifield of Beechgrove; a brother, R.K. Milks, Ottawa; two sisters, Mrs. W. Rowe, Beechgrove and Mrs. A. Craig, Fitzroy Harbour and three grandchildren.

The funeral will be held from his daughter's residence, Beechgrove, on Friday, to St. Luke's church, Eardley, for service at 3 pm. Interment will be in the adjoining cemetery.

Children of WILLIAM MILKS and FRANCES BOUCHER are:

957.   i. LEAH ETHEL[9] MILKS, b. 24 May 1889, March Township, Carleton, Ontario, Canada; d. 03 Mar 1962, Ottawa, Carleton, Ontario, Canada.
958.   ii. VERA MILKS, b. 26 Apr 1891, Portage-du-Fort, Quebec, Canada; d. 1983, Eardley, Quebec.
       iii. IDA CAROLINE MILKS, b. 17 Nov 1895, Eardley, Quebec; d. 15 Jul 1929, Ottawa, Ontario, Canada[1355,1356].

        Ottawa Citizen - 1929 - Miss Ida Milks

        OBITUARY

The death occurred yesterday at a local hospital of Ida C. Milks, daughter of Mr. and Mrs. William Milks, 154 Primrose Avenue, after an illness of about 15 years. She was in her 34th year.

Born in Eardley, Quebec, the late Miss Milks came to Ottawa with her parents when very young and has spent the past 23 years in the Capital. She was educated at Wellington Public School, and at the School of Higher English and Applied Arts, Kent Street. An Anglican in religion, Miss Milks attended St.

Luke's Church. She was well-known in the city and her passing will be deeply mourned by her many friends.

Surviving besides her parents are two sisters, Mrs. E.H. Hall, Ottawa, Mrs. Ira Merrifield, Beach Grove, Quebec and brother, Hibbert at home. The funeral will be from the home of her parents, 154 Primrose Avenue, on Wednesday at 12:30 pm daylight savings time. Interment will be in St. Luke's cemetery, Eardley, Quebec.

iv. EDMUND 'EDDIE' HECTOR MILKS[1357], b. 13 Aug 1897, Ottawa, Ontario, Canada[1358]; d. 27 Aug 1918, France (WW I) (unmarried). First World War, Force: Army, Regiment: Canadian Field Artillery, Unit: 5th Bde. Burial Information: Cemetery: WANCOURT BRITISH CEMETERY, France. Wancourt is a village about 8 kilometres south-east of Arras. It is 2 kilometres south of the main road from Arras to Cambria. The WANCOURT BRITISH CEMETERY is a short distance south-east of the village just off the D 35 road.

Information courtesy of the Commonwealth War Graves Commission

v. HIBBERT HENRY "HIB" MILKS, b. 01 Apr 1899, Eardley, Quebec[1359]; d. 21 Jan 1949, unmarried[1359].

Professional Hockey Player. A native of Eardley, Quebec, he played for teams in the OCJHL, OCHL, USAHA, and the NHL Hockey Leagues. Milks played for the Ottawa Lansdownes from 1917 to 1918, Ottawa West-Enders from 1918 to 1919, Ottawa Gunners from 1919 to 1922, Pittsburgh Yellowjackets from 1922 to 1923, and 1924 to 1925, Philadelphia Quakers from 1930 to 1931, and the Ottawa Senators from 1932 to 1933. After World War II, Milks moved to Shawville, Quebec, for his health, but turned to alcohol and he died at the age of 49 in January 1949. (bio by: K)

Played for Pittsburgh Pirates, Philadelphia Quakers, Ottawa Senators, New York Rangers, Ottawa Gunners, and others.

Burial: Zion United Cemetery, Upper Eardley, Eardley Twp, Pontiac County, Quebec

423. ROBERT KENNETH[8] MILKS *(BENJAMIN[7], FREEBORN GARRETTSON[6], JOB[5] MILK, JONATHAN[4], JOB[3], JOHN[2], JOHN[1])*[1360] was born 20 Aug 1864 in Eardley, Quebec[1361,1362], and died 20 Oct 1945 in Ottawa, Carleton, Ontario, Canada[1362]. He married AGNES CUTHBERTSON 06 Jun 1888 in Ottawa, Ontario, Canada. She was born 10 Dec 1866 in Bristol, Quebec, Canada[1363,1364], and died 30 Jul 1948 in Goderich, Ontario, Canada[1365,1366].

OBITUARY - Ottawa Citizen - October 20, 1945 - Robert K. Milks

Robert Kenneth Milks, for the past 40 years a resident of Ottawa and district, died at a local hospital yesterday, after a short illness. He was 82 years of age.

A son of the late Benjamin Milks and Deborah Lusk of Eardley, Quebec, his family came to Canada from Pennsylvania with the UEL's and settled near Brockville. They later moved to the Ottawa district. He is the last of a family of nine.

Engaged in mining, he married the former Agnes Cuthbertson of Bristol, Quebec, who survives him. He is survived in addition to his wife by two daughters; Mrs. J.A. Sully, Goderich, Mrs. J.R. Acheson, Oyen, Alta. In addition, he leaves two sons, Mr. Earle K. Milks, Chelsea and Mr. E.A. Milks of Edmonton.

Funeral will be held on Monday from Hulse and Playfair Ltd., 315 McLeod Street, where service will be conducted in the chapel at 11 am. Interment will take place at Beechwood cemetery.

OBITUARY

MILKS - At the home of her daughter, Mrs. J. A. Sully, Rosny Manor, Goderich, Ontario, on Friday, July 30, 1948, Agnes C. Milks, widow of Robert C. Milks, in her 83rd year. Resting at Hulse and Playfair Ltd., 315 McLeod street, where services will be held in the chapel on Monday, August 2 at 2 pm. Interment Beechwood cemetery, Friends may call after 1 pm Sunday.

Children of ROBERT MILKS and AGNES CUTHBERTSON are:
959.   i.   ERLE KENNETH[9] MILKS, b. 21 Dec 1888; d. 1967.
       ii. EDWARD MAYNE 'ERSKINE' MILKS[1368,1369], b. 24 Apr 1891; d. Bef. 1956; m. LILLIAN FOSTER. Residence: Saskatchewan, Canada
960.   iii. ELODIE MARGUERITE MILKS, b. 27 Sep 1893, Renfrew, Renfrew, Ontario.
961.   iv. MARIAN ISABELLA LUSK MILKS, b. 07 Apr 1899, Renfrew County, Ontario, Canada; d. 14 Oct 1999, Calgary, Alberta, Canada.

424. IDA MATILDA[8] MILKS *(BENJAMIN[7], FREEBORN GARRETTSON[6], JOB[5] MILK, JONATHAN[4], JOB[3], JOHN[2], JOHN[1])* was born 03 Mar 1867 in Eardley, Quebec[1370], and died 24 Jul 1945 in Fitzroy Harbour, Ontario, Canada[1371]. She married ARCHIBALD CRAIG. He was born 05 Aug 1859 in Fitzroy Harbour, Ontario, Canada[1371], and died 14 Jan 1943 in Fitzroy Harbour, Ontario, Canada[1371]. They are buried in Whyte Cemetery, Fitzroy, Carleton, Ontario, Canada

Children of IDA MILKS and ARCHIBALD CRAIG are:
   i.   PEARL LILLIAN[9] CRAIG, b. 21 Jun 1899, Fitzroy Harbour, Ontario, Canada; m. RUGGLES COUGHLAN, 22 Dec 1921, Windsor, Ontario, Canada[1372]; b. 1888, Quebec, Canada.
   ii. BENJAMIN MILKS CRAIG, b. 29 Jul 1891, Fitzroy Harbour, Ontario, Canada; d. 05 Apr 1966; m. MYRTLE E. ARMSTRONG, 14 Dec 1929, Ottawa, Ontario, Canada; b. 26 Nov 1905; d. 20 Apr 1991.
   iii. DEBORA M. CRAIG, b. 15 Aug 1894, Fitzroy Harbour, Ontario, Canada; d. 08 May 1978.
   iv. ISAAC HOWARD CRAIG, b. 23 Apr 1899, Carleton, Ontario, Canada; d. 18 Aug 1987, Fitzroy Harbour, Ontario, Canada; m. M. LILLIAN WILSON; b. 1907; d. 1998, Fitzroy Harbour, Ontario, Canada.
   v.   GLADYS ALMIRA CRAIG, b. 06 Jan 1904, Carleton, Ontario, Canada; d. 18 Nov 1983.
   vi. GEORGE ARTHUR CRAIG, b. 15 Aug 1906, Fitzroy Harbour, Ontario, Canada; d. 11 Aug 1916, Fitzroy Harbour, Ontario, Canada.

Carp Review - August 19, 1915 - Boy Drowned at the Harbour

Fitzroy Harbour people were deeply grieved on Wednesday when news spread about the sudden death by drowning of little George Craig, the bright and loveable nine-year-old son of Mr. and Mrs. Archie Craig of that village.

The child was playing about the wharf with a number of other companions when he slipped backwards into the water, and before assistance arrived, he was drowned. The body was soon recovered and Thursday at 2 o'clock, the funeral took place.

Sincere sympathy is extended to the bereaved parents and to the three sisters and two brothers, Pearl, Howard, Gladys and Bennie at home and Ora, professional nurse of Ottawa.

425. CATHERINE "KATE"[8] MILKS *(AMBROSE[7], FREEBORN GARRETTSON[6], JOB[5] MILK, JONATHAN[4], JOB[3], JOHN[2], JOHN[1])* was born Abt. 1846 in Quebec, Canada. She married UNKNOWN BULLIS. He was born Abt. 1845. Lived in: Gracefield, Quebec, Canada

Child of CATHERINE MILKS and UNKNOWN BULLIS is:
   i.   DAUGHTER[9] BULLIS, b. Abt. 1865; m. UNKNOWN DAVIS.

426. GARRISON[8] MILKS *(AMBROSE[7], FREEBORN GARRETTSON[6], JOB[5] MILK, JONATHAN[4], JOB[3], JOHN[2], JOHN[1])* was born 20 Feb 1852 in Onslow, Quebec, Canada, and died 24 Aug 1916 in Bristol Mines, Quebec, Canada. He married JEMINA BROWNLEE Abt. 1873, daughter of NATHANIEL BROWNLEE and MARY RICHARDSON. She was born 07 Jun 1847 in Clarendon Tp., Pontiac Co., Quebec, Canada. They are buried in Bristol Mines, Quebec

Children of GARRISON MILKS and JEMINA BROWNLEE are:
962.   i.   ANDREW[9] MILKS, b. 02 Aug 1874, Clarendon Tp., Pontiac Co., Quebec, Canada.
963.   ii. MARY ALICE MILKS, b. 16 Jun 1877, Clarendon Tp., Pontiac Co., Quebec, Canada; d. 07 Oct 1948,

		Quebec, Canada.
964.	iii.	AMBROSE MILKS, b. 01 May 1883, Onslow, Quebec, Canada.
965.	iv.	WILLIAM ALEXANDER WILSON MILKS, b. 30 Jul 1889, Onslow, Quebec, Canada.
	v.	GERALDINE MILKS[1373], b. 02 Apr 1899, Pontiac, Quebec, Canada[1374,1374]; d. 17 Apr 1976, Bristol, New Brunswick, Canada[1374]. Burial: Norway Bay Anglican Cemetery, Bristol, New Brunswick, Canada[1375]

Geraldine is listed in the 1901 census as a daughter of Garrison & Jemima, even though Jemima would have been almost 52 yrs old at the time.

In the 1911 census Geraldine is listed as a grand-daughter.

Speculating: she could be a daughter, out of wedlock, of Garrison & Jemima's dau., Mary, who would have been 21 at the time and single.

427. PATRICK 'PATT' ALBERT THOMAS[8] MILKS *(JOHN[7], FREEBORN GARRETTSON[6], JOB[5] MILK, JONATHAN[4], JOB[3], JOHN[2], JOHN[1])*[1376,1377,1378,1379,1380] was born 16 Mar 1848 in Cantley, Quebec, Canada[1381], and died 04 Dec 1927 in Ottawa, Carleton, Ontario, Canada[1382,1383]. He married (1) THERESA JANE 'JENNY JESSIE' QUINN 01 Jan 1878 in Quebec, Canada[1384,1385], daughter of JOHN QUINN and ELLEN CREATON. She was born 23 May 1859 in Ontario, Canada, and died Abt. 1912 in Laval, Quebec. He married (2) JULIA KENNY 16 Nov 1912 in Saint Elizabeth, Cantley, Quebec, Canada, daughter of JOSEPH KENNY and LIZZIE LAFOND. She was born May 1868 in Maniwaki Indian Reservation, Gracefield, Quebec[1385].

Much of the information on the family of Patrick Albert Thomas Milks was generously contributed by Jennifer Lisle Nathan in 2012

He was a millwright for years; installed the machinery at Table Rock, where the Gatineau Power Co. now is situated on the Ottawa River between Ottawa, Ont. and Hull, Que; he was also employed as head millwright for the firm of J. R. Booth in Ottawa. Chn. b. in Wrightville, Que. 3.

Patrick 'Patt' Albert Thomas Milks was born 16 March 1848 in Cantley, Quebec, Canada to John Milks (1822) and Mary MacLinden (there are variations on the spelling, McLinden, McAlinden, etc.; her grave marker in Ste. Elizabeth Cemetery, Cantley reads: In Memory of Mary MacLinden wife of John Milks died Jan. 11, 1887 aged 60 Yrs.). Patrick remained in the Milks Homestead, a one story log house until he moved to a neighboring lot in abt. 1877. ["Father McGoey established himself in Cantley not in a rectory but rather in his own house on the main road (now known as the Milks' house, across from Blackburn Rd.)".] Both Patrick and John were farmers for many years while his brothers were shanty men. Patrick married twice and had a total of 10 children.

Patrick spent many years employed with the Public Works Department in Aylmer, Quebec. He worked as a millwright, installing the machinery at Table Rock, where the Gatineau Power Co. now stands on the Ottawa River between Ottawa, Ontario and Hull, Quebec. He also worked as head millwright for the firm of J. R. Booth in Ottawa.

Patrick Albert Thomas Milks died 4 December 1927 in the Ottawa General Hospital of Nephritis and various complications of multiple inflamed organs. His death was preceded by a surgery. He was 79 years old and 9 months. He had been an Ontario resident for 40 years and was buried in the cemetery at Notre Dame 7 December 1927. His son Victor was the informant of his death.

Patrick's first wife, Theresa 'Jessie' Jane Quinn was born 23 May 1859. She was baptized 13 December 1877 at Ste. Elizabeth Parish in Cantley. Her parents, John Quinn and Ellen Creaton were witnesses, as well as the godparents, Alexander Prudhomme and Jane Johnston. A proclamation of marriage was made that day as well. Patrick and Theresa were then married 1 January 1878. The baptism and marriage were officiated by the Parish Priest John MacFinnis (the spelling of his last name is in question as the records are difficult to read). Census records show Theresa as "black" and therefore it is assumed she was a Native Indian to the area; explaining why she would have been baptized prior to marriage. Patrick and Theresa had 6 children: Isabella Louise, born 14 August 1878 (died 15 September 1883, buried in Ste. Elizabeth Cemetery with a number of other ancestors); James Edward, born 1885; Albert Thomas, born 11 November 1888; Robert T. and Herbert, born 1889; David Victor Williams, born 11 October 1892. In 1901 Theresa is listed as an inmate of unsound mind at the Longue Pointe Asylum in Longue Pointe, Laval, Quebec. She is not listed in any further census reports.. (Jennifer Lisle Nathan)

Patrick's second wife, Julia Kenny (also referred to as Kelly) was born May 1868, in Gracefield, Quebec on the Maniwaki Reservation being of the Algonquin Tribe. Her parents were Joseph Kenny and Lizzie Lafond. Her first husband was James Brennan who died in 1895. She had four children with James. Their youngest son, Robert Allen, lived with Patrick and Julia in 1911. Patrick and Julia had 4 children: Laurence Patrick, born February 1902; Margaret Isabel, born 1904; Pearl, born December 1905; Herbert Joseph, born March 1907. Although they already had children, Patrick and Julia's marriage was not officiated until 16 November 1912 at Ste. Elizabeth Church, Cantley, Quebec. On the marriage certificate Patrick is named as the widow of Theresa Jane Quinn; this lends to suspicions that although Theresa lived in the Asylum, Patrick and Julia were living as man and wife until Theresa's death, which must have been shortly before the marriage in 1912.   At this time, Patrick was Roman Catholic and divorce would not have been allowed, however special permissions could be granted dependent on the circumstances, such as Theresa's incarceration in the "mad house".

[Jennifer Lisle Nathan]   JULIA KENNY Nationality: Algonquin Indian Tribe[1385]

Children of PATRICK MILKS and THERESA JESSIE' QUINN are:
- i. ISABELLA LOUISE[9] MILKS, b. 14 Aug 1878, Cantley, Quebec, Canada[1386]; d. 15 Sep 1883, Cantley, Quebec, Canada[1387].
  Burial: Ste. Elizabeth Cemetery, Cantley, Hull Township, Gatineau County, Quebec, Canada
- ii. JAMES EDWARD MILKS, b. 1885, Wrightville, Quebec, Canada.
- 966. iii. ALBERT THOMAS MILKS, b. 11 Nov 1888, Ottawa, Carleton, Ontario, Canada.
- iv. HERBERT MILKS[1388], b. 1889, Hull, Ottawa, Quebec, Canada; d. Prob dy (not in 1911 census).
- v. ROBERT T. MILKS, b. 1889, Hull, Ottawa, Quebec, Canada.
- 967. vi. DAVID VICTOR WILLIAM MILKS, b. 11 Oct 1892, Wrightville, Quebec, Canada; d. 31 Aug 1990, March, Carleton, Ontario, Canada.

Children of PATRICK MILKS and JULIA KENNY are:
- vii. ROBERT ALEX[9] ALLEN BRENNAN-MILKS, b. Nov 1892, Quebec, Canada.   Robert was a son of Julia's from a prior marriage.\
- viii. LAURENCE PATRICK MILKS, b. 16 Feb 1903, Ottawa, Carleton County, Ontario, Canada; m. LORNA MARGARET DESLIPPE, 19 Oct 1926, Maidstone, Essex North, Ontario, Canada.
- ix. MARGARET ISABEL MILKS, b. 23 Dec 1905, Quebec, Canada?; d. 15 Apr 1995, Detroit, Wayne County, Michigan; m. JAMES EDWARD CURREN, 22 Oct 1923, Cantley, Quebec, Canada.
- x. PEARL MILKS, b. Dec 1905, Quebec, Canada.
- 968. xi. HERBERT JOSEPH MILKS, b. 17 Mar 1907, Aylmergace, Quebec, Canada; d. 1988, Hamilton, Ontario.

428. PETER[8] MILKS *(JOHN[7], FREEBORN GARRETTSON[6], JOB[5] MILK, JONATHAN[4], JOB[3], JOHN[2], JOHN[1])* was born 1854 in Hull, Ottawa, Quebec[1389,1390], and died Bef. 1911 in Hull, Ottawa, Quebec, Canada[1391]. He married CATHERINE DACEY Abt. 1882 in Hull, Ottawa, Quebec, Canada, daughter of PATRICK DACEY and BRIDGET HOLMES. She was born 11 Jul 1859[1392,1393].

Children of PETER MILKS and CATHERINE DACEY are:
- i. BRIDGET[9] MILKS, b. 28 May 1883, Hull, Ottawa, Quebec, Canada[1394]; m. GILIS GILMOUR.
- ii. MARY ANN 'ANNIE' MILKS, b. 07 Jun 1885, Hull, Ottawa, Quebec, Canada[1394]; m. ARTHUR GOODE.
- iii. CATHERINE CECILIA MILKS, b. 11 May 1887, Hull, Ottawa, Quebec, Canada[1394]; m. JOHN POWERS.
- iv. ANTHONY MILKS, b. 07 Jan 1891, Hull, Ottawa, Quebec, Canada[1395].
- v. MARTHA LOUISE MILKS, b. 08 Apr 1892, Hull, Ottawa, Quebec, Canada[1396]; m. JOSEPH LEGER, 17 May 1910, Saint Patrick, Ottawa, Carleton County, Ontario, Canada[1396]; b. Abt. 1883.
- vi. WILLIAM EDWARD MILKS, b. 19 Feb 1894, Hull, Ottawa, Quebec, Canada[1397].
- 969. vii. ALMIRA MILKS, b. 27 Jan 1896, Hull, Ottawa, Quebec, Canada.
- 970. viii. MALINDA MARTHA MILKS, b. 29 Jul 1898, Hull, Ottawa, Quebec, Canada.

429. MARY ANN[8] MILKS *(JOHN[7], FREEBORN GARRETTSON[6], JOB[5] MILK, JONATHAN[4], JOB[3], JOHN[2], JOHN[1])* was born 15 Feb 1858 in Cantley, Quebec[1398], and died 1914 in Cantley, Quebec[1399]. She married MARTIN LYNOTT, son of JAMES LYNOTT and ELLEN CAVANAGH. He was born 23 Oct 1839 in Quebec, Canada[1400], and died 1919[1401]. They are buried in Ste Elizabeth's Cemetery, Cantley, Quebec, Canada

Children of MARY MILKS and MARTIN LYNOTT are:
- i. WILLIAM[9] LYNOTT, b. 30 Mar 1881, Quebec, Canada[1402,1403]; d. 1948[1403]. Burial: Ste Elizabeth's Cemetery, Cantley, Quebec, Canada
- ii. JOHN THOMAS LYNOTT, b. 24 Dec 1882, Quebec, Canada[1404]; d. 1948, Cantley, Quebec, Canada[1405]; m. MARY ELLEN HOLMES; b. 1889[1405]; d. 1963, Cantley, Quebec, Canada[1405]. They are buried in Ste Elizabeth's Cemetery, Cantley, Quebec, Canada

iii. DAVID MARTIN LYNOTT, b. 05 Jul 1887, Quebec, Canada[1406].
iv. ALVINA GRAVELLE, b. Dec 1901, Quebec, Canada (adopted).

Anthony & Mary Frances Milks house in Cantley, Quebec, Canada

430. ANTHONY[8] MILKS *(JOHN[7], FREEBORN GARRETTSON[6], JOB[5] MILK, JONATHAN[4], JOB[3], JOHN[2], JOHN[1])*[1407] was born 17 May 1859 in Cantley, Quebec[1408,1409], and died 09 Apr 1937 in Cantley, Quebec[1409]. He married MARY FRANCES BURKE[1410] 14 Oct 1885 in St. Elizabeth's Church in Cantley, Quebec[1411], daughter of EDWARD BURKE and BRIDGET MCANDREW. She was born 18 Jul 1863 in Cantley, Quebec[1412,1413], and died 31 Dec 1949 in Cantley, Quebec[1413]. They are buried in Ste Elizabeth's Cemetery, Cantley, Quebec, Canada

OBITUARY - Ottawa Citizen April 10, 1937
- Late Anthony Milks on Nile Expedition

With the death at Cantley, Quebec yesterday of Anthony Milks, another member of that now diminishing band of loyal and intrepid rivermen from Ottawa and district who responded to the call of their country to play a part in the attempted rescue of General Gordon at Khartoum, passed on.

Born at Cantley, 77 years ago, the son of John Milks and his wife, Mary McAlinden, he was a life-long resident of that community. He was a carpenter and millwright, and many of the barns and mills in and around Cantley are the result of his labors.

When the call came for volunteers to go to the river Nile to handle the boats being used in the attempted rescue of General Gordon, he was among the first to offer his services. Mr. Milks was away on this expedition for about a year, and upon his return to Canada, again took up residence in Cantley and continued his work as a carpenter and millwright.

He married Frances Burke, who survives him, at Cantley and the 50th anniversary of the wedding was celebrated on October 14th, 1935.

Surviving besides his wife are two brothers, Dan Milks of Hull and Ned Milks of Seattle, Wash., three sons, Herbert and Bernard of Sudbury and Hector of Cantley, two daughters, Mrs. C. Holmes of Cantley and Mrs. H. Thibaudeau of Ottawa and 14 grandchildren.

The funeral will be held from the late residence on Monday to St. Elisabeth's Church, of which he was a member, for requiem high mass. Interment will be in the parish cemetery.

Children of ANTHONY MILKS and MARY BURKE are:
- 971. i. FLORENCE[9] MILKS, b. 24 Jul 1886, Cantley, Quebec; d. 1965, Cantley, Quebec.
- 972. ii. HERBERT MILKS, b. 17 Jan 1889, Cantley, Quebec; d. 09 Dec 1943, Sudbury, Ontario (while working at International Nickel Co.).
- iii. ROSELLA MILKS[1414], b. 25 May 1892, Cantley, Quebec[1415,1416]; d. 05 Dec 1928, Hull, Quebec, Canada[1417,1418]; m. ANDREW FOLEY[1419], 1917, Hull, Quebec, Canada[1419]; b. Abt. 1890. Burial: Ste Elizabeth's Cemetery, Cantley, Quebec, Canada

973.	iv.	LAURA MILKS, b. 19 Feb 1894, Cantley, Quebec; d. 07 May 1966, Cantley, Quebec.
	v.	LILLIAN MILKS, b. 20 Nov 1896, Cantley, Quebec[1420]; d. 07 Aug 1908, Cantley, Quebec[1420]. Burial: Ste Elizabeth's Cemetery, Cantley, Quebec, Canada
	vi.	HENRY HILIARY MILKS[1421,1422], b. 01 Jan 1898, Cantley, Quebec[1423,1424]; d. 01 Mar 1919, Madoc, Quebec (in a mine)[1424]. Burial: Ste Elizabeth's Cemetery, Cantley, Quebec, Canada
	vii.	EDNA MILKS[1425], b. 25 May 1900, Cantley, Quebec[1426]; d. 20 Jun 1901, Cantley, Quebec[1426]. Burial: Ste Elizabeth's Cemetery, Cantley, Quebec, Canada
974.	viii.	OWEN BERNARD MILKS, b. 10 Jun 1902, Cantley, Quebec; d. 26 Aug 1986, Cantley, Quebec.
975.	ix.	HENRY ACTOR GERALD 'HECTOR' MILKS, b. 30 Aug 1905, Cantley, Quebec, Canada; d. 11 Jan 1982, Cantley, Quebec, Canada.

431. DAVID[8] MILKS (JOHN[7], FREEBORN GARRETTSON[6], JOB[5] MILK, JONATHAN[4], JOB[3], JOHN[2], JOHN[1]) was born 31 Mar 1861 in Cantley, Quebec, Canada, and died 13 Sep 1918 in Ottawa, Ontario[1427,1428]. He married CATHERINE LACHARITY, daughter of AUGUSTINE LACHARITY. She was born 08 Oct 1865 in Chelsea, Quebec[1429], and died 17 Dec 1935 in Ottawa, Ontario[1430,1431]. David was a farmer, millwright, and carpenter. They are buried in Ste. Elizabeth Cemetery, Cantley, Hull Township, Gatineau County, Quebec, Canada

Children of DAVID MILKS and CATHERINE LACHARITY are:

	i.	MARY ELIZABETH[9] MILKS, b. 19 Jul 1887, Quebec, Canada[1432]; d. 20 Jun 1888, Quebec, Canada.
976.	ii.	JAMES THOMAS MILKS, b. 14 Jun 1888, Cantley, Quebec, Canada; d. 1950.
977.	iii.	JOHN AUSTIN MILKS, b. 11 Oct 1889, Quebec, Canada; d. 31 May 1945, Hull Twp, Quebec, Canada.
978.	iv.	DAVID AMBROSE MILKS, b. 18 May 1891, Cantley, Quebec; d. 1950, Cantley, Quebec.
979.	v.	MARIA EVA ISABELLA ABIGAIL MILKS, b. 03 Dec 1893, Cantley, Quebec, Canada; d. 04 Aug 1974, Ottawa, Ontario, Canada.
980.	vi.	JOSEPH EDWARD MILKS, b. 14 Nov 1895, Cantley, Quebec, Canada; d. 26 Jul 1976, Cantley, Quebec, Canada.
	vii.	DANIEL BENJAMIN LAWRENCE MILKS, b. 14 Feb 1898, Cantley, Quebec[1433]; d. 1961, No children[1433]; m. ALEXANDRA ALBERT; b. 1902[1433]; d. 1975, Cantley, Quebec[1433]. Daniel was Chief Machinist, Govt. Printing Bureau, Ottawa. They are buried in Ste. Elizabeth Cemetery, Cantley, Hull Township, Gatineau County, Quebec, Canada
981.	viii.	ALBERT FRANCIS "FRANK" MILKS, b. 09 Jul 1900, Cantley, Quebec; d. 1968, Cantley, Quebec.
982.	ix.	RAYMOND PETER MILKS, b. 22 Nov 1903, Cantley, Quebec, Canada; d. 09 Aug 1983, Cantley, Quebec, Canada.
983.	x.	RICHARD ANTHONY MILKS, b. 03 Jul 1905, Cantley, Quebec; d. 1964.

432. PETER FELIX[8] MILKS (JOHN[7], FREEBORN GARRETTSON[6], JOB[5] MILK, JONATHAN[4], JOB[3], JOHN[2], JOHN[1])[1434] was born Bet. 1863 - 1864 in Hull, Ottawa, Quebec[1435,1436,1437], and died Abt. 1910 in Lac des Iles, Quebec[1438]. He married (1) BARBERAH DAICEY[1439] Abt. 1888, daughter of PATRICK DACEY and BRIDGET HOLMES. She was born Bet. 1867 - 1868 in Hull Twp, Quebec[1439], and died 27 Aug 1895 in Cantley, Quebec[1440]. He married (2) MARIE MCKANABE[1441] 16 Nov 1903 in Kiamika, LaBelle County, Quebec[1441]. She was born Jan 1869[1442]. Barberah is buried in Ste. Elizabeth Cemetery, Cantley, Hull Township, Gatineau County, Quebec, Canada

Children of PETER MILKS and BARBERAH DAICEY are:

	i.	ROSE[9] MILKS[1443], b. 14 May 1886, Cantley, Quebec[1444].
984.	ii.	PATRICK AMBROSE MILKS, b. 20 Aug 1890, Cantley, Quebec; d. 15 Apr 1956, Hull Twp, Quebec.
	iii.	WILLIAM J. MILKS[1445], b. Abt. Aug 1895, Cantley, Quebec; d. 20 Jan 1896, Cantley, Quebec[1446]. Burial: Ste Elizabeth Cemetery, Cantley, Hull Township, Gatineau County, Quebec, Canada

Children of PETER MILKS and MARIE MCKANABE are:

985.	iv.	JAMES THOMAS[9] MILKS, b. Apr 1904, Cantley, Quebec, Canada.
	v.	MARIE ELISABETH MILKS[1447], b. May 1906, Cantley, Quebec, Canada[1448].
	vi.	EMILE ABRAHAM MILKS[1449], b. 30 Dec 1907, Cantley, Quebec, Canada[1450]; d. 1972, La Tuque, Quebec[1451].

433. DANIEL[8] MILKS *(JOHN[7], FREEBORN GARRETTSON[6], JOB[5] MILK, JONATHAN[4], JOB[3], JOHN[2], JOHN[1])* was born 11 Aug 1871[1452]. He married MARIE JEANNE LANGLOIS[1453,1454] 1908 in LaPasse, Ontario[1455]. She was born 1875[1456]. They lived on Frontenac Street, Hull, Quebec[1457]

Children of DANIEL MILKS and MARIE LANGLOIS are:
- i. FLORENCE[9] MILKS[1458].
- ii. WILFRED MILKS[1458].
- 986. iii. DAVID MILKS, b. 09 Mar 1909; d. 04 Aug 1960.

434. SARAH JANE[8] MILKS *(DAVID[7], FREEBORN GARRETTSON[6], JOB[5] MILK, JONATHAN[4], JOB[3], JOHN[2], JOHN[1])* was born 05 Feb 1858 in Quebec, Canada, and died 1937 in Eardley, Quebec[1459]. She married SAMUEL FINDLEY 16 Jun 1885. He was born 1855[1459], and died 1935 in Eardley, Quebec[1459]. They are buried in St. Luke's Anglican Cemetery, Eardley, Quebec, Canada

Children of SARAH MILKS and SAMUEL FINDLEY are:
- 987. i. GEORGE DAVID[9] FINDLEY, b. 1886, Beech Grove, Quebec, Canada.
- 988. ii. FRED BALMER FINDLEY, b. 1887, Beech Grove, Quebec, Canada.
- 989. iii. FLORENCE MAY FINDLEY, b. 1890, Beech Grove, Quebec, Canada.
- iv. SAMUEL EDISON FINDLEY, b. 1891, Beech Grove, Quebec, Canada; d. 1961, Eardley, Quebec. Burial: St. Luke's Anglican Cemetery, Eardley, Quebec, Canada
- 990. v. ANNIE AZELDA FINDLEY, b. 1893, Beech Grove, Quebec, Canada.
- 991. vi. SADIE LULA FINDLEY, b. 1895, Beech Grove, Quebec, Canada.
- 992. vii. CLARA 'JENNIE' FINDLEY, b. 1897, Beech Grove, Quebec, Canada.
- 993. viii. JOSEPH HECTOR FINDLEY, b. 1898, Beech Grove, Quebec, Canada.
- ix. ESTHER MARTENA FINDLEY, b. 1900, Beech Grove, Quebec, Canada; d. 1903, Beech Grove, Quebec, Canada. Burial: St. Luke's Anglican Cemetery, Eardley, Quebec, Canada

435. JOSEPH FINLEY[8] MILKS *(DAVID[7], FREEBORN GARRETTSON[6], JOB[5] MILK, JONATHAN[4], JOB[3], JOHN[2], JOHN[1])* was born 24 Jul 1859 in Eardley, Quebec, Canada, and died 13 Jul 1930 in Rochester, Minnesota[1460]. He married AMELIA M. POEHL 05 Sep 1893 in Florence, Wisconsin. She was born 07 Aug 1874 in Alginia, Wisconsin, and died 24 Oct 1962 in Norway, Dickinson County, Michigan[1461]. Joseph was a Bookkeeper for Oliver Iron Mining Co.. Lived in Norway, Michigan. They are buried in Norway Township Cemetery, Norway, Dickinson County, Michigan[1462]

Children of JOSEPH MILKS and AMELIA POEHL are:
- i. VIOLA MARGUERITE[9] MILKS, b. 20 Apr 1895, Florence, Wisconsin; d. 19 Nov 1976, Ypsilanti, Michigan ?[1463,1464].
  Viola was a school teacher in Ypsilanti, Washtenaw County, Michigan. She is buried in Norway Township Cemetery, Norway, Dickinson County, Michigan
- ii. HAZEL IRENE MILKS, b. 26 Mar 1897, Florence, Wisconsin; d. 17 May 1949, Ypsilanti, Michigan ?.
  Hazel was a school teacher in Ypsilanti, Washtenaw County, Michigan. She is buried in Norway Township Cemetery, Norway, Dickinson County, Michigan
- iii. DAISY ETHEL MILKS, b. 26 Jan 1899, Norway, Michigan; d. 14 Mar 1989, Norway, Dickinson County, Michigan.

436. DUNCAN WILLIAM HECTOR[8] MILKS *(DAVID[7], FREEBORN GARRETTSON[6], JOB[5] MILK, JONATHAN[4], JOB[3], JOHN[2], JOHN[1])* was born 06 Mar 1862 in Onslow, Quebec, Canada[1465], and died 10 Jan 1927 in Carleton, Ontario, Canada[1466,1467]. He married EDITH FRANCES EMMA BARNES 14 Nov 1892 in Quebec, Canada[1468]. She was born 30 Jan 1875 in Lower Eardley, Quebec, Canada, and died 21 Oct 1918 in Eardley, Quebec, Canada[1469]. They are buried in St. Luke's Anglican Cemetery, Eardley, Quebec, Canada

Children of DUNCAN MILKS and EDITH BARNES are:
- 994. i. WILLIAM FREDERICK 'FRED' R.[9] MILKS, b. 11 Aug 1894, Beech Grove, Quebec, Canada; d. 1971, Eardley, Quebec.
- ii. VIOLET EDITH MILKS, b. 28 Mar 1896, Eardley, Quebec, Canada; d. 06 Jul 1896, Mcnab, Renfrew,

		Ontario.
995.	iii.	PEARL ANNIE MILKS, b. 07 Sep 1897, Braeside, Ontario, Canada; d. 1992, Ottawa, Ontario, Canada.
996.	iv.	GEORGE EARL MILKS, b. 25 Mar 1899, Eardley, Quebec, Canada; d. 1983, Ottawa, Ontario, Canada.
997.	v.	HECTOR ERNEST MILKS, b. 21 Oct 1901, Arnprior, Ontario, Canada; d. 04 Dec 1964, Eardley, Quebec.
998.	vi.	KATHLEEN EDITH MILKS, b. 18 Sep 1907, Ottawa, Canada; d. 1997.
	vii.	HAROLD GARRED MILKS, b. 15 Aug 1910, Ottawa, Canada[1470]; m. AGNES CATHERINE FOX; b. Abt. 1910, Ottawa, Ontario, Canada.
	viii.	HORACE MCALLISTER MILKS, b. 20 Jan 1914, Ottawa, Ontario, Canada; d. 25 Aug 1914, Ottawa, Ontario, Canada.
999.	ix.	CLARA LOUISE MILKS, b. 06 Oct 1915, Ottawa, Canada; d. 1982, Eardley, Quebec.

437. ISAAC JAMES[8] NEWMARCH *(MELISSA[7] MILKS, FREEBORN GARRETTSON[6], JOB[5] MILK, JONATHAN[4], JOB[3], JOHN[2], JOHN[1])* was born 10 Apr 1854 in Quebec, Canada, and died 1937 in Grand Traverse County, Michigan. He married (1) ELLEN MONTIETH 22 Apr 1873 in Montreal, Quebec, Canada[1471], daughter of JOHN MONTIETH and MARY DEVINE. She was born 03 Feb 1850 in Quebec, Canada, and died 25 Jul 1909 in Fife Lake, Grand Traverse County, Michigan. He married (2) JOSEPHINE MARGARET (MANIGOLD) POTTER 25 Dec 1912 in Kingsley, Grand Traverse County, Michigan[1472], daughter of PIERRE MANIGOLD and MARGARET BRODERICK. She was born 02 Oct 1873 in Kingsley, Grand Traverse County, Michigan, and died 30 Jul 1951 in Detroit, Wayne County, Michigan. Isaac, Ellen, and Josephine are buried in Evergreen Cemetery, Kingsley, Grand Traverse County, Michigan

Children of ISAAC NEWMARCH and ELLEN MONTIETH are:

	i.	ANDREW[9] NEWMARCH, d. d.y..
1000.	ii.	MARY ELLEN NEWMARCH, b. 1875, Quebec, Canada; d. 1944.
1001.	iii.	MELISSA SARAH EMILY NEWMARCH, b. Jan 1878, Montreal, Quebec, Canada; d. 28 Apr 1956, Grand Traverse County, Michigan.
1002.	iv.	JAMES JOHN NEWMARCH, b. 1880, Quebec, Canada; d. 1925, Grand Traverse County, Michigan.
	v.	WILLIAM HOWARD NEWMARCH, b. 30 Mar 1883, Paradise Twp., Grand Traverse County, Michigan[1473]; m. SUSANNA DAISY KALNDORFER[1474], 27 Feb 1909, Traverse City, Grand Traverse County, Michigan[1474]; b. 1888, Paradise Twp., Grand Traverse County, Michigan.

438. ANDREW THOMPSON[8] NEWMARCH *(MELISSA[7] MILKS, FREEBORN GARRETTSON[6], JOB[5] MILK, JONATHAN[4], JOB[3], JOHN[2], JOHN[1])* was born 27 Jul 1855 in Grand Traverse County, Michigan[1475], and died 11 Jun 1921 in Grand Traverse County, Michigan[1475]. He married MARGARET E. 'MAGGIE' HALSTEAD Bet. 1877 - 1878. She was born 6 April 1863 in New Jersey[1476] and died 31 July 1951 in Grand Traverse County, Michigan. Both are buried in Evergreen Cemetery, Kingsley, Grand Traverse County, Michigan

Children of ANDREW NEWMARCH and MARGARET HALSTEAD are:

1003.	i.	LAURA VIENA[9] NEWMARCH, b. Abt. Jan 1880, Paradise Twp., Grand Traverse County, Michigan; d. Bef. 1966.
1004.	ii.	CORA NEWMARCH, b. 22 Mar 1884, Paradise Twp., Grand Traverse County, Michigan; d. 07 Dec 1966, Grand Traverse County, Michigan.
1005.	iii.	EARL ROY NEWMARCH, b. 13 Jun 1886, Paradise Twp., Grand Traverse County, Michigan; d. 24 Sep 1978, Traverse City, Grand Traverse County, Michigan.
1006.	iv.	ERNEST LEE 'ERNIE' NEWMARCH, b. 21 Aug 1888, Paradise Twp., Grand Traverse County, Michigan; d. May 1978, Buckley, Wexford County, Michigan.
	v.	CECILE M. NEWMARCH, b. Aft. 01 Jun 1900, Paradise Twp., Grand Traverse County, Michigan; m. (1) MISTER COURTADE; m. (2) SAMUEL H. LEONARD, 28 Sep 1920, Traverse City, Grand Traverse County, Michigan[1477]; b. 1893, Antrim County, Michigan.

439. DAVID[8] NEWMARCH *(MELISSA[7] MILKS, FREEBORN GARRETTSON[6], JOB[5] MILK, JONATHAN[4], JOB[3], JOHN[2], JOHN[1])* was born Oct 1857 in Quebec, Canada[1478]. He married HATTIE PAULINA PELTZ 09 Dec 1889 in Paradise Twp., Grand Traverse County, Michigan[1479], daughter of G. PELTZ and SUSANNA ____. She was born May 1866 in Germany[1480].

Children of DAVID NEWMARCH and HATTIE PELTZ are:

	i.	MELISSA M.[9] NEWMARCH, b. Aug 1894, Fife Lake, Grand Traverse County, Michigan; m. ALFRED

ZEIGLER, 24 Dec 1912, Traverse City, Grand Traverse County, Michigan[1481]; b. 1891, Traverse City, Grand Traverse County, Michigan.
ii. ARTHUR L. NEWMARCH, b. Aug 1896, Fife Lake, Grand Traverse County, Michigan.
iii. TILDA I. NEWMARCH, b. Abt. Aug 1900, Fife Lake, Grand Traverse County, Michigan.

440. WILLIAM C.[8] NEWMARCH *(MELISSA[7] MILKS, FREEBORN GARRETTSON[6], JOB[5] MILK, JONATHAN[4], JOB[3], JOHN[2], JOHN[1])* was born Apr 1859 in Quebec, Canada. He married NELLIE COLE 1881 in Grand Traverse County, Michigan[1482], daughter of SAMUEL COLE and RACHEL CORBETT. She was born Mar 1856 in Canada, and died Bef. 1930 in Grand Rapids, Kent County, Michigan. William immigrated in 1873.

Child of WILLIAM NEWMARCH and NELLIE COLE is:
1007. i. ARTHUR E.[9] NEWMARCH, b. 25 Nov 1891, Traverse City, Grand Traverse County, Michigan.

441. HOWARD B.[8] NEWMARCH *(MELISSA[7] MILKS, FREEBORN GARRETTSON[6], JOB[5] MILK, JONATHAN[4], JOB[3], JOHN[2], JOHN[1])* was born 1862, and died 1931. He married ORA N. WOODWARD WOODRUFF 09 Oct 1894 in Summit City, Grand Traverse County, Michigan[1483], daughter of JERRET WOODRUFF and MARY DELL. She was born 1877, and died 1950. They are buried in Evergreen Cemetery, Kingsley, Grand Traverse County, Michigan

Children of HOWARD NEWMARCH and ORA WOODRUFF are:
i. RALPH B.[9] NEWMARCH, b. Abt. 1895, Paradise Twp., Grand Traverse County, Michigan; d. 1899, Paradise Twp., Grand Traverse County, Michigan. Burial: Evergreen Cemetery, Kingsley, Grand Traverse County, Michigan
ii. IDA M. NEWMARCH, b. Abt. 1897, Paradise Twp., Grand Traverse County, Michigan.

442. ANNA ADA[8] MILKS *(CHARLES[7], FREEBORN GARRETTSON[6], JOB[5] MILK, JONATHAN[4], JOB[3], JOHN[2], JOHN[1])* was born 17 Jan 1869 in Ottawa, Canada[1484], and died 11 Nov 1918 in Ottawa, Carleton, Ontario, Canada[1485,1486]. She married JOHN CHUGG 13 Jan 1886 in Ontario, Canada[1487], son of PHILIP CHUGG and CATHERINE DAVIS. He was born 1866 in Canada, and died 1959 in Ottawa, Ontario, Canada. John was a member of the International Order of Odd Fellows (IOOF). They are buried in :
Burial: Beachwood Cemetery - Section 39, Ottawa East of the Rideau, Ottawa, Canada

Children of ANNA MILKS and JOHN CHUGG are:
i. ALEX[9] CHUGG, b. Ottawa, Ontario, Canada; d. Ottawa, Ontario, Canada (dy).
ii. HAYTHORNE CHUGG, b. Ottawa, Ontario, Canada; d. Ottawa, Ontario, Canada (dy).
iii. ADA BEATRICE CHUGG, b. 1892, Ottawa, Ontario, Canada[1488]; d. 1970, Ottawa, Ontario, Canada[1488]. Burial: Beachwood Cemetery - Section 39, Ottawa East of the Rideau, Ottawa, Canada
iv. GRACE LOUISE CHUGG, b. 1896, Ottawa, Ontario, Canada[1488]; d. 1974, Ottawa, Ontario, Canada[1488]; m. MISTTER PEAKE. Burial: Beachwood Cemetery - Section 39, Ottawa East of the Rideau, Ottawa, Canada
v. EARL M. CHUGG, b. Abt. 1898, Ottawa, Ontario, Canada[1488]; d. 05 May 1961, Ottawa, Ontario, Canada[1488].
:Military service: WWI, Private, 21 Battalion, Canadian Expeditionary Forces. Burial: Beachwood Cemetery - Section 39, Ottawa East of the Rideau, Ottawa, Canada

443. JOHN SMITH[8] MILKS *(PETER[7], FREEBORN GARRETTSON[6], JOB[5] MILK, JONATHAN[4], JOB[3], JOHN[2], JOHN[1])* was born 07 Sep 1859 in Canada[1489], and died 11 Jun 1922 in Trenton, Wayne County, Michigan[1490]. He married ELLA MAE LYTLE 04 Nov 1916 in Fife Lake, Grand Traverse County, Michigan[1491,1492], daughter of JAMES LYTLE and CORA DAVIS. She was born 04 Sep 1882 in Michigan[1493,1494], and died 11 Nov 1964 in Trenton, Wayne County, Michigan[1494]. John immigrated in 1868. In 1900 and 1910 they lived in Paradise, Grand Traverse County, Michigan. They are buried in Bloomdale Cemetery, Trenton, Wayne County, Michigan

Child of JOHN MILKS and ELLA LYTLE is:
1008. i. DOROTHY ELIZABETH[9] MILKS, b. 29 Apr 1918, Trenton, Wayne County, Michigan; d. 14 Sep 1997, Trenton, Wayne County, Michigan.

444. MARTHA[8] MILKS *(PETER[7], FREEBORN GARRETTSON[6], JOB[5] MILK, JONATHAN[4], JOB[3], JOHN[2], JOHN[1])* was born 22 Nov 1860 in Eardley, Quebec, Canada[1496,1497,1498], and died 07 May 1948 in East Jordan, Michigan[1499,1500]. She married GEORGE NELSON CAMPBELL 26 Nov 1876 in Paradise Township, GT County, Michigan, by Alvah K. Wynkoop, J.P.[1501], son of LEMUEL CAMPBELL and HANNAH ATWELL. He was born 09 Mar 1838 in New York[1502], and died 11 Feb 1908 in Fife Lake, Grand Traverse County, Michigan. George served during the Civil War as a PVT Co B, 8th Ill. Cavalry. They are buried in : Fife Lake Cemetery, Fife Lake, Grand Traverse County, Michigan

Children of MARTHA MILKS and GEORGE CAMPBELL are:
- i. VIOLA[9] CAMPBELL, b. 1877, Fife Lake, Grand Traverse County, Michigan.
- ii. ROSE CAMPBELL, b. 1879, Fife Lake, Grand Traverse County, Michigan.
- iii. JAY L. CAMPBELL, b. 22 Apr 1881, Fife Lake, Grand Traverse County, Michigan[1504]; d. 18 Apr 1975, Fife Lake, Grand Traverse County, Michigan[1504]; m. (1) DOLLIE SPAULDING; b. 15 Feb 1889, Grand Traverse County, Michigan[1505]; d. 02 Feb 1975, Fife Lake, Grand Traverse County, Michigan[1505]; m. (2) BESSIE S. LEAVELL, 1907, Grand Traverse County, Michigan; b. Abt. 1887, Indiana. They are buried in Fife Lake Cemetery, Fife Lake, Grand Traverse County, Michigan
- iv. HANNAH MAE CAMPBELL, b. Nov 1883, Fife Lake, Grand Traverse County, Michigan[1506]; m. EDGAR LEE SAYERS[1507], 12 Apr 1905, Grand Traverse County, Michigan[1508,1509]; b. 28 May 1885, Grand Traverse County, Michigan[1510,1511]; d. 09 Nov 1949. Edgar was a Grinder at Ford Motor Company
- v. AMELIA ALICE CAMPBELL, b. 1887, Fife Lake, Grand Traverse County, Michigan; d. 1888, Fife Lake, Grand Traverse County, Michigan. Burial: Fife Lake Cemetery, Grand Traverse County, Michigan
- vi. FRANCIS M. CAMPBELL, b. Jul 1888, Fife Lake, Grand Traverse County, Michigan.
- 1009. vii. WAYNE A. CAMPBELL, b. 10 Feb 1892, Fife Lake, Grand Traverse County, Michigan; d. 15 Dec 1970, Lansing, Ingham County, Michigan.
- 1010. viii. MILDRED L. CAMPBELL, b. Nov 1896, Fife Lake, Grand Traverse County, Michigan.
- 1011. ix. GEORGE DEWEY CAMPBELL, b. 27 Jan 1899, Fife Lake, Grand Traverse County, Michigan; d. Sep 1962.

445. HENRY[8] MILKS *(PETER[7], FREEBORN GARRETTSON[6], JOB[5] MILK, JONATHAN[4], JOB[3], JOHN[2], JOHN[1])* was born 27 Dec 1862 in Quebec, Canada[1512], and died 18 Oct 1942 in Cadillac, Wexford County, Michigan. He married SELINA E. FORTON[1513] 03 Jul 1902 in Traverse City, Grand Traverse County, Michigan[1514], daughter of FRANK FORTON and MARY DEFFER. She was born 27 Aug 1883 in Michigan[1515]. Henry immigrated in 1870 and was naturalized in 1875.

Child of HENRY MILKS and SELINA FORTON is:
- 1012. i. HAZEL LEONA[9] MILKS, b. 04 Feb 1904, Grand Traverse County, Michigan; d. 29 Oct 1972, Cadillac, Wexford County, Michigan.

446. SARAH EMMA[8] MILKS *(PETER[7], FREEBORN GARRETTSON[6], JOB[5] MILK, JONATHAN[4], JOB[3], JOHN[2], JOHN[1])* was born 21 Aug 1868 in Quebec, Canada, and died 07 Feb 1946. She married (1) JOHN B. PRICE 31 Jan 1888 in Fife Lake, Grand Traverse County, Michigan[1516], son of JEREMIAH PRICE and EMMA SMITH. He was born Abt. 1868, and died Abt. 1930 in Michigan. She married (2) PATRICK 'PETE' PETERSON Bet. 1930 - 1940 in Michigan. He was born Abt. 1864 in Sweden. They lived in Hulbert, Chippewa, Michigan

Child of SARAH MILKS and JOHN PRICE is:
- i. CARL[9] PRICE, b. 12 Nov 1888, Grand Traverse County, Michigan[1517]. Never married.

447. WILLIAM RUGLESS[8] HODGINS *(ALMIRA[7] MILKS, FREEBORN GARRETTSON[6], JOB[5] MILK, JONATHAN[4], JOB[3], JOHN[2], JOHN[1])* was born Bet. 1868 - 1869 in Canada, and died 27 Apr 1951 in Everett, Snohomish County, Washington[1518]. He married ALICE ETHELYN HAVERCROFT[1519] 02 May 1894, daughter of THOMAS HAVERCROFT and SARAH COLLINS. She was born 1875 in Nebraska[1519], and died 1948 in Snohomish County, Washington[1519]. William is buried in Grand Army of the Republic Cemetery, Plot: Addition #6. Alice is buried in Evergreen Cemetery, Everett, Snohomish County, Washington [Plot: Block 48]

Children of WILLIAM HODGINS and ALICE HAVERCROFT are:
- i. GLADYS M.[9] HODGINS, b. Abt. 1894, Everett, Snohomish County, Washington; m. CHARLES AUSTIN WILSON; b. 24 Oct 1895, Cheney, Washington[1520]. Lived Bet. 1918 - 1930, in Everett, Snohomish County, Washington

1013. ii. ROLAND DEO HODGINS, b. 08 Nov 1896, Everett, Snohomish County, Washington; d. Sep 1962, Washington.

448. ETHEL MAUDE[8] HODGINS *(ALMIRA[7] MILKS, FREEBORN GARRETTSON[6], JOB[5] MILK, JONATHAN[4], JOB[3], JOHN[2], JOHN[1])* was born Apr 1874 in Canada[1521], and died 22 May 1946 in Sedro Woolley Rural, Skagit, Washington[1522]. She married JOHN FRANCIS BIRNEY 1893 in Washington[1523], son of WILLIAM BIRNEY and FANNIE TREGER. He was born 16 Feb 1865 in Ireland[1523,1524], and died 05 Dec 1935 in Seattle, King County, Washington[1524].

Children of ETHEL HODGINS and JOHN BIRNEY are:
  i. MAUD[9] BIRNEY, b. Nov 1894, Snohomish, Washington[1525,1526].
  ii. MAE BIRNEY, b. Nov 1895, Snohomish, Washington[1527,1528].

449. ASA F.[8] HODGINS *(ALMIRA[7] MILKS, FREEBORN GARRETTSON[6], JOB[5] MILK, JONATHAN[4], JOB[3], JOHN[2], JOHN[1])* was born 04 Apr 1878 in Canada[1529], and died 15 Sep 1912 in Snohomish, Washington[1529]. He married EMMA VIOLA LARSON Abt. 1905 in Everett, Snohomish County, Washington ?[1530], daughter of OSCAR LARSON and ANNIE MARCUSON. She was born 31 Aug 1886 in McCook County, South Dakota[1531], and died Aft. 1930.

Child of ASA HODGINS and EMMA LARSON is:
  i. PERCY F.[9] HODGINS, b. 15 Dec 1906, Everett, Snohomish County, Washington[1532]; d. Aug 1969, Greenbank, Island, Washington[1532].

450. MARK C.[8] MILKS *(GILES[7], SAMUEL[6] MILK, JOB[5], JONATHAN[4], JOB[3], JOHN[2], JOHN[1])*[1533] was born Abt. 1862 in New York, and died 24 Mar 1928 in San Diego, California[1534]. He married (1) CORA E. HOUR[1535,1536] 30 Mar 1882 in Wilson Twp, Kalkaska County, Michigan[1537]. She was born Abt. 1866 in Indiana[1538]. He married (2) MINNIE C. _____ Abt. 1891. She was born Abt. 1872 in Michigan/Indiana.

MARK MILKS and CORA HOUR had two children.

451. OSCAR E.[8] BEMUS *(HELEN L.[7] MILKS, SAMUEL[6] MILK, JOB[5], JONATHAN[4], JOB[3], JOHN[2], JOHN[1])* was born Oct 1863 in Buffalo, New YorK. He married (1) MARY LOUISE MCGEE 14 Sep 1890 in Kalkaska, Kalkaska County, Michigan[1538], daughter of WILLIAM MCGEE and NOT NAMED. She was born Mar 1874 in Syracuse, New York. He married (2) MINA (SAWYER) LINCOLN 13 Mar 1903 in Traverse City, Grand Traverse County, Michigan[1538], daughter of NELSON SAWYER and CAROLINE WELTON. She was born 1864 in Paris, Michigan. Oscar was a Hotel Proprietor in Traverse City in 1910

Children of OSCAR BEMUS and MARY MCGEE are:
1014. i. LLOYD G.[9] BEMUS, b. 09 Mar 1891, Kalkaska, Kalkaska County, Michigan; d. Nov 1973, Houghton Lake Heights, Roscommon County, Michigan.
1015. ii. DONNA LOUISE BEMUS, b. 09 Aug 1895, Traverse City, Grand Traverse County, Michigan.
  iii. FAY BEMUS, b. Jan 1897, Traverse City, Grand Traverse County, Michigan.

452. ELIZABETH 'LIBBIE'[8] BEMUS *(HELEN L.[7] MILKS, SAMUEL[6] MILK, JOB[5], JONATHAN[4], JOB[3], JOHN[2], JOHN[1])* was born Jul 1868 in New York, and died 1949 in Osceola County, Michigan. She married TILLMAN ADAMS 25 Dec 1889 in Kalkaska, Kalkaska County, Michigan[1538], son of LEWIS ADAMS and SARAH ROWLEY. He was born Apr 1863 in Michigan, and died 1943 in Osceola County, Michigan. They are buried in Osceola Township Cemetery, Evart, Osceola County, Michigan

Children of ELIZABETH BEMUS and TILLMAN ADAMS are:
  i. HELEN J.[9] ADAMS, b. 1893, Michigan; d. 1899. Burial: Osceola Township Cemetery, Evart, Osceola County, Michigan
  ii. RUTH ADAMS, b. 1902, Michigan.
  iii. LEE W. ADAMS, b. 1906, Michigan.

453. HARRY J.[8] WILLIAMS *(ESTHER ANN (HESTER)[7] MILKS, SAMUEL[6] MILK, JOB[5], JONATHAN[4], JOB[3], JOHN[2], JOHN[1])* was born 02 May 1872 in Cattaraugus County, New York, and died 10 Aug 1934 in Fremont, Isabella County, Michigan. He married EUSTACE H. 'STACE' CONLEY Abt. 1902 in Michigan, daughter of MICHAEL ARTHUR CONLEY. She was born

1884 in Michigan, and died 1953 in Isabella County, Michigan. They are buried in Union Cemetery, Blanchard, Isabella County, Michigan

Children of HARRY WILLIAMS and EUSTACE CONLEY are:
- i. RUTH[9] WILLIAMS, b. Abt. 1903, Fremont, Isabella County, Michigan.
- ii. JOHN E. WILLIAMS, b. 09 Nov 1904, Fremont, Isabella County, Michigan; d. 19 Sep 1969. Military service: Mich. Tec. 5 15 CML Maint. Co. WWI. Burial: Union Cemetery, Blanchard, Isabella County, Michigan
- iii. HUBERT E. WILLIAMS, b. Abt. 1906, Fremont, Isabella County, Michigan.
- iv. ESTHER R. WILLIAMS, b. Abt. 1908, Fremont, Isabella County, Michigan.
- v. MICHAEL A. WILLIAMS, b. 12 May 1909, Fremont, Isabella County, Michigan[1539,1540]; d. 23 May 1971, Saginaw, Saginaw County, Michigan[1541,1542]. Military service: PFC Military Police Corps, WWII. Burial: Union Cemetery, Blanchard, Isabella County, Michigan
- vi. FRANCIS E. WILLIAMS, b. Abt. 1911, Fremont, Isabella County, Michigan.
- vii. MARY ANNE WILLIAMS, b. 03 May 1914, Fremont, Isabella County, Michigan[1543]; d. 28 May 2003, Traverse City, Grand Traverse County, Michigan[1543]; m. BERYL R. WOODS; b. 19 Sep 1913; d. 29 Nov 1990. They are buried in Forest Hill Cemetery, Haines City, Polk County, Florida
- viii. CATHERINE M. WILLIAMS, b. Abt. Sep 1915, Fremont, Isabella County, Michigan.
- ix. MARGARET E. WILLIAMS, b. Abt. May 1917, Fremont, Isabella County, Michigan.
- x. HELEN WILLIAMS, b. Abt. 1920, Fremont, Isabella County, Michigan.
- xi. HARRY J. WILLIAMS, b. 21 Oct 1922, Fremont, Isabella County, Michigan[1543,1544]; d. 13 Mar 1974, Montcalm County, Michigan[1545,1546]. Burial: Union Cemetery, Blanchard, Isabella County, Michigan

454. HELEN E.[8] WILLIAMS *(ESTHER ANN (HESTER)[7] MILKS, SAMUEL[6] MILK, JOB[5], JONATHAN[4], JOB[3], JOHN[2], JOHN[1])* was born 02 May 1872 in New York[1546], and died 17 Dec 1917 in Coe Township, Isabella County, Michigan (married)[1546]. She married GEORGE B. HAWKINS. He was born 1861 in Ohio, and died 1924 in Isabella County, Michigan. They are buried in : Salt River Cemetery, Shepherd, Isabella County, Michigan

Children of HELEN WILLIAMS and GEORGE HAWKINS are:
- i. BURTON W.[9] HAWKINS, b. 21 Jul 1902, Michigan[1547]; d. Feb 1988, Shepherd, Isabella County, Michigan[1547].
  Burial: Salt River Cemetery, Shepherd, Isabella County, Michigan
- ii. ELWOOD E. HAWKINS, b. 08 Apr 1907, Michigan[1547]; d. 14 Nov 1999, Shepherd, Isabella County, Michigan[1547].
  Burial: Salt River Cemetery, Shepherd, Isabella County, Michigan

455. CATHERINE[8] WILLIAMS *(ESTHER ANN (HESTER)[7] MILKS, SAMUEL[6] MILK, JOB[5], JONATHAN[4], JOB[3], JOHN[2], JOHN[1])* was born Jan 1874 in New York, and died 1961 in Riverdale, Gratiot County, Michigan. She married CORNELIUS D. 'NEIL' VAN ALSTINE 05 Feb 1896 in Dushville, Isabella County, Michigan[1548], son of ALEX VAN ALSTINE and DIODAZY ZAFELT. He was born Oct 1862 in Canada, and died 1947 in Riverdale, Gratiot County, Michigan[1549]. They are buried in Riverdale Cemetery, Gratiot County, Michigan

Children of CATHERINE WILLIAMS and CORNELIUS VAN ALSTINE are:
- i. RUBY A.[9] VAN ALSTINE, b. Oct 1891, Isabella County, Michigan (dau. of Cornelius's 1st wife).
- ii. FRANCIS C. 'FRANK' VAN ALSTINE, b. Nov 1896, Isabella County, Michigan; d. 1986.
  Burial: Riverdale Cemetery, Gratiot County, Michigan
- iii. HELEN N. VAN ALSTINE, b. May 1899, Isabella County, Michigan.
- iv. MARY VAN ALSTINE, b. Abt. 1907, Michigan.
- v. PAUL VAN ALSTINE, b. Abt. 1913, Seville, Gratiot County, Michigan.
- vi. MARGARET VAN ALSTINE, b. Abt. Oct 1917, Seville, Gratiot County, Michigan.

456. MARY[8] MOOERS *(CYNTHIA[7] MILK, JONATHAN[6], BENJAMIN[5], JONATHAN[4], JOB[3], JOHN[2], JOHN[1])* was born Bet. 1835 - 1836 in Ithaca, Tompkins County, New York, and died 20 Mar 1891 in Toledo, Lucas County, Ohio[1550]. She married ALBERT COOKE. He was born Jun 1833 in New York.

Children of MARY MOOERS and ALBERT COOKE are:
- i. CHARLES H.[9] COOKE, b. 1860, Toledo, Lucas County, Ohio.
- ii. WALTER A. COOKE, b. 1862, Toledo, Lucas County, Ohio.
- iii. ALICE A. COOKE, b. 1865, Toledo, Lucas County, Ohio.
- iv. GEORGE H. COOKE, b. 1865, Toledo, Lucas County, Ohio.
- v. SIDNEY S. COOKE, b. 1867, Toledo, Lucas County, Ohio.
- vi. ALBERT M. COOKE, b. 1878, Toledo, Lucas County, Ohio.

457. CYNTHIA[8] MOOERS *(CYNTHIA[7] MILK, JONATHAN[6], BENJAMIN[5], JONATHAN[4], JOB[3], JOHN[2], JOHN[1])* was born Bet. 1842 - 1843 in Ithaca, Tompkins County, New York. She married WARREN W. COOK 28 Sep 1865 in Lucas County, Ohio[1551]. He was born Abt. 1840.

Child of CYNTHIA MOOERS and WARREN COOK is:
- i. FRANK S.[9] COOK, b. 1867, Ohio; m. EMMA F. PETE, 03 Mar 1896, Detroit, Wayne County, Michigan[1552]; b. 1866, Ohio.

458. ESTHER[8] MOOERS *(CYNTHIA[7] MILK, JONATHAN[6], BENJAMIN[5], JONATHAN[4], JOB[3], JOHN[2], JOHN[1])* was born Bet. 1844 - 1845 in Ithaca, Tompkins County, New York[1553], and died 11 May 1875 in Toledo, Lucas County, Ohio[1553]. She married HENRY BLAKE. He was born Oct 1841 in Ohio[1554]. Henry's father was born in Ireland and his mother was born in Ohio.

Children of ESTHER MOOERS and HENRY BLAKE are:
- i. EDWARD[9] BLAKE, b. Jun 1864, Virginia.
- ii. WILMOT BLAKE, b. Jul 1865, Ohio.

459. HENRY CLAY[8] MOOERS *(CYNTHIA[7] MILK, JONATHAN[6], BENJAMIN[5], JONATHAN[4], JOB[3], JOHN[2], JOHN[1])* was born 16 Nov 1849 in Ithaca, Tompkins County, New York[1554,1555], and died 30 Jul 1920 in Flint, Genesee County, Michigan[1555]. He married (1) ESTHER BLAKE[1556] Abt. 1870 in Toledo, Lucas County, Ohio. She was born Abt. 1850. He married (2) MAYME BELL BEARD[1557] 04 Jun 1890 in Toledo, Lucas County, Ohio[1558]. She was born Aug 1869 in Indiana[1559], and died Aft. 1925 in Michigan ???. Henry was a Foreman in an auto factory. They lived in Flint, Genesee County, Michigan. He is buried in Grace Lawn Cemetery, Flint, Michigan

Child of HENRY MOOERS and ESTHER BLAKE is:
- 1016. i. FRANK C.[9] MOOERS, b. Feb 1874, Toledo, Lucas County, Ohio.

Child of HENRY MOOERS and MAYME BEARD is:
- 1017. ii. ARTHUR BEARD[9] MOOERS, b. 26 Apr 1892, Toledo, Lucas County, Ohio; d. Jun 1970, Youngtown, Maricopa County, Arizona.

460. WILLIAM JEWETT[8] MILK *(WILLIAM JEWETT[7], JONATHAN[6], BENJAMIN[5], JONATHAN[4], JOB[3], JOHN[2], JOHN[1])* was born 05 Nov 1842 in Varna, Tompkins County, New York[1560,1561], and died 1943 in Candor, Tioga County, New York. He married (1) MARTHA H. MIDDAUGH Abt. 1864. She was born Abt. 1845, and died 17 Feb 1873 in Dryden, Tompkins County, New York. He married (2) SARAH MATILDA SMITH Abt. 1878, daughter of WILLIAM SMITH and ELEANOR SLATE. She was born 14 May 1858 in New York, and died 10 Dec 1929 in Owego, Tioga County, New York. William was a farmer, leasing 90 acres from Alfred Willie. William and Sarah are buried in Maple Grove Cemetery, Candor, Tioga County, New York

Children of WILLIAM MILK and MARTHA MIDDAUGH are:
- i. ELMER[9] MILK, b. 23 Apr 1865, Dryden, Tompkins County, New York; d. 30 Apr 1891, Cortland, New York (Unmarried). Military service: Co. G, U. S. Regulars. Occupation: 1889, Blacksmith, Village of Cortland, New York
- ii. MAUD MILK, b. 21 Apr 1869, Dryden, Tompkins County, New York; d. 29 Apr 1921; m. EDWARD F. VAN VORHIS, 1888; b. Abt. 1869.. Lived in: Owego, New York. Occupation: Veterinarian
- iii. WILLIAM O. MILK, b. 17 Apr 1872, Dryden, Tompkins County, New York; d. 1908, Cortland, New York (unmarried). Occupation: 1889, Baker, Village of Cortland, New York

Children of WILLIAM MILK and SARAH SMITH are:

1018. iv. HOWARD JAY⁹ MILKS, b. 25 Jun 1879, Dryden, Tompkins County, New York; d. 30 Mar 1954, Ithaca, Tompkins County, New York.
1019. v. LENA AMANDA MILKS, b. 04 Oct 1881.
1020. vi. HARLEY H. MILKS, b. 13 Sep 1883.
    vii. VIDA MAY MILKS, b. 09 Jan 1886, Candor, Tioga County, New York[1562,1563]; d. Jun 1967, Falls Church, Fairfax County, Virginia[1564,1565]; m. FREDERICK GARDNER BEHRENDS, 05 Jan 1918; b. 23 Feb 1894, Buffalo, New York; d. Jul 1958. Vida was a Teacher, Hope Farm School, Unionvale, Dutchess County, New York. Burial: Maple Grove Cemetery, Candor, Tioga County, New York. No children. Frederick was Superintendent, Hope Farm School, Unionvale, Dutchess County, New York
1021. viii. HAROLD CLIFFORD MILKS, b. 27 Aug 1889, Dryden, Tompkins County, New York; d. 1961.

461. BENJAMIN F.⁸ MILK (*WILLIAM JEWETT⁷, JONATHAN⁶, BENJAMIN⁵, JONATHAN⁴, JOB³, JOHN², JOHN¹*) was born 1842[1566], and died 04 Jan 1897 in Dryden, Tompkins County, New York[1567]. He married CORNELIA L. BELNAP. She was born 1839[1567], and died 1913 in Dryden, Tompkins County, New York[1567]. They are buried in Ellis Hollow Cemetery, Ellis Hollow Road, Dryden, New York

Children of BENJAMIN MILK and CORNELIA BELNAP are:

1022. i. MINNIE⁹ MILKS, b. 1873, Dryden, Tompkins County, New York; d. 1940.
1023. ii. LENA MILKS, b. Abt. 1875, Dryden, Tompkins County, New York.
1024. iii. GRACE MILKS, b. Abt. 1877, Dryden, Tompkins County, New York.
1025. iv. MYRTLE MILKS, b. Dec 1882, Dryden, Tompkins County, New York.

462. ANN JANE⁸ MILK (*WILLIAM JEWETT⁷, JONATHAN⁶, BENJAMIN⁵, JONATHAN⁴, JOB³, JOHN², JOHN¹*) was born 1845 in Dryden, Tompkins County, New York[1568], and died 20 May 1916. She married IRIS DANIEL MANNING 1878, son of DANIEL MANNING and SAVILLA BROWN. He was born Abt. 1850 in Tompkins County, New York, and died 27 May 1913.

Children of ANN MILK and IRIS MANNING are:

1026. i. PEARL ETHEL⁹ MANNING, b. Feb 1879, Dryden, Tompkins County, New York.
1027. ii. LELAND BROWN MANNING, b. 23 Feb 1880, Dryden, Tompkins County, New York; d. 1918, Auburn, Cayuga County, New York.
    iii. RAYMOND DANIEL MANNING[1569,1570], b. 18 Aug 1882, Dryden, Tompkins County, New York[1571]; d. 1918, Cayuga County, New York[1572]; m. ELIZABETH 'BESS' BRIGHTMAN, Jul 1907; b. 20 Mar 1881, New York.

463. GEORGE HENRY⁸ MILK (*WILLIAM JEWETT⁷, JONATHAN⁶, BENJAMIN⁵, JONATHAN⁴, JOB³, JOHN², JOHN¹*) was born 14 Mar 1847 in Dryden, Tompkins County, New York[1572,1573], and died 04 Apr 1926 in Town of Kirkwood, Broome County, New York. He married (1) HELEN E. MILLER Abt. 1874, daughter of ABRAM MILLER and SUSAN HORTON. She was born 09 Jul 1845 in Town of Dryden, Tompkins County, New York, and died 05 Dec 1881 in Ithaca, Tompkins County, New York. He married (2) CLARA BRAMAN 15 May 1890. She was born Feb 1870 in New Hampshire.

Children of GEORGE MILK and HELEN MILLER are:

1028. i. GEORGIA BELLE⁹ MILKS, b. 03 Aug 1875, New York; d. 14 Jun 1961, Dryden, Tompkins County, New York.
1029. ii. FRED A. MILKS, b. 07 Feb 1878, Ellis Hollow, Dryden, Tompkins Co., NY; d. 24 Jul 1945, Ithaca, New York.
    iii. GLENN MILKS, b. 22 May 1880, Dryden, Tompkins County, New York[1574]; d. 27 Aug 1950, Minneapolis, Hennepin County, Minnesota; m. UNNAMED, Bet. 1920 - 1930, Minneapolis, Hennepin County, Minnesota[1575]; d. Bet. 1920 - 1930.

Children of GEORGE MILK and CLARA BRAMAN are:

1030. iv. LEROY ST. CLAIR⁹ MILKS, b. 20 Sep 1892, Candor, Tioga County, New York; d. Oct 1964.
    v. EDWARD MERLE MILKS, b. 23 Jul 1897, Candor, Tioga County, New York[1576]; d. 29 Jan 1956, Columbus, Ohio[1577]; m. EVA M. CONNOLLY, 23 Oct 1941[1578]; b. 05 Jun 1907, New York[1579]; d. 02 Dec 1985, Springfield, Clark County, Ohio,[1579]. Military service: 26 Oct 1945, Enlisted at Fort Hayes, Columbus, Ohio. Edward is buried in Green Lawn Cemetery, Columbus, Franklin County, Ohio

vi. GEORGE W. MILKS, b. Oct 1899, Candor, Tioga County, New York[1580]; d. Prob. d.y.

464. LYDIA[8] MILK *(ISAAC[7], JONATHAN[6], BENJAMIN[5], JONATHAN[4], JOB[3], JOHN[2], JOHN[1])* was born 1845. She married JAMES R. SMYTHE. He was born Abt. 1845 in Of Newark, Ohio. Lived in: 1907, Galena, Ohio

Children of LYDIA MILK and JAMES SMYTHE are:
    i. CHARLES[9] SMYTHE, d. d.y..
    ii. LOLA A. SMYTHE. Lived in: Galena, Ohio
    iii. MYRTLE SMYTHE.
    iv. CLAUDE L. SMYTHE, b. Abt. 1874, Galena, Ohio; m. DAISY P. COCHRAN, 10 Nov 1901, Delaware County, Ohio[1581]; b. Abt. 1875, Harlem, Delaware County, Ohio.
    v. DAISIE SMYTHE, m. HAROLD STILES.. Lived in: Ames, Iowa[1582]
    vi. JAMES HUBERT SMYTHE, b. 19 Feb 1884, Ohio[1583]; d. 30 Dec 1917, Columbus, Ohio[1583].

465. EDGAR ROMAIN[8] MILK *(ISAAC[7], JONATHAN[6], BENJAMIN[5], JONATHAN[4], JOB[3], JOHN[2], JOHN[1])* was born 12 Jun 1850 in Tompkins County, New York, and died 15 Sep 1931 in Galena, Delaware County, Ohio. He married EMMA MARY RUGG Abt. 1879. She was born 20 Sep 1858, and died 06 Jul 1940 in Galena, Delaware County, Ohio. They are buried in Galena Cemetery, Galena, Delaware County, Ohio

Children of EDGAR MILK and EMMA RUGG are:
    i. ARTHUR[9] MILKS, b. 08 Sep 1880, Ohio[1584]; d. Feb 1974, Ohio (No children)[1584]; m. JENNIE THORNTON; b. 02 Nov 1879, Kingsmills, Ohio; d. 15 Jul 1926, Columbus, Ohio. Lived in: Galena, Ohio[1585]
    ii. RALPH MILKS, b. 18 Oct 1887, Galena, Ohio[1586]; d. 28 Oct 1958, Los Angeles, California (No children)[1586,1587]; m. HAZEL SMITH; b. 13 Aug 1893, Blissfield, Michigan. Lived in: Pasadena, California

466. MARY KIZIAH[8] MILK *(ISAAC[7], JONATHAN[6], BENJAMIN[5], JONATHAN[4], JOB[3], JOHN[2], JOHN[1])* was born Jul 1869 in South Milford, Ind.[1588], and died 07 Apr 1936 in Columbus, Ohio. She married JAMES BUFORD MCKNIGHT Abt. 1893[1588], son of JAMES MCKNIGHT and ELECTRA QUINN. He was born 03 Jan 1872 in Wright County, Minnesota[1588], and died 25 Dec 1965 in Minneapolis, Minnesota. James was a railroad conductor. They were divorced: Bet. 1900 - 1910, Minneapolis, Minnesota Mary is buried in Minneapolis, Minn.[1589]

Children of MARY MILK and JAMES MCKNIGHT are:
1031. i. EDNA MYRTLE[9] MCKNIGHT, b. 02 Feb 1894, Wright County, Minn.; d. 20 Dec 1984, Minneapolis, Minn..
    ii. NINA LORA MCKNIGHT, b. 22 Jul 1895, Minneapolis, Minn.[1590]; d. 02 Feb 1896, Minneapolis, Minn.[1591]. Burial: Buffalo, Minnesota
1032. iii. JAMES IAN MCKNIGHT, b. 06 Mar 1897, Minneapolis, Minn.; d. Jan 1963, California.
1033. iv. EUNICE CONSTANCE MCKNIGHT, b. 06 Jul 1898, Minneapolis, Minn.; d. 24 Oct 1965, Hennepin County, Minnesota.
1034. v. GEORGE MCKNIGHT, b. 03 May 1900, Minneapolis, Minn.; d. 21 May 1949, Weber, Utah.
    vi. BERNICE CLARE MCKNIGHT, b. 20 Mar 1902, Minneapolis, Minn.; d. 17 Jan 1981, Lynnfield, Massachusetts.
Lived in: 1925, Des Moines, Polk County, Iowa

467. JOHN WESLEY[8] MILKS *(HENRY[7] MILK, JONATHAN[6], BENJAMIN[5], JONATHAN[4], JOB[3], JOHN[2], JOHN[1])* was born 19 Mar 1843 in Tompkins County, NY, and died 26 Jan 1929 in South Milford, Indiana. He married ALMIRA C. "MINA" LEARNED[1592] 01 Mar 1866 in Kendallville, Indiana, daughter of SAMUEL LEARNED and JEMIMA BEARD. She was born Jun 1846 in Indiana, and died 04 Mar 1916 in South Milford, Lagrange County, Indiana[1593]. They are buried in South Milford Cemetery, Lagrange County, Indiana
    John enlisted 24 Sept. 1861 in Civil War: Wm. Dawson's Co. G, 30 Regt. Ind. Inf. Volunteers, discharged 29 Sept. 1864; also served as 1st Sgt, 1865 in McGregor's Co. B, 152d Regt. Ind. Volunteers

Children of JOHN MILKS and ALMIRA LEARNED are:
    i. ALBERT[9] MILKS, b. 1867, South Milford, Lagrange County, Indiana[1594]; d. 1868, South Milford, Lagrange County, Indiana[1594]. Burial: Section 1, row 4, South Milford Cemetery, South Milford, Lagrange County, Indiana

| 1035. | ii. | LELIA BELLE MILKS, b. 24 Dec 1868, South Milford, Lagrange County, Indiana; d. 20 Jan 1942, Coral Gables, Florida. |
| 1036. | iii. | LEONARD "LEN" H. MILKS, b. 02 Feb 1875, South Milford, Lagrange County, Indiana; d. 23 Jul 1951, Kalamazoo, Michigan. |

468. CHARLES H.[8] MILK *(HENRY[7], JONATHAN[6], BENJAMIN[5], JONATHAN[4], JOB[3], JOHN[2], JOHN[1])* was born 25 Mar 1845 in Tompkins Co., NY[1595], and died 26 Sep 1917 in South Milford, Ind.[1595,1596]. He married CAROLINE LEWIS. She was born 11 Dec 1847 in South Milford, Ind., and died 01 Apr 1919 in Kendallville, Ind. Charles was a farmer and a horse trader. Charles is buried in South Milford, Lagrange County, Indiana, Plot: Section 3, row 3

Charles served in the Civil War as a private in Co.B, 152nd Indiana Volunteers. His mother, Almira Summers Milk was also buried in South Milford, IN

Children of CHARLES MILK and CAROLINE LEWIS are:

    i. HERBERT E.[9] MILK, b. Sep 1870, Indiana[1597]; d. 23 Oct 1913, North Liberty, Indiana[1598]; m. STELLA E. ALLEN, 04 Jan 1896, Lagrange County, Indiana[1599]; b. Sep 1868, Indiana[1600]. Lived in: Superior, Williams County, Ohio

1037. ii. MARGARET MAY 'MAGGIE' MILKS, b. 22 Jun 1878, Indiana; d. 1959, South Milford, Lagrange County, IN.

469. ELIZABETH 'BETSEY' A.[8] MILK *(HENRY[7], JONATHAN[6], BENJAMIN[5], JONATHAN[4], JOB[3], JOHN[2], JOHN[1])* was born 25 Jul 1849 in Tompkins Co., New York[1601], and died 30 Jun 1918 in Adrian, Hillsdale, Michigan[1601]. She married (1) FRANKLIN E. STRONG Abt. 1870. He was born Abt. 1844 in Ohio[1602]. Franklin was a Saw Mill Engineer. She married (2) LUCIUS A. DANIELS[1603] 20 Feb 1896 in Lagrange County, Indiana[1604,1605]. He was born Aug 1847 in Michigan[1606]. Elizabeth is buried in Lake View Cemetery, Hillsdale, Hillsdale County, Michigan[1607]

ELIZABETH MILK and FRANKLIN STRONG had one child who died before 1900.

470. CYNTHIA[8] MILK *(HENRY[7], JONATHAN[6], BENJAMIN[5], JONATHAN[4], JOB[3], JOHN[2], JOHN[1])* was born Jul 1853 in South Milford, LaGrange County, Indiana[1608], and died Bet. 1900 - 1910 in Portland, Multnomah County, Oregon. She married IRWIN IRVIN E. RABER 1877 in LaGrange County, Indiana, son of ANDREW RABER and MARY _____. He was born Aug 1857 in LaGrange County, Indiana.

Child of CYNTHIA MILK and IRWIN IRVIN E. RABER is:

1038. i. FERN L.[9] RABER, b. Dec 1879, LaGrange County, Indiana; d. 18 Mar 1966, Portland, Multnomah County, Oregon.

471. ASA BENJAMIN[8] RODMAN *(DEBORAH[7] MILK, BENJAMIN[6], BENJAMIN[5], JONATHAN[4], JOB[3], JOHN[2], JOHN[1])* was born 31 Jan 1832 in Fulton, Schoharie County, New York[1608], and died 05 Apr 1902 in Clinton County, Iowa. He married (1) ADELINE _____. She was born Abt. 1830. He married (2) HANNAH _____ Abt. 1846 in New York. She was born Abt. 1827 in New York. He married (3) MARY JANE _____ Abt. 1852. She was born 31 Jan 1830 in New York, and died 13 Jan 1893 in Clinton County, Iowa. Asa, Hannah, and Mary Jane are buried in Oakland Cemetery, Clinton County, Iowa

U.S. Civil War Soldier Record for Asa B Rodman: Age at enlistment: 36; Enlistment Date: 23 Sep 1864 Rank at enlistment: Private; State Served: Iowa; Survived the War?: Yes; Service Record: Enlisted in Company C, Iowa 14th Infantry Regiment on 23 Sep 1864. Mustered out on 13 May 1865 at Davenport, IA.

Children of ASA RODMAN and HANNAH _____ are:

    i. MARTIN R.[9] RODMAN, b. Abt. 1847, New York.
    ii. ANALIZA RODMAN, b. Abt. 1850, New York.

Children of ASA RODMAN and MARY _____ are:

1039. iii. MENZO W.[9] RODMAN, b. 1853, Iowa; d. 1920, Clinton County, Iowa.
    iv. HARLIN E. RODMAN, b. Abt. 1857, Iowa.
    v. NETTIE A. RODMAN, b. Abt. 1865, Iowa.

472. MARY[8] RODMAN *(DEBORAH[7] MILK, BENJAMIN[6], BENJAMIN[5], JONATHAN[4], JOB[3], JOHN[2], JOHN[1])* was born 1827 in Fulton, Schoharie County, New York. She married SEBASTIAN COLE 1845 in Schoharie County, New York?. He was born Abt. 1825. Moved to Clinton County, Iowa abt. 1856,

Children of MARY RODMAN and SEBASTIAN COLE are:
- i. PERMILLA A.[9] COLE, b. 1845, Schoharie County, New York; d. Bef. 10 Nov 1931.
- ii. JOHN HENRY COLE, b. 1849, Schoharie County, New York; d. Bef. 10 Nov 1931.
- iii. MARY A. COLE, b. 1851, Schoharie County, New York; d. Bef. 10 Nov 1931.
- 1040. iv. JOEL SEBASTIAN COLE, b. 04 Mar 1853, Schoharie County, New York; d. 10 Nov 1931, Corning, Adams County, Iowa.
- 1041. v. HANNAH AMANDA 'MANDY' COLE, b. 16 Dec 1854, Schoharie County, New York; d. 11 Aug 1944, Douglas, Adams County, Iowa.
- 1042. vi. GEORGE E. COLE, b. Apr 1867, Clinton County, Iowa; d. 1939, Adams County, Iowa.

473. WILLIAM HENRY[8] RODMAN *(DEBORAH[7] MILK, BENJAMIN[6], BENJAMIN[5], JONATHAN[4], JOB[3], JOHN[2], JOHN[1])* was born 04 May 1830 in Fulton, Schoharie County, New York (date ???), and died 28 Nov 1915 in Sutter, Sacramento, California. He married MELISSA JANE RODMAN[1609], daughter of ROBERT RODMAN and REBECCA HERSAN. She was born 25 Jun 1838 in Schoharie County, New York[1609], and died 04 Feb 1901 in Walworth, Walworth County, Wisconsin[1609]. Melissa is buried in Brick Church Cemetery, Walworth, Wisconsin

Children of WILLIAM RODMAN and MELISSA RODMAN are:
- i. MARY[9] RODMAN, b. Abt. 1857, Wisconsin.
- ii. REBECCA RODMAN, b. Abt. 1859, Iowa.
- iii. SETH RODMAN, b. Abt. 1862, Iowa.
- iv. SARAH RODMAN, b. Abt. 1865, California.
- v. KATY MELISSA RODMAN, b. 28 Aug 1867, California[1610]; d. 10 Feb 1954, Los Angeles, California[1610]; m. MISTTER MERRILL.
- vi. GEORGE RODMAN, b. Abt. 1873, California.
- vii. HARRIET 'HATTIE' RODMAN, b. Abt. 1876, California.
- viii. FRANK RODMAN, b. Abt. 1879, California.

474. LEVI GALLOP[8] RODMAN *(DEBORAH[7] MILK, BENJAMIN[6], BENJAMIN[5], JONATHAN[4], JOB[3], JOHN[2], JOHN[1])* was born 29 Apr 1832 in Fulton, Schoharie County, New York[1611], and died 30 Sep 1898 in San Francisco, California[1612]. He married (1) ASINATH _____. She was born Abt. 1834 in New York. He married (2) MELVINA H. BALDWIN 15 Feb 1874 in Sacramento, California[1613]. She was born 1838 in New York, and died 01 Sep 1876 in Napa, Napa County, California. Lived in: 1860, Deep Creek, Clinton County, Iowa. Levi is buried in Kilgore Cemetery, Rancho Cordova, Sacramento County, California

Children of LEVI RODMAN and ASINATH _____ are:
- i. ASA B.[9] RODMAN, b. Abt. 1854, New York; d. 22 Jan 1922, Sacramento County, California[1614].
- ii. JULIA A. RODMAN, b. Abt. 1855, New York.
- iii. IDA RODMAN, b. 1859, Iowa.
- iv. DEBORAH RODMAN, b. Abt. 1861, Iowa.

475. EZRA COOK[8] RODMAN *(DEBORAH[7] MILK, BENJAMIN[6], BENJAMIN[5], JONATHAN[4], JOB[3], JOHN[2], JOHN[1])* was born Jul 1836 in Fulton, Schoharie County, New York[1615,1616,1617], and died 02 Aug 1908 in Hawleyton, Broome County, New York[1618]. He married MARY JOSEPHINE _____. She was born May 1840[1618,1619], and died 1920 in Hawleyton, Broome County, New York[1620]. They are buried in Spring Forest Cemetery, Binghamton, Broome County, NY.

Children of EZRA RODMAN and MARY _____ are:
- 1043. i. FRANCES MARIE[9] RODMAN, b. 20 Jul 1855, Callicoon, Sullivan County, New York; d. 21 Nov 1941, Binghamton, Broome County, New York.
- ii. MARY ANN 'MINNIE' RODMAN, b. Abt. 1857, Callicoon, Sullivan County, New York.
- iii. MARTHA ANN 'ANNA' RODMAN, b. Abt. 1859, Callicoon, Sullivan County, New York.
- 1044. iv. CECILE RODMAN, b. 05 Dec 1863, Callicoon, Sullivan County, New York; d. 1945, Binghamton, Broome

		County, New York.
	v.	EZRA RODMAN, b. Apr 1866, Pennsylvania.
1045.	vi.	GRANT A. RODMAN, b. Oct 1867, Pennsylvania; d. 1945, Binghamton, Broome County, New York.
	vii.	ARTHUR RODMAN, b. Abt. 1871, Binghamton, Broome County, New York; d. Bet. 1880 - 1900, New York.
1046.	viii.	HARRY E. RODMAN, b. May 1873, Binghamton, Broome County, New York; d. 1959.
	ix.	BELLE RODMAN, b. Feb 1883, Binghamton, Broome County, New York.

476. DAVID E.[8] RODMAN (*DEBORAH[7] MILK, BENJAMIN[6], BENJAMIN[5], JONATHAN[4], JOB[3], JOHN[2], JOHN[1]*) was born 05 Jun 1841 in Fulton, Schoharie County, New York, and died 24 Aug 1914 in Adams County, Iowa. He married (1) JULIA ANN DOING 03 May 1862 in Clinton County, Iowa[1621]. She was born Abt. 1841. He married (2) MARTHA ANN GARSIDE 25 Sep 1868 in Clinton County, Iowa. She was born Abt. 1847 in New York[1622], and died 1884 in Santa Rosa, Sonoma County, California. He married (3) AMELIA JANE 'MILLIE' PLETCHER 27 Jun 1892 in Coming, Adams County, Iowa[1623]. She was born Apr 1833 in Ohio.

Children of DAVID RODMAN and MARTHA GARSIDE are:
    i. CLARA MAY[9] RODMAN, b. Apr 1870, Waterford, Clinton County, Iowa[1624].
    ii. IDA RODMAN, b. Abt. 1876, Waterford, Clinton County, Iowa.
    iii. MARY RODMAN, b. Jul 1879, Santa Rosa, Sonoma County, California[1625].

477. PERMELIA ELIZABETH[8] RODMAN (*DEBORAH[7] MILK, BENJAMIN[6], BENJAMIN[5], JONATHAN[4], JOB[3], JOHN[2], JOHN[1]*) was born 06 Jun 1844 in Fulton, Schoharie County, New York, and died 26 Jan 1921 in Shasta County, California. She married WILLIAM JOEL JOHNSON 08 Aug 1862 in Salt Lake City, Utah. He was born 18 Apr 1840 in Kentucky, and died 12 Jul 1901 in Round Mountain, Shasta County, California.

Children of PERMELIA RODMAN and WILLIAM JOHNSON are:
    i. ALICE JOSEPHINE[9] JOHNSON, b. 1863, Sutter County, California; d. 1937.
    ii. MARY ELIZABETH JOHNSON, b. 1865, Sutter County, California; d. 1953.
    iii. WILLIAM JOEL JOHNSON, JR., b. 1868, Sutter County, California.
    iv. EUGENE FRANKLIN JOHNSON, b. 1870, Sutter County, California; d. 1955.
    v. ROBERT LARKIN JOHNSON, b. 1873, Sutter County, California; d. 1932.
    vi. HARLIN EWING JOHNSON, b. 1877, Sutter County, California; d. 1925.
    vii. LEILA RUBY JOHNSON, b. 1878, Sutter County, California; d. 1954.

478. MARY E. 'POLLY'[8] MILK (*STEPHEN[7], BENJAMIN[6], BENJAMIN[5], JONATHAN[4], JOB[3], JOHN[2], JOHN[1]*) was born 28 Nov 1829 in Schoharie County, New York[1626], and died 29 Oct 1901 in Cazenovia, Madison County, New York[1626]. She married (1) JOHN S. CLARK[1627]. He was born 23 Jun 1828 in New York[1628], and died 01 Sep 1865 in Cazenovia, Madison County, New York[1628]. She married (2) WILLIAM GILES SHEPHERD. He was born Abt. 1831 in New York[1629], and died 24 Mar 1898 in Cazenovia, Madison County, New York[1629]. William served Bet. 11 Jun 1861 - 05 Jun 1863, Civil War; 35th Regiment, New York Infantry, Co. H. (Madison County)[1632] Mary, John, and William are buried in Evergreen Cemetery, Cazenovia, Madison County, New York[1630]

Child of MARY MILK and JOHN CLARK is:
    i. MARY E.[9] CLARK, b. 16 Sep 1856, Cazenovia, Madison County, New York[1633,1634]; d. 14 Jun 1938, Cazenovia, Madison County, New York[1634]; m. CHARLES H. MANN; b. May 1855, New York[1635]. No children. Mary is buried in Evergreen Cemetery, Cazenovia, Madison County, New York[1636]

479. JOHN B.[8] MILK (*STEPHEN[7], BENJAMIN[6], BENJAMIN[5], JONATHAN[4], JOB[3], JOHN[2], JOHN[1]*) was born 04 Mar 1831 in New York[1637], and died 12 Jan 1866 in Cazenovia, Madison County, New York[1638,1639]. He married MARION H. _____ Abt. 1854 in Madison County, New York. She was born Abt. 1835 in New York. John was a blacksmith. He is buried in Evergreen Cemetery, Cazenovia, Madison County, New York. His tombstone says that he was 30 yrs, 10 mos. old at the time of his death. This has to be an error, because he is not shown in the 1830 census (official date of 1 June 1830), but he is shown in the 1840 census as being between 5 and 9 years old. I am assuming a birth year of 1931.

Children of JOHN MILK and MARION _____ are:
- i. ELLEN E.[9] MILK, b. Abt. 1856, Georgetown, Madison County, New York.
- ii. ELIZA 'LIZZIE' MILK, b. Abt. Mar 1860, Georgetown, Madison County, New York.

480. PERLINA[8] DIBBLE *(BETSEY[7] MILK, BENJAMIN[6], BENJAMIN[5], JONATHAN[4], JOB[3], JOHN[2], JOHN[1])* was born 16 Dec 1825 in Fulton, Schoharie County, New York, and died 12 Sep 1874 in Schoharie County, New York. She married HIRAM MEYERS 1849 in Schoharie County, New York, son of HENRY MEYERS and PHOBE FINEHORET. He was born Abt. 1827, and died Abt. 1905.

Children of PERLINA DIBBLE and HIRAM MEYERS are:
1047. i. REUBEN[9] MEYERS, b. Abt. 1850.
       ii. SARAH MEYERS.
       iii. CALEB MEYERS, b. 1851; d. 13 Dec 1889.

481. POLLY MARGARET[8] DIBBLE *(BETSEY[7] MILK, BENJAMIN[6], BENJAMIN[5], JONATHAN[4], JOB[3], JOHN[2], JOHN[1])* was born 23 Oct 1827 in Fulton, Schoharie County, New York, and died 11 Oct 1915 in Schoharie County, New York. She married WILLIAM ALBRO FANCHER 1851, son of JOSEPH FANCHER and NANCY POTTER. He was born 13 Sep 1823 in Berne, New York, and died 29 Dec 1914 in Eminence, New York. Lived in: Fulton, Schoharie County, New York. William was a farmer and a carpenter. They are buried in H.W. Ploss Cemetery, Blenheim/Eminence, Schoharie County, New York.

Children of POLLY DIBBLE and WILLIAM FANCHER are:
1048. i. MARVIN R.[9] FANCHER, b. 21 Oct 1851, Schoharie County, New York; d. 28 Oct 1928.
1049. ii. ADELINE FANCHER, b. 30 Aug 1853, Schoharie County, New York; d. 17 May 1931, Summit, Schoharie County, New York.
       iii. RACHAEL FANCHER, b. 13 Feb 1855, Schoharie County, New York; d. 02 Apr 1918, West Richmondville, New York; m. CHARLES HILSINGER; b. Abt. 1855; d. 30 Jun 1936.
1050. iv. HIRAM J. FANCHER, b. 24 Sep 1857, Schoharie County, New York; d. 17 May 1946, Schenectady, New York.
1051. v. CALEB FANCHER, b. 19 Dec 1859, Schoharie County, New York; d. 21 Oct 1951, Schoharie County, New York.
1052. vi. PERLINA FANCHER, b. 14 Sep 1861, Schoharie County, New York; d. 1952.
       vii. BETHIAR FANCHER, b. 06 Feb 1864, Schoharie County, New York; d. 06 Dec 1890.
1053. viii. JAMES RUSSELL FANCHER, b. 14 Aug 1866, Schoharie County, New York; d. 14 Dec 1954, West Fulton, Schoharie County, New York.
1054. ix. FANNIE ESTHER FANCHER, b. 19 Sep 1869, Schoharie County, New York; d. 26 May 1952, Warnerville, New York.

482. JAMES PATRICK[8] DIBBLE *(BETSEY[7] MILK, BENJAMIN[6], BENJAMIN[5], JONATHAN[4], JOB[3], JOHN[2], JOHN[1])* was born 09 Apr 1830 in Fulton, Schoharie County, New York[1640], and died 31 Dec 1874 in Putnam County, Illinois[1641]. He married CATHERINE E. 'KATY' PROPER. She was born Abt. 1830 in New York, and died Bet. 1880 - 1885. James is buried in Union Grove Cemetery, Florid, Putnam County, Illinois

Children of JAMES DIBBLE and CATHERINE PROPER are:
       i. MALE[9] DIBBLE, b. Bet. 1860 - 1865, Putnam County, Illinois[1642]; d. d.y..
1055. ii. SARAH ELIZABETH DIBBLE, b. 15 Mar 1865, Putnam County, Illinois; d. 1931, Page County, Iowa.
       iii. FRANCIS C. DIBBLE, b. Nov 1872, Putnam County, Illinois. Lived in: Sac County, Iowa

473. ADELINE[8] DIBBLE *(BETSEY[7] MILK, BENJAMIN[6], BENJAMIN[5], JONATHAN[4], JOB[3], JOHN[2], JOHN[1])* was born 21 Mar 1833 in West Fulton, Schoharie County, New York, and died 08 Jun 1910 in Schenectady, New York. She married JOSEPH VAN VORIS 09 Sep 1849, son of JOHN VAN VORIS and HANNAH CARY. He was born 25 Dec 1823 in New Baltimore, New York, and died 18 Mar 1904 in Eminence, New York. Lived in West Fulton, Schoharie County, New York

Children of ADELINE DIBBLE and JOSEPH VAN VORIS are:
1056. i. HANNAH ELIZABETH[9] VAN VORIS, b. 10 Aug 1850, West Fulton, Schoharie County, New York; d. 15 Apr

		1924, Stamford, Delaware County, New York.
1057.	ii.	CATHERINE 'KATE' VAN VORIS, b. 07 Apr 1854, West Fulton, Schoharie County, New York; d. 16 Apr 1939, Schenectady, New York.
1058.	iii.	EMMA VAN VORIS, b. 11 Apr 1856, West Fulton, Schoharie County, New York.
1059.	iv.	ANDREW VAN VORIS, b. 07 Mar 1858, West Fulton, Schoharie County, New York; d. 06 Apr 1946, San Francisco, California.
	v.	JANE VAN VORIS, b. 06 Apr 1864, West Fulton, Schoharie County, New York; d. 26 Oct 1926, Clarksville, New York; m. FRANK WHITLOCK, 24 Sep 1897, Eminence, Schoharie County, New York; b. Abt. 1864, Indian Falls, Albany County, New York; d. Clarksville, New York.
	vi.	ELLA E. VAN VORIS, b. 14 Mar 1866, West Fulton, Schoharie County, New York; m. (1) ELLIOT KNIFFEN, 14 Mar 1890; b. Abt. 1866; m. (2) BENJAMIN MILLER, 28 Nov 1918; b. 22 Jul 1865; d. 26 Nov 1926, Schenectady, New York.
	vii.	ROXIE E. VAN VORIS, b. 26 Dec 1876, West Fulton, Schoharie County, New York; d. 14 Nov 1945; m. WILLIAM MILLETT, 22 May 1898; b. 22 Jul 1874; d. 04 May 1946.

484. ISAAC[8] DIBBLE *(BETSEY[7] MILK, BENJAMIN[6], BENJAMIN[5], JONATHAN[4], JOB[3], JOHN[2], JOHN[1])* was born 21 May 1836 in Fulton, Schoharie County, New York[1643], and died 25 Dec 1918 in Schoharie County, New York. He married (1) CAROLINE _____[1644] Abt. 1855 in Schoharie County, New York. She was born Abt. 1836. He married (2) BETHIER JUMP[1645,1646] Bet. 1860 - 1870 in Schoharie County, New York. She was born 09 Dec 1831 in New York?[1647], and died 09 Jun 1877 in Schoharie County, New York[1647]. He married (3) LOUISA HILSINGER 1878 in Schoharie County, New York. She was born Abt. 1852.. Isaac and Bethier are buried in H.W. Ploss Cemetery, Blenheim/Eminence, Schoharie County, New York

Children of ISAAC DIBBLE and LOUISA HILSINGER are:

	i.	EVERETT[9] DIBBLE, b. 07 Jul 1879, Schoharie County, New York.
	ii.	MARTIN DIBBLE, b. May 1882, Schoharie County, New York.
	iii.	LEROY DIBBLE, b. 16 Dec 1883, Schoharie County, New York.
1060.	iv.	MAY A. DIBBLE, b. Jul 1888, Schoharie County, New York.

485. BENJAMIN[8] DIBBLE *(BETSEY[7] MILK, BENJAMIN[6], BENJAMIN[5], JONATHAN[4], JOB[3], JOHN[2], JOHN[1])* was born 04 Jul 1838 in Fulton, Schoharie County, New York, and died 12 Apr 1918 in Dibble Hollow, Schoharie County, New York. He married EMMA WILDAY Abt. 18 Aug 1869 in Schoharie County, New York. She was born Aug 1849 in Schoharie County, New York?[1648,1649], and died 24 Oct 1919 in Cobleskill, New York[1650].

Children of BENJAMIN DIBBLE and EMMA WILDAY are:

	i.	GEORGE W.[9] DIBBLE, b. 28 Sep 1872, Fulton, Schoharie County, New York[1651]; d. 30 Mar 1960, Schoharie County, New York; m. CLARA LAPE, 1899, Schoharie County, New York; b. 04 Oct 1865, New York; d. 05 Jun 1949, Schoharie County, New York. Lived in: Richmondville, Schoharie County, New York
	ii.	DAVID C. DIBBLE, b. 14 Oct 1879, Fulton, Schoharie County, New York[1651,1652]; d. Apr 1967, Richmondville, Schoharie County, New York; m. LELIA S. FELTER; b. 15 Apr 1887, Richmondville, Schoharie County, New York[1653]; d. Apr 1982, Cobleskill, New York[1653].

486. SARAH EMELINE[8] DIBBLE *(BETSEY[7] MILK, BENJAMIN[6], BENJAMIN[5], JONATHAN[4], JOB[3], JOHN[2], JOHN[1])* was born 10 Sep 1844 in Fulton, Schoharie County, New York, and died 06 Sep 1912 in Eminence, New York. She married GEORGE WILDAY Abt. 1874. He was born 05 May 1851, and died 23 Apr 1901.

Children of SARAH DIBBLE and GEORGE WILDAY are:

1061.	i.	MARION CALEB[9] WILDAY, b. 07 Jul 1875, Eminence, New York; d. 24 Mar 1927.
	ii.	HOWARD EMORY WILDAY, b. 21 Aug 1881, Eminence, New York; d. 06 Oct 1901.

487. MARION G.[8] DIBBLE *(BETSEY[7] MILK, BENJAMIN[6], BENJAMIN[5], JONATHAN[4], JOB[3], JOHN[2], JOHN[1])* was born 30 Oct 1847 in West Fulton, Schoharie County, New York, and died 12 Jul 1928 in Schoharie County, New York. He married CATHERINE ZIMMER 27 Dec 1871. She was born 06 Jun 1852, and died 24 Oct 1896.

Children of MARION DIBBLE and CATHERINE ZIMMER are:

1062. i. CORA[9] DIBBLE, b. 01 Oct 1872; d. 08 Feb 1951.
1063. ii. ROBIE DIBBLE, b. 10 Nov 1874; d. 15 Mar 1949.
1064. iii. BETHIAR DIBBLE, b. 07 Sep 1877.
1065. iv. ETTA DIBBLE, b. 30 Dec 1879.
1066. v. JENNIE DIBBLE, b. 06 Feb 1882; d. 08 Nov 1943.
1067. vi. MARY DIBBLE, b. 25 Apr 1884; d. 15 Nov 1950.
1068. vii. HARLAN DIBBLE, b. 28 Aug 1886; d. 14 Aug 1949, Richmondville, Schoharie County, New York.

488. PHEBE[8] DYER *(PERLINA[7] MILK, BENJAMIN[6], BENJAMIN[5], JONATHAN[4], JOB[3], JOHN[2], JOHN[1])* was born 27 Mar 1837 in Jefferson, Schoharie County, New York[1654], and died 17 Jul 1873 in Jefferson, Schoharie County, New York[1654]. She married JOEL SEBASTIAN MILLIAS Abt. 1858, son of SEBASTIAN MILLIAS and HANNAH CLARK. He was born 05 Jun 1836 in Worcester, Otsego County, New York, and died 28 Nov 1898 in Worcester, Otsego County, New York.

Phebe is shown in the 1870 census, living with her parents, listed as Phebe Dyer, and with the notation "Insane".
Burial: Old School Baptist Church Cemetery, East Jefferson, Schoharie County, New York
Sebastian was a carpenter. He is buried in Maple Grove Cemetery, Worcester, Otsego County, New York

Children of PHEBE DYER and JOEL MILLIAS are:

1069. i. WINTHROP L.[9] MILLIAS, b. 15 Feb 1859; d. Valatie, New York.
1070. ii. JENNIE B. MILLIAS, b. 1862; d. 1927.
1071. iii. WILLIAM EUGENE 'WILLIY' MILLIAS, b. 21 Mar 1864, Jefferson, Schoharie County, New York; d. 19 Jul 1948, Fox Hospital, Oneonta, Otsego County, New York.

489. LEWIS[8] DYER *(PERLINA[7] MILK, BENJAMIN[6], BENJAMIN[5], JONATHAN[4], JOB[3], JOHN[2], JOHN[1])* was born 09 Feb 1848 in Jefferson, Schoharie County, New York, and died 27 Dec 1926. He married (1) CARRIE KENYON 25 Oct 1873. She was born 1852, and died 19 May 1874. He married (2) EMMA KENYON Sep 1879. She was born 15 Jul 1855, and died 08 Dec 1927.

Child of LEWIS DYER and CARRIE KENYON is:

i. MYRON[9] DYER, b. 12 May 1874; d. Sep 1947, East Worcester, New York; m. (1) VIOLA VAN DEBOE; b. 1874; m. (2) MARY SMITH VAN BUREN RYDER.

Children of LEWIS DYER and EMMA KENYON are:

1072. ii. GEORGE ALFRED[9] DYER, b. 05 Sep 1880.
1073. iii. MARY DYER, b. 29 Jun 1883.

490. NATHANIEL EZRA[8] COOK *(PERMELIA[7] MILK, BENJAMIN[6], BENJAMIN[5], JONATHAN[4], JOB[3], JOHN[2], JOHN[1])* was born 26 Mar 1836 in West Fulton, Schoharie County, New York, and died 14 Dec 1901 in Winters, California. He married (1) MINERVA STEARN. She was born Abt. 1836. He married (2) MARIAH GRANT 21 Oct 1860. She was born 02 Dec 1845.

Children of NATHANIEL COOK and MINERVA STEARN are:

i. GEORGE ALBERT EASTMOND[9] COOK, b. Kelseyville, California.
ii. BEULAH SOPHINA MINERVA COOK, b. 22 Oct 1880, Kelseyville, California.
iii. ROSE ELIZABETH PERMELIA COOK, b. 22 Oct 1880, Kelseyville, California.
iv. FRANK EUGENE BLANCHARD COOK, b. 15 Jul 1883, Christine, California.

Children of NATHANIEL COOK and MARIAH GRANT are:

v. WILLIAM EZRA[9] COOK, b. 20 Aug 1861, Aurora, Illinois.
vi. REUBEN NATHANIEL COOK, b. 18 Aug 1863, Wheaton, Illinois.

491. LOUISE DESIRE[8] COOK *(PERMELIA[7] MILK, BENJAMIN[6], BENJAMIN[5], JONATHAN[4], JOB[3], JOHN[2], JOHN[1])* was born 03 Feb 1839 in Coxsackie, New York. She married EDWIN H. HEMENWAY 15 Sep 1864. He was born 27 Mar 1837.

Children of LOUISE COOK and EDWIN HEMENWAY are:

i. EZRA EDWARD[9] HEMENWAY, b. 14 Oct 1873, Wayne Center, DuPage County, Illinois; d. 01 Feb 1878,

ii. ESTHER LOUISE HEMENWAY, b. 09 Dec 1876, Wayne Center, DuPage County, Illinois; m. FRANK E. RUSSELL, 04 Sep 1900, Sacramento, California; b. Abt. 1876.

492. EZRA ASHER[8] COOK *(PERMELIA[7] MILK, BENJAMIN[6], BENJAMIN[5], JONATHAN[4], JOB[3], JOHN[2], JOHN[1])* was born 05 Nov 1841 in Windsor, Connecticut, and died 1911. He married MARIA ELIZABETH BLANCHARD 05 Aug 1869 in Wheaton, Illinois, daughter of JONATHAN BLANCHARD and MARY BENT. She was born 30 Oct 1846 in Galesburg, Illinois, and died 05 Mar 1916 in Wheaton, Illinois. Ezra served during the Civil War, between 1861 and 1864 in Company G., Thirty-ninth Illinois Volunteers

Children of EZRA COOK and MARIA BLANCHARD are:
i. LILLIAN[9] COOK, b. 1870, Chicago, Illinois; d. d.y..
ii. MARY AMELIA COOK, b. Sep 1871, Chicago, Illinois; m. GEORGE CHAFFEE; b. Abt. 1871.
iii. JULIA ELIZABETH COOK, b. 05 Nov 1872, Chicago, Illinois; m. C. WILL AVELING; b. Abt. 1872, Holland (Europe); d. 1947, Wheaton, Illinois.
iv. BLANCHARD COOK, b. 1874, Chicago, Illinois; d. d.y..
v. EZRA ALBERT COOK, b. 14 Jul 1875, Wheaton, Illinois; m. (1) IDA BRODE; b. Abt. 1875; d. 1939; m. (2) MAUDE _____; b. Abt. 1875. Residence: New Boston, Illinois
vi. HANNAH IDA WILLISTON 'JEAN' COOK, b. 05 Oct 1877, Chicago, Illinois; d. 1934, Latona, Seattle County, Washington; m. HARVEY K. BOYER; b. Abt. 1877.
vii. GRACE ELOISE COOK, b. 30 Oct 1879, Chicago, Illinois; m. KARL E. ZAHN; b. Abt. 1879, Of Warsaw, Wisconsin.
Residence: Sacramento, California

1074 viii. DR. JONATHAN BLANCHARD COOK, b. 11 Sep 1881, Chicago, Illinois.
ix. DAVID MAURICE COOK, b. 09 Oct 1883, Chicago, Illinois; d. 1929; m. EDNA COOPER; b. Abt. 1883.
x. LYMAN JOSEPH COOK, M.D., b. 13 Sep 1885, Chicago, Illinois; m. EDITH MARKS; b. Abt. 1885. Residence: Omaha, Nebraska
xi. ETHEL MARGUERITE COOK, b. 14 Aug 1887, Chicago, Illinois; d. 1924, Elgin, Illinois; m. WALTER J. HARTMAN; b. Abt. 1887. Lived in Elgin, Illinois, where Walter was an Attorney.
xii. HELEN GERALDINE COOK, b. 16 Apr 1889, Chicago, Illinois; d. 1929, Bellflower, California; m. EDWARD D. WILLING, Abt. 1910; b. Abt. 1889. Helen was Superintendent of Art in Santa Ana public schools

493. MARY AMELIA[8] COOK *(PERMELIA[7] MILK, BENJAMIN[6], BENJAMIN[5], JONATHAN[4], JOB[3], JOHN[2], JOHN[1])* was born 11 Mar 1844 in Great Barrington, Massachusetts. She married DWIGHT L. HEMENWAY 04 Jul 1864 in Naperville, Illinois. He was born Abt. 1844.

Children of MARY COOK and DWIGHT HEMENWAY are:
i. HENRY LEWELLYN[9] HEMENWAY, b. 04 Jan 1866, Wheaton, Illinois.
ii. DAVID HEMENWAY, b. 25 Mar 1869, Wayne, Illinois; m. ERNESTINE LAGER; b. Abt. 1869, Of Winters, California.
iii. LIZZIE HEMENWAY, b. 25 Aug 1871, Chicago, Illinois.
iv. CHESTER EDWIN HEMENWAY, b. 27 May 1875, Chicago, Illinois; m. EVA COOPER; b. Abt. 1875, Of San Francisco, California.
v. MAYBELL C. HEMENWAY, b. 03 Jan 1882, Lakeview, Illinois; m. GEORGE MOLAR; b. Abt. 1882, Of Berkley, California.

494. DAVID CALEB[8] COOK *(PERMELIA[7] MILK, BENJAMIN[6], BENJAMIN[5], JONATHAN[4], JOB[3], JOHN[2], JOHN[1])* was born 28 Aug 1850 in East Worcester, New York, and died 30 Jul 1927 in Elgin, Illinois. He married MARGUERITE MURAT 06 May 1874. She was born 07 Jun 1852 in Chicago, Illinois, and died 10 Jul 1941.

David attended Wheaton College. In 1871 he was a successful salesman of sewing machines and accessories. He invested his entire capital of $1,000 in sewing machine needles and put them in a safe. That night Mrs. O'Leary's cow kicked over a lantern and his savings were lost.

He became greatly interested in religious work by organizing missions in the poorer sections of Chicago and starting Sunday Schools. He found that he, as well as other teachers, needed help in presenting lessons. At that time there were no such helps as illustrations, stimulating literature, hymns, and other equipment for Sunday School workers. Consequently he set himself to writing and then by setting his own type, he printed aids for his work. His Our Sunday School Quarterly was the first publication of its kind in the world. These helps became so popular that he was forced to devote all his time in preparing and printing Sunday School supplies. His first plant was at Lake View, Ill., later a larger plant was established in Elgin, Ill.

Ill health for a time forced him to retire in California. He bought a ranch in Piru Canyon, made famous by Helen Hunt Jackson in "Ramona". Oil was discovered on the property. He accepted the first fair offer for his property and put the money in his publishing business: the David C. Cook Publishing Co. When he died, the newspapers estimated his wealth at $3,000,000.

DAVID C. COOK
"Godfather of the Sunday School"

In an article on David C. Cook entitled "Godfather of the Sunday School," written by Clarence W. Hall and printed in the Christian Herald, are some statistics as of 1942. "Today the David C. Cook Publishing Co. is the world's largest concern catering exclusively to the Sunday School and its needs. Through its big presses in Elgin, Ill., there annually flow 100,000,000 copies of publications . . . six to ten tons of Sunday School literature are shipped every weekday of the year. More than 60,000 Sunday Schools the world around use its twenty-seven different papers and magazines, which are read by millions of every race and color where the English language is spoken or taught." Only Sunday School aids are published. The company has never passed out of the control of the Cook family. Today, David C. Cook III continues the work of his father, David C. Cook Jr. and the founder David C. Cook.

Children of DAVID COOK and MARGUERITE MURAT are:
      i.   GEORGE EVANS^9 COOK, b. 28 Feb 1875, Elgin, Illinois; m. UNA HOWELL; b. Abt. 1875. Residence: Elgin, Illinois
1075.   ii.   DAVID CHARLES COOK, b. 20 Jun 1881, Elgin, Illinois; d. 16 Mar 1932, Elgin, Illinois.

495. RACHAEL^8 JUDD *(JANET^7 MILK, BENJAMIN^6, BENJAMIN^5, JONATHAN^4, JOB^3, JOHN^2, JOHN^1)* was born 18 Sep 1844 in Schoharie County, New York. She married WILLIAM GAULT 22 Nov 1868. He was born Abt. 1844.

Child of RACHAEL JUDD and WILLIAM GAULT is:
1076.   i.   VIRA^9 GAULT, b. 19 Mar 1878.

496. GEORGE H.^{8} MILK *(DAVID^7, BENJAMIN^6, BENJAMIN^5, JONATHAN^4, JOB^3, JOHN^2, JOHN^1)* was born 11 Oct 1850 in Delaware County, New York[1655,1656], and died 11 Mar 1917 in Hancock, Delaware Co., NY[1657]. He married AMELIA BIEDEKAPP 04 Oct 1876, daughter of JOHN BIEDEKAPP and CATHERINE _____. She was born 14 May 1860 in

Plainfield, PA[1657,1658], and died 30 Dec 1954 in Hancock, Delaware Co., NY[1659].

George was elected purchasing agent for the Rock Valley, Delaware County grange in 1889, 1890. George was a firm believer in the cooperative movements, preferring to share with his neighbors the profits he might have had from the annual shipment of their lambs to the New York City market. He was treasurer of the Mutual County Fire Insurance for many years. He was also a director of the Agriculture Insurance Co. Burial: Marysville Cemetery, Goulds, Delaware County, New York

OBITUARY

Mrs. Amelia Biedekapp Milk, 94, of Goulds died in Hancock Hospital on December 30, 1954. She had been hospitalized about a month. Funeral services were held Sunday at the Goulds Methodist Church, Rev. Roger Riley officiating. Interment was made in Marysville Cemetery by Henderson's.

The deceased was born at Plainfield, Pa. on May 14, 1860, the daughter of John Biedekapp and Katherine Klauss. She was united in marriage with George H. Milk on April 10, 187, at Long Eddy. Mrs. Milk had been a Goulds resident for over 90 years.

Surviving are two sons, Arlyn R. Milk, Goulds, and Lee Milk of Walton. Seventeen grandchildren and 42 great-grandchildren also survive.

The oldest member of the community, Mrs. Milk was a member of the Goulds Mutual Society. She had a remarkable memory and was fond of reciting poems and verses of Scripture. She devoted her life to the care of her family. Burial: Marysville Cemetery, Goulds, Delaware County, New York

Children of GEORGE MILK and AMELIA BIEDEKAPP are:

1077. i. JOHN A.⁹ MILK, b. 12 Oct 1878, Hancock, Delaware County, New York; d. 09 May 1909, Hancock, Delaware County, New York.

1078. ii. LENA VIOLA MILK, b. 26 Apr 1880, Hancock, Delaware County, New York; d. 22 Feb 1920, Binghamton, Broome County, New York.

1079. iii. LEE B. MILK, b. 05 Sep 1882, Hancock, Delaware County, New York; d. 22 Dec 1959, Walton, Delaware County, NY.

1080. iv. ARLYN RAY MILK, b. 09 Aug 1891, Hancock, Delaware County, New York; d. 02 Jul 1993, Long Eddy, Sullivan, NY 12760.

497. ANNA SARAH⁸ MILK *(DAVID⁷, BENJAMIN⁶, BENJAMIN⁵, JONATHAN⁴, JOB³, JOHN², JOHN¹)* was born 16 May 1854 in Delaware County, New York[1659,1660], and died 19 Sep 1935 in Boonville, NY[1661,1662]. She married MELVIN BRAZIE[1663] 19 Oct 1872 in Delaware County, NY[1664], son of ABRAM BRAZIE and NANCY LIVINGSTON. He was born 19 Oct 1851 in Hancock, Delaware County, New York[1665,1666], and died 25 Apr 1927 in East Branch, Delaware County, New York[1667,1668]. Melvin was Commissioner of Highways in Hancock, NY[1669]. They are buried in East Branch Cemetery, Hancock, Delaware Co., NY

Children of ANNA MILK and MELVIN BRAZIE are:

1081. i. CHARLES EDWOND⁹ BRAZIE, b. 14 Jun 1873, Hancock, Delaware County, New York; d. 22 Dec 1955, Hancock, Delaware County, New York.

1082. ii. EMMET A. BRAZIE, b. 30 Apr 1886, Hancock, Delaware County, New York.

498. ABRAM LINCOLN⁸ MILK *(DAVID⁷, BENJAMIN⁶, BENJAMIN⁵, JONATHAN⁴, JOB³, JOHN², JOHN¹)* was born 14 Oct 1860 in Delaware County, New York[1670], and died 26 Mar 1925 in Goulds, Delaware County, New York[1670,1671]. He married MARY CATHERINE 'CASSIE' BIEDEKAPP Bet. 1877 - 1878[1672], daughter of JOHN BIEDEKAPP and CATHERINE _____. She was born 22 Sep 1863 in New York[1672,1673], and died 28 Sep 1951 in Goulds, Delaware County, New York[1674]. They are buried in Marysville Cemetery, Goulds, Delaware County, New York[1674]

OBITUARY

Death of Abram MILK of Goulds

--died March 26, 1925 --daughter is Mrs. John RUTZ of Rock Valley is listed as a survivor--A team of horses ran away and he was thrown from the wagon. He was 64 years old. Abram was a potato farmer and was noted for killing foxes on his property.

Abram L. Milk, after his marriage to Mary Catherine, a daughter of John Biedekapp, had started farming on the place his grandfather, Philip Neer, had originally cleared. "Abe" and "Cassie" has a large family, eight children, all growing up on the place except Della, who died in infancy. The other seven, most of whom remained in the neighborhood after marriage, were Leslie (m. Louise Rutz); Minnie (m. Clarence Hoolihan); Nellie (m.John Rutz); Lester

(m. Flossie Klinegardner); Earl (m. Sylvia Jones); Goldie (m. John Hendricks); and Janette (m. John May).

Children of ABRAM MILK and MARY BIEDEKAPP are:
- 1083. i. MINNIE ANN[9] MILK, b. 25 Dec 1878, Hancock, Delaware County, New York; d. 13 Jun 1901.
- 1084. ii. IRVIN "LESLIE" D. MILK, b. 12 Jun 1881, Hancock, Delaware County, New York; d. 14 Aug 1956, Delaware County, NY.
- 1085. iii. NELLIE MAY MILK, b. 31 Oct 1883, Hancock, Delaware County, New York.
- iv. MABEL G. "GOLDIE" MILK[1675], b. 06 Jun 1887, Hancock, Delaware County, New York[1675,1676]; d. 01 Mar 1911, Hancock, Delaware County, New York[1676]; m. JOHN HENDRICKS[1676], 16 Oct 1907; b. Abt. 1885. Mabel is buried in Marysville Cemetery, Hancock, NY
- v. DAVID EARL MILK, b. 15 Apr 1891, Hancock, Delaware County, New York[1677,1678,1679]; d. 15 Mar 1969, San Francisco, California[1680]; m. SYLVIA E. JONES[1681], 15 Nov 1920[1681]; b. Bet. 1896 - 1897, Pennsylvania[1681]. Lived in: 1920, Walton, New York. Military service: WWI - Militia
- vi. DELLA CATHERINE MILK[1682], b. 16 Oct 1897, Hancock, Delaware County, New York[1682]; d. 01 Mar 1898, Hancock, Delaware Co., NY (measles)[1682]. Burial: Marysville Cemetery, Goulds, Delaware County, NY Cause of Death: Measles
- 1086. vii. JANETTE A. MILK, b. 20 Feb 1899, Hancock, Delaware County, New York.
- 1087. viii. LESTER L. MILK, b. 20 Jan 1902, Hancock, Delaware County, New York; d. 24 May 1987, Long Eddy, Sullivan County, New York.

499. WILLIAM[8] MILK *(DAVID[7], BENJAMIN[6], BENJAMIN[5], JONATHAN[4], JOB[3], JOHN[2], JOHN[1])* was born 16 Aug 1865 in Delaware County, New York[1682], and died 03 Jan 1952 in Hancock, Delaware County, New York[1682]. He married MARY ELIZABETH HOFFMAN 05 Mar 1890 in Rock Valley, Delaware Co., NY[1683], daughter of JOHN HOFFMAN and KATHERINE SHERMAN. She was born 19 Jan 1870[1684], and died 10 Feb 1963 in Hancock, Delaware County, New York[1684]. They are buried in Rock Valley Cemetery, Hancock, New York.

William put up a new barn in late May 1898. He bought a new touring car in May 1913.

Children of WILLIAM MILK and MARY HOFFMAN are:
- 1088. i. JOHN WILLIAM[9] MILK, b. 03 Jun 1892; d. 21 Feb 1977, Long Eddy, Sullivan, NY 12760.
- 1089. ii. CHARLES CORBETT MILK, b. 19 Aug 1894, Sullivan County, New York; d. 27 Oct 1960, Hancock, Delaware County, New York.
- iii. CATHERINE A. MILK[1685], b. Jan 1896, Hancock, Delaware County, New York[1686]; d. 09 Feb 1910, Hancock, Delaware County, New York[1687]. Burial: Rock Valley Cemetery, Hancock, NY
- 1090. iv. MARGARET L. MILK, b. 24 Aug 1898, Hancock, Delaware County, New York; d. 20 Feb 1965, Hancock, Delaware County, New York.
- 1091. v. LETTIE "MAE" MILK, b. 01 Apr 1903.
- vi. ARTHUR MILK[1688], b. 17 Jul 1905, Hancock, Delaware County, New York[1689]; d. 19 Oct 1905, Hancock, Delaware County, New York[1689]. Burial: Rock Valley Cemetery, Hancock, NY
- vii. WALTER MILK[1690], b. 1915, Hancock, Delaware County, New York[1690]; d. 1929, Hancock, Delaware County, New York[1690]. Burial: Rock Valley Cemetery, Hancock, NY

500. PEARL[8] MILKS *(LEVI 'STEPHEN'[7], BENJAMIN[6] MILK, JR., BENJAMIN[5], JONATHAN[4], JOB[3], JOHN[2], JOHN[1])* was born Abt. 1881 in Town of Jefferson, Schoharie County, New York. She married MELVIN D. WARD, son of DEXTER WARD and ZERNA _____. He was born Abt. 1871.

Children of PEARL MILKS and MELVIN WARD are:
- 1092. i. GLADYS M.[9] WARD, b. Abt. 1904, New York; d. Prob. 1930-1940 Otsego County, NY.
- ii. MARJORIE R. WARD, b. Abt. 1908.

501. CHRISTCHANA[8] VAN VALKENBURGH *(LYDIA JANE[7] MILK, TROWBRIDGE[6], BENJAMIN[5], JONATHAN[4], JOB[3], JOHN[2], JOHN[1])* was born 24 May 1836, and died 18 Apr 1921. She married JUDSON KIRKE 05 Nov 1856. He was born 04 Sep 1832, and died 23 Feb 1904.

Children of CHRISTCHANA VAN VALKENBURGH and JUDSON KIRKE are:
- 1093. i. VAN RENSSELAER[9] KIRKE, b. Abt. 1858.

1094.   ii.   ANGELO KIRKE, b. 28 Sep 1860; d. 31 Aug 1928.
- iii. CHARLES KIRKE, d. 20 Sep 1905, (unmarried).
- iv. PERCY OKLEY KIRKE, d. 25 Jul 1887, Killed by a train, unmarried
- v. DEMA LINDA KIRKE, b. 02 Apr 1871; m. EUGENE E. HOWE, 19 Feb 1908; b. May 1867, New York; d. 14 Sep 1932. No children. Dema attended Wesleyan University, Lincoln, Nebraska. She was a teacher in Lincoln County, Nebraska. Eugene had at least three children by an earlier marriage. He graduated from Middlebury College & Albany Law School. Occupation: Attorney, Fleischmanns, New York; Deputy Attorney General

502. GEORGE ANGELO^8 VAN VALKENBURGH *(LYDIA JANE^7 MILK, TROWBRIDGE^6, BENJAMIN^5, JONATHAN^4, JOB^3, JOHN^2, JOHN^1)* was born 24 Feb 1838, and died 01 Jan 1903 in New York. He married (1) CYLINDA DECKER 23 Oct 1861. She was born Abt. 1838. He married (2) HARRIET 'HATTIE' WINTERS 11 Jan 1871. She died Mar 1905 in New York. George served several terms as Supervisor of the Town of Lexington, Green County, New York, in the Catskills. He had a large boarding house at Spruceton, Green County, New York

Child of GEORGE VAN VALKENBURGH and CYLINDA DECKER is:
- i. CHARLES^9 VAN VALKENBURGH, d. d.y..

Children of GEORGE VAN VALKENBURGH and HARRIET WINTERS are:
1095.   ii.   NINA L.^{9} VAN VALKENBURGH, b. Apr 1873, Jewett, Greene County, New York.
- iii. MORGAN A. VAN VALKENBURGH, b. Abt. 1874, Jewett, Green County, New York; d. Bef. 1900.
1096.   iv.   CYRUS WILBUR VAN VALKENBURGH, b. 15 Jul 1878, Jewett, Green County, New York.
1097.   v.   GEORGE A. VAN VALKENBURGH, b. 25 Jun 1889, Jewett, Greene County, New York.

503. BENJAMIN^8 VAN VALKENBURGH *(LYDIA JANE^7 MILK, TROWBRIDGE^6, BENJAMIN^5, JONATHAN^4, JOB^3, JOHN^2, JOHN^1)* was born 24 Aug 1845. He married MARIA BUTLER 28 Aug 1864. She was born Abt. 1845.

Children of BENJAMIN VAN VALKENBURGH and MARIA BUTLER are:
1098.   i.   ALVERETTA^9 VAN VALKENBURGH.
- ii. ALFRED VAN VALKENBURGH.

504. LODEMA^8 VAN VALKENBURGH *(LYDIA JANE^7 MILK, TROWBRIDGE^6, BENJAMIN^5, JONATHAN^4, JOB^3, JOHN^2, JOHN^1)* was born 16 Feb 1847, and died Dec 1905. She married CHARLES SPEENBURG 25 Nov 1868. He was born Abt. 1847, and died 1916.

Children of LODEMA VAN VALKENBURGH and CHARLES SPEENBURG are:
1099.   i.   DELMAR^9 SPEENBURG, b. 1871.
- ii. GEORGE A. SPEENBURG, b. 1876; m. GERTRUDE SMITH; b. Abt. 1876. Lived in Fleischmanns, Delaware County, New York

505. WESLEY^8 VAN VALKENBURGH *(LYDIA JANE^7 MILK, TROWBRIDGE^6, BENJAMIN^5, JONATHAN^4, JOB^3, JOHN^2, JOHN^1)* was born 21 Jun 1848, and died 09 Jan 1906. He married (1) OLLIE HUGGINS. She was born Abt. 1850. He married (2) JULIA PLANK Sep 1877.

Children of WESLEY VAN VALKENBURGH and JULIA PLANK are:
1100.   i.   DAYTON^9 VAN VALKENBURGH.
1101.   ii.   LYDIA VAN VALKENBURGH, b. 1883.

506. LYDIA JANE^8 SMITH *(CATHERINE^7 MILK, TROWBRIDGE^6, BENJAMIN^5, JONATHAN^4, JOB^3, JOHN^2, JOHN^1)*[1691] was born 25 Apr 1841 in Lexington, Greene County, New York[1691], and died 22 May 1881 in Westkill, Greene County, New York[1691]. She married ISAAC J. VAN VALKENBURGH[1691] 25 Nov 1859 in Greene County, New York. He was born 31 Jul 1839 in Lexington, Greene County, New York, and died 21 Jul 1911 in Chichester, Ulster County, New York.

Children of LYDIA SMITH and ISAAC VAN VALKENBURGH are:
- i. ANGELINE^9 VAN VALKENBURGH.

ii. SARAH KATHERINE "KATIE" VAN VALKENBURGH.
iii. FERNANDO VAN VALKENBURGH.
iv. MARY J. VAN VALKENBURGH.
v. ORLANDO VAN VALKENBURGH.
vi. WILBUR J. VAN VALKENBURGH.
vii. JESSE VAN VALKENBURGH.
viii. GEORGE BENJAMIN VAN VALKENBURGH.
ix. ROMAINE VAN VALKENBURGH, b. 09 Oct 1878, Lexington, Greene County, New York; d. Abt. 1919.
x. AMANDA "MANDY" VAN VALKENBURGH.

507. VIOLA[8] SHARPE *(ANN ELIZA[7] MILK, TROWBRIDGE[6], BENJAMIN[5], JONATHAN[4], JOB[3], JOHN[2], JOHN[1])* was born 10 Apr 1856, and died 27 Apr 1901 in Griffin Corners/Fleischmanns, Delaware County, New York. She married HON. DEWITT GRIFFIN 30 Mar 1879, son of MATTHEW GRIFFIN and CLARISSA DODGE. He was born 27 Mar 1836.

DeWitt was a lawyer, member of the New York State Legislature, and the first Postmaster of Griffin Corners/Fleischmanns, New York.

Children of VIOLA SHARPE and DEWITT GRIFFIN are:
1102. i. DEWITT CLINTON[9] GRIFFIN, b. 22 Sep 1882, New York.
1103. ii. MATTHEW SHARPE GRIFFIN, b. 22 Feb 1886, New York; d. 12 Feb 1914, Brooklyn, New York.
1104. iii. WARNER MILLER GRIFFIN, b. 19 Nov 1889, Griffin Corners/Fleischmanns, Delaware County, New York.

508. LENA A.[8] MILK *(BENJAMIN[7], TROWBRIDGE[6], BENJAMIN[5], JONATHAN[4], JOB[3], JOHN[2], JOHN[1])* was born 28 Nov 1862, and died 12 Apr 1899. She married ROMAINE W. VAN VALKENBURGH 06 Oct 1883 in West Kill, Greene County, New York, son of WATSON VAN VALKENBURGH and MARY _____. He was born 08 May 1860 in Spruceton, Greene County, New York[1692], and died 17 Jan 1917.

Child of LENA MILK and ROMAINE VAN VALKENBURGH is:
1105. i. PEARL[9] VAN VALKENBURGH, b. Jun 1884, Lexington, Greene County, New York.

509. MARIAN ALICE[8] MILK *(BENJAMIN[7], TROWBRIDGE[6], BENJAMIN[5], JONATHAN[4], JOB[3], JOHN[2], JOHN[1])* was born 23 Apr 1870 in Lexington, New York[1693], and died 12 Sep 1944 in Los Angeles, California[1693]. She married JOHN LEWIS REEDER 25 Feb 1901 in Concepción, Concepción, Chile[1694], son of JAMES MCMAHON REEDER and SARA JACOBY. He was born 22 Sep 1859 in Madison County, Ohio, and died 18 Jan 1932 in Syracuse, New York.

Marian graduated from Barnard College. She was a Missionary teacher and Principal of Colegio Americana, Conception, Chile

John graduated: Ohio Wesleyan University & Sacred School of Theology, Boston, Mass., Masters Degree of Sacred Theology. He was a Minister of Methodist Church in Mass. and VT. & 20 yr missionary service in Chile.

Child of MARIAN MILK and JOHN REEDER is:
1106. i. PAUL ASBURY[9] REEDER, b. 11 Mar 1903, Milan, Ohio; d. 14 Oct 1984, Los Angeles, California.

510. SAMANTHA[8] VAN VALKENBURGH *(JULIA ANN[7] MILK, TROWBRIDGE[6], BENJAMIN[5], JONATHAN[4], JOB[3], JOHN[2], JOHN[1])* was born 17 Feb 1859, and died 1906. She married CHARLES DUNHAM 1878. He was born Jul 1856 in New York.

Children of SAMANTHA VAN VALKENBURGH and CHARLES DUNHAM are:
1107. i. WARD JAMES[9] DUNHAM, b. 28 Mar 1880, New York; d. Mar 1963, Volusia County, Florida.
1108. ii. CLARENCE E. DUNHAM, b. 23 Nov 1884.
1109. iii. JULIA DUNHAM, b. Abt. 1888, Lexington, Greene County, New York.
1110. iv. CORYDON BUSHNELL DUNHAM, b. 01 Sep 1890, Lexington, Greene County, New York; d. 09 Nov 1966, Yonkers, Westchester County, New York.

511. JANE[8] VAN VALKENBURGH *(JULIA ANN[7] MILK, TROWBRIDGE[6], BENJAMIN[5], JONATHAN[4], JOB[3], JOHN[2], JOHN[1])* was born 04 Jun 1861, and died 22 Dec 1915. She married JAMES HERDMAN Abt. 1881. He was born 24 Sep 1859, and died 30 Nov 1936.

Children of JANE VAN VALKENBURGH and JAMES HERDMAN are:
- i. FERRIS[9] HERDMAN, b. 25 Nov 1883; m. GRACE PLANK, 25 Nov 1914; b. Abt. 1885.
- ii. MAUDE HERDMAN.
- iii. CARRIE HERDMAN, m. MORGAN VAN VALKENBURGH.
- iv. CLIFFORD HERDMAN.

512. CARRIE[8] VAN VALKENBURGH *(JULIA ANN[7] MILK, TROWBRIDGE[6], BENJAMIN[5], JONATHAN[4], JOB[3], JOHN[2], JOHN[1])* was born 15 Mar 1863, and died 21 Jun 1940. She married ADDISON PERSONS 25 May 1882. He was born 03 Feb 1853, and died 17 Dec 1916.

Children of CARRIE VAN VALKENBURGH and ADDISON PERSONS are:
- 1111. i. OLIVE MAY[9] PERSONS, b. 26 Apr 1883.
- 1112. ii. DR. ALFRED OTIS PERSONS, b. 25 Aug 1886.
- iii. JAY D. PERSONS, b. 14 Nov 1890; d. 28 Dec 1890.
- 1113. iv. RAY EUGENE PERSONS, b. 14 Nov 1890; d. 29 Sep 1948.

513. JAMES[8] VAN VALKENBURGH *(JULIA ANN[7] MILK, TROWBRIDGE[6], BENJAMIN[5], JONATHAN[4], JOB[3], JOHN[2], JOHN[1])* was born 11 Jan 1867, and died 23 Dec 1939 in Lexington, Greene County, New York. He married BERTHA KIRK 14 May 1885. She was born 05 May 1868, and died 17 Apr 1912.

Children of JAMES VAN VALKENBURGH and BERTHA KIRK are:
- 1114. i. CHARLES W.[9] VAN VALKENBURGH, b. 05 Dec 1887, Lexington, Greene County, New York.
- ii. ADDISON P. VAN VALKENBURGH, b. 23 Apr 1889, Lexington, Greene County, New York; m. ELIZABETH FOUNTAIN, 15 Aug 1915; b. Abt. 1890. Residence: Spruceton, Greene County, New York
- iii. LEON 'LEE' VAN VALKENBURGH, b. 04 Mar 1891, Lexington, Greene County, New York.
    Leon lived at home with his father, until sometime between 1920 and 1930, when he was admitted to the Hudson River State (Psychiatric) Hospital in Poughkeepsie, New York, where he is shown as a patient in the 1930 census.
- iv. CHARLOTTE M. 'LOTTIE' VAN VALKENBURGH, b. 11 May 1894, Lexington, Greene County, New York; m. FRANK W. COUGHTRY, 02 Feb 1950; b. Abt. 1894.
    Lottie was Proprietor, Van Valkenburgh Guest House at Spruceton, New York. Frank was an Albany businessman.
- v. JAMES K. VAN VALKENBURGH, b. Dec 1899, Lexington, Greene County, New York; d. Bef. 1910, Lexington, Greene County, New York.
- 1115. vi. GLENN M. VAN VALKENBURGH, b. 06 Jun 1901, Lexington, Greene County, New York.
- vii. ALFRED J. VAN VALKENBURGH, b. 20 Jan 1908, Lexington, Greene County, New York; m. GERTURDE VAN VALKENBURGH. Alfred was a veteran of WWII. He was a High School Custodian, and lived in Westkill, Greene County, New York

514. ELLA[8] VAN VALKENBURGH *(JULIA ANN[7] MILK, TROWBRIDGE[6], BENJAMIN[5], JONATHAN[4], JOB[3], JOHN[2], JOHN[1])* was born 15 Jul 1871, and died 12 Dec 1947. She married EDGAR BUTLER 31 Oct 1887. He was born 31 Oct 1866 in of Westkill, Greene County, New York, and died 18 Aug 1952. Residence: Hunter, Greene County, New York

Children of ELLA VAN VALKENBURGH and EDGAR BUTLER are:
- 1116. i. ELIZABETH[9] BUTLER, b. 15 Aug 1890, Greene County, New York.
- ii. RENSSELAER BUTLER, b. 21 Apr 1894, Spruceton, Greene County, New York; m. (1) FLORENCE VERMELYA; b. Abt. 1894; m. (2) MARJORIE LYNCH; b. Abt. 1894. RENSSELAER was a Salesman in Kingston, New York
- 1117. iii. MARIA JULIA BUTLER, b. 31 Jul 1900, Spruceton, Greene County, New York.

515. JENNIE[8] MARTIN *(CYNTHIA JANE[7] MILK, TROWBRIDGE[6], BENJAMIN[5], JONATHAN[4], JOB[3], JOHN[2], JOHN[1])* was born 1867 in Spruceton, New York, and died Abt. 1938 in San Diego, California[1695]. She married EUGENE KILLIAN KLEINER Aft. 25 Apr 1910[1696]. He was born 31 Jul 1876 in Ohio[1697], and died 17 May 1948 in Napa, California[1697].

Eugene served in the army: Bet. 28 Sep 1907 - 27 Sep 1910, Fort Rosencrans, Pt. Loma Military Reservation, San Diego, California

Child of JENNIE MARTIN and EUGENE KLEINER is:

1118.   i.   EUGENE WESLEY[9] KLEINER, b. 30 Sep 1912, San Diego, California; d. 11 Jul 1990, San Mateo, California.

516. CHARLES BRIGGS[8] MARTIN *(CYNTHIA JANE[7] MILK, TROWBRIDGE[6], BENJAMIN[5], JONATHAN[4], JOB[3], JOHN[2], JOHN[1])* was born 23 Dec 1872 in Spruceton, New York, and died Aft. 1940 in Parsons, Labette County, Kansas ?. He married AMELIA MYRIA MYERS Abt. 1895. She was born Oct 1871 in Illinois[1698], and died 31 Aug 1940 in Parsons, Labette County, Kansas.

from: *History of Labette County, Kansas and representative citizens* - 1901

CHARLES BRIGGS MARTIN, the genial separating clerk at the post office in Parsons, Kansas, has been a resident of the city since 1884, and has had considerable experience in post office business. He was born December 2 3, 1872, at Catskill, Greene county, New York, and is a son of Augustus and Cynthia (Milk s) Martin.

Augustus Martin is a member of a company manufacturing fuel in Parsons, with a plant located near the Davison elevator. He is a member of the city council, and takes a great interest in local affairs. He served during the Civil War, in the Union army, and was wounded in the right arm, August 21, 1862, at the crossing of the Rappahannock river. He was taken to Bellevue Hospital, New York, for treatment, and was discharged as cured December 8, 1862.

Charles B. Martin attended the public schools of his native county, and also the schools of Parsons, Kansas, whither his parents removed in 1884. His first work was in the capacity of a molder at Skelton's foundry, where he worked two years. He then joined a party of surveyors on the Missouri, Kansas & Texas Railway, and made the trip through the ""Nation," in charge of A. B. Thurston. Returning to Parsons, he entered the government service as sub-mail-carrier, in 1892. In June, of the following year, he was transferred to t he clerical department, and acted as general delivery clerk until March, 1894. He was then promoted to be mailing clerk, and made up all outgoing mail,—also separating all incoming mail. Under the Democratic administration, he was "set back" for a short time to general delivery clerk, but in 1896 he was again promoted, and became assistant postmaster under Frank W. Frye. He served also under his successor, H. H. Lusk, who advanced him to his present position as mailing and separating clerk. He works from 7 A M to 7:30 P M

Mr. Martin was joined in marriage with Amelia Myers, a daughter of W. P. and Elizabeth (Corbett) Martin. That ceremony being performed on June 17, 1894. Mrs. Myers is deceased.

Mr. Myers, who is engaged in the transfer business at Parsons, contracted a second matrimonial alliance by wedding Annie L. McKinstry. Five children were the result of this union, name ly: Nellie, Luella, Alice, Oscar, and Ethel,—aged, respectively, twenty-four, twenty- two, twenty, seventeen, and thirteen years. Mrs. Martin also has one brother, Ernest Myers, who is a prominent farmer in Illinois.

Mr. and Mrs. Martin have one little son, Raymond W., who was born December 25, 1898, and was indeed a blessed Christmas gift. Fraternally, Mr. Martin affiliates with the Knights and Ladies of Security, and the Sons of Veterans, and both he and Mrs. Martin are members of the Knights and Ladies of America. They show a decided preference for the Presbyterian faith. In his political opinions, Mr. Martin is a Republican, and believes the principles of that party to be the most advantageous to the country. He is a capable and trustworthy public servant, and is highly esteemed by his fellow citizens.

Children of CHARLES MARTIN and AMELIA MYERS are:

      i.   RAYMOND WADSWORTH[9] MARTIN, b. 25 Dec 1898, Parsons, Labette County, Kansas; m. CLEDA WIDUP, 25 Dec 1928; b. Abt. 1898. Raymond graduated from Illinois University. Residence: Toledo, Ohio

      ii.   CLARENCE ARTHUR MARTIN, b. 05 Apr 1904, Parsons, Labette County, Kansas; m. LOIS NAURINE HAYDEN, 26 Dec 1931; b. Abt. 1904.   Clarence graduated from Illinois University. Occupation: Mgr. Barrows-Wade-Guthrie Accountant Co., Tulsa, Oklahoma

1119.   iii.   DR. EARL AUGUSTUS MARTIN, b. 06 Apr 1907, Parsons, Labette County, Kansas.

517. CALVIN HARVY[8] MILKS *(AMOS MARSH[7], EZRA[6], DAVID[5] MILK, JONATHAN[4], JOB[3], JOHN[2], JOHN[1])*[1699] was born 28 Aug 1825 in Ithaca, Tompkins County, New York, and died 1864 in Libby Prison (Civil War). He married HARRIET S. BUTLER[1700] Abt. 1847, daughter of EARL BUTLER and HANNAH _____. She was born 11 Aug 1828 in Pennsylvania[1701], and died 01 Aug 1859 in Girard, Erie County, Pennsylvania?[1701]. Harriet is buried in Platea Cemetery, Girard Township, Erie County, Pennsylvania

    U.S. Civil War Soldiers, 1861-1865 about Calvin H. Milks
    Side: Union,   Regiment Name: 83rd Regiment, Pennsylvania Infantry, Company: H

Rank In: Drummer, Rank Out: Private
Cause of Death: Starved to death in prison

Children of CALVIN MILKS and HARRIET BUTLER are:
1120.   i.   LOVINA P.[9] MILKS, b. 1848, Franklin, Erie County, Pennsylvania.
1121.   ii.   ABIGAIL "ABBIE" LETITIA MILKS, b. 23 Mar 1850, Franklin, Erie County, Pennsylvania; d. 23 May 1919, Sharon, Medina County, Ohio.
1122.   iii.   WILLIAM LEANDER MILKS, b. 1852, Franklin, Erie County, Pennsylvania; d. 16 Oct 1920, Erie County, Pennsylvania.
1123.   iv.   CLARENCE G. MILKS, b. 06 Jan 1854, Franklin, Erie County, Pennsylvania; d. 29 Aug 1932, Kansas City, Jackson County, Missouri.
        v.   JAMES MILKS, b. Abt. 1856, Franklin, Erie County, Pennsylvania. Never married.

518. CAROLINE C.[8] MILKS *(AMOS MARSH[7], EZRA[6], DAVID[5] MILK, JONATHAN[4], JOB[3], JOHN[2], JOHN[1])* was born 04 Jul 1832 in Ithaca, Tompkins County, New York, and died 04 Feb 1917 in Erie County, Pennsylvania. She married JOHN W. CLARK. He was born 1837, and died 1911.

Child of CAROLINE MILKS and JOHN CLARK is:
        i.   HATTIE[9] CLARK, b. Adopted.

519. DAVID BENJAMIN[8] MILKS *(AMOS MARSH[7], EZRA[6], DAVID[5] MILK, JONATHAN[4], JOB[3], JOHN[2], JOHN[1])* was born 15 Feb 1835 in Erie County, Pennsylvania, and died 01 Oct 1902 in Erie County, Pennsylvania. He married ALICE AURORA OLNEY 05 Aug 1866 in Lockport, PA, daughter of HENRY OLNEY and AURELIA CASTLE. She was born 18 Nov 1846 in Weedsport, Cayuga County, New York, and died 26 Oct 1931 in Livermore Falls, Androscoggin County, Maine. David served during the Civil War Bet. Aug 1862 - Mar 1863, Pvt., Co. D, 145th Pennsylvania Volunteers, Infantry. Burial: Francis Cemetery, Cranesville, Franklin Township, Erie County, Pennsylvania

After her husband, David Milks, died, Alice lived with her daughter, Grace and her family (McEwards) in Maine. She is buried there in a family plot.

Children of DAVID MILKS and ALICE OLNEY are:
1124.   i.   NELLIE CAROLINE[9] MILKS, b. 15 Jan 1869, Erie County, Pennsylvania; d. 27 Jun 1954, Villenova, Chautauqua County, New York.
1125.   ii.   GRACE AURELIA MILKS, b. 07 Feb 1877, Erie County, Pennsylvania; d. 25 Aug 1961, Cuba, Allegany County, New York.

520. PARTHENIA ANN[8] MILKS *(AMOS MARSH[7], EZRA[6], DAVID[5] MILK, JONATHAN[4], JOB[3], JOHN[2], JOHN[1])* was born Dec 1844 in Elk Creek, Erie County, Pennsylvania, and died 1929 in Cranesville, Erie County, Pennsylvania. She married THERON E. RICE Abt. 1864 in Erie Co., Pennsylvania[1703]. He was born 11 Jun 1840 in New York[1704,1705], and died 03 Sep 1922 in Cranesville, Erie County, Pennsylvania. They are buried in Francis Cemetery, Cranesville, Erie County, Pennsylvania

Children of PARTHENIA MILKS and THERON RICE are:
1126.   i.   WILLIAM BURDELL[9] RICE, b. Jun 1865; d. 1928.
1127.   ii.   MABEL JOSEPHINE RICE, b. Dec 1878, Erie County, Pennsylvania.

521. SYLVESTER REESE[8] STEPHENS *(SARAH "SALLY" ANN[7] MILKS, EZRA[6], DAVID[5] MILK, JONATHAN[4], JOB[3], JOHN[2], JOHN[1])* was born 22 Sep 1822 in Enfield, Tompkins County, New York[1707,1708], and died 03 May 1909 in Juda, Green County, Wisconsin[1709]. He married WEALTHY BALL 16 Oct 1844 in Green County, Wisconsin[1710], daughter of GARY BALL and POLLY DAVIS. She was born 18 May 1823 in Springfield, Erie County, Pennsylvania[1711,1712], and died 21 May 1911 in Juda, Green County, Wisconsin[1713,1714].

Commemorative Biographical Record of the Counties of Rock, Green, Grant, Iowa and Lafayette, Wisconsin...
(Chicago: J. H. Beers, 1901), pp. 461-62.
    SYLVESTER REUBEN [REESE] STEPHENS, one of the old and highly respected pioneer farmers of Green county, is now spending his last years in a well-deserved freedom from the cares and burdens of active business life.

Mr. Stephens is a son of Reuben D. and Sallie (Milk) Stephens, both natives of the State of New York, where he was born Sept. 22, 1822. At the age of twelve he accompanied his parents into Erie county, Penn., and in 1844 they came to Green county, Wis. This was in the early days, when the country was wild and rough, and six years before the admission of the Territory as a State into the Federal Union. He drove a team and wagon from Erie county to Green county, and two years later made a return trip to Erie county, driving over the route three times in all. For seven years he was engaged in teaming between Green county and Milwaukee, and he has also drawn wheat to market at Chicago. After his marriage he entered 160 acres of government land, including the site of the present railroad station at Juda, there being not a single house where that thriving village now stands. He helped to build a log school house there, which was the first building in the place. His father was the prime mover in organizing the school and putting up the building. Mr. Stephens is a musician of considerable local repute. He has a violin which has been in his possession nearly three-score years, and has played for many parties and entertainments including the first 4th of July celebration in Monroe, held in 1843.

Mr. Stephens and Miss Wealthy Ball were married in Green county, Wis., Oct. 16, 1844. Mrs. Stephens was born in Springfield, Erie Co., Penn., the daughter of Gary Ball, who settled at Joliet, Ill., in 1836, and granddaughter of Daniel Ball, who came from England, and first settled in Maryland. He died in Erie county, Penn., aged about eighty years. His bachelor brother left a large estate in Philadelphia and Virginia, of which the descendants of Daniel Ball are the rightful heirs, though they have never come into possession. To Mr. and Mrs. Stephens were born ten children: Alfred, now a farmer near Flandreau, S. Dak.; Susan, widow of Quincy David, of Shenandoah, Iowa; Wilder, who died at David City, Neb., Jan. 30, 1901, aged fifty-two years; Alba, a resident of Henderson, Neb.; Edward, living in Juda, Wis.; James, in Juda; Theo R., wife of Jehiel Davis; a farmer of Sylvester township; Malvina, who died Nov. 24, 1886, aged thirty-six years; Ezra and Etta, who both died in infancy. Mr. and Mrs. Stephens have thirteen grandchildren and fourteen great-grandchildren.

Mr. Stephens started out in life a poor man, and when he was married was rich only in courage and in hope of the future. After many years he became the owner of a choice Wisconsin farm of 160 acres, which he has recently sold, that he might move into the village of Juda, and be care-free. For some forty years he owned and operated a threshing machine in the county. Mr. Stephens is a honored veteran of the war of the Rebellion, having served as a member of Company K, 22d Wis. V. I., and is now in receipt of a liberal pension for injuries sustained during his service. With is wife he belongs to the Methodist Church. He is a Republican, and a good citizen. During his years of active life he was a hard-working an, and was known to be very honorable and upright in all his transactions.

Brodhead Independent (Brodhead, Wisconsin), May 13, 1909, p. 8, col. 3   OBITUARY

OBITUARY

Sylvester Reese Stephens was born near Ithaca, New York state on September 20th, 1822. When he was twenty years of age he came to Green county, Wisconsin and around this vicinity he spent the remainder of his life.

He was married to Miss Wealthy Ball (on the Lyman place near Juda) on October 16, 1844. To this union were born ten children, six of whom survive. He also leaves his wife, two brothers and one sister.

He enlisted in Company K 22nd Wisconsin Regiment in August 1862. After serving about a year he was discharged on account of disabilities.

He was converted in 1869 and united with the Methodist church. Mr. Stephens along with his wife have lived within a mile of Juda since 1844 and at the time of the former's death they were the oldest couple in Green county having over sixty-four years of married life. They took up a government claim on the Moldenhauer place and lived there over thirty years. About fourteen years ago they moved to Juda and at his home on the hill

Mr. Stephens passed away on Monday morning May 3, 1909 at the advanced age of 86 years, 7 months and 13 days. Few are permitted to live as long as Grandma [sic] Stephens as he was familiarly called.

He was well known to the community and loved by all who knew him.

He was a loving husband, a kind father, a cheery neighbor and a true citizen, and we mourn his death but not without hope of a sure and certain resurrection.

The funeral service was held on Wednesday, May 5 at the Methodist Episcopal church, Juda conducted by the pastor who took for his text: "And Israel said unto Joseph, Behold, I die; but God shall be with you and bring you again unto the land of your fathers." The song service was by Albert Matzke, Frank Matzke, Mrs. A. Matzke and Mrs. W. Bagley, with Mrs. Kryder at the organ. The church was very tastefully decorated with potted plants and flags emblematic of a soldiers' life and death. There were present the old soldiers of Brodhead and Juda. The pall bearers were: Dr. Hilliard, Frank Milks, A. A. Gillett, Frank Montgomery, John Binger and M. Martin. Five of the pall bearers were relatives of the deceased.

Burial: Mount Vernon Cemetery, Juda, Green County, Wisconsin

~~~~~~~~~~~~~~~~~~~~~~~~~~

OBITUARY - *Brodhead Independent* (Brodhead, Wisconsin), May 21, 1911, p. 8, col. 5

Mrs. Wealthy B. Stevens passed away at the home of her daughter, Mrs. J.Z. Davis on Sunday morning at five o'clock.

Mrs. Stevens was born near Erie, Pa., on May 18th, 1823. In 1842 she came with her parents to Green County. On October 15th, 1844, she was married to Sylvester Stevens. To this union were born ten children, six of whom are living: Alfred, of Henderson, Neb.; James, of Boaz, Wis.; Edward, of Juda, Wis.; and Mrs. Susan Davis, and Mrs. J.Z. Davis also of Juda. Sylvester Stevens died in 1909. [NOTE: Alfred was a resident of Eagan, South Dakota; Alba, who is not mentioned, lived in Henderson, Neb.]

Mrs. Stevens was converted at the age of fifteen years. She was one of the charter members of the Juda M.E. Church which was organized in 1862, and has been a prominent worker and loyal supporter of the church ever since. She has always been held in the very highest esteem by all who knew her.

The funeral services were held on Wednesday, May 31st, in the home at one o'clock, and in the church at 1:30. The Pastor, Rev. W.J. Marshfield, officiated, preaching from Phil. 1:21, "To me to live is Christ, and to die is gain." The songs were sung by Mrs. Bagley, Miss Gifford, F.E. Matzke and J. Wolgast; Mrs. Kryder presided at the organ.

The remains were interred in Mount Vernon Cemetery, Juda, Green County, Wisconsin.

Children of SYLVESTER STEPHENS and WEALTHY BALL are:

- i. ALFRED REUBEN[9] STEPHENS, b. 1845, Juda, Green County, Wisconsin. Lived in: Flandreau, South Dakota
- 1128. ii. SUSAN E. STEPHENS, b. 24 Aug 1847, Juda, Green County, Wisconsin; d. 28 Sep 1911, Shenandoah, Page County, Iowa.
- iii. DAVID 'WILDER' STEPHENS, b. 1849, Juda, Green County, Wisconsin; d. 30 Jan 1901, David City, Butler County, Nebraska.
- iv. AMANDA MALVINA STEPHENS, b. 1851, Juda, Green County, Wisconsin; d. 24 Nov 1886, Juda, Green County, Wisconsin.
- v. ALBA H. STEPHENS, b. Abt. 1853, Juda, Green County, Wisconsin; m. UNKNOWN, 03 Oct 1875, Green County, Wisconsin[1715]. Lived in Henderson, Nebraska. Burial: Mount Vernon Cemetery, Juda, Green County, Wisconsin
- vi. EDWARD EDMUND WALDO 'ED' STEPHENS, b. Abt. 1856, Juda, Green County, Wisconsin; d. 1941, Green County, Wisconsin. Lived in: 1911, Juda, Green County, Wisconsin
- vii. JAMES S. STEPHENS, b. Abt. 1859, Juda, Green County, Wisconsin. Lived in: 1911, Boaz, Wisconsin
- viii. THEO R. STEPHENS, b. Abt. 1862, Juda, Green County, Wisconsin; m. JEHIEL Z. DAVIS, 21 Feb 1892, Sylvester, Green County, Wisconsin[1715]; b. Spring Grove, Wisconsin. Lived in: 1911, Juda, Green County, Wisconsin
- ix. EZRA STEPHENS[1716], b. Abt. 1865, Juda, Green County, Wisconsin; d. Abt. 1865, Juda, Green County, Wisconsin (d.y.).
- x. ETTA STEPHENS[1716], b. Abt. 1865, Juda, Green County, Wisconsin; d. Abt. 1865, Juda, Green County, Wisconsin (d.y.).

522. CLARISSA[8] STEPHENS *(SARAH "SALLY" ANN[7] MILKS, EZRA[6], DAVID[5] MILK, JONATHAN[4], JOB[3], JOHN[2], JOHN[1])*[1717] was born 1824 in Enfield, Tompkins County, New York[1717], and died 14 Oct 1885 in David City, Butler County, Nebraska. She married IRA EDDIE BALL 04 Feb 1844 in Green County, Wisconsin, son of GARY BALL and POLLY DAVIS. He was born 31 Aug 1820 in Erie, Erie County, Pennsylvania, and died 29 Nov 1853 in Sauk City, Sauk County, Wisconsin. Ira is buried in Pioneer Cemetery, Sauk County, Wisconsin

OBITUARY - *David City Tribune* (David City, Nebraska), October 22, 1885, p. 5, col. 1

BALL - On Wednesday, October 14, 1885, at the residence of C.M. Ball, of internal cancer, Mrs. Clarissa Ball, at the age of 61 years.

Mrs. Ball is the mother of C. M. and J. D. Ball, two of Butler county's most esteemed citizens.

She had been a resident of this county for about a dozen years, and made a large circle of appreciative friends, won by her sterling worth, who mourn her departure and sympathize with the bereaved friends.

Funeral services were held at the Baptist church in this city on Friday, Rev. Webb officiating.

Burial: David City Cemetery, David City, Butler County, Nebraska. Plot: 22 13 SW 1/4

Children of CLARISSA STEPHENS and IRA BALL are:

- i. JAMES DEMETRIUS[9] BALL, b. Abt. 1846, Kingston, Sauk County, Wisconsin.

1129. ii. CURTIS MACK BALL, b. 02 Sep 1849, Kingston, Sauk County, Wisconsin; d. 15 Aug 1919, Butler County, Nebraska.
   iii. FRANCIS J. 'FRANK' BALL, b. Abt. 1851, Sauk County, Wisconsin.
   iv. EDDY BALL, b. 29 Nov 1853, Wisconsin; d. 30 Dec 1853, Sauk County?, Wisconsin. Burial: Pioneer Cemetery, Sauk County, Wisconsin

523. EZRA MILKS[8] STEPHENS *(SARAH "SALLY" ANN[7] MILKS, EZRA[6], DAVID[5] MILK, JONATHAN[4], JOB[3], JOHN[2], JOHN[1])*[1718,1719] was born 08 Jan 1831 in Enfield, Tompkins County, New York[1719,1720], and died 16 Jun 1917 in David City, Butler County, Nebraska[1720]. He married MARGERY MORSE DECKER 19 Dec 1854 in Sylvester, Green County, Wisconsin. She was born 30 May 1835[1720], and died 11 May 1916 in David City, Butler Co., Nebraska[1720].

Civil War veteran - Enlisted as a Private on August 13, 1862 (the day after his son Parker's birth); joined Company A, 27th Infantry Regiment, Iowa September 3, 1862; promoted to Full 5th Corporal May 29, 1863; mustered out August 8, 1865 at Clinton, Iowa.

OBITUARY - People's Banner (David City, Nebr.), June 21, 1917, p. 6, col. 5

EZRA M. STEPHENS

Ezra M. Stephens was born January 8, 1831, in Erie County, New York. He died at the home of his daughter, Mrs. George McKnight, in David City, Nebraska, June 16, 1917, at the age of 86 years.

When a small boy he removed with his parents to Pennsylvania, and from there later to Wisconsin and to Iowa.

He was married to Margery Decker, December 19, 1854, at Julian, Wisconsin. To this union were born four children, all of whom survive their father. With his wife and children he moved to Butler County in 1873, and settled on a farm two miles south of David City, where he farmed for many years. He moved to David City a number of years ago, and for several years past has made his home with Mr. and Mrs. George McKnight. His wife passed away May 11, 1916. Since her death Mr. Stephens has been in very poor health probably the result of old age.

He was a soldier of the civil war, belonging to the 27th Iowa Regiment, Co. A, and served three years. He was a life-long member of the Baptist church and always tried to do his duty as a Christian man. Mr. Stephens was a great home man and it was a rare thing for him to be away from his home unless called by business.

His children are scattered over a wide territory, R.D. Stephens, living in Chaplin, Canada, Mrs. Chas. Blackman in White Water, Montana, E.P. Stephens in St. Edwards, Nebraska, and Mrs. George McKnight in David City. E.P. Stephens and family are the only ones of the children who were able to reach here for the funeral which was held from the Baptist church on Tuesday afternoon at 2 o'clock, Rev. J.J. Bell, the pastor, conducting the services.

The body was laid to rest beside that of his wife in the David City cemetery.

The pall bearers were Elmer Haight, A.M. Walling, I.J. West, J.G. Ross, A.B. Roys and S. Clingman.

Ezra Stephens was one of the pioneers of Nebraska and of Butler County. He was here during the grasshopper days and suffered with the rest, but was made of that material that sticks and when the hard times passed over he was one of those who were here to do his mite in building the country up to its present standard. He had a large circle of acquaintances, especially among the early settlers, who will be sorry to know of his passing away. He had lived his life and his work was done and his maker had called him to come home.

OBITUARY - Butler County Press (David City, Nebr.), June 21, 1917, p. 1, col. 5

PASSING OF EZRA STEPHENS

Aged Civil War Veteran Laid to Rest Tuesday, June 19

Ezra M. Stephens, aged civil war veteran and long-time resident of Butler county passed to the great beyond Saturday, June 16, at 11 p.m. Death was from la grippe, and his illness was of only a few days duration. Owing to his advanced age he was unable to withstand the disease. He died in the home of his daughter, Mrs. George S. McKnight.

The body of the aged veteran was laid to rest in the David City cemetery Tuesday afternoon by the side of his wife, who departed this life May 11, 1916, and who lived to be nearly 81 years of age. Funeral services were held at 2 o'clock in the Baptist church and were conducted by Rev. J.J. Bell, pastor of that church. There were three songs, "Rock of Ages," "Jesus, Lover of My Soul" and "Nearer My God to Thee," given by a male quartet, H.L. Boston, Hugo Hahn, W.S. Rosenstock and Guy Walling. The pall bearers were S. Clingman, L.J. Eberly, E.E. Haight, A.B. Roys, J.J. West and A.M. Walling.

Mr. Stephens served in the civil war nearly three years. He enlisted in August, 1862, and was honorably discharged on account of illness in July, 1865. He was a member of Company A, 27th Iowa Infantry, which was in the Southern states during most of the war.

On January 8, 1917, he was 86 years of age.

Mr. Stephens was born in New York state, in Tompkins county. He left New York with his parents when three years *of age going to Pennsylvania and eight years later to Green county, Wisconsin.*

It was in Green county that his marriage to Miss Marjory Decker took place, on December 19, 1854. In the fifth year of their marriage they moved to Allamakee county, Iowa, on a farm near Rossville, living there ten years. They then came to Nebraska (this was in the year of 1869) and located on a farm three miles from David City. In 1897 they bought a home in David City and moved here. On account of failing age they went to the McKnight home to live five years ago. Mr. and Mrs. Stephens enjoyed nearly 62 years of a happy and companionable married life.

Four children were born to Mr. and Mrs. Stephens and they are all living. They are Mrs. Clara McKnight, Mrs. Laura Blackman of Whitewater, Mont., Reuben D. Stephens, living in Saskatchewan, Canada, and E.P. Stephens of St. Edwards.

Mr. and Mrs. Stephens also raised two boys, Philander Martin and George Davis. Mr. Stephens leaves 15 grandchildren and 22 great grandchildren.

They are buried in David City Cemetery, David City, Butler County, Nebraska. Plot: 3 20 SW 1/4

Children of EZRA STEPHENS and MARGERY DECKER are:
- 1130. i. LAURA^9 STEPHENS, b. Sep 1856, Green County, Wisconsin.
- ii. REUBEN D. STEPHENS, b. Abt. 1858, Green County, Wisconsin.
- 1131. iii. EZRA PARKER STEPHENS, b. 12 Aug 1862, Allamakee County, Iowa; d. 16 Sep 1942, Bellwood, Butler County, Nebraska.
- 1132. iv. CLARISSA 'CLARA' B. STEPHENS, b. Aug 1868, Allamakee County, Iowa; d. 1942, David City, Butler County, Nebraska.

524. JAMES PARKER^8 STEPHENS *(SARAH "SALLY" ANN^7 MILKS, EZRA^6, DAVID^5 MILK, JONATHAN^4, JOB^3, JOHN^2, JOHN^1)^{1721}* was born 27 Apr 1833 in Enfield, Tompkins County, New York^{1721}, and died 21 Oct 1921 in David City, Butler County, Nebraska. He married ESTHER ANNA MARTIN 13 Mar 1856 in Juda, Green County, Wisconsin. She was born 16 Oct 1837 in Cayuga, Cayuga County, New York, and died 20 Jan 1888 in David City, Butler County, Nebraska.

Children of JAMES STEPHENS and ESTHER MARTIN are:
- 1133. i. HARRIE ELLIS^9 STEPHENS, b. 18 Jan 1866, Allamakee County, Iowa; d. 14 Apr 1946, Loup City, Sherman County, Nebraska.
- ii. CARRIE MAE STEPHENS, b. 20 Jan 1869, Allamakee County, Iowa; d. 05 Dec 1931, Horton, Brown County, Kansas.
- iii. EFFIE GRACE STEPHENS, b. 29 May 1871, Allamakee County, Iowa; d. 06 Nov 1956, Wood, Melletta County, South Dakota.
- iv. TOMMIE STEPHENS, b. 05 Mar 1880, David City, Butler County, Nebraska; d. 05 Mar 1880, David City, Butler County, Nebraska.

525. RUTH ANN^8 MILKS *(DANIEL^7, EZRA^6, DAVID^5 MILK, JONATHAN^4, JOB^3, JOHN^2, JOHN^1)* was born 1840 in Erie County, Pennsylvania. She married ALBERT A. BURTON 27 Nov 1864 in Green County, Wisconsin^{1722}, son of JOHN BURTON and ELIZABETH _____. He was born Abt. 1840 in Dutchess County, New York.

Child of RUTH MILKS and ALBERT BURTON is:
- i. ANGIE M.^{9} BURTON, b. Abt. 1867; m. ROBERT M. RAND, 13 Jan 1892, Butte, Silver Bow County, Montana^{1723}; b. Abt. 1863.

526. CALVIN S.^{8} LOVELACE *(PRUDENCE^7 MILKS, EZRA^6, DAVID^5 MILK, JONATHAN^4, JOB^3, JOHN^2, JOHN^1)* was born 1832 in New York, and died Bet. 1880 - 1900. He married MARTHA JANE _____. She was born Jul 1835 in Indiana^{1724}, and died Aft. 1910.

Children of CALVIN LOVELACE and MARTHA _____ are:
- i. WHEELER^9 LOVELACE, b. Abt. 1862, Green County, Wisconsin; d. d.y..
- 1134. ii. HATTIE B. LOVELACE, b. Abt. 1865, Green County, Wisconsin.
- iii. CHARLES GEORGE LOVELACE, b. Apr 1870, Green County, Wisconsin^{1725}; m. LOTTIE C. LEONHARDT , Abt. Dec 1909, Sturgeon Bay, Door County, Wisconsin; b. Abt. 1878, Wisconsin. Charles was Manager - Telephone Exchange, Sturgeon Bay, Door County, Wisconsin
- iv. AMY AIMEE LOVELACE, b. 07 Aug 1875, Green County, Wisconsin; d. 19 May 1965, Hennepin County,

Minnesota; m. CASSIUS WILLARD REYNOLDS, Abt. 1906; b. Nov 1865, New York[1726]; d. 20 Oct 1940, Hennepin County, Minnesota[1727]. No children. They are buried in Plot: SECTION 18 LOT 58 GRAVE 5; Lakewood Cemetery, Minneapolis, Hennepin County, Minnesota

527. JEFFERSON[8] LOVELACE *(PRUDENCE[7] MILKS, EZRA[6], DAVID[5] MILK, JONATHAN[4], JOB[3], JOHN[2], JOHN[1])* was born 1837 in Erie County, Pennsylvania, and died 07 Oct 1869 in Jefferson, Green County, Wisconsin[1728]. He married (1) SARAH JORDAN 11 Jun 1859 in Green County, Wisconsin. She was born 04 May 1837 in Pennsylvania[1728], and died 06 May 1860 in Sylvester, Green County, Wisconsin[1728]. He married (2) HARRIET RAYMOND 21 Dec 1863 in Green County, Wisconsin, daughter of ENOCH RAYMOND and REBECCA _____. She was born 13 Apr 1842 in Holmes County, Ohio, and died 02 Mar 1920 in Monroe, Green County, Ohio. Jefferson died of Typhoid Fever. Jefferson, Sarah, and Harriet are buried in Mount Vernon Cemetery, Juda, Green County, Wisconsin

Civil War veteran - Enlisted as a Private in Company C, 3rd Infantry Regiment, Wisconsin on April 22 1861; received a disability discharge on April 6, 1863; enlisted in Company M, 2nd Cavalry Regiment, Wisconsin on 5 January 5, 1864; mustered out November 15, 1865 at Austin, Texas. Member of Lebanon Lodge No. 127 (Masons)

Child of JEFFERSON LOVELACE and SARAH JORDAN is:
- 1135. i. GEORGE NELSON[9] LOVELACE, b. 02 Feb 1860, Green County, Wisconsin; d. 19 Jun 1936, Green County, Wisconsin.

Children of JEFFERSON LOVELACE and HARRIET RAYMOND are:
- 1136. ii. STEWART ANSON[9] LOVELACE, b. Oct 1866, Green County, Wisconsin; d. 05 Apr 1946, Atchison County, Kansas.
- iii. HARRY LOVELACE, b. Abt. 1868, Green County, Wisconsin.

528. HARRISON 'HANK'[8] LOVELACE *(PRUDENCE[7] MILKS, EZRA[6], DAVID[5] MILK, JONATHAN[4], JOB[3], JOHN[2], JOHN[1])* was born Feb 1839 in Erie County, Pennsylvania. He married MARY C. WITMER 1870[1729]. She was born Dec 1850 in Pennsylvania[1730], and died Bet. 1910 - 1919. Lived in: Bet. 1919 - 1923, U.S. National Homes for Disabled Volunteer Soldiers, Sawtelle, Los Angeles County, California

Children of HARRISON LOVELACE and MARY WITMER are:
- 1137. i. ETHELYN 'ETHEL'[9] LOVELACE, b. Abt. 1872, Grant City, Worth County, Missouri; d. 10 Jan 1952, Clarkston, Asotin County, Washington.
- ii. LULU LOVELACE, b. Abt. 1873, Grant City, Worth County, Missouri.
- iii. RUTH LOVELACE[1730], b. 28 Apr 1875, Grant City, Worth County, Missouri[1731]; d. 06 Nov 1955, Los Angeles, California[1731]; m. ELMER F. SMITH, Abt. 1904, Worth County, Missouri; b. 19 Jul 1870, Missouri[1731]; d. 17 May 1944, Los Angeles, California[1731]. No children. Lived in: 1930, Grant City, Worth County, Missouri

529. ELIZABETH RUTH[8] LOVELACE *(PRUDENCE[7] MILKS, EZRA[6], DAVID[5] MILK, JONATHAN[4], JOB[3], JOHN[2], JOHN[1])* was born 04 Oct 1843 in Erie County, Pennsylvania. She married SETH RAYMOND 16 Jan 1864 in Janesville, Wisconsin. He was born 09 Sep 1835 in Ohio, and died 10 Jun 1910. Military service: Bet. 03 Apr 1861 - Feb 1865, Co. G, Third Wisconsin Volunteer Infantry

Children of ELIZABETH LOVELACE and SETH RAYMOND are:
- 1138. i. JEREMIAH L. 'JAY'[9] RAYMOND, b. Sep 1864, Wisconsin.
- ii. CHARLES RAYMOND, b. Abt. 1865, Wisconsin; d. Bef. 1885.
- 1139. iii. HOWARD RAYMOND, b. Abt. 1867, Iowa.
- 1140. iv. ANNA RAYMOND, b. Abt. 1868, Iowa.
- 1141. v. LEWIS L. RAYMOND, b. 19 Oct 1871, Butler County, Nebraska; d. 02 Oct 1935, Nebraska.
- vi. SETH RAYMOND, b. Abt. 1872, Nebraska.
- vii. JOSEPH RAYMOND, b. Abt. 1874, Nebraska.
- viii. WHEELER A. RAYMOND, b. Jul 1876, Nebraska.
- ix. CHLOE RAYMOND, b. Abt. 1881, Nebraska.
- x. THOMAS RAYMOND, b. Apr 1885, Nebraska.

530. NELSON R.[8] LOVELACE *(PRUDENCE[7] MILKS, EZRA[6], DAVID[5] MILK, JONATHAN[4], JOB[3], JOHN[2], JOHN[1])* was born Feb

1846 in Green County, Wisconsin. He married MARY ALICE LORE in 1872. She was born 04 Jan 1851 in Pennsylvania[1732], and died 11 Jan 1925 in Scotts Bluff, Nebraska[1732]. In 1930, Nelson was living in the Gering Hotel, in Gering, Scotts Bluff Count, Nebraska. We have no record of his burial, although he probably is buried in West Lawn Cemetery next to his wife. Alice is buried in West Lawn Cemetery, Gering, Scotts Bluff, Nebraska.

Children of NELSON LOVELACE and MARY LORE are:
1142. i.   EDNA A.[9] LOVELACE, b. Dec 1873, Wisconsin; d. 30 Sep 1964, Weld County, Colorado.
       ii. LEROY LOVELACE, b. Abt. 1877, Wisconsin. Lived in: 1940, Bird, Jackson County, Arkansas
1143. iii. OSCAR ROY LOVELACE, b. 04 Feb 1880, Grant City, Worth County, Missouri; d. 28 Nov 1932, Scotts Bluff, Nebraska.
       iv. PEARL B. LOVELACE, b. Jul 1882, Missouri.

531. LEANDER MILKS[8] STEPHENS *(PATIENCE[7] MILKS, EZRA[6], DAVID[5] MILK, JONATHAN[4], JOB[3], JOHN[2], JOHN[1])*[1733] was born 08 Feb 1824 in Tompkins County, New York[1733], and died 09 May 1902 in Jennings, Louisiana. He married JULIANA ANN ROSE 23 Dec 1846. She was born 19 Sep 1826 in New York, and died 17 Jun 1886 in Black Earth, Wisconsin (Cancer)[1733]. Juliana is buried in Oak Hill Cemetery, Black Earth, Wisconsin[1733] Leander is buried in Jennings, Louisiana.

Children of LEANDER STEPHENS and JULIANA ROSE are:
       i.   EMMA RUTH[9] STEPHENS, b. 07 Jan 1848, Ithaca, New York; d. 17 Jul 1895, Jennings, Louisiana; m. MARTIN V. MARSH. Burial: Jennings, La.
       ii.   MALISSIE PATIENCE STEPHENS, b. 21 Oct 1850, Tioga County, New York; d. 20 Feb 1922, Black Earth, Wisconsin; m. MILTON FOYE.
       iii. GEORGE FRANKLIN STEPHENS, b. 27 Mar 1853, Tioga County, New York; d. 16 Jan 1937, Eunice, , St. Landry, Louisiana; m. LAURA CROOK.
       iv.   PRUDENCE ANN STEPHENS, b. 16 Feb 1857, Dane County, Wisconsin; d. 18 Aug 1857, Black Earth, Wisconsin.
1144. v.   ELIZABETH EFFIE STEPHENS, b. 09 May 1858, Dane County, Wisconsin; d. 18 Apr 1940, Mazomnie?, Wisconsin.
       vi.   WILLIAM EZRA STEPHENS, b. 29 Nov 1861, Dane County, Wisconsin; d. 16 Oct 1949, Madison, Wisconsin; m. CLARA MAUDE SHOLTS, 18 Feb 1886, Grand Island, Nebraska. Burial: Oak Hill Cemetery, Black Hill, Wis.
       vii. LEANDER GRAND STEPHENS, b. 03 Mar 1864, Dane County, Wisconsin; d. 07 Mar 1940, Jennings, Louisiana.
       viii. DELBERT SHERMAN STEPHENS, b. 18 Jan 1868, Dane County, Wisconsin; d. 13 Aug 1943, San Benito, Cameron County, Texas; m. OLER MILLER, 1895, Louisiana; b. May 1880, Louisiana; d. 1970. Number of Children (Facts: 1900, 2 children, 0 living

532. BENJAMIN FRANKLIN[8] MILKS *(DAVID B.[7], EZRA[6], DAVID[5] MILK, JONATHAN[4], JOB[3], JOHN[2], JOHN[1])* was born 14 Jan 1857 in Ithaca, Tompkins County, New York, and died 06 Jul 1929 in Ithaca, Tompkins County, New York. He married ALICE BELLE MCWHORTER 21 Aug 1878 in Ithaca, NY[1734], daughter of SMITH MCWHORTER and FRANCES SNYDER. She was born 22 May 1859 in Ithaca, Tompkins County, New York, and died 12 Feb 1941 in Ithaca, Tompkins County, New York. They are buried in East Lawn Cemetery, Ithaca, Tompkins County, New York

Children of BENJAMIN MILKS and ALICE MCWHORTER are:
1145. i.   FANNY[9] MILKS, b. 27 Jun 1879, Ithaca, Tompkins County, New York.
       ii. HARRIET L. MILKS, b. 11 Oct 1881, Ithaca, Tompkins County, New York; m. SHERMAN COLLINS, 16 Dec 1908, Bradford, McKean County, Pennsylvania[1735]; b. Bet. 1864 - 1865[1736]. No children.
1146. iii. MARY S. 'MAYME' MILKS, b. 12 Dec 1883, Ithaca, Tompkins County, New York.
1147. iv. WILLIAM S. MILKS, b. 01 Dec 1884, Ithaca, Tompkins County, New York; d. Jul 1964, Ithaca, Tompkins County, New York.

533. LEGRANDE[8] MILKS *(DAVID B.[7], EZRA[6], DAVID[5] MILK, JONATHAN[4], JOB[3], JOHN[2], JOHN[1])* was born 20 Dec 1865 in

Ithaca, Tompkins County, New York, and died 26 Aug 1934. He married EDITH SPAULDING. She was born Abt. 1865.

Child of LEGRANDE MILKS and EDITH SPAULDING is:
    i. VERA ESTELL[9] MILKS, b. 18 Feb 1900; m. CARLOS A. FURMAN. No children.

534. AMOS E.[8] MILKS *(EZRA[7], EZRA[6], DAVID[5] MILK, JONATHAN[4], JOB[3], JOHN[2], JOHN[1])* was born Bet. 1847 - 1848 in Sylvester Township, Green Co., Wisconsin[1737], and died 10 Jul 1926 in Pueblo, Pueblo County, Colorado[1738]. He married JOSEPHINE E. RUTLEDGE 03 Jul 1867 in Green County, Wisconsin[1739], daughter of PETER RUTLEDGE and CHARLOTTE _____. She was born Abt. 1850 in Wisconsin, and died 07 May 1930 in Pueblo, Pueblo County, Colorado[1740].

    Service Record: Enlisted in Company I, 40th Infantry Regiment Wisconsin on 02 June 1864. Mustered out Company I, 40th Infantry Regiment Wisconsin on 16 September 1864 in Milwaukee, WI

Children of AMOS MILKS and JOSEPHINE RUTLEDGE are:
    i. LILLIAN HARRIET[9] MILKS, b. Abt. 1868, Clay, Harrison County, Missouri.
    ii. RUEY C. MILKS[1741], b. Abt. 1870, Clay, Harrison County, Missouri; m. JAMES A. DAVIS[1741], 17 Dec 1887, Philips County, Kansas[1741]; b. Abt. 1870.
    iii. ERNEST ERWIN MILKS, b. 14 Sep 1873, Missouri[1742]; d. 23 May 1885, Phillips County, Kansas[1742]. Burial: Pleasant View Cemetery, Gretna, Phillips County, Kansas
    iv. ELLA M. MILKS, b. Abt. 1877, Missouri[1743]; m. (1) ERNEST L. HOWARD; b. Abt. 1897, Texas; m. (2) BENJAMIN KERNS[1744], 15 May 1893, Philips County, Kansas[1744]. No children. Lived at 1430 E. 8th, Pueblo, Colorado
    v. NINA DOROTHY MILKS, b. Abt. 1879, Missouri. Lived in: Denver, Colorado
    vi. LAWRENCE WILLIAM MILKS, b. 03 Jan 1882, Missouri[1745,1746]; d. 19 Dec 1946, Pueblo, Pueblo County, Colorado[1747]; m. NANCY _____[1748]; b. Abt. 1887, Nebraska[1748]; d. Bet. 1920 - 1930, Pueblo, Colorado. No children. Occupation: 1930, Mine Operator, Pueblo, Colorado

535. THOMAS W.[8] MILKS *(EZRA[7], EZRA[6], DAVID[5] MILK, JONATHAN[4], JOB[3], JOHN[2], JOHN[1])* was born 28 Oct 1850 in Green County, Wisconsin[1749], and died Mar 1928 in Burchard, Pawnee County, Nebraska. He married ELIZABETH M. PLACE 15 Dec 1872 in Stephenson County, Illinois[1750], daughter of JACOB PLACE and SARAH BIVENS. She was born 29 Sep 1854 in Durand, Winnebago County, Illinois[1751], and died Apr 1934 in Burchard, Pawnee County, Nebraska. They are buried in Burchard Cemetery, Burchard, Pawnee County, Nebraska; Plot: block 2, Lot 125

Children of THOMAS MILKS and ELIZABETH PLACE are:
1148.   i. CHARLES EVERETT[9] MILKS, b. 16 Sep 1873, Rock Run, Stephenson County, Illinois; d. 1952, Lincoln, Nebraska?.
1149.   ii. FLORA A. MILKS, b. 02 Dec 1877, Rock Run, Stephenson County, Illinois; d. Aft. 1940, Hastings, Adams County, Nebraska.
    iii. GEORGE WHITWORTH MILKS[1752], b. 05 Aug 1885, New York (adopted)[1752].

536. HARRIET "HATTIE"[8] MILKS *(EZRA[7], EZRA[6], DAVID[5] MILK, JONATHAN[4], JOB[3], JOHN[2], JOHN[1])* was born 1853 in Sylvester, Green County, Wisconsin, and died 1888 in Kansas. She married SCOTT BARKER Abt. 1877. He was born Jul 1854 in Stephenson County, Illinois[1753], and died 1908.

Children of HARRIET MILKS and SCOTT BARKER are:
1150.   i. MABEL[9] BARKER, b. 1878, Stephenson County, Illinois.
1151.   ii. JAY THOMAS BARKER, b. 1880, Stephenson County, Illinois.
    iii. KATE BARKER, b. 1882, Kansas; m. MISTRE WRIGHT; b. Abt. 1882. Lived in: Rockford, Illinois
    iv. FRED BARKER, b. 1884, Kansas; d. Bet. 1920 - 1930.

537. FRANK WHEELER[8] MILKS *(EZRA[7], EZRA[6], DAVID[5] MILK, JONATHAN[4], JOB[3], JOHN[2], JOHN[1])* was born 12 Mar 1857 in Green County, Wisconsin, and died Apr 1934 in Juda, Green County, Wisconsin. He married (1) ELIZABETH 'LIZZIE' IVERSON[1754] 12 Oct 1890 in Dane County, Wisconsin, daughter of J. IVERSON. She was born 25 Jun 1872 in Wisconsin[1754], and died 21 Jun 1921 in Freeport, Stephenson County, Illinois[1754]. He married (2) ALICE M. _____

Bet. 1921 - 1930 in Green County, Wisconsin. She was born Abt. 1861 in Wisconsin. Frank and Elizabeth are buried in Mount Vernon Cemetery, Juda, Green County, Wisconsin

Child of FRANK MILKS and ELIZABETH IVERSON is:
1152.   i.   RUTH KATHRYN^9 MILKS, b. 16 Aug 1892, Fitchburg Township, Dane County, Wisconsin; d. 12 Nov 1979, Monroe, Green County, Wisconsin.

538. RUTH^8 MILKS *(EZRA^7, EZRA^6, DAVID^5 MILK, JONATHAN^4, JOB^3, JOHN^2, JOHN^1)* was born 1859 in Green County, Wisconsin, and died Abt. 1889 in Green County, Wisconsin. She married JOHN SHAFFER. He was born Abt. 1859.

Child of RUTH MILKS and JOHN SHAFFER is:
         i.   CHARLES^9 SHAFFER, b. Abt. 1888, Albany, Wisconsin.

539. DAVID^8 MILKS *(EZRA^7, EZRA^6, DAVID^5 MILK, JONATHAN^4, JOB^3, JOHN^2, JOHN^1)* was born 03 Apr 1861 in Albany, Green County, Wisconsin, and died 06 Dec 1923. He married MARIA E. ABLEY^{1755,1756} 25 Dec 1886 in Green County, Wisconsin^{1757,1758}, daughter of JACOB ABLEY and ANGELINE MINERT. She was born 09 Jul 1860, and died 05 Mar 1935. They are buried in Circle Cemetery, Hudson, Steuben County, Indiana

----

Biography of David Milks, pages 788/789/790. *History of DeKalb County, Indiana;* B. F. Bowen & Company, Inc., Indianapolis, 1914.

The following is a brief sketch of the life of one who, by close attention to business, has achieved marked success in the world's affairs and risen to an honorable position among the enterprising men of the county with which his interests are identified. It is a plain record, rendered remarkable by no strange or mysterious adventure, no wonderful or lucky accident and no tragic situation. Mr. Milks is one of those estimable characters whose integrity and strong personality must force them into and admirable notoriety, which their modesty never seeks, who command the respect of their contemporaries and their posterity and leave the impress of their individuality upon the age in which they live. David Milks was born on April 3, 1861, in Green county, Wisconsin, a son of Ezra and Sarah (Ronds) Milks. Ezra Milks, who was a native of New York state, went to Pennsylvania with his parents in young manhood and soon afterwards migrated to Wisconsin, where he followed agricultural pursuits during practically his entire life.

He was born in 1820, and died at the Soldier's Home in Leavenworth, Kansas, in 1907, having been a veteran of the Civil war. His wife, whose maiden name was Sarah Ronds, was born in Massachusetts in 1827 and died in Wisconsin on June 7, 1909. Mr. Milks was the father of seven children, of whom three, Amos, Thomas and Hattie were born of his first union, and four, Frank, Ruth, David and Ella (Mrs. Estes), to the second union. Mrs. Milks, the subject's mother, had a child, Martha, by a former marriage, she being now deceased. David Milks was reared on the paternal homestead, receiving a common school education and following the vocation of farming during his early manhood years. In the spring of 1887 he went to Kansas, where he remained until 1902, being engaged in farming operations, and then came to Smithfield township, DeKalb county, Indiana, and bought the Kimmel farm of one hundred and forty acres. In the fall of 1911 he bought a residence property in Ashley, this county, remodeling the same and moving into it in the spring of the following year, his son Bert, taking charge of the farm. The latter place is one of the best farms in Smithfield township, being well drained and practically all under cultivation, very little timber being on the place. From the age to twenty years until he attained his majority Mr. Milks was reared by Arnold Bennett, who gave to him the same careful attention that he would have given to a son of his own blood. Mr. Milks has proven to be a man of broad, humanitarian impulses, and he has not only achieved a large success in this own personal affairs, but has also been successful as a citizen, giving the proper care and attention to those things which have for their object the advancement of the general welfare of the community. On Christmas day, 1886, Mr. Milks was married to Maria, the daughter of Jacob and Angeline (Minert) Abley. Jacob Abley was a native of the little republic of Switzerland, where he remained until twenty-four years of age, when he emigrated to the United States and he followed the trade of a carpenter until his marriage, in September, 1859, to Angeline Minert.

He was married in Wisconsin and there he settled on a farm. He followed agricultural pursuits there until his death, which occurred on April 18, 1897. By this union Mr. Abley became the father of six children. Mrs. Maria Milks, Cassie, Ida, Mrs. Lizzie Lewis, William and Mrs. Vera Marlcook, the mother of these children was a native of Indiana, born near Covington, Vermilion county, and died in Albany, Wisconsin, on July 28, 1906. To Mr. and Mrs. Milks were born two children, Bert and George. The former married Georgia Conrad and lives on his father's farm, which he operates. Politically, David Milks gives his earnest support to the Republican party, in the counsels of which he was a prominent figure for many years. Fraternally, he is a member of the Independent Order of Odd Fellows at Ashley.

Religiously, he has for a number of years been a member of the Christian church, of which he has served as treasurer and is now one of the deacons. A man of kindly and charitable impulses, he breathes a spirit of optimism whereever he goes, and those who know him best hold him in the highest regard. A man of clean character, a good business manager and keenly alive to the highest and best interests of his community, he is entitled to that measure of confidence and regard in which he is held by his fellow citizens. David was a member of the International Order of Odd Fellows (IOOF).

Children of DAVID MILKS and MARIA ABLEY are:
1153.   i.   BERT ABLEY[9] MILKS, b. 30 Mar 1890, Chepstow, Kansas; d. Jul 1970, Garrett, De Kalb County, Indiana.
1154.   ii.   GEORGE ARNOLD MILKS, b. 08 Aug 1895, Greenleaf, Washington County, Kansas; d. 14 May 1963, Dekalb County, Indiana?.

540. ELLA[8] MILKS *(EZRA[7], EZRA[6], DAVID[5] MILK, JONATHAN[4], JOB[3], JOHN[2], JOHN[1])* was born Abt. 1863 in Green County, Wisconsin, and died Abt. 1937 in No children. She married THOMAS LUKE ESTES[1759,1760,1761] 23 Mar 1898 in Green County, Wisconsin[1761]. He was born Aug 1869 in Wisconsin.

Child of ELLA MILKS and THOMAS ESTES is:
       i.   ALBERT L.[9] ESTES, b. Abt. 1908, Wisconsin (adopted).

541. HETTY[8] MILKS *(EZRA[7], EZRA[6], DAVID[5] MILK, JONATHAN[4], JOB[3], JOHN[2], JOHN[1])* was born Jun 1872 in Missouri[1762], and died Aft. 14 Mar 1907. She married MARK SHAFFER Abt. 1893, son of ADAM SHAFFER and ISABELLE BLUNT. He was born 01 Apr 1873 in Muskingum County, Ohio[1763], and died 26 Oct 1943 in San Bernardino, California.

Child of HETTY MILKS and MARK SHAFFER is:
       i.   CARL[9] SHAFFER, b. Aug 1894, Oklahoma; d. Bet. 1900 - 1910, Oklahoma.

542. DANIEL MARENOS[8] HILLIARD *(PHOEBE ANN[7] MILKS, EZRA[6], DAVID[5] MILK, JONATHAN[4], JOB[3], JOHN[2], JOHN[1])* was born 01 Feb 1846 in Illinois, and died in California. He married RENA _____. She was born Abt. 1850.

Child of DANIEL HILLIARD and RENA _____ is:
1155.   i.   MAUD[9] HILLIARD.

543. EZRA MILKS[8] HILLIARD *(PHOEBE ANN[7] MILKS, EZRA[6], DAVID[5] MILK, JONATHAN[4], JOB[3], JOHN[2], JOHN[1])* was born 22 Mar 1849 in Green County, Wisconsin, and died 09 Jun 1929 in Warren, Jo Daviess County, Illinois. He married (1) CHARLOTTE M. CLARK. She was born Abt. 1850 in Of Brodhead, Wisconsin. He married (2) GRACE VAN EPPS. She was born Abt. 1850 in Of Euclid, New York. Ezra was a salesman. He is buried in Elmwood Cemetery, Warren, Jo Davies County, Illinois

Children of EZRA HILLIARD and CHARLOTTE CLARK are:
       i.   EDITH[9] HILLIARD, m. MISTRE BATES.
1156.   ii.   LORENZO MERRILL HILLIARD, b. Aug 1870, Wisconsin; d. Bet. 1900 - 1910, California.

Child of EZRA HILLIARD and GRACE VAN EPPS is:
1157.   iii.   GRACE[9] HILLIARD.

544. LONSON DARIUS[8] HILLIARD *(PHOEBE ANN[7] MILKS, EZRA[6], DAVID[5] MILK, JONATHAN[4], JOB[3], JOHN[2], JOHN[1])*[1764] was born 22 Mar 1849 in Oakley, Green County, Wisconsin, and died 23 Nov 1903 in Albany, Green County, Wisconsin. He married HARRIET ANN WILSON 06 Nov 1870, daughter of PETER WILSON and SARAH FOSTER. She was born 17 Dec 1857 in Monticello, Green County, Wisconsin, and died 06 Mar 1934 in Albany, Green County, Wisconsin.
OBITUARY - *Albany Vindicator* (Albany, Wisconsin), December 3, 1903, p. 5, col. 2-3
    Lonson Hilliard was born March 22, 1849, at Oakley, Wis.
    He was married Nov. 6, 1870 to Miss Harriette Wilson. To them were born five children, three girls and two boys. For the past twenty-seven years they have lived in Albany.
    His occupation was that of city drayman, which brought him into close relation with the public, so that both young and old, all knew and revered this genial soul and kindly countenance of "Lon," who, whether storm or shine, was

always at his post of duty. He has been a patient sufferer for many months. Though all was done that skill and care and love could do, on the 23rd of November, 1903, his spirit passed from its prolonged suffering to rest.

The funeral obsequies were held from the M.E. church Thursday, Nov. 26, at 2 p.m., Rev. H.B. Brenaman of Kilbourn City speaking the words of comfort from the Scripture: "That Disciple whom Jesus loved." The services were under the auspices of the I.O.O.F. and Rebekah lodges, of which Mr. Hilliard was a respected and honored member.

That "Lon" was revered, we need but say that the city turned out en masse to do him homage and shed tears and bestow flowers upon his casket until he was buried under a mound of flowers and the tomb was filled with the perfume. Lon leaves behind in the land of sunshine and shadow his beloved wife and five children, all of whom were present.

Brother Hilliard was baptized into the Christian faith at the age of eighteen at Oakley, Wis., by Rev. P.K. Jones. He was perfectly resigned to go, and wrapping the drapery of his couch about him lay down to pleasant dreams.

Dear "Lon" has crossed the river,
Returning to the Giver
A pure and stainless soul;
He has passed the tide before us
To join the angel chorus
And reached the peaceful goal.

And he, so slowly dying,
Whose years of pain and sighing,
Were weary with unrest,
Hath passed with the pure spirits
Forever to inherit
A home among the blest.

H.B. BRENAMAN

Occupation: City Drayman. Burial: Hillcrest Cemetery, Albany, Green County, Wisconsin

----

OBITUARY - Albany Herald (Albany, Wisconsin), March 15, 1934, p. 1, col. 2

Mrs. Harriet Ann Hilliard, daughter of Peter and Sarah Foster Wilson, was born Dec. 17, 1857 [sic], at Monticello, Wisconsin.

She was united in marriage to Lonson Hilliard, Nov. 6, 1870. She died March 6, 1934, at the age of 82 years, two months and 17 days.

Mrs. Hilliard is survived by four children, Mrs. Fred Morton, Albany, Ellis, of Janesville, Frank and Mrs. Trella Webb of Albany. Her daughter, Mrs. Ethel O'Brien, preceded her in death on December 6, 1933.

Mrs. Hilliard is survived by six grandchildren and other relatives and friends.

The funeral services were held last Thursday afternoon, Rev. H.A. Erickson officiating.

Burial was in the Hillcrest cemetery.

Children of LONSON HILLIARD and HARRIET WILSON are:
- i. MYRTLE^9 HILLIARD, b. 1871, Albany, Green County, Wisconsin; d. 1936; m. FRED MORTON; b. Abt. 1870. No children.
- ii. ELLIS HILLIARD, b. 1874, Albany, Green County, Wisconsin; d. 1938.
- 1158. iii. FRANK HILLIARD, b. 26 Jun 1879, Albany, Green County, Wisconsin; d. 1949.
- 1159. iv. TRELLA HILLIARD, b. 04 Apr 1884, Albany, Green County, Wisconsin; d. 26 Nov 1975, Albany, Green County, Wisconsin.
- 1160. v. ETHEL HILLIARD, b. Abt. 1889, Albany, Green County, Wisconsin; d. 06 Dec 1933.

545. CLARA CLARINDA^8 HILLIARD *(PHOEBE ANN^7 MILKS, EZRA^6, DAVID^5 MILK, JONATHAN^4, JOB^3, JOHN^2, JOHN^1)* was born 19 Apr 1855 in Green County, Wisconsin. She married GEORGE KNIGHT.

Child of CLARA HILLIARD and GEORGE KNIGHT is:
- 1161. i. CHARLES S.^{9} KNIGHT, b. 28 Sep 1879, Cedar Falls, Iowa.

546. DR. SUMNER HALE[8] HILLIARD *(PHOEBE ANN[7] MILKS, EZRA[6], DAVID[5] MILK, JONATHAN[4], JOB[3], JOHN[2], JOHN[1])* was born 05 May 1858 in Green County, Wisconsin, and died 29 Mar 1917 in Miami, Florida?. He married MARY BAYNE 04 May 1897. She was born Abt. 1860.

Children of SUMNER HILLIARD and MARY BAYNE are:
  i. MERRITT[9] HILLIARD, b. Adopted.
  ii. JOSEPHINE HILLIARD, b. Adopted.

547. JOHN W.[8] MYLKS *(DAVID[7] MILKS, DAVID[6], DAVID[5] MILK, JONATHAN[4], JOB[3], JOHN[2], JOHN[1])* was born 1833 in Augusta, Leeds, Ontario, Canada[1765]. He married BATHIAH TIMPSON. She was born 1836 in Ireland[1766], and died 31 Oct 1889 in Brockville, Leeds, Ontario[1766].

Children of JOHN MYLKS and BATHIAH TIMPSON are:
  i. MOSES[9] MILKS[1767], b. 1858, Grenville, Ontario.
  ii. AMELIA MILKS[1767], b. 1860, Grenville, Ontario.
  iii. ALBERT B. MILKS, b. 1862, Brockville, Ontario[1768]; d. 25 Feb 1900, Brantford, Brant, Ontario[1768].
  iv. LOVEDAY F. MILKS, b. 1862, Brockville, Ontario.
  v. ANNIE J. MILKS, b. 1869, Brockville, Ontario.

548. HARMON WILLIAM[8] MYLKS *(DAVID[7] MILKS, DAVID[6], DAVID[5] MILK, JONATHAN[4], JOB[3], JOHN[2], JOHN[1])* was born 23 Mar 1836 in Augusta, Grenville, Ontario, Canada[1769], and died 19 May 1917 in Wellington County, Ontario, Canada[1770]. He married MARY ANN JACKSON. She was born 25 Sep 1847 in Ontario, Canada[1771], and died 07 Aug 1932 in Wellington County, Ontario, Canada[1772]. Harmon was a Baker. They are buried in Greenfield Cemetery, Trinity-Victoria, Wellington Peel, Ontario

Children of HARMON MYLKS and MARY JACKSON are:
1162. i. HATTIE[9] MYLKS, b. 19 Aug 1868, Ontario, Canada; d. 25 Feb 1933, Brandon, Manitoba, Canada.
  ii. CARRIE MYLKS[1773], b. 09 Jun 1876, Ontario, Canada.
  iii. WILLIAM HARMON MYLKS, JR.[1773], b. 07 Jul 1876, Ontario, Canada; d. 04 Jun 1951, Wellington County, Ontario, Canada; m. ELIZABETH HEWITT; b. 17 Mar 1873; d. 12 May 1956, Wellington County, Ontario, Canada. They are buried in Arthur Greenfield Cemetery, Wellington North, Ontario, Canada

549. DAVID SHEPHERD[8] MYLKS *(DAVID[7] MILKS, DAVID[6], DAVID[5] MILK, JONATHAN[4], JOB[3], JOHN[2], JOHN[1])* was born 1838 in Augusta, Grenville, Ontario, Canada[1774], and died 17 May 1909 in Elizabethtown, Leeds, Ontario, Canada[1775]. He married EVA COLE 06 May 1885 in Rowe Corners, Leeds, Ontario, Canada[1776], daughter of HENRY COLE and MARY STEWART. She was born Bet. 1857 - 1858 in Elizabethtown, Leeds, Ontario, Canada, and died 02 Aug 1893 in Augusta, Grenville/Leeds, Ontario, Canada[1777]. They are buried in Read Cemetery, Augusta, Ontario, Canada

Children of DAVID MYLKS and EVA COLE are:
  i. ELENA[9] MYLKS, b. 24 Nov 1886, Augusta, Grenville/Leeds, Ontario, Canada; d. 30 Mar 1887, Augusta, Grenville/Leeds, Ontario, Canada.
  ii. ELICIA MYLKS, b. 24 Nov 1886, Augusta, Grenville/Leeds, Ontario, Canada.
  iii. MYRTLE MYLKS, b. 28 Oct 1888, Augusta, Grenville/Leeds, Ontario, Canada.

550. MANUEL[8] MYLKS *(DAVID[7] MILKS, DAVID[6], DAVID[5] MILK, JONATHAN[4], JOB[3], JOHN[2], JOHN[1])*[1778] was born Abt. 1843 in Augusta, Grenville, Ontario, Canada[1779], and died 26 Feb 1933 in Kingston, Ontario. He married (1) UNKNOWN. She died Bet. 1908 - 1912. He married (2) CLARA ADAMS. He married (3) EMILY HELEN WRIGHT[1780] 15 Oct 1873 in Augusta, Leeds and Grenville, Ontario, Canada, daughter of ISAIAH JACOB WRIGHT and ELIZA KEAYS. She was born 08 Jun 1849 in Augusta, Grenville, Ontario, Canada, and died 31 Dec 1938 in Kingston, Ontario. Manuel and Emily are buried in Cataraqui Cemetery, Frontenac, Kingston, Ontario

Children of MANUEL MYLKS and EMILY WRIGHT are:
1163. i. DR. GORDON WRIGHT[9] MYLKS, b. 14 Aug 1874, Augusta Township, Grenville County, Ontario, Canada; d. 13 Feb 1957, Pinellas County, Florida.

1164. ii. LEONARD EUGENE MYLKS, b. 14 Feb 1876, Augusta Township, Grenville County, Ontario; d. Dec 1955, Kingston, Ontario.

551. CHARLES BARNEY[8] MILKS *(EZRA[7], DAVID[6], DAVID[5] MILK, JONATHAN[4], JOB[3], JOHN[2], JOHN[1])*[1781,1782] was born Dec 1839 in Erie County, Pennsylvania[1783]. He married LAURA CHAPMAN Abt. 1865 in Pennsylvania[1784]. She was born Oct 1841 in Pennsylvania[1784].

Children of CHARLES MILKS and LAURA CHAPMAN are:
    i. BESSIE[9] MILKS, b. Bet. 1878 - 1879, Elk Creek, Erie County, Pennsylvania[1785].
    ii. FLETCHER MILKS?.

552. SILAS E.[8] MILKS *(EZRA[7], DAVID[6], DAVID[5] MILK, JONATHAN[4], JOB[3], JOHN[2], JOHN[1])* was born Abt. 1841 in Erie County, Pennsylvania[1786], and died 1920 in Conneaut, Ohio[1786]. He married MARY DAILY 1866 in Crossingville Church, Crawford County, Pennsylvania[1787], daughter of MISTTER DAILY and WIFE. She was born Bet. 1843 - 1844 in Pennsylvania[1788], and died 1908 in Conneaut, Ohio[1789]. They are buried in City Cemetery, Conneaut, Ohio
    U.S., Civil War Soldier Records and Profiles, 1861-1865 about Silas E Milks
Rank at enlistment: Corporal;   State Served:Wisconsin;   Survived the War?: Yes
Service Record: Enlisted in Company G, Wisconsin 13th Infantry Regiment on 31 Aug 1861.Mustered out on 24 Nov 1865 at San Antonio, TX. Sources: *Roster of Wisconsin Volunteers: War of the Rebellion*
    Silas lived Bet. 1890 - 1920, in the Pennsylvania Soldiers' and Sailors' Home, Erie, Erie County, Pennsylvania
Military service: Bet. 31 Aug 1861 - 04 Nov 1865, Corporal, Co. G. 13th Volunteer Infantry, Wisconsin[1790]
Occupation: 1870, Canal Boatman

Children of SILAS MILKS and MARY DAILY are:
1165. i. JAMES E.[9] MILKS, b. 28 Oct 1867, Elk Creek, Erie County, Pennsylvania; d. 20 Jul 1954, Terra Haute, Vigo County, Indiana.
    ii. CHARLES S. "CHARLIE" MILKS[1791], b. 08 Aug 1869, Elk Creek, Erie County, Pennsylvania[1792]; d. 11 Mar 1947, Terra Haute, Vigo County, Indiana[1793,1794]; m. MARGARET FRANCES LONG; b. 1872, Rochester, New York[1795,1796]; d. 17 Jul 1932, Terre Haute, Vigo County, Indiana[1797,1798]. They are buried in Calvary Cemetery, Terra Haute, Vigo County, Indiana
    iii. NELLIE MILKS[1799], b. 1874, Elk Creek, Erie County, Pennsylvania[1799]; d. 1894, Conneaut, Ohio[1799]. Never married. Burial: City Cemetery, Conneaut, Ohio

553. ADELAIDE "ADDIE"[8] MILKS *(EZRA[7], DAVID[6], DAVID[5] MILK, JONATHAN[4], JOB[3], JOHN[2], JOHN[1])*[1800] was born 22 Aug 1843 in Erie County, Pennsylvania[1801], and died 20 Nov 1928 in Manchester, Delaware County, Iowa. She married WILLIAM C. CAWLEY[1802], son of JOHN CAWLEY and EVALINE CAMPBELL. He was born Bet. 1831 - 1832 in Pennsylvania[1802], and died Bet. 1925 - 1930 in Manchester, Delaware County, Iowa. They are buried in Oakland Cemetery, Manchester, Delaware

Child of ADELAIDE MILKS and WILLIAM CAWLEY is:
    i. CHARLES[9] CAWLEY[1802], b. Bet. 1865 - 1866, Iowa; d. Aft. 1940, Manchester, Delaware County, Iowa; m. MARJORIE _____, Bet. 1925 - 1940, Manchester, Delaware County, Iowa; b. Abt. 1906, Iowa.

554. SARAH ANNA[8] MILKS *(ALBERT[7], DAVID[6], DAVID[5] MILK, JONATHAN[4], JOB[3], JOHN[2], JOHN[1])* was born 14 Aug 1858 in Cranesville, Erie County, Pennsylvania[1803], and died 09 Jan 1929 in Erie, Erie County, Pennsylvania[1803]. She married AARON F. BUSH Abt. 1882 in Pennsylvania[1804]. He was born 30 Mar 1856 in Pennsylvania[1805], and died 14 Apr 1921 in Erie, Erie County, Pennsylvania[1805]. They are buried in Erie Cemetery, Erie, Erie County, Pennsylvania; Lot #107, Section MM. Number of Children (Facts: 1900, 5 children, 4 living

Children of SARAH MILKS and AARON BUSH are:
    i. LEWIS A.[9] BUSH, b. 28 Aug 1883, Erie County, Pennsylvania; d. 01 Oct 1883, Erie, Erie County, PA. Burial: Erie Cemetery, Erie, Erie County, Pennsylvania (in the same Section & Lot # as Sarah Anna Bush)
1166. ii. ARTHUR BLAINE BUSH, b. 17 Sep 1884, Erie, Erie County, Pennsylvania; d. 08 May 1960, Milford, New Haven, Connecticut.
1167. iii. CHESTER A. BUSH, b. 21 Sep 1887, Erie, Erie County, Pennsylvania; d. Feb 1966, Berea, Cuyahoga County,

		Ohio.
1168.	iv.	DOROTHY K. BUSH, b. 19 Apr 1895, Erie, Erie County, Pennsylvania; d. Jun 1984, Erie, Erie County, Pennsylvania.
	v.	ROSALIND S. BUSH, b. 09 Jan 1898, Erie, Erie County, Pennsylvania; d. 09 Feb 1987. Never married. Burial: Erie Cemetery, Erie, Erie County, Pennsylvania

555. MARY E.[8] MILKS *(ALBERT[7], DAVID[6], DAVID[5] MILK, JONATHAN[4], JOB[3], JOHN[2], JOHN[1])* was born 13 Nov 1861 in Cranesville, Erie County, Pennsylvania, and died 30 Apr 1928 in Erie, Erie County, Pennsylvania. She married (1) GEORGE J. HEYBECK Abt. 1880 in Erie County, Pennsylvania. He was born Abt. 1855 in Pennsylvania. She married (2) PHILIP W. DIETLEY 22 Oct 1891 in Erie County, Pennsylvania[1806], son of URAS DIETLY and CAROLINE REASER. He was born 26 Sep 1861 in Erie County, Pennsylvania[1807], and died 17 Sep 1939 in Erie County, Pennsylvania[1807]. Mary and Philip are buried in Erie Cemetery, Erie, Erie County, Pennsylvania; As Mary E. Dietley
Philip was Proprietor/owner of Erie Machine Shop, Erie, Pennsylvania

Children of MARY MILKS and PHILIP DIETLEY are:

1169.	i.	HAZEL S.[9] DIETLEY, b. 02 Dec 1892, Erie County, Pennsylvania.
1170.	ii.	URAS A. DIETLEY, b. 18 May 1894, Erie County, Pennsylvania; d. 08 Jul 1953, Erie, Erie County, Pennsylvania.
1171.	iii.	PHILIP W. DIETLEY, b. 03 Feb 1897, Erie County, Pennsylvania; d. 20 Sep 1934.
1172.	iv.	MARY E. DIETLEY, b. 16 Mar 1900, Erie County, Pennsylvania.

556. WARREN "JACK"[8] MILKS *(HARRIS[7], SILAS W.[6], DAVID[5] MILK, JONATHAN[4], JOB[3], JOHN[2], JOHN[1])* was born 09 Nov 1850 in Pittstown, NY (See Croft, p155)[1808,1809], and died 21 Feb 1915 in Farrel, Clare County, Michigan[1810]. He married PHOEBE SMITH 12 Aug 1874 in Morley, Mecosta County, Michigan, daughter of JOHN SMITH. She was born 03 Apr 1857 in Chatham, Ontario, Canada[1810], and died 11 Feb 1916 in Grayling, Crawford County, Michigan[1811]. "Jack" was a farmer. They are buried in Mount View Cemetery, McBain, Missaukee County, Michigan

Children of WARREN MILKS and PHOEBE SMITH are:

1173.	i.	FRANKLIN HORACE[9] MILKS, b. 20 Mar 1877, Morley, Mecosta County, Michigan; d. May 1966, Augusta, Kalamazoo, Michigan.
1174.	ii.	CLARA MILKS, b. 09 May 1879, Morley, Mecosta County, Michigan.
1175.	iii.	ALFRED WARREN MILKS, b. 02 Jul 1883, Morley, Mecosta County, Michigan; d. 26 Mar 1976, Midland, Michigan.
1176.	iv.	WALTER H. MILKS, b. 13 May 1886, Morley, Mecosta County, Michigan; d. 04 Nov 1916, Midland, Michigan.
	v.	FLOSSIE MAY MILKS, b. 02 Jul 1889, Morley, Mecosta County, Michigan; d. 31 Jul 1913, McBain, Missaukee County, Michigan[1812]; m. JOHN FITZPATRICK, 31 Aug 1909; b. Abt. 1889. Flossie is buried in Mount View Cemetery, McBain, Missaukee County, Michigan. Cause of Death: Uremic Poisoning
1177.	vi.	LYLE N. MILKS, b. 30 May 1900, Tustin, Michigan; d. 28 Dec 1966, Saginaw, Saginaw Co., Michigan.

557. CHRISTINA[8] MILKS *(HARRIS[7], SILAS W.[6], DAVID[5] MILK, JONATHAN[4], JOB[3], JOHN[2], JOHN[1])* was born Bet. 1852 - 1853 in Pittstown, NY[1813], and died 07 Oct 1886 in Morley, Mecosta County, Michigan. She married FRANKLIN J. 'FRANK' WILSON 28 Jul 1870 in Hope, Midland County, Michigan[1814], son of CHARLES WILSON and MARY MARIA WINFIELD. He was born 27 Apr 1850 in Michigan, and died 17 Feb 1907 in Winfield Township, Montcalm County, Michigan. They are buried in Boyd Cemetery, Morley, Mecosta County, Michigan

Child of CHRISTINA MILKS and FRANKLIN WILSON is:

	i.	FRANCIS[9] FRED E. WILSON, b. 23 Jul 1870, Barry County, Michigan; m. JENNIER M. GRIFFIN; b. Abt. 1871, Michigan.

558. ERNEST L.[8] MILKS *(HARRIS[7], SILAS W.[6], DAVID[5] MILK, JONATHAN[4], JOB[3], JOHN[2], JOHN[1])* was born 01 Jan 1856 in Pittstown, NY[1815,1816], and died 24 May 1941 in Barry County, Michigan[1816]. He married ELNA R. CHARLES[1817] 1882 in Kalamazoo County, Michigan[1818,1819], daughter of FATHER CHARLES. She was born 1861 in Michigan[1820,1821], and died 1946 in Barry County, Michigan[1821]. Ernest was a farmer. They are buried in East Hickory Corners Cemetery, Hickory Corners, Barry County, Michigan

Children of ERNEST MILKS and ELNA CHARLES are:
1178. i. JOHN HARRIS 'HARRY'[9] MILKS, b. 13 Nov 1883, Howard City, Michigan; d. 23 May 1938, Augusta, Kalamazoo, Michigan.
1179. ii. CHARLES EDWARD MILKS, b. 09 Jan 1887, Howard City, Montcalm County, Michigan; d. 04 Dec 1958, Barry County, Michigan.
iii. IRMA B. MILKS[1822], b. Sep 1894, Michigan; m. PETER NELSON[1822]. Lived in: Morley, Michigan

559. JESSE[8] MILKS (HARRIS[7], SILAS W.[6], DAVID[5] MILK, JONATHAN[4], JOB[3], JOHN[2], JOHN[1]) was born Sep 1858 in Pittstown, Rensselaer County, New York[1823], and died 1941. He married IDA L. CHARLES 1883 in Kalamazoo County, Michigan[1824], daughter of MARIE CHARLES She was born Dec 1857 in Michigan[1825], and died 1951.

Children of JESSE MILKS and IDA CHARLES are:
1180. i. BERTHA M.[9] MILKS, b. Dec 1883, Michigan; d. 1942, Battle Creek, Calhoun County, Michigan.
ii. FLOYD HARRIS MILKS, b. 25 Nov 1888, Michigan[1826]; m. CLARA J. TODD, 06 Jun 1912, Lee County, Iowa; b. 1896, Illinois. Lived in: Ft. Madison, Lee County, Iowa. No children.

560. FRANKLIN GRANT[8] MILKS (HARRIS[7], SILAS W.[6], DAVID[5] MILK, JONATHAN[4], JOB[3], JOHN[2], JOHN[1])[1827] was born 30 Dec 1863 in Pittstown, New York[1828,1829], and died Bef. 1930 in Michigan. He married MINNIE MARIAN MARTIN 14 Mar 1886 in Morley, Mecosta County, Michigan[1830,1831], daughter of FATHER MARTIN and MOTHER. She was born 16 Apr 1869 in Cortland, Illinois[1832].

Children of FRANKLIN MILKS and MINNIE MARTIN are:
1181. i. LEO LEROY[9] MILKS, b. 18 Sep 1887, Reynolds, Montcalm County, Michigan.
1182. ii. VIRGIE M. MILKS, b. 12 May 1891, Reynolds, Montcalm County, Michigan.
iii. EVA MAY MILKS, b. 30 Mar 1893, Reynolds, Montcalm County, Michigan[1833]; d. Bet. 1920 - 1930, Howard City, Montcalm County, Michigan[1834]; m. FRED ZENK, 19 Jan 1917, Howard City, Montcalm County, Michigan[1835]; b. 22 Dec 1893, Sheboygan, Wisconsin; d. Aug 1982, Howard City, Montcalm County, Michigan. No children.
1183. iv. LILLIAN GRACE MILKS, b. 10 Jun 1895, Reynolds, Montcalm County, Michigan; d. 1963, Montcalm County, Michigan.

561. JULIA ANN[8] MILKS (HARRIS[7], SILAS W.[6], DAVID[5] MILK, JONATHAN[4], JOB[3], JOHN[2], JOHN[1]) was born 26 May 1872 in Hope, Barry County, Michigan. She married (1) JACK DOXTATER. He was born Abt. 1870. She married (2) CHARLES HILL. He was born 1870. JULIA MILKS and JACK DOXTATER had a son.

JULIA MILKS and CHARLES HILL had three sons, one of whom was named HENRY[9] HILL.

562. ANNA[8] MILK (DAVID[7], SILAS W.[6] MILKS, DAVID[5] MILK, JONATHAN[4], JOB[3], JOHN[2], JOHN[1]) was born 1861 in Valley Falls (Pittstown), New York, and died 1942. She married BYRON CENTER. He was born Abt. 1860.

Child of ANNA MILK and BYRON CENTER is:
i. ROY[9] CENTER, b. 1881, Valley Falls (Pittstown), NY; d. 1949; m. LOIS TRUESDALE; b. 1891; d. 20 Jun 1945. No children.

563. EMMA A.[8] MILKS (MATTHEW G.[7], SILAS W.[6], DAVID[5] MILK, JONATHAN[4], JOB[3], JOHN[2], JOHN[1]) was born 1849 in Valley Falls (Pittstown), Rensselaer County, New York, and died 1909 in Troy, New York. She married JOHN WESLEY STOVER, son of JOHN STOVER and SALLY SNYDER. He was born 1846 in New York, and died 1919 in Troy, New York. Emma is buried in Elmwood Cemetery, Schaghticoke, Rensselaer County, New York

Children of EMMA MILKS and JOHN STOVER are:
i. JACOB A.[9] STOVER, b. 1871, New York; d. 1933.
ii. HOWARD ELLIS STOVER, b. 27 Sep 1875, New York[1836]; d. 1928, New York; m. CLARA EDWARDS; b. 06 Oct 1874, Rock City Falls, Saratoga County, New York; d. 10 Jul 1947, New York. They are buried in Elmwood Cemetery, Schaghticoke, Rensselaer County, NY.

iii. LAURA E. STOVER, b. 1876, New York; d. 1952.
iv. IRVING ALLEN STOVER, b. 19 Dec 1878, New York[1836]; d. 1947.

564. ELLIS DAVID[8] MILKS *(MATTHEW G.[7], SILAS W.[6], DAVID[5] MILK, JONATHAN[4], JOB[3], JOHN[2], JOHN[1])* was born 1855 in Valley Falls (Pittstown), Rensselaer County, New York[1837], and died 1914 in Valley Falls (Pittstown), Rensselaer County, New York[1837]. He married EMMA LODUSKA LOTTRIDGE 05 Sep 1879 in North Hoosick, Rensselaer County, New York, daughter of ALVIN LOTTRIDGE and ELLEN SEARS. She was born 08 Oct 1860 in Hoosick Falls, Rensselaer County, New York, and died 29 Jul 1929 in Englewood, New Jersey. They are buried in Elmwood Cemetery, Schaghticoke, Rensselaer County, New York. Emma was a member of the D.A.R. (#239532)

Child of ELLIS MILKS and EMMA LODUSKA LOTTRIDGE

i. MARGARET LODUSKA[9] MILKS, b. 09 Mar 1880, Hoosick Falls, Rensselaer County, New York[1838]; d. 09 Jan 1965, Old Lyme, New London County, Connecticut[1839,1840]; m. JUDSON LEO PUFFER, 14 Jun 1911, Hoosick Falls, Rensselaer County, New York; b. 22 Jan 1883, New York[1841,1842]; d. Jul 1969, Old Lyme, New London County, Connecticut[1842].
Lived in: 1917, Hoosick Falls, Rensselaer County, New York

565. ALLEN EDGAR[8] MILKS *(MATTHEW G.[7], SILAS W.[6], DAVID[5] MILK, JONATHAN[4], JOB[3], JOHN[2], JOHN[1])* was born 13 Jul 1856 in Valley Falls (Pittstown), New York[1843], and died 23 Apr 1924 in Valley Falls (Pittstown), New York[1843]. He married MARY JANE 'JENNIE' THOMPSON 19 Feb 1880 in New York, daughter of JAMES THOMPSON and ISABELLE CURRAN. She was born 09 Jun 1857 in New York, New York County, New York[1844], and died 30 Jan 1917 in Valley Falls (Pittstown), Rensselaer County, New York[1844]. They are buried in Elmwood Cemetery, Schaghticoke, Rensselaer County, New York

Children of ALLEN MILKS and MARY THOMPSON are:

i. CLARENCE ALLEN[9] MILKS, b. 27 Jul 1882, Valley Falls (Pittstown), New York[1845]; d. 1928, Newark, New Jersey; m. MARY FRANCES ROESNER[1845], 06 May 1906, Manhattan, New York[1846,1847]; b. 1884, New York.
Lived in: 1917, Newark, New Jersey
Occupation: Dental Surgeon. No children.

1184. ii. ELLIS CLYDE MILKS, b. 17 Dec 1890, Valley Falls, Rensselaer County, New York; d. 09 Mar 1940, Bensonhurst, Kings County, New York.

566. JULIA FRANCES[8] MILKS *(MATTHEW G.[7], SILAS W.[6], DAVID[5] MILK, JONATHAN[4], JOB[3], JOHN[2], JOHN[1])* was born 1857 in Valley Falls (Pittstown), Rensselaer County, New York. She married WILLIAM A. ALEXANDER.

Children of JULIA MILKS and WILLIAM ALEXANDER are:

i. FRED W.[9] ALEXANDER.
ii. MONTGOMERY ALEXANDER, b. 26 Sep 1887, Troy, New York[1848]; m. MARTHA F. _____; b. Abt. 1892, Delaware. Lived in: 1917, Wilmington, Delaware
Occupation: 1917, Chemist, Water Department

567. ANGELINA[8] WAITE *(ISAAC[7], MARY[6] MILKS, JONATHAN[5] MILK, JONATHAN[4], JOB[3], JOHN[2], JOHN[1])* was born Nov 1849 in Rensselaer County, New York, and died 1931 in Bangor, Van Buren County, Michigan. She married JAMES A. HOWARD. He was born Abt. 1841 in Massachusetts.

Child of ANGELINA WAITE and JAMES HOWARD is:

1185. i. HARRY W.[9] HOWARD, b. 14 May 1872, Bangor, Van Buren County, Michigan; d. 03 May 1948, Hartford, Van Buren County, Michigan.

568. FRANK[8] MILKS *(PERRY M.[7], BENJAMIN[6], DAVID[5] MILK, JONATHAN[4], JOB[3], JOHN[2], JOHN[1])* was born Dec 1857 in Scio, Allegany County, New York, and died Bet. 1900 - 1910 in Train Wreck. He married RACHEL ESTHER _____. She was born Nov 1857 in Iowa. They lived in 1885, in Eldon, Wapello County, Iowa. Frank was a Locomotive Engineer - C.R.I. & P. Railroad

Child of FRANK MILKS and RACHEL _____ is:

1186. i. MABEL⁹ MILKS, b. Aug 1889, Wapello County, Iowa.

569. GEORGE MARTIN⁸ WOOLMAN *(GEORGE W.⁷, PATIENCE⁶ MILK, LEMUEL⁵, JONATHAN⁴, JOB³, JOHN², JOHN¹)* was born Abt. 1847 in Michigan, and died 1920 in Arenac County, Michigan. He married ELIZA J. LEE Abt. 1871. She was born Jul 1853 in England, and died Bet. 1910 - 1920.

George was a carpenter and a mason. He served during the Civil War as a Private in Co F 30 Reg Mich Inf Vol. He is buried in Cedar Valley Cemetery, Twining, Arenac County, Michigan

Children of GEORGE WOOLMAN and ELIZA LEE are:
- 1187. i. BARTON G.⁹ WOOLMAN, b. Abt. 1873, Ortonville, Oakland County, Michigan; d. 01 Mar 1917, Ortonville, Oakland County, Michigan.
- 1188. ii. URBAN VICTOR WOOLMAN, b. 27 Oct 1879, Ortonville, Oakland County, Michigan.
- 1189. iii. EVAN L. WOOLMAN, b. 26 Jun 1886, Ortonville, Oakland County, Michigan; d. 09 Sep 1939, Montana.

570. NELSON JOSEPH⁸ WOOLMAN *(GEORGE W.⁷, PATIENCE⁶ MILK, LEMUEL⁵, JONATHAN⁴, JOB³, JOHN², JOHN¹)* was born Aug 1859 in Michigan[1849]. He married (1) CLARA E. FERRIS, daughter of MISTTER and MISSUS. She was born 01 Dec 1864 in Canada (English)[1850], and died 23 Oct 1910 in Oakland County, Michigan. He married (2) ADDIE (CLARK) HAWKINS 18 Oct 1916 in Oxford, Oakland County, Michigan. Clara is buried in Ortonville Cemetery, Brandon Gardens, Oakland

Children of NELSON WOOLMAN and CLARA FERRIS are:
- i. JAMES HENRY⁹ WOOLMAN, b. 30 Apr 1886, Lakefield, Saginaw County, Michigan (surname given as Sam.[1851,1852].
- ii. ELSIE MAY WOOLMAN, b. 05 Apr 1891, Saginaw, Oakland County, Michigan[1853].
- iii. MELVIN C. WOOLMAN, b. 20 Nov 1893, Brandon, Oakland County, Michigan[1853,1854].
- iv. MORTON E. WOOLMAN, b. 20 Nov 1893, Brandon, Oakland County, Michigan[1855,1856].

571. ANNETTE ADELIA⁸ WHIPPLE *(ADELIA⁷ PROSSER, MARY⁶ MILK, LEMUEL⁵, JONATHAN⁴, JOB³, JOHN², JOHN¹)* was born 26 Feb 1846 in Bloomingdale, Illinois, and died 19 Jun 1938 in Seattle, Washington. She married REV. CHARLES ANDERSON 27 Dec 1863 in Waupaca, Waupaca County, Wisconsin. He was born 24 Jul 1843 in Kallundborg, Zeeland, Denmark, and died 21 Aug 1910 in Coeur d'Alene, Idaho.

Annette, granddaughter of grief-stricken Mary Milk, wrote in her memoirs: "Mother was positive in her statement that the name of Milk should not have an 's.' The neighbors called us 'Milks' but we were careful not to add an 's' when signing our name . . . . One of my earliest recollections is the visit of my mother's uncles, Uncle Ben and Uncle Job. I can remember our going out into the door-yard to watch the passenger pigeons. The sky was filled with them. These uncles were large men and very jolly. They were only taking a trip through the West with no inclination to move there. Their name was Milk."

Children of ANNETTE WHIPPLE and CHARLES ANDERSON are:
- 1190. i. JAMES ELMER⁹ ANDERSON, b. 11 May 1868, Mt. Carroll, Illinois; d. 01 Oct 1942, Long Beach, California.
- 1191. ii. REV. FRANK HOWARD ANDERSON, b. 22 Oct 1870, Galesburg, Illinois; d. 30 Jun 1945, Omaha, Nebraska.
- iii. DELIA IRENE ANDERSON, b. 20 Apr 1874, Keokuk, Iowa; d. 01 Sep 1889, Potter, Nebraska.
- iv. RALPH WHIPPLE ANDERSON, b. 03 Jul 1876, Knoxville, Illinois; d. 18 Oct 1954; m. (1) ALICE PEARL KINNEY, 26 Jun 1906, Milford, Nebraska; b. Abt. 1876; d. Milford, Nebraska; m. (2) HENRIETTA (ALFORD) COSLETT, 30 Nov 1923; b. Abt. 1876.
  Lived in: Portland, Oregon (2nd marriage)
- v. MABEL ANDERSON, b. 21 Dec 1878, Knoxville, Illinois; d. Aft. 1956; m. WILLIS HAMILTON WARNER, 03 Jul 1905; b. Abt. 1878.
  Mabel was an assistant author of "History and Genealogy of the Milk-Milks Family".
  Lived in: Orlando, Florida
- vi. ETHEL ANDERSON, b. 23 Nov 1880, Omaha, Nebraska; d. 03 Sep 1881, Omaha, Nebraska.
- vii. MARJORIE LEILA ANDERSON, b. 18 Sep 1883, Rockford, Illinois[1857]; d. Sep 1966, Orange County, Florida[1857]. Never married. Lived in: 1910, Lincoln, Nebraska
- viii. CLYDE ANDERSON, b. 26 Aug 1887; d. 02 Apr 1889, Potter, Nebraska.

572. IRA FRANK[8] WHIPPLE *(ADELIA[7] PROSSER, MARY[6] MILK, LEMUEL[5], JONATHAN[4], JOB[3], JOHN[2], JOHN[1])* was born 26 Feb 1849 in Clayton, Winnebago County, Wisconsin, and died 15 Jun 1905 in Waupaca, Wisconsin?. He married FLORENCE E. HOOKER. She was born Feb 1852 in New York.

Children of IRA WHIPPLE and FLORENCE HOOKER are:
1192.   i.   ERLE INMAN[9] WHIPPLE, b. 21 Oct 1876, Spencer, Marathon County, Wisconsin.
           ii.   ERWIN WHIPPLE, b. Abt. 1878, Spencer, Marathon County, Wisconsin; d. Bet. 1880 - 1900, Wisconsin.

573. ADDISON[8] MOORE *(MARIA LYNDIA[7] PROSSER, ELIZABETH 'BETSEY'[6] MILK, LEMUEL[5], JONATHAN[4], JOB[3], JOHN[2], JOHN[1])* was born Abt. 1831 in Bolton, Warren County, New York, and died 1900. He married MARIA 'RIA' FRANCIS. She was born Abt. 1831.

Children of ADDISON MOORE and MARIA FRANCIS are:
           i.   MARY[9] MOORE, m. AMOS REYNOLDS. No children. Burial: Glens Falls, Warren County, New York
           ii.   ED MOORE, m. JENNIE HOWE. No children.

574. MASSENA[8] MOORE *(MARIA LYNDIA[7] PROSSER, ELIZABETH 'BETSEY'[6] MILK, LEMUEL[5], JONATHAN[4], JOB[3], JOHN[2], JOHN[1])* was born 1833 in Bolton, Warren County, New York. He married (1) CYNTHIA DICKINSON. She was born Abt. 1833. He married (2) FRANCES DICKINSON Abt. 1870. She was born Abt. 1835, and died 1926.

Children of MASSENA MOORE and FRANCES DICKINSON are:
1193.   i.   CHARLES D.[9] MOORE, b. Feb 1872; d. Nov 1949, Glens Falls, Warren County, New York ?.
           ii.   CORDELIA MOORE, b. 1875; d. 1944; m. CHARLES DURRIN; b. Abt. 1875; d. 1941. They are buried in Bolton, Warren County, New York

575. BETSEY[8] MOORE *(MARIA LYNDIA[7] PROSSER, ELIZABETH 'BETSEY'[6] MILK, LEMUEL[5], JONATHAN[4], JOB[3], JOHN[2], JOHN[1])* was born 11 Mar 1842 in Bolton, Warren County, New York, and died 04 Jan 1911 in Diamond Point (Hill View), New York. She married MARVIN TRUESDALE 01 Jan 1863, son of SETH TRUESDALE and EUNICE HARRINGTON. He was born 08 Nov 1840 in Caldwell, New York, and died 21 Feb 1934 in Diamond Point (Hill View), New York.

Children of BETSEY MOORE and MARVIN TRUESDALE are:
           i.   FRED ELMER[9] TRUESDALE, b. 02 Aug 1864, Diamond Point (Hill View), New York; m. ELLIOTT S. STILES, 08 Jan 1893; b. Abt. 1864.
           ii.   WILLIAM SHERMAN TRUESDALE, b. 1867, Diamond Point (Hill View), New York; d. 1868, Diamond Point (Hill View), New York.
           iii.   BERTRAND TRUESDALE, b. 1869, Diamond Point (Hill View), New York; d. 1871, Diamond Point (Hill View), New York.
1194.   iv.   EMMA GERTRUDE TRUESDALE, b. 06 Nov 1871, Diamond Point (Hill View), New York.
           v.   ETHEL MAY TRUESDALE, b. 07 May 1874, Diamond Point (Hill View), New York; m. GEORGE M. KINNEY; b. Abt. 1874. Lived in: Diamond Point (Hill View), New York.
Ethel May Truesdale Kinney contributed records of the descendants of Elizabeth Milk Prosser.
           vi.   CHARLES S. TRUESDALE, b. 12 Oct 1878, Diamond Point (Hill View), New York; d. 28 Aug 1950; m. MILDRED L. WRIGHT, 1908; b. Abt. 1880.
           vii.   GRACE P. TRUESDALE, b. 22 Dec 1880, Diamond Point (Hill View), New York; d. 25 Apr 1912.
           viii.   MAUDE ELIZABETH TRUESDALE, b. 20 May 1888, Diamond Point (Hill View), New York; m. GORDON G. SAMPSON; b. Abt. 1888, Of Glens Falls, New York. Lived in: Diamond Point (Hill View), New York

576. EMILY[8] MOORE *(MARIA LYNDIA[7] PROSSER, ELIZABETH 'BETSEY'[6] MILK, LEMUEL[5], JONATHAN[4], JOB[3], JOHN[2], JOHN[1])* was born 27 Oct 1844 in Bolton, Warren County, New York[1858], and died 08 Oct 1924 in Little River, Rice County, Kansas[1858]. She married LINUS BRAYTON Abt. 1869. He was born 01 Aug 1841[1858], and died 18 Jun 1925 in Little River, Rice County, Kansas[1858]. They are buried in Bean Cemetery, Little River, Rice County, Kansas

Children of EMILY MOORE and LINUS BRAYTON are:
1195.   i.   WILLIAM D.[9] BRAYTON, b. 22 Mar 1870, Diamond Point (Hill View), New York; d. 10 Jul 1949, Kansas.
1196.   ii.   ROBERT LINUS BRAYTON, b. 23 Sep 1874; d. 23 Jun 1965, Kansas.

      iii. EDGAR B. 'EDDIE' BRAYTON, b. 28 Dec 1877, Little River, Rice County, Kansas; d. 28 Sep 1880, Little River, Rice County, Kansas. Burial: Bean Cemetery, Little River, Rice County, Kansas

1197. iv. FRANK ERNEST BRAYTON, b. 02 Oct 1881; d. 28 Aug 1961.

577. MARIA FRANCES[8] MOORE *(MARIA LYNDIA[7] PROSSER, ELIZABETH 'BETSEY'[6] MILK, LEMUEL[5], JONATHAN[4], JOB[3], JOHN[2], JOHN[1])* was born 26 Feb 1847 in Bolton, Warren County, New York, and died 1927. She married CHATLES T. PENFIELD Abt. 1879. He was born 1840, and died 1927.

Children of MARIA MOORE and CHATLES PENFIELD are:
1198. i. AGNES[9] PENFIELD, b. 04 May 1880.
1199. ii. CHARLES E. PENFIELD, b. 13 Oct 1883.
      iii. WALTER E. PENFIELD, b. 09 Nov 1886; m. LULU LANFAIR; b. 1890; d. 1936. No children.

578. ELMINA M.[8] PROSSER *(JAMES LEMUEL 'NELSON'[7], ELIZABETH 'BETSEY'[6] MILK, LEMUEL[5], JONATHAN[4], JOB[3], JOHN[2], JOHN[1])* was born 21 Oct 1851 in New York. She married JOHN BURT. He was born Abt. 1850.

Children of ELMINA PROSSER and JOHN BURT are:
      i. OTON J.[9] BURT, b. 26 Jan 1869, Warren County, New York; d. 06 Jan 1946; m. ADA _____, Abt. 1897[1859]; b. Jul 1860. Lived in: 1900, Pawlet, Rutland County, Vermont. No children.
      ii. GRACE M. BURT, b. 07 Apr 1871, Warren County, New York.
      iii. NELLIE L. BURT, b. 26 Oct 1873, Warren County, New York; d. 18 Aug 1948; m. MISTTER WOOD; b. Abt. 1873.
      iv. EMMA F. BURT, b. 01 Sep 1875, Warren County, New York; d. 08 Apr 1915.
      v. HELEN L. BURT, b. 21 Nov 1877, Warren County, New York.

579. ELLEN A.[8] BABCOCK *(ROXCENA[7] BATES, SARAH 'SALLY'[6] MILK, LEMUEL[5], JONATHAN[4], JOB[3], JOHN[2], JOHN[1])* was born 1840 in Otto, Cattaraugus Co., New York, and died 09 Nov 1879 in East Otto, Cattaraugus County, New York[1860,1861]. She married OEL D. SATTERLEE Abt. 1860, son of JOSEPH SATTERLEE and DORCAS BABCOCK. He was born Dec 1833 in Otto, Cattaraugus Co., New York[1862], and died 1907 in East Otto, Cattaraugus County, New York[1862]. Buried. in East Otto Cemetery next to his mother; m. 1.) abt. 1860, Ellen A. Babcock (b. 1840 in Otto, N.Y.; d. 9 Nov. 1879 in East Otto, N.Y.; bur. in East Otto Cemetery; dau. of Darius A. and Roxcena [Bates] Babcock of Otto, N.Y.); m. 2.) abt. 1884, Alice M. Spaulding (b. Feb. 1850 in New York State). Ellen Babcock's mother, Roxcena Bates, was the sister of Nelson and Charles W. Bates. Oel Satterlee was a blacksmith and served in the Civil War in Co. K of the 9th Regiment, N.Y. Volunteer Cavalry. He mustered on 2 Sept. 1864 and was appointed Company blacksmith on 1 Jan. 1865. He was discharged on 1 June 1865 at Winchester, VA. Oel and Ellen Satterlee settled in East Otto and Oel served as the Town Clerk of that town in 1877-78. After Ellen's death, Oel boarded in the Allman Gooderick home in East Otto. Mr. Gooderick was also a blacksmith. Oel and Alice Satterlee remained in East Otto. Oel and Ellen (Babcock) Satterlee had 2 daughters: May Della (b. 1862; d. 1875; bur. in East Otto Cemetery with her parents); Anna Crystal (b. 1872. After Ellen [Babcock] Satterlee's death, their daughter, Anna was adopted by Ellen's sister and her husband, Adelia [Babcock] and Allen A. Bates. Allen and Adelia Bates were living on Franklin Street in Springville, Erie Co., N.Y. at the time. Anna eventually married _____ Prill and removed to Scio, Oregon).

Children of ELLEN BABCOCK and OEL SATTERLEE are:
      i. MAY DELLA[9] SATTERLEE, b. 1862, East Otto, Cattaraugus County, New York; d. 1875.
      ii. ANNA CRYSTAL SATTERLEE BATES, b. 24 Jun 1872, East Otto, Cattaraugus County, New York; d. 02 May 1950, Scio, Linn County, Oregon; m. DR. ALBERT GREGORY PRILL, 06 Jul 1890, West Valley, Cattaraugus County, New York; b. 05 May 1869, Springville, Erie County, New York; d. 26 Jan 1958, Scio, Linn County, Oregon.
          After her mother, Ellen Satterlee, died, Anna was adopted by Ellen's sister and her husband, Adelia (Babcock) & Allen A. Bates.
          Mrs Prill taught two years at the Mineral Springs College at Sodaville. She received a degree of Bachelor of English Literature while at that institute on or about June 3,1897. She also taught five years in the Scio school in the elementary department. She held a life diploma from the Department of Public Instruction, State of Oregon. She also gave music lessons for a number of years.
          Source: 'Scio in the Forks of the Santiam' book by Carol Bates. Burial: Franklin Butte Masonic Cemetery,

Scio, Linn County, Oregon

Who's Who on the Pacific Coast, *1913* forAlbert G Prill

Prill, Albert G., Physician and Surgeon; born, New York State, May 5, 1869; son, John and Mary (Tardell) P. Edu. Univ. of Buffalo, 1886-1890; Univ of Vermont, summer, 1889; M.D., N.Y. School Clinical Med., 1892; licensed Ore. State Med. Board, 1892;

post grad. course, 3 months, N.Y. City, 1900. Special work in Gynecology, Surgery. Married, Anna C. Satterlee Bates, July 6, 1890, at West Valley, N.Y. Secy., Scio Condensed Milk Co.; Mayor, City of Scio, three terms; Health officer, Scio, 10 years; Surgeon, Sou. Pac. R.R.; Pres., Linn County Fair Assn. 6 years. Member: Central Willamette Valley Med. Soc., Oregon State Med. Soc., N.Y. Medico Legal Soc. Res,: Race St.; Office: Main St., Scio, Ore. Burial: Franklin Butte Masonic Cemetery, Scio, Linn County, Oregon

580. JULIA CATHERINE[8] BABCOCK *(ROXCENA[7] BATES, SARAH 'SALLY'[6] MILK, LEMUEL[5], JONATHAN[4], JOB[3], JOHN[2], JOHN[1])* was born 1846 in Otto, Cattaraugus Co., New York, and died 1934 in Otto, Cattaraugus Co., New York. She married MARK COLVIN Abt. 1866 in Cattaraugus County, New York[1863]. He was born 1840[1864], and died 1917 in Otto, Cattaraugus Co., New York[1864]. They are buried in North Otto Cemetery, Otto, Cattaraugus County, New York

Children of JULIA BABCOCK and MARK COLVIN are:
    i. CHILD[9] COLVIN, b. Abt. 1869, Otto, Cattaraugus County, New York; d. Aft. 1910.
1200. ii. BERT COLVIN, b. 29 Jan 1873, Otto, Cattaraugus County, New York; d. 13 Nov 1941, Cattaraugus County, New York.

581. DAVID B.[8] SATTERLEE *(MARY ANN[7] BATES, SARAH 'SALLY'[6] MILK, LEMUEL[5], JONATHAN[4], JOB[3], JOHN[2], JOHN[1])* was born 17 Feb 1847 in Otto, Cattaraugus Co., New York, and died Bet. 1910 - 1920 in East Otto, Cattaraugus County, New York. He married SOPHRONIA WHALEY Feb 1870 in East Otto, Cattaraugus County, New York. She was born Jul 1854 in Herkimer County, New York, and died Bet. 1910 - 1920 in East Otto, Cattaraugus County, New York.

Children of DAVID SATTERLEE and SOPHRONIA WHALEY are:
    i. MARY E.[9] SATTERLEE, b. Dec 1872, East Otto, Cattaraugus County, New York.
    ii. MABEL H. SATTERLEE, b. Dec 1876, East Otto, Cattaraugus County, New York; m. (1) JOHN ALLENS, 1899; b. Apr 1878; d. Bef. 1909; m. (2) FLOYD COLE, 1909; b. Abt. 1876.

582. SARAH L.[8] SATTERLEE *(MARY ANN[7] BATES, SARAH 'SALLY'[6] MILK, LEMUEL[5], JONATHAN[4], JOB[3], JOHN[2], JOHN[1])* was born 12 Jul 1850 in Otto, Cattaraugus County, New York. She married FRANK G. HAWKINS Abt. 1866. He was born Nov 1845 in New York.

Children of SARAH SATTERLEE and FRANK HAWKINS are:
    i. ZINA F.[9] HAWKINS, b. Abt. 1867, Springville, Erie County, New York.
    ii. CHARLES L. HAWKINS, b. Abt. 1869, Springville, Erie County, New York.
    iii. BURT J. HAWKINS, b. Abt. 1874, Springville, Erie County, New York.
    iv. LETTY L. HAWKINS, b. Abt. 1876, Springville, Erie County, New York.

583. EMER DARIUS[8] SATTERLEE *(MARY ANN[7] BATES, SARAH 'SALLY'[6] MILK, LEMUEL[5], JONATHAN[4], JOB[3], JOHN[2], JOHN[1])* was born 11 Nov 1855 in East Otto, Cattaraugus County, New York, and died 1939 in East Otto, Cattaraugus County, New York. He married DEHLIA A. _____. She was born Jun 1856 in Monroe County, New York, and died 1936 in East Otto, Cattaraugus County, New York. Emer was a Blacksmith and a Trucker. They are buried in East Otto Cemetery, Cattaraugus County, New York

Children of EMER SATTERLEE and DEHLIA _____ are:
    i. CLARENCE[9] SATTERLEE, b. Abt. 1872, East Otto, Cattaraugus County, New York; d. 03 Sep 1878, East Otto Cemetery, Cattaraugus County, New York.
    ii. NELLIE A. SATTERLEE, b. 1877, Otto, Cattaraugus County, New York.
    iii. UNKNOWN SATTERLEE, b. Abt. 1880, Otto, Cattaraugus County, New York; d. 27 Apr 1884, Otto, Cattaraugus County, New York.
1201. iv. ZINA E. SATTERLEE, b. Oct 1885, Otto, Cattaraugus County, New York.

584. ALICE J.[8] SATTERLEE *(MARY ANN[7] BATES, SARAH 'SALLY'[6] MILK, LEMUEL[5], JONATHAN[4], JOB[3], JOHN[2], JOHN[1])* was born 30 Jun 1861 in East Otto, Cattaraugus County, New York, and died 19 Oct 1919 in Cattaraugus County, New York. She married AMBROSE HENSIE BROOKS 16 Sep 1875, son of PHILO BROOKS and SALLY BOUTWELL. He was born 19 Jan 1855 in Otto, Cattaraugus County, New York, and died 17 Apr 1932.

Children of ALICE SATTERLEE and AMBROSE BROOKS are:
    i. LOLA MAE[9] BROOKS, b. 19 Aug 1876, Cattaraugus County, New York; d. 06 Jul 1965, Cleveland, Ohio.
    ii. ARCHIE J. BROOKS, b. 15 Sep 1878, East Otto, Cattaraugus County, New York; d. 06 Apr 1955; m. ELEANOR MCKEAN.
    iii. CARL ELMER BROOKS, b. 24 Sep 1880, Cattaraugus County, New York; m. EZZIE HYSLIP; b. Jun 1880, New York. Carl worked for the Erie Railway Depot
    iv. PAUL AMBROSE BROOKS, b. 13 Mar 1893, Cattaraugus County, New York; d. Mar 1978, Wellsburg, New York; m. ERMA MAE PRINCE, 06 Sep 1916, Cattaraugus County, New York; b. 08 Sep 1895, New York; d. Mar 1986, Binghamton, Broome County, New York.

585. CHARLES FRANKLIN[8] BATES *(CHARLES W.[7], SARAH 'SALLY'[6] MILK, LEMUEL[5], JONATHAN[4], JOB[3], JOHN[2], JOHN[1])* was born 08 Mar 1878 in Forestville\Hanover, Chautauqua County, New York[1865,1866], and died 16 Feb 1977 in Brocton, Plymouth County, Massachusetts[1867,1868]. He married BESSIE C. _____. She was born Abt. 1877 in New York. Lived in: 1917, Plymouth, Massachusetts

Child of CHARLES BATES and BESSIE _____ is:
    i. CARLINE[9] BATES.

586. FLORA M.[8] BATES *(CHARLES W.[7], SARAH 'SALLY'[6] MILK, LEMUEL[5], JONATHAN[4], JOB[3], JOHN[2], JOHN[1])* was born Mar 1880 in Forestville\Hanover, Chautauqua County, New York. She married (1) GUS L. DEAN Abt. 1898 in Cattaraugus County, New York[1869]. He was born Abt. 1875 in New York. She married (2) CLAUDE R LEBECK 30 Jul 1914 in Cuyahoga County, Ohio, son of THEODORE LEBECK and ALICE HIXON. He was born Abt. 1880 in Olmsted Falls, Ohio.

Child of FLORA BATES and GUS DEAN is:
1202.   i. ARTHUR LEWIS[9] DEAN, b. 03 Mar 1900, Cattaraugus County, New York; d. Nov 1980, Jamestown, Chautauqua County, New York.

587. SUSAN MARIA[8] PIERCE *(MARY JANE[7] MILKS, BENJAMIN[6], LEMUEL[5] MILK, JONATHAN[4], JOB[3], JOHN[2], JOHN[1])* was born 27 Feb 1849 in West Seneca, Erie County, New York, and died 08 Jun 1874. She married ROYAL ASA GOULD 29 Nov 1870. He was born 19 Jan 1846 in Hamburg, Erie County, New York, and died 22 Aug 1909 in Hamburg, Erie County, New York.

Child of SUSAN PIERCE and ROYAL GOULD is:
1203.   i. FRANK ARNOLD[9] GOULD, b. 09 Sep 1871, Hamburg, Erie County, New York; d. 01 Dec 1948, Hamburg, Erie County, New York.

588. LAURA A.[8] PIERCE *(MARY JANE[7] MILKS, BENJAMIN[6], LEMUEL[5] MILK, JONATHAN[4], JOB[3], JOHN[2], JOHN[1])* was born 27 Sep 1850 in West Seneca, Erie County, New York, and died 22 Oct 1931. She married WORTHY MASON PATRIDGE, son of MASON PATRIDGE and ANNA GOULD. He was born 02 Apr 1848 in Erie County, New York. Moved 1887 to Owosso, Michigan[1870]

Children of LAURA PIERCE and WORTHY PATRIDGE are:
1204.   i. CARRIE DELL[9] PATRIDGE, b. 09 May 1872, Erie County, New York; d. 10 May 1935, Owosso, Shiawassee County, Michigan ?.
1205.   ii. SUSAN MAY PATRIDGE, b. 02 Feb 1879, West Seneca, Erie County, New York; d. 08 Jul 1943, Owosso, Shiawassee County, Michigan.

589. HERBERT DOUGLAS[8] PIERCE *(MARY JANE[7] MILKS, BENJAMIN[6], LEMUEL[5] MILK, JONATHAN[4], JOB[3], JOHN[2], JOHN[1])*

was born 02 May 1863 in West Seneca, Erie County, New York, and died 12 Dec 1928 in Water Valley, Erie County, New York. He married PHOEBE L. PHILLIPS, daughter of JOHN PHILLIPS and SARAH _____. She was born 02 Sep 1859.

Children of HERBERT PIERCE and PHOEBE PHILLIPS are:
- 1206. i. LAURA SARAH[9] PIERCE, b. 29 Apr 1884, Erie County, New York; d. 27 Jul 1949, Water Valley, Erie County, New York.
- 1207. ii. HOWARD ARNOLD PIERCE, b. 02 Jul 1886, Erie County, New York.
- iii. LESLIE PIERCE, b. 15 Nov 1895, Water Valley, Erie County, New York; d. 19 Nov 1895, Water Valley, Erie County, New York.

590. JEROME[8] MILKS *(HENRY BENJAMIN[7], BENJAMIN[6], LEMUEL[5] MILK, JONATHAN[4], JOB[3], JOHN[2], JOHN[1])* was born 17 Nov 1854 in Erie County, New York, and died Bef. 30 Apr 1910 in Lone Star, Wagoner County, Oklahoma[1871]. He married HANNAH E. PLYMALE Abt. 1873, daughter of HUEY PLYMALE and MARY _____. She was born Sep 1856 in Indiana[1872], and died 05 Jan 1930 in Sioux City, Woodbury County, Iowa[1873]. Jerome lived in 1880 in Dardenne, St Charles County, Missouri. Occupation: 1880, Farmer

Hannah lived in: 1900, Hutton Valley, Howell, Missouri. Burial: 08 Jan 1930, Graceland Cemetery, Sioux City, Iowa

Children of JEROME MILKS and HANNAH PLYMALE are:
- 1208. i. ESTHER ROSETTA[9] MILKS, b. 18 Aug 1874, St. Charles, Missouri.
- 1209. ii. SHERIDAN IRA MILKS, b. 25 Mar 1876, St. Charles, Missouri.
- 1210. iii. HENRY EDWARD MILKS, b. 16 Jan 1878, St. Charles, Missouri; d. 27 Mar 1947, Little Rock, Pulaski County, Arkansas.
- 1211. iv. JEROME FRANKLIN MILKS, b. 18 Oct 1879, Willow Springs, Howell County, Missouri; d. 23 Nov 1945, Little Rock, Pulaski County, Arkansas.
- 1212. v. ANNA MAY MILKS, b. 18 Oct 1883, Missouri.
- 1213. vi. CHARLES ARNOLD MILKS, b. 03 Jun 1885, Pomona, Missouri; d. 07 May 1977, Orange County, Florida.
- 1214. vii. DELLA MACIE MILKS, b. 01 Dec 1887, Willow Springs, Howell County, Missouri; d. Abt. 1908, Willow Springs, Howell County, Missouri.
- 1215. viii. DAVID LEWIS MILKS, b. 03 Oct 1890, Pomona, Missouri; d. 23 Jun 1970, Marysville, Snohomish, Washington.
- 1216. ix. JOSEPH HIRAM MILKS, b. 01 Jun 1892, Willow Springs, Howell County, Missouri; d. 19 Oct 1933, Quincy, Norfolk County, Massachusetts.
- 1217. x. ERNEST OSCAR MILKS, b. 12 Jun 1895, Howell Co., Missouri; d. 22 Jun 1990, Sioux City, Woodbury County, Iowa (SSDI).
- 1218. xi. WILLIAM WESLEY MILKS, b. 29 Sep 1897, Willow Springs, Missouri; d. 23 Oct 1921, Walnut Lake, Arkansas.
- xii. GEORGE ALMA MILKS, b. 29 Jul 1899, Willow Springs, Missouri[1874]; d. Feb 1962, Sioux City, Woodbury County, Iowa. Never married. Burial: Graceland Park Cemetery, Sioux City, Woodbury County, Iowa

591. LEWIS LYONS[8] MILKS *(HENRY BENJAMIN[7], BENJAMIN[6], LEMUEL[5] MILK, JONATHAN[4], JOB[3], JOHN[2], JOHN[1])* was born 15 Jul 1861 in Jonesburg, St. Louis, Missouri[1875,1876,1877], and died 10 Sep 1928 in Cincinnati, Ohio[1878]. He married (1) KATE B. BALDWIN 18 Mar 1885 in Valley Park, St. Louis, Missouri, daughter of SMITH BALDWIN and SUSAN PAGE. She was born Oct 1859 in St. Louis, Missouri[1879], and died 15 Feb 1938. He married (2) LAAMMA (WHITNEY) ROBINSON 07 Mar 1912 in Marion County, Indiana[1880], daughter of DAVID WHITNEY and MARY VANMETER. She was born 16 Jul 1863 in Sunbury, Ohio.

At the time of his death, Lewis was divorced. He was a Salesman for International Harvester & had an agency for Maxwell Automobiles. Burial: 12 Sep 1928, Sec. 23, Lot 23 (or Lot 1), Grave 262, Spring Grove Cemetery, Cincinnati, Ohio

Kate was class poet of Stephens College, Columbia, Missouri

Children of LEWIS MILKS and KATE BALDWIN are:
- 1219. i. WILLIAM CLAUDE[9] MILKS, b. 02 Jan 1886, Valley Park, St. Louis County, Missouri; d. Feb 1967, St. Louis, Missouri.
- 1220. ii. FRANK CRAYCROFT MILKS, b. 16 May 1887, Valley Park, Missouri; d. 01 Aug 1948.

1221.   iii. FLORENCE ANN MILKS, b. 10 Oct 1891, Valley Park, Missouri.
          iv. HAROLD BENJAMIN MILKS, b. 16 Dec 1894, Valley Park, Missouri; d. Bef. 1910, St Louis County, Missouri[1881].

592. HARRY J.[8] MILKS (*HENRY BENJAMIN*[7], *BENJAMIN*[6], *LEMUEL*[5] *MILK*, *JONATHAN*[4], *JOB*[3], *JOHN*[2], *JOHN*[1]) was born Jun 1869 in Meramec, St. Louis County, Missouri[1882]. He married (1) EFFIE LEIDY Feb 1890, daughter of ABRAM LEIDY and MARTHA STITH. She was born Abt. 1866 in Leon, Kansas[1883], and died Bet. 1895 - 1898 in Leon, Kansas (25 Feb.?). He married (2) LENA C. ADAMS 26 Feb 1897. She was born Abt. 1876 in Of Springfield, Missouri.

Child of HARRY MILKS and EFFIE LEIDY is:
1222.   i. HERBERT HARRY[9] MILKS, b. 24 Mar 1892, Monett, Missouri; d. 20 Jun 1969, Fallon, Churchill County, Nevada.

Child of HARRY MILKS and LENA ADAMS is:
          ii. EARL LEWIS 'JACK'[9] MILKS, b. 04 Feb 1899, Neodesha, Kansas[1884,1885]; d. 26 Aug 1945, Solano County, California[1885]; m. (1) VERA WINIFIELD COLEMAN, 17 Oct 1921, Solano County, California[1886]; b. Abt. 1900; m. (2) ELMA FLORENCE THOMPSON, Bet. 1930 - 1940, California; b. 18 Aug 1907, Eureka, Mitchell County, Kansas[1887]; d. 01 Dec 1994, Sacramento County, California[1887]. EARL LEWIS 'JACK' MILKS: lived in: 1910, Rainier, Columbia County, Oregon (with his mother). Military service: 1920, US Navy

593. IDA A.[8] MILKS (*CHARLES JONATHAN*[7], *BENJAMIN*[6], *LEMUEL*[5] *MILK*, *JONATHAN*[4], *JOB*[3], *JOHN*[2], *JOHN*[1]) was born 09 Mar 1855 in West Seneca, Erie County, New York[1888]. She married LOUIS A. SMITH[1889] 05 Feb 1890 in Magnolia, Rock County, Wisconsin[1889], son of AARON SMITH and HELLEN DENNY. He was born Apr 1862 in Magnolia, Rock County, Wisconsin[1890].

Children of IDA MILKS and LOUIS SMITH are:
          i. NEVA M.[9] SMITH, b. Nov 1890, Rock County, Wisconsin[1890]; d. Bef. 1956.
1223.   ii. SARAH HELEN SMITH, b. 23 Mar 1897, Magnolia, Rock County, Wisconsin; d. 04 Jun 1921, Spring Valley, Rock County, Wisconsin.

594. FREEMAN B.[8] MILKS (*CHARLES JONATHAN*[7], *BENJAMIN*[6], *LEMUEL*[5] *MILK*, *JONATHAN*[4], *JOB*[3], *JOHN*[2], *JOHN*[1]) was born 09 Jul 1864 in Magnolia, Rock County, Wisconsin[1891], and died 18 Oct 1893 in Magnolia, Rock County, Wisconsin[1891]. He married CORA MAY DAVIS 06 Jun 1889 in Rock County, Wisconsin[1892], daughter of E. DAVIS and MS. KLINE. She was born Abt. 1865. Burial: Spring Valley, Rock County, Wisconsin

Child of FREEMAN MILKS and CORA DAVIS is:
1224.   i. MABEL M.[9] MILKS, b. 27 Feb 1890, Magnolia, Rock County, Wisconsin; d. Bef. 1956.

595. JESSIE EDNA[8] MILKS (*CHARLES JONATHAN*[7], *BENJAMIN*[6], *LEMUEL*[5] *MILK*, *JONATHAN*[4], *JOB*[3], *JOHN*[2], *JOHN*[1]) was born 07 Dec 1865 in Magnolia, Rock County, Wisconsin, and died 27 Nov 1935 in Brodhead, Wisconsin. She married WILLIAM BAKER CHASE 01 Mar 1894 in Rock County, Wisconsin[1892], son of JOHN CHASE and MARTHA BAKER. He was born 09 May 1862, and died 11 May 1922 in Brodhead, Wisconsin.

Children of JESSIE MILKS and WILLIAM CHASE are:
1225.   i. MAY MABEL[9] CHASE, b. 09 Jan 1895, Brodhead, Green County, Wisconsin.
          ii. CHARLES MILKS CHASE, b. 05 May 1897, Brodhead, Green County, Wisconsin; m. LOIS (HEWITT) MILLER, 02 Apr 1932, Alma, Wisconsin (no children); b. 08 Oct 1896.
1226.   iii. FLOYD MILKS CHASE, b. 10 May 1899, Brodhead, Green County, Wisconsin.
          iv. BENJAMIN MILKS CHASE, b. 13 May 1902, Brodhead, Green County, Wisconsin; m. MARJORIE MATHISON, (No children); b. Abt. 1902. Occupation: Gas Station operator
1227.   v. ROY MILKS CHASE, b. 29 May 1904, Brodhead, Green County, Wisconsin.
          vi. CORA CHASE, b. Abt. 1907, Brodhead, Green County, Wisconsin.
          vii. MARJORIE CHASE, b. 1909, Brodhead, Green County, Wisconsin; d. 1909, Brodhead, Green County, Wisconsin.

596. JOSEPH EDWIN[8] MILKS *(DAVID WESLEY[7], BENJAMIN[6], LEMUEL[5] MILK, JONATHAN[4], JOB[3], JOHN[2], JOHN[1])* was born 01 Aug 1851 in Buffalo, New York, and died 22 Jan 1932 in Albee Township, Saginaw County, Michigan[1893]. He married ADDIE ELLEN SLOAN 25 Dec 1879[1894], daughter of HORACE SLOAN and JULIA MALONE. She was born 20 Dec 1863 in Albee Twp., Saginaw County, Michigan[1895], and died 07 Feb 1940 in Albee Twp., Saginaw County, Michigan[1895,1896]. They are buried in Pine Grove Cemetery, Saginaw Co., Michigan'

Children of JOSEPH MILKS and ADDIE SLOAN are:
- i. STANLEY M.[9] MILKS, b. 24 Jun 1881, Saginaw County, Michigan[1897]; d. 11 Aug 1893, Saginaw County, Michigan[1897].
- 1228. ii. MILDRED MILKS, b. 12 May 1884, Albee, Saginaw County, Michigan.
- 1229. iii. ADA H. MILKS, b. 24 Aug 1886, Michigan.
- iv. DORTHA 'DORIS' MILKS[1898], b. 07 Oct 1890, Saginaw County, Michigan[1898,1899]; d. 29 Nov 1897, Albee, Saginaw, Michigan[1900,1901]. Burial: Pine Grove Cemetery, Saginaw Co., Michigan'
- 1230. v. EDWIN A. MILKS, b. 02 Apr 1893, Saginaw, Michigan; d. 20 Jul 1985, Lansing, Ingham County, Michigan.
- 1231. vi. MALCOLM HORACE MILKS, b. 28 Mar 1896, Saginaw, Michigan; d. 26 Mar 1978, Meridian, Ingham County, Michigan.

597. POLLIE ALPHA[8] MILKS *(DAVID WESLEY[7], BENJAMIN[6], LEMUEL[5] MILK, JONATHAN[4], JOB[3], JOHN[2], JOHN[1])*[1902] was born 18 Apr 1854 in Hamburg, Erie County, New York[1902], and died 20 Nov 1940 in Chesaning, Saginaw County, Michigan[1902]. She married GEORGE DELOS ACKLEY 25 Nov 1875 in Chesaning, Saginaw County, Michigan, son of JAMES B. ACKLEY. He was born 10 Aug 1853 in Byron, Michigan[1903], and died 27 Sep 1911 in Saginaw County, Michigan. George was a Blacksmith. Burial: Wildwood Cemetery, Chesaning, Saginaw County, Michigan

Child of POLLIE MILKS and GEORGE DELOS ACKLEY is:
- 1232. i. MYRTLE[9] ACKLEY, b. 08 Jul 1879.

598. PARNA ROZELIA[8] MILKS *(DAVID WESLEY[7], BENJAMIN[6], LEMUEL[5] MILK, JONATHAN[4], JOB[3], JOHN[2], JOHN[1])*[1904] was born 30 Mar 1864 in Saginaw County, Michigan[1904], and died 16 May 1954 in Chesaning, Saginaw County, Michigan[1904]. She married WARD H. STUART 20 Aug 1888 in Corunna, Shiawassee, Michigan[1905], son of WILISTON STUART and ELLEN LIVERMORE. He was born 26 Jun 1866[1906], and died 10 May 1956 in Chesaning, Saginaw County, Michigan[1906]. They are buried in Wildwood Cemetery, Chesaning, Saginaw County, Michigan

Child of PARNA MILKS and WARD STUART is:
- 1233. i. MILDRED A.[9] STUART, b. 02 Aug 1889, Chesaning, Saginaw County, Michigan.

599. MARA ELEANOR[8] BURCHARD *(CALISTA ELIZABETH[7] MILKS, BENJAMIN[6], LEMUEL[5] MILK, JONATHAN[4], JOB[3], JOHN[2], JOHN[1])* was born 07 Apr 1862 in East Otto, Cattaraugus County, New York[1907], and died 03 Nov 1941 in Alhambra, Los Angeles County, California[1907]. She married ABRAHAM GAMPP Abt. 1888. He was born Jul 1849 in New York[1908,1909].

Children of MARA BURCHARD and ABRAHAM GAMPP are:
- 1234. i. MAMIE DOROTHEA CHRISTINE[9] GAMPP, b. 23 Aug 1889, East Otto, Cattaraugus County, New York.
- ii. LESLIE B. GAMPP, b. 22 Apr 1892, East Otto, Cattaraugus County, New York[1910,1911]; d. 26 Sep 1985, San Diego County, California[1912,1913]; m. UNNAMED, Abt. 1923[1914]. Lived in: 1930, Alhambra, Los Angeles County, California. Occupation: 1930, Sign writer
- 1235. iii. GENEVIEVE ALICE GAMPP, b. 30 Mar 1894, East Otto, Cattaraugus County, New York; d. 01 Dec 1975, San Diego County, California.
- 1236. iv. GEORGE ELMER GAMPP, b. 28 May 1898, East Otto, Cattaraugus County, New York; d. May 1982, NY.

600. GRACE ANNA[8] BURCHARD *(CALISTA ELIZABETH[7] MILKS, BENJAMIN[6], LEMUEL[5] MILK, JONATHAN[4], JOB[3], JOHN[2], JOHN[1])* was born 07 May 1869 in East Otto, Cattaraugus County, New York. She married ISAAC GAMPP Abt. 1895. He was born 31 May 1853 in Westfalls, New York. Isaac was a Cheese Maker. Grace studied Medicine.

Child of GRACE BURCHARD and ISAAC GAMPP is:
- 1237. i. GERTRUDE[9] GAMPP, b. 11 Oct 1896, Kane, Pennsylvania; d. 1966, Cambridge Springs, Pennsylvania.

601. BEATRICE A. E.[8] BURCHARD *(CALISTA ELIZABETH[7] MILKS, BENJAMIN[6], LEMUEL[5] MILK, JONATHAN[4], JOB[3], JOHN[2], JOHN[1])* was born 14 Jan 1877 in East Otto, Cattaraugus County, New York. She married ELTON CURTIS. He was born Abt. 1877. Lived in: Stockton, Chautauqua County, New York

Child of BEATRICE BURCHARD and ELTON CURTIS is:
    i. DAUGHTER[9] CURTIS, d. d. aged 7 mos..

602. EDITH SOPHIA[8] BURCHARD *(CALISTA ELIZABETH[7] MILKS, BENJAMIN[6], LEMUEL[5] MILK, JONATHAN[4], JOB[3], JOHN[2], JOHN[1])* was born 27 Dec 1864 in East Otto, Cattaraugus County, New York. She married EDGAR ALLEN DARLING 1885 in New York, son of JOHN DARLING and ALTERIA PRATT. He was born 28 Mar 1862.

    Edith composed the lyrics and music for many songs, such as, "Back to the North", "We Are Never Parted", "Up the Steeps of Time We're Climbing". She composed a book of campaign songs and sang them, with her rich contralto voice, during the Bryan and McKinley campaigns. When her youngest son, Dale, was 5 years of age, she resumed teaching in district schools near Springville, Erie County, New York. Graduated: Fredonia Normal and Baxter Conservatory of Music

Children of EDITH BURCHARD and EDGAR DARLING are:
    i. LEAL ALLEN[9] DARLING, b. 01 May 1886, Lilly Dale, Chautauqua County, New York; d. Jun 1912, Springville, New York (no children); m. BERTHA TANNEBAUM; b. Abt. 1886, Of Brooklyn, New York.
        At the age of 26 years he was drowned while rescuing his wife from treacherous cold springs in Cattaraugus Creek, near Springville, New York
        Leal was High School Principal at Panama, Chautauqua County, New York
1238. ii. GRACE IRENE DARLING, b. 08 May 1892, Vineland, New Jersey; d. 31 Oct 1977, El Monte, California.
1239. iii. ALTON BURCHARD DARLING, b. 25 Dec 1893, East Otto, Cattaraugus County, New York; d. 1941, Akron, New York.
1240. iv. ESMARIE DARLING, b. 11 Jun 1897, East Otto, Cattaraugus County, New York.
1241. v. JESSIE LUCILE DARLING, b. 12 Mar 1899, East Otto, Cattaraugus County, New York.
1242. vi. WINIFRED MARGUERITE DARLING, b. 28 Dec 1901.
1243. vii. KENNETH CLARK DARLING, b. 19 Feb 1903.
1244. viii. EDGAR DALE DARLING, b. 26 Jan 1905.

603. ELBERT B.[8] MILKS *(MERRITT SIDWAY[7], BENJAMIN[6], LEMUEL[5] MILK, JONATHAN[4], JOB[3], JOHN[2], JOHN[1])* was born 14 Oct 1870 in Green County, Wisconsin[1915,1916,1917]. He married (1) MARGARET ELIZABETH RICHMOND 24 Oct 1894 in Green County, Wisconsin[1918,1919], daughter of THOMAS RICHMOND and ELIZABETH _____. She was born 02 Jul 1869 in Wisconsin[1920,1921], and died Aft. 1920. He married (2) MARY _____ Aft. 1920. Elbert was a Miller in a Grist Mill.

Child of ELBERT MILKS and MARGARET RICHMOND is:
1245. i. MERRL THOMAS[9] MILKS, b. 08 Apr 1898; d. 1958, Brodhead, Green County, Wisconsin.

604. ELMER F.[8] MILKS *(JAMES FRANKLIN[7], BENJAMIN[6], LEMUEL[5] MILK, JONATHAN[4], JOB[3], JOHN[2], JOHN[1])* was born 19 May 1873 in Buffalo, New York[1922], and died May 1963 in Buffalo, New York[1922]. He married HELEN M. POTTER[1923], daughter of JAMES POTTER and MARY _____. She was born Nov 1881 in New York[1924], and died Aft. 1942. Elmer was a Truck Gardner.

Child of ELMER MILKS and HELEN POTTER is:
1246. i. DR, ROBERT FRANKLIN[9] MILKS, b. 25 Dec 1923, Buffalo, New York; d. 23 Oct 2008, Buffalo, New York.

605. DANIEL BENJAMIN[8] MILKS *(JAMES FRANKLIN[7], BENJAMIN[6], LEMUEL[5] MILK, JONATHAN[4], JOB[3], JOHN[2], JOHN[1])* was born 18 Mar 1875 in Buffalo, New York[1924], and died 08 May 1953 in Erie County, New York. He married HARRIETT M. LEWIS Apr 1899 in Buffalo, New York[1925], daughter of GEORGE LEWIS and MARY _____. She was born 22 Mar 1876 in Buffalo, New York.

Children of DANIEL MILKS and HARRIETT LEWIS are:
    i. RUSSELL DANIEL[9] MILKS[1926,1927], b. 29 Oct 1899, Buffalo, New York[1928]; d. 18 Jul 1974, Orchard Park, New

York[1928,1929]; m. CLARABEL GEITTER, 07 Dec 1953; b. 28 May 1925.
Military service: Bet. 22 Oct 1942 - 16 Mar 1944, WWII

1247. ii. GERTRUDE E. MILKS, b. 12 Nov 1900, Buffalo, New York; d. Aug 1982, Orchard Park, New York.

iii. MARION L. MILKS, b. 22 Feb 1903, Buffalo, New York; d. unmarried.

606. WILLIAM H.[8] MILKS *(JAMES FRANKLIN[7], BENJAMIN[6], LEMUEL[5] MILK, JONATHAN[4], JOB[3], JOHN[2], JOHN[1])* was born 21 Feb 1878 in Buffalo, New York[1930], and died Sep 1965 in Buffalo, New York[1931]. He married EDNA CALDWELL 1901, daughter of TAYLOR CALDWELL and MARY GETTY. She was born 04 Oct 1879 in West Seneca, New York[1931], and died Jun 1978 in Buffalo, New York[1931].

Children of WILLIAM MILKS and EDNA CALDWELL are:

i. HOWARD WILLIAM[9] MILKS, b. 22 Aug 1902, Buffalo, New York; m. LOUISE BEETON, 15 Nov 1931; b. 25 Jan 1903, Canada. They lived, in 1941, in Long Beach, California, where Howard was a Police Lt.

1248. ii. RICHARD JAMES MILKS, b. 11 Jan 1908, Buffalo, New York; d. Mar 1981, Snyder, New York.

607. MERRILL V.[8] MILKS *(JAMES FRANKLIN[7], BENJAMIN[6], LEMUEL[5] MILK, JONATHAN[4], JOB[3], JOHN[2], JOHN[1])* was born 07 Mar 1880 in Buffalo, New York, and died Bef. Apr 1930. He married (1) EDNA MAY WILLGANSZ 1903, daughter of WILLIAM WILLGANSZ and MARGARET _____. She was born Abt. 1881 in New York. He married (2) LOUISE BEETON Abt. 1928, daughter of WILLIAM BEETON and HALLIE CHAMBERS. She was born 25 Jan 1903 in Canada.

Children of MERRILL MILKS and EDNA WILLGANSZ are:

i. MAY MERLE[9] MILKS, b. 17 Oct 1904, Buffalo, NY.

1249. ii. ELMER WILLIAM MYLKS, b. 10 Mar 1908, Buffalo, NY; d. Feb 1973, Ridgewood, New Jersey.

Child of MERRILL MILKS and LOUISE BEETON is:

1250. iii. WILLIAM FISHER[9] MILKS, b. 14 Mar 1929, Buffalo, New York.

608. GEORGE RICHARD[8] MILKS *(IRA NELSON[7], BENJAMIN[6], LEMUEL[5] MILK, JONATHAN[4], JOB[3], JOHN[2], JOHN[1])* was born 23 Oct 1871 in West Seneca, New York, and died 1935. He married ELIZABETH TANNER 28 Oct 1903. She was born Abt. 1871.

Child of GEORGE MILKS and ELIZABETH TANNER is:

1251. i. ROLLIN CHARLES[9] MILKS, b. 19 Aug 1904; d. Jan 1950.

609. CLARA MAHALA[8] MILKS *(IRA NELSON[7], BENJAMIN[6], LEMUEL[5] MILK, JONATHAN[4], JOB[3], JOHN[2], JOHN[1])* was born 19 Sep 1875 in West Seneca, New York. She married FRANK J. FISHER Abt. 1901, son of CHARLES FISHER and HARRIET BEDFORD. He was born 26 Jul 1877 in West Seneca, New York, and died 25 Mar 1949 in Orchard Park, New York.

Children of CLARA MILKS and FRANK FISHER are:

1252. i. JESSIE BEDFORD[9] FISHER, b. 17 Sep 1902, Los Angeles, California.

1253. ii. FLORENCE FISHER, b. 13 Sep 1908, West Seneca, New York.

610. NELSON CLARENCE[8] MILKS *(IRA NELSON[7], BENJAMIN[6], LEMUEL[5] MILK, JONATHAN[4], JOB[3], JOHN[2], JOHN[1])* was born 03 Sep 1879 in West Seneca, NY, and died 30 Aug 1953. He married SOPHIA A. KRAKOW 03 Dec 1903, daughter of CHARLES KRAKOW and SOPHIA _____. She was born 09 Jul 1879 in So. Buffalo, NY, and died 12 Sep 1953.

Nelson was a builder of homes; one of the founders of the City of Lackawanna, New York, and its Chamber of Commerce; a co-founder and Past Master of Lackawanna Masonic Lodge; editor of Milks calendar, published 1909; assistant author of History and Genealogy of the Milk-Milks Family.

Children of NELSON MILKS and SOPHIA KRAKOW are:

1254. i. IRA CHARLES[9] MILKS, b. 10 Oct 1904, Hamburg, Erie County, New York; d. Apr 1944, Hamburg, Erie County, New York.

1255. ii. ARNOLD RICHARD MILKS, b. 15 Sep 1907, Lackawanna, NY; d. Sep 1973, Beaver Dams, Schuyler Co, NY 14812.

1256. iii. ADELINE MILDRED MILKS, b. 14 Jan 1909, New York.

1257.   iv.   ELEANOR SOPHIA MILKS, b. 22 Aug 1915, New York.

611. ANNA ALFREDINE[8] MORRIS *(ELIZABETH A. "BETSEY"[7] MILKS, JOB[6] MILK, LEMUEL[5], JONATHAN[4], JOB[3], JOHN[2], JOHN[1])* was born 26 Dec 1851 in Cattaraugus County, New York, and died 15 Aug 1909 in Stutsman, North Dakota. She married THOMAS RAE NEGUS 20 Aug 1875, son of WEST NEGUS and LUCINDA SARGENT. He was born 23 Feb 1851 in Oil City, Crawford County, Pennsylvania, and died 07 May 1929 in Minneapolis, Hennepin County, Minnesota.

Children of ANNA MORRIS and THOMAS NEGUS are:

            i.   CECILE MAY[9] NEGUS, b. 24 Mar 1878; d. 15 Aug 1893.
1258.   ii.   LENDAL DEAN NEGUS, b. 05 Apr 1887, Hurley, Turner County, S. Dakota; d. 18 Jun 1952, Grant, Oregon.
1259.   iii.   ARTHUR NEGUS, b. 10 Jan 1883, South Dakota; d. 01 Aug 1966, Mount Vernon, Grant, Oregon.
           iv.   ELIZABETH LUCINDA NEGUS, b. 01 Jan 1884; d. 11 Aug 1893.
1260.   v.   CLARENCE W. NEGUS, b. 24 Jun 1886, Buena Vista, Meade County, South Dakota; d. 16 Sep 1961, Deschutes, Oregon.
           vi.   CLIFFORD NEGUS, b. 24 Oct 1887, Turner County, South Dakota; d. 15 Jan 1976, Mount Vernon, Grant, Oregon.
           vii.   HARRY THOMAS NEGUS, b. 19 Jan 1890, Turner County, South Dakota; d. 10 Jan 1917, Turner County, South Dakota.
1261.   viii.   HARVEY MYRL NEGUS, b. 10 Aug 1891, Turner County, South Dakota; d. 03 Jun 1965, Glendive, Dawson County, Montana.

612. MARY ETTA[8] MORRIS *(ELIZABETH A. "BETSEY"[7] MILKS, JOB[6] MILK, LEMUEL[5], JONATHAN[4], JOB[3], JOHN[2], JOHN[1])* was born Apr 1860 in Iowa, and died in Missouri. She married WALTER WILLIAM WARBURTON Abt. 1880 in South Dakota ?. He was born Aug 1856 in Wisconsin

Children of MARY MORRIS and WALTER WARBURTON are:

           i.   VERNA L.[9] WARBURTON, b. Jan 1882, Dakota Territory (South).
           ii.   RALPH WARBURTON, b. 10 Dec 1883, Dakota Territory (South); d. Jan 1968, Summersville, Texas County, Missouri.
           iii.   PEARL PURL WARBURTON, b. Aug 1886, Dakota Territory (South).
           iv.   SARAH ANN WARBURTON, b. 07 Nov 1888, Turner County, South Dakota.
           v.   JESSIE WARBURTON, b. Jul 1890, North Dakota.
           vi.   OWEN WARBURTON, b. 11 Apr 1894, Spring Valley, Shannon County, Missouri; d. May 1973, Summersville, Texas County, Missouri. Prob. never married. Still single at age 44 in 1940 census.
           vii.   CLIFFORD WARBURTON, b. 17 Feb 1896, Spring Valley, Shannon County, Missouri; d. Nov 1981, Mountain View, Howell County, Missouri.
1262.   viii.   FRED WARBURTON, b. 22 Jun 1899, Spring Valley, Shannon County, Missouri; d. Nov 1980, McCook, Red Willow County, Nebraska.
           ix.   RAY WARBURTON, b. Abt. 1901, Spring Valley, Shannon County, Missouri.

613. WEBSTER CYRUS[8] MORRIS *(ELIZABETH A. "BETSEY"[7] MILKS, JOB[6] MILK, LEMUEL[5], JONATHAN[4], JOB[3], JOHN[2], JOHN[1])* was born Sep 1873 in South Dakota, and died 18 Jan 1944 in Deschutes, Oregon. He married MAY E. TAYLOR Abt. 1895. She was born Sep 1873 in Illinois.

Children of WEBSTER MORRIS and MAY TAYLOR are:

           i.   BERTHA G.[9] MORRIS, b. Jan 1898, Kansas.
           ii.   FRED F. MORRIS, b. 26 Mar 1899, Missouri; d. 08 Jul 1966, Prineville, Crook County, Oregon. Single at age of 31 yrs.
           iii.   MABLE M. MORRIS, b. Abt. 1901, Kansas.
           iv.   EMMA G. MORRIS, b. Abt. 1905, Kansas.
           v.   GLADYS MORRIS, b. Abt. 1907, Kansas.
           vi.   RAYMOND A. MORRIS, b. Abt. 1909, Kansas. Still living with his mother in 1940 and single at age 31.

614. JAMES EBENEZER[8] CULLINGS *(CAROLINE "PHEBE" E.[7] MILKS, JOB[6] MILK, LEMUEL[5], JONATHAN[4], JOB[3], JOHN[2], JOHN[1])* was born 24 Jun 1858 in Fredericksburg, Iowa, and died 25 Feb 1944 in Wahoo, Nebraska. He married ALICE

KIDDER 21 May 1885 in Fredericksburg, Iowa, daughter of RUSSELL KIDDER and HANNAH MARSH. She was born 13 Sep 1864 in Fredericksburg, Iowa.

Children of JAMES CULLINGS and ALICE KIDDER are:
- 1263. i. CLIFFORD RUSSELL[9] CULLINGS, b. 11 Mar 1886, Grand Island, Nebraska; d. 23 Apr 1927, Colorado.
- 1264. ii. NELLIE E. CULLINGS, b. 20 Mar 1888, Fredericksburg, Iowa.
- iii. NEAL CULLINGS, b. 13 Jan 1892, Osceola, Nebraska; d. 28 Sep 1892, Osceola, Nebraska.

615. CLARA F.[8] CULLINGS *(CAROLINE "PHEBE" E.[7] MILKS, JOB[6] MILK, LEMUEL[5], JONATHAN[4], JOB[3], JOHN[2], JOHN[1])* was born 1868 in Fredericksburg, Iowa, and died 23 Feb 1945 in Riceville, Iowa. She married ISAAC S. DUNCAN, son of JOHN DUNCAN and MARY SHANE. He was born 21 Nov 1874 in Beaver County, Pennsylvania.

Child of CLARA CULLINGS and ISAAC DUNCAN is:
- 1265. i. KENNETH[9] DUNCAN, b. Sep 1910, Riceville, Iowa.

616. MARY ETTOLA[8] PETTIT *(JEMIMA DIANTHA[7] MILKS, JOB[6] MILK, LEMUEL[5], JONATHAN[4], JOB[3], JOHN[2], JOHN[1])* was born 01 Jun 1859 in Mt. Ida, Grant County, Wisconsin, and died 05 Nov 1930 in Joliet, Will County, Illinois. She married (1) MR. HOPKINS. He was born Abt. 1860. She married (2) JOSEPH E. STULTZ.

Children of MARY PETTIT and MR. HOPKINS are:
- i. CLYDE[9] HOPKINS, b. Abt. 1880.
- ii. VIVA HOPKINS, b. Abt. 1882; d. Abt. 1898.

617. FRANK BURR[8] PETTIT *(JEMIMA DIANTHA[7] MILKS, JOB[6] MILK, LEMUEL[5], JONATHAN[4], JOB[3], JOHN[2], JOHN[1])* was born 16 Jul 1862 in Mt. Ida, Grant County, Wisconsin, and died 01 Mar 1929 in Walnut Grove, Minnesota. He married AURA MONROE 25 Mar 1885 in Mt. Ida, Grant County, Wisconsin. She was born 25 Sep 1860 in Howell, Michigan, and died 10 Jan 1938 in Sioux Falls, South Dakota.

Children of FRANK PETTIT and AURA MONROE are:
- i. SON[9] PETTIT, b. 03 May 1888, Mt. Ida, Grant County, WI.; d. 05 May 1888, Mt. Ida, Grant County, WI.
- 1266. ii. PEARL RHEA PETTIT, b. 11 May 1889, Mt. Ida, Grant County, Wisconsin.

618. FRED SILAS[8] PETTIT *(JEMIMA DIANTHA[7] MILKS, JOB[6] MILK, LEMUEL[5], JONATHAN[4], JOB[3], JOHN[2], JOHN[1])* was born 13 Jul 1865 in Mt. Ida, Grant County, Wisconsin, and died 29 Apr 1954 in Kalispell, Montana. He married (1) EMMA HUTCHESON. She was born Abt. 1865. He married (2) NELLIE JANE BRAY 21 Jun 1893. She was born 29 Jan 1872 in Mt. Ida, Grant County, Wisconsin.

Child of FRED PETTIT and EMMA HUTCHESON is:
- i. EWELL[9] PETTIT.

Children of FRED PETTIT and NELLIE BRAY are:
- 1267. ii. MAMIE ESTELLA[9] PETTIT, b. 23 Sep 1894, Mt. Ida, Grant County, Wisconsin; d. 08 Oct 1984, Bigfork, Flathead County, Montana.
- iii. ADA FLORENCE PETTIT, b. 28 Nov 1898, Mt. Ida, Grant County, Wisconsin; d. (no children); m. JAMES A. DURNING; b. Abt. 1898, Of Kalispell, Montana.
- 1268. iv. HARRY LLOYD PETTIT, b. 04 Jan 1900, Mt. Ida, Grant County, Wisconsin.
- v. VERA FERN PETTIT, b. 04 Apr 1902, Mt. Ida, Grant County, Wisconsin; d. 03 Sep 1925, Butte, Montana; m. DAVID LUNSFORD YANDELL, 15 Mar 1922, Missoula, Missoula County, Montana; b. 25 Dec 1884, Mississippi; d. 17 Mar 1927, Montana.
- 1269. vi. HAROLD GEORGE PETTIT, b. 28 May 1905, Mt. Ida, Grant County, Wisconsin; d. 02 Feb 1933, Kalispell, Flathead County, Montana.

619. WILL D.[8] PETTIT *(JEMIMA DIANTHA[7] MILKS, JOB[6] MILK, LEMUEL[5], JONATHAN[4], JOB[3], JOHN[2], JOHN[1])* was born Abt. 1867 in Mt. Ida, Grant County, Wisconsin. He married JANE CROW. She was born Abt. 1867.

Child of WILL PETTIT and JANE CROW is:
  i. MERRILL D.[9] PETTIT, b. Abt. 1890, Mt. Ida, Grant County, Wisconsin.

620. CHARLES NELSON[8] MILKS *(DAVID FRANKLIN[7], JOB[6] MILK, LEMUEL[5], JONATHAN[4], JOB[3], JOHN[2], JOHN[1])* was born 10 Apr 1866 in New Albin, Iowa, and died 27 Jul 1940 in Lennox, South Dakota. He married MAMIE MCGREGOR 1889 in Lennox, South Dakota. She was born 01 Mar 1871 in Wisconsin, and died 1967 in Lincoln County, South Dakota.

Children of CHARLES MILKS and MAMIE MCGREGOR are:
1270. i. FLOYD EDWIN[9] MILKS, b. 03 Jun 1890, Hurley, Turner County, South Dakota; d. 21 Feb 1978, Faith, Meade County, South Dakota.
1271. ii. CARRIE M. MILKS, b. 20 Aug 1892, Turner County, South Dakota.
1272. iii. GUY STANLEY MILKS, b. 13 Jan 1898, Turner County, South Dakota; d. 05 Mar 1976, Beltrami County, Minnesota.

621. PEARL MELISSA[8] MILKS *(DAVID FRANKLIN[7], JOB[6] MILK, LEMUEL[5], JONATHAN[4], JOB[3], JOHN[2], JOHN[1])* was born 06 Feb 1871 in New Albin, Allamakee, Iowa, and died 28 Apr 1972 in Hurley, Turner, South Dakota. She married GEORGE MARTIN BENSON 20 Jul 1889 in Kellogg, Jasper County, Iowa, son of HENRY BENSON and MARY ELDRIDGE. He was born 20 Jul 1868 in Kellogg, Jasper, Iowa, and died 07 Jun 1931 in Hurley, Turner, South Dakota. Pearl assisted in gathering some of the family records.

Children of PEARL MILKS and GEORGE BENSON are:
1273. i. LEROY ELLIS 'SLIM'[9] BENSON, b. 08 Nov 1890, Parsons, Kansas; d. 24 Dec 1950, Viborg, Turner County, South Dakota.
1274. ii. EMMET H. BENSON, b. 1892, South Dakota.
1275. iii. ERNEST CLIFFORD BENSON, b. 04 Oct 1894, Parsons, Kansas; d. Dec 1982, Freeman, Hutchinson County, South Dakota.
1276. iv. RUTH ANNA BENSON, b. 20 Feb 1898, Parsons, Kansas; d. 19 Apr 1977, Turner County, South Dakota.
1277. v. GLADYS IRENE BENSON, b. 31 Jan 1900, South Dakota; d. 14 Mar 1971, Turner County, South Dakota.
       vi. EDITH M. BENSON, b. 09 May 1901, South Dakota; m. RICHARD J. JOHNSON, Abt. 1927; b. Abt. 1903, Minnesota.
1278. vii. FRANK M. BENSON, b. 1903, South Dakota.
1279. viii. HAROLD G. BENSON, b. 1905, South Dakota.
1280. ix. VIOLET M. BENSON, b. 1907, South Dakota.
1281. x. HOWARD BENSON, b. 1914, South Dakota.

622. HARRY STREATOR[8] MILKS *(DAVID FRANKLIN[7], JOB[6] MILK, LEMUEL[5], JONATHAN[4], JOB[3], JOHN[2], JOHN[1])* was born 10 Apr 1878 in New Albin, Iowa, and died Aft. 1956. He married BERTIE V. ELLIDGE 10 Nov 1900 in Parsons, Labette County, Kansas, daughter of MICHAEL ELLIDGE and MARY DAVIS. She was born 30 Sep 1881 in Parsons, Kansas, and died 11 Nov 1952 in Parsons, Kansas.

Harry contributed many records on the Milks family.

Children of HARRY MILKS and BERTIE ELLIDGE are:
1282. i. LLOYD ALBERT[9] MILKS, b. 24 Jul 1901, Parsons, Kansas.
1283. ii. NELLIE 'BLANCHE' MILKS, b. 02 Aug 1903, Parsons, Kansas.
1284. iii. MARY DENZEL MILKS, b. 21 Jun 1905, Parsons, Kansas; d. 27 May 1990, Los Angeles, California.
1285. iv. INEZ IRENE MILKS, b. 01 Apr 1908, Parsons, Kansas; d. 23 Mar 1936.
1286. v. HELEN BERTIE MILKS, b. 19 Dec 1910, Parsons, Kansas.
       vi. MAX HARRY MILKS, b. 19 Jan 1912, Parsons, Kansas; m. IRMA G. VANCE; b. 25 Sep 1913, Kansas; d. Jun 1987, Parsons, Labette County, Kansas.
1287. vii. DORA ALEENE MILKS, b. 09 Jun 1914, Parsons, Kansas.
1288. viii. GLENN HOWARD MILKS, b. 13 Aug 1916, Parsons, Kansas; d. 08 Mar 1986, Parsons, Labette County, KS.

623. DAVID HARTMAN[8] MILKS *(DAVID FRANKLIN[7], JOB[6] MILK, LEMUEL[5], JONATHAN[4], JOB[3], JOHN[2], JOHN[1])* was born 05 Oct 1883 in New Albin, Iowa, and died Oct 1967 in Parsons, Labette County, Kansas. He married MARY ELLEN CLARY Abt. 1914, daughter of WILLIAM CLARY and SYLVIA MCCASLIN. She was born 29 May 1895 in Crawford, Kansas, and died Feb 1984 in Parsons, Labette County, Kansas.

Children of DAVID MILKS and MARY CLARY are:
- 1289. i. IDA GWENDOLE^9 MILKS, b. 24 Oct 1915, Parsons, Labette County, Kansas; d. Nov 1991, Parsons, Labette County, Kansas.
- 1290. ii. DOROTHY LORRAINE MILKS, b. 25 Oct 1919, Viborg, South Dakota; d. 15 Feb 2012, Chanute, Neosho County, Kansas.
- 1291. iii. ERNEST DAVID MILKS, b. 23 Oct 1923, Parsons, Labette County, Kansas; d. 19 Apr 1990, Labette County, Kansas.
- 1292. iv. BETTY JUNE MILKS, b. 17 Jun 1933, Parsons, Labette County, Kansas.

624. SHERMAN GEORGE^8 MILKS *(DAVID FRANKLIN^7, JOB^6 MILK, LEMUEL^5, JONATHAN^4, JOB^3, JOHN^2, JOHN^1)* was born 14 Apr 1886 in New Albin, Iowa. He married BLANCHE ELLIS Abt. 1920, daughter of BERT ELLIS and LENA BOYLES. She was born 12 Sep 1899 in Springdale, Washington.

Children of SHERMAN MILKS and BLANCHE ELLIS are:
- i. MAXINE PEARL^9 MILKS, b. 01 Jun 1921, Viborg, S. Dak..
- 1293. ii. LOIS ELLEN MILKS, b. 21 Jan 1923, Parsons, Kansas; d. 29 May 2004, Labette County, Kansas.
- iii. NOLA MARIE MILKS, b. 18 Jul 1927, Parsons, Kansas; d. 21 Dec 2008, Topeka, Shawnee County, Kansas; m. MELVIN 'BILL' DWAYNE CARTER, 06 Jan 1946, Parsons, Kansas; b. 01 Jul 1921, Parsons, Kansas; d. 27 Feb 1999, Topeka, Shawnee County, Kansas.

    `OBITUARY
    Nola M. Carter, 81, of Topeka, passed away Sun., Dec. 21, 2008 at Plaza West Care Center. She was born July 18, 1927 in Parsons, KS, the daughter of Sherman G. and Blanche E. Milks.
    On Jan. 6, 1946 she married Melvin "Bill" Carter in Parsons, KS. She worked for the Kansas Department of Revenue in the Titles and Registration. She was a member of the University United Methodist Church and United Methodist Women.
    Funeral service will be at 11:00 a.m. on Sat., Dec. 27 at University United Methodist Church.
    Private family burial will be at Mt. Hope Cemetery.
    Mrs. Carter will lie in state after 2:00 p.m. on Fri., Dec. 26 at Penwell-Gabel Mid Town with visitation from 6:00 to 8:00 p.m.
    Memorial contributions may be made to University United Methodist Church, 1621 SW College, Topeka, KS 66604 or Helping Hands Humane Society 2625 NW Rochester Rd, Topeka, KS 66617.

    OBITUARY
    Services will be at 10 a.m. Tuesday at University United Methodist Church for Melvin Dwayne "Bill" Carter, 77, Topeka, who died Saturday, Feb. 27, 1999, at home.
    He was born July 1, 1921, in Parsons, to George A. and Kittie Perkel Carter. He lived in Leavenworth before he moved to Topeka in 1966. He worked for Hallmark Cards nearly 38 years before he retired in 1986.
    He was an Army veteran of World War II, having served in Europe with the 507th Parachute Regiment in the 82nd Airborne Division. He participated in the Battle of the Bulge and received the Purple Heart and Bronze Star medals. He was a member of University United Methodist Church and Capitol Post No. 1 of the American Legion.
    He married Nola Milks on Jan. 6, 1946, in Parsons. She survives.
    Burial will be in Mount Hope Cemetery.
    Mr. Carter will lie in state after 8 a.m. today at Penwell-Gabel Mid-Town Funeral Home where relatives and friends will meet from 7 to 8 p.m.
    Memorial contributions may be made to University United Methodist Church, 1621 College, 66604, or to Midland Hospice Care, 200 Frazier Circle, 66606.
    Parents: George Alexander Carter (1881 - 1947); Kittie May Perkel Carter (1888 - 1981)
- 1294. iv. ROBERT GLENN MILKS, b. 21 Jan 1934, Parsons, Kansas.

625. GLADYS ANNA^8 MILKS *(DAVID FRANKLIN^7, JOB^6 MILK, LEMUEL^5, JONATHAN^4, JOB^3, JOHN^2, JOHN^1)* was born 25 Apr 1889 in New Albin, Iowa. She married EBERT S. SMITH 06 May 1907 in Parsons, Labette County, Kansas, son of

THOMAS LARKIN and SARAH SANDERS. He was born 25 Dec 1884 in Greenfield, Illinois.

Children of GLADYS MILKS and EBERT SMITH are:
1295.   i. HAROLD LARKIN[9] SMITH, b. 24 Feb 1908, Parsons, Labette County, Kansas.
       ii. EBERT EUGENE SMITH, b. 12 Jan 1916, Parsons, Labette County, Kansas; m. GLADYS A. EMERY, 09 Feb 1946; b. Abt. 1916.

626. ALVIN LUCIUS[8] MILKS *(DAVID FRANKLIN[7], JOB[6] MILK, LEMUEL[5], JONATHAN[4], JOB[3], JOHN[2], JOHN[1])* was born 16 Jan 1892 in New Albin, Iowa, and died 25 Jul 1927 in Parsons, Labette County, Kansas. He married NONA I. RUSSELL Abt. 1916, daughter of WARREN RUSSELL and MINNIE SPRINGER. She was born 08 Jun 1895 in Dunlap, Kansas.

Children of ALVIN MILKS and NONA RUSSELL are:
1296.   i. LUELLA EVELYN[9] MILKS, b. 30 Oct 1917, Parsons, Labette County, Kansas; d. 19 Mar 1986, Santa Barbara, California.
1297.   ii. VIRGINIA ROSE MILKS, b. 30 Sep 1919, Parsons, Labette County, Kansas.
       iii. NONA ALLE MILKS, b. 02 Jan 1921, Parsons, Labette County, Kansas; d. 01 Feb 2005, Parsons, Labette County, Kansas; m. KENNETH E. PEAK, 04 Aug 1951; b. Abt. 1920; d. 03 Mar 1995.

OBITUARY

PARSONS - Nona A. Peak, 84, Parsons, died Tuesday, Feb. 1, 2005, at Labette County Medical Center.

She was born Jan. 2, 1921, in Parsons, the daughter of Alvin L. and Nona Russell Milks.

She attended Parsons High School, Parsons Business College and a photography school in Indiana.

She worked in the field of photography throughout her career, including jobs at D. Peterson Studio, Kansas Ordnance Plant and Leon Crooks Studio. She retired in 1981.

She was a member of First Christian Church, Parsons.

On Aug. 4, 1951, she married Kenneth E. Peak. He died March 3, 1995.

Survivors include a step-daughter, Barbara Clark, Owasso, Okla., a step-sister, Mary Roberts, Coffeyville, and two step-grandchildren and two step-great-grandchildren.

She was preceded in death by a brother and four sisters.

Funeral services will be at 10:30 a.m. Thursday, Feb. 3, at the funeral home, led by the Rev. Robert Brown. Burial will be in Memorial Lawn Cemetery.

Memorials to Labette County Medical Center Foundation may be left at the funeral home, where visitation will be today.

627. CORA ANNABELLE[8] MILKS *(HUMPHREY W.[7], JOB[6] MILK, LEMUEL[5], JONATHAN[4], JOB[3], JOHN[2], JOHN[1])* was born 08 Dec 1873 in Chickasaw, Iowa, and died 29 Sep 1945 in Boise, Idaho. She married ERNEST W. HEATH 01 Jan 1914 in Ada County, Idaho, son of SETH HEATH and MARY JOLLEY. He was born 26 May 1869 in Paola, Kansas, and died 20 Nov 1932 in Boise, Ada County, Idaho.

Child of CORA MILKS and ERNEST HEATH is:
       i. HAROLD[9] HEATH, b. 17 Oct 1914, Boise, Ada County, Idaho; d. 14 Sep 1934, Nampa, Canyon County, ID.

628. ELENORE 'ELLA' MARY[8] MILKS *(HUMPHREY W.[7], JOB[6] MILK, LEMUEL[5], JONATHAN[4], JOB[3], JOHN[2], JOHN[1])* was born May 1876 in Atlantic, Cass County, Iowa. She married (1) OTTO ZEHRENDT Abt. 1894. He was born 1863 in Germany. She married (2) MISTRE THAYER Abt. 1897. He was born Abt. 1875. She married (3) ALBERT RUFUS BIXBY 22 May 1906 in Ellsworth, Wisconsin, son of SAMUEL BIXBY and SABRINA TOZER. He was born in Stanton, St. Croix County, Wisconsin.

Child of ELENORE MILKS and OTTO ZEHRENDT is:
       i. BERTHA H.[9] ZEHRENDT, b. 06 Jul 1895, Elma, Howard County, Iowa. Bertha was in the Holy Angels Academy in Minneapolis, Hennepin County, Minnesota in 1910.

629. HUMPHREY[8] MILKS *(HUMPHREY W.[7], JOB[6] MILK, LEMUEL[5], JONATHAN[4], JOB[3], JOHN[2], JOHN[1])* was born 13 Aug 1879 in Cass County, Iowa. He married MARGARET 'MADGE' REED 1898 in Desoto, Wisconsin, daughter of FATHER and MOTHER. She was born 1879 in Iowa, and died 1939. Burial: Saint Gabriel Cemetery, Prairie du Chine, Crawford County, Wisconsin

Child of HUMPHREY MILKS and MARGARET REED is:
> i. ALLEN ARTHA[9] MILKS, b. 27 Oct 1901, Waukon Corp, Allamakee County, Iowa; d. Mar 1969, Elkader, Clayton County, Iowa; m. ONA J. SEBASTIAN, Abt. 1935; b. Abt. 1916, Wisconsin.

630. GEORGE THEODORE[8] MILCKS *(HUMPHREY W.[7] MILKS, JOB[6] MILK, LEMUEL[5], JONATHAN[4], JOB[3], JOHN[2], JOHN[1])* was born 24 Dec 1882 in Pottawattamie County, Iowa. He married (1) CLARA BRAKKE Abt. 1900. She was born 07 May 1883 in St. James, Minnesota, and died Feb 1979 in Quincy, Adams County, Illinois. He married (2) MABEL C. SMITH Bef. 1930, daughter of WILLIAM SMITH and LOUISA GATTS. She was born Abt. 1899 in Iowa.

George is shown, in the 1920 census (and later censuses) living with Mabel C., even though his first wife Clara had a child, Loraine, in 1926. Curious.

Illinois, Cook County Marriages, 1871-1920
Mrs. Clara Milcks marriage: 28 October 1920 Chicago, Cook, Illinois, spouse: Charles J. Miller

In spite of this marriage record for Clara, her daughter Lorraine, b: 1926, still carried the Milcks surname in the 1940 Census.

Waukon Democrat, December 22, 1943

Leap from R.R. Bridge Results in Death of Two Horses - Two horses belonging to Ed DONAHUE and Leo WARD, farmers residing between Waukon Junction and Waterville, received injuries last week when they jumped from the bridge on the Milwaukee branch road that spans Paint Creek four miles north of the Junction. The morning train from Marquette to Waukon was approaching the bridge when Engineer George MILCKS saw two horses standing on the trestle, their feet caught between the ties. He stopped the train and Brakeman Ambrose O'NIELL went to the nearest farm home to telephone the section boss for help in removing the trapped animals.

Before he returned the Ward horse loosened it's feet and jumped to the bank of the creek 15 feet below, breaking its neck. The other animal also jumped, picked itself up from the bank after a few moments and was seen to walk off down the pasture to the DONAHUE farm a half mile away, but dropped dead an hour later.

Children of GEORGE MILCKS and CLARA BRAKKE are:
> i. ALICE C.[9] MILCKS, b. 26 Apr 1904, Iowa; d. 20 Jan 1940, Melrose Park, Cook County, Illinois; m. FRED FESTNER; b. Abt. 1902, Illinois. Alice is buried in Woodlawn Cemetery, Forest Park, Cook County, Illinois

1298. ii. CLARENCE A. MILCKS, b. 02 Mar 1906, Minnesota; d. 28 Sep 1936, Berwyn, Cook County, Illinois.

1299. iii. DELBERT CHARLES MILCKS, b. 28 Mar 1908, N. McGregor, Clayton County, Iowa; d. 06 Jan 1989, Hayward, Alameda County, California.

> iv. GRACE VICTORIA MILCKS, b. 03 Jul 1910, N. McGregor, Clayton County, Iowa. Grace is shown as a servant in the household of Joseph D. Solon, in Maywood, Cook County, Illinois, in the 1930 census.

1300. v. LORRAINE HARRIET MILCKS, b. 28 Mar 1926, Cook County, Illinois.

631. ANNA H.[8] MILKS *(JAMES HARTMAN[7], JOB[6] MILK, LEMUEL[5], JONATHAN[4], JOB[3], JOHN[2], JOHN[1])* was born 28 Jul 1884 in New Albin, Allamakee County, Iowa, and died 1946 in Huron, South Dakota. She married JOSEPH UTTER 1911. He was born Abt. 1885 in South Dakota.

Children of ANNA MILKS and JOSEPH UTTER are:
1301. i. KATHERINE[9] UTTER, b. 07 Jul 1912, Iroquois, South Dakota.
> ii. JOHN UTTER, b. Abt. 1914.
> iii. JAMES AMOS UTTER, b. 23 Dec 1916, South Dakota; d. 20 Nov 1980, Los Angeles, California.
> iv. MABEL E. UTTER, b. 15 Dec 1918, South Dakota; d. 09 May 1962, Los Angeles, California; m. CLIFFORD TILBURY; b. Abt. 1918.

632. FRANK[8] MILKS *(JAMES HARTMAN[7], JOB[6] MILK, LEMUEL[5], JONATHAN[4], JOB[3], JOHN[2], JOHN[1])* was born 07 Mar 1887 in New Albin, Iowa. He married RUTH "BESSIE" TARR 14 Aug 1909 in Bowman, North Dakota, daughter of WILLIAM TARR and ALICE _____. She was born 28 Feb 1892 in Clinton, Iowa.

Children of FRANK MILKS and RUTH TARR are:
> i. HAZEL IRENE[9] MILKS, b. 07 Nov 1910, Scranton, North Dakota; d. 25 Mar 2001, Newberg, Oregon (Bowman County, ND?); m. KENNETH TAYLOR GOE; b. 14 Feb 1917; d. 04 Oct 1992, Newberg, Yamhill, Oregon.

1302. ii. FLORENCE 'FLOSSIE' LUCILLE MILKS, b. 27 Dec 1911, Scranton, North Dakota; d. 03 Dec 1988, Yamhill

		County, Oregon.
1303.	iii.	JAMES WILLIAM MILKS, b. 02 Feb 1913, Haley, North Dakota; d. 14 Oct 2005, McMinnville, Yamhill County, Oregon.
1304.	iv.	ATOLA OLIVE 'DONNA' MILKS, b. 03 Dec 1914, Scranton, North Dakota; d. 16 May 2005, Austin, Mower County, Minnesota.
1305.	v.	MARGARET NEOMA MILKS, b. 08 Mar 1916, Scranton, North Dakota; d. 19 Mar 1997, Las Vegas, Nevada.
	vi.	MILDRED KATHRYN MILKS, b. 04 Feb 1918, Scranton, North Dakota; d. 11 Dec 2006, Portland, Multnomah, OR; m. (1) UNKNOWN JOHNSON; m. (2) MISTTER KINDLE.
	vii.	CLIFFORD DALLAS MILKS, b. 29 Nov 1919, Scranton, North Dakota; d. 19 Jun 1987, Portland, Multnomah County, Oregon; m. OPAL L. _____; b. 17 Apr 1924, Kansas; d. 21 Mar 2006, Portland, Multnomah County, Oregon.
	viii.	CLAYTON MILKS, b. 25 Aug 1921, Scranton, North Dakota; d. 10 Jul 1987, Brookings, Curry County, Oregon; m. (1) NATALIE _____; b. Abt. 1926; d. 1997; m. (2) MABEL C. GRIMSTAD, 15 Jun 1946, Mower County, Minnesota; b. Abt. 1921. Clayton was a PFC US ARMY, Plot: W 649, and is buried in Willamette National Cemetery, Multnomah County, Oregon
	ix.	GLADYS RUTH MILKS, b. 09 Apr 1923, Scranton, North Dakota; m. RAY R. BESCO, 28 May 1949, Mower County, Minnesota; b. 31 May 1925, Gravity, Iowa; d. 10 Jun 1997, Austin, Mower County, Minnesota.
	x.	JOHNIE CHESTER MILKS, b. 27 Apr 1925, Scranton, North Dakota; d. 06 Dec 1944, Leyte Island (WWII).
1306.	xi.	DONALD LESTER MILKS, SR., b. 11 Jun 1930, Scranton, North Dakota; d. 26 Sep 1972, Mower County, Minnesota.
1307.	xii.	DUANE LEROY MILKS, b. 23 Mar 1933, Scranton, North Dakota; d. 10 Dec 2007, Union Gap, Washington.

633. ALEX[8] MILKS-COX *(JAMES HARTMAN[7] MILKS, JOB[6] MILK, LEMUEL[5], JONATHAN[4], JOB[3], JOHN[2], JOHN[1])* was born 16 Sep 1888 in New Albin, Allamakee County, Iowa. He married AGNES DUFFY. She was born Abt. 1890.

Child of ALEX MILKS-COX and AGNES DUFFY is:
    i. MARION[9] MILKS-COX.

634. ANDREW HARTMAN[8] MILKS *(JAMES HARTMAN[7], JOB[6] MILK, LEMUEL[5], JONATHAN[4], JOB[3], JOHN[2], JOHN[1])* was born 16 Dec 1889 in DeSmet, South Dakota, and died 1966 in Dubuque County, Iowa. He married MARY MULLIGAN, daughter of PATRICK MULLIGAN and ELIZABETH MCGIFFNEY. She was born 11 Jan 1892 in Dubuque, Iowa.

Children of ANDREW MILKS and MARY MULLIGAN are:

	i.	PATRICIA ELIZABETH[9] MILKS, b. 20 Dec 1921, Dubuque, Iowa.
1308.	ii.	MARY KATHLEEN MILKS, b. 03 Jul 1923, Dubuque, Iowa.
	iii.	ZITA ROSE MILKS, b. 11 Jan 1929, Dubuque, Iowa.
1309.	iv.	WILLIAM PATRICK MILKS, b. 17 Mar 1932, Dubuque, Iowa; d. 13 Mar 1996, Merriam, Kansas.
1310.	v.	JOHN JOSEPH MILKS, b. 19 Jan 1934, Dubuque, Iowa.

635. WILLIAM JOB[8] MILKS *(JAMES HARTMAN[7], JOB[6] MILK, LEMUEL[5], JONATHAN[4], JOB[3], JOHN[2], JOHN[1])* was born 04 Oct 1892 in Manchester, Kingsbury County, So. Dakota, and died 07 Jan 1968 in Los Angeles, California. He married EMMA FONDA 29 May 1914, daughter of MISTTER FONDA and MS BARTLESON. She was born 01 Mar 1896 in South Dakota, and died 24 Aug 1980 in Long Beach, Los Angeles, California.

Children of WILLIAM MILKS and EMMA FONDA are:

1311.	i.	JOHN DALLAS[9] MILKS, b. 20 Dec 1915, Kingsbury, So. Dakota; d. 03 Sep 1966, San Francisco, California.
	ii.	NELSON LORENZO MILKS, b. 09 Jan 1917, Kingsbury, So. Dakota; d. Abt. 1927, Kingsbury County, South Dakota.
1312.	iii.	MARY ELIZABETH MILKS, b. 01 Mar 1918, Kingsbury, So. Dakota.
1313.	iv.	RICHARD JEROME MILKS, b. 12 Jul 1920, Kingsbury, So. Dakota.
1314.	v.	DOROTHY MAXINE MILKS, b. 21 Aug 1922, Kingsbury, So. Dakota.
	vi.	THERESSA MILKS, b. 01 Mar 1930, Kingsbury, So. Dakota (twin); d. Bef. 1956.
	vii.	PATHRESA MILKS, b. 01 Mar 1930, Kingsbury, So. Dakota (twin); d. Bef. 1956.
1315.	viii.	BEVERLY ROSE THERESE MILKS, b. 05 Nov 1932.

636. GILBERT DOUGLAS[8] SIDWAY *(GEORGE[7], WILLIAM[6], REBECCA[5] MILK, JONATHAN[4], JOB[3], JOHN[2], JOHN[1])* He married MARY CAROLINE CRANS.

Child of GILBERT SIDWAY and MARY CRANS is:
  i. ERNESTINE ALBERTI[9] SIDWAY.

637. WILLIAM HENRY[8] SIDWAY *(JONATHAN[7], JONATHAN[6], REBECCA[5] MILK, JONATHAN[4], JOB[3], JOHN[2], JOHN[1])* was born 07 Mar 1860 in Buffalo, Erie County, New York. He married IDA ADELE LITTLEFIELD 1885 in Buffalo, Erie County, New York ?, daughter of JOHN LITTLEFIELD and ROSELL JOHNSON. She was born 24 Sep 1860 in Buffalo, Erie County, New York.

Children of WILLIAM SIDWAY and IDA LITTLEFIELD are:
  i. EDNA[9] SIDWAY, b. 02 Apr 1884, Montclair Heights, NJ.
  ii. CHESTER EUGENE SIDWAY, b. 04 Sep 1886, New York City; m. GRACE _____; b. 28 Aug 1897, Oyster Bay, Nassau County, New York; d. May 1976, Oyster Bay, Nassau County, New York. No children.
1316. iii. KENNETH L. SIDWAY, b. 09 Sep 1891, Batavia, New York.
1317. iv. DOROTHY SIDWAY, b. Oct 1896, New York City.
  v. GERTRUDE SIDWAY, b. Dec 1898, New York City.

638. KATE BALDWIN[8] SIDWAY *(JONATHAN[7], JONATHAN[6], REBECCA[5] MILK, JONATHAN[4], JOB[3], JOHN[2], JOHN[1])* was born 24 Apr 1861 in Buffalo, Erie County, New York, and died Aft. 26 Apr 1929. She married EDWIN HASTINGS MULFORD 16 Sep 1884 in Grace Episcopal Church, Buffalo, Erie County, New York. He was born 05 Nov 1855 in Montour Falls, New York, and died Aft. 26 Apr 1929.

Children of KATE SIDWAY and EDWIN MULFORD are:
  i. GERTRUDE[9] MULFORD, b. Jan 1889, New York.
  ii. ELMER S. MULFORD, b. Nov 1890, New York.

639. HAROLD SPAULDING[8] SIDWAY *(FRANKLIN[7], JONATHAN[6], REBECCA[5] MILK, JONATHAN[4], JOB[3], JOHN[2], JOHN[1])* was born 26 Apr 1868 in Buffalo, Erie County, New York. He married (1) MARY SARGENT CHASE 20 Dec 1897 in London, England. She was born Aug 1872 in Syracuse, New York. He married (2) MAUD LOVE Bef. Dec 1922, daughter of DWIGHT WHEELER LOVE. She was born 15 Feb 1878 in New York, and died 1934 in Whitney Point, Broome County, New York.

Children of HAROLD SIDWAY and MARY CHASE are:
1318. i. JAMES[9] SIDWAY, b. 29 Dec 1898, Pittsfield, Berkshire County, Massachusetts.
1319. ii. FRANKLIN SIDWAY, b. 23 May 1900, Pittsfield, Berkshire County, Massachusetts.

640. FRANK ST. JOHN[8] SIDWAY *(FRANKLIN[7], JONATHAN[6], REBECCA[5] MILK, JONATHAN[4], JOB[3], JOHN[2], JOHN[1])* was born 05 Dec 1869 in Buffalo, Erie County, New York, and died 17 Jan 1938 in Buffalo, Erie County, New York. He married AMELIA MINIRVA ROBERTS 16 Apr 1903, daughter of JAMES ROBERTS and MINIRVA PINEO. She was born 04 Dec 1881, and died 06 Jan 1972 in Buffalo, Erie County, New York.

Children of FRANK SIDWAY and AMELIA ROBERTS are:
  i. ARTHUR ROBERTS[9] SIDWAY, b. 18 Feb 1904, Buffalo, Erie County, New York; d. 05 Apr 1905, Buffalo, Erie County, New York.
  ii. CHARLOTTE SIDWAY, b. 02 Mar 1905, Buffalo, Erie County, New York; d. 26 Jun 1905, Buffalo, Erie County, New York.
1320. iii. MARGARET ST. JOHN SIDWAY, b. 16 May 1907, Buffalo, Erie County, New York.
1321. iv. MARTHA ROBERTS SIDWAY, b. 01 Oct 1908, Buffalo, Erie County, New York; d. 24 Feb 1999, Buffalo, Erie County, New York.
1322. v. EDITH SIDWAY, b. 22 Feb 1913, Buffalo, Erie County, New York.

641. EDITH[8] SIDWAY (*FRANKLIN[7], JONATHAN[6], REBECCA[5] MILK, JONATHAN[4], JOB[3], JOHN[2], JOHN[1]*) was born 12 Jan 1872 in Buffalo, Erie County, New York. She married WILLIAM ALLAN GARDNER 26 Apr 1892. He was born 18 Mar 1869 in Buffalo, Erie County, New York.

Children of EDITH SIDWAY and WILLIAM GARDNER are:
- i. WILLIAM HAMILTON[9] GARDNER.
- ii. NANCY STRONG GARDNER.

642. CLARENCE SPAULDING[8] SIDWAY (*FRANKLIN[7], JONATHAN[6], REBECCA[5] MILK, JONATHAN[4], JOB[3], JOHN[2], JOHN[1]*) was born 12 Feb 1877 in Buffalo, Erie County, New York, and died Bet. 1941 - 1956. He married (1) GENEVIEVE CLARK HINGSTON 16 Oct 1901. She was born Abt. 1880, and died 20 Oct 1939. He married (2) CLARA MARIE COLLINS 30 May 1941. She was born Abt. 1880, and died Aft. 1956.

Children of CLARENCE SIDWAY and GENEVIEVE HINGSTON are:
- i. ELBRIDGE SPAULDING[9] SIDWAY, b. 22 Sep 1903; d. Abt. 26 Mar 1972, Pinehurst, Moore County, North Carolina; m. MABEL COLEMAN.
- ii. CHARLOTTE MARY SIDWAY, b. 21 Mar 1906.

643. RALPH HUNTINGTON[8] SIDWAY (*FRANKLIN[7], JONATHAN[6], REBECCA[5] MILK, JONATHAN[4], JOB[3], JOHN[2], JOHN[1]*) was born 15 Dec 1884 in Buffalo, Erie County, New York, and died 12 Dec 1936 in Buffalo, Erie County, New York. He married STEPHANA OSTRUM BARNUM 16 Sep 1908 in Buffalo, Erie County, New York , daughter of THEODORE BARNUM and SARAH AVERY. She was born 23 Apr 1882 in Buffalo, Erie County, New York, and died Aft. 1956.

Child of RALPH SIDWAY and STEPHANA BARNUM is:
- i. RALPH HUNT[9] SIDWAY, JR., b. 11 Aug 1913, Buffalo, Erie County, New York; d. 11 May 1977, Shelby, Kentucky; m. (1) AVIS _____, Abt. 1935; b. 01 Jun 1915, Beverly, Massachusetts; m. (2) MARION _____, Aft. 1935; b. Abt. 1915.

644. WILLIAM ALONZO[8] MILKS (*CHARLES[7], DAVID[6] MILK, GEORGE[5], JONATHAN[4], JOB[3], JOHN[2], JOHN[1]*) was born Feb 1845 in New York, and died 1905 in Hamburg, NY??. He married MARY SCHAMBERS 1874 in New York. She was born May 1855 in New York, and died 1911 in Hamburg, NY??.

Children of WILLIAM MILKS and MARY SCHAMBERS are:
- 1323. i. WILLIAM EDWARD[9] MILKS, b. 10 Aug 1874, East Eden, Erie County, New York; d. 29 May 1950, Buffalo, Erie County, New York.
- 1324. ii. CHARLES ALBERT MILKS, b. 20 Oct 1875, East Eden, Erie County, New York; d. 13 Mar 1943, Buffalo, Erie County, New York.
- 1325. iii. EMMA MILKS, b. 1877, East Eden, NY; d. 1916.
- 1326. iv. JULIA M. MILKS, b. Aug 1880, East Eden, NY; d. 1920, Buffalo, Erie County, New York.
- 1327. v. GEORGE J. MILKS, b. 13 Mar 1882, East Eden, New York; d. 1960, Erie County, New York.
- vi. HARRY MILKS, b. Oct 1884, East Eden, NY; d. 1902, New York.
- vii. GILBERT FREEMAN MILKS, b. 18 Sep 1888, East Eden, Erie County, New York; d. 10 Nov 1955, Seattle, King County, Washington (unmarried). Gilbert's WWI Draft Reg. Card says that he was married. He lived at 916 Third Ave, Seattle, Wash.
- 1328. viii. EDGAR H. MILKS, b. 19 Feb 1889, East Eden, NY; d. Jun 1973.
- ix. CLARENCE F. MILKS, b. 21 Apr 1891, East Eden, NY; d. 17 Dec 1925, Hamburg, Erie County, New York; m. JESSIE ANDREWS, 31 Oct 1915, New York; b. 1891, New York; d. 17 Oct 1925, Hamburg, Erie County, New York (no children). Clarence is shown as a grocer in Hamburg, NY, in both the 1920 and 1925 censuses. Perhaps he was in business with his brother Edgar.

645. HARRIET LOUISE[8] MILKS (*CHARLES[7], DAVID[6] MILK, GEORGE[5], JONATHAN[4], JOB[3], JOHN[2], JOHN[1]*) was born 1848 in New York (Mar 1851). She married JAMES BULL, son of JOHN BULL and HANNAH MASDEN. He was born 1851 in Freehold, Warren County, Pennsylvania, and died 20 Jul 1927 in Dunkirk, Chautauqua County, New York.

Children of HARRIET MILKS and JAMES BULL are:
- i. CHARLES[9] BULL, b. Jan 1877, New York.
- ii. ETTA BULL, b. 1878, New York.
- 1329. iii. ARCHIE JOHN BULL, b. 05 May 1884, New York; d. 23 Sep 1961.
- iv. MERTAL BULL, b. Feb 1892, New York.

646. TERESSA L.[8] MILKS *(CHARLES[7], DAVID[6] MILK, GEORGE[5], JONATHAN[4], JOB[3], JOHN[2], JOHN[1])* was born 1852, and died Abt. Jul 1880. She married JOSEPH THOMAS. He was born Jun 1842 in New York.

Children of TERESSA MILKS and JOSEPH THOMAS are:
- i. MINNIE THERESSA[9] THOMAS, b. Abt. 1875; d. unmarried.
- 1330. ii. GERTRUDE THOMAS, b. 29 Sep 1876, Gowanda, Cattaraugus County, New York; d. 07 Mar 1955, Tionesta, Forest County, Pennsylvania.
- iii. MABEL THERESSA THOMAS, b. 25 Jul 1880, Cattaraugus County, New York; d. 09 May 1952, San Mateo, California.

647. DENCY M.[8] MILKS *(CHARLES[7], DAVID[6] MILK, GEORGE[5], JONATHAN[4], JOB[3], JOHN[2], JOHN[1])* was born 06 May 1854. She married OEL BAILEY. He was born Abt. 1854.

Children of DENCY MILKS and OEL BAILEY are:
- 1331. i. HERMAN[9] BAILEY, b. 26 Aug 1883, Cattaraugus County, New York.
- ii. BERTHA BAILEY, b. 07 Nov 1890, Cattaraugus County, New York.
- iii. LEE BAILEY, b. 21 Jan 1894, Cattaraugus County, New York.

648. CHARLES "NEWMAN"[8] MILKS *(CHARLES[7], DAVID[6] MILK, GEORGE[5], JONATHAN[4], JOB[3], JOHN[2], JOHN[1])* was born May 1856 in Cattaraugus County, New York. He married ALICE LOVELLA CRANDALL, daughter of WILLIAM CRANDALL and LEAFY HILL. She was born 09 Dec 1860 in Persia, Cattaraugus County, New York, and died 28 Jul 1925 in South Dayton, Cattaraugus County, New York.

Children of CHARLES MILKS and ALICE CRANDALL are:
- 1332. i. ETHEL[9] MILKS, b. 13 Feb 1882, Dayton, Cattaraugus County, New York; d. Bet. 1920 - 1930.
- ii. CHESTER CHARLES MILKS, b. 26 Nov 1889, Dayton, Cattaraugus County, New York; d. 31 Oct 1918, World War I casualty; m. JEANETTE H. BERG BIELAWSKI, Questionable marriage. see Chester's notes.; b. 01 Aug 1889, Buffalo, New York; d. Jul 1978, Buffalo, New York (no children).
    Chester lists himself as 'Single' on 5 June 1917 on his WWI draft registration card. also shown as single living with his parents in the 1910 census. NY Pvt Btry B 27th FA, Died Pneumonia.
- 1333. iii. LETTIE M. MILKS, b. 11 Nov 1891, Persia, Cattaraugus County, New York.

649. SARAH SOPHRONIA[8] MILKS *(CHARLES[7], DAVID[6] MILK, GEORGE[5], JONATHAN[4], JOB[3], JOHN[2], JOHN[1])* was born 1858. She married MENZO EDMUNDS. He was born Abt. 1858, and died in of Collins, NY.

Child of SARAH MILKS and MENZO EDMUNDS is:
- i. CORA[9] EDMUNDS.

650. MARY J.[8] MILKS *(CHARLES[7], DAVID[6] MILK, GEORGE[5], JONATHAN[4], JOB[3], JOHN[2], JOHN[1])* was born 1860 in New York. She married GEORGE CROUSE. He was born Abt. 1860 in Germany.

Children of MARY MILKS and GEORGE CROUSE are:
- 1334. i. JOHN CHARLES[9] CROUSE, b. 08 Dec 1882, Cattaraugus County, New York.
- 1335. ii. RAYMOND CROUSE, b. 15 Apr 1882, Cattaraugus County, New York; d. 02 Oct 1948.

651. DAVID W.[8] MILKS *(ALEXANDER B.[7] MILK, DAVID[6], GEORGE[5], JONATHAN[4], JOB[3], JOHN[2], JOHN[1])* was born Mar 1848 in Persia, Cattaraugus County, New York, and died 27 Oct 1931 in Salamanca, Cattaraugus County, New York. He married (1) UNKNOWN. She was born Abt. 1850. He married (2) JEANETTE AUGUSTA "NETTIE" MEACHAM Abt. 1877, daughter of DANIEL MEACHAM and EMILY BOWEN. She was born Sep 1856 in New York, and died 16 May 1916 in

Killbuck, New York. He married (3) ALICE M. WHITTAKER 26 Oct 1917 in Great Valley, Cattaraugus County, New York, daughter of DANIEL WHITTAKER and JULIA MEIGS. She was born Bet. 1850 - 1851 in Delaware County, New York. He married (4) HARRIET J. 'HATTIE' ROSS 19 Oct 1925 in Cattaraugus County, New York, daughter of ALFRED ROSS and MINERVA HENDERSON. She was born 1857 in Venango County, Pennsylvania, and died Aft. 1931.

OBITUARY - Salamanca Press Oct 28, 1931

" David Milks, 83, dies; was ill eight weeks. David Milks, 83 years old , died Tuesday evening at 9:30 , at his home at 419 Center St. after having been ill the past eight weeks.

He was born in Persia, New York , and had lived in this vicinity , nearly his entire life.

Besides his widow Mrs. Hattie Milks, he is survived by five daughters, Mrs. Harry Williams of Great Valley, Mrs. Albert Winsor of Center St., Mrs. George Webster of Great Valley, Mrs. Charles Chapman of Franklinville and Mrs. Leo Terhune of Center St.; by three brothers, Robert milks of Rochester, Michigan, and care milks of Great Valley and Frank milks of East Otto; by 26 grandchildren, 25 great-grandchildren , and several nieces and nephews.

The funeral will be held from the family home at 419 Center St., Saturday afternoon at 1:45, and from the UB church of West Salamanca at two o'clock. Rev. H. S. Kissinger , will officiate.

Burial level be in the family plot and Chamberlain Cemetery, Great Valley."

OBITUARY - Salamanca Press Nov 2, 1931

"Funeral of David Milks. The funeral of David Milks was held from the family home at 419 Center St. Saturday afternoon at 1:45 o'clock and from the West Salamanca UB church at two o'clock. Several local selections were given by Mrs. Fred Rettburg, accompanied by Mrs. Dan Sweet. Rev. H. S. Kissinger officiated. Internment was made in the family plot and Chamberlain Cemetery, Great Valley.

The bearers were David Christian, Walter Chapman, Carol Webster, William Terhune, Lagerne Winsor and Harry Winsor. Out of town relatives and friends attending were Mr. and Mrs. Charles Chapman of Franklinville, Mr. and Mrs. Hiram Clark, Mr. and Mrs. George Webster, Mr. and Mrs. Harry Williams and Mr. and Mrs. Edgar Milks and family of Great Valley, Mr. and Mrs. Harold Creeley and Mr. and Mrs. Lagerne Winsor of Olean, Mr. and Mrs. Lloyd Edison and Mr. and Mrs. Frank Milks of Bradford, PA, Mr. and Mrs. Charles Shaw and family of Coudersport, PA, Mr. and Mrs. Edison Marble of Buffalo, Mr. and Mrs. John Metcalf , and Mr. and Mrs. Ernest Haas of Ashtabula, Ohio."

OBITUARY - Ellicottville Post - May 10, 1916

" Mrs. Augusta Milks. Mrs. Augusta Milks, wife of David Milks of Killbuck died at the family home Monday noon following a prolonged illness, at the age of 59 years.

She was born at Mansfield and practically her entire life was spent in this part of Cattaraugus County, the last three years having lived at Killbuck and for five years previous at Ellicottville.

She is survived by her husband, five daughters, Mrs. Gertrude Williams of Great Valley, Mrs. Jenny Winsor of Delevan, Mrs. George Webster of Franklinville, Mrs. Helen Chapman of Franklinville, Mrs. Georgia Terhune of Salamanca, one stepdaughter, Mrs. Chloe Christian of Expedit, PA., two sons, Glenn Milks and Hastings Milks at home; four sisters, Mrs. Chandler Chamberlain, Machias, Mrs. May Leyman, West Valley, Mrs. Frank Chamberlain, Little Valley, and Mrs. Peter Williams , Springville, and one brother Lewis Meacham of Machias.

A prayer service will be held from the family home at Killbuck Thursday morning at 10:30 after which the funeral party will go to the UB church at Great Valley where the funeral will be held at one o'clock, Rev. Baker officiating.

The Ladies of the Maccabees of Great Valley Tent will attend in a body after which internment will be made in the family plot of Chamberlain Cemetery nearby."

Child of DAVID MILKS and UNKNOWN is:

1336.   i.   CHLOE B.[9] MILKS, b. Jun 1872, Mansfield, NY; d. 22 Dec 1925.

Children of DAVID MILKS and JEANETTE MEACHAM are:

1337.   ii.   GERTRUDE P.[9] MILKS, b. 09 Jun 1879, Mansfield, Cattaraugus County, New York; d. 28 Jan 1962, Great Valley, Cattaraugus County, New York.

1338.   iii.   JENNIE MILKS, b. 06 Dec 1880, Great Valley, Cattaraugus County, New York; d. 18 Feb 1969, New York.

1339.   iv.   LOLA A. MILKS, b. 1882, Great Valley, Cattaraugus County, New York; d. Apr 1963, Cattaraugus County, New York.

1340.   v.   HELEN ELIZABETH MILKS, b. 18 Jul 1885, Great Valley, Cattaraugus County, New York; d. 17 Apr 1978, Olean, Cattaraugus County, New York.

1341.   vi.   GEORGIA AMERICA MILKS, b. 03 Jun 1893, Great Valley, Cattaraugus County, New York; d. 08 Feb 1978,

Salamanca, Cattaraugus County, New York.
- vii. GLENN DAVID MILKS, b. 22 Sep 1895, Mansfield, NY; d. 16 Oct 1918, World War I casualty, Killed in Action..
  Fought and died in Europe during World War One. Company K, 325th Regiment, 82nd Division.
- 1342. viii. CHARLES HASTINGS MILKS, b. 29 Oct 1897, Great Valley, Cattaraugus County, New York; d. 08 Apr 1921.

652. GEORGE PRINCE[8] MILKS *(ALEXANDER B.[7] MILK, DAVID[6], GEORGE[5], JONATHAN[4], JOB[3], JOHN[2], JOHN[1])* was born 15 Jul 1850 in Mansfield, Cattaraugus County, New York, and died 27 Jun 1917 in Cattaraugus County, New York. He married MARY A. HICKS. She was born 1853 in New York, and died 1918 in Cattaraugus County, New York.

Child of GEORGE MILKS and MARY HICKS is:
- 1343. i. GORDON JOSEPH[9] MILKS, b. 08 Jan 1898, Salamanca, NY; d. 23 Feb 1989, Asheboro, Randolph County, North Carolina.

653. ROBERT S.[8] MILK *(ALEXANDER B.[7], DAVID[6], GEORGE[5], JONATHAN[4], JOB[3], JOHN[2], JOHN[1])* was born 07 Apr 1852 in Mansfield, NY, and died 07 Jan 1937 in Great Valley, Cattaraugus County, NY. He married (1) ORDELIA EVA CALKINS Abt. 1874. She was born Jun 1857 in New York, and died Abt. 1903 in Cattaraugus County, New York. He married (2) EDITH SIMMONDS Bet. 1885 - 1886 in Cattaraugus County, New York. She was born Abt. 1855 in Olean, Cattaraugus Co., NY, and died 02 Feb 1929 in Great Valley, Cattaraugus County, NY.

After Robert Milks and Ordelia divorced, Merritt, Burt, and Edward lived with their mother and her new husband, Lambert Corthell.

Children of ROBERT MILK and ORDELIA CALKINS are:
- i. MERRITT WELLINGTON[9] MILKS, b. 24 Sep 1875, New York; d. Aft. 1942, (No children); m. ELLA MAY HOWES, Bet. 1900 - 1901, Oswego County, New York; b. 1874, New York; d. 21 Nov 1952.
- 1344. ii. BURTON HENRY MILKS, b. 30 Nov 1879, Great Valley, Chautauqua Co., NY; d. 16 May 1958, Riverside Hospital, Toledo, Ohio.
- iii. ALEXANDER EDWARD MILKS, b. Dec 1880, New York; d. 04 Jun 1933.

Children of ROBERT MILK and EDITH SIMMONDS are:
- 1345. iv. REV. RALPH P.[9] MILKS, b. 25 Mar 1889, East Leon, Cattaraugus County, New York; d. 06 Feb 1973, Flint, Genesee County, Michigan.
- v. IRA T. MILK, b. 1891; d. 1898, East Leon, Cattaraugus Co., NY.
- vi. FRANCIS M. MILKS, b. 05 May 1894, New York; d. 01 Jun 1967, Seattle, Washington (no children); m. CHARLOTTE SMITH, Aft. 1930; b. 07 Dec 1902, Gratiot County, Michigan; d. Nov 1970, Snohomish, Snohomish County, Washington.
- vii. ARTHUR R. MILKS, b. 05 Apr 1896, New York; d. 25 Jun 1958, Milwaukee, Wisconsin (unmarried).
  PVT BTRY B 6 FA, Plot: 37 15/16, bur. 06/30/1958 in Wood National Cemetery, Milwaukee County, Wisconsin
- 1346. viii. HOWARD A. MILKS, b. 19 Jul 1898, Leon, Cattaraugus County, New York; d. Jul 1970, Carsonville, Sanilac County, Michigan.
- 1347. ix. ALVAN L. MILKS, b. 10 Nov 1901, Leon, Cattaraugus County, NY; d. 29 May 1997, Gerry, Chautauqua, NY 14740.
- 1348. x. RUTH MILKS, b. 22 Dec 1903, Cattaraugus County, New York; d. 04 Aug 1997, Miami, Dade County, Florida.
- xi. GENEVA P. MILKS, b. 25 Apr 1906, Gladwin Co., Michigan; d. 28 Aug 1908, Bentley, Gladwin, Michigan.
- xii. MARY NAOMI MILKS, b. 30 Jun 1911, Gladwin Co., Michigan; d. 10 Jul 1911, Gladwin Co., Michigan.

654. ELIZABETH[8] MILK *(ALEXANDER B.[7], DAVID[6], GEORGE[5], JONATHAN[4], JOB[3], JOHN[2], JOHN[1])* was born 16 Aug 1853 in Mansfield, Cattaraugus County, NY, and died 24 Apr 1896 in Cattaraugus County, New York?. She married WARREN E. BROCKITT Abt. 1875, son of TUNIS BROCKITT and LUCINDA MEACHAM. He was born 24 Feb 1854 in New York, and died 16 Jun 1931 in Bradford, McKean County, Pennsylvania.

Children of ELIZABETH MILK and WARREN BROCKITT are:
- i. ARTHUR[9] BROCKITT, b. 04 Jul 1880, Cattaraugus County, New York; d. 23 Apr 1957; m. (1) LYDIA

		_____, Bet. 1904 - 1905; b. Abt. 1880, Pennsylvania; m. (2) MARIE _____, Aft. 1918; b. Abt. 1882.
1349.	ii.	MARY L. BROCKITT, b. May 1882, Cattaraugus County, New York; d. 1964.
1350.	iii.	JOSEPHINE BROCKITT, b. 18 Apr 1884, Cattaraugus County, New York; d. 23 Dec 1944.
1351.	iv.	NORMAN ALEXANDER BROCKITT, b. 01 Jan 1886, Orlando, Cattaraugus County, New York; d. 23 Sep 1949.
1352.	v.	WILLIAM BROCKITT, b. Jun 1887, Cattaraugus County, New York.

655. JOHN OSCAR[8] MILKS (ALEXANDER B.[7] MILK, DAVID[6], GEORGE[5], JONATHAN[4], JOB[3], JOHN[2], JOHN[1]) was born Aug 1858 in Mansfield, NY, and died 1922 in Pike, Wyoming County, New York. He married CECILIA J. PRATT, daughter of AMOS PRATT and JOHANNA PERKINS. She was born 09 Aug 1869, and died 23 Dec 1964 in Elba, Genesee County, New York.

OBITUARY
Cecilia Milks, age 95, died at the home of a daughter, Mrs. Ella Boudreau of Orchard Road, Elba. Widow of John O. Milks who died in 1922.
Born in Pike, daughter of the late Amos and Johanna Perkins Pratt.
Member of 1st Baptist Church.
Survived besides the daughter is another daughter, Mrs. George Morgan of Warsaw; 6 grandchildren; 10 great grandchildren.
Burial: Warsaw Cemetery, Warsaw, Wyoming County, New York

Children of JOHN MILKS and CECILIA PRATT are:

	i.	CLOVER B.[9] MILKS, b. Mar 1890, Pike, Wyoming County, New York; d. 1907, Pike, Wyoming County, NY.
	ii.	BABY MILKS, b. 1894, Pike, Wyoming County, New York; d. 1894, Pike, Wyoming County, New York.
	iii.	ELLA F. MILKS, b. Sep 1896, Pike, Wyoming County, New York; d. Lived Elba & Warsaw, NY (no children); m. OLIVER C. BOUDREAU; b. 1886, Massachusetts.
1353.	iv.	AGNES E. MILKS, b. 1902, Pike, Wyoming County, New York; d. Lived Warsaw, NY.

656. EDGAR[8] MILKS (ALEXANDER B.[7] MILK, DAVID[6], GEORGE[5], JONATHAN[4], JOB[3], JOHN[2], JOHN[1]) was born 19 Feb 1861 in Mansfield, NY, and died 04 May 1939 in New York. He married ETTA ANN SIMMONS. She was born 10 May 1871 in Great Valley, Cattaraugus County, New York, and died 10 Feb 1955 in New York.

Children of EDGAR MILKS and ETTA SIMMONS are:

	i.	BERTHA[9] MILKS, b. 1889, Mansfield, Cattaraugus County, New York; d. 1905, Mansfield, Cattaraugus County, New York.
	ii.	GRANT S. MILKS, b. 18 Apr 1892, Mansfield, Cattaraugus County, New York; d. 04 Apr 1978, De Ruyter, Madison, NY; m. FRANCES ELEANOR STODDARD, 19 May 1918, Madison, New York; b. 28 Mar 1892; d. 11 Mar 1991, De Ruyter, Madison County, NY (no children).
1354.	iii.	ETTA A. MILKS, b. Bet. 1898 - 1899, Great Valley, Cattaraugus County, New York; d. 03 Nov 1948, S. Dayton, NY.
	iv.	MARY ANNA MILKS, b. Bet. 1901 - 1902, Great Valley, Cattaraugus County, New York; m. WALLACE STRONG, 21 Oct 1920, Great Valley, Cattaraugus County, New York; b. 23 Aug 1901, Elton, New York; d. 03 Nov 1989, New York.
1355.	v.	FRANCES A. MILKS, b. 18 Mar 1912, Great Valley, Cattaraugus County, New York; d. 15 Dec 1993, Cattaraugus County, New York.

657. DAISEY[8] MILKS (ALEXANDER B.[7] MILK, DAVID[6], GEORGE[5], JONATHAN[4], JOB[3], JOHN[2], JOHN[1]) was born Sep 1887 in Mansfield, Cattaraugus County, New York. She married UNKNOWN SMITH.

Children of DAISEY MILKS and UNKNOWN SMITH are:

	i.	JOHN[9] SMITH.
	ii.	ELLEN M. SMITH, m. UNKNOWN BRIDENBAKER.

658. MANLEY H.[8] MILKS (DAVID W.[7], DAVID[6] MILK, GEORGE[5], JONATHAN[4], JOB[3], JOHN[2], JOHN[1]) was born Abt. 1857 in Cattaraugus County, New York, and died Bef. 17 Sep 1913. He married (1) MARY PETERS Abt. 1876. She was born Abt.

1860. He married (2) ROSIE B. L. WOLFE Bet. 1888 - 1889, daughter of MORTOMAN WOLFE and ELIZABETH WOOD. She was born Bet. 1863 - 1864 in Illinois.

Rosie may have been married before her marriage to Manley. The marriage license for her son, George A. Milks says her maiden name was Rose Benton.

Children of MANLEY MILKS and MARY PETERS are:

1356. i. MYRTLE B.^{9} MILKS, b. 24 Oct 1877, Salamanca, Cattaraugus County, New York; d. 1954, Norway, Herkimer County, New York.

1357. ii. JUDSON DAVID MILKS, b. 24 Mar 1879, Salamanca, Cattaraugus County, New York; d. 22 Sep 1931, Truxton, Cortland County, New York.

iii. LETTIE L. MILKS, b. 24 Oct 1880; d. No children; m. JOSEPH B. 'JOE' MAPES, 1902, Cattaraugus County, New York?; b. 12 Dec 1872, New York.

Grace Croft wrote that George A. Milks was a son of Lettie Milks, but no data has been found that supports this statement. On George's marriage certificate, he lists his parents as Manley H. and Rosie B. Milks, and he is shown as their son in the 1900 census and the 1910 census

1358. iv. LESLIE B. MILKS, b. 17 Dec 1884, Salamanca, Cattaraugus Co, NY; d. 18 Feb 1965, Randolph, Cattaraugus Co, NY.

Child of MANLEY MILKS and ROSIE WOLFE is:

1359. v. GEORGE ALFRED^9 MILKS, b. 18 Feb 1895, Salamanca, Cattaraugus County, New York; d. 03 Sep 1956, Cattaraugus County, New York.

659. EVA^8 MILKS *(DAVID W.^{7}, DAVID^6 MILK, GEORGE^5, JONATHAN^4, JOB^3, JOHN^2, JOHN^1)* was born Oct 1859 in Cattaraugus County, New York. She married GEORGE B. ROOD Bet. Jun - Jul 1888 in New York, son of GREELEY ROOD and ANN _____. He was born Oct 1862 in New York.

Children of EVA MILKS and GEORGE ROOD are:

i. FRED^9 ROOD, b. Apr 1889, New York; d. 19 May 1951, Herkimer, Herkimer County, New York.
OBITUARY
Cold Brook - Fred Rood died May 19 in Herkimer Hospital after a short illness. He was 62.
Born in 1889, he was the son of the late George and Eva Milks Rood. He had been a farming man during most of his life.
He is survived by three brothers, William, Spinnerville, NY; Robert, Mt. Vision, NY and George, Town of Ohio; one sister, Mrs. Harvey Everson, Ilion, and a half sister, Grace Frazier, Town of Ohio; also, several nieces and nephews.
The funeral will be held from the Autenrith Funeral Home, Newport, at 2 p.m. today. The Rev. Walter J. Suits will officiate.
Burial will be in the Town of Ohio. Utica Daily Press, Monday, May 21, 1951

1360. ii. WILLIAM ROOD, b. Jan 1891, New York.

1361. iii. MAY ROOD, b. 11 Oct 1893, New York; d. 06 Dec 1977, Herkimer, Herkimer County, New York.

iv. ODELL ROOD, b. 21 Dec 1896, New York; d. 04 Nov 1950, Herkimer, Herkimer County, New York.
OBITUARY - *Utica Daily Press, November 6, 1950*
Cold Brook - Odell Rudd (sic), 53, Town of Ohio, died Nov. 4, 1950, in Herkimer County Hospital, after a brief illness.
He was born Dec. 21, 1896, in the Town of Russia, a son of George and Eva Milks Rudd (sic).
Surviving are three brothers, Fred, Ohio; William, Ilion and Robert, Mount Vision; a sister, Mrs. Harvey Everson, Ilion and several nieces and nephews.
The funeral will be at 3 p.m. tomorrow from the Autenrith Funeral Home, Newport. The Rev. Walter J. Suits, pastor of the Newport Methodist Church, will officiate.
Burial: Ohio Cemetery, Ohio, Herkimer County, New York, USA

v. ROBERT G. ROOD, b. Dec 1898, New York.

vi. GEORGE ROOD, b. 1903, Remsen, Oneida County, New York.

vii. DAVID ROOD, b. Mar 1887, New York; d. Step-son to George Rood, Sr..

660. FRED A.[8] MILKS (DAVID W.[7], DAVID[6] MILK, GEORGE[5], JONATHAN[4], JOB[3], JOHN[2], JOHN[1]) was born Abt. 1873 in Cattaraugus County, New York, and died 1898. He married MAMIE ROOD Abt. 1895 in Cattaraugus County, New York ??, daughter of RANSOM ROOD and ELIZABETH _____. She was born Mar 1874 in Ohio, Herkimer County, N Y.

Child of FRED MILKS and MAMIE ROOD is:
    i. RAYMOND G.[9] MILKS, b. 12 Nov 1895, Cattaraugus County, New York; d. 05 Nov 1981, Cold Brook, Herkimer County, New York; m. ELLEN W. 'NELLIE' _____; b. 07 Nov 1901, New York; d. Oct 1989, New York (no children).

661. JEROME BONAPARTE[8] MILKS (MONTERVILLE[7], DAVID[6] MILK, GEORGE[5], JONATHAN[4], JOB[3], JOHN[2], JOHN[1]) was born 1 Dec 1856 in Mansfield, Cattaraugus Co., NY, and d. 06 May 1934 in Santa Cruz County, CA . He married LOUISE DOROTHEA ALBRECHT 1888 in California, daughter of JACOB and DORA ALBRECHT. She was born 01 Jul 1864 in Maine and died 11 Aug 1937 in Santa Cruz County, California.

  California, Voter Registers, Jerome Bonapart Milks,
  1884   Residence Place: Santa Cruz, California
  1888   Event Place: Corralitos, Santa Cruz, California, United States
  1890   Event Place: Westport, Mendocino, California, United States
  1898   Residence Place: Humboldt, California

Child of JEROME MILKS and LOUISE ALBRECHT is:
    i. DOROTHY L.[9] MILKS, b. 05 Jan 1902, Santa Cruz County, California; d. Nov 1978, Watsonville, Santa Cruz County, California; m. DUARD GEORGE NISONGER, Bet. 1930 - 01 Apr 1940; b. 17 Jun 1898, California; d. 28 Jan 1982, Watsonville, Santa Cruz County, California.

662. FRANK EDWIN[8] MILKS (MONTERVILLE[7], DAVID[6] MILK, GEORGE[5], JONATHAN[4], JOB[3], JOHN[2], JOHN[1]) was born 17 Mar 1859 in Napoli, Cattaraugus Co, NY, and died 09 Oct 1938 in Tuna, McKean County, Pennsylvania. He married (1) HATTIE B. WILLIAMS Abt. 1882, daughter of SOLOMON WILLIAMS and LORETTA SMITH. She was born Jan 1863 in Mansfield, Cattaraugus Co., NY, and died 1916. He married (2) BESSIE FANNIE GREEN 16 Apr 1918 in Salamanca, Cattaraugus County, New York, daughter of CHARLES GREENE and LOUISA MEACHAM. She was born 04 Sep 1880 in Mansfield, Cattaraugus Co., NY, and died 15 May 1966 in Bradford, McKean County, Pennsylvania.

Children of FRANK MILKS and HATTIE WILLIAMS are:
1362.   i.   RUIE CAROLINE[9] MILKS, b. Feb 1885; d. Bet. 1930 - 1940, Los Angeles, California.
1363.   ii.   LLOYD ELMER MILKS, b. 08 Jan 1887, Ellicottville, Cattaraugus County, New York; d. 13 Oct 1954, Asheboro, Randolph County, North Carolina.
1364.   iii.   MONTEVILLE SAMUEL MILKS, b. 02 Sep 1888, Devereux, New York; d. 03 Oct 1961, Bradford, McKean County, Pennsylvania.
    iv.   HAROLD ARCHIE MILKS, b. 30 Sep 1891, Ellicottville, Cattaraugus Co, NY; d. 29 May 1954, Bradford, McKean County, Pennsylvania; m. ETHEL MAE HILLS, 12 Aug 1913, Salamanca, Cattaraugus County, New York; b. 1890, De Golia, PA; d. 23 Mar 1954, Bradford, McKean County, Pennsylvania (no children).
    v.   CHILDA MILKS, b. Abt. 1894; d. Bef. 1900.
    vi.   FLOSSIE LORETTA MILKS, b. Oct 1896; d. 1968, Bradford, McKean County, Pennsylvania; m. MR. PRICE, Aft. 1940.
    vii.   CHILDB MILKS, b. Bet. 1900 - 1910; d. Bef. 1910.

Children of FRANK MILKS and BESSIE GREEN are:
1365.   viii.   HENRY EDWIN[9] MILKS, b. 22 May 1919, Bradford, PA; d. 15 Feb 1998, Bradford, McKean Co., PA.
1366.   ix.   ARLENE BESSIE MILKS, b. 25 Sep 1921, Bradford, McKean County, Pennsylvania (no children).
1367.   x.   FRANK ELMER MILKS, b. 25 Mar 1923, Bradford, PA; d. 20 Jun 1992, Bradford, McKean Co., PA.

663. HENRY JOSEPH[8] MILKS (MONTERVILLE[7], DAVID[6] MILK, GEORGE[5], JONATHAN[4], JOB[3], JOHN[2], JOHN[1]) was born 1862 in Mansfield, Cattaraugus Co., NY, and died Feb 1949 in Ellicottville, Cattaraugus Co, NY. He married IDA AMANDA DROWN 1889, daughter of ALPHONSO DROWN and NANCY BATT. She was born 28 Jun 1866 in Ellicottville, Cattaraugus County, New York, and died 1952 in Cattaraugus County, New York.

Children of HENRY MILKS and IDA DROWN are:

1368.   i.   CAROL JOSEPH[9] MILKS, b. 24 Mar 1890, Ellicottville, Cattaraugus County, New York; d. May 1969, Ellicottville, Cattaraugus County, New York.
1369.   ii.   ORSON L. MILKS, b. 14 Nov 1891, Cattaraugus County, New York; d. Jul 1966, Ellicottville, Cattaraugus Co., NY.
          iii.   ALVAN M. MILKS, b. Jan 1894, Cattaraugus County, New York; d. 1901, Cattaraugus County, New York.

664. ORSON LEROY[8] MILKS *(MONTERVILLE[7], DAVID[6] MILK, GEORGE[5], JONATHAN[4], JOB[3], JOHN[2], JOHN[1])* was born 16 Jan 1871 in Mansfield, Cattaraugus Co., NY, and died 24 Jun 1960 in Yamhill County, Oregon. He married (1) JESSIE MANAHAN 31 Jul 1895 in Buffalo, NY. She was born 1873 in Canada, and died 09 Nov 1899 in Cattaraugus County, New York. He married (2) SADIE MCDONALD Mar 1905, daughter of RONALD MCDONALD and MARGARET. She was born 07 Dec 1878, and died 17 Dec 1922 in Seattle, King County, Washington. He married (3) IVA FORBES Abt. 1925, daughter of WILLIAM FORBES and MARY UNDERWOOD. She was born 13 Apr 1891 in Mt. Vernon, Washington.

    Orson graduated from high school at Ellicottville, NY, 1889, and thereafter followed the farming and lumbering trades. In 1894 he moved to Buffalo and learned the machinist and engineering trade, which work subsequently took him to Denver and Boulder, Colo, and Oil City, Pa. In 1913 he commenced a 13-year grocery business in Seattle, Washington, and recalls that his first day's sales totaled 13 cents, 2 cents of which was the purchase of a postage stamp. Orson also recalls his visit at the Pan American Fair in Buffalo in 1901 and his shaking hands with Pres. William McKinley some five minutes before he was shot. Res. 215 - 9th St., McMinnville, Ore.

Children of ORSON MILKS and JESSIE MANAHAN are:

1370.   i.   GLADYS I.[9] MILKS, b. 25 Aug 1896, Buffalo, NY; d. Aft. 1941.
          ii.   EDWIN MILKS, b. Aug 1898; d. Oct 1898, Boulder, Colorado.

Child of ORSON MILKS and IVA FORBES is:

          iii.   MARGARET[9] MILKS, b. Abt. 1912, New York (gr-daughter, adopted).
                Margaret was a grand-daughter of Orson, by his daughter Gladys, prior to her marriage to Nathaniel M. Stewart.

665. FRANK ALBERT[8] MILKS *(WASHINGTON G.[7], DAVID[6] MILK, GEORGE[5], JONATHAN[4], JOB[3], JOHN[2], JOHN[1])* was born 13 Oct 1863 in Persia, Cattaraugus County, New York. He married FLORA ISABELL WOOD, daughter of DANIEL WOOD and SARAH WELLS. She was born 23 Jul 1866 in Leon, Cattaraugus County, New York, and died 18 Apr 1912 in Dayton, Cattaraugus County, New York.

Children of FRANK MILKS and FLORA WOOD are:

1371.   i.   GEORGE DANIEL[9] MILKS, b. 13 Sep 1885, Leon, Cattaraugus County, NY; d. 18 May 1970, Fredonia, Chautauqua Co, NY.
1372.   ii.   HERBERT ALBERT MILKS, b. 09 Feb 1894, Leon, Cattaraugus County, New York; d. 13 Nov 1927, Pomfret, Chautauqua County, New York.
          iii.   SARAH AMANDA MILKS, b. 26 Apr 1896, Leon, Cattaraugus Co., NY; d. 04 Nov 1896, Town of Dayton, Cattaraugus Co., NY.
1373.   iv.   CLAYTON FREDERICK MILKS, b. 18 Mar 1903, Dayton, Cattaraugus County, New York; d. Oct 1987, South Dayton, Cattaraugus County, New York.
1374.   v.   MYRTLE ISOBEL MILKS, b. 15 Nov 1904, Dayton, Cattaraugus County, New York; d. 05 Jan 2004, South Dayton, Cattaraugus County, New York.

666. ESTHER[8] MILKS *(WASHINGTON G.[7], DAVID[6] MILK, GEORGE[5], JONATHAN[4], JOB[3], JOHN[2], JOHN[1])* was born 11 Jul 1871 in Little Valley, Cattaraugus County, New York, and died 25 Feb 1933 in South Dayton, Cattaraugus County, New York ?. She married BERT HALLENBECK, son of MATHIAS HALLENBECK and AMELIA WOOD. He was born 03 Sep 1870 in Leon, Cattaraugus County, New York, and died 18 Aug 1936 in South Dayton, Cattaraugus County, New York ?.

Child of ESTHER MILKS and BERT HALLENBECK is:

1375.   i.   HAZEL[9] HALLENBECK, b. 22 Apr 1895, Leon, Cattaraugus County, New York.

667. MARTIN B.⁸ WAITE *(MARTIN⁷, MARY⁶ MILKS, JONATHAN⁵ MILK, JONATHAN⁴, JOB³, JOHN², JOHN¹)* was born 1841 in Dayton, Cattaraugus County, New York, and died 1923 in Winnebago County, Wisconsin. He married (1) PHEBE _____ Abt. 1870. She was born Abt. 1841 in New York. He married (2) HANNAH HOUGH 03 Nov 1874 in Winchester, Winnebago County, Wisconsin, daughter of NATHAN HOUGH and DENNISE _____. She was born Oct 1854 in Wisconsin, and died 1930 in Winnebago County, Wisconsin.

Name: Martin V. B. Wait, Residence: Hortonville, Wisconsin
Enlistment Date: 9 May 1861 Rank at enlistment: Private
State Served: Wisconsin
Service Record: Enlisted in Company D, Wisconsin 1st Infantry Regiment on 05 Sep 1861. Promoted to Full Corporal. Mustered out on 14 Oct 1864.
Was POW?: Yes, Survived the War?:   Yes
Sources: Roster of Wisconsin Volunteers: War of the Rebellion

First Infantry. -- Cols., John C. Starkweather, George B. Bingham; Lieut.- Cols., Charles L. Harris, David H. Lane, George B. Bingham, Henry A. Mitchell; Majs., David H. Lane, George B. Bingham, Henry A. Mitchell, Donald C. McVean, Thomas H. Green.
Regiment: 1st Infantry Regiment Wisconsin
Officers Killed or Mortally Wounded: 6
Officers Died of Disease or Accident: 1
Enlisted Killed or Mortally Wounded: 151
Enlisted Died of Disease or Accident: 142

This regiment was organized as a 90-day regiment under the proclamation of April 16, 1861, with a numerical strength of 810, and left the state June 9. It led the advance on Martinsburg, participated in the battle of Falling Waters, and was mustered out Aug. 22, 1861.

It was reorganized as a three year regiment and mustered in Oct. 19, with a strength of 945. Col. Starkweather was placed in command of the 28th brigade, Sept. 3, 1862, and Lieut.-Col. Bingham was advanced to colonel, Maj. Mitchell to lieutenant- colonel, and Capt. Donald C. McVean was appointed major.

The regiment participated in the battles of Perryville, Stone's River, Chickamauga and Missionary Ridge. It was mustered out Oct. 21, 1864.

The original organization of 810 lost 91 by death, desertion, transfer and discharge, and mustered out, 719.

The reorganization numbering 945, was increased by recruiting, drafting and reenlistment of veterans to 1,508; losses, by death, 235; by desertion, 57; by transfer, 47- by discharge, 298; mustered out, 871.
Source: The Union Army, vol. 4

Battles Fought
Fought on 9 Mar 1862 at Nashville, TN.
Fought on 20 Jul 1862.
Fought on 8 Oct 1862 at Chaplin Hills, KY.
Fought on 9 Oct 1862.
Fought on 30 Dec 1862 at Jefferson, TN.
Fought on 31 Dec 1862 at Stones River, TN.
Fought on 11 Sep 1863 at Dug Gap, GA.
Fought on 19 Sep 1863 at Chickamauga, GA.
Fought on 20 Sep 1863 at Chickamauga, GA.
Fought on 9 May 1864.
Fought on 15 May 1864.
Fought on 24 May 1864.
Fought on 25 May 1864 at Altoona Hills, GA.
Fought on 27 May 1864 at Dallas, GA.
Fought on 28 May 1864 at Dallas, GA.
Fought on 29 May 1864 at Dallas, GA.

Fought on 31 May 1864 at Pumpkin Vine Creek, GA.
Fought on 31 May 1864 at Atlanta, GA.
Fought on 1 Jun 1864 at Pumpkin Vine Creek, GA.
Fought on 6 Jun 1864 at Big Shanty, GA.
Fought on 21 Jun 1864 at Kennesaw Mountain, GA.
Fought on 22 Jun 1864 at Kennesaw Mountain, GA.
Fought on 23 Jun 1864 at Kennesaw Mountain, GA.
Fought on 2 Jul 1864.
Fought on 4 Jul 1864.
Fought on 6 Jul 1864 at Atlanta, GA.
Fought on 18 Jul 1864 at Atlanta, GA.
Fought on 20 Jul 1864 at Peach Tree Creek, GA.
Fought on 21 Jul 1864 at Atlanta, GA.
Fought on 8 Aug 1864 at Atlanta, GA.
Fought on 12 Aug 1864 at Atlanta, GA.
Fought on 15 Aug 1864 at Atlanta, GA.
Fought on 20 Aug 1864 at Atlanta, GA.
Fought on 1 Sep 1864 at Jonesboro, GA.

Children of MARTIN WAITE and HANNAH HOUGH are:
- i. LUKE^9 WAITE, b. Mar 1876, Winchester, Winnebago County, Wisconsin.
- ii. PHEBE A. WAITE, b. Abt. 1877, Winchester, Winnebago County, Wisconsin.
- iii. NANCY A. WAITE, b. 1879, Winchester, Winnebago County, Wisconsin.
- iv. EARLE L. WAITE, b. Jun 1881, Winnebago County, Wisconsin; d. 1907, Winnebago County, Wisconsin.
- v. EDITH M. WAITE, b. Mar 1884, Winnebago County, Wisconsin.
- vi. SUMNER R. WAITE, b. Jan 1886, Winnebago County, Wisconsin.
- vii. EDNA WAITE, b. Sep 1887, Winnebago County, Wisconsin.
- viii. WEALTHA WAITE, b. May 1889, Winnebago County, Wisconsin; d. 1963, Winnebago County, Wisconsin.
- ix. LOLA WAITE, b. Feb 1891, Winnebago County, Wisconsin.
- x. GLADYS R. WAITE, b. Jan 1893, Winnebago County, Wisconsin.
- xi. TIMOTHY B. WAITE, b. Jun 1895, Winnebago County, Wisconsin.
- xii. OLIVE G. WAITE, b. 07 Nov 1897, Winnebago County, Wisconsin; d. 10 Oct 1900, Winnebago County, WI.

668. JONATHAN^8 WAITE *(MARTIN^7, MARY^6 MILKS, JONATHAN^5 MILK, JONATHAN^4, JOB^3, JOHN^2, JOHN^1)* was born 10 Oct 1845 in Dayton, Cattaraugus County, New York, and died Abt. 15 Mar 1932 in Hortonville, Outagamie County, Wisconsin. He married ALTHERA 'ELLA' JONES 11 Apr 1873 in Hortonville, Wisconsin. She was born Mar 1857 in Wisconsin, and died 20 Apr 1924.

OBITUARY - Appleton (WI) Post-Crescent, Fri., March 18, 1932, Page 12:

"CONDUCT SERVICES FOR OLD PIONEER *"Jonathan Waite, 86, Buried in Union Cemetery at Hortonville*

"Hortonville - Jonathan Waite, 86, one of Hortonia's oldest pioneers, was buried Tuesday at Hortonville, in the Union cemetery, the Rev. Mr. F. P. Raby of the Methodist church, officiating.

He was born Oct. 10, 1845 in Dayton, Cattaraugus Co. N.Y., a son of Martin and Lavina Waite.

He was married April 11, 1873 to Miss Althera Jones of Hortonville. To this union 12 children [were] born, five sons and seven daughters.

He was preceded in death by his wife, who died April 20, 1924, also two sons, 4 daughters.

Survivors are three sons: Irvin and John of Hortonia, Marion of Appleton: three daughters, Mrs. Mary Bowe of Marysville, Wash; Mrs. Reyna Olson, Navarino; Mrs. Martha Larson, Hortonville; 28 grandchildren, 22 great grandchildren; one brother, Frank Waite, Leeman.

"Martin Waite and family came to Wisconsin when Jonathan was 10 years of age. They came by boat from Buffalo, they settled in Hortonville for two years. Then they moved to Stephensville where they lived for a number of years. Jonathan bought the old homestead in Hortonia but very little clearing had been done. He lived on this farm for 65 years. For several years Mr. Waite was on the town board served as town treasurer one year and for 22 years was school clerk.

Children of JONATHAN WAITE and ALTHERA JONES are:
1376. i. ROSA E.⁹ WAITE, b. Feb 1874, Outagamie County, Wisconsin; d. 1928, Outagamie County, Wisconsin.
ii. NETTTIE WAITE, b. Abt. 1877, Outagamie County, Wisconsin.
iii. MARY WAITE, b. Jan 1879, Outagamie County, Wisconsin; m. MISTTER BOWE.
iv. VENE WAITE, b. Feb 1881, Outagamie County, Wisconsin.
v. WILLIAM WAITE, b. Mar 1883, Outagamie County, Wisconsin.
vi. IRVIN WAITE, b. May 1885, Outagamie County, Wisconsin; d. Six more children.
vii. BERTHA WAITE, b. Feb 1887, Outagamie County, Wisconsin.
viii. REYNA WAITE, b. Apr 1889, Outagamie County, Wisconsin; m. MISTTER OLSON.
ix. JOHN WAITE, b. Oct 1891, Outagamie County, Wisconsin.
x. MARTHA WAITE, b. Nov 1895, Outagamie County, Wisconsin; m. MISTTER LARSON.
xi. MARION WAITE, b. Apr 1898, Outagamie County, Wisconsin.

669. HORACE⁸ WAITE *(MARTIN⁷, MARY⁶ MILKS, JONATHAN⁵ MILK, JONATHAN⁴, JOB³, JOHN², JOHN¹)* was born 22 Jul 1850 in Dayton, Cattaraugus County, New York, and died 17 Oct 1913. He married CLARA R. _____ Abt. 1875 in Wisconsin. She was born 17 Aug 1859 in Wisconsin, and died 31 Dec 1923 in New London, Wisconsin.

Children of HORACE WAITE and CLARA _____ are:
i. GUY V.⁹ WAITE, b. 28 Oct 1875, Wisconsin; d. 04 Oct 1878, Wisconsin.
ii. MYOCTEE WAITE, b. Nov 1880, Wisconsin.
iii. CORTNEY J. WAITE, b. 03 Oct 1882, Wisconsin; d. 26 Sep 1955, Wisconsin; m. ELIZABETH "LIZZIE" RIEDEL; b. 28 Apr 1897; d. 02 Nov 1986, Wisconsin.

670. FRANKLIN⁸ WAITE *(MARTIN⁷, MARY⁶ MILKS, JONATHAN⁵ MILK, JONATHAN⁴, JOB³, JOHN², JOHN¹)* was born Abt. 1856 in Ellington, Outagamie County, Wisconsin. He married OSCA _____ Abt. 1878. She was born Abt. 1861 in Wisconsin.

Children of FRANKLIN WAITE and OSCA _____ are:
i. CLEORA⁹ WAITE, b. Oct 1879, Ellington, Outagamie County, Wisconsin; d. Bef. 1900, Ellington, Outagamie County, Wisconsin.
ii. LUCILLE WAITE, b. Abt. 1882, Ellington, Outagamie County, Wisconsin.

671. CLARA⁸ WAITE *(MARTIN⁷, MARY⁶ MILKS, JONATHAN⁵ MILK, JONATHAN⁴, JOB³, JOHN², JOHN¹)* was born Mar 1867 in Ellington, Outagamie County, Wisconsin. She married ROBERT CAVNER. He was born Jan 1861 in Missouri.

Child of CLARA WAITE and ROBERT CAVNER is:
i. LAUREL FRANK⁹ CAVNER, b. 02 Sep 1891, Seneca, Missouri.

672. WILLIAM⁸ POTTER *(MARY ANN⁷ WAITE, MARY⁶ MILKS, JONATHAN⁵ MILK, JONATHAN⁴, JOB³, JOHN², JOHN¹)* was born May 1857 in Machias, Cattaraugus County, New York. He married LINDA _____ 1879 in New York. She was born Jan 1856 in New York.

Children of WILLIAM POTTER and LINDA _____ are:
i. EDWARD⁹ POTTER, b. Aug 1879, New York.
ii. CLAYTON POTTER, b. Apr 1881, New York.
iii. LAMONT POTTER, b. Jun 1884, New York.

673. EMMA JANELLA 'NELLIE'⁸ BARKER *(JANE⁷ WAITE, MARY⁶ MILKS, JONATHAN⁵ MILK, JONATHAN⁴, JOB³, JOHN², JOHN¹)* was born 1868 in Leon, Cattaraugus County, New York, and died 1923. She married FRANK MOSHER, son of HENRY MOSHER and BETSEY LOWE. He was born 25 Aug 1866 in Leon, Cattaraugus County, New York, and died 25 Dec 1948.

Children of EMMA BARKER and FRANK MOSHER are:
1377. i. ANNA⁹ MOSHER, b. 30 Nov 1886, Leon, Cattaraugus County, New York.
1378. ii. RAYMOND MOSHER, b. 1888, Leon, Cattaraugus County, New York.

1379.   iii.   IRVING HENRY MOSHER, b. 27 Aug 1896, New Albion, Cattaraugus County, New York.
1380.   iv.   LELAND MOSHER, b. 14 May 1899, New Albin, Allamakee County, Iowa; d. 1946.

674. ALBERT[8] WAITE (BENJAMIN[7], MARY[6] MILKS, JONATHAN[5] MILK, JONATHAN[4], JOB[3], JOHN[2], JOHN[1]) was born 07 Mar 1857 in Concord, Erie County, New York, and died 04 Dec 1936 in Leon, Cattaraugus County, New York. He married (1) ELLA O. PACK 1882 in Cattaraugus County, New York. She was born 1863 in New York, and died Abt. 1923 in Cattaraugus County, New York. He married (2) MARY J. (CHURCH) PLARK 22 Apr 1925 in Chautauqua County, New York, daughter of REUBEN CHURCH and ALICE NICHOLS. She was born 1865.

Children of ALBERT WAITE and ELLA PACK are:
1381.   i.   MERTIE MAE[9] WAITE, b. 04 Feb 1883, Dayton, Cattaraugus County, New York; d. 23 Aug 1955.
1382.   ii.   NETTIE M. WAITE, b. 12 Jun 1888, East Leon, Cattaraugus County, New York.
1383.   iii.   GLADYS WAITE, b. 21 Aug 1906, East Leon, Cattaraugus County, New York.

675. FRED[8] WAITE (BENJAMIN[7], MARY[6] MILKS, JONATHAN[5] MILK, JONATHAN[4], JOB[3], JOHN[2], JOHN[1]) was born 13 May 1863 in East Leon, Cattaraugus County, New York. He married ETTA SHELDON. She was born Abt. 1865.

Children of FRED WAITE and ETTA SHELDON are:
   i.   CLIFFORD L.[9] WAITE, b. 25 Jan 1893, Leon, Cattaraugus County, New York.
   ii.   MAURICE W. WAITE, b. 13 Nov 1897, Leon, Cattaraugus County, New York.
   iii.   PEARL VERA WAITE, b. 24 Oct 1899, Leon, Cattaraugus County, New York.
   iv.   HAROLD O. WAITE, b. 13 Apr 1904, Cattaraugus County, New York.
   v.   LELAND WAITE, b. East Leon, Cattaraugus County, New York.

676. LUCY J.[8] WAITE (BENJAMIN[7], MARY[6] MILKS, JONATHAN[5] MILK, JONATHAN[4], JOB[3], JOHN[2], JOHN[1]) was born 19 May 1868 in East Leon, Cattaraugus County, New York. She married GEORGE WATSON. He was born Abt. 1865.

Children of LUCY WAITE and GEORGE WATSON are:
1384.   i.   ELVA L.[9] WATSON, b. 09 May 1896, East Leon, Cattaraugus County, New York.
   ii.   LEON WATSON, b. 14 Jun 1903, East Leon, Cattaraugus County, New York.

677. GEORGE B.[8] WAITE (BUTLER R.[7], MARY[6] MILKS, JONATHAN[5] MILK, JONATHAN[4], JOB[3], JOHN[2], JOHN[1]) was born 29 Oct 1859 in Leon, Cattaraugus County, New York. He married ANNA SISSON. She was born Abt. 1860 in New York.

Child of GEORGE WAITE and ANNA SISSON is:
   i.   FRANK[9] WAITE, b. Leon, Cattaraugus County, New York; m. ELIZABETH SHELDON.

678. WILLIAM A.[8] WAITE (BUTLER R.[7], MARY[6] MILKS, JONATHAN[5] MILK, JONATHAN[4], JOB[3], JOHN[2], JOHN[1]) was born 02 Feb 1861 in Leon, Cattaraugus County, New York. He married FRANCES FENTON. She was born Abt. 1861.

Child of WILLIAM WAITE and FRANCES FENTON is:
1385.   i.   FLORENCE E.[9] WAITE, b. 06 Mar 1897, Kennedy, Chautauqua County, New York.

679. EMILY[8] HUBBARD (JEMIMA[7] MILKS, JOHN[6] MILK, JONATHAN[5], JONATHAN[4], JOB[3], JOHN[2], JOHN[1]) was born 1834 in Napoli, Cattaraugus County, New York, and died 05 Aug 1857. She married JESSE WORDEN CASE, son of WILLIAM CASE and SOPHIA ARNOLD. He was born 23 Jul 1823, and died 09 Aug 1870 in Fredonia, Chautauqua County, NY.

Children of EMILY HUBBARD and JESSE CASE are:
   i.   FRANK[9] CASE, b. Abt. 1855, Napoli, Cattaraugus County, New York; d. 1855, Cattaraugus County, NY.
   ii.   EVA CASE, b. 13 Oct 1855, Napoli, Cattaraugus County, New York; d. 22 Mar 1938, New York; m. (1) GEORGE W. WRIGHT, Abt. 1879, New York; b. 16 Feb 1856, Of Dunkirk, New York; d. 04 Jul 1921, Dunkirk, Chautauqua County, New York; m. (2) JOHN BROWN, Abt. 1911, New York; b. Abt. 1851, New York; d. Bet. 1920 - 1930, Little Valley, Cattaraugus County, New York.
1386.   iii.   FREDERICK CASE, b. 06 Jul 1857, Napoli, Cattaraugus County, New York; d. 02 Aug 1927, Fredonia, Chautauqua County, New York.

680. NEWTON[8] MILKS *(JOHN[7], JOHN[6] MILK, JONATHAN[5], JONATHAN[4], JOB[3], JOHN[2], JOHN[1])* was born 09 Jan 1842 in Napoli, Cattaraugus County, New York, and died 16 May 1917 in New Albion, Cattaraugus Co, NY. He married MELVINA PLOUGH, daughter of MARTIN PLOUGH and PHEBE _____. She was born 20 Aug 1852 in Napoli, Cattaraugus Co, NY, and died 04 Apr 1926 in New Albion, Cattaraugus Co, NY.

Children of NEWTON MILKS and MELVINA PLOUGH are:
1387. i. WARREN[9] MILKS, b. 06 Apr 1872, Napoli, New York; d. 27 Apr 1948, Cattaraugus County, New York.
ii. FLORENCE MILKS, b. 1874, Napoli, New York; d. 1890.
1388. iii. HENRY JOHN MILKS, b. 20 Feb 1880, Napoli, Cattaraugus Co, NY; d. 21 Apr 1947, Cattaraugus County, New York.
1389. iv. BLANCHE MILKS, b. 21 Jun 1885, Napoli, Cattaraugus County, New York; d. 13 Feb 1965, Cattaraugus, Cattaraugus County, NY.

681. WILLARD[8] MILKS *(JOHN[7], JOHN[6] MILK, JONATHAN[5], JONATHAN[4], JOB[3], JOHN[2], JOHN[1])* was born Jun 1844 in Napoli, Cattaraugus County, New York, and died 17 May 1911 in Napoli, Cattaraugus County, New York. He married LUCY WILCOX 1868 in Napoli, Cattaraugus Co., New York. She was born 1847 in Chautauqua County, New York, and died 10 Feb 1905 in Napoli, New York

In the 1900 census, Lucy reported that she had 9 children, but only one was still living. All of the children who died early, died of diphtheria.

Children of WILLARD MILKS and LUCY WILCOX are:
i. FAYETTE[9] MILKS, b. 1870, Napoli, New York; d. 11 Jan 1888, Napoli, New York.
1390. ii. ANNA BELL MILKS, b. 20 Oct 1871, Napoli, New York; d. 19 Feb 1911, New Albion, New York.
iii. LAFRANCE MILKS, b. 1874, Napoli, New York; d. 03 Jan 1888, Napoli, New York.
iv. CORA MILKS, b. 1876, Napoli, New York; d. 10 Jan 1888, Napoli, New York.
v. MALINDA MILKS, b. 1878, Napoli, New York; d. 15 Jan 1888, Napoli, New York.
vi. LIDA MILKS, b. 1881, Napoli, New York; d. 13 Jan 1888, Napoli, New York.
vii. EVA MILKS, b. 1884, Napoli, New York; d. 16 Jan 1888, Napoli, New York.
viii. CHILD8 MILKS, b. Bef. 1890, Napoli, New York; d. Bef. 1900, Napoli, New York.
ix. CHILD9 MILKS, b. Bef. 1890, Napoli, New York; d. Bef. 1900, Napoli, New York.

682. JOHN D.[8] MILKS *(JOHN[7], JOHN[6] MILK, JONATHAN[5], JONATHAN[4], JOB[3], JOHN[2], JOHN[1])* was born 14 Jan 1849 in Napoli, Cattaraugus County, New York, and died Bef. 1900 in Napoli, Cattaraugus County, New York. He married LYDIA FOX, daughter of MR. FOX and ANN _____. She was born Nov 1854 in New York.

Children of JOHN MILKS and LYDIA FOX are:
1391. i. MYRTLE A.[9] MILKS, b. 25 Dec 1874, Napoli, Cattaraugus County, New York; d. 11 Feb 1966, Cattaraugus County, New York.
1392. ii. JENNIE E. MILKS, b. Sep 1876, Napoli, Cattaraugus County, New York.
1393. iii. DAVID MILKS, b. 05 Jun 1883, Napoli, Cattaraugus County, New York.

683. NANCY S.[8] MILKS *(JOHN[7], JOHN[6] MILK, JONATHAN[5], JONATHAN[4], JOB[3], JOHN[2], JOHN[1])* was born 12 Mar 1858 in Napoli, Cattaraugus County, New York, and died 24 Jul 1928 in East Randolph, Cattaraugus Co., NY. She married FRANK E. MERCHANT 02 Dec 1875 in Cattaraugus County, New York, son of TRUMAN MERCHANT and MARY BIGLER. He was born 17 Mar 1854, and died 28 Jul 1930 in East Randolph, Cattaraugus Co., NY.

Children of NANCY MILKS and FRANK MERCHANT are:
1394. i. EDNA E.[9] MERCHANT, b. 03 Jan 1877, East Randolph Cemetery, East Randolph, Cattaraugus Co., NY; d. 01 Jul 1947, Cattaraugus Co., New York.
1395. ii. ORA V. MERCHANT, b. 22 Nov 1879, East Randolph, Cattaraugus Co., NY; d. Dec 1965.
iii. EMERELDA A. MERCHANT, b. 24 Nov 1881, East Randolph, Cattaraugus Co., NY; d. 1975, East Randolph, Cattaraugus Co., NY; m. CASMER DYER CHURCHILL, 14 Mar 1914, Cattaraugus County, New York; b. 06 Nov 1881, Randolph, Cattaraugus County, NY; d. Feb 1963, East Randolph, Cattaraugus Co., NY.

	iv.	JOHNNIE T. MERCHANT, b. 1885, East Randolph Cemetery, East Randolph, Cattaraugus Co., NY; d. 1887, East Randolph Cemetery, East Randolph, Cattaraugus Co., NY.
1396.	v.	PEARL M. MERCHANT, b. 1888, East Randolph, Cattaraugus Co., NY; d. 1983, Conewango, Cattaraugus Co., NY.

684. HENRY BENSON[8] MILKS *(BENJAMIN B.[7], JOHN[6] MILK, JONATHAN[5], JONATHAN[4], JOB[3], JOHN[2], JOHN[1])* was born 22 Oct 1844 in Napoli, Cattaraugus Co, NY, and died 09 Nov 1910 in Bainbridge Twp., Geauga County, Ohio. He married LYDIA A. BOSWELL 30 Sep 1885 in Geauga County, Ohio, daughter of HENRY BOSWELL and ELIZABETH CHAPMAN. She was born 29 Feb 1860 in Russell, Ohio, and died 17 Dec 1943 in Mantua, Portage County, Ohio.

Child of HENRY MILKS and LYDIA BOSWELL is:
   i.   BESSIE[9] MILKS, b. Abt. 1886, Geauga County, Ohio; d. Bef. 1900, Geauga County, Ohio.

685. ELEANOR R.[8] MILKS *(BENJAMIN B.[7], JOHN[6] MILK, JONATHAN[5], JONATHAN[4], JOB[3], JOHN[2], JOHN[1])* was born Dec 1847 in Napoli, New York, and died 1925 in Geauga County, Ohio. She married AMASA S. BOSWELL, son of HENRY BOSWELL and ELIZA CHAPMAN. He was born 24 Jun 1849, and died 25 Dec 1918 in Geauga County, Ohio (Bronchial Pneumonia).

Child of ELEANOR MILKS and AMASA BOSWELL is:
1397.   i.   BENJAMIN "BENNIE" M.[9] BOSWELL, b. 23 Aug 1879; d. 16 Dec 1918, Russell, Geauga County, Ohio (Bronchial Pneumonia).

686. ALVIN L.[8] MILKS *(BENJAMIN B.[7], JOHN[6] MILK, JONATHAN[5], JONATHAN[4], JOB[3], JOHN[2], JOHN[1])* was born 14 Jul 1849 in Napoli, Cattaraugus County, New York, and died 10 Dec 1924 in Springfield, Sarpy County, Nebraska. He married (1) LILLIE DIANA BORDMAN 27 Sep 1880 in Springfield, Sarpy County, Nebraska, daughter of ALONZO BORDMAN and OLIVE _____. She was born 25 Jun 1862 in Randolph, New York, and died 05 Feb 1914 in Springfield, Sarpy County, Nebraska. He married (2) GERTRUDE STEPANEK Aft. 1914 in Sarpy County, Nebraska. She was born 1880, and died 1926 in Springfield, Sarpy County, Nebraska.

Children of ALVIN MILKS and LILLIE BORDMAN are:
1398.   i.   ZADIE ANN[9] MILKS, b. 14 Jul 1881, Springfield, Nebraska; d. 15 Aug 1941, Omaha, Nebraska.
1399.   ii.   NORA OLIVE MILKS, b. 18 Feb 1883, Napoli, Cattaraugus Co, NY; d. 1927, Little Valley, Cattaraugus Co., NY.
1400.   iii. DUARD ALVIN MILKS, b. 17 Aug 1884, Napoli, Cattaraugus County, New York; d. 08 Dec 1930, Springfield, Nebraska.
1401.   iv.   CORA DIANE MILKS, b. 20 Feb 1887.
1402.   v.   GLEN C. MILKS, b. 22 Dec 1891, Springfield, Nebraska; d. 06 Dec 1950.
1403.   vi.   ANNA LILLIE MILKS, b. 06 Jul 1893.

687. EUGENE BENJAMIN[8] MILKS *(BENJAMIN B.[7], JOHN[6] MILK, JONATHAN[5], JONATHAN[4], JOB[3], JOHN[2], JOHN[1])* was born 1851 in Napoli, New York, and died Bet. 1930 - 1940 in Cattaraugus County, New York. He married LAURA DEVOE, daughter of JAMES DEVOE and ANN _____. She was born Abt. Apr 1856.

   Laura was married, once, before she married Eugene, and she had 2 children, according to both the 1900 and the 1910 census records, where she states that she had 4 children, and all 4 were living. It is possible that her first marriage was to Wm. Wilcox, and that her children were Mary Wilcox, b. 1874, and Sherman L. Wilcox, b. 1876, both prob. born in Chautauqua County, New York.

Children of EUGENE MILKS and LAURA DEVOE are:
1404.   i.   BESSIE IRENE[9] MILKS, b. 1889, Randolph, Cattaraugus County, New York.
1405.   ii. ROSE MILKS, b. 1893, Ellington, Chautauqua County, New York.

688. EMILY H.[8] MILKS *(BENJAMIN B.[7], JOHN[6] MILK, JONATHAN[5], JONATHAN[4], JOB[3], JOHN[2], JOHN[1])* was born 1855 in Napoli, New York. She married HANNIBLE LADOW. He was born Abt. 1855.

Child of EMILY MILKS and HANNIBLE LADOW is:
  i. ZEPHIA[9] LADOW, b. Abt. 1871, Cattaraugus County, New York; d. Abt. 1876, Cattaraugus County, N Y.

689. ELMER F.[8] MILKS *(DAVID[7] MILK, JOHN[6], JONATHAN[5], JONATHAN[4], JOB[3], JOHN[2], JOHN[1])* was born Jul 1843 in Napoli, Cattaraugus Co., NY. He married CHLOE _____ Abt. 1865.

Child of ELMER MILKS and CHLOE _____ is:
  i. NELLIE[9] MILKS, b. 1868.

690. EDWARD R.[8] MILKS *(DAVID[7] MILK, JOHN[6], JONATHAN[5], JONATHAN[4], JOB[3], JOHN[2], JOHN[1])* was born Apr 1846 in Napoli, Cattaraugus Co, NY, and died Bet. 1920 - 1930 in Olean, Cattaraugus County, New York ??. He married (1) AMELIA OAKES 16 Sep 1872 in Cattaraugus County, New York, daughter of LYMAN OAKS and LYDIA _____. She was born 1854 in New York, and died 12 Sep 1875 in Coldspring, Cattaraugus County, New York. He married (2) FIDELIA 'DELIA' OAKES Bef. 16 Jun 1880, daughter of LYMAN OAKS and LYDIA _____. She was born 1860, and died Bef. 01 Jun 1900 in Edward is shown in the 1900 census as 'Widowed'.

Child of EDWARD MILKS and AMELIA OAKES is:
  i. CORA[9] MILKS, b. Abt. 1873, Cattaraugus County, New York.

Children of EDWARD MILKS and FIDELIA OAKES are:
1406. ii. DAVID WESLEY[9] MILKS, b. 10 Jun 1881, Red House, Cattaraugus County, New York; d. 06 Dec 1929, Red House, Cattaraugus County, New York.
1407. iii. BERTHA MABEL MILKS, b. 20 May 1882, Red House, Cattaraugus County, New York; d. 10 Oct 1960, Cuba, Allegany County, New York.

691. EVELINE LOUISE[8] MILKS *(DAVID[7] MILK, JOHN[6], JONATHAN[5], JONATHAN[4], JOB[3], JOHN[2], JOHN[1])* was born 10 Jan 1849 in Napoli, Cattaraugus Co., NY, and died 13 Jan 1928 in Valmont, Boulder County, Colorado. She married LUTHER N. HIXSON 25 Jun 1873 in Boulder, Colorado. He was born 19 Oct 1843 in Ohio, and died 08 Oct 1910 in Valmont, Boulder County, Colorado.

Children of EVELINE MILKS and LUTHER HIXSON are:
1408. i. HOWARD HARDEN[9] HIXSON, b. 24 Apr 1874, Valmont, Boulder County, Colorado; d. 05 Dec 1955, Seattle, King County, Washington.
1409. ii. THOMAS EDSON 'TED' HIXSON, b. 24 Dec 1875, Valmont, Boulder County, Colorado; d. 03 May 1941, Valmont, Boulder County, Colorado.
       iii. ALICE M. HIXSON, b. Aug 1879, Valmont, Boulder County, Colorado.

692. MANLEY DAVID[8] MILKS *(DAVID[7] MILK, JOHN[6], JONATHAN[5], JONATHAN[4], JOB[3], JOHN[2], JOHN[1])* was born Nov 1852 in Napoli, Cattaraugus Co., NY, and died 1937 in Reynoldsville, Jefferson County, Pennsylvania. He married (1) ADALINE RHUAMY "AMY" THOMA 08 Jan 1874 in Randolph, Cattaraugus County, NY, daughter of DOMINICUS THOMA and MARY SMITH. She was born 28 Apr 1852 in Cattaraugus County, New York, and died 22 Apr 1932 in East Randolph, Cattaraugus County, NY. He married (2) DORA F. SIBLEY 1886, daughter of AMENZO SIBLEY and ALZINA _____. She was born Feb 1866 in New York, and died 1932 in Reynoldsville, Jefferson County, Pennsylvania.

Children of MANLEY MILKS and ADALINE THOMA are:
1410. i. MARY EMELINE[9] MILKS, b. 19 Sep 1881, Conewango, Cattaraugus County, New York.
1411. ii. MILFORD PENROSE MILKS, b. 17 Jun 1888, Cattaraugus County, New York; d. 04 Mar 1922, Dallas, Texas.
       iii. PERCY HOWARD MILKS, b. 19 Sep 1891, East Randolph, Cattaraugus Co., NY; d. Oct 1966, Gloversville, Fulton County, New York; m. (1) LILLIAN M. SPRUNG, Bet. 1917 - 1918; b. Bet. 1876 - 1877, New York; m. (2) MARTHA SCHRAY, Aft. 1940; b. 13 Jun 1894. No children.

Children of MANLEY MILKS and DORA SIBLEY are:
  iv. SILFORD M.[9] MILKS, b. Jun 1890, Jefferson County, Pennsylvania; d. 1908, Jefferson County, Pennsylvania.
   v. EVELYN D. MILKS, b. Jun 1892, Jefferson County, Pennsylvania.

	vi.	VIVIAN MILKS, b. Feb 1895, Jefferson County, Pennsylvania.
1412.	vii.	LOUIS ELMER MILKS, b. 31 Dec 1896, Jefferson County, Pennsylvania; d. 26 Mar 1974, Westmoreland County, Pennsylvania.
	viii.	DOROTHY A. MILKS, b. Bet. 1901 - 1902, Jefferson County, Pennsylvania.

693. ANNA VIRGINIA[8] CASE *(DEBORAH[7] MILKS, JOHN[6] MILK, JONATHAN[5], JONATHAN[4], JOB[3], JOHN[2], JOHN[1])* was born 17 May 1844 in Napoli, Cattaraugus County, New York, and died 06 May 1914 in Little Valley, Cattaraugus County, New York. She married (1) MISTTER WATKINS. He was born Abt. 1844. She married (2) IRA ASA J. REED. He was born Abt. 1844 in Ellington, Cattaraugus County, New York, and died Bet. 1880 - 1900 in Little Valley, Cattaraugus County, New York.

Child of ANNA CASE and IRA ASA J. REED is:
    i. EUGENE L. 'JEAN'[9] REED, b. 05 Mar 1870, Little Valley, Cattaraugus County, New York; d. 28 Aug 1934; m. CARRIE SCHIER. No children.

694. THERESA MARY[8] CASE *(DEBORAH[7] MILKS, JOHN[6] MILK, JONATHAN[5], JONATHAN[4], JOB[3], JOHN[2], JOHN[1])* was born 16 Jul 1845 in Napoli, Cattaraugus County, New York, and died 10 Jan 1893 in Buffalo, New York. She married JOHN BROWN FRANCIS CHAMPLIN, son of JOHN CHAMPLIN and HANNAH COTTRELL. He was born 17 Jul 1841 in New York, and died 21 Mar 1903 in Little Valley, Cattaraugus County, New York.

    John Champlin started a cutlery business in New York City in 1864, moved it to Little Valley in 1880, incorporated the Cattaraugus Cutlery Co. in 1886.

Children of THERESA CASE and JOHN CHAMPLIN are:
1413.	i.	JOHN B. 'TINT'[9] CHAMPLIN, b. 12 Aug 1866, Little Valley, Cattaraugus County, New York; d. 1938, Little Valley, Cattaraugus County, New York.
	ii.	JESSIE CHAMPLIN, b. 1878, Little Valley, Cattaraugus County, New York.
	iii.	WALTER VALENTINE CHAMPLIN, b. 1874, Little Valley, Cattaraugus County, New York.
	iv.	ALLEN CHAMPLIN, b. Little Valley, Cattaraugus County, New York.

695. WILLIAM R.[8] CASE *(DEBORAH[7] MILKS, JOHN[6] MILK, JONATHAN[5], JONATHAN[4], JOB[3], JOHN[2], JOHN[1])* was born Aug 1847 in Napoli, Cattaraugus County, New York. He married (1) JULIA _____. She was born Abt. 1847. He married (2) MARGARET _____. She was born Abt. 1847. He married (3) LINA TANNER. She was born Abt. 1847. He married (4) ADDIE MARY FOX Abt. 1869. She was born Abt. 1847, and died in Furnas County, Nebraska. He married (5) CAROLINE C. JOHNS Abt. 1892. She was born Dec 1847 in Ohio.

    In the 1920 census, William is listed as "President W. R. Case Cutlery".

W. R. CASE & SONS CUTLERY COMPANY

    W.R. Case & Sons Cutlery Company is an American manufacturer of traditional pocketknives, fixed blades/sporting knives, limited edition commemoratives and collectibles. The company originated in Little Valley, New York around the turn of the 20th century before relocating to its current home, Bradford, Pennsylvania, in 1905. The company's namesake, William Russell Case, first made knives with his brothers under the name, Case Brothers Cutlery Company. His son, John Russell ("Russ") Case, worked as a salesman for his father's company before founding W.R. Case & Sons.

Classic Case pocket knife

History

The company's roots extend back to 1889, when the Case brothers – William Russell (W.R.), Jean, John and

Andrew Case, formerly of the Cattaraugus Cutlery Company – began selling cutlery from the back of a wagon in various small western New York villages. In January 1900, the brothers incorporated to form Case Brothers Cutlery Company.

John Russell Case, who named the company after his father, William Russell ("W.R."), formed W.R. Case & Sons as it is known today. By the time the company moved to Bradford, PA in 1905, the four Case brothers had established their brands.

Beginning with World War I, Case has made military knives for U.S. servicemen and women including the USMC's Ka-bar knife and the V-42 Stiletto for the Devil's Brigade. During the 1965 flight of the Molly Brown, astronauts Gus Grissom and John Young used special Case knives on a NASA space mission.

The Case Company is currently owned by Zippo Manufacturing Company, another business based in Bradford

Case knives are made with blades stamped from domestic steel and hardened using proprietary heat treatment methods. Knife handles are shaped using a variety of natural materials like Brazilian cattle bone, genuine India Stag, Buffalo horn, ancient Mammoth Ivory, Mother-of-Pearl, exotic hardwoods and precious stones. Brass, nickel, and silver metals are used to make the knives' other component parts.

Many people collect Case knives as a hobby. This practice arose from the unique tang stamp dating systems employed by the company beginning in the late 19th century. Today's Case Collectors Club is made up of 18,000 members.

Children of WILLIAM CASE and ADDIE FOX are:

1414.   i.   DEBORAH[9] CASE, b. Abt. 1870, Furnas County, Nebraska; d. 26 May 1950, Boulder, Colorado.

1415.   ii.   THERESA CASE, b. Abt. 1875, Furnas County, Nebraska; d. Bradford, Pennsylvania.

        iii.   MAUD CASE, b. Furnas County, Nebraska.

        iv.   J. RUSSELL CASE, b. 1878, Furnas County, Nebraska; m. (1) EFFIE KROUSE; d. Bradford, Pennsylvania; m. (2) FLORENCE LIGHTY.

696. JEAN J.[8] CASE *(DEBORAH[7] MILKS, JOHN[6] MILK, JONATHAN[5], JONATHAN[4], JOB[3], JOHN[2], JOHN[1])* was born 10 Aug 1853 in Napoli, Cattaraugus County, New York, and died 19 Aug 1935 in Napoli, Cattaraugus County, New York. He married IDA MAY AINSWORTH, daughter of JOSEPH AINSWORTH and ABIGAIL BEARDSLY. She was born 13 Nov 1858 in St. Henry, Ohio, and died 07 Jan 1940 in Little Valley, Cattaraugus County, New York.

Children of JEAN CASE and IDA AINSWORTH are:

1416.   i.   ELLIOTT JEAN[9] CASE, b. 30 Mar 1876, Furnas County, Nebraska; d. 08 Sep 1903, Little Valley, Cattaraugus County, New York.

1417.   ii.   DEAN JOSEPH CASE, b. 19 Sep 1883, Napoli, Cattaraugus County, New York; d. 03 Apr 1951, Ocean City, Maryland.

1418.   iii.   LINA CASE, b. 21 Jul 1888, Little Valley, Cattaraugus County, New York.

1419.   iv.   ADDIE MAY CASE, b. 09 Feb 1892, Furnas County, Nebraska.

697. EMMA E.[8] CASE *(DEBORAH[7] MILKS, JOHN[6] MILK, JONATHAN[5], JONATHAN[4], JOB[3], JOHN[2], JOHN[1])* was born 1855 in Napoli, Cattaraugus County, New York, and died 1901 in Little Valley, Cattaraugus County, New York. She married JOHN W. BROWN, son of DAVID BROWN and LANNY LORY. He was born 17 Jul 1850, and died 1924 in Little Valley, Cattaraugus County, New York.

Children of EMMA CASE and JOHN BROWN are:

1420.   i.   WALLACE E.[9] BROWN, b. Sep 1875, Little Valley, Cattaraugus County, New York; d. 1924.

1421.   ii.   ANNA BROWN, b. 1880, Little Valley, Cattaraugus County, New York.

1422.   iii.   R. EMERSON BROWN, b. Feb 1883, Little Valley, Cattaraugus County, New York; d. 1934, Olean, Cattaraugus County, New York.

1423.   iv.   ETHEL E. BROWN, b. 10 Nov 1887, Little Valley, Cattaraugus County, New York.

        v.   EVERETT BROWN, b. 1901, Little Valley, Cattaraugus County, New York; d. 1918.

698. JESSIE[8] CASE *(DEBORAH[7] MILKS, JOHN[6] MILK, JONATHAN[5], JONATHAN[4], JOB[3], JOHN[2], JOHN[1])* was born 1856 in Napoli, Cattaraugus County, New York. She married JAMES BARNARD. He was born 1855, and died 1925 in Little Valley, Cattaraugus County, New York.

Children of JESSIE CASE and JAMES BARNARD are:

1424.   i.   MILLIE[9] BARNARD, b. 1877, Little Valley, Cattaraugus County, New York; d. 1899, Little Valley, Cattaraugus County, New York.

        ii.   HARLAND BARNARD, b. Abt. 1879, Little Valley, Cattaraugus County, New York; m. BESSIE GREEN; b. 18 Jan 1885.
No children.

699. JOHN DEBORAH[8] CASE *(DEBORAH[7] MILKS, JOHN[6] MILK, JONATHAN[5], JONATHAN[4], JOB[3], JOHN[2], JOHN[1])* was born 12 Jul 1858 in Napoli, Cattaraugus County, New York, and died 15 Jul 1929 in Little Valley, Cattaraugus County, New York. He married (1) ADELINE 'ADDIE' WYATT 19 Feb 1881, daughter of ELITHLIT WYATT and JANE SMITH. She was born Jun 1861 in Brantford, Canada, and died 23 Jun 1930 in Olean, Cattaraugus County, New York. He married (2) MINNIE MAUD MILLER 15 Mar 1909 in Cuyahoga County, Ohio, daughter of WILLIAM MILLER and MARY CLARK. She was born Mar 1874 in Iowa. He married (3) MYRTLE E. LARDIE Bet. 1910 - 1920, daughter of JOSEPH LARDIE and MARGRETTE TOBIN. She was born 24 Aug 1882 in Traverse City, Grand Traverse County, Michigan, and died 03 May 1971 in Lily Dale, Chautauqua County, New York.

    John D. Case married the widow of Elliott Jean Case (a nephew), Minnie Maud Miller.

Children of JOHN CASE and ADELINE WYATT are:

1425.   i.   EMMA V.[9] CASE, b. Apr 1882, Furnas County, Nebraska.

        ii.   MARGARETT L. CASE, b. 26 Nov 1883, Little Valley, Cattaraugus County, New York; m. CHARLES HARRINGTON; b. Abt. 1883.

1426.   iii.   JAY WYATT CASE, b. 06 Oct 1885, Little Valley, Cattaraugus County, New York; d. Mar 1968, Tucson, Arizona.

1427.   iv.   CLIFTON CLINTON CASE, b. 14 Dec 1888, Little Valley, Cattaraugus County, New York; d. 05 Dec 1960.

1428.   v.   ARNOLD D. CASE, b. Oct 1889, Little Valley, Cattaraugus County, New York.

1429.   vi.   MINA M. CASE, b. Nov 1892, Furnas County, Nebraska; d. 1959, Olean, Cattaraugus County, New York.

        vii.   GERTRUDE H. CASE, b. 19 Apr 1900, Little Valley, Cattaraugus County, New York; d. Nov 1901, Little Valley, Cattaraugus County, New York.

700. ANDREW J.[8] CASE *(DEBORAH[7] MILKS, JOHN[6] MILK, JONATHAN[5], JONATHAN[4], JOB[3], JOHN[2], JOHN[1])* was born 04 Mar 1862 in Napoli, Cattaraugus County, New York, and died 15 Jan 1940 in Little Valley, Cattaraugus County, New York. He married (1) SARAH JANE WYATT 22 Mar 1881 in Norton, Norton County, Kansas, daughter of ELITHLIT WYATT and JANE SMITH. She was born 23 Jun 1865 in Brockville, Leeds, Ontario, Canada, and died 07 May 1941 in Little Valley, Cattaraugus County, New York. He married (2) MYRTLE C. CASE 21 Apr 1917 in Erie, Pennsylvania, daughter of ALVIN CASE and CLEORA FERRIS. She was born 1879.

Children of ANDREW CASE and SARAH WYATT are:

        i.   JACKSON[9] CASE, b. 10 Mar 1883, Norton, Norton County, Kansas; m. CARRIE HIGBEE. No children.

1430.   ii.   JAMES ANDREW CASE, b. 06 Apr 1884, Little Valley, Cattaraugus County, New York.

1431.   iii.   LELA CASE, b. 31 Jul 1886, Little Valley, Cattaraugus County, New York; d. Salamanca, Cattaraugus County, New York.

1432.   iv.   ALLAN A. CASE, b. 18 Sep 1888, Little Valley, Cattaraugus County, New York.

701. SUSAN J.[8] MILKS *(GEORGE[7], JOHN[6] MILK, JONATHAN[5], JONATHAN[4], JOB[3], JOHN[2], JOHN[1])* was born 26 Jan 1844 in Napoli, Cattaraugus County, New York, and died 11 Sep 1913 in New Albion, Cattaraugus County, New York. She married ALFRED PADDOCK MOSHER Abt. 1867, son of JOHN MOSHER and ELIZA POTTER. He was born 18 Sep 1827 in Leon, Cattaraugus County, New York, and died 1904 in New Albion, Cattaraugus County, New York. Susan was listed as a servant in Alfred's house in the 1865 NY state census (June 1, 1865)

Children of SUSAN MILKS and ALFRED MOSHER are:

1433.   i.   ETTIE ANN[9] MOSHER, b. 01 Nov 1867, Leon, Cattaraugus County, New York; d. 06 May 1944.

1434.   ii.   FREDERICK HERBERT MOSHER, b. Jan 1870, Leon, Cattaraugus County, New York; d. 09 May 1935, Leon, Cattaraugus County, New York.

        iii.   ELTON ALFRED MOSHER, b. 22 Jan 1875, Cattaraugus County, New York; d. 30 Sep 1959, New York; m. JENNIE BARKER, 1895, New York; b. Abt. 1876, Wayne County, New York. No children.

iv. HAROLD MOSHER, b. 22 Jan 1875, Cattaraugus County, New York; d. Bef. 1900, Cattaraugus County, New York.
v. BLANCHE MOSHER, b. Abt. 1880, Cattaraugus County, New York; d. Bef. 1900, Cattaraugus County, New York.
1435. vi. SHERMAN ANDREW MOSHER, b. 22 May 1888, New Albion, Cattaraugus County, New York; d. 01 Aug 1954, Lake County, Ohio.

702. SARAH JANE^8 MILKS (*GEORGE^7, JOHN^6 MILK, JONATHAN^5, JONATHAN^4, JOB^3, JOHN^2, JOHN^1*) was born 25 Nov 1846 in Napoli, Cattaraugus Co., NY, and died 16 Nov 1929 in Great Valley, Cattaraugus County, New York. She married OTIS DIMMOCK RHOADES 1868, son of ASAHEL RHOADES and AGNES FAIR. He was born 03 Oct 1840 in Napoli, Cattaraugus County, New York, and died 27 Apr 1928 in Great Valley, Cattaraugus County, NY

Children of SARAH MILKS and OTIS RHOADES are:
1436. i. GEORGE O.^{9} RHOADES, b. 19 Sep 1869, Cattaraugus County, New York.
1437. ii. FRANK A. RHOADES RHODES, b. Abt. 1872, Cattaraugus County, New York.
1438. iii. GRACE RHOADES, b. 08 May 1880, Cattaraugus County, New York.
1439. iv. CARRIE RHOADES, b. 29 Aug 1889, Cattaraugus County, New York.

703. GEORGE WILSON^8 MILKS (*GEORGE^7, JOHN^6 MILK, JONATHAN^5, JONATHAN^4, JOB^3, JOHN^2, JOHN^1*) was born 06 Nov 1848 in Napoli, Cattaraugus County, New York, and died 29 Aug 1931 in New Albion, Cattaraugus County, New York. He married (1) CARRIE WATKINS Abt. 1877 in Cattaraugus County, New York, daughter of EDWARD WATKINS and JULIA _____. She was born 1856. He married (2) BERTHA M. WITT Abt. 1895 in Cattaraugus County, New York, daughter of HENRY WITT and MARY LAU. She was born 1878 in Germany, and died 28 Apr 1906 in New Albion, Cattaraugus County, NY. He married (3) CORA EARLE Abt. 1907 in Cattaraugus County, New York. She was born 1864 in New York, and died in No children.

Children of GEORGE MILKS and BERTHA WITT are:
i. GEORGE RICHARD^9 MILKS, b. 30 Oct 1895, New Albion, Cattaraugus County, NY; d. 17 Nov 1895, New Albion, Cattaraugus County, NY.
ii. BERTHA MILKS, b. 03 Nov 1896, New Albion, Cattaraugus County, NY; d. Bef. 1900, New Albion, Cattaraugus County, New York.
1440. iii. ELLA MARIE MILKS, b. 03 Nov 1896, New Albion, Cattaraugus County, NY.
1441. iv. HAROLD GEORGE MILKS, b. 23 Jan 1898, New Albion, Cattaraugus County, NY; d. May 1968, Little Valley, Cattaraugus County, New York.
v. WILSON MCKINLEY MILKS, b. 02 Aug 1900, New Albion, Cattaraugus County, NY; d. Nov 1973, Little Valley, Cattaraugus County, New York. In 1942, Wilson records that he is single with no dependents.

704. HARVEY R. 'DADE'^{8} MILKS (*GEORGE^7, JOHN^6 MILK, JONATHAN^5, JONATHAN^4, JOB^3, JOHN^2, JOHN^1*) was born 16 Oct 1850 in Napoli, Cattaraugus County, New York, and died 08 Aug 1932 in Napoli, Cattaraugus County, New York. He married ADDIE LEONA FRARY 23 Jul 1876 in Cattaraugus County, New York, daughter of WILLIAM FRARY and ELECTA BUSHNELL. She was born 18 Jun 1860 in South Valley, Cattaraugus County, New York, and died 26 Jul 1933 in Napoli, Cattaraugus County, New York.

Children of HARVEY MILKS and ADDIE FRARY are:
1442. i. BLANCHE ELVIRA^9 MILKS, b. 12 Feb 1880, Napoli, Cattaraugus County, New York; d. Abt. 1954.
1443. ii. ARA LYNN MILKS, b. 16 Aug 1889, Napoli, Cattaraugus Co, NY; d. 15 Jan 1956, Little Valley, Cattaraugus County, NY.

705. LYDIA^8 MILKS (*GEORGE^7, JOHN^6 MILK, JONATHAN^5, JONATHAN^4, JOB^3, JOHN^2, JOHN^1*) was born 06 Jun 1853 in Napoli, Cattaraugus Co., NY, and died 1940 in Cattaraugus County, New York. She married (1) AUSTIN S. GARDNER Abt. 1878, son of STEPHEN GARDNER and HANNAH CROSSFIELD. He was born 1850 in New York, and died 1885 in Cattaraugus County, New York. She married (2) THADDEUS S. PHILLIPS Abt. 1895 in Chautauqua County, New York, son of LEONARD PHILLIPS and MARY _____. He was born 17 Sep 1850 in New Albion, Cattaraugus County, New York, and died 27 Dec 1922 in Fredonia, Chautauqua County, New York.

Child of LYDIA MILKS and AUSTIN GARDNER is:
1444. i. BERYL MAY^9 GARDNER, b. Jun 1879, New York; d. 25 Jun 1962, Chautauqua County, New York.

706. FRANK W.^{8} MILKS *(GEORGE^7, JOHN^6 MILK, JONATHAN^5, JONATHAN^4, JOB^3, JOHN^2, JOHN^1)* was born 07 Nov 1856 in Napoli, Cattaraugus Co, NY, and died 06 Sep 1927. He married GERTRUDE HERRICK. She was born 17 Jan 1870 in Napoli, Cattaraugus Co, NY.

Children of FRANK MILKS and GERTRUDE HERRICK are:
     i. GEORGIA ALTA^9 MILKS, b. 17 Oct 1888, Napoli, Cattaraugus Co, NY; m. GEORGE SHEARER; b. Abt. 1888. No children.
1445. ii. MARJORIE MILKS, b. 12 Dec 1889, Napoli, Cattaraugus Co, NY; d. 03 Feb 1948.
1446. iii. BEULAH MILKS, b. 18 Jun 1893, Napoli, Cattaraugus Co, NY.
1447. iv. HARLAN PORTER MILKS, b. 08 Jan 1907, Salamanca, Cattaraugus County, New York; d. 26 Apr 1971, Guilderland, New York.

707. FRED^8 MILKS *(GEORGE^7, JOHN^6 MILK, JONATHAN^5, JONATHAN^4, JOB^3, JOHN^2, JOHN^1)* was born 27 Jul 1860 in Napoli, Cattaraugus Co., NY, and died 13 Jan 1931 in Cattaraugus County, New York. He married CARRIE ESTHER COMSTOCK 20 Aug 1892, daughter of ALONZO COMSTOCK and RUTH HOLDRIDGE. She was born 06 Sep 1872 in Napoli, Cattaraugus County, New York, and died 1936 in Cattaraugus County, New York.

Child of FRED MILKS and CARRIE COMSTOCK is:
1448. i. ELVA OLIVE^9 MILKS, b. 27 Apr 1897, Napoli, Cattaraugus Co, NY.

708. NETTIE^8 MILKS *(GEORGE^7, JOHN^6 MILK, JONATHAN^5, JONATHAN^4, JOB^3, JOHN^2, JOHN^1)* was born 14 Oct 1865 in Napoli, Cattaraugus County, New York, and died 30 Nov 1942 in Buffalo, Erie County, New York. She married ARCHIE B. MILKS, son of LUTHER MILKS and MARY WILLIAMS. He was born 17 Feb 1867 in Napoli, Cattaraugus County, New York, and died 20 May 1930 in East Randolph, Cattaraugus County, New York.

Child of NETTIE MILKS and ARCHIE MILKS is:
1449. i. AUDRA^9 MILKS, b. 05 Dec 1888, Napoli, Cattaraugus County, New York.

709. FRANCES ELLEN^8 MILKS *(GILES^7, JOHN^6 MILK, JONATHAN^5, JONATHAN^4, JOB^3, JOHN^2, JOHN^1)* was born Feb 1854 in Napoli, Cattaraugus County, New York. She married MALCOM NELSON FREEMAN. He was born Sep 1853 in Pennsylvania.

Children of FRANCES MILKS and MALCOM FREEMAN are:
1450. i. MARK F.^{9} FREEMAN, b. Mar 1875, Salamanca, Cattaraugus County, New York.
1451. ii. FRANK N. FREEMAN, b. Jul 1879, Salamanca, Cattaraugus County, New York.
     iii. HARRY LEROY FREEMAN, b. 13 Mar 1891, Salamanca, Cattaraugus County, New York; m. MILDRED B. ACHENBACH, 25 Dec 1918, Cattaraugus County, New York; b. 31 Aug 1887, Cattaraugus County, New York; d. Jul 1972, Fredonia, Chautauqua County, New York.

710. JAMES^8 MILKS *(GILES^7, JOHN^6 MILK, JONATHAN^5, JONATHAN^4, JOB^3, JOHN^2, JOHN^1)* was born Dec 1863 in Napoli, Cattaraugus County, New York. He married ACHSA CLARK. She was born Abt. 1862 in Of Leon, New York.

Children of JAMES MILKS and ACHSA CLARK are:
1452. i. CLARK BURNELL^9 MILKS, b. 29 Nov 1895, Leon, Cattaraugus County, New York; d. 1962, McKean County, Pennsylvania.
1453. ii. CLARENCE LELAND MILKS, b. 09 Nov 1899, Leon, Cattaraugus County, New York; d. Jan 1985, Angola, Erie County, New York.

711. BERT^8 MILKS *(GILES^7, JOHN^6 MILK, JONATHAN^5, JONATHAN^4, JOB^3, JOHN^2, JOHN^1)* was born 22 Oct 1874 in Napoli, Cattaraugus County, New York. He married (1) ISOLENE L. TATE Bet. 1907 - 1908 in Cattaraugus County, New York. She was born 1879 in Pennsylvania. He married (2) NOT KNOWN Abt. 1894. She was born Abt. 1875, and died Bef. 1900 in Napoli, Cattaraugus County, New York. Bert was an accomplished violinist.

Child of BERT MILKS and ISOLENE TATE is:
- i. HARRY[9] MILKS, b. 26 Nov 1911, Little Valley, Cattaraugus County, NY; d. 26 Nov 1911, Little Valley, Cattaraugus County, NY.

712. ADELBERT[8] MILKS *(HIRAM[7], JOHN[6] MILK, JONATHAN[5], JONATHAN[4], JOB[3], JOHN[2], JOHN[1])* was born 7 June 1854 in Napoli, Cattaraugus County, New York, and died 19 Feb. 1923 in Napoli, Cattaraugus County, New York. He married ADA MILES. She was born 14 Apr 1864 in Watertown, Jefferson County, New York, and died 18 Oct 1932 in Cattaraugus County, New York.

Children of ADELBERT MILKS and ADA MILES are:
- i. ERNEST M.[9] MILKS, b. 11 Oct 1884, Cattaraugus Co, NY; d. 28 Jun 1907, Salamanca, NY (railway accident) (unmarried).
- 1454. ii. ARTHUR GLENN MILKS (aka: Hiram Glenn Milks), b. 18 Jul 1886, Napoli, Cattaraugus County, New York; d. Jan 1966, New York.
- iii. JULIAN MILKS, b. 19 Apr 1889; d. 22 Feb 1963, Frewsburg, Chautauqua County, New York (unmarried).
  When Julian registered for the World War 1 draft in 1917, he lived in Napoli, Cattaraugus Co., New York, where he worked on the farm of George R. Simpson. He was single and reported the loss of one eye. He does not seem to be included in any Federal Census after 1910, when he was living with his parents. He died in February 1963 in Cattaraugus County, New York.
- 1455. iv. HAROLD E. MILKS, b. 06 Jun 1891, Randolph, Cattaraugus County, New York; d. Jul 1968, Horseheads, Chemung County, New York.
- 1456. v. GEORGE WASHINGTON MILKS, b. 06 Apr 1894, Napoli, Cattaraugus Co, NY; d. 25 Jul 1963, Napoli, Cattaraugus Co, NY.
- 1457. vi. WILLIAM HENRY MILKS, b. 18 Jul 1896, Red House, Cattaraugus County, New York; d. 19 Dec 1986, Hudson, Fremont County, Wyoming.
- vii. ESTHER HELEN MILKS, b. 22 Dec 1902, Cattaraugus Co, NY; d. 09 Sep 1909, Cattaraugus Co, NY.

713. SIDNEY DAVID[8] MILKS *(HIRAM[7], JOHN[6] MILK, JONATHAN[5], JONATHAN[4], JOB[3], JOHN[2], JOHN[1])* was born 05 Mar 1858 in Cattaraugus County, New York, and died 04 Dec 1931 in Mt. Pleasant, Iowa. He married (1) ETTIE _____ Abt. 1880 in Cattaraugus County, New York. She was born 1863 in New York. He married (2) LOVINA BAUSMAN 26 Jan 1886 in Mt. Pleasant, Henry County, Iowa, daughter of ISAAC BAUSMAN and MARY SPINGLER. She was born 01 Dec 1859 in Sheffield, Tippecanoe County, Indiana, and died 30 Jan 1941 in Mt. Pleasant, Iowa.

Children of SIDNEY MILKS and LOVINA BAUSMAN are:
- 1458. i. ELIZABETH 'LIZZY'[9] MILKS, b. Jan 1888, East Randolph, Cattaraugus County, New York; d. 15 Oct 1962, Salina, Jefferson County, Iowa.
- ii. LAURA ANNA MILKS, b. 03 Jan 1890, Mt. Pleasant, Iowa; d. 09 Jul 1897, Mt. Pleasant, Iowa (died young of spinal meningitis.).
- 1459. iii. WALTER BAUSMAN MILKS, b. 12 Jan 1893, Mt. Pleasant, Iowa; d. Apr 1964, Iowa.

714. WALLACE H.[8] MILKS *(HIRAM[7], JOHN[6] MILK, JONATHAN[5], JONATHAN[4], JOB[3], JOHN[2], JOHN[1])* was born 12 Jan 1863, and died 19 Sep 1932 in East Randolph, Cattaraugus County, New York. He married LOULIE B. EDDY 10 Jun 1886 in Napoli, NY, daughter of JOHN EDDY and MARIA CATLIN. She was born 09 Jun 1868, and died Feb 1937 in East Randolph, Cattaraugus County, New York.

Children of WALLACE MILKS and LOULIE EDDY are:
- 1460. i. IRENE BESSIE[9] MILKS, b. 09 Sep 1888, Napoli, Cattaraugus Co, NY.
- 1461. ii. CLIFFORD PAUL MILKS, b. 26 May 1897, Napoli, Cattaraugus Co, NY; d. 28 Mar 1969, East Randolph, Cattaraugus, NY 14730.

715. MARY B.[8] MILKS *(HIRAM[7], JOHN[6] MILK, JONATHAN[5], JONATHAN[4], JOB[3], JOHN[2], JOHN[1])* was born 20 Jun 1870 in Napoli, Cattaraugus County, New York. She married STANLEY E. HAAS 10 Feb 1897 in Napoli, Cattaraugus County, New York, son of PIERRE HAAS and HANNAH PFLUEGER. He was born 07 May 1876 in Cattaraugus County, New York, and died 14 Jan 1948.

Mary Milks Haas contributed many records of her family for Grace Croft's book.

Children of MARY MILKS and STANLEY HAAS are:

      i. WALTER S.[9] HAAS, b. 30 Jan 1903, Napoli, Cattaraugus County, New York; d. Nov 1978, Niagara County, New York; m. MAUDE F. GREEN, 19 Apr 1930; b. 04 Aug 1906, Chautauqua County, New York; d. 08 May 2000, Sinclairville, Chautauqua County, New York. No children.

1462.   ii. HELEN D. HAAS, b. 19 Nov 1904, Napoli, Cattaraugus County, New York; d. 18 Apr 1998, Ithaca, Tompkins County, New York.

716. SIBYL[8] MILKS (*HIRAM[7], JOHN[6] MILK, JONATHAN[5], JONATHAN[4], JOB[3], JOHN[2], JOHN[1]*) was born 07 Dec 1876 in Napoli, Cattaraugus County, New York, and died Aft. Jan 1930 in Cattaraugus County, New York. She married EDWARD RHODES 12 Aug 1896, son of WILLIAM RHODES and SARAH WATENPAN. He was born Abt. 1878 in Napoli, Cattaraugus County, New York, and died Aft. Jan 1930 in Cattaraugus County, New York.

Children of SIBYL MILKS and EDWARD RHODES are:

1463.   i. AUDRA[9] RHODES, b. 07 Apr 1900, Conewango, Cattaraugus County, New York; d. 18 Aug 1999, Melbourne, Brevard County, Florida.

1464.   ii. RALPH E. 'DUSTY' RHODES, b. 26 Nov 1904, Conewango, Cattaraugus County, New York; d. 02 Jun 2004, Santa Barbara, California.

717. MANLEY KENNETH[8] MILKS (*HIRAM[7], JOHN[6] MILK, JONATHAN[5], JONATHAN[4], JOB[3], JOHN[2], JOHN[1]*) was born 26 May 1880 in Napoli, Cattaraugus Co., NY, and died 14 Mar 1941. He married LENA A. FLAGG 1904, daughter of DAVID FLAGG and SARAH EVERETTS. She was born 31 Jul 1886 in Michigan, and died 1939.

Children of MANLEY MILKS and LENA FLAGG are:

1465.   i. KENNETH WALLACE[9] MILKS, b. 09 Dec 1907, Frewsburg, Chautauqua County, New York; d. 25 Oct 1980, Jamestown, Chautauqua Co, NY.

1466.   ii. JOHN HIRAM MILKS, b. 25 Feb 1910, Frewsburg, NY; d. 30 Jan 2004, Cattaraugus Co., NY.

1467.   iii. OLDICE HOMER ALTON MILKS, b. 16 May 1912, Frewsburg, Chautauqua County, New York; d. 07 Jul 2008, Danville, Montour County, Pennsylvania.

718. ANNIE J.[8] MILKS (*MARTIN[7], JOHN[6] MILK, JONATHAN[5], JONATHAN[4], JOB[3], JOHN[2], JOHN[1]*) was born 28 Jan 1860 in Napoli, Cattaraugus County, New York, and died 1915 in Cattaraugus County, New York. She married WILLIAM H. MCELWAIN, son of REUBEN MCELWAIN and MARY CHAMPLAIN. He was born 18 Nov 1858 in Conewango, Cattaraugus County, New York, and died 1936 in Cattaraugus County, New York.

Children of ANNIE MILKS and WILLIAM MCELWAIN are:

1468.   i. ROBERT LEE[9] MCELWAIN, b. 10 Apr 1879, Conewango, Cattaraugus County, New York.

1469.   ii. MARY ALICE MCELWAIN, b. 02 Sep 1880, Cattaraugus County, New York.

1470.   iii. ALBERT DOUGLAS MCELWAIN, b. 12 Feb 1883, Little Valley, Cattaraugus County, New York; d. Sep 1970, Cattaraugus County, New York.

1471.   iv. BENJAMIN CLAYTON MCELWAIN, b. 13 Jun 1885, Conewango, Cattaraugus County, New York; d. 30 Dec 1966, Randolph, Cattaraugus County, New York.

      v. JESSIE E. MCELWAIN, b. 07 Jul 1887, Napoli, Cattaraugus County, New York; d. 12 May 1968; m. BENJAMIN FRANK BARBER, 22 Apr 1914, Kennedy, Chautauqua County, New York; b. 27 Jan 1883; d. Dec 1971, Ovid, Seneca County, New York. No children.

1472.   vi. HARRIET J. 'HATTIE' MCELWAIN, b. 13 Jun 1889, Conewango, Cattaraugus County, New York.

1473.   vii. HESTER DOROTHY 'HETTIE' MCELWAIN, b. 13 Jan 1892, Conewango, Cattaraugus County, New York; d. Jan 1974, Falconer, Chautauqua County, New York.

1474.   viii. GEORGE EARL MCELWAIN, b. 10 Jan 1893, Conewango, Cattaraugus County, New York; d. Apr 1966, Randolph, Cattaraugus County, New York.

1475.   ix. WILLIAM H. MCELWAIN, JR., b. 24 Jul 1895, Napoli, Cattaraugus County, New York.

1476.   x. PAUL OAKLEY MCELWAIN, b. 24 Sep 1899, Randolph, Cattaraugus County, New York; d. Jun 1983, Warsaw, Wyoming County, New York.

1477.   xi. WALTER MCELWAIN, b. Oct 1903, Randolph, Cattaraugus County, New York; d. 26 Dec 1961, Randolph, Cattaraugus County, New York.

719. MARY A.⁸ MILKS *(MARTIN⁷, JOHN⁶ MILK, JONATHAN⁵, JONATHAN⁴, JOB³, JOHN², JOHN¹)* was born 11 Jul 1861 in Napoli, Cattaraugus County, New York. She married FRED SPENCER COMSTOCK 15 Feb 1883 in Little Valley, Cattaraugus, NY, son of ALONZO COMSTOCK and RUTH HOLDRIDGE. He was born 06 Sep 1861 in Napoli, Cattaraugus County, New York, and died Bef. 1943.

Children of MARY MILKS and FRED COMSTOCK are:
- i. GLENN E.⁹ COMSTOCK, b. 16 Apr 1886, Napoli, Cattaraugus County, New York; d. 1943, Issue, Charles County, Maryland; m. ANNA QUIGLEY, 30 Oct 1911, Salamanca, Cattaraugus County, New York; b. Abt. 1886. No children.
- ii. FLORA "FLOSSIE" COMSTOCK, b. 12 May 1888; d. No children; m. FRED HILDRETH; b. Abt. 1888.
- iii. HERBERT COMSTOCK, d. d.y..

720. HARVEY C.⁸ MILKS *(MARTIN⁷, JOHN⁶ MILK, JONATHAN⁵, JONATHAN⁴, JOB³, JOHN², JOHN¹)* was born 19 Dec 1863 in Napoli, Cattaraugus County, New York, and died 22 Feb 1942. He married OLIVE HOLDREDGE 19 Sep 1889 in Cattaraugus County, New York, daughter of JEFFERSON HOLDREDGE and ADDIE BEEBE. She was born 14 Oct 1869 in Napoli, Cattaraugus County, New York.

Children of HARVEY MILKS and OLIVE HOLDREDGE are:
- i. ADDIE⁹ MILKS, b. 30 Jan 1890, Napoli, Cattaraugus County, New York; d. 1907, Napoli, Cattaraugus County, New York.
- ii. MARVIN J. MILKS, b. 07 Feb 1891, Napoli, Cattaraugus County, New York; d. 31 Aug 1925, Los Angeles, Calif.; m. ERNESTINE ROWLEY, Sep 1924, Los Angeles, Calif.; b. 22 Aug 1895, Formerly of Little Valley; d. 15 Dec 1966, Winter Haven, Polk Co., Florida. No children.
- iii. ALLEN G. MILKS, b. Bet. 1893 - 1894, Napoli, Cattaraugus County, New York; m. (1) HENRIETTA C. MCCLUSKEY, 22 Jul 1920, Salamanca, Cattaraugus County, New York; b. 04 Sep 1897, Little Valley, Cattaraugus County, New York; d. 30 Jun 1990; m. (2) NINA (WAITE) MEACHAM, Bet. 1949 - 1950. No children.
- 1478. iv. ROSS JENNINGS MILKS, b. 25 Jul 1896, Napoli, Cattaraugus County, New York; d. 15 Mar 1971, McCain, Hoke County, North Carolina.
- v. ALICE MILKS, b. 1900, Napoli, Cattaraugus County, New York; d. 1912, Napoli, Cattaraugus County, NY.

721. CLAUDIA E.⁸ MILKS *(MARTIN⁷, JOHN⁶ MILK, JONATHAN⁵, JONATHAN⁴, JOB³, JOHN², JOHN¹)* was born 1865 in Napoli, Cattaraugus County, New York, and died in In Childbirth. She married WILLIAM TOWN.

Child of CLAUDIA MILKS and WILLIAM TOWN is:
- i. BABY⁹ TOWN, d. At birth.

722. GEORGE B.⁸ MILKS *(MARTIN⁷, JOHN⁶ MILK, JONATHAN⁵, JONATHAN⁴, JOB³, JOHN², JOHN¹)* was born 17 Nov 1867 in Napoli, Cattaraugus County, New York, and died 02 Jul 1949 in Jamestown, New York. He married MARY A. GAST 11 Oct 1893 in Dunkirk, NY, daughter of JOHN GAST and MARGARET _____. She was born 24 Apr 1870 in Dunkirk, New York, and died 28 Jul 1948 in Dunkirk, New York.

Children of GEORGE MILKS and MARY GAST are:
- 1479. i. HOWARD GEORGE⁹ MILKS, b. 18 Jun 1895, Dunkirk, New York; d. Feb 1966, Columbus, Franklin County, Ohio.
- 1480. ii. EARLE DONALD MILKS, b. 03 Feb 1900, Dunkirk, New York; d. 13 Mar 1965, Chautauqua, New York.
- iii. WALTER C. MILKS, b. 17 Jan 1906, Dunkirk, New York; d. 25 Sep 1971, Dunkirk, New York. Never married.

723. ELIZABETH "LIZZIE"⁸ MILKS *(MARTIN⁷, JOHN⁶ MILK, JONATHAN⁵, JONATHAN⁴, JOB³, JOHN², JOHN¹)* was born Apr 1870 in Napoli, Cattaraugus County, New York. She married WILLIAM J. FOX Abt. 1891 in Cattaraugus County, New York. He was born Aug 1868.

Child of ELIZABETH MILKS and WILLIAM FOX is:

1481. i. WILLIAM MILKS[9] FOX, b. 08 Dec 1898, Leon, Cattaraugus County, New York; d. Apr 1973, Leon, Cattaraugus County, New York.

724. ALMYRA "MYRA"[8] MILKS *(MARTIN[7], JOHN[6] MILK, JONATHAN[5], JONATHAN[4], JOB[3], JOHN[2], JOHN[1])* was born 01 Apr 1872 in Napoli, Cattaraugus County, New York, and died 1954 in Salamanca, Cattaraugus County, New York. She married ELMER OWEN COMSTOCK 15 Oct 1890 in New Albion, Cattaraugus County, New York, son of ALONZO COMSTOCK and RUTH HOLDRIDGE. He was born 12 Mar 1864 in Napoli, Cattaraugus County, New York, and died 17 Mar 1931 in Napoli, Cattaraugus County, New York.

Children of ALMYRA MILKS and ELMER COMSTOCK are:

1482. i. EULA ALETHA[9] COMSTOCK, b. 24 Oct 1891, Cattaraugus County, New York.
ii. HAZEL MILDRED COMSTOCK, b. 28 Dec 1897, Napoli, Cattaraugus County, New York; d. 17 Apr 1906, Little Valley, Cattaraugus County, New York.
1483. iii. CLAUDIA RUTH COMSTOCK, b. 09 May 1899, Napoli, Cattaraugus County, New York; d. 13 Jun 1922, Napoli, Cattaraugus County, New York (in Childbirth).

725. MARTIN "VAN"[8] MILKS *(MARTIN[7], JOHN[6] MILK, JONATHAN[5], JONATHAN[4], JOB[3], JOHN[2], JOHN[1])* was born 1875 in Napoli, Cattaraugus County, New York, and died 01 Jul 1953 in Little Valley, Cattaraugus County, New York. He married INA WHITCOMB Abt. 1895. She died 1950 in Little Valley, Cattaraugus County, New York.

Children of MARTIN MILKS and INA WHITCOMB are:

i. JOSEPHINE E. 'JOSIE'[9] MILKS, b. Sep 1891, New Albion, Cattaraugus County, New York.
ii. FLOYD MARTIN MILKS, b. 12 Jan 1896, New Albion, Cattaraugus County, New York; d. 10 Oct 1918, Fort Dix, New Jersey.

726. EMMET EARL[8] MILKS *(MARTIN[7], JOHN[6] MILK, JONATHAN[5], JONATHAN[4], JOB[3], JOHN[2], JOHN[1])* was born 23 Oct 1876 in Napoli, Cattaraugus County, New York, and died 18 Mar 1946 in Cattaraugus County, New York. He married (1) WINIFRED SHAW 1899 in Cattaraugus, NY, daughter of ERVIN SHAW and ELIZABETH _____. She was born Jun 1879 in Dayton, NY, and died 1913 in Cattaraugus County, New York. He married (2) ETTIE E. WAITE 29 Oct 1914 in Little Valley, Cattaraugus, NY, daughter of GEORGE WAITE and ADELINE JONES. She was born Bet. 1866 - 1867 in Napoli, Cattaraugus Co, NY.

Children of EMMET MILKS and WINIFRED SHAW are:

i. CLAYTON E.[9] MILKS, b. 13 Nov 1900, Conewango; d. 04 Oct 1902, Conewango.
ii. FENTON ERVIN MILKS, b. 28 Jan 1904, Mansfield, New York; d. 12 Apr 1988, Plant City, Hillsborough Co., Florida; m. RUTH SIMPSON MCALLISTER, 31 Oct 1925, Fredonia, Chautauqua Co, NY, by A. L. Prosens, Priest; b. 04 May 1904, Fredonia, NY; d. 03 Oct 1979, Cattaraugus, NY. No children.
1484. iii. ELLSWORTH M. MILKS, b. 04 Dec 1906, Conewango, NY; d. May 1953, Little Valley, Cattaraugus County, NY.

727. HORACE 'LEE'[8] MILKS *(MARTIN[7], JOHN[6] MILK, JONATHAN[5], JONATHAN[4], JOB[3], JOHN[2], JOHN[1])* was born 10 Oct 1878 in Little Valley, Cattaraugus County, New York, and died 10 Nov 1936 in Salamanca, Cattaraugus County, New York. He married MAUDE GIBSON Abt. 1901 in Cattaraugus County, New York, daughter of DANIEL GIBSON and ELIZA ELLIS. She was born 23 Aug 1883 in Cooper Tract, Pennsylvania, and died 03 Sep 1945 in Salamanca, Cattaraugus County, New York.

OBITUARY

Rev. H. S. Kissinger will officiate at the funeral of Lee Milks of Salamanca, which will be held Saturday afternoon at 2 o'clock from Middleton's funeral home in Little Valley. Mr. Milks, who died Tuesday night at the age of 58, leaves two sons, Clifton and Kenneth Milks of Little Valley; two daughters, Mrs. Theodore Carlson of Randolph and Mrs. Lee Whitcomb of Little Valley; four brothers, Emmitt, Harvey and Van Milks of Little Valley and George Milks of Dunkirk, and three sisters, Mrs. Myra Comstock of Little Valley, Mrs. Ruby Drew of Randolph and Mrs. Lizzie Fox of Leon.

Children of HORACE MILKS and MAUDE GIBSON are:

1485.   i.   CLIFTON LEE[9] MILKS, b. 06 Oct 1901, Little Valley, Cattaraugus County, New York; d. May 1975, Latrobe, Westmoreland County, Pennsylvania.

1486.   ii.   HAZEL G. MILKS, b. 07 Aug 1903, Little Valley, Cattaraugus County, New York; d. Jun 1980, Little Valley, Cattaraugus County, NY.

1487.   iii.   MARGUERITE ARLENE MILKS, b. 19 Sep 1906, New York.

1488.   iv.   KENNETH LEE MILKS, b. 08 Jan 1913, Little Valley, Cattaraugus County, New York; d. Apr 1976, Cattaraugus County, New York.

728. RUBY C.[8] MILKS *(MARTIN[7], JOHN[6] MILK, JONATHAN[5], JONATHAN[4], JOB[3], JOHN[2], JOHN[1])* was born 1883 in Napoli, Cattaraugus Co, NY. She married BENJAMIN DREW 01 Sep 1908 in Little Valley, Cattaraugus, NY, son of CLARK DREW and DORA PULSE. He was born 03 Jul 1887 in Little Valley, Cattaraugus County, New York, and died Oct 1973 in Machias, Cattaraugus County, New York.

Children of RUBY MILKS and BENJAMIN DREW are:
    i.   JOHN C.[9] DREW, b. Abt. Feb 1914, Salamanca, Cattaraugus County, NY.
    ii.   HENRY M. DREW, b. Abt. Apr 1918, Salamanca, Cattaraugus County, NY.
    iii.   EMMETT DREW, b. Abt. Aug 1924, Salamanca, Cattaraugus County, NY.

729. CYNTHIA[8] HARRINGTON *(JOB[7], DEBORAH[6] MILKS, JONATHAN[5] MILK, JONATHAN[4], JOB[3], JOHN[2], JOHN[1])* was born 16 Oct 1862 in Easton, Washington County, New York, and died in Greenwich, Washington County, New York. She married BARBER WATERS. He was born 09 Sep 1859.

Children of CYNTHIA HARRINGTON and BARBER WATERS are:
    i.   HENRY J.[9] WATERS, b. Greenwich, Washington County, New York.
    ii.   NATHAN C. WATERS, b. Greenwich, Washington County, New York.
    iii.   BARBARA L.. WATERS, b. Greenwich, Washington County, New York.
    iv.   ESTHER E. WATERS, b. Greenwich, Washington County, New York.
    v.   IRWIN M. WATERS, b. Greenwich, Washington County, New York.

730. LUCY[8] HARRINGTON *(JOB[7], DEBORAH[6] MILKS, JONATHAN[5] MILK, JONATHAN[4], JOB[3], JOHN[2], JOHN[1])* was born 15 Jul 1865 in Easton, Washington County, New York, and died 20 Jan 1932 in Greenwich, Washington County, New York. She married ALBERT ENGLISH. He was born Abt. 1863.

Children of LUCY HARRINGTON and ALBERT ENGLISH are:
    i.   BERTHA[9] ENGLISH, b. Greenwich, Washington County, New York.
    ii.   RENA ENGLISH, b. Greenwich, Washington County, New York.
    iii.   ADELAIDE ENGLISH, b. Greenwich, Washington County, New York.
    iv.   MYRTLE ENGLISH, b. Greenwich, Washington County, New York.

731. HOWARD[8] HARRINGTON *(BENJAMIN[7], DEBORAH[6] MILKS, JONATHAN[5] MILK, JONATHAN[4], JOB[3], JOHN[2], JOHN[1])* was born 24 Feb 1860 in Easton, Washington County, New York, and died 18 Feb 1903. He married LOTTIE OLIVER. She was born Abt. 1860.

Child of HOWARD HARRINGTON and LOTTIE OLIVER is:
    i.   HANNAH[9] HARRINGTON, b. 09 Oct 1897, Cambridge, Washington County, New York; m. JAMES BEVERIDGE; b. Abt. 1897.

732. DORA[8] HARRINGTON *(BENJAMIN[7], DEBORAH[6] MILKS, JONATHAN[5] MILK, JONATHAN[4], JOB[3], JOHN[2], JOHN[1])* was born 11 Mar 1862 in Cambridge, Washington County, New York, and died 04 Mar 1930 in Easton, Washington County, New York. She married RICHARD LYONS. He was born 30 May 1861.

Children of DORA HARRINGTON and RICHARD LYONS are:
    i.   MALCOMB[9] LYONS.
    ii.   FOREST LYONS.

733. THOMAS A.[8] HARRINGTON *(DAVID W.[7], DEBORAH[6] MILKS, JONATHAN[5] MILK, JONATHAN[4], JOB[3], JOHN[2], JOHN[1])* was born 04 Oct 1858 in Greenwich, Washington County, New York, and died 30 Oct 1935 in Flagler Beach, Florida. He married LENA VAN NORMAN. She was born Abt. 1858, and died 1925.

Child of THOMAS HARRINGTON and LENA VAN NORMAN is:
1489.   i.   BYRON[9] HARRINGTON, b. 1894, Greenwich, Washington County, New York.

734. MERRITT R.[8] HARRINGTON *(DAVID W.[7], DEBORAH[6] MILKS, JONATHAN[5] MILK, JONATHAN[4], JOB[3], JOHN[2], JOHN[1])* was born 13 Dec 1863 in Greenwich, Washington County, New York, and died 13 May 1927 in Greenwich, Washington County, New York. He married MARGARET WILKINSON Abt. 1887. She was born 30 Jul 1864.

Children of MERRITT HARRINGTON and MARGARET WILKINSON are:
1490.   i.   MAUD[9] HARRINGTON, b. 30 Aug 1888, Greenwich, Washington County, New York.
           ii.   DAVID W. HARRINGTON, b. 09 Apr 1890, Greenwich, Washington County, New York; m. HELEN DUDA; b. Oct 1893, Bayonne, New Jersey.

735. GEORGE[8] HARRINGTON *(ALLEN[7], DEBORAH[6] MILKS, JONATHAN[5] MILK, JONATHAN[4], JOB[3], JOHN[2], JOHN[1])* was born 30 Oct 1865 in Greenwich, Washington County, New York, and died 09 Jun 1902. He married EMMA SPRINGER. She was born Nov 1867.

Children of GEORGE HARRINGTON and EMMA SPRINGER are:
           i.   VOLNEY G.[9] HARRINGTON, b. Jan 1888, Greenwich, Washington County, New York; m. MATTIE F (WILLIAMS) BURGESS, 23 Mar 1913, Washington County, New York; b. Abt. 1883.
           ii.   MARY 'MATTIE' HARRINGTON, b. May 1892, Easton, Washington County, New York; d. 2 children; m. MISTTER DEVOY; b. Abt. 1886.
           iii.   RUTH E. HARRINGTON, b. Oct 1899, Easton, Washington County, New York.

736. LEWIS[8] HARRINGTON *(ALLEN[7], DEBORAH[6] MILKS, JONATHAN[5] MILK, JONATHAN[4], JOB[3], JOHN[2], JOHN[1])* was born 1871 in Easton, Washington County, New York, and died 13 Feb 1951 in Dorset, Bennington County, Vermont. He married (1) EMMA WILKINSON. He married (2) PEARL SERILLA FISHER Abt. 1914, daughter of MARK FISHER and BERTHA BROOKS. She was born 13 Nov 1886 in Dorset, Bennington County, Vermont, and died 08 Jan 1959 in Burlington, Chittenden County, Vermont. No children.

Child of LEWIS HARRINGTON and PEARL FISHER is:
           i.   MARGORY[9] HARRINGTON, b. Abt. 1915, Vermont.

737. WILLIAM[8] HARRINGTON *(ALLEN[7], DEBORAH[6] MILKS, JONATHAN[5] MILK, JONATHAN[4], JOB[3], JOHN[2], JOHN[1])* was born 1872 in Easton, Washington County, New York. He married HARRIET A. 'HATTIE' SPRINGER. She was born 1879.

Child of WILLIAM HARRINGTON and HARRIET SPRINGER is:
           i.   LUCY J.[9] HARRINGTON, b. Abt. 1892, Easton, Washington County, New York.

738. EDWARD[8] HARRINGTON *(ALLEN[7], DEBORAH[6] MILKS, JONATHAN[5] MILK, JONATHAN[4], JOB[3], JOHN[2], JOHN[1])* was born 1874 in Jackson, New York. He married ANNA IRONS. She was born in Of Greenwich, New York.

Child of EDWARD HARRINGTON and ANNA IRONS is:
           i.   RAYMOND[9] HARRINGTON, b. Abt. 1908, Easton, Washington County, New York.

739. HENRY[8] MILKS-HOWARD *(LEONARD[7] MILKS, BENJAMIN[6], JONATHAN[5] MILK, JONATHAN[4], JOB[3], JOHN[2], JOHN[1])* was born Apr 1844 in Cattaraugus County, New York, and died 1914 in Cattaraugus County, New York. He married (1) EMMA ACKLEY, daughter of WILLARD ACKLEY and BETSEY _____. She was born Abt. 1857 in Cattaraugus County, New York. He married (2) MELISSA M. SNYDER 1865 in Cattaraugus County, New York. She was born 1842, and died 1906 in Cattaraugus County, New York.

     Henry Milks changed his surname to Howard after his mother died, and his grandfather Howard reared him.
     [In order to keep mindful of Henry and his descendants actually being blood of the Milks family, I am going to

keep their surname as Milks-Howard, rather than just Howard.]

Children of HENRY MILKS-HOWARD and MELISSA SNYDER are:

1491. i. FRED H.[9] MILKS-HOWARD, b. 21 Jul 1865, Dayton, Cattaraugus County, New York; d. 17 May 1926, Leon, Cattaraugus County, New York.
1492. ii. HARRIET A. 'HATTIE' MILKS-HOWARD, b. 10 May 1869, Dayton, Cattaraugus County, New York; d. 12 Dec 1953, Chester, Orange County, New York.
1493. iii. JAMES HENRY 'JIMMY' MILKS-HOWARD, b. 24 Jan 1875, Dayton, Cattaraugus County, New York; d. 21 Apr 1955, South Dayton, Cattaraugus County, New York.

740. EDGAR[8] MILKS *(LEONARD[7], BENJAMIN[6], JONATHAN[5] MILK, JONATHAN[4], JOB[3], JOHN[2], JOHN[1])* was born 05 Dec 1849 in Mansfield, Cattaraugus County, New York, and died 12 Oct 1917 in Gowanda, Cattaraugus County, New York. He married (1) LUELLA CAMERON in Cattaraugus County, New York, daughter of DOCTOR CAMERON and SARAH SMITH. She was born Abt. 1850 in New York ?, and died 1886 in Cattaraugus County, New York. He married (2) ELLEN MARIE PINE 29 Sep 1887 in New York, daughter of JOSHUA PINE and SARAH BARNHART. She was born 24 Jul 1851 in Hoosick Falls, New York, and died 26 May 1926 in New York.

Children of EDGAR MILKS and LUELLA CAMERON are:

i. MABEL[9] MILKS, d. d. aged 5 yrs.
ii. SON MILKS, d. d.y..
iii. EDGAR EUGENE MILKS, b. Abt. 1873, Cattaraugus County, New York; d. d.y..
1494. iv. LEONARD GLENN MILKS, b. 12 Mar 1877, Cattaraugus County, New York; d. 20 May 1951, Yankton County, South Dakota.

Children of EDGAR MILKS and ELLEN PINE are:

1495. v. PORTIA EDNA[9] MILKS, b. 17 Aug 1888, Franklinville, Cattaraugus County, New York; d. 25 Jul 1955, Pittsburgh, Pennsylvania.
1496. vi. MERVA ERDEN MILKS, b. 03 Apr 1890, Franklinville, Cattaraugus County, New York.
1497. vii. GRETCHEN IRENE MILKS, b. 22 Dec 1891, Gowanda, Cattaraugus County, New York; d. 22 Nov 1984, Gowanda, NY.
1498. viii. LEROY ETHELBERT MILKS, b. 06 Nov 1894, Collins, NY; d. 1960, Collins, Erie County, New York.

741. FRANCIS JAMES 'FRANK'[8] MILKS *(LEONARD[7], BENJAMIN[6], JONATHAN[5] MILK, JONATHAN[4], JOB[3], JOHN[2], JOHN[1])* was born 13 Jul 1851 in Persia, Cattaraugus County, New York, and died Nov 1929 in Cattaraugus County, New York. He married PHENIE A. BUFFINGTON, daughter of JEREMIAH BUFFINGTON and PHEBE _____. She was born 1852 in Cattaraugus County, New York, and died Nov 1939 in Cattaraugus County, New York.

Grace Croft stated that PHENIE A. BUFFINGTON was a direct descendant of Capt. Miles Standish

Children of FRANCIS MILKS and PHENIE BUFFINGTON are:

1499. i. FRED JAMES[9] MILKS, b. 31 Mar 1874, Mansfield, Cattaraugus County, New York; d. 1953, Cattaraugus County, New York.
1500. ii. CHARLES H. MILKS, b. 23 May 1877, Otto, Cattaraugus County, New York; d. 15 Apr 1943, Ellicottville, Cattaraugus County, New York.
1501. iii. FRANK W. MILKS, b. 12 Nov 1879, New Albion, Cattaraugus County, NY; d. 15 Feb 1968, Machias, Cattaraugus County, New York.
iv. EDITH M. MILKS, b. 10 Dec 1880, Cattaraugus County, New York; m. JOHN W. MORSE, 1904, New Albion, Cattaraugus County, New York; b. 17 Dec 1881, Cattaraugus County, New York; d. May 1972, Delevan, Cattaraugus County, New York. No children.
1502. v. ROLAND MILKS, b. 10 Jan 1883, Leon, New York.
1503. vi. JAY E. MILKS, b. 04 May 1885, Leon, Cattaraugus County, New York; d. 1961, Cattaraugus County, New York.
1504. vii. ROBERT MILKS, b. 20 Sep 1886, Conewango, Cattaraugus County, New York; d. 05 Jun 1970, Covington, Miami County, Ohio.
viii. TWIN CHILD A. MILKS, b. 1890; d. Died young.
ix. TWIN CHILD B. MILKS, b. 1890; d. Died young.

742. ELIZA JANE 'ALIDA'[8] LOOP *(CORDELIA[7] MILKS, BENJAMIN[6], JONATHAN[5] MILK, JONATHAN[4], JOB[3], JOHN[2], JOHN[1])* was born 1848 in Hubbard, Dodge County, Wisconsin, and died 1924 in Carrollton, Cattaraugus County, New York. She married DAVID SAMUEL JONES Abt. 1870 in Cattaraugus County, New York, son of SIMON JONES and RUTH OWEN. He was born 12 Nov 1834 in Utica, New York, and died Bet. 01 Jan - 10 Feb 1911 in Carrollton, Cattaraugus County, New York.

Children of ELIZA LOOP and DAVID JONES are:
- i. ASAHEL[9] JONES, b. Abt. 1871, Leon, Cattaraugus County, New York.
- 1505. ii. EDWARD TRUMAN JONES, b. 15 Mar 1877, Leon, Cattaraugus County, New York.
- iii. ALVIN O. JONES, b. May 1880, Leon, Cattaraugus County, New York.
- iv. RUTH C. JONES, b. Abt. 1883, Leon, Cattaraugus County, New York.

743. GEORGE HENRY[8] MILKS *(GARRETT T.[7], BENJAMIN[6], JONATHAN[5] MILK, JONATHAN[4], JOB[3], JOHN[2], JOHN[1])* was born 1854 in Persia, Cattaraugus Co., NY, and died Bef. 05 May 1913. He married FRANCELIA G. 'CELIA' COMSTOCK Aft. 01 Jun 1880 in Cattaraugus County, New York, daughter of DAVID COMSTOCK and EMERY REMINGTON. She was born Feb 1862 in Dayton, Cattaraugus County, New York, and died 1914 in Cattaraugus County, New York.

from "**Death Notices** 1819-1899" Fredonia Censor, vol. II, p370 by Lois Barris 1994.
   "Milks, John Lavern d: 1 Feb 1890, murdered by his brother, George Henry, during a quarrel in the Southern part of the town of Persia. George was arrested and taken to Gowanda."

Nineteen YEARS IN PRISON. - Buffalo Express, June 6, 1890
   George Henry Milks Sentenced for the Murder of His Brother. LITTLE VALLEY, June 5.—At the opening of the court this morning District-Attorney Warring moved sentence on George Henry Milks.
The defense asked for a suspension of sentence until an appeal could be taken. The motion was denied. The prisoner was sworn, and stated to the Court that he was born in the town of Persia, was 80 years old, a farmer, and had a family.
   When asked if he had anything to say. the prisoner talked in a disconnected manner for about
20 minutes. and then was sentenced to 19 years and 6 months' confinement at Auburn Prison at
hard labor. The prisoner was entirely unmoved by his sentence.

Children of GEORGE MILKS and FRANCELIA COMSTOCK are:
- 1506. i. GARRETT LANSING[9] MILKS, b. 30 Oct 1881, Dayton, Cattaraugus County, New York; d. 10 Feb 1964, Cattaraugus County, New York.
- ii. HELEN MILKS, b. Abt. 1883. Croft says that Helen was adopted out. I can find no record of her, and it may be that she took the surname of the adopting family.
- 1507. iii. FREEMAN MILKS, b. 07 Aug 1885, Persia, Cattaraugus County, New York; d. 04 Aug 1955, Madera, California.

744. ALEDA[8] MILKS *(GARRETT T.[7], BENJAMIN[6], JONATHAN[5] MILK, JONATHAN[4], JOB[3], JOHN[2], JOHN[1])* was born 11 Jul 1860 in Persia, Cattaraugus County, New York, and died 13 Oct 1955 in Los Angeles, California. She married LOUIE H. MORGAN Bet. 1879 - 1889 in Cattaraugus County, New York. He was born Jun 1854 in New York, and died Bef. 1930.

Children of ALEDA MILKS and LOUIE MORGAN are:
- i. MARY A.[9] MORGAN, b. 31 Aug 1880, Cattaraugus County, New York; d. 1949; m. FRED ALMON STEWARD, 1900, Cattaraugus County, New York; b. 05 Mar 1879, Mansfield, Cattaraugus County, New York.
- 1508. ii. FRANCES D. MORGAN, b. 18 Oct 1891, Cattaraugus County, New York.

745. DELPHINE[8] MILKS *(GARRETT T.[7], BENJAMIN[6], JONATHAN[5] MILK, JONATHAN[4], JOB[3], JOHN[2], JOHN[1])* was born 18 Oct 1871 in Persia, Cattaraugus County, New York, and died 1920 in Randolph, Cattaraugus County, New York. She married HERBERT ROLFE, son of GILBERT MILKS and CLARISSA PAYNE. He was born 06 Sep 1867 in Perrysburg, Cattaraugus County, New York (adopted son), and died 10 Jun 1944 in Randolph, Cattaraugus County, New York.
   Delphine married the adopted son of her uncle, Gilbert Milks.

Child of DELPHINE MILKS and HERBERT ROLFE is:
1509. i. RAYMOND HERBERT[9] ROLFE, b. 02 Apr 1888, Persia, Cattaraugus County, New York; d. 26 Jul 1953, Salamanca, Cattaraugus County, New York.

746. JOANNAH DAISY[8] MILKS *(GARRETT T.[7], BENJAMIN[6], JONATHAN[5] MILK, JONATHAN[4], JOB[3], JOHN[2], JOHN[1])* was born 22 Jul 1879 in Persia, Cattaraugus County, New York. She married JOHN CHARLESWORTH 1896, son of JOSEPH CHARLESWORTH and ROSANNA HIGBEE. He was born 01 Aug 1875 in Salamanca, Cattaraugus County, New York.

Children of JOANNAH MILKS and JOHN CHARLESWORTH are:
  i. HAZEL[9] CHARLESWORTH, b. 22 Feb 1898, Toledo, Lucas County, Ohio; d. 22 Feb 1919, Gowanda, Cattaraugus County, New York; m. HAROLD A. HOWARD, 16 Nov 1917, South Dayton, Cattaraugus County, New York; b. 10 Sep 1894, Wesley, Cattaraugus County, New York; d. May 1981, Cattaraugus County, New York.
1510. ii. JOHN CHARLESWORTH, b. 13 Dec 1903, Persia, Cattaraugus County, New York; d. Feb 1970, Little Valley, Cattaraugus County, New York.

747. GILBERT WALLACE[8] ALLEN *(JOANNA IRENE[7] MILKS, BENJAMIN[6], JONATHAN[5] MILK, JONATHAN[4], JOB[3], JOHN[2], JOHN[1])* was born Abt. 1851 in Wisconsin. He married HARRIET A. HALLOCK 1877 in Wisconsin, daughter of JAMES D. HALLOCK. She was born Jan 1855 in Wisconsin.

Children of GILBERT ALLEN and HARRIET HALLOCK are:
1511. i. ETHEL[9] ALLEN, b. Sep 1878, Loyal, Clark County, Wisconsin; d. Bet. 1907 - 1910, Loyal, Clark County, Wisconsin.
  ii. FREEMAN ALLEN, b. 1879, Loyal, Clark County, Wisconsin.

748. ROSALIE 'ROSE'[8] ALLEN *(JOANNA IRENE[7] MILKS, BENJAMIN[6], JONATHAN[5] MILK, JONATHAN[4], JOB[3], JOHN[2], JOHN[1])* was born Feb 1858 in Wisconsin, and died 1928 in Loyal, Clark County, Wisconsin. She married ARTHUR MILES 01 Nov 1874 in Pine Valley, Clark County, Wisconsin, son of SAMUEL MILES and SARAH _____. He was born May 1850 in Verona, Dane County, Wisconsin, and died 1916 in Loyal, Clark County, Wisconsin.

Children of ROSALIE ALLEN and ARTHUR MILES are:
  i. BERTHA[9] MILES, b. 1875, Loyal, Clark County, Wisconsin.
  ii. FLORENCE MILES, b. Jul 1877, Loyal, Clark County, Wisconsin.
1512. iii. LOIS MILES, b. 25 Aug 1880, Loyal, Clark County, Wisconsin; d. 25 Jul 1957, Winona County, Minnesota.
  iv. ROY MILES, b. Feb 1884, Loyal, Clark County, Wisconsin.
  v. LINNIE MILES, b. Apr 1888, Loyal, Clark County, Wisconsin; d. 1914, Loyal, Clark County, Wisconsin.

749. S. JACKSON[8] FULLER *(DEBORAH[7] MILKS, BENJAMIN[6], JONATHAN[5] MILK, JONATHAN[4], JOB[3], JOHN[2], JOHN[1])* was born Oct 1861 in Dayton, Cattaraugus County, New York, and died 1925 in Cattaraugus County, New York. He married CORA RICH 1885 in Cattaraugus County, New York. She was born Jan 1870 in New York, and died 1942 in Cattaraugus County, New York.

Child of S. FULLER and CORA RICH is:
  i. MAUD[9] FULLER, b. Nov 1885, Cattaraugus County, New York.

750. HERBERT[8] ROLFE *(GILBERT[7] MILKS, BENJAMIN[6], JONATHAN[5] MILK, JONATHAN[4], JOB[3], JOHN[2], JOHN[1])* was born 06 Sep 1867 in Perrysburg, Cattaraugus County, New York (adopted son), and died 10 Jun 1944 in Randolph, Cattaraugus County, New York. He married DELPHINE MILKS, daughter of GARRETT MILKS and MARIA KENYON. She was born 18 Oct 1871 in Persia, Cattaraugus County, New York, and died 1920 in Randolph, Cattaraugus County, New York.

Child is listed above under (745) Delphine Milks.

751. ABBIE J.[8] MILKS *(LUTHER P.[7], PRINCE WILLIAM[6], JONATHAN[5] MILK, JONATHAN[4], JOB[3], JOHN[2], JOHN[1])* was born 20 May 1861 in Napoli, Cattaraugus County, New York, and died 1945 in Erie, Pennsylvania. She married WILLIAM SMITH Abt. 1880, son of JAMES SMITH. He was born 1856 in Napoli, Cattaraugus County, New York.

Children of ABBIE MILKS and WILLIAM SMITH are:
- i. ROBERT[9] SMITH, b. 17 Mar 1882.
- ii. ROLLIN SMITH.
- iii. LILLIAN SMITH, m. (1) HARRY WHIPPLE; m. (2) WILLARD PHILLIPS.
- iv. JESSIE SMITH, m. MERLE QUAY.
- v. JENNIE SMITH.

752. ARCHIE B.[8] MILKS *(LUTHER P.[7], PRINCE WILLIAM[6], JONATHAN[5] MILK, JONATHAN[4], JOB[3], JOHN[2], JOHN[1])* was born 17 Feb 1867 in Napoli, Cattaraugus County, New York, and died 20 May 1930 in East Randolph, Cattaraugus County, New York. He married NETTIE MILKS, daughter of GEORGE MILKS and MAHALA ARNOLD. She was born 14 Oct 1865 in Napoli, Cattaraugus County, New York, and died 30 Nov 1942 in Buffalo, Erie County, New York.

Archie B. MILKS died 20 May 1930 in Town of Napoli, NY at the age of 63 yrs, 3 mos, 3 days. (Source: Myers & Myers Funeral Home Records, 1930, p. 66)

A farmer he was married to Nettie MILKS who survived him. A resident of the area his entire life, his funeral was held 23 May 1930 at The House with Rev. Dellbridge officiating. His burial the same day in East Randolph, NY.

Child is listed above under (708) Nettie Milks.

753. WILLIAM A.[8] MILKS *(LUTHER P.[7], PRINCE WILLIAM[6], JONATHAN[5] MILK, JONATHAN[4], JOB[3], JOHN[2], JOHN[1])* was born 10 Jun 1872 in New York, and died 04 Feb 1920 in East Randolph, Cattaraugus County, New York. He married WINIFRED WOODS Abt. 1909, daughter of MICHAEL WOODS and WINIFRED COLWELL. She was born 1878 in Onoville, Cattaraugus County, New York, and died 12 Apr 1933 in East Randolph, Cattaraugus County, New York.

Children of WILLIAM MILKS and WINIFRED WOODS are:
- 1513. i. WILLIAM WOODS[9] MILKS, b. 23 Aug 1910, East Randolph, Cattaraugus County, New York; d. 17 Oct 1968, Bradford, McKean County, Pennsylvania.
- 1514. ii. WINIFRED MAY MILKS, b. 18 Aug 1913, East Randolph, Cattaraugus County, New York; d. 15 Apr 1991, WCA Hospital, Jamestown, Chautauqua County, New York.
- 1515. iii. MARY ANN MILKS, b. 25 Sep 1915, East Randolph, Cattaraugus County, New York; d. 23 Jun 2009, Texas.

754. MARY ELIZABETH[8] LYON *(MARY ELIZABETH[7] MILKS, PRINCE WILLIAM[6], JONATHAN[5] MILK, JONATHAN[4], JOB[3], JOHN[2], JOHN[1])* was born 1856 in Cattaraugus Co., NY, and died 1918. She married CHARLES H. DEWEY. He was born Abt. 1856.

Children of MARY LYON and CHARLES DEWEY are:
- i. GERTRUDE[9] DEWEY, m. MISTTER WELCH.
- ii. DR. EDWIN DEWEY.
- iii. MARION DEWEY, m. MISTTER BOLTON.

755. JAMES B.[8] LYON *(MARY ELIZABETH[7] MILKS, PRINCE WILLIAM[6], JONATHAN[5] MILK, JONATHAN[4], JOB[3], JOHN[2], JOHN[1])* was born 04 Jun 1858 in Cattaraugus Co., NY, and died Apr 1924 in Fairbank, Iowa. He married MARY C. KANE Abt. 1883. She was born 08 Dec 1856 in Ohio, and died 04 Jul 1919 in Fairbank, Iowa.

Children of JAMES LYON and MARY KANE are:
- 1516. i. CASSIE[9] LYON, b. 24 Apr 1884, Fairbank, Iowa; d. 02 Jun 1947, Fairbank, Iowa.
- ii. WILLIAM H. LYON, b. 04 Nov 1885, Fairbank, Iowa; d. 04 Oct 1947; m. IRENE ZIMMER; b. Abt. 1885; d. No children.
- iii. EDWIN J. LYON, b. 24 May 1893, Fairbank, Iowa; d. unm.. Edwin contributed records on the Lyon family.
- 1517. iv. JESSE J. LYON, b. 17 Jan 1896, Fairbank, Iowa; d. 06 Sep 1947, Los Angeles, California.

756. CHARLES H.[8] LYON *(MARY ELIZABETH[7] MILKS, PRINCE WILLIAM[6], JONATHAN[5] MILK, JONATHAN[4], JOB[3], JOHN[2], JOHN[1])* was born 02 Aug 1860 in Cattaraugus Co., NY, and died Jun 1912. He married SARAH E. (FARNSWORTH) FELT. She was born Abt. 1860 in Columbia County, Wisconsin, and died 13 Sep 1954 in Fairbank, Iowa?.

Children of CHARLES LYON and SARAH FELT are:
1518.   i.   ANN^9 LYON.
       ii.   BELVA ORINDA LYON, d. d. aged 15 mos..
       iii. JAMES LYON, d. No children.
       iv. ELIZABETH LYON, d. No children.
       v.   FRED LYON, d. 1 daughter.
       vi. CHARLES LYON, d. No children.

757. JESSE^8 LYON *(MARY ELIZABETH^7 MILKS, PRINCE WILLIAM^6, JONATHAN^5 MILK, JONATHAN^4, JOB^3, JOHN^2, JOHN^1)* was born 11 Nov 1862 in Cattaraugus Co., NY, and died 29 Nov 1914 in Fairbank, Iowa. He married MARY NEAL Abt. 1885 in Fairbank, Iowa. She was born Abt. 1862, and died 16 May 1951 in Fairbank, Iowa ?.

Children of JESSE LYON and MARY NEAL are:
1519.   i.   DELLA^9 LYON, b. 06 Oct 1887, Fairbank, Iowa; d. 09 Jul 1954, Fairbank, Iowa.
1520.   ii. HARRY NEAL LYON, b. 18 Nov 1890, Fairbank, Iowa.
1521.   iii. HAROLD LYON, b. Abt. 1901, Fairbank, Iowa.

758. NORA R.^{8} LYON *(MARY ELIZABETH^7 MILKS, PRINCE WILLIAM^6, JONATHAN^5 MILK, JONATHAN^4, JOB^3, JOHN^2, JOHN^1)* was born 03 Aug 1867 in Cattaraugus Co., NY, and died 24 Apr 1917. She married PORT WALKER.

Children of NORA LYON and PORT WALKER are:
       i.   ABBIE^9 WALKER, d. 2 sons, 2 daus.; m. MISTTER FETTKETHER.
       ii. JAMES WALKER, d. unm..
       iii. FRANK WALKER.
       iv. JESSE WALKER, d. No children.
1522.   v.   WILMA WALKER.

759. PRINCE ARTHUR "TIMOTHY"^{8} LYON *(MARY ELIZABETH^7 MILKS, PRINCE WILLIAM^6, JONATHAN^5 MILK, JONATHAN^4, JOB^3, JOHN^2, JOHN^1)* was born Jun 1874 in Fairbank, Iowa, and died 1926 in Steamburg, Cattaraugus County, New York. He married (1) EMMA ETSEL 16 Dec 1893 in Cattaraugus County, New York. She was born Abt. 1875. He married (2) GRACE WATERS 20 Dec 1897 in Cattaraugus County, New York. She was born Sep 1876 in Cattaraugus County, New York. He married (3) EDITH E. BURR 09 Nov 1910 in Cattaraugus County, New York, daughter of STEPHEN BURR and UNKNOWN HATCH. She was born 1876, and died 1931.

Children of PRINCE LYON and GRACE WATERS are:
       i.   MARY^9 LYON, b. Mar 1898, Cattaraugus Co., NY; d. 24 Apr 1934, Cattaraugus County, New York; m. EDWARD O'BRIEN, Cattaraugus County, New York.
1523.   ii. HOWARD R. LYON, b. 07 Jul 1900, Cattaraugus County, New York; d. Mar 1971, Falconer, Chautauqua County, New York.

760. MARY E.^{8} BOTHWELL *(CAROLINE P.^{7} SEELEY, BATHSHEBA^6 MILKS, JONATHAN^5 MILK, JONATHAN^4, JOB^3, JOHN^2, JOHN^1)* was born 1849 in Jones County, Iowa, and died Abt. 1939 in Harlan, Iowa. She married DANIEL W. ALLEN. He was born Abt. 1849.

Children of MARY BOTHWELL and DANIEL ALLEN are:
       i.   CORA^9 ALLEN, b. 03 Jun 1871, Harlan, Iowa; m. H. J. WILCOX; b. Abt. 1871.
       ii. DR. GILBERT ALLEN, b. 19 Apr 1873, Harlan, Iowa; m. LOUISE BAREN; b. Abt. 1873.
       iii. SADIE ALLEN, b. 16 Aug 1876, Harlan, Iowa; m. J. T. NEWBY; b. Abt. 1876. No children. Sadie contributed family records.
       iv. DR. GEORGE ALLEN, b. Harlan, Iowa; m. HOPE MOLAR. No children.
1524.   v.   DAISY ALLEN, b. 03 Mar 1884, Harlan, Iowa.
       vi. MAYMIE ALLEN, b. 10 Jan 1887, Harlan, Iowa; m. ED GUERIN; b. Abt. 1887.
       vii. CLEO ALLEN, m. E. F. ZOERB.

761. CAROLINE A.[8] BOTHWELL *(CAROLINE P.[7] SEELEY, BATHSHEBA[6] MILKS, JONATHAN[5] MILK, JONATHAN[4], JOB[3], JOHN[2], JOHN[1])* was born 1851 in Jones County, Iowa. She married (1) TRACEY D. MACE 28 Apr 1869 in Anamosa, Jones County, Iowa. She married (2) ROBERT KENNEY 31 Aug 1872 in Anamosa, Jones County, Iowa. He was born Abt. 1851.

Child of CAROLINE BOTHWELL and TRACEY MACE is:
   i. KELLY[9] MACE, b. Abt. 1869, Rome, Jones County, Iowa.

Child of CAROLINE BOTHWELL and ROBERT KENNEY is:
   ii. ADA[9] KENNEY, d. Had 10 children; m. J. W. REBER.

762. FLORA J.[8] BOTHWELL *(CAROLINE P.[7] SEELEY, BATHSHEBA[6] MILKS, JONATHAN[5] MILK, JONATHAN[4], JOB[3], JOHN[2], JOHN[1])* was born 1857 in Jones County, Iowa. She married J. P. MILLER. He was born Abt. 1857.

Children of FLORA BOTHWELL and J. MILLER are:
   i. GEORGE[9] MILLER, b. Of Harlan, Iowa.
   ii. LILLIAN MILLER, b. Of Omaha, Nebraska.
   iii. LEONA MILLER, b. Of Cedar Rapids, Iowa.
   iv. GROVER MILLER.
   v. VERNA MILLER, b. Of Omaha, Nebraska.

763. JOHN J.[8] BOTHWELL *(CAROLINE P.[7] SEELEY, BATHSHEBA[6] MILKS, JONATHAN[5] MILK, JONATHAN[4], JOB[3], JOHN[2], JOHN[1])* was born 1859 in Jones County, Iowa. He married MARY BAKER. She was born Abt. 1859.

Children of JOHN BOTHWELL and MARY BAKER are:
   i. MABLE[9] BOTHWELL, b. Of Omaha, Nebraska.
   ii. AGNES BOTHWELL, b. Of Omaha, Nebraska.
   iii. MARIE BOTHWELL, b. Of Omaha, Nebraska.
   iv. JOHN BOTHWELL, b. Of Shelby, Iowa.
   v. LEONARD BOTHWELL, b. Of Minnesota.

764. LYDIA ZERUIE 'ADA'[8] BOTHWELL *(CAROLINE P.[7] SEELEY, BATHSHEBA[6] MILKS, JONATHAN[5] MILK, JONATHAN[4], JOB[3], JOHN[2], JOHN[1])* was born 15 Dec 1865 in Olin, Jones County, Iowa, and died 14 Mar 1935 in McGraw, Cortland County, New York. She married (1) GEORGE ANTHONY 24 Oct 1880 in Iowa. He was born Abt. 1865. She married (2) ABRAM C. WILKINS 08 Jan 1882 in Olin, Jones County, Iowa, son of A. WILKINS and ANN SMEAH. He was born 1855. She married (3) BUTLER WEBSTER MILKS May 1885, son of BENJAMIN MILKS and ORINDA LAWRENCE. He was born 12 Sep 1862 in Black Hawk County, Iowa, and died 27 Mar 1943 in Peace River, Alberta, Canada. She married (4) JOHN H. GRIMM 27 Feb 1909 in Brown County, Nebraska, son of LUDWIG GRIMM and CHRISTINA _____. He was born Abt. 1855 in Wisconsin. She married (5) MERRITT NORTON LAMB 08 Oct 1910 in Council Bluffs, Pottawattamie, Iowa, son of GEORGE LAMB and CHARLETT WARDEN. He was born 02 Aug 1853 in New London, Oneida County, New York, and died 27 Sep 1932 in Cedar Rapids, Linn County, Iowa. She married (6) GEORGE COX Abt. 1925. Lydia Bothwell Cox is buried in Ainsworth Cemetery, Ainsworth. Brown County, Nebraska

Compendium of History Reminiscence & Biography of Western Nebraska
Alden Publishing Company, 1909   page 447-448
MRS. LYDIA MILKS.
The management of an extensive tract of land has fallen to the lot of the lady above mentioned, and the prosperity apparent is evidence of her ability and good judgment. Mrs. Milks is one of the early settlers in Brown County, where she has spent the best part of her life in building up her farm and home. She has had the care of a family of children, and exerted her energies for their support and education, and is now the owner of a valuable ranch.

Mrs. Milks was born in Olin, Jones county, Iowa, in 1864. Her father, John Bothwell, was a native of Scotland, and her mother of Yankee stock. She was raised and educated in Jones County, attending the common schools and later moved to Nebraska, locating in Cherry county in May, 1885. She married B. W. Milks. The home was ninety miles south of Valentine. Their first dwelling was a house built of sods, with a sod roof, and in this place all but their youngest child was born. They proved up on the homestead, remaining on it for twelve or thirteen years, and in 1899 moved to

Lakeland, Brown County, settling on a ranch on Moon Lake, where their children would have a better chance to attend good schools. Mrs. Milks lived on this ranch until 1905, and she has had the entire management of the place, the ranch comprising one thousand one hundred and twenty acres, stocked with horses and cattle, and improved with good buildings. There was a fine grove of trees on this place, the grove including twenty-five acres, which added greatly to the value of the ranch.

At first this place only contained three hundred and twenty acres, and it was added to gradually and improved, until a comfortable home has been built up, which at present is under the management of Mrs. Milks' son and daughter, she now living on three hundred and twenty acres of land located near Ainsworth, which she purchased after getting the ranch established and running in good shape. She has improved this property until it is now one of the most valuable in this locality, the farm being used for a dairy and hay farm.

Mrs. Milks deserves much praise for the success which she has attained through her own unaided efforts, for many years doing a man's work in running the farm, besides raising her family of children and directing their education, few men have accomplished as much as she. Her family consists of eight children, as follows: Clyde D., Clarence L., Burney B., Gertrude May Vera E., Lillian T., Percy L., and Gerald R.

Child of LYDIA BOTHWELL and ABRAM WILKINS is:
    i. CLYDE D.^{9} WILKINS, b. Nov 1880, Iowa.

Children of LYDIA BOTHWELL and BUTLER MILKS are:
    ii. CLYDE D. WILKINS^9 MILKS, b. Nov 1880, Iowa.
1525. iii. CLARENCE LUKE MILKS, b. 28 Mar 1886, Fairbank, Iowa; d. Oct 1962, New York.
    iv. BURNEY B. MILKS, b. 01 Sep 1887, Pullman, Nebraska; d. 24 Jun 1911.
1526. v. GERTRUDE MAY MILKS, b. 12 May 1889, Pullman, Cherry County, Nebraska; d. 09 Mar 1968, Norfolk, Madison, Nebraska.
1527. vi. VERA ELAINE MILKS, b. 17 Apr 1892, Pullman, Nebraska; d. 13 Feb 1984, Scottsbluff, Nebraska.
1528. vii. LILLIAN TRESSIE MILKS, b. 27 Feb 1895, Pullman, Nebraska; d. 20 Oct 1991, Alachua County, Florida.
1529. viii. PERCIE L. MILKS, b. 22 Jan 1898, Nebraska; d. Sep 1983, Cortland County, New York.
    ix. GERALD ROOSEVELT MILKS, b. 30 May 1905, Ainsworth, Nebraska; d. 19 Aug 1907, Ainsworth, Brown County, Nebraska.

765. GEORGE GRANT^8 BOTHWELL *(CAROLINE P.^{7} SEELEY, BATHSHEBA^6 MILKS, JONATHAN^5 MILK, JONATHAN^4, JOB^3, JOHN^2, JOHN^1)* was born 1867 in Jones County, Iowa. He married BELLE FENNELSON.

Child of GEORGE BOTHWELL and BELLE FENNELSON is:
    i. MILBERT^9 BOTHWELL, b. Of Bassett, Nebraska; d. 2 daughters.

766. LUCIUS^8 BACON *(ZERUAH^7 MILKS, JONATHAN^6, JONATHAN^5 MILK, JONATHAN^4, JOB^3, JOHN^2, JOHN^1)* was born 1855 in Chautauqua County, New York, and died 14 Apr 1888 in Napoli, Cattaraugus County, New York. He married JANE FOX, daughter of WILLIAM FOX and ANNA SUTTON. She was born 15 Apr 1858, and died Dec 1931.

Children of LUCIUS BACON and JANE FOX are:
1530. i. MABEL^9 BACON, b. 04 Jul 1877, Cattaraugus County, New York.
1531. ii. ANNA ZERUAH BACON, b. 14 May 1885, Leon, Cattaraugus County, New York.

767. DEFOREST^8 BENTLEY *(LYDIA A.^{7} MILKS, JONATHAN^6, JONATHAN^5 MILK, JONATHAN^4, JOB^3, JOHN^2, JOHN^1)* was born 26 Feb 1854 in Ellington, Chautauqua County, New York, and died 31 Dec 1922 in Wichita Falls, Wichita County, Texas. He married ELIZA TEMPLE 04 Jul 1876 in Pike County, Illinois, daughter of JAMES TEMPLE and SARAH HAWKER. She was born 23 Sep 1855 in Griggsville, Pike County, Illinois, and died 15 Dec 1934 in Wichita Falls, Wichita County, Texas.

Children of DEFOREST BENTLEY and ELIZA TEMPLE are:
    i. CHARLES H.^{9} BENTLEY, b. 1877; d. 1960.
    ii. MARGARET E. BENTLEY, b. 1878.
    iii. HARRIETT S. BENTLEY, b. 1880.
    iv. JAMES HARVEY BENTLEY, b. 31 Oct 1882, Illinois; d. 25 Feb 1953, Wichita Falls, Wichita County, Texas;

       m. TENNESSEE WALLER; b. 18 Sep 1882, Charlie, Clay County, Texas; d. 28 Jul 1976, Burkburnett, Wichita County, Texas.
- v. GEORGE J. BENTLEY, b. 1888; d. 1973.
- vi. MARY ANN BENTLEY, b. 1892; d. 1929.
- vii. JOHN PERRY BENTLEY, b. 1893.
- viii. LLOYD H. BENTLEY, b. 1895; d. 1954.
- ix. RUTH ELIZA BENTLEY, b. 18 Nov 1897, Thornberry, Clay County, Texas; d. 11 Oct 1972, Wichita Falls, Wichita County, Texas; m. LESLIE HOWARD; d. 20 Jul 1966, Wichita Falls, Wichita County, Texas.

768. GEORGE W.[8] SATTERLEE *(MARY JANE[7] BENSON, SARAH[6] MILKS, JONATHAN[5] MILK, JONATHAN[4], JOB[3], JOHN[2], JOHN[1])* was born 16 Feb 1852 in Grundy County, Illinois, and died 16 Sep 1911 in Elk County, Kansas. He married LORA ELLA CARTER 1875. She was born 27 Mar 1853 in Illinois, and died 14 Jul 1927 in Elk County, Kansas.

Children of GEORGE SATTERLEE and LORA CARTER are:
- i. W. H.[9] SATTERLEE, b. Abt. 1878; d. Bef. 1900.
- 1532. ii. MARY AMANDA SATTERLEE, b. 08 May 1879, Moline, Elk County, Kansas; d. Jun 1964, Moline, Elk County, Kansas.
- iii. HOWARD F. SATTERLEE, b. Abt. 1883, Kansas.
- iv. RAY SATTERLEE, b. Abt. 1893, Kansas.
- v. EVA LORA SATTERLEE, b. Abt. 1897, Center, Chautauqua County, Kansas.

769. MARY[8] WHITE *(LYDIA[7] BENSON, SARAH[6] MILKS, JONATHAN[5] MILK, JONATHAN[4], JOB[3], JOHN[2], JOHN[1])* was born Jul 1852 in Grundy County, Illinois. She married JOHN ROBINSON 1867. He was born Jan 1833 in New York.

Children of MARY WHITE and JOHN ROBINSON are:
- 1533. i. JOHN J.[9] ROBINSON, b. 29 Jan 1870, Illinois; d. 04 Feb 1961, Chisago County, Minnesota.
- ii. ALICE ROBINSON, b. Bet. 1877 - 1878, Iowa.
- iii. EDGAR E. ROBINSON, b. 21 Oct 1881, Stratford, Iowa; d. 24 Sep 1951, San Francisco, California.
- iv. KENNETH WILLIAM ROBINSON, b. 08 Jun 1892, Webster City, Hamilton County, Iowa.

770. SARAH[8] WHITE *(LYDIA[7] BENSON, SARAH[6] MILKS, JONATHAN[5] MILK, JONATHAN[4], JOB[3], JOHN[2], JOHN[1])* was born 25 Jun 1854 in Grundy County, Illinois, and died 01 Mar 1934 in Kansas. She married WILLIAM JUNE 16 Jul 1876 in Morris, Grundy County, Illinois, son of CYRUS JUNE and LUTHERA PIERCE. He was born 08 Jul 1850 in Calhoun County, Michigan, and died 04 Aug 1936 in Kansas.

Children of SARAH WHITE and WILLIAM JUNE are:
- i. MARY 'MINNIE'[9] JUNE, b. Abt. 1877, Kansas.
- ii. FRANK JUNE, b. 1879, Kansas; d. 1950, Kansas.
- 1534. iii. CHARLES JUNE, b. Sep 1882, Kansas; d. 1948, Kansas.
- iv. EDITH JUNE, b. Jan 1884, Kansas; d. x.
- 1535. v. GLENN JUNE, b. 26 Sep 1887, Udall, Cowley County, Kansas; d. 04 May 1975, Kansas.
- vi. BESSIE JUNE, b. Sep 1888, Kansas; d. x.
- 1536. vii. HOWARD HENRY JUNE, b. 17 Oct 1889, Kansas; d. 07 Mar 1961, Kansas.
- viii. WILLIAM JUNE, b. Abt. 1892, Kansas; d. Bef. 1900, Kansas.
- ix. ROY JUNE, b. Abt. 1895, Kansas; d. x.

771. CHARLES[8] WHITE *(LYDIA[7] BENSON, SARAH[6] MILKS, JONATHAN[5] MILK, JONATHAN[4], JOB[3], JOHN[2], JOHN[1])* was born 1856 in Grundy County, Illinois, and died in Kansas. He married HALLIE (TRAVIS) SHOCK 19 Jul 1884 in Dallas County, Iowa, daughter of HENRY TRAVIS and _____ HUNTER. She was born Abt. 1860 in Pennsylvania, and died in Washington.

Children of CHARLES WHITE and HALLIE SHOCK are:
- i. HARRY TRAVIS[9] WHITE, b. 12 Oct 1887, Morris, Illinois; d. 10 Jun 1975, Burlington, Skagit County, Washington; m. HELEN C. _____; b. 10 Apr 1895, South Dakota; d. 05 Jun 1965, Yakima, Washington.
- 1537. ii. PHILLIP TRAVIS WHITE, b. 12 Oct 1887, Morris, Illinois; d. Aug 1964, Washington.

772. LYDIA[8] WHITE *(LYDIA[7] BENSON, SARAH[6] MILKS, JONATHAN[5] MILK, JONATHAN[4], JOB[3], JOHN[2], JOHN[1])* was born 18 Dec 1867 in Grundy County, Illinois, and died 1945 in Morris, Illinois. She married ROBERT W. PEACOCK 18 Mar 1885 in Morris, Grundy County, Illinois, son of JOHN PEACOCK and REBECCA ANDERSON. He was born 23 Jun 1856 in Morris, Illinois.

Children of LYDIA WHITE and ROBERT PEACOCK are:
- i. MARGARET BLANCHE 'MAGGIE'[9] PEACOCK, b. 11 Aug 1886, Morris, Grundy County, Illinois; d. d.y..
- 1538. ii. EDWARD H. PEACOCK, b. 11 Dec 1887, Morris, Grundy County, Illinois.
- 1539. iii. FLORENCE E. PEACOCK, b. 11 Jul 1892, Morris, Grundy County, Illinois.
- iv. RUTH PEACOCK, b. 23 Dec 1897, Morris, Grundy County, Illinois; d. no children.; m. ARNIE FLATTNESS; b. Abt. 1897.
- 1540. v. LESLIE PEACOCK, b. 22 Aug 1901, Morris, Grundy County, Illinois.
- vi. J. AUSTIN PEACOCK, b. 22 Feb 1904, Morris, Grundy County, Illinois; d. 1904, Morris, Grundy County, Illinois.

773. WILLIAM J.[8] WHITE *(RUTH[7] BENSON, SARAH[6] MILKS, JONATHAN[5] MILK, JONATHAN[4], JOB[3], JOHN[2], JOHN[1])* was born 23 Feb 1855 in Grundy County, Illinois, and died 27 May 1937 in Morris, Grundy County, Illinois. He married JENNIE ELYEA 30 Sep 1877, daughter of WILLIAM ELYEA and JANE BEESON. She was born 07 Apr 1859 in Kankakee, Illinois, and died 03 Feb 1947 in Morris, Grundy County, Illinois.

Children of WILLIAM WHITE and JENNIE ELYEA are:
- 1541. i. MINNIE M.[9] WHITE, b. 16 Jan 1880, Grundy County, Illinois.
- 1542. ii. JAMES LAWRENCE WHITE, b. 14 May 1882, Grundy County, Illinois.

774. CAROLINE[8] WHITE *(RUTH[7] BENSON, SARAH[6] MILKS, JONATHAN[5] MILK, JONATHAN[4], JOB[3], JOHN[2], JOHN[1])* was born 25 Feb 1858 in Grundy County, Illinois, and died 04 Nov 1930. She married GEORGE EDWARD SEVERNS 25 Dec 1876. He was born 1852, and died 1926.

Child of CAROLINE WHITE and GEORGE SEVERNS is:
- 1543. i. HORACE[9] SEVERNS, b. 14 Apr 1878, Morris, Grundy County, Illinois.

775. ALMIRA D.[8] WHITE *(RUTH[7] BENSON, SARAH[6] MILKS, JONATHAN[5] MILK, JONATHAN[4], JOB[3], JOHN[2], JOHN[1])* was born 12 Feb 1861 in Grundy County, Illinois, and died 28 Dec 1931 in Morris, Grundy County, Illinois. She married BARTIN V. PATTISON 13 Feb 1884 in Morris, Grundy County, Illinois, son of WILLIAM PATTISON and JANE ROGERS. He was born 14 Feb 1854, and died 24 Jun 1921.

Children of ALMIRA WHITE and BARTIN PATTISON are:
- i. SUSIE ALMIRA[9] PATTISON, b. 23 Jun 1885, Morris, Grundy County, Illinois; d. no children.; m. FRANK H. ELDRED; b. 31 May 1883, Bourne, England; d. 21 Oct 1943, Morris, Grundy County, Illinois.
- 1544. ii. JAMES LAWRENCE PATTISON, b. 19 Feb 1890, Morris, Grundy County, Illinois.

776. SUSAN LINDSEY[8] WHITE *(RUTH[7] BENSON, SARAH[6] MILKS, JONATHAN[5] MILK, JONATHAN[4], JOB[3], JOHN[2], JOHN[1])* was born 07 Sep 1864 in Grundy County, Illinois, and died 01 Mar 1944 in Morris, Grundy County, Illinois. She married ARTHUR AMOS DEWEY 18 Feb 1891, son of JOSEPH DEWEY and SARAH _____. He was born 21 Sep 1865 in Grundy County, Illinois, and died 04 Sep 1945 in Morris, Grundy County, Illinois.

Children of SUSAN WHITE and ARTHUR DEWEY are:
- 1545. i. JAMES LAWRENCE[9] DEWEY, b. 17 Feb 1892.
- 1546. ii. FRED DEWEY, b. 21 May 1900.

777. SAMUEL HOLDERMAN[8] WHITE *(RUTH[7] BENSON, SARAH[6] MILKS, JONATHAN[5] MILK, JONATHAN[4], JOB[3], JOHN[2], JOHN[1])* was born 07 Apr 1866 in Grundy County, Illinois, and died 12 Dec 1945 in Morris, Grundy County, Illinois. He married KATE WINZENBURG Mar 1898. She was born 22 Nov 1871 in St. Louis, Missouri, and died 14 Nov 1906 in Grundy County, Illinois.

Children of SAMUEL WHITE and KATE WINZENBURG are:
1547. i. AGNES[9] WHITE, b. 16 Feb 1900, Grundy County, Illinois.
1548. ii. SAMUEL HOLDERMAN WHITE, JR., b. 24 Jun 1904, Grundy County, Illinois.
iii. RUTH WHITE, b. 10 Nov 1906, Grundy County, Illinois; d. 1906, Grundy County, Illinois.

778. GEORGE PERRY[8] WHITE *(RUTH[7] BENSON, SARAH[6] MILKS, JONATHAN[5] MILK, JONATHAN[4], JOB[3], JOHN[2], JOHN[1])* was born 05 Jul 1874 in Grundy County, Illinois, and died 14 Mar 1940. He married MARIE JOHNSON 10 Feb 1897 in Morris, Grundy County, Illinois. She was born Abt. 1875.

Children of GEORGE WHITE and MARIE JOHNSON are:
i. MAE[9] WHITE, b. 21 May 1898, Morris, Grundy County, Illinois; d. no children.; m. ROY BEESLEY; b. Abt. 1898.
1549. ii. ORVILLE WHITE, b. 09 Sep 1899, Morris, Grundy County, Illinois.
1550. iii. BESSIE WHITE, b. 28 Feb 1900, Morris, Grundy County, Illinois.
iv. ELMER WHITE, b. 23 Nov 1902, Morris, Grundy County, Illinois.
v. RUTH WHITE, b. 21 Aug 1906, Morris, Grundy County, Illinois.

779. SARAH[8] MARSHALL *(CAROLINE SARAH[7] BENSON, SARAH[6] MILKS, JONATHAN[5] MILK, JONATHAN[4], JOB[3], JOHN[2], JOHN[1])* was born 24 Aug 1864 in Grundy County, Illinois, and died 09 Aug 1941 in Morris, Grundy County, Illinois. She married WILLIAM F. BARTLETT, son of JONAS BARTLETT and LUNA WILKINS. He was born 16 Jul 1859 in New York, and died 29 Nov 1927.

Children of SARAH MARSHALL and WILLIAM BARTLETT are:
1551. i. EVA ESTELLA[9] BARTLETT, b. 07 Nov 1885, Coal City, Illinois; d. 10 Mar 1948, Antigo, Langlade County, Wisconsin.
1552. ii. ALICE HESTER BARTLETT, b. 31 Aug 1888, Coal City, Illinois.
iii. WILLIAM JONAS BARTLETT, b. 05 Jul 1891, Coal City, Illinois; d. 17 Mar 1907, unmarried.
1553. iv. ETHEL DOVY BARTLETT, b. 19 Nov 1897, Grundy County, Illinois.

780. HESTER[8] MARSHALL *(CAROLINE SARAH[7] BENSON, SARAH[6] MILKS, JONATHAN[5] MILK, JONATHAN[4], JOB[3], JOHN[2], JOHN[1])* was born 21 Apr 1867 in Grundy County, Illinois, and died 15 Jul 1908 in Morris, Grundy County, Illinois. She married SOLOMON M. ROSE Abt. 1884 in Grundy County, Illinois. He was born 18 Feb 1860 in Morris, Grundy County, Illinois, and died 19 Feb 1910 in Morris, Grundy County, Illinois.

Children of HESTER MARSHALL and SOLOMON ROSE are:
1554. i. FRANK CALVIN[9] ROSE, b. 16 Sep 1885, Morris, Grundy County, Illinois; d. 09 Aug 1943, Hamilton, Butler County, Ohio.
ii. NETTIE BELLE ROSE, b. Nov 1886, Morris, Grundy County, Illinois; d. 25 Dec 1888, Morris, Grundy County, Illinois.
1555. iii. IDA MAY ROSE, b. 21 Jan 1888, Morris, Grundy County, Illinois.
iv. GEORGE WILLIAM ROSE, b. 09 Jul 1890, Morris, Grundy County, Illinois; d. 1933, no children.; m. PEARL _____.
1556. v. LELA HESTER ROSE, b. 02 Sep 1892, Morris, Grundy County, Illinois.
1557. vi. CAROLINE ADELINE ROSE, b. 22 Mar 1895, Morris, Grundy County, Illinois.
1558. vii. FERN AGNES ROSE, b. 09 Mar 1898, Morris, Grundy County, Illinois.

781. GEORGE W.[8] MARSHALL *(CAROLINE SARAH[7] BENSON, SARAH[6] MILKS, JONATHAN[5] MILK, JONATHAN[4], JOB[3], JOHN[2], JOHN[1])* was born 01 Feb 1869 in Grundy County, Illinois, and died Sep 1931. He married ANGIE WINZENBURG 01 Jan 1895, daughter of ANDREW WINZENBURG and MARGARET STAUB. She was born Abt. 1870 in St. Louis, Missouri.

Children of GEORGE MARSHALL and ANGIE WINZENBURG are:
1559. i. JEANETTE CATHERINE[9] MARSHALL, b. 10 Jul 1901.
1560. ii. LOUIS WINZENBURG MARSHALL, b. 04 Apr 1917.

782. BENJAMIN J.[8] BENSON *(ARVILLA[7], SARAH[6] MILKS, JONATHAN[5] MILK, JONATHAN[4], JOB[3], JOHN[2], JOHN[1])* was born 31 Aug 1870 in Grundy County, Illinois. He married ANNIE CARNEGIE, daughter of WILLIAM CARNEGIE and ANNIE FRASER. She was born 20 Jun 1875 in Dumfarlin, Scotland.

Children of BENJAMIN BENSON and ANNIE CARNEGIE are:
- i. RAYMOND[9] BENSON, b. 15 Oct 1893, Grundy County, Illinois; d. 09 Sep 1906, Grundy County, Illinois.
- 1561. ii. CORA A. BENSON, b. 24 Jan 1896, Grundy County, Illinois; d. Jan 1977, Braceville, Grundy County, Illinois.
- 1562. iii. HERBERT BENSON, b. 24 Jul 1898, Grundy County, Illinois.
- 1563. iv. MILDRED BENSON, b. 19 Sep 1900, Grundy County, Illinois.
- 1564. v. BERTHA BENSON, b. 09 Jan 1904, Grundy County, Illinois.
- vi. ALICE BENSON, b. 27 Apr 1906, Grundy County, Illinois; d. 15 Jun 1934; m. HENRY NELSON; b. Abt. 1905.
- vii. DOROTHY BENSON, b. 24 Aug 1908, Grundy County, Illinois; m. LOUIS PIANO; b. Abt. 1908.
- viii. MAY BENSON, b. 01 Apr 1912, Grundy County, Illinois; m. CHARLIE KELLER; b. Abt. 1912.
- 1565. ix. RUSSELL BENSON, b. 26 May 1916, Grundy County, Illinois; d. Nov 1983, Morris, Grundy County, Illinois.
- x. RODNEY K. BENSON, b. 22 Aug 1919, Grundy County, Illinois; d. 27 Jul 1980, Morris, Grundy County, Illinois.

783. JOHN RIAL[8] BENSON *(JOHN MILKS[7], SARAH[6] MILKS, JONATHAN[5] MILK, JONATHAN[4], JOB[3], JOHN[2], JOHN[1])* was born 04 Jan 1883 in Grundy County, Illinois, and died 29 Dec 1954 in Morris, Grundy County, Illinois. He married ELIZABETH AGNES BORN, daughter of JACOB BORN and CATHERINE WIO. She was born 10 Jul 1890 in Rhine, Germany.

Children of JOHN BENSON and ELIZABETH BORN are:
- 1566. i. VIOLET GERTRUDE[9] BENSON, b. 18 Apr 1913, Grundy County, Illinois.
- 1567. ii. FLOYD ERNEST BENSON, b. 14 Feb 1916, Grundy County, Illinois.
- iii. HELEN LOUISE BENSON, b. 11 Oct 1918, Grundy County, Illinois; d. No children; m. HAROLD CLARENCE JOHNSON, 08 Feb 1941; b. 15 Jan 1916, Morris, Grundy County, Illinois.
- iv. KLINTON DOUGLAS BENSON, b. 20 Apr 1926, Grundy County, Illinois; d. 02 Jun 1926, Grundy County, Illinois.
- 1568. v. QUENTEN EUGENE BENSON, b. 20 Apr 1926, Grundy County, Illinois.

784. GRACE MAE[8] BENSON *(JOHN MILKS[7], SARAH[6] MILKS, JONATHAN[5] MILK, JONATHAN[4], JOB[3], JOHN[2], JOHN[1])* was born 30 Dec 1885 in Grundy County, Illinois, and died 17 Feb 1952 in Pasadena, California. She married CHARLES EDWARD HILDY 21 Dec 1904 in Morris, Grundy County, Illinois, son of JOHN HILDY and SARAH BARKER. He was born 30 Jun 1880 in Cullom, Illinois, and died 09 May 1953 in Huntington Park, California.

Grace was an artist, musician, and writer.

Children of GRACE BENSON and CHARLES HILDY are:
- 1569. i. CORNELIUS WALLACE[9] HILDY, b. 21 Oct 1907, Morris, Grundy County, Illinois.
- 1570. ii. GRACE OLIVIA ELSIE HILDY, b. 24 Jan 1910, Chicago, Illinois; d. 18 Mar 2006, Provo, Utah County, Utah.

785. ROY EDWARD[8] BENSON *(JOHN MILKS[7], SARAH[6] MILKS, JONATHAN[5] MILK, JONATHAN[4], JOB[3], JOHN[2], JOHN[1])* was born 22 Mar 1891 in Grundy County, Illinois, and died 06 Apr 1955 in Morris, Grundy County, Illinois. He married GRACE DOCKERY, daughter of JOHN DOCKERY and GRACE TALBOT. She was born 09 Apr 1893 in Oldham, England, and died Apr 1980 in Morris, Grundy County, Illinois.

Children of ROY BENSON and GRACE DOCKERY are:
- i. RONALD R.[9] BENSON, b. 16 Feb 1917, Morris, Grundy County, Illinois; d. Oct 1980, Morris, Grundy County, Illinois; m. MINNIE FRESCHI.
- ii. CHARLOTTE LORRAINE BENSON, b. 20 Jan 1923, Morris, Grundy County, Illinois; d. 12 Feb 1923, Morris, Grundy County, Illinois.
- iii. NORMA JEAN BENSON, b. 17 Sep 1924, Morris, Grundy County, Illinois; d. Oct 1998, Morris, Grundy County, Illinois; m. WILLIS WEST; b. 14 Nov 1924, Morris, Grundy County, Illinois; d. 15 May 1991, Morris, Grundy County, Illinois.

786. MYRTLE OLIVIA[8] BENSON *(JOHN MILKS[7], SARAH[6] MILKS, JONATHAN[5] MILK, JONATHAN[4], JOB[3], JOHN[2], JOHN[1])* was born 27 Feb 1894 in Pine Grove, Grundy County, Illinois, and died 30 Apr 1966 in Morris, Grundy County, Illinois. She married HAROLD FOREST WEBSTER, son of EDMUND WEBSTER and MINNIE SMITH. He was born 31 Mar 1891 in Seattle, Washington, and died Mar 1970 in Morris, Grundy County, Illinois.

Children of MYRTLE BENSON and HAROLD WEBSTER are:
- 1571. i. ELMA MAE[9] WEBSTER, b. 21 Jun 1917, Morris, Grundy County, Illinois; d. 02 Feb 1998, Morris, Grundy County, Illinois.
- 1572. ii. WAYNE EDMUND WEBSTER, b. 20 Apr 1919, Morris, Grundy County, Illinois.
- 1573. iii. MARILYN EUNICE WEBSTER, b. 07 Dec 1923, Morris, Grundy County, Illinois.
- 1574. iv. ROGER DANIEL WEBSTER, b. 16 Jul 1926, Morris, Grundy County, Illinois; d. 30 Oct 1988, Morris, Grundy County, Illinois.

787. CLARENCE EUGENE[8] BENSON *(JOHN MILKS[7], SARAH[6] MILKS, JONATHAN[5] MILK, JONATHAN[4], JOB[3], JOHN[2], JOHN[1])* was born 08 Jan 1900 in Grundy County, Illinois. He married DOROTHY MAY WILLIAMS, daughter of WILLIAM WILLIAMS and MARGARET CONDON. She was born 06 Jul 1904 in Morris, Grundy County, Illinois.

Children of CLARENCE BENSON and DOROTHY WILLIAMS are:
- i. WILLIAM EUGENE[9] BENSON, b. 27 Jan 1942, Chicago, Illinois.
- ii. JOHN HAROLD BENSON, b. 03 Feb 1948, Oshkosh, Wisconsin.

788. EFFIE ADELLA[8] BENSON *(JOHN MILKS[7], SARAH[6] MILKS, JONATHAN[5] MILK, JONATHAN[4], JOB[3], JOHN[2], JOHN[1])* was born 24 Nov 1904 in Grundy County, Illinois. She married PAUL JAMES BARNEY 1923, son of EUGENE BARNEY and DORA GREEN. He was born 22 Apr 1893 in Vicksburg, Michigan.

Child of EFFIE BENSON and PAUL BARNEY is:
- i. ALAN PAUL[9] BARNEY, b. 08 Nov 1939, Jacksonville, Florida.

789. FRED ERNEST[8] BENSON *(JOHN MILKS[7], SARAH[6] MILKS, JONATHAN[5] MILK, JONATHAN[4], JOB[3], JOHN[2], JOHN[1])* was born 14 Feb 1907 in Grundy County, Illinois. He married STELLA EDITH LARDI 22 Aug 1936, daughter of DANTE LARDI and OLYMPIA ZINANNI. She was born 12 Mar 1910 in South Wilmington, Illinois.

Fred and Stella lived on the original homestead of Sarah Milks Benson.

Children of FRED BENSON and STELLA LARDI are:
- i. FREDDIE JOHN[9] BENSON, b. 10 Jun 1937, Grundy County, Illinois.
- ii. PAUL WAYNE BENSON, b. 04 Mar 1942, Grundy County, Illinois.

790. ADELBERT THEODORE[8] BENSON *(JOHN MILKS[7], SARAH[6] MILKS, JONATHAN[5] MILK, JONATHAN[4], JOB[3], JOHN[2], JOHN[1])* was born 27 Mar 1910 in Grundy County, Illinois. He married EVELYN WILLS 23 Aug 1941, daughter of RAY WILLS and ANNA OLSON. She was born 22 Dec 1917 in Morris, Grundy County, Illinois.

Children of ADELBERT BENSON and EVELYN WILLS are:
- i. JAMES ADELBERT[9] BENSON, b. 23 Jan 1946, Morris, Grundy County, Illinois.
- ii. THOMAS BENSON, b. 31 Mar 1950, Morris, Grundy County, Illinois.

791. LUKE WINFIELD[8] RANNEY *(NANCY MARIA[7] MILKS, LUKE[6] MILK, JONATHAN[5], JONATHAN[4], JOB[3], JOHN[2], JOHN[1])* was born 30 Jul 1850 in Perrysburg, Cattaraugus County, New York, and died 01 Oct 1916 in Humbolt, Iowa. He married (1) ELLEN E. HIGBY 10 Jul 1872 in Buchanan County, Iowa. She was born Abt. 1850 in Iowa, and died Bet. 1879 - 1880 in Fairbank, Buchanan\Black Hawk County, Iowa. He married (2) IDA LUZINA ADAMS 12 May 1886 in Black Hawk County, Iowa, daughter of HORACE ADAMS and RACHEL HILL. She was born May 1867 in Lester, Iowa.

Children of LUKE RANNEY and ELLEN HIGBY are:
- i. GRACE[9] RANNEY, b. Abt. 1878, Fairbank, Buchanan\Black Hawk County, Iowa.
- ii. MYRA RANNEY, b. Dec 1879, Fairbank, Buchanan\Black Hawk County, Iowa; m. WILLIAM WALLACE GALLUP, 17 Mar 1897, Grant, Wisconsin; b. 26 Aug 1875.

Children of LUKE RANNEY and IDA ADAMS are:
- iii. DOROTHY[9] RANNEY, b. ?.
- iv. ALBERT H. RANNEY, b. Jan 1887, Iowa.
- 1575. v. JESSIE MARIA RANNEY, b. 14 Apr 1889, Waverly Bremer County, Iowa; d. 16 Mar 1943, Coos Bay, Coos County, Oregon.
- 1576. vi. ELLA RACHEL RANNEY, b. 09 May 1894, of Havelock, Pocohontas County, Iowa (divorced); d. 14 Jun 1956, Los Angeles, California.
- 1577. vii. WILLIAM FOSTER RANNEY, b. 19 Mar 1896, Pocohantas, Iowa; d. 25 Nov 1975, Coos County, Oregon.
- viii. MARGARET K. 'MADGE' RANNEY, b. 08 Mar 1900, Trosky, Pipestone, Minnesota.
- 1578. ix. FRANKIE HELENE RANNEY, b. 15 Jun 1902, Beadle County, South Dakota; d. 22 Feb 1989, Riverside, California.

792. NATHAN AMES[8] RANNEY (*NANCY MARIA[7] MILKS, LUKE[6] MILK, JONATHAN[5], JONATHAN[4], JOB[3], JOHN[2], JOHN[1]*) was born 27 Aug 1853 in Perrysburg, Cattaraugus County, New York, and died 03 May 1925 in Glasgow, Montana. He married ELLA JANE VAUGHN, daughter of FREEMAN VAUGHN and CORDELIA MCDOUGALL. She was born 16 Oct 1863 in New Auburn, Minnesota, and died 17 Apr 1914 in Nashua, Montana.

Children of NATHAN RANNEY and ELLA VAUGHN are:
- 1579. i. BLANCHE[9] RANNEY, b. 30 Aug 1887, McLeod County, Minnesota.
- ii. CECIL JUSTIN RANNEY, b. 12 May 1889, Mitchell Gulch, Montana.
- 1580. iii. RUSSELL RAY RANNEY, b. 23 Feb 1892, New Auburn, Minnesota; d. 01 Sep 1947, Sheldon, North Dakota.
- 1581. iv. LOLA VAUGHN RANNEY, b. 04 Dec 1894, New Auburn, Minnesota; d. 14 Feb 1984, San Bernardino County, California.
- v. AGNES GERALDINE RANNEY, b. 06 Jun 1897, New Auburn, Minnesota; d. Sep 1918, Harlem, Montana.
- vi. NOEL DELORNE RANNEY, b. 22 Sep 1903, New Auburn, Minnesota; d. 11 Dec 1966, Hennepin County, Minnesota; m. MARION PAULINE PETERSON; b. 13 Feb 1906, Chicago, Cook County, Illinois; d. 15 Feb 1987, Hennepin County, Minnesota.
- vii. WILFRED IVAN RANNEY, b. 29 Nov 1899, New Auburn, Sibley County, Minnesota; d. 25 May 1902, New Auburn, Sibley County, Minnesota.

793. ALFRED HERRICK[8] RANNEY (*NANCY MARIA[7] MILKS, LUKE[6] MILK, JONATHAN[5], JONATHAN[4], JOB[3], JOHN[2], JOHN[1]*) was born 03 Oct 1858 in Perrysburg, Cattaraugus County, New York, and died 30 Sep 1934 in Cerro Gordo County, Iowa. He married CASSIE _____. She was born Abt. 1858.

Child of ALFRED RANNEY and CASSIE _____ is:
- i. GLENN[9] RANNEY, b. Abt. 1878.

794. HERMAN[8] RANNEY (*NANCY MARIA[7] MILKS, LUKE[6] MILK, JONATHAN[5], JONATHAN[4], JOB[3], JOHN[2], JOHN[1]*) was born 08 Jul 1863 in Cattaraugus County, New York, and died 12 Jun 1919 in Maynard, Fayette County, Iowa. He married CORA A. PAYNE. She was born 19 Jun 1865 in Maynard, Iowa, and died 07 Jul 1935 in Maynard, Fayette County, Iowa.

Children of HERMAN RANNEY and CORA PAYNE are:
- i. ETHEL MAYE[9] RANNEY, b. 01 Oct 1886, Maynard, Fayette County, Iowa; d. 04 Jan 1943, No children.; m. J. A. CARSON, 24 Dec 1913, Tacoma, Washington; b. Abt. 1886.
- 1582. ii. GOLDA RUTH RANNEY, b. 09 Apr 1888, Maynard, Fayette County, Iowa; d. 18 Jul 1959, Maynard, Fayette County, Iowa.
- iii. LYLE VANCE RANNEY, b. 24 Dec 1892, Maynard, Fayette County, Iowa; d. Feb 1893, Maynard, Iowa.
- iv. RAYMOND ROBERT RANNEY, b. 25 Apr 1894, Maynard, Fayette County, Iowa; d. 15 Dec 1943, Unmarried..
- 1583. v. LAURA PALMYRA RANNEY, b. 10 Sep 1896, Maynard, Fayette County, Iowa; d. 05 Feb 1971, Maynard, Fayette County, Iowa.
- vi. INEZ PAULINA RANNEY, b. 30 May 1898, Maynard, Fayette County, Iowa; d. 15 Mar 1919, Maynard, Fayette County, Iowa.
- 1584. vii. MILDRED MARY RANNEY, b. 25 Oct 1901, Maynard, Fayette County, Iowa.

795. EVALINE SALOME[8] RANNEY *(NANCY MARIA[7] MILKS, LUKE[6] MILK, JONATHAN[5], JONATHAN[4], JOB[3], JOHN[2], JOHN[1])* was born 22 Nov 1867 in Pennsylvania, and died Bet. 1910 - 1918 in South Dakota. She married LAUREL J. BARNES 1885 in Iowa, son of TAURSON BARNES and HESTER _____. He was born Jul 1867 in Harlan, Fayette County, Iowa.

Children of EVALINE RANNEY and LAUREL BARNES are:

- 1585. i. BURR T.[9] BARNES, b. 16 Aug 1888, Maynard, Iowa; d. 07 Feb 1970, Fergus County, Montana.
- ii. VAIL BARNES, b. Feb 1891, Iowa.
- iii. FLOYD BARNES, b. Feb 1893, Iowa.
- iv. HESTER MAY BARNES, b. May 1900, Iowa.
- v. ALFRED BARNES, b. 1902, Iowa.
- vi. LILA BARNES, b. 1905, South Dakota.
- vii. MARIE BARNES, b. 1907, South Dakota.

796. JUSTIN WARREN[8] RANNEY *(NANCY MARIA[7] MILKS, LUKE[6] MILK, JONATHAN[5], JONATHAN[4], JOB[3], JOHN[2], JOHN[1])* was born 08 Dec 1870 in Fairbank, Black Hawk County, Iowa, and died 28 Apr 1941 in Maynard, Fayette County, Iowa. He married CHARLOTTE ANGELINE 'LOTTIE' PACKARD 31 Mar 1895 in Maynard, Fayette County, Iowa, daughter of EDMUND PACKARD and CALISTA CARPENTER. She was born 22 Jan 1874 in Edgewood, Clayton County, Iowa, and died 23 Nov 1967 in Maynard, Fayette County, Iowa.

Obituary

Justin Warren Ranney

Justin Warren Ranney has gone on, but the kind deeds that he performed, his kindly words and the warm clasp of his hand are still with us.

Justin Warren Ranney, son of Julius Caesar and Nancy M. Ranney, was born at Fairbank, Iowa on December 8th 1870 and passed peacefully away in the early morning of April 28th, 1941 at the age of 70 years, 4 months, and 8 days.

The Ranney family came to Maynard in 1885 when Justin Ranney was 15 years of age. With the exception of about 10 years when he was employed by the Bell Telephone company, he has made his home in Maynard. While away he and his family resided in Iowa Falls, Alden, Ackley, Cedar Falls and Fredericksburg, Ia.

On March 31st, 1895, Justin Ranney was united in marriage to Charlotte Packard, also of Maynard, Iowa. To this union were born nine children: Grace, Mrs. Clayton Morse of Maynard; Ruth, Mrs. Robert Ponsar of West Union, Ia.; Fern, Mrs. Earl Shemick of St. Paul, Minn.; Helen, Mrs. Max Hedrick of Glen Ellen, Ill.; Mary, Mrs. Elmer Moen of Kewanee, Ill.; Ardath, Mrs. Louis Garnier of Maynard and Kathryn at home; Dale Charles who died in 1902 and an infant son Byron Edmund who passed away in 1904. The seven daughters, with their beloved mother, Justin's devoted wife, were all with him to grant his every wish when the end came. He also leaves three grandchildren and several nieces and nephews.

Justin Ranney's philosophy of life was that, we pass through life but once, therefore if there was any kindly act that he could do, he must do it at once. If there was any kindly word that he could say, he must say it when the opportunity arose. Such a philosophy of life has left a multitude of friends, grieved at his passing, but glad that he knew and loved them. The many flowers heaped about his casket bear mute but loving tribute of his good neighborliness.

Endowed with a keen mind Justin Ranney held patents for a number of his inventions. Some of which were manufactured at a profit to himself at Maynard, where he engaged in business for many years.

During the latter years of his life he filled the office of Justice of the Peace at Maynard, Iowa.

Both Mr. and Mrs. Ranney were members of the Presbyterian church and were regular attendants at Sunday School and church services. At these services Justin Ranney will be missed. But he has left behind memories that make life richer and sweeter, because he lived and worked among the people of Maynard. For if each doorway that he entered was happier because he came that way, and each one smiled more tenderly he would count that a perfect day. Riches take wings and fame is comfortless but friendship is a jewel that still binds with a clasp of hand, and smiles, and sometimes tears the hands and hearts of all mankind.

Funeral services were held at the Maynard Presbyterian church on Wednesday afternoon. Purley Jennison officiating, assisted by Rev. D. E. Freeman. A trio consisting of E. H. Stewart, Dr. C. C. Hall and Gerald Warnke sang "One by One" and "Shall We Meet", with Mrs. H. Malven accompanist. Those having charge of the flowers were Mrs. George Mears, Mrs. George Maynard and Frances Mears. The pall bears were Mr. Henry Garnier, George Mears, Henry Henniges, L. C. Surfus, Oscar Gilley and George McLeish.

Interment was in Long Grove Cemetery.

Children of JUSTIN RANNEY and CHARLOTTE PACKARD are:
- i. GRACE M.[9] RANNEY, b. May 1896, Fayette County, Iowa; m. CLAYTON MORSE; d. Of Maynard.
- ii. DALE CHARLES RANNEY, b. 03 Jul 1897, Fayette County, Iowa; d. 15 Sep 1902.
- iii. RUTH E. RANNEY, b. Dec 1899, Fayette County, Iowa; m. ROBERT PONSAR; d. Of West Union, IA..
- iv. FERN FRANCES RANNEY, b. 25 Jun 1902, Maynard, Fayette County, Iowa; d. 29 Jul 1947, Dowagiac, Cass County, Michigan (no children); m. EARL ERWIN SCHEMICK, 03 Aug 1927; b. 21 Aug 1894, Menominee, Michigan; d. Mar 1967, Ft. Lauderdale, Broward County, Florida.

  OBITUARY

  Fern Frances Shemick

  MAYNARD (Special) *Fern Frances Ranney, fourth child of Justin W. and Charlotte A. Ranney, was born at Maynard June 25, 1902, and died July 29, 1947 in Dowagiac, Mich., at the age of 45.*

  She was graduated from the Maynard High School with the class of 1921 and had employment with the Western Electric Co. at Chicago until her marriage to Earl Shemick Aug. 3, 1927. She was one of a family of seven sisters.

  Survivors are her husband, her mother, Mrs. J. W. Ranney of Maynard, her sisters, Mrs. Clay ton Morse and Mrs. Robert Ponsar of Long Beach, Calif.; Mrs. Max Hedrick of Polo, Ill,; Mrs. Elmer Moen of Urbana, Ill.; Mrs. Louis Garnier and Mrs. Hugo Fick of Maynard and other relatives and friends.

  Funeral services were held Fri day afternoon at 1:30 at the home of her mother and 2 o'clock at Maynard Presbyterian church with the Rev. L. W. Hauter of Oelwein officiating, assisted by P. E. Jennison.

  The casket-bearers were Dale Mears, George Buenneke, Henry Kappmeyer, Walter Warnke, Herbert Malven and Gerald Warnke . Interment was in the family lot in Long Grove cemetery.

  Obituary appeared Aug. 7, 1947 Oelwein Daily Register
- v. BYRON EDMUND RANNEY, b. 1904; d. 1904.
- vi HFLFN G. RANNEY, b. 1907; m. MAX HEDRICK; d. Of Glen Ellen, IL.
- vii. MARY H. RANNEY, b. Jan 1910; m. ELMER MOEN; d. Of Kewanee, IL.

1586. viii. ARDATH ARLOENE RANNEY, b. 05 Jun 1913, Alden, Hardin County, Iowa; d. 25 Feb 2001, Maynard, Fayette County, Iowa.

1587. ix. KATHRYN BLANCHE RANNEY, b. 24 Mar 1916, Iowa; d. 15 Sep 2007, Fayette County, Iowa.

797. JENNIE[8] MILKS *(BENJAMIN FRANKLIN[7], LUKE[6] MILK, JONATHAN[5], JONATHAN[4], JOB[3], JOHN[2], JOHN[1])* was born 1857 in Cattaraugus County, New York, and died 06 Jan 1946 in Oelwein, Fayette County, Iowa. She married JOSEPH HANSON. He was born 1827 in Yorkshire, England, and died 1909 in Oelwein, Fayette County, Iowa.

Children of JENNIE MILKS and JOSEPH HANSON are:
1588. i. JOSEPH WILLIAM[9] HANSON, b. 27 Dec 1874, Oelwein, Fayette County, Iowa; d. Saco, Montana.
- ii. JOHN P. HANSON, b. 15 Jan 1884, Oelwein, Fayette County, Iowa; d. Jan 1968, Malta, Phillips County, Montana [Unmarried.].

798. IDA LOUISE[8] MILKS *(BENJAMIN FRANKLIN[7], LUKE[6] MILK, JONATHAN[5], JONATHAN[4], JOB[3], JOHN[2], JOHN[1])* was born 27 Mar 1858 in Cattaraugus County, New York, and died 12 Aug 1947 in Lynch, Nebraska. She married JOHN S. HIGGINS 06 May 1885 in Independence, Iowa. He was born 1860 in Waterloo, Iowa, and died 24 Jul 1902 in Lynch, Boyd County, Nebraska.

Children of IDA MILKS and JOHN HIGGINS are:
1589. i. BENJAMIN JOHN 'BEN'[9] HIGGINS, b. 19 Feb 1886, Lester, Black Hawk County, Iowa; d. Aug 1969, Niobrara, Knox County, Nebraska.
- ii. GAIL ELWIN HIGGINS, b. 26 Oct 1887, Oelwein, Fayette County, Iowa; d. 06 Feb 1951, Lived Spencer, Neb.; m. MINNIE STORJOHANN; b. 1891, Nebraska. No children.

1590. iii. BESSIE E. HIGGINS, b. May 1890, Iowa; d. 1966, Lynch, Boyd County, Nebraska.

1591. iv. MABEL GRACE HIGGINS, b. Oct 1891, Nebraska; d. 1970, Lynch, Boyd County, Nebraska.

1592. v. EDNA RUTH HIGGINS, b. 18 Feb 1893, Nebraska; d. 12 Nov 1979, Rapid City, Pennington County, SD.
- vi. EDITH MAE HIGGINS, b. May 1895, Nebraska; d. 28 Apr 1913.

1593. vii. HAZEL LENNIE HIGGINS, b. Mar 1898, Nebraska.

1594. viii. GERTRUDE LILA HIGGINS, b. Feb 1900, Lynch, Boyd County, Nebraska.

1595. ix. VERA ELLA HIGGINS, b. 15 Mar 1903, Lynch, Boyd County, Nebraska; d. 12 Apr 1995, Nebraska.

799. BUTLER WEBSTER[8] MILKS *(BENJAMIN FRANKLIN[7], LUKE[6] MILK, JONATHAN[5], JONATHAN[4], JOB[3], JOHN[2], JOHN[1])* was born 12 Sep 1862 in Black Hawk County, Iowa, and died 27 Mar 1943 in Peace River, Alberta, Canada. He married LYDIA ZERUIE 'ADA' BOTHWELL May 1885, daughter of JOHN BOTHWELL and CAROLINE SEELEY. She was born 15 Dec 1865 in Olin, Jones County, Iowa, and died 14 Mar 1935 in McGraw, Cortland County, New York.

Children are listed above under (764) Lydia Zeruie 'Ada' Bothwell.

800. NANCY MARIA[8] MILKS *(BENJAMIN FRANKLIN[7], LUKE[6] MILK, JONATHAN[5], JONATHAN[4], JOB[3], JOHN[2], JOHN[1])* was born 10 May 1865 in Black Hawk County, Iowa, and died 15 Aug 1913 in Fairbank, Iowa. She married FRANK LAWRENCE BOND 27 May 1882 in Buchanan County, Iowa, son of SAMUEL BOND and ALMIRA HYDE. He was born 01 Aug 1860 in Naperville, Illinois, and died 19 Apr 1907 in Fairbank, Iowa.

OBITUARY

    Nancy Marie Milk was born in Black Hawk County, May 10,1865, died August 15,1913, aged 48 years,3 months and 5 days.

    The immediate cause of her death was heart trouble.

    She was united in marriage in 1883 to Mr. Frank Bond, who preceded her in death, April 19, 1907. To this union was born twelve children all living, except one who died in infancy. They are: Earl T. Bond, Fairbank, Iowa; Mrs. C.E. DeWald. Dunkerton, Iowa; Mrs. W.F. Kraft, Fairbank; Mr. H.E. Bond, Waterloo; Mrs. J.A. Platt, Aurora; Mrs. W.B. Ervin, Oelwein; Mrs. F.W. Sherwood, Oelwein; Miss Lenora Bond, Des Moines; Frankie, Thomas and Doretha at home.

    Besides her children she leaves to mourn her loss her aged mother, three sisters, two brothers and six grandchildren together with a host of friends.

    The funeral was held in the Methodist Church Saturday.   SOURCE: Cleda Blumenrader

Children of NANCY MILKS and FRANK BOND are:
- i. EARL F.[9] BOND, b. 02 Feb 1884, Fairbank, Iowa; d. Nov 1936; m. IDA BENDER; b. Abt. 1885; d. No children.
- ii. RUTH E. BOND, b. 16 Apr 1886, Fairbank, Iowa; d. 07 Jan 1934, Hazelton, Buchanan County, Iowa; m. CHARLES E. DEWALD; b. Abt. 1885.
- 1596. iii. MYRA O. BOND, b. 22 Jan 1888, Fairbank, Iowa.
- 1597. iv. HARRY ELWIN BOND, b. 02 Mar 1890, Lester Township, Black Hawk County, Iowa; d. Jan 1978, Waterloo, Black Hawk County, Iowa.
- 1598. v. LUCY ORINDA BOND, b. 04 Aug 1892, Fairbank, Iowa; d. 07 Jun 1944.
- 1599. vi. OLIVE HAZEL BOND, b. 13 Mar 1894, Fairbank, Iowa; d. 15 Feb 1920, Salt Lake City, Utah.
- 1600. vii. CORA ELIZABETH BOND, b. 17 May 1896, Fairbank, Iowa; d. 1949, Austin, Minnesota.
- 1601. viii. LENORA BOND, b. 06 May 1898, Fairbank, Iowa.
- ix. FRANK BOND, b. 11 Jan 1900, Fairbank, Iowa; d. No children.
- 1602. x. THOMAS BONNELL BOND, b. 31 Mar 1904, Fairbank, Iowa; d. 24 Apr 1993, Independence, Buchanan County, Iowa.
- 1603. xi. DOROTHY MARGUERITE BOND, b. 27 Jul 1906, Lester Township, Blackhawk County, Iowa; d. 15 Nov 1986, Corona, Riverside County, California.

801. RUTH ANN[8] MILKS *(BENJAMIN FRANKLIN[7], LUKE[6] MILK, JONATHAN[5], JONATHAN[4], JOB[3], JOHN[2], JOHN[1])* was born 15 Jul 1869, and died 07 Dec 1959. She married (1) JAMES VAN ETTEN, son of CHRIS ETTEN and ELIZABETH LITZ. He was born 02 Aug 1862 in Clayton County, Iowa, and died 1942 in Oelwein, Fayette County, Iowa. She married (2) WILLIAM BUMPUS. Ruth contributed many records for her family.

Child of RUTH MILKS and JAMES VAN ETTEN is:
- 1604. i. IONE[9] VAN ETTEN, b. 28 Nov 1896, Iowa; d. 09 Apr 1977.

802. THOMAS BENJAMIN[8] MILKS *(BENJAMIN FRANKLIN[7], LUKE[6] MILK, JONATHAN[5], JONATHAN[4], JOB[3], JOHN[2], JOHN[1])* was born 26 Apr 1876 in Lester Township, Black Hawk Co., Iowa, and died 07 Feb 1936 in Waterloo, Iowa. He married (1) LOUISA ELIZABETH 'LIZZIE' FRIEDMANN 22 Mar 1894 in Black Hawk Co, Iowa, daughter of CHRISTIAN FRIEDMANN and BERTHA KLEGIN. She was born 28 Jan 1874 in Black Hawk Co., Iowa, and died 08 Nov 1950 in Malta, Montana. He married (2) MINNIE HEINEMANN, daughter of WILLIAM HEINEMANN and FRIEDERIKE SUHR. She was born 26 May 1897 in Iowa, and died 15 Dec 1975 in Waterloo, Black Hawk County, Iowa.

The 1930 census for Cedar Falls, Black Hawk County, Iowa show Thomas and Elizabeth still living together. Elizabeth died after Thomas and according to the gravestone in the Fairbank Lutheran Cemetery, they are buried side-by-side.

I have searched diligently for a marriage record for Thomas and Minnie, but have been unable to locate one.

Aug 14, 1933, Waterloo Daily Courier Elizabeth W. Milks has filed suit for divorce against Thomas P. Milks, to whom she was married at Dunkerton, Iowa, March 22, 1894. She states that they separated in November 1927.

Divorce Granted: Feb 6, 1934. Waterloo Daily Courier. Mrs. Elizabeth W. Milks is granted a divorce from Thomas B. Milks in an order signed by Judge A. B. Lovejoy, on file Tuesday in district court.

OBITUARY

Funeral services for Thomas B Milks, 59, 320 Eleventh street east, Waterloo, who died at 1:30 pm, Friday, Feb 7 at St Francis hospital of heart disease, were at the Kistner chapel, Rev Mark Shock the pastor of the Free Methodist church officiating Burial was in the Fairbank cemetery

Thomas B Milks son of Benjamin and Orinda Milks, was born April 26 1876 in Lester township Black Hawk county Iowa.

Surviving besides his widow Minnie Milks are four sons Verne and Russell of Fairbank and Don and Victor at home one daughter Lottie at home three stepchildren Fred, William, and Irene at home. 14 grandchildren two great-children, one brother B W Milks of Alberta Canada and four sisters Mrs William Birmpus, Spokane Wash., Mrs Frank Higgins, Lynch Neb, Mrs. Joseph Hansen West Union Iowa and Mrs Leila Oxart of Saco Montana.

Five children preceded him in death.

Mr. Milks was a former Fairbank resident and well known here

OBITUARY - Newspaper: Waterloo Courier, Waterloo, Iowa; Publication Date: Dec 16, 1975

Mrs. Minnie M. Berry

Services for Mrs. Minnie M. Berry, 82, formerly of 521 Fowler St., who died at Parkview Nursing Home Monday (Dec. 15), will be 1 pm, Wednesday at Grace Lutheran Church.

Burial will be in the Garden of Memories.

She was born May 26, 1893, in Minnesota, the daughter of Will and Charlotte Suhr Heinemann.

Survivors include three sons, William Jurgens of 1557 Byron Ave, Victor Milks of Woodvale, Ill., and Donald Milks of Orlando, Fla.; two daughters, Mrs. Irene Mixdorf of 1017 Kingsley Ave., and Mrs. Charlotte Marsh of 1110 Wisner Dr.; a brother, Fred Heinemann of Readlyn; and a sister, Mrs. Lydia Nielsen of Hawthorne, Calif.

Friends may call at Parrott & Wood Funeral Home until 11 am Wednesday and for an hour preceding the services at the church.

Children of THOMAS MILKS and LOUISA FRIEDMANN are:

1605.   i.   VERN LEO[9] MILKS, b. 03 Nov 1895, Black Hawk County, Iowa; d. 07 Aug 1969, Buchanan Co., Iowa.
1606.   ii. CHARLES WILLIAM MILKS, b. 05 Jan 1897, Lester Township, Black Hawk County, Iowa; d. 24 Apr 1931, Fairbank, Iowa.
        iii. LYLE RONALD MILKS, b. 20 Dec 1898, Black Hawk County, Iowa; d. 27 Feb 1904.
        iv. DELPHA HAZEL MILKS, b. 01 Dec 1900, Black Hawk County, Iowa; d. 05 Mar 1904.
        v.   SON MILKS, b. 15 Mar 1906, Black Hawk County, Iowa; d. 15 Mar 1906, Black Hawk County, Iowa.
1607.   vi. LEILA MARJORIE MILKS, b. 13 Jul 1907, Black Hawk County, Iowa; d. 19 Dec 1997, Malta, Phillips County, Montana.
1608.   vii. RUSSELL HAROLD MILKS, b. 27 Aug 1909, Black Hawk County, Iowa; d. 08 May 1994, Phillips, Phillips County, Montana.

Children of THOMAS MILKS and MINNIE HEINEMANN are:

1609.   viii. CHARLOTTE JOHANNA 'LOTTIE'[9] MILKS, b. 19 Feb 1927, Fairbank, Bremer County, Iowa; d. 09 May 1984, Waterloo, Black Hawk County, Iowa.
1610.   ix.   DONALD PAUL MILKS, b. 26 Mar 1928, Iowa?; d. 27 Jun 2000, Orlando, Orange County, Florida.
1611.   x.   VICTOR KENNETH MILKS, b. 30 Apr 1930, Waterloo, Black Hawk County, Iowa; d. 21 Nov 2003, Princeton, Bureau County, Illinois.

803. MARY[8] GILMAN *(URSULA[7] ROGERS, ISAAC[6], RHODA[5] CHASE, ABIGAIL[4] MILK, JOB[3], JOHN[2], JOHN[1])* was born 14 Dec 1840 in Brownville, Jefferson County, New York, and died 19 May 1929 in Palermo, Oswego County, New York. She married HENRY KNIGHT 03 Mar 1873 in Volney, New York, son of CALEB KNIGHT and SALLY ADAMS. He was born Abt.

1840, and died 1901 in Oswego County, New York.

Children of MARY GILMAN and HENRY KNIGHT are:
1612.   i.   DORA[9] KNIGHT, b. 08 Aug 1880, Palermo, Oswego County, New York.
          ii.   GEORGE KNIGHT, b. 1883, Palermo, Oswego County, New York; m. VERA BERRY; b. Abt. 1885.

804. SULLIVAN G.[8] HOLMES *(ALZINA BIANCA[7] CHASE, ORRIN[6], JOHN[5], ABIGAIL[4] MILK, JOB[3], JOHN[2], JOHN[1])* was born 10 May 1862 in Georgetown, Madison County, New York, and died Dec 1938 in Newport, Herkimer County, New York. He married ALICE KELLOGG 07 Nov 1882 in Remsen, Oneida County, New York. She was born 22 Oct 1866 in Georgetown, Madison County, New York, and died Apr 1930 in Newport, Herkimer County, New York.

Child of SULLIVAN HOLMES and ALICE KELLOGG is:
          i.   MABLE A.[9] HOLMES, b. 31 May 1884, Georgetown, Madison County, New York; d. 1950; m. STANLEY A. WALLACE; b. 29 Mar 1884, Texas Valley, Cortland County, New York; d. 25 Apr 1946. Mable grad. Syracuse Univ., Ph.B., author of Blackberry Mountain a novel of the Kentucky Hills, and 40 short stories. Contributed fam. Records.

805. WILLIAM EDWIN[8] MILK *(JOHN[7], JOHN[6], JOHN[5], JOHN[4], JOHN[3], JOHN[2], JOHN[1])* was born 22 Nov 1849 in Boston, Massachusetts, and died 12 Apr 1905 in Boston, Suffolk, Mass.. He married ELLEN F. MAHONEY 23 Jan 1878 in Boston, Massachusetts, daughter of JOHN MAHONEY and JULIA _____. She was born 1852 in Massachusetts.

Child of WILLIAM MILK and ELLEN MAHONEY is:
          i.   HARRIET ELIZABETH[9] MILK, b. 28 Feb 1880, Boston, Massachusetts; m. BIRKET F LETSON, 20 Sep 1909, Medford, Massachusetts; b. Bet. 1878 - 1879, Halifax, Nova Scotia, Canada.

806. JAMES MADISON[8] MILK, JR. *(JAMES MADISON[7], JOHN[6], JOHN[5], JOHN[4], JOHN[3], JOHN[2], JOHN[1])* was born 03 Jun 1855 in Boston, Massachusetts, and died 09 Nov 1882 in Boston, Massachusetts. He married MARY JUSTINA SHEDD 01 May 1877 in Boston, Massachusetts, daughter of LUTHER SHEDD and SARAH _____. She was born Jan 1855 in Massachusetts. Mary J. Parkman was living with Edwin and Mary Milk in 1910

Child of JAMES MILK and MARY SHEDD is:
1613.   i.   EDWIN AUGUSTUS[9] MILK, b. 15 Mar 1878, Charleston, Massachusetts; d. 09 Dec 1947, Beverly, Essex County, Massachusetts.

807. JOHN HENRY[8] MILK *(JAMES MADISON[7], JOHN[6], JOHN[5], JOHN[4], JOHN[3], JOHN[2], JOHN[1])* was born 19 Jul 1864 in Boston, Massachusetts. He married (1) MARGARET S. GILBERT 05 May 1881 in Boston, Massachusetts, daughter of CHARLES GILBERT and MARY _____. She was born Abt. 1862 in Waterloo, Illinois. He married (2) EDNA T. WELLER 23 Nov 1892 in Boston, Massachusetts, daughter of EDWARD WELLER and ELIZABETH _____. She was born Feb 1869 in Boston, Suffolk, Mass..

Child of JOHN MILK and MARGARET GILBERT is:
          i.   MARY A.[9] MILK, b. 26 Jun 1881, Boston, Suffolk, Mass.; d. 12 Aug 1881, Boston, Suffolk, Mass..

Child of JOHN MILK and EDNA WELLER is:
1614.   ii.   HERBERT ATWOOD[9] MILK, b. 18 Jun 1897, Boston, Massachusetts; d. 07 Jan 1987, Norton, Bristol Co., Massachusetts.

GENERATION NO. 9

808. ELIZABETH BROWNELL^9 WHITE *(GEORGE MILK^8, HOLDER^7, CYNTHIA^6 MILK, LEMUEL^5, DAVID^4, JOB^3, JOHN^2, JOHN^1)* was born 10 Oct 1871 in Westport, Massachusetts. She married ALBERT DARLING MILLIKEN 03 Mar 1897 in Westport, Massachusetts ?. He was born 30 Jul 1870 in Westport, Massachusetts ?.

Child of ELIZABETH WHITE and ALBERT MILLIKEN is:
1615.   i.   ARNOLD WHITE^{10} MILLIKEN, b. 30 Aug 1899, Westport, Massachusetts.

809. MARY V.^{9} MILK *(OBED H.^{8}, WILLIAM W.^{7}, WILLIAM^6, LEMUEL^5, DAVID^4, JOB^3, JOHN^2, JOHN^1)* was born Feb 1873 in Auburn, Cayuga County, New York, and died Apr 1958 in Auburn, Cayuga County, New York. She married ALFRED 'LOBAR' BOLGER 1900 in Cayuga County, New York. He was born Jul 1863 in New York, and died Jul 1917 in Auburn, Cayuga County, New York.

Children of MARY MILK and ALFRED BOLGER are:
    i.   MARY E.^{10} BOLGER, b. Bet. 1903 - 1904, Auburn, Cayuga County, New York.
    ii.   WILLIAM HOWARD BOLGER, b. Bet. 1906 - 1907, Auburn, Cayuga County, New York.
    iii.   IDA E. BOLGER, b. May 1907, Auburn, Cayuga County, New York; d. May 1907, Auburn, Cayuga County, New York (3 days old).

810. KATHERINE ELIZABETH^9 KELLY *(HARRIET^8 MILK, WILLIAM W.^{7}, WILLIAM^6, LEMUEL^5, DAVID^4, JOB^3, JOHN^2, JOHN^1)* was born 25 Aug 1863 in Port Byron, Cayuga County, New York, and died 19 Nov 1942 in Syracuse, Onondaga County, New York. She married DR. GEORGE HENRY SWIFT 12 Jul 1883 in Port Byron, New York, son of LANSING SWIFT and EUNICE PRIME. He was born 10 Aug 1853 in Morris, Otsego County, New York, and died 16 Jan 1906 in Niagara Falls, New York.

    DR. GEORGE HENRY SWIFT: from: **Mary-Louise Clary**, Date: Aug 24, 2012
    I wrote you earlier with information on my Milk line relatives - Harriet Milk who married Augustus Kelly. I have an update on their son-in-law's year of death after receiving a copy of his death certificate. George Henry Swift b1853 in Hamilton, NY died in Niagara Falls, 16 Jan 1906 (not 1905). He is buried in Syracuse, New York at Oakwood cemetery.

Children of KATHERINE KELLY and GEORGE SWIFT are:
    i.   JEANNETTE HARDY^{10} SWIFT, b. 11 Nov 1885, Syracuse, New York; d. 24 Jan 1887, Syracuse, Onondaga County, New York.
1616.   ii.   HARRIET HARDY SWIFT, b. 25 Mar 1888, Syracuse, New York; d. 03 Oct 1948, Syracuse, Onondaga County, New York.
1617.   iii.   AMY LOUISA SWIFT, b. 25 Sep 1890, Syracuse, New York; d. 19 Nov 1968, Syracuse, Onondaga County, New York.
1618.   iv.   MARY EUNICE SWIFT, b. 06 Aug 1893, Syracuse, New York.
    v.   WILLIAM KELLY SWIFT, b. 24 Mar 1898, Syracuse, New York; d. 01 Feb 1950, Utica, New York; m. FLORENCE _____; b. Abt. 1900. No children
    vi.   JAMES TAUNT SWIFT, b. 23 Feb 1901, Syracuse, New York; d. 12 Apr 1958, Syracuse, Onondaga County, New York.
    Unmarried.
1619.   vii.   ROBERT LYNN SWIFT, b. 20 Nov 1904, Syracuse, New York; d. 16 Feb 1967, Greer. Greenville County, South Carolina.

811. CYNTHIA BLANCHE^9 MILK *(SILAS WRIGHT^8, WILLIAM W.^{7}, WILLIAM^6, LEMUEL^5, DAVID^4, JOB^3, JOHN^2, JOHN^1)* was born 10 Jan 1887 in Waldron, Kankakee County, Illinois. She married ARTHUR L. LEWIS 22 Sep 1914. He was born Abt. 1885.

Children of CYNTHIA MILK and ARTHUR LEWIS are:
    i.   RUTH ELIZABETH^{10} LEWIS, b. 10 Feb 1916, Kerrville, Texas; d. Bef. 04 May 2010; m. JARREL G. HAMILTON.
    ii.   JOHN WRIGHT LEWIS, b. 25 Aug 1918, Kerrville, Texas; d. 25 May 1919, Kerrville, Texas.

1620. iii. JANE MARGARET LEWIS, b. 10 Jul 1922, Syracuse, Onondaga County, New York; d. 04 Mar 2010, San Antonio, Bexar County, Texas.
        iv. CHARLES ARTHUR LEWIS, b. 28 Feb 1927, Kerrville, Texas/N. Syracuse, NY; m. JUANITA ELAINE COOK; b. Abt. 1927.

812. LEMUEL^9 MILK *(GEORGE WASHINGTON^8, WILLIAM W.^{7}, WILLIAM^6, LEMUEL^5, DAVID^4, JOB^3, JOHN^2, JOHN^1)* was born 29 May 1884 in Clifton, Iroquois County, Illinois, and died 26 Sep 1968 in Kankakee, Illinois. He married LURA BEATRICE STABLER Jun 1904 in St. Joseph, Michigan, daughter of FREDERICK STABLER and EMMA KENDALL. She was born 05 May 1883, and died 14 Jan 1976 in Kankakee, Illinois.

Lemuel was an assistant author of Grace Croft's "History and Genealogy of the MILK-MILKS Family"
He toured extensively, visiting old Milk-Milks home sites, landmarks, and relatives.

Children of LEMUEL MILK and LURA STABLER are:
1621. i. EDITH FRANCES^{10} MILK, b. 24 Mar 1905, Chebanse, Illinois.
1622. ii. HAROLD SHERWOOD MILK, b. 08 Jul 1906, Kankakee, Illinois.
        iii. CLARENCE LEMUEL MILK, b. 16 Jan 1908, Kankakee, Illinois; d. 26 May 1968, Kankakee, Illinois (Unmarried).
1623. iv. ROSS FREDERICK MILK, b. 29 Jul 1911, Kankakee, Illinois.
1624. v. RUTH VIVIAN MILK, b. 04 Feb 1913, Kankakee, Illinois.
1625. vi. MARVIN ELWOOD MILK, b. 17 Jan 1915, Franklin Park, Illinois.
1626. vii. DONALD LEROY MILK, b. 21 Jan 1916, Kankakee, Illinois.
1627. viii. DARRELL DELBERT MILK, b. 05 Aug 1917, Kankakee, Illinois.
1628. ix. ROYAL GEORGE MILK, b. 25 Sep 1918, Kankakee, Illinois; d. 04 Dec 2004, Watseka, Iroquois County, Illinois
1629. x. ARDYS LUCILLE MILK, b. 14 Apr 1920, Kankakee, Illinois; d. 04 Feb 2007, Kankakee, Illinois.
1630. xi. MARILYN LOUISE MILK, b. 01 Jul 1923, Kankakee, Illinois; d. 30 May 2010, Conway, Faulkner County, Arkansas.
        xii. ROBERT VERNON MILK, b. 10 Jul 1925, Kankakee, Illinois; d. 20 Feb 2010, Kankakee, Illinois.
        OBITUARY
        A memorial service for Robert V. "Bob" Milk, 84, of Kankakee, will be held at 10 a.m. Saturday at the Kankakee Chapel of the Schreffler Funeral Homes.

        In lieu of flowers, memorials may be made to the Alzheimer's Association or Guiding Eyes for the Blind. He passed away Saturday (Feb. 20, 2010) following a short illness.

        Mr. Milk retired from Kankakee Roper after 25 years of service. He was born July 10, 1925, the son of Lemuel and Lura Stabler Milk. He was a World War II veteran. Affectionately known as "UB" to his great-nieces and great-nephews, Bob enjoyed fishing along the Kankakee River, shooting a game of pool, playing cards, bowling, cheering on Brett Favre and throwing back-to-back ringers while playing Lawn Jarts.

        In his later years, Bob was challenged by the loss of his sight. Although facing a great challenge, he remained optimistic and continued to live life to its fullest until his death. His smile and hearty chuckle will be missed by everyone who knew him.

        He is survived by a sister, Marilyn Smith of Arkansas; sisters-in-law, Millie Milk of Manteno, Jackie Milk of Watseka and Sylvia Milk of Missouri. Several nieces and nephews survive, including: Richard (Margie) Elam of Bourbonnais, Marlene (Daryl) Albers of Kankakee, Lee (Karen) Elam of Texas, Russ (Betsy) Elam of California, Glen (Vicky) Elam of Idaho, Rebecca (Michael) Patchett of Kankakee, Marsha Adrian of Arkansas, Marla Porter Fitzpatrick of Chebanse, Leslie Porter and Gary Porter, both of Wisconsin; and a special niece, Cindy Elam of Bourbonnais. In addition, several great-nieces and great-nephews survive, including: Jessica (Rodger) Fehland of Watseka, Todd Albers of Kankakee, Chad (Julie) Albers of El Dorado, Denise (Kevin) DeCarlo of Indiana, Brad Elam of Indiana and Cara Leonard of Kentucky. Special friends who survive include, Cecelia Schekerke, Mary Kripple and Pam Brav of Kankakee.

        In addition to his parents, he was preceded in death by his longtime companion, Bea Frechette; his brothers, Harold, Clarence, Ross, Royal, Donald, Darrell and Marvin; and sisters, Edith Thompson, Ruth Elam and Ardys Porter.

        Burial: Cremated, Location of ashes is unknown.

813. FAYE ELIZABETH[9] MILK *(GEORGE WASHINGTON[8], WILLIAM W.[7], WILLIAM[6], LEMUEL[5], DAVID[4], JOB[3], JOHN[2], JOHN[1])* was born 13 Aug 1888 in Clifton, Illinois. She married CLIFFORD RAY BROWN 15 Jun 1910 in Kankakee, Illinois, son of WILLIAM BROWN and MARIAN KELLY. He was born 19 Oct 1885 in Randolph, Cattaraugus County, New York.

Children of FAYE MILK and CLIFFORD BROWN are:
1631.   i.   ANITA MAY[10] BROWN, b. 22 Jan 1912, Kankakee, Illinois.
1632.   ii.   GENE LYLE BROWN, b. 18 May 1926, Kankakee, Illinois.
1633.   iii.   ROBERT LAURELLE BROWN, b. 23 Feb 1929, Kankakee, Illinois.

814. ELLA MAE[9] MILK *(GEORGE WASHINGTON[8], WILLIAM W.[7], WILLIAM[6], LEMUEL[5], DAVID[4], JOB[3], JOHN[2], JOHN[1])* was born 21 Sep 1892 in Clifton, Illinois. She married CHESTER LEE KESSLER 15 Jan 1915 in Kankakee, Illinois. He was born 29 Apr 1892 in Morocco, Indiana, and died 24 Oct 1937 in Morocco, Indiana.

Children of ELLA MILK and CHESTER KESSLER are:
       i.   WILLIAM GEORGE[10] KESSLER, b. 09 Feb 1917, Morocco, Indiana; d. 23 Mar 1922, Morocco, Indiana.
1634.   ii.   ROBERT NOBLE KESSLER, b. 22 Oct 1918, Morocco, Indiana.
1635.   iii.   RUTH ANN KESSLER, b. 29 Nov 1920, Morocco, Indiana.

815. ELIZABETH COOLEY[9] MANRO *(HELEN M.[8] COOLEY, CYNTHIA[7] MILK, WILLIAM[6], LEMUEL[5], DAVID[4], JOB[3], JOHN[2], JOHN[1])* was born 30 Sep 1860 in Auburn, Cayuga County, New York, and died 18 Jun 1927 in Auburn, Cayuga County, New York. She married ASA RANDALL BARNES. He was born 20 Aug 1858 in Evans Mills, Jefferson County, New York, and died 18 Aug 1926 in Auburn, Cayuga County, New York.

Children of ELIZABETH MANRO and ASA BARNES are:
       i.   PEARL WOODWORTH[10] BARNES, b. 1887; d. 1972.
       ii.   GERTRUDE COOLEY BARNES, b. 1895; d. 1983.

816. FRED JONATHAN[9] MANRO *(HELEN M.[8] COOLEY, CYNTHIA[7] MILK, WILLIAM[6], LEMUEL[5], DAVID[4], JOB[3], JOHN[2], JOHN[1])* was born 10 Oct 1863 in Aurelius, Cayuga County, New York, and died 03 Jun 1942 in Auburn, Cayuga County, New York. He married TEMMA CASTNER. She was born 1866 in Penn Yan, Yates County, New York, and died 11 May 1936 in Auburn, Cayuga County, New York.

Children of FRED MANRO and TEMMA CASTNER are:
       i.   HELEN MIRIAM[10] MANRO, b. 1885; d. 1978.
       ii.   MILDRED LOIS MANRO, b. 1890; d. 1971.

817. JENNIE BELL[9] MANRO *(HELEN M.[8] COOLEY, CYNTHIA[7] MILK, WILLIAM[6], LEMUEL[5], DAVID[4], JOB[3], JOHN[2], JOHN[1])* was born 17 Sep 1866 in Throop, Cayuga County, New York, and died 18 Feb 1962 in Auburn, Cayuga County, New York. She married FRANK AUGUSTUS ELDREDGE Abt. 1887 in Cayuga County, New York. He was born 13 Jan 1863 in Slaterville Springs, Tompkins County, New York, and died 15 Jan 1928 in Auburn, Cayuga County, New York.
Obituary:
    Fair Haven, New York, The Register newspaper. Thursday, February 22, 1962, Page 8, Column 3
    Services Held for Jennie Eldredge
    Mrs. Jennie Manrow Eldredge, 95, widow of Frank A. Eldredge, died Sunday morning in an Auburn nursing home after a long illness.
    Her former husband was a former Cayuga County treasurer and one of the founders of the Auburn Trust Co. He also owned and operated the Garrett Coal and Ice Co. for many years. He died in 1928.
    Mrs. Eldredge lived for many years at 17 Orchard St., Auburn. She was born in Throop but spent 70 years in Auburn. For many years, she spent her summers at Eldredge Point, Fair Haven. Mrs. Eldredge was an active member of the First Presbyterian Church for many years.
    She was the mother of the late Allan M., C. Fred and Edward B. Eldredge. The survivors are grandchildren and six great-grandchildren.
    Services were Tuesday from the Lester E. Brew Funeral Chapel with the Rev. Ralph H. Wagner, pastor of the First Presbyterian Church officiating. Burial in Fort Hill Cemetery.

Children of JENNIE MANRO and FRANK ELDREDGE are:
- i. ALLEN MANRO[10] ELDREDGE, b. 1889; d. 1957.
- ii. CHARLES FREDERICK ELDREDGE, b. 1894; d. 1957.
- iii. EDWARD BALL ELDREDGE, b. 1896; d. 1947.

818. CHARLES HENRY[9] MANRO *(HELEN M.[8] COOLEY, CYNTHIA[7] MILK, WILLIAM[6], LEMUEL[5], DAVID[4], JOB[3], JOHN[2], JOHN[1])* was born 28 March 1871 in Throop, Cayuga County, New York, and died 17 June 1934 in Syracuse, Onondaga County, New York. He married EDITH ABBOTT CASE 1899. She was born Abt. 1871.

They divorced at some point, and she married Loomis Hutchinson.

Obituary: Auburn, New York, The Citizen-Advertiser newspaper, Monday, June 18, 1934, Page 5, Column 4

DEATH TAKES CHARLES H. MANRO AT 63

Operation Fails to Save Life of Well Known Auburnian - Served Many Years As Soldier

Charles H. Manro, 63, well-known Auburnian, died Sunday morning at the Hospital of the Good Shepherd in Syracuse after a an operation performed about one week ago. For a time after the operation his recovery seemed assured but a kidney infection developed and he failed to rally.

Mr. Manro was born in the Town of Aurelius but had lived practically all his life in Auburn. He served in the National Guard for a quarter century and for many years he was active in the affairs of Auburn Lodge of Elks.

He enlisted in the old Wheeler Rifles as a private, November 25, 1890, at the age of 19 years, and served with the Guard until his full and honorable discharge on December 15, 1906.

He enlisted May 1, 1898, with Company M, Third New York Volunteer Infantry during the Spanish-American War and left with the company for Camp Black. He was promoted to corporal May 24, 1898. When Company M was mustered out of the U. S. service December 2, 1898, he remained with the National Guard unit in Auburn. He was promoted to corporal March 1, 1899, and then to sergeant February 3, 1900. He was made first sergeant of Company M November 19, 1904 and took his discharge December 15, 1906. He always retained great interest in the local National Guard companies.

Mr. Manro was also an active member of Auburn Lodge of Elks, serving for many years as chairman of the Sick Committee.

He was especially interested in Major Louis B. Lawton Camp, United Spanish War Veterans, of which he was a past commander. In the days of the bicycle in the Nineties he was a member of the old Auburn Cyclers.

For many years Mr. Manro had been bookkeeper for the Hewitt-Wilcox Coal Company and prior to taking that position had served in a similar capacity with the Manro and Hugg Coal Company.

Surviving are a son, Philip Manro of Oswego; a brother, Fred J. Manro of Auburn; a sister, Mrs. Frank E. Eldredge of Auburn; a niece, Mrs. Howard Nicholson of Syracuse.

The funeral will be held at 2:30 o'clock Wednesday afternoon from Bradley Memorial Chapel, Rev. Dr. Malcolm L. MacPhail, pastor of the First Presbyterian Church, will officiate. Burial will be in Fort Hill cemetery.

The body was brought to Auburn by Undertaker Howard M. Cameron. Friends may call at the Cameron funeral parlors in William Street.

Child of CHARLES MANRO and EDITH CASE is:
- i. PHILIP CHAPIN[10] MANRO.

819. ADELLE 'DELLA'[9] ROBINSON *(LOUISE CAROLINE[8] MILK, CHARLES G.[7], WILLIAM[6], LEMUEL[5], DAVID[4], JOB[3], JOHN[2], JOHN[1])* was born 1874 in Cayuga County, New York, and died 1934. She married FLOYD ADDISON COLE Abt. 1905 in New York, son of ADDISON COLE and ELIZABETH _____. He was born 24 Aug 1877 in New York, and died 1965.

Child of ADELLE ROBINSON and FLOYD COLE is:
1636.   i. IRENE[10] COLE, b. Abt. 1906, Cayuga County, New York; d. 1993.

820. FRANCES A.[9] GUION *(AUGUSTA FRANCES[8] MILK, CHARLES G.[7], WILLIAM[6], LEMUEL[5], DAVID[4], JOB[3], JOHN[2], JOHN[1])* was born Feb 1866 in Auburn, Cayuga County, New York. She married FRED N. WHALEY Abt. 1886 in Cayuga County, New York. He was born Apr 1861 in New York.

Children of FRANCES GUION and FRED WHALEY are:
- i. FREDRICK G.[10] WHALEY, b. May 1892, Auburn, Cayuga County, New York.
- ii. HARROLD R. WHALEY, b. Oct 1897, Auburn, Cayuga County, New York.

iii. DONALD C. WHALEY, b. Abt. 1905, Auburn, Cayuga County, New York.

821. ELIZABETH IVES[9] GUION *(AUGUSTA FRANCES[8] MILK, CHARLES G.[7], WILLIAM[6], LEMUEL[5], DAVID[4], JOB[3], JOHN[2], JOHN[1])* was born 29 Sep 1875 in Auburn, Cayuga County, New York, and died Dec 1969 in Auburn, Cayuga County, New York. She married HAROLD FELD HUTCHINSON 08 Aug 1900 in Cayuga County, New York, son of GARRY HUTCHINSON and JULIA NICHOLS. He was born May 1879 in Auburn, Cayuga County, New York, and died 17 Nov 1937 in Frankfort, Clinton County, Indiana.

Elizabeth was the youngest daughter of Charles Frederick Guion and Frances Augusta Milk. She married Harold Feld Hutchinson 8 Aug 1900. Unfortunately by the mid-1920s, Harold left the family and moved to Indiana where he re-married and had one son. Elizabeth remained in Auburn for the rest of her life, working for the Columbian Rope Co as an office worker.

Burial: Fort Hill Cemetery, Auburn, Cayuga County, New York; Plot: Glen Alpine Lot 17 Grave 7

Children of ELIZABETH GUION and HAROLD HUTCHINSON are:

1637. i. ELIZABETH GUION[10] HUTCHINSON, b. 04 May 1901, Rochester, Monroe County, New York; d. Jul 1992, Cayuga County, New York; m.. JAMES JACOBS
      ii. MARGARET FRANCES HUTCHINSON, b. 1903, Rochester, Monroe County, New York; d. 01 Aug 1921, Long Lake, Hamilton County, New York (drowned).
     iii. GARRY CHARLES HUTCHINSON, b. 03 Oct 1904, Rochester, Monroe County, New York; d. 04 Nov 1970, Staten Island, New York. Never married.
      iv. ADA ELINOR HUTCHINSON, b. Abt. 1906, Rochester, Monroe County, New York; m. EARLE CLINTON.
       v. JULIA AUGUSTA HUTCHINSON, b. 1910, Rochester, Monroe County, New York; m. (1) BYRON BIBBENS; m. (2) JOHN JOSHANSKI.

822. HUBERT CRAMPTON[9] BARTON *(MARY SHERWOOD[8] MILK, LEMUEL[7], WILLIAM[6], LEMUEL[5], DAVID[4], JOB[3], JOHN[2], JOHN[1])* was born 12 Jan 1910 in Chicago, Illinois, and died Jul 1985 in San Juan, Puerto Rico. He married (1) ROSAMOND CHURCHILL 1929 in Amherst, Massachusetts. He married (2) MARIE A. GRAMMER 1944. She was born 30 Sep 1917, and died 27 Jan 2008 in Manatee, Florida.

Children of HUBERT BARTON and ROSAMOND CHURCHILL are:
1638. i. SHERWOOD 'SHERRY'[10] BARTON, b. 27 Jul 1936.
1639. ii. NORA BARTON, b. 16 Feb 1941.

Child of HUBERT BARTON and MARIE GRAMMER is:
  iii. HUBERT C.[10] BARTON III, b. 23 Dec 1951, Puerto Rico; d. 26 Apr 2010, Atlanta, Georgia; m. AUDREY MARCELLIS.

Death Notice Published in The Atlanta Journal-Constitution on May 2, 2010
BARTON, Hubert, III Hubert C. Barton, III, 1951 - 2010 Hubert Crampton Barton III, 58 of Atlanta, GA died at home on Monday, April26, 2010.
Known to his friends as "Hugh" or "Hubert".
He was born on December 23, 1951, in Rio Piedras, Puerto Rico. He was the son of Hubert and Marie Barton, Jr.
He attended Windham College in Putney, Vermont, graduating with a degree in accounting. Hubert first worked as a Certified Public Accountant for accounting firms located in New England and Atlanta, Georgia .. Hubert left public accounting to work as a credit specialist with General Electric Credit Corporation. Hubert was known for his generosity, and for his love of animals, especially cats. As a youth, he often adopted pets and he had great concern for the welfare of stray cats and dogs in Puerto Rico. Hubert was preceded in death by his wife, Audrey Marcellis . He is survived by his half-sisters, Sherwood Barton Bromley of Marlboro, Vermont and Nora Barton Bryant of Jaffrey, New Hampshire, nieces Nevada Knight Bromley of Putney, Vermont and Bethany Dyer of Jaffrey, New Hampshire; his nephew, Barton Bryant of Mont Vernon, New Hampshire; his grand-nieces, Morgan Rose and Sarah Jane Dyer and grand-nephews, Arden Bromley of Manhattan, New York and Kyle Bryant of Jaffrey, New Hampshire; his aunt, Thyrza Barton White of State College, Pennsylvania and uncle, William Barton, of Concord, Massachusetts, various cousins and host of friends who were all but family to him. A memorial service celebrating his life will be held at 2:30 p.m. at his residence on

May 16, 2010. Expressions of sympathy should be made in the form of donations to the Atlanta Humane Society. Arrangements by the Cremation Society of Georgia 404- 355-7627

823. DR. PRESTON NICHOLS[9] BARTON (*MARY SHERWOOD*[8] *MILK, LEMUEL*[7]*, WILLIAM*[6]*, LEMUEL*[5]*, DAVID*[4]*, JOB*[3]*, JOHN*[2]*, JOHN*[1]) was born 14 Jun 1913 in Amherst, Massachusetts, and died Sep 1978 in Mountain Side, Union County, New Jersey. He married (1) BARBARA JORDON 04 Jun 1939. She died 15 Sep 1950. He married (2) LYDIA JORDON Jan 1951.

Children of PRESTON BARTON and BARBARA JORDON are:
  i. PRESTON NICHOLS[10] BARTON, JR., b. 21 Jul 1942, Terryville, Connecticut.
  ii. WILLIAM HALE BARTON, b. 26 Mar 1949, Terryville, Connecticut.

824. ELIZABETH SHERWOOD[9] BARTON (*MARY SHERWOOD*[8] *MILK, LEMUEL*[7]*, WILLIAM*[6]*, LEMUEL*[5]*, DAVID*[4]*, JOB*[3]*, JOHN*[2]*, JOHN*[1]) was born 15 Jul 1916 in Amherst, Massachusetts, and died 17 May 1999 in Amherst, Hampshire County, Massachusetts. She married GEORGE F. CRAMER, JR. 02 Jan 1939. He was born 08 Apr 1915, and died 01 Sep 2006 in Amherst, Hampshire County, Massachusetts.

Children of ELIZABETH BARTON and GEORGE CRAMER are:
  i. GEORGE F.[10] CRAMER III, b. 25 Aug 1941, Amherst, Massachusetts.
  ii. ELIZABETH S. CRAMER, b. 29 Jul 1943, Amherst, Massachusetts.
  iii. ROBERT CRAMER, b. 22 Mar 1946, Amherst, Massachusetts.

825. THYRZA STEVENS[9] BARTON (*MARY SHERWOOD*[8] *MILK, LEMUEL*[7]*, WILLIAM*[6]*, LEMUEL*[5]*, DAVID*[4]*, JOB*[3]*, JOHN*[2]*, JOHN*[1]) was born 23 Jul 1921 in Amherst, Massachusetts. She married HAROLD B. WHITE, JR. 05 May 1942. He was born 28 Feb 1919, and died 10 May 2008 in State College, Centre County, Pennsylvania.

Children of THYRZA BARTON and HAROLD WHITE are:
  i. HAROLD B.[10] WHITE III, b. 26 Feb 1943, State College, Pennsylvania; m. JEAN S. _____; b. 1943.
  ii. HUBERT BARTON WHITE, b. 28 Feb 1946, State College, Pennsylvania.
  iii. HEBRON BRYANT WHITE, b. 07 Jul 1949, State College, Pennsylvania.
  iv. DANIEL SHERWOOD WHITE, b. 19 Sep 1954, State College, Pennsylvania.

826. MARY HATHAWAY[9] BARTON (*MARY SHERWOOD*[8] *MILK, LEMUEL*[7]*, WILLIAM*[6]*, LEMUEL*[5]*, DAVID*[4]*, JOB*[3]*, JOHN*[2]*, JOHN*[1]) was born 24 May 1923 in Amherst, Massachusetts, and died 24 Nov 2002 in Silver Spring, Montgomery County, Maryland. She married STUART PHILIP BROCK 29 May 1947. He was born 09 Jul 1917, and died Sep 1982 in Silver Spring, Montgomery, Maryland.

Children of MARY BARTON and STUART BROCK are:
  i. LOREN P.[10] BROCK, b. 04 Jun 1950, Wheaton, Maryland.
  ii. MARY BROCK, b. 05 May 1953, Wheaton, Maryland.

827. URA MAE/MAY[9] STEPHENSON (*FRANCES ALMEDA*[8] *WILKINS, LAURA ANN*[7] *MILKS, JOHN*[6]*, LEMUEL*[5] *MILK, DAVID*[4]*, JOB*[3]*, JOHN*[2]*, JOHN*[1]) was born Abt. 1872 in Joliet, Will County, Illinois, and died 27 May 1950 in Joliet, Illinois. She married GEORGE R. EASTWOOD. He was born Abt. 1870.

Children of URA STEPHENSON and GEORGE EASTWOOD are:
  i. FRANCIS ARCHIBALD[10] EASTWOOD.
  ii. STEVENSON EASTWOOD.

828. ALTA MAE[9] STEPHENSON (*FRANCES ALMEDA*[8] *WILKINS, LAURA ANN*[7] *MILKS, JOHN*[6]*, LEMUEL*[5] *MILK, DAVID*[4]*, JOB*[3]*, JOHN*[2]*, JOHN*[1]) was born 15 Nov 1876 in Joliet, Will County, Illinois, and died 04 Jan 1929 in Evanston, Cook County, Illinois. She married MELVIN CHARLES TOWNSEND Abt. 1905 in Cook County, Illinois, son of AUGUSTAV TOWNSEND and ELIZABETH KERNAN. He was born 28 Jan 1872 in Hinsdale, Illinois, and died 14 Mar 1939 in Cook County, Illinois.

Children of ALTA STEPHENSON and MELVIN TOWNSEND are:
- i. THEODORE[10] TOWNSEND, b. Abt. 1906, DuPage County, Illinois.
- ii. FLORA TOWNSEND, b. Abt. 1908, DuPage County, Illinois.
- iii. ALTA MAE TOWNSEND, b. Abt. 1910, Illinois.

829. ALTA MAE[9] DESELMA *(HARRIET M. 'HATTIE'[8] WILKINS, LAURA ANN[7] MILKS, JOHN[6], LEMUEL[5] MILK, DAVID[4], JOB[3], JOHN[2], JOHN[1])* was born 07 Oct 1879 in Kankakee County, Illinois, and died 01 Dec 1958 in Santa Barbara, California. She married CHARLES O. MONTAGUE 1905 in Kankakee, Illinois. He was born Abt. 1877.

Child of ALTA DESELMA and CHARLES MONTAGUE is:
- i. GLADYS HOPE[10] MONTAGUE, b. 29 Jun 1915, Cook County, Illinois; d. 02 Jun 1954, Santa Barbara, California; m. MR. BOMAR.

830. HOWARD W.[9] WEEKS *(EDWIN L.[8], MARIAH E.[7] MILKS, JOHN[6], LEMUEL[5] MILK, DAVID[4], JOB[3], JOHN[2], JOHN[1])* was born 29 Feb 1888 in Will County, Illinois, and died 18 Aug 1947 in Cameron County, Texas. He married EUPTRA B. 'FAY' BEADLE Abt. 1913, daughter of CHARLES BEADLE and CLARA SNOW. She was born 20 Dec 1890 in Toledo, Lucas County, Ohio.

Child of HOWARD WEEKS and EUPTRA BEADLE is:
- i. CHARLES EDWIN[10] WEEKS, b. Abt. 1915, Illinois; d. 13 Nov 1956, Cameron County, Texas.

831. ANN ELIZA[9] PORTER *(MINERVA ADELINE[8] DEUEL, WILLIAM HENRY[7], LEWIS[6], PATIENCE[5] MILK, DAVID[4], JOB[3], JOHN[2], JOHN[1])* was born 22 Oct 1862 in Porterville, Utah, and died 12 Jun 1927 in Farmington, Davis County, Utah. She married HYRUM DON CARLOS CLARK 11 Nov 1880 in Salt Lake City, Utah, son of EZRA THOMPSON CLARK and MARY STEVENSON. He was born 13 Feb 1856 in Farmington, Davis County, Utah, and died 02 Jul 1938 in Ogden, Weber County, Utah.

OBITUARY - Star Valley Independent, 17 Jun 1927

Mrs. Eliza Porter Clark, beloved wife of Hyrum D. Clark, for twenty years a resident of Auburn died at her home at Farmington, Utah, Sunday morning June 12th after a period of ill health extending over the past two years.

Surviving is her husband who was just completing a short term mission in California, and the following children: Mrs. Avery C. Lambert of Salt Lake City, Mrs. Mary Bennion of Farmington, Heber D. Clark of Monroe, Utah, Mrs. Edna C. Erickson of Salt Lake, A. Portor Clark of Auburn, Thelma Rachel Kjarr of Salt Lake, Rhoda C. Burningham of Farmington, R. Elwin Clark of Salt Lake, Mrs. Zula C. Higgs of Layton, Utah, Mrs. Blanche C. Wilcox, O. Morrell and A. Ivins Clark all of Farmington.

The eldest son, Hyrum T. Clark was killed in an accident in Star Valley in 1911.

The living descendants of Mrs. Clark number twelve children and 42 grandchildren. She also has three brothers Chas. W., Orson M., and Myron Porter all of Wyoming and all bishops and one sister Mary Porter of Arizona. She was a sister also of the late Vilate White of Thayne.

Funeral services were held at Farmington Tuesday the 14th. Bp. A. L. Clark presided. The speakers were Stake President J. H. Robinson, President Joseph W. McMurrin of the California mission, Bishop Nicholas G. Smith of Salt Lake, a long time neighbor, Bishop Heber C. Iverson of the M.I.A. general board and Bishop Clark. All paid beautiful and fitting tributes to the character and activities of the deceased. Her cheerful and loving disposition being especially emphasized.

Special musical numbers were rendered by Mrs. Thomas of the Primary general board and by the Farmington male quartet and choir.

The invocation was by Henry Wilcox of Farmington and the benediction by Thomas F. Burton of Afton.

Mrs. Eliza Clark was an active church worker all her life serving as president of Auburn primary for some thirteen years and as a Relief society president for six years. After removing to Farmington in 1908 she was made president of the Y.L.M.I.A. She also did extensive temple and genealogical work.

The floral offerings were extensive and beautiful and were sent from far and near. Interment was in the Farmington cemetery. Dedicatory prayer was offered by her son Heber.

H. D. Clark married Mary Alice Robinson, 27 Dec 1903, Salt Lake City, Salt Lake, Utah (1878 - 1942)
Children - Herma Clark, Weston Robinson Clark, Jasper Clark, Carlos Robinson Clark, Hazel Clark

Obituary

H.D. Clark Passes Away

H. D. Clark, who passed away recently at his home in Farmington was one of the early pioneers of Star Valley. He settled in Auburn in 1888 and has owned real estate there continuously since that time. Until recently he owned upward of 1200 acres of land in the meadow near Auburn.

He was always active in civic affairs and also church affairs. He served two terms as County Commissioner. He was a member of the Auburn Bishopric and a Stake High Councilman in Star Valley. A year ago he completed a two year mission to California as an L.D.S. missionary.

He was always strong and robust and never had any serious illness until four weeks before his death. While crossing the street he was struck by a boy on a bicycle, and received injuries from which he never recovered. He passed peacefully away at the Dee Hospital, in Ogden July 2, 1938.

Surviving him are his widow, Mary Robinson Clark, seventeen children, 64 grandchildren and several great grand-children.

He was buried in the Farmington Cemetery.

Children of ANN PORTER and HYRUM CLARK are:
- i. ELIZA AVERY^{10} CLARK, b. 1882, Utah; d. 1953; m. MR. LAMBERT.
- ii. MARY MINERVA CLARK, b. 1883, Utah; d. 1978; m. MR. BENNION.
- iii. HYRUM TAYLOR CLARK, b. Feb 1885, Idaho; d. 1911, Star Valley, Uinta County, Wyoming.
- iv. HEBER DON CARLOS CLARK, b. Jul 1887, Idaho; d. 1986.
- v. EDNA CLARK, b. Nov 1889, Star Valley, Uinta County, Wyoming; d. 1983; m. MR. ERICKSON.
- vi. ALMA PORTER CLARK, b. Jan 1892, Utah; d. 1953.
- vii. THELMA RACHEL CLARK, b. Jan 1894, Wyoming Star Valley, Uinta County, Wyoming; d. 1990; m. MR. KJARR.
- viii. RHODA CLARK, b. May 1896, Star Valley, Uinta County, Wyoming; m. MR. BURNINGHAM.
- ix. ROSEL ELWIN CLARK, b. May 1899, Star Valley, Uinta County, Wyoming; d. 1977.
- x. ZULA CLARK, b. 1901, Star Valley, Uinta County, Wyoming; m. MR. HIGGS.
- xi. BLANCHE CLARK, b. 1904, Star Valley, Uinta County, Wyoming; d. 1997; m. MR. WILCOX.
- xii. OWEN MORRELL CLARK, b. 1906, Star Valley, Uinta County, Wyoming; d. 1996.
- xiii. ANTHONY IVINS CLARK, b. 1908, Star Valley, Uinta County, Wyoming.

832. ORSON MERRITT^9 PORTER *(MINERVA ADELINE^8 DEUEL, WILLIAM HENRY^7, LEWIS^6, PATIENCE^5 MILK, DAVID^4, JOB^3, JOHN^2, JOHN^1)* was born 26 Jul 1869 in Porterville, Utah, and died 08 May 1935 in Otto, Wyoming. He married MAGGIE BELLE TOLMAN 03 Jan 1894, daughter of CYRUS TOLMAN and MARGARET UTLEY. She was born 26 Apr 1877 in Tooele, Utah.

Children of ORSON PORTER and MAGGIE TOLMAN are:
- i. WINNIFRED BELLE^{10} PORTER, b. 13 Aug 1895, Fairview, Wyoming; m. LELAND HARRIS.
- ii. VIOLA LORETTA PORTER, b. 20 Sep 1897, Fairview, Wyoming; d. 29 Sep 1898, Fairview, Wyoming.
- 1640. iii. VALERIA PORTER, b. 07 Jul 1899, Fairview, Wyoming.
- iv. RHEA ELIZA PORTER, b. 10 Mar 1902, Otto, Wyoming; m. WILLIS FRANKLIN WHITE; b. Abt. 1900.
- v. ALMA ORSON PORTER, b. 06 Oct 1904, Porterville, Utah; m. JENNIE ORR; b. Abt. 1904.
- vi. ELWOOD MYRON PORTER, b. 17 Jun 1907, Porterville, Utah; m. JEAN WHEELER; b. Abt. 1907.
- vii. REX TOLMAN PORTER, b. 16 Apr 1910, Porterville, Utah; m. MARCA LYNN; b. Abt. 1910.
- viii. DEUEL ERNEST PORTER, b. 21 Oct 1913, Lovell, Wyoming; m. ELLIE MCCARNEY; b. Abt. 1913.
- ix. MAGGIE MAYE PORTER, b. 15 May 1918, Basin, Wyoming; m. LYNN MESERVEY.

833. KATIE ROSILLA^9 DEUEL *(LEWIS^8, WILLIAM HENRY^7, LEWIS^6, PATIENCE^5 MILK, DAVID^4, JOB^3, JOHN^2, JOHN^1)* was born 05 Mar 1884 in Escalante, Utah. She married JOSEPH COLEMAN LAY 11 May 1902 in Escalante, Utah, son of JOHN LAY and RACHEL WILTBANK. He was born 12 Nov 1881 in Santa Clara, Utah.

Children of KATIE DEUEL and JOSEPH LAY are:
- i. OTHELLO^{10} LAY, b. 22 Apr 1903, Nibbley, Oregon; m. (1) MAY HALLINGTON; b. Abt. 1903; m. (2) BERNICE ELEANOR ORD; b. Abt. 1903.
- ii. URDEL WANDEL LAY, b. 21 Jun 1905, Nibbley, Oregon; m. MILDRED IONE WANKER; b. Abt. 1905.

iii. GUILD DEUEL LAY, b. 08 Dec 1906, Nibbley, Oregon; m. (1) EDNA BRADSHAW; b. Abt. 1906; m. (2) LOIS DEARDORFF; b. Abt. 1906.
iv. CLARA FONTELLA LAY, b. 28 Nov 1908, Union, Oregon; m. ALVA WARREN ORTON; b. Abt. 1908.
v. LAUREL EASTON LAY, b. 13 Jul 1910, Union, Oregon; d. 29 Nov 1936; m. CLETA MARY MICKEY; b. Abt. 1910.
vi. DESHLER COLEMAN LAY, b. 01 Jun 1912, Union, Oregon; m. MYRTLE YVONNE INMAN; b. Abt. 1912.
vii. RETHA GAY LAY, b. 17 Jun 1915, Union, Oregon; m. PAGE LERWILL; b. Abt. 1915.
viii. MASYL WILLMERTH LAY, b. 05 Dec 1917, Union, Oregon; m. (1) ELMER R. VAN LEUVEN; b. Abt. 1917; m. (2) JAY E. BOWEN; b. Abt. 1917.
ix. BEVERLY ROSE LAY, b. 03 Mar 1922, Union, Oregon; m. ROBERT LEE WORLEY, 10 Oct 1941; b. Abt. 1922.
x. PAULA ERROLO LAY, b. 25 Mar 1926, Union, Oregon; m. CLIFFORD EDWIN BURFORD, 16 Sep 1949; b. Abt. 1926.

834. MARY ELLA^9 BLOSSOM *(ELI WALTER^8, CLARISSA^7, ALICE^6 MILK, JOB^5, DAVID^4, JOB^3, JOHN^2, JOHN^1)* was born 06 Jul 1879. She married WALDO A. SHERMAN Abt. 1900. He was born Abt. 1879.

Children of MARY BLOSSOM and WALDO SHERMAN are:
1641. i. WILSON R.^{10} SHERMAN, b. 13 Nov 1902, North Westport, Massachusetts.
1642. ii. WENDELL B. SHERMAN, b. 11 Aug 1907, North Westport, Massachusetts.

835. SUSAN MILLER^9 BLOSSOM *(ELI WALTER^8, CLARISSA^7, ALICE^6 MILK, JOB^5, DAVID^4, JOB^3, JOHN^2, JOHN^1)* was born 20 Jul 1887. She married ERNEST F. PETTEY. He was born Abt. 1887.

Child of SUSAN BLOSSOM and ERNEST PETTEY is:
i. ERNEST F.^{10} PETTEY, JR., b. Abt. 1910; d. 17 Jul 1944, Italy. Killed in Italy in WWII

836. JULIA EVALYN^9 WOODRUFF *(MARGARET^8 MILKS, JOHN^7, ELI S.^{6} MILK, JOB^5, DAVID^4, JOB^3, JOHN^2, JOHN^1)* was born 17 Jul 1884 in Binghamton, Broome County, NY. She married HARRY EDWIN PRENTICE 12 Oct 1916 in Binghamton, NY. He was born 05 Mar 1888 in Brandt, PA. Raymond E. Prentice was a step-son to Julia.

Child of JULIA WOODRUFF and HARRY PRENTICE is:
i. RAYMOND E.^{10} PRENTICE.

837. ELIZABETH^9 MILKS *(DEWITT WILLIAM^8, DAVID^7, ELI S.^{6} MILK, JOB^5, DAVID^4, JOB^3, JOHN^2, JOHN^1)* was born 29 Jul 1905 in Broome County, New York, and died 17 May 1938 in Broome County, New York. She married RUDOLPH TAPKEN ELLSWORTH Abt. 1922 in Binghamton, Broome County, New York, son of ORRIN ELLSWORTH and HATTIE ___. He was born 20 May 1905 in Ulster County, New York, and died 15 Sep 1987 in Kernersville, Forsyth County, NC.

Child of ELIZABETH MILKS and RUDOLPH ELLSWORTH is:
1643. i. EMMA LOUISE^{10} ELLSWORTH, b. Abt. 1923, Binghamton, Broome County, New York.

838. ESTHER J.^{9} MILKS *(DEWITT WILLIAM^8, DAVID^7, ELI S.^{6} MILK, JOB^5, DAVID^4, JOB^3, JOHN^2, JOHN^1)* was born Abt. 1908 in Broome County, New York. She married B. OLIVER. He was born Abt. 1908.

Child of ESTHER MILKS and B. OLIVER is:
i. CAROLYN JEAN^{10} OLIVER.

839. HARLEY EDWARD^9 MILKS *(FRANCIS "FRANK" ELI^8, BENJAMIN B.^{7}, ELI S.^{6} MILK, JOB^5, DAVID^4, JOB^3, JOHN^2, JOHN^1)* was born 14 Apr 1908 in Hawleyton, Broome County, New York, and died 09 Mar 1995 in Hawleyton, Broome County, New York. He married KATHRYN MARIE ZELLERS 27 Sep 1930 in Johnson City, Broome County, New York, daughter of HARRY ZELLERS and ALICE HOOVER. She was born 23 Jun 1912 in Williamsport, Lycoming County, Pennsylvania, and died 22 Mar 2002 in Johnson City, Broome County, New York.
MATERIAL PROVIDED BY JOHN & MIRIAM (MILKS) KOBUSKIE
Harley had four years of formal education. He worked on the family farm as a child, raising potatoes and producing butter and eggs which he sold to distributors in Binghamton. He left home at 16 and took a job with the

Vulcan shoe company. He later went to Sisson Brothers and then Morris Distributing Company, where he retired in June 1973 after 32 years of service.

In his youth be helped build the Hawleyton Turnpike (now Pennsylvania Avenue), removing stone fences and spreading stone for 40 cents an hour. During a part of WWI, when food was being rationed for the forces, the family subsisted on potatoes and milk produced on the farm because they could not afford other foodstuffs.

Harley lived in Johnson City and for a short time in Binghamton before retuning to the Town of Binghamton. In order to pay for the funeral of his mother Grace in 1942, he and his brother Charles cut 250 cord of maple from the farm and sold it at $1.25 a cord. He served as a school trustee in the Town until the time the school district was consolidated.

He was a member of the Binghamton Elks Lodge #852, Binghamton Amateur Radio Association, Town of Binghamton Historical Society and the Hawleyton United Methodist Church.
- He worked as an appliance repairman, many years for Morris Distributing Company, Binghamton.
- He was buried at the Milks Hill Cemetery, Hawleyton, NY.

Reminiscing about Dad by his kids

Harley Milks was a husband, father, grandfather and friend. He was a devoted husband and companion to our Mom for over 64 years. Together they raised three children in a warm and secure home. Dad and Mom also made a home for their foster son, whom they loved and treated as their own.

Dad lived most of his life in Hawleyton on the land where his family had lived before him. He loved his land and cared for it until he was no longer able. When that time came, he watched over his children and grandchildren as they mowed and trimmed and cared for his lawn. On the days he felt strong enough, he would hop on his riding lawn mower and take a spin around his yard, and you could tell he was happy to be there.

For many years, he relaxed by hunting and fishing. He often shared those times with his son or his brother, Charlie, who was also his closest friend. Dad liked gadgets and electronics. He had the first television set in the area and friends and neighbors would come to the top of Milks Hill to watch TV in a tent. He supported the Ham radio operators in the area and lent them land to use for their operations. He could fix anything using whatever odds and ends were available. He was a genius with bailing wire.

He liked a good party and was a good host. He liked to dance - with or without a partner. Often his idea of a good time was just sitting around telling stories and laughing over things that had happened in his lifetime. He was a great storyteller who remembered every name and every detail. His sense of humor was well honed and he never lost his knack for making us laugh, even in the final days of his life.

Dad enjoyed his pets. He always had dogs, mostly beagles, and he named at least two of them Buster. His faithful companion for the last 12 years was his cat Buffy.

He had very definite opinions regarding life and politics, but he never forced his beliefs on anyone. He was honest and hardworking and he set a good example for all of us.

Mom and Dad were married for almost 64 years. They enjoyed the good times and weathered the bad times together. In their later years, they faced the annoyances of aging with love and good humor. When mother had trouble seeing, Dad became her eyes and when Dad sometimes found walking painful, Mom became his legs. They joined their strengths and became a formidable team.

It's hard to lose someone you love. But we must comfort ourselves with the fact that Dad lived a happy life on the land he loved with the people he loved.

Good bye Dad

KATHRYN MARIE ZELLERS:
Remembering Mom   Eulogy by Miriam (Milks) Kobuskie March 25, 2002

Carol, Chum and I would like to share some memories of Mother. During the eighty nine years that she lived she was known by many names. Our father called her Kathryn, as did most of her family and friends. Some called her Kate. To her children she was Mom and sometimes Ma (which she wasn't particularly fond of), and she was Grandma to her seven grandchildren and five great-grandchildren.

She was the Kool-Aid Lady without the Kool-Aid. She provided the neighborhood kids with dill pickles - they were wonderful and there were quarts of them in our cellar.

She fried up her famous peanuts, baked wonderful pies and breads, grew vegetables, and planted flowers.

She could sew a party dress and crochet wonderful afghans. She could create a magical sight with a few

Christmas ornaments on one of Dad's famous pine trees with three branches! One year she insisted we keep the Christmas tree up until February so we could celebrate with Jerry when he came home from Japan where he was in the Army. To make more time for things she liked to do she usually slacked off a little on things such as dusting! She didn't like to dust much, and besides, there were so many neighborhood kids running around the house that the dust barely had time to settle.

In the early years that she and Dad lived in their beloved house in the country she existed without electricity, running water or indoor plumbing. Things improved over the years and became cozier for her and Dad, but the one constant was their love for the house and the land, and their love for each other. In their last few years together they would spend days in the late summer and early fall sawing wood and hauling it down to the house for the furnace. How she loved those days and loved working with Dad.

She was a wonderful mother. She went beyond just raising us. She strong-armed the high school principal into making Chum finish high school, and when that was accomplished she wrote letters to her "Chummie" almost every day of the three years he served in the Army. She also sent some pretty nifty care packages to him and his fellow soldiers. She helped Carol finance her first beauty parlor and helped Miriam buy her first car. Sorry about the car Chum, but you did get letters for three years!

When we were all married and had children, Mom provided Sunday and holiday dinners for us and for our families for over thirty years. Mom had a mind of her own. She and Dad had a wonderful marriage for sixty four years, and they usually agreed on most things. However, Mom wasn't above threatening to knock out part of the pantry wall with a sledgehammer (which she actually did) to encourage some remodeling, or threatening to burn the old beds (which she didn't do) to get new ones. Last summer, shortly after she turned eighty nine years old, we told her we didn't think she should be swimming in the eight foot deep end of the swimming pool. She informed us that she wouldn't be going in the pool anymore because she wasn't going to swim in the baby end. We have to understand this is a woman who chose to swim across the Susquehanna River in her younger years. She was going to do it right or not at all.

As recently as last fall she was going apple picking. She loved going to the orchard. We were a sight! It would begin with my friend Bev, Bev's sister Joyce, and me boosting Mom into Bev's van with much joking and laughter. The trip always ended with Mom buying donuts at the farm store. Mom had a large family of brothers and sisters. The brothers, Glen, Mack, and Tommy, were all handsome, and the sisters, Verna-deen, Miriam, Florence and Kathryn, were all beautiful --- and feisty! These were women who survived the difficult times and relished the good ones. Florence now survives to carry on the legacy. She was at Mom's side for those last few weeks and was there when she passed on.

You can tell by what your have heard here this morning that Mom's life was full of loving family, friends and happiness. Over the years Mom's sight and hearing failed, and her memory wasn't all she had hoped it would be, but the one thing that never diminished was her love for Dad and for her family.

As she leaves us to join Dad, we comfort ourselves with the knowledge that she had a long and truly wonderful life.

- She was buried at the Milks Hill Cemetery, Hawleyton.
- She worked as a homemaker, and as an employee of Morris Distributing Company, Binghamton for 15 years.

She was a member of the Cooperative Extension, the Hawleyton Grange and the Hawleyton United Methodist Church.

Goodbye Mom, we'll miss you.

Children of HARLEY MILKS and KATHRYN ZELLERS are:
1644. i. HARLEY GLENN[10] MILKS, SR., b. 26 Oct 1936, Johnson City, Broome County, New York; d. 21 Oct 2002, Hawleyton, Broome County, New York.
1645. ii. MIRIAM HARLENE MILKS, b. 24 Aug 1943, Binghamton, Broome County, New York.
1646. iii. CAROL MARIE MILKS, b. 12 Feb 1945, Binghamton, Broome County, New York.

840. EVERETT W.[9] MILKS, SR. *(FRANCIS "FRANK" ELI[8], BENJAMIN B.[7], ELI S.[6] MILK, JOB[5], DAVID[4], JOB[3], JOHN[2], JOHN[1])* was born 18 Dec 1921 in Hawleyton, Broome Co., NY, and died 12 Apr 1998 in Chenango County, New York. He married (1) AVIS RUNYON Abt. 1944, daughter of LEWIS RUNYON and DELTA STONE. She was born 16 Apr 1924 in Broome Co., NY, and died 27 Nov 2001 in Broome Co., NY. He married (2) ESTHER HEATH 1949 in Broome County, NY. He married (3) CARRIE BARNUM Abt. 1960 in Broome County, NY?.

Children of EVERETT MILKS and AVIS RUNYON are:
1647. i. JONATHAN (JON) ELWOOD[10] MILKS, b. 17 Jun 1945, Binghamton, NY; d. 27 Nov 2008, Binghamton, NY.
1648. ii. RUTH AMANDA MILKS, b. 15 Oct 1947, Binghamton, NY.
1649. iii. RETHA ANN MILKS, b. 15 Oct 1947, Binghamton, NY.

Child of EVERETT MILKS and ESTHER HEATH is:
1650. iv. EVERETT W.[10] MILKS, JR., b. 20 Jun 1950, Broome County, NY.

Child of EVERETT MILKS and CARRIE BARNUM is:
1651. v. HOWARD[10] MILKS, b. Abt. 1962, Broome Co., NY.

841. BETTY E.[9] MILKS *(FRANCIS "FRANK" ELI[8], BENJAMIN B.[7], ELI S.[6] MILK, JOB[5], DAVID[4], JOB[3], JOHN[2], JOHN[1])* was born Bet. 1924 - 1925 in Hawleyton, Broome Co., NY, and died Abt. 1985 in Tennessee. She married (1) DONALD FLAHERTY Abt. 1944. He was born Abt. 1920. She married (2) TIMOTHY ELLIOTT Aft. 1950. He was born Abt. 1924.

Children of BETTY MILKS and DONALD FLAHERTY are:
    i. DONALD[10] FLAHERTY, JR..
    ii. GERALD "JERRY" FLAHERTY.

Children of BETTY MILKS and TIMOTHY ELLIOTT are:
    iii. BETTY[10] ELLIOTT.
    iv. JOSEPH ELLIOTT.

842. ALBERT R.[9] BROWNELL *(STEPHEN A.[8], EZRA PLUMMER[7], JIRAH[6], ABIGAIL[5] MILK, DAVID[4], JOB[3], JOHN[2], JOHN[1])* was born Jun 1865 in New Bedford, Massachusetts. He married MARY H. _____. She was born Sep 1866 in Massachusetts.

Children of ALBERT BROWNELL and MARY _____ are:
    i. STELLA A.[10] BROWNELL, b. May 1885, New Bedford, Massachusetts.
    ii. RALPH M. BROWNELL, b. May 1886, New Bedford, Massachusetts.
    iii. HILDA BROWNELL, b. Feb 1900, New Bedford, Massachusetts.

843. EMMA LODUSKA[9] LOTTRIDGE *(ALVIN DURHAM[8], THOMAS[7], ESTHER[6] BULL, AMY[5] CHASE, SARAH[4] MILK, JOB[3], JOHN[2], JOHN[1])* was born 08 Oct 1860 in Hoosick Falls, Rensselaer County, New York, and died 29 Jul 1929 in Englewood, New Jersey. She married ELLIS DAVID MILKS 05 Sep 1879 in North Hoosick, Rensselaer County, New York, son of MATTHEW MILKS and MARGARET ALLEN. He was born 1855 in Valley Falls (Pittstown), Rensselaer County, New York, and died 1914 in Valley Falls (Pittstown), Rensselaer County, New York.
    Notes for EMMA LODUSKA LOTTRIDGE: D.A.R. #239532

844. ARTHUR CLIFFORD[9] LOTTRIDGE *(ALVIN DURHAM[8], THOMAS[7], ESTHER[6] BULL, AMY[5] CHASE, SARAH[4] MILK, JOB[3], JOHN[2], JOHN[1])* was born 01 Jun 1862 in Hoosic Falls, New York. He married (1) SARAH E. MILLSON 18 Dec 1889. She was born 1867, and died 1890. He married (2) MAYTE G. WOOD 26 Oct 1892. She was born 16 Jun 1868, and died 26 Apr 1899.

Child of ARTHUR LOTTRIDGE and SARAH MILLSON is:
    i. SARAH E.[10] LOTTRIDGE, b. 1890; d. 1923.

Children of ARTHUR LOTTRIDGE and MAYTE WOOD are:
    ii. C. WOOD[10] LOTTRIDGE, b. 30 Jun 1894; m. NOT KNOWN, 1950.
    iii. MARY M. LOTTRIDGE, b. 25 May 1896; m. WALTER SANDS, 1927; b. Abt. 1895.

845. ETTA[9] LOTTRIDGE *(ALVIN DURHAM[8], THOMAS[7], ESTHER[6] BULL, AMY[5] CHASE, SARAH[4] MILK, JOB[3], JOHN[2], JOHN[1])* was born 18 Aug 1867 in Hoosic Falls, New York, and died 26 Aug 1949 in Shaftsbury, Vermont. She married CURT REYNOLDS ARMSTRONG 04 Feb 1890 in North Hoosick, New York. He was born 08 Aug 1867 in North Hoosick, New York, and died 06 Dec 1933 in Bennington, Vermont.

Child of ETTA LOTTRIDGE and CURT ARMSTRONG is:
1652. i. HAZEL LOTTRIDGE[10] ARMSTRONG, b. 09 Mar 1896, Hoosic, New York.

846. STEPHEN SMITH[9] LOTTRIDGE *(ALVIN DURHAM[8], THOMAS[7], ESTHER[6] BULL, AMY[5] CHASE, SARAH[4] MILK, JOB[3], JOHN[2], JOHN[1])* was born 26 Apr 1873 in Hoosic Falls, New York, and died 08 Feb 1950 in Stillwater, New York. He married KATE L. WOOD 21 Jun 1902. She was born 07 Mar 1876.

Child of STEPHEN LOTTRIDGE and KATE WOOD is:
 i. RICHARD WOOD[10] LOTTRIDGE, b. 22 May 1903; m. CLARA USHUR; b. Abt. 1905.

847. HARRY LAUSON[9] PRESCOTT *(FRANCES CAROLINE[8] LOTTRIDGE, ISAAC BULL[7], ESTHER[6] BULL, AMY[5] CHASE, SARAH[4] MILK, JOB[3], JOHN[2], JOHN[1])* was born 29 Jul 1852 in Stillwater, New York, and died 28 Feb 1887. He married KATHARINE T. HOOPER 14 Jun 1876. She was born 1851 in Maine.

Child of HARRY PRESCOTT and KATHARINE HOOPER is:
1653. i. AMY LAUSON[10] PRESCOTT, b. 01 Feb 1886, North Dakota.

848. GERTRUDE C.[9] JAMES *(MARY ELLEN[8] LOTTRIDGE, ISAAC BULL[7], ESTHER[6] BULL, AMY[5] CHASE, SARAH[4] MILK, JOB[3], JOHN[2], JOHN[1])* was born 19 Dec 1846, and died 03 Nov 1873 in Kansas City, Missouri. She married CHARLES D. ROCKWOOD 1871. He was born Abt. 1846.

Child of GERTRUDE JAMES and CHARLES ROCKWOOD is:
 i. ALICE MARY[10] ROCKWOOD, b. 01 May 1872, Kansas City, Missouri; m. (1) JOSEPH HOOKER LEW, 20 Aug 1890, Chicago, Illinois; b. Abt. 1870; m. (2) CLIFFORD L. GAGE, 12 Apr 1913, Washington, D.C.; b. Abt. 1870.

849. RICHARD[9] ROSA, JR. *(JANIE ESTHER[8] LOTTRIDGE, MORDECAI[7], ESTHER[6] BULL, AMY[5] CHASE, SARAH[4] MILK, JOB[3], JOHN[2], JOHN[1])* was born 06 Dec 1863 in Schenectady, New York, and died 27 Jun 1918. He married JENNIE KELLOCK 15 Nov 1898 in Schenectady, New York ?. She was born Abt. 1865.

Children of RICHARD ROSA and JENNIE KELLOCK are:
1654. i. RICHARD[10] ROSA III, b. 14 Oct 1899, Schenectady, New York.
1655. ii. ESTHER TAYLOR ROSA, b. 04 Sep 1901, Schenectady, New York.
1656. iii. FRANCIS YATES ROSA, b. 09 Dec 1906, Schenectady, New York.
1657. iv. ROBERT JAMES ROSA, b. 24 Sep 1914, Schenectady, New York.

850. GERTRUDE BANKER[9] ROSA *(JANIE ESTHER[8] LOTTRIDGE, MORDECAI[7], ESTHER[6] BULL, AMY[5] CHASE, SARAH[4] MILK, JOB[3], JOHN[2], JOHN[1])* was born 01 Jul 1869 in Schenectady, New York, and died 02 Jun 1889. She married CHAUNCEY BARHYDT 1888 in Schenectady, New York. He was born Abt. 1869.

Child of GERTRUDE ROSA and CHAUNCEY BARHYDT is:
 i. CHAUNCEY ROSA[10] BARHYDT, b. 22 May 1889; d. 04 Jul 1889.

851. LIBBIE[9] IRWIN *(ESTHER[8] LOTTRIDGE, ROBERT[7], ESTHER[6] BULL, AMY[5] CHASE, SARAH[4] MILK, JOB[3], JOHN[2], JOHN[1])* was born 1851, and died 23 Mar 1926. She married CYRUS ALTMAN. He was born Abt. 1850.

Children of LIBBIE IRWIN and CYRUS ALTMAN are:
 i. RAY[10] ALTMAN, b. 1866; d. 1917; m. ARLETTA EDLEMAN; b. Abt. 1866.
 ii. OTIS ALTMAN, b. 1872; m. LOIS F. NEWTON; b. Abt. 1872.
 iii. MYRON ALTMAN, b. 1877; m. RENA _____; b. Abt. 1877.

852. WILLIS[9] IRWIN *(ESTHER[8] LOTTRIDGE, ROBERT[7], ESTHER[6] BULL, AMY[5] CHASE, SARAH[4] MILK, JOB[3], JOHN[2], JOHN[1])* was born 1857. He married EMMA WEBSTER. She was born Abt. 1860.

Children of WILLIS IRWIN and EMMA WEBSTER are:
- i. GRACE[10] IRWIN, b. 1880; m. MISTER VAN SYCKLES; b. Abt. 1880.
- ii. GERTRUDE IRWIN, b. 1882; m. MR. MCCARTNEY; b. Abt. 1880.
- iii. LEVERNE IRWIN, b. 1886; m. HILDA SEARLS; b. Abt. 1886.

853. ALICE[9] IRWIN (ESTHER[8] LOTTRIDGE, ROBERT[7], ESTHER[6] BULL, AMY[5] CHASE, SARAH[4] MILK, JOB[3], JOHN[2], JOHN[1]) was born 1860. She married (1) WILLIAM SHEARS Abt. 1880. He was born Abt. 1860. She married (2) CHARLES WARD Aft. 1880. He was born Abt. 1860.

Child of ALICE IRWIN and WILLIAM SHEARS is:
- i. NELSON[10] SHEARS, b. Abt. 1880.

854. CHARLOTTE ELIZA[9] BOTHWELL (SARAH MARIA[8] WOLF, ELIZA[7] LOTTRIDGE, ESTHER[6] BULL, AMY[5] CHASE, SARAH[4] MILK, JOB[3], JOHN[2], JOHN[1]) was born 01 May 1858 in McArthur, Ohio, and died 09 Aug 1927 in Wilmington, New Jersey. She married JOHN BANCROFT 30 Nov 1881. He was born 1856.

Children of CHARLOTTE BOTHWELL and JOHN BANCROFT are:
- i. PAULINE[10] BANCROFT, b. 1885; m. WILLIAM CHADWICK; b. Abt. 1885.
- ii. JOHN BANCROFT, JR., b. 1887; m. (1) MADELINE DUPOINT, Abt. 1910; b. Abt. 1887; m. (2) FRANCES HUSELTON, Aft. 1910; b. Abt. 1890.
- iii. ESTHER A. BANCROFT, b. 1897; m. GORDON MATTHEWS; b. Abt. 1895.

855. HELENA DORR[9] RANNELLS (LYDIA M.[8] WOLF, ELIZA[7] LOTTRIDGE, ESTHER[6] BULL, AMY[5] CHASE, SARAH[4] MILK, JOB[3], JOHN[2], JOHN[1]) was born 11 Aug 1861. She married MCCLELLAN POSTON 1883. He was born Abt. 1860.

Children of HELENA RANNELLS and MCCLELLAN POSTON are:
- i. DONALD R.[10] POSTON.
- ii. ANNA R. POSTON.
- iii. JOHN B. R. POSTON.

856. ANNA KING[9] RANNELLS (LYDIA M.[8] WOLF, ELIZA[7] LOTTRIDGE, ESTHER[6] BULL, AMY[5] CHASE, SARAH[4] MILK, JOB[3], JOHN[2], JOHN[1]) was born 02 Apr 1867, and died 14 Feb 1904 in Oakland, California. She married WILLIAM F. KELLY. He was born Abt. 1865.

Child of ANNA RANNELLS and WILLIAM KELLY is:
- i. SON[10] KELLY.

857. PAULINE WOLF[9] RANNELLS (LYDIA M.[8] WOLF, ELIZA[7] LOTTRIDGE, ESTHER[6] BULL, AMY[5] CHASE, SARAH[4] MILK, JOB[3], JOHN[2], JOHN[1]) was born 28 Oct 1868, and died 01 Feb 1930. She married CHARLES P. BAUMAN. He was born Abt. 1865.

Child of PAULINE RANNELLS and CHARLES BAUMAN is:
- i. SON[10] BAUMAN, b. Columbus, Ohio.

858. DELIA LOTTRIDGE[9] MOSES (CATHRYNE 'KATIE'[8] TEASDALE, DELIA[7] LOTTRIDGE, ESTHER[6] BULL, AMY[5] CHASE, SARAH[4] MILK, JOB[3], JOHN[2], JOHN[1]) was born 28 Sep 1872, and died 31 Jan 1942. She married FRED ALVIN ROBERTS 25 Jun 1901.

Child of DELIA MOSES and FRED ROBERTS is:
- i. WILLIAM MOSES[10] ROBERTS, b. 03 May 1908.

859. EDITH[9] MOORE (LESTER J.[8], DAVID[7], DUDLEY[6], SARAH[5] MILK, JOB[4], JOB[3], JOHN[2], JOHN[1]) was born Abt. 1911 in Weber County, Utah. She married GERALD SEAMONS, son of JOSEPH SEAMMONS and ANNIE ____. He was born Abt. 1910 in Utah.

Child of EDITH MOORE and GERALD SEAMONS is:
  i. DARWIN[10] SEAMONS, b. Abt. 1929.

860. ANTONIA WILLIAM[9] FRONK *(CLARA DIANA[8] MOORE, DAVID[7], DUDLEY[6], SARAH[5] MILK, JOB[4], JOB[3], JOHN[2], JOHN[1])* was born Sep 1890 in Utah. He married MAE ____.

Child of ANTONIA FRONK and MAE ____ is:
  i. S. VIOLET[10] FRONK, b. Abt. 1911, Utah.

861. DAVID[9] FRONK *(CLARA DIANA[8] MOORE, DAVID[7], DUDLEY[6], SARAH[5] MILK, JOB[4], JOB[3], JOHN[2], JOHN[1])* was born 30 Apr 1899 in Utah, and died Apr 1973 in Ogden, Weber County, Utah. He married JESSIE P. ____, daughter of _____ CRISTENSEN. She was born 03 Apr 1906 in Denmark, and died 16 Jan 1993 in Hemet, Riverside, California.

Children of DAVID FRONK and JESSIE ____ are:
  i. PEARL C.[10] FRONK, b. Abt. Feb 1926, Ogden, Weber County, Utak.
  ii. DAVID C. FRONK, b. Abt. Nov 1928, Ogden, Weber County, Utak.

862. HAROLD RAYMOND[9] MOORE *(PARLEY PARKER[8], DAVID[7], DUDLEY[6], SARAH[5] MILK, JOB[4], JOB[3], JOHN[2], JOHN[1])* was born 01 Apr 1891 in Salt Lake County, Utah, and died 12 Nov 1946 in Los Angeles County, California. He married ELIZABETH ____. She was born Abt. 1900 in Germany.

Child of HAROLD MOORE and ELIZABETH ____ is:
  i. RAYMOND[10] MOORE, b. Abt. 1922, Utah.

863. DOROTHY E.[9] MOORE *(PARLEY PARKER[8], DAVID[7], DUDLEY[6], SARAH[5] MILK, JOB[4], JOB[3], JOHN[2], JOHN[1])* was born May 1895 in Salt Lake County, Utah. She married MISTER BRIGGS. He was born Abt. 1895 in Utah.

Child of DOROTHY MOORE and MISTER BRIGGS is:
  i. DONNA[10] BRIGGS, b. 29 Apr 1913, Utah; d. 28 Jan 1983, Los Angeles, California; m. MISTER YUKI; b. Abt. 1910.

864. PARLEY EUGENE[9] MOORE *(PARLEY PARKER[8], DAVID[7], DUDLEY[6], SARAH[5] MILK, JOB[4], JOB[3], JOHN[2], JOHN[1])* was born 30 Jan 1897 in Ogden, Weber County, Utah, and died 03 Apr 1987 in Orange County, California. He married RUTH C. NIELSON Abt. 1916, daughter of SAM NIELSON and ANNENA PETERSON. She was born 29 Mar 1897 in Utah, and died 17 Oct 1980 in Orange County, California.

Children of PARLEY MOORE and RUTH NIELSON are:
  i. DONALD[10] MOORE, b. Abt. Oct 1916, Utah.
  ii. HAROLD MOORE, b. Abt. Nov 1918, Utah.
  iii. NORMA MOORE, b. Abt. 1922, Utah.

865. EVA ELIZABETH[9] MOORE *(PARLEY PARKER[8], DAVID[7], DUDLEY[6], SARAH[5] MILK, JOB[4], JOB[3], JOHN[2], JOHN[1])* was born 25 Jan 1899 in Salt Lake County, Utah, and died 26 Oct 1990 in Los Angeles, California. She married (1) CHARLES ROLLINS DAVEY, son of DAVID DAVEY and MARY OSBORNE. He was born 19 Jul 1884 in Utah. She married (2) MISTER TAYLOR Abt. 1918 in Utah. He was born Abt. 1899.

Child of EVA MOORE and MISTER TAYLOR is:
  i. MELVIN[10] TAYLOR, b. Jan 1919, Salt Lake County, Utah.

866. HATTIE E.[9] HARVEY *(MARY IDA[8] BAINWAY, SALLY[7] ANDREWS, AMY[6] MILKS, JONATHAN[5] MILK, JOB[4], JOB[3], JOHN[2], JOHN[1])* was born 27 Sep 1875 in Pittsfield, Berkshire County, Massachusetts, and died 07 Feb 1906 in Meriden, New Haven County, Connecticut. She married WALTER GORDON WILSON 29 May 1896 in Westfield, Hampden County, Massachusetts, son of WALTER WILSON and SARAH SAMSON. He was born 20 Dec 1873 in West Dummerston, Windham County, Vermont, and died 20 Mar 1914 in Springfield, Hampden County, Massachusetts.

Hattie died at the young age of 30 of heart trouble and Anemia. She left behind her husband, Walter Wilson and two daughters, Helen and Dora. Hattie was connected with the Esther Rebekah Lodge and the Daughters of Liberty.

Walter died a rather mysterious death. His obituary indicates he wandered away from his home one morning and later was found frozen to death in a shallow pool of water. He was a member of the Masonic Temple. His first wife was Hattie Harvey and his second wife, who was left behind, was Amy Mayhew.

Children of HATTIE HARVEY and WALTER WILSON are:
- i. MABEL[10] WILSON, b. 14 Aug 1896, Meriden, New Haven County, Connecticut; d. 20 Jun 1899, Pittsfield, Berkshire County, Massachusetts.
- 1658. ii. HELEN ELIZABETH WILSON, b. 14 Apr 1899, Meriden, New Haven County, Connecticut; d. 15 Apr 1959, Springfield, Hampden County, Massachusetts.
- iii. DORA EMELINE WILSON, b. 14 Oct 1901, Meriden, New Haven County, Connecticut; d. 16 Dec 1989, Springfield, Hampden County, Massachusetts; m. (1) SAMUEL HICKSON; b. 1864; d. 1936; m. (2) JAMES KELLY O'NEAL, 05 Feb 1921, West Springfield, Hampden County, Massachusetts; b. 10 Jul 1898, Watertown, Middlesex County, Massachusetts; d. 31 May 1929, Boston, Suffolk County, Massachusetts.
  Dora Married James on February 5, 1921 in West Springfield, Massachusetts. After the death of James, Dora married Samuel Hickson.

867. HOMER P.[9] MILKS *(HERMAN[8], ICHABOD[7], JOB[6], JONATHAN[5] MILK, JOB[4], JOB[3], JOHN[2], JOHN[1])* was born 15 May 1877 in Watson, Lewis County, New York, and died 29 Nov 1957 in Lewis County, New York. He married DELIA HONORA ROGERS 31 Jul 1905 in St. Regis Falls, NY, by Rev. C. M. Smith, daughter of LESLIE ROGERS and JANE TRIMM. She was born 29 Sep 1886 in Dickenson Center, NY, and died 22 Nov 1947 in Miami, Florida.

Children of HOMER MILKS and DELIA ROGERS are:
- 1659. i. VIOLET L.[10] MILKS, b. 07 May 1906, Santa Clara, NY; d. Jun 1992, Highlands, Florida.
- 1660. ii. LESLIE ROGER MILKS, b. 29 May 1910, Tupper Lake, NY; d. 06 Dec 1974, Opa Locka, Miami-Dade County, FL.

868. ALBERT ROBERT[9] LOSEE *(SARAH ERSULA[8] MILKS, JOHN/JONATHAN L.[7], JOB[6], JONATHAN[5] MILK, JOB[4], JOB[3], JOHN[2], JOHN[1])* was born 16 Jul 1880 in Hurricane, W. Va.. He married CLARA MCABOY Abt. 1900 in West Virginia. She was born Abt. 1880.

Children of ALBERT LOSEE and CLARA MCABOY are:
- i. ELSIE IRENE[10] LOSEE, b. 10 Nov 1902, Huntington, Cabell County, West Virginia; d. 11 Sep 1909, Huntington, Cabell County, West Virginia.
- ii. WILLIAM RAY LOSEE, b. 17 Jan 1905, Huntington, Cabell County, West Virginia; d. 24 Apr 1927, Huntington, Cabel County, West Virginia; m. DOROTHY E. LANGFITT; b. Abt. 1905. No children.
- 1661. iii. ROBERT LAWRENCE LOSEE, b. 08 Aug 1910, Huntington, Cabell County, West Virginia.
- iv. C. TRUMAN 'JACK' LOSEE, b. 02 Oct 1913, Huntington, Cabell County, West Virginia; m. LOIS JEAN DAMRON; b. Abt. 1913. Jack served as Specialist Classifications Officer, 1st Class at U.S. Naval Training Station, Sampson, NY, World War II; he was with the U.S. Government as Chief Investigator for the Labor and Contract Div. of the Wage and Hour Dept. Res. Tampa, Florida.

869. WILLIAM GUY[9] LOSEE *(SARAH ERSULA[8] MILKS, JOHN/JONATHAN L.[7], JOB[6], JONATHAN[5] MILK, JOB[4], JOB[3], JOHN[2], JOHN[1])* was born 28 Aug 1884 in Hurricane, W. Va., and died 06 May 1950 in Boyd, Kentucky. He married ROSE HELEN KENNY 1909 in Putnam, West Virginia. She was born Abt. 1882.

Children of WILLIAM LOSEE and ROSE KENNY are:
- 1662. i. LAWRENCE KENNY[10] LOSEE, b. 26 Sep 1910, West Virginia.
- 1663. ii. THELMA IRENE LOSEE, b. 10 Apr 1913, West Virginia.

870. LIZZIE[9] HOWLAND *(EMMA[8] MILKS, EBENEZER[7], JOB[6], JONATHAN[5] MILK, JOB[4], JOB[3], JOHN[2], JOHN[1])* was born 10 Apr 1883 in Delaware County, New York. She married REV. WILLIAM V. ALLEN, JR. 10 Sep 1907 in Delaware County, New York, son of REV. WILLIAM ALLEN. He was born 10 Apr 1884 in Walton, Delaware County, NY.

Children of LIZZIE HOWLAND and WILLIAM ALLEN are:
      i. ERWIN[10] ALLEN, b. 02 Nov 1908; d. unm..
1664.   ii. JANET ALLEN, b. 24 Feb 1922.

871. SETH ADAN[9] HOWLAND *(EMMA[8] MILKS, EBENEZER[7], JOB[6], JONATHAN[5] MILK, JOB[4], JOB[3], JOHN[2], JOHN[1])* was born 29 Aug 1885 in Delaware County, New York, and died Nov 1964 in Oxford, Chenango County, New York. He married (1) ELLA CLOSE 18 Dec 1910. She was born 18 Sep 1890, and died 01 Feb 1921. He married (2) MARY E. HILLIKER 14 Jun 1921 in Margaretville, Delaware County, New York. She was born 09 Sep 1902, and died Mar 1978 in Greene, Chenango County, New York.

Children of SETH HOWLAND and ELLA CLOSE are:
1665.   i. MILTON E.[10] HOWLAND, b. 28 Apr 1913, Walton, Delaware County, New York.
1666.   ii. VERA HOWLAND, b. 20 Jan 1920, Arena, Delaware County, New York.

Children of SETH HOWLAND and MARY HILLIKER are:
1667.   iii. CHARLES S.[10] HOWLAND, b. 23 May 1922, Arena, Delaware County, New York.
1668.   iv. HAZEL E. HOWLAND, b. 14 Dec 1925, Arena, Delaware County, New York.
      v. EMMA F. HOWLAND, b. 01 Sep 1926; d. 03 Jan 1927.
1669.   vi. ELSIE L. HOWLAND, b. 23 Aug 1929, Andes, Delaware County, New York.
1670.   vii. ETHEL MAE HOWLAND, b. 30 Dec 1931, Andes, Delaware County, New York.
      viii. HARRY G. HOWLAND, b. 24 Jul 1936, Andes, Delaware County, New York.
      ix. ROGER E. HOWLAND, b. 25 Jun 1939.
      x. WANDA LOU HOWLAND, b. 01 Sep 1944; d. 24 Dec 1944.

872. MINNIE M.[9] CURTIS *(CLARA[8] MILKS, EBENEZER[7], JOB[6], JONATHAN[5] MILK, JOB[4], JOB[3], JOHN[2], JOHN[1])* was born 19 Aug 1888 in New York, and died Dec 1983 in Sidney, Delaware County, New York. She married ELMER J. DANN 04 Mar 1909. He was born 14 Sep 1887.

Children of MINNIE CURTIS and ELMER DANN are:
1671.   i. ELMER J.[10] DANN, JR., b. 13 Aug 1912, Sidney, Delaware County, New York; d. 1969, Sidney, Delaware County, New York.
1672.   ii. CHARLES C. DANN, b. 26 Sep 1914, Sidney, Delaware County, New York; d. 16 Dec 2000, Veterans' Home, Oxford, Chenango County, New York.

873. RAYMOND[9] CURTIS *(CLARA[8] MILKS, EBENEZER[7], JOB[6], JONATHAN[5] MILK, JOB[4], JOB[3], JOHN[2], JOHN[1])* was born 21 Oct 1898 in West Exeter, Otsego County, New York. He married (1) MINNIE SILVERY 12 May 1928 in Otsego County, New York ?. She was born Abt. 1900. He married (2) NAOMI BELNAPP 12 Jun 1934 in Unadilla, New York. She was born Abt. 1900.

Children of RAYMOND CURTIS and MINNIE SILVERY are:
      i. KATHRYN[10] CURTIS, b. 18 May 1929, Unadilla, Chenango/Otsego Count, New York; m. MILFORD OSTRANDER, 27 Nov 1949, Unadilla, New York; b. Abt. 1929.
      ii. CLARA MAE CURTIS, b. 17 Apr 1930, Unadilla, Chenango/Otsego Count, New York; m. FREDERIC MOHRIEN, 12 May 1951, Geneva, New York; b. Abt. 1930.

Children of RAYMOND CURTIS and NAOMI BELNAPP are:
      iii. GEORGE[10] CURTIS, b. 05 Aug 1935, Unadilla, Chenango/Otsego Count, New York.
      iv. ROBERT CURTIS, b. 24 Oct 1937, Unadilla, Chenango/Otsego Count, New York.
      v. BETTY CURTIS, b. 26 Nov 1939, Unadilla, Chenango/Otsego Count, New York.
      vi. RAYMOND CURTIS, b. 24 Oct 1941, Unadilla, Chenango/Otsego Count, New York.

874. REXFORD[9] CURTIS *(CLARA[8] MILKS, EBENEZER[7], JOB[6], JONATHAN[5] MILK, JOB[4], JOB[3], JOHN[2], JOHN[1])* was born 20 Dec 1902 in Richfield, Otsego County, New York. He married (1) LEONE DANN 22 Mar 1927 in Sidney, Delaware County, New York. She was born Abt. 1907 in New York. He married (2) CHARLOTTE HYATT 29 Apr 1950 in Utica, New York. She was born Abt. 1902.

Rexford served 3 years in Medical Detachment of Air Force, World War II; he after-wards took an electronics course in Chicago, Ill.

Child of REXFORD CURTIS and LEONE DANN is:
　　i. RICHARD[10] CURTIS, b. Abt. Jun 1928, Otsego County, New York.

875. ARTHUR ROLLAND[9] MILKS *(RICHARD GRAVES[8], CHARLES ROLLAND[7], JOHN[6], JONATHAN[5] MILK, JOB[4], JOB[3], JOHN[2], JOHN[1])* was born 29 Oct 1863 in New York, and died Jul 1947 in Denver, Colorado. He married (1) MATILDA 'TILLIE' REESE Abt. 1890 in New York, daughter of BENJAMIN REESE and CORNELIA _____. She was born Mar 1870 in Albany, New York. He married (2) MARY B. _____ Bet. 1910 - 1920 in Denver, Colorado ?. She was born Bet. 1884 - 1885 in New York. He married (3) CORRINE _____ Abt. 1927 in Denver, Colorado ?. She was born 19 Sep 1888 in Gloucester, Massachusetts, and died Aug 1983 in Denver, Colorado.

Children of ARTHUR MILKS and MATILDA REESE are:
　　i. JANE ELIZABETH[10] MILKS, b. Abt. 1891, Albany, New York; m. HARRY HARVEY.
　　ii. ARTHUR ROLLAND MILKS, JR., b. 07 Aug 1893, Albany, New York; d. 17 Jan 1958; m. HARRIETT L. _____; b. 17 Aug 1894, New York; d. 17 Mar 1959.

876. RICHARD GRAVES[9] MILKS *(RICHARD GRAVES[8], CHARLES ROLLAND[7], JOHN[6], JONATHAN[5] MILK, JOB[4], JOB[3], JOHN[2], JOHN[1])* was born Bet. 1876 - 1877 in New York, and died 19 Jul 1947 in Penfield, NY. He married (1) FIRST WIFE Abt. 1897. She was born Abt. 1877. He married (2) MERTELLA _____ Bet. 1920 - 1921. She was born Bet. 1878 - 1879 in Ohio.

Child of RICHARD MILKS and FIRST WIFE is:
1673.　i. HELEN ELDREDGE[10] MILKS, b. Abt. 1898, New York; d. 30 Aug 1949.

877. WILLIAM G.[9] CHASE *(CHARLOTTE H. 'LOTTIE'[8] MILKS, CHARLES ROLLAND[7], JOHN[6], JONATHAN[5] MILK, JOB[4], JOB[3], JOHN[2], JOHN[1])* was born 02 Aug 1869 in Waterford, Saratoga County, New York. He married ABBIE W. _____. She was born Abt. 1869 in Michigan.

Child of WILLIAM CHASE and ABBIE _____ is:
　　i. CHARLOTTE[10] CHASE, b. Abt. 1907, Massachusetts.

878. MARTHA 'MATTIE' SCOVIL[9] CHASE *(CHARLOTTE H. 'LOTTIE'[8] MILKS, CHARLES ROLLAND[7], JOHN[6], JONATHAN[5] MILK, JOB[4], JOB[3], JOHN[2], JOHN[1])* was born 21 Oct 1878 in Lowville, Columbia County, Wisconsin. She married FREDERICK E. BACHMAN 08 May 1901 in Columbia County, Wisconsin, son of FRANCIS BACHMAN and CAROLINE DURON. He was born Jun 1875 in Michigan.

Children of MARTHA CHASE and FREDERICK BACHMAN are:
1674.　i. FREDERICK DIAMOND[10] BACHMAN, b. 18 Nov 1903, Appleton, Calumet County, Wisconsin.
　　ii. JAMES BACHMAN, b. Abt. 1906, Wisconsin. Probably adopted, because he was not shown in the 1910 census, and Mattie is shown with 1 child and 1 child living.

879. CLARA[9] MILKS *(HORACE B.[8], ELKANAH B.[7], JONATHAN[6], JONATHAN[5] MILK, JOB[4], JOB[3], JOHN[2], JOHN[1])* was born 06 Dec 1864 in Westford, Otsego County, New York, and died 27 Sep 1950 in Milford, New York. She married (1) EDWARD NELLIS 1883 in Westford, Otsego County, New York. He was born 28 Nov 1863 in Westford, Otsego County, New York, and died 09 Nov 1896 in Westford, Otsego County, New York. She married (2) JACOB BALDWIN 21 Jun 1913 in Westford, Otsego County, New York, son of HENRY BALDWIN and EVA NELLIS. He was born 14 May 1863 in Westford, Otsego County, New York, and died 22 Dec 1949 in Milford, New York.
OBITUARY - Friday, September 29, 1950 - The Otsego Farmer, page 2
Mrs. Clara Baldwin of Milford died September 27 at the Wheeler Nursing Home in Oneonta, where she had been a patient for nearly two years. She was 85 years old.
Mrs. Baldwin was born in Westford December 6, 1864, daughter of Horace and Lena Milks. She was twice married. Her first husband was Edward P. Nellis, to whom she was married in 1883. He died in 1896. She was married to Jacob Baldwin in 1913. He died December 22, 1949.

She is survived by a daughter, Mrs. M.B. Dewey, Milford and a son, Jesse L. Nellis, Schenevus; two grandchildren, Byron N. Dewey, East Aurora, and Mrs. E.J. Butler, Rochester, and six great-grandchildren.

She had lived in Elk Creek, Westville and Milford. She was a member of the Westville Methodist Church and a former member of the Westville Grange.

Funeral services will be held at 2 p.m. Saturday at the Tillapaugh Funeral Home in Milford, with the Rev. Philip Pitcher, pastor, and the Rev. Wilber Dodge, retiring pastor, of the Milford Methodist Church, officiating.

Burial will be in Westville. Friends may call at the funeral home Friday night.

OBITUARY - Dec 28, 1949 ""The Freeman's Journal", Cooperstown, NY

Jacob M. Baldwin, a retired farmer died Thursday at his home in this village.

Funeral services were held at the Tillapagh Funeral Home, Milford, on Tuesday afternoon at 2 o'clock. The Rev. Philip N. Pitcher of the M.E. Church, assisted by the Rev. Wilbur C. Dodge, officiated. Burial was in the Westville Cemetery.

Mr Baldwin was born in the town of Westford May 14, 1863, a son of Henry W. and Eva (Nellis) Baldwin.

He married Nora Osborn on December 16, 1891. She died April 8, 1912.

On June 21, 1913 he married Clara Milks Nellis, who survives.

Mr Baldwin owned and operated a large farm near Westville until 1925, when he retired and moved to Milford where he has since resided. Mr Baldwin was a member of the Westville Methodist church, where he sang in the choir for many years. He was also a member of the Westville Grange.

Besides his wife he is survived by a step-daughter, Mrs. M.B. Dewey, who resides at the Baldwin home, a step-son, Jesse Nellis of Westford, two nieces, Mrs Ella Joslyn of Cooperstown and Mrs Viola Ellett of Oneonta, a nephew, Vernon Baldwin of Cooperstown, and two step-grandchildren, Mrs. E.J. Butler of Rochester and Byron Dewey of East Aurora.

Children of CLARA MILKS and EDWARD NELLIS are:
1675.   i.   MARCIA BELLE^{10} NELLIS, b. 10 Dec 1885, Westford, Otsego County, New York.
         ii.   JESSE LEROY NELLIS, b. 25 Apr 1890, Westford, Otsego County, New York. Never married.

880. MARGARET^9 CRIPPIN *(SARAH ANN^8 MILKS, ELKANAH B.^{7}, JONATHAN^6, JONATHAN^5 MILK, JOB^4, JOB^3, JOHN^2, JOHN^1)* was born 10 Feb 1865 in Worcester, Otsego County, New York, and died 1947. She married JOHN N. CLARK?. He was born Abt. 1865 in Wisconsin.

Child of MARGARET CRIPPIN and JOHN CLARK? is:
         i.   ROY^{10} CLARK, b. Monroe, Butler, Iowa.

881. MARY L.^{9} CRIPPIN *(SARAH ANN^8 MILKS, ELKANAH B.^{7}, JONATHAN^6, JONATHAN^5 MILK, JOB^4, JOB^3, JOHN^2, JOHN^1)* was born 29 May 1866 in Worcester, Otsego County, New York, and died Sep 1943. She married (1) JONATHAN W. DYE 01 Jan 1885 in Des Moines, Polk County, Iowa, son of RUEBEN DYE and ANNA BOOTH. He was born Jun 1847 in Illinois. She married (2) ALFRED GLENN 06 Feb 1913 in Des Moines, Polk County, Iowa, son of WESLEY GLENN and EMMA WILLIAMS. He was born Abt. 1866 in Marion County, Iowa.

Children of MARY CRIPPIN and JONATHAN DYE are:
         i.   ETHEL^{10} DYE, b. Jan 1886, Polk County, Iowa; m. C. W. STRODLEY, 23 Dec 1904, Des Moines, Iowa; b. 1876, Spring Hill, Iowa.
         ii.   NORA DYE, b. Apr 1887, Polk County, Iowa; m. R. A. TRIPP, 04 Jul 1908, Des Moines, Iowa; b. 1878, Jasper County, Iowa.

882. JOHN R.^{9} CRIPPIN *(SARAH ANN^8 MILKS, ELKANAH B.^{7}, JONATHAN^6, JONATHAN^5 MILK, JOB^4, JOB^3, JOHN^2, JOHN^1)* was born 06 Nov 1880 in Brighton, Washington County, Iowa, and died Feb 1925. He married ADA MURPHY 03 Nov 1902. She was born 19 Nov 1879, and died 15 Feb 1945 in Death year?.

Child of JOHN CRIPPIN and ADA MURPHY is:
1676.   i.   JOHN SIDNEY^{10} CRIPPIN, b. 07 Aug 1903, Winterset, Iowa.

883. OSCAR^9 MILKS *(CHARLES B.^{8}, ELKANAH B.^{7}, JONATHAN^6, JONATHAN^5 MILK, JOB^4, JOB^3, JOHN^2, JOHN^1)* was born 24 May 1877 in Otsego Co., NY, and died 10 Jun 1911 in Worcester, Otsego County, New York. He married EVA ALBERT 07 Jan 1903, daughter of JOHN ALBERT and EVA VAN VALKENBURG. She was born Mar 1874 in Ireland, and died 17 Sep 1953 in Worcester, Otsego Co., NY.

Child of OSCAR MILKS and EVA ALBERT is:
1677.   i.   IRENE^{10} MILKS, b. 04 Apr 1904, Schenevus, Otsego Co., NY; d. 1969, Otsego County, New York.

884. LUELLA B.^{9} MILKS (*CHARLES B.^{8}, ELKANAH B.^{7}, JONATHAN^6, JONATHAN^5 MILK, JOB^4, JOB^3, JOHN^2, JOHN^1*) was born 08 Sep 1880 in Otsego County, New York, and died 1970 in Otsego County, New York. She married FRANK EDWARD CHICKERING 18 Nov 1908 in Schenevus, Otsego County, New York, son of FINLEY CHICKERING and AUGUSTA LYON. He was born 26 Sep 1881 in Otsego County, New York, and died Jul 1964 in Otsego County, New York.

Child of LUELLA MILKS and FRANK CHICKERING is:
1678.   i.   RUTH LOUISE^{10} CHICKERING, b. 28 Oct 1918.

885. WICKHAM H.^{9} GRISWOLD (*JOHN J.^{8}, MARY ANN^7 MILKS, JONATHAN^6, JONATHAN^5 MILK, JOB^4, JOB^3, JOHN^2, JOHN^1*) was born 27 Mar 1876 in Otsego County, New York, and died 10 Mar 1950 in Schenevus, Otsego County, New York. He married NETTIE ETHEL ALBERT 26 Jan 1914 in Worcester, Otsego County, New York, daughter of L. ALBERT and ELVA _____. She was born 15 Feb 1891 in East Worcester, Otsego County, New York, and died 16 Feb 1966 in Schenevus, Otsego Co., NY.

Children of WICKHAM GRISWOLD and NETTIE ALBERT are:
    i.   MARJORIE A.^{10} GRISWOLD, b. 1914.
    ii.   ANITA E. GRISWOLD, b. 1918.

886. CORA^9 CRIPPEN (*JOHN A.^{8}, CHRISTINE^7 MILKS, JONATHAN^6, JONATHAN^5 MILK, JOB^4, JOB^3, JOHN^2, JOHN^1*) was born 27 Oct 1869 in Otsego County, New York, and died 07 Oct 1955 in Oneonta, Otsego County, New York. She married CLARENCE WILLIAM PATRICK 23 Dec 1891, son of THOMAS PATRICK and SARAH CHASE. He was born Abt. 1869 in of Elk Creek, NY.

Children of CORA CRIPPEN and CLARENCE PATRICK are:
    i.   LELA MAY^{10} PATRICK, b. 10 Aug 1893.
    ii.   DORIS LOUISE PATRICK, b. 16 Apr 1901.

887. GRACE^9 CRIPPEN (*JOHN A.^{8}, CHRISTINE^7 MILKS, JONATHAN^6, JONATHAN^5 MILK, JOB^4, JOB^3, JOHN^2, JOHN^1*) was born 18 May 1876 in Otsego County, New York, and died 14 Jul 1900 in Otsego County, New York. She married FLOYD BRAZEE Abt. 1895. He was born Abt. 1875 in of Wolcott, NY.

Children of GRACE CRIPPEN and FLOYD BRAZEE are:
    i.   LOLA^{10} BRAZEE, b. 31 Jul 1896.
    ii.   CLIFTON BRAZEE, b. 14 Jul 1900.

888. CHARLES FULLER^9 BARNARD (*GEORGE^8, GEORGE^7, RUTH^6 MILKS, JOB^5 MILK, JONATHAN^4, JOB^3, JOHN^2, JOHN^1*) was born 11 Dec 1859 in Rome, Oneida County, New York, and died 27 Oct 1905 in Rome, Oneida County, New York. He married ANNA MAE ALDRIDGE 21 Nov 1889, daughter of DAVID ALDRIDGE and HARRIET COMSTOCK. She was born 07 Jun 1869 in New York, and died 12 Feb 1962 in Rome, Oneida County, New York.

Children of CHARLES BARNARD and ANNA ALDRIDGE are:
    i.   GEORGE A.^{10} BARNARD, b. Sep 1890, Rome, Oneida County, New York; d. 09 Aug 1963, Canandaigua, Ontario County, New York.
    ii.   DEAN S. BARNARD, b. Aug 1892, Rome, Oneida County, New York.
    iii.   BRADLEY CUTTING BARNARD, b. Oct 1894, Rome, Oneida County, New York.
1679.   iv.   JULIA FULLER BARNARD, b. 13 Jan 1897, Rome, Oneida County, New York; d. 15 Mar 1973, Orange County, California.
    v.   HOWARD BARNARD, b. Apr 1899, Rome, Oneida County, New York.
    vi.   DONALD COLE BARNARD, b. 1901, Rome, Oneida County, New York; d. 24 Feb 1967.
    vii.   EDWARD F. BARNARD, b. Abt. 1904, Rome, Oneida County, New York.

889. GEORGE HENRY[9] KELLOGG *(ELIZABETH ANN 'BETSY'[8] MILKS, GEORGE[7], FREEMAN[6], JOB[5] MILK, JONATHAN[4], JOB[3], JOHN[2], JOHN[1])* was born 1861 in Trenton, Ontario, Canada, and died 25 Dec 1925 in Bon Homme County, South Dakota. He married IDA MAY MCCOLLUM Abt. 1887 in Tyndall, Bon Homme County, South Dakota, daughter of JOHN MCCOLLUM and ELIZABETH RIGGS. She was born 1871 in Carroll, Iowa, and died 08 May 1944 in Bon Homme County, South Dakota.

Children of GEORGE KELLOGG and IDA MCCOLLUM are:
- i. BELLE[10] KELLOGG, b. 1889, Bon Homme County, South Dakota; d. Bet. 1900 - 1910, Bon Homme County, South Dakota.
- ii. VINA KELLOGG, b. 1890, Bon Homme County, South Dakota; d. Bet. 1900 - 1910, Bon Homme County, South Dakota.
- iii. BESSIE M. KELLOGG, b. 1894, Bon Homme County, South Dakota; d. Aft. 1910; m. JOSEPH E. VANDEMARK, 23 Mar 1916, Minnehaha, South Dakota; b. 30 May 1879, South Dakota.
- iv. CHESTER EARL KELLOGG, b. 15 Jan 1899, Bon Homme County, South Dakota; d. Nov 1986, Spearfish, Lawrence County, South Dakota.
- 1680. v. STELLA KELLOGG, b. 1911, Bon Homme County, South Dakota.

890. JAMES MONROE[9] KELLOGG *(ELIZABETH ANN 'BETSY'[8] MILKS, GEORGE[7], FREEMAN[6], JOB[5] MILK, JONATHAN[4], JOB[3], JOHN[2], JOHN[1])* was born 1863 in Ontario, Canada, and died Aft. 1930 in Missouri. He married NELLIE MAUD PERKINS Abt. 1891. She was born 1868 in Wisconsin, and died Bef. 1930 in Missouri.

Children of JAMES KELLOGG and NELLIE PERKINS are:
- i. EDWARD BYRON[10] KELLOGG, b. 08 Jul 1893, Bon Homme County, South Dakota; d. 30 Aug 1956, Missouri.
- ii. BENJAMIN F. KELLOGG, b. 20 Feb 1897, St. Louis, Missouri; d. 08 Nov 1962, Missouri.

891. EVA LOUISE[9] KELLOGG *(ELIZABETH ANN 'BETSY'[8] MILKS, GEORGE[7], FREEMAN[6], JOB[5] MILK, JONATHAN[4], JOB[3], JOHN[2], JOHN[1])* was born 1869 in Putnam, Fayette County, Iowa, and died 11 Nov 1945 in Wapato, Yakima County, Washington. She married JAMES GOODMAN WEEKS, son of RICHARD WEEKS and MARY GOODMAN. He was born 1853 in Canada, and died 19 Jul 1911 in Lincoln, Ontario, Canada.

Children of EVA KELLOGG and JAMES WEEKS are:
- i. ELMER L.[10] WEEKS, b. 07 Mar 1887, Bon Homme County, South Dakota; d. Oct 1964, Yakima County, Washington; m. MALINDA MCCOLLUM; b. 24 Sep 1896, South Dakota (step-child); d. 16 Jul 2000, Benton County, Washington.
- 1681. ii. GEORGE CLARENCE WEEKS, b. 09 Sep 1891, Lake County, South Dakota; d. 02 Dec 1971, Tacoma, Pierce County, Washington.
- 1682. iii. STELLA R. WEEKS, b. Sep 1892, Lake County, South Dakota.
- 1683. iv. WILLIAM JAMES 'WILLIE' WEEKS, b. 07 Nov 1894, Lake County, South Dakota; d. 06 Jan 1984, Yakima, Yakima County, Washington.
- 1684. v. HARRIET E. 'HATTIE' WEEKS, b. 21 Apr 1895, Lake County, South Dakota; d. 05 Aug 1971, Bremerton, Kitsap County, Washington.
- 1685. vi. BLANCHE WEEKS, b. Feb 1897, Lake County, South Dakota; d. 25 Jul 1965, Yakima County, Washington.
- vii. ELGIN GLEN 'DOC' WEEKS, b. 07 Jul 1899, Lake County, South Dakota; d. 24 Mar 1965, Walla Walla, Washington; m. BERTHA M. _____; b. 23 Oct 1902, Washington; d. 20 Aug 1988, Pasco, Franklin County, Washington.
- viii. THELMA KELLOGG WEEKS, b. 18 Jan 1901, Lake County, South Dakota.
- ix. FRED O. WEEKS, b. 31 Oct 1903, Lake County, South Dakota; d. 30 Jun 1993, Yakima County, Washington; m. ROWENA E. _____, Abt. 1930; b. 27 May 1912, Texas; d. 15 Apr 1997, Yakima County, Washington.
- x. LUCILLA WEEKS, b. Abt. 1907, Lake County, South Dakota.
- xi. RUTH WEEKS, b. Abt. 1911, Yakima County, Washington; m. JOHN E. HOFF.

892. MATILDA MELISSA[9] KELLOGG *(ELIZABETH ANN 'BETSY'[8] MILKS, GEORGE[7], FREEMAN[6], JOB[5] MILK, JONATHAN[4], JOB[3], JOHN[2], JOHN[1])* was born Dec 1870 in Iowa, and died 1935 in Fayetteville, Washington County, Arkansas. She married HARRY OTIS SANFORD 22 Jun 1890, son of JOHN HENRY SANFORD. He was born 13 Apr 1871 in Byron, Ogle County, Illinois, and died 05 Feb 1928 in Bon Homme County, South Dakota.

Mr. Sanford graduated from the Chicago Veterinary College and practiced several years at Beresford, South Dakota, and later established a veterinary hospital at Tyndall, South Dakota. His health failing him, he removed to Fayetteville, Arkansas, in August 1908.

Child of MATILDA KELLOGG and HARRY SANFORD is:
1686.   i.   HARRY WHITTIMORE[10] SANFORD, b. 23 Mar 1893, Bon Homme County, South Dakota; d. 1952, Arkansas.

893. BENJAMIN F.[9] KELLOGG *(ELIZABETH ANN 'BETSY'[8] MILKS, GEORGE[7], FREEMAN[6], JOB[5] MILK, JONATHAN[4], JOB[3], JOHN[2], JOHN[1])* was born 1873 in Iowa, and died 05 May 1949 in Yakima County, Washington. He married NORA SCOTT 1900 in Hancock, Bon Homme County, South Dakota. She was born 1872 in Iowa, and died 1917 in Yakima County, Washington.

Children of BENJAMIN KELLOGG and NORA SCOTT are:
- i.   ROBERT[10] MCCOLLUM, b. 1891, South Dakota (step-child).
- ii.   CLOA MCCOLLUM, b. 1893, South Dakota (step-child).
- iii.   MALINDA MCCOLLUM, b. 24 Sep 1896, South Dakota (step-child); d. 16 Jul 2000, Benton County, Washington; m. ELMER L. WEEKS; b. 07 Mar 1887, Bon Homme County, South Dakota; d. Oct 1964, Yakima County, Washington.
- iv.   MATILDA KELLOGG, b. 1902, South Dakota.
- v.   LILLIAN E. KELLOGG, b. 16 Feb 1903, South Dakota; d. 27 Jul 1982, San Francisco, California; m. (1) LORIN LEROY COATES, Abt. 1923; b. 26 Jun 1901, California; d. 19 Feb 1946, San Francisco, California; m. (2) MR. STERUD, Aft. 1946, California.
- vi.   JESSIE F. KELLOGG, b. 1905, South Dakota.
- vii.   CHARLES H. KELLOGG, b. 1907, South Dakota.
- viii.   GEORGE KELLOGG, b. 1909, South Dakota.

894. BERTHA MAY[9] KELLOGG *(ELIZABETH ANN 'BETSY'[8] MILKS, GEORGE[7], FREEMAN[6], JOB[5] MILK, JONATHAN[4], JOB[3], JOHN[2], JOHN[1])* was born 31 Jul 1879 in Iowa, and died 24 Sep 1934 in Prob. Sioux County, Nebraska. She married JOSEPH WILLIAM ADAMS Abt. 1898. He was born Jan 1872 in North Carolina, and died 28 May 1957 in Prob. Sioux County, Nebraska.

Children of BERTHA KELLOGG and JOSEPH ADAMS are:
- i.   ALBERT CHESTER[10] ADAMS, b. 02 Dec 1899, Charles Mix County, South Dakota; d. 28 Dec 1987, Harrison, Sioux County, Nebraska; m. ELVA MAE WIDGER; b. 18 Feb 1910, Geddes, Charles Mix County, South Dakota; d. 24 May 1999, Harrison, Sioux County, Nebraska.

1687.   ii.   LAWRENCE W. ADAMS, b. 20 Dec 1901, Geddes, Charles Mix County, South Dakota; d. 05 Mar 1988, Van Tassell, Niobrara County, Wyoming.
- iii.   RALPH H. ADAMS, b. 1917, Sioux County, Nebraska; d. 05 Mar 1942, Nebraska; m. BETTY M. ADAMS; b. Abt. 1922, Nebraska.

895. GEORGE HENRY[9] MYLKES *(BENJAMIN L.[8] MILKS, GEORGE[7], FREEMAN[6], JOB[5] MILK, JONATHAN[4], JOB[3], JOHN[2], JOHN[1])* was born 25 Nov 1875 in Rome, New York, and died 01 Feb 1936 in Burlington, Chittenden County, Vermont. He married LUCIA DAY PETERSON 17 Jun 1903 in Burlington, Vermont, daughter of CHARLES PETERSON and LAURA MARTIN. She was born 24 Jul 1875 in Vermont, and died 05 Oct 1950 in Burlington, Chittenden County, Vermont.
Vermont, Vital Records, 1760-1954: Marriage for Geo H. Mylkes to Lucia Day Peterson states that Geo. parents are Benj. L. Mylkes & Sarah Smith

In 1930 and 1935, George Mylkes owned a gift and antiques shop in Burlington, Vermont. Lucia was a buyer for the gift shop. It appears, from the directory listing that the gift shop was at the corner of Church St. and Hyde St.

Neola lived at home with her parents at 341 Pearl St., as did Reginald, who was employed in Washington, D.C.

Children of GEORGE MYLKES and LUCIA PETERSON are:
1688.   i.   ZERELDA PETERSON[10] MYLKES, b. 29 Sep 1904, Burlington, Chittenden County, Vermont; d. Aug 1977,

Buffalo, Erie County, New York.
1689. ii. REGINALD 'ROGER' GEORGE MYLKES, b. 23 Oct 1907, Burlington, Chittenden County, Vermont; d. 03 May 1993, Jacksonville Beach, Duval County, Florida.
1690. iii. MARCIA DAY MYLKES, b. 15 Dec 1908, Burlington, Chittenden County, Vermont; d. 30 Oct 1968, Alexandria, Virginia.
1691. iv. NEOLA INA MYLKES, b. 03 Mar 1910, Burlington, Chittenden County, Vermont.

896. HARRIETT 'HATTIE' MELISSA[9] MYLKES *(BENJAMIN L.[8] MILKS, GEORGE[7], FREEMAN[6], JOB[5] MILK, JONATHAN[4], JOB[3], JOHN[2], JOHN[1])* was born 27 Jun 1878 in Belleville, Hastings, Ontario, Canada. She married HARRY C. 'HENRY' FOSTER 27 Dec 1899 in Moira, Hastings, Ontario, Canada, son of JAMES FOSTER and HANNAH WOOD. He was born 26 Jun 1870 in Ontario, Canada.

Children of HARRIETT MYLKES and HARRY FOSTER are:
  i. EARL DEWITT[10] FOSTER, b. 11 Jan 1903, Huntingdon, Hastings West, Ontario, Canada.
  ii. JAMES BENJAMIN DOUGLAS FOSTER, b. 20 Nov 1905, Huntingdon, Hastings West, Ontario, Canada.
  iii. STEWART M. FOSTER, b. Feb 1908, Huntingdon, Hastings West, Ontario, Canada.
  iv. ALVINA L. FOSTER, b. Apr 1911, Huntingdon, Hastings West, Ontario, Canada.
  v. ALETHEA DOREEN FOSTER, b. Aft. 1911, Huntingdon, Hastings West, Ontario, Canada; m. CHARLES WILLIAM GOLDBOURNE JACKSON, Ontario, Canada.
  vi. CLINTON RALPH FOSTER, b. Huntingdon, Hastings West, Ontario, Canada.

897. CHARLES FREDERICK 'FRED'[9] MYLKES *(BENJAMIN L.[8] MILKS, GEORGE[7], FREEMAN[6], JOB[5] MILK, JONATHAN[4], JOB[3], JOHN[2], JOHN[1])* was born 11 Sep 1882 in Hastings, Ontario, Canada, and died Apr 1964 in New York. He married MAUD ETHEL RUSHNELL 16 Oct 1908 in Hastings County, Ontario, Canada, daughter of ADAM RUSHNELL and ANNIE ALCOMBRACK. She was born 21 Feb 1885 in Belleville, Hastings County, Ontario, Canada, and died 26 Nov 1958 in Watertown, Jefferson County, New York.

Children of CHARLES MYLKES and MAUD RUSHNELL are:
1692. i. VERA ALTHEA[10] MYLKES, b. 06 Sep 1908, Hastings, Ontario, Canada; d. 30 May 1990, New York.
1693. ii. ROSS ELMER MYLKES, b. 25 Jul 1916, Hastings, Ontario, Canada; d. 28 Aug 1987, Oswego, Oswego County, New York.

898. MELISSA VIRGINIA 'JENNIE'[9] ROBINSON *(ORA AMELIA 'AMY'[8] MILKS, GEORGE[7], FREEMAN[6], JOB[5] MILK, JONATHAN[4], JOB[3], JOHN[2], JOHN[1])* was born 1871 in New York, and died Abt. 1930 in Saltville, Smyth County, Virginia. She married FAYETTE 'JAMES' DAVIDSON 12 Oct 1891 in Smyth County, Virginia. He was born 1870 in Smyth County, Virginia, and died Aft. 1940 in Saltville, Smyth County, Virginia.

Children of MELISSA ROBINSON and FAYETTE DAVIDSON are:
  i. JACOB 'JAKE'[10] DAVIDSON, b. 01 Dec 1892, Smyth County, Virginia; d. 30 Mar 1949, Saltville, Smyth County, Virginia; m. MARY A. MCKENNY; b. 16 Dec 1898, Virginia; d. 31 Dec 1971, Saltville, Smyth County, Virginia.
1694. ii. JOSEPH W. DAVIDSON, b. 27 Oct 1893, Smyth County, Virginia; d. 03 Feb 1951, Smyth County, Virginia.
1695. iii. HARRIET DAVIDSON, b. 17 Mar 1899, Smyth County, Virginia; d. 23 Feb 1983, Smyth County, Virginia.
1696. iv. HENRY DAVIDSON, b. 1900, Smyth County, Virginia; d. Bef. 29 Mar 1997, Virginia.
  v. SONNIE ERNEST DAVIDSON, b. 1902, Smyth County, Virginia; d. Virginia; m. MABEL OLINGER; b. 1906, Virginia.
1697. vi. MARIA DAVIDSON, b. 22 May 1903, Smyth County, Virginia; d. 17 Nov 1976, Smyth County, Virginia.
1698. vii. HELEN V. DAVIDSON, b. 28 Oct 1908, Smyth County, Virginia; d. 30 Dec 1926, Saltville, Smyth County, Virginia.
  viii. LEONARD 'LEN' DAVIDSON, b. 1909, Smyth County, Virginia; d. 1952, Smyth County, Virginia; m. LUCY HELTON; b. 1911, Virginia.
1699. ix. WILLIAM MONTE 'BUSTER' DAVIDSON, b. 1913, Smyth County, Virginia; d. Virginia.
1700. x. ALICE DAVIDSON, b. 11 Jun 1915, Smyth County, Virginia; d. 11 Apr 2004, Abington, Virginia.

899. WILLIAM[9] ROBINSON, JR. *(ORA AMELIA 'AMY'[8] MILKS, GEORGE[7], FREEMAN[6], JOB[5] MILK, JONATHAN[4], JOB[3], JOHN[2], JOHN[1])* was born 1873 in New York, and died Aft. 1930 in Virginia. He married EVALINE FANNIE NUTTER. She was born Abt. 1871 in Tazewell County, Virginia, and died Aft. 1930 in Virginia.

Children of WILLIAM ROBINSON and EVALINE NUTTER are:

	i.	JENNY[10] ROBINSON, b. 1892, Washington County, Virginia; m. MR. JACKSON.
1701.	ii.	HUBERT R. ROBINSON, b. 1893, Washington County, Virginia.
1702.	iii.	EULA MAE ROBINSON, b. 13 Jun 1898, Washington County, Virginia; d. 15 Jun 1988, Washington County, Virginia.
	iv.	DAVID ROBINSON, b. 06 Apr 1890, Washington County, Virginia; d. Jul 1975, Dublin, Pulaski County, Virginia.
1703.	v.	JAMES ROBINSON, b. 24 Sep 1901, Washington County, Virginia; d. Jul 1978, Smyth County, Virginia.
	vi.	GEORGE ROBINSON, b. 1905, Washington County, Virginia.
	vii.	JACOB 'JAKE' ROBINSON, b. 1908, Washington County, Virginia.
	viii.	ORA ROBINSON, b. 02 Apr 1911, Washington County, Virginia; d. 01 May 1996, Washington County, Virginia; m. (1) GEORGE BUCHANAN; b. 1898, Washington County, Virginia; d. 1981, Washington County, Virginia; m. (2) RAY GOAD; b. 08 Mar 1919, Virginia; d. 25 Jan 1997, Washington County, Virginia.
	ix.	STUART ROBINSON, b. 09 Jul 1914, Washington County, Virginia; d. Mar 1980, Washington County, Virginia.

900. EMMETT RAY[9] GILBERT *(ORA AMELIA 'AMY'[8] MILKS, GEORGE[7], FREEMAN[6], JOB[5] MILK, JONATHAN[4], JOB[3], JOHN[2], JOHN[1])* was born 28 Apr 1879 in Saltville, Smyth County, Virginia, and died 10 Feb 1940 in Mt. Hope, Fayette County, West Virginia. He married ANNA COLE Abt. 1908. She was born in Virginia.

Children of EMMETT GILBERT and ANNA COLE are:
    i. ORA ELIZABETH[10] GILBERT, b. 06 Jul 1909, Virginia; d. 22 Oct 1970, Florida; m. HERBERT R. GWINN; b. 13 Jun 1903; d. 15 Jun 1989, Florida. Ora was living in Mantua, Ohio in April 1966.
    ii. EDWARD GILBERT, b. 16 Apr 1913, Virginia; d. May 1980, Pennsylvania.
    iii. ROBERT GILBERT, b. 25 Oct 1921, West Virginia; d. Oct 1977, West Virginia.
    iv. JUANITA ROSE GILBERT, b. 07 Jun 1925, West Virginia; d. 20 May 1997, Blythe, Riverside County, California; m. HERSCHEL LOUIS LAZENBY; b. 05 May 1907; d. 18 Jan 1991, Blythe, Riverside County, California.

901. EMORY HENRY[9] GILBERT *(ORA AMELIA 'AMY'[8] MILKS, GEORGE[7], FREEMAN[6], JOB[5] MILK, JONATHAN[4], JOB[3], JOHN[2], JOHN[1])* was born 28 Apr 1879 in Saltville, Smyth County, Virginia, and died 21 Apr 1951 in Palatka, Putnam County, Florida. He married ALMEDA COLE 29 Dec 1904. She was born 1890 in Virginia, and died Sep 1956 in Duval County, Florida.

Child of EMORY GILBERT and ALMEDA COLE is:
    i. ILEADA[10] GILBERT, b. 1922, West Virginia (adopted).

902. MAUDE[9] GILBERT *(ORA AMELIA 'AMY'[8] MILKS, GEORGE[7], FREEMAN[6], JOB[5] MILK, JONATHAN[4], JOB[3], JOHN[2], JOHN[1])* was born 04 Nov 1882 in Saltville, Smyth County, Virginia, and died 1945 in Tennessee. She married SAMUEL J. HUTTON 27 Apr 1905 in Saltville, Smyth County, Virginia. He was born Abt. 1872 in Virginia, and died Aft. 1930 in Tennessee.

Children of MAUDE GILBERT and SAMUEL HUTTON are:

	i.	HENRY[10] HUTTON, b. 1906, Virginia.
1704.	ii.	MYRTLE HUTTON, b. 11 Oct 1907, Virginia; d. 27 Aug 1988, Tennessee.
	iii.	ELEANOR HUTTON, b. 1910, Virginia.

903. CARRIE MYRTLE[9] GILBERT *(ORA AMELIA 'AMY'[8] MILKS, GEORGE[7], FREEMAN[6], JOB[5] MILK, JONATHAN[4], JOB[3], JOHN[2], JOHN[1])* was born 30 Oct 1884 in Saltville, Smyth County, Virginia, and died Nov 1974 in Indiana. She married (1) DAVID A. GEER 18 Oct 1899 in Smyth County, Virginia, son of THOMAS M. GEER. He was born 1866 in Virginia, and died 25 May 1910 in Virginia. She married (2) LUCIEN MINOR KING Abt. 1920. He was born 16 Nov 1882 in Hanover

County, Virginia, and died 01 Apr 1954 in Virginia.

Ora Gilbert was living with Lucien and Myrtle in 1930 in Saltville.

Child of CARRIE GILBERT and DAVID GEER is:
1705. i. SUSAN LEE 'SUSIE'[10] GEER, b. 28 Jul 1900, Smyth County, Virginia; d. Mar 1987, Indianapolis, Marion County, Indiana.

904. REBECCA[9] GILBERT *(ORA AMELIA 'AMY'[8] MILKS, GEORGE[7], FREEMAN[6], JOB[5] MILK, JONATHAN[4], JOB[3], JOHN[2], JOHN[1])* was born Oct 1886 in Saltville, Smyth County, Virginia, and died Abt. 1954 in Saltville, Smyth County, Virginia. She married KING TOLBERT 24 Jun 1907 in Saltville, Smyth County, Virginia, son of WILLIAM TOLBERT and MARY HOLMES. He was born 1882 in Washington County, Virginia, and died 20 May 1916 in Smyth County, Virginia.

It appears that Rebecca either adopted Pearl or had her out of wedlock. Pearl doesn't appear in the 1920 census, and in the 1930 and 1940 censuses she is listed as 9 and 19 respectively.

Children of REBECCA GILBERT and KING TOLBERT are:
1706. i. HOWARD DUNKLEY[10] TOLBERT, b. 28 Mar 1909, Saltville, Smyth County, Virginia; d. 12 Jul 1950, Abingdon, Virginia.
1707. ii. PEARL EDITH TOLBERT, b. 11 Oct 1920, Saltville, Smyth County, Virginia; d. 06 Dec 2005, Alliance, Ohio.

905. MARY[9] GILBERT *(ORA AMELIA 'AMY'[8] MILKS, GEORGE[7], FREEMAN[6], JOB[5] MILK, JONATHAN[4], JOB[3], JOHN[2], JOHN[1])* was born 20 Mar 1889 in Saltville, Smyth County, Virginia, and died May 1968 in Tennessee. She married JAMES POORE Abt. 1903 in Virginia. He was born Abt. 1875 in Tennessee, and died in Tennessee.

Children of MARY GILBERT and JAMES POORE are:
  i. JOSEPH[10] POORE, b. Abt. 1903, Tennessee.
  ii. SAM POORE, b. Abt. 1910, Tennessee.
  iii. JOHN POORE, b. Abt. 1914, Tennessee.
  iv. BONNIE POORE, b. Abt. 1919, Tennessee.
  v. HENRY POORE, b. Abt. 1925, Tennessee.
  vi. MYRTLE POORE, b. Abt. 1928, Tennessee.

906. FRED[9] GILBERT *(ORA AMELIA 'AMY'[8] MILKS, GEORGE[7], FREEMAN[6], JOB[5] MILK, JONATHAN[4], JOB[3], JOHN[2], JOHN[1])* was born 30 Nov 1891 in Saltville, Smyth County, Virginia, and died 17 Jul 1959 in Saltville, Smyth County, Virginia. He married ELLA GAY BARTON 15 Nov 1909 in Saltville, Smyth County, Virginia. She was born 04 Apr 1896 in Virginia, and died 15 Jan 1965 in Saltville, Smyth County, Virginia.

Child of FRED GILBERT and ELLA BARTON is:
1708. i. HENRY DUNKLEY 'ROBERT'[10] GILBERT, b. 02 Nov 1910, Saltville, Smyth County, Virginia; d. 17 Feb 1945, Saltville, Smyth County, Virginia.

907. ALBERT[9] GILBERT *(ORA AMELIA 'AMY'[8] MILKS, GEORGE[7], FREEMAN[6], JOB[5] MILK, JONATHAN[4], JOB[3], JOHN[2], JOHN[1])* was born 05 Sep 1896 in Saltville, Smyth County, Virginia, and died May 1973 in Abingdon, Virginia. He married (1) DOLLIE ELIZABETH PROFFITT 21 Oct 1915 in Saltville, Smyth County, Virginia, daughter of WILLIAM PROFFITT and MARY WALSH. She was born 17 Oct 1899 in North Carolina, and died 14 May 1926 in Saltvile, Smyth County, Virginia. He married (2) DAISY IRENE WALSH 1926 in Mountain City, Tennessee, daughter of THOMAS WALSH and RAWSA ASHLEY. She was born 11 Oct 1905 in Tennessee, and died Nov 1972 in Saltvile, Smyth County, Virginia.

Children of ALBERT GILBERT and DOLLIE PROFFITT are:
  i. JOHN W. 'WHICK'[10] GILBERT, b. 21 Sep 1916, Saltville, Smyth County, Virginia; d. 30 Sep 1991, Marion, Smyth County, Virginia; m. BEULAH HARPER; b. 07 Sep 1918, Washington County, Virginia; d. Apr 1982, Abingdon, Virginia.
1709. ii. ORA JUANITA GILBERT, b. 14 Jan 1920, Saltville, Smyth County, Virginia; d. 16 May 1981, Hopewell, VA.
  iii. R. C. GILBERT, b. 1922, Saltville, Smyth County, Virginia; d. 1923, Saltville, Smyth County, Virginia.
1710. iv. MARYLAND 'MARILYN' VIRGINIA GILBERT, b. 14 Oct 1924, Saltville, Smyth County, Virginia; d. 18 Mar 1989, Abingdon, Virginia.

Children of ALBERT GILBERT and DAISY WALSH are:

1711. v. RALPH JUNIOR[10] GILBERT, b. 04 Jul 1927, Saltville, Smyth County, Virginia; d. 16 May 2013, Saltville, Smyth County, Virginia.

1712. vi. DAPHNE HELEN GILBERT, b. 28 Aug 1930, Saltville, Smyth County, Virginia; d. 23 Jun 2008, Abingdon, Virginia.

908. HATTIE[9] GILBERT *(ORA AMELIA 'AMY[8] MILKS, GEORGE[7], FREEMAN[6], JOB[5] MILK, JONATHAN[4], JOB[3], JOHN[2], JOHN[1])* was born 24 Jul 1897 in Saltville, Smyth County, Virginia, and died 09 Mar 1918 in Virginia. She married ERNEST A. BARTON. He was born 19 Dec 1891 in Virginia, and died 30 Dec 1916 in Virginia.

Child of HATTIE GILBERT and ERNEST BARTON is:

1713. i. MINNIE BELLE[10] BARTON, b. 14 Oct 1915, Saltville, Smyth County, Virginia; d. Abt. 1955, Tazewell County, Virginia.

909. HAZEL VIOLET[9] KILE *(CHESTER PIERCE[8], SARAH S.[7] MILKS, DAVID[6], JOB[5] MILK, JONATHAN[4], JOB[3], JOHN[2], JOHN[1])* was born 18 Oct 1887 in Greenwich, Huron County, Ohio, and died 24 Oct 1946 in Rocky River, Cuyahoga County, Ohio. She married EARL L. LOCKE. He was born Abt. 1885 in Ohio, and died Bef. 24 Oct 1946 in Ohio.

Children of HAZEL KILE and EARL LOCKE are:

1714. i. DALE M.[10] LOCKE, b. 07 Aug 1906, Norwalk, Ohio; d. 30 Nov 1953, Rocky River, Cuyahoga County, Ohio.

ii. DONALD E. LOCKE, b. Abt. 1910, Ohio.

910. CORA E.[9] KIMBALL *(FRANCES LAVERN[8] MILKS, ROBERT DUDLEY[7], DAVID[6], JOB[5] MILK, JONATHAN[4], JOB[3], JOHN[2], JOHN[1])* was born Bet. 1870 - 1871 in Rollin, Lenawee County, Michigan. She married (1) ARTHUR E. CRANDALL 27 Apr 1889 in Adrian, Lenawee County, Michigan, son of CHARLES CRANDALL and AUGUSTA RUDE. He was born 24 Aug 1867 in Rollin, Lenawee County, Michigan, and died Bet. 1910 - 1920. She married (2) HOMER W. COOLEY 14 Jan 1922 in Coldwater, Branch County, Michigan, son of JACOB COOLEY and MARY HAMILTON. He was born 1869 in Michigan.

Children of CORA KIMBALL and ARTHUR CRANDALL are:

i. AIDEN BURR[10] CRANDALL, b. 13 Mar 1891, Hudson, Michigan; m. (1) SARAH GERTRUDE MOTT, 02 Jan 1913, Manistee Lake, Kalkaska County, Michigan; b. Jun 1892, Barryton, Mecosta County, Michigan; m. (2) EMMA (LAMERAUX) WAGNER, 30 Sep 1930, Miles City, Custer County, Montana; b. 1883, New York (divorced).

ii. LAURA I. CRANDALL, b. Feb 1893, Michigan; m. (1) WINFIELD O. LARRABEE, 08 Mar 1909, Coldwater, Branch County, Michigan; b. 1889, Michigan; m. (2) L. J. ERDLE, 28 Nov 1912, Coldwater, Branch County, Michigan; b. 1892, Michigan.

iii. EARL R. CRANDALL, b. 09 Dec 1896, Adrian, Lenawee County, Michigan; m. ISABELLE MERRIFIELD, 23 Oct 1913, Tekonsha Twp, Calhoun County, Michigan; b. 1895, Michigan.

iv. NELLIE E. CRANDALL, b. Aug 1898, Michigan; m. JOSEPH ANTOINE, 28 Nov 1914, Kalkaska, Kalkaska County, Michigan; b. 1887, Leelanau County, Michigan.

v. RAY B. CRANDALL, b. 03 Jun 1900, Orient Twp., Osceola County, Michigan.

vi. ERMA L. CRANDALL, b. Bet. 1903 - 1904, Michigan; m. WILLIAM A. LAKE, 02 Sep 1921, Coldwater, Branch County, Michigan; b. 16 Jan 1899, Springport, Jackson County, Michigan.

1715. vii. HOMER GREGORY CRANDALL, b. 05 Jul 1905, Michigan; d. 01 Nov 1993, Kalamo Twp, Eaton County, Michigan.

viii. IRVING C. CRANDALL, b. Bet. 1907 - 1908, Michigan.

911. MINNIE M.[9] KIMBALL *(FRANCES LAVERN[8] MILKS, ROBERT DUDLEY[7], DAVID[6], JOB[5] MILK, JONATHAN[4], JOB[3], JOHN[2], JOHN[1])* was born Mar 1873 in Rollin, Lenawee County, Michigan. She married ABIJAH EUGENE WALTER 07 Nov 1894 in Quincy, Branch County, Michigan, son of GEORGE WALTER and HANNAH BENNETT. He was born 21 Jan 1869 in Branch County, Michigan.

Children of MINNIE KIMBALL and ABIJAH WALTER are:

i. MAUD LAVERNE[10] WALTER, b. Oct 1895, Michigan.

ii. GEORGE E. WALTER, b. Oct 1897, Michigan; m. MILDRED _____; b. Bet. 1900 - 1901, Indiana.

    iii. CHILD WALTER, b. Abt. 1899, Michigan; d. d.y..
    iv. GRACE A. WALTER, b. Bet. 1901 - 1902, Michigan.
    v. ILA C. WALTER, b. Bet. 1902 - 1903, Michigan.
    vi. ROLLAND WALTER, b. Bet. 1914 - 1915, Michigan.

912. ROBERT HOMER[9] KIMBALL *(FRANCES LAVERN[8] MILKS, ROBERT DUDLEY[7], DAVID[6], JOB[5] MILK, JONATHAN[4], JOB[3], JOHN[2], JOHN[1])* was born Bet. 1876 - 1877 in Rollin, Lenawee County, Michigan, and died Bet. 1896 - 1900 in Michigan.

Children of ROBERT HOMER KIMBALL are:
    i. LORA I.[10] KIMBALL, b. Feb 1893, Michigan.
    ii. EARL R. KIMBALL, b. Dec 1896, Michigan.

913. ADA A.[9] MILKS *(EDWIN H.[8], ROBERT DUDLEY[7], DAVID[6], JOB[5] MILK, JONATHAN[4], JOB[3], JOHN[2], JOHN[1])* was born Apr 1876 in Coldwater, Branch County, Michigan. She married OTTO R. SHORT 24 Feb 1900 in Coldwater, Branch County, Michigan, son of WILLIAM SHORT and ELIZABETH SMITH. He was born Aug 1877 in Indiana.

Child of ADA MILKS and OTTO SHORT is:
    i. REX F.[10] SHORT, b. Bet. 1904 - 1905, Coldwater, Branch County, Michigan.

914. HARRIET B.[9] MILKS *(EDWIN H.[8], ROBERT DUDLEY[7], DAVID[6], JOB[5] MILK, JONATHAN[4], JOB[3], JOHN[2], JOHN[1])* was born 29 Feb 1884 in Indiana, and died 14 Apr 1951 in Berkley, Oakland County, Michigan. She married BERT CLARENCE BALL 05 Nov 1904 in Coldwater, Branch County, Michigan, son of CLINTON BALL and MARTHA DAVIS. He was born 15 Nov 1883 in Coldwater, Branch County, Michigan, and died 07 Nov 1937 in Branch County, Michigan.

Children of HARRIET MILKS and BERT BALL are:
    i. ARTHUR E.[10] BALL, b. Abt. 1907, Coldwater, Branch County, Michigan; m. BERTHA _____; b. Abt. 1907, Michigan.
    ii. JACK C. BALL, b. Abt. 1913, Coldwater, Branch County, Michigan.

915. HAZEL TURNER[9] MILKS *(EDWIN H.[8], ROBERT DUDLEY[7], DAVID[6], JOB[5] MILK, JONATHAN[4], JOB[3], JOHN[2], JOHN[1])* was born 30 Dec 1888 in Hudson, Lenawee County, Michigan, and died Oct 1974 in Aberdeen, Brown County, South Dakota. She married ROY CHRISTOPHER LETHERER 08 Jun 1911 in Coldwater, Branch County, Michigan, son of O. LETHERER and ETTA DILLON. He was born 19 Jul 1892 in Hillsdale, Michigan, and died Jul 1968 in Aberdeen, Brown County, South Dakota.

Children of HAZEL MILKS and ROY LETHERER are:
    i. ALICE[10] LETHERER, b. Abt. 1912, Michigan.
    ii. ROY C. LETHERER, b. 05 Feb 1914, Chicago, Illinois; d. d.y..
    iii. BEVERLY LETHERER, b. Abt. 1916, South Dakota; m. HAROLD JESSIE VAN SCOY, 21 Jun 1935, Day County, South Dakota; b. Abt. 1915.

916. WILLIAM EZRA[9] HILLIARD *(SARAH ELIZABETH[8] MILKS, GEORGE JEROME[7], DAVID[6], JOB[5] MILK, JONATHAN[4], JOB[3], JOHN[2], JOHN[1])* was born 26 May 1885 in Manistee County, Michigan, and died 06 Sep 1954 in Kaleva, Manistee County, Michigan. He married GENIE HAZEL BUMP 1912 in Michigan, daughter of GEORGE BUMP and JULIA SHABKNAUGH. She was born 25 Aug 1892 in Michigan, and died 29 Jun 1979 in Flint, Genesee County, Michigan.

Children of WILLIAM HILLIARD and GENIE BUMP are:
    i. HAROLD E.[10] HILLIARD, b. 1913, Wisconsin.
1716. ii. VIOLET IRENE HILLIARD, b. 10 Aug 1915, Manistee County, Michigan; d. 13 Feb 2004, Burton, Genesee County, Michigan.
    iii. VELMA R. HILLIARD, b. Abt. Feb 1919, Michigan.
    iv. FLOYD W. HILLIARD, b. Abt. Sep 1928, Michigan.

917. HAZEN I.[9] HILLIARD *(SARAH ELIZABETH[8] MILKS, GEORGE JEROME[7], DAVID[6], JOB[5] MILK, JONATHAN[4], JOB[3], JOHN[2], JOHN[1])* was born May 1898 in Michigan. He married NELLIE _____. She was born Abt. 1902 in Michigan.

Child of HAZEN HILLIARD and NELLIE _____ is:
    i. HAZEN I.[10] HILLIARD, JR, b. Abt. 1925, Michigan.

918. HERBERT JAMES[9] MILKS *(DAVID TILDEN[8], GEORGE JEROME[7], DAVID[6], JOB[5] MILK, JONATHAN[4], JOB[3], JOHN[2], JOHN[1])* was born 10 Apr 1901 in Kaleva, Manistee County, Michigan, and died 17 Sep 1974 in Kaleva, Manistee Co., Michigan. He married (1) BEATRICE M. PAPPE 09 Oct 1920 in Ludington, Michigan, by Holden A. Putnam, Minister, daughter of CHARLES PAPPE and ANNA SCOTT. She was born Abt. 1900. He married (2) THURESA A. PARKER Bet. 1922 - 1930, daughter of MERRITT PARKER and ELLEN HIGGINS. She was born 13 May 1894 in Decker, Michigan, and died 28 Mar 1971 in Kaleva, Michigan.

Child of HERBERT MILKS and BEATRICE PAPPE is:
    i. SCOTT TILDEN[10] MILKS, b. Abt. 1922.

919. HUBERT EMANUEL 'JACK'[9] MILKS *(DAVID TILDEN[8], GEORGE JEROME[7], DAVID[6], JOB[5] MILK, JONATHAN[4], JOB[3], JOHN[2], JOHN[1])* was born 16 Jun 1912 in Kaleva, Michigan, and died 04 Feb 1994 in Garfield, Grand Traverse Co., Mich. He married (1) MARY YEDNIK 21 Mar 1936. He married (2) VIVIEN VIOLET JOHNS 1948 in Michigan, daughter of JOHN JOHNS and LEONA WORDEN. She was born 02 Mar 1911 in Valley City, Medina, Ohio, and died 28 Feb 2004 in Traverse City, Grand Traverse County, Michigan.

OBITUARY

BEULAH - *Vivien Violet Miner, 92, of Beulah, died Saturday, Feb. 28, 2004, at Munson Medical Center in Traverse City.*

She was born March 2, 1911, in Valley City, Ohio, the daughter of John and Leona (Worden) Johns.

A 1931 graduate of Mount Pleasant Teachers College (now CMU), Vivien taught in a one-room schoolhouse in Benzie County. She also worked with the WPA, establishing the first libraries in Beulah, Frankfort and Elberta. In later years, she owned and operated The Honeymoon Lodge. She also served as Beulah's village treasurer from 1976 until 1986.

Vivien was the oldest living member of the First Congregational Church of Benzonia, where she attended services for 78 years. She volunteered with many church and community organizations, including the Red Cross, Stephen's Ministry, The Order of the Eastern Star, Friends of the Library, Benzie Area Historical Society, Dorothy Rice Singers, Church Choir, and the Monday Study and Garden Clubs. In addition, as the mother of a veteran, she often repaired flags for tribal government buildings.

Vivien was a lifelong scholar who enjoyed reading, traveling, and cultural events. She also liked playing Scrabble, knitting, playing piano, and spending time with her family and friends.

Vivien always took great joy in life and loved trying anything new. She was always smiling and saw only the best in other people. Her adventurous spirit and loving nature will continue to inspire all those who were blessed to know her.

Vivien is survived by her son, John Milks of Beulah; her step-daughter, Janice Heniser of Grand Rapids; five grandchildren, Johnna Lee Milks of Honor, Shantel (Anthony) Sellers of Jacksonville, Fla., Katrina (Owen) Smith of Honor, John (Erica) Milks II of Benzonia, and Heather Heniser of Seattle, Wash.; 10 great-grandchildren, Edward Milks, Robin Sellers, Austin Sellers, Haiven Sellers, Calvin Smith, Mercedes Smith, Gabriella Milks, Jared Milks, Evan Milks and Colin Milks; and many beloved friends and family.

Vivien was preceded in death by her husband, K. Wesley Miner in 1975; her former husband, Hubert "Father Jack" Milks; and her brother, Percy Johns, during infancy.

Funeral services will be conducted at 1 p.m. today, March 2, 2004, at the First Congregational Church in Benzonia, with Reverend Stephen J. Davidson officiating. Interment will be in the Benzonia Township Cemetery in the spring.

The Bennett-Barz Funeral Home is in charge of arrangements.

Child of HUBERT MILKS and VIVIEN JOHNS is:
1717.   i. JOHN WORDEN[10] MILKS, b. 30 Dec 1948, Frankfort, Michigan.

920. HOWARD 'ESTLE'[9] MILKS *(DAVID TILDEN[8], GEORGE JEROME[7], DAVID[6], JOB[5] MILK, JONATHAN[4], JOB[3], JOHN[2], JOHN[1])* was born 13 Jul 1914 in Kaleva, Michigan, and died 29 Mar 1995 in Traverse City, Michigan. He married ANNA ELIZABETH ROMSEK 25 Dec 1935 in Copemish, Michigan. She was born 10 May 1913, and died 05 May 1994 in Springdale, Manistee Co., Michigan.

Children of HOWARD MILKS and ANNA ROMSEK are:
1718.   i.   HERBERT GORDON[10] MILKS, b. 29 Jun 1937, Copemish, Michigan; d. 04 Mar 2008, Empire, Michigan.
1719.   ii. DAVID ESTLE MILKS, SR., b. 19 Apr 1939, Copemish, MI; d. 31 Oct 1997, Thompsonville, Benzie Co., MI
1720.   iii. ROBERT LAVERNE MILKS, b. 03 Oct 1941, Copemish, Michigan.

921. HATTIE[9] MCCLELLAND *(MILLIE MAY[8] MILKS, GEORGE JEROME[7], DAVID[6], JOB[5] MILK, JONATHAN[4], JOB[3], JOHN[2], JOHN[1])* was born Jul 1893 in Michigan, and died in White Cloud, Newaygo County, Michigan. She married GEORGE GLEN NEWLAND 09 Mar 1912 in St. Ignace, Mackinac County, Michigan, son of ROBERT NEWLAND and PAULINA BROINA. He was born 11 Oct 1890 in Wexford County, Michigan.

Children of HATTIE MCCLELLAND and GEORGE NEWLAND are:
   i.   RUTH J.[10] NEWLAND, b. Bet. 1912 - 1913, Michigan.
   ii. DORTHEA F. NEWLAND, b. 1917, Michigan.
   iii. MILDRED M. NEWLAND, b. Aug 1919, Wexford County, Michigan.
   iv. GLENN NEWLAND, b. Bet. 1921 - 1922, Michigan.
   v.   HAZEL NEWLAND, b. Feb 1926, Michigan.
   vi. VIVIAN NEWLAND, b. Jan 1928, Michigan.

922. BERTHA GLADYS[9] MILKS *(GEORGE JEROME[8], GEORGE JEROME[7], DAVID[6], JOB[5] MILK, JONATHAN[4], JOB[3], JOHN[2], JOHN[1])* was born 19 Nov 1902 in Bear Lake, Manistee County, Michigan, and died 12 Apr 1989 in Frankfort, Benzie County, Michigan. She married ELMER LEWIS MATTHEWS 06 Jul 1920 in Manistee, Manistee County, Michigan, son of JOHN MATTHEWS and EMMA LYMAN. He was born 12 Jun 1896 in Wellston, Manistee County, Michigan, and died 06 Jun 1958 in Bear Lake, Manistee County, Michigan.

Children of BERTHA MILKS and ELMER MATTHEWS are:
   i.   ELSWORTH LYLE[10] MATTHEWS, b. 18 Dec 1920, Bear Lake, Manistee County, Michigan.
   ii. ELSIE KATHERINE MATTHEWS, b. 08 Feb 1922, Bear Lake, Manistee County, Michigan; m. BILL MONK.
   iii. ROLAND ELMER MATTHEWS, b. 07 Oct 1925, Bear Lake, Manistee County, Michigan; m. JANET _____.
1721.   iv. DARLENE JOYCE MATTHEWS, b. 18 Jan 1934, Bear Lake, Manistee County, Michigan; d. 21 Oct 2003, Beulah, Benzie County, Michigan.

923. EVA[9] MILKS *(BERT LEROY[8], GEORGE JEROME[7], DAVID[6], JOB[5] MILK, JONATHAN[4], JOB[3], JOHN[2], JOHN[1])* was born 20 Dec 1903 in Michigan. She married (1) UNKNOWN CLAYTON Abt. 1922. She married (2) DEWEY M. OAKFIELD Bef. 1929. He was born 07 Jul 1897, and died 03 Sep 1950.

Children of EVA MILKS and DEWEY OAKFIELD are:
   i.   LORRAINE[10] OAKFIELD, b. Abt. 1928, Iowa.
   ii. MELVIN OAKFIELD, b. Abt. Nov 1929, Michigan.

924. ROBERT BART[9] MILKS *(BERT LEROY[8], GEORGE JEROME[7], DAVID[6], JOB[5] MILK, JONATHAN[4], JOB[3], JOHN[2], JOHN[1])* was born 13 Mar 1907 in Michigan, and died 04 Dec 1992 in Beverly Hills, Oakland Co., Michigan. He married (1) ETHEL ESKURI 05 Oct 1925 in Detroit, Wayne County, Michigan, daughter of ISAAC ESKURI and TECKLA LINGREN. She was born Bet. 1905 - 1906 in Michigan. He married (2) JOSEPHINE C. _____ Aft. 1940 in Michigan. She was born 10 Mar 1904 in Michigan, and died 20 May 1988 in Beverly Hills, Oakland County, Michigan.

Child of ROBERT MILKS and ETHEL ESKURI is:
   i.   BETTY[10] MILKS, b. 1927, Michigan.

925. WILLIAM[9] WILLARD W. MILKS *(BERT LEROY[8] MILKS, GEORGE JEROME[7], DAVID[6], JOB[5] MILK, JONATHAN[4], JOB[3], JOHN[2], JOHN[1])* was born 07 Sep 1909 in Kaleva, Michigan, and died 17 Mar 1988 in Garden City, Wayne Co., Michigan. He married JAMESINA BIRRELL. She was born 21 Jul 1910, and died Aug 1993 in Redford, Wayne Co., Michigan.

Child of WILLIAM WILLARD W. MILKS and JAMESINA BIRRELL is:
1722.   i.   WILLIAM ANN 'BILL'[10] MILKS, b. 13 Jan 1950, Detroit, Michigan; d. 17 Feb 2011, Glendale (Peoria), Maricopa County, Arizona.

926. LORIN CHARLES[9] MILKS *(EDWIN ELMER[8], GEORGE JEROME[7], DAVID[6], JOB[5] MILK, JONATHAN[4], JOB[3], JOHN[2], JOHN[1])* was born 31 Jul 1913 in Michigan, and died Oct 1978 in Lebanon, New London, CT. He married MARY MAY SWICK Abt. 1936, daughter of BURTON SWICK and ALVINA. She was born Abt. 1919 in Michigan.

Children of LORIN MILKS and MARY SWICK are:
- 1723. i. EDWIN CHARLES[10] MILKS, SR., b. 22 Dec 1937, Michigan; d. 10 Sep 2000, Lansing, Ingham County, Michigan.
- 1724. ii. STEPHEN ALBERT MILKS, b. 28 May 1940, Michigan; d. 09 Mar 2006, Lapeer, Lapeer County, Michigan.
- 1725. iii. MARY KATHRYN MILKS, b. 20 Mar 1947.
- 1726. iv. LORIN ANDREW MILKS, b. 02 Oct 1951, Michigan.
- 1727. v. SUSANNE ALVINA 'SUSIE' MILKS, b. 15 Oct 1954, Michigan.
- 1728. vi. DEBRA ANN 'DEBBIE' MILKS, b. 06 Oct 1956.

927. ARLENE E.[9] MILKS *(WILLIAM HENRY[8], GEORGE JEROME[7], DAVID[6], JOB[5] MILK, JONATHAN[4], JOB[3], JOHN[2], JOHN[1])* was born 26 Jul 1915 in Brethren, Manistee County, Michigan, and died 25 Feb 2003 in Flint, Genesee County, Michigan. She married (2) OTTO O. RYKER May 1941. He was born 1902, and died 20 Feb 1977.

  Burial: Montrose Cemetery, Montrose, Genesee County, Michigan, USA

Child of ARLENE E. MILKS and Mr. Simms is:
- i. FREDERICK[10] SIMMS, b. Bet. 1939 - 1940, Manistee, Michigan.

Children of ARLENE MILKS and OTTO RYKER are:
- ii. WAYNE O.[10] RYKER, b. 19 May 1942, Michigan; m. BARBARA _____; b. 27 Feb 1945.
- iii. WILLIAM H. RYKER, b. 25 May 1948, Michigan; m. DEBORAH J. 'DEBBIE' _____; b. 05 Nov 1952.

928. WARREN W.[9] MILKS *(WILLIAM HENRY[8], GEORGE JEROME[7], DAVID[6], JOB[5] MILK, JONATHAN[4], JOB[3], JOHN[2], JOHN[1])* was born 28 Nov 1922 in Brethren, Manistee County, Michigan, and died 06 Jul 2012 in Winter Haven, Florida. He married BETTY C. _____ Abt. 1946 in Michigan?. She was born 23 Nov 1922.

OBITUARY
  - WARREN W. MILKS, 89
  WINTER HAVEN - *Mr. Warren W. Milks of Winter Haven, Florida, passed away Friday, July 6, 2012 at home from cancer. He was 89.*
  A native of Flint, MI, born November 28, 1922, to William and Emma Schmidt Milks, Warren moved here 35 years ago from Fenton, MI.
  He retired from General Motors as a pipe fitter, was a World War II veteran, serving in the US Navy; he was a member of the American Legion Post #8 of Winter Haven; and he was a member of the U.A.W.
  Warren was preceded in death by his son, Richard, who was killed in Vietnam in 1968, his parents, and his sisters, Rhenetta & Arlene.
  He is survived by his loving wife of 66 years, Betty of Winter Haven; his daughter, Karen and her husband Jerry of Winter Haven; his sister, Charlotte Lambert of Montrose, MI; five grandchildren: Heather McCrimmon (Marco) Pena, Richard McCrimmon, Kim Wallace, Cindy Little, and Kathy Valencia; and 8 great-grandchildren.
  Memorial services will be Tuesday, July 10, 2012 at 6:00 P.M. at Oak Ridge Funeral Care, Winter Haven.

Children of WARREN MILKS and BETTY _____ are:
- i. RICHARD ALLEN[10] MILKS, b. 18 Sep 1946, Fenton, Michigan; d. 23 Nov 1968, Vietnam (unmarried). Tour Start Date: 16 Apr 1968
- 1729. ii. KAREN E. MILKS, b. 08 Jun 1952, Fenton, Michigan.

929. SILAS EDGAR[9] MILKS *(LEONARD[8], RICHARD[7], FREEBORN GARRETTSON[6], JOB[5] MILK, JONATHAN[4], JOB[3], JOHN[2], JOHN[1])* was born 02 Jun 1878 in Fife Lake, Michigan, and died 30 Jun 1959 in Grand Traverse County, Michigan. He married MAY E. BOWMAN 22 May 1900 in Kingsley, Grand Traverse County, Michigan, daughter of ALONZO BOMAN and DORA COHOON. She was born 27 Mar 1882 in Crofton, Michigan, and died 24 Nov 1956 in Grand Traverse County, Michigan.

Children of SILAS MILKS and MAY BOWMAN are:
- i. CARROLL A.¹⁰ MILKS, b. 16 Apr 1901, Kingsley, Michigan; d. 22 Jul 1917, East Bay, Grand Traverse County, Michigan.
- 1730. ii. THELMA IRENE MILKS, b. 12 Aug 1912, Kingsley, Michigan; d. 10 Nov 1996, Sacramento, California.
- 1731. iii. MERRILL W. MILKS, b. 28 Apr 1916, Detroit, Michigan; d. 19 Mar 1986, Acme, Grand Traverse Co., Michigan.

930. DONALD HENRY⁹ MILKS *(LEONARD⁸, RICHARD⁷, FREEBORN GARRETTSON⁶, JOB⁵ MILK, JONATHAN⁴, JOB³, JOHN², JOHN¹)* was born 22 May 1881 in Fife Lake, Grand Traverse County, Michigan, and died 19 Dec 1946 in Grand Traverse County, Michigan. He married (1) LULU B. LAMBKIN 25 Dec 1905 in Grand Traverse County, Michigan, daughter of CURTIS LAMBKIN and CARRIE _____. She was born May 1888 in Michigan. He married (2) GRACE B. LYDELL 26 Nov 1912 in Grand Traverse County, Michigan, daughter of FRANK LYDELL and EMMA BROWN. She was born 06 Feb 1893 in Missouri, and died Dec 1969 in Traverse City, Michigan.

Child of DONALD MILKS and LULU LAMBKIN is:
- i. BESSIE ALPHA¹⁰ MILKS, b. 17 Jan 1907, Kingsley, Michigan; d. 17 Jan 1907, Kingsley, Michigan.

Child of DONALD MILKS and GRACE LYDELL is:
- ii. LLOYD D.¹⁰ MILKS, b. 07 Jun 1915, Paradise Township, Grand Traverse County, Michigan; d. 26 Mar 1945, Luzon, Philippine Islands.

931. MAGGIE OLIVIA⁹ CASE *(MELINDA A.⁸ MILKS, RICHARD⁷, FREEBORN GARRETTSON⁶, JOB⁵ MILK, JONATHAN⁴, JOB³, JOHN², JOHN¹)* was born 12 Aug 1873 in Grand Traverse County, Michigan, and died 13 May 1936 in Traverse City, Grand Traverse County, Michigan. She married (1) EDWIN SIMEON ADAMS 30 Jul 1891 in Traverse City, Grand Traverse County, Michigan, son of GILBERT ADAMS and SUSAN DECKER. He was born 20 Nov 1867 in Manchester, Delaware County, Iowa, and died 20 Jul 1955 in Traverse City, Grand Traverse County, Michigan. She married (2) LINLEY MOSES HUDSON 24 Mar 1917 in Traverse City, Grand Traverse County, Michigan, son of JOHN HUDSON and SARAH SCOTT. He was born 10 Apr 1886 in Wexford County, Michigan, and died 21 Jul 1951 in Wexford County, MI.

Children of MAGGIE CASE and EDWIN ADAMS are:
- 1732. i. GILBERT DANIEL¹⁰ ADAMS, b. 10 Sep 1892, Grawn, Blair Twp., Grand Traverse County, Michigan; d. 23 Sep 1972, Reed City, Osceola County, Michigan.
- 1733. ii. HATTIE LENORE ADAMS, b. 25 Jan 1895, Blair Twp., Grand Traverse County, Michigan; d. 01 Jun 1954, Traverse City, Grand Traverse County, Michigan.
- iii. ROBERT (WILLIAM) ERNEST ADAMS, b. 15 Jun 1898, Grawn, Blair Twp., Grand Traverse County, Michigan; m. (1) ELLEN R. (DUNNING) MICHAM, 05 Mar 1920, Traverse City, Grand Traverse County, Michigan; b. 1893, Fife Lake, Grand Traverse County, Michigan; m. (2) BERTHA A. (RUSSELL) MELLAR, 15 Jul 1935, Elkhart, Indiana; b. 30 May 1903, Traverse City, Grand Traverse County, Michigan.
- 1734. iv. ARCHIE ADAMS, b. 08 Jul 1899, Blair Twp., Grand Traverse County, Michigan; d. 15 Nov 1968, Traverse City, Grand Traverse County, Michigan.
- v. RAYMOND ADAMS, b. 15 Mar 1903, Blair Twp., Grand Traverse County, Michigan; d. 28 Dec 1918, Traverse City, Grand Traverse County, Michigan.
- 1735. vi. LEROY ADAMS, b. 12 May 1904, Blair Twp., Grand Traverse County, Michigan; d. 10 Dec 1972, Detroit, Wayne County, Michigan.
- vii. CELIA IRENE ADAMS, b. Aug 1912; d. 19 Dec 1912, Monroe Center, Traverse City, Michigan.

932. FLORENCE⁹ RILEY *(EMALINE⁸ MILKS, RICHARD⁷, FREEBORN GARRETTSON⁶, JOB⁵ MILK, JONATHAN⁴, JOB³, JOHN², JOHN¹)* She married OLE ENGER.

Child of FLORENCE RILEY and OLE ENGER is:
- 1736. i. WILLIAM HENRY¹⁰ ENGER, b. 1898; d. 1952.

933. WILLIAM J.⁹ RILEY *(EMALINE⁸ MILKS, RICHARD⁷, FREEBORN GARRETTSON⁶, JOB⁵ MILK, JONATHAN⁴, JOB³, JOHN², JOHN¹)* was born Bet. 1868 - 1869 in Quebec, Canada, and died 28 Aug 1941 in Grand Traverse County, Michigan. He married KATIE PERHALL 29 Sep 1890 in Elk Rapids, Antrim County, Michigan, daughter of JOHN PERHALL and MARY

JELENECK. She was born Aug 1873 in Leelanau County, Michigan.

Children of WILLIAM RILEY and KATIE PERHALL are:

1737. i. JESSIE INEZ[10] RILEY, b. 15 Apr 1899, Kingsley, Grand Traverse County, Michigan; d. 12 Jul 1988, Traverse City, Grand Traverse County, Michigan.

1738. ii. LOTTIE J. RILEY, b. 24 Jul 1890, Traverse City, Grand Traverse County, Michigan; d. 04 Feb 1965, Grand Traverse County, Michigan.

iii. JOHN JAMES RILEY, b. 11 Jun 1893, Grand Traverse County, Michigan; d. 24 Feb 1947, Grand Traverse County, Michigan.

1739. iv. WILLIAM LEROY RILEY, b. 28 Jun 1895, Traverse City, Grand Traverse County, Michigan; d. 10 Oct 1966, Grand Traverse County, Michigan.

1740. v. MELVIN M. RILEY, b. 02 Oct 1901, Paradise Twp., Grand Traverse County, Michigan; d. 17 Oct 1992, Traverse City, Grand Traverse County, Michigan.

1741. vi. ELSIE A. RILEY, b. Bet. 1903 - 1904, Paradise Twp., Grand Traverse County, Michigan.

vii. ORVILLE E. RILEY, b. 26 Aug 1907, Paradise Twp., Grand Traverse County, Michigan; d. 29 Apr 1992, Garfield, Grand Traverse County, Michigan; m. PEARL (HENCY) SMITH, 25 Dec 1931, Traverse City, Grand Traverse County, Michigan; b. 02 Aug 1905, Kingsley, Grand Traverse County, Michigan; d. 10 May 1998, Grand Traverse County, Michigan.

    1930 census: divorced: Elsie M Smith   F   4

viii. WILMA I. RILEY, b. Bet. 1913 - 1914, Paradise Twp., Grand Traverse County, Michigan.

ix. VELMA K. RILEY, b. Bet. 1913 - 1914, Paradise Twp., Grand Traverse County, Michigan; m. MILO HENCY, 07 Dec 1932, Traverse City, Grand Traverse County, Michigan; b. 1899, Grand Traverse County, Michigan.

x. HAROLD C. RILEY, b. 17 Sep 1915, Paradise Twp., Grand Traverse County, Michigan; d. 30 May 1998, Kingsley, Grand Traverse County, Michigan.

934. EDITH REBECCA[9] RILEY *(EMALINE[8] MILKS, RICHARD[7], FREEBORN GARRETTSON[6], JOB[5] MILK, JONATHAN[4], JOB[3], JOHN[2], JOHN[1])* was born 09 Oct 1883 in Paradise Twp., Grand Traverse County, Michigan, and died Bet. 1913 - 12 Sep 1918 in Traverse City, Grand Traverse County, Michigan. She married JOHN (NMI) OLMAN 28 Mar 1899 in Traverse City, Grand Traverse County, Michigan, son of PETER OLMAN and MARY MANDEL. He was born 28 Jul 1875 in Mecosta County, Michigan.

Children of EDITH RILEY and JOHN OLMAN are:

1742. i. MABEL R.[10] OLMAN, b. 14 Apr 1900, Traverse City, Grand Traverse County, Michigan; d. 19 Jan 1977, Traverse City, Grand Traverse County, Michigan.

ii. WILLIAM J. OLMAN, b. Bet. 1902 - 1903, Traverse City, Grand Traverse County, Michigan; m. LENA M. (BREWER) SAXTON, 14 Mar 1923, Traverse City, Grand Traverse County, Michigan; b. 08 Oct 1896, Elmira, New York; d. 23 Sep 1991, Garfield, Grand Traverse County, Michigan.

1743. iii. HAZEL MARIE OLMAN, b. 24 Sep 1908, Traverse City, Grand Traverse County, Michigan; d. 13 Aug 1989, Traverse City, Grand Traverse County, Michigan.

iv. EARL OLMAN, b. 08 Aug 1912, Traverse City, Grand Traverse County, Michigan; d. Nov 1966, Traverse City, Grand Traverse County, Michigan.

v. INFANT OLMAN, b. Abt. 1911, Traverse City, Grand Traverse County, Michigan; d. 30 Jan 1912, Traverse City, Grand Traverse County, Michigan.

vi. HARRY OLMAN, b. 1915, Traverse City, Grand Traverse County, Michigan; d. 06 Mar 1915, Traverse City, Grand Traverse County, Michigan.

935. CHAUNCY EMORY[9] ILIFF *(LYDIA ANN[8] MILKS, RICHARD[7], FREEBORN GARRETTSON[6], JOB[5] MILK, JONATHAN[4], JOB[3], JOHN[2], JOHN[1])* was born 01 Mar 1875 in Kingsley, Grand Traverse County, Michigan, and died 19 May 1950. He married (1) ROSA DENNIS 08 May 1897 in Springfield, Grand Traverse County, Michigan, daughter of JOHN DENNIS and EVA HUSKNANO. She was born 1879 in Kalkaska, Michigan. He married (2) HARRIETT TROCKS Abt. 1899 in Michigan ?. She was born Abt. 1875. He married (3) MAGGIE (SAUNDERS) NICHOLS 17 Dec 1917 in Otsego, Michigan, daughter of ALEX SAUNDERS and ANNIE PAYNE. She was born 1888 in West Virginia.

Children of CHAUNCY ILIFF and HARRIETT TROCKS are:
- i. BOWDEN LAFAYETTE[10] ILIFF, b. 22 Apr 1900, Antrim County, Michigan; d. 06 Dec 1979, Big Rapids, Mecosta County, Michigan; m. LILLIAN LARABEE, 27 Dec 1921, Interlocken, Grand Traverse County, Michigan; b. 1904, Muskegon, Michigan.
- ii. BERT S. ILIFF, b. 06 May 1906, Michigan; d. 28 Oct 1988, Munising, Alger, Michigan; m. CAROLINE (PATRICK) GALLARD, 31 Jul 1926, Traverse City, Grand Traverse County, Michigan; b. 1902, Columbus, Indiana.

936. DAISY ELLEN[9] MILKS *(EZRA[8], RICHARD[7], FREEBORN GARRETTSON[6], JOB[5] MILK, JONATHAN[4], JOB[3], JOHN[2], JOHN[1])* was born 27 Jan 1880 in Kingsley, Grand Traverse County, Michigan, and died Mar 1941 in Kingsley, Grand Traverse County, Michigan. She married (1) BENJAMIN E. WILSON 1901 in Grand Traverse County, Michigan. He was born 1868 in Traverse City, Grand Traverse County, Michigan, and died 1943 in Kingsley, Grand Traverse County, Michigan. She married (2) ERNEST LUPER 1911 in Grand Traverse County, Michigan. He died 21 Jan 1919 in Grand Traverse County, Michigan. She remarried (3) BENJAMIN E. WILSON 24 Dec 1921 in Grand Traverse County, Michigan, son of WILLIAM WILSON and CLARISSA CHAPEL. He was born 11 May 1868 in Grand Traverse Co., Michigan, and died 23 Jul 1943 in Kingsley, Michigan.

Children of DAISY MILKS and ERNEST LUPER are:
1744. i. IRVIN EZRA[10] LUPER, b. 28 Sep 1912, Traverse City, Mich; d. 06 Sep 2000, Traverse City, Mich.
1745. ii. MINETTA LUPER, b. 24 Oct 1913, Traverse City, Mich; d. 16 Oct 2000, Elkhart, Indiana.

Child of DAISY MILKS and BENJAMIN WILSON is:
1746. iii. GEORGE B. 'PETE'[10] WILSON, b. 05 Jan 1923, Kingsley, Mich; d. 18 Sep 2000, Traverse City, Mich.

OBITUARY
Died September 18, 2000

TRAVERSE CITY - On Sept. 18, 2000, surrounded by his family and friends at Grand Traverse Pavilions, George B. "Pete" Wilson left this world to enter one free of pain.

George was born on Jan. 5, 1923, to Benjamin and Daisy (Milks) Wilson of Kingsley. Drawn in by her ever present smile, he married the love of his life, Rose Marie Ockert, on Aug. 2, 1941. In their 59 years together, they raised seven daughters and two sons.

George loved spending time outdoors, working with his hands, growing beautiful flowers and feeding wild life. Animals also piqued his interest, and he spent many years of his life raising, breeding and showing Arabian horses. He was especially interested in the 4-H horse program to which he donated breeding and foals. But above all, George was a dedicated husband, father and grandfather whose pride and joy were his children and grandchildren.

George lived and gave back to the Grand Traverse area all of his life, except ten years which he spent in Port Orchard, Wash. where he worked as a carpenter and also worked as a logger. During World War II, he worked at a naval ship yard in Bremerton, Wash., as well as other military installations in the area. And, in 1955, George and his growing family returned home where he continued to spread his warm ways; kindness, honesty, generosity and strong work ethic. George retired in 1983 as chief engineer at Traverse City Area Public Schools after working there 28 years.

George will be greatly missed by his wife, Rosie; all of his children, Beverly Causey of Longs, SC, Barbara and Rob Trevena of Athens, Ga., Gary and Christine Wilson of Kalkaska, Carol and Kip Newell and Kay and Greg Lyon - all of Kingsley; Linda and Dave Bugai, Wenda and Gary Warren and Deb and Dave Sexton - all of Traverse City, and Benjamin Wilson and his fiancé Meg Peterson of Evart; 32 grandchildren; 31 great-grandchildren; plus many others who also lovingly called him Grandpa; three nieces, two nephews; one sister-in-law, Fern Luper, of Traverse City; and a special aunt, Sadie Milks, of Buckley.

George will join both his parents; a sister, Xena Cunningham; a brother, Irvin Luper; a grandson, Cory Wilson; two nephews; one niece; two infant sisters; and two beloved companions, Lexi and Laddie, who all predeceased him.

Services will be at Reynolds-Jonkhoff Funeral Home in Traverse City at 11 a.m. Saturday, Sept. 23, with Rev. Char Minger of Kingsley United Methodist Church officiating, with interment in the Evergreen Cemetery in Kingsley. Visitations will be Friday, Sept. 22, from 2 to 4 p.m. and 6 to 8 p.m. at the funeral home.

937. OSCAR WYAN[9] MILKS *(EZRA[8], RICHARD[7], FREEBORN GARRETTSON[6], JOB[5] MILK, JONATHAN[4], JOB[3], JOHN[2], JOHN[1])* was born 12 Oct 1883 in Kingsley, Michigan. He married (1) JENNIE ARMINA WATSON 21 Jan 1905 in Kingsley, Grand Traverse County, Michigan, daughter of HOLDEN WATSON and THRESSA PAYNE. She was born 30 Jun 1886 in Millington, Michigan, and died 05 Mar 1934 in Owosso, Michigan. He married (2) JULIA (STURGIS) BENNETT 01 Jun

1922 in Cadillac, Wexford, Michigan, daughter of FRED STURGIS and EMILY _____. She was born 21 Oct 1877 in Gaines, Michigan, and died 16 Feb 1950 in Cadillac, Michigan.

Children of OSCAR MILKS and JENNIE WATSON are:
1747.   i.   DOROTHEA LILLY^{10} MILKS, b. 08 Jun 1906; d. 1991.
1748.   ii.   THONON WAYNE MILKS, b. 08 Aug 1909, Kingsley, Michigan; d. 13 Aug 1982, Saginaw County, Mich.
1749.   iii.   ORVILLE WALTER MILKS, b. 21 Jun 1913, Kingsley, Mich; d. 09 Sep 1995, Clare, Clare Co., Michigan.

938. LOTTIE ZELLA^9 MILKS (*EZRA^8, RICHARD^7, FREEBORN GARRETTSON^6, JOB^5 MILK, JONATHAN^4, JOB^3, JOHN^2, JOHN^1*) was born 24 Aug 1886 in Kingsley, Michigan, and died 10 May 1969 in Hamilton, Butler County, Ohio. She married (1) ELDA SURRELL YORKS 14 Jun 1905 in Grand Traverse County, Michigan. He was born 20 Apr 1883 in Paradise Twp., Grand Traverse County, Michigan, and died 23 Jan 1919 in Grand Traverse County, Michigan. She married (2) EDWARD DARWIN DRONE 15 Apr 1925 in Grand Traverse County, Michigan, son of ANDREW DRONE and ANGELINA CLARK. He was born Jun 1871 in Muscoda, Grant County, Wisconsin, and died 25 Aug 1942 in Grand Traverse County, Michigan. He was a son of Andrew and Angeline Drone.

Lottie was stricken in the 1918 Influenza Epidemic, along with her husband Elda, and one daughter Marie. Elda died in 1919 from the flu, but Lottie and Marie survived.

Children of LOTTIE MILKS and ELDA YORKS are:
1750.   i.   GERALD ALBERT RUSSELL^{10} YORKS, b. 25 Jun 1906, Kingsley, Grand Traverse County, Michigan; d. 08 Oct 1984, Cedar Creek, Muskegon County, Michigan.
1751.   ii.   DAISY EDWINA CHRISTINA BELLE YORKS, b. 25 Dec 1907, Traverse City, Grand Traverse County, Michigan; d. 02 Nov 1997, Franklin, North Carolina.
1752.   iii.   MARIE MAXINE YORKS, b. 13 Dec 1917, Traverse City, Grand Traverse County, Michigan; d. 15 Apr 2011, Kalamazoo, Kalamazoo County, Michigan.

Children of LOTTIE MILKS and EDWARD DRONE are:
1753.   iv.   EDWARD ARTHUR^{10} DRONE, b. 04 Sep 1926, Williamsburg, Grand Traverse County, Michigan; d. 26 Oct 2003, Suttons Bay, Leelanau County, Michigan.
1754.   v.   CHARLOTTE ANGELINE DRONE, b. 14 Dec 1927, Traverse City, Grand Traverse County, Michigan; d. 14 Jan 2005, Bridgman, Michigan.

939. WESLEY JONATHON 'DOAD'^{9} MILKS (*EZRA^8, RICHARD^7, FREEBORN GARRETTSON^6, JOB^5 MILK, JONATHAN^4, JOB^3, JOHN^2, JOHN^1*) was born 08 Jul 1892 in Kingsley, Mich, and died 27 May 1972 in Grand Traverse County, Mich. He married (1) LAURA E. DEAN 1914 in Grand Traverse Co, Mich. She was born Abt. 1892 in Michigan, and died 06 Nov 1957 in Grand Traverse County, Mich. He married (2) SADIE F. HUNT 1957 in Grand Traverse Co, Mich. She was born 10 Jul 1913, and died 14 Nov 2007 in Buckley, Wexford, Michigan.

Sadie F. (Hunt) Milks was the second wife of Wesley Jonathan Milks (Uncle Dode), b. 1892 in Traverse City, a brother of my grandmother, Lottie Milks Yorks Drone, and son of Ezra Milks and Minerva Swain, and grandson of Richard Milks and Margaret Corbitt. Many people thought that they were 'living in sin', but they were married in Grand Traverse County in 1957. Uncle Dode and Aunt Sadie owned a farm just north of Buckley on Rte 37, where Sadie lived until her death in 2007.

Uncle Dode and Aunt Sadie were two of my favorite people. My first memories of Uncle Dode were when he worked at a small dairy and ice cream parlor on the corner of E. Front St and Rose Street. My sister Geraldine also worked there and made super Banana Split sundaes for us. We lived only a couple of blocks away, after WWII, and used to go down to the dairy and visit Dode. Sadie was one of the most loving and gentle women I have known. She worked for quite a few years at Gerry Olson's first store on W. Front St. Dode and Sadie had one child, Juanita, who married Vernon L. Duff. I believe they still live in Buckley on Dode and Sadie's old farm.

Children of WESLEY MILKS and LAURA DEAN are:
    i.   LAWRENCE REXAL^{10} MILKS, b. 26 Jul 1914, Buckley, Michigan; d. 25 May 1931, Mackinaw City, Cheboygan, Michigan.
    ii.   LEROY HORTON MILKS, b. 04 Mar 1917, Buckley, Michigan; d. 11 May 1951; m. (1) JEANN EVA BELLOWS, 1937, Grand Traverse County, Michigan; b. Abt. 1917; m. (2) ELSIE BECKER, 1945, Grand Traverse County, Michigan; b. Abt. 1917.

1755. iii. FLOYD WESLEY MILKS, b. 30 Dec 1918, Buckley, Michigan; d. 10 Apr 1966, Grand Traverse County, MI.
iv. KENNETH WALTER MILKS, b. 07 Aug 1920, Buckley, Michigan; d. 07 Feb 1921, Michigan.
1756. v. IRENE MAY MILKS, b. 07 Nov 1924, Traverse City, Mich; d. 30 May 2000, Traverse City, Mich.
vi. ELMER DEAN MILKS, b. 19 Jan 1929, Buckley, Michigan; d. 29 Jun 1950, Tacoma, Washington (Drowned).

Child of WESLEY MILKS and SADIE HUNT is:
1757. vii. JUANITA JOYCE[10] HUNT, b. 29 Sep 1932, Petoskey, Michigan; d. 02 Mar 2012, Grand Traverse County, Michigan.

940. MABEL ROSE[9] MILKS *(RICHARD AMBROSE[8], RICHARD[7], FREEBORN GARRETTSON[6], JOB[5] MILK, JONATHAN[4], JOB[3], JOHN[2], JOHN[1])* was born 16 Apr 1881 in Michigan, and died 31 Mar 1942 in Grand Traverse County, Michigan. She married (1) FRANK N. FREEMAN 03 Jul 1899 in Grand Traverse County, Michigan, son of GEORGE FREEMAN and EMMA BROWN. He was born Bet. 1871 - 1872 in Michigan, and died Bef. 1920. She married (2) ALBERT ANTHONY CLOUS 29 May 1920 in Grand Traverse County, Michigan, son of MATHEW CLOUS and MARY _____. He was born 21 Sep 1883 in Bingham, Leelanau, Michigan, and died 15 Dec 1961 in Grand Traverse County, Michigan.

Child of MABEL MILKS and FRANK FREEMAN is:
1758. i. GERTRUDE IRENE[10] FREEMAN, b. 23 Apr 1900, Traverse City, Grand Traverse County, Michigan.

941. NELSON LESLIE[9] MILKS *(RICHARD AMBROSE[8], RICHARD[7], FREEBORN GARRETTSON[6], JOB[5] MILK, JONATHAN[4], JOB[3], JOHN[2], JOHN[1])* was born 04 Mar 1884 in Traverse City, Michigan, and died 30 Dec 1963 in Grand Traverse County, Michigan. He married ELSIE CRONKHITE 04 Aug 1920 in Grand Traverse County, Michigan, daughter of BYRON CRONKHITE and ELIZABETH WILCOX. She was born Bet. 1898 - 1899 in Kingsley, Grand Traverse County, Michigan, and died 23 Jul 1967 in Grand Traverse County, Michigan ?.
Linda Lou Milks Lile has supplied a lot of data for this family.

Children of NELSON MILKS and ELSIE CRONKHITE are:
1759. i. BRIAN CLEMENT[10] MILKS, b. 27 Mar 1920, Traverse City, Michigan; d. 08 Mar 1974, Lakeside, Navajo County, Arizona.
ii. ERNEST JOHN MILKS, b. 07 Apr 1921, Traverse City, Michigan; d. 29 Nov 1923, Traverse City, Michigan.
1760. iii. OLIVE MELVINA MILKS, b. 04 Jul 1923, Traverse City, Michigan; d. 05 Jun 2003, Traverse City, Grand Traverse County, Michigan.
1761. iv. NELSON LESLIE MILKS, JR., b. 24 Sep 1925, Traverse City, Michigan.
v. BYRON AMBROSE MILKS, b. 19 Jul 1927, Traverse City, Michigan; d. 21 Nov 1927, Traverse City, MI.
1762. vi. FORD LEROY MILKS, b. 16 Aug 1928, Traverse City, Grand Traverse County, Michigan; d. 24 Apr 2003, Platte County Memorial Hospital, Wheatland, Wyoming.
1763. vii. ELSIE MYRTLE MILKS, b. 08 Oct 1932, Traverse City, Grand Traverse County, Michigan.

942. MARGARET EURETTA "RETTA"[9] MILKS *(RICHARD AMBROSE[8], RICHARD[7], FREEBORN GARRETTSON[6], JOB[5] MILK, JONATHAN[4], JOB[3], JOHN[2], JOHN[1])* was born 28 Jun 1886 in Traverse City, Michigan, and died 27 Dec 1969 in Grand Traverse County, Michigan. She married (1) CLAUDE SKUTT 1907 in Grand Traverse County, Michigan, son of FRANK SKUTT and NORA BLANCHARD. He was born Aug 1882 in Traverse City?, Michigan, and died 17 Oct 1950. She married (2) GEORGE L. KNAPP 16 Jul 1914 in Traverse City, Grand Traverse County, Michigan?. He was born Bet. 1890 - 1891 in Michigan. She married (3) ERNEST J. WERY Abt. 1924 in Grand Traverse County, Michigan?, son of FELIX WERY and ALEXANDRA DECAMP. He was born 25 Feb 1893 in Stephenson, Michigan, and died 12 Mar 1981 in Peshtigo, Marinette, Wisconsin.

Children of MARGARET MILKS and CLAUDE SKUTT are:
i. MAY BELL[10] SKUTT, b. 13 Mar 1908, Traverse City, Michigan; d. 13 Mar 1908, East Bay, Grand Traverse County, Michigan.
ii. CHARLOTTE IONE SKUTT, b. 25 Aug 1909, Traverse City, Michigan; d. 09 Oct 1953, Traverse City, MI.

943. BLANCHE LUELLA[9] MILKS *(RICHARD AMBROSE[8], RICHARD[7], FREEBORN GARRETTSON[6], JOB[5] MILK, JONATHAN[4], JOB[3], JOHN[2], JOHN[1])* was born 10 Apr 1892 in Traverse City, Michigan, and died 09 Aug 1974 in Plainwell, Allegan County, Michigan,. She married (1) ROY F. AMES 01 Jul 1911 in Grand Traverse County, Michigan, son of DAVID AMES and BEULAH MCFARLIN. He was born 1887 in Dublin, Ireland. She married (2) ERNEST NELSON GARRETSON 25 Aug 1921 in Bessemer, Gogebic County, Mich., son of CHARLES GARRETSON and JULIA CLARK. He was born 08 Jun 1884, and died 19 Feb 1932 in Ontanogon, Michigan. She married (3) JOSEPH CLOUSE 22 Nov 1932 in Traverse City, Michigan, son of MATHIAS CLOUSE and FREDERICKA SLICKENMYER. He was born 15 Apr 1895 in Traverse City, Michigan, and died 20 Mar 1983 in Grand Rapids, Kent County, Michigan.

Children of BLANCHE MILKS and ERNEST GARRETSON are:
- i. THOMAS[10] GARRETSON, b. Abt. 1922.
- 1764. ii. RICHARD CHARLES 'DICK' GARRETSON, b. 30 Jan 1924, Traverse City, Michigan; d. 12 Oct 2000, Traverse City, Grand Traverse County, Michigan.

944. AGNES IDA[9] MILKS *(RICHARD AMBROSE[8], RICHARD[7], FREEBORN GARRETTSON[6], JOB[5] MILK, JONATHAN[4], JOB[3], JOHN[2], JOHN[1])* was born 22 Jun 1895 in Traverse City, Michigan, and died 15 Nov 1962 in Niles, Berrien County, Michigan. She married CLAUDE SYLVESTER HAVENER 17 Oct 1914 in Kingsley, Grand Traverse County, Michigan, son of ARTHUR HAVENER and LILLIAN GOODE. He was born 02 Aug 1895 in Eau Claire, Michigan, and died Feb 1982 in Niles, Berrien County, Michigan.

Child of AGNES MILKS and CLAUDE HAVENER is:
- 1765. i. EVA LEONA[10] HAVENER, b. 17 Sep 1917, Michigan.

945. ERNEST AMBROSE[9] MILKS *(RICHARD AMBROSE[8], RICHARD[7], FREEBORN GARRETTSON[6], JOB[5] MILK, JONATHAN[4], JOB[3], JOHN[2], JOHN[1])* was born 30 Apr 1898 in Traverse City, Michigan, and died 09 Sep 1974 in Traverse City, Michigan. He married ETHEL MAE PFISTHNER 09 Jun 1920 in Honor, Benzie County, Michigan, daughter of ELLIS PFISTHNER and BESSIE GRIFFEN. She was born 22 May 1904 in Homestead, Benzie County, Michigan, and died 02 Aug 1960 in Traverse City, Grand Traverse County, Michigan.

Children of ERNEST MILKS and ETHEL PFISTHNER are:
- 1766. i. ERNEST ELLIS[10] MILKS, b. 02 Feb 1922, Grawn, Michigan; d. 08 Sep 1995, Au Gres, Arenac, Michigan.
- 1767. ii. GILBERT JAMES PFISTHNER, b. 15 Jun 1923, Benzie County, Michigan.
- 1768. iii. GERALD 'JERRY' ERWIN MILKS, b. 17 Jul 1924, Grawn, Grand Traverse County, Michigan; d. 22 Oct 2008, Saginaw, Michigan.

946. IRA ELDIE[9] MILKS *(RICHARD AMBROSE[8], RICHARD[7], FREEBORN GARRETTSON[6], JOB[5] MILK, JONATHAN[4], JOB[3], JOHN[2], JOHN[1])* was born 08 Aug 1900 in Traverse City, Grand Traverse County, Michigan, and died 24 May 1964 in Saginaw County, Michigan. He married (1) ELSIE ELVENA JOHNSON 15 Jul 1919 in Traverse City, Grand Traverse County, Michigan, daughter of JOHN JOHNSON and WILHELMINA OLSON. She was born 28 Sep 1903 in Wallin, Michigan, and died 01 Feb 1980 in Muskegon, Michigan. He married (2) GLADYS I. BRIMMER 30 Dec 1925 in Hart, Oceana County, Michigan, daughter of LOUIS BRIMMER and EDNA PHILLIPS. She was born 19 Nov 1907 in Hart, Michigan, and died 25 Dec 1992 in Traverse City, Grand Traverse County, Michigan. ELSIE JOHNSON MILKS married (2) ERNEST W. GEETING in 1924 and had at least 8 children with him. After ERNEST died, she married (3) Mr. ELDERS.

Child of IRA MILKS and ELSIE JOHNSON is:
- 1769. i. IRA RICHARD[10] MILKS, b. 13 Jun 1920, Traverse City, Grand Traverse County, Michigan; d. 23 Oct 2009, Turner, Arenac County, Michigan.

Children of IRA MILKS and GLADYS BRIMMER are:
- 1770. ii. ILLA JEAN[10] MILKS, b. 29 Nov 1926, Saginaw, Michigan; d. 15 Oct 2005, St. Charles, Saginaw County, Michigan.
- 1771. iii. DORIS MAXINE MILKS, b. 08 Mar 1929, Saginaw, Michigan; d. 06 May 2010, Buckley, Grand Traverse County, Michigan.
- 1772. iv. DOROTHY MAE MILKS, b. 09 Nov 1930, Saginaw, Michigan.
- 1773. v. MARGARET MARILYN MILKS, b. 29 Jun 1932, Saginaw, Michigan.
- 1774. vi. LEWIS ELDIE 'LOU' MILKS, b. 19 Oct 1935, Saginaw, Michigan; d. 12 Dec 1992, Tacoma, Pierce County, Washington.
- 1775. vii. GERALDINE DIANNE MILKS, b. 30 Jan 1943, Saginaw, Michigan.

1776. viii. JOYCE EDNA MILKS, b. 06 Oct 1944, Saginaw, Michigan; d. 16 Jan 2001, Thompsonville, Benzie Co, Mich.

947. MYRTLE ORINDA[9] SAYERS *(ZADIA ELLA[8] MILKS, RICHARD[7], FREEBORN GARRETTSON[6], JOB[5] MILK, JONATHAN[4], JOB[3], JOHN[2], JOHN[1])* was born 02 Mar 1883 in Kingsley, Michigan, and died 15 Dec 1940 in Grand Traverse County, Michigan. She married (1) JOHN PERHALL 04 Apr 1899 in Grand Traverse County, Michigan, son of JOHN PERHALL and MARY YELNICK. He was born Aug 1869 in Austria, and died 09 Mar 1935 in Grand Traverse County, Michigan. She married (2) ADAM MANG 1936 in Grand Traverse County, Michigan. He was born 26 Sep 1872 in Canada, and died 25 Apr 1946 in Grand Traverse County, Michigan.

Children of MYRTLE SAYERS and JOHN PERHALL are:
1777. i. MARY ELLA[10] PERHALL, b. 29 Jun 1903; d. 16 Sep 1971.
1778. ii. LETTIE IRENE PERHALL, b. 02 Jul 1907; d. 1992, Warren, Macomb County, Michigan.
1779. iii. DEALIA ALICE PERHALL, b. 11 Mar 1920, Kingsley, Michigan; d. 31 Mar 1991, Kingsley, GT Co., Michigan.
       iv. AUDREY BERNICE PERHALL, b. 08 Aug 1921; d. 13 Nov 2005, Grand Traverse County, Michigan; m. ROBERT M. DILS, 1938, Grand Traverse County, Michigan; b. Abt. 1921; d. 02 Oct 1994, Grand Traverse County, Michigan.

948. BRUCE ALVIN[9] SAYERS *(ZADIA ELLA[8] MILKS, RICHARD[7], FREEBORN GARRETTSON[6], JOB[5] MILK, JONATHAN[4], JOB[3], JOHN[2], JOHN[1])* was born 04 Apr 1890 in Grand Traverse County, Michigan, and died 21 Jul 1973 in Grand Traverse County, Michigan. He married LYDIA ALICE JONES 11 Nov 1913 in Grand Traverse County, Michigan. She was born Abt. 1895, and died 23 May 1970 in Grand Traverse County, Michigan.

Children of BRUCE SAYERS and LYDIA JONES are:
1780. i. LOUISE EMMA[10] SAYERS, b. 03 Jun 1916, Bates, Michigan.
       ii. IRENE ALICE SAYERS, b. 18 Apr 1918, Williamsburg, Michigan; m. LORAIN G. ECKEL; b. Abt. 1918.
1781. iii. EVA MARIE SAYERS, b. 15 Jan 1921, Midland, Michigan; d. 21 Dec 2000, Dryden, Michigan.

949. BERNICE ISABELLE[9] SAYERS *(ZADIA ELLA[8] MILKS, RICHARD[7], FREEBORN GARRETTSON[6], JOB[5] MILK, JONATHAN[4], JOB[3], JOHN[2], JOHN[1])* was born 21 May 1893 in Grand Traverse County, Michigan. She married REUBEN JAMES MITCHELL 05 Oct 1911 in Grand Traverse County, Michigan, son of JAMES MITCHELL and MARY COLEMAN. He was born 22 Jul 1888 in Michigan.

Children of BERNICE SAYERS and REUBEN MITCHELL are:
       i. ROBERT WILLIAM[10] MITCHELL, b. 25 Oct 1916, Kingsley, Grand Traverse County, Michigan; d. 27 Oct 1916, Kingsley, Grand Traverse County, Michigan.
       ii. KENNETH LEE MITCHELL, b. 07 Jul 1919, Detroit, Michigan; m. ALMA RICE.

950. WALTER PAUL[9] SAYERS *(ZADIA ELLA[8] MILKS, RICHARD[7], FREEBORN GARRETTSON[6], JOB[5] MILK, JONATHAN[4], JOB[3], JOHN[2], JOHN[1])* was born 27 Jul 1895 in Kingsley, Grand Traverse County, Michigan, and died Dec 1970 in Shelby, Oceana County, Michigan. He married (1) ELSIE CRONKHITE 09 Aug 1915 in Grand Traverse County, Michigan, daughter of BYRON CRONKHITE and ELIZABETH WILCOX. She was born Bet. 1898 - 1899 in Kingsley, Grand Traverse County, Michigan, and died 23 Jul 1967 in Grand Traverse County, Michigan ?. He married (2) VASHIT H. TUCKER Abt. 04 Sep 1926 in Kalamazoo County, Michigan, daughter of HIRAM TUCKER and MAY MCCULLOUGH. She was born Abt. 1900 in Michigan. He married (3) ADALINE DUMAS 20 Apr 1934. She was born Abt. 1895.

Child of WALTER SAYERS and ELSIE CRONKHITE is:
1782. i. EMERETTA JUNE[10] SAYERS, b. 29 Jan 1916, Michigan; d. 26 May 1988, Grand Traverse County, Michigan.

Children of WALTER SAYERS and ADALINE DUMAS are:
       ii. PAUL ALVIN[10] SAYERS, b. 30 Sep 1937.
       iii. MARION ALINE SAYERS, b. 02 Jan 1943.

951. MILDRED M.[9] MILKS *(LEWIS ETHIL[8], RICHARD[7], FREEBORN GARRETTSON[6], JOB[5] MILK, JONATHAN[4], JOB[3], JOHN[2], JOHN[1])* was born 06 Sep 1899 in Michigan, and died 22 Apr 1994 in Menominee, Menominee Co., Michigan. She married JOHN ALFRED DAHL Abt. 1920 in Michigan, son of MATTHEW DAHL and BETH ____. He was born 30 Mar 1900 in Delta County, Michigan, and died 28 Mar 1981 in Escanaba, Delta Co., Michigan.

Children of MILDRED MILKS and JOHN DAHL are:
1783.   i.   ALFRED L.[10] DAHL, b. 17 May 1922, Cornell, Delta Co., Michigan.
          ii.   RUDOLPH M. DAHL, b. 01 Jan 1929, Cornell, Delta Co., Michigan; d. 11 Jun 1976, Wisconsin; m. MARY T.

952. LENA ALMIRA[9] MILKS *(JOSEPH[8], BENJAMIN[7], FREEBORN GARRETTSON[6], JOB[5] MILK, JONATHAN[4], JOB[3], JOHN[2], JOHN[1])* was born 27 Apr 1884 in Eardley, Quebec, and died 1975 in Ottawa, Carleton, Ontario, Canada. She married JOSEPH FREDERICK ALLAN MULLIGAN 27 Oct 1909 in Ottawa, Carleton, Ontario, Canada, son of DAVID MULLIGAN and ELLEN CASSELLS. He was born 07 Oct 1884 in Ottawa, Carleton, Ontario, Canada, and died 23 Jun 1949 in Ottawa, Carleton, Ontario, Canada.

OBITUARY - Ottawa Citizen - June 25, 1949 - F.A. Mulligan Dies Suddenly

A well-known figure in automobile agency circles in the Capital, Frederick Allan Mulligan, manager of Federal Motors Limited for the past 20 years, died suddenly Thursday at his home at 107 Broadway Avenue. He was in his 65th year.

Mr. Mulligan was the son of the late David Mulligan and Ellen Cassels and was born in Ottawa on October 7, 1884. He was educated in Ottawa schools and in 1907 married Lena A. Milks. He attended St. James United Church and was a member of Builder's Lodge, AF and AM.

Surviving are one son, Alan of Schumacher, Ont., two daughters, Mrs. A.G. Marshall and Mrs. C.E. Spence, both of Toronto and a brother, J.E. Mulligan of the Department of National Revenue.

A public service will be held at the A.E. Veitch parlors, 338 Somerset Street on Saturday at 3 pm with Rev. Robert W. McLauchlin of St. James United Church conducting. Interment will be in Upper Eardley United Church cemetery.

Children of LENA MILKS and JOSEPH MULLIGAN are:
1784.   i.   EDITH CLARISSA[10] MULLIGAN, b. 28 Sep 1910, Ottawa, Carleton, Ontario, Canada.
          ii.   ALAN FREDERICK MULLIGAN, b. 31 Oct 1912, Ottawa, Carleton, Ontario, Canada.
1785.   iii. ANNA AUDREY MULLIGAN.

953. JOSEPH OSBORNE[9] MILKS *(JOSEPH[8], BENJAMIN[7], FREEBORN GARRETTSON[6], JOB[5] MILK, JONATHAN[4], JOB[3], JOHN[2], JOHN[1])* was born 25 Jul 1886 in Eardley, Quebec, and died 1965. He married MARY LOUISE DOWE 17 Sep 1913. She was born 1885, and died 1965.

Children of JOSEPH MILKS and MARY DOWE are:
1786.   i.   LESLIE OSBORNE[10] MILKS, b. 25 Jun 1914, Schreiber, Ontario; d. 28 Aug 2000, Thunder Bay, Ontario.
1787.   ii.   JOHN 'JACK' STANLEY MILKS, b. 21 Jun 1916, Schreiber, Ontario; d. Bef. 28 Aug 2000.
1788.   iii. ANNIE MILKS, b. 12 Sep 1917, Schreiber, Ontario; d. Bef. 28 Aug 2000.
1789.   iv. GWYNNETH MILKS, b. 26 Jan 1920, Schreiber, Ontario; d. 09 Nov 1972, Nanaimo, British Columbia, Canada.

954. WILLIAM ASAHEL "ACE"[9] MILKS *(JOSEPH[8], BENJAMIN[7], FREEBORN GARRETTSON[6], JOB[5] MILK, JONATHAN[4], JOB[3], JOHN[2], JOHN[1])* was born 27 Nov 1888 in Eardley, Quebec, and died 05 Jul 1955 in Ottawa, Carleton, Ontario. He married FLORENCE GERTRUDE SCOTT 06 Sep 1922 in Toronto, Canada, daughter of WILLIAM SCOTT and ELIZABETH WATSON. She was born 20 Apr 1891 in Lisburn, N. Ireland, and died 1984.

Ace was a veteran YMCA worker; director of Golden Lake Camp for 34 yrs.; Ottawa Collegiate Institute attendance officer; treas. Ottawa and District Boys Work Board; elder at St. James United Church and Sunday School teacher for boys. He was greatly interested in family history and he and his wife, Gertrude, provided many family records.

Children of WILLIAM MILKS and FLORENCE SCOTT are:
1790.   i.   WILLIAM JOSEPH[10] MILKS, b. 08 Aug 1924, Ottawa, Canada; d. 26 Feb 2010, Ontario, Canada.
1791.   ii.   DR. JOHN EDWARD MILKS, b. 01 Jul 1926, Ottawa, Canada.

955. CHARLES HECTOR[9] MILKS *(JOSEPH[8], BENJAMIN[7], FREEBORN GARRETTSON[6], JOB[5] MILK, JONATHAN[4], JOB[3], JOHN[2], JOHN[1])* was born 16 Feb 1895 in Eardley, Quebec, Canada, and died 28 Jul 1972 in Lakeland, Polk County, Florida. He married GRACE AUDREY KEYES 03 Sep 1932, daughter of JOSEPH KEYES and EVA WRIGHT. She was born 15 May 1905 in Westmeath, Ontario, Canada, and died 1977 in Lakeland, Polk County, Florida.

Children of CHARLES MILKS and GRACE KEYES are:
    i. GRACE A.[10] MILKS, b. 31 Dec 1935, New Rochelle, NY.
    ii. DOROTHY H. MILKS, b. 29 Nov 1937, New Rochelle, NY.

956. HECTOR H.[9] DOWE *(ALMIRA[8] MILKS, BENJAMIN[7], FREEBORN GARRETTSON[6], JOB[5] MILK, JONATHAN[4], JOB[3], JOHN[2], JOHN[1])* was born 24 May 1891 in Eardley, Quebec. He married MABEL R. COCHRANE, daughter of JOSEPH COCHRANE and ELIZA _____. She was born 29 Jan 1889 in Eardley, Quebec.

Child of HECTOR DOWE and MABEL COCHRANE is:
    i. OLGA ELIZABETH[10] DOWE, b. Abt. 1924; d. 19 Jun 1927, Carleton, Ontario, Canada.

957. LEAH ETHEL[9] MILKS *(WILLIAM THOMAS[8], BENJAMIN[7], FREEBORN GARRETTSON[6], JOB[5] MILK, JONATHAN[4], JOB[3], JOHN[2], JOHN[1])* was born 24 May 1889 in March Township, Carleton, Ontario, Canada, and died 03 Mar 1962 in Ottawa, Carleton, Ontario, Canada. She married EDGAR HAROLD HALL 19 Feb 1925 in Ottawa, Carleton, Ontario, Canada. He was born 21 Sep 1889 in Ottawa, Carleton, Ontario, Canada, and died 25 Mar 1978 in Ottawa, Carleton, Ontario, Canada.

Children of LEAH MILKS and EDGAR HALL are:
    i. DOROTHY GWENDOLIN[10] HALL. Never married.
1792. ii. HAMLYN 'SONNY' ROBERT HALL, b. 26 Jun 1928, Ottawa, Canada; d. 15 Nov 1998, Ottawa, Canada.

958. VERA[9] MILKS *(WILLIAM THOMAS[8], BENJAMIN[7], FREEBORN GARRETTSON[6], JOB[5] MILK, JONATHAN[4], JOB[3], JOHN[2], JOHN[1])* was born 26 Apr 1891 in Portage-du-Fort, Quebec, Canada, and died 1983 in Eardley, Quebec. She married IRA MERRIFIELD 17 Mar, son of THOMAS MERRIFIELD and MARY WILSON. He was born 19 Oct 1888 in Eardley, Quebec, and died 1982 in Eardley, Quebec.

Children of VERA MILKS and IRA MERRIFIELD are:
    i. ERIC HIBBERT[10] MERRIFIELD, b. 29 Jun 1921, Eardley, Quebec; d. 19 Aug 1921, Eardley, Quebec.
    ii. LORNA SHIRLEY MERRIFIELD, b. 19 May 1923, Eardley, Quebec; m. REV. FRANK L. STONE, 15 Jun 1946; b. Abt. 1923.

959. ERLE KENNETH[9] MILKS *(ROBERT KENNETH[8], BENJAMIN[7], FREEBORN GARRETTSON[6], JOB[5] MILK, JONATHAN[4], JOB[3], JOHN[2], JOHN[1])* was born 21 Dec 1888, and died 1967. He married HELEN CATHERINE CHRISTIE Bef. 1924. She was born 1900, and died 31 May 1970.

Children of ERLE MILKS and HELEN CHRISTIE are:
    i. ERLE MAYNE[10] MILKS, b. 1924, Chelsea, Quebec, Canada; d. 23 Sep 1944, Netherlands (WW II).
        ERLE MAYNE MILKS:
        MILKS, E M Flight Sergeant R/180687 23 September 1944 20 Royal Canadian Air Force Canadian Debt of Honour Register
        In Memory of ERLE MAYNE MILKS Flight Sergeant R/180687 Air Bomber 570 (R.A.F.) Sqdn, Royal Canadian Air Force who died on Saturday 23 September 1944 . Age 20 .
        Son of Erle Kenneth and Helen Catherine Milks, of Chelsea, Province of Quebec, Canada. Cemetery: HETEREN GENERAL CEMETERYGelderland, Netherlands Grave or Reference Panel Number: Plot 2. Row A. Grave 15A.
        Location: Heteren is a small village 12 kilometres south-west of Arnhem, on the south bank of the Neder (Lower) Rhine. The cemetery is 800 metres south of the village, at the junction of the roads leading to Randwijk and Homort. The graves are on the western side of the main path.
    ii. HELEN ELODIE MILKS, b. 1929, Carleton, Ontario, Canada; d. 28 Aug 1929, Carleton, Ontario, Canada.
1793. iii. AGNES IRENE MILKS, b. Canada.
    iv. MARIAN MILKS, b. Canada; m. WILLIAM 'BILL' ANDERSON, Bef. 1964, Canada.
    v. JOHN MILKS, b. Canada.
    vi. ROBERT MILKS, b. Canada.
    vii. NORMAN MILKS, b. Canada.
    viii. AUDREY MILKS, b. Canada; m. (1) FRED WARD, Bef. 1964; m. (2) BERNARD TRUDEAU, Bet. 1964 - 1970,

		Canada.
1794.	ix.	SHEILA MILKS, b. 1941, Canada.
	x.	HAROLD MILKS, b. Canada.
	xi.	JEAN ALMA MILKS, b. Abt. 1937, Canada; d. 18 May 2004, Ottawa, Ontario, Canada.

          OBITUARY - Ottawa Citizen - May 20, 2004

            MILKS, Alma

            Peacefully at Island Lodge on Tuesday, May 18th, 2004 at age 67 years.

          Predeceased by her parents Earl Milks and Helen Christie. Dear sister of Marian, Irene, John, Robert, Norman, Audrey, Sheila, Harold and predeceased by Erle Jr., James and Beatrice. Also survived by numerous nieces, nephews and cousins. Friends may visit at the McGarry Memorial Chapel, 139 Valley Road, Wakefield on Saturday, May 22nd, 2004 after 10:00 a.m. until service time in the Chapel at 11:00 a.m. Memorial donations to Island Lodge would be appreciated.

      xii. JAMES DAVID MILKS, b. 1943, Canada; d. 23 Jan 1964, Quebec, Canada.

          OBITUARY - *1964*

          Milks, James David - Accidentally, Thursday January 23, James David Milks, aged 20 of Chelsea Que., son of Earl Kenneth Milks and Ellen Christie, brother of John of Ottawa, Robert of Stittsville, Norman and Harold of Chelsea, Mrs. William Anderson (Marian) Burlington, Ont., Mrs. Edward Sheriden (Irene) Rivers Manitoba, Mrs. Fred Ward (Audrey) Richmond Que., Alma of Ottawa, Mrs. George Skokos (Beatrice) Ottawa, Mrs Harold Townsend (Sheila), Stevansville Ont., Reting at Emond's Funeral Home, St. Joseph Blvd., Hull where funeral service will be held Monday Jan. 27 at 2 o'clock. Internment Hall cemetery, Wakefield. Rev. R. L. Bacon will officiate.

1795.   xiii. BEATRICE CATHERINE MILKS, b. 23 Sep 1938, Canada; d. 17 Mar 2003, Wakefield, Quebec, Canada.

960. ELODIE MARGUERITE[9] MILKS *(ROBERT KENNETH[8], BENJAMIN[7], FREEBORN GARRETTSON[6], JOB[5] MILK, JONATHAN[4], JOB[3], JOHN[2], JOHN[1])* was born 27 Sep 1893 in Renfrew, Renfrew, Ontario. She married JOHN ALFRED SULLY 28 Sep 1912 in Ontario, Canada, son of JOHN SULLY and MARY KYLE. He was born 19 Nov 1892 in Carleton, Ontario, Canada, and died 23 Jun 1968.

    Air Vice Marshal, Royal Canadian Air Force, entrepreneur, President of Dominion Road Machinery Company and Champion Motor Graders Limited, builders of "Big Mudder", until that time the largest earth-moving device ever constructed in the world, etc.

Children of ELODIE MILKS and JOHN SULLY are:
1796.	i.	ELODIE MARGUERITE[10] SULLY, b. 20 Nov 1914, Winnipeg, Manitoba, Canada; d. 09 Jan 2005, Florida.
	ii.	JOHN KENNETH SULLY, b. 11 Nov 1920.
	iii.	BRUCE ALLENBY SULLY, b. 21 Mar 1926.

961. MARIAN ISABELLA LUSK[9] MILKS *(ROBERT KENNETH[8], BENJAMIN[7], FREEBORN GARRETTSON[6], JOB[5] MILK, JONATHAN[4], JOB[3], JOHN[2], JOHN[1])* was born 07 Apr 1899 in Renfrew County, Ontario, Canada, and died 14 Oct 1999 in Calgary, Alberta, Canada. She married JOSEPH ROBERT ROSS ACHESON 03 Jan 1922 in Ottawa, Ontario, Canada, son of SAMUEL ACHESON and LUCINDA PATTERSON. He was born 26 Jan 1891 in Westport, Ontario, Canada, and died 09 May 1933 in Oyen, Alberta, Canada.

Children of MARIAN MILKS and JOSEPH ACHESON are:
- i. ROSS KENNETH[10] ACHESON, b. Abt. 1923, Canada.
- ii. SHIRLEY ELSIE ACHESON, b. Abt. 1925, Canada.

962. ANDREW[9] MILKS *(GARRISON[8], AMBROSE[7], FREEBORN GARRETTSON[6], JOB[5] MILK, JONATHAN[4], JOB[3], JOHN[2], JOHN[1])* was born 02 Aug 1874 in Clarendon Tp., Pontiac Co., Quebec, Canada. He married AGNES MCNEILL 02 Jul 1897. She was born 15 Jun 1873, and died 1949 in Ontario, Canada.

Children of ANDREW MILKS and AGNES MCNEILL are:
- i. GARRISON[10] MILKS, b. 23 Dec 1897, Bristol Mines, Pontiac, Quebec, Canada; m. FLORENCE SCAFE.
- ii. BEULAH MILKS, b. 25 Jan 1900, Bristol Mines, Quebec, Canada; d. 19 Aug 1945; m. NICHOLL TRIP; b. Abt. 1900.
- iii. MINA MILKS, b. 13 Nov 1904, Bristol Mines, Quebec, Canada; m. HILLIARD PROPHET; b. Abt. 1900.

1797. iv. ANDREW LLOYD MILKS, b. 12 Dec 1906, Bristol Mines, Quebec, Canada; d. 1988, Ontario, Canada.
   v. CHRISTOPHER EARL MILKS, b. 27 Jan 1908, North Cobalt, Ontario; d. 1974, Ontario, Canada. Unmarried.
   vi. MARGARET MILKS, b. 06 May 1913, Bristol Mines, Quebec, Canada; m. AUSTIN HAYES; b. Abt. 1910.

963. MARY ALICE^9 MILKS *(GARRISON^8, AMBROSE^7, FREEBORN GARRETTSON^6, JOB^5 MILK, JONATHAN^4, JOB^3, JOHN^2, JOHN^1)* was born 16 Jun 1877 in Clarendon Tp., Pontiac Co., Quebec, Canada, and died 07 Oct 1948 in Quebec, Canada. She married JOHN MILLER 04 Sep 1901 in Quebec, Canada?. He was born 1877, and died 1950 in Quebec, Canada.

Children of MARY MILKS and JOHN MILLER are:
1798. i. CECIL C.^{10} MILLER, b. 02 Jan 1904, Bristol Mines, Quebec, Canada.
   ii. LILLIAN E. MILLER, b. 25 Mar 1911, Bristol Mines, Quebec, Canada; m. BEN CRAIG; b. Abt. 1910.
   iii. WILLIAM J. MILLER, b. 10 Nov 1912, Bristol Mines, Quebec, Canada; m. MARY FARRELL; b. Abt. 1912.

964. AMBROSE^9 MILKS *(GARRISON^8, AMBROSE^7, FREEBORN GARRETTSON^6, JOB^5 MILK, JONATHAN^4, JOB^3, JOHN^2, JOHN^1)* was born 01 May 1883 in Onslow, Quebec, Canada. He married ELIZABETH MILLER 12 Aug 1903 in Quebec, Canada?. She was born Apr 1883 in Canada.

Children of AMBROSE MILKS and ELIZABETH MILLER are:
   i. NORA^{10} MILKS, b. 28 Feb 1905, Bristol Mines, Quebec, Canada; m. PERCY RICHARDSON; b. Abt. 1905.
   ii. HAROLD A. MILKS, b. 25 Jan 1908, Bristol Mines, Quebec, Canada; d. 1992, Ontario, Canada; m. MARY E. SILVERTHORNE; b. 1918; d. 1999, Ontario, Canada.
   iii. MABEL MILKS, b. 25 Feb 1911, Bristol Mines, Quebec, Canada; m. DANNIE OTT; b. Abt. 1909.
1799. iv. VERNA MILKS, b. 25 Jan 1913, Bristol Mines, Quebec, Canada; d. Jun 1964.

965. WILLIAM ALEXANDER WILSON^9 MILKS *(GARRISON^8, AMBROSE^7, FREEBORN GARRETTSON^6, JOB^5 MILK, JONATHAN^4, JOB^3, JOHN^2, JOHN^1)* was born 30 Jul 1889 in Onslow, Quebec, Canada. He married MARY IDA MAYHEW 26 Mar 1907 in Quyon, Quebec, Canada, daughter of LOUIS MAYHEW and ARLENE PROULX. She was born 01 May 1887 in Masham, Quebec, Canada, and died 11 Aug 1955 in Capreol, Ontario.

Children of WILLIAM MILKS and MARY MAYHEW are:
1800. i. WINNIFRED J. L.^{10} MILKS, b. 28 Aug 1911, Canoe Lake, Ontario.
1801. ii. BYTHEA MILKS, b. 19 Mar 1914, Bristol Mines, Quebec, Canada.
1802. iii. WILLIAM L. L. MILKS, b. 30 Nov 1916, Bristol Mines, Quebec, Canada; d. 1979.
1803. iv. JOHN EBERT MILKS, b. 17 Feb 1920, Desaulniers, Ontario; d. 1979, Sudbury, Ontario, Canada.
1804. v. RALPH CLINTON MILKS, b. 28 Jan 1922, Sudbury, Ontario; d. 28 Dec 1972, Vancouver, British Columbia, Canada.
   vi. GERALDINE MILKS, b. 02 Jul 1924, Desaulniers, Ontario; d. 06 Apr 1926, Desaulniers, Ontario.
1805. vii. GERALD A. C. MILKS, b. 18 Apr 1927, Desaulniers, Ontario, Canada; d. 1996, Ontario, Canada.
1806. viii. LLEWELLYN 'LOU' W. G. MILKS, b. 12 Nov 1932, Desaulniers, Ontario; d. Feb 9, 198?; Sudbury, Ontario, Canada?.

966. ALBERT THOMAS^9 MILKS *(PATRICK 'PATT' ALBERT THOMAS^8, JOHN^7, FREEBORN GARRETTSON^6, JOB^5 MILK, JONATHAN^4, JOB^3, JOHN^2, JOHN^1)* was born 11 Nov 1888 in Ottawa, Carleton, Ontario, Canada. He married LAURA FARRELL, daughter of PHILIP W. FARRELL. She was born 1894, and died 1976.

Child of ALBERT MILKS and LAURA FARRELL is:
   i. CLARENCE^{10} MILKS, b. 1915, Ottawa, Carleton, Ontario; d. 24 Dec 1920, Ottawa, Carleton, Ontario.

967. DAVID VICTOR WILLIAM^9 MILKS *(PATRICK 'PATT' ALBERT THOMAS^8, JOHN^7, FREEBORN GARRETTSON^6, JOB^5 MILK, JONATHAN^4, JOB^3, JOHN^2, JOHN^1)* was born 11 Oct 1892 in Wrightsville, Quebec, Canada, and died 31 Aug 1990 in March, Carleton, Ontario, Canada. He married MURIEL MARY ELIZA PAPPIN. She was born 1889 in Beachburg, Quebec, Canada, and died 1974 in March, Carleton, Ontario, Canada.

Children of DAVID MILKS and MURIEL PAPPIN are:
   i. ERVAN V.^{10} MILKS, b. 19 Dec 1916, Ottawa, Ontario; d. 01 Sep 1936, Ottawa, Carleton, Ontario; m.

		VIOLET A. SULLIVAN; b. 26 Apr 1919; d. 06 Nov 1991, Ottawa, Carleton, Ontario.
	ii.	VERNA MILKS, b. 16 Sep 1918, Ottawa, Ontario; m. GORDON MUNRO; b. Abt. 1918.
1807.	iii.	GERALD ELMER MILKS, b. 10 Dec 1919, Ottawa, Ontario.
	iv.	MALE MILKS, b. 1922, Ottawa, Carleton, Ontario; d. 25 Jan 1922, Ottawa, Carleton, Ontario.
	v.	GWYNNETH 'GWEN' MILKS, b. 16 Jan 1923, Ottawa, Ontario; m. PHILIP SCANTLAND; b. Abt. 1920.
	vi.	IRA LESLIE MILKS, b. 1924; d. 10 Dec 1945, England.

MILKS, I L, Signalman C/100285 10 December 1945 21 Royal Canadian Corps of Signals

Debt of Honour Register

In Memory of IRA LESLIE MILKS Signalman C/100285 Royal Canadian Corps of Signals who died on Monday 10 December 1945 . Age 21 .

Additional Information: Son of Victor and Muriel Milks, of Ottawa, Ontario, Canada.

Cemetery: BROOKWOOD MILITARY CEMETERY Surrey, United Kingdom

Grave or Reference Panel Number: 58. A. 8.

Location: Brookwood is 30 miles from London (M3 to Bagshot and then A322). The main entrance to Brookwood Military Cemetery is on the A324 from the village of Pirbright.

1808.	vii.	REGINALD VINCENT MILKS, b. 22 Nov 1927, Ottawa, Ontario, Canada; d. 15 Mar 2003, Ottawa, Ontario (age 75).
	viii.	MALETWO MILKS, b. 1931, Ottawa, Carleton, Ontario; d. 16 May 1931, Ottawa, Carleton, Ontario.

968. HERBERT JOSEPH^9 MILKS *(PATRICK 'PATT' ALBERT THOMAS^8, JOHN^7, FREEBORN GARRETTSON^6, JOB^5 MILK, JONATHAN^4, JOB^3, JOHN^2, JOHN^1)* was born 17 Mar 1907 in Aylmergace, Quebec, Canada, and died 1988 in Hamilton, Ontario, Canada. He married LISLE WILCOX 21 May 1927 in Church of England, Windsor, Ontario, Canada, daughter of THOMAS WILCOX and BELLA COONS. She was born 29 Dec 1909 in Lincoln County, Grimsby, Ontario, Canada, and died 28 Aug 1991 in Hamilton, Ontario, Canada.

U.S. Naturalization Records Indexes, 1794-1995 about Herbert Joseph Milks

Name: Herbert Joseph Milks Birth Date: 17 Mar 1907 State: Michigan

Locality, Court: Detroit, District Court [Sept 19, 1928]

OBTUARY

Herbert "Herb" Joseph Milks was born 17 March 1907 in Aylmer, Quebec, Canada to Patrick Albert Thomas Milks (1848) and Julia Kenny. He resided in Aylmer until his marriage to Lisle Wilcox. Lisle was born 29 December 1909 Lincoln County, Grimsby, Ontario, Canada. Her birth wasn't registered until 21 April 1927. Her father is listed as Thomas Wilcox and mother as Bella Wilcox (nee Coons). One month later, 21 May 1927, Herbert and Lisle were married by the Church of England in Windsor, Ontario. His brother Laurence and his wife of 510 Caron Avenue, Windsor, Ontario signed as witnesses. Herbert was 20 years old, working as a shipping clerk and Lisle was just 17 years old. At this time, Thomas Wilcox gave his permission in a signed note for the two of them to marry. They had 2 daughters; Helen born abt. 1926 and Shirley** born 26 August 1928. Both girls were born and raised in Grimsby. Throughout the end of the 1920s and early 1930s, Herbert travelled extensively between Canada and Detroit, Michigan with his brother Laurence. Laurence was a hockey player, he may have played for the Hamilton Tigers, and Herbert travelled with him as a skate sharpener. Herbert was naturalized as a U.S. citizen 19 September 1928. While Herbert was away, Lisle raised the children with the help of her parents and siblings on Grimsby Beach. Lisle helped her mother who ran a little concession stand on the beach. Shirley and Helen remember the days at the beach filled with fun and excitement. When WWII broke out, Herbert served as a cook in the Canadian Armed Forces. These records are still sealed. He was discharged from the war after sustaining an injury leaving him blind in one eye. (Although the army believed it was a war injury, he actually got glass in his eye from a bar fight during the war!)

Following his war time, Herbert found work as a butcher and cook for the St. Joseph's Hospital in Hamilton, Ontario. While working for the hospital he cut off at least 2 fingers and sliced open his abdomen. After leaving the hospital Herbert and Lisle ran the concession stand at Sportsman Lanes in Hamilton until retiring to their apartment in St. John's Place on Wellington Street in Hamilton, Ontario. After Herbert's death, Lisle moved to a nursing home. Helen married William "Bill" West (and moved to Stratford, Ontario) and Shirley married John "Jack" Hall Weir Heugh. Helen and Bill West had 8 children: Faye, Heather, Jack, Joseph, Julia, twins Paul and Pauline, and Shirley. Shirley and Jack Heugh had 2 children: Herbert John and Nancy Jean. Herbert's grandson (and namesake) John remembers taking a trip to Ottawa with him to visit Julia Kenny abt. 1960. John was very close to Lisle and spent many days and nights at their apartment at 593 ½ King Street East in Hamilton (this apartment was above a Credit Union). "Having some drinks (beer for Herbert and apricot brandy for Lisle), doing a little arguing and playing cards is what kept them together", Lisle would say about her and Herb.

Herbert Joseph Milks died from a stroke in the winter of 1988 in Hamilton, Ontario, Canada. Lisle Milks (nee Wilcox) died of pulmonary disease and emphysema 28 Aug 1991 in Townsview Nursing Home, Hamilton, Ontario, Canada. Lisle and Herbert are buried side by side in Holy Sepulchre Catholic Cemetery on Plains Road in Burlington, Ontario, Canada.

Children of HERBERT MILKS and LISLE WILCOX are:
1809.   i.   HELEN[10] MILKS, b. Abt. 1930, Grimsby, Ontario, Canada [Date ????].
1810.   ii.   SHIRLEY BELLE MILKS, b. 26 Aug 1928, Grimsby, Ontario, Canada; d. 02 Jun 2008, Hamilton, Ontario, Canada.

969. ALMIRA[9] MILKS *(PETER[8], JOHN[7], FREEBORN GARRETTSON[6], JOB[5] MILK, JONATHAN[4], JOB[3], JOHN[2], JOHN[1])* was born 27 Jan 1896 in Hull, Ottawa, Quebec, Canada. She married GILBERT CHOQUETTE 28 Feb 1922 in Ottawa, Ontario, Canada. He was born 03 Jul 1894, and died 18 Aug 1974.

Child of ALMIRA MILKS and GILBERT CHOQUETTE is:
         i.   WILLIAM JOHN ULRIC[10] CHOQUETTE, b. 1926, Ottawa, Carleton, Ontario; d. 17 Oct 1926, Ottawa, Carleton, Ontario.

970. MALINDA MARTHA[9] MILKS *(PETER[8], JOHN[7], FREEBORN GARRETTSON[6], JOB[5] MILK, JONATHAN[4], JOB[3], JOHN[2], JOHN[1])* was born 29 Jul 1898 in Hull, Ottawa, Quebec, Canada. She married JAMES KYLE.

Child of MALINDA MILKS and JAMES KYLE is:
1811.   i.   LOLA[10] KYLE.

971. FLORENCE[9] MILKS *(ANTHONY[8], JOHN[7], FREEBORN GARRETTSON[6], JOB[5] MILK, JONATHAN[4], JOB[3], JOHN[2], JOHN[1])* was born 24 Jul 1886 in Cantley, Quebec, and died 1965 in Cantley, Quebec. She married CHRISTOPHER C. HOLMES. He was born 1874, and died 1959 in Cantley, Quebec.

Children of FLORENCE MILKS and CHRISTOPHER HOLMES are:
1812.   i.   ROMA[10] HOLMES, b. Abt. 1910.
         ii.   J. VIVIAN HOLMES, b. 1912; d. 1981, Cantley, Quebec; m. IMELDA MARY TRUDEAU; b. 1914; d. 1997, Cantley, Quebec.
         iii.   MARY HOLMES, b. Abt. 1913; d. Abt. 1913, Died at birth.
1813.   iv.   LILLIAN HOLMES, b. Abt. 1915.
         v.   JEAN HOLMES, b. Abt. 1917; d. No children; m. EDWARD LAWLOR.
1814.   vi.   MARY MORNA HOLMES.
1815.   vii.   HILIARY HOLMES.
1816.   viii.   MARY HOLMES.

972. HERBERT[9] MILKS *(ANTHONY[8], JOHN[7], FREEBORN GARRETTSON[6], JOB[5] MILK, JONATHAN[4], JOB[3], JOHN[2], JOHN[1])* was born 17 Jan 1889 in Cantley, Quebec, and died 09 Dec 1943 in Sudbury, Ontario (while working at International Nickel Co.). He married (1) THERESA FLEMING. She was born 26 Dec 1891, and died 09 Jun 1915. He married (2) CATHERINE THERESA MULCAHEY, daughter of JAMES MULCAHEY and MARGARET HOLMES. She was born 11 Oct 1899 in Wakefield, Ottawa West, Quebec, Canada, and died 04 Apr 1993.
OBITUARY - Ottawa Citizen - December 10, 1943 - Herbert Milks, Former Ottawa, Killed In Mine

Herbert Milks, former resident of Ottawa and brother of Mrs. Henry Thibaudeau, 134 Henderson Avenue, was killed instantly yesterday noon at the Frood Mine in Sudbury, where he was employed as underground foreman for the past 15 years.

There were no witnesses to the accident, but it is believed that he was crushed by one of the large ventilation doors which apparently slammed shut by the concussion of a dynamite blast. The accident occurred on the 1,800 foot level of the mine.

Mr. Milks, who resided in Ottawa for several years before going to Northern Ontario, was born in Cantley, a son of Mrs. Frances Milks and the late Anthony Milks. For about 10 years after leaving Ottawa he was employed at the McIntyre Mines at Schumacher and then accepted the position at the Frood Mines. He was twice married, and was of Catholic faith.

Surviving in addition to his widow, the former Theresa Mulcahey, whom he married 18 years ago, are two sons, Garnet Milks (by his first marriage) and Basil Milks, 14 of Sudbury, a daughter Patricia, 9 at home; two brothers, Hector of Cantley and Bernard Milks of Sudbury, and two sisters, Mrs. Henry Thibaudeau of Ottawa and Mrs. Christopher Holmes of Cantley.

The body will arrive in Ottawa tomorrow morning at 8:30 o'clock and will rest at the parlors of McEvoy Brothers, 235 Kent Street. The funeral arrangements have not been completed.

Children of HERBERT MILKS and CATHERINE MULCAHEY are:
- i. GARNET[10] MILKS, b. Abt. 1925, Timmins, Ontario.
- 1817. ii. BASIL MILKS, b. 16 Jun 1929, Sudbury, Ontario, Canada; d. 30 Oct 2011, Sudbury, Ontario, Canada.
- iii. PATRICIA MILKS, b. Abt. 1934, Sudbury, Ontario.

973. LAURA[9] MILKS (ANTHONY[8], JOHN[7], FREEBORN GARRETTSON[6], JOB[5] MILK, JONATHAN[4], JOB[3], JOHN[2], JOHN[1]) was born 19 Feb 1894 in Cantley, Quebec, and died 07 May 1966 in Cantley, Quebec. She married HENRY C. THIBAUDEAU. He was born 27 Jun 1891, and died 28 Oct 1948 in Cantley, Quebec.

Children of LAURA MILKS and HENRY THIBAUDEAU are:
- 1818. i. BERNARD[10] THIBAUDEAU.
- 1819. ii. BERNICE THIBAUDEAU.
- iii. JANNET THIBAUDEAU.
- iv. LILLIAN THIBAUDEAU, b. Jan 1920, Cantley, Quebec; d. 21 Jul 1920, Cantley, Quebec.
- v. HELENA THIBAUDEAU, b. 31 Mar 1921, Cantley, Quebec; d. 08 Apr 1921, Cantley, Quebec.
- vi. PHYLLIS THIBAUDEAU, b. 10 May 1922, Cantley, Quebec; d. 17 May 1922, Cantley, Quebec.

974. OWEN BERNARD[9] MILKS (ANTHONY[8], JOHN[7], FREEBORN GARRETTSON[6], JOB[5] MILK, JONATHAN[4], JOB[3], JOHN[2], JOHN[1]) was born 10 Jun 1902 in Cantley, Quebec, and died 26 Aug 1986 in Cantley, Quebec. He married JANE BERNADETTE HORAN 24 Jul 1927 in Quinnville, Quebec, daughter of JAMES HORAN and HANNAH PRUDHOMME. She was born 13 Sep 1906 in Quinnville, Quebec, and died 06 Aug 1983 in Cantley, Quebec.

Bernard worked as a carpenter, contractor, and was engaged in the real estate business. He had extensive property holdings in Quebec. Owen contributed many records for the Milks family history.

Child of OWEN MILKS and JANE HORAN is:
- 1820. i. ANTHONY RONALD JAMES[10] MILKS, b. 20 Sep 1934, Ottawa, Ontario; d. 10 May 1979.

975. HENRY ACTOR GERALD 'HECTOR'[9] MILKS (ANTHONY[8], JOHN[7], FREEBORN GARRETTSON[6], JOB[5] MILK, JONATHAN[4], JOB[3], JOHN[2], JOHN[1]) was born 30 Aug 1905 in Cantley, Quebec, Canada, and died 11 Jan 1982 in Cantley, Quebec, Canada. He married ANNE ELIZABETH ELLEN 'NELLIE' MULCAHEY 24 Nov 1931 in St. Elisabeth's Church, Cantley, Quebec, daughter of JAMES MULCAHEY and MARGARET HOLMES. She was born 14 Jul 1908 in Cantley, Quebec, Canada, and died 24 Sep 2003 in Cantley, Quebec, Canada.

OBITUARY - Ottawa Citizen - 1982 - Hector Milks
HENRY ACTOR GERALD 'HECTOR' MILKS:

In Gatineau Memorial Hospital in Wakefield on Monday, January 11, 1982, Hector Gerald Milks of Cantley, Quebec. Dearly loved husband of Ellen (Nellie) Mulcahey. Dear father of Audrey McNulty of Hull, Arnold of Cantley, Ellard of Ottawa, Elva (Mrs. John Perron) of Poltimore, Quebec, Bernadette of Quyon, Helen (Mrs. Danny Scissons) of Richmond, Ontario and Marion Verdon of Cantley.

Dear brother of Bernard Milks of Ottawa. Loving grandfather of 30 grandchildren and 8 great-grandchildren. Predeceased by a granddaughter, Mary Milks.

Friends may call at the McEvoy-Shields Funeral Home, 235 Kent Street, from 2 to 10 Tuesday and Wednesday. Funeral Thursday to St. Elisabeth's Church, Cantley for mass at 10 am. Interment parish cemetery. Those desiring may make donations to the Gatineau Memorial Hospital, Wakefield, Quebec.

Children of HENRY MILKS and ANNE MULCAHEY are:
- 1821. i. AUDREY MARGARET GRACE[10] MILKS, b. 01 Sep 1932, Hull, Quebec, Canada; d. 13 Oct 1989, Hull, Quebec, Canada.
- 1822. ii. JOSEPH ARNOLD HECTOR MILKS, b. 26 Jul 1933; d. 02 Jul 2006.

	iii.	ELLARD ANTHONY MILKS, b. 06 Nov 1934, Cantley, Quebec, Canada; d. 18 Dec 2009.
1823.		
1824.	iv.	ELVA MILKS, b. 08 May 1936.
1825.	v.	BERNADETTE CATHERINE GRACE ANNE MILKS, b. 24 Oct 1939, Hull, Quebec, Canada.
1826.	vi.	HELEN MILKS, b. 02 Jan 1941, Canada.
1827.	vii.	MARION MILKS, b. 30 Sep 1942, Cantley, Que.; d. Bef. 18 Dec 2009.

976. JAMES THOMAS[9] MILKS *(DAVID[8], JOHN[7], FREEBORN GARRETTSON[6], JOB[5] MILK, JONATHAN[4], JOB[3], JOHN[2], JOHN[1])* was born 14 Jun 1888 in Cantley, Quebec, Canada, and died 1950. He married CATHERINE ROSE 'KATIE' LAVELLE, daughter of ANTHONY LAVELLE. She was born 1889 in Mayo, Quebec, Canada, and died 1991.

Child of JAMES MILKS and CATHERINE LAVELLE is:
  i. HAROLD ANTHONY DAVID AMBROSE[10] MILKS, b. 07 Dec 1917, Hull, Quebec, Canada; d. 29 Nov 1925, Ottawa, Ontario, Canada.

977. JOHN AUSTIN[9] MILKS *(DAVID[8], JOHN[7], FREEBORN GARRETTSON[6], JOB[5] MILK, JONATHAN[4], JOB[3], JOHN[2], JOHN[1])* was born 11 Oct 1889 in Quebec, Canada, and died 31 May 1945 in Hull Twp, Quebec, Canada. He married MARY MAUD MILDRED BLANCHFIELD 1914, daughter of WILLIAM BLANCHFIELD and MARY BURKE. She was born 05 May 1893 in Cantley, Quebec, Canada, and died 06 Apr 1944 in Hull Twp, Quebec, Canada.

OBITUARY - Ottawa Citizen - April 7, 1944 - Milks

At her residence, 36 Lois St., Hull on Thursday, April 6, 1944, Mildred Blanchfield, aged 50 years, beloved wife of John Milks. Resting at the parlors of McEvoy Bros., 235 Kent Street (cor. Nepean). Funeral on Saturday, the 8th inst. at 2 o'clock to St. Joseph's Church, Wrightsville, for Libera service at 2:30 pm, thence to Notre Dame vault Ottawa. Burial at Cantley in May.

Ottawa Citizen - April 7, 1944 - Mrs. John Milks

A resident of Hull for 20 years, Mrs. John Milks, the former Mildred Blanchfield, died early yesterday at her home, 36 Lois Street, Hull. She was in her 51st year.

Born at Cantley, Quebec, she had lived there until coming to Hull in 1923. She was a member of St. Joseph's Roman Catholic Church at Wrightsville. Her husband, John Milks, survives.

Also surviving, besides her father, William Blanchfield, are three sons, Maynard with the RCAF at Mount Joli and Keith and Lorne of Hull, six daughters; Gladys, Evelyn, Phyliss, Eileen, Lois and Bernice, all at home, three brothers; Maynard of Ottawa, Herman and Kevin of Montreal, two sisters; Mrs. E. Horne of Sudbury and Mrs. N. Spiers of Detroit and several nieces and nephews.

The body is resting at the parlors of McEvoy Brothers, 235 Kent Street.

Children of JOHN MILKS and MARY BLANCHFIELD are:
  i. JOSEPH KENNETH LORNE[10] MILKS, b. 03 Jan, Quebec, Canada.
  ii. JOSEPH MAYNARD GERALD MILKS, b. 24 May, Quebec, Canada.
  iii. MARY FRANCIS BERNICE MILKS, b. 27 May, Quebec, Canada; m. GERALD MCLEAN.
  iv. MARY VELMA GLADYS MILKS, b. 31 Jul 1915, Quebec, Canada; d. 30 Aug 1998, Cantley, Quebec.
  v. MARY EVELYN PAMELLA MILKS, b. 07 Jul 1917, Hull, Quebec, Canada; d. 13 Mar 1947, Hull, Cantley, Quebec (Unmarried).

1828. vi. MARY MYRTLE PHYLLIS MILKS, b. 20 Oct 1920, Quebec, Canada; d. 12 Nov 2001, Cantley, Quebec.
  vii. MARY CATHERINE LOIS MILKS, b. 03 Aug 1926, Hull, Quebec, Canada; d. 28 Apr 1969, Ottawa, Ontario, Canada; m. RONALD KIRBY.

  DEATH NOTICE:

  Ottawa Citizen - April 30, 1969 - Kirby, Lois

  In hospital on Monday, April 28, 1969, Lois Milks, age 42 of 566 Lisgar St., beloved wife of Ronald Kirby, daughter of the late Mr. and Mrs. John Milks, dear sister to Keith, Lorne, Gladys, Phyllis (Mrs. Donald Campbell), Bernice (Mrs. Gerald McLean). Resting at the Kelly Funeral Home, 585 Somerset St. (center town). Funeral Thursday to St. Patrick's Church for mass at 10 am. Interment St. Elizabeth's cemetery, Cantley.

  viii. MARY MAVIS EILEEN MILKS, b. 03 Aug 1926, Cantley, Quebec; d. 16 Nov 1944, Cantley, Quebec.
1829. ix. JOSEPH JOHN KEITH MILKS, b. 16 Aug 1931, Quebec, Canada; d. 10 Jun 1980, Hull, Quebec, Canada.

978. DAVID AMBROSE[9] MILKS *(DAVID[8], JOHN[7], FREEBORN GARRETTSON[6], JOB[5] MILK, JONATHAN[4], JOB[3], JOHN[2], JOHN[1])* was born 18 May 1891 in Cantley, Quebec, and died 1950 in Cantley, Quebec. He married EMILY "EMMA" LLOYD 04 Nov 1913 in St. Francis Assizi Church, Ottawa, Canada, daughter of WILLIAM LLOYD and MARY EVANS. She was born 1894, and died 1975 in Cantley, Quebec.

Children of DAVID MILKS and EMILY LLOYD are:
  i. FEMALE[10] MILKS, b. 13 Dec 1914, Ottawa, Carleton, Ontario; d. 13 Dec 1914, Ottawa, Carleton, Ontario.
  ii. MALE MILKS, b. 1922, Ottawa, Carleton, Ontario; d. 19 Jan 1922, Ottawa, Carleton, Ontario.

979. MARIA EVA ISABELLA ABIGAIL[9] MILKS *(DAVID[8], JOHN[7], FREEBORN GARRETTSON[6], JOB[5] MILK, JONATHAN[4], JOB[3], JOHN[2], JOHN[1])* was born 03 Dec 1893 in Cantley, Quebec, Canada, and died 04 Aug 1974 in Ottawa, Ontario, Canada. She married PATRICK JAMES CULLEN 26 Aug 1913 in Cantley, Quebec, Canada. He was born 12 Jul 1890 in Quebec, Canada, and died 26 Nov 1962 in Ottawa, Ontario, Canada.

DEATH NOTICE

Ottawa Citizen - August 6, 1974 - Mrs. Abigail Cullen

In hospital, on Sunday, August 4, 1974, Abigail Milks widow of Patrick James Cullen, dear mother of David, Orville and Mrs. Doris McEwen. Dear sister of Joseph Milks of Ottawa and Raymond Milks of Montreal. Also survived by 9 grandchildren. Resting at the Kelly Funeral Home, 585 Somerset Street W. (center town). Funeral Wednesday to Our Lady of Perpetual Help Church for mass at 7:45 am. Interment Notre Dame Cemetery.

Children of MARIA MILKS and PATRICK CULLEN are:

1830. i. WILBERT JAMES[10] CULLEN, b. Aug 1914, Ottawa, Ontario, Canada; d. 04 Aug 1965, Ottawa, Ontario, Canada.
  ii. MARY ELIZABETH KATHLEEN LILLIAN CULLEN, b. 20 Jul 1916, Quebec, Canada; d. 11 Jan 1944, Ottawa, Ontario, Canada; m. PAUL BURKE, Jul 1943; b. Abt. 1915. No children.

  Ottawa Citizen - January 13, 1944 - Burke

  At a local hospital on Tuesday, January 11, 1944, Kathleen Lillian Cullen, aged 26 years, beloved wife of Paul Burke, 535 Albert Street. Resting at the parlors of McEvoy Brothers, 235 Kent Street (cor. Nepean). Funeral Friday, 14th inst. at 8:45 am to Our Lady of Perpetual Help church for requiem mass at 9 o'clock. Thence to Notre Dame vault.

  Ottawa Citizen - January 13, 1944 - Mrs. Paul Burke

  A host of friends in the Capital will learn with deep regret of the passing at a local hospital Tuesday of Mrs. Paul Burke, a well-known member of Our Lady of Perpetual Help Church and the Ottawa branch of the Canadian National Institute for the Blind. Mrs. Burke, who was 26 years of age, had been ill for only a week.

  The funeral will be held on Friday morning from the parlors of McEvoy Brothers, 235 Kent Street to Our Lady of Perpetual Help Church for requiem high mass at nine o'clock. The body will be placed in the Notre dame vault for burial in the spring.

  The former Lillian 'Kay' Cullen, she was born in Hull, a daughter of Mr. and Mrs. James P. Cullen, who reside at 535 Albert Street. She moved to Ottawa with her parents when she was still a child, and last July married Mr. Burke.

  iii. DAVID ALBERT JOSEPH CULLEN, b. 30 Mar 1919, Ontario, Canada; d. 1990; m. UNNAMED, 24 Jul 1948, Ottawa, Ontario, Canada.
  iv. JOSEPH PATRICK LEONARD CULLEN, b. 30 Mar 1919, Ontario, Canada; d. 28 Dec 1944, Sandefjord, Vestfold, Norway.
1831. v. ORVILLE JOSEPH GERALD CULLEN, b. 06 Sep 1923, Ottawa, Ontario, Canada; d. 26 Aug 2002, Carleton County, Ontario, Canada.
  vi. DORIS ANNIE ABIGAIL CULLEN, b. 16 May 1925, Ottawa, Ontario, Canada; d. 01 Mar 1994; m. KENNETH MCEWEN; b. 25 Sep 1924; d. 21 Jul 1988.
  vii. JOSEPH PATRICK ELDON CULLEN, b. 11 Mar 1930, Ottawa, Ontario, Canada; d. 23 Jun 1945, Ottawa, Ontario, Canada [Drowned at Bathing Island, Rideau River, while attempting to rescue others].
  viii. JAMES ROBERT BERNARD CULLEN, b. 03 Feb 1932, Ottawa, Ontario, Canada; d. 1970.

980. JOSEPH EDWARD[9] MILKS *(DAVID[8], JOHN[7], FREEBORN GARRETTSON[6], JOB[5] MILK, JONATHAN[4], JOB[3], JOHN[2], JOHN[1])* was born 14 Nov 1895 in Cantley, Quebec, Canada, and died 26 Jul 1976 in Cantley, Quebec, Canada. He married LILLIAN THERESA COOGAN 28 Jun 1922 in Ottawa, Ontario, Canada, daughter of RICHARD COOGAN and MARY BRENMAN. She was born 1900 in Masham, Quebec, Canada, and died 1992 in Cantley, Quebec, Canada.

Children of JOSEPH MILKS and LILLIAN COOGAN are:
- i. DOROTHY^{10} MILKS, m. ROBERT BELIER.
- 1832. ii. CHARLOTTE MARY T. MILKS, b. 1927; d. 23 Oct 2004.
- 1833. iii. JOSEPH GERALD CECIL MILKS, b. 31 Mar 1933, Ottawa, Ontario, Canada; d. 18 Jan 2013, Ottawa, Ontario, Canada.
- iv. MARY MILKS, b. 15 Apr 1923, Ottawa, Ontario, Canada; d. 15 Apr 1923, Ottawa, Ontario, Canada.

981. ALBERT FRANCIS "FRANK"^{9} MILKS *(DAVID^8, JOHN^7, FREEBORN GARRETTSON^6, JOB^5 MILK, JONATHAN^4, JOB^3, JOHN^2, JOHN^1)* was born 09 Jul 1900 in Cantley, Quebec, and died 1968 in Cantley, Quebec. He married CORA VANASSE 05 Nov 1921, daughter of OLIVER VANASSE and ELIZABETH _____. She was born 1900 in Chapeau, Quebec, and died 1977 in Cantley, Quebec.

Children of ALBERT MILKS and CORA VANASSE are:
- 1834. i. DOREEN^{10} MILKS, b. 04 Nov 1922.
- 1835. ii. MARVEL MILKS, b. 07 Feb 1925, Ottawa, Ontario.
- iii. F. LORRAINE 'PEGGY' MILKS, b. 11 Jun 1927, Ottawa, Ontario; d. 1972; m. WILLIAM J. CAMPBELL; b. Abt. 1925.
- 1836. iv. DONALD MILKS, b. 19 Feb 1930.
- v. LYNDA MILKS, b. 12 Sep 1944.

982. RAYMOND PETER^9 MILKS *(DAVID^8, JOHN^7, FREEBORN GARRETTSON^6, JOB^5 MILK, JONATHAN^4, JOB^3, JOHN^2, JOHN^1)* was born 22 Nov 1903 in Cantley, Quebec, Canada, and died 09 Aug 1983 in Cantley, Quebec, Canada. He married EDNA ANNA HAWLEY. She was born 04 Nov 1905, and died 18 Jan 1993.

Children of RAYMOND MILKS and EDNA HAWLEY are:
- i. THREE DAUGHTERS^{10} MILKS.
- 1837. ii. MARGARET ANN MILKS, b. 1934, Cantley, Quebec, Canada; d. 1989.

983. RICHARD ANTHONY^9 MILKS *(DAVID^8, JOHN^7, FREEBORN GARRETTSON^6, JOB^5 MILK, JONATHAN^4, JOB^3, JOHN^2, JOHN^1)* was born 03 Jul 1905 in Cantley, Quebec, and died 1964. He married GWENDOLYN THERESA LATHEM 27 Oct 1923 in Carleton, Ontario, Canada, daughter of ROBERT LATHEM and BARBARA NICHOL. She was born 1905 in Ottawa, Ontario, and died 1959 in Aylmer (Gatineau), Quebec.

Children of RICHARD MILKS and GWENDOLYN LATHEM are:
- 1838. i. VIOLA RETA^{10} MILKS, b. 18 Jul 1924, Ottawa, Ontario.
- 1839. ii. CATHELINE MILKS, b. 23 Jul 1925, Ottawa, Ontario.
- 1840. iii. VIDA BERNADETTE MILKS, b. 28 Mar 1927, Ottawa, Ontario.
- 1841. iv. BEVERLY BARBARA MILKS, b. 28 Feb 1929, Ottawa, Ontario.
- 1842. v. WALLACE 'WALLY' JOSEPH MILKS, b. 18 Jun 1930, Ottawa, Ontario; d. 08 Apr 2011, Ottawa, Canada.
- vi. ROBERT ANDREW MILKS, b. 28 Aug 1931, Ottawa, Ontario.
- vii. RICHARD ANTHONY MILKS, b. 03 Jul 1936, Ottawa, Ontario; d. 26 Nov 1978, Ontario, Canada; m. MARIE SUSIE _____; b. 1938.
- viii. GWENDOLYN THERESA MILKS, b. 02 Jun 1938, Ottawa, Ontario; m. EDWARD D. TACHNYK, 07 Jan 1956; b. Abt. 1938.
- ix. DIANE MARGARET MILKS, b. 03 Dec 1941, Ottawa, Ontario; m. MISTRE FORD.

984. PATRICK AMBROSE^9 MILKS *(PETER FELIX^8, JOHN^7, FREEBORN GARRETTSON^6, JOB^5 MILK, JONATHAN^4, JOB^3, JOHN^2, JOHN^1)* was born 20 Aug 1890 in Cantley, Quebec, and died 15 Apr 1956 in Hull Twp, Quebec. He married RUTH AGNES MILES 23 Jan 1917 in Ottawa, Ontario, daughter of WILLIAM MILES and HANNAH WHITE. She was born 20 Oct 1897 in Ottawa, Ontario, and died 10 Sep 1959 in Hull Twp, Quebec.

Children of PATRICK MILKS and RUTH MILES are:
1843. i. CLARA ROSE[10] MILKS, b. 26 Jun 1918, Ottawa, Ontario; d. 05 May 1960, Ottawa, Ontario.
1844. ii. WILLIAM JOHN MILKS, b. 16 Aug 1919, Ottawa, Ontario; d. 1981.
iii. AUDREY RUTH MILKS, b. 08 Apr 1921, Ottawa, Ontario; d. Abt. 1983, Hull Twp, Quebec; m. RONALD DUFOUR; b. Abt. 1920.
iv. ELDON MILKS, b. 1922; d. 1922, Ottawa, Ontario.
1845. v. GERALDINE ABIGAIL MILKS, b. 13 Jun 1923, Ottawa, Ontario.
1846. vi. THORAH HANNAH MILKS, b. 28 Apr 1925, Ottawa, Ontario.
vii. GARNET THOMAS MILKS, b. 04 Aug 1927, Ottawa, Ontario; m. GAYE CANNING; b. Abt. 1930.
viii. MERLE MILKS, b. 07 Apr 1931, Ottawa, Ontario.
ix. STERLING ARNOLD MILKS, b. 30 Oct 1931, Ottawa, Ontario; d. 08 Jun 1987.
x. MILES "BO" MILKS, b. Sep, Ottawa, Ontario.
1847. xi. HILARY MILKS, b. 19 Jan, Ottawa, Ontario.
1848. xii. NEELIN MILKS, b. 03 Apr, Ottawa, Ontario.
xiii. MARILYN THERESA MILKS, b. 24 Sep 1939, Ottawa, Ontario.
1849. xiv. IVAN "JOE" EDWARD MILKS, b. 22 Mar, Ottawa, Ontario; d. Bef. 07 May 2007.

985. JAMES THOMAS[9] MILKS (PETER FELIX[8], JOHN[7], FREEBORN GARRETTSON[6], JOB[5] MILK, JONATHAN[4], JOB[3], JOHN[2], JOHN[1]) was born Apr 1904 in Cantley, Quebec, Canada. He married CECILE LEONARD 07 Jul 1943 in Notre Dame de, Pontmain, Quebec.

Children of JAMES MILKS and CECILE LEONARD are:
1850. i. MADELEINE[10] MILKS, b. 29 May 1944.
1851. ii. MARIE MARTHE MILKS, b. 08 Sep 1945.
iii. MARKI MILKS, b. 25 Jan 1951, Ontario?, Quebec?; d. 1977; m. MURIELLE LYNESS; b. Abt. 1951.
iv. MARJOLAINE MILKS, b. 19 Mar 1956; m. ROBERT VIENNEAU.

986. DAVID[9] MILKS (DANIEL[8], JOHN[7], FREEBORN GARRETTSON[6], JOB[5] MILK, JONATHAN[4], JOB[3], JOHN[2], JOHN[1]) was born 09 Mar 1909, and died 04 Aug 1960. He married FERNANDE PORTELANCE 1932. She was born 21 Feb 1910, and died 12 May 1973.

Children of DAVID MILKS and FERNANDE PORTELANCE are:
1852. i. JOSEPH RICHARD EMILE[10] MILKS, b. 1933.
1853. ii. MARCEL MILKS, b. 04 Mar 1944, Hull, Quebec, Canada.

987. GEORGE DAVID[9] FINDLEY (SARAH JANE[8] MILKS, DAVID[7], FREEBORN GARRETTSON[6], JOB[5] MILK, JONATHAN[4], JOB[3], JOHN[2], JOHN[1]) was born 1886 in Beech Grove, Quebec, Canada. He married EVA ERWIN. She was born Abt. 1886.

Children of GEORGE FINDLEY and EVA ERWIN are:
1854. i. ALLAN[10] FINDLEY.
1855. ii. EVELYN FINDLEY.
1856. iii. HAZEL FINDLEY.
1857. iv. BERYL FINDLEY.
1858. v. GERALD FINDLEY.
1859. vi. ERIC FINDLEY.

988. FRED BALMER[9] FINDLEY (SARAH JANE[8] MILKS, DAVID[7], FREEBORN GARRETTSON[6], JOB[5] MILK, JONATHAN[4], JOB[3], JOHN[2], JOHN[1]) was born 1887 in Beech Grove, Quebec, Canada. He married (1) WINIFRED SHELDON. She was born Abt. 1887. He married (2) NETTIE BARNES.

Children of FRED FINDLEY and WINIFRED SHELDON are:
1860. i. EDNA[10] FINDLEY.
1861. ii. ERNEST FINDLEY.
1862. iii. ELMER FINDLEY.
1863. iv. KEITH FINDLEY.

1864. v. ELLEN FINDLEY.
1865. vi. LEONARD FINDLEY.

989. FLORENCE MAY^9 FINDLEY *(SARAH JANE^8 MILKS, DAVID^7, FREEBORN GARRETTSON^6, JOB^5 MILK, JONATHAN^4, JOB^3, JOHN^2, JOHN^1)* was born 1890 in Beech Grove, Quebec, Canada. She married WILLIAM DRAPER. He was born Abt. 1890.

Children of FLORENCE FINDLEY and WILLIAM DRAPER are:
1866. i. EDWARD^{10} DRAPER.
1867. ii. VIOLA DRAPER.
       iii. EDITH DRAPER.
1868. iv. KENNETH DRAPER, b. Twin.
1869. v. KEITH DRAPER, b. Twin.
1870. vi. CLIFTON DRAPER.
1871. vii. MYRTLE DRAPER.
1872. viii. SYBIL DRAPER.
1873. ix. SHIRLEY DRAPER.
1874. x. LORNA DRAPER.
1875. xi. MARJORIE DRAPER.
       xii. LORNE DRAPER, m. ANITA GRAHAM.

990. ANNIE AZELDA^9 FINDLEY *(SARAH JANE^8 MILKS, DAVID^7, FREEBORN GARRETTSON^6, JOB^5 MILK, JONATHAN^4, JOB^3, JOHN^2, JOHN^1)* was born 1893 in Beech Grove, Quebec, Canada. She married ALFRED MCMILLAN. He was born Abt. 1893.

Children of ANNIE FINDLEY and ALFRED MCMILLAN are:
1876. i. LESLIE^{10} MCMILLAN.
1877. ii. ENID MCMILLAN.
1878. iii. CHESLEY MCMILLAN.
1879. iv. HARTLEY MCMILLAN.
1880. v. ELMER MCMILLAN.
1881. vi. DOROTHY MCMILLAN.

991. SADIE LULA^9 FINDLEY *(SARAH JANE^8 MILKS, DAVID^7, FREEBORN GARRETTSON^6, JOB^5 MILK, JONATHAN^4, JOB^3, JOHN^2, JOHN^1)* was born 1895 in Beech Grove, Quebec, Canada. She married HAROLD BRADLEY. He was born Abt. 1895.

Children of SADIE FINDLEY and HAROLD BRADLEY are:
1882. i. MELVILLE^{10} BRADLEY.
1883. ii. CRAIG BRADLEY.

992. CLARA 'JENNIE'^{9} FINDLEY *(SARAH JANE^8 MILKS, DAVID^7, FREEBORN GARRETTSON^6, JOB^5 MILK, JONATHAN^4, JOB^3, JOHN^2, JOHN^1)* was born 1897 in Beech Grove, Quebec, Canada. She married HAROLD T. POOLE.

Children of CLARA FINDLEY and HAROLD POOLE are:
1884. i. JOHN^{10} POOLE.
1885. ii. LAURA POOLE.

993. JOSEPH HECTOR^9 FINDLEY *(SARAH JANE^8 MILKS, DAVID^7, FREEBORN GARRETTSON^6, JOB^5 MILK, JONATHAN^4, JOB^3, JOHN^2, JOHN^1)* was born 1898 in Beech Grove, Quebec, Canada. He married EMILY TABER. She was born 1898.

Child of JOSEPH FINDLEY and EMILY TABER is:
1886. i. CLIFTON^{10} FINDLEY.

994. WILLIAM FREDERICK 'FRED' R.[9] MILKS (*DUNCAN WILLIAM HECTOR[8], DAVID[7], FREEBORN GARRETTSON[6], JOB[5] MILK, JONATHAN[4], JOB[3], JOHN[2], JOHN[1]*) was born 11 Aug 1894 in Beech Grove, Quebec, Canada, and died 1971 in Eardley, Quebec. He married SOPHIA BAILEY WALTERS 02 Aug 1921, daughter of JAMES WALTERS and MARY DUNN. She was born 1895, and died 1977 in Eardley, Quebec.

Children of WILLIAM MILKS and SOPHIA WALTERS are:
1887.   i.   EDITH ELIZABETH[10] MILKS, b. 11 Jun 1922, Ottawa, Ontario, Canada; d. 2005, Kensington, Maryland.
         ii.   JOAN MILKS, b. 17 Aug 1926, Ottawa, Ontario, Canada; m. NORMAN BEATON; b. Abt. 1925.
1888.   iii.   WILLIAM JAMES MILKS, b. 27 Nov 1927, Ottawa, Ontario, Canada.
         iv.   ELEANOR MILKS, b. 11 May 1933, Ottawa, Ontario, Canada; m. BERNARD HUGHES; b. Abt. 1930.

995. PEARL ANNIE[9] MILKS (*DUNCAN WILLIAM HECTOR[8], DAVID[7], FREEBORN GARRETTSON[6], JOB[5] MILK, JONATHAN[4], JOB[3], JOHN[2], JOHN[1]*) was born 07 Sep 1897 in Braeside, Ontario, Canada, and died 1992 in Ottawa, Ontario, Canada. She married EDWARD SIDNEY BISHOP, son of RICHARD JOHN BISHOP. He was born 1892 in Kinburn, Ontario, Canada, and died 1964 in Ottawa, Ontario, Canada.

Children of PEARL MILKS and EDWARD BISHOP are:
1889.   i.   LLOYD[10] BISHOP, b. 20 Aug 1921, Westboro, Ontario, Canada.
1890.   ii.   VELMA STOREY BISHOP, b. 14 Dec 1922, Westboro, Ontario, Canada; d. 2002, Lakewood, Ohio.
1891.   iii.   BERNICE BISHOP, b. 31 May 1932, Montreal, Quebec, Canada.
         iv.   SYLVIA BISHOP, b. 17 Dec 1937, Barrie, Ontario, Canada; m. H. FRANK LLOYD, 29 Nov 1955, Ontario, Canada ??; b. Abt. 1935.

996. GEORGE EARL[9] MILKS (*DUNCAN WILLIAM HECTOR[8], DAVID[7], FREEBORN GARRETTSON[6], JOB[5] MILK, JONATHAN[4], JOB[3], JOHN[2], JOHN[1]*) was born 25 Mar 1899 in Eardley, Quebec, Canada, and died 1983 in Ottawa, Ontario, Canada. He married MARY LOUISE GRACE WILLIAMS 1923 in Ontario, Canada ??. She was born 1903, and died 1991 in Ottawa, Ontario, Canada.

Children of GEORGE MILKS and MARY WILLIAMS are:
         i.   BETTY ELEANOR[10] MILKS, b. 23 Nov 1930, Ottawa, Ontario, Canada; d. 07 Oct 1933, Ottawa, Ontario, Canada.
         ii.   KATHLEEN EDITH MILKS, b. 22 Jun 1933, Ottawa, Ontario, Canada.
         iii.   PETER EARL MILKS, b. 12 Jun 1936, Ottawa, Ontario, Canada.

997. HECTOR ERNEST[9] MILKS (*DUNCAN WILLIAM HECTOR[8], DAVID[7], FREEBORN GARRETTSON[6], JOB[5] MILK, JONATHAN[4], JOB[3], JOHN[2], JOHN[1]*) was born 21 Oct 1901 in Arnprior, Ontario, Canada, and died 04 Dec 1964 in Eardley, Quebec. He married MILDRED SUSAN LONSDALE 30 Aug 1923 in Quebec, daughter of ARNOLD LONSDALE and AGNES COTTRELL. She was born 01 Jun 1903 in Quyon, Quebec, and died 01 May 1995 in Eardley, Quebec.

Child of HECTOR MILKS and MILDRED LONSDALE is:
1892.   i.   ROBERT ERNEST[10] MILKS, b. 07 Aug 1926, Ottawa.

998. KATHLEEN EDITH[9] MILKS (*DUNCAN WILLIAM HECTOR[8], DAVID[7], FREEBORN GARRETTSON[6], JOB[5] MILK, JONATHAN[4], JOB[3], JOHN[2], JOHN[1]*) was born 18 Sep 1907 in Ottawa, Canada, and died 1997. She married ROBERT CHARLES MULVAGH 30 Jun 1931 in Ontario, Canada ??, son of ROBERT MULVAGH and ANNIE NELSON. He was born 1897 in City View, Ontario, Canada, and died 1955.

Children of KATHLEEN MILKS and ROBERT MULVAGH are:
         i.   ROBERT WILLIAM[10] MULVAGH, b. 01 Jan 1933, Ottawa, Ontario, Canada; m. JOAN E. BUCK; b. Abt. 1935.
         ii.   DONALD MAYNARD MULVAGH, b. 09 May 1935, Ottawa, Ontario, Canada.
         iii.   DAVID MAYNARD MULVAGH, b. 03 Jun 1941, Ottawa, Ontario, Canada.
         iv.   JAMES GORDON MULVAGH, b. 10 Jun 1944, Ottawa, Ontario, Canada.

999. CLARA LOUISE[9] MILKS (*DUNCAN WILLIAM HECTOR[8], DAVID[7], FREEBORN GARRETTSON[6], JOB[5] MILK, JONATHAN[4], JOB[3], JOHN[2], JOHN[1]*) was born 06 Oct 1915 in Ottawa, Canada, and died 1982 in Eardley, Quebec. She married

NORMAN HENRY MCAULEY, son of HENRY MCAULEY and FRANCES HARGRAVES. He was born 1908 in Kingston, Canada, and died 1982.

Child of CLARA MILKS and NORMAN MCAULEY is:
    i. DAVID EDWARD[10] MCAULEY, b. 16 Apr 1946, Ottawa, Ontario, Canada; d. Ottawa, Ontario, Canada (d.y.).

1000. MARY ELLEN[9] NEWMARCH *(ISAAC JAMES[8], MELISSA[7] MILKS, FREEBORN GARRETTSON[6], JOB[5] MILK, JONATHAN[4], JOB[3], JOHN[2], JOHN[1])* was born 1875 in Quebec, Canada, and died 1944. She married ADAM SEEGMILLER 27 Dec 1893 in Summit City, Grand Traverse County, Michigan, son of JACOB SEEGMILLER and EMMA MORT. He was born 1867 in Canada.

Children of MARY NEWMARCH and ADAM SEEGMILLER are:
    i. HARRY EUGENE[10] SEEGMILLER, b. 1906, Paradise Twp., Grand Traverse County, Michigan; d. 21 Mar 1906, Paradise Twp., Grand Traverse County, Michigan.
    ii. VIRGINIA E. G. SEEGMILLER, b. 1902, Paradise Twp., Grand Traverse County, Michigan; m. JOHN DEWARD, 23 Dec 1922, Flint, Genesee County, Michigan; b. 1896, Kalamazoo, Michigan.
    iii. AMY M. SEEGMILLER, b. 1895, Paradise Twp., Grand Traverse County, Michigan; m. WILLIAM C. SCHANKS, 02 Sep 1912, Kingsley, Grand Traverse County, Michigan; b. 1890, Port Huron, Michigan.
    iv. WILLIAM I. J. SEEGMILLER, b. 1898, Summit City, Grand Traverse County, Michigan; m. ADA MAY WALKER, 25 Apr 1922, Flint, Genesee County, Michigan; b. 1902, Charlevoix, Michigan.

1001. MELISSA SARAH EMILY[9] NEWMARCH *(ISAAC JAMES[8], MELISSA[7] MILKS, FREEBORN GARRETTSON[6], JOB[5] MILK, JONATHAN[4], JOB[3], JOHN[2], JOHN[1])* was born Jan 1878 in Montreal, Quebec, Canada, and died 28 Apr 1956 in Grand Traverse County, Michigan. She married WILLIAM SAMUEL SAXTON 15 Oct 1901 in Paradise Twp., Grand Traverse County, Michigan, son of WILLIAM SAXTON and CLARISSA TIBBITS. He was born 02 Apr 1868 in Quebec, Canada, and died 01 Nov 1941 in Grand Traverse County, Michigan.

Children of MELISSA NEWMARCH and WILLIAM SAXTON are:
    i. JESSE RUSSELL[10] SAXTON, b. 14 Jun 1906, Grand Traverse County, Michigan; d. 14 Dec 1971, Grand Traverse County, Michigan; m. LAVERNA MARGARET SEEGMILLER; b. 01 Dec 1908, Summit City, Grand Traverse County, Michigan; d. 20 Feb 1987, Grand Traverse County, Michigan.
    ii. OLIVER J. SAXTON, b. 04 Feb 1910, Kingsley, Grand Traverse County, Michigan; d. 28 Feb 1986, Grand Traverse County, Michigan.
    iii. PAUL CARLTON SAXTON, b. 19 Aug 1912, Grand Traverse County, Michigan; d. 09 Jun 1929, Fife Lake, Grand Traverse County, Michigan.
    iv. FLOYD MELVIN SAXTON, b. 05 Jul 1914, Grand Traverse County, Michigan; d. 09 Jun 1929, Fife Lake, Grand Traverse County, Michigan.
    Paul & Floyd Saxton sons of William & Sarah (Newmarch) Saxton of Kingsley died on the same day. Paul (16yrs) attempted to save his brother, Floyd (14) while they were swimming in a pond near their farm. There were 4 boys swimming at the time; actually Floyd & a neighbor boy were in an old canoe & paddling across the pond when it tipped over near the center of the pond. The neighbor boy managed to swim to the shore (30 ft) & Paul went to rescue his brother; Paul reached him quickly but Floyd panicked & they both went under. (Ref. taken from obit, The Traverse City Record Eagle 10Jun1929).

1002. JAMES JOHN[9] NEWMARCH *(ISAAC JAMES[8], MELISSA[7] MILKS, FREEBORN GARRETTSON[6], JOB[5] MILK, JONATHAN[4], JOB[3], JOHN[2], JOHN[1])* was born 1880 in Quebec, Canada, and died 1925 in Grand Traverse County, Michigan. He married JENNIE RAI LANCE 30 Nov 1903 in Kingsley, Grand Traverse County, Michigan, daughter of ALBERT LANCE and MARY PRINGLE. She was born 1885.

Children of JAMES NEWMARCH and JENNIE LANCE are:
    i. LEVI JAMES[10] NEWMARCH, b. 05 Mar 1909, Kingsley, Grand Traverse County, Michigan; m. (1) MADGE CARMIEN, 05 Apr 1930, Traverse City, Grand Traverse County, Michigan; b. Abt. 1912, Benzonia, Michigan; m. (2) BRIDE TWO, Abt. 1933; b. Abt. 1910; m. (3) MYRTLE ESTHER (BLAISDELL) GOODMAN, 11 Oct 1937, Allen County, Indiana; b. 16 Dec 1904, Cadillac, Michigan.

ii. NITA P. NEWMARCH, b. 1905, Grand Traverse County, Michigan; m. EARL C. LOUNSBERG, 16 Jul 1923, Traverse City, Grand Traverse County, Michigan; b. 1893, Howell, Michigan.

1003. LAURA VIENA[9] NEWMARCH *(ANDREW THOMPSON[8], MELISSA[7] MILKS, FREEBORN GARRETTSON[6], JOB[5] MILK, JONATHAN[4], JOB[3], JOHN[2], JOHN[1])* was born Abt. Jan 1880 in Paradise Twp., Grand Traverse County, Michigan, and died Bef. 1966. She married (1) CHARLES ANSON 05 Jul 1908 in Kingsley, Grand Traverse County, Michigan, son of JOEL ANSON and EMMA WEATHERS. He was born 1880 in Battle Creek, Michigan. She married (2) EMMET WILBERT CORNELL 24 May 1917 in Paradise Twp., Grand Traverse County, Michigan. He was born 24 Mar 1895 in Wexford County, Michigan, and died Nov 1965 in Michigan.

Child of LAURA NEWMARCH and EMMET CORNELL is:
   i. JAMES C.[10] CORNELL, b. 23 Aug 1922, Paradise Twp., Grand Traverse County, Michigan; d. 12 Aug 1990, Fife Lake, Grand Traverse County, Michigan.

1004. CORA[9] NEWMARCH *(ANDREW THOMPSON[8], MELISSA[7] MILKS, FREEBORN GARRETTSON[6], JOB[5] MILK, JONATHAN[4], JOB[3], JOHN[2], JOHN[1])* was born 22 Mar 1884 in Paradise Twp., Grand Traverse County, Michigan, and died 07 Dec 1966 in Grand Traverse County, Michigan. She married JAMES ELTON DELANCEY 20 Aug 1902 in Grand Traverse County, Michigan. He was born 16 Nov 1883 in New York, and died 09 Sep 1952 in Grand Traverse County, Michigan.

OBITUARY

Mrs. Cora D. Delancey, 82, of Kingsley died Thursday morning at Traverse City Osteopathic Hospital after a lingering illness.

Mrs. Delancey was born Mar 22, 1884 at Kingsley, the daughter of Thompson and Margaret Newmarch, and later lived on a farm at Hodges Corners near Kingsley for many years before moving to the village a few years ago.

On August 20, 1902, she was married to James E Delancey, who died in 1952 and she was also preceded in death by a sister Laura Cornell in 1965.

Surviving are: Clarence of Traverse City and Lee of Kingsley; a daughter Mrs. Lester (Dorothy) Davis of Kingsley and Palmetto, Florida; eight grandchildren and twenty-five great-grandchildren; a sister, Mrs. Cecile Courtade of Traverse City; and two brothers Earl Newmarch of Florida and Ernie Newmarch of Buckley.

Funeral services will be held at 2:00p.m., Saturday at Smith Funeral Home in Kingsley, the Reverend Alfred Nelson officiating. Burial will follow in Evergreen Cemetery in Kingsley.

Children of CORA NEWMARCH and JAMES DELANCEY are:
1893.   i. CLARENCE H.[10] DELANCEY, b. 15 Dec 1903, Fife Lake, Grand Traverse County, Michigan; d. 27 Aug 1985, Traverse City, Grand Traverse County, Michigan.
1894. ii. LEE R. DELANCEY, b. 02 Sep 1906, Fife Lake, Grand Traverse County, Michigan; d. Nov 1974, Kingsley, Grand Traverse County, Michigan.
      iii. DOROTHY G. DELANCEY, b. Abt. Oct 1909, Fife Lake, Grand Traverse County, Michigan; m. LESTER DAVIS.

1005. EARL ROY[9] NEWMARCH *(ANDREW THOMPSON[8], MELISSA[7] MILKS, FREEBORN GARRETTSON[6], JOB[5] MILK, JONATHAN[4], JOB[3], JOHN[2], JOHN[1])* was born 13 Jun 1886 in Paradise Twp., Grand Traverse County, Michigan, and died 24 Sep 1978 in Traverse City, Grand Traverse County, Michigan. He married MILDRED MAY SMITH. She was born 1898 in Walton Junction, Grand Traverse County, Michigan, and died 08 Dec 1955 in Grand Traverse County, Michigan.

Children of EARL NEWMARCH and MILDRED SMITH are:
         i. VERA[10] NEWMARCH, b. Mar 1917, Fife Lake, Grand Traverse County, Michigan.
        ii. HAROLD L. NEWMARCH, b. Jan 1919, Fife Lake, Grand Traverse County, Michigan.
       iii. LENA M. NEWMARCH, b. 28 Feb 1921, Fife Lake, Grand Traverse County, Michigan; d. 05 Nov 1988.
1895. iv. FLOYD LEE NEWMARCH, b. 11 Oct 1922, Fife Lake, Grand Traverse County, Michigan; d. 15 Sep 1986, Traverse City, Grand Traverse County, Michigan.
        v. DORIS M. NEWMARCH, b. Bet. 1926 - 1927, Fife Lake, Grand Traverse County, Michigan.
       vi. KENNETH LEROY NEWMARCH, b. 1928, Fife Lake, Grand Traverse County, Michigan; d. 1928, Fife Lake, Grand Traverse County, Michigan.

1006. ERNEST LEE 'ERNIE'[9] NEWMARCH *(ANDREW THOMPSON[8], MELISSA[7] MILKS, FREEBORN GARRETTSON[6], JOB[5] MILK, JONATHAN[4], JOB[3], JOHN[2], JOHN[1])* was born 21 Aug 1888 in Paradise Twp., Grand Traverse County, Michigan, and died May 1978 in Buckley, Wexford County, Michigan. He married (1) ETTA E. SMITH Abt. Sep 1909 in Grand Traverse County, Michigan. She was born 1892 in Michigan, and died 1918 in Michigan. He married (2) FRANCES B. LANCE Aft. Jan 1920 in Michigan, daughter of ALBERT LANCE and MARY ____. She was born 28 Jul 1889 in Michigan, and died 06 Dec 1984 in Buckley, Wexford County, Michigan.

Children of ERNEST NEWMARCH and ETTA SMITH are:
- i. LLOYD ERNEST[10] NEWMARCH, b. 16 Feb 1914, Michigan; d. 24 Oct 1989, Tampa, Hillsborough County, Florida.
- ii. HELEN NEWMARCH, b. Dec 1917, Michigan.
   Helen Steed, 89, of Traverse City, died Nov. 17 (2005); Reynolds-Jonkhoff Funeral Home, Traverse City. TC Record Eagle, Nov 20, 2005. b. 12 Mar 1916

1007. ARTHUR E.[9] NEWMARCH *(WILLIAM C.[8], MELISSA[7] MILKS, FREEBORN GARRETTSON[6], JOB[5] MILK, JONATHAN[4], JOB[3], JOHN[2], JOHN[1])* was born 25 Nov 1891 in Traverse City, Grand Traverse County, Michigan. He married EDNA FAY CHESSHIRE 18 May 1913 in Traverse City, Grand Traverse County, Michigan, daughter of E. CHESSHIRE and JENNIE CROOK. She was born 1895 in Kalkaska, Michigan.

Children of ARTHUR NEWMARCH and EDNA CHESSHIRE are:
- i. ARTHUR[10] NEWMARCH, b. 1914, Detroit, Wayne County, Michigan.
- ii. WILLIAM C. NEWMARCH, b. Bet. 1917 - 1918, Detroit, Wayne County, Michigan.

1008. DOROTHY ELIZABETH[9] MILKS *(JOHN SMITH[8], PETER[7], FREEBORN GARRETTSON[6], JOB[5] MILK, JONATHAN[4], JOB[3], JOHN[2], JOHN[1])* was born 29 Apr 1918 in Trenton, Wayne County, Michigan, and died 14 Sep 1997 in Trenton, Wayne County, Michigan. She married MICHAEL 'MIKE' ZAWOYSKY, son of WASYL ZAWOYSKI and MARY HNAT. He was born 22 Jan 1909 in Allegheny County, Pennsylvania, and died 26 Aug 1984 in Trenton, Wayne County, Michigan.

Child of DOROTHY MILKS and MICHAEL ZAWOYSKY is:
1896.   i. CHARLENE MARIE[10] ZAWOYSKY, b. 07 Sep 1956, Trenton, Wayne County, Michigan.

1009. WAYNE A.[9] CAMPBELL *(MARTHA[8] MILKS, PETER[7], FREEBORN GARRETTSON[6], JOB[5] MILK, JONATHAN[4], JOB[3], JOHN[2], JOHN[1])* was born 10 Feb 1892 in Fife Lake, Grand Traverse County, Michigan, and died 15 Dec 1970 in Lansing, Ingham County, Michigan. He married NELLIE CELIA STAMPHTON 1917 in Grand Traverse County, Michigan. She was born 1894 in Michigan, and died 1952 in Michigan.

Children of WAYNE CAMPBELL and NELLIE STAMPHTON are:
- i. WILLIAM A.[10] CAMPBELL, b. Abt. 1923, Michigan.
- ii. JEANETTE C. CAMPBELL, b. 1926, Michigan.
- iii. EDWARD CAMPBELL, b. Abt. 1930, Michigan.

1010. MILDRED L.[9] CAMPBELL *(MARTHA[8] MILKS, PETER[7], FREEBORN GARRETTSON[6], JOB[5] MILK, JONATHAN[4], JOB[3], JOHN[2], JOHN[1])* was born Nov 1896 in Fife Lake, Grand Traverse County, Michigan. She married WILLIAM O. BREAKEY. He was born Abt. 1891 in Michigan.

Child of MILDRED CAMPBELL and WILLIAM BREAKEY is:
- i. THOMAS O.[10] BREAKEY, b. Abt. Nov 1919, Pontiac, Oakland County, Michigan.

1011. GEORGE DEWEY[9] CAMPBELL *(MARTHA[8] MILKS, PETER[7], FREEBORN GARRETTSON[6], JOB[5] MILK, JONATHAN[4], JOB[3], JOHN[2], JOHN[1])* was born 27 Jan 1899 in Fife Lake, Grand Traverse County, Michigan, and died Sep 1962. He married MABEL B. _____. She was born 1904, and died 1975.

Children of GEORGE CAMPBELL and MABEL _____ are:
- i. GEORGE N.[10] CAMPBELL, b. Abt. 1926, Grand Traverse County, Michigan.
- ii. ELAINE J. CAMPBELL, b. Abt. 1929, Grand Traverse County, Michigan.
- iii. JERRY CAMPBELL, b. Abt. 1938, Grand Traverse County, Michigan.

1012. HAZEL LEONA^9 MILKS *(HENRY^8, PETER^7, FREEBORN GARRETTSON^6, JOB^5 MILK, JONATHAN^4, JOB^3, JOHN^2, JOHN^1)* was born 04 Feb 1904 in Grand Traverse County, Michigan, and died 29 Oct 1972 in Cadillac, Wexford County, Michigan. She married JOSIAH CHRISTIAN MERKLE 17 Sep 1924 in Cadillac, Wexford County, Michigan, son of JONATHAN MERKLE and KATHERINE BROWER. He was born 17 Sep 1892 in Missaukee County, Michigan, and died Feb 1969 in Cadillac, Wexford County, Michigan.

Child of HAZEL MILKS and JOSIAH MERKLE is:
  i. WILLIAM H.^{10} MERKLE, b. 30 Dec 1937, Cadillac, Wexford County, Michigan; d. Abt. 1937, Cadillac, Wexford County, Michigan.

1013. ROLAND DEO^9 HODGINS *(WILLIAM RUGLESS^8, ALMIRA^7 MILKS, FREEBORN GARRETTSON^6, JOB^5 MILK, JONATHAN^4, JOB^3, JOHN^2, JOHN^1)* was born 08 Nov 1896 in Everett, Snohomish County, Washington, and died Sep 1962 in Washington. He married UNA GREENER, daughter of MISTER GREENER and GEORGINA ____. She was born 19 Oct 1896 in Bolden, Colliery, England, and died 16 Jul 1991 in Seattle, King County, Washington.

Child of ROLAND HODGINS and UNA GREENER is:
  i. CAROL MAY^{10} HODGINS, b. Abt. 1924, Seattle, King County, Washington.

1014. LLOYD G.^{9} BEMUS *(OSCAR E.^{8}, HELEN L.^{7} MILKS, SAMUEL^6 MILK, JOB^5, JONATHAN^4, JOB^3, JOHN^2, JOHN^1)* was born 09 Mar 1891 in Kalkaska, Kalkaska County, Michigan, and died Nov 1973 in Houghton Lake Heights, Roscommon County, Michigan. He married (1) MYRTLE E. DRAKE 22 Apr 1914 in Jackson, Ingham County, Michigan. She was born 1896 in Eaton County, Michigan. He married (2) JUNE _____ Bet. 1920 - 1930. She was born 1895 in Indiana. He married (3) THERESA _____ Bet. 1930 - 1940. She was born 1901 in Pennsylvania.

Child of LLOYD BEMUS and MYRTLE DRAKE is:
  i. CHILD^{10} BEMUS, b. Abt. 1915, Michigan.

1015. DONNA LOUISE^9 BEMUS *(OSCAR E.^{8}, HELEN L.^{7} MILKS, SAMUEL^6 MILK, JOB^5, JONATHAN^4, JOB^3, JOHN^2, JOHN^1)* was born 09 Aug 1895 in Traverse City, Grand Traverse County, Michigan. She married CLARENCE LEONARD ANDERSON 25 Jul 1917 in Traverse City, Grand Traverse County, Michigan, son of ANDREW ANDERSON and SOPHIA CARLSON. He was born 1896 in Traverse City, Grand Traverse County, Michigan.

Child of DONNA BEMUS and CLARENCE ANDERSON is:
  i. FAYE JEANNE^{10} ANDERSON, b. Jun 1919, Detroit, Wayne County, Michigan.

1016. FRANK C.^{9} MOOERS *(HENRY CLAY^8, CYNTHIA^7 MILK, JONATHAN^6, BENJAMIN^5, JONATHAN^4, JOB^3, JOHN^2, JOHN^1)* was born Feb 1874 in Toledo, Lucas County, Ohio. He married IRENE M. CANARY 11 Jun 1904 in Detroit, Wayne County, Michigan, daughter of JOHN CANARY and CELIA DUNCAN. She was born 1884 in Ohio.

Child of FRANK MOOERS and IRENE CANARY is:
  i. CELIA E.^{10} MOOERS, b. 1911, Ohio.

1017. ARTHUR BEARD^9 MOOERS *(HENRY CLAY^8, CYNTHIA^7 MILK, JONATHAN^6, BENJAMIN^5, JONATHAN^4, JOB^3, JOHN^2, JOHN^1)* was born 26 Apr 1892 in Toledo, Lucas County, Ohio, and died Jun 1970 in Youngtown, Maricopa County, Arizona. He married (1) FLORENCE ZISSLER Abt. 1914 in Toledo, Lucas County, Ohio ??. She was born Abt. 1892 in Galesburg, Illinois. He married (2) ELSIE A. FRITSCH 11 Jun 1919 in Flint, Genesee County, Michigan, daughter of HERMAN FRITSCH and LOVINA FAULKNER. She was born 10 Oct 1898 in Hersey, Michigan, and died Nov 1985 in Sun City, Maricopa County, Arizona.

Child of ARTHUR MOOERS and FLORENCE ZISSLER is:
  i. INFANT^{10} MOOERS, b. 15 Jul 1915, Toledo, Lucas County, Ohio; d. 15 Jul 1915, Toledo, Lucas County, Ohio.

Child of ARTHUR MOOERS and ELSIE FRITSCH is:
  ii. DONALD JUSTIN^{10} MOOERS, b. 23 Sep 1920, Flint, Genesee County, Michigan; d. 08 May 2010, Orange

Park, Clay County, Florida.

1018. HOWARD JAY[9] MILKS *(WILLIAM JEWETT[8] MILK, WILLIAM JEWETT[7], JONATHAN[6], BENJAMIN[5], JONATHAN[4], JOB[3], JOHN[2], JOHN[1])* was born 25 Jun 1879 in Dryden, Tompkins County, New York, and died 30 Mar 1954 in Ithaca, Tompkins County, New York. He married LENA MABEL VOSE 12 Jul 1906, daughter of SYLVANUS VOSE and PHOEBE CLARK. She was born 1884 in Spencer, Tioga County, New York, and died 1961 in Tioga County, New York.

Children of HOWARD MILKS and LENA VOSE are:
1897. i. CLIFFORD HOWARD[10] MILKS, b. 29 Apr 1907, Louisiana; d. 14 Aug 1955.
1898. ii. RAYMOND CLAUDE MILKS, b. 15 Sep 1910, New York; d. 14 Sep 1992.
1899. iii. RICHARD VOSE MILKS, b. 01 Sep 1917, New York; d. 26 Dec 1991.

1019. LENA AMANDA[9] MILKS *(WILLIAM JEWETT[8] MILK, WILLIAM JEWETT[7], JONATHAN[6], BENJAMIN[5], JONATHAN[4], JOB[3], JOHN[2], JOHN[1])* was born 04 Oct 1881. She married HERMAN PERELLA 16 Sep 1908. He was born Abt. 1880.

Child of LENA MILKS and HERMAN PERELLA is:
  i. DARWIN HERMAN[10] PERELLA, b. 19 Nov 1909; m. ISABEL NUSS, 10 Oct 1932; b. Abt. 1910.

1020. HARLEY H.[9] MILKS *(WILLIAM JEWETT[8] MILK, WILLIAM JEWETT[7], JONATHAN[6], BENJAMIN[5], JONATHAN[4], JOB[3], JOHN[2], JOHN[1])* was born 13 Sep 1883. He married ELLA T. HAGGERTY 28 Jul 1915. She was born Abt. 1885.

Children of HARLEY MILKS and ELLA HAGGERTY are:
1900. i. MARIE AGNES[10] MILKS, b. 11 Oct 1917, Binghamton, New York; d. 30 Dec 2004, Worcester, Maryland.
1901. ii. JAMES EDWARD MILKS, b. 13 Oct 1919.

1021. HAROLD CLIFFORD[9] MILKS *(WILLIAM JEWETT[8] MILK, WILLIAM JEWETT[7], JONATHAN[6], BENJAMIN[5], JONATHAN[4], JOB[3], JOHN[2], JOHN[1])* was born 27 Aug 1889 in Dryden, Tompkins County, New York, and died 1961. He married AUGUSTA MARGARET GOURLEY 27 Sep 1917 in New York, daughter of JAMES GOURLEY and AUGUSTA HICKS. She was born 1891 in Pennsylvania, and died 1959.

Children of HAROLD MILKS and AUGUSTA GOURLEY are:
1902. i.   WILLIAM JAY[10] MILKS, b. 26 Aug 1918, New York; d. 04 May 1999, Tampa, Florida.
1903. ii. ROSEMARY MILKS, b. 1921, New York; d. 23 Oct 2002, Burnet, Texas (Seton Highland Lakes Hospital).
       iii. HAROLD FREDERICK MILKS, b. Abt. Jan 1928, New York; d. 1998, Broome County, New York ?.

1022. MINNIE[9] MILKS *(BENJAMIN F.[8] MILK, WILLIAM JEWETT[7], JONATHAN[6], BENJAMIN[5], JONATHAN[4], JOB[3], JOHN[2], JOHN[1])* was born 1873 in Dryden, Tompkins County, New York, and died 1940. She married ARTHUR G. ROBSON Abt. 1892. He was born 1864, and died 1939.

Child of MINNIE MILKS and ARTHUR ROBSON is:
  i. STANLEY BENJAMIN[10] ROBSON, b. 22 Dec 1893, New York; d. 1944, unmarried.

1023. LENA[9] MILKS *(BENJAMIN F.[8] MILK, WILLIAM JEWETT[7], JONATHAN[6], BENJAMIN[5], JONATHAN[4], JOB[3], JOHN[2], JOHN[1])* was born Abt. 1875 in Dryden, Tompkins County, New York. She married OTIS SMITH. He was born Abt. 1875.

Child of LENA MILKS and OTIS SMITH is:
  i. ALICE[10] SMITH, b. 17 Sep 1910.

1024. GRACE[9] MILKS *(BENJAMIN F.[8] MILK, WILLIAM JEWETT[7], JONATHAN[6], BENJAMIN[5], JONATHAN[4], JOB[3], JOHN[2], JOHN[1])* was born Abt. 1877 in Dryden, Tompkins County, New York. She married EDWARD HUGHSON FREAR 1898 in Ithaca, NY. He was born Abt. 1875.

Child of GRACE MILKS and EDWARD FREAR is:
  i. DONALD[10] FREAR, b. Abt. 1899.

1025. MYRTLE^9 MILKS *(BENJAMIN F.^{8} MILK, WILLIAM JEWETT^7, JONATHAN^6, BENJAMIN^5, JONATHAN^4, JOB^3, JOHN^2, JOHN^1)* was born Dec 1882 in Dryden, Tompkins County, New York. She married VERNON AYERS. He was born Abt. 1880.

Children of MYRTLE MILKS and VERNON AYERS are:
- 1904. i. KENNETH EMORY^{10} AYERS, b. Abt. 1904, Cortland, New York.
- 1905. ii. LAURENCE L. AYERS, b. 21 Aug 1908, Cortland, New York; d. Apr 1976, Cortland, New York.
- iii. MARION AYERS, b. Abt. 1917, Cortland, New York.

1026. PEARL ETHEL^9 MANNING *(ANN JANE^8 MILK, WILLIAM JEWETT^7, JONATHAN^6, BENJAMIN^5, JONATHAN^4, JOB^3, JOHN^2, JOHN^1)* was born Feb 1879 in Dryden, Tompkins County, New York. She married GEORGE ALFRED METZGER 1901. He was born 29 Apr 1876.

Child of PEARL MANNING and GEORGE METZGER is:
- i. CHARLES R.^{10} METZGER, b. 16 Jan 1907, Auburn, Cayuga County, New York; d. Sep 1927, Auburn, Cayuga County, New York.

1027. LELAND BROWN^9 MANNING *(ANN JANE^8 MILK, WILLIAM JEWETT^7, JONATHAN^6, BENJAMIN^5, JONATHAN^4, JOB^3, JOHN^2, JOHN^1)* was born 23 Feb 1880 in Dryden, Tompkins County, New York, and died 1918 in Auburn, Cayuga County, New York. He married ELSIE ASHLEY 1905. She was born 1885, and died 1918 in Auburn, Cayuga County, New York.

Child of LELAND MANNING and ELSIE ASHLEY is:
- 1906. i. GLADYS^{10} MANNING, b. 13 Dec 1906, Auburn, Cayuga County, New York.

1028. GEORGIA BELLE^9 MILKS *(GEORGE HENRY^8 MILK, WILLIAM JEWETT^7, JONATHAN^6, BENJAMIN^5, JONATHAN^4, JOB^3, JOHN^2, JOHN^1)* was born 03 Aug 1875 in New York, and died 14 Jun 1961 in Dryden, Tompkins County, New York. She married ALBERT JEM FRANCIS 24 Oct 1894 in Snyder Hill, Dryden, Tompkins County, New York. He was born 14 Jun 1868 in England, and died 10 Mar 1947 in Dryden, Tompkins County, New York.

Children of GEORGIA MILKS and ALBERT FRANCIS are:
- 1907. i. ORALLA^{10} FRANCIS, b. 04 Aug 1895, Dryden, Tompkins County, New York.
- 1908. ii. PERCY G. FRANCIS, b. 06 Oct 1897, Dryden, Tompkins County, New York.
- 1909. iii. FRANK WILSON FRANCIS, b. 16 Nov 1899, Dryden, Tompkins County, New York.
- 1910. iv. ALBERT LAWRENCE FRANCIS, b. 19 Feb 1902, Dryden, Tompkins County, New York.
- 1911. v. MARY EMILY FRANCIS, b. 10 Aug 1904, Dryden, Tompkins County, New York.
- vi. WINIFRED HELEN FRANCIS, b. 29 Jan 1907, Dryden, Tompkins County, New York.
- vii. GLENN A. FRANCIS, b. 17 Aug 1910, Dryden, Tompkins County, New York; m. (1) LENA MYRTLE FROST, 30 Sep 1934, Tompkins County, New York; b. Abt. 1913; m. (2) LILLIAN KELLOGG, Feb 1951; b. Sep 1910.
- 1912. viii. ROBERT MERLE FRANCIS, b. 24 Sep 1920, Dryden, Tompkins County, New York.

1029. FRED A.^{9} MILKS *(GEORGE HENRY^8 MILK, WILLIAM JEWETT^7, JONATHAN^6, BENJAMIN^5, JONATHAN^4, JOB^3, JOHN^2, JOHN^1)* was born 07 Feb 1878 in Ellis Hollow, Dryden, Tompkins Co., NY, and died 24 Jul 1945 in Ithaca, New York. He married CORA M. ONAN 17 Oct 1900 in Caroline, Tompkins Co., NY, daughter of SAMUEL ONAN and ALICE WAITE. She was born Bet. 1881 - 1882 in Caroline, Tompkins Co., NY.

DEATH NOTICE

MILKS, Fred A. d. July 24, 1945. Survived by wife, Mrs. Cora O. MILKS; dau., Mrs. James F. FRANCIS of Ithaca; a bro. Roy of Union; sister, Mrs. Belle FRANCIS of Willseyville, several nieces and nephews. Interment in East Lawn Cemetery

ELLIS HOLLOW SCHOOL NO. 10

Located in the Town of Dryden, Tompkins County, NY On Ellis Hollow Creek Road, near the intersection of Ellis Hollow Road. The Ellis Hollow School contained one room. A teacher's desk was at the front and behind it there was a large blackboard and some cupboards. In the corner of the room there was an old metal stove fed by firewood provided by the parents of the students. The school house is still there today, but has been made into a home.

Students around the Year 1890 : Milks, Fred

Child of FRED MILKS and CORA ONAN is:
    i. HELEN M.[10] MILKS, b. 07 Mar 1902, Ithaca, NY; d. 03 Feb 1997, Ithaca, Tompkins County, New York; m. JAMES F. FRANCIS, 10 Aug 1923, Dryden, Tompkins Co., New York; b. Bet. 1896 - 1897, Shemokin, Penn.; d. 05 Aug 1945.

1030. LEROY ST. CLAIR[9] MILKS *(GEORGE HENRY[8] MILK, WILLIAM JEWETT[7], JONATHAN[6], BENJAMIN[5], JONATHAN[4], JOB[3], JOHN[2], JOHN[1])* was born 20 Sep 1892 in Candor, Tioga County, New York, and died Oct 1964. He married HAZEL V. FISH 20 Jul 1913. She was born 02 Oct 1894.

Children of LEROY MILKS and HAZEL FISH are:
1913.   i. DOROTHY H.[10] MILKS, b. 12 Jan 1915, Lestershire, Broome County, New York.
1914.   ii. DONALD EDWARD MILKS, b. 23 Sep 1919, Broome County, New York; d. 01 Dec 1977, Memphis, TN.

1031. EDNA MYRTLE[9] MCKNIGHT *(MARY KIZIAH[8] MILK, ISAAC[7], JONATHAN[6], BENJAMIN[5], JONATHAN[4], JOB[3], JOHN[2], JOHN[1])* was born 02 Feb 1894 in Wright County, Minn., and died 20 Dec 1984 in Minneapolis, Minn.. She married HELGE MARTIN MARTIALIS EMANUEL OLSON. He was born 15 Jun 1887 in Sundsvall, Sweden, and died 18 Oct 1955 in Mille Lacs, Minnesota.

Children of EDNA MCKNIGHT and HELGE OLSON are:
1915.   i. LYNN HELGE[10] OLSON, b. 07 Jan 1917, Minnesota; d. 27 Feb 1999, Berkeley, California.
1916.   ii. JEANNETTE MERLE OLSON, b. 09 Mar 1919, Seattle, Washington; d. 31 Jan 2002, Simi Valley, Ventura County, California.
    iii. DONALD CLAIR OLSON, b. 20 Feb 1924, Minnesota; d. 20 Feb 1924.
    iv. REYNARD GEORGE OLSON, b. 16 Feb 1925, Minneapolis, Minnesota; d. 08 Jul 1998, Wright County, Minn.; m. NELLIE D. RICI; b. 1926.
    v. PAUL OLSON, b. Sep 1928, Minnesota.
    vi. PATRICIA OLSON.

1032. JAMES IAN[9] MCKNIGHT *(MARY KIZIAH[8] MILK, ISAAC[7], JONATHAN[6], BENJAMIN[5], JONATHAN[4], JOB[3], JOHN[2], JOHN[1])* was born 06 Mar 1897 in Minneapolis, Minn., and died Jan 1963 in California. He married (1) CLARICE Abt. 1917 in South Dakota ?. She was born 22 Aug 1895 in South Dakota, and died 13 Oct 1986 in Minneapolis, Minnesota. He married (2) LILLIAN HENLY Abt. 1922 in California ?. She was born 14 Aug 1901 in Canada, and died 09 Apr 1994 in Marin County, California.

Children of JAMES MCKNIGHT and CLARICE are:
    i. JOYCE D.[10] MCKNIGHT, b. Bet. 1918 - 1919, Watertown, Codington County, S. Dakota.
    ii. JAMES MCKNIGHT, b. Bet. 1921 - 1922, Minnesota.

Children of JAMES MCKNIGHT and LILLIAN HENLY are:
    iii. JAMES[10] MCKNIGHT, b. 10 Mar 1924, California; d. 29 Aug 1994, San Francisco, California.
    iv. JEANNE ILLENE MCKNIGHT, b. 28 Jan 1926, California. Lived in San Mateo, California

1033. EUNICE CONSTANCE[9] MCKNIGHT *(MARY KIZIAH[8] MILK, ISAAC[7], JONATHAN[6], BENJAMIN[5], JONATHAN[4], JOB[3], JOHN[2], JOHN[1])* was born 06 Jul 1898 in Minneapolis, Minn., and died 24 Oct 1965 in Hennepin County, Minnesota. She married (1) WILLIAM BURNHAM TIBBETS Abt. 1916 in Minnesota?, son of WILLIAM TIBBETS and NETTIE BOYD. He was born 06 May 1891, and died 02 Nov 1962 in Koochiching County, Minnesota. She married (2) EDWARD CHARLES HUGHES Abt. 1936 in Minnesota?, son of FRANK HUGHES and MILLIE _____. He was born Abt. 1908 in Minnesota.

Child of EUNICE MCKNIGHT and WILLIAM TIBBETS is:
    i. WALLACE BURNHAM[10] TIBBETS, b. 09 Nov 1918, Minneapolis, Hennepin County, Minnesota; d. 03 Mar 1988, Itasca County, Minnesota; m. HAZEL J. GLADUE, 27 May 1939, Moody County, South Dakota; b. Abt. 1920.

Child of EUNICE MCKNIGHT and EDWARD HUGHES is:
   ii. KATHRYN MARY[10] HUGHES, b. 11 Jun 1938, Hennepin County, Minnesota.

1034. GEORGE[9] MCKNIGHT *(MARY KIZIAH[8] MILK, ISAAC[7], JONATHAN[6], BENJAMIN[5], JONATHAN[4], JOB[3], JOHN[2], JOHN[1])* was born 03 May 1900 in Minneapolis, Minn., and died 21 May 1949 in Weber, Utah. He married (1) ANNA P. _____ Abt. 1920 in Minnesota?, daughter of _____ OLSON. She was born 22 Oct 1894 in Sweden, and died 16 Mar 1967 in Hennepin County, Minnesota. He married (2) ELEANOR LOUISA HOPKIN 11 Jun 1943 in Salt Lake City, Utah, daughter of JOSEPH HOPKIN and BERTHA _____. She was born 31 Oct 1910, and died 27 May 1995 in Coalville, Utah.

Children of GEORGE MCKNIGHT and ANNA _____ are:
   i. PHYLLIS[10] MCKNIGHT, b. Abt. 1921, Minnesota?.
   ii. CONSTANCE LOU ELLEN MC KNIGHT, b. Abt. 1920, Minnesota?.
   iii. UNKNOWN MCKNIGHT, b. Minnesota?.

1035. LELIA BELLE[9] MILKS *(JOHN WESLEY[8], HENRY[7] MILK, JONATHAN[6], BENJAMIN[5], JONATHAN[4], JOB[3], JOHN[2], JOHN[1])* was born 24 Dec 1868 in South Milford, Lagrange County, Indiana, and died 20 Jan 1942 in Coral Gables, Florida. She married OLIVER PERRY WILKINS 28 Sep 1887 in Noble County, Indiana, son of WILLIAM WILKINS and HELEN LEARNED. He was born 20 Apr 1864 in Hamilton, DeKalb County, Indiana, and died 06 Oct 1936 in Coral Gables, Florida.

Children of LELIA MILKS and OLIVER WILKINS are:
   i. LELAND A[10] WILKINS, b. 16 Aug 1893, Ft. Wayne, Indiana; d. Jan 1977, Coral Gables, Florida. Never married.
   ii. RALPH L. WILKINS, b. 12 Mar 1896, South Milford, Lagrange County, Indiana, d. May 1977, Coral Gables, Florida. Never married.

1036. LEONARD "LEN" H.[9] MILKS *(JOHN WESLEY[8], HENRY[7] MILK, JONATHAN[6], BENJAMIN[5], JONATHAN[4], JOB[3], JOHN[2], JOHN[1])* was born 02 Feb 1875 in South Milford, Lagrange County, Indiana, and died 23 Jul 1951 in Kalamazoo, Michigan. He married FLOSSIE GLENN SMITH 13 Jan 1908 in Lagrange County, Indiana, daughter of MISTRE SMITH and 'WILLIAM' _____. She was born 27 Sep 1886 in LaGrange, Indiana, and died 15 May 1935 in Kendalville, Indiana.

Children of LEONARD MILKS and FLOSSIE SMITH are:
   i. LEONARD R.[10] MILKS, b. 15 May 1907, Milford Township, Lagrange County, Indiana; d. Bef. 1910, Milford Township, Lagrange County, Indiana.
1917. ii. HAROLD KEITH MILKS, b. 28 Jun 1908, Milford Township, Lagrange County, Indiana; d. 12 Dec 1979, Paradise Valley, Maricopa County, Arizona.
1918. iii. MAX LEON MILKS, b. 19 May 1914, South Milford, Indiana; d. 28 Jul 1968, Garrett, De Kalb, Indiana.
1919. iv. JOHN WESLEY MILKS II, b. 15 May 1917, South Milford, Indiana; d. 01 Aug 1978, Lafayette, Tippecanoe Co., Indiana.
1920. v. ARTHUR LYNN "JACK" MILKS, b. 09 Mar 1927, Kendallville, Indiana; d. 14 Feb 1995, Battle Creek, Calhoun Co., Michigan.

1037. MARGARET MAY 'MAGGIE'[9] MILKS *(CHARLES H.[8] MILK, HENRY[7], JONATHAN[6], BENJAMIN[5], JONATHAN[4], JOB[3], JOHN[2], JOHN[1])* was born 22 Jun 1878 in Indiana, and died 1959 in South Milford, Lagrange County, Indiana. She married (1) GUY FREDERICK FAILOR Abt. 1916 in Noble County, Indiana?, son of MARION FAILOR and LAURA _____. He was born 09 Feb 1885 in Indiana, and died 1937 in South Milford, Lagrange County, Indiana. She married (2) JAMES PERRY EMERICK 20 Jan 1898 in Lagrange County, Indiana. He was born 10 Jul 1875 in Indiana, and died 15 Jun 1952 in Indiana.

Children of MARGARET MILKS and GUY FAILOR are:
   i. BEVERLY M.[10] FAILOR, b. Abt. Aug 1918, Kendallville, Noble County, Indiana.
   ii. RICHARD GUY FAILOR, b. 20 Aug 1920, Kendallville, Noble County, Indiana; m. BETTY JANE JEFFERIES, 24 Jan 1942, Ft. Wayne, Indiana; b. 09 Feb 1921, Ft. Wayne, Indiana.
   iii. JUNE MAXINE FAILOR, b. 26 Jun 1922, Kendallville, Noble County, Indiana; m. CARL WALDEN, 01 Nov 1941, Allen County, Indiana; b. 02 Nov 1917, Indianapolis, Marion County, Indiana.

Child of MARGARET MILKS and JAMES EMERICK is:
    iv. CHARLES P.^{10} EMERICK, b. Abt. 1906, Indiana.

1038. FERN L.^{9} RABER *(CYNTHIA^8 MILK, HENRY^7, JONATHAN^6, BENJAMIN^5, JONATHAN^4, JOB^3, JOHN^2, JOHN^1)* was born Dec 1879 in LaGrange County, Indiana, and died 18 Mar 1966 in Portland, Multnomah County, Oregon. She married LUCIEN BRACY 1905 in Portland, Multnomah County, Oregon. He was born 1878 in Kentucky.

Child of FERN RABER and LUCIEN BRACY is:
    i. LUCIEN E.^{10} BRACY, b. Abt. 1914, Portland, Multnomah County, Oregon.

1039. MENZO W.^{9} RODMAN *(ASA BENJAMIN^8, DEBORAH^7 MILK, BENJAMIN^6, BENJAMIN^5, JONATHAN^4, JOB^3, JOHN^2, JOHN^1)* was born 1853 in Iowa, and died 1920 in Clinton County, Iowa. He married THEKLA J. GUTH GOUTH, daughter of EDWARD GUTH and DORIS _____. She was born Feb 1855 in Iowa, and died 1942 in Clinton County, Iowa.

Children of MENZO RODMAN and THEKLA GOUTH are:
    i. GERTRUDE^{10} RODMAN, b. Abt. 1885, Clinton County, Iowa.
    ii. DOROTHEA RODMAN, b. Abt. 1887, Clinton County, Iowa.
    iii. RUSSEL G. RODMAN, b. Abt. 1889, Clinton County, Iowa.
    iv. MENZO J. RODMAN, b. Abt. 1894, Clinton County, Iowa; d. 27 Aug 1894, Clinton County, Iowa.

1040. JOEL SEBASTIAN^9 COLE *(MARY^8 RODMAN, DEBORAH^7 MILK, BENJAMIN^6, BENJAMIN^5, JONATHAN^4, JOB^3, JOHN^2, JOHN^1)* was born 04 Mar 1853 in Schoharie County, New York, and died 10 Nov 1931 in Corning, Adams County, Iowa. He married CHARLOTTE VIRGINIA PALMER 10 Jan 1877 in Adams County, Illinois, daughter of ABEL PALMER and JANE _____. She was born 16 Aug 1858 in Henry County, Illinois, and died 05 Aug 1949 in Corning, Adams County, Iowa.

OBITUARY - Adams County Free Press, November 19, 1931

Joel Sebastian Cole was born to Sebastian and Mary Cole, was born in Schoharie county, New York, March 4 , 1853 and passed away at his home in Corning, Iowa November 10, 1931, at the age of 78 years, 8 months and 6 days, after four weeks illness. He was tenderly cared for by loving hands, but on Tuesday at one o'clock he suffered a heart collapse, and passed quietly into the "Great Beyond". Funeral services were held at the Carbon M. S. church Thursday at 2 p. m. Rev. E. L. Stone of Chariton, who is an old friend of the family, conducted the services, assisted by Rev. Herman, pastor of the Carbon church. Interment was made in the Quincy cemetery.

Mr. Cole came to Clinton county in Iowa with his parents when he was only three years old, and remained there until 1871, when he came to Adams county, where he has since resided.

He was married to Miss Charlotte Palmer of Brooks, Iowa, January 10, 1877, and they spent almost 55 years together. Ten children were born to this union, these being Mrs. Bessie Sundstrom of Corning, Iowa; Mrs. George Powell of Rouleau, Sask., Can.: Fred, of Carroll, Iowa; Arthur, Floyd and Harry, of Massena; Perry, of Bridgewater; Mrs. Minnie Johnson, Smith and Frank, the three latter named having preceded their father in death.

He is also survived by his widow: a. grandson. Russell Johnson, whom he had loved and cared for as one of his own children; 13 other grandchildren; one sister, Mrs. Amanda Hartsock, of Carbon; and one brother, George Cole, of Corning, Iowa. Two sisters and one brother preceded him in death.

Mr. Cole was one of the pioneers of Adams county, having lived here sixty years. On September 2. 1S31, he moved from his old home at Carbon to Corning, where he passed away. He was a loving husband and a kind and indulgent father, one who found his greatest happiness in his home and among his friends. He was highly respected in the community where he has always lived, was a good neighbor and friend, always willing to lend a helping hand to others. His door was always open to others less fortunate and many found shelter under his roof.

He believed in, and practiced the "Golden Rule". He was a member of the Carbon Methodist church and often told his family and friends, while he was ill. that he was prepared and is ready to meet his maker.

    Gone to his rest, where there is no is more toiling,
    Where the cares of the world never try or annoy.
    He may not come back, but his loved ones may follow.
    And see him and greet him and share in his joy.

OBITUARY - Adams County Free Press, August 11, 1949

Charlotte Virginia Palmer Cole, oldest daughter of Abel and Jane Palmer passed away at the home of her son,

Arthur, in Prescott, at 12:30 o'clock Friday morning, August 5, at the age of 90 years. 11 months and 19 days. She was born in Henry County, Illinois, on August 16, 1858. She came to Adams county at the of 12 years with her parents and they settled near Brooks.

She was united in marriage to Joel S. Cole on January 10, 1877, and they made their home in and around Carbon until 1931, when they moved to Corning. To this union 10 children were born, Bessie E. Sundstrom of Corning, Ladye Powell of Rouleau, Canada, Fred of Indianola, Arthur of Prescott, Harry of Massena, Floyd of Bridgewater. She was preceded in death by her husband and four children. Mrs Minnie Johnson. Frank. Smith and Perry. She is survived by her six children, a grandson, Russell Johnson, whom she cared for as her own, 15 grandchildren, 21 great-grandchildren, and 2 great-great-grandchildren. She is also survived by two sisters, Mrs. D. T. Odell of Brooks, and Ida King, and one brother, Frank Palmer, both of Corning, and a host on nieces, nephews and friends.

Mrs. Cole was one of the pioneers of this community having lived here for 79 years. After the death of her husband in 1931 she made her home with her children. She was a kind and loving wife and mother and the community will remember her for her loving and kindly nature. She was a member of the Methodist Church in Carbon.

Funeral services were held August 7 at the Methodist Church in Carbon with burial in Quincy Cemetery.

Children of JOEL COLE and CHARLOTTE PALMER are:

    i. BESSIE E.[10] COLE, b. Abt. 1878, Adams County, Iowa; m. MISTRE SUNDSTROM.
    ii. FREDERICK A. COLE, b. Nov 1878, Adams County, Iowa.
    iii. SMITH COLE, b. Abt. 1881, Adams County, Iowa; d. Bef. 10 Nov 1931.
1921. iv. MINNIE BELL COLE, b. Oct 1883, Adams County, Iowa; d. Bef. 10 Nov 1931.
    v. FRANK E. COLE, b. Abt. 1885, Adams County, Iowa; d. Bef. 10 Nov 1931.
    vi. ARTHUR BENJAMIN COLE, b. Feb 1887, Adams County, Iowa.
    vii. HARRY COLE, b. Feb 1889, Adams County, Iowa.
    viii. LYDIA COLE, b. Feb 1891, Adams County, Iowa; m GEORGE POWELL; b. Abt. 1890.
    ix. PERRY AARON COLE, b. Oct 1893, Adams County, Iowa; d. Bef. 05 Aug 1949.
    x. FLOYD M. COLE, b. Oct 1897, Adams County, Iowa.

1041. HANNAH AMANDA 'MANDY'[9] COLE *(MARY[8] RODMAN, DEBORAH[7] MILK, BENJAMIN[6], BENJAMIN[5], JONATHAN[4], JOB[3], JOHN[2], JOHN[1])* was born 16 Dec 1854 in Schoharie County, New York, and died 11 Aug 1944 in Douglas, Adams County, Iowa. She married GEORGE HARTSOCK 02 Oct 1872, son of WILLIAM HARTSOCK and REBECCA _____. He was born 09 Feb 1851 in Ohio, and died 07 Sep 1921 in Douglas, Adams County, Iowa.

OBITUARY

Hannah Amanda Hartsock, daughter of Sabastian & Mary Cole, was born in Schohara County, New York Dec,16, 1854 and passed away at the home of her daughter, Mrs. J.H Killough,

She had been a resident of Adams County since 1871, having moved at that time with her parents from Clinton County Iowa.

Married to George Hartsock, their home was in Carbon, Where six children were born; Willie & Frankie who died in infancy, Vernie Ellen, died 1927, Mrs J.H killough, who lives in Corning Iowa, Roy E Hartsock of Sioux City IA. and Charlie of Libby Montana. She also made a home for Cyrus, now of Stockton California, and Orla (Mrs. F.M Mounts) New Port Richie Florida, they are children of Roy, who's wife died in 1910, She leaves 14 grandchildren, 25 great grandchildren and 3 gr-grandchildren. Amanda was the last of a family of seven children, and is survived by seven half brohters and sisters.

Mrs Hartsock was one of the first members of the Carbon Free Methodist Church when it was orginized more than 30 years ago. She has been a devoted worker for her lord ever since. Thirteen years ago she moved to live in the home of her daughter Mrs. Killough in Nov of 1939 she lost her eyesight. Although nearly 85 years old she learned to find her way in the house, dress herself and eat at the table. On July 16th 1944 she suffered a stroke, leaving her nearly helpless but still able to enjoy the visits of her friends and relatives, She was especially happy to have Orla and her husband with her before and during her last illness.

The funeral service was held at lines funeral home in Corning, Aug, 12 with burial in the family plot at Quincy Cemetery. Her children were present except Charlie, who was unable to make the trip.

Children of HANNAH COLE and GEORGE HARTSOCK are:

    i. WILLIAM[10] HARTSOCK, b. 1873, Douglas, Adams County, Iowa; d. 22 Oct 1877, Douglas, Adams County, Iowa.
    ii. FRANK HARTSOCK, b. 1876, Douglas, Adams County, Iowa; d. 22 Oct 1877, Douglas, Adams County,

   Iowa.
- iii. VERNICE ELLEN HARTSOCK, b. Abt. 1878, Douglas, Adams County, Iowa; d. 1927.
- iv. ROY E. HARTSOCK, b. Abt. 1881, Douglas, Adams County, Iowa.
- v. CHARLES E. HARTSOCK, b. Abt. 1884, Douglas, Adams County, Iowa.
- vi. BESSIE A. HARTSOCK, b. Abt. 1887, Douglas, Adams County, Iowa.

1042. GEORGE E.^{9} COLE (MARY^8 RODMAN, DEBORAH^7 MILK, BENJAMIN^6, BENJAMIN^5, JONATHAN^4, JOB^3, JOHN^2, JOHN^1) was born Apr 1867 in Clinton County, Iowa, and died 1939 in Adams County, Iowa. He married EVA MAUD 'EVVIE' GOODWIN Abt. 1885 in Iowa. She was born Nov 1866 in Wisconsin, and died 1940 in Adams County, Iowa.

Child of GEORGE COLE and EVA GOODWIN is:
- i. ORRIE E.^{10} COLE, b. Aug 1886, Iowa.

1043. FRANCES MARIE^9 RODMAN (EZRA COOK^8, DEBORAH^7 MILK, BENJAMIN^6, BENJAMIN^5, JONATHAN^4, JOB^3, JOHN^2, JOHN^1) was born 20 Jul 1855 in Callicoon, Sullivan County, New York, and died 21 Nov 1941 in Binghamton, Broome County, New York. She married EDWARD SNYDER HARDING. He was born 24 Jul 1854 in Binghamton, Broome County, New York, and died 06 Dec 1941 in Binghamton, Broome County, New York.

Children of FRANCES RODMAN and EDWARD HARDING are:
- i. LILLA B.^{10} HARDING, b. Abt. 1879, New York.
- ii. RENA M. HARDING, b. Abt. 1881, New York.
- iii. ALBERT H. HARDING, b. Abt. 1886, New York.
- iv. FRED LESLIE HARDING, b. Abt. 1891, New York.
- v. GRANT M. HARDING, b. Abt. 1898, New York.
- vi. EZRA G. HARDING, b. Abt. 1894, New York.

1044. CECILE^9 RODMAN (EZRA COOK^8, DEBORAH^7 MILK, BENJAMIN^6, BENJAMIN^5, JONATHAN^4, JOB^3, JOHN^2, JOHN^1) was born 05 Dec 1863 in Callicoon, Sullivan County, New York, and died 1945 in Binghamton, Broome County, New York. She married REILEY W. SAMPSON. He was born Dec 1859 in Pennsylvania, and died 1915 in Binghamton, Broome County, New York.

Children of CECILE RODMAN and REILEY SAMPSON are:
- i. MARION^{10} SAMPSON, b. Abt. 1902, New York.
- ii. EDGAR SAMPSON, b. Sep 1887, New York.
- iii. DEAN SAMPSON, b. Dec 1891, New York.
- iv. LAURA SAMPSON, b. Mar 1897, New York.
- v. CARROL L. SAMPSON, b. Jun 1898, New York.

1045. GRANT A.^{9} RODMAN (EZRA COOK^8, DEBORAH^7 MILK, BENJAMIN^6, BENJAMIN^5, JONATHAN^4, JOB^3, JOHN^2, JOHN^1) was born Oct 1867 in Pennsylvania, and died 1945 in Binghamton, Broome County, New York. He married (1) BERTHA J. LANDON Abt. 1885, daughter of ISAAC LANDON and SABRINA _____. She was born 1867, and died 1900 in Binghamton, Broome County, New York. He married (2) AMA MAY _____ Abt. 1903 in New York. She was born 1866 in New York, and died 1936 in Binghamton, Broome County, New York.

Children of GRANT RODMAN and BERTHA LANDON are:
- i. HAZEL^{10} RODMAN, b. Oct 1888, New York.
- ii. ERNEST L. RODMAN, b. Mar 1895, Pennsylvania.

Children of GRANT RODMAN and AMA _____ are:
- iii. SARAH CECILE^{10} RODMAN, b. Abt. 1906, New York.
- iv. RUTH ELIZABETH RODMAN, b. Abt. 1909, New York.

1046. HARRY E.^{9} RODMAN (EZRA COOK^8, DEBORAH^7 MILK, BENJAMIN^6, BENJAMIN^5, JONATHAN^4, JOB^3, JOHN^2, JOHN^1) was born May 1873 in Binghamton, Broome County, New York, and died 1959. He married MAUDE B. _____ Abt. 1891. She was born Feb 1871 in Pennsylvania, and died 1931.

Children of HARRY RODMAN and MAUDE _____ are:
- i. MARE J.[10] RODMAN, b. May 1892, Pennsylvania.
- ii. ARTHUR G. RODMAN, b. Nov 1893, Pennsylvania.
- iii. DONALD H. RODMAN, b. Sep 1896, Pennsylvania.
- iv. HARRY G. RODMAN, b. Abt. 1901, Pennsylvania.
- v. RENA B. RODMAN, b. Abt. 1907, Pennsylvania.

1047. REUBEN[9] MEYERS *(PERLINA[8] DIBBLE, BETSEY[7] MILK, BENJAMIN[6], BENJAMIN[5], JONATHAN[4], JOB[3], JOHN[2], JOHN[1])* was born Abt. 1850. He married ELIZABETH BECKER Abt. 1876. She was born Abt. 1855.

Children of REUBEN MEYERS and ELIZABETH BECKER are:
- i. RODELTHA A.[10] MEYERS, b. 20 Jul 1877; d. 18 Nov 1952, Cobleskill, New York; m. ORIE BROWN, 24 Nov 1902, Cobleskill, New York; b. Abt. 1875.
- 1922. ii. EDNA MEYERS, b. 04 May 1886, Richmondville, Schoharie County, New York; d. 21 Aug 1954, Warnerville, New York.
- 1923. iii. JOHN MEYERS, d. 1933, Cobleskill, New York.

1048. MARVIN R.[9] FANCHER *(POLLY MARGARET[8] DIBBLE, BETSEY[7] MILK, BENJAMIN[6], BENJAMIN[5], JONATHAN[4], JOB[3], JOHN[2], JOHN[1])* was born 21 Oct 1851 in Schoharie County, New York, and died 28 Oct 1928. He married CATHERINE A. STROH 17 Feb 1874 in Cobleskill, New York. She was born 04 Oct 1858 in Blenheim, Schoharie County, New York, and died 16 Jun 1937.

Children of MARVIN FANCHER and CATHERINE STROH are:
- 1924. i. BERTHA J.[10] FANCHER, b. 03 Aug 1884, Fulton, Schoharie County, New York.
- ii. WILLIS LAVERNE FANCHER, b. 21 Jul 1887, Fulton, Schoharie County, New York; d. 18 Nov 1945.
- iii. JENNIE MAY FANCHER, b. 23 Aug 1891, Fulton, Schoharie County, New York; d. 10 Nov 1903, Fulton, Schoharie County, New York.
- 1925. iv. ROBERT MORRIS FANCHER, b. 31 May 1898, Fulton, Schoharie County, New York; d. 01 Feb 1991, Schenectady, New York.

1049. ADELINE[9] FANCHER *(POLLY MARGARET[8] DIBBLE, BETSEY[7] MILK, BENJAMIN[6], BENJAMIN[5], JONATHAN[4], JOB[3], JOHN[2], JOHN[1])* was born 30 Aug 1853 in Schoharie County, New York, and died 17 May 1931 in Summit, Schoharie County, New York. She married CHARLES BANKS 09 Feb 1875. He was born Aug 1853, and died Bet. 1920 - 1930 in Schoharie County, New York.

Children of ADELINE FANCHER and CHARLES BANKS are:
- 1926. i. CAROLINE 'CARRIE'[10] BANKS, b. 13 Mar 1876, Blenheim, Schoharie County, New York; d. 01 Feb 1953, Cooperstown, New York.
- 1927. ii. MYRON JAMES BANKS, b. 12 Jun 1878, Blenheim, Schoharie County, New York; d. Aft. 01 Feb 1953.
- iii. LEROY BANKS, b. Jul 1881, Schoharie County, New York; d. 24 Aug 1945. Never married.
- 1928. iv. MARVIN W. BANKS, b. 19 Aug 1882, Schoharie County, New York; d. 03 Nov 1958, New York.
- v. STEPHEN BANKS, b. Nov 1889, Schoharie County, New York; d. 1916, Schoharie County, New York; m. ANNA _____.

1050. HIRAM J.[9] FANCHER *(POLLY MARGARET[8] DIBBLE, BETSEY[7] MILK, BENJAMIN[6], BENJAMIN[5], JONATHAN[4], JOB[3], JOHN[2], JOHN[1])* was born 24 Sep 1857 in Schoharie County, New York, and died 17 May 1946 in Schenectady, New York. He married OLIVE COOK 10 Mar 1881 in West Fulton, Schoharie County, New York. She was born 21 Feb 1864 in Schenectady, New York, and died 20 Mar 1934 in Schenectady, New York.

Children of HIRAM FANCHER and OLIVE COOK are:
- i. LIZZIE[10] FANCHER, d. d.y..
- ii. DORA FANCHER, d. d.y..
- iii. MYRTLE FANCHER, d. d.y..
- iv. ELVA FANCHER, d. d.y..
- 1929. v. STEPHEN FANCHER, b. Abt. 1890.

vi. MAGGIE FANCHER.

1051. CALEB[9] FANCHER *(POLLY MARGARET[8] DIBBLE, BETSEY[7] MILK, BENJAMIN[6], BENJAMIN[5], JONATHAN[4], JOB[3], JOHN[2], JOHN[1])* was born 19 Dec 1859 in Schoharie County, New York, and died 21 Oct 1951 in Schoharie County, New York. He married EMMA P. MYERS 13 Jan 1885. She was born 22 Jul 1863 in Schoharie County, New York, and died 25 Sep 1948 in Summit, Schoharie County, New York.

Children of CALEB FANCHER and EMMA MYERS are:
- 1930. i. VIOLA[10] FANCHER, b. 10 Dec 1885, Fulton, Schoharie County, New York; d. 18 Apr 1963, Stamford, Delaware County, New York.
- 1931. ii. ERNEST CALEB FANCHER, b. 11 May 1887, Schoharie County, New York; d. 06 Jan 1971, Schoharie County, New York.
- 1932. iii. GORDON FANCHER, b. 03 Apr 1891, Schoharie County, New York; d. 07 Dec 1962, Schoharie County, New York.
- iv. DONOVAN LOURGHN FANCHER, b. 08 Apr 1893, Schoharie County, New York; d. 09 Apr 1949, Schoharie County, New York.
- v. FRANK FANCHER, b. 10 Jan 1895, Schoharie County, New York; d. 24 Nov 1956, Schoharie County, New York; m. ETHEL STEVENS, 10 Nov 1915; b. Abt. 1895; d. 19 Feb 1926, Schoharie County, New York.
- 1933. vi. MABEL FANCHER, b. 13 Feb 1896, Schoharie County, New York; d. 29 Dec 1957, Schoharie County, New York.
- 1934. vii. BYRON FANCHER, b. 29 Aug 1897, Schoharie County, New York; d. 01 Nov 1950, Schoharie County, New York.
- viii. MARCUS FANCHER, b. 23 May 1899, Schoharie County, New York; d. 13 Oct 1915, Schoharie County, New York.
- 1935. ix. EUNICE FANCHER, b. 08 Dec 1900, Eminence, Schoharie County, New York; d. 05 Apr 1987, West Fulton, Schoharie County, New York.
- 1936. x. ALBRO WILLIAM FANCHER, b. 27 Feb 1902, Schoharie County, New York; d. 02 Oct 1981, Richmondville, Schoharie County, New York.
- 1937. xi. FLORENCE E. FANCHER, b. 27 Sep 1905, Schoharie County, New York; d. 03 Jan 1989, Schoharie County, New York.

1052. PERLINA[9] FANCHER *(POLLY MARGARET[8] DIBBLE, BETSEY[7] MILK, BENJAMIN[6], BENJAMIN[5], JONATHAN[4], JOB[3], JOHN[2], JOHN[1])* was born 14 Sep 1861 in Schoharie County, New York, and died 1952. She married SPENCER MEAD Abt. 1880. He was born Abt. 1860 in Richmondville, Schoharie County, New York, and died 1926.

Children of PERLINA FANCHER and SPENCER MEAD are:
- 1938. i. LORISSA[10] MEAD, b. 27 Feb 1883.
- 1939. ii. GROVER E. MEAD, b. 30 Nov 1888.

1053. JAMES RUSSELL[9] FANCHER *(POLLY MARGARET[8] DIBBLE, BETSEY[7] MILK, BENJAMIN[6], BENJAMIN[5], JONATHAN[4], JOB[3], JOHN[2], JOHN[1])* was born 14 Aug 1866 in Schoharie County, New York, and died 14 Dec 1954 in West Fulton, Schoharie County, New York. He married IOLA WHEELER 01 Jan 1889. She was born 19 Jul 1866, and died 10 Apr 1945.

Children of JAMES FANCHER and IOLA WHEELER are:
- 1940. i. ETHEL[10] FANCHER, b. 08 Jan 1890.
- ii. HAZEL FANCHER, b. 24 May 1894; m. RAYMOND MYERS, 28 Dec 1921; b. Abt. 1894; d. Bef. 1956.
- iii. BERNICE FANCHER, b. 08 May 1898.
- 1941. iv. ARKEL FANCHER, b. 25 Feb 1900.
- 1942. v. ORIEN FANCHER, b. 19 Nov 1903.
- 1943. vi. SANFORD FANCHER, b. 01 Apr 1906.

1054. FANNIE ESTHER[9] FANCHER *(POLLY MARGARET[8] DIBBLE, BETSEY[7] MILK, BENJAMIN[6], BENJAMIN[5], JONATHAN[4], JOB[3], JOHN[2], JOHN[1])* was born 19 Sep 1869 in Schoharie County, New York, and died 26 May 1952 in Warnerville, New York. She married MARVIN DAULEY 18 Jun 1890 in West Fulton, Schoharie County, New York. He was born 1861, and died 05 Sep 1938.

Children of FANNIE FANCHER and MARVIN DAULEY are:
- i. ELLA[10] DAULEY, b. 02 Jul 1890, Fulton, Schoharie County, New York; m. WILL CAIN; b. Abt. 1890.
- 1944. ii. JOHN DAULEY, b. 01 Dec 1891, Fulton, Schoharie County, New York.
- iii. RAYMOND DAULEY, b. 27 Oct 1897, Fulton, Schoharie County, New York.
- 1945. iv. NELLIE DAULEY, b. 1900, Fulton, Schoharie County, New York.
- 1946. v. HELEN DAULEY, b. 13 Nov 1902, Fulton, Schoharie County, New York.
- 1947. vi. FORD DAULEY, b. 14 Sep 1904, Fulton, Schoharie County, New York.
- vii. MARGARET E. DAULEY, b. 17 Aug 1906, Fulton, Schoharie County, New York.
- viii. GEORGE W. DAULEY, b. 10 Jun 1908, Fulton, Schoharie County, New York; d. 1953, Richmondville, Schoharie County, New York; m. ADDIE ESTER BANKS; b. 1916, New York; d. 1984, New York.
- ix. HIRAM DAULEY, b. 18 Oct 1910, Fulton, Schoharie County, New York; m. MARRIETTA HELLIGAS; b. Abt. 1910.

1055. SARAH ELIZABETH[9] DIBBLE *(JAMES PATRICK[8], BETSEY[7] MILK, BENJAMIN[6], BENJAMIN[5], JONATHAN[4], JOB[3], JOHN[2], JOHN[1])* was born 15 Mar 1865 in Putnam County, Illinois, and died 1931 in Page County, Iowa. She married NATHAN NAPOLEAN 'NATE' WALDRON 17 Jun 1882 in Sac City, Iowa. He was born 18 Dec 1859, and died 30 Dec 1944 in Page County, Iowa.

Children of SARAH DIBBLE and NATHAN WALDRON are:
- i. JAMES N.[10] WALDRON, b. 1883, Iowa.
- ii. BESSIE L. WALDRON, b. 1884, Iowa.
- iii. ELLA L. WALDRON, b. 1885, Iowa.
- iv. EVERETT C. WALDRON, b. 1887, Iowa.
- v. NATHAN C. WALDRON, b. 1888, Iowa.
- vi. GLENN G. WALDRON, b. 1891, Iowa.
- vii. BERTHA C. WALDRON, b. 1895, Iowa.

1056. HANNAH ELIZABETH[9] VAN VORIS *(ADELINE[8] DIBBLE, BETSEY[7] MILK, BENJAMIN[6], BENJAMIN[5], JONATHAN[4], JOB[3], JOHN[2], JOHN[1])* was born 10 Aug 1850 in West Fulton, Schoharie County, New York, and died 15 Apr 1924 in Stamford, Delaware County, New York. She married CORNELIUS DENNY 14 Nov 1871 in Eminence, Schoharie County, New York, son of HORACE DENNY and ELEANOR TERK. He was born 12 Oct 1849, and died 21 Mar 1892 in Eminence, Schoharie County, New York.

Children of HANNAH VAN VORIS and CORNELIUS DENNY are:
- i. MINNIE E.[10] DENNY, b. 18 Oct 1872, Eminence, New York.
- 1948. ii. CARY J. DENNY, b. 23 Jul 1874, Eminence, New York; d. 10 Apr 1950.
- iii. EMERY R. DENNY, b. 23 May 1877, Eminence, New York; m. NINA HEYWOOD, 16 Sep 1916, Harpersfield, New York; b. 03 May 1898, North Harpersfield, New York.
- iv. MARY V. DENNY, b. 05 May 1879, Eminence, New York; d. 31 Mar 1941, Hyndsville, New York.
- v. MAUD A. DENNY, b. 13 Apr 1885, Eminence, New York; m. GEORGE FITZPATRICK, 08 Jun 1908, Summit, Schoharie County, New York; b. 12 Aug 1889, Guilderland, New York.
- vi. ELLA MAE DENNY, b. 17 Aug 1887, Eminence, New York; d. 27 Jun 1903, Eminence, New York.
- vii. BELLE A. DENNY, b. 31 Mar 1890, Eminence, New York; m. LAWRENCE HOLLENBECK, 30 Jun 1929, Stamford, Delaware County, New York; b. 17 Apr 1876, Blenheim, New York. No children.

1057. CATHERINE 'KATE'[9] VAN VORIS *(ADELINE[8] DIBBLE, BETSEY[7] MILK, BENJAMIN[6], BENJAMIN[5], JONATHAN[4], JOB[3], JOHN[2], JOHN[1])* was born 07 Apr 1854 in West Fulton, Schoharie County, New York, and died 16 Apr 1939 in Schenectady, New York. She married PETER J. HENNESS 04 Jul 1878. He was born Abt. 1854.

Child of CATHERINE VAN VORIS and PETER HENNESS is:
- 1949. i. HARRY V.[10] HENNESS, b. Abt. 1879.

1058. EMMA[9] VAN VORIS *(ADELINE[8] DIBBLE, BETSEY[7] MILK, BENJAMIN[6], BENJAMIN[5], JONATHAN[4], JOB[3], JOHN[2], JOHN[1])* was born 11 Apr 1856 in West Fulton, Schoharie County, New York. She married ALEC JOHNSON 11 Nov 1890. He was born Abt. 1856.

Children of EMMA VAN VORIS and ALEC JOHNSON are:
    i. EDYTH[10] JOHNSON, b. Feb 1880; m. BURR SOURS; b. 08 Oct 1886.
    ii. FLOYD JOHNSON, m. GRACE VANDERBILT.

1059. ANDREW[9] VAN VORIS *(ADELINE[8] DIBBLE, BETSEY[7] MILK, BENJAMIN[6], BENJAMIN[5], JONATHAN[4], JOB[3], JOHN[2], JOHN[1])* was born 07 Mar 1858 in West Fulton, Schoharie County, New York, and died 06 Apr 1946 in San Francisco, California. He married IDA CRASPER 04 Mar 1881, daughter of PETER CRASPER and JANE DECKER. She was born Abt. 1858, and died in San Francisco, California.

Children of ANDREW VAN VORIS and IDA CRASPER are:
    i. EARL[10] VAN VORIS.
    ii. RAY VAN VORIS.
    iii. GRACE VAN VORIS.

1060. MAY A.[9] DIBBLE *(ISAAC[8], BETSEY[7] MILK, BENJAMIN[6], BENJAMIN[5], JONATHAN[4], JOB[3], JOHN[2], JOHN[1])* was born Jul 1888 in Schoharie County, New York.

Child of MAY A. DIBBLE is:
    i. LLOYD L.[10] DIBBLE, b. Abt. Feb 1909, Unadilla, Otsego County, New York.

1061. MARION CALEB[9] WILDAY *(SARAH EMELINE[8] DIBBLE, BETSEY[7] MILK, BENJAMIN[6], BENJAMIN[5], JONATHAN[4], JOB[3], JOHN[2], JOHN[1])* was born 07 Jul 1875 in Eminence, New York, and died 24 Mar 1927. He married FLORA BEACH COOK 17 Mar 1897. She was born 14 Nov 1878.

Children of MARION WILDAY and FLORA COOK are:
1950.   i. CHARLES GEORGE[10] WILDAY, b. 27 Dec 1897.
1951.   ii. GRACE MARIE WILDAY, b. 07 Feb 1899.
1952.   iii. RUTH EMELINE WILDAY, b. 29 Dec 1902.
1953.   iv. HOWARD MARION WILDAY, b. 17 Dec 1922; d. Aug 1968, New York.

1062. CORA[9] DIBBLE *(MARION G.[8], BETSEY[7] MILK, BENJAMIN[6], BENJAMIN[5], JONATHAN[4], JOB[3], JOHN[2], JOHN[1])* was born 01 Oct 1872, and died 08 Feb 1951. She married ARTHUR VAN BUREN 22 Mar 1891. He was born 1870.

Children of CORA DIBBLE and ARTHUR VAN BUREN are:
    i. LULU[10] VAN BUREN, b. Abt. 1892; m. MISTRE VAN WORMER, Central Bridge, New York; b. Abt. 1890.
    ii. KATHLEEN VAN BUREN, b. Aft. 1892.
    iii. JULIETTE VAN BUREN, b. Aft. 1892; m. ARCHIE SHAFER, Schenectady, New York.

1063. ROBIE[9] DIBBLE *(MARION G.[8], BETSEY[7] MILK, BENJAMIN[6], BENJAMIN[5], JONATHAN[4], JOB[3], JOHN[2], JOHN[1])* was born 10 Nov 1874, and died 15 Mar 1949. She married TOBIAS WAYMAN 1910. He was born Apr 1877 in Schenectady, New York.

Child of ROBIE DIBBLE and TOBIAS WAYMAN is:
1954.   i. VIRGINIA[10] WAYMAN, b. Abt. 1926, (adopted).

1064. BETHIAR[9] DIBBLE *(MARION G.[8], BETSEY[7] MILK, BENJAMIN[6], BENJAMIN[5], JONATHAN[4], JOB[3], JOHN[2], JOHN[1])* was born 07 Sep 1877. She married JOHN A. MORSE 1900. He was born 1879 in Of Halcottville, New York, and died 17 Jul 1953.

Child of BETHIAR DIBBLE and JOHN MORSE is:
1955.   i. HARRY B.[10] MORSE, b. Abt. 1905, Middletown, Delaware County, New York.

1065. ETTA[9] DIBBLE *(MARION G.[8], BETSEY[7] MILK, BENJAMIN[6], BENJAMIN[5], JONATHAN[4], JOB[3], JOHN[2], JOHN[1])* was born 30 Dec 1879. She married VIRGIL SPAULDING 1896. He was born 1876.

Children of ETTA DIBBLE and VIRGIL SPAULDING are:
    i. HOWARD[10] SPAULDING, b. 09 Feb 1898, Richmondville, Schoharie County, New York.
    ii. DONALD SPAULDING, b. 03 Jun 1915, Richmondville, Schoharie County, New York; d. 1924, Richmondville, Schoharie County, New York.

1066. JENNIE[9] DIBBLE *(MARION G.[8], BETSEY[7] MILK, BENJAMIN[6], BENJAMIN[5], JONATHAN[4], JOB[3], JOHN[2], JOHN[1])* was born 06 Feb 1882, and died 08 Nov 1943. She married FORD G. CHASE 1903. He was born 1877.

Children of JENNIE DIBBLE and FORD CHASE are:
    i. WALTER[10] CHASE.
    ii. ELIZABETH CHASE, m. MISTRE HENDERSON.

1067. MARY[9] DIBBLE *(MARION G.[8], BETSEY[7] MILK, BENJAMIN[6], BENJAMIN[5], JONATHAN[4], JOB[3], JOHN[2], JOHN[1])* was born 25 Apr 1884, and died 15 Nov 1950. She married BERT CASPER 1902. He was born 1878.

Child of MARY DIBBLE and BERT CASPER is:
    i. CLIFFORD[10] CASPER, b. Abt. 1903.

1068. HARLAN[9] DIBBLE *(MARION G.[8], BETSEY[7] MILK, BENJAMIN[6], BENJAMIN[5], JONATHAN[4], JOB[3], JOHN[2], JOHN[1])* was born 28 Aug 1886, and died 14 Aug 1949 in Richmondville, Schoharie County, New York. He married (1) ESTHER MCNEIL. He married (2) GRACE PITCHER 1908. She was born Abt. 1886.

Children of HARLAN DIBBLE and GRACE PITCHER are:
    i. GLENN[10] DIBBLE, b. Abt. 1913, Fulton, Schoharie County, New York; m. MISS RURY.
1956. ii. MARGARET DIBBLE, b. 1909, Fulton, Schoharie County, New York.

1069. WINTHROP L.[9] MILLIAS *(PHEBE[8] DYER, PERLINA[7] MILK, BENJAMIN[6], BENJAMIN[5], JONATHAN[4], JOB[3], JOHN[2], JOHN[1])* was born 15 Feb 1859, and died in Valatie, New York. He married BURNESINA D. _____. She was born Oct 1862.

Child of WINTHROP MILLIAS and BURNESINA _____ is:
    i. DR. WARD WINTHROP[10] MILLIAS, b. 05 Jan 1888, Schoharie County, New York; d. Oct 1974, Rome, Oneida County, New York; m. FLORENCE S. _____, Abt. 1918; b. Abt. 1891, New York.

1070. JENNIE B.[9] MILLIAS *(PHEBE[8] DYER, PERLINA[7] MILK, BENJAMIN[6], BENJAMIN[5], JONATHAN[4], JOB[3], JOHN[2], JOHN[1])* was born 1862, and died 1927. She married HARRISON MICKLE. He was born 1862, and died 1928.

Child of JENNIE MILLIAS and HARRISON MICKLE is:
1957. i. PEARL[10] MICKLE, b. Abt. 1885.

1071. WILLIAM EUGENE 'WILLIY'[9] MILLIAS *(PHEBE[8] DYER, PERLINA[7] MILK, BENJAMIN[6], BENJAMIN[5], JONATHAN[4], JOB[3], JOHN[2], JOHN[1])* was born 21 Mar 1864 in Jefferson, Schoharie County, New York, and died 19 Jul 1948 in Fox Hospital, Oneonta, Otsego County, New York. He married LOUIE TEN BROECK 21 Mar 1888 in Richmondville, Schoharie County, New York, daughter of JEREMIAH TEN BROECK and ANNA ALLEN. She was born 04 Jul 1869 in Simpsonville, Delaware County, New York, and died 17 Jan 1937 in Brighton, Otsego County, New York.
    LOUIE TEN BROECK: Said to be a descendant of Ethan Allen
    Some information on this family was provided by Annette Morgan.
    OBITUARY
    "WORCESTER - *Mrs. W. E. Millias passed away at her home in Brighton, Sunday evening at 7:40, following an illness of eleven months.*
    Funeral services will be held from the home, Thursday afternoon at 2 o'clock, the Rev. L. C. Jones of the Baptist church officiating, with burial in Maple Grove cemetery.

Louie Nevada was born July 4th, 1869, at Simpsonville, a daughter of Jeremiah and Ann Elisa (Allen) Tenbroeck. She was married March 21st, 1888, at Richmondville to Willie Eugene Millias.

Surviving are her husband; two sons, Otho J. Millias of Center Valley and Joel S. Millias of this village; two daughters, Mrs. Paul Gage of Worcester, and Mrs. Orie Jenkins of Cobleskill; seventeen grandchildren; a sister-in-law, Mrs. Elnora Tenbroeck, and a niece, Mrs. Clarence Hathaway, both of Deposit.

Mrs. Millias had been a respected resident of this community her entire life and a faithful and loving mother and wife. A member of the Worcester Second Baptist church, the Circo of Ruth, and the Missionary society, she was loyal and active in these organizations and ever ready to serve when needed." ["The Otsego Farmer & Republican" (Cooperstown, NY), Fri., Jan. 22, 1937, Page Six]

Children of WILLIAM MILLIAS and LOUIE TEN BROECK are:

    i. RALPH^{10} MILLIAS, b. Apr 1890, Worcester, Otsego County, New York; d. Feb 1907, In RR accident.

    DEATH NOTICE

    "WORCESTER - *Ralph Millias, a Worcester boy and a Delaware and Hudson brakeman was killed by his train in the Oneonta yards Sunday morning. He had only been in the employ of the company for three or four weeks, and was only about seventeen years old. His remains were brought here Monday morning."* ["The Otsego Farmer" (Cooperstown, NY), Feb. 15, 1907, p. 3]

    ii. OTHO JEREMIAH MILLIAS, b. 04 Jan 1895, Worcester, Otsego County, New York; d. 05 May 1976, Worcester, Otsego County, New York.

1959.   iii. JOEL SEBASTIAN MILLIAS, b. 31 Aug 1898, Worcester, Otsego County, New York; d. 31 Jan 1988, Sidney, Delaware County, New York.

    iv. RUBY M. MILLIAS, b. 08 Jan 1903, Worcester County, New York; d. Feb 1911, Worcester, Otsego County, New York.

    DEATH NOTICE

    Richfield Springs NY Mercury

    Joel Millias, the 10 year old son of Mr. and Mrs. William Millias, of Worcester, accidently shot and killed his eight year old sister, Ruby, Friday while playing with a 32 caliber rifle.

    The family had finished dinner and the children were playing in the kitchen.

    The boy took down from the wall the rifle, not knowing it was loaded, and in trying to manipulate it the gun was accidently discharged the bullet entering the girl's body under the left arm.

    She died in less than 15 minutes and before medical aid could be summoned.

1960.   v. LAURA A. MILLIAS, b. 12 Nov 1904, Worcester, Otsego County, New York.

1961.   vi. PHEBE G. MILLIAS, b. 09 May 1907, Worcester, Otsego County, New York.

    vii. HELEN D. MILLIAS, b. 1910, Worcester, Otsego County, New York; d. 11 Feb 1919, Oneonta, Otsego County, New York.

1072. GEORGE ALFRED^9 DYER *(LEWIS^8, PERLINA^7 MILK, BENJAMIN^6, BENJAMIN^5, JONATHAN^4, JOB^3, JOHN^2, JOHN^1)* was born 05 Sep 1880. He married ELVA VAUGHN. She was born 11 Aug 1883.

Children of GEORGE DYER and ELVA VAUGHN are:

    i. FLORENCE^{10} DYER, b. 15 Feb 1907, Schenevus, New York; m. WARREN ENGLISH, 08 Oct 1927; b. Abt. 1907.

1962.   ii. JOHN LEWIS DYER, b. 05 Jun 1917, Schenevus, New York.

1073. MARY^9 DYER *(LEWIS^8, PERLINA^7 MILK, BENJAMIN^6, BENJAMIN^5, JONATHAN^4, JOB^3, JOHN^2, JOHN^1)* was born 29 Jun 1883. She married JAMES WILLIAM WEBBER 1905. He was born 04 Jul 1883.

Child of MARY DYER and JAMES WEBBER is:

1963.   i. MABEL LOUISE^{10} WEBBER, b. 07 Nov 1906.

1074. DR. JONATHAN BLANCHARD^9 COOK *(EZRA ASHER^8, PERMELIA^7 MILK, BENJAMIN^6, BENJAMIN^5, JONATHAN^4, JOB^3, JOHN^2, JOHN^1)* was born 11 Sep 1881 in Chicago, Illinois. He married ADAH MILLER Abt. 1919, daughter of JOHN MILLER and ELIZA STRASBURGER. She was born Abt. 1881, and died 10 Jun 1920 in Chicago, Illinois.

Child of JONATHAN COOK and ADAH MILLER is:
- i. JONATHAN MILLER[10] COOK, b. 08 Jun 1920, Chicago, Illinois.

1075. DAVID CHARLES[9] COOK *(DAVID CALEB[8], PERMELIA[7] MILK, BENJAMIN[6], BENJAMIN[5], JONATHAN[4], JOB[3], JOHN[2], JOHN[1])* was born 7 Jun 1881 in Elgin, Illinois, and died 16 Mar 1932 in Elgin, Illinois. He married FRANCES LOIS KERR Abt. 1905. She was born 24 Sep 1880 in Iowa, and died 12 Aug 1950 in Los Angeles, California.

Cook County, Illinois, Birth Certificates Index, 1871-1922 about David Charles Cook
Name: David Charles Cook, Birth Date: 7 Jun 1881, Birth Place: Worth, Cook, Illinois

Children of DAVID COOK and FRANCES KERR are:
- i. LOIS[10] COOK, b. 1907, Elgin, Illinois; d. 1931, Elgin, Illinois; m. G. I. H. PERRY; b. Abt. 1907.
- 1964. ii. FRANCES COOK, b. 1910, Elgin, Illinois.
- 1965. iii. DAVID C. COOK III, b. 11 Jun 1912, Elgin, Illinois; d. 06 Apr 1990, Cook County, Illinois.

1076. VIRA[9] GAULT *(RACHAEL[8] JUDD, JANET[7] MILK, BENJAMIN[6], BENJAMIN[5], JONATHAN[4], JOB[3], JOHN[2], JOHN[1])* was born 19 Mar 1878. She married IRVING DAYTON 16 Sep 1896. He was born Abt. 1878, and died Jun 1928 in Slingerlands, New York?.

Children of VIRA GAULT and IRVING DAYTON are:
- 1966. i. HOWARD[10] DAYTON, b. 20 Sep 1897.
- 1967. ii. MILDRED DAYTON, b. 24 Jun 1899.
- 1968. iii. ELDRED DAYTON, b. 24 Jun 1899.
- 1969. iv. HARVEY DAYTON, b. 30 Nov 1903.
- 1970. v. HILTON DAYTON, b. 31 Jul 1916.

1077. JOHN A.[9] MILK *(GEORGE H.[8], DAVID[7], BENJAMIN[6], BENJAMIN[5], JONATHAN[4], JOB[3], JOHN[2], JOHN[1])* was born 12 Oct 1878 in Hancock, Delaware County, New York, and died 09 May 1909 in Hancock, Delaware County, New York. He married CALLA A. PEAKE 21 Dec 1899 in Callicoon Depot, Delaware County, NY, daughter of WILLIAM PEAKE and JULIA HITCHCOCK. She was born 14 Feb 1869 in Of Long Eddy, and died 15 Mar 1926 in Hancock, Delaware Co., NY.

Children of JOHN MILK and CALLA PEAKE are:
- 1971. i. JULIA MARION[10] MILK, b. 20 Jun 1901, Delaware County, NY.
- 1972. ii. DOROTHY GRACE MILK, b. 17 Jan 1905; d. Jul 1968, Long Island City, Queens, New York.

1078. LENA VIOLA[9] MILK *(GEORGE H.[8], DAVID[7], BENJAMIN[6], BENJAMIN[5], JONATHAN[4], JOB[3], JOHN[2], JOHN[1])* was born 26 Apr 1880 in Hancock, Delaware County, New York, and died 22 Feb 1920 in Binghamton, Broome County, New York. She married GEORGE SMITH 30 Oct 1901 in Delaware County, New York, son of LEWIS SMITH and ELIZABETH WAGNER. He was born 07 Jul 1879, and died 06 Apr 1907 in Delaware County, New York.

George Smith was killed by an explosion while opening a stone quarry.

Children of LENA MILK and GEORGE SMITH are:
- 1973. i. MILTON RAY[10] SMITH, b. 20 Aug 1904, Delaware County, New York.
- 1974. ii. GEORGE WALTER SMITH, b. 05 Jan 1907, New York.

1079. LEE B.[9] MILK *(GEORGE H.[8], DAVID[7], BENJAMIN[6], BENJAMIN[5], JONATHAN[4], JOB[3], JOHN[2], JOHN[1])* was born 05 Sep 1882 in Hancock, Delaware County, New York, and died 22 Dec 1959 in Walton, Delaware County, NY. He married MARTHA PRISCILLA HENDRICKS 21 Sep 1911 in Delaware County, NY, daughter of ISAAC HENDRICKS and MARY GOULD. She was born 14 Jan 1886 in Hancock, Delaware County, NY, and died 29 May 1962 in Walton, Delaware County, NY.

Lee Milk was historian of the David and Lucinda Milk family and was an assistant author of History and Genealogy of the Milk-Milks Family, and was treasurer of the Wm. B. Ogden Free Library in Walton, New York.

Lee was elected Librarian for the Sunday school on April 7, 1898.

Lee is referred to as Prof. Lee Milk of Fleischmanns in excerpts from the Hancock Herald on Oct 13, 1927

Martha Priscilla Hendricks was a teacher, D.A.R. regent, a daughter of Isaac Newton Hendricks and Mary Gould, a descendant of Sir William Cranston and of Governors Jeremy Clark and John Cranston of R.I.

Children of LEE MILK and MARTHA HENDRICKS are:

1975. i. HELEN MARGARET[10] MILK, b. 22 Jun 1912, Newfield, Tompkins County, New York.
1976. ii. ROBERT HENDRICKS MILK, b. 04 Nov 1913, Newfield, Tompkins County, New York; d. May 1978, Greene, Chenango Co., New York.
1977. iii. RICHARD GEORGE MILK, b. 28 Sep 1915, Munnsville, Madison County, New York; d. May 1980, Petersburg City, Petersburg Co., Virginia.
1978. iv. PRISCILLA ANN MILK, b. 23 Nov 1917, Munnsville, Madison County, New York; d. 16 Mar 1987, Oakland, Alameda County, California.
1979. v. RUTH LOUISE MILK, b. 19 Nov 1921, East Bloomfield, Ontario County, New York.

1080. ARLYN RAY[9] MILK *(GEORGE H.[8], DAVID[7], BENJAMIN[6], BENJAMIN[5], JONATHAN[4], JOB[3], JOHN[2], JOHN[1])* was born 09 Aug 1891 in Hancock, Delaware County, New York, and died 02 Jul 1993 in Long Eddy, Sullivan, NY 12760. He married VICTORIA MARY "DORA" SHEA 12 Feb 1915 in Delaware County, NY, daughter of EDWARD SHEA and MARY MEYERS. She was born Bet. 1886 - 1887, and died 06 Aug 1952 in Sullivan County, New York.

Children of ARLYN MILK and VICTORIA SHEA are:

1980. i. GERALD A.[10] MILK, b. 15 Jun 1915, Hancock, Delaware County, New York; d. Jan 1980.
1981. ii. MARY "ARLENE" MILK, b. 01 May 1916, Hancock, Delaware County, New York; d. Bef. Oct 2002.
1982. iii. KATHRYN A. MILK, b. 17 Jul 1917, Hancock, Delaware County, New York; d. Bef. Oct 2002.
 iv. GERTRUDE M. MILK, b. 13 Sep 1918, Hancock, Delaware County, New York; d. 22 Oct 1982, Kirkwood, Broome County, New York; m. CARL B. JOHNS, 02 Sep 1939; b. 20 Sep 1906, Stanton, Pennsylvania; d. 23 May 1999, Kirkwood, Broome County, New York.

   DEATH NOTICE

   Carl B. Johns, 92, of Kirkwood, passed away peacefully in his home on May 23, 1999. Mr. Johns was a heavy equipment operator of many projects such as the Dream Highway of Pa., and the St. Lawrence Seaway.

   He was a member of local # 410 Operating Engineers. Carl married Gertrude Milk of Long Eddy, NY. in 1939. She preceded him in death in 1982.

   He was the youngest son of Eli C. and Martha VanLeer Johns of Stanton, Pa. and was also predeceased by his five brothers and five sisters. Carl will be missed by his many nephews, nieces, dear friends and caring neighbors.

   Services will be held at the Thomas J. Shea Funeral Home Inc. Rev Gerald Buckley officiated. Entombment was in Vestal Hills Memorial Park

1983. v. VERONICA MILK, b. 15 Sep 1919, Hancock, Delaware County, New York; d. Oct 1986, Deposit, Broome County, New York.
1984. vi. DONALD GEORGE MILK, b. 23 Nov 1920, Hancock, Delaware County, New York; d. 30 Oct 2006, Long Eddy, Sullivan County, New York.
1985. vii. MARION T. MILK, b. 12 Jan 1924, Hancock, Delaware County, New York; d. 20 Oct 2002, Long Eddy, Sullivan County, New York.
1986. viii. EDWARD H. MILK, b. 28 Mar 1928, Hancock, Delaware County, New York; d. 24 Oct 2010, Long Eddy, Sullivan County, New York.

1081. CHARLES EDWOND[9] BRAZIE *(ANNA SARAH[8] MILK, DAVID[7], BENJAMIN[6], BENJAMIN[5], JONATHAN[4], JOB[3], JOHN[2], JOHN[1])* was born 14 Jun 1873 in Hancock, Delaware County, New York, and died 22 Dec 1955 in Hancock, Delaware County, New York. He married ROSIELEAN DUNN Bet. 1892 - 1893 in Hancock, Delaware County, New York. She was born Sep 1873 in Hancock, Delaware County, New York, and died 1958 in Hancock, Delaware County, New York.

Rosielean and Charles also had a child born 1893-1900 who died young.

Children of CHARLES BRAZIE and ROSIELEAN DUNN are:

1987. i. ROYAL MELVIN[10] BRAZIE, b. 18 Sep 1894, Hancock, Delaware County, New York; d. 12 Aug 1973, Deposit, Broome County, New York.
 ii. ETHEL MAE BRAZIE, b. 27 Jul 1897, Hancock, Delaware County, New York; m. (1) JOHN R SCHOONMAKER, 20 Nov 1923, Sullivan County, New York; b. 07 Jan 1888; d. 07 Sep 1952; m. (2) RUFUS BULLIS, 01 May 1954; b. Abt. 1897.

	iii.	CLYDE A. BRAZIE, b. 13 Sep 1904, Delaware County, New York; d. Oct 1927, Pontiac, Michigan.
1988.	iv.	SUSAN MILDRED BRAZIE, b. 04 Jan 1910, Delaware County, New York.
1989.	v.	KENNETH CHARLES BRAZIE, b. 11 Jan 1912, Delaware County, New York; d. 1968, Delaware County, NY.

1082. EMMET A.^{9} BRAZIE *(ANNA SARAH^8 MILK, DAVID^7, BENJAMIN^6, BENJAMIN^5, JONATHAN^4, JOB^3, JOHN^2, JOHN^1)* was born 30 Apr 1886 in Hancock, Delaware County, New York. He married (1) BLANCHE RICKARD 1903, daughter of CORNELIUS RICKARD and JENNIE _____. She was born Abt. 1885. He married (2) LYDIA ROBERTS 25 Apr 1923, daughter of GRIFFITH ROBERTS and SARAH DAVIS. She was born 24 Apr 1898.

Child of EMMET BRAZIE and BLANCHE RICKARD is:
1990.	i.	CLAYTON P.^{10} BRAZIE, b. 29 Jan 1904, Delaware County, New York; d. 19 Apr 1972, Boonville, Oneida County, NY.

1083. MINNIE ANN^9 MILK *(ABRAM LINCOLN^8, DAVID^7, BENJAMIN^6, BENJAMIN^5, JONATHAN^4, JOB^3, JOHN^2, JOHN^1)* was born 25 Dec 1878 in Hancock, Delaware County, New York, and died 13 Jun 1901. She married CLARENCE HOOLIHAN 1898, son of REV. RICHARD HOOLIHAN. He was born 16 Mar 1871.

Child of MINNIE MILK and CLARENCE HOOLIHAN is:
1991.	i.	ALMA MINNIE^{10} HOOLIHAN, b. 03 Oct 1900.

1084. IRVIN "LESLIE" D.^{9} MILK *(ABRAM LINCOLN^8, DAVID^7, BENJAMIN^6, BENJAMIN^5, JONATHAN^4, JOB^3, JOHN^2, JOHN^1)* was born 12 Jun 1881 in Hancock, Delaware County, New York, and died 14 Aug 1956 in Delaware County, NY. He married LOUISA RUTZ 14 Feb 1901, daughter of PETER RUTZ and LOUISE GABRIEL. She was born 30 Nov 1881 in New York, and died 08 Jul 1947 in Callicoon, Sullivan County, New York.

Children of IRVIN MILK and LOUISA RUTZ are:
1992.	i.	LAWRENCE R.^{10} MILK, b. 18 Jan 1902, Brooklyn, NY City, New York; d. 1959, Sullivan County, New York.
	ii.	FRIEDA MILK, b. 27 Oct 1903, Brooklyn, NY City, New York; d. 08 May 1925; m. TONY GRIEBLE, 19 Sep 1922; b. Abt. 1898, New York.
1993.	iii.	ARTHUR L. MILK, b. 01 Nov 1905, Brooklyn, NY City, New York; d. Oct 1962.
	iv.	WILLIAM L. MILK, b. 25 Sep 1910, New York; d. 24 May 1993, Callicoon, Sullivan County, New York; m. BERTHA MCGUIRE, 01 Apr 1934; b. 03 Aug 1910, Callicoon, Sullivan County, New York; d. 30 Apr 2004, Callicoon, Sullivan County, New York. No children.

OBITUARY

Bertha M. Milk, Ret. Teacher, 93

Bertha M. Milk of Callicoon, a lifelong area resident and a retired elementary teacher at the Delaware Valley Central School, died Friday, April 30, 2004, at her home. She was 93 years of age.

The daughter of the late Edward and Amanda Engert McGuire, she was born August 2, 1910, in Callicoon. She was the widow of William Milk.

A 1928 graduate of Callicoon High School, she attended Delhi Training Class and New Paltz and Oneonta colleges. She received her B.S. from New Paltz and spent 40 years teaching in many local rural schools and Callicoon High School before it became Delaware Valley Central School, retiring in 1973.

She was a charter member of Delta Kappa Gamma, Tau Chapter, an honorary society for outstanding teachers, organized in Liberty in 1952, and recommended by her principal, the late Charles E. Lewis. She was loved by her hundreds of students and her co-workers.

After retirement, "Bert" and her husband enjoyed wintering in Florida. They were members of the former Happy Wanderers Trailer Club and enjoyed many fishing trips to Canada.

Mrs. Milk was a member of Holy Cross Church in Callicoon, the Delaware Valley Senior Citizens and Court Father Raphael Chapter #1542 of Catholic Daughters of the Americas, all in Callicoon. She was also a member of the Jeffersonville Senior Citizens, the Sullivan County Retired Teachers and the New York State Retired Teachers.

She is survived by three sisters, Agnes Spielmann of Youngsville, Florence Bauer of Callicoon and Dorothy Gottschalk and her husband, Philip, of Hankins; several nieces, nephews, grand-nieces and grand-nephews; and a sister-in-law, Genevieve Hughs of Goulds. She was predeceased by a sister, Helen Walters

> *A funeral Mass will be offered at 11 a.m. on Tuesday at Holy Cross Church in Callicoon with Father Ignatius Smith, O.F.M., officiating.*
> *Burial will be made in Holy Cross Cemetery in Callicoon.*
> *Memorial contributions may be made to the Upper Delaware Ambulance Corps, P.O. Box 238, Hankins, N.Y. 12741 or to Holy Cross Church, P.O. Box 246, Callicoon, N.Y. 12723.*
> *Funeral arrangements were made by the Stewart-Murphy Funeral Home in Callicoon.*

1994. v. GENEVIEVE H. MILK, b. 08 Nov 1915, New York; d. 11 Oct 2005, Long Eddy, Sullivan County, New York.

1085. NELLIE MAY^9 MILK *(ABRAM LINCOLN^8, DAVID^7, BENJAMIN^6, BENJAMIN^5, JONATHAN^4, JOB^3, JOHN^2, JOHN^1)* was born 31 Oct 1883 in Hancock, Delaware County, New York. She married JOHN F. RUTZ 09 Jan 1901 in Delaware County, NY, son of PETER RUTZ and LOUISE GABRIEL. He was born 15 Dec 1878 in Of Eminence, New York.

Children of NELLIE MILK and JOHN RUTZ are:
1995. i. LETTIE L.^{10} RUTZ, b. 13 Aug 1901.
1996. ii. JOHN L. RUTZ, b. 30 May 1903.

1086. JANETTE A.^{9} MILK *(ABRAM LINCOLN^8, DAVID^7, BENJAMIN^6, BENJAMIN^5, JONATHAN^4, JOB^3, JOHN^2, JOHN^1)* was born 20 Feb 1899 in Hancock, Delaware County, New York. She married JOHN D. MAY, JR. 23 Oct 1916 in Delaware County, NY, son of CHARLES MAY and ELIZABETH RICKARD-STEVENS. He was born 10 Aug 1892.

Children of JANETTE MILK and JOHN MAY are:
1997. i. ELDA IRENE^{10} MAY, b. 12 Mar 1919.
ii. NORMAN ABRAM MAY, b. 13 May 1922.

1087. LESTER L.^{9} MILK *(ABRAM LINCOLN^8, DAVID^7, BENJAMIN^6, BENJAMIN^5, JONATHAN^4, JOB^3, JOHN^2, JOHN^1)* was born 20 Jan 1902 in Hancock, Delaware County, New York, and died 24 May 1987 in Long Eddy, Sullivan County, New York. He married FLOSSIE KLEINGARDNER 07 Dec 1926 in Delaware County, NY, daughter of JOHN KLEINGARDNER and NORA SANDERSON. She was born 12 Oct 1907, and died Jan 1977 in Long Eddy, Sullivan County, New York.

Children of LESTER MILK and FLOSSIE KLEINGARDNER are:
1998. i. GWENDOLYN NORA^{10} MILK, b. 04 Nov 1927, Long Eddy, Sullivan Co., NY.
1999. ii. STEWART LIONEL MILK, b. 16 Aug 1929; d. 19 Jan 2011, Deposit, New York.
iii. GAIL IRVING MILK, b. 04 Jul 1931.
2000. iv. DEWAIN ELMER MILK, b. 18 Aug 1934.
v. SHIRLEY DAWN MILK, b. 10 Apr 1936.

1088. JOHN WILLIAM^9 MILK *(WILLIAM^8, DAVID^7, BENJAMIN^6, BENJAMIN^5, JONATHAN^4, JOB^3, JOHN^2, JOHN^1)* was born 03 Jun 1892, and died 21 Feb 1977 in Long Eddy, Sullivan, NY 12760. He married (1) LAURA LOUISE KNAPP 17 Nov 1917 in Delaware County, NY, daughter of WILLIAM KNAPP and CLARA LAYMAN. She was born 09 Dec 1897, and died 27 Feb 1946 in Hancock, Delaware Co., NY. He married (2) TALINA ANDERSON 31 Mar 1948. She was born 07 Apr 1906, and died 26 Jan 1998 in Delhi, Delaware Co, NY 13753.

Children of JOHN MILK and LAURA KNAPP are:
2001. i. KATHLEEN CHARLOTTE^{10} MILK, b. 11 Feb 1921, Delaware County, New York.
2002. ii. ROBERT WILLIAM MILK, b. 25 Apr 1926, Delaware County, New York.

1089. CHARLES CORBETT^9 MILK *(WILLIAM^8, DAVID^7, BENJAMIN^6, BENJAMIN^5, JONATHAN^4, JOB^3, JOHN^2, JOHN^1)* was born 19 Aug 1894 in Sullivan County, New York, and died 27 Oct 1960 in Hancock, Delaware County, New York. He married ALICE MARJORIE GEER 27 Apr 1918 in Callicoon, Delaware County, NY, daughter of SAMPSON GEER and EUNICE CARPENTER. She was born 17 Sep 1896, and died 21 Feb 1982 in Long Eddy, Sullivan, NY 12760.

Child of CHARLES MILK and ALICE GEER is:
2003. i. THEODORE^{10} MILK, b. 16 Oct 1924, Long Eddy, Sullivan County, New York; d. 11 Mar 1964, Long Eddy, Sullivan County, New York.

1090. MARGARET L.[9] MILK *(WILLIAM[8], DAVID[7], BENJAMIN[6], BENJAMIN[5], JONATHAN[4], JOB[3], JOHN[2], JOHN[1])* was born 24 Aug 1898 in Hancock, Delaware County, New York, and died 20 Feb 1965 in Hancock, Delaware County, New York. She married MAURICE K. 'MORRIS' PEAKE 04 Aug 1919, son of CYRUS PEAKE and MARCIA KELLAM. He was born 04 Jul 1893, and died 03 Oct 1972.

Children of MARGARET MILK and MAURICE PEAKE are:
- 2004. i. CAROLYN M.[10] PEAKE, b. 17 May 1920, Binghamton, Broome County, New York; d. 06 Feb 2002, Unadilla, Otsego County, New York.
- ii. JUNE W. PEAKE, b. 21 Jun 1921, Franklin, Delaware County, New York; d. 16 Nov 1995, Delaware County, New York; m. ALBERT D. HAMMOND, 1945; b. 05 Aug 1917, Walton, Delaware County, New York; d. 28 May 1981, Ft. Lauderdale, Dade County, Florida.
- 2005. iii. ELIZABETH PEAKE, b. Abt. 1923, Franklin, Delaware County, New York.
- 2006. iv. JEANE J. PEAKE, b. 25 Jun 1926, Franklin, Delaware County, New York.
- v. JACOB M. 'JAKE' PEAKE, b. 25 Jun 1926, Franklin, Delaware County, New York; d. 15 Jan 2012.

1091. LETTIE "MAE"[9] MILK *(WILLIAM[8], DAVID[7], BENJAMIN[6], BENJAMIN[5], JONATHAN[4], JOB[3], JOHN[2], JOHN[1])* was born 01 Apr 1903. She married (1) RAYMOND MACCLURE 23 Apr 1922. He was born Abt. 1903. She married (2) HARRY E. BOLLMAN 26 Nov 1929. He was born Abt. 1903.

Child of LETTIE MILK and RAYMOND MACCLURE is:
- 2007. i. ELIZABETH ARDIS[10] MACCLURE, b. 10 Feb 1923.

1092. GLADYS M.[9] WARD *(PEARL[8] MILKS, LEVI 'STEPHEN'[7], BENJAMIN[6] MILK, JR., BENJAMIN[5], JONATHAN[4], JOB[3], JOHN[2], JOHN[1])* was born Abt. 1904 in New York, and died in Prob. 1930-1940 Otsego County, NY. She married RAYMOND FRED COLLIER Abt. 1923, son of JACOB COLLIER and PEARL _____. He was born 1903 in New York, and died 1971 in Greene, Chenango County, New York?.

Child of GLADYS WARD and RAYMOND COLLIER is:
- i. ELIZABETH I.[10] COLLIER, b. 08 Aug 1924, Otsego County, New York.

1093. VAN RENSSELAER[9] KIRKE *(CHRISTCHANA[8] VAN VALKENBURGH, LYDIA JANE[7] MILK, TROWBRIDGE[6], BENJAMIN[5], JONATHAN[4], JOB[3], JOHN[2], JOHN[1])* was born Abt. 1858. He married MARY HERDMAN.

Child of VAN KIRKE and MARY HERDMAN is:
- i. MARION OKLEY[10] KIRKE.

1094. ANGELO[9] KIRKE *(CHRISTCHANA[8] VAN VALKENBURGH, LYDIA JANE[7] MILK, TROWBRIDGE[6], BENJAMIN[5], JONATHAN[4], JOB[3], JOHN[2], JOHN[1])* was born 28 Sep 1860, and died 31 Aug 1928. He married ANNA FOWLER 09 Dec 1885. She was born Abt. 1860, and died Jan 1931.

Child of ANGELO KIRKE and ANNA FOWLER is:
- 2008. i. JUDSON FABIAN 'JAY'[10] KIRKE, b. 16 Jun 1888, Fleischmanns, Delaware County, New York; d. 01 Sep 1968, New Orleans, Orleans Parish, Louisiana.

1095. NINA L.[9] VAN VALKENBURGH *(GEORGE ANGELO[8], LYDIA JANE[7] MILK, TROWBRIDGE[6], BENJAMIN[5], JONATHAN[4], JOB[3], JOHN[2], JOHN[1])* was born Apr 1873 in Jewett, Greene County, New York. She married AARON JACOB VAN VALKENBURGH 16 Jun 1897 in Greene County, New York. He was born 26 Apr 1874 in Greene County, New York.

Child of NINA VAN VALKENBURGH and AARON VAN VALKENBURGH is:
- i. ROGER[10] VAN VALKENBURGH, d. d.y..

1096. CYRUS WILBUR[9] VAN VALKENBURGH *(GEORGE ANGELO[8], LYDIA JANE[7] MILK, TROWBRIDGE[6], BENJAMIN[5], JONATHAN[4], JOB[3], JOHN[2], JOHN[1])* was born 15 Jul 1878 in Jewett, Green County, New York. He married MINNIE VAN VALKENBURGH Abt. 1898. She was born Feb 1880.

Children of CYRUS VAN VALKENBURGH and MINNIE VAN VALKENBURGH are:
- i. RITA A.[10] VAN VALKENBURGH, b. Abt. 1901, Jewett, Green County, New York.
- ii. CHRISTINA H. VAN VALKENBURGH, b. Abt. 1906, Jewett, Green County, New York.

1097. GEORGE A.[9] VAN VALKENBURGH *(GEORGE ANGELO[8], LYDIA JANE[7] MILK, TROWBRIDGE[6], BENJAMIN[5], JONATHAN[4], JOB[3], JOHN[2], JOHN[1])* was born 25 Jun 1889 in Jewett, Greene County, New York. He married LULU DOUGLAS 16 Sep 1908. She was born Abt. 1890.

Children of GEORGE VAN VALKENBURGH and LULU DOUGLAS are:
- 2009. i. GEORGE ARLINGTON[10] VAN VALKENBURGH, b. Abt. 1910, Jewett, Greene County, New York.
- ii. DOUGLAS VAN VALKENBURGH, b. 26 Jan 1921, Jewett, Greene County, New York.

1098. ALVERETTA[9] VAN VALKENBURGH *(BENJAMIN[8], LYDIA JANE[7] MILK, TROWBRIDGE[6], BENJAMIN[5], JONATHAN[4], JOB[3], JOHN[2], JOHN[1])* She married JOHN BUCKLEY.

Children of ALVERETTA VAN VALKENBURGH and JOHN BUCKLEY are:
- i. NELLIE MAY[10] BUCKLEY, m. S. PARKER ROCKEFELLER; b. of Hudson, New York.
- 2010. ii. ETHELYN MARIA BUCKLEY.

1099. DELMAR[9] SPEENBURG *(LODEMA[8] VAN VALKENBURGH, LYDIA JANE[7] MILK, TROWBRIDGE[6], BENJAMIN[5], JONATHAN[4], JOB[3], JOHN[2], JOHN[1])* was born 1871. He married JESSIE DEYO.

Children of DELMAR SPEENBURG and JESSIE DEYO are:
- i. VERA[10] SPEENBURG, m. MAURICE PLATT.
- ii. GLEASON SPEENBURG, m. DOROTHY REGAN.
- iii. PERRY SPEENBURG.

1100. DAYTON[9] VAN VALKENBURGH *(WESLEY[8], LYDIA JANE[7] MILK, TROWBRIDGE[6], BENJAMIN[5], JONATHAN[4], JOB[3], JOHN[2], JOHN[1])* He married BERTHA DUNHAM.

Children of DAYTON VAN VALKENBURGH and BERTHA DUNHAM are:
- i. HAROLD[10] VAN VALKENBURGH, m. RUTH _____.
- 2011. ii. EVELYN VAN VALKENBURGH.
- 2012. iii. ADELAIDE VAN VALKENBURGH.
- iv. GERTURDE VAN VALKENBURGH, m. ALFRED J. VAN VALKENBURGH; b. 20 Jan 1908, Lexington, Greene County, New York.

1101. LYDIA[9] VAN VALKENBURGH *(WESLEY[8], LYDIA JANE[7] MILK, TROWBRIDGE[6], BENJAMIN[5], JONATHAN[4], JOB[3], JOHN[2], JOHN[1])* was born 1883. She married JAY TRUESDELL. He was born Abt. 1880.

Children of LYDIA VAN VALKENBURGH and JAY TRUESDELL are:
- i. OLIVE[10] TRUESDELL, m. PAUL FORD.
- ii. FLORA TRUESDELL, m. MISTRE GRAHAM.
- iii. LOUISE TRUESDELL, m. MIKE SOKOLL.
- iv. LEVI TRUESDELL.
- v. DOROTHY TRUESDELL.
- vi. DONALD TRUESDELL.

1102. DEWITT CLINTON[9] GRIFFIN *(VIOLA[8] SHARPE, ANN ELIZA[7] MILK, TROWBRIDGE[6], BENJAMIN[5], JONATHAN[4], JOB[3], JOHN[2], JOHN[1])* was born 22 Sep 1882 in New York. He married ADA GAY MILLER 19 Mar 1910. She was born Abt. 1882.

Child of DEWITT GRIFFIN and ADA MILLER is:
- 2013. i. DEWITT JAMES[10] GRIFFIN, b. 26 Aug 1914.

1103. MATTHEW SHARPE[9] GRIFFIN *(VIOLA[8] SHARPE, ANN ELIZA[7] MILK, TROWBRIDGE[6], BENJAMIN[5], JONATHAN[4], JOB[3], JOHN[2], JOHN[1])* was born 22 Feb 1886 in New York, and died 12 Feb 1914 in Brooklyn, New York. He married ELIZABETH MIAENHULDER in Kingston, Ulster County, New York. She was born 20 Jul 1885 in Kingston, Ulster County, New York, and died 10 Feb 1944.

Child of MATTHEW GRIFFIN and ELIZABETH MIAENHULDER is:
2014.   i.   DONALD V.[10] GRIFFIN, b. 19 May 1907.

1104. WARNER MILLER[9] GRIFFIN *(VIOLA[8] SHARPE, ANN ELIZA[7] MILK, TROWBRIDGE[6], BENJAMIN[5], JONATHAN[4], JOB[3], JOHN[2], JOHN[1])* was born 19 Nov 1889 in Griffin Corners/Fleischmanns, Delaware County, New York. He married ELIZABETH LOUISE SCHAEFER Abt. 1915. She was born 21 Jun 1889 in Brooklyn, New York.
    Warner was manager of Holmes Electric Protection Company; member of Boy Scout Council of Queens County, and other civic organizations.

Children of WARNER GRIFFIN and ELIZABETH SCHAEFER are:
2015.   i.   VIOLA CATHERINE[10] GRIFFIN, b. 14 Feb 1916, Brooklyn, New York.
2016.   ii.   WARNER GEORGE GRIFFIN, b. 05 May 1920, Brooklyn, New York.

1105. PEARL[9] VAN VALKENBURGH *(LENA A.[8] MILK, BENJAMIN[7], TROWBRIDGE[6], BENJAMIN[5], JONATHAN[4], JOB[3], JOHN[2], JOHN[1])* was born Jun 1884 in Lexington, Greene County, New York. She married GEORGE OGDEN RILEY 24 Dec 1902 in Greene County, New York. He was born Nov 1881 in Lexington, Greene County, New York.

Child of PEARL VAN VALKENBURGH and GEORGE RILEY is:
2017.   i.   CLAUDE A.[10] RILEY, b. 10 Oct 1905, Lexington, Greene County, New York.

1106. PAUL ASBURY[9] REEDER *(MARIAN ALICE[8] MILK, BENJAMIN[7], TROWBRIDGE[6], BENJAMIN[5], JONATHAN[4], JOB[3], JOHN[2], JOHN[1])* was born 11 Mar 1903 in Milan, Ohio, and died 14 Oct 1984 in Los Angeles, California. He married MARJORIE EDITH ROSINE 16 Jul 1938, daughter of HOWARD ROSINE and LABLANCHE SIMPSON. She was born 06 Aug 1910 in Evanston, Illinois.

Children of PAUL REEDER and MARJORIE ROSINE are:
    i.   PAUL ASBURY[10] REEDER, b. 15 Mar 1941, Palos Verdes Estates, California.
    ii.   JOHN LEWIS HOWARD REEDER, b. 31 Dec 1942, Palos Verdes Estates, California.
    iii.   CHARLES DONALD REEDER, b. 16 Apr 1946, Palos Verdes Estates, California.

1107. WARD JAMES[9] DUNHAM *(SAMANTHA[8] VAN VALKENBURGH, JULIA ANN[7] MILK, TROWBRIDGE[6], BENJAMIN[5], JONATHAN[4], JOB[3], JOHN[2], JOHN[1])* was born 28 Mar 1880 in New York, and died Mar 1963 in Volusia County, Florida. He married (1) KATHERINE KATHLEEN 'KITTY' MIX. She was born 10 Sep 1897 in New York. He married (2) FLORENCE MARY PELHAM Abt. 1928 in Kingston, Ulster County, New York ?. She was born 10 Sep 1897 in New York, and died 15 Nov 1981 in Raleigh, Wake County, North Carolina.

Child of WARD DUNHAM and FLORENCE PELHAM is:
2018.   i.   WARD JAMES[10] DUNHAM, JR., b. Abt. Aug 1929, Kingston, Ulster County, New York.

1108. CLARENCE E.[9] DUNHAM *(SAMANTHA[8] VAN VALKENBURGH, JULIA ANN[7] MILK, TROWBRIDGE[6], BENJAMIN[5], JONATHAN[4], JOB[3], JOHN[2], JOHN[1])* was born 23 Nov 1884. He married NELLIE BLY HOMEL 30 Mar 1907 in New York.

Children of CLARENCE DUNHAM and NELLIE HOMEL are:
2019.   i.   AUGUSTA SAMANTHA[10] DUNHAM.
2020.   ii.   CHARLES C. DUNHAM.
2021.   iii.   HOMMELL E. DUNHAM.
    iv.   WARD J. DUNHAM, d. Tunisia (WWII).
    v.   CLARENCE C. DUNHAM, m. ELLEN MARY KELLY.
    vi.   NASH E. DUNHAM.

1109. JULIA[9] DUNHAM *(SAMANTHA[8] VAN VALKENBURGH, JULIA ANN[7] MILK, TROWBRIDGE[6], BENJAMIN[5], JONATHAN[4], JOB[3], JOHN[2], JOHN[1])* was born Abt. 1888 in Lexington, Greene County, New York. She married THOMAS JANSEN.

Children of JULIA DUNHAM and THOMAS JANSEN are:
- 2022. i. EVELYN[10] JANSEN.
- 2023. ii. JOHN DUNHAM JANSEN.
- 2024. iii. RUTH JANSEN.
- iv. JEAN JANSEN, m. HERBERT SHULTIS, JR., 22 Oct 1955.
- 2025. v. WILLIAM D. JANSEN.
- 2026. vi. CLARENCE ROBERT JANSEN.

1110. CORYDON BUSHNELL[9] DUNHAM *(SAMANTHA[8] VAN VALKENBURGH, JULIA ANN[7] MILK, TROWBRIDGE[6], BENJAMIN[5], JONATHAN[4], JOB[3], JOHN[2], JOHN[1])* was born 01 Sep 1890 in Lexington, Greene County, New York, and died 09 Nov 1966 in Yonkers, Westchester County, New York. He married MARION HOWE 10 Apr 1925, daughter of EUGENE HOWE and FLORENCE EATON. She was born 04 May 1898 in New York, and died 13 Mar 1984 in Ridgefield, Fairfield County, Connecticut.

Children of CORYDON DUNHAM and MARION HOWE are:
- i. CORYDON BUSHNELL[10] DUNHAM, JR., b. 14 Nov 1927.
- ii. JOAN HOWE DUNHAM, b. Abt. 1931; m. MISTRE DEAN.

1111. OLIVE MAY[9] PERSONS *(CARRIE[8] VAN VALKENBURGH, JULIA ANN[7] MILK, TROWBRIDGE[6], BENJAMIN[5], JONATHAN[4], JOB[3], JOHN[2], JOHN[1])* was born 26 Apr 1883. She married MILTON O. BAILEY 04 Jan 1905 in Greene County, New York ?. He was born Abt. 1883.

Child of OLIVE PERSONS and MILTON BAILEY is:
- i. DR. ORVILLE T.[10] BAILEY, b. 28 May 1909, Greene County, New York.
  Taught at Harvard University, then Professor of Neurology & Pathology, Indiana University.

1112. DR. ALFRED OTIS[9] PERSONS *(CARRIE[8] VAN VALKENBURGH, JULIA ANN[7] MILK, TROWBRIDGE[6], BENJAMIN[5], JONATHAN[4], JOB[3], JOHN[2], JOHN[1])* was born 25 Aug 1886. He married HAZEL ELIZA MAKELY 12 Jan 1911, daughter of FREDERICK MAKELY and MARY ALLEN. She was born Abt. 1886.

Dr. Otis was the 1950 Outstanding General Practitioner in New York State.

Children of ALFRED PERSONS and HAZEL MAKELY are:
- 2027. i. ADDISON FREDERICK[10] PERSONS, b. 08 Mar 1912, New York.
- 2028. ii. FRANCES ELIZABETH PERSONS, b. 07 Jul 1913, New York.

1113. RAY EUGENE[9] PERSONS *(CARRIE[8] VAN VALKENBURGH, JULIA ANN[7] MILK, TROWBRIDGE[6], BENJAMIN[5], JONATHAN[4], JOB[3], JOHN[2], JOHN[1])* was born 14 Nov 1890, and died 29 Sep 1948. He married (1) GRACE DOCHTERMANN. She was born Abt. 1890. He married (2) LULU PATTERSON Abt. 1919. She was born Abt. 1890, and died 05 Mar 1927.

Children of RAY PERSONS and LULU PATTERSON are:
- i. RAY EUGENE[10] PERSONS, JR., b. 26 Feb 1920.
- ii. HELEN OLIVE PERSONS, b. 08 Jun 1923.

1114. CHARLES W.[9] VAN VALKENBURGH *(JAMES[8], JULIA ANN[7] MILK, TROWBRIDGE[6], BENJAMIN[5], JONATHAN[4], JOB[3], JOHN[2], JOHN[1])* was born 05 Dec 1887 in Lexington, Greene County, New York. He married GLADYS E. WAKEFIELD 07 Jun 1916. She was born Abt. 1887 in of Olean, New York.

Children of CHARLES VAN VALKENBURGH and GLADYS WAKEFIELD are:
- 2029. i. ELEANOR MAE[10] VAN VALKENBURGH, b. 17 Apr 1922, Cairo, New York.
- ii. INA CLAUDIA VAN VALKENBURGH, b. 10 Mar 1924, Catskill, Greene County, New York. Art student.

1115. GLENN M.[9] VAN VALKENBURGH *(JAMES[8], JULIA ANN[7] MILK, TROWBRIDGE[6], BENJAMIN[5], JONATHAN[4], JOB[3], JOHN[2], JOHN[1])* was born 06 Jun 1901 in Lexington, Greene County, New York. He married ELIZABETH GRASMUK 28 Dec 1926. She was born Abt. 1901.

Children of GLENN VAN VALKENBURGH and ELIZABETH GRASMUK are:
- i. KARL[10] VAN VALKENBURGH, b. 18 Nov 1927.
- ii. MARIAH VAN VALKENBURGH, b. 03 Apr 1931, New York City.

1116. ELIZABETH[9] BUTLER *(ELLA[8] VAN VALKENBURGH, JULIA ANN[7] MILK, TROWBRIDGE[6], BENJAMIN[5], JONATHAN[4], JOB[3], JOHN[2], JOHN[1])* was born 15 Aug 1890 in Greene County, New York. She married EARL MEAD 14 Nov 1907 in Greene County, New York ?. He was born 12 Nov 1882 in of Westkill, Greene County, New York.

Child of ELIZABETH BUTLER and EARL MEAD is:
- 2030. i. KENNETH EARL[10] MEAD, b. 21 Jul 1909, Westkill, Greene County, New York.

1117. MARIA JULIA[9] BUTLER *(ELLA[8] VAN VALKENBURGH, JULIA ANN[7] MILK, TROWBRIDGE[6], BENJAMIN[5], JONATHAN[4], JOB[3], JOHN[2], JOHN[1])* was born 31 Jul 1900 in Spruceton, Greene County, New York. She married (1) SELA LEANDER COLE 05 Nov 1918. He was born 23 Sep 1891 in Prattville, New York. She married (2) CHARLES RAVER 31 Oct 1940. He was born Abt. 1900 in of Averill Park, New York.

Children of MARIA BUTLER and SELA COLE are:
- 2031. i. ELIDA MAE[10] COLE, b. 10 Nov 1919, Windham, Greene County, New York.
- ii. EDWARD COLE, b. 26 Oct 1921, Windham, Greene County, New York; m. MADELINE MARTIN, 1946; b. Abt. 1921.
- 2032. iii. ESTHER MARIE COLE, b. 13 Jan 1923, Windham, Greene County, New York.
- iv. KENNETH DEVERE COLE, b. 24 Jul 1924, Windham, Greene County, New York; m. EDITH REYNOLDS.
- 2033. v. SELA EARL COLE, b. 15 Feb 1926, Windham, Greene County, New York.

1118. EUGENE WESLEY[9] KLEINER *(JENNIE[8] MARTIN, CYNTHIA JANE[7] MILK, TROWBRIDGE[6], BENJAMIN[5], JONATHAN[4], JOB[3], JOHN[2], JOHN[1])* was born 30 Sep 1912 in San Diego, California, and died 11 Jul 1990 in San Mateo, California. He married MARJORIE _____. She was born Abt. 1913 in California.

Child of EUGENE KLEINER and MARJORIE _____ is:
- i. BARBARA[10] KLEINER, b. Abt. 1937, California.

1119. DR. EARL AUGUSTUS[9] MARTIN *(CHARLES BRIGGS[8], CYNTHIA JANE[7] MILK, TROWBRIDGE[6], BENJAMIN[5], JONATHAN[4], JOB[3], JOHN[2], JOHN[1])* was born 06 Apr 1907 in Parsons, Labette County, Kansas. He married ELIZABETH ALBERTA MOSS 10 May 1936. She was born Abt. 1907.

Children of EARL MARTIN and ELIZABETH MOSS are:
- i. JERRY LEE[10] MARTIN, b. 15 Oct 1937, Topeka, Kansas.
- ii. PEGGY SUE MARTIN, b. 15 Sep 1941, Parsons, Labette County, Kansas ?.

1120. LOVINA P.[9] MILKS *(CALVIN HARVY[8], AMOS MARSH[7], EZRA[6], DAVID[5] MILK, JONATHAN[4], JOB[3], JOHN[2], JOHN[1])* was born 1848 in Franklin, Erie County, Pennsylvania. She married FRANK CHAPMAN 08 Mar 1866. He was born Abt. 1848

Children of LOVINA MILKS and FRANK CHAPMAN are:
- i. GEORGE[10] CHAPMAN.
- ii. INEZ CHAPMAN, m. (1) MISTRE EBERT; m. (2) UNKNOWN.
- 2034. iii. IVAH DOROTHY CHAPMAN, b. 1888, Kansas.
- iv. BERT CHAPMAN.

1121. ABIGAIL "ABBIE" LETITIA[9] MILKS *(CALVIN HARVY[8], AMOS MARSH[7], EZRA[6], DAVID[5] MILK, JONATHAN[4], JOB[3], JOHN[2], JOHN[1])* was born 23 Mar 1850 in Franklin, Erie County, Pennsylvania, and died 23 May 1919 in Sharon, Medina County, Ohio. She married ABRAHAM W. CHAPMAN 27 Jan 1870. He was born Aug 1849 in Ohio, and died 31 May

1921 in Medina County, Ohio.

The Ohio death record lists her mother's maiden name as 'Burton'

Children of ABIGAIL MILKS and ABRAHAM CHAPMAN are:
- 2035. i. CLARENCE H.[10] CHAPMAN, b. Aug 1872, Copley, Summit County, Ohio.
- 2036. ii. FRED E. CHAPMAN, b. 1874, Copley, Summit County, Ohio; d. 18 Nov 1959, Medina, Medina County, Ohio.
- iii. EDWARD O. CHAPMAN, b. Oct 1877, Copley, Summit County, Ohio.
- 2037. iv. AUGUSTA ELIZABETH 'LIZZIE' CHAPMAN, b. 02 May 1880, Summit County, Ohio.
- v. ALICE CHAPMAN, b. Abt. 1882, Copley, Summit County, Ohio.
- 2038. vi. LEONA A. CHAPMAN, b. 25 Sep 1884, Copley, Summit County, Ohio; d. 13 Mar 1950, Akron, Summit County, Ohio.
- vii. LEON A. CHAPMAN, b. Sep 1887, Copley, Summit County, Ohio.
- viii. RAY V. CHAPMAN, b. 08 Sep 1895, Copley, Summit County, Ohio; d. 19 May 1947, Cambridge Township, Guernsey County, Ohio. Never married.

1122. WILLIAM LEANDER[9] MILKS *(CALVIN HARVY[8], AMOS MARSH[7], EZRA[6], DAVID[5] MILK, JONATHAN[4], JOB[3], JOHN[2], JOHN[1])* was born 1852 in Franklin, Erie County, Pennsylvania, and died 16 Oct 1920 in Erie County, Pennsylvania. He married FLORILLA KELLOGG. She was born Bet. 1854 - 1855 in Illinois, and died 10 May 1937 in Erie County, Pennsylvania. William was left in an orphanage after his father's death.

Children of WILLIAM MILKS and FLORILLA KELLOGG are:
- 2039. i. ETTA MAE[10] MILKS, b. 1875, Erie County, Pennsylvania; d. 03 May 1946.
- 2040. ii. JENNIE RUTH MILKS, b. 1877, Erie County, Pennsylvania.
- iii. CALVIN ELIAS MILKS, b. Jun 1879, Erie County, Pennsylvania; d. 1879, Aged 4 days.
- 2041. iv. CHARLES CHAPPLE MILKS, b. 26 Aug 1882, Franklin Center, Erie County, Pennsylvania; d. 1954, Erie County, Pennsylvania.
- v. ARTHUR IVAL MILKS, b. 27 Apr 1885, Erie County, Pennsylvania; d. Jul 1964, Pennsylvania. Never married.
- vi. BENJAMIN DAVID MILKS, b. 30 Jan 1888, Erie County, Pennsylvania; d. 22 May 1896, Erie County, Pennsylvania.
- 2042. vii. IVAH LOVINA MILKS, b. 04 May 1891, Erie County, Pennsylvania; d. Jul 1982, Edinboro, Erie County, PA.

1123. CLARENCE G.[9] MILKS *(CALVIN HARVY[8], AMOS MARSH[7], EZRA[6], DAVID[5] MILK, JONATHAN[4], JOB[3], JOHN[2], JOHN[1])* was born 06 Jan 1854 in Franklin, Erie County, Pennsylvania, and died 29 Aug 1932 in Kansas City, Jackson County, Missouri. He married LOUISE CATHERINE CADLIN, daughter of JOHN CADLIN and MARTHA JUNKINS. She was born 20 Feb 1861 in Indiana, and died 23 May 1918 in Kansas City, Jackson County, Missouri.

Children of CLARENCE MILKS and LOUISE CADLIN are:
- 2043. i. ROE EDWIN[10] MILKS, b. 30 Apr 1883, Missouri; d. 1958, Kansas City, Jackson County, Missouri.
- ii. JAY GOULD MILKS, b. 22 Jan 1886, Missouri; d. 23 Jul 1973, Costa Mesa, Orange County, California; m. ELSIE LILLIAN DEAN; b. 01 Sep 1886, Kansas; d. 16 Jan 1990, Orange County, California.
- iii. MERRILL E. MILKS, b. 07 Oct 1889, Missouri; m. (1) JULIA MAUER, 28 May 1912, Jackson County, Missouri; b. Abt. 1893; m. (2) LENA W. _____, Bet. 1930 - 1940, Kansas City, Missouri.

1124. NELLIE CAROLINE[9] MILKS *(DAVID BENJAMIN[8], AMOS MARSH[7], EZRA[6], DAVID[5] MILK, JONATHAN[4], JOB[3], JOHN[2], JOHN[1])* was born 15 Jan 1869 in Erie County, Pennsylvania, and died 27 Jun 1954 in Villenova, Chautauqua County, New York. She married REVERAND CHARLES LESLIE SMITH 10 Sep 1890 in Ivarea, Erie County, Pennsylvania. He was born 14 Feb 1868 in Erie County, Pennsylvania, and died 27 Nov 1947 in Hanover, Chautauqua County, New York.

Children of NELLIE MILKS and CHARLES SMITH are:
- i. OLIVER OLNEY[10] SMITH, b. 1891, Ivarea, Erie County, Pennsylvania; d. 1891, Ivarea, Erie County, Pennsylvania.
- 2044. ii. OPAL LENORE SMITH, b. 22 Oct 1892, Pittsburg, Allegheny County, Pennsylvania; d. 30 Nov 1994, Houghton, Allegany County, New York.

1125. GRACE AURELIA[9] MILKS *(DAVID BENJAMIN[8], AMOS MARSH[7], EZRA[6], DAVID[5] MILK, JONATHAN[4], JOB[3], JOHN[2], JOHN[1])* was born 07 Feb 1877 in Franklin Township, Erie County, Pennsylvania, and died 25 Aug 1961 in Cuba, Allegany County, New York. She married JAMES DAVIDSON CLEOPHASE MCEDWARD 17 Mar 1895 in Franklin Township, Erie County, Pennsylvania. He was born 18 Aug 1867 in St. Anicet, Huntingdon, Quebec, Canada, and died 03 Oct 1932 in Livermore Falls, Androscoggin County, Maine.

OBITUARY

The Cuba Patriot, Cuba, NY, Aug 30, 1961

Mrs. McEdward Passes away

Mrs. Grace McEdward, 11 N. Park St., widow of James McEdward, passed away Friday, Aug. 25, 1961, at Cuba Memorial Hospital, following a short illness. Mrs. McEdward had lived in Cuba the past two years, making her home with the Rev. Miss Mary Bennett, pastor of the Wesleyan Methodist Church.

Surviving are her daughter, Mrs. Alice Smith, Wetumka, Ala., seven grandchildren and several great-grandchildren.

Funeral services were held Monday, Aug 28, 1961, at the Cuba Wesleyan Methodist Church. The Rev. Daniel Heinz, president of the Lockport Conference of the Wesleyan Methodist Church officiated, assisted by the Rev. Milton Putnam, pastor of the Higgins Wesleyan Methodist Church, Freedom, and the Rev. Maurice A. Gibbs, Houghton.

Burial was in Mt. Pleasant Cemetery, Houghton (NY).

Children of GRACE MILKS and JAMES MCEDWARD are:

2045.   i.   DONALD DAVID[10] MCEDWARD, b. 21 Sep 1896, Ivarea, Franklin Township, Erie County, Pennsylvania; d. 13 Jun 1953, Orwell, Addison County, Vermont.

            ii.   ALICE OLNEY MCEDWARD, b. 10 Jul 1901, Livermore Falls, Androscoggin County, Maine; d. 20 Dec 1974, Lewiston, Maine; m. ARCHIE EUGENE SMITH; b. Abt. 1900, Livermore Falls, Androscoggin County, Maine. No children.

            iii.   JAMES LESLIE MCEDWARD, b. 1903, Livermore Falls, Androscoggin County, Maine; d. 27 Dec 1903, Livermore Falls, Androscoggin County, Maine.

1126. WILLIAM BURDELL[9] RICE *(PARTHENIA ANN[8] MILKS, AMOS MARSH[7], EZRA[6], DAVID[5] MILK, JONATHAN[4], JOB[3], JOHN[2], JOHN[1])* was born Jun 1865, and died 1928. He married HATTIE EASTMAN. She was born Nov 1861 in of Ivarea, Pennsylvania.

Child of WILLIAM RICE and HATTIE EASTMAN is:

            i.   THEODORE EZRA[10] RICE, b. 30 Aug 1895, Erie County, Pennsylvania; d. 06 Sep 1966, Erie County, Pennsylvania; m. MARGUERITE _____; b. Abt. 1894, Pennsylvania.

1127. MABEL JOSEPHINE[9] RICE *(PARTHENIA ANN[8] MILKS, AMOS MARSH[7], EZRA[6], DAVID[5] MILK, JONATHAN[4], JOB[3], JOHN[2], JOHN[1])* was born Dec 1878 in Erie County, Pennsylvania. She married (1) DANA S. MARSH 1897 in Erie County, Pennsylvania, son of WILLIAM MARSH and DELLA COOPER. He was born Aug 1877 in Pennsylvania, and died 1901 in Denver, Colorado. She married (2) ARCHIE B. EASTMAN 24 Jan 1905 in Erie County, Pennsylvania, son of LEVI EASTMAN and ELIZABETH _____. He was born 1875 in Pennsylvania, and died 1937 in Erie County, Pennsylvania. She married (3) FRED MORRIS LYON Bet. 1930 - 1940 in Erie County, Pennsylvania. He was born 16 Jan 1873 in of Cranesville, Pennsylvania.

Child of MABEL RICE and DANA MARSH is:

2046.   i.   DOROTHEA LOUISE[10] MARSH, b. 26 Aug 1898, Erie County, Pennsylvania; d. 20 Jan 1995, Warren, Trumbull County, Ohio.

Children of MABEL RICE and ARCHIE EASTMAN are:

            ii.   LLOYD O. (WINDSOR)[10] EASTMAN, b. Abt. 1913, North Dakota (adopted son).

            iii.   SHELDEN P. (SANSELLA) EASTMAN, b. Abt. 1913, North Dakota (adopted son).

1128. SUSAN E.[9] STEPHENS *(SYLVESTER REESE[8], SARAH "SALLY" ANN[7] MILKS, EZRA[6], DAVID[5] MILK, JONATHAN[4], JOB[3], JOHN[2], JOHN[1])* was born 24 Aug 1847 in Juda, Green County, Wisconsin, and died 28 Sep 1911 in Shenandoah, Page County, Iowa. She married JOHN QUINCY DAVIS 24 Nov 1867 in Green County, Wisconsin, son of DAVID DAVIS and MARY WOODLE. He was born Abt. 1847, and died 11 Nov 1878 in Green Lake County, Wisconsin.

Children of SUSAN STEPHENS and JOHN DAVIS are:

        i. CLARISSA[10] DAVIS, b. 1868, Green County, Wisconsin.

2047.   ii. ALBA Z. DAVIS, b. 27 May 1870, Green County, Wisconsin; d. 17 Apr 1952.

       iii. GEORGE E. DAVIS, b. 04 Apr 1872, Iowa?; d. 12 Mar 1893, David City, Butler County, Iowa.

2048.   iv. GERTRUDE ESTELLE DAVIS, b. 19 Jan 1874, Green County, Wisconsin; d. 31 Aug 1950, Norfolk, Madison County, Nebraska.

       v. IDA DAVIS, b. Abt. 1876, Green County, Wisconsin.

1129. CURTIS MACK[9] BALL *(CLARISSA[8] STEPHENS, SARAH "SALLY" ANN[7] MILKS, EZRA[6], DAVID[5] MILK, JONATHAN[4], JOB[3], JOHN[2], JOHN[1])* was born 02 Sep 1849 in Kingston, Sauk County, Wisconsin, and died 15 Aug 1919 in Butler County, Nebraska. He married NANCY J. BRAMMER 1873. She was born 20 Dec 1855 in Kentucky, and died 05 Aug 1962 in Butler County, Nebraska.

Children of CURTIS BALL and NANCY BRAMMER are:

       i. WILLIAM[10] BALL, b. 17 Oct 1874, David City, Butler County, Nebraska; d. 06 Feb 1963, David City, Butler County, Nebraska; m. JENNY WILGUS; b. 07 Dec 1879, West Liberty, Muscatine County, Iowa; d. 15 Jul 1964, David City, Butler County, Nebraska.

About William Ball Family History, Written by Doris F (Dollison) Ball

There have been Balls living on the Herman and Doris Ball farm for over a hundred years until 2008 when it was sold to Karen and Randy Fendrich. Karen is the granddaughter of Herman and Doris. Herman's grandfather, Curtis Mack Ball bought the 320 acres of land from the Union Pacific Railroad in 1871. Curtis Mack, son of Ira and Clarissa (Stephens) Ball was born September 2, 1849, at Baraboo, Wisconsin. He came to Nebraska with his brother in a wagon and made a couple trips back to Wisconsin by wagon. He went to Schuyler for supplies.

On November 13, 1873, he married Nancy Brammer, daughter of William and Mary Ann (Offil) Brammer, born December 20, 1855 in Kentucky. Nancy had been keeping house for her father on a nearby farm. To this union six children were born: William, Curtis (Pat), George, Wealthy, Winnie, and Ethel. All but Pat, Wealthy, and George lived out their lives in Butler County. Curtis Mack and Nancy retired to David City where Curtis Mack died August 15, 1919, and Nancy died August 5, 1932.

William Ball, born October 17, 1874, attended East Olive Elementary School close to David City, Nebraska, and Bryant Business College at Stromsburg, Nebraska. He loved music and baseball and engaged in both activities as a youth and young adult. On September 17, 1900, William married Jenny Wilgus. Daughter of James and Adeline (Gedney) Wilgus, Jenny was born December 7, 1879, at West Liberty, Iowa. William was leading the David City Concert Band at the time of their marriage. The band played at their wedding, held at the bride's farm home near Rising City, Nebraska. Their gift was a silver service engraved with the monogram "B" and the words "D.C. Concert Band". The teapot is a treasured family memento.

William and Jenny lived on the farm. Over the years William shipped livestock to Omaha, and was one of the first to be honored when the Omaha livestock industry began honoring pioneer livestock shippers. He was a pioneer Butler County sheep man, and belonged to the Purebred Shropshire Association. He also served for a time on the County Board of Supervisors.

William's wife, Jenny, joined the Owls Club in David City as a bride and was a lifelong member of the Women's Society of Christian Service. One of her most vivid memories was of the Blizzard of '88 – the so-called "School Children's Storm". Her family was living in Holt County and she had to spend the night in the schoolhouse with her school mates. Jenny had great taste and their home was filled with lovely things from furniture to dishes. She also spent the late summers canning her wonderful crops of fruits and vegetables.

Two sons, Herman and Harold, were born, but Harold died at the age of seven from appendicitis. Harold had lost his sight in one eye. He and Herman had been playing with a stick. Herman never forgave himself for this tragic accident and loss of his little brother.

William Ball died February 6, 1963 at the age of 88 years. Jenny died the next year on July 15, 1964, at the age of 84 years. Herman Ball, born November 12, 1908, in the same room in which his father was born, married Doris Dollison in 1939. His parents retired to David City and the newlyweds took over the home place.

       ii. WEALTHY BALL, b. 1877, David City, Butler County, Nebraska; d. 19 Feb 1925.

2049. iii. WINIFRED 'WINEY' BALL, b. 22 Jul 1880, David City, Butler County, Nebraska; d. 22 Dec 1926, David City, Butler County, Nebraska.
iv. ETHEL BALL, b. 20 Nov 1881, David City, Butler County, Nebraska; d. Feb 1944.
v. CURTIS MACK BALL, JR., b. 27 Nov 1886, David City, Butler County, Nebraska; d. 12 Sep 1948, Fremont, Dodge County, Nebraska; m. IDA MAY MYATT, 23 Oct 1913, David City, Butler County, Nebraska; b. 18 May 1888, David City, Butler County, Nebraska; d. 14 Jun 1973, Omaha, Dodge County, Nebraska.
vi. GEORGE W. BALL, b. Jul 1894, David City, Butler County, Nebraska; d. 10 Oct 1962, Portland, Multnomah County, Oregon.
vii. LITTLE BENNY BALL, b. 1896, David City, Butler County, Nebraska; d. 1899, David City, Butler County, Nebraska.

1130. LAURA[9] STEPHENS (*EZRA MILKS[8], SARAH "SALLY" ANN[7] MILKS, EZRA[6], DAVID[5] MILK, JONATHAN[4], JOB[3], JOHN[2], JOHN[1]*) was born Sep 1856 in Green County, Wisconsin. She married CHARLES H. BLACKMAN 1880. He was born Feb 1856 in Illinois.

Children of LAURA STEPHENS and CHARLES BLACKMAN are:
  i. FLOYD[10] BLACKMAN, b. Dec 1881, Nebraska.
  ii. MYRTLE BLACKMAN, b. Oct 1883, Nebraska.
  iii. CHILDTHREE BLACKMAN, b. Abt. 1886, Nebraska.
  iv. ELBERT BLACKMAN, b. Jul 1890, Nebraska.

1131. EZRA PARKER[9] STEPHENS (*EZRA MILKS[8], SARAH "SALLY" ANN[7] MILKS, EZRA[6], DAVID[5] MILK, JONATHAN[4], JOB[3], JOHN[2], JOHN[1]*) was born 18 Aug 1862 in Allamakee County, Iowa, and died 16 Sep 1942 in Bellwood, Butler County, Nebraska. He married MARY AMANDA MCKNIGHT 16 May 1884 in David City, Butler County, Nebraska. She was born 28 Nov 1858 in Mercer County, Pennsylvania, and died 02 Feb 1963 in Council Bluffs, Pottawattamie County, Iowa.

Ezra's gravestone mistakenly gives his birth date as 1860.

OBITUARY
A LONG TIME RESIDENT DIED WEDNESDAY, SEPT. 16
Funeral of Ezra Parker Stephens Held Friday Afternoon
Ezra Parker Stephens, long-time resident of Butler county, died at 10:35 a.m. Wednesday, Sept. 16, at his home eight miles south of Columbus, from complications after illness of eight months. He was 80 years of age.

Funeral services were conducted at the Stephens home at 2 o'clock Friday afternoon by a Jehovah speaker from Columbus. The pallbearers were George Cady, Wolford Hiatt, John Minnick, Roy McKnight, Ben Snyder and Maurice Snyder. Burial was in Watke Hill cemetery.

In attendance at the funeral from elsewhere were Mr. and Mrs. Orval Stephens and children, Mr. and Mrs. David Johnson, Mr. and Mrs. George Holmstedt and Miss Edna Holmstedt of Fullerton; Mr. and Mrs. Ivan Stephens and children and Mr. and Mrs. Arnold Mahoney, of St. Edward, Mr. and Mrs. Tom Boyer, Mr. and Mrs. Leo Brown and son, Larry, Mr. and Mrs. Will Kealy and sons Dean and Patrick, and Mrs. Flower, of Council Bluffs, Ia.; Mrs. E.J. Whitmore, Irvin McKnight, Mrs. Blanche Powell, Mr. and Mrs. Roy McKnight and children and Mrs. and Mrs. Will Campbell, of David City; George McKnight, Mr. and Mrs. Ben Snyder and children and Mr. and Mrs. Carl Hall, of Rising City; and Mrs. Alfred Sells and son, Larry, of Dumont, Colo.

Ezra Parker Stephens, son of Ezra and Margery Stephens, was born at Rossville, Ia., August 18, 1862. He engaged in farming as his life occupation. He was married at David City May 16, 1885, to Amanda McKnight, and they resided near St. Edward, moving to the farm in Butler county in February, 1918.

Six children were born to Mr. and Mrs. Stephens, of whom three, two daughters and one son, have passed away. The surviving children are Orval Stephens, of Fullerton, Ivan Stephens of St. Edward and Mrs. Thomas A. Boyer of Council Bluffs, Iowa. Mrs. Stephens also survives as do 22 grandchildren and eight great grandchildren.

Butler County Press (David City, Nebr.), September 24, 1942, p. 1, col. 3

OBITUARY
St. Edward Advance (St. Edward, Nebr.), February 7, 1963, p. 1, col. 6
Services Held Monday for Mrs. Stephens
Amanda Stephens, daughter of Robert and Margaret Hahn McKnight, was born November 28, 1858, in a log cabin near Clarksville, Pa., and passed away at the home of her daughter, Mrs. Ruby Smith, at Council Bluffs, Iowa, on Saturday, February 2, 1963, at the age of 104 years, 2 months and 4 days.

She was united in marriage to Ezra Parker Stephens at David City, Nebraska on May 16, 1884. To this union six children were born, three of whom survive. Those living are Mrs. Ruby Smith of Council Bluffs, Ia., Ivan of St. Edward, Nebr., and Orval of Portland, Ore.

There are 23 grandchildren, 64 great grandchildren and 7 great great- grandchildren.

She was preceded in death by her husband, three children, and by her brothers and sisters.

Mrs. Stephens remained active even in her advanced years, and during the past winter she pieced together more than 20 lap robes for the Veterans' Hospital in Omaha.

Her places of residence included David City, Bellwood, St. Edward, Dumont, Colo., and the last three and a half years in Council Bluffs.

Services were held from the Miller Funeral Home Monday, February 4th, at 1:30 p.m. with the Rev. Ralph Allen in charge.

Mrs. Ivan Maricle and Mrs. Hazel Condreay sang "Beautiful Garden of Prayer" and "Softly and Tenderly." Mrs. Fay Smith accompanied at the organ.

Pallbearers were Lewis Wilson, Robert Johnson, Richard Francis, Bruce Condreay, Harold Denman and Lawrence Collins. Interment was at Rising City, Nebraska.

Children of EZRA STEPHENS and MARY MCKNIGHT are:
- i. IVA A.[10] STEPHENS, b. 1886, Nebraska; d. 1886, Nebraska.
- ii. ORVAL IRVIN STEPHENS, b. May 1888, Nebraska.
- 2050. iii. IRMA V. STEPHENS, b. May 1890, Nebraska; d. Bet. 1927 - 1930, Council Bluffs, Pottawattamie County, Iowa.
- iv. IVAN LEROY STEPHENS, b. Feb 1892, Nebraska.
- v. ROYAL I. STEPHENS, b. 1893, Nebraska; d. 1893, Nebraska.
- 2051. vi. RUBY STEPHENS, b. Nov 1894, Nebraska.

1132. CLARISSA 'CLARA' B.[9] STEPHENS *(EZRA MILKS[8], SARAH "SALLY" ANN[7] MILKS, EZRA[6], DAVID[5] MILK, JONATHAN[4], JOB[3], JOHN[2], JOHN[1])* was born Aug 1868 in Allamakee County, Iowa, and died 1942 in David City, Butler County, Nebraska. She married GEORGE S. MCKNIGHT 1890. He was born Oct 1862 in Pennsylvania, and died 1959 in David City, Butler County, Nebraska.

Children of CLARISSA STEPHENS and GEORGE MCKNIGHT are:
- i. VELMA Z.[10] MCKNIGHT, b. Jan 1891, Nebraska.
- ii. CLEO L. MCKNIGHT, b. Jan 1894, Nebraska.
- iii. LUZETTA V. MCKNIGHT, b. May 1895, Nebraska.

1133. HARRIE ELLIS[9] STEPHENS *(JAMES PARKER[8], SARAH "SALLY" ANN[7] MILKS, EZRA[6], DAVID[5] MILK, JONATHAN[4], JOB[3], JOHN[2], JOHN[1])* was born 18 Jan 1866 in Allamakee County, Iowa, and died 14 Apr 1946 in Loup City, Sherman County, Nebraska. He married CORA ELIZABETH FOX 05 Mar 1890 in David City, Butler County, Nebraska. She was born 19 Feb 1869 in Butler, Butler County, Nebraska, and died 02 Mar 1944 in Arnold, Custer County, Nebraska.

Children of HARRIE STEPHENS and CORA FOX are:
- i. ERNES[10] STEPHENS, b. 27 Dec 1890, David City, Butler County, Nebraska; d. 30 Dec 1955, Loup City, Sherman County, Nebraska.
- ii. ROY EDGAR STEPHENS, b. 02 Dec 1892, David City, Butler County, Nebraska; d. 23 Jul 1967, Grand Island, Hall County, Nebraska.
- iii. IRA EZRA STEPHENS, b. 14 Jan 1895, David City, Butler County, Nebraska; d. 10 Jun 1954, Montpelier, Bear Lake County, Idaho.
- 2052. iv. MARY OLIVE STEPHENS, b. 05 Oct 1899, David City, Butler County, Nebraska; d. 14 Sep 1946, Nampa, Canyon County, Idaho.

1134. HATTIE B.[9] LOVELACE *(CALVIN S.[8], PRUDENCE[7] MILKS, EZRA[6], DAVID[5] MILK, JONATHAN[4], JOB[3], JOHN[2], JOHN[1])* was born Abt. 1865 in Green County, Wisconsin. She married JAMES J. CALLISON.

Child of HATTIE LOVELACE and JAMES CALLISON is:
- 2053. i. OSCAR LOVELACE[10] CALLISON, b. 25 May 1893, Wisconsin; d. 28 Sep 1972, Janesville, Rock County, WI..

1135. GEORGE NELSON[9] LOVELACE *(JEFFERSON[8], PRUDENCE[7] MILKS, EZRA[6], DAVID[5] MILK, JONATHAN[4], JOB[3], JOHN[2], JOHN[1])* was born 02 Feb 1860 in Green County, Wisconsin, and died 19 Jun 1936 in Green County, Wisconsin. He married EVA KIBBE 08 Dec 1884 in Rock County, Wisconsin. She was born 10 Feb 1863 in Magnolia, Rock County, Wisconsin, and died 27 Dec 1944 in Janesville, Rock County, Wisconsin.

DEATH NOTICE - Thursday, January 4, 1945, Evansville Review, p. 1, Evansville, Wisconsin

    NATIVE OF MAGNOLIA DIES IN JANESVILLE

    Funeral services For Mrs. Eva Lovelace, 81, Are Held In Evansville Saturday

Funeral services for Mrs. Eva Lovelace, who died at 7 a.m. last week Wednesday in Mercy hospital, Janesville, where she had been a patient for four weeks as a result of a hip fracture, were held at 2 p.m. Saturday in the Allen funeral home, the Rev. Grant V. Clark officiating. Burial was in Hillcrest cemetery, Albany.

Eva Kibbie was born Feb. 10, 1863, in Magnolia. She was married to George Lovelace Dec. 8, 1884, and they made their home in this vicinity.

Surviving are three daughters, Mrs. Lambert Furseth, Evansville, Mrs. Orrie Lee, Spooner, Mrs. George Newhall, Evanston, Ill; a son, Eugene Lovelace, Evanston, Ill.; 12 grandchildren and four great-grandchildren. Mr. Lovelace died June 19, 1936.

Children of GEORGE LOVELACE and EVA KIBBE are:

2054.   i.   ORRIN EUGENE[10] LOVELACE, b. 29 Sep 1886, Rock County, Wisconsin; d. 06 Dec 1966, Preston, Fillmore County, Minnesota.
       ii.   DAUONE LOVELACE, b. Abt. 1890, Rock County, Wisconsin; d. Bef. 1900, Rock County, Wisconsin.
2055.   iii.   MARCIA M. LOVELACE, b. Jan 1894, Rock County, Wisconsin.
2056.   iv.   SARAH FLORENCE LOVELACE, b. 14 May 1896, Rock County, Wisconsin; d. Nov 1973, Tucson, Pima County, Arizona.
2057.   v.   LILA M. LOVELACE, b. Abt. 1901, Rock County, Wisconsin.

1136. STEWART ANSON[9] LOVELACE *(JEFFERSON[8], PRUDENCE[7] MILKS, EZRA[6], DAVID[5] MILK, JONATHAN[4], JOB[3], JOHN[2], JOHN[1])* was born Oct 1866 in Green County, Wisconsin, and died 05 Apr 1946 in Atchison County, Kansas. He married MARY ARMENIA 'MINNIE' CALVIN 03 Jan 1891 in Juda, Green County, Wisconsin. She was born Mar 1867 in Wisconsin, and died 11 Jul 1954 in Atchison County, Kansas.

Children of STEWART LOVELACE and MARY CALVIN are:

       i.   PERCY JEFFERSON[10] LOVELACE, b. 10 Oct 1891, Carrol County, Illinois; d. 15 Mar 1958, Atchison County, Kansas; m. MARY ABEL, Abt. 1917; b. Abt. 1896, Kansas.
       ii.   JESSIE LOVELACE, b. Jan 1894, Carrol County, Illinois.
       iii.   PRUDENCE LOVELACE, b. Sep 1895, Carrol County, Illinois.
       iv.   MARGURITE MARGARET LOVELACE, b. Mar 1899, Carrol County, Illinois.
       v.   MARIE LOVELACE, b. Abt. 1900, Carrol County, Illinois; d. 30 Jan 1922, Atchison County, Kansas.
       vi.   MELVIN LOVELACE, b. Abt. 1902, Atchison County, Kansas.
2058.   vii.   HARRY EUGENE LOVELACE, b. 06 May 1906, Atchison County, Kansas; d. 19 Jun 1986, Atchison, Atchison County, Kansas.
       viii.   RAYMOND LOVELACE, b. Abt. 1908, Atchison County, Kansas.
       ix.   CALVIN C. LOVELACE, b. 1911, Atchison County, Kansas; d. 1990, Atchison County, Kansas; m. MARY H. _____; b. 1917; d. 1989, Atchison County, Kansas.

1137. ETHELYN 'ETHEL'[9] LOVELACE *(HARRISON 'HANK'[8], PRUDENCE[7] MILKS, EZRA[6], DAVID[5] MILK, JONATHAN[4], JOB[3], JOHN[2], JOHN[1])* was born Abt. 1872 in Grant City, Worth County, Missouri, and died 10 Jan 1952 in Clarkston, Asotin County, Washington. She married GEORGE H. BULFINCH Abt. 1893 in Worth County, Missouri. He was born Mar 1859 in Wisconsin, and died 12 Jul 1933 in Klamath Falls, Klamath County, Oregon.

Children of ETHELYN LOVELACE and GEORGE BULFINCH are:

       i.   GLADYS E.[10] BULFINCH, b. Mar 1894, Worth County, Missouri.
       ii.   FREDRICK H. BULFINCH, b. Dec 1895, Worth County, Missouri.
2059.   iii.   RUTH E. BULFINCH, b. Mar 1897, Worth County, Missouri.
       iv.   KALE D. BULFINCH, b. Feb 1899, Worth County, Missouri.

1138. JEREMIAH L. 'JAY'^{9} RAYMOND *(ELIZABETH RUTH^8 LOVELACE, PRUDENCE^7 MILKS, EZRA^6, DAVID^5 MILK, JONATHAN^4, JOB^3, JOHN^2, JOHN^1)* was born Sep 1864 in Wisconsin. He married LAURA M. _____ Abt. 1903 in Nebraska. She was born Abt. 1882.

Children of JEREMIAH RAYMOND and LAURA _____ are:
         i. LEWIS SETH^{10} RAYMOND, b. 05 May 1905, Scotts Bluff County, Nebraska; d. 04 Apr 1985, Scotts Bluff County, Nebraska; m. KATHRYNE MILLER; b. 24 Sep 1912, Iowa; d. Mar 1972, Scotts Bluff County, Nebraska.
2060.   ii. HELEN RAYMOND, b. 29 Oct 1918, Scotts Bluff County, Nebraska; d. 10 Mar 2006, Denver, Colorado.

1139. HOWARD^9 RAYMOND *(ELIZABETH RUTH^8 LOVELACE, PRUDENCE^7 MILKS, EZRA^6, DAVID^5 MILK, JONATHAN^4, JOB^3, JOHN^2, JOHN^1)* was born Abt. 1867 in Iowa. He married NELLIE M. _____ Abt. 1896. She was born Abt. 1876 in Iowa.

Children of HOWARD RAYMOND and NELLIE _____ are:
2061.   i. MARIE^{10} RAYMOND, b. 1898, Nebraska; d. 1988, Scotts Bluff County, Nebraska.
         ii. FRANCES RAYMOND, b. Abt. 1902, Nebraska.
         iii. RUTH RAYMOND, b. Abt. 1904, Nebraska.
         iv. SHIRLEY RAYMOND, b. Abt. 1907, Nebraska.

1140. ANNA^9 RAYMOND *(ELIZABETH RUTH^8 LOVELACE, PRUDENCE^7 MILKS, EZRA^6, DAVID^5 MILK, JONATHAN^4, JOB^3, JOHN^2, JOHN^1)* was born Abt. 1868 in Iowa. She married MISTRE HASTING.

Child of ANNA RAYMOND and MISTRE HASTING is:
         i. JOSEPH E.^{10} HASTING, b. Aug 1891, Nebraska.

1141. LEWIS L.^{9} RAYMOND *(ELIZABETH RUTH^8 LOVELACE, PRUDENCE^7 MILKS, EZRA^6, DAVID^5 MILK, JONATHAN^4, JOB^3, JOHN^2, JOHN^1)* was born 19 Oct 1871 in Butler County, Nebraska, and died 02 Oct 1935 in Nebraska. He married MABLE G. SHUMWAY 01 Sep 1897 in Nebraska. She was born Abt. 1878.

From - **"History of Western NE & Its People"**, Vol III; Page 013
     LEWIS L. RAYMOND, whose name carries with it the high regard that comes of honorable achievement, is a leader of the bar at Scottsbluff, and a citizen of the county who has served in numerous important official capacities with marked efficiency and great public spirit. A native son of Nebraska, he is a representative of an old pioneer family that settled within its borders almost a half century ago. Mr. Raymond was born October 19, 1871, in Butler county, the son of Seth and Elizabeth (Lovelace) Raymond.
     Seth Raymond was born at Millersburg, Ohio, September 9, 1835, but was a resident of Wisconsin when the Civil War came on. He enlisted April 3, 1861, in Company G, Third Wisconsin volunteer infantry and served faithfully as a soldier until he was honorably discharged at Beaufort, North Carolina, in February, 1865. Until the day of his death, June 10, 1910, he bore the marks of the wounds he received at the battle of Winchester, Virginia. On January 16, 1864, he was united in marriage, at Janesville, Wisconsin, to Elizabeth Lovelace, who was born October 4, 1843, at Erie, Pennsylvania. She resides at Scottsbluff, where she is active in the Methodist Episcopal church, to which her husband also belonged. Of their family of nine children, Lewis L. was the fifth in order of birth. In October, 1870, Seth Raymond and his family came to Nebraska and he homesteaded in Butler county, remaining on his land there until August, 1884, when he moved to Dawson county, from there coming to Scottsbluff county in March, 1887. He took up land five miles southwest of Gering and remained on that farm until March, 1892, when he moved into Gering, where he lived a somewhat retired life until 1905. In the spring of that year he came to Scottsbluff, where his remaining years were passed. He was a man of sterling character, was somewhat active in the Republican party and a Mason in good standing in his lodge.
     Lewis L. Raymond had public school advantages in early youth and later spent four years in study in the normal school at Fremont. Like many another intellectual young man, he began business life in the schoolroom and more or less continuously taught school for the following fourteen years in Scottsbluff county, during a part of this time devoting himself to the study of law, F. A. Wright being his preceptor. Mr. Raymond was admitted to the bar, November 17, 1902, and soon afterward started practice in this county, where since then he has been identified with many of the most important cases that have come before the courts. He has not, however, been able to devote his

entire time to his profession for his fellow citizens have often called him into public life. He served one term as deputy county clerk, two terms as county superintendent, two terms as county attorney, and one term as county judge, while in 1909 he was elected to the state senate. Since retiring from the political field his law practice has absorbed his attention to a great extent and his high standing at the bar is unquestioned.

On September 1, 1897, Mr. Raymond was united in marriage to Miss Mable Shumway, a member of the prominent Shumway family of this section of the state, and they have three children, two sons and one daughter: Charles R., Jack L., and Evelyn. The daughter is still in school. Both sons entered military service as volunteers in 1918, neither of them being of military age, but loyal and patriotic American youths to the core. Charles R. is a sergeant in the Four Hundred Forty-seventh Labor battalion, at Camp Humphrey, Virginia, and Jack L. is a member of the United States Marines. Mr. Raymond and his family are members of the Methodist Episcopal church. In his political convictions he is a Republican.

Children of LEWIS RAYMOND and MABLE SHUMWAY are:
    i. CHARLES R.^{10} RAYMOND, b. Abt. 1899, Gering, Scotts Bluff, Nebraska.
    ii. JACK L. RAYMOND, b. Abt. 1902, Scotts Bluff County, Nebraska.
    iii. EVELYN RAYMOND, b. Abt. 1905, Scotts Bluff County, Nebraska.

1142. EDNA A.^{9} LOVELACE *(NELSON R.^{8}, PRUDENCE^7 MILKS, EZRA^6, DAVID^5 MILK, JONATHAN^4, JOB^3, JOHN^2, JOHN^1)* was born Dec 1873 in Wisconsin, and died 30 Sep 1964 in Weld County, Colorado. She married JAMES HARVEY FERGUSON Abt. 1898. He was born 27 Jun 1875 in Clarence, Cedar County, Iowa, and died 17 Jan 1948 in Ault, Weld County, Colorado.

James H. Ferguson was the husband of Edna A. Lovelace and he was the son of James and Isabella (Anthony) Ferguson. He was the 1st Register of Deeds of Scotts Bluff Co. (1916-1918) and was also County Clerk at one time. He was very active in church and community affairs.

Child of EDNA LOVELACE and JAMES FERGUSON is:
    i. RUTH^{10} FERGUSON, b. 25 Jun 1907, Stettler, Alberta, Canada; d. 03 Jul 1907, Stettler, Alberta, Canada.

1143. OSCAR ROY^9 LOVELACE *(NELSON R.^{8}, PRUDENCE^7 MILKS, EZRA^6, DAVID^5 MILK, JONATHAN^4, JOB^3, JOHN^2, JOHN^1)* was born 04 Feb 1880 in Grant City, Worth County, Missouri, and died 28 Nov 1932 in Scotts Bluff, Nebraska. He married GERTRUDE L. FORD Abt. 1908, daughter of CHARLES FORD and JENNIE _____. She was born 10 Mar 1884 in Colorado, and died 28 Dec 1959 in Scotts Bluff, Nebraska.

History of Western Nebraska and Its People, Vol. 3, by Grant Lee Shumway
OSCAR R. LOVELACE, vice president of the American Bank of Mitchell, Nebraska, is one of the younger bankers who are making financial history in the Panhandle as his management of the bank has placed him in the front rank in the commercial circles of the northwest. His business career has been characterized by self -reliance, initiative and executive ability of a high order, all qualities which bring normally in their train a great measure of success. His integrity and conservatism have begotten public confidence for the bank and he is held in high esteem by the citizens of Mitchell, which is necessary in the furtherance of success in the line of enterprise which Mr. Lovelace has chosen. As a banker, Mr. Lovelace has shown great constructive talent and it has been largely through his policies and efforts as manager, that the American Bank has made such rapid progress since its organization in 1919.

Mr. Lovelace is practically a son of Scottsbluff county, though he was born in Grant City, Missouri, February 4, 1880, the son of N. R. and Alice (Lore) Lovelace, the former a native of the Badger state, while the mother was born in Pennsylvania. In 1883, N. R. Lovelace came to Dawson county, Nebraska, being one of the earliest settlers, of that section. He took a pre-emption on which he proved up but learning of the fine land to be had in the upper valley of the Platte came to Scottsbluff county in 1889. After arriving here he took a tree claim near Gering but gave it up in 1893, to go to California where he engaged in fruit raising near Fresno. The family, however, did not like California as well as the high prairie country so returned to Nebraska, when Mr. Lovelace filed on a homestead and bought an additional quarter section of land adjoining, six miles southwest of Gering, where the family still make their home. This farm has been highly developed and today is one of the most valuable and productive tracts of land in the county.

Oscar was practically reared in Scottsbluff county as he was but a small child when the family first located here. He received his educational advantages in the excellent public schools and then graduated from the high school at Gering. As the cattle industry was still one of the largest in this section of the country at that time, the boy naturally craved to join in the free life, with the adventures afforded by the cow camps of the great cattle barons and became a cowboy, spending four years on the ranges in western Nebraska and Wyoming. When he had exhausted all the various phases of outdoor life he began to give thought and attention to the question of a career. By the life in the open Mr. Lovelace had become robust and hearty and he soon saw that muscle alone did not bring in the greatest returns for the amount of work expended but when guided by a well -trained mind, the combination won. Realizing the value of a higher education he deserted the cattle business and went to Lincoln, Nebraska, to take a special course in the Lincoln Business College, having decided that a business career best suited his inclinations. On the completion of his studies, Mr. Lovelace returned to Scottsbluff county and Mitchell, accepting a position as bookkeeper in the Mitchell State Bank, when it was organized in 1907. Here he displayed such marked ability in finance, learning the banking business from the ground up, that when the American Bank was organized in 1919, he was made executive officer and vice-president of the institution; in fact, he was one of the prime movers in its inception and organization. He became one of the heavy stockholders and so has their interests ever at heart. From its start the bank has had a phenomenal (sic) success, due to the men who have shaped its policies and especially Mr. Lovelace, who has proved a most efficient manager. Mr. Lovelace has made many worth- while business acquaintances and associations which have been valuable to the bank; he is popular personally and when the bank was organized told all the employees that the slogan of the institution was to be "Service." Patrons are treated courteously, their interests are considered as well as those of the bank and as a result the deposits are constantly increasing. From first entering business Mr. Lovelace has also entered actively into the civic and communal life of the county and town of Mitchell, he advocates and helps "boost" everything that tends to the development and up-building of this section of the valley, giving liberally of time and money, in support of all the progressive movements that are placing the Panhandle "on the map," and is the originator of many of them. He firmly believes in living his Americanism and citizenship and personally attains the high standard that he sets for others. During the war he aided in every way in its prosecution, being one of the prominent figures in raising money during all the drives for Liberty Bonds and for the Red Cross.

In politics he is a member of the Republican party, while his church affiliations are with the Federated church. For some time Mr. Lovelace has been secretary of the school board, which has led to many modem equipments being introduced and he is now serving as a member of the city council.

On April 15, 1909, Mr. Lovelace married Miss Gertrude Ford, born in Colorado, but practically reared in Scottsbluff county, as she is the daughter of C. W. Ford, who was clerk of the county for more than six years, and is one of the prominent pioneer settlers. Three sons, have been born to Mr. and Mrs. Lovelace, Ross C., Charles Ford, and Joseph Nelson.

Children of OSCAR LOVELACE and GERTRUDE FORD are:
2062.   i.   ROSS CRAIG^{10} LOVELACE, b. 10 Dec 1909, Scotts Bluff, Nebraska; d. 07 Mar 1969, Santa Clara, California.
2063.   ii.   CHARLES FORD LOVELACE, b. 02 Dec 1914, Scotts Bluff, Nebraska; d. 09 Sep 1993, Scotts Bluff, Nebraska.
2064.   iii.   JOE NELSON LOVELACE, b. 24 Dec 1916, Scotts Bluff, Nebraska; d. 07 Mar 2006, Scotts Bluff, Nebraska.
        iv.   HELEN C. LOVELACE, b. Abt. 1921, Scotts Bluff, Nebraska.

1144. ELIZABETH EFFIE^9 STEPHENS *(LEANDER MILKS^8, PATIENCE^7 MILKS, EZRA^6, DAVID^5 MILK, JONATHAN^4, JOB^3, JOHN^2, JOHN^1)* was born 09 May 1858 in Dane County, Wisconsin, and died 18 Apr 1940 in Mazomanie, Wisconsin. She married GEORGE HUES REEVE 03 Mar 1885 in Town of Vermont, Wis.. He was born 1858, and died 1916.

Children of ELIZABETH STEPHENS and GEORGE REEVE are:
        i.   LOTTIE E.^{10} REEVE, b. 1889.
2065.   ii.   EMILY ISBELLE REEVE, b. 1894; d. 1980.
2066.   iii.   MYRTLE MELISSA REEVE, b. 1898; d. 1986.
2067.   iv.   BELLE BURDETA REEVE, b. 1902.
        v.   BLANCHE R. REEVE, b. 1905; m. JOSEPH LOY; b. 1903; d. 1959.

1145. FANNY^9 MILKS *(BENJAMIN FRANKLIN^8, DAVID B.^{7}, EZRA^6, DAVID^5 MILK, JONATHAN^4, JOB^3, JOHN^2, JOHN^1)* was born 27 Jun 1879 in Ithaca, Tompkins County, New York. She married FRANK I. CUNNINGHAM 23 Jul 1900, son of JOHN CUNNINGHAM and MARGARET SPAULDING. He was born Abt. 1879 in St. Catherines, Ontario, Canada.

Children of FANNY MILKS and FRANK CUNNINGHAM are:
2068.   i.   MARGARET E.^{10} CUNNINGHAM, b. 02 Aug 1901, St. Catherines, Ontario, Canada; d. Sep 1979, Niagara County, New York.
2069.   ii.   ISABELLE CUNNINGHAM, b. 04 Apr 1903, St. Catherines, Ontario, Canada.
        iii.   FRANCES A. CUNNINGHAM, b. 24 Jan 1907, Ithaca, Tompkins County, New York.

iv. RUTH CUNNINGHAM, b. 15 Jul 1910, Ithaca, Tompkins County, New York; d. 14 Feb 1937.
v. JOSEPH B. CUNNINGHAM, b. 28 Nov 1914, Rochester, New York; m. NEVE BRIDGMAN, Washington, D.C.; b. Abt. 1914.
vi. CHARLES E. CUNNINGHAM, b. 26 May 1920, Rochester, New York; m. BEVERLY E. ECHRICK; b. Abt. 1920.

1146. MARY S. 'MAYME'^{9} MILKS *(BENJAMIN FRANKLIN^8, DAVID B.^{7}, EZRA^6, DAVID^5 MILK, JONATHAN^4, JOB^3, JOHN^2, JOHN^1)* was born 12 Dec 1883 in Ithaca, Tompkins County, New York. She married RALPH C. MANDEVILLE. He was born Abt. 1883.

Children of MARY MILKS and RALPH MANDEVILLE are:
2070. i. ESTHER LUCILE^{10} MANDEVILLE, b. 14 Aug 1913.
2071. ii. CHARLES MANDEVILLE, b. 14 Apr 1919.

1147. WILLIAM S.^{9} MILKS *(BENJAMIN FRANKLIN^8, DAVID B.^{7}, EZRA^6, DAVID^5 MILK, JONATHAN^4, JOB^3, JOHN^2, JOHN^1)* was born 01 Dec 1884 in Ithaca, Tompkins County, New York, and died Jul 1964 in Ithaca, Tompkins County, New York. He married GRACE B. NORTHRUP Abt. 1912, daughter of J. NORTHRUP and MARY SELLEY. She was born 20 Oct 1888 in Ithaca, Tompkins County, New York.
William contributed many records of the family.

Child of WILLIAM MILKS and GRACE NORTHRUP is:
2072. i. JAMES B.^{10} MILKS, b. 30 Oct 1913, Ithaca, Tompkins County, New York; d. 17 Dec 2005, Sodus, Wayne County, NY.

1148. CHARLES EVERETT^9 MILKS *(THOMAS W.^{8}, EZRA^7, EZRA^6, DAVID^5 MILK, JONATHAN^4, JOB^3, JOHN^2, JOHN^1)* was born 16 Sep 1873 in Rock Run, Stephenson County, Illinois, and died 1952 in Lincoln, Nebraska?. He married EDNA MARY BROWN 29 Jan 1899 in Pawnee County, Nebraska, daughter of JOHN BROWN and MARY CLARK. She was born 05 Sep 1878 in Burlington Junction, Nodaway County, Missouri, and died 07 Dec 1944 in Lincoln, Nebraska.

Children of CHARLES MILKS and EDNA BROWN are:
i. CLYDE WILLIS^{10} MILKS, b. 24 Nov 1899, Burchard, Pawnee County, Nebraska; d. Aug 1968, Omaha, Douglas County, Nebraska; m. (1) BETTY POULSTON, 25 Aug 1923, Lincoln, Nebraska; b. Abt. 1899; m. (2) HELEN SELLS, Abt. 1928, Nebraska; b. Abt. 1905, Nebraska; m. (3) HELEN G. PETERSON-FERGUSON, Bet. 1928 - 1940; b. Abt. 1907, Indiana.
ii. CYRIL CARLTON MILKS, b. 1905, Burchard, Pawnee County, Nebraska; d. 1938, Burchard, Pawnee County, Nebraska. Never married.
iii. ETHEL VIVIAN MILKS, b. 16 Mar 1908, Palisade, Nebraska; m. ROBERT LAMBERT; b. 16 Jan 1909, Stella, Nebraska.
iv. VIRGINIA BEA MILKS, b. 06 May 1913, Osceola, Nebraska; m. EARL JENSON; b. 07 Jan 1909, Filley, Nebraska. No children.

1149. FLORA A.^{9} MILKS *(THOMAS W.^{8}, EZRA^7, EZRA^6, DAVID^5 MILK, JONATHAN^4, JOB^3, JOHN^2, JOHN^1)* was born 02 Dec 1877 in Rock Run, Stephenson County, Illinois, and died Aft. 1940 in Hastings, Adams County, Nebraska. She married FRANKLIN B. HUNT 03 Jul 1899 in Burchard, Pawnee County, Nebraska. He was born 15 Dec 1874 in Lenox, Iowa, and died 30 May 1939 in Hastings, Adams County, Nebraska.

Children of FLORA MILKS and FRANKLIN HUNT are:
2073. i. MARVEL LILLIAN^{10} HUNT, b. 04 Sep 1901, Nebraska; d. 20 Sep 1988, Cincinnati, Ohio.
2074. ii. DOROTHY HUNT, b. 31 May 1905, Nebraska.

1150. MABEL^9 BARKER *(HARRIET "HATTIE"^{8} MILKS, EZRA^7, EZRA^6, DAVID^5 MILK, JONATHAN^4, JOB^3, JOHN^2, JOHN^1)* was born 1878 in Stephenson County, Illinois. She married FRANK STONEWALL. He was born Aug 1865 in Sweden.

Children of MABEL BARKER and FRANK STONEWALL are:
2075. i. EFFIE V.^{10} STONEWALL, b. Jul 1899, Illinois.
2076. ii. RALPH C. STONEWALL, b. Abt. 1901, Illinois.

2077. iii. HARRY A. STONEWALL, b. Abt. Jan 1910, Faulkton, Faulk County, South Dakota.
       iv. MARGARET STONEWALL, b. Abt. 1914, Faulk County, South Dakota.
       v. MELVIN STONEWALL, b. 31 Mar 1918, Faulk County, South Dakota; d. 10 Apr 1972, Pontiac, Oakland County, Michigan.

1151. JAY THOMAS^9 BARKER *(HARRIET "HATTIE"^{8} MILKS, EZRA^7, EZRA^6, DAVID^5 MILK, JONATHAN^4, JOB^3, JOHN^2, JOHN^1)* was born 1880 in Stephenson County, Illinois. He married ANNIE KIESTER Dec 1901. She was born Abt. 1880.

Children of JAY BARKER and ANNIE KIESTER are:
2078. i.   ESTHER^{10} BARKER, b. 1903, Freeport, Stephenson County, Illinois.
2079. ii.   VIVA BARKER, b. 1905, Freeport, Stephenson County, Illinois.
2080. iii. HELEN BARKER, b. 1907, Freeport, Stephenson County, Illinois.
       iv.   HAZEL BARKER, b. 1910, Faulk County, South Dakota; d. 1911, South Dakota.
2081. v.   CLYDE BARKER, b. 1912, Freeport, Stephenson County, Illinois.
       vi.   VELMA BARKER, b. 1913, Freeport, Stephenson County, Illinois; d. 1913, Freeport, Stephenson County, Illinois.
2082. vii. ETHEL BARKER, b. 1915, Freeport, Stephenson County, Illinois.
2083. viii. DALE E. BARKER, b. 30 Jun 1918, Freeport, Stephenson County, Illinois; d. Dec 1983, Davis, Stephenson County, Illinois.
       ix.   CLIFFORD BARKER, b. 1921, Freeport, Stephenson County, Illinois; d. 1921, Freeport, Stephenson County, Illinois.

1152. RUTH KATHRYN^9 MILKS *(FRANK WHEELER^8, EZRA^7, EZRA^6, DAVID^5 MILK, JONATHAN^4, JOB^3, JOHN^2, JOHN^1)* was born 16 Aug 1892 in Fitchburg Township, Dane County, Wisconsin, and died 12 Nov 1979 in Monroe, Green County, Wisconsin. She married CLAUDE ELMER WIDEMAN 25 Nov 1914 in Rock Grove Township, Stephenson County, Illinois, son of JOHN WIDEMAN and CORILLA FRANKEBERGER. He was born 04 Jun 1890 in Rock Grove Township, Stephenson County, Illinois, and died 29 Nov 1954 in Monroe, Green County, Wisconsin. Ruth contributed many records of the descendants of Ezra (1781)

Children of RUTH MILKS and CLAUDE WIDEMAN are:
2084. i. ELIZABETH ELEANOR^{10} WIDEMAN, b. 23 Aug 1917, Jefferson Township, Green County, Wisconsin; d. 25 Nov 1992, Madison, Dane County, Wisconsin.
2085. ii. JOHN FRANK WIDEMAN, b. 02 Feb 1922, Jefferson Township, Green County, Wisconsin.

1153. BERT ABLEY^9 MILKS *(DAVID^8, EZRA^7, EZRA^6, DAVID^5 MILK, JONATHAN^4, JOB^3, JOHN^2, JOHN^1)* was born 30 Mar 1890 in Chepstow, Kansas, and died Jul 1970 in Garrett, De Kalb County, Indiana. He married GEORGIA MAY CONRAD Abt. 13 Apr 1912 in Ashley, Indiana, daughter of WILLIAM CONRAD and EFFIE SALANDER. She was born 30 Nov 1890 in Southfield Township, Indiana, and died 1982 in Garrett, De Kalb, Indiana.

Children of BERT MILKS and GEORGIA CONRAD are:
2086. i.   DOROTHY RUTH^{10} MILKS, b. 12 Oct 1913, De Kalb County, Indiana.
2087. ii. LUCILLE JOSEPHINE MILKS, b. 31 Dec 1916, De Kalb County, Indiana; d. 18 Sep 2009, Heritage Pointe, Warren, Huntington County, Indiana.
2088. iii. MARY ELIZABETH MILKS, b. 13 Aug 1923, De Kalb County, Indiana.
2089. iv. MARGARET JOANNE MILKS, b. 10 Apr 1925, De Kalb County, Indiana.

1154. GEORGE ARNOLD^9 MILKS *(DAVID^8, EZRA^7, EZRA^6, DAVID^5 MILK, JONATHAN^4, JOB^3, JOHN^2, JOHN^1)* was born 08 Aug 1895 in Greenleaf, Washington County, Kansas, and died 14 May 1963 in DeKalb County, Indiana?. He married HADDY MANILA ROBINETT 31 Mar 1913 in Hillsdale, Michigan, daughter of THOMAS ROBINETT and SADIE HARRIS. She was born 16 Sep 1896 in Edon, Ohio, and died 04 Oct 1971 in Auburn, DeKalb County, Indiana.

Children of GEORGE MILKS and HADDY ROBINETT are:
2090. i. ARNOLD R.^{10} MILKS, b. 26 Oct 1914, Ashley, De Kalb County, Indiana; d. 09 Nov 1983, Ashley, De Kalb County, Indiana.
2091. ii. HELEN BERTA MILKS, b. 13 May 1918, Ashley, Indiana.

2092. iii. MILDRED MARIE MILKS, b. 24 Dec 1922, Ashley, De Kalb County, Indiana.

1155. MAUD^9 HILLIARD *(DANIEL MARENOS^8, PHOEBE ANN^7 MILKS, EZRA^6, DAVID^5 MILK, JONATHAN^4, JOB^3, JOHN^2, JOHN^1)* She married MISTRE DEAN.

Child of MAUD HILLIARD and MISTRE DEAN is:
    i. DOROTHY^{10} DEAN, m. MISTRE ANKLIN.

1156. LORENZO MERRILL^9 HILLIARD *(EZRA MILKS^8, PHOEBE ANN^7 MILKS, EZRA^6, DAVID^5 MILK, JONATHAN^4, JOB^3, JOHN^2, JOHN^1)* was born Aug 1870 in Wisconsin, and died Bet. 1900 - 1910 in California. He married CLARISA MAY 'CLARA' HARRIS 1894 in California, daughter of MISTRE HARRIS and ZARELDA STUART. She was born Oct 1871 in California, and died 30 May 1959 in Kern County, California.

Children of LORENZO HILLIARD and CLARISA HARRIS are:
    i. COLEEN M.^{10} HILLIARD, b. Jun 1895, California.
    ii. LORITA M. HILLIARD, b. Apr 1897, California.
    iii. LAVENE M. HILLIARD, b. Oct 1899, California.

1157. GRACE^9 HILLIARD *(EZRA MILKS^8, PHOEBE ANN^7 MILKS, EZRA^6, DAVID^5 MILK, JONATHAN^4, JOB^3, JOHN^2, JOHN^1)* She married FAY F. WELTY 26 Jun 1913.

Children of GRACE HILLIARD and FAY WELTY are:
2093. i. MARDA^{10} WELTY, b. 24 Apr 1916, Illinois.
2094. ii. JACK WELTY, b. 24 Apr 1924, Illinois.

1158. FRANK^9 HILLIARD *(LONSON DARIUS^8, PHOEBE ANN^7 MILKS, EZRA^6, DAVID^5 MILK, JONATHAN^4, JOB^3, JOHN^2, JOHN^1)* was born 26 Jun 1879 in Albany, Green County, Wisconsin, and died 1949. He married OLIVE JACOBSON. She was born Abt. 1880.

Children of FRANK HILLIARD and OLIVE JACOBSON are:
2095. i. SHIRL^{10} HILLIARD, b. 22 Mar 1908, Albany, Green County, Wisconsin; d. 24 Mar 1976, Warren, Jo Daviess County, Illinois.
2096. ii. DEAN HILLIARD, b. Albany, Green County, Wisconsin.

1159. TRELLA^9 HILLIARD *(LONSON DARIUS^8, PHOEBE ANN^7 MILKS, EZRA^6, DAVID^5 MILK, JONATHAN^4, JOB^3, JOHN^2, JOHN^1)* was born 04 Apr 1884 in Albany, Green County, Wisconsin, and died 26 Nov 1975 in Albany, Green County, Wisconsin. She married HOMER DE WAYNE WEBB 19 Oct 1904 in Green County, Wisconsin, son of WILLIAM ROSWELL WEBB and ADELPHA EUDORA BUMP. He was born 24 Aug 1882 in Green County, Wisconsin, and died 16 Jan 1921 in Milwaukee, Milwaukee County, Wisconsin.
OBITUARY
    Albany Vindicator (Albany, WI) January 27, 1921
    Homer Duane Webb, whose death was mentioned last week, was born in Albany on August 24, 1882 and died January 16, 1921 at Milwaukee after a brief illness from pneumonia at the age of 38 years, 4 months and 22 days. He married Trella Hilliard of Albany on October 19, 1904. To this union were born ten (I only found proof of 4 children) children: Wayne, Ila, La Verne and Helen. They lived in Albany the greater part of their married life, moving to Iowa a few years ago where they lived a short time, returning to Albany where they resided until about three years ago when they went to Milwaukee where they have since lived. He leaves to mourn his death a wife, four children, a father and mother, three brothers W.A. Webb and R. G. Webb of Princeton, Minnesota; and F.D. Webb of Windsor, New York; and a sister Mrs. Hazel Kullenbeck of Wallace, Idaho. The funeral was held from the Baptist Church in Albany on Wednesday, Jan. 19, 1921 at 2:00, conducted by G.M. King and the remains laid to rest in Hillcrest Cemetery. Relatives were here to attend the funeral from Evansville, Janesville, Monroe, Brodhead and Madison; his father and mother, Mr. and Mrs. W.R. Webb of Spencer, Iowa; and his brother R.G. Webb and wife of Princeton, Minnesota. Mrs. Webb and children will return to Albany to make their future home after disposing of their machinery stock and farm produce in Milwaukee.

Children of TRELLA HILLIARD and HOMER WEBB are:
2097. i.   WAYNE J.[10] WEBB, b. 14 Nov 1907, Albany, Green County, Wisconsin; d. 01 Aug 1979, Beloit, Rock County, Wisconsin.
       ii. ILA C. WEBB, b. Abt. Mar 1909, Albany, Green County, Wisconsin; m. MISTRE GILLIES.
       iii. LA VERNE WEBB, b. 1912, Iowa; d. 1927, Wisconsin.
2098. iv. HELEN L. WEBB, b. 05 Apr 1916, Iowa; d. 18 Dec 1996, Monroe, Green County, Wisconsin.

1160. ETHEL[9] HILLIARD *(LONSON DARIUS[8], PHOEBE ANN[7] MILKS, EZRA[6], DAVID[5] MILK, JONATHAN[4], JOB[3], JOHN[2], JOHN[1])* was born Abt. 1889 in Albany, Green County, Wisconsin, and died 06 Dec 1933. She married (1) EDWARD O'BRIEN. He was born Abt. 1889. She married (2) ALLIE BREESE Abt. 1910. He was born Abt. 1889.

Child of ETHEL HILLIARD and ALLIE BREESE is:
       i. KENNETH[10] BREESE, b. 1912.

1161. CHARLES S.[9] KNIGHT *(CLARA CLARINDA[8] HILLIARD, PHOEBE ANN[7] MILKS, EZRA[6], DAVID[5] MILK, JONATHAN[4], JOB[3], JOHN[2], JOHN[1])* was born 28 Sep 1879 in Cedar Falls, Iowa.

Children of CHARLES S. KNIGHT are:
       i. OPAL[10] KNIGHT, m. MISTRE BASSETT.
       ii. LOUISE KNIGHT.

1162. HATTIE[9] MYLKS *(HARMON WILLIAM[8], DAVID[7] MILKS, DAVID[6], DAVID[5] MILK, JONATHAN[4], JOB[3], JOHN[2], JOHN[1])* was born 19 Aug 1868 in Ontario, Canada, and died 25 Feb 1933 in Brandon, Manitoba, Canada. She married JOHN CHRISTIE IRVING Abt. 1887 in Ontario, Canada. He was born 06 Dec 1864 in Winchester, Ontario, Canada, and died 27 Jan 1937 in Brandon, Manitoba, Canada. They are buried in Maple Ridge Cemetery, Chesterville, Ontario, Canada

Children of HATTIE MYLKS and JOHN IRVING are:
       i.   MARY BESSIE MAUD[10] IRVING, b. 27 Jun 1888, Arthur Village, Wellington North, Ontario, Canada.
       ii. MABEL JENNIE READ IRVING, b. 01 Apr 1890, Arthur Village, Wellington North, Ontario, Canada.
       iii. DONALD SMITH IRVING, b. Mar 1907, Brandon, Manitoba, Canada; d. 1934, Brandon, Manitoba, Canada.

1163. DR. GORDON WRIGHT[9] MYLKS *(MANUEL[8], DAVID[7] MILKS, DAVID[6], DAVID[5] MILK, JONATHAN[4], JOB[3], JOHN[2], JOHN[1])* was born 14 Aug 1874 in Augusta Township, Grenville County, Ontario, Canada, and died 13 Feb 1957 in Pinellas County, Florida. He married (1) LUCY HAMILTON ROWE 09 Sep 1903 in Jefferson, Jefferson County, Kentucky. She was born 1878, and died 1940. He married (2) MAY HAYDON Aft. 1940.

Children of GORDON MYLKS and LUCY ROWE are:
2099. i.   DR. GORDON WRIGHT[10] MYLKS II, b. 15 Jun 1904, Kingston, Ontario; d. 23 Feb 1973, Kingston, Ontario.
       ii. HENRY SAYLES MYLKS, b. 1909, Kingston, Ontario; d. 16 Oct 1928, Frontenac, Ontario, Canada. Shot himself, and died, while he was a medical student.
2100. iii. HELEN ISABELLE MYLKS, b. 04 Jun 1912, Kingston, Ontario; d. 1943, Kingston, Ontario.

1164. LEONARD EUGENE[9] MYLKS *(MANUEL[8], DAVID[7] MILKS, DAVID[6], DAVID[5] MILK, JONATHAN[4], JOB[3], JOHN[2], JOHN[1])* was born 14 Feb 1876 in Augusta Township, Grenville County, Ontario, and died Dec 1955 in Kingston, Ontario. He married (1) MARY EVELINE GRAY 19 Jul 1911. She was born Abt. 1888 in Chater, Manitoba, and died 19 Apr 1913 in Calgary. He married (2) CATHERINE LAUREL SHAW 03 Jun 1914 in St. James Church, Dufferin, Ontario. She was born 05 Nov 1883 in Mono Twp, Simcoe, Ontario, and died 30 Jul 1939 in Shelburne, MT, DC, Ontario. He married (3) CLARA ADAMS Aft. 1939. She was born in Beamsville, Ontario.

Children of LEONARD MYLKS and CATHERINE SHAW are:
2101. i.   NORMA[10] MYLKS, b. 29 Dec 1914.
2102. ii. CATHERINE LENORE MYLKS, b. 04 Jan 1917, Prince Albert, Sask.; d. 06 Apr 1988, Niagara Falls, Ontario, Canada.
2103. iii. MIRIAM ELIZABETH "BETTY" MYLKS, b. 09 Feb 1920, Niagara Falls, Ontario.

1165. JAMES E.[9] MILKS *(SILAS E.[8], EZRA[7], DAVID[6], DAVID[5] MILK, JONATHAN[4], JOB[3], JOHN[2], JOHN[1])* was born 28 Oct 1867 in Elk Creek, Erie County, Pennsylvania, and died 20 Jul 1954 in Terra Haute, Vigo County, Indiana. He married SIBYL E. GREEN 27 Oct 1892 in Cleveland, Ohio. She was born 03 Oct 1868 in Kingsville, Ohio, and died 02 Feb 1957 in Terra Haute, Vigo County, Indiana.

Children of JAMES MILKS and SIBYL GREEN are:
- i. PETER[10] MILKS, b. Abt. 1894; d. Bef. 1900.
- 2104. ii. HELEN G. MILKS, b. 28 Jun 1898, Indianapolis, Indiana; d. 1986, Terra Haute, Vigo County, Indiana.
- 2105. iii. ELIZABETH CAWLEY MILKS, b. 03 Feb 1907, Terra Haute, Indiana; d. 31 Mar 2000, Delray Beach, Florida.

1166. ARTHUR BLAINE[9] BUSH *(SARAH ANNA[8] MILKS, ALBERT[7], DAVID[6], DAVID[5] MILK, JONATHAN[4], JOB[3], JOHN[2], JOHN[1])* was born 17 Sep 1884 in Erie, Erie County, Pennsylvania, and died 08 May 1960 in Milford, New Haven, Connecticut. He married (1) GERTRUDE _____ Abt. 1904 in Erie County, Pennsylvania. She was born Abt. 1889 in Pennsylvania. He married (2) HELEN K. BAINK Abt. 1912. She was born 17 Jul 1890 in Winona, Winona County, Minnesota.

Children of ARTHUR BUSH and GERTRUDE _____ are:
- i. RUTH[10] BUSH, b. Abt. 1905, Pennsylvania.
- ii. FLORENCE BUSH, b. Abt. 1908, Pennsylvania.

Child of ARTHUR BUSH and HELEN BAINK is:
- 2106. iii. HELEN K.[10] BUSH, b. Abt. 1913, Manhattan, New York.

1167. CHESTER A.[9] BUSH *(SARAH ANNA[8] MILKS, ALBERT[7], DAVID[6], DAVID[5] MILK, JONATHAN[4], JOB[3], JOHN[2], JOHN[1])* was born 21 Sep 1887 in Erie, Erie County, Pennsylvania, and died Feb 1966 in Berea, Cuyahoga County, Ohio. He married MARGARET V. _____. She was born Abt. 1885 in New York.

Children of CHESTER BUSH and MARGARET _____ are:
- i. CHESTER A.[10] BUSH, JR., b. Abt. 1912, Pennsylvania.
- ii. RANDOLPH E BUSH, b. Abt. 1914, Pennsylvania.
- iii. MARLIN E. BUSH, b. Abt. 1915, Pennsylvania.
- iv. HARRISON A. BUSH, b. Abt. 1920, New York.
- v. THEODORE A. BUSH, b. Abt. 1922, New York.

1168. DOROTHY K.[9] BUSH *(SARAH ANNA[8] MILKS, ALBERT[7], DAVID[6], DAVID[5] MILK, JONATHAN[4], JOB[3], JOHN[2], JOHN[1])* was born 19 Apr 1895 in Erie, Erie County, Pennsylvania, and died Jun 1984 in Erie, Erie County, Pennsylvania. She married GEORGE ERNEST MIDDLETON Abt. 1923 in Erie County, Pennsylvania. He was born 26 May 1892 in Pennsylvania, and died 05 Mar 1979 in Erie, Erie County, Pennsylvania.

Child of DOROTHY BUSH and GEORGE MIDDLETON is:
- i. GLORIA E.[10] MIDDLETON, b. 04 Jul 1924, Erie, Erie County, Pennsylvania; m. PAUL R. AMIDON, 22 Sep 1948, Union City, Erie County, Pennsylvania; b. 10 Nov 1924, Erie, Erie County, Pennsylvania; d. May 1980, Erie, Erie County, Pennsylvania.

1169. HAZEL S.[9] DIETLEY *(MARY E.[8] MILKS, ALBERT[7], DAVID[6], DAVID[5] MILK, JONATHAN[4], JOB[3], JOHN[2], JOHN[1])* was born 02 Dec 1892 in Erie County, Pennsylvania. She married FRANKLIN P. KINCADE 02 Jan 1915. He was born Abt. 1890.

Children of HAZEL DIETLEY and FRANKLIN KINCADE are:
- i. FRANKLIN D.[10] KINCADE, b. 05 Apr 1916, Erie, Erie County, Pennsylvania; d. 31 Mar 1945, Zeitz, Germany; m. MARGARET HAGERTY; b. Abt. 1916.
- 2107. ii. MARY JANE KINCADE, b. 26 Dec 1920, Erie, Erie County, Pennsylvania.
- iii. RUSSELL KINCADE, b. 29 Sep 1922, Erie, Erie County, Pennsylvania; d. Bef. 1956.
- iv. THOMAS KINCADE, b. 16 Aug 1924, Erie, Erie County, Pennsylvania; m. PATRICIA WATERS; b. Abt. 1925.
- v. PHILLIP W. KINCADE, b. 18 Apr 1928, Buffalo, New York; m. BARBARA BIUTSHOLTS; b. Abt. 1930.

1170. URAS A.[9] DIETLEY *(MARY E.[8] MILKS, ALBERT[7], DAVID[6], DAVID[5] MILK, JONATHAN[4], JOB[3], JOHN[2], JOHN[1])* was born 18 May 1894 in Erie County, Pennsylvania, and died 08 Jul 1953 in Erie, Erie County, Pennsylvania. He married MAGDALINE C. KRAMER 12 Dec 1917 in Erie, Erie County, Pennsylvania, daughter of PHILIP KRAMER and CATHERINE RICHTCHEIDT. She was born 28 Dec 1888 in Erie, Erie County, Pennsylvania, and died 07 Nov 1969 in Erie, Erie County, Pennsylvania.

Children of URAS DIETLEY and MAGDALINE KRAMER are:
- i. URAS PHILIP[10] DIETLEY, b. 12 Mar 1920, Erie, Erie County, Pennsylvania; d. 18 Apr 1927, Erie Cemetery, Erie, Erie County, Pennsylvania.
- 2108. ii. RICHARD WILLIAM DIETLEY, b. 27 Mar 1922, Erie, Erie County, Pennsylvania.
- iii. ROBERT KRAMER DIETLEY, b. 26 Dec 1923, Erie, Erie County, Pennsylvania; m. PATRICIA STRICKLER, 10 Jun 1950; b. Abt. 1923.

1171. PHILIP W.[9] DIETLEY *(MARY E.[8] MILKS, ALBERT[7], DAVID[6], DAVID[5] MILK, JONATHAN[4], JOB[3], JOHN[2], JOHN[1])* was born 03 Feb 1897 in Erie County, Pennsylvania, and died 20 Sep 1934. He married MILDRED DIXON. She was born Abt. 1900 in Of Buffalo, New York.

Children of PHILIP DIETLEY and MILDRED DIXON are:
- 2109. i. PHYLLIS A.[10] DIETLEY.
- ii. MARY ALICE DIETLEY, b. Of Pittsburgh.

1172. MARY E.[9] DIETLEY *(MARY E.[8] MILKS, ALBERT[7], DAVID[6], DAVID[5] MILK, JONATHAN[4], JOB[3], JOHN[2], JOHN[1])* was born 16 Mar 1900 in Erie County, Pennsylvania. She married CHESTER W. NICHOLS 14 Mar 1929 in Erie County, Pennsylvania, son of CHESTER NICHOLS and SOPHIA LINK. He was born Abt. 1905 in Pennsylvania.

Child of MARY DIETLEY and CHESTER NICHOLS is:
- i. CHESTER C.[10] NICHOLS, JR., b. Abt. 1932, Erie, Erie County, Pennsylvania.

1173. FRANKLIN HORACE[9] MILKS *(WARREN "JACK"[8], HARRIS[7], SILAS W.[6], DAVID[5] MILK, JONATHAN[4], JOB[3], JOHN[2], JOHN[1])* was born 20 Mar 1877 in Morley, Mecosta County, Michigan, and died May 1966 in Augusta, Kalamazoo, Michigan. He married (1) EDNA E. MINZIE 21 Jun 1902 in Cadillac, Osceola County, Michigan, daughter of ANDREW MINZIE. She was born 1881 in Michigan, and died 1928 in Oakland County, Michigan. He married (2) MARJORIE HELEN PULLIN Bet. 1930 - 1932, daughter of ALFRED PULLIN and MARY LEWIS. She was born 02 Feb 1900 in Avon, Ontario, Canada.

Child of FRANKLIN MILKS and MARJORIE PULLIN is:
- 2110. i. DONALD FRANK[10] MILKS, b. 19 Oct 1932, Highland Park, Michigan; d. 15 Aug 1978, Kalamazoo, Michigan.

1174. CLARA[9] MILKS *(WARREN "JACK"[8], HARRIS[7], SILAS W.[6], DAVID[5] MILK, JONATHAN[4], JOB[3], JOHN[2], JOHN[1])* was born 09 May 1879 in Morley, Mecosta County, Michigan. She married THOMAS FRANK PETTIE 22 Nov 1900. He was born Abt. 1879.

Children of CLARA MILKS and THOMAS PETTIE are:
- i. MARSHALL W.[10] PETTIE, b. 12 Nov 1909, Tustin, Michigan; d. 13 Apr 2001, Kent County, Michigan.
- 2111. ii. JERRINE PETTIE, b. 18 Oct 1912, Tustin, Michigan; d. 23 Jun 2004, Kent County, Michigan.

1175. ALFRED WARREN[9] MILKS *(WARREN "JACK"[8], HARRIS[7], SILAS W.[6], DAVID[5] MILK, JONATHAN[4], JOB[3], JOHN[2], JOHN[1])* was born 02 Jul 1883 in Morley, Mecosta County, Michigan, and died 26 Mar 1976 in Midland, Michigan. He married SARAH M. JOHNSON 28 Nov 1911, daughter of FATHER JOHNSON and MOTHER. She was born 1885 in Michigan, and died 1968 in Midland, Michigan.

Children of ALFRED MILKS and SARAH JOHNSON are:
- i. PATRICIA[10] MILKS, b. 23 Jun 1913, Santa Rosa, Calif.; m. OLIVER E. BEUTEL; b. Abt. 1910.
- 2112. ii. WARREN NELSON MILKS, b. 22 Feb 1916, Jennings, Michigan; d. 22 Jun 2011, Miami, Florida.

iii. ROY FRANKLIN MILKS, b. 31 Oct 1921, Midland, Michigan; m. (1) HELEN E. NEBRIG; b. 08 Apr 1928; d. Dec 1978, Littleton, Arapahoe, Colorado,; m. (2) IRMA B. _____; b. 10 Mar 1933.

iv. FRANCES MILKS, b. 26 May 1928, Midland, Michigan; m. MISTRE ALDRICH; b. Abt. 1928.

1176. WALTER H.^{9} MILKS *(WARREN "JACK"^{8}, HARRIS^7, SILAS W.^{6}, DAVID^5 MILK, JONATHAN^4, JOB^3, JOHN^2, JOHN^1)* was born 13 May 1886 in Morley, Mecosta County, Michigan, and died 04 Nov 1916 in Midland, Michigan. He married BESSIE MAY LEAF 21 Oct 1907. She was born 04 Apr 1891 in Michigan.

Children of WALTER MILKS and BESSIE LEAF are:
   i. ALFRED WARREN^{10} MILKS, b. 29 Jun 1911, Yakima County, Washington; d. 16 Oct 1911, Granger, Yakima County, Washington.
   ii. WALTER EDWIN MILKS, b. 01 Aug 1912, Yakima, Washington; d. 30 Oct 1973, Pontiac, Oakland County, Michigan; m. MARTHA S. ERICKSON, Aft. 1940; b. 25 Nov 1916, Michigan; d. 26 Nov 2000, Birmingham, Oakland County, Michigan.

1177. LYLE N.^{9} MILKS *(WARREN "JACK"^{8}, HARRIS^7, SILAS W.^{6}, DAVID^5 MILK, JONATHAN^4, JOB^3, JOHN^2, JOHN^1)* was born 30 May 1900 in Tustin, Michigan, and died 28 Dec 1966 in Saginaw, Saginaw Co., Michigan. He married (1) ELSIE ALBERTA ZALSMAN 13 Sep 1921 in Holland, Ottawa County, Michigan, daughter of PHILIP ZALSMAN and FLORENCE LYDELL. She was born 1902 in Paris, Michigan, and died 02 Feb 1954 in Grayling, Crawford Co., Mich.. He married (2) VIRGINIA B. (KLITZ) BROTT 1953, daughter of EARL KLITZ and LAURA _____. She was born 29 Jan 1911 in Ohio, and died 09 Jul 1991 in Saginaw County, Michigan.

Child of LYLE MILKS and ELSIE ZALSMAN is:
   i. PHYLLIS MARIE^{10} MILKS, b. 29 Dec 1931, Grayling, Crawford County, Michigan; d. 17 Nov 2011, Clare, Clare County, Michigan (never married).
      OBITUARY
      Phyllis Marie Milks, age 79, of Clare, passed away at Tendercare of Clare. She was born the daughter of Lyle and Alberta (Zalsman) Milks.
      After graduating High School in Grayling in 1949, she cared for her ailing mother until her passing in 1954. Phyllis attended a Christian School in Grand Rapids and worked as a counsellor in several bible camps in northern Michigan and in the upper peninsula. She then attended college in Flint to become an X-ray technician and was employed in the Alpena area. She moved to Clare from Grand Rapids in 1976 and served as a caregiver for elderly residents and also house-sat for people who liked to travel. Upon retiring as a caregiver, Phyllis became a very faithful servant in many childrens ministries within the Baptist Church. She had a heart for little children in Awana, bible school, release time classes, and was a teacher for beginners and junior church for years.
      Funeral services were held on Monday, Nov. 21, at 11:00 AM at the First Baptist Church in Clare, with Pastor Randy Emmory officiating.
      Burial: Elmwood Cemetery, Grayling, Crawford County, Michigan, USA

1178. JOHN HARRIS 'HARRY'^{9} MILKS *(ERNEST L.^{8}, HARRIS^7, SILAS W.^{6}, DAVID^5 MILK, JONATHAN^4, JOB^3, JOHN^2, JOHN^1)* was born 13 Nov 1883 in Howard City, Michigan, and died 23 May 1938 in Augusta, Kalamazoo, Michigan. He married CARLENE AMELIA DOUGHERTY 1921 in Michigan. She was born Abt. 1885.

Children of JOHN MILKS and CARLENE DOUGHERTY are:
2113.   i. JACK K.^{10} MILKS, b. 04 Sep 1922, Augusta Township, Kalamazoo County, Michigan; d. 10 Apr 1994, Johnstown, Barry County, Michigan.
2114.   ii. GERALD K. MILKS, b. Bet. 1923 - 1924, Augusta Township, Kalamazoo County, Michigan; d. Abt. 1950.
        iii. MARYTA MILKS, m. MISTRE HOLBERT.

1179. CHARLES EDWARD^9 MILKS *(ERNEST L.^{8}, HARRIS^7, SILAS W.^{6}, DAVID^5 MILK, JONATHAN^4, JOB^3, JOHN^2, JOHN^1)* was born 09 Jan 1887 in Howard City, Montcalm County, Michigan, and died 04 Dec 1958 in Barry County, Michigan. He married (1) SARAH A. BROWN 01 Nov 1909 in Kalamazoo County, Michigan, daughter of FATHER BROWN and MOTHER _____. She was born 26 Aug 1881 in Barry, Michigan, and died 18 Oct 1931 in Galesburg, Kalamazoo Co., Michigan. He married (2) ANNE HAYNES 1949 in Kalamazoo County, Michigan. She was born Abt. 1890.

Sarah died suddenly while motoring near Galesburg, MI

Children of CHARLES MILKS and SARAH BROWN are:
- i. MARGARET ELNA[10] MILKS, b. 15 Jan 1911, Ross Twp., Kalamazoo Co., Michigan; d. 21 Jan 1911, Ross Twp., Kalamazoo Co., Michigan.
- 2115. ii. MILDRED B. MILKS, b. 27 Jan 1912, Michigan; d. 25 Jul 1995, Barton Lake, Vicksburg, Kalamazoo Co., Michigan.
- 2116. iii. HAROLD J. MILKS, b. 27 Jan 1913, Michigan; d. 23 Jul 2001, Holt, Ingham Co., Michigan.
- iv. GLADYS E. MILKS, b. 1915; m. REYNOLD L. HAAS, 1937, Kalamazoo County, Michigan.
- 2117. v. ALICE IRENE MILKS, b. 02 Mar 1921, Michigan; d. 18 Oct 2011, Kalamazoo, Michigan.

1180. BERTHA M.[9] MILKS *(JESSE[8], HARRIS[7], SILAS W.[6], DAVID[5] MILK, JONATHAN[4], JOB[3], JOHN[2], JOHN[1])* was born Dec 1883 in Michigan, and died 1942 in Battle Creek, Calhoun County, Michigan. She married ALLEN POTTER MANWARREN, son of SCEMILIOUS MANWARREN and SARAH _____. He was born 13 Jun 1886 in Michigan, and died Jan 1967 in Battle Creek, Calhoun County, Michigan.

Children of BERTHA MILKS and ALLEN MANWARREN are:
- i. NOLA M.[10] MANWARREN, b. Bet. 1918 - 1919, Calhoun County, Michigan.
- ii. THELMA MANWARREN, b. Abt. 1921, Calhoun County, Michigan.

1181. LEO LEROY[9] MILKS *(FRANKLIN GRANT[8], HARRIS[7], SILAS W.[6], DAVID[5] MILK, JONATHAN[4], JOB[3], JOHN[2], JOHN[1])* was born 18 Sep 1887 in Reynolds, Montcalm County, Michigan. He married (1) MARIE LOUISE RACINE 15 Sep 1909 in Manistee, Manistee County, Michigan, daughter of CHARLES RACINE and TURVILLE FILIAN. She was born 1888 in Canada, and died 1960. He married (2) EDITH BAKER 19 Jul 1919 in Manistee, Manistee County, Michigan, daughter of ALBERT BAKER and MARTHA _____. She was born 04 Feb 1892 in Manistee County, Michigan, and died Jun 1971 in Dearborn, Wayne County, Michigan.

Children of LEO MILKS and MARIE RACINE are:
- i. VIRGINIA[10] MILKS, b. 04 May 1910, Manistee, Michigan; d. 18 May 1910, Manistee, Michigan.
- 2118. ii. GRACE O. MILKS, b. 17 May 1911, Manistee, Manistee County, Michigan (twin); d. 07 Jul 1987, Manistee, Manistee County, Michigan.
- iii. UNNAMED MILKS, b. 17 May 1911, Manistee, Michigan (twin); d. 17 May 1911, Manistee, Michigan (twin).
- 2119. iv. LEROY JOSEPH MILKS, b. 04 Feb 1913, Manistee, Michigan; d. 11 Jun 1982, Manistee County, Michigan.
- 2120. v. CHARLES L. MILKS, b. 1915, Manistee, Michigan.

Children of LEO MILKS and EDITH BAKER are:
- 2121. vi. RONALD JAMES[10] MILKS, b. 30 Jul 1921, Manistee, Mich; d. 05 May 2000, North Port, Sarasota, Florida.
- vii. DOUGLAS DAVID MILKS, b. 22 May 1932; d. 12 Feb 1994, Onekama, Manistee County, Michigan.

1182. VIRGIE M.[9] MILKS *(FRANKLIN GRANT[8], HARRIS[7], SILAS W.[6], DAVID[5] MILK, JONATHAN[4], JOB[3], JOHN[2], JOHN[1])* was born 12 May 1891 in Reynolds, Montcalm County, Michigan. She married MISTRE SPEARS. He was born Abt. 1890.

Children of VIRGIE MILKS and MISTRE SPEARS are:
- i. BEATRICE[10] SPEARS.
- ii. LILLIAN SPEARS, b. 16 Aug 1926; d. Sep 1976, Howard City, Montcalm County, Michigan. Maybe married to Donald L. Chaffee, b: 1911, d:

1183. LILLIAN GRACE[9] MILKS *(FRANKLIN GRANT[8], HARRIS[7], SILAS W.[6], DAVID[5] MILK, JONATHAN[4], JOB[3], JOHN[2], JOHN[1])* was born 10 Jun 1895 in Reynolds, Montcalm County, Michigan, and died 1963 in Montcalm County, Michigan. She married ALBERT TRONSON 30 Oct 1915 in Grand Rapids, Michigan, son of OLE TRONSON and REGINA OLSEN. He was born 1897 in Michigan, and died 1962.

Child of LILLIAN MILKS and ALBERT TRONSON is:
- 2122. i. RONALD LEROY[10] TRONSON, b. 15 Mar 1916, Reynolds Township, Montcalm County, Michigan; d. 16 Dec

1999, Morley, Montcalm County, Michigan.

1184. ELLIS CLYDE[9] MILKS *(ALLEN EDGAR[8], MATTHEW G.[7], SILAS W.[6], DAVID[5] MILK, JONATHAN[4], JOB[3], JOHN[2], JOHN[1])* was born 17 Dec 1890 in Valley Falls, Rensselaer County, New York, and died 09 Mar 1940 in Bensonhurst, Kings County, New York. He married HEDWIG ALBERTA ADELAIDE WACKER 29 Nov 1916 in Brooklyn, New York (at Hedwig's home), daughter of HEINRICH WACKER and ANNA HAESLOP. She was born 05 Apr 1888 in Bronx County, New York, and died 27 Sep 1973 in Bronx County, New York.

Children of ELLIS MILKS and HEDWIG WACKER are:

2123. i. ALLEN HENRY[10] MILKS, b. 28 Oct 1917, Bensonhurst, Kings County, New York; d. 10 Jun 1996, Bay Ridge, Kings County, New York.
2124. ii. JEANNETTE ADELAIDE MILKS, b. 16 Jun 1919, Bensonhurst, Kings County, New York; d. 06 Mar 1988, Melbourne, Brevard County, Florida.

1185. HARRY W.[9] HOWARD *(ANGELINA[8] WAITE, ISAAC[7], MARY[6] MILKS, JONATHAN[5] MILK, JONATHAN[4], JOB[3], JOHN[2], JOHN[1])* was born 14 May 1872 in Bangor, Van Buren County, Michigan, and died 03 May 1948 in Hartford, Van Buren County, Michigan. He married (1) ELLA _____ 1890 in Van Buren County, Michigan ?. She was born Sep 1872 in Indiana. He married (2) BELLE (OXLEY) LATHBERY Abt. 1904. She was born Abt. 1876 in Michigan.

Ella and son, Guy, were living with Angelina Howard (widow) in 1900 in South Haven, Van Buren County, Michigan.

Child of HARRY HOWARD and ELLA _____ is:

2125. i. GUY L.[10] HOWARD, b. 22 Feb 1895, South Haven, Van Buren County, Michigan; d. 17 Oct 1954, Kalamazoo, Michigan.

1186. MABEL[9] MILKS *(FRANK[8], PERRY M.[7], BENJAMIN[6], DAVID[5] MILK, JONATHAN[4], JOB[3], JOHN[2], JOHN[1])* was born Aug 1889 in Wapello County, Iowa. She married SYLVESTER STEELE 1910 in Iowa. He was born 08 Jul 1887 in Minnesota.

Child of MABEL MILKS and SYLVESTER STEELE is:
i. MAXINE[10] STEELE, b. Abt. 1912, Polk County, Iowa.

1187. BARTON G.[9] WOOLMAN *(GEORGE MARTIN[8], GEORGE W.[7], PATIENCE[6] MILK, LEMUEL[5], JONATHAN[4], JOB[3], JOHN[2], JOHN[1])* was born Abt. 1873 in Ortonville, Oakland County, Michigan, and died 01 Mar 1917 in Ortonville, Oakland County, Michigan. He married FLOY FLAGLER 25 Jul 1895 in Ortonville, Oakland County, Michigan, daughter of ALONZO FLAGLER and JANE LEMON. She was born 03 Mar 1876 in Ortonville, Oakland County, Michigan.

Children of BARTON WOOLMAN and FLOY FLAGLER are:
i. LYNN F.[10] WOOLMAN, b. 21 Jan 1897, Ortonville, Oakland County, Michigan; d. 28 Apr 1982, Ft. Lauderdale, Broward County, Florida; m. DOROTHY _____; b. 16 Nov 1902, Patterson, New Jersey; d. 12 Apr 1989, Ft. Lauderdale, Broward County, Florida.
ii. VOYLE VERNELL WOOLMAN, b. 17 Jul 1903, Ortonville, Oakland County, Michigan; d. 02 Oct 1983, Laguna Hills, Orange County, California; m. (1) JEANNE HAMILTON, 14 Jul 1930, Seneca County, Ohio; b. Abt. 1908, Westley, California; m. (2) FRANCES ELVIRA GOODWIN, Aft. 1940, California; b. 26 Dec 1898, Texas; d. 20 Dec 1999, Orange County, California.
iii. RUTHALEE WOOLMAN, b. Abt. 1911, Ortonville, Oakland County, Michigan.

1188. URBAN VICTOR[9] WOOLMAN *(GEORGE MARTIN[8], GEORGE W.[7], PATIENCE[6] MILK, LEMUEL[5], JONATHAN[4], JOB[3], JOHN[2], JOHN[1])* was born 27 Oct 1879 in Ortonville, Oakland County, Michigan. He married KATHERINE L. SKINNER 06 May 1913 in Ortonville, Oakland County, Michigan, daughter of ROBERT SKINNER and LUCY RUDD. She was born 16 Apr 1881 in Orion Township, Oakland County, Michigan.

Children of URBAN WOOLMAN and KATHERINE SKINNER are:
i. ELIZABETH[10] WOOLMAN, b. Abt. 1914, Brazil.
ii. GEORGIA WOOLMAN, b. Abt. 1917, Brazil.

1189. EVAN L.[9] WOOLMAN *(GEORGE MARTIN[8], GEORGE W.[7], PATIENCE[6] MILK, LEMUEL[5], JONATHAN[4], JOB[3], JOHN[2], JOHN[1])* was born 26 Jun 1886 in Ortonville, Oakland County, Michigan, and died 09 Sep 1939 in Montana. He married (1) VERA W. _____. She was born Abt. 1895 in Oregon. He married (2) MAGDELINE A. 'LENA' RHORSON Abt. 1923 in Montana. She was born Abt. 1900 in Iowa.

Child of EVAN WOOLMAN and VERA _____ is:
- i. KEITH L.[10] WOOLMAN, b. 18 Oct 1918, Montana; d. 02 Dec 1995, Myrtle Beach, Horry County, South Carolina.

Child of EVAN WOOLMAN and MAGDELINE RHORSON is:
- ii. KATHERINE L.[10] WOOLMAN, b. Abt. Apr 1924, Butte, Silver Bow, Montana; m. (1) MONTANA HAROLD KAMPS, 17 Jul 1943, Dillon, Beaverhead, Montana; b. Abt. 1923; m. (2) ROBERT O. CUNNINGHAM, 31 Jul 1946, Yellowstone County, Montana; b. Abt. 1923.

1190. JAMES ELMER[9] ANDERSON *(ANNETTE ADELIA[8] WHIPPLE, ADELIA[7] PROSSER, MARY[6] MILK, LEMUEL[5], JONATHAN[4], JOB[3], JOHN[2], JOHN[1])* was born 11 May 1868 in Mt. Carroll, Illinois, and died 01 Oct 1942 in Long Beach, California. He married CORA B. SMITH 15 Aug 1894 in Omaha, Nebraska. She was born Abt. 1868.

Child of JAMES ANDERSON and CORA SMITH is:
2126.   i. RUTH[10] ANDERSON, b. 31 Aug 1895.

1191. REV. FRANK HOWARD[9] ANDERSON *(ANNETTE ADELIA[8] WHIPPLE, ADELIA[7] PROSSER, MARY[6] MILK, LEMUEL[5], JONATHAN[4], JOB[3], JOHN[2], JOHN[1])* was born 22 Oct 1870 in Galesburg, Illinois, and died 30 Jun 1945 in Omaha, Nebraska. He married ADA STONE 30 Jun 1900 in Omaha, Nebraska. She was born Abt. 1870.

Child of FRANK ANDERSON and ADA STONE is:
2127.   i. REV. HOWARD STONE[10] ANDERSON, b. 02 Jul 1905, Durand, Wisconsin.

1192. ERLE INMAN[9] WHIPPLE *(IRA FRANK[8], ADELIA[7] PROSSER, MARY[6] MILK, LEMUEL[5], JONATHAN[4], JOB[3], JOHN[2], JOHN[1])* was born 21 Oct 1876 in Spencer, Marathon County, Wisconsin. He married GEORGIA GHOCA Abt. 1902 in Wisconsin. She was born Abt. 1880 in Wausau, Wisconsin.

Child of ERLE WHIPPLE and GEORGIA GHOCA is:
2128.   i. FORD GHOCA[10] WHIPPLE, b. 21 May 1904, Waupaca, Waupaca County, Wisconsin; d. Apr 1978, Izard,? Arkansas.

1193. CHARLES D.[9] MOORE *(MASSENA[8], MARIA LYNDIA[7] PROSSER, ELIZABETH 'BETSEY'[6] MILK, LEMUEL[5], JONATHAN[4], JOB[3], JOHN[2], JOHN[1])* was born Feb 1872, and died Nov 1949 in Glens Falls, Warren County, New York ?. He married LENA ELDRIDGE. She was born Abt. 1872.

Child of CHARLES MOORE and LENA ELDRIDGE is:
2129.   i. DR. ELDRIDGE[10] MOORE.

1194. EMMA GERTRUDE[9] TRUESDALE *(BETSEY[8] MOORE, MARIA LYNDIA[7] PROSSER, ELIZABETH 'BETSEY'[6] MILK, LEMUEL[5], JONATHAN[4], JOB[3], JOHN[2], JOHN[1])* was born 06 Nov 1871 in Diamond Point (Hill View), New York. She married REV. GORDON L. THOMPSON 06 Jun 1894, son of ORLO THOMPSON and EMMA PRESTON. He was born 02 Mar 1869 in Ticonderoga, New York, and died in Hempstead, New York.

Children of EMMA TRUESDALE and GORDON THOMPSON are:
- i. ETHEL TRUESDALE[10] THOMPSON, b. 16 May 1895, Diamond Point (Hill View), New York; d. Aft. 1956.
- ii. HAROLD ORLO THOMPSON, b. 19 Sep 1897, Hartford, New York; m. (1) ELIZABETH STRICKLER; b. Abt. 1900, Of California; m. (2) HELEN HARTER; b. Abt. 1900, Of Washington, D.C..

1195. WILLIAM D.[9] BRAYTON *(EMILY[8] MOORE, MARIA LYNDIA[7] PROSSER, ELIZABETH 'BETSEY'[6] MILK, LEMUEL[5], JONATHAN[4], JOB[3], JOHN[2], JOHN[1])* was born 22 Mar 1870 in Diamond Point (Hill View), New York, and died 10 Jul 1949 in Kansas. He married LENA TRUESDALE Oct 1895 in Diamond Point (Hill View) Warren County, New York. She was born 20 Sep 1878, and died 05 Mar 1971 in Kansas.

Children of WILLIAM BRAYTON and LENA TRUESDALE are:
2130.   i.   MABEL[10] BRAYTON, b. 20 Jul 1897, Kansas; d. 02 Feb 1970, Kansas.
2131.   ii. ALTHA BRAYTON, b. 1900.
2132.   iii. DAN L. BRAYTON, b. 07 Feb 1907, Kansas; d. 21 Dec 1991, Kansas.

1196. ROBERT LINUS[9] BRAYTON *(EMILY[8] MOORE, MARIA LYNDIA[7] PROSSER, ELIZABETH 'BETSEY'[6] MILK, LEMUEL[5], JONATHAN[4], JOB[3], JOHN[2], JOHN[1])* was born 23 Sep 1874, and died 23 Jun 1965 in Kansas. He married FLORA GRACE PECK Abt. 1895 in Kansas. She was born 04 Sep 1876 in Galesburg, Knox County, Illinois, and died 10 Jul 1940 in Kansas.

Children of ROBERT BRAYTON and FLORA PECK are:
2133.   i.   HELEN L.[10] BRAYTON, b. Aug 1896, Rice County, Kansas; d. 21 Jun 1982, Longview, Washington.
        ii. DOROTHY BRAYTON, b. Abt. 1900, Rice County, Kansas.
2134.   iii. ROBERT VIVIAN BRAYTON, b. 29 Mar 1906, Rice County, Kansas; d. 07 Oct 1977.
        iv. KENNETH BRAYTON, b. Abt. Nov 1909, Rice County, Kansas.

1197. FRANK ERNEST[9] BRAYTON *(EMILY[8] MOORE, MARIA LYNDIA[7] PROSSER, ELIZABETH 'BETSEY'[6] MILK, LEMUEL[5], JONATHAN[4], JOB[3], JOHN[2], JOHN[1])* was born 02 Oct 1881, and died 28 Aug 1961. He married MAYBELLE CLARA STUART. She was born 04 Nov 1884, and died 21 Mar 1964 in Kansas.

Children of FRANK BRAYTON and MAYBELLE STUART are:
2135.   i.   BISHIP ELTON[10] BRAYTON, b. 14 Dec 1905; d. 15 Dec 1989, Kansas.
        ii. GERALDINE E. BRAYTON, b. 07 Jul 1907.

1198. AGNES[9] PENFIELD *(MARIA FRANCES[8] MOORE, MARIA LYNDIA[7] PROSSER, ELIZABETH 'BETSEY'[6] MILK, LEMUEL[5], JONATHAN[4], JOB[3], JOHN[2], JOHN[1])* was born 04 May 1880. She married PERCY A. LYNNE. He was born Abt. 1880 in Of Connecticut.

Child of AGNES PENFIELD and PERCY LYNNE is:
2136.   i.   DOROTHY[10] LYNNE, b. 30 Mar 1908.

1199. CHARLES E.[9] PENFIELD *(MARIA FRANCES[8] MOORE, MARIA LYNDIA[7] PROSSER, ELIZABETH 'BETSEY'[6] MILK, LEMUEL[5], JONATHAN[4], JOB[3], JOHN[2], JOHN[1])* was born 13 Oct 1883. He married ANN COOLIDGE. She was born Abt. 1883.

Child of CHARLES PENFIELD and ANN COOLIDGE is:
        i.   MARJORIE[10] PENFIELD.

1200. BERT[9] COLVIN *(JULIA CATHERINE[8] BABCOCK, ROXCENA[7] BATES, SARAH 'SALLY'[6] MILK, LEMUEL[5], JONATHAN[4], JOB[3], JOHN[2], JOHN[1])* was born 29 Jan 1873 in Otto, Cattaraugus County, New York, and died 13 Nov 1941 in Cattaraugus County, New York. He married LUTIE E. FOSTER, daughter of ALBERT FOSTER and JULIA _____. She was born 09 Jun 1875, and died 16 Feb 1948 in Cattaraugus County, New York.

Children of BERT COLVIN and LUTIE FOSTER are:
        i.   EDNA J.[10] COLVIN, b. 25 Aug 1895, Otto, Cattaraugus County, New York; d. Aug 1974, Springville, Erie County, New York; m. (1) LYNN ATWOOD THURBER, Abt. 1916, New York; b. 01 Dec 1892, Springville, Erie County, New York; d. 27 Sep 1918, France; m. (2) NELSON RALPH WOODWORTH, 07 Sep 1940; b. 13 Oct 1888, Java Center, Cattaraugus County, New York; d. 05 Dec 1966, Buffalo, Erie County, New York. No children.
2137.   ii. LILLIAN M. COLVIN, b. 19 Oct 1897, Otto, Cattaraugus County, New York.

1201. ZINA E.⁹ SATTERLEE *(EMER DARIUS⁸, MARY ANN⁷ BATES, SARAH 'SALLY'⁶ MILK, LEMUEL⁵, JONATHAN⁴, JOB³, JOHN², JOHN¹)* was born Oct 1885 in Otto, Cattaraugus County, New York. He married XENIA S. GAYLORD Abt. 1906 in Cattaraugus County, New York, daughter of WINTON GAYLORD and LILLIAN AUSTIN. She was born 14 Jun 1887 in New York, and died 31 Dec 1974 in Randolph, Cattaraugus County, New York.

Child of ZINA SATTERLEE and XENIA GAYLORD is:
    i. OEL WARD¹⁰ SATTERLEE, b. Abt. 1907, East Otto, Cattaraugus County, New York; m. ONA _____; b. Abt. 1900, New York.

1202. ARTHUR LEWIS⁹ DEAN *(FLORA M.⁸ BATES, CHARLES W.⁷, SARAH 'SALLY'⁶ MILK, LEMUEL⁵, JONATHAN⁴, JOB³, JOHN², JOHN¹)* was born 03 Mar 1900 in Cattaraugus County, New York, and died Nov 1980 in Jamestown, Chautauqua County, New York. He married PEARL ELIZABETH BRUNNER 28 Apr 1922 in Chautauqua County, New York, daughter of ANTHONY BRUNNER and EMMA DUGAN. She was born Abt. 1903 in New York.

Children of ARTHUR DEAN and PEARL BRUNNER are:
    i. LEWIS B.¹⁰ DEAN, b. Abt. 1922, New York.
    ii. HARRY W. DEAN, b. Abt. 1932, New York.

1203. FRANK ARNOLD⁹ GOULD *(SUSAN MARIA⁸ PIERCE, MARY JANE⁷ MILKS, BENJAMIN⁶, LEMUEL⁵ MILK, JONATHAN⁴, JOB³, JOHN², JOHN¹)* was born 09 Sep 1871 in Hamburg, Erie County, New York, and died 01 Dec 1948 in Hamburg, Erie County, New York. He married ANNA CARRIE KEHR 27 Feb 1902 in Niagara Falls, New York, daughter of JOHN KEHR and ELIZABETH SYON. She was born 22 Feb 1874 in New Oregon, Erie County, NY.

Children of FRANK GOULD and ANNA KEHR are:
2138.   i. CHARLOTTE ELIZABETH¹⁰ GOULD, b. 13 Apr 1907, Hamburg, Erie County, New York.
2139.   ii. LAURA LOUISE GOULD, b. 04 Mar 1909, Hamburg, Erie County, New York.
2140.   iii. DORIS ANNA GOULD, b. 04 Nov 1912, Hamburg, Erie County, New York.
2141.   iv. ROYAL FRANK GOULD, b. 16 Jun 1914, Hamburg, Erie County, New York.

1204. CARRIE DELL⁹ PATRIDGE *(LAURA A.⁸ PIERCE, MARY JANE⁷ MILKS, BENJAMIN⁶, LEMUEL⁵ MILK, JONATHAN⁴, JOB³, JOHN², JOHN¹)* was born 09 May 1872 in Erie County, New York, and died 10 May 1935 in Owosso, Shiawassee County, Michigan ?. She married GEORGE MASON GETMAN 14 Jan 1890 in New York. He was born 27 Oct 1866 in Syracuse, Onondaga County, New York, and died 18 Feb 1948 in Owosso, Shiawassee County, Michigan ?.

Children of CARRIE PATRIDGE and GEORGE GETMAN are:
2142.   i. MATTIBELL¹⁰ GETMAN, b. 24 Oct 1890, Owosso, Shiawassee County, Michigan .
    ii. CLARA ELLEN GETMAN, b. 12 Mar 1894, Owosso, Shiawassee County, Michigan ; m. HERBERT JAY DREHER; b. 23 Apr 1893, Owosso, Shiawassee County, Michigan . No children.
2143.   iii. GEORGE ARNOLD GETMAN, b. 17 Sep 1899, Owosso, Shiawassee County, Michigan .
    iv. DAU GETMAN, b. 11 May 1905, Owosso, Shiawassee County, Michigan ?; d. 11 May 1905, Owosso, Shiawassee County, Michigan ?.

1205. SUSAN MAY⁹ PATRIDGE *(LAURA A.⁸ PIERCE, MARY JANE⁷ MILKS, BENJAMIN⁶, LEMUEL⁵ MILK, JONATHAN⁴, JOB³, JOHN², JOHN¹)* was born 02 Feb 1879 in West Seneca, Erie County, New York, and died 08 Jul 1943 in Owosso, Shiawassee County, Michigan. She married CHARLES M. MILLER 01 Jan 1900 in Shiawassee County, Michigan. He was born 1865 in Michigan, and died 1916 in Owosso, Shiawassee County, Michigan.

Children of SUSAN PATRIDGE and CHARLES MILLER are:
    i. LAURA LUZENE¹⁰ MILLER, b. 02 Dec 1902, Owosso, Michigan; d. 25 May 1930, Owosso, Shiawassee County, Michigan.
2144.   ii. CHARLES M. MILLER, b. 24 Jul 1914, Owosso, Michigan ?; d. 1962, Shiawassee County, Michigan.

1206. LAURA SARAH⁹ PIERCE *(HERBERT DOUGLAS⁸, MARY JANE⁷ MILKS, BENJAMIN⁶, LEMUEL⁵ MILK, JONATHAN⁴, JOB³, JOHN², JOHN¹)* was born 29 Apr 1884 in Erie County, New York, and died 27 Jul 1949 in Water Valley, Erie County, New York. She married PETER M. FRANK 26 Jan 1907 in Buffalo, New York. He was born 29 Jun 1881 in

Washington, D.C..

Child of LAURA PIERCE and PETER FRANK is:
2145. i. SUSAN M.^{10} FRANK, b. 26 Jan 1910, Water Valley, Erie County, New York.

1207. HOWARD ARNOLD^9 PIERCE *(HERBERT DOUGLAS^8, MARY JANE^7 MILKS, BENJAMIN^6, LEMUEL^5 MILK, JONATHAN^4, JOB^3, JOHN^2, JOHN^1)* was born 02 Jul 1886 in Erie County, New York. He married OLIVE SHERO 23 Dec 1913 in Hamburg, Erie County, New York, daughter of PHILLIP SHERO and LOUISE HERMAN. She was born 05 Apr 1888 in Hamburg, Erie County, New York.

Children of HOWARD PIERCE and OLIVE SHERO are:
 i. PHYLLIS JUNE^{10} PIERCE, b. 11 Nov 1916, Hamburg, Erie County, New York; m. NORMAN E. WILLIAMS, JR, 20 Feb 1948, Hamburg, Erie County, New York; b. 22 Jul 1919, Hamburg, Erie County, New York.
 ii. JAMES ARNOLD PIERCE, b. 13 Feb 1923, Hamburg, Erie County, New York; m. BEVERLY JEAN PFAFFENBACH, 04 Jun 1948, Hamburg, Erie County, New York; b. 16 May 1929, Hamburg, Erie County, New York.

1208. ESTHER ROSETTA^9 MILKS *(JEROME^8, HENRY BENJAMIN^7, BENJAMIN^6, LEMUEL^5 MILK, JONATHAN^4, JOB^3, JOHN^2, JOHN^1)* was born 18 Aug 1874 in St. Charles, Missouri. She married (1) EDWARD TAYLOR. She married (2) JOHN RASTEN JONES 14 Aug 1893 in Batesville, Arkansas. He was born Abt. 1874. She married (3) ANDREW AMES 02 Sep 1900 in Mammoth Springs, Fulton County, Arkansas. He was born 12 Jan 1864 in Germany. She married (4) ERNEST PANZEER 17 Jul 1911 in Jackson County, Arkansas. He was born Abt. 1877 in Minnesota ?.

Children of ESTHER MILKS and JOHN JONES are:
 i. JAMES ALVA^{10} JONES, b. 17 Jul 1895, Batesville, Independence County, Arkansas; m. CAROLINE .
 ii. GEORGE MYLAN JONES, b. 12 Jun 1897, Batesville, Independence County, Arkansas.

Children of ESTHER MILKS and ANDREW AMES are:
2146. iii. ESTHER MARY 'MAYME'^{10} AMES, b. 09 Jul 1901, Mammoth Springs, Arkansas.
2147. iv. MINNIE PEARL AMES, b. 07 Feb 1904, Springfield, Minnesota.
2148. v. ETTA MACIE AMES, b. 11 Nov 1906, Springfield, Minnesota; d. 29 Nov 1990, Monroe, Ouachita Parish, Louisiana,.

1209. SHERIDAN IRA^9 MILKS *(JEROME^8, HENRY BENJAMIN^7, BENJAMIN^6, LEMUEL^5 MILK, JONATHAN^4, JOB^3, JOHN^2, JOHN^1)* was born 25 Mar 1876 in St. Charles, Missouri. He married MARTHA ELIZABETH 'LIZZIE' JONES 11 Aug 1902 in Newport, Jackson County, Arkansas, daughter of ANDREW JONES and SUZANNE NANEY. She was born 04 Jul 1880 in Dexter, Missouri.

Children of SHERIDAN MILKS and MARTHA JONES are:
2149. i. PEARLA ALMA^{10} MILKS, b. 26 Jan 1904, Newport, Arkansas; d. 09 Mar 1976, Amity, Clark County, Arkansas.
 ii. ETTA MAY MILKS, b. 04 Jul 1906, Newport, Arkansas; d. 1910, Newport, Arkansas.
 iii. EDGAR FRANKLIN MILKS, b. 13 Nov 1908, Newport, Arkansas; d. 1912, St. Charles, Arkansas.
 iv. FLORA BELLE MILKS, b. 30 Jul 1911, Newport, Arkansas; m. (1) JOHN GASSEIN; b. Abt. 1911; m. (2) CHARLES MCCUMPSEY, 1934; b. Abt. 1911; d. Abt. 1948; m. (3) WILLIAM DRAFFIN, 01 Nov 1949; b. Abt. 1911. No children.

1210. HENRY EDWARD^9 MILKS *(JEROME^8, HENRY BENJAMIN^7, BENJAMIN^6, LEMUEL^5 MILK, JONATHAN^4, JOB^3, JOHN^2, JOHN^1)* was born 16 Jan 1878 in St. Charles, Missouri, and died 27 Mar 1947 in Little Rock, Pulaski County, Arkansas. He married (1) SARAH CLEMENTINE (ROBERTS) HECHINGER 22 Mar 1901 in Minturn, Lawrence County, Arkansas. She was born 1879 in Missouri, and died 25 Mar 1919 in Clarendon, Arkansas. He married (2) TINEY JONES 07 Oct 1919 in Clarendon, Monroe County, Arkansas. She was born Abt. 1901 in Pine Bluff, Jefferson County, Arkansas. He married (3) KALLIE _____ Bet. 1924 - 1930 in Arkansas ?. She was born Abt. 1882 in Arkansas. He married (4) SALLIE GOODRUM Bet. 1940 - 1942 in Arkansas ?.

Children of HENRY MILKS and SARAH HECHINGER are:
- i. CHARLIE[10] MILKS, b. Arkansas; d. d.y..
- ii. HANNAH ETTA MILKS, b. Arkansas (twin); d. d.y..
- iii. HENRY EDWARD MILKS, b. Arkansas (twin); d. d.y..
- iv. MABEL MILKS, b. Arkansas; d. d.y..
- 2150. v. CLARENCE BENJAMIN MILKS, b. 06 Jun 1906, Clarendon, Arkansas; d. 10 Aug 1999, Knoxville, Knox County, Tennessee.
- 2151. vi. LILLIE MAE MILKS, b. 18 Mar 1908, Georgetown, Arkansas; d. 11 Apr 1983, North Little Rock, Pulaski County, Arkansas.

1211. JEROME FRANKLIN[9] MILKS (*JEROME*[8], *HENRY BENJAMIN*[7], *BENJAMIN*[6], *LEMUEL*[5] *MILK*, *JONATHAN*[4], *JOB*[3], *JOHN*[2], *JOHN*[1]) was born 18 Oct 1879 in Willow Springs, Howell County, Missouri, and died 23 Nov 1945 in Little Rock, Pulaski County, Arkansas. He married (1) MARY BLACKMAN 08 Jun 1900 in White County, Arkansas. She was born 1864. He married (2) PEARL JOHNSON 10 Apr 1909 in Little Rock, Arkansas, daughter of JAMES JOHNSON and LUEY _____. She was born 28 Jun 1894 in Arkansas, and died 15 Sep 1958 in Little Rock, Pulaski County, Arkansas.

Children of JEROME MILKS and PEARL JOHNSON are:
- 2152. i. MABLE MAY[10] MILKS, b. 02 Feb 1910, Coesta, Oklahoma; d. 29 Jan 1970, Floydada, Floyd County, Texas (may have had 5 children).
- 2153. ii. ERNEST THURMAN MILKS, b. 02 Aug 1912, Keo, Arkansas; d. 12 Apr 1947, Los Angeles, California.
- 2154. iii. HENRY W. MILKS, b. 29 Dec 1914, Grady, Arkansas; d. May 1979, North Little Rock, Pulaski, Arkansas.
- iv. EDNA M. MILKS, b. 09 Feb 1918, Gould, Arkansas; d. 22 Jul 2004, Morongo Valley, San Bernardino, California (3 children); m. JOHN SHANDOR BOHN; b. 27 Jun 1912, Baker, Fallon County, Montana; d. 09 Dec 1983, Morongo Valley, San Bernardino, California.
- v. EDGAR JEROME MILKS, b. 16 Dec 1920, Gould, Arkansas; d. Aug 1983, Rodeo, Contra Costa, California; m. EDNA KNIGHT; b. Abt. 1921.
- 2155. vi. CHARLES ARNOLD MILKS, b. 31 May 1925, Little Rock, Arkansas; d. 27 Oct 1983, Contra Costa, California.
- 2156. vii. RAMONA MILKS, b. 26 Jul 1928, Little Rock, Arkansas.
- viii. IRA RAYMOND MILKS, b. 13 Jun 1931, Little Rock, Arkansas; d. 10 Dec 1999, Raeford, Hoke County, North Carolina; m. (1) PEGGY TURNER; m. (2) SHIRLEY JEAN _____; b. 19 Aug 1937, Robeson, North Carolina; d. 20 Jan 2003, Raeford, Hoke County, North Carolina.

1212. ANNA MAY[9] MILKS (*JEROME*[8], *HENRY BENJAMIN*[7], *BENJAMIN*[6], *LEMUEL*[5] *MILK*, *JONATHAN*[4], *JOB*[3], *JOHN*[2], *JOHN*[1]) was born 18 Oct 1883 in Missouri. She married JOHN M. SMOTHERMAN 23 Oct 1897 in Willow Springs, Howell County, Missouri, son of J. C. SMOTHERMAN. He was born 13 Sep 1871 in Missouri.

Children of ANNA MILKS and JOHN SMOTHERMAN are:
- i. ETHEL H.[10] SMOTHERMAN, b. 14 Mar 1900, Iowa; m. OSCAR H. GRAY, 05 Sep 1917, Leon, Decatur County, Iowa; b. Abt. 1899, Iowa. No children.
- 2157. ii. VERONA BETHEL SMOTHERMAN, b. 01 Mar 1905, Leon, Decatur County, Iowa; d. 1962, Ottawa, Franklin County, Kansas.

1213. CHARLES ARNOLD[9] MILKS (*JEROME*[8], *HENRY BENJAMIN*[7], *BENJAMIN*[6], *LEMUEL*[5] *MILK*, *JONATHAN*[4], *JOB*[3], *JOHN*[2], *JOHN*[1]) was born 03 Jun 1885 in Pomona, Missouri, and died 07 May 1977 in Orange County, Florida. He married (1) PHOEBE EMILY MCCUNE, daughter of JESSE MCCUNE and MARTHA MCGRIFF. She was born 08 Feb 1895 in Hutchinson, Kansas, and died 04 Jul 1941 in Omaha, Nebraska. He married (2) FLORENCE ELIZABETH (O'BRIEN) LAKIN 10 Mar 1928 in Duval County, Florida, daughter of JOHN O'BRIEN and CAROLINE MCLEAN. She was born Abt. 1881 in Massachusetts, and died Jan 1963 in Orange County, Florida.

Children of CHARLES MILKS and PHOEBE MCCUNE are:
- 2158. i. ANNA LOUISE[10] MILKS, b. 24 Mar 1916, Skoby, Montana; d. 10 Mar 1993, Orange County, Florida.
- 2159. ii. GOLDA EVA MILKS, b. 26 Jul 1917, Sioux City, Woodbury County, Iowa.
- iii. LAWRENCE LEROY MILKS, b. Sioux City, Woodbury County, Iowa; d. Sioux City, Iowa   d.y..

1214. DELLA MACIE^9 MILKS *(JEROME^8, HENRY BENJAMIN^7, BENJAMIN^6, LEMUEL^5 MILK, JONATHAN^4, JOB^3, JOHN^2, JOHN^1)* was born 01 Dec 1887 in Willow Springs, Howell County, Missouri, and died Abt. 1908 in Willow Springs, Howell County, Missouri. She married ROBERT AUSTIN POTTLE 24 Dec 1906 in Howell County, Missouri, son of THOMAS POTTLE and SARAH NORTHCUT. He was born 19 Aug 1881 in Willow Springs, Howell County, Missouri, and died 12 Oct 1961 in Tumwater, Thurston County, Washington.

Children of DELLA MILKS and ROBERT POTTLE are:
- i. HENRY THOMAS^{10} POTTLE, b. 11 Oct 1908, Howell County, Missouri; d. 09 Jul 1933, Tumwater, Thurston, Washington; m. ROSALIE F. _____; b. Abt. 1910, Iowa.
  Originally interred in Odd Fellows Cemetery in Tumwater on 7/11/1933. Removed to Mt. View in Tacoma Aug. 2, 1933
- ii. JEROME POTTLE, d. d.y..

1215. DAVID LEWIS^9 MILKS *(JEROME^8, HENRY BENJAMIN^7, BENJAMIN^6, LEMUEL^5 MILK, JONATHAN^4, JOB^3, JOHN^2, JOHN^1)* was born 03 Oct 1890 in Pomona, Missouri, and died 23 Jun 1970 in Marysville, Snohomish, Washington. He married (1) MARTHA ELIZABETH 'MATTIE' FINE 11 Sep 1908 in Howell County, Missouri, daughter of CHARLES FINE and INDIANA GREGORY. She was born 15 May 1888 in Howell County, Missouri, and died 12 Jul 1974 in Olden, Howell County, Missouri. He married (2) ALICE LYDIA M. SALA Bet. 1930 - 1935, daughter of FRANK SALA and ANNA _____. She was born 25 Mar 1911, and died 19 Sep 1996 in Marysville, Snohomish, Washington.

Children of DAVID MILKS and MARTHA FINE are:
- i. INFANT SON1^{10} MILKS, b. 04 May 1909, Pomona, Howell County, Missouri; d. 04 May 1909, Pomona, Howell County, Missouri.
- ii. INFANT SON2 MILKS, b. 21 Mar 1912, Pomona, Howell County, Missouri; d. 21 Mar 1912, Pomona, Howell County, Missouri.
- 2160. iii. EVA LIONELL MILKS, b. 02 Jul 1915, Olden, Howell County, Missouri; d. 02 Dec 2002, Warrensburg, Johnson County, Missouri.

1216. JOSEPH HIRAM^9 MILKS *(JEROME^8, HENRY BENJAMIN^7, BENJAMIN^6, LEMUEL^5 MILK, JONATHAN^4, JOB^3, JOHN^2, JOHN^1)* was born 01 Jun 1892 in Willow Springs, Howell County, Missouri, and died 19 Oct 1933 in Quincy, Norfolk County, Massachusetts. He married MARTHA JULIA MORRELL Abt. 1918, daughter of WILLIAM MORRELL and MARY WHITE. She was born 24 Jul 1898 in Quincy, Norfolk County, Massachusetts, and died 08 Apr 1989 in Rockland, Plymouth County, Massachusetts.

Children of JOSEPH MILKS and MARTHA MORRELL are:
- 2161. i. MARTHA JANE^{10} MILKS, b. 02 Mar 1919, Quincy, Norfolk County, Massachusetts; d. 14 Sep 1998, Raymond, New Hampshire.
- ii. MARION TERESA MILKS, b. 13 Mar 1922, Lynn, Essex County, Massachusetts; d. 21 Feb 1926, Lynn, Essex County, Massachusetts.
- iii. WILLIAM JEROME MILKS, b. 07 Aug 1925, Quincy, Norfolk County, Massachusetts; d. 01 Feb 1926, Lynn, Essex County, Massachusetts.
- 2162. iv. JOSEPH PAUL MILKS, b. 05 Jul 1927, Quincy, Norfolk County, Massachusetts; d. 09 Feb 1998, Brockton, Plymouth County, Massachusetts.
- 2163. v. ERNEST ARNOLD MILKS, b. 29 Nov 1928, East Braintree, Norfolk County, Massachusetts; d. 12 Aug 1993, Milton, Norfolk County, Massachusetts.

1217. ERNEST OSCAR^9 MILKS *(JEROME^8, HENRY BENJAMIN^7, BENJAMIN^6, LEMUEL^5 MILK, JONATHAN^4, JOB^3, JOHN^2, JOHN^1)* was born 12 Jun 1895 in Howell Co., Missouri, and died 22 Jun 1990 in Sioux City, Woodbury County, Iowa (SSDI). He married ROWENA HELEN JONES 17 May 1919 in Sioux City, Woodbury County, Iowa, daughter of SAMUEL JONES and ELIZABETH MARTIN. She was born 20 Aug 1901 in Onawa, Iowa, and died 29 May 1973 in Alexander, Pulaski, Arkansas.

Children of ERNEST MILKS and ROWENA JONES are:
- 2164. i. IRA CLAYTON^{10} MILKS, b. 07 Dec 1920, Sioux City, Woodbury County, Iowa; d. 17 Jul 1994, Benton, Saline County, Arkansas.

  ii. LEWIS ERNEST MILKS, b. 22 Oct 1924, Sioux City, Woodbury County, Iowa; d. 18 Jul 1944, France.
    Milks, Lewis E Iowa Staff Sergeant 816th Bomber Squadron 483rd Bomber Jul 18 1944 Lorraine, France Buried Purple Heart Medal, Air Medal, Additional Army Awards
  iii. ERVIN LEROY MILKS, b. 22 Nov 1926, Sioux City, Woodbury County, Iowa; d. Jan 1992; m. JANELLA _____.

2165. iv. ORVILLE JOSEPH MILKS, b. 26 Jun 1930, Sioux City, Woodbury County, Iowa; d. 28 Nov 2003, Benton, Saline County, Arkansas.
  v. VIRGINIA BETTY MILKS, b. 10 Apr 1939, Sioux City, Woodbury County, Iowa; m. MISTRE HOLCOMB.
  vi. WILLIAM FRANKLIN MILKS, b. 27 Nov 1940, Sioux City, Woodbury County, Iowa; d. 15 Mar 1991, Mabelvale, Pulaski, Arkansas.

1218. WILLIAM WESLEY^9 MILKS *(JEROME^8, HENRY BENJAMIN^7, BENJAMIN^6, LEMUEL^5 MILK, JONATHAN^4, JOB^3, JOHN^2, JOHN^1)* was born 29 Sep 1897 in Willow Springs, Missouri, and died 23 Oct 1921 in Walnut Lake, Arkansas. He married BESSIE ROLMAN 26 Jun 1917 in Pine Bluff, Arkansas, daughter of JOHN ROLMAN and LIZZY GOLDSMITH. She was born 24 Aug 1902 in Maldon, Missouri.

Children of WILLIAM MILKS and BESSIE ROLMAN are:
2166. i. THERMAN FRANKLIN^{10} MILKS, b. 18 Sep 1919, Gould, Arkansas; d. 29 May 2002, Loraine, Ohio.
  ii. GOLDY MILKS, b. 06 Nov 1921, Walnut Lake, Arkansas; d. 11 Mar 1923, Walnut Lake, Arkansas.

1219. WILLIAM CLAUDE^9 MILKS *(LEWIS LYONS^8, HENRY BENJAMIN^7, BENJAMIN^6, LEMUEL^5 MILK, JONATHAN^4, JOB^3, JOHN^2, JOHN^1)* was born 02 Jan 1886 in Valley Park, St. Louis County, Missouri, and died Feb 1967 in St. Louis, Missouri. He married NINA OCKERHAUSEN, daughter of JOHN OCKERHAUSEN and THERESA _____. She was born 03 Oct 1897 in Jonesburg, Missouri, and died Jan 1982 in St. Louis, Missouri.

Children of WILLIAM MILKS and NINA OCKERHAUSEN are:
2167. i. WILLIAM CLAUDE^{10} MILKS, JR., b. 27 May 1924, St. Louis, Missouri; d. 10 Dec 2007, Riverside, California.
  ii. JEANE CLAIRE MILKS, b. 19 Nov 1926, St. Louis, Missouri; m. UNKNOWN MILLER; b. Abt. 1925.

1220. FRANK CRAYCROFT^9 MILKS *(LEWIS LYONS^8, HENRY BENJAMIN^7, BENJAMIN^6, LEMUEL^5 MILK, JONATHAN^4, JOB^3, JOHN^2, JOHN^1)* was born 16 May 1887 in Valley Park, Missouri, and died 01 Aug 1948. He married IRENE E. SOMMERS 01 Aug 1913 in St. Louis, Missouri, daughter of HENRY SOMMERS and ELIZABETH POHLMAN. She was born 06 Jun 1888 in St. Louis, Missouri.

Children of FRANK MILKS and IRENE SOMMERS are:
2168. i. MARGERY^{10} MILKS, b. 26 Apr 1914, St. Louis, Missouri; d. 20 Sep 2007, Concord, Cabarrus, North Carolina.
2169. ii. MARIAN F. MILKS, b. 21 Aug 1916, St. Louis, Missouri; d. 07 Aug 2008, St. Louis, Missouri.

1221. FLORENCE ANN^9 MILKS *(LEWIS LYONS^8, HENRY BENJAMIN^7, BENJAMIN^6, LEMUEL^5 MILK, JONATHAN^4, JOB^3, JOHN^2, JOHN^1)* was born 10 Oct 1891 in Valley Park, Missouri. She married WALTER WARREN 12 Jul 1924 in St Popeia, St Louis, Missouri, son of VALENTI WURZYNIAK and EVA CIESLAK. He was born Abt. 1900 in Poland.
An article appearing in the Los Angeles Evening Express, 17 Nov. 1923, reads:
 "She's So. Cal's only Woman Engineer. Miss Florence A. Milks has invaded man's world of business and action a little bit farther than any other member of her sex in Southern California. She works as strenuously, physically, as any of the sterner sex, tramping miles and lugging loads, but she remains bright and pretty, and a real woman despite the old myth that man's toils roughen and deplete the feminite.
 "Miss Milks may be seen any day if the observer is in the right place, hiking and carrying a transit level, chains, target or whatnot of engineering paraphernalia. For she's an honest-to-goodness engineer, putting on every one of man's tricks in that arduous line.
 "She graduated from the engineering school of Washington University, St. Louis, in 1918. Since leaving school she was four years with the Frisco in St. Louis, and a year and a half with the Roxana Petroleum Corp. During both employments Miss Milks held her own alongside veteran men in her field. She is now on the Victor Girard engineering staff."

Florence's name is linked with the platting of the town of Girard, Calif., known for its unique and picturesque civic center of modern Persian design. She was also an artist and musician.

Children of FLORENCE MILKS and WALTER WARREN are:
2170. i. WALTER WALLACE[10] WARREN, b. 29 Apr 1925, St. Louis, Missouri.
2171. ii. FLORENCE WANDA WARREN, b. 17 Jul 1926, Indianapolis, Marion County, Indiana.

1222. HERBERT HARRY[9] MILKS *(HARRY J.[8], HENRY BENJAMIN[7], BENJAMIN[6], LEMUEL[5] MILK, JONATHAN[4], JOB[3], JOHN[2], JOHN[1])* was born 24 Mar 1892 in Monett, Missouri, and died 20 Jun 1969 in Fallon, Churchill County, Nevada. He married MURIEL LYDIA _____ Abt. 1918 in Nevada ?. She was born 28 Aug 1900 in Nebraska, and died 07 Apr 1971 in Fallon, Churchill County, Nevada.

Pvt. Herbert H. Milks. Served with the U.S. Army during WW1 of 1917-18. He died in Fallon NV in June of 1969 at the age of 82.

Children of HERBERT MILKS and MURIEL _____ are:
2172. i. HARRY W.[10] MILKS, b. 02 Feb 1920, Nevada; d. 23 Jun 1996, Fallon, Churchill County, Nevada.
ii. EFFIE M. MILKS, b. Abt. 1922, Nevada.

1223. SARAH HELEN[9] SMITH *(IDA A.[8] MILKS, CHARLES JONATHAN[7], BENJAMIN[6], LEMUEL[5] MILK, JONATHAN[4], JOB[3], JOHN[2], JOHN[1])* was born 23 Mar 1897 in Magnolia, Rock County, Wisconsin, and died 04 Jun 1921 in Spring Valley, Rock County, Wisconsin. She married WALTER CHRIST GEMPELER 24 Oct 1917 in Rock County, Wisconsin. He was born 13 Jan 1895 in Argyle, Lafayette County, Wisconsin, and died 27 Apr 1970 in Brodhead, Green County, Wisconsin.
OBITUARY

Evansville Review, Evansville, WI dated June 9, 1921

Sarah Helen Smith, was born in Magnolia March 23rd, 1897, and passed away at her home in Spring Valley, at a quarter of twelve o'clock Saturday evening, June 4th, 1921, after an illness of some duration. At the age of seven years she was baptized by Rev. Churm with water taken from the River Jordan, and always lived a consistent Christian life. At the age of fifteen she graduated from the Evansville high school and taught a class in Sunday School. October 24, 1917, she was united in matrimony with Walter Gempeler and resided on the farm in Spring Valley.

She leaves to mourn her early demise a daughter and son, Margaret Ruth and Robert Arthur, besides her husband and many relatives and friends.

Funeral services were conducted Tuesday, a short service being, held at the home and from there the remains were taken to Evansville where services were held in the Methodist Church, Rev. A. W. Barnlund assisting Rev. Fraser. The large number of friends present from Brodhead, as also from Evansville, was a noble tribute of love to the departed and to the sorrowing. Interment was at Maple Hill cemetery.

Children of SARAH SMITH and WALTER GEMPELER are:
i. MARGARET RUTH[10] GEMPELER, b. Abt. 1917, Rock County, Wisconsin.
ii. ROBERT ARTHUR GEMPELER, b. 1921, Rock County, Wisconsin.

1224. MABEL M.[9] MILKS *(FREEMAN B.[8], CHARLES JONATHAN[7], BENJAMIN[6], LEMUEL[5] MILK, JONATHAN[4], JOB[3], JOHN[2], JOHN[1])* was born 27 Feb 1890 in Magnolia, Rock County, Wisconsin, and died Bef. 1956. She married EDWARD A. EISELE Abt. 1911. He was born Abt. 1890.

Children of MABEL MILKS and EDWARD EISELE are:
i. CORA[10] EISELE, b. 02 May 1912.
2173. ii. DOROTHY EISELE, b. 02 Apr 1914.
2174. iii. ALBERT E. EISELE, b. 16 Apr 1915; d. 27 Jun 1987, South Beloit, Winnebago County, Illinois.
2175. iv. MARJORIE M. EISELE, b. 27 Dec 1919.
2176. v. EVELYN J. EISELE, b. 21 Sep 1923.
vi. EDWARD O. EISELE, b. 18 Sep 1928.

1225. MAY MABEL[9] CHASE *(JESSIE EDNA[8] MILKS, CHARLES JONATHAN[7], BENJAMIN[6], LEMUEL[5] MILK, JONATHAN[4], JOB[3], JOHN[2], JOHN[1])* was born 09 Jan 1895 in Brodhead, Green County, Wisconsin. She married (1) MARVIN LEE 24 Dec 1912, son of EDWARD LEE and CAROLINE THURMAN. He was born Abt. 1895. She married (2) ROY NEILLY 03 Feb

1916. He was born Abt. 1895.

Child of MAY CHASE and MARVIN LEE is:
2177.   i.   JESSIE BETH[10] LEE, b. 26 Jul 1913, Brodhead, Green County, Wisconsin.

Children of MAY CHASE and ROY NEILLY are:
2178.   ii.   ANNA MAY[10] NEILLY, b. 27 Nov 1916, Wisconsin.
2179.   iii.   GRACE NEILLY, b. 08 Jun 1918, Wisconsin.
2180.   iv.   WILLIAM ALEXANDER NEILLY, b. 19 Jan 1920, Wisconsin.

1226. FLOYD MILKS[9] CHASE *(JESSIE EDNA[8] MILKS, CHARLES JONATHAN[7], BENJAMIN[6], LEMUEL[5] MILK, JONATHAN[4], JOB[3], JOHN[2], JOHN[1])* was born 10 May 1899 in Brodhead, Green County, Wisconsin. He married ETHEL CAROLINE LETTS Abt. 1935, daughter of WILLIAM LETTS and ETTA WORTHING. She was born 16 Apr 1899 in Magnolia, Rock County, Wisconsin.

Children of FLOYD CHASE and ETHEL LETTS are:
    i.   JOYCE KAY[10] CHASE, b. 11 Jul 1936, Beloit, Wisconsin.
    ii.   GERALD EUGENE CHASE, b. 04 Oct 1941, Janesville, Wisconsin.

1227. ROY MILKS[9] CHASE *(JESSIE EDNA[8] MILKS, CHARLES JONATHAN[7], BENJAMIN[6], LEMUEL[5] MILK, JONATHAN[4], JOB[3], JOHN[2], JOHN[1])* was born 29 May 1904 in Brodhead, Green County, Wisconsin. He married LEONA GRACE WEBB 28 May 1927 in Rockford, Illinois, daughter of CLARK WEBB and JULIA WOLFE. She was born Abt. 1904.

Children of ROY CHASE and LEONA WEBB are:
    i.   MARLENE ELEANOR[10] CHASE, b. 19 May 1926.
    ii.   CHARLOTTE MARIE CHASE, b. 16 Feb 1930, Janesville, Wisconsin.
    iii.   CHARLES WILLIAM CHASE, b. 05 May 1932, Janesville, Wisconsin; d. 05 May 1932, Janesville, Wisconsin.
    iv.   KENNETH WEBB CHASE, b. 02 Feb 1936, Janesville, Wisconsin.
    v.   GERALD ROY CHASE, b. 16 Oct 1938, Janesville, Wisconsin.

1228. MILDRED[9] MILKS *(JOSEPH EDWIN[8], DAVID WESLEY[7], BENJAMIN[6], LEMUEL[5] MILK, JONATHAN[4], JOB[3], JOHN[2], JOHN[1])* was born 12 May 1884 in Albee, Saginaw County, Michigan. She married T. EDWARD JOHNSON 07 Aug 1907. He was born 1883.

Children of MILDRED MILKS and T. JOHNSON are:
2181.   i.   STANLEY H.[10] JOHNSON, b. 23 Jan 1912, Stockbridge, Michigan.
2182.   ii.   PATRICIA JOHNSON, b. 03 May 1916.

1229. ADA H.[9] MILKS *(JOSEPH EDWIN[8], DAVID WESLEY[7], BENJAMIN[6], LEMUEL[5] MILK, JONATHAN[4], JOB[3], JOHN[2], JOHN[1])* was born 24 Aug 1886 in Michigan. She married JOHN M. MCCORMICK 26 Aug 1908. He was born Abt. 1886 in Michigan.

Children of ADA MILKS and JOHN MCCORMICK are:
2183.   i.   ADDIE H.[10] MCCORMICK, b. 02 Sep 1909, Saginaw County, Michigan.
2184.   ii.   JEDD MCCORMICK, b. 26 Jun 1913.
2185.   iii.   FREDERICK MICHAEL MCCORMICK, b. 11 Aug 1929, (adopted).

1230. EDWIN A.[9] MILKS *(JOSEPH EDWIN[8], DAVID WESLEY[7], BENJAMIN[6], LEMUEL[5] MILK, JONATHAN[4], JOB[3], JOHN[2], JOHN[1])* was born 02 Apr 1893 in Saginaw, Michigan, and died 20 Jul 1985 in Lansing, Ingham County, Michigan. He married (1) GRACE E. MILLER 05 Nov 1919, daughter of JAMES MILLER and ELLEN COOK. She was born 26 Jul 1893 in Cadillac, Michigan. He married (2) AGNES PFUND Aft. 1926. She was born Abt. 1895.

Children of EDWIN MILKS and GRACE MILLER are:
2186.   i.   ERMA DORIS[10] MILKS, b. 11 Sep 1920, Saginaw, Michigan; d. 27 Jan 2013, Tucson, Pima County, Arizona.
2187.   ii.   MILDRED EVELYN MILKS, b. 10 Mar 1926, Michigan; d. 04 Mar 2006, Ocala, Marion County, Florida.

1231. MALCOLM HORACE[9] MILKS *(JOSEPH EDWIN[8], DAVID WESLEY[7], BENJAMIN[6], LEMUEL[5] MILK, JONATHAN[4], JOB[3], JOHN[2], JOHN[1])* was born 28 Mar 1896 in Saginaw, Michigan, and died 26 Mar 1978 in Meridian, Ingham County, Michigan. He married HAZEL M. FRY 1922 in Grand Traverse County, Michigan. She was born 31 Oct 1896, and died 15 Nov 1975 in Lansing, Ingham County, Michigan.

Children of MALCOLM MILKS and HAZEL FRY are:
2188. i. MALCOLM L. 'MACK'[10] MILKS, b. 31 Oct 1924, Michigan; d. 15 Dec 1991, Lansing, Ingham County, Michigan.
2189. ii. MARJORIE MILKS, b. 11 Jan 1934, Michigan.

1232. MYRTLE[9] ACKLEY *(POLLIE ALPHA[8] MILKS, DAVID WESLEY[7], BENJAMIN[6], LEMUEL[5] MILK, JONATHAN[4], JOB[3], JOHN[2], JOHN[1])* was born 08 Jul 1879. She married ALBERT V. CANTWELL 01 Aug 1905, son of GEORGE CANTWELL and MARY EDWARDS. He was born 26 Nov 1878 in Michigan, and died 18 Jul 1954 in Lakeview, Michigan.

Children of MYRTLE ACKLEY and ALBERT CANTWELL are:
2190. i. VAUGHN E.[10] CANTWELL, b. 20 Jun 1908, Saginaw County, Michigan.
2191. ii. ESTHER CANTWELL, b. 04 Apr 1912, Saginaw County, Michigan.

1233. MILDRED A.[9] STUART *(PARNA ROZELIA[8] MILKS, DAVID WESLEY[7], BENJAMIN[6], LEMUEL[5] MILK, JONATHAN[4], JOB[3], JOHN[2], JOHN[1])* was born 02 Aug 1889 in Chesaning, Saginaw County, Michigan. She married RALPH AGNEW Abt. 1919, son of A. AGNEW and LILLY CRITTENDEN. He was born 29 Aug 1880.

Children of MILDRED STUART and RALPH AGNEW are:
2192. i. LESLIE W.[10] AGNEW, b. 19 Sep 1920.
2193. ii. BETTY G. AGNEW, b. 11 Oct 1923.

1234. MAMIE DOROTHEA CHRISTINE[9] GAMPP *(MARA ELEANOR[8] BURCHARD, CALISTA ELIZABETH[7] MILKS, BENJAMIN[6], LEMUEL[5] MILK, JONATHAN[4], JOB[3], JOHN[2], JOHN[1])* was born 23 Aug 1889 in East Otto, Cattaraugus County, New York. She married GEORGE WELLINGTON FREEMAN Abt. 1913, son of LEON FREEMAN and MARY GIBBS. He was born 19 Feb 1885 in Smiths Mills, New York.

Children of MAMIE GAMPP and GEORGE FREEMAN are:
2194. i. HALYCONE CALISTA[10] FREEMAN, b. 25 Apr 1914, Gerry, Chautauqua County, New York.
 ii. SILVION BEVERLY FREEMAN, b. 24 Jan 1921, Liverpool, Onondaga County, New York; m. ELAINE LARUE SMITH, 28 Dec 1954; b. Abt. 1921, Manchester, Pennsylvania.

1235. GENEVIEVE ALICE[9] GAMPP *(MARA ELEANOR[8] BURCHARD, CALISTA ELIZABETH[7] MILKS, BENJAMIN[6], LEMUEL[5] MILK, JONATHAN[4], JOB[3], JOHN[2], JOHN[1])* was born 30 Mar 1894 in East Otto, Cattaraugus County, New York, and died 01 Dec 1975 in San Diego County, California. She married HENRY WARD SOULE 29 Feb 1916, son of CHARLES SOULE and ALICE SHACKFORD. He was born 14 Apr 1892 in Portland, Maine, and died 25 Feb 1968 in San Diego County, California.

Children of GENEVIEVE GAMPP and HENRY SOULE are:
 i. MAXINE ELEANOR[10] SOULE, b. 21 Mar 1919, Altadena, California; m. EMIL HRUBIK, 20 Apr 1942; b. 27 Aug 1911, Akron, Ohio.
2195. ii. VALERIA ALICE SOULE, b. 05 Mar 1920, Pasadena, California.
 iii. MILTON THOMPSON SOULE, b. 08 Aug 1926, Alhambra, California; d. 23 Sep 1998, Vista, San Diego County, California; m. BARBARA SEFERT, 15 Aug 1947; b. 11 Mar 1926, San Francisco, California.

1236. GEORGE ELMER[9] GAMPP *(MARA ELEANOR[8] BURCHARD, CALISTA ELIZABETH[7] MILKS, BENJAMIN[6], LEMUEL[5] MILK, JONATHAN[4], JOB[3], JOHN[2], JOHN[1])* was born 28 May 1898 in East Otto, Cattaraugus County, New York, and died May 1982 in New York. He married ESMARIE DARLING 18 Aug 1927 in Buffalo, New York, daughter of EDGAR DARLING and EDITH BURCHARD. She was born 11 Jun 1897 in East Otto, Cattaraugus County, New York.

Children of GEORGE GAMPP and ESMARIE DARLING are:
- i. MARON EUGENE^{10} GAMPP, b. 04 Jun 1928, Kenmore, New York; m. ANN HARRINGTON, 25 Apr 1953, Frankfort, Germany; b. 25 Feb 1926.
- ii. BARBARA JANE GAMPP, b. 24 Jan 1930, Niagara Falls, New York.
- iii. ROLYN GEORGE GAMPP, b. 20 Dec 1932, Niagara Falls, New York.

1237. GERTRUDE^9 GAMPP *(GRACE ANNA^8 BURCHARD, CALISTA ELIZABETH^7 MILKS, BENJAMIN^6, LEMUEL^5 MILK, JONATHAN^4, JOB^3, JOHN^2, JOHN^1)* was born 11 Oct 1896 in Kane, Pennsylvania, and died 1966 in Cambridge Springs, Pennsylvania. She married FRED WADE 22 Sep 1923 in Meadville, Pennsylvania, son of ARTHUR WADE and ELIZABETH APPLEBY. He was born 11 Jan 1890 in Birch, England, and died 1982 in Cambridge Springs, Pennsylvania. Both Gertrude and Fred were chiropractors in Cambridge Springs, Pennsylvania

Children of GERTRUDE GAMPP and FRED WADE are:
- i. ELIZABETH JANE^{10} WADE, b. 06 Nov 1926, Cambridge Springs, Pennsylvania; d. 28 Jan 1929, Cambridge Springs, Pennsylvania.
- ii. BEATRICE WADE, b. 17 Feb 1930, Cambridge Springs, Pennsylvania.

1238. GRACE IRENE^9 DARLING *(EDITH SOPHIA^8 BURCHARD, CALISTA ELIZABETH^7 MILKS, BENJAMIN^6, LEMUEL^5 MILK, JONATHAN^4, JOB^3, JOHN^2, JOHN^1)* was born 08 May 1892 in Vineland, New Jersey, and died 31 Oct 1977 in El Monte, California. She married ELDRED WELLINGTON BARNHART 12 Dec 1914 in Buffalo, New York, son of SYLVESTER BARNHART and HELEN GRAY. He was born 21 Aug 1884 in Brocton, New York, and died 23 Aug 1953 in El Monte, California.

Grace Irene has taught school and followed practical nursing. She has specialized in child psychology, having studied under Jessie Fowler at N. Y. Institute; recently she has worked with juvenile children of Los Angeles. She is an assistant author of History and Genealogy of Milk-Milks Family.

Children of GRACE DARLING and ELDRED BARNHART are:
- i. VIRGINIA MAY^{10} BARNHART, b. 13 Dec 1915, Springville, New York; d. 23 Oct 1953, El Monte, California. Virginia was an invalid.
- 2196. ii. LAUREL ELDRENE BARNHART, b. 04 Jul 1917, Emsworth, Pennsylvania; d. 12 Jun 2000, Wallace, Shoshone County, Idaho.
- 2197. iii. KENNETH ALLEN BARNHART, b. 23 Jun 1921, Springville, New York; d. 30 Sep 1992, Victorville, San Bernardino, California.
- 2198. iv. CAROLEE IRENE BARNHART, b. 16 May 1925, Hillsdale, New Jersey.

1239. ALTON BURCHARD^9 DARLING *(EDITH SOPHIA^8 BURCHARD, CALISTA ELIZABETH^7 MILKS, BENJAMIN^6, LEMUEL^5 MILK, JONATHAN^4, JOB^3, JOHN^2, JOHN^1)* was born 25 Dec 1893 in East Otto, Cattaraugus County, New York, and died 1941 in Akron, New York. He married AMY REGINA FRANZ 04 Sep 1919 in Springville, New York. She was born 18 Jul 1901 in Sardinia, New York.

Children of ALTON DARLING and AMY FRANZ are:
- 2199. i. JUNE AMY^{10} DARLING, b. 06 Sep 1922, Buffalo, New York.
- 2200. ii. DAWN AUDREY DARLING, b. 13 Aug 1924, Akron, New York; d. 10 May 2010, Lady Lake, Lake County, Florida.
- 2201. iii. DENIS ALTON DARLING, b. 07 Mar 1927, Akron, New York.
- 2202. iv. BRADLEY ROSS DARLING, b. 17 May 1934, Akron, New York.

1240. ESMARIE^9 DARLING *(EDITH SOPHIA^8 BURCHARD, CALISTA ELIZABETH^7 MILKS, BENJAMIN^6, LEMUEL^5 MILK, JONATHAN^4, JOB^3, JOHN^2, JOHN^1)* was born 11 Jun 1897 in East Otto, Cattaraugus County, New York. She married (1) NATHANIEL SMITH Abt. 1921. He was born Abt. 1897 in Millerton, Pennsylvania. She married (2) GEORGE ELMER GAMPP 18 Aug 1927 in Buffalo, New York, son of ABRAHAM GAMPP and MARA BURCHARD. He was born 28 May 1898 in East Otto, Cattaraugus County, New York, and died May 1982 in New York.

Child of ESMARIE DARLING and NATHANIEL SMITH is:
- 2203. i. MALCOLM DARLING^{10} SMITH, b. 10 Aug 1922, Buffalo, New York.

Children of Esmarie Darling and George Elmer Gampp are listed above under (1236) George Elmer Gampp.

1241. JESSIE LUCILE[9] DARLING *(EDITH SOPHIA[8] BURCHARD, CALISTA ELIZABETH[7] MILKS, BENJAMIN[6], LEMUEL[5] MILK, JONATHAN[4], JOB[3], JOHN[2], JOHN[1])* was born 12 Mar 1899 in East Otto, Cattaraugus County, New York. She married ALFRED WILLIAM HALLETT 27 Jun 1929 in Buffalo, New York, son of ALFRED HALLETT and EMILY DOWDELL. He was born 10 Mar 1899 in Buffalo, New York.

Children of JESSIE DARLING and ALFRED HALLETT are:
- i. RICHARD DARLING[10] HALLETT, b. 16 Jun 1930, Buffalo, New York.
- ii. WILLIAM JESSE HALLETT, b. 21 Aug 1934, Orchard Park, New York.
- iii. SYLVIA EMILY HALLETT, b. 08 Jun 1936, Orchard Park, New York.
- iv. MARCIA MARIE HALLETT, b. 26 Dec 1942, Orchard Park, New York.

1242. WINIFRED MARGUERITE[9] DARLING *(EDITH SOPHIA[8] BURCHARD, CALISTA ELIZABETH[7] MILKS, BENJAMIN[6], LEMUEL[5] MILK, JONATHAN[4], JOB[3], JOHN[2], JOHN[1])* was born 28 Dec 1901. She married THOMAS GERARD HUGHES 04 Jul 1925 in Kenmore, New York, son of ALBERT HUGHES and CATHERINE GERARD. He was born 14 May 1902 in Elmira, New York.

Children of WINIFRED DARLING and THOMAS HUGHES are:
- i. DOUGLAS GERARD[10] HUGHES, b. 28 Mar 1927, Kenmore, New York; d. 02 Apr 1927, Kenmore, New York.
- 2204. ii. LOIS KATHRYN HUGHES, b. 09 Jul 1929, Columbus, Ohio.
- iii. SHIRLEY WINIFRED HUGHES, b. 14 Feb 1931, Kenmore, New York.
- 2205. iv. FRANCES MARIAN HUGHES, b. 08 Sep 1932, Kenmore, New York.
- v. HELEN JANICE HUGHES, b. 20 Dec 1935, Wichita, Kansas.

1243. KENNETH CLARK[9] DARLING *(EDITH SOPHIA[8] BURCHARD, CALISTA ELIZABETH[7] MILKS, BENJAMIN[6], LEMUEL[5] MILK, JONATHAN[4], JOB[3], JOHN[2], JOHN[1])* was born 19 Feb 1903. He married HAZEL MARGARITE BISHOP Abt. 1931, daughter of ALBERT BISHOP and ELIZABETH GAMEL. She was born 29 May 1903 in Cresco, Iowa.

Children of KENNETH DARLING and HAZEL BISHOP are:
- i. PAUL KENNETH[10] DARLING, b. 24 Jan 1932, Oradell, New Jersey.
- ii. PATRICIA HAZEL DARLING, b. 16 May 1933, Valley Stream, New York.
- iii. CLARK ALBERT DARLING, b. 10 Nov 1935, Valley Stream, New York.
- iv. MARY ELIZABETH DARLING, b. 19 Jan 1940, Valley Stream, New York.

1244. EDGAR DALE[9] DARLING *(EDITH SOPHIA[8] BURCHARD, CALISTA ELIZABETH[7] MILKS, BENJAMIN[6], LEMUEL[5] MILK, JONATHAN[4], JOB[3], JOHN[2], JOHN[1])* was born 26 Jan 1905. He married (1) MARGARET LOUISA PAYNE 15 Feb 1932 in Buffalo, New York, daughter of EARL PAYNE and LOUISA WEAVER. She was born 12 Oct 1912. He married (2) ALICE LILLIAN BARTLOW 23 Feb 1946 in Lancaster, New York, daughter of ALBERT BARTLOW and LILLIAN KAUFMAN. She was born 10 Aug 1919.

Children of EDGAR DARLING and MARGARET PAYNE are:
- 2206. i. ANN PHYLLIS[10] DARLING, b. 14 Dec 1933, Gardenville, New York.
- ii. SANDRA ELLEN DARLING, b. 15 Feb 1935, Springville, New York; m. CHARLES WESLEY HAMPTON, 18 Jun 1955; b. Abt. 1935, Of Springville, New York.
- 2207. iii. JEAN ELLEN DARLING, b. 05 Jan 1937, Kenmore, New York.

Children of EDGAR DARLING and ALICE BARTLOW are:
- iv. ERIC JOHN[10] DARLING, b. 01 Feb 1949, Fort Dodge, Iowa.
- v. KAREN DALE DARLING, b. 08 Mar 1951, Fort Dodge, Iowa.

1245. MERRL THOMAS[9] MILKS *(ELBERT B.[8], MERRITT SIDWAY[7], BENJAMIN[6], LEMUEL[5] MILK, JONATHAN[4], JOB[3], JOHN[2], JOHN[1])* was born 08 Apr 1898, and died 1958 in Brodhead, Green County, Wisconsin. He married GERTRUDE FAYE BROBST 12 Aug 1919 in Wisconsin, daughter of ALVIN BROBST and MINNIE MARTIN. She was born 27 Sep 1897 in

Janesville, Green County, Wisconsin, and died 1971 in Brodhead, Green County, Wisconsin.

DEATH NOTICE - Wisconsin State Journal, Madison Wisconsin, May 18, 1971 pg 40

Mrs G Faye Milks

Brodhead - Mrs G Faye Milks, 73, died unexpectedly Monday (May 17) in a Monroe Hospital after an apparent heart attack. The former G Faye Brobst lived in Spring Grove Township until September 1970 when she moved to Brodhead.

She was married to Merrill Milks in 1919. She was a member of the Congregational Church, the Eastern Star, and Spring Grove Farmerettes.

Surviving are three sons, Merritt and James both of Brodhead, and Joe Davies, Ill. three daughters, Marilyn and Mrs Margaret Wischer, both of Monroe, and Mrs Ralph Hammerly of Monticello. A sister, Mrs Bess Hopkins, Brodhead, and 15 grandchildren.

Children of MERRL MILKS and GERTRUDE BROBST are:

    i. MARILYN^{10} MILKS, b. 21 Aug 1920, Brodhead, Wisconsin; d. 1971, Brodhead, Green County, Wisconsin.

2208.   ii. MERRITT THOMAS 'PUTT' MILKS, b. 21 Feb 1926, Janesville, Wisconsin; d. 07 Nov 1988, Rock County, Wisconsin.

2209.   iii. BARBARA FAYE MILKS, b. 11 Feb 1928, Janesville, Wisconsin.

2210.   iv. JAMES WALKER MILKS, b. 02 May 1930, Janesville, Wisconsin; d. 15 Nov 1988, Wisconsin.

    v. MARGARET MAE MILKS, b. 01 Nov 1931, Janesville, Wisconsin.

    vi. JOE BROBST MILKS, b. 15 Jul 1933, Brodhead, Wisconsin; m. ESTHER M. _____; b. Abt. 1939.

1246. DR, ROBERT FRANKLIN^9 MILKS *(ELMER F.^{8}, JAMES FRANKLIN^7, BENJAMIN^6, LEMUEL^5 MILK, JONATHAN^4, JOB^3, JOHN^2, JOHN^1)* was born 25 Dec 1923 in Buffalo, New York, and died 23 Oct 2008 in Buffalo, New York.

Child of DR, ROBERT FRANKLIN MILKS is:

    i. KATHERINE E.^{10} MILKS, b. Abt. 1979, Buffalo, New York.

1247. GERTRUDE E.^{9} MILKS *(DANIEL BENJAMIN^8, JAMES FRANKLIN^7, BENJAMIN^6, LEMUEL^5 MILK, JONATHAN^4, JOB^3, JOHN^2, JOHN^1)* was born 12 Nov 1900 in Buffalo, New York, and died Aug 1982 in Orchard Park, New York. She married FRED WALTER HODSON, son of JOHN HODSON and MINNIE _____. He was born 26 Jun 1899, and died Oct 1971 in Orchard Park, New York.

Children of GERTRUDE MILKS and FRED HODSON are:

2211.   i. RUSSELL BLAKE^{10} HODSON, b. 14 Oct 1930, Buffalo, New York; d. 14 Apr 2005, Vero Beach, Indian River County, Florida.

2212.   ii. MARY LOU HODSON, b. 12 May 1933, Orchard Park, New York.

    iii. JOHN DANIEL HODSON, b. 31 Dec 1938, Buffalo, New York.

1248. RICHARD JAMES^9 MILKS *(WILLIAM H.^{8}, JAMES FRANKLIN^7, BENJAMIN^6, LEMUEL^5 MILK, JONATHAN^4, JOB^3, JOHN^2, JOHN^1)* was born 11 Jan 1908 in Buffalo, New York, and died Mar 1981 in Snyder, New York. He married RUTH MCCREADIE 16 Aug 1934, daughter of ALBERT MCCREADIE and CAROLINE ROBINSON. She was born 15 Jan 1911 in Buffalo, New York, and died 11 May 2013 in Aiken, South Carolina.

OBITUARY - Family-Placed Death Notice

MILKS, Ruth E.

Dateline: Aiken, SC Mrs. Ruth E. Milks, 102, of Aiken, SC, formerly of Dunwoody, GA died Saturday, May 11, 2013 at her residence.

A memorial service will be held this Friday, May 17th, 2013 at 2pm at Dunwoody United Methodist Church, 1548 Mount Vernon Rd., Dunwoody. January 15, 1911 marked the arrival of a feisty girl now named Ruth Milks.

For 67 years, she went to school, worked, married, raised two children, volunteered and lived most of her life in Buffalo, NY and then Dunwoody, GA.

Ruth, the lone survivor among her siblings, lost her husband Richard in 1981 and a son Roger, in 2009.

She is survived by her daughter, Nancy Tisdale, Aiken; grandson, Andy and Erica Tisdale, Aiken; daughter in law, Laurie Milks and granddaughter Jody and Todd Miller. There is another generation now, too: four great grandchildren, Adam, Zachary, Sara, and the youngest, five year-old Waylon. When asked about a philosophy of life, she just "kept going" and enjoys life, extending a cheerful personal style, piercing eyes, and a good, hearty laugh. Expressions of

sympathy may be left at www.georgefuneralhomes.com
Published in The Atlanta Journal-Constitution on May 15, 2013

Children of RICHARD MILKS and RUTH MCCREADIE are:
2213.   i.   NANCY[10] MILKS, b. 18 Dec 1938, Snyder, New York; d. Of Aiken, SC.
2214.   ii. ROGER ALAN MILKS, b. 02 Jul 1941, Snyder, New York; d. 04 Jan 2009, Woodland Hills, Los Angeles County, California.

1249. ELMER WILLIAM[9] MYLKS *(MERRILL V.[8] MILKS, JAMES FRANKLIN[7], BENJAMIN[6], LEMUEL[5] MILK, JONATHAN[4], JOB[3], JOHN[2], JOHN[1])* was born 10 Mar 1908 in Buffalo, NY, and died Feb 1973 in Ridgewood, New Jersey. He married MARGUERITE LUCILLE IRVING. She was born 26 Jul 1910 in Cartersville, VA, and died 27 Apr 2000 in Ridgewood, NJ.

Children of ELMER MYLKS and MARGUERITE IRVING are:
2215.   i.   HERBERT WILLIAM[10] MYLKS, b. 09 Oct 1938, New York; d. 09 May 1980, Private passenger car accident, passenger in car..
        ii. ELMER W. MYLKS, b. 01 Sep 1952, Ridgewood, New Jersey.

1250. WILLIAM FISHER[9] MILKS *(MERRILL V.[8], JAMES FRANKLIN[7], BENJAMIN[6], LEMUEL[5] MILK, JONATHAN[4], JOB[3], JOHN[2], JOHN[1])* was born 14 Mar 1929 in Buffalo, New York. He married FRANCES WATSON 06 Oct 1951 in New York. She was born Abt. 1930 in Of Niagara Falls, New York, and died Bef. 09 Nov 2011.

Children of WILLIAM MILKS and FRANCES WATSON are:
        i.   WILLIAM FISHER[10] MILKS, JR., b. 15 Jul 1952, Niagara Falls, New York; d. 09 Nov 2011, Niagara Falls, New York; m. CONNIE L. _____; b. Abt. 1954.
             OBITUARY
             William F. Milks, Jr., age 59 of Niagara Falls died unexpectedly on Wednesday November 9, 2011 at his residence after a brief illness.
             William was born July 15, 1952 in Niagara Falls, NY, the son of William F. Milks, Sr. of Sedona, AZ and the late Frances (Watson) Milks and had attended Lewiston Porter High School. A veteran of Vietnam, he served in the U.S. Marine Corps from 1970 to his honorable discharge in 1971. William enjoyed the outdoors, fishing and camping.
             In addition to his father he is survived by a sister, Mary Ferchen of Lewiston; a brother, James "Jamie" Milks of Niagara Falls; two nieces, Michele (Sean) Hausauer and Cindi Ferchen both of Lewiston; and two nephews, Robert Milks of Buffalo and Patrick Milks of Lewiston. He was predeceased by a brother, Robert P. Milks.
             A memorial service will be held at a later date. There will be no calling hours. Memorials may be made to the Heart & Soul Food Pantry 939 Ontario Ave., Niagara Falls, NY 14305 or to the
             Leukemia Society of America WNY Chapter, 4053 Maple Rd., Suite 110, Amherst, NY 14226. Arrangements have been entrusted to HARDISON FUNERAL HOME, N. Fourth & Ridge Sts., Lewiston.

2216.   ii. MARY LOUISE MILKS, b. 07 Aug 1953, Niagara Falls, New York.
2217.   iii. ROBERT PETER MILKS, b. 21 Oct 1955, Niagara Falls, New York; d. Apr 1982, Lewiston, New York.
        iv. JAMES 'JAMIE' GERARD MILKS, b. 16 Oct 1969, Niagara Falls, New York.

1251. ROLLIN CHARLES[9] MILKS *(GEORGE RICHARD[8], IRA NELSON[7], BENJAMIN[6], LEMUEL[5] MILK, JONATHAN[4], JOB[3], JOHN[2], JOHN[1])* was born 19 Aug 1904, and died Jan 1950. He married (1) ELISSA DOLAN Abt. 1932 in New York. She was born Abt. 1905. He married (2) VERA MCNIFF Abt. 1934 in New York. She was born Abt. 1905. He married (3) ALICE C. HAMM Abt. 1937 in New York. She was born 18 Apr 1908, and died 30 Aug 2010 in New York.

Child of ROLLIN MILKS and ELISSA DOLAN is:
        i.   MARJORIE H.[10] MILKS, b. 22 Dec 1932, New York; m. MICHAEL HAGGERTY; b. Abt. 1932.

Children of ROLLIN MILKS and ALICE HAMM are:
        ii. MEIL R.[10] MILKS, b. 26 Nov 1937, Lackawanna, New York; m. DONNA _____; b. Abt. 1937.
        iii. MARILYN A. MILKS, b. 14 May 1940, Lackawanna, New York; m. RICHARD CORCORAN; b. Abt. 1940.

iv. DAN R. MILKS, b. 21 Jan 1944, Lackawanna, New York.
v. ELIZABETH A. MILKS, b. 06 Feb 1946, Lackawanna, New York; m. KEN BARNES; b. Abt. 1946.

1252. JESSIE BEDFORD[9] FISHER *(CLARA MAHALA[8] MILKS, IRA NELSON[7], BENJAMIN[6], LEMUEL[5] MILK, JONATHAN[4], JOB[3], JOHN[2], JOHN[1])* was born 17 Sep 1902 in Los Angeles, California. She married RICHARD A. WALBURG 08 Jun 1924 in Orchard Park, New York, son of JOHN WALBURG and ANNA CARLSON. He was born 06 Mar 1898 in Chicago, Illinois.
Material on this family is primarily from the History of Niagara Frontier, Vol. III (Biographical) , pgs, 556 and 559

Children of JESSIE FISHER and RICHARD WALBURG are:
      i. SHIRLEY FISHER[10] WALBURG, b. 18 Jan 1926, Orchard Park, New York; m. ALEXANDER BRYSON, 10 Dec 1945; b. Abt. 1926. Shirley kept name of Bryson after annulment of marriage. No children.
2218. ii. DORIS JANE WALBURG, b. 29 Nov 1930, Hamburg, Erie County, New York.

1253. FLORENCE[9] FISHER *(CLARA MAHALA[8] MILKS, IRA NELSON[7], BENJAMIN[6], LEMUEL[5] MILK, JONATHAN[4], JOB[3], JOHN[2], JOHN[1])* was born 13 Sep 1908 in West Seneca, New York. She married GEORGE E. WILLARD 19 Dec 1929, son of JOSEPH WILLARD and FLORENCE MARSHALL. He was born 27 Oct 1903 in Orchard Park, New York.

Children of FLORENCE FISHER and GEORGE WILLARD are:
      i. BEVERLY CLAIRE[10] WILLARD, b. 09 Sep 1930, Orchard Park, New York.
      ii. GEORGE FISHER WILLARD, b. 21 Oct 1932, Orchard Park, New York.
      iii. JOAN BEATRICE WILLARD, b. 04 Dec 1935, Orchard Park, New York.

1254. IRA CHARLES[9] MILKS *(NELSON CLARENCE[8], IRA NELSON[7], BENJAMIN[6], LEMUEL[5] MILK, JONATHAN[4], JOB[3], JOHN[2], JOHN[1])* was born 10 Oct 1904 in Hamburg, Erie County, New York, and died Apr 1944 in Hamburg, Erie County, New York. He married INEZ GRASSMEYER Abt. 1929, daughter of HARRY GRASSMEYER and LAURA _____. She was born 04 Dec 1901, and died 1963 in Erie County, New York.

Children of IRA MILKS and INEZ GRASSMEYER are:
2219. i. IRA CHARLES[10] MILKS, JR., b. 19 Jul 1930, Akron, Ohio; d. 29 Apr 2001, Deltona, FL.
2220. ii. JAMES I. MILKS, b. 02 Jul 1936, Ohio.
      iii. NELSA INEZ MILKS, b. 19 Dec 1937, New York; m. (1) ?? VOIGHT; m. (2) ALBERT E. SPONHOLZ, 29 Jan 1955; b. Abt. 1935, Of Orchard Park, New York.
      iv. LAURA MAY MILKS, b. 10 Aug 1942, New York; m. ?? JOHNSON.

1255. ARNOLD RICHARD[9] MILKS *(NELSON CLARENCE[8], IRA NELSON[7], BENJAMIN[6], LEMUEL[5] MILK, JONATHAN[4], JOB[3], JOHN[2], JOHN[1])* was born 15 Sep 1907 in Lackawanna, NY, and died Sep 1973 in Beaver Dams, Schuyler Co, NY 14812. He married ERMA WEILER 27 Oct 1929 in Buffalo, NY. She was born 17 Aug 1908 in New York, and died May 1979 in Hamburg, Erie County, New York.

Children of ARNOLD MILKS and ERMA WEILER are:
      i. JOAN ERMA[10] MILKS, b. 17 Jan 1932; m. EDWARD HESCHKE, 16 Sep 1950; b. 19 Mar 1927.
      ii. ANNA MARIE MILKS, b. 17 Mar 1934, New York; m. FLOYD O'NEIL, 28 Oct 1955; b. Abt. 1934.

1256. ADELINE MILDRED[9] MILKS *(NELSON CLARENCE[8], IRA NELSON[7], BENJAMIN[6], LEMUEL[5] MILK, JONATHAN[4], JOB[3], JOHN[2], JOHN[1])* was born 14 Jan 1909 in New York. She married ELWOOD WILLIAM LAND 12 Jul 1930 in Chautauqua County, New York, son of ARTHUR LAND and JULIA PECK. He was born 15 Dec 1907, and died 2003.

Children of ADELINE MILKS and ELWOOD LAND are:
      i. ELWOOD WILLIAM[10] LAND, JR., b. 11 Jun 1932; m. KATHLINE B. _____, 26 Nov 1954; b. Abt. 1928.
      ii. KURT VAN DORN LAND, b. 29 Aug 1937; m. PATRICIA H. _____.

1257. ELEANOR SOPHIA[9] MILKS *(NELSON CLARENCE[8], IRA NELSON[7], BENJAMIN[6], LEMUEL[5] MILK, JONATHAN[4], JOB[3], JOHN[2], JOHN[1])* was born 22 Aug 1915 in New York. She married ERNEST E. PERRIN 10 Jun 1935, son of ALFRED PERRIN and ELLEN _____. He was born 17 Jun 1910 in New York, and died Dec 1962.

Children of ELEANOR MILKS and ERNEST PERRIN are:
- i. DAVID NELSON[10] PERRIN, b. 08 Jul 1936.
- ii. DONNA ELEANOR PERRIN, b. 28 Nov 1938.
- iii. LOIS ELLEN PERRIN, b. 23 Jul 1943.
- iv. DANIEL L. PERRIN, b. 07 Apr 1946.
- v. LESLIE ANN PERRIN, b. 12 Aug 1954.

1258. LENDAL DEAN[9] NEGUS *(ANNA ALFREDINE[8] MORRIS, ELIZABETH A. "BETSEY"[7] MILKS, JOB[6] MILK, LEMUEL[5], JONATHAN[4], JOB[3], JOHN[2], JOHN[1])* was born 05 Apr 1887 in Hurley, Turner County, S. Dakota, and died 18 Jun 1952 in Grant, Oregon. He married GRACE EMELINE STOTTS Abt. 1913, daughter of WILLIAM STOTTS and ROSA LEWELLEN. She was born 21 Feb 1893 in Iowa, and died 28 Feb 1987 in Tulare, California.

Children of LENDAL NEGUS and GRACE STOTTS are:
- i. DEAN HENRY[10] NEGUS, b. 07 Jul 1914; d. 17 Jun 1992, Clackamas, Oregon; m. EVELYN _____.
- ii. HENRY T. NEGUS, b. Abt. 1916.
- iii. ERNEST W. NEGUS, b. Abt. 1919, Stevens County, Minnesota.
- iv. ARTHUR EUGENE NEGUS, b. Abt. 1921.
- v. LENDAL T. NEGUS, b. 28 Jul 1924; d. 26 Aug 1951, Portland, Oregon.

1259. ARTHUR[9] NEGUS *(ANNA ALFREDINE[8] MORRIS, ELIZABETH A. "BETSEY"[7] MILKS, JOB[6] MILK, LEMUEL[5], JONATHAN[4], JOB[3], JOHN[2], JOHN[1])* was born 10 Jan 1883 in South Dakota, and died 01 Aug 1966 in Mount Vernon, Grant, Oregon. He married OCTAVIA _____. She was born Abt. 1884 in Wisconsin.

Child of ARTHUR NEGUS and OCTAVIA _____ is:
- i. ELOISE[10] NEGUS, b. Abt. 1900, Wisconsin.

1260. CLARENCE W.[9] NEGUS *(ANNA ALFREDINE[8] MORRIS, ELIZABETH A. "BETSEY"[7] MILKS, JOB[6] MILK, LEMUEL[5], JONATHAN[4], JOB[3], JOHN[2], JOHN[1])* was born 24 Jun 1886 in Buena Vista, Meade County, South Dakota, and died 16 Sep 1961 in Deschutes, Oregon. He married FLORENCE 'FLOSS' ROSE ASLIN 05 Feb 1906 in Turner, South Dakota. She was born 03 Jul 1887 in Davis, South Dakota, and died 10 Jul 1976 in Bend, Deschutes County, Oregon.

Children of CLARENCE NEGUS and FLORENCE ASLIN are:
- 2221. i. WAYNE A.[10] NEGUS, b. 16 Jan 1907, Davis, South Dakota; d. 29 Jun 1991, Oregon.
- ii. MILDRED V. NEGUS, b. 06 Nov 1909, Jamestown, North Dakota; d. 17 Sep 1998; m. LES LUTTON; d. 23 Sep 1985, Aberdeen Washington.
- iii. THOMAS JOHN NEGUS, b. 25 Mar 1913, Davis, South Dakota; d. Apr 1983, Grant County, Oregon; m. FLORA _____.
- iv. DOROTHY DIONE NEGUS, b. 1916, Jamestown, North Dakota; d. 27 Apr 1999, Bend, Oregon; m. OREN BOWMAN.
- v. KENNETH JOHN NEGUS, b. 1919, Jamestown, North Dakota; d. Aft. 1953, Oregon??.
- vi. EUGENE LAMONT NEGUS, b. 1921, Jamestown, North Dakota; d. Aft. 1971, Oregon??.

1261. HARVEY MYRL[9] NEGUS *(ANNA ALFREDINE[8] MORRIS, ELIZABETH A. "BETSEY"[7] MILKS, JOB[6] MILK, LEMUEL[5], JONATHAN[4], JOB[3], JOHN[2], JOHN[1])* was born 10 Aug 1891 in Turner County, South Dakota, and died 03 Jun 1965 in Glendive, Dawson County, Montana. He married ELOISE CECIL SMITH 19 May 1915. She was born 19 May 1897 in Cadott, Chippewa County, Wisconsin, and died 27 Apr 1954 in Glendive, Dawson County, Montana.

Children of HARVEY NEGUS and ELOISE SMITH are:
- i. PARKER W.[10] NEGUS, b. 09 Jul 1918, Severn, Stutsman, North Dakota; d. 15 Jun 2003, Carlsbad, San Diego County, California.
- ii. AUDRE E. NEGUS, b. Abt. 1925, Glendive, Dawson County, Montana.
- iii. DR. MILTON K. NEGUS, b. 19 Oct 1930, Glendive, Dawson County, Montana.

1262. FRED[9] WARBURTON *(MARY ETTA[8] MORRIS, ELIZABETH A. "BETSEY"[7] MILKS, JOB[6] MILK, LEMUEL[5], JONATHAN[4], JOB[3], JOHN[2], JOHN[1])* was born 22 Jun 1899 in Spring Valley, Shannon County, Missouri, and died Nov 1980 in McCook,

Red Willow County, Nebraska. He married GOLDIE LARREAU Abt. 1928, daughter of FRANK LARREAU and ELLA WALLACE. She was born 10 Sep 1912 in Kansas, and died 20 Feb 1995 in Martell, Lancaster County, Nebraska.

Children of FRED WARBURTON and GOLDIE LARREAU are:

2222. i. ROBERT LEE 'RED'[10] WARBURTON, b. 13 Jun 1929, Oberlin, Decatur County, Kansas; d. 07 Oct 2011, Gering, Scotts Bluff County, Nebraska.
2223. ii. CLAUD D. 'ROCKY' WARBURTON, b. 11 Sep 1931, Oberlin, Decatur County, Kansas; d. 31 Jan 1996, McCook, Red Willow County, Nebraska.
2224. iii. WALTER R. 'PINKY' WARBURTON, b. 22 Aug 1933, Oberlin, Decatur County, Kansas; d. 19 Dec 2004, McCook, Red Willow County, Nebraska.
     iv. PAULINE 'POLLY' WARBURTON, b. 17 Dec 1935, Oberlin, Decatur County, Kansas; m. RAYMOND LEE CHILDS, Abt. 1981; b. 24 Nov 1919, Missouri; d. 27 Oct 2003, Martell, Lancaster County, Nebraska.

1263. CLIFFORD RUSSELL[9] CULLINGS *(JAMES EBENEZER[8], CAROLINE "PHEBE" E.[7] MILKS, JOB[6] MILK, LEMUEL[5], JONATHAN[4], JOB[3], JOHN[2], JOHN[1])* was born 11 Mar 1886 in Grand Island, Nebraska, and died 23 Apr 1927 in Colorado. He married NORA REED 12 Apr 1912. She was born Abt. 1888.

Children of CLIFFORD CULLINGS and NORA REED are:

     i. CLIFFORD REED[10] CULLINGS, b. 25 May 1913, Colorado; d. 02 May 1957, Conta Costa, California.
     ii. DAVID J. CULLINGS, b. 17 Mar 1916, Colorado; d. Dec 1944, Germany.
     iii. SADIE MARIE CULLINGS, b. Jul 1925, Colorado.

1264. NELLIE E.[9] CULLINGS *(JAMES EBENEZER[8], CAROLINE "PHEBE" E.[7] MILKS, JOB[6] MILK, LEMUEL[5], JONATHAN[4], JOB[3], JOHN[2], JOHN[1])* was born 20 Mar 1888 in Fredericksburg, Iowa. She married EMIL A. LEURS 07 Apr 1907. He was born Abt. 1888.

Children of NELLIE CULLINGS and EMIL LEURS are:

2225. i. LEROY J.[10] LEURS, b. 26 Apr 1908.
     ii. RUTH A. LEURS, b. 01 Dec 1910.

1265. KENNETH[9] DUNCAN *(CLARA F.[8] CULLINGS, CAROLINE "PHEBE" E.[7] MILKS, JOB[6] MILK, LEMUEL[5], JONATHAN[4], JOB[3], JOHN[2], JOHN[1])* was born Sep 1910 in Riceville, Iowa. He married EDNA FALLON 22 Feb 1935. She was born Abt. 1910.

Children of KENNETH DUNCAN and EDNA FALLON are:

     i. JAMES[10] DUNCAN.
     ii. JOHN DUNCAN.
     iii. KATHRYN DUNCAN.

1266. PEARL RHEA[9] PETTIT *(FRANK BURR[8], JEMIMA DIANTHA[7] MILKS, JOB[6] MILK, LEMUEL[5], JONATHAN[4], JOB[3], JOHN[2], JOHN[1])* was born 11 May 1889 in Mt. Ida, Grant County, Wisconsin. She married ADOLPH H. KEMPER 01 Jun 1910 in Mt. Ida, Grant County, Wisconsin. He was born 06 Sep 1880 in Lancaster, Wisconsin, and died 02 Jul 1954 in Sioux Falls, South Dakota.

Children of PEARL PETTIT and ADOLPH KEMPER are:

2226. i. DR. CARLOS E.[10] KEMPER, b. 09 Apr 1911, Walnut Grove, Minnesota.
2227. ii. EVELYN ELAINE KEMPER, b. 30 Jul 1912, Walnut Grove, Minnesota.
2228. iii. ARDYS MARION KEMPER, b. 04 Aug 1914, Walnut Grove, Minnesota.
2229. iv. KATHRYN ELIZABETH KEMPER, b. 04 Sep 1919, Walnut Grove, Minnesota.

1267. MAMIE ESTELLA[9] PETTIT *(FRED SILAS[8], JEMIMA DIANTHA[7] MILKS, JOB[6] MILK, LEMUEL[5], JONATHAN[4], JOB[3], JOHN[2], JOHN[1])* was born 23 Sep 1894 in Mt. Ida, Grant County, Wisconsin, and died 08 Oct 1984 in Bigfork, Flathead County, Montana. She married WALTER HENDERSON FARRIS 01 May 1915 in Sidney, Montana, son of JOHN FARRIS and SARAH KIELLEY. He was born 22 Nov 1888 in Wisconsin, and died 15 Sep 1975 in Kalispell, Flathead County, Montana.

Children of MAMIE PETTIT and WALTER FARRIS are:

2230. i. FORREST EDWARD[10] FARRIS, b. 30 Mar 1916, Richland, Montana; d. 22 Mar 2002.
2231. ii. GLADYS MAY FARRIS, b. 21 Sep 1917, Richland, Montana; d. 29 Dec 1974, Flathead County, Montana.
iii. WALTER WOODROW FARRIS, b. 13 Aug 1919, Richland, Montana; d. 12 Mar 1991, 3 children.
iv. NELLIE J. FARRIS, b. Abt. 1921, Montana; d. 2 daughters; m. WILLIAM CLYDE 'BILL' HUBBARD; b. Abt. 1916; d. 1996, Fontana, California.
v. ADA F. FARRIS, b. Abt. 1923, Montana; d. 1991, Libby, Montana (3 children); m. LEO A. SCHMAUCH; b. Abt. 1919.
vi. DELORES E. FARRIS, b. Abt. 1933, Montana.

1268. HARRY LLOYD[9] PETTIT *(FRED SILAS[8], JEMIMA DIANTHA[7] MILKS, JOB[6] MILK, LEMUEL[5], JONATHAN[4], JOB[3], JOHN[2], JOHN[1])* was born 04 Jan 1900 in Mt. Ida, Grant County, Wisconsin. He married MARY MILLER Abt. 1927. She was born Abt. 1900.

Children of HARRY PETTIT and MARY MILLER are:

2232. i. VERA ANN[10] PETTIT, b. 21 May 1928, Kalispell, Flathead County, Montana.
ii. JOYCE ELAINE PETTIT, b. 06 Aug 1929, Kalispell, Flathead County, Montana; d. 29 Nov 1934, Kalispell, Flathead County, Montana.
2233. iii. DONALD LLOYD PETTIT, b. 21 Apr 1931, Kalispell, Flathead County, Montana.
iv. LYLE RAY PETTIT, b. 03 May 1937, Kalispell, Flathead County, Montana.

1269. HAROLD GEORGE[9] PETTIT *(FRED SILAS[8], JEMIMA DIANTHA[7] MILKS, JOB[6] MILK, LEMUEL[5], JONATHAN[4], JOB[3], JOHN[2], JOHN[1])* was born 28 May 1905 in Mt. Ida, Grant County, Wisconsin, and died 02 Feb 1933 in Kalispell, Flathead County, Montana. He married OLGA M. PANICO. She was born Abt. 1907 in Northern Italy.

Child of HAROLD PETTIT and OLGA PANICO is:

i. ROBERT GEORGE[10] PETTIT, b. 28 Jun 1930, Kalispell, Flathead County, Montana; d. 16 Nov 1950, San Joaquin County, California,.

1270. FLOYD EDWIN[9] MILKS *(CHARLES NELSON[8], DAVID FRANKLIN[7], JOB[6] MILK, LEMUEL[5], JONATHAN[4], JOB[3], JOHN[2], JOHN[1])* was born 03 Jun 1890 in Hurley, Turner County, South Dakota, and died 21 Feb 1978 in Faith, Meade County, South Dakota. He married (1) CAROLINE M. 'CARRIE' STEWART Abt. 1912. She was born Abt. 1886 in Scotland. He married (2) LILLIAN (WHITE) DOUGHTERTY 25 Jan 1939 in Glasgow, Valley County, Montana, daughter of EDWARD WHITE and CAROLINE FLAKOI. She was born 1902. He married (3) GLADYS REYNOLDS Aft. 1939. She was born 20 Feb 1908, and died 29 Jan 1976 in Sturgis, Meade County, South Dakota.

Children of FLOYD MILKS and CAROLINE STEWART are:

2234. i. MINA MARIE[10] MILKS, b. 12 Dec 1913, Millerton, North Dakota.
ii. INEZ IONE MILKS, b. 20 Aug 1915, Millerton, North Dakota.
iii. ROBERT CHARLES MILKS, b. 04 Mar 1917, Millerton, North Dakota; d. 09 Jan 1945, South Pacific on a Japanese POW ship..

1271. CARRIE M.[9] MILKS *(CHARLES NELSON[8], DAVID FRANKLIN[7], JOB[6] MILK, LEMUEL[5], JONATHAN[4], JOB[3], JOHN[2], JOHN[1])* was born 20 Aug 1892 in Turner County, South Dakota. She married HENRY C. PIPER. He was born 13 Dec 1891 in Worcester, Massachusetts.

Child of CARRIE MILKS and HENRY PIPER is:

i. REGINA[10] PIPER, b. Adopted.

1272. GUY STANLEY[9] MILKS *(CHARLES NELSON[8], DAVID FRANKLIN[7], JOB[6] MILK, LEMUEL[5], JONATHAN[4], JOB[3], JOHN[2], JOHN[1])* was born 13 Jan 1898 in Turner County, South Dakota, and died 05 Mar 1976 in Beltrami County, Minnesota. He married ELLA MABEL DEBOER 08 Jun 1936 in Lake County, South Dakota. She was born 25 Feb 1908.

Children of GUY MILKS and ELLA DEBOER are:

i. STANLEY ALLEN[10] MILKS, b. 11 Nov 1925, Hurley, Turner County, South Dakota; d. 15 Nov 1925, Lincoln

		County, South Dakota.
2235.	ii.	FERNELLA MAY MILKS, b. 24 Dec 1927, Lennox, Lincoln County, South Dakota.
2236.	iii.	FLOYD LEROY MILKS, b. 11 Jul 1931; d. 13 Dec 1978, Bemidji, Beltrami County, Minnesota.
2237.	iv.	SHIRLEY ANN MILKS, b. 09 Jan 1933; d. 21 May 2008, Bemidji, Minnesota.

1273. LEROY ELLIS 'SLIM'^{9} BENSON *(PEARL MELISSA^8 MILKS, DAVID FRANKLIN^7, JOB^6 MILK, LEMUEL^5, JONATHAN^4, JOB^3, JOHN^2, JOHN^1)* was born 08 Nov 1890 in Parsons, Kansas, and died 24 Dec 1950 in Viborg, Turner County, South Dakota. He married HENRIETTA WIBBENS 26 May 1915 in Canton, Lincoln County, South Dakota, daughter of HENRY WIBBENS and JOHANNA KRUGER. She was born 18 Apr 1898 in Little Rock, Nobles County, Minnesota, and died 09 Jun 1983 in Viborg, Turner County, South Dakota.

Children of LEROY BENSON and HENRIETTA WIBBENS are:

2238.	i.	RUSSELL LEROY^{10} BENSON, b. 23 Jan 1917, South Dakota; d. 04 Apr 1995, Seattle, King County, WA.
2239.	ii.	RUTH BENSON, b. Abt. 1918, Turner County, South Dakota.
2240.	iii.	JACK OWEN BENSON, b. 17 May 1921, South Dakota; d. 05 Aug 1999, Cass, Michigan (1 dau., 2 sons).
2241.	iv.	DR. DONALD BENSON, b. 08 Dec 1924, South Dakota; d. 24 Jun 2000, South Dakota.
	v.	AVIS IRENE BENSON, b. Abt. 1933, Spring Valley, Turner County, South Dakota.
	vi.	JANIS BENSON, b. Abt. 1935, Spring Valley, Turner County, South Dakota.

1274. EMMET H.^{9} BENSON *(PEARL MELISSA^8 MILKS, DAVID FRANKLIN^7, JOB^6 MILK, LEMUEL^5, JONATHAN^4, JOB^3, JOHN^2, JOHN^1)* was born 1892 in South Dakota. He married ELLOWENE PIPER. She was born Abt. 1892.

Child of EMMET BENSON and ELLOWENE PIPER is:

2242.	i.	KEITH M.^{10} BENSON.

1275. ERNEST CLIFFORD^9 BENSON *(PEARL MELISSA^8 MILKS, DAVID FRANKLIN^7, JOB^6 MILK, LEMUEL^5, JONATHAN^4, JOB^3, JOHN^2, JOHN^1)* was born 04 Oct 1894 in Parsons, Kansas, and died Dec 1982 in Freeman, Hutchinson County, South Dakota. He married ELVA BLANCHE LAKINGS 28 Mar 1917 in Turner County, South Dakota, daughter of JOHN LAKINGS and MARIA MOTLEY. She was born 26 Mar 1894 in Turner County, South Dakota, and died Oct 1982 in Turner Co., SD.

Children of ERNEST BENSON and ELVA LAKINGS are:

2243.	i.	PHYLLIS M.^{10} BENSON, b. 14 Jan 1918, Swan Lake, Turner County, South Dakota; d. 17 Jun 2000, South Dakota.
2244.	ii.	MARILYN E. BENSON, b. Abt. 1923, Swan Lake, Turner County, South Dakota.
2245.	iii.	HELEN J. BENSON, b. Abt. 1925, Swan Lake, Turner County, South Dakota.

1276. RUTH ANNA^9 BENSON *(PEARL MELISSA^8 MILKS, DAVID FRANKLIN^7, JOB^6 MILK, LEMUEL^5, JONATHAN^4, JOB^3, JOHN^2, JOHN^1)* was born 20 Feb 1898 in Parsons, Kansas, and died 19 Apr 1977 in Turner County, South Dakota. She married MAXWELL RUNDELL FARRAR 23 Mar 1921 in Turner County, South Dakota, son of PERCY FARRAR and LUCRETIA HAMILTON RUNDELL. He was born 03 Dec 1897 in South Dakota, and died Mar 1980 in Turner County, South Dakota. Ruth was born in Parsons, Kansas. She moved to South Dakota with her family in 1900 and settled in Hurley. After attending Madison Normal in Madison, SD, she taught school for several years before her marriage.

In 1889, Maxwell's parents came to South Dakota from Wisconsin with his sister Clara and brother Orville, where the family bought a farm in Spring Valley. Max was born in 1897 while they lived on the farm. They built a home in Hurley in 1902 and moved from the farm.

Max married Ruth Anna Benson on March 23, 1921. They farmed in Swan Lake for a number of years, and later moved to a farm near Hurley. In 1963, they retired and moved to a home in Hurley.

Max was an original incorporator and served as an officer and director of the Turner-Hutchinson Electric Cooperative of Marion, SD from 1941 to March 1980.

They are buried in Hurley Cemetery, Hurley, Turner County, South Dakota, USA

Children of RUTH BENSON and MAXWELL FARRAR are:

2246.	i.	GORDON MAXWELL^{10} FARRAR, b. 1923, Turner County, South Dakota; d. 2004, Turner County, S D.
2247.	ii.	MURIEL JEAN FARRAR, b. Abt. 1926, Turner County, South Dakota.
2248.	iii.	SHIRLEY R. FARRAR, b. 28 Jun 1930, Turner County, South Dakota.

1277. GLADYS IRENE[9] BENSON *(PEARL MELISSA[8] MILKS, DAVID FRANKLIN[7], JOB[6] MILK, LEMUEL[5], JONATHAN[4], JOB[3], JOHN[2], JOHN[1])* was born 31 Jan 1900 in South Dakota, and died 14 Mar 1971 in Turner County, South Dakota. She married ELDO OMER FRIMAN 04 Mar 1922 in Turner County, South Dakota, son of JOHN FRIMAN and JENNIE DAY. He was born 06 Mar 1901 in Douglas Township, Adams County, Iowa, and died Jun 1983 in Hurley, Turner County, SD.

Children of GLADYS BENSON and ELDO FRIMAN are:

	i.	EUGENE E. 'GENE'[10] FRIMAN, b. 12 Jun 1922, Turner County, South Dakota; d. 21 Nov 1996, Hurley, Turner County, South Dakota; m. PHYLLIS E. LONG, 02 Dec 1965; b. 1919.
2249.	ii.	DOROTHY J. FRIMAN, b. 1923, Turner County, South Dakota; d. 2006, South Dakota.
2250.	iii.	KENNETH J. 'JIM' FRIMAN, b. 14 Aug 1924, Turner County, South Dakota; d. 13 May 2002.
2251.	iv.	GERALDINE FRIMAN, b. 09 Dec 1925, Turner County, South Dakota.
	v.	VIVIAN MAE FRIMAN, b. 14 Feb 1927, Turner County, South Dakota; d. 21 Jul 2008, Yankton, Yankton County, South Dakota (unmarried).

DEATH NOTICE

Vivian M. Friman, 81, died Monday, July 21, 2008 at Avera St. Jams Care Center, Yankton.

Vivian Mae Friman was born on February 14, 1927 near Hurley, SD to Eldo and Gladys (Benson) Friman. She took care of her parents and many others in the Hurley, Parker, and Viborg areas.

She was a member of the United Methodist Church, American Legion Auxiliary, and the Senior Citizens, all of Hurley.

Grateful for having shared her life are 9 sisters, Geraldine Letchner, Madison, Marion Straw, Mitchell, Edith (Donald) Moe, Letcher, Doris (Victor) Cordell, Huron, Audrey (George) Sample, Flandreau, Margaret Adel, Lake Andes, Eleanor Bjerkaas, Irene, Genette (Kenneth) Rusk, Flandreau, and Carolyn McMahon, Flandreau; 2 brother in laws, Lester Hansen, Viborg and Herbert Gossel, Kimball, and 2 sister in laws, Phyllis Friman, Lennox and Dorothy Friman, Tripp; and many nieces and nephews.

She was preceded in death by her parents, sisters Dorothy and Frances, and 3 brothers, Gene, Jim, and Richard.

	vi.	FRANCES FRIMAN, b. 1929, Turner County, South Dakota; m. HERBERT WALTER GOSSEL; b. Abt. 1924.
	vii.	MARION FRIMAN, b. 1931, Turner County, South Dakota; m. DUANE STRAW; b. Abt. 1930.
	viii.	EDITH FRIMAN, b. 1932, Turner County, South Dakota; m. DONALD MOE; b. Abt. 1928.
2252.	ix.	DORIS FRIMAN, b. 1934, Turner County, South Dakota.
	x.	AUDREY FRIMAN, b. 1936, Turner County, South Dakota; m. GEORGE SAMPLE.
2253.	xi.	MARGARET E. FRIMAN, b. 1938, Turner County, South Dakota.
2254.	xii.	ELEANOR J. FRIMAN, b. 1938, Turner County, South Dakota.
2255.	xiii.	GENETTE FRIMAN, b. 1940, Turner County, South Dakota.
2256.	xiv.	CAROLYN FRIMAN, b. 15 Mar 1943, Turner County, South Dakota.
	xv.	RICHARD FRIMAN, b. Abt. 1928, Turner County, South Dakota; d. 10 Feb 1930, Turner County, South Dakota.

1278. FRANK M.[9] BENSON *(PEARL MELISSA[8] MILKS, DAVID FRANKLIN[7], JOB[6] MILK, LEMUEL[5], JONATHAN[4], JOB[3], JOHN[2], JOHN[1])* was born 1903 in South Dakota. He married (1) VERA MARTINSON. She died 1940. He married (2) IRENE LUNDGREN 1943.

Children of FRANK BENSON and VERA MARTINSON are:
- i. FRANK M.[10] BENSON, JR..
- ii. ROGER BENSON.
- iii. CAROL BENSON, m. MISTTER BERG.
- iv. BOB BENSON.

Child of FRANK BENSON and IRENE LUNDGREN is:
- v. SHARON[10] BENSON.

1279. HAROLD G.[9] BENSON *(PEARL MELISSA[8] MILKS, DAVID FRANKLIN[7], JOB[6] MILK, LEMUEL[5], JONATHAN[4], JOB[3], JOHN[2], JOHN[1])* was born 1905 in South Dakota. He married HAZEL NEIMEIER. She was born Abt. 1905.

Children of HAROLD BENSON and HAZEL NEIMEIER are:
- i. KENNETH[10] BENSON, d. Abt. 1954, Killed in action in Korea.
- ii. DEAN BENSON.
- iii. HAROLD G. BENSON, JR..
- iv. GARY BENSON.
- v. DONNA G. BENSON.
- vi. ROBERT BENSON.

1280. VIOLET M.[9] BENSON *(PEARL MELISSA[8] MILKS, DAVID FRANKLIN[7], JOB[6] MILK, LEMUEL[5], JONATHAN[4], JOB[3], JOHN[2], JOHN[1])* was born 1907 in South Dakota. She married LORRAIN C. PAULSON. He was born Abt. 1907.

Child of VIOLET BENSON and LORRAIN PAULSON is:
- i. SARA JEAN[10] PAULSON, b. Abt. 1945, Sioux Falls, Minnehaha County, South Dakota.

1281. HOWARD[9] BENSON *(PEARL MELISSA[8] MILKS, DAVID FRANKLIN[7], JOB[6] MILK, LEMUEL[5], JONATHAN[4], JOB[3], JOHN[2], JOHN[1])* was born 1914 in South Dakota. He married SHIRLEY CALSBEEK. She was born Abt. 1914.

Children of HOWARD BENSON and SHIRLEY CALSBEEK are:
- i. TERRY[10] BENSON.
- ii. ROCHELLE BENSON.

1282. LLOYD ALBERT[9] MILKS *(HARRY STREATOR[8], DAVID FRANKLIN[7], JOB[6] MILK, LEMUEL[5], JONATHAN[4], JOB[3], JOHN[2], JOHN[1])* was born 24 Jul 1901 in Parsons, Kansas. He married LEONA DODD. She was born 01 Jun 1912, and died Sep 1974 in Parsons, Labette County, Kansas.

Child of LLOYD MILKS and LEONA DODD is:
- i. GARY STEVENS[10] MILKS, b. Adopted.

1283. NELLIE 'BLANCHE'[9] MILKS *(HARRY STREATOR[8], DAVID FRANKLIN[7], JOB[6] MILK, LEMUEL[5], JONATHAN[4], JOB[3], JOHN[2], JOHN[1])* was born 02 Aug 1903 in Parsons, Kansas. She married (1) DR. JACOB WATSON HUGHES, son of JACOB HUGHES and MARTHA MINNICK. He was born 11 Nov 1885 in Ottawa, Kansas. She married (2) WILLIAM W. MORRIS Abt. 1923. He was born Abt. 1900.

Child of NELLIE MILKS and WILLIAM MORRIS is:
2257. i. WILLIAM W.[10] MORRIS, b. 27 Jul 1924.

1284. MARY DENZEL[9] MILKS *(HARRY STREATOR[8], DAVID FRANKLIN[7], JOB[6] MILK, LEMUEL[5], JONATHAN[4], JOB[3], JOHN[2], JOHN[1])* was born 21 Jun 1905 in Parsons, Kansas, and died 27 May 1990 in Los Angeles, California. She married DELBERT EARL ELLIOTT 17 Oct 1923 in Topeka, Kansas, son of JAMES ELLIOTT and ELLA KING. He was born 19 Jul 1900 in Valencia, Kansas.

Children of MARY MILKS and DELBERT ELLIOTT are:
- i. GEORGE EARL[10] ELLIOTT, b. 14 Sep 1924, Topeka, Kansas; d. 21 Jul 1925, Topeka, Kansas.
- 2258. ii. LLOYD OTTO ELLIOTT, b. 03 Dec 1925, Topeka, Kansas.
- iii. EUNICE JOYCE ELLIOTT, b. 19 Apr 1927, Topeka, Kansas; m. JOHN RODNEY NEISWENDER, 18 Apr 1948, Topeka, Kansas; b. Abt. 1925.
- 2259. iv. PATRICAI LOUISE ELLIOTT, b. 04 Dec 1928, Topeka, Kansas.
- v. DELBERT GENE ELLIOTT, b. 23 Sep 1937, Topeka, Kansas.

1285. INEZ IRENE[9] MILKS *(HARRY STREATOR[8], DAVID FRANKLIN[7], JOB[6] MILK, LEMUEL[5], JONATHAN[4], JOB[3], JOHN[2], JOHN[1])* was born 01 Apr 1908 in Parsons, Kansas, and died 23 Mar 1936. She married EARL PICKERILL Abt. 1924, son of ADDISON PICKERILL and MARY WARD. He was born 26 Jul 1896 in Enid, Oklahoma.

Children of INEZ MILKS and EARL PICKERILL are:
- i. MAX EARL[10] PICKERILL, b. 26 Jun 1925, Parsons, Labette County, Kansas; m. DOLLY WINTERS, Jun 1948;

                    b. Abt. 1925.
2260.   ii.   DENZEL MAXINE PICKERILL, b. 17 Sep 1926, Parsons, Labette County, Kansas.
2261.   iii.   DONALD RAY PICKERILL, b. 23 Nov 1928, Parsons, Labette County, Kansas.
2262.   iv.   DELORES ANN PICKERILL, b. 26 Aug 1931, Parsons, Labette County, Kansas.
2263.   v.   JEANETTE ELLEN PICKERILL, b. 05 Oct 1932, Parsons, Labette County, Kansas.
2264.   vi.   GRACE LORRAINE PICKERILL, b. 01 Jan 1935, Parsons, Labette County, Kansas.

1286. HELEN BERTIE^9 MILKS *(HARRY STREATOR^8, DAVID FRANKLIN^7, JOB^6 MILK, LEMUEL^5, JONATHAN^4, JOB^3, JOHN^2, JOHN^1)* was born 19 Dec 1910 in Parsons, Kansas. She married KENNETH PEAK Abt. 1932, son of GEORGE PEAK and LURA GOOD. He was born 11 Dec 1909 in Parsons, Labette County, Kansas.

Child of HELEN MILKS and KENNETH PEAK is:
2265.   i.   BARBARA LOOU^{10} PEAK, b. 05 Jan 1934, Parsons, Labette County, Kansas.

1287. DORA ALEENE^9 MILKS *(HARRY STREATOR^8, DAVID FRANKLIN^7, JOB^6 MILK, LEMUEL^5, JONATHAN^4, JOB^3, JOHN^2, JOHN^1)* was born 09 Jun 1914 in Parsons, Kansas. She married (1) MARVIN SHAFER Abt. 1932, son of ROLL SHAFER and FLORA VALENTINE. He was born 1910 in Parsons, Labette County, Kansas. She married (2) BOYCE EDWARD PRICE 1941, son of JOHN PRICE and LILLIE KIDD. He was born 10 Jan 1910.

Child of DORA MILKS and MARVIN SHAFER is:
            i.   MARVIN WAYNE^{10} SHAFER, b. 15 Jun 1933, Parsons, Labette County, Kansas; m. DANNA DEANE, 1953; b. Abt. 1933.

1288. GLENN HOWARD^9 MILKS *(HARRY STREATOR^8, DAVID FRANKLIN^7, JOB^6 MILK, LEMUEL^5, JONATHAN^4, JOB^3, JOHN^2, JOHN^1)* was born 13 Aug 1916 in Parsons, Kansas, and died 08 Mar 1986 in Parsons, Labette County, Kansas. He married GENEVIEVE R. DEVINE. She was born 24 Jan 1921, and died 15 Jul 2000 in Parsons, Labette Co., KS.
   DEATH NOTICE:
   Milks, Genevieve, 79, retired J C Penney employee, died Saturday, July 15, 2000. Service 2 p.m. today, Carson-Wall Funeral Home.
   Survivors: son, Michael of Parsons; daughter, Diane Roberts of Harrison, Ark.; brothers, Bob Divine of Parsons, Bill Divine of Pittsburg; sisters, Thelma Shields, Fernita Heiskell, Patricia Cosby all of Parsons; four grandchildren. Memorial has been established with Operation Bright Touch.

Children of GLENN MILKS and GENEVIEVE DEVINE are:
2266.   i.   MICHAEL GLENN 'MIKE'^{10} MILKS, b. 25 Oct 1953, Kansas City, Missouri (Adopted?); d. 22 Feb 2004, Wichita, Kansas.
            ii.   DIANE LOUISE MILKS, b. 17 May 1951, Adopted?; d. Of Harrison, AR; m. AUSTIN ROBERTS; b. 01 Sep 1938.

1289. IDA GWENDOLE^9 MILKS *(DAVID HARTMAN^8, DAVID FRANKLIN^7, JOB^6 MILK, LEMUEL^5, JONATHAN^4, JOB^3, JOHN^2, JOHN^1)* was born 24 Oct 1915 in Parsons, Labette County, Kansas, and died Nov 1991 in Parsons, Labette County, Kansas. She married THOMAS L. CRAMER Abt. 1936. He was born 17 Jan 1917, and died 20 Apr 1997 in Parsons, Labette County, Kansas.

Children of IDA MILKS and THOMAS CRAMER are:
            i.   VERNA SUE^{10} CRAMER, b. 06 Jan 1937, Parsons, Labette County, Kansas; m. DAVID KARL CLAPSADDLE, 01 Jul 1955, Parsons, Labette County, Kansas; b. 09 Oct 1934.
            ii.   SON CRAMER, b. 07 Oct 1955, Parsons, Labette County, Kansas.

1290. DOROTHY LORRAINE^9 MILKS *(DAVID HARTMAN^8, DAVID FRANKLIN^7, JOB^6 MILK, LEMUEL^5, JONATHAN^4, JOB^3, JOHN^2, JOHN^1)* was born 25 Oct 1919 in Viborg, South Dakota, and died 15 Feb 2012 in Chanute, Neosho County, Kansas. She married LELAND ROY TROUT 04 Apr 1939 in Oswego, Kansas, son of EARL TROUT and ALICE TREADWELL. He was born 14 Nov 1913 in Labette County, Kansas, and died 11 Jul 1982 in Parsons, Labette County, Kansas.
   OBITUARY
   Dorothy L. Trout, 92, a former Galesburg and Parsons resident, died at 6:20 a.m. Wednesday, Feb. 15, 2012, at the

Heritage Healthcare Center in Chanute.

She was born on Oct. 25, 1919, Viborg, S.D., to David and Mary Ellen (Clary) Milks. She moved to Parsons at age 2, where the family lived east of Parsons and then moved to rural Galesburg when the Kansas Ordnance Plant was established. She attended Parsons High School.

She married Leland R. Trout on April 4, 1939, at Oswego. He preceded her in death on July 11, 1982.

She and her husband farmed for many years at rural Galesburg. She moved to Parsons a couple years after her husband's death.

She loved to garden, make birthday cakes and cards. She was active in SCOOP and TOPS in Parsons.

Survivors include two sons, Leland Duane Trout and his wife, Donna, and Donald Trout and his wife, Sharon, all of Chanute; two grandchildren, Darren Trout and his wife, Nancy, of Thayer and Angie Hess and her husband, Doug, of Lecompton; seven great-grandchildren, Cheyenne Trout, Dakota Trout, Madison Hess, Hunter Hess, Shelby Trout, Sydney Trout and Sabry Trout; a granddaughter-in-law, Wendy Trout of Chanute; and a sister, Betty Gearhiser of Parsons.

In addition to her husband she was preceded in death by an infant daughter, Margaret Louise "Peggy" Trout; two grandsons, Jeff Trout and Greg Trout; a brother, Ernest Milks; and a sister, Gwendola Cramer

The service will be at 10:30 a.m. Saturday at Carson-Wall Funeral Home. Burial will follow in Memorial Lawn Cemetery. The casket will remain closed at the service. Friends may call at the funeral home at their convenience.

Children of DOROTHY MILKS and LELAND TROUT are:
2267.   i.   LELAND DUANE[10] TROUT, b. 22 Feb 1940, Parsons, Labette County, Kansas.
       ii.   DONALD RAY TROUT, b. 04 May 1944, Parsons, Labette County, Kansas; m. SHARON K. _____; b. 09 Jul 1946.
       iii.   MARGARET LOUISE TROUT, b. 03 Dec 1947, Parsons, Labette County, Kansas; d. 03 Dec 1947, Parsons, Labette County, Kansas.

1291. ERNEST DAVID[9] MILKS *(DAVID HARTMAN[8], DAVID FRANKLIN[7], JOB[6] MILK, LEMUEL[5], JONATHAN[4], JOB[3], JOHN[2], JOHN[1])* was born 23 Oct 1923 in Parsons, Labette County, Kansas, and died 19 Apr 1990 in Labette County, Kansas. He married CARRIE LEE CHRISTINE Abt. 1942. She was born Abt. 1925, and died 02 Nov 1970 in Labette County, Kansas.

Children of ERNEST MILKS and CARRIE CHRISTINE are:
2268.   i.   DAVID LEE[10] MILKS, b. 02 Dec 1942, Parsons, Labette County, Kansas; d. 14 Mar 2012, ???.
       ii.   WARREN ANDREW MILKS, b. 25 Jul 1946, Parsons, Labette County, Kansas; m. BARBARA J. _____; b. 27 Mar 1951.
       iii.   PAUL LESLIE MILKS, b. 23 Oct 1947, Parsons, Labette County, Kansas; m. CARLITA JOLEEN _____; b. 1952.
       iv.   SYLVIA RAE MILKS, b. 27 Oct 1950, Parsons, Labette County, Kansas.
       v.   CAROL SUE MILKS, b. 21 Sep 1952, Parsons, Labette County, Kansas.

1292. BETTY JUNE[9] MILKS *(DAVID HARTMAN[8], DAVID FRANKLIN[7], JOB[6] MILK, LEMUEL[5], JONATHAN[4], JOB[3], JOHN[2], JOHN[1])* was born 17 Jun 1933 in Parsons, Labette County, Kansas. She married (1) MISTTER PARSONS. She married (2) JOHN RICHARD GEARHISER 26 Nov 1953 in Parsons, Labette County, Kansas. He was born Abt. 1933, and died 1991.

Children of BETTY MILKS and JOHN GEARHISER are:
       i.   DAVID LEON[10] GEARHISER, b. 21 Jan 1954, Wichita, Kansas; d. 2001.
       ii.   JUDY BETH GEARHISER, b. 28 Aug 1964, Parsons, Kansas; d. 19 Jun 2005, Tulsa, Oklahoma; m. (1) MISTTER FRAKER; m. (2) RICK MYERS, 1992; b. Abt. 1964.
             OBITUARY
             Judy Beth Gearhiser-Fraker, 40, of Parsons, died at 8:25 a.m., Sunday, June 19, 2005, at the Hillcrest Medical Center Burn Unit in Tulsa, Oklahoma, from injuries sustained in a house fire at her home on Saturday.
             She was born August 28, 1964, in Parsons, to Richard and Betty (Milks) Gearhiser. She attended Altamont Grade School and graduated from Labette County High School in 1982.
             She worked at the Kansas Army Ammunition Plant for a number of years. She then attended the Franklin Institute in Joplin, Missouri and received her Licensed Practical Nursing Degree.

Judy loved working with the elderly and caring for them and was currently employed at the Presbyterian Manor in Parsons as an LPN. She had a wonderful sense of humor and had a special way of making you laugh and feel good. She enjoyed swimming and water sports.

She married Rick Myers in 1992 and they later divorced.

SURVIVORS: Mother Betty (Milks) Gearhiser Parsons; Three Sisters June Cooper and her husband, Gary New Braunfels, Texas, Janet Gearhiser San Antonio, Texas, Jo Dixon and her husband, Ron Parsons

She was preceded in death by her father, Richard Gearhiser, in 1991, and a brother, David Gearhiser, in 2001.

Memorial Services will be held at 11:00 a.m., Saturday, June 25, 2005, at the Forbes-Hoffman Funeral Home, with Rev. Rodney Howell officiating. The body has been cremated. Friends may call at the home of Judy s mother at 3113 Chess, Parsons.

Memorials are suggested to the Safehouse for Women in Pittsburg. These may be left at or mailed to the Forbes-Hoffman Funeral Home, 405 Main, Parsons.

    iii.   JUNE GEARHISER, d. Of New Braunfels, Texas; m. GARY COOPER.
    iv.   JANET GEARHISER, d. Of San Antonio, Texas.
    v.   JO GEARHISER, m. RON PARSONS.

1293. LOIS ELLEN^9 MILKS *(SHERMAN GEORGE^8, DAVID FRANKLIN^7, JOB^6 MILK, LEMUEL^5, JONATHAN^4, JOB^3, JOHN^2, JOHN^1)* was born 21 Jan 1923 in Parsons, Kansas, and died 29 May 2004 in Labette County, Kansas. She married CLIFF DIEDIKER 10 Oct 1941 in Parsons, Kansas. He was born Abt. 1919.

OBITUARY
Published June 1, 2004 - Parsons, KS

Lois E. Diediker, 81, of rural Parsons, Kansas, died at her home at 5:32 p.m. Saturday, May 29, 2004. She had been in failing health for several months.

She was born Jan. 21, 1923, in Parsons, Kansas, to Sherman G. and Blanche E. (Ellis) Milks.

She grew up in Parsons and graduated from Parsons High School.

She married Cliff Diediker on Oct. 10, 1941, in Parsons, Kansas.

They moved to rural Parsons, where they farmed and raised livestock. He survives of the home.

She enjoyed bowling and had been a member of Parsons Women's Bowling Association for many years. She also enjoyed playing golf and had been active in the Ladies Golf Association at the Katy Golf Course for many years. She enjoyed fishing and being outdoors.

She was a member of the Church of the Brethren in Parsons.

Other survivors include one son, John Diediker of rural Parsons, KS; one daughter, Judy Vitt and husband, Jim, of rural Parsons, KS; one daughter-in-law, Carla Diediker of Joplin, MO; 10 grandchildren; 27 great-grandchildren; one great-great-granddaughter; one brother, Bob and wife, Lou, of Greenleaf, KS; and one sister, Nola Carter of Topeka, KS.

She was preceded in death by a son, Donald, in 1986; one sister; and one great great-granddaughter.

The service will be at Forbes-Hoffman Funeral Home with the Rev. Tom Smith officiating. Burial will be in Valley Cemetery near Parsons Lake, in Neosho County, Kansas.

Memorials may be made to Church of the Brethren or to American Cancer Society.

Children of LOIS MILKS and CLIFF DIEDIKER are:
    i.   JOHN^{10} DIEDIKER, b. Parsons, Kansas.
    ii.   JUDY DIEDIKER, b. Parsons, Kansas; m. JAMES VITT.
    iii.   DONALD DIEDIKER, b. Parsons, Kansas; d. 1986, Parsons, Kansas.

1294. ROBERT GLENN^9 MILKS *(SHERMAN GEORGE^8, DAVID FRANKLIN^7, JOB^6 MILK, LEMUEL^5, JONATHAN^4, JOB^3, JOHN^2, JOHN^1)* was born 21 Jan 1934 in Parsons, Kansas. He married MARY LOUISE. She was born Abt. 1942.

Child of ROBERT MILKS and MARY LOUISE is:
    i.   DENNIS GLENN^{10} MILKS, b. Abt. 1965; m. BECKY A. PENN; b. Abt. 1969.

1295. HAROLD LARKIN^9 SMITH *(GLADYS ANNA^8 MILKS, DAVID FRANKLIN^7, JOB^6 MILK, LEMUEL^5, JONATHAN^4, JOB^3, JOHN^2, JOHN^1)* was born 24 Feb 1908 in Parsons, Labette County, Kansas. He married VIOLA MAXWELL 23 Dec 1940. She was born Abt. 1908.

Children of HAROLD SMITH and VIOLA MAXWELL are:
- i. DUANE MARSHALL[10] SMITH, b. 17 Apr 1944, Kansas City, Missouri.
- ii. ERIC LYNN SMITH, b. 18 Jul 1949, Kansas City, Missouri.

1296. LUELLA EVELYN[9] MILKS *(ALVIN LUCIUS[8], DAVID FRANKLIN[7], JOB[6] MILK, LEMUEL[5], JONATHAN[4], JOB[3], JOHN[2], JOHN[1])* was born 30 Oct 1917 in Parsons, Labette County, Kansas, and died 19 Mar 1986 in Santa Barbara, California. She married (1) WILBUR PAPE Abt. 1934. He was born Abt. 1917. She married (2) W. E. GOLDEN Abt. 1946. He was born Abt. 1917. She married (3) MISTTER ERICKSON Aft. 1947.

Child of LUELLA MILKS and WILBUR PAPE is:
- i. REGINA ANNETTE[10] PAPE, b. 22 Aug 1935, Kansas City, Missouri.

Child of LUELLA MILKS and W. GOLDEN is:
- ii. ETHIE JACQUELINE[10] GOLDEN, b. 02 Nov 1947, Los Angeles, California.

1297. VIRGINIA ROSE[9] MILKS *(ALVIN LUCIUS[8], DAVID FRANKLIN[7], JOB[6] MILK, LEMUEL[5], JONATHAN[4], JOB[3], JOHN[2], JOHN[1])* was born 30 Sep 1919 in Parsons, Labette County, Kansas. She married PAUL OVERLY Abt. 1943. He was born Abt. 1919.

Child of VIRGINIA MILKS and PAUL OVERLY is:
- i. PATRICIA[10] OVERLY, b. 22 Jul 1944, Parsons, Labette County, Kansas.

1298. CLARENCE A.[9] MILCKS *(GEORGE THEODORE[8], HUMPHREY W.[7] MILKS, JOB[6] MILK, LEMUEL[5], JONATHAN[4], JOB[3], JOHN[2], JOHN[1])* was born 02 Mar 1906 in Minnesota, and died 28 Sep 1936 in Berwyn, Cook County, Illinois. He married MARY J. EPPERSON Abt. 1930 in Illinois, daughter of ARTHUR EPPERSON and MATTIE _____. She was born Abt. 1909 in Illinois.

Children of CLARENCE MILCKS and MARY EPPERSON are:
- i. CONRAD[10] MILCKS, b. Abt. 1931, Oak Park, Cook County, Illinois.
- ii. DAU MILCKS, b. 28 Oct 1933, West Lake Hospital, Melrose Park, Cook County, Illinois; d. 28 Oct 1933, West Lake Hospital, Melrose Park, Cook County, Illinois.

1299. DELBERT CHARLES[9] MILCKS *(GEORGE THEODORE[8], HUMPHREY W.[7] MILKS, JOB[6] MILK, LEMUEL[5], JONATHAN[4], JOB[3], JOHN[2], JOHN[1])* was born 28 Mar 1908 in N. McGregor, Clayton County, Iowa, and died 06 Jan 1989 in Hayward, Alameda County, California. He married DORIS COLLESEL. She was born 18 Jan 1913 in Illinois, and died 24 Jan 1997 in Hayward, Alameda County, California.

Children of DELBERT MILCKS and DORIS COLLESEL are:
- i. ALAN[10] DEL MILCKS, b. 24 Aug 1944, Maywood, Cook County, Illinois; d. 22 Aug 2010, Hayward, Alameda County, California.

  OBITUARY - Published in Inside Bay Area on August 25, 2010

  Alan Del Milcks, 65, of Castro Valley, California formerly of San Leandro, California, and of Maywood, Illinois, died on August 22, 2010, at his home.

  He was born in Maywood, Illinois, on August 24, 1944, to Delbert and Doris (Collesel) Milcks.

  He worked for many years for Bay Area Rapid Transit (BART) in the Treasury Department. Alan will be remembered for his generous spirit, his all-embracing thoughtfulness, and his good humor.

  His parents and his sister Gayle preceded him in death.

  He is survived by his aunt Lorraine; numerous cousins - among them Franklin Hider, John Scalet, Jean (Scalet) Kibler, Richard Collesel, Edward Collesel, Mary Lou (Collesel) Whiting, and Christopher Collesel; numerous second cousins; and his dear friends, Charles Moseley and Diane Ludwig.

  Private services will be held. Memorials in Alan's honor may be made to the American Cancer Society. Grissom's Chapel & Mortuary 510-278-2800 www.grissomsmortuary.com
- ii. GAYLE LYNN MILCKS, b. 11 Feb 1949, Illinois; d. 10 Nov 1958, Hayward, Alameda County, California.

1300. LORRAINE HARRIET[9] MILCKS *(GEORGE THEODORE[8], HUMPHREY W.[7] MILKS, JOB[6] MILK, LEMUEL[5], JONATHAN[4], JOB[3], JOHN[2], JOHN[1])* was born 28 Mar 1926 in Cook County. She married CLARENCE JOSEPH GENENBACHER, son of JOHN GENENBACHER and ANNA KLAUSER. He was born 28 Mar 1918, and died 27 Mar 1997 in Quincy, Adams County, Illinois.

Lorraine H Milcks: U.S., World War II Cadet Nursing Corps; Educational Institution: St Mary's Hospital Training School for Nurses, Quincy, Illinois.

CLARENCE JOSEPH GENENBACHER: U.S. Veterans Gravesites: Calvary Cemetery, 1730 North 18th Street Quincy, IL 62301; Service Info.: TEC 4 US ARMY WORLD WAR II

Children of LORRAINE MILCKS and CLARENCE GENENBACHER are:
- i. STANLEY DALE[10] GENENBACHER, b. 11 Apr 1948, Quincy, Adams County, Illinois; d. 15 Apr 1948, Quincy, Adams County, Illinois.
- ii. DIANNE MARIE GENENBACHER.
- iii. DELVAN ROBERT GENENBACHER, b. 04 Jan 1951, Quincy, Adams County, Illinois; d. 20 Jun 1962, Quincy, Adams County, Illinois.
- iv. CHARLES JOSEPH GENENBACHER.
- v. VICTORIA LEE GENENBACHER.
- 2269. vi. STEVEN DALE GENENBACHER, b. 03 Jul 1957, Quincy, Adams County, Illinois.
- vii. THERESA LYNN GENENBACHER.

1301. KATHERINE[9] UTTER *(ANNA H.[8] MILKS, JAMES HARTMAN[7], JOB[6] MILK, LEMUEL[5], JONATHAN[4], JOB[3], JOHN[2], JOHN[1])* was born 07 Jul 1912 in Iroquois, South Dakota. She married GLEN SELMER LEE 1930 in Huron, South Dakota, son of GUS LEE and JULIA FORN. He was born 17 Sep 1907 in Colman, South Dakota.

Children of KATHERINE UTTER and GLEN LEE are:
- i. ROBERT GLEN[10] LEE, b. 17 Dec 1931, Huron, Beadle County, South Dakota.
- 2270. ii. JOHN LAWRENCE LEE, b. 27 Mar 1934, Huron, Beadle County, South Dakota.
- iii. JULIA ANN LEE, b. 24 Dec 1938, Huron, Beadle County, South Dakota.
- iv. MABEL MAY LEE, d. d.y..

1302. FLORENCE 'FLOSSIE' LUCILLE[9] MILKS *(FRANK[8], JAMES HARTMAN[7], JOB[6] MILK, LEMUEL[5], JONATHAN[4], JOB[3], JOHN[2], JOHN[1])* was born 27 Dec 1911 in Scranton, North Dakota, and died 03 Dec 1988 in Yamhill County, Oregon. She married (1) ALFRED IRA OPHEIM 15 May 1934 in Sturgis, Meade County, South Dakota, son of SAM OPHEIM and EZIBEL _____. He was born 01 Jan 1908 in North Dakota, and died 29 Jan 1989 in Carlton, Yamhill County, Oregon. She married (2) JAMES HAMMOND Aft. 1940. He was born Abt. 1910.

Children of FLORENCE MILKS and ALFRED OPHEIM are:
- i. LESLIE[10] OPHEIM, b. 1935, North Dakota.
- ii. BEVERLY OPHEIM, b. Abt. Sep 1939, North Dakota.

1303. JAMES WILLIAM[9] MILKS *(FRANK[8], JAMES HARTMAN[7], JOB[6] MILK, LEMUEL[5], JONATHAN[4], JOB[3], JOHN[2], JOHN[1])* was born 02 Feb 1913 in Haley, North Dakota, and died 14 Oct 2005 in McMinnville, Yamhill County, Oregon. He married CLARA M. STRUVER 14 Oct 1936 in Huron, South Dakota. She was born 18 May 1918 in Zell, South Dakota, and died 13 Jul 2000 in McMinnville, Yamhill County, Oregon.

OBITUARY

Published: October 18, 2005

Services for James W. Milks of McMinnville will be held at 11 a.m. Wednesday, Oct. 19, in the chapel of Macy & Son Funeral Directors. The Rev. Steve Ross will officiate.

Visitation is set for 4 to 7 p.m. today, Oct. 18, in the chapel. Private family interment is planned in Evergreen Memorial Park.

Mr. Milks died Friday, Oct. 14, 2005, at Alterra Villas in McMinnville. He was 92.

Born Feb. 2, 1913, in Haley, N.D., he was the son of James and Ruth (Tarr) Milks. He moved to Huron, S.D., at the age of 17. After high school, he enlisted in the Civilian Conservation Corps at Camp Crook in Pierre, S.D.

He married Clara M. Struver on Oct. 14, 1936, in Huron. He farmed South Dakota until 1956, when he moved to Oregon. He worked at the newsprint mill in Newberg until his retirement in 1975.

He enjoyed square dancing, ballroom dancing and outdoor activities. He also enjoyed woodcrafting, cardplaying, bowling and watching baseball and boxing.

His family said he was a wonderful husband, father and grandfather who loved to tell jokes and make people smile.

Survivors include two sons, Donald J. Milks of McMinnville and Douglas L. Milks of Buckeye, Ark.; three daughters, Sharon K. Yates and Rosita F. Seibel, both of McMinnville, and Doris J. Berkey of Rickreall; a brother, Duane Milks of Prineville; two sisters, Mildred Kandel of Portland and Gladys Besco of Austin, Minn.; 11 grandchildren, 19 great-grandchildren and one great-grandchild. He was preceded in death by his wife in 2001 and by four brothers and four sisters.

Memorial contributions may be made to the Legacy VNA Hospice, care of Macy & Son Funeral Directors, 135 N.E. Evans St., McMinnville, OR 97128.

OBITUARY

McMINNVILLE — *Clara Milks, 82, died Thursday at home.*

Born in Zell, S.D., she moved to Pierre, S.D., when she was 16. She later lived in the Huron area for 16 years, and in 1956 settled in McMinnville.

She was a cook for the McMinnville School District for many years, and was a member of the United Methodist Church. She enjoyed dancing, hiking, swimming, sewing and crafts.

She was preceded in death by five sisters and four brothers.

Survivors include her husband, James, whom she married in 1936; daughters, Doris Berkey of Rickreall, Rosita Seibel and Sharon Yates, both of McMinnville; sons, Donald of McMinnville and Douglas of Salem; 11 grandchildren; and 16 great-grandchildren.

Visiting will be noon to 6 p.m. Sunday and noon to 7 p.m. Monday at Macy & Son Funeral Directors. Services are 10:30 a.m. Tuesday at the mortuary. Interment will be at Evergreen Memorial Park Cemetery.

Contributions: Rock of Ages, care of the mortuary.

Children of JAMES MILKS and CLARA STRUVER are:

2271.   i.   DONALD J.^{10} MILKS, b. 03 Jun 1937, South Dakota.
2272.   ii.   DOUGLAS L. MILKS, b. 20 Dec 1938, South Dakota.
2273.   iii.   DORIS J. MILKS, b. 25 Apr 1947, Oregon.
2274.   iv.   SHARON K. MILKS, b. 05 Jan 1949, Oregon.
         v.   ROSITA F. MILKS, b. 25 Oct 1954; m. EDWARD SEIBEL; b. 1950. Manager First Federal Savings & Loan Newberg, OR 97132-2812

1304. ATOLA OLIVE 'DONNA'^{9} MILKS *(FRANK^8, JAMES HARTMAN^7, JOB^6 MILK, LEMUEL^5, JONATHAN^4, JOB^3, JOHN^2, JOHN^1)* was born 03 Dec 1914 in Scranton, North Dakota, and died 16 May 2005 in Austin, Mower County, Minnesota. She married DUDLEY NORMAN ROSENTHAL, son of PETER ROSENTHAL and MILLIE WIGGINS. He was born 07 Jan 1906 in Owatonna, Steele County, Minnesota, and died 25 Jan 1942 in Austin, Mower County, Minnesota.

OBITUARY-

Atola O. "Donna" Rosenthal, age 90, of Austin, died Monday, May 16, 2005, at the Austin Medical Center.
Donna was born Dec. 3, 1914, on a farm near Scranton, N.D., to Frank and Bessie (Tarr) Milks. She was the fourth oldest of 12 children and attended rural schools. Donna moved to Austin in 1936 and was employed by the George A. Hormel Company. She soon met and married Dudley Rosenthal. Years later she went to work at the Austin Medical Center in the housekeeping department, retiring in 1980. She was residing at Sacred Heart Care Center at the time of her death.

Donna was a quiet and private person who enjoyed homemaking, cooking, baking, long phone conversations, needle work and spending time with her children and grandchildren.

Survivors include a son, Darrell (Lorraine) Rosenthal, Austin, Minn.; daughters: Marlene (Gene) Seavey, Austin, Minn.; Bonnie (Frank) Karnes, Austin, Minn.; 13 grandchildren; 30 great grandchildren; sisters: Gladys (Ray) Besco, Austin, Minn.; Mildred Krandell, Portland, Ore.; brothers: James Milks, Portland, Ore.; Duane (Esther) Milks, Portland, Ore.; sister-in-law, Bessie May Rosenthal, Austin, Minn.; many nieces and nephews.

She is preceded in death by her parents; husband, Dudley Rosenthal; brothers-in-law: Harland and Lloyd Rosenthal; sisters-in-law: Clarice Stedman, Cleo Erwin, Maude Windorf; brothers: Donald, Johnny, Clifford and Clayton Milks; sisters: Hazel Goe, Margaret Ryan and Florence Hammond; grandson, Stephen Walker; great grandsons: Rob Walker Jr., Andrew Karnes, James Anderson and Tylor Anderson.

A funeral mass will be celebrated 10:30 a.m. on Thursday, May 19, 2005, at the Church of St. Augustine with Father John Traufler officiating. There will be a 4 p.m. CCW rosary on Wednesday at Mayer Funeral Home where friends may call from 4-6 p.m. and also from 9-10 a.m. on Thursday. Interment will be in Enterprise Cemetery.

The casket bearers will be David Rosenthal, Thomas Rosenthal, Frank Karnes Jr., Mike Karnes, Matt Karnes, and Robert Walker.

Burial: Rose Creek Enterprise Cemetery, Varco, Mower County, Minnesota, USA

Children of ATOLA MILKS and DUDLEY ROSENTHAL are:
- i. DARRELL DEAN[10] ROSENTHAL, b. 28 May 1938, Austin, Minnesota; d. 16 Apr 2010, Austin, Minnesota; m. LORRAINE _____; b. Abt. 1940.
- 2275. ii. MARLENE K. ROSENTHAL, b. 1943, White Pages shows age as 68 (Jan 2012); d. Marriage to Ellis Walker says she was 16 yrs old.
- 2276. iii. BONNIE SHARON ROSENTHAL, b. 1946, White Pages shows age as 65 (Jan 2012).

1305. MARGARET NEOMA[9] MILKS *(FRANK[8], JAMES HARTMAN[7], JOB[6] MILK, LEMUEL[5], JONATHAN[4], JOB[3], JOHN[2], JOHN[1])* was born 08 Mar 1916 in Scranton, North Dakota, and died 19 Mar 1997 in Las Vegas, Nevada. She married (1) THURLO RYAN Abt. 1935. He was born Abt. 1915. She married (2) UNKNOWN ARNOLDT Aft. 1936.

Child of MARGARET MILKS and THURLO RYAN is:
- i. LEROY THOMAS[10] RYAN, b. 21 Jun 1936, Iowa; d. 23 Jun 1991, Los Angeles, California.

1306. DONALD LESTER[9] MILKS, SR. *(FRANK[8], JAMES HARTMAN[7], JOB[6] MILK, LEMUEL[5], JONATHAN[4], JOB[3], JOHN[2], JOHN[1])* was born 11 Jun 1930 in Scranton, North Dakota, and died 26 Sep 1972 in Mower County, Minnesota. He married RUTH ELLEN MILLER Abt. 1958 in Mower County, Minnesota, daughter of LOU MILLER and AGNES NOBLE. She was born 25 Aug 1937 in Mower County, Minnesota.

Children of DONALD MILKS and RUTH MILLER are:
- 2277. i. DONALD LESTER[10] MILKS, JR., b. 16 Jan 1959, Mower County, Minnesota; d. 10 Apr 2011, Austin, Mower County, Minnesota.
- ii. BRENDA LOU RUTH MILKS, b. 29 Nov 1960, Mower County, Minnesota.
- iii. RONALD FRANK MILKS, b. 07 Apr 1962, Mower County, Minnesota; m. PATRICIA ANN HAMILTON, 08 Oct 1994, Mower County, Minnesota; b. Abt. 1962.
- iv. BRYAN LOU MILKS, b. 03 Dec 1963, Mower County, Minnesota; m. (1) PATRICIA ANN TATE, 28 Sep 1982, Wabasha County, Minnesota; b. Abt. 1963; m. (2) SHERYL ANN HANSON, 10 Feb 1987, Winona County, Minnesota; b. Abt. 1963.

1307. DUANE LEROY[9] MILKS *(FRANK[8], JAMES HARTMAN[7], JOB[6] MILK, LEMUEL[5], JONATHAN[4], JOB[3], JOHN[2], JOHN[1])* was born 23 Mar 1933 in Scranton, North Dakota, and died 10 Dec 2007 in Union Gap, Washington. He married (1) ALICE MAE ETHERINGTON Abt. 1953, daughter of FRANK and RUTH ETHERINGTON. She was born Abt. 1936 in North Dakota. He married (2) HESTER MAY PETITT Abt. 2966. She was born 1945 in Rapid City, South Dakota, and died 29 Jul 2008 in Yakima, Washington.

OBITUARY

Duane LeRoy Milks, 74, of Yakima died Monday in Union Gap.

Mr. Milks was born in North Dakota.

Survivors include his wife, Hester Milks of Union Gap; two sons, David Milks of Union Gap and Johnny Milks of Las Vegas, Nev.; five daughters, Iona Milks of Las Vegas, Elizabeth Montgomery of Redmond, Ore., Sharlene Tarula of Toppenish, Gloria Pina and Carolyn Milks of Yakima; two sisters, Mildred Kindle of Portland and Gladys Besico of Austin, Minn.; 17 grandchildren and five great-grandchildren.

Visitation will be from 10 a.m. to 5 p.m. Thursday and from 9 a.m. to 2 p.m. Friday at Valley Hills Funeral Home, Yakima. The funeral will be at 2 p.m. Friday at the Yakima Chapel of Valley Hills Funeral Home. Burial will follow in Tahoma Cemetery.

Valley Hills Funeral Home and Crematory, Yakima, is in charge of arrangements.

OBITUARY

Hester May Milks, 63, of Yakima died Thursday at Yakima Valley Memorial Hospital.

Mrs. Milks was born in Rapid City, S.D. She worked as a waitress in Kah-Nee-Ta, in nursing homes as an a NAC in a Portland hospital.

Survivors include a son, David Milks of Yakima; three daughters, Sharlene Tarula of Toppenish, Gloria Pena of Indiana and Carolyn Milks of Yakima; three stepchildren, Elizabeth Montgomery of Redmond, Ore., Johnny Milks and Iona Milks, both of Las Vegas; 12 siblings, Chris Petitt of Kingsville, Mo., Henry Petitt of Nevada, Mo., Rosy Thomas of Rochester, N.Y., Edith Zibriskie of Shorthills, N.J., Shirley Sneed of Longview, Texas, Larry Petitt and Toni Kidd of Nezland, S.D., Edward Petitt of Grand Junction, Colo., Sharon Henderson of Nevada, Mo., Sheila Berry of Tobyhanna, Pa., Patt Petitt of Spearfish, S.D. and Barbie Sweet of Rhinelander, Wis.; 22 grandchildren.

Viewing will be today from 1-6 p.m. and Wednesday from 9 a.m. to noon at the Yakima Chapel of Valley Hills Funeral Home. Graveside funeral service will be at 2 p.m. Wednesday at Tahoma Cemetery.

Valley Hills Funeral Home and Crematory is in charge of the arrangements.

Children of DUANE MILKS and HESTER PETITT are:
- i. DAVID[10] MILKS, b. Abt. 1970, Of Union Gap, Washington; d. *.
- 2278. ii. SHARLENE S. MILKS, b. 24 May 1967, Of Toppenish, Washington; d. *.
- iii. CAROLYN M MILKS, b. 11 Jan 1970, Prineville, Oregon; d. *.
- iv. GLORIA E. MILKS, b. Abt. 1972, Of Yakima, Washington; d. *; m. MISTTER PINA.

Children of DUANE MILKS and ALICE ETHERINGTON are:
- v. JOHNNY LEE[10] MILKS, b. 28 Dec 1953, Freeborn County, Minnesota.
- vi. ELIZABETH MILKS, b. Of Redmond, Oregon; m. MISTTER MONTGOMERY.
- vii. IONA MILKS, b. Of Las Vegas, Nevada.

1308. MARY KATHLEEN[9] MILKS *(ANDREW HARTMAN[8], JAMES HARTMAN[7], JOB[6] MILK, LEMUEL[5], JONATHAN[4], JOB[3], JOHN[2], JOHN[1])* was born 03 Jul 1923 in Dubuque, Iowa. She married WILLIAM JUNGBLUT 30 Sep 1950. He was born Abt. 1923.

Child of MARY MILKS and WILLIAM JUNGBLUT is:
- i. SUSAN MARY[10] JUNGBLUT, b. 10 Jul 1951.

1309. WILLIAM PATRICK[9] MILKS *(ANDREW HARTMAN[8], JAMES HARTMAN[7], JOB[6] MILK, LEMUEL[5], JONATHAN[4], JOB[3], JOHN[2], JOHN[1])* was born 17 Mar 1932 in Dubuque, Iowa, and died 13 Mar 1996 in Merriam, Kansas.

Children of WILLIAM PATRICK MILKS are:
- i. MICHAEL P.[10] MILKS, b. 1961; m. DEBORAH K. _____; b. 1961.
- ii. PATRICK J. MILKS, b. 1963.

1310. JOHN JOSEPH[9] MILKS *(ANDREW HARTMAN[8], JAMES HARTMAN[7], JOB[6] MILK, LEMUEL[5], JONATHAN[4], JOB[3], JOHN[2], JOHN[1])* was born 19 Jan 1934 in Dubuque, Iowa.

Child of JOHN JOSEPH MILKS is:
- i. JOHN KEVIN[10] MILKS, b. Abt. 1955.

1311. JOHN DALLAS[9] MILKS *(WILLIAM JOB[8], JAMES HARTMAN[7], JOB[6] MILK, LEMUEL[5], JONATHAN[4], JOB[3], JOHN[2], JOHN[1])* was born 20 Dec 1915 in Kingsbury, So. Dakota, and died 03 Sep 1966 in San Francisco, California. He married OROL EVELYN (JOHNSON) HOLT Abt. 1941, daughter of CLIFTON JOHNSON and ANN BLOMQUIST. She was born Bet. 1916 - 1917.

Children of JOHN MILKS and OROL HOLT are:
- 2279. i. WILLIAM CLIFTON[10] MILKS, b. 14 Jan 1942.
- 2280. ii. JOHN FRANCIS 'JACK' MILKS, b. 17 Oct 1943.
- iii. ROBERT JAMES MILKS, b. 08 Mar 1945; d. 19 Feb 1998, Norwalk, Los Angeles, California.
- 2281. iv. THOMAS PATRICK MILKS, b. 21 Dec 1946.
- 2282. v. DONALD JOSEPH MILKS, b. 15 Jul 1954, Whittier, Orange County, California; d. 12 Jun 2011, Valley Center, California.

1312. MARY ELIZABETH[9] MILKS *(WILLIAM JOB[8], JAMES HARTMAN[7], JOB[6] MILK, LEMUEL[5], JONATHAN[4], JOB[3], JOHN[2], JOHN[1])* was born 01 Mar 1918 in Kingsbury, So. Dakota. She married CARL CLEMA. He was born Abt. 1918.

Children of MARY MILKS and CARL CLEMA are:
    i. RICHARD DALLAS[10] CLEMA, b. 13 Nov 1938.
    ii. WILLIAM JAMES CLEMA, b. 15 Dec 1941.

1313. RICHARD JEROME[9] MILKS *(WILLIAM JOB[8], JAMES HARTMAN[7], JOB[6] MILK, LEMUEL[5], JONATHAN[4], JOB[3], JOHN[2], JOHN[1])* was born 12 Jul 1920 in Kingsbury, So. Dakota. He married MARCELLA KHURT. She was born Abt. 1920.

Children of RICHARD MILKS and MARCELLA KHURT are:
    i. RICHELLE DIANE[10] MILKS, b. 21 Aug 1943.
    ii. DARCY LYNN MILKS, b. 13 Dec 1950.

1314. DOROTHY MAXINE[9] MILKS *(WILLIAM JOB[8], JAMES HARTMAN[7], JOB[6] MILK, LEMUEL[5], JONATHAN[4], JOB[3], JOHN[2], JOHN[1])* was born 21 Aug 1922 in Kingsbury, So. Dakota. She married INGRID HILLESTAD. He was born Abt. 1920.

Children of DOROTHY MILKS and INGRID HILLESTAD are:
    i. SHIRLEY JEAN[10] HILLESTAD, b. 10 Aug 1941.
    ii. RODGER LEE HILLESTAD, b. 14 Oct 1942.
    iii. KAYLEEN MAY HILLESTAD, b. 22 Jul 1949.

1315. BEVERLY ROSE THERESE[9] MILKS *(WILLIAM JOB[8], JAMES HARTMAN[7], JOB[6] MILK, LEMUEL[5], JONATHAN[4], JOB[3], JOHN[2], JOHN[1])* was born 05 Nov 1932. She married THOMAS JOHN MEIGHEN 23 Feb 1952, son of THOMAS MEIGHEN and MARGARET GALLAGHER. He was born 02 Dec 1930 in Glendale, California.

Children of BEVERLY MILKS and THOMAS MEIGHEN are:
    i. DEBRA ANN[10] MEIGHEN, b. 28 Aug 1955, California; d. 26 Mar 1982, Los Angeles, California; m. ROBERT M. THURSTON; b. Abt. 1955.
    ii. THOMAS JOHN MEIGHEN, b. 21 Sep 1957, Los Angeles, California.

1316. KENNETH L.[9] SIDWAY *(WILLIAM HENRY[8], JONATHAN[7], JONATHAN[6], REBECCA[5] MILK, JONATHAN[4], JOB[3], JOHN[2], JOHN[1])* was born 09 Sep 1891 in Batavia, New York. He married HAZEL _____ 1920 in New York. She was born 1897 in New York.

Children of KENNETH SIDWAY and HAZEL _____ are:
    i. WINIFRED GRANT[10] SIDWAY, b. Bet. 1921 - 1922, New York; d. 2005.
    ii. GARDNER HUGHSON SIDWAY, b. 30 Sep 1926, New York; d. 05 Jan 1991, Palm Beach County, Florida.

1317. DOROTHY[9] SIDWAY *(WILLIAM HENRY[8], JONATHAN[7], JONATHAN[6], REBECCA[5] MILK, JONATHAN[4], JOB[3], JOHN[2], JOHN[1])* was born Oct 1896 in New York City. She married NOT NAMED Abt. 1923 in New York. He was born Abt. 1896.

Child of DOROTHY SIDWAY and NOT NAMED is:
    i. WALLACE[10] SIDWAY, b. 26 May 1924, New York, NY.

1318. JAMES[9] SIDWAY *(HAROLD SPAULDING[8], FRANKLIN[7], JONATHAN[6], REBECCA[5] MILK, JONATHAN[4], JOB[3], JOHN[2], JOHN[1])* was born 29 Dec 1898 in Pittsfield, Berkshire County, Massachusetts. He married JANE _____ 1925. She was born 1904 in Buffalo, Erie County, New York.

Children of JAMES SIDWAY and JANE _____ are:
    i. MARY JANE[10] SIDWAY, b. 1926, Utica, New York.
2283.   ii. PETER SIDWAY, b. 21 Sep 1929, Cleveland, Cuyahoga County, Ohio; d. 13 Feb 2011, Exmore, Northampton County, Virginia.

1319. FRANKLIN[9] SIDWAY *(HAROLD SPAULDING[8], FRANKLIN[7], JONATHAN[6], REBECCA[5] MILK, JONATHAN[4], JOB[3], JOHN[2], JOHN[1])* was born 23 May 1900 in Pittsfield, Berkshire County, Massachusetts. He married FRANCES M. _____. She was born Abt. 1900 in New York.

Children of FRANKLIN SIDWAY and FRANCES _____ are:
      i. FRANKLIN ST. JOHN[10] SIDWAY, b. Bet. 1921 - 1922, Syracuse, Onondaga County, New York.
      ii. F. MIRIANA SIDWAY, b. Bet. 1922 - 1923, Syracuse, Onondaga County, New York.

1320. MARGARET ST. JOHN[9] SIDWAY *(FRANK ST. JOHN[8], FRANKLIN[7], JONATHAN[6], REBECCA[5] MILK, JONATHAN[4], JOB[3], JOHN[2], JOHN[1])* was born 16 May 1907 in Buffalo, Erie County, New York. She married JAMES KENT AVERILL. He was born 15 Oct 1904, and died 26 Mar 1944.

Child of MARGARET SIDWAY and JAMES AVERILL is:
      i. JAMES KENT[10] AVERILL, JR., b. 31 Dec 1935.

1321. MARTHA ROBERTS[9] SIDWAY *(FRANK ST. JOHN[8], FRANKLIN[7], JONATHAN[6], REBECCA[5] MILK, JONATHAN[4], JOB[3], JOHN[2], JOHN[1])* was born 01 Oct 1908 in Buffalo, Erie County, New York, and died 24 Feb 1999 in Buffalo, Erie County, New York. She married ROGER KEATING ADAMS. He was born 19 Jul 1905.

Child of MARTHA SIDWAY and ROGER ADAMS is:
      i. JANET AMELIA[10] ADAMS, b. 06 Jul 1947.

1322. EDITH[9] SIDWAY *(FRANK ST. JOHN[8], FRANKLIN[7], JONATHAN[6], REBECCA[5] MILK, JONATHAN[4], JOB[3], JOHN[2], JOHN[1])* was born 22 Feb 1913 in Buffalo, Erie County, New York. She married STEVAN I. STEVENS. He was born 14 Feb 1900.

Children of EDITH SIDWAY and STEVAN STEVENS are:
      i. STEFANIE[10] STEVENS, b. 26 May 1937.
      ii. GABRIELLE STEVENS, b. 06 Sep 1938.

1323. WILLIAM EDWARD[9] MILKS *(WILLIAM ALONZO[8], CHARLES[7], DAVID[6] MILK, GEORGE[5], JONATHAN[4], JOB[3], JOHN[2], JOHN[1])* was born 10 Aug 1874 in East Eden, Erie County, New York, and died 29 May 1950 in Buffalo, Erie County, New York. He married MAMIE TIBBITS, daughter of WILLIAM TIBBITS. She was born 1889 in New York, and died 11 Dec 1957 in Buffalo, Erie County, New York.

Children of WILLIAM MILKS and MAMIE TIBBITS are:
      i. EDGAR A.[10] MILKS, b. Abt. 1913, Montana; d. No further data found..
          It is assumed, by the author, that Edgar died between 1930 and 1940 as no further records of any type have been found for him.
      ii. MARGURITE MARY MILKS, b. 08 Jan 1915, Snohomish County, Washington; d. No further data found.; m. ARTHUR THIMM.
2284. iii. WINIFRED L. MILKS, b. 13 Sep 1921, Los Angeles, California; d. 07 Dec 1999, Buffalo, Erie County, New York.
      iv. SHIRLEY MILKS, b. Abt. 1934, New York; d. No further data found..

1324. CHARLES ALBERT[9] MILKS *(WILLIAM ALONZO[8], CHARLES[7], DAVID[6] MILK, GEORGE[5], JONATHAN[4], JOB[3], JOHN[2], JOHN[1])* was born 20 Oct 1875 in East Eden, Erie County, New York, and died 13 Mar 1943 in Buffalo, Erie County, New York. He married EDNA MAY (FINAN?) BOWDEN Abt. 1903, daughter of ELIZABETH BOWDEN. She was born 13 Jun 1887 in Toronto, Canada?/New York, and died 03 Aug 1948 in Buffalo, Erie County, New York.

    It is certain that Edna was not born to Elizabeth Bowden. In the 1900 census she is described as a "Ward" of Elizabeth. Also in the 1900 & the 1910 census records, Elizabeth says that she had only
1 child, and that was Hazel, b. July 1895. Also in the 1910 census, Hazel is described as an adopted sister to Edna.
    One researcher, Elaine Culling?, believes she was born a Finan in Canada, but has no proof of that yet. There is some possible support for that name, since Edna's second child, Earl was given the middle name of Finan. However, the 1891 Canada census does not show any Edna or May Finan.
    Edna met Ernest Lee, because Ernest was married to Charles's sister, Julia M. Milks, who died in Buffalo in 1920.

Edna and Charles divorced in the early 1920s and Edna married Ernest. They moved to Detroit, Michigan and had two children there. It is believed, however, that Edna is buried in the same cemetery as Charles Milks. Hopefully we will get confirmation from the Cemetery office, and a photo confirmation of the headstone.

Children of CHARLES MILKS and EDNA BOWDEN are:
- 2285. i. HORACE WAYNE[10] MILKS, b. 13 Jun 1904, Hamburg, Erie County, New York; d. 09 May 1979, Saint Augustine, Saint Johns, FL.
- 2286. ii. EARL FINAN MILKS, b. 09 Jan 1907, Hamburg, Erie County, New York; d. Dec 1967, Buffalo, Erie County, New York.
- 2287. iii. FRANCES ELIZABETH MILKS, b. 21 Dec 1910, Hamburg, Erie County, New York.
- 2288. iv. ELEANOR MAY MILKS, b. 10 May 1914, Hamburg, Erie County, New York; d. 05 Feb 1997, Tonawanda, Erie County, New York.
- v. LORRAINE EDNA MILKS, b. 19 Dec 1916, Buffalo, Erie County, New York; d. 03 Jan 2007, Ocala, Marion County, Florida; m. DONALD LEE KOHN; b. 02 Feb 1923, New York; d. 03 Jan 2007, Ocala, Marion County, Florida.

1325. EMMA[9] MILKS *(WILLIAM ALONZO[8], CHARLES[7], DAVID[6] MILK, GEORGE[5], JONATHAN[4], JOB[3], JOHN[2], JOHN[1])* was born 1877 in East Eden, NY, and died 1916. She married JOHN NEWMAN. He was born Abt. 1877.

Children of EMMA MILKS and JOHN NEWMAN are:
- i. BERNICE[10] NEWMAN, m. EDWARD DUCHMAN; b. of Hamburg, NY.
- 2289. ii. DOROTHY NEWMAN, b. 07 Dec 1911, New York; d. 15 Feb 1993, Erie County, New York.

1326. JULIA M.[9] MILKS *(WILLIAM ALONZO[8], CHARLES[7], DAVID[6] MILK, GEORGE[5], JONATHAN[4], JOB[3], JOHN[2], JOHN[1])* was born Aug 1880 in East Eden, NY, and died 1920 in Buffalo, Erie County, New York. She married ERNEST DEAN LEE 1906, son of GEORGE LEE and JANNIE STANLEY. He was born 15 Apr 1878 in Paducah, KY, and died 24 Aug 1963 in Detroit, Wayne County, Michigan.

Julia M. Milks was a sister to Charles Albert Milks (husband of Edna Bowden).

Children of JULIA MILKS and ERNEST LEE are:
- i. STANLEY[10] LEE, b. Mar 1910, Buffalo, Erie County, New York.
  Stanley was a 'delivery boy' for a retail grocery store, living in Hamburg, NY in 1940.
- ii. IRVING LEE, b. 1912, Buffalo, Erie County, New York.
  Irving was a steel worker, living in Hamburg, NY in 1940.

1327. GEORGE J.[9] MILKS *(WILLIAM ALONZO[8], CHARLES[7], DAVID[6] MILK, GEORGE[5], JONATHAN[4], JOB[3], JOHN[2], JOHN[1])* was born 13 Mar 1882 in East Eden, New York, and died 1960 in Erie County, New York. He married DELIA SCHMITZ, daughter of NICKLAS SCHMITZ and MARGARET KOHNNA. She was born 28 Feb 1883 in Collins, New York, and died 1958 in Erie County, New York.

Children of GEORGE MILKS and DELIA SCHMITZ are:
- i. MILDRED A.[10] MILKS, b. 03 Sep 1910, Concord, New York; d. 12 Dec 2001, Springville, Erie County, New York; m. RODNEY F. NELSON, 24 Jan 1934; b. 01 May 1908, New York; d. Dec 1984, Springville, Erie County, New York.
- 2290. ii. HAROLD F. MILKS, b. 22 Apr 1913, Concord, New York; d. 11 May 2003, East Aurora, Erie County, New York.
- 2291. iii. IRMA E. MILKS, b. 30 Dec 1915, Concord, New York; d. 09 Dec 1997, Buffalo, Erie County, New York.
- 2292. iv. WILMA R. MILKS, b. 09 Mar 1918, Concord, New York; d. 1983, Concord, Erie County, New York.
- 2293. v. MARIE L. MILKS, b. 14 Mar 1920, Concord, New York; d. 26 Jan 1996.
- vi. MARJORIE A. MILKS, b. 20 Jun 1923, Concord, New York; d. 2005, Erie County, New York (never married).
- 2294. vii. GEORGE R. MILKS, b. 18 Jan 1926, Concord, New York; d. 05 Apr 2012, Morton's Corners, Erie County, New York.

1328. EDGAR H.[9] MILKS *(WILLIAM ALONZO[8], CHARLES[7], DAVID[6] MILK, GEORGE[5], JONATHAN[4], JOB[3], JOHN[2], JOHN[1])* was born 19 Feb 1889 in East Eden, NY, and died Jun 1973. He married VIOLET (ANDRES) CARR 26 Aug 1931 in Buffalo, New York, daughter of GEORGE ANDRES and MINNIE NORTON. She was born 01 Aug 1894 in Buffalo, Erie County, New York.

Edgar owned and operated a retail grocery store in Hamburg, New York. His nephew, Stanley Lee, worked for him, at least, from 1930 to 1940 as a clerk and delivery man.

When Edgar married Violet in 1931, her two sons, Russell and Robert, from her first marriage to Thomas Carr lived with them and they are recorded in the 1940 census with the surname of Milks.

Children of EDGAR MILKS and VIOLET CARR are:
- i. RUSSELL T.[10] CARR-MILKS, b. 01 Oct 1919, Erie County, New York; d. 13 Dec 1988, Suitland, Prince Georges County, Maryland.
  Russell enlisted in the army, on 25 Oct 1940, for duty in Alaska with the Corps of Engineers.
- ii. ROBERT J. CARR-MILKS, b. 14 Mar 1921, Erie County, New York; d. 22 Jun 2008, Erie County, New York.

1329. ARCHIE JOHN[9] BULL *(HARRIET LOUISE[8] MILKS, CHARLES[7], DAVID[6] MILK, GEORGE[5], JONATHAN[4], JOB[3], JOHN[2], JOHN[1])* was born 05 May 1884 in New York, and died 23 Sep 1961. He married BESSIE HAGERDON 18 Dec 1907 in Collins, Erie County, New York. She was born 1885, and died 1931.

Children of ARCHIE BULL and BESSIE HAGERDON are:
- 2295. i. CLIFFORD JAMES[10] BULL, b. 12 Sep 1908, New York; d. Nov 1986, Perry, Wyoming County, New York.
- ii. LUCILLE MARION BULL, b. 1910; d. 1981; m. MISTRE WAKENHUT.
- iii. MAURICE H. BULL, b. Nov 1916, New York; d. 1964.

1330. GERTRUDE[9] THOMAS *(TERESSA L.[8] MILKS, CHARLES[7], DAVID[6] MILK, GEORGE[5], JONATHAN[4], JOB[3], JOHN[2], JOHN[1])* was born 29 Sep 1876 in Gowanda, Cattaraugus County, New York, and died 07 Mar 1955 in Tionesta, Forest County, Pennsylvania. She married JAMES N. ALLIO 1894, son of JOSEPH ALLIO and MARY KNISLEY. He was born 24 Feb 1862 in Forest County, Pennsylvania, and died 03 Sep 1943 in Tionesta, Forest County, Pennsylvania.

Children of GERTRUDE THOMAS and JAMES ALLIO are:
- i. PEARL M.[10] ALLIO, b. Mar 1898, Forest County, Pennsylvania.
- ii. MARGARET P. 'MAGGIE' ALLIO, b. Jan 1900, Forest County, Pennsylvania.
- iii. JULIA MARIE ALLIO, b. 1902, Forest County, Pennsylvania.
- iv. JOSEPH ALLIO, b. 1904, Forest County, Pennsylvania.
- v. MYRTLE ALLIO, b. 1906, Forest County, Pennsylvania.
- vi. MABEL ALLIO, b. 1908, Forest County, Pennsylvania.
- 2296. vii. JAMES RAYMOND ALLIO, b. 27 Aug 1910, Forest County, Pennsylvania; d. Aug 1980, Tionesta, Forest County, Pennsylvania.
- viii. GERTRUDE ALLIO, b. 1912, Forest County, Pennsylvania.

1331. HERMAN[9] BAILEY *(DENCY M.[8] MILKS, CHARLES[7], DAVID[6] MILK, GEORGE[5], JONATHAN[4], JOB[3], JOHN[2], JOHN[1])* was born 26 Aug 1883 in Cattaraugus County, New York.

Children of HERMAN BAILEY are:
- 2297. i. BEATRICE[10] BAILEY, b. 10 Sep 1906, Cattaraugus County, New York.
- ii. ARLETTA L. BAILEY, b. 04 Jan 1914, Cattaraugus County, New York.
- 2298. iii. MARGARET M. BAILEY, b. 08 Jul 1921, Cattaraugus County, New York.

1332. ETHEL[9] MILKS *(CHARLES "NEWMAN"[8], CHARLES[7], DAVID[6] MILK, GEORGE[5], JONATHAN[4], JOB[3], JOHN[2], JOHN[1])* was born 13 Feb 1882 in Dayton, Cattaraugus County, New York, and died Bet. 1920 - 1930. She married MILES ELBRIDGE FANCHER 1898 in Cattaraugus County, New York. He was born 21 May 1878 in New York, and died Aug 1968 in Springville, Erie County, New York.

Children of ETHEL MILKS and MILES FANCHER are:
- i. BESSIE[10] FANCHER, b. 1899, Dayton, Cattaraugus County, New York; d. 1899, d.y..

2299.	ii.	DORA BELLE FANCHER, b. 23 Jul 1900, Erie County, New York.
	iii.	ALICE CLARISSA FANCHER, b. 03 Mar 1902.
	iv.	ALANSON NEWMAN FANCHER, b. 14 Apr 1904.
	v.	IVA FANCHER, b. 1906; d. 1910.
2300.	vi.	GERTRUDE MARION FANCHER, b. 18 Jan 1908; d. Apr 1984, Watkins Glen, Schuyler County, New York.

1333. LETTIE M.^{9} MILKS *(CHARLES "NEWMAN"^{8}, CHARLES^7, DAVID^6 MILK, GEORGE^5, JONATHAN^4, JOB^3, JOHN^2, JOHN^1)* was born 11 Nov 1891 in Persia, Cattaraugus County, New York. She married FRED LUTHER VAN ETTEN 14 Apr 1915 in Hamburg, New York, by Alfred R. Spencer, son of STEPHEN VAN ETTEN and CAROLINE COTTINGTON. He was born 19 Nov 1888 in Woodstock, New York, and died Jun 1969 in Gowanda, Cattaraugus County, New York.

Children of LETTIE MILKS and FRED VAN ETTEN are:

2301.	i.	CHARLES FREDERICK^{10} VAN ETTEN, b. 03 Nov 1918, Dayton, Cattaraugus County, New York.
	ii.	CLAIR CHESTER VAN ETTEN, b. 04 Jan 1921, Dayton, Cattaraugus County, New York; d. Jul 1985, Phoenix, Maricopa County, Arizona; m. MARJORIE H. ROTH, 25 Sep 1945; b. 27 Jul 1920; d. 30 Oct 2009, Phoenix, Maricopa County, Arizona.
	iii.	DONALD VAN ETTEN, b. 1925, Dayton, Cattaraugus County, New York; d. Bet. 1930 - 1940, Dayton, Cattaraugus County, New York. Donald wasn't shown in the 1925 census, so must have been born in 1925 or later.

1334. JOHN CHARLES^9 CROUSE *(MARY J.^{8} MILKS, CHARLES^7, DAVID^6 MILK, GEORGE^5, JONATHAN^4, JOB^3, JOHN^2, JOHN^1)* was born 08 Dec 1882 in Cattaraugus County, New York. He married GOLDIE SADIE BOYER 04 Mar 1911. She was born 06 Dec 1890 in Indiana, and died Dec 1981 in Gowanda, Cattaraugus County, New York.

Children of JOHN CROUSE and GOLDIE BOYER are:

2302.	i.	GEORGE^{10} CROUSE, b. 17 Mar 1912, Golden Valley County, North Dakota; d. Bef. 06 Dec 2004.
2303.	ii.	MARY CROUSE, b. 08 Jul 1913, Beach, Golden Valley County, North Dakota; d. 06 Dec 2004, Gowanda, Cattaraugus County, New York.
2304.	iii.	CHARLES H. CROUSE, b. 15 Jul 1915, Golden Valley County, North Dakota; d. Bef. 06 Dec 2004.
	iv.	ROBERT J. CROUSE, b. 05 Jan 1919, Golden Valley County, North Dakota; d. Abt. 1990, Buffalo, Erie County, New York??? date ???; m. JOAN NELSON, Aft. 28 Apr 1941; b. Abt. 1918. World War II, Enlistment Date: Apr 28, 1941, Enlistment Place: Buffalo New York Occupation: Semiskilled Occupations In Fabrication Of Textile Products, N.E.C.
	v.	DOROTHY M. CROUSE, b. Abt. 1920, Golden Valley County, North Dakota; d. Aft. 06 Dec 2004, of Perrysburg, NY; m. MISTRE CLARK.
2305.	vi.	KATHERINE T. CROUSE, b. 30 Mar 1923, Golden Valley County, North Dakota; d. Abt. 1950, Appleton, Calumet County, Wisconsin.
	vii.	GLADYS U. CROUSE, b. 25 Jan 1927, Cattaraugus County, New York; d. 1935.
2306.	viii.	JOHN C. CROUSE, JR., b. 07 May 1929, Cattaraugus County, New York; d. 27 Jul 1998, Perrysburg, Cattaraugus County, New York.

1335. RAYMOND^9 CROUSE *(MARY J.^{8} MILKS, CHARLES^7, DAVID^6 MILK, GEORGE^5, JONATHAN^4, JOB^3, JOHN^2, JOHN^1)* was born 15 Apr 1882 in Cattaraugus County, New York, and died 02 Oct 1948. He married MAGDALENE 'LENA' T. GETZ 1902 in New York. She was born Bet. 1882 - 1885 in New York.

Child of RAYMOND CROUSE and MAGDALENE GETZ is:

2307.	i.	RAYMOND JOHN^{10} CROUSE, JR., b. 06 Apr 1903, New York; d. 19 Jun 1981, Manhattan Beach, Los Angeles County, California.

1336. CHLOE B.^{9} MILKS *(DAVID W.^{8}, ALEXANDER B.^{7} MILK, DAVID^6, GEORGE^5, JONATHAN^4, JOB^3, JOHN^2, JOHN^1)* was born Jun 1872 in Mansfield, NY, and died 22 Dec 1925. She married ADELBERT LINCOLN 'BERT' CHRISTIAN 29 Oct 1889 in Cattaraugus County, New York, son of DARIUS CHRISTIAN and HANNAH PICKETT. He was born Jan 1867 in NY.

Children of CHLOE MILKS and ADELBERT CHRISTIAN are:

2308.	i.	DORA E.^{10} CHRISTIAN, b. 07 Jun 1891, Soldier, Jefferson County, Pennsylvania; d. 26 Feb 1962, Lock

         Haven, Pennsylvania.
2309. ii. FRANK A. CHRISTIAN, b. 26 Mar 1893, Pennsylvania; d. Dec 1984, West Virginia.
2310. iii. DAVID DARIUS CHRISTIAN, b. 08 Jan 1895, Clearfield County, Pennsylvania; d. 27 Aug 1981, Cleveland, Cuyahoga County, Ohio.
       iv. MILDRED P. CHRISTIAN, b. 10 Dec 1896, Clearfield County, Pennsylvania; d. 22 Feb 1901, Clearfield County, Pennsylvania.

1337. GERTRUDE P.^{9} MILKS *(DAVID W.^{8}, ALEXANDER B.^{7} MILK, DAVID^6, GEORGE^5, JONATHAN^4, JOB^3, JOHN^2, JOHN^1)* was born 09 Jun 1879 in Mansfield, Cattaraugus County, New York, and died 28 Jan 1962 in Great Valley, Cattaraugus County, New York. She married HARRY ANDREW WILLIAMS 23 Jun 1895 in Ellicottville, Cattaraugus County, New York, son of GEORGE WILLIAMS and ANNA. He was born 03 Apr 1875 in Great Valley, Cattaraugus County, New York, and died 09 Feb 1956 in Great Valley, Cattaraugus County, New York.

Children of GERTRUDE MILKS and HARRY WILLIAMS are:
2311. i. CAROLINE M.^{10} WILLIAMS, b. 30 Jul 1898, Great Valley, Cattaraugus County, New York; d. 03 Nov 1992, Wellsville, Allegany County, New York.
2312. ii. EDITH M. WILLIAMS, b. 25 Mar 1902, Great Valley, Cattaraugus County, New York; d. 17 Jun 1985, Buffalo, New York.

1338. JENNIE^9 MILKS *(DAVID W.^{8}, ALEXANDER B.^{7} MILK, DAVID^6, GEORGE^5, JONATHAN^4, JOB^3, JOHN^2, JOHN^1)* was born 06 Dec 1880 in Great Valley, Cattaraugus County, New York, and died 18 Feb 1969 in New York. She married ALBERT VINCENT WINSOR 20 Feb 1898 in Great Valley, Cattaraugus County, New York, son of MARCUS WINSOR and SARAH FLISHER. He was born 06 May 1866 in Venango, Crawford County, Pennsylvania, and died 08 Oct 1942 in Salamanca, Cattaraugus County, New York.

Children of JENNIE MILKS and ALBERT WINSOR are:
2313. i. LEGURN ADELBERT^{10} WINSOR, b. 12 Jan 1899, Mansfield, Cattaraugus County, New York; d. 29 Apr 1949, New York.
       ii. WELTHY ADDIE WINSOR, b. 21 Mar 1900, Mansfield, Cattaraugus County, New York; d. 1983, New York; m. EDSON J. MARBLE; b. 1896; d. 1941.
       iii. HARRY VINCENT WINSOR, b. 05 Feb 1902, Cattaraugus County, New York.
       iv. LYLE H. WINSOR, b. 07 Nov 1918, Cattaraugus County, New York; d. 01 Jul 1988, Cattaraugus County, New York; m. MARGARET NEAMON; b. 09 Jul 1907, Java Village, Wyoming County, New York; d. 24 May 2002, Warsaw, Wyoming County, New York.
       OBITUARY
       Mrs. Winsor, of Warsaw, formerly of Great Valley, was a daughter of Henry & Mamie Bremiller Neamon.
       She had worked at the East Aurora Basket Factory and Mileham's Restaurant and Drug Store.
       Her first husband, Erwin Pingrey, died in June 1949 and her second husband, Lyle winsor, died in Jan. 1988.
       Surviving are 4 sons, Harold (Arlene)Neamon, Richard (Dorothy) Neamon, Lester (Mildred) Neamon and Robert (Jane) Neamon; a daughter, Marian (Elman) Holmes; a sister, Doris Carlisle; a brother, Lloyd (Caroline) Neamon; 26 grandchildren; 80 great-grandchildren and 46 great-great-grandchildren.
       She was grandmother of the late Gary Neamon and Michael Pingrey and sister of the late Arthur, Robert and Kenneth Neamon, Francis Richey, Agnes Rosier and Mabel Mathewson.
       Burial: Maple Grove Cemetery, Machias, Cattaraugus County, New York, USA

1339. LOLA A.^{9} MILKS *(DAVID W.^{8}, ALEXANDER B.^{7} MILK, DAVID^6, GEORGE^5, JONATHAN^4, JOB^3, JOHN^2, JOHN^1)* was born 1882 in Great Valley, Cattaraugus County, New York, and died Apr 1963 in Cattaraugus County, New York. She married GEORGE L. WEBSTER 1901, son of LUCY. He was born 03 Feb 1873 in New York, and died 28 Jan 1949 in Cattaraugus County, New York.

Child of LOLA MILKS and GEORGE WEBSTER is:
       i. G. CARROLL^{10} WEBSTER, b. 09 Dec 1914, Farmersville, Cattaraugus County, New York (adopted); d. 29 Mar 1941, Salamanca, Cattaraugus County, New York; m. MARY HILL.

Adopted son of George Webster and Lola Milks.

Carroll's birth mother was Elizabeth Bain, daughter of Andrew Bain and Matilda Lawson.

1340. HELEN ELIZABETH[9] MILKS *(DAVID W.[8], ALEXANDER B.[7] MILK, DAVID[6], GEORGE[5], JONATHAN[4], JOB[3], JOHN[2], JOHN[1])* was born 18 Jul 1885 in Great Valley, Cattaraugus County, New York, and died 17 Apr 1978 in Olean, Cattaraugus County, New York. She met CHARLES AARON CHAPMAN 31 Dec 1904 in ???? Need more data on this marriage., son of JOHN CHAPMAN and LAURA _____. He was born 11 Apr 1881 in Humphrey, Cattaraugus County, New York, and died 24 Apr 1965 in Salamanca, Cattaraugus County, New York.

Children of HELEN MILKS and CHARLES CHAPMAN are:

2314.	i.	PAULINE MABEL[10] CHAPMAN, b. 02 Jun 1908, Cattaraugus County, New York; d. 14 Feb 1978.
2315.	ii.	GRACE MAE CHAPMAN, b. 31 May 1910, Cattaraugus County, New York; d. 20 Apr 1999, Portville, Cattaraugus, New York.
	iii.	NORA MILDRED CHAPMAN, b. 26 Nov 1911, Cattaraugus County, New York; d. 18 Jul 2012, Du Bois, Clearfield County, Pennsylvania; m. (1) LLOYD EDSON; b. Abt. 1910; m. (2) MILES H. BECK; b. 20 Jan 1910; d. 29 Aug 1994, Du Bois, Clearfield County, Pennsylvania.
	iv.	WALTER JAMES CHAPMAN, b. 07 Oct 1913, Cattaraugus County, New York; d. 02 Jul 1982, Wyoming County, New York; m. ALICE FEDUSKI; b. 11 Mar 1923; d. 04 May 2005, Wyoming County, New York.
2316.	v.	FRANK EDWARD CHAPMAN, b. 18 Jan 1920, Salamanca, Cattaraugus County, New York; d. 01 Jul 2000, Olean, Cattaraugus County, New York.

1341. GEORGIA AMERICA[9] MILKS *(DAVID W.[8], ALEXANDER B.[7] MILK, DAVID[6], GEORGE[5], JONATHAN[4], JOB[3], JOHN[2], JOHN[1])* was born 03 Jun 1893 in Great Valley, Cattaraugus County, New York, and died 08 Feb 1978 in Salamanca, Cattaraugus County, New York. She married LEO GEORGE TERHUNE 13 Aug 1911 in Great Valley, Cattaraugus County, New York, son of D. TERHUNE and DELLA AUSTIN. He was born 19 Apr 1891 in Franklinville, Cattaraugus County, New York, and died 12 Jul 1957 in Cattaraugus County, New York.

Children of GEORGIA MILKS and LEO TERHUNE are:

2317.	i.	WILLIAM A.[10] TERHUNE, b. 27 Jan 1912, Cattaraugus County, New York; d. Apr 1967, Cattaraugus County, New York.
	ii.	THELMA TERHUNE, b. 13 Jul 1914, Cattaraugus County, New York; d. 10 Feb 1990, Cattaraugus County, New York; m. GILBERT PARR; b. 15 Dec 1924; d. Jan 1987, Cattaraugus County, New York.
	iii.	KENTON H. TERHUNE, b. 23 Jul 1915, Cattaraugus County, New York; d. 31 Mar 1997, Malakoff, Henderson County, Texas; m. ALICE F. _____, 04 Jun 1945; b. 30 Sep 1918; d. 31 Jan 2004, Texas.
2318.	iv.	LEO D. TERHUNE, b. 10 Feb 1920, Cattaraugus County, New York; d. Jul 1985, Little Valley, Cattaraugus County, New York.
	v.	PAUL L. TERHUNE, b. 02 Oct 1922, Cattaraugus County, New York; d. Jul 1979, Salamanca, Cattaraugus County, New York.
	vi.	ROBERT SIDLER TERHUNE, b. 31 Dec 1923, Cattaraugus County, New York; d. 26 Sep 1988, Salamanca, Cattaraugus County, New York; m. DOROTHY JOHNSON; b. 22 Aug 1928; d. 19 Dec 1998, Salamanca, Cattaraugus County, New York.
2319.	vii.	GLEN M. TERHUNE, b. 16 Mar 1926, Salamanca, Cattaraugus County, New York; d. 30 Dec 2007, Olean, Cattaraugus County, New York.
2320.	viii.	DAVID A. TERHUNE, b. 11 Aug 1928, Cattaraugus County, New York; d. Dec 1986, Allegany, Cattaraugus County, New York.
	ix.	LOUIS N. TERHUNE, b. 07 Oct 1930, Cattaraugus County, New York; d. Jul 1992, Cattaraugus County, New York; m. ALBERTA J. _____; b. 1931.
2321.	x.	JOSEPH R TERHUNE, b. 29 Sep 1934, Cattaraugus County, New York; d. 10 Apr 2011, Salamanca, Cattaraugus County, New York.
2322.	xi.	RICHARD T. TERHUNE, b. 28 Feb 1937, Salamanca, Cattaraugus County, New York; d. 02 Jun 2009, Olean, Cattaraugus County, New York.

1342. CHARLES HASTINGS[9] MILKS *(DAVID W.[8], ALEXANDER B.[7] MILK, DAVID[6], GEORGE[5], JONATHAN[4], JOB[3], JOHN[2], JOHN[1])* was born 29 Oct 1897 in Great Valley, Cattaraugus County, New York, and died 08 Apr 1921. He married FRANCES ROCKWELL 29 Dec 1917 in Salamanca, Cattaraugus County, New York, daughter of MERTON ROCKWELL and

MAUD JACOBS. She was born 1901 in Cherry Creek, NY.

Children of CHARLES MILKS and FRANCES ROCKWELL are:
- i. HERBERT[10] MILKS, b. Mar 1919, Salamanca, Cattaraugus County, New York.
- 2323. ii. ALBERTA GENEVIEVE MILKS, b. 02 Apr 1920, Salamanca, Cattaraugus County, New York; d. 19 Jan 1990, Vallejo, Solana County, California.

1343. GORDON JOSEPH[9] MILKS (*GEORGE PRINCE*[8], *ALEXANDER B.*[7] *MILK, DAVID*[6], *GEORGE*[5], *JONATHAN*[4], *JOB*[3], *JOHN*[2], *JOHN*[1]) was born 08 Jan 1898 in Salamanca, NY, and died 23 Feb 1989 in Asheboro, Randolph County, North Carolina. He married (1) MARIE C. MORRIS 06 Aug 1921 in Dunkirk, New York, daughter of CHARLES MORRIS and FLORA CARNAHAN. She was born Bet. 1895 - 1896 in Dayton, Ohio. He married (2) ROSA ETTA SHEFFIELD Abt. 1937. She was born 20 Feb 1907 in North Carolina, and died 24 Dec 1991 in Asheboro, Randolph County, North Carolina.

Children of GORDON MILKS and ROSA SHEFFIELD are:
- 2324. i. GORDON JOSEPH[10] MILKS, JR., b. 28 Jun 1939, Abingdon Shores, Calvert County, Maryland; d. 25 Nov 2012, Randolph Hospital, Randolph County, North Carolina.
- 2325. ii. GEORGE VERNON MILKS, b. 1941, Abingdon, Maryland; d. Of Asheboro.
- iii. MARY RUTH MILKS, b. 29 Jun 1947, Asheboro, Randolph County, North Carolina; m. HAROLD LEE BREWER; b. 26 May 1950; d. 15 Aug 2012.

1344. BURTON HENRY[9] MILKS (*ROBERT S.*[8] *MILK, ALEXANDER B.*[7], *DAVID*[6], *GEORGE*[5], *JONATHAN*[4], *JOB*[3], *JOHN*[2], *JOHN*[1]) was born 30 Nov 1879 in Great Valley, Chautauqua Co., NY, and died 16 May 1958 in Riverside Hospital, Toledo, Ohio. He married (1) MARY JOSEPHINE BALDWIN Bet. 1905 - 1906. She was born Abt. 1880 in Kansas. He married (2) LILLIE THURMAN BOWDEN 19 May 1920 in Lucas County, Ohio, daughter of WILLIAM BOWDEN and MOLLIE VOOCH. She was born 27 Oct 1888 in North Carolina, and died 29 Nov 1966 in Flower Hospital, Toledo, Ohio.

Children of BURTON MILKS and MARY BALDWIN are:
- 2326. i. MARY BEATRICE[10] MILKS, b. 10 Dec 1908, Kiowa County, Colorado; d. 10 Jul 1997, Kansas City, Jackson County, Missouri.
- 2327. ii. WINONA MILKS, b. 12 Jan 1912, Toledo, Lucas County, Ohio; d. 18 Aug 1999, Westland, Wayne County, Michigan.
- iii. LAURA AIELIE MILKS, b. 15 Feb 1914, Toledo, Lucas County, Ohio; d. 09 Aug 1914, Toledo, Lucas County, Ohio.

Children of BURTON MILKS and LILLIE BOWDEN are:
- 2328. iv. HERMA ANN[10] MILKS, b. 01 Mar 1921, Lucas County, Ohio; d. 22 Feb 1986, San Diego, California.
- 2329. v. BURTON 'BERT' HENRY MILKS, JR., b. 02 Jun 1924, Toledo, Lucas County, Ohio; d. 18 May 1998, Bradenton Beach, Manatee, Florida.

1345. REV. RALPH P.[9] MILKS (*ROBERT S.*[8] *MILK, ALEXANDER B.*[7], *DAVID*[6], *GEORGE*[5], *JONATHAN*[4], *JOB*[3], *JOHN*[2], *JOHN*[1]) was born 25 Mar 1889 in East Leon, Cattaraugus County, New York, and died 06 Feb 1973 in Flint, Genesee County, Michigan. He married EVA C. ELLIS 15 Jul 1910 in Flint, Michigan, daughter of WILLIAM ELLIS and ELLEN HOWARD. She was born 07 Jul 1892 in Mt. Morris, Michigan, and died 05 Apr 1978 in Port Huron, St. Clair County, Michigan.

Children of RALPH MILKS and EVA ELLIS are:
- 2330. i. GENEVA[10] MILKS, b. 23 Jul 1911, Michigan.
- 2331. ii. ORVAL ROBERT MILKS, b. 18 Dec 1912, Michigan; d. Oct 1983, Las Vegas, NV 89104.
- iii. HESTER AILEEN MILKS, b. 20 Aug 1917, Grand Bay, Alabama; d. 07 Apr 1951, Port Huron, St Clair County, Michigan,.
- 2332. iv. HOWARD RALPH MILKS, b. 18 Dec 1918, Grand Bay, Alabama; d. 03 Jul 1990, Flint, Genesee County, MI.
- v. OLIVE M. MILKS, b. 29 Mar 1920, Summerville, Louisiana; m. HERSEY DORMAN; b. Abt. 1920.
- 2333. vi. RALPH P. MILKS, JR., b. 26 Jan 1926, Fowlerville, Michigan.

1346. HOWARD A.[9] MILKS (*ROBERT S.*[8] *MILK, ALEXANDER B.*[7], *DAVID*[6], *GEORGE*[5], *JONATHAN*[4], *JOB*[3], *JOHN*[2], *JOHN*[1]) was born 19 Jul 1898 in Leon, Cattaraugus County, New York, and died Jul 1970 in Carsonville, Sanilac County,

Michigan. He married DOROTHY MAY WELSH 01 Jun 1940 in Croswell, Michigan, daughter of NICHOLAS WELSH and MARTHA BLOOMFIELD. She was born 01 Mar 1908 in Alonson, Michigan.

Child of HOWARD MILKS and DOROTHY WELSH is:
    i. BARBARA JEAN[10] MILKS, b. 13 Sep 1940, Tower, Michigan.

1347. ALVAN L.[9] MILKS *(ROBERT S.[8] MILK, ALEXANDER B.[7], DAVID[6], GEORGE[5], JONATHAN[4], JOB[3], JOHN[2], JOHN[1])* was born 10 Nov 1901 in Leon, Cattaraugus County, NY, and died 29 May 1997 in Gerry, Chautauqua, NY 14740. He married INA E. SLOCUM 12 Dec 1928, daughter of FRED SLOCUM and JEANNETTE ELLIS. She was born 04 Oct 1910 in Allegany, NY, and died 23 Aug 2006 in Tucson, Arizona.

OBITUARY
    ALVAN L. MILKS
Surviving are his wife of 68 years, Ina Slocum Milk, whom he married Dec 12, 1928; a daughter, Esther Howard of Tucson, AZ; two sons, Robert Milk and David Milk, both of Gerry, seven grandchildren: Jeane Milk, Gary Miller, Deborah Milk, and Lisa Milk, all of Gerry, Gary Slocum of Mesquite, Texas, Dawn Lockwood of Rochester and Sandra Erb of Lima, NY. seven great-grandchildren, a sister, Ruth Beman of Lancaster, NY

DEATH NOTICE
Ina S. Milk9/1/2006 - Ina S. Milk, 95, of Tucson, AZ, formerly of Route 60, Gerry, died Aug. 23, 2006. Born Oct. 4, 1910 in Allegany, daughter of the late Fred and Jeanette Slocum.
A Gerry resident from 1946 until 1990 she was a housekeeper for Gerry Homes for over 20 years. Ina belonged to Gerry Free Methodist Church for over 60 years.
Wife of late Alvan L. Milk; Mother of Esther Howard, Robert Milk. and David Milk; 7 grandchildren;
9 great grandchildren and 1 great great- granddaughter survive.

Children of ALVAN MILKS and INA SLOCUM are:
    i. ROBERT ALVAN[10] MILKS, b. 27 Apr 1930, Romeo, Michigan; m. ELAINE GROTH.
    ii. ESTHER MARIAM MILKS, b. 12 Jan 1933; m. ?? HOWARD.
    iii. DAVID BURDETTE MILKS, b. 23 Apr 1947, Gerry, Chautauqua Co., NY?; m. PATRICIA A. ___; b. Abt. 1948.

1348. RUTH[9] MILKS *(ROBERT S.[8] MILK, ALEXANDER B.[7], DAVID[6], GEORGE[5], JONATHAN[4], JOB[3], JOHN[2], JOHN[1])* was born 22 Dec 1903 in Cattaraugus County, New York, and died 04 Aug 1997 in Miami, Dade County, Florida. She married JOHN LEO BEMAN 15 Mar 1925 in Castile, New York. He was born 29 Nov 1897 in New York, and died 12 Apr 1985 in Miami, Dade County, Florida.

Children of RUTH MILKS and JOHN BEMAN are:
    i. JOHN LAURENCE 'JACK'[10] BEMAN, b. 1927, New York (Adopted?).
    ii. MARJORIE RUTH BEMAN, b. 24 Feb 1929, Ellicottville, Cattaraugus County, New York.
    iii. KATHERINE ANN BEMAN, b. 09 Aug 1931, Ellicottville, Cattaraugus County, New York.

1349. MARY L.[9] BROCKITT *(ELIZABETH[8] MILK, ALEXANDER B.[7], DAVID[6], GEORGE[5], JONATHAN[4], JOB[3], JOHN[2], JOHN[1])* was born May 1882 in Cattaraugus County, New York, and died 1964. She married FRANK E. GOULD 1902 in Cattaraugus County, New York, son of CARL GOULD and MARY _____. He was born Nov 1874 in Cattaraugus County, New York (twin).

Child of MARY BROCKITT and FRANK GOULD is:
    i. OLIVE G.[10] GOULD, b. 1903, Cattaraugus County, New York.

1350. JOSEPHINE[9] BROCKITT *(ELIZABETH[8] MILK, ALEXANDER B.[7], DAVID[6], GEORGE[5], JONATHAN[4], JOB[3], JOHN[2], JOHN[1])* was born 18 Apr 1884 in Cattaraugus County, New York, and died 23 Dec 1944. She married JAY CARROLL GOULD, son of CARL GOULD and MARY _____. He was born 28 Nov 1881 in Farmersville, Cattaraugus County, New York, and died 09 Apr 1942.

Children of JOSEPHINE BROCKITT and JAY GOULD are:
    i. HAROLD[10] GOULD, b. Bet. 1903 - 1904, Cattaraugus County, New York.

    ii. LOLA GOULD, b. Bet. 1905 - 1906, Cattaraugus County, New York.
    iii. ETHEL M. GOULD, b. Bet. 1907 - 1908, Cattaraugus County, New York.
    iv. CARROLL J. GOULD, b. 1909, Allegany County, New York?.
    v. DONALD W. GOULD, b. Bet. 1911 - 1912, Allegany County, New York?.
    vi. EARL D. GOULD, b. Bet. 1914 - 1915, Allegany County, New York?.
    vii. THELMA I. GOULD, b. Bet. 1916 - 1917, Allegany County, New York?.
    viii. GLADYS J. GOULD, b. Bet. 1918 - 1919, Cattaraugus County, New York?.

1351. NORMAN ALEXANDER^9 BROCKITT *(ELIZABETH^8 MILK, ALEXANDER B.^{7}, DAVID^6, GEORGE^5, JONATHAN^4, JOB^3, JOHN^2, JOHN^1)* was born 01 Jan 1886 in Orlando, Cattaraugus County, New York, and died 23 Sep 1949. He married (1) FIRST WIFE _____ Abt. 1903. He married (2) SUSAN M. 'SUSIE' WHITNEY 04 Apr 1915 in Cattaraugus, New York, daughter of ELIAS WHITNEY and _____ STAFFORD. She was born Bet. 1888 - 1889 in Pennsylvania, and died 08 Apr 1930 in Rixford, McKean, Pennsylvania. He married (3) BLANCHE M. GRANDIN Aft. 1930 in Pennsylvania?. She was born 24 Dec 1890, and died 08 Dec 1955.

Children of NORMAN BROCKITT and FIRST _____ are:
    i. DORIS G.^{10} BROCKITT, b. Bet. 1903 - 1904, Pennsylvania.
2334. ii. ORVAL E. BROCKITT, b. 05 Jun 1907, New York; d. 19 Jul 1970, Pittsburgh, Allegheny County, Pennsylvania.
    iii. BEATRICE BROCKITT, b. Bet. 1908 - 1909, New York.

Child of NORMAN BROCKITT and BLANCHE GRANDIN is:
    iv. NORMA^{10} BROCKITT, b. 18 Mar 1931, Bradford, McKean County, Pennsylvania; d. May 1994, Pittsburgh, Allegheny County, Pennsylvania; m. GALE WORTH SMITH; b. 01 Sep 1924, Bradford, McKean County, Pennsylvania; d. 24 Jul 2002, Clarion County, Pennsylvania.

1352. WILLIAM^9 BROCKITT *(ELIZABETH^8 MILK, ALEXANDER B.^{7}, DAVID^6, GEORGE^5, JONATHAN^4, JOB^3, JOHN^2, JOHN^1)* was born Jun 1887 in Cattaraugus County, New York. He married NETTIE _____ Bet. 1905 - 1906. She was born Bet. 1884 - 1885 in New York.

Children of WILLIAM BROCKITT and NETTIE _____ are:
    i. ELIZABETH M.^{10} BROCKITT, b. Bet. 1907 - 1908, Franklinville Village, Cattaraugus County, NY, as a farm laborer for Benjamin Pratt.
       In 1920, Elizabeth was an living at the Randolph Children's Home in East Randolph, Cattaraugus County, New York
    ii. BERTHA BROCKITT, b. Bet. 1908 - 1909, Franklinville Village, Cattaraugus County, NY.

1353. AGNES E.^{9} MILKS *(JOHN OSCAR^8, ALEXANDER B.^{7} MILK, DAVID^6, GEORGE^5, JONATHAN^4, JOB^3, JOHN^2, JOHN^1)* was born 1902 in Pike, Wyoming County, New York, and died in Lived Warsaw, NY. She married GEORGE W. MORGAN, son of CHARLES MORGAN and MARY _____. He was born Apr 1899 in Covington, Wyoming County, New York.

Children of AGNES MILKS and GEORGE MORGAN are:
    i. CHARLOTTE C.^{10} MORGAN, b. 1922, Warsaw, Wyoming County, New York.
    ii. SHIRLEY P. MORGAN, b. 1924, Warsaw, Wyoming County, New York.
    iii. MARY VIRGINIA MORGAN, b. Jul 1925, Warsaw, Wyoming County, New York.
    iv. MICHAEL MORGAN, b. 1932, Warsaw, Wyoming County, New York.

1354. ETTA A.^{9} MILKS *(EDGAR^8, ALEXANDER B.^{7} MILK, DAVID^6, GEORGE^5, JONATHAN^4, JOB^3, JOHN^2, JOHN^1)* was born Bet. 1898 - 1899 in Great Valley, Cattaraugus County, New York, and died 03 Nov 1948 in S. Dayton, NY. She married ROSS F. ESTUS 13 Jan 1919 in Great Valley, Cattaraugus County, New York, son of ALBERT ESTUS and IDA RASTOPHER. He was born 16 May 1897 in Little Valley, Cattaraugus County, NY, and died May 1971 in Ellicottville, Cattaraugus County, New York.

Children of ETTA MILKS and ROSS ESTUS are:
2335. i. EDGAR A.^{10} ESTUS, b. 04 Oct 1919, Great Valley, Cattaraugus County, New York; d. 28 Nov 1962, NY.

2336.	ii.	ROSS F. ESTUS, JR., b. 14 Oct 1923, Great Valley, Cattaraugus County, New York; d. Aug 1976, South Dayton, Cattaraugus County, New York.
	iii.	MARY ESTUS, b. May 1927, Great Valley, Cattaraugus County, New York.
	iv.	MARION E. ESTUS, b. Abt. Oct 1929, Great Valley, Cattaraugus County, New York.
	v.	HELENA ESTUS, b. Abt. 1931.

1355. FRANCES A.^{9} MILKS *(EDGAR^8, ALEXANDER B.^{7} MILK, DAVID^6, GEORGE^5, JONATHAN^4, JOB^3, JOHN^2, JOHN^1)* was born 18 Mar 1912 in Great Valley, Cattaraugus County, New York, and died 15 Dec 1993 in Cattaraugus County, New York. She married THEODORE C. BURLESON 05 May 1935 in Salamanca, Cattaraugus County, New York, son of GEORGE BURLESON and CARRIE DAILEY. He was born 09 Jul 1902 in Freedom, Cattaraugus County, New York, and died Jan 1977 in Cattaraugus County, New York.

Child of FRANCES MILKS and THEODORE BURLESON is:

2337.	i.	CHARLES F.^{10} BURLESON, b. 26 Feb 1939, Cattaraugus County, New York; d. 1999, Cattaraugus County, New York.

1356. MYRTLE B.^{9} MILKS *(MANLEY H.^{8}, DAVID W.^{7}, DAVID^6 MILK, GEORGE^5, JONATHAN^4, JOB^3, JOHN^2, JOHN^1)* was born 24 Oct 1877 in Salamanca, Cattaraugus County, New York, and died 1954 in Norway, Herkimer County, New York. She married SYLVESTER STANLEY 1897 in New York. He was born 1872 in New York, and died 1952 in Norway, Herkimer County, New York.

Children of MYRTLE MILKS and SYLVESTER STANLEY are:

2338.	i.	GEORGE^{10} STANLEY, b. 22 Sep 1898, Herkimer County, New York; d. 1961, Norway, Herkimer County, New York.
2339.	ii.	MILDRED M. 'MILLIE' STANLEY, b. 1903, Herkimer County, New York.
	iii.	FLORENCE A. STANLEY, b. 1909, Herkimer County, New York.
	iv.	FREDA STANLEY, b. Jun 1916, Herkimer County, New York.

1357. JUDSON DAVID^9 MILKS *(MANLEY H.^{8}, DAVID W.^{7}, DAVID^6 MILK, GEORGE^5, JONATHAN^4, JOB^3, JOHN^2, JOHN^1)* was born 24 Mar 1879 in Salamanca, Cattaraugus County, New York, and died 22 Sep 1931 in Truxton, Cortland County, New York. He married ELLA M. ROOD 29 Jun 1903 in Prospect, Oneida County, New York. She was born 13 Feb 1883 in Ohio, Herkimer County, New York, and died 19 Apr 1948 in Barneveld, Oneida County, New York.

Children of JUDSON MILKS and ELLA ROOD are:

2340.	i.	JESSIE M.^{10} MILKS, b. 08 Apr 1907, Ohio, Herkimer County, New York; d. 19 Nov 2000, Port Jervis, Orange County, New York.
2341.	ii.	LESTER JUDSON MILKS, b. 26 May 1908, Ohio, Herkimer County, New York; d. 29 May 1989, Onondaga County, New York.
2342.	iii.	MARJORIE E. MILKS, b. 09 Jun 1912, Fairfield, New York; d. 11 Aug 1949.
2343.	iv.	MARIAN MILKS, b. 29 Dec 1913, Norway, Herkimer County, New York; d. 02 Oct 2012, Clemson, Pickens County, South Carolina.
2344.	v.	FREDERICK E. MILKS, b. 05 May 1916, Gray, New York; d. Oct 1984, Jordan, Onondaga, NY.
2345.	vi.	ELSIE MILKS, b. 07 Apr 1919, Gray, NY.
2346.	vii.	THADDEUS RAYMOND 'TED' MILKS, b. 08 Dec 1921, Ohio, Herkimer County, New York; d. 04 Apr 2004, Fabius, Onondaga County, New York.

1358. LESLIE B.^{9} MILKS *(MANLEY H.^{8}, DAVID W.^{7}, DAVID^6 MILK, GEORGE^5, JONATHAN^4, JOB^3, JOHN^2, JOHN^1)* was born 17 Dec 1884 in Salamanca, Cattaraugus Co, NY, and died 18 Feb 1965 in Randolph, Cattaraugus Co, NY. He married MILDRED BEERS 27 Nov 1912 in Randolph, New York, daughter of WILLIAM BEERS and CORNELIA LAWRENCE. She was born 12 May 1894 in Randolph, Cattaraugus Co, NY, and died 27 Jun 1986 in Jamestown, Chautauqua Co, NY.

Child of LESLIE MILKS and MILDRED BEERS is:

	i.	EVELYN MARY^{10} MILKS, b. 19 Jul 1919; d. 25 Aug 1928, Randolph, Cattaraugus Co, NY.

1359. GEORGE ALFRED⁹ MILKS *(MANLEY H.⁸, DAVID W.⁷, DAVID⁶ MILK, GEORGE⁵, JONATHAN⁴, JOB³, JOHN², JOHN¹)* was born 18 Feb 1895 in Salamanca, Cattaraugus County, New York, and died 03 Sep 1956 in Cattaraugus County, New York. He married (1) HILA SCHRECKINGAST 22 Jun 1913 in Killbuck, New York, daughter of PAUL SCHRECKINGAST and LIZZIE BEAN. She was born 1895 in Meadville, Pennsylvania, and died Abt. 1932 in Town of Allegany, Cattaraugus County, New York. He married (2) DEMA EMILY PIERCE 14 Jul 1934 in Allegany, Cattaraugus County, New York, daughter of JESSE PIERCE and EMILY THOMPSON. She was born 14 Sep 1914 in Gowanda, Cattaraugus County, New York, and died 1958 in Cattaraugus County, New York.

In Croft's 1956 2nd Edition, George is shown as a son of Lettie Milks (which is possible, of course), but on his marriage certificate, he lists his parents as Manley H. and Rosie B. Milks, and he is shown living with them in the 1900 and 1910 census records.

Children of GEORGE MILKS and HILA SCHRECKINGAST are:
2347. i. ALMA ELIZABETH¹⁰ MILKS, b. 09 Jul 1914, East Salamanca, Cattaraugus County, New York.
2348. ii. FRANCES MILKS, b. 1917, Bradford, Pennsylvania.
 iii. JANE MILKS, m. DONALD RADLINSKI.

Children of GEORGE MILKS and DEMA PIERCE are:
 iv. ROBERT LEROY¹⁰ PIERCE-MILKS, b. 02 Aug 1934, Buffalo, Erie County, New York; d. 1962.
 v. RICHARD EDMOND MILKS, b. 31 Jul 1935, Vandalia, NY; d. Abt. 1960. No children.
 vi. DONALD DOUGLAS MILKS, b. 12 Nov 1936, Salamanca, NY; d. 1972. No children.
 vii. ALBERTA MILKS, b. 12 Aug 1938, Salamanca, NY; d. 24 Nov 1938.

1360. WILLIAM⁹ ROOD *(EVA⁸ MILKS, DAVID W.⁷, DAVID⁶ MILK, GEORGE⁵, JONATHAN⁴, JOB³, JOHN², JOHN¹)* was born Jan 1891 in New York. He married IDA _____. She was born 1890 in New York.

Children of WILLIAM ROOD and IDA _____ are:
 i. HAROLD¹⁰ ROOD, b. 1911, New York.
 ii. RICHARD ROOD, b. 1912, New York.
 iii. CLARENCE ROOD, b. 1915, New York.
 iv. BAYARD ROOD, b. 1918, New York.

1361. MAY⁹ ROOD *(EVA⁸ MILKS, DAVID W.⁷, DAVID⁶ MILK, GEORGE⁵, JONATHAN⁴, JOB³, JOHN², JOHN¹)* was born 11 Oct 1893 in New York, and died 06 Dec 1977 in Herkimer, Herkimer County, New York. She married HARVEY L. EVERSON 10 Jun 1909 in Ohio, Herkimer County, New York. He was born 17 Mar 1888 in Newburgh, Orange County, New York, and died 05 Oct 1977 in Ilion, Herkimer County, New York.
OBITUARY
Ilion - Harvey Everson, 89, of 160 East Main St., died Wednesday, Oct. 5 at his home.

He was born March 17, 1888 in Newburgh. On June 10, 1909 he married Mae Rood in the Town of Ohio.

Mr. Everson had resided most of his life in Ilion and was employed for 18 years as a foreman for the Ilion Sanitation Department, retiring in 1957. He was also a self-employed farmer.

He was a member of the Ilion Presbyterian Church.

Besides his wife he is survived by six sons, Harry of Ilion; Ernest of Herkimer, Harvey Jr. of Fitchburg, Mass.; Leon of Seattle Wash.; Roy and Warren, both of Ilion; four daughters, Mrs. Ruth Flanders, Canastota; Mrs. Earl (Edna) Mathis, Boonville; Mrs. Marjorie Renodin, Ilion and Mrs. Floyd (Lillian) Parmer of East Herkimer; 75 grandchildren; more than 100 great grandchildren and three great great grandchildren.

Burial in Mountainview Memorial Gardens, Little Falls. Boonville Herald, October 20, 1977

Children of MAY ROOD and HARVEY EVERSON are:
 i. HAROLD 'HARRY'¹⁰ EVERSON, b. 1911, Herkimer County, New York; d. Bef. 16 Dec 2011, of Ilion.
 ii. ERNEST WILLIAM EVERSON, b. 04 Feb 1913, Norway, Herkimer County, New York; d. 14 Jan 1979, Herkimer, Herkimer County, New York.
 iii. RUTH EVERSON, b. 1914, Herkimer County, New York; d. Bef. 16 Dec 2011, of Canastota; m. MISTRE FLANDER.
 iv. ROY J. EVERSON, b. 1919, Herkimer County, New York; d. Bef. 16 Dec 2011, of Ilion.
2349. v. EDNA EVERSON, b. 18 May 1920, Newport, Herkimer County, New York; d. 09 Jul 2011, Lewis County

General Hospital, Lewis County, New York.
2350. vi. HARVEY L. EVERSON, JR., b. 18 May 1920, Newport, Herkimer County, New York; d. 16 Dec 2011, Lowville, Lewis County, New York.
vii. LEON C. EVERSON, b. 1924, Herkimer County, New York; d. Bef. 16 Dec 2011, of Seattle, Wash..
viii. LILLIAN J. EVERSON, b. Jun 1925, Herkimer County, New York; d. Bef. 16 Dec 2011, of East Herkimer; m. FLOYD FALMER.
ix. MARJORIE JEAN EVERSON, b. 1928, Herkimer County, New York; d. Bef. 16 Dec 2011, of Ilion; m. MISTRE RENODIN.
x. WARREN E. EVERSON, b. Jun 1929, Herkimer County, New York; d. Bef. 16 Dec 2011, of Ilion.
xi. GEORGE? EVERSON, d. Bef. 16 Dec 2011, Prob. d.y..

1362. RUIE CAROLINE^9 MILKS *(FRANK EDWIN^8, MONTERVILLE^7, DAVID^6 MILK, GEORGE^5, JONATHAN^4, JOB^3, JOHN^2, JOHN^1)* was born Feb 1885, and died Bet. 1930 - 1940 in Los Angeles, California. She married CLYDE GERALD WALLEY, son of THOMAS WALLEY and CAROLINE NELLIS. He was born 22 Apr 1886 in New York, and died 07 Feb 1950 in Los Angeles, California.

Child of RUIE MILKS and CLYDE WALLEY is:
i. CLIFFORD J.^{10} WALLEY, b. 09 Sep 1907, Pennsylvania; d. 21 Mar 1965, Sherman Oaks, Los Angeles County, California; m. (1) VIRGINIA I FEE, 04 Jul 1931, Los Angeles, California; b. 1908; m. (2) RUTH S. _____, Bet. 1932 - 1940; b. Abt. 1914, Michigan.

1363. LLOYD ELMER^9 MILKS *(FRANK EDWIN^8, MONTERVILLE^7, DAVID^6 MILK, GEORGE^5, JONATHAN^4, JOB^3, JOHN^2, JOHN^1)* was born 08 Jan 1887 in Ellicottville, Cattaraugus County, New York, and died 13 Oct 1954 in Asheboro, Randolph County, North Carolina. He married LEDIAH HARDY 21 Feb 1912 in Olean, New York, daughter of GILBERT HARDY and MARY GOOL. She was born 07 Nov 1887 in Lewis Run, Pennsylvania, and died 03 Jul 1950 in Greensboro, Guilford County, North Carolina.

Children of LLOYD MILKS and LEDIAH HARDY are:
2351. i. DORIS IONA^{10} MILKS, b. 13 Sep 1913, Bradford County, Pennsylvania; d. 06 Aug 1996, Asheboro, Randolph County, North Carolina.
2352. ii. MILDRED MAE MILKS, b. 05 Jul 1915, Bradford County, Pennsylvania; d. 29 Sep 1994, Greensboro, Guilford County, North Carolina.
2353. iii. EDITH ELIZABETH MILKS, b. 23 Jun 1917, Bradford County, Pennsylvania; d. 30 Jun 2000, Randolph Hospital, Asheboro, North Carolina.
2354. iv. LLOYD ELMER MILKS, JR., b. 09 Mar 1919, Bradford County, Pennsylvania; d. 14 Aug 1988, Asheboro, Randolph County, North Carolina.
2355. v. RICHARD PAUL MILKS, b. 11 Mar 1921, Bradford County, Pennsylvania.
2356. vi. ROBERT LEROY MILKS, b. 02 Jan 1923, Bradford County, Pennsylvania; d. 21 Aug 2004, Cary, North Carolina.
2357. vii. CLAYTON HOWARD MILKS, b. 02 Sep 1924, Bradford County, Pennsylvania; d. 21 Jul 2007, Asheboro, Randolph County, North Carolina.
2358. viii. GILBERT LYLE MILKS, b. 19 Jul 1926, Bradford County, Pennsylvania.

1364. MONTEVILLE SAMUEL^9 MILKS *(FRANK EDWIN^8, MONTERVILLE^7, DAVID^6 MILK, GEORGE^5, JONATHAN^4, JOB^3, JOHN^2, JOHN^1)* was born 02 Sep 1888 in Devereux, New York, and died 03 Oct 1961 in Bradford, McKean County, Pennsylvania. He married MABLE MAY DUNKLE 04 Jul 1908 in Niagara Falls, NY, daughter of DANIEL DUNKLE and CATHERINE BIGLER. She was born 08 Nov 1888 in Dubois, Pennsylvania, and died 02 Aug 1971 in Bradford, McKean County, Pennsylvania.

Children of MONTEVILLE MILKS and MABLE DUNKLE are:
2359. i. HELEN LORETTA^{10} MILKS, b. 20 May 1911, Pennsylvania; d. 23 Jan 1988, Pennsylvania.
ii. LEONA M. MILKS, b. Bet. 1912 - 1913, Pennsylvania; m. JOSEPH EDWARD PERROTT; b. 05 Oct 1897, NY.

1365. HENRY EDWIN^9 MILKS *(FRANK EDWIN^8, MONTERVILLE^7, DAVID^6 MILK, GEORGE^5, JONATHAN^4, JOB^3, JOHN^2, JOHN^1)* was born 22 May 1919 in Bradford, PA, and died 15 Feb 1998 in Bradford, McKean Co., PA. He married

MARTHA A. FRANKLIN. She was born 10 May 1920, and died 27 Feb 2001 in Bradford, McKean Co., PA.

Children of HENRY MILKS and MARTHA FRANKLIN are:
        i. HENRY EDWIND[10] MILKS, JR., b. 28 Jul 1948, Bradford, PA; d. 06 Apr 2003, Bradford, PA (unmarried).
2360. ii. CARL L. MILKS, b. 11 Nov 1955, Bradford, PA.

1366. ARLENE BESSIE[9] MILKS *(FRANK EDWIN[8], MONTERVILLE[7], DAVID[6] MILK, GEORGE[5], JONATHAN[4], JOB[3], JOHN[2], JOHN[1])* was born 25 Sep 1921 in Bradford, McKean County, Pennsylvania (no children). She married KENNETH WILLIAM MORRIS 29 Jun 1945 in Bradford, PA, son of SYDNEY MORRIS and BINA MCKEE. He was born 05 Oct 1910 in Olean, New York.

Child of ARLENE MILKS and KENNETH MORRIS is:
        i. CAROL ANNE[10] MORRIS, b. 21 Aug 1947.

1367. FRANK ELMER[9] MILKS *(FRANK EDWIN[8], MONTERVILLE[7], DAVID[6] MILK, GEORGE[5], JONATHAN[4], JOB[3], JOHN[2], JOHN[1])* was born 25 Mar 1923 in Bradford, PA, and died 20 Jun 1992 in Bradford, McKean Co., PA. He married MARY ENID WEAVER 22 Jun 1942, daughter of OTTO WEAVER and P. SMITH. She was born 01 Jun 1925 in Muncy, Lycoming County, Pennsylvania, and died 18 May 2001 in Bradford, McKean Co., PA.

Children of FRANK MILKS and MARY WEAVER are:
2361. i. FRANK E.[10] MILKS III, b. 03 Nov 1947, Bradford, McKean County, Pennsylvania (no children).
        ii. JUDITH ANN MILKS, b. Jun 1945, Bradford, McKean County, Pennsylvania (no children).

1368. CAROL JOSEPH[9] MILKS *(HENRY JOSEPH[8], MONTERVILLE[7], DAVID[6] MILK, GEORGE[5], JONATHAN[4], JOB[3], JOHN[2], JOHN[1])* was born 24 Mar 1890 in Ellicottville, Cattaraugus County, New York, and died May 1969 in Ellicottville, Cattaraugus County, New York. He married WINIFRED C. FAY 19 Jun 1914 in Salamanca, Cattaraugus, NY, daughter of ASA FAY and MARY HITCHCOCK. She was born 11 Dec 1895 in Great Valley, Cattaraugus County, New York, and died Apr 1981 in Ellicottville, Cattaraugus County, New York.

Children of CAROL MILKS and WINIFRED FAY are:
        i. CAROL FAY[10] MILKS, b. 1916, Ellicottville, Cattaraugus County, New York; d. 1932.
        ii. NEIL DENTON MILKS, b. 1919, Ellicottville, Cattaraugus County, New York; d. 1935.
        iii. BARBARA ELIZABETH MILKS, b. 1931, Ellicottville, Cattaraugus County, New York; d. 1952.
           Barbara was a prominent musician and senior at Geneseo State Normal Teachers College.

1369. ORSON L.[9] MILKS *(HENRY JOSEPH[8], MONTERVILLE[7], DAVID[6] MILK, GEORGE[5], JONATHAN[4], JOB[3], JOHN[2], JOHN[1])* was born 14 Nov 1891 in Cattaraugus County, New York, and died Jul 1966 in Ellicottville, Cattaraugus Co., NY. He married FLORENCE MAY HERBST 30 May 1913 in Salamanca, Cattaraugus County, New York, daughter of FRANK HERBST and MARGARET LORCH. She was born Bet. 1893 - 1894 in Machias, Cattaraugus County, New York, and died 1960.

Child of ORSON MILKS and FLORENCE HERBST is:
        i. DORIS[10] MILKS, b. 23 Aug 1914, Ellicottville, Cattaraugus Co, NY; d. 20 Sep 1999, Cattaraugus County, New York; m. JAMES SOUTHWICK, 23 Sep 1943; b. Jun 1915, Cattaraugus County, New York; d. 07 Jan 1993, Cattaraugus County, New York. Apparently, Doris and James had no children, since none were mentioned in Doris's obituary.

1370. GLADYS I.[9] MILKS *(ORSON LEROY[8], MONTERVILLE[7], DAVID[6] MILK, GEORGE[5], JONATHAN[4], JOB[3], JOHN[2], JOHN[1])* was born 25 Aug 1896 in Buffalo, NY, and died Aft. 1941. She married (1) NATHANIEL M. STEWART. He was born Abt. 1895 in Massachusetts. She married (3) EDWIN ALBERT TYLER 1926. He was born 19 May 1891 in Corvallis, Oregon, and died 18 Jan 1969 in Portland, Multnomah County, Oregon. No children.

Child of GLADYS I. MILKS is:
        i. MARGARET[10] MILKS, b. Abt. 1912, New York (adopted by her grandfather, Orson Milks).

1371. GEORGE DANIEL[9] MILKS *(FRANK ALBERT[8], WASHINGTON G.[7], DAVID[6] MILK, GEORGE[5], JONATHAN[4], JOB[3], JOHN[2], JOHN[1])* was born 13 Sep 1885 in Leon, Cattaraugus County, NY, and died 18 May 1970 in Fredonia, Chautauqua Co, NY. He married CAROL JEWELL ALLEN Abt. 1905, daughter of DEWITT ALLEN. She was born Abt. 1883 in Pennsylvania, and died 02 Nov 1958 in Erie, PA (aged 80 yrs).

Children of GEORGE MILKS and CAROL ALLEN are:
2362.   i.   EDITH S.[10] MILKS, b. 02 Oct 1907, Cattaraugus County, New York; d. Mar 1979, Erie, Erie County, Pennsylvania.
2363.   ii.   GEORGE CLINTON MILKS, JR., b. 14 Feb 1910, Leon, Cattaraugus County, NY; d. 25 Mar 1985, Brocton, Chautauqua Co, NY.
2364.   iii.   ALLEN ALBERT MILKS, b. 07 Apr 1917, Perrysburg, Cattaraugus County, New York; d. 27 Apr 1991, Soldiers & Sailors Memorial Hospital, Wellsboro, Tioga County, Pennsylvania.

1372. HERBERT ALBERT[9] MILKS *(FRANK ALBERT[8], WASHINGTON G.[7], DAVID[6] MILK, GEORGE[5], JONATHAN[4], JOB[3], JOHN[2], JOHN[1])* was born 09 Feb 1894 in Leon, Cattaraugus County, New York, and died 13 Nov 1927 in Pomfret, Chautauqua County, New York. He married ANNA VIOLA PRATT 28 Oct 1914 in Dayton, Cattaraugus County, New York, daughter of JOHN D. PRATT and CORA WILCOX. She was born 30 Aug 1893 in Little Valley, Cattaraugus County, New York, and died 30 Aug 1961 in Cottage, Cattaraugus County, New York.

OBITUARY - The Randolph Register, Friday, November 18, 1927. Page 3.
   Pimple on Nose Fatal to Man in Few Days
   Herbert Milks, 34 years old, died in the home of Carl Prosser, near Fredonia. A pimple on his nose developed an infection and he was sick only five days.
   Mr. Milks was the son of Frank and Flora Milks, born near South Dayton, and had always lived in that vicinity. The body was taken to his father's house where the funeral was held Wednesday at 1 p.m., with interment in Villenova cemetery.
   He is survived by four children, Fenton, Flora, Donald and Doris; a sister, Mrs. George Volk; two brothers, George of Dunkirk, and Clayton, who lives with his father, Frank Milks, between Cottage and Markhams.

   Anna married Herbert Albert Milks, the son of Frank Albert Milks and Flora Isabell Wood, on October 26, 1914. The couple lived in Dayton, Cattaraugus, New York. They had four children: Fenton J 1915, Flora 1918, Donald and Doris 1921. Herbert died in 1928.
   Anna married second Charles Freeman Darbee, the son of John Augustus Darbee and Malvina, about 1828. The couple lived in Dayton, Cattaraugus, New York. They had two children, Beverly 1929 and Ardis 1936.

DARBEE, ANNA V.
b. 8-30-1893 Jamestown, NY d. 8-30-1961 68y of carcinoma of rectum
Burial: Cottage Cemetery, Cottage, Cattaraugus County, New York, USA
Plot: Row 27 Sec. C lot 84 grave
 Parents: John D Pratt (1866 - 1938); Cora Wilcox Pratt (1866 - 1932)
 Spouses: Charles Freeman Darbee (1877 - 1954); Herbert Albert Milks (1894 - 1927)*

Children of HERBERT MILKS and ANNA PRATT are:
      i.   FENTON J.[10] MILKS, b. 15 May 1915, Leon, Cattaraugus County, New York; d. 12 Sep 1928, Dayton, Cattaraugus County, New York.
2365.   ii.   FLORA ELIZABETH MILKS, b. 16 Mar 1918, Leon, Cattaraugus County, New York; d. 11 Jun 2002, Visalia, Tulare County, California.
2366.   iii.   DONALD HERBERT MILKS, b. 12 Jul 1921, Leon, Cattaraugus County, New York; d. 30 Nov 2008, Brooksville, Florida.
2367.   iv.   DORIS HELEN MILKS, b. 12 Jul 1921, Dayton, Cattaraugus County, New York; d. 21 Oct 1989, Oklahoma City, Oklahoma.

1373. CLAYTON FREDERICK[9] MILKS *(FRANK ALBERT[8], WASHINGTON G.[7], DAVID[6] MILK, GEORGE[5], JONATHAN[4], JOB[3], JOHN[2], JOHN[1])* was born 18 Mar 1903 in Dayton, Cattaraugus County, New York, and died Oct 1987 in South Dayton, Cattaraugus County, New York. He married CLARA MINNIE VOLK 24 Dec 1924 in S. Dayton, Cattaraugus County, New York, daughter of JACOB VOLK and ANNA HOLTZ. She was born 02 Dec 1895 in Dayton, Cattaraugus County, New

York, and died Mar 1977 in South Dayton, Cattaraugus County, New York.

Children of CLAYTON MILKS and CLARA VOLK are:
2368. i.   CLAYTON FREDERICK[10] MILKS, JR., b. 24 Jan 1926, Dayton, Cattaraugus County, New York.
       ii. ALBERT MILKS, b. 04 Jan 1928, Dayton, Cattaraugus County, New York; d. 04 Jan 1928, Dayton, Cattaraugus County, New York.
2369. iii. JOYCE FERN MILKS, b. 11 Mar 1932, Dayton, Cattaraugus County, New York.

1374. MYRTLE ISOBEL[9] MILKS *(FRANK ALBERT[8], WASHINGTON G.[7], DAVID[6] MILK, GEORGE[5], JONATHAN[4], JOB[3], JOHN[2], JOHN[1])* was born 15 Nov 1904 in Dayton, Cattaraugus County, New York, and died 05 Jan 2004 in South Dayton, Cattaraugus County, New York. She married CHARLES CARL VOLK 29 Nov 1924 in S. Dayton, Cattaraugus County, New York, son of JACOB VOLK and ANNA HOLTZ. He was born 18 Jan 1902 in Dayton, Cattaraugus County, New York, and died 21 Sep 2004 in South Dayton, Cattaraugus County, New York.

OBITUARY

SOUTH DAYTON - *Charles Carl Volk, 102, of South Dayton, a maintenance worker for Gowanda Central School, died on Tuesday, Sept. 21, 2004 He was born on January 18, 1902 to Jacob & Anna (Holtz) Volk.*

Mr. Volk worked at the South Dayton Canning Factory for 14 years.

He also owned and operated a dairy farm in Cottage for many years.

He was a charter member of the Cottage Grange 609 and a Councilman for the Town of Dayton for 30 years.

He loved farming and making maple syrup.

He is survived by a son, Kenneth C. Volk of South Dayton; five grandchildren, six great-grandchildren and two great-great-grandchildren.

Besides his parents, he was preceded in death by his wife, Myrtle I. Volk, whom he married on Nov. 29, 1924; two brothers, George Volk and Floyd Volk; and two sisters, Clara Milks and Bertha Ruckh.

Child of MYRTLE MILKS and CHARLES VOLK is:
2370. i.   KENNETH CHARLES[10] VOLK, b. 13 Oct 1925; d. 5 children.

1375. HAZEL[9] HALLENBECK *(ESTHER[8] MILKS, WASHINGTON G.[7], DAVID[6] MILK, GEORGE[5], JONATHAN[4], JOB[3], JOHN[2], JOHN[1])* was born 22 Apr 1895 in Leon, Cattaraugus County, New York. She married (1) FITZHUGH JEMISON 17 Apr 1922, son of NICHOLAS JEMISON and CORA SILVERHEELS. He was born 21 Feb 1898 in Irving, New York, and died 01 Sep 1938 in Manhattan, New York City, New York. She married (2) EDWARD DEAN JIMERSON 19 Mar 1949. He was born 27 Aug 1894 in Irving, New York.

Child of HAZEL HALLENBECK and FITZHUGH JEMISON is:
2371. i.   JOAN[10] JEMISON, b. 19 Nov 1927, Manhattan, New York City, New York.

1376. ROSA E.[9] WAITE *(JONATHAN[8], MARTIN[7], MARY[6] MILKS, JONATHAN[5] MILK, JONATHAN[4], JOB[3], JOHN[2], JOHN[1])* was born Feb 1874 in Outagamie County, Wisconsin, and died 1928 in Outagamie County, Wisconsin. She married GEORGE MODER 1897 in Wisconsin. He was born 11 Aug 1874 in Wisconsin, and died 1944 in Outagamie County, Wisconsin.

Children of ROSA WAITE and GEORGE MODER are:
       i.   ARNIE A.[10] MODER, b. Dec 1897, Outagamie County, Wisconsin.
       ii. ELLA MODER, b. Jan 1899, Outagamie County, Wisconsin.
       iii. GEORGE E. MODER, b. Abt. 1903, Outagamie County, Wisconsin.
       iv. ROCK IRVIN MODER, b. 14 Jan 1905, Outagamie County, Wisconsin; d. 22 Apr 1987, Outagamie County, Wisconsin; m. BEATRICE MCGLIN; b. 10 Mar 1907, Bear Creek, Outagamie County, Wisconsin; d. 17 Feb 1984, Hortonville, Outagamie County, Wisconsin.
       v.   EMMA F. MODER, b. Abt. 1908, Outagamie County, Wisconsin.
       vi. JOHN H. MODER, b. Abt. 1911, Outagamie County, Wisconsin.

1377. ANNA[9] MOSHER *(EMMA JANELLA 'NELLIE'[8] BARKER, JANE[7] WAITE, MARY[6] MILKS, JONATHAN[5] MILK, JONATHAN[4], JOB[3], JOHN[2], JOHN[1])* was born 30 Nov 1886 in Leon, Cattaraugus County, New York. She married JAY WOLFE. He was born Abt. 1886.

Child of ANNA MOSHER and JAY WOLFE is:
    i. DOROTHY^{10} WOLFE.

1378. RAYMOND^9 MOSHER *(EMMA JANELLA 'NELLIE'^{8} BARKER, JANE^7 WAITE, MARY^6 MILKS, JONATHAN^5 MILK, JONATHAN^4, JOB^3, JOHN^2, JOHN^1)* was born 1888 in Leon, Cattaraugus County, New York. He married EMMA HINTZ. She was born Abt. 1890.

Children of RAYMOND MOSHER and EMMA HINTZ are:
    i. MARIAN^{10} MOSHER.
    ii. LESTER MOSHER.
    iii. GERALD MOSHER.
    iv. MERLIN MOSHER.

1379. IRVING HENRY^9 MOSHER *(EMMA JANELLA 'NELLIE'^{8} BARKER, JANE^7 WAITE, MARY^6 MILKS, JONATHAN^5 MILK, JONATHAN^4, JOB^3, JOHN^2, JOHN^1)* was born 27 Aug 1896 in New Albion, Cattaraugus County, New York. He married HELEN PINGLETON. She was born Abt. 1900.

Child of IRVING MOSHER and HELEN PINGLETON is:
    i. MARGARET^{10} MOSHER.

1380. LELAND^9 MOSHER *(EMMA JANELLA 'NELLIE'^{8} BARKER, JANE^7 WAITE, MARY^6 MILKS, JONATHAN^5 MILK, JONATHAN^4, JOB^3, JOHN^2, JOHN^1)* was born 14 May 1899 in New Albin, Allamakee County, Iowa, and died 1946. He married HELEN COURTER. She was born Abt. 1900.

Child of LELAND MOSHER and HELEN COURTER is:
    i. ROBERT^{10} MOSHER.

1381. MERTIE MAE^9 WAITE *(ALBERT^8, BENJAMIN^7, MARY^6 MILKS, JONATHAN^5 MILK, JONATHAN^4, JOB^3, JOHN^2, JOHN^1)* was born 04 Feb 1883 in Dayton, Cattaraugus County, New York, and died 23 Aug 1955. She married RALPH F. ALLEN 04 Dec 1903 in Cattaraugus County, New York. He was born Abt. 1883.

Children of MERTIE WAITE and RALPH ALLEN are:
2372.   i. FRANCES A.^{10} ALLEN, b. 28 Mar 1906, Cattaraugus County, New York.
2373.   ii. HELEN L. ALLEN, b. 23 Nov 1907, Cattaraugus County, New York.
2374.   iii. DORIS I. ALLEN, b. 19 Aug 1912, Cattaraugus County, New York; d. Dec 1981, South Dayton, Cattaraugus County, New York.
2375.   iv. ALBERT CLINTON ALLEN, b. 08 Jun 1917, Cattaraugus County, New York.

1382. NETTIE M.^{9} WAITE *(ALBERT^8, BENJAMIN^7, MARY^6 MILKS, JONATHAN^5 MILK, JONATHAN^4, JOB^3, JOHN^2, JOHN^1)* was born 12 Jun 1888 in East Leon, Cattaraugus County, New York. She married (1) JONATHAN POWELL 05 Dec 1906. He was born Abt. 1876 in Iowa. She married (2) ELTON L. GATES 30 Oct 1922 in Butte, Silver Bow County, Montana, son of T. GATES and MILDRED NEWKIRK. He was born Abt. 1882. She married (3) CHARLES E. GILL 18 Feb 1929 in Helena, Lewis and Clark County, Montana, son of GEORGE GILL and MARTHA STEARNS. He was born Abt. 1888 in Of Butte, Montana.

Children of NETTIE WAITE and JONATHAN POWELL are:
2376.   i. KENNETH^{10} POWELL, b. 01 Sep 1907, Cardwell, Montana.
2377.   ii. DONALD POWELL, b. 17 Jun 1912, Cardwell, Montana.
2378.   iii. CATHERINE O. POWELL, b. 01 Jan 1918, Whitehall, Montana.

1383. GLADYS^9 WAITE *(ALBERT^8, BENJAMIN^7, MARY^6 MILKS, JONATHAN^5 MILK, JONATHAN^4, JOB^3, JOHN^2, JOHN^1)* was born 21 Aug 1906 in East Leon, Cattaraugus County, New York. She married NELSON RICHTER 03 Nov 1928 in New York. He was born Abt. 1906 in Of Forestville, New York.

Children of GLADYS WAITE and NELSON RICHTER are:
- i. ROBERT[10] RICHTER, b. 15 Nov 1929, South Dayton, Cattaraugus County, New York; d. 1948.
- ii. RAYMOND RICHTER, b. 02 Jan 1936, South Dayton, Cattaraugus County, New York.

1384. ELVA L.[9] WATSON *(LUCY J.[8] WAITE, BENJAMIN[7], MARY[6] MILKS, JONATHAN[5] MILK, JONATHAN[4], JOB[3], JOHN[2], JOHN[1])* was born 09 May 1896 in East Leon, Cattaraugus County, New York. She married GEORGE NELSON. He was born Abt. 1896.

Children of ELVA WATSON and GEORGE NELSON are:
- i. ELINOR[10] NELSON, b. 07 Jul 1920, Cattaraugus County, New York.
- ii. EDWARD NELSON, b. 31 Jan 1922, Cattaraugus County, New York.

1385. FLORENCE E.[9] WAITE *(WILLIAM A.[8], BUTLER R.[7], MARY[6] MILKS, JONATHAN[5] MILK, JONATHAN[4], JOB[3], JOHN[2], JOHN[1])* was born 06 Mar 1897 in Kennedy, Chautauqua County, New York. She married HAROLD BROWN. He was born Abt. 1897 in Of Cattaraugus County, New York.

Children of FLORENCE WAITE and HAROLD BROWN are:
- i. FENTON[10] BROWN.
- ii. FRANCES BROWN.

1386. FREDERICK[9] CASE *(EMILY[8] HUBBARD, JEMIMA[7] MILKS, JOHN[6] MILK, JONATHAN[5], JONATHAN[4], JOB[3], JOHN[2], JOHN[1])* was born 06 Jul 1857 in Napoli, Cattaraugus County, New York, and died 02 Aug 1927 in Fredonia, Chautauqua County, New York. He married (1) LUCY F. PETIT 10 May 1876, daughter of M. S. PETIT. She was born Abt. 1857, and died 31 May 1877. He married (2) IDA SMITH 01 Sep 1880. She was born Abt. 1857.

Child of FREDERICK CASE and LUCY PETIT is:
- i. JESSE M.[10] CASE, b. 06 Feb 1877, Fredonia, Chautauqua County, New York.

Child of FREDERICK CASE and IDA SMITH is:
- ii. EVA LOUINE[10] CASE, b. 25 Jun 1883, Fredonia, Chautauqua County, New York.

1387. WARREN[9] MILKS *(NEWTON[8], JOHN[7], JOHN[6] MILK, JONATHAN[5], JONATHAN[4], JOB[3], JOHN[2], JOHN[1])* was born 06 Apr 1872 in Napoli, New York, and died 27 Apr 1948 in Cattaraugus County, New York. He married THERESA EDDY 08 May 1895 in New Albion, Cattaraugus County, New York, daughter of ALBERT EDDY and JULIA BATES. She was born 17 Jul 1879 in New York, and died 27 Nov 1946 in Cattaraugus County, New York.

Children of WARREN MILKS and THERESA EDDY are:
- i. VERNON[10] MILKS, b. 08 May 1896, Napoli, Cattaraugus County, New York.
- ii. KENNETH MILKS, b. 10 Jan 1898, Napoli, Cattaraugus County, New York; d. 17 Mar 1958, Cattaraugus County, New York.
- 2379. iii. VICTOR J. MILKS, b. 27 Mar 1901, Napoli, Cattaraugus Co, NY; d. 17 Jun 1962, Cattaraugus County, New York.

1388. HENRY JOHN[9] MILKS *(NEWTON[8], JOHN[7], JOHN[6] MILK, JONATHAN[5], JONATHAN[4], JOB[3], JOHN[2], JOHN[1])* was born 20 Feb 1880 in Napoli, Cattaraugus Co, NY, and died 21 Apr 1947 in Cattaraugus County, New York. He married ZANA IONE NIEMAN Abt. 1908, daughter of HENRY NIEMAN and MINNIE PLOUGH. She was born 19 Jan 1891 in Ypsilanti, Michigan, and died 1957.

Children of HENRY MILKS and ZANA NIEMAN are:
- i. MINNIE "IONE"[10] MILKS, b. 14 Aug 1909, Cattaraugus County, New York; d. Nov 1983, Randolph, Cattaraugus County, New York; m. KLINE F. DIETER, 17 Dec 1938; b. 19 Sep 1906, East Randolph, Cattaraugus County, New York; d. 05 Mar 1985, Randolph, Cattaraugus County, New York.
- 2380. ii. BESSIE ETTA MILKS, b. 07 Dec 1911, Coldspring, Cattaraugus County, New York; d. 27 May 1990, Cattaraugus County, New York.
- iii. CLEO H. MILKS, b. 04 Nov 1914, Cattaraugus County, New York; d. 17 Jan 1989, NY?.

2381.　iv.　ALMA CELIA MILKS, b. 20 Oct 1916, Cattaraugus County, New York; d. 22 May 1991, Kennedy, Chautauqua County, New York.

2382.　v.　MERLE DOUGLAS MILKS, b. 05 Mar 1919, Napoli, Cattaraugus County, New York; d. 17 Feb 1945.

1389. BLANCHE[9] MILKS *(NEWTON[8], JOHN[7], JOHN[6] MILK, JONATHAN[5], JONATHAN[4], JOB[3], JOHN[2], JOHN[1])* was born 21 Jun 1885 in Napoli, Cattaraugus County, New York, and died 13 Feb 1965 in Cattaraugus, Cattaraugus County, NY. She married JAMES MONTELL "MONTY" KILBY, son of JOSEPH KILBY and ALICE ROOT. He was born 02 Sep 1880 in New Albion, Cattaraugus County, New York, and died 22 Oct 1930 in New Albion, Cattaraugus County, NY.

Children of BLANCHE MILKS and JAMES KILBY are:

2383.　i.　FLORENCE LEOLA[10] KILBY, b. 19 Dec 1906, New Albion, Cattaraugus County, NY; d. 03 Feb 1968, New Albion, Cattaraugus County, NY.

　　ii.　FLOYD HENRY KILBY, b. 17 Jul 1912, New Albion, Cattaraugus County, New York; m. VIRGINIA HAWKINS; b. Abt. 1912.

　　iii.　JAMES LESTER KILBY, b. 26 Apr 1918, New Albion, Cattaraugus County, New York; m. ELEANOR BOARDMAN; b. Abt. 1918.

2384.　iv.　DOROTHY IRENE KILBY, b. 12 Mar 1926, New Albion, Cattaraugus County, New York; d. 27 Sep 2000, Falconer, Chautauqua County, New York.

1390. ANNA BELL[9] MILKS *(WILLARD[8], JOHN[7], JOHN[6] MILK, JONATHAN[5], JONATHAN[4], JOB[3], JOHN[2], JOHN[1])* was born 20 Oct 1871 in Napoli, New York, and died 19 Feb 1911 in New Albion, New York. She married MORTIMER A. NILES Abt. 1897. He was born 1847 in New Albion, Cattaraugus County, New York.

Children of ANNA MILKS and MORTIMER NILES are:

2385.　i.　EVA MAY[10] NILES, b. 12 Mar 1899, New Albion, Cattaraugus County, New York; d. Mar 1981, Perrysburg, Cattaraugus County, New York.

2386.　ii.　LUCY MALINDA NILES, b. 17 Aug 1900, New Albion, Cattaraugus County, New York; d. Apr 1978, Angola, Erie County, New York.

2387.　iii.　WILLIAM MORTIMER NILES, b. 29 Dec 1902, New Albion, Cattaraugus County, New York; d. 13 Mar 1990.

2388.　iv.　HERBERT ALBERT NILES, b. 07 Jul 1905, New York.

1391. MYRTLE A.[9] MILKS *(JOHN D.[8], JOHN[7], JOHN[6] MILK, JONATHAN[5], JONATHAN[4], JOB[3], JOHN[2], JOHN[1])* was born 25 Dec 1874 in Napoli, Cattaraugus County, New York, and died 11 Feb 1966 in Cattaraugus County, New York. She married FRED S. MONROE Abt. 1894. He was born 04 Jul 1870 in Steamburg, Cattaraugus County, New York, and died 11 Mar 1917 in Napoli, Cattaraugus County, New York.

Child of MYRTLE MILKS and FRED MONROE is:

2389.　i.　JOHN S.[10] MONROE, b. 21 Feb 1897, Little Valley, Cattaraugus County, New York; d. 03 Jun 1977, Randolph, Cattaraugus County, New York.

1392. JENNIE E.[9] MILKS *(JOHN D.[8], JOHN[7], JOHN[6] MILK, JONATHAN[5], JONATHAN[4], JOB[3], JOHN[2], JOHN[1])* was born Sep 1876 in Napoli, Cattaraugus County, New York. She married CLARENCE H. COVEDILL, son of JOHN COVEDILL. He was born 03 Apr 1876 in New York.

Children of JENNIE MILKS and CLARENCE COVEDILL are:

2390.　i.　ETTA P.[10] COVEDILL, b. Jul 1899, Coldspring, Cattaraugus County, New York.

　　ii.　MYRTLE A. COVEDILL, b. Abt. 1903, Cold Spring, Cattaraugus County, New York; m. RUTHERFORD WHITCOMB.

　　iii.　CLAIR D. COVEDILL, b. Abt. 1905, Cold Spring, Cattaraugus County, New York; d. d.y..

2391.　iv.　PEARL D. COVEDILL, b. 18 Mar 1908, Cold Spring, Cattaraugus County, New York; d. Nov 1974, Randolph, Cattaraugus County, New York.

2392.　v.　FREDERICK C. COVEDILL, b. 31 Aug 1911, Cold Spring, Cattaraugus County, New York; d. Sep 1964.

2393.　vi.　LEO D. COVEDILL, b. Abt. Jul 1913, Cold Spring, Cattaraugus County, New York.

2394.　vii.　ROBERT C. COVEDILL, b. Abt. Jun 1918, Cold Spring, Cattaraugus County, New York.

1393. DAVID[9] MILKS *(JOHN D.[8], JOHN[7], JOHN[6] MILK, JONATHAN[5], JONATHAN[4], JOB[3], JOHN[2], JOHN[1])* was born 05 Jun 1883 in Napoli, Cattaraugus County, New York. He married (1) VELMA _____. He married (2) FLORENCE SHEDD Abt. 1903, daughter of JOHN SHEDD and REBECCA KYLER. She was born Jun 1887, and died 25 Dec 1933 in Napoli, Cattaraugus County, New York.

Children of DAVID MILKS and FLORENCE SHEDD are:
- i. LEROY[10] MILKS, b. 13 Feb 1905, Napoli, Cattaraugus County, New York; d. 13 Feb 1905, Napoli, Cattaraugus County, New York.
- 2395. ii. JOHN D. MILKS, b. 05 Aug 1906, Napoli, Cattaraugus Co, NY; d. Bet. 1956 - 1977.
- 2396. iii. EMERSON S. MILKS, b. 23 Apr 1909, Napoli, Cattaraugus County, New York; d. 19 Jan 1977, W.C.A Hospital, Jamestown, Chautauqua County, New York.
- 2397. iv. NORRIS D. MILKS, b. 11 Jul 1911.
- 2398. v. HUGH LINCOLN MILKS, b. 12 Feb 1916; d. 30 Jul 1987.
- 2399. vi. JESSE DAVID MILKS, b. 08 May 1920, Cattaraugus County, New York; d. 06 May 1990, Cherry Creek, Chautauqua County, New York.

1394. EDNA E.[9] MERCHANT *(NANCY S.[8] MILKS, JOHN[7], JOHN[6] MILK, JONATHAN[5], JONATHAN[4], JOB[3], JOHN[2], JOHN[1])* was born 03 Jan 1877 in East Randolph Cemetery, East Randolph, Cattaraugus Co., NY, and died 01 Jul 1947 in Cattaraugus Co., New York. She married (1) CLINTON E. REEVES, son of DANIEL REEVES and SOPHRONIA _____. He was born Dec 1872, and died 1902 in Cattaraugus County, New York. She married (2) JAMES HARVEY BURR 15 Jul 1903 in Cattaraugus County, New York, son of STEPHEN BURR and LYDIA WILSON. He was born 1869 in Cattaraugus Co., New York, and died 20 Oct 1931 in Cattaraugus Co., New York.

Child of EDNA MERCHANT and CLINTON REEVES is:
- 2400. i. LLOYD VINTON[10] REEVES, SR., b. 11 Dec 1899, Cattaraugus Co., New York.

Children of EDNA MERCHANT and JAMES BURR are:
- ii. MILDRED LOUISE[10] BURR, b. Abt. 1904, Cattaraugus Co., New York; d. 1970.
- 2401. iii. LOUISA N. BURR, b. 19 Oct 1907, Coldspring, Cattaraugus Co., New York; d. 13 Dec 2001, Coldspring, Cattaraugus Co., New York.
- 2402. iv. ODESSA P. BURR, b. 22 Jul 1909, Cattaraugus Co., New York; d. 08 Feb 2004, Cattaraugus Co., New York.
- v. LELAND J. BURR, b. Abt. 1912, Cattaraugus Co., New York; d. 1996.

1395. ORA V.[9] MERCHANT *(NANCY S.[8] MILKS, JOHN[7], JOHN[6] MILK, JONATHAN[5], JONATHAN[4], JOB[3], JOHN[2], JOHN[1])* was born 22 Nov 1879 in East Randolph, Cattaraugus Co., NY, and died Dec 1965. She married CHARLES G. MC ELWAINE 27 Jun 1908 in Cattaraugus County, New York, son of BENJAMIN MC ELWAINE and ANNA WAGER. He was born Jan 1869 in Cattaraugus Co., New York.

Child of ORA MERCHANT and CHARLES MC ELWAINE is:
- i. CATHERINE M.[10] MC ELWAINE, b. Abt. 1911, Conewango, Cattaraugus Co., NY.

1396. PEARL M.[9] MERCHANT *(NANCY S.[8] MILKS, JOHN[7], JOHN[6] MILK, JONATHAN[5], JONATHAN[4], JOB[3], JOHN[2], JOHN[1])* was born 1888 in East Randolph, Cattaraugus Co., NY, and died 1983 in Conewango, Cattaraugus Co., NY. She married LEIGH E TINGUE. He was born 06 Oct 1886 in Leon, Cattaraugus Co., NY, and died 1947 in Conewango, Cattaraugus Co., NY.

Child of PEARL MERCHANT and LEIGH TINGUE is:
- 2403. i. FRANK LEE[10] TINGUE, b. 03 Jan 1917, Conewango, Cattaraugus Co., NY; d. 17 Mar 2001, Newark, New York.

1397. BENJAMIN "BENNIE" M.[9] BOSWELL *(ELEANOR R.[8] MILKS, BENJAMIN B.[7], JOHN[6] MILK, JONATHAN[5], JONATHAN[4], JOB[3], JOHN[2], JOHN[1])* was born 23 Aug 1879, and died 16 Dec 1918 in Russell, Geauga County, Ohio (Bronchial Pneumonia). He married SARAH MANSON Abt. 1912 in Geauga County, Ohio. She was born 1880, and died 1962 in Russell, Geauga County, Ohio.

Child of BENJAMIN BOSWELL and SARAH MANSON is:
    i. BABY BOY[10] BOSWELL, b. 14 Jan 1914, Russell, Geauga County, Ohio (premature); d. 14 Jan 1914, Russell, Geauga County, Ohio (14 hours old).

1398. ZADIE ANN[9] MILKS *(ALVIN L.[8], BENJAMIN B.[7], JOHN[6] MILK, JONATHAN[5], JONATHAN[4], JOB[3], JOHN[2], JOHN[1])* was born 14 Jul 1881 in Springfield, Nebraska, and died 15 Aug 1941 in Omaha, Nebraska. She married EDMOND R. PARKS 01 Sep 1901 in Randolph, NY. He was born 26 Jul 1877 in Randolph, NY, and died 14 Jun 1940 in Nebraska.

Child of ZADIE MILKS and EDMOND PARKS is:
2404. i. HELEN I.[10] PARKS, b. 30 Aug 1902, Nebraska; d. 19 Sep 1998, Omaha, Douglas County, Nebraska.

1399. NORA OLIVE[9] MILKS *(ALVIN L.[8], BENJAMIN B.[7], JOHN[6] MILK, JONATHAN[5], JONATHAN[4], JOB[3], JOHN[2], JOHN[1])* was born 18 Feb 1883 in Napoli, Cattaraugus Co, NY, and died 1927 in Little Valley, Cattaraugus Co., NY. She married WILLIAM ERNEST TIMME 09 Jun 1907 in Cattaraugus, NY, son of CARL TIMME and MISS BROCKMAN. He was born Apr 1887.

Children of NORA MILKS and WILLIAM TIMME are:
2405. i. AUTUMN EVA[10] TIMME, b. 08 Jul 1908, Mansfield, Cattaraugus County, New York; d. 14 Jan 1992, Olean, NY.
    ii. DOROTHEA TIMME, b. 29 Nov 1913, Little Valley, Cattaraugus County, New York; d. 31 Jul 1916, Little Valley, Cattaraugus County, New York.
    iii. GLEN TIMME, b. 04 Dec 1919, Cattaraugus County, New York.

1400. DUARD ALVIN[9] MILKS *(ALVIN L.[8], BENJAMIN B.[7], JOHN[6] MILK, JONATHAN[5], JONATHAN[4], JOB[3], JOHN[2], JOHN[1])* was born 17 Aug 1884 in Napoli, Cattaraugus County, New York, and died 08 Dec 1930 in Springfield, Nebraska. He married MAUDE MAE WHITCOMB 10 Feb 1915, daughter of EDWIN WHITCOMB and MARY SATTLER. She was born 21 Jun 1889 in Randolph, Cattaraugus County, New York.

Children of DUARD MILKS and MAUDE WHITCOMB are:
2406. i. DUARD ALVIN[10] MILKS, JR., b. 25 Sep 1917, Springfield, Nebraska; d. 19 Jun 2000, San Bruno, California.
    ii. MARY JOSEPHINE MILKS, b. 21 Jul 1920.
    iii. MILDRED MAE MILKS, b. 03 Jan 1923.

1401. CORA DIANE[9] MILKS *(ALVIN L.[8], BENJAMIN B.[7], JOHN[6] MILK, JONATHAN[5], JONATHAN[4], JOB[3], JOHN[2], JOHN[1])* was born 20 Feb 1887. She married JAMES 'WORTHY' ECKERT 25 Jun 1912, son of HIRAM ECKERT and FRANCES EDDY. He was born 30 Jan 1885 in Little Valley, Cattaraugus County, New York.

Children of CORA MILKS and JAMES ECKERT are:
    i. JAMES ROBERT[10] ECKERT, b. 24 May 1918, Springfield, Sarpy County, Nebraska; d. 22 Dec 1918, Springfield, Sarpy County, Nebraska.
    ii. LILLIAN ECKERT, b. 12 Sep 1920, Springfield, Sarpy County, Nebraska; m. BILL MEACHAM.
    iii. DONALD ECKERT, b. 12 Jan 1922, Springfield, Sarpy County, Nebraska; d. 1929, Springfield, Sarpy County, Nebraska.
    iv. MARILYN ECKERT, b. 17 Oct 1923, Springfield, Sarpy County, Nebraska; m. LYNN PHILLIPS; b. Abt. 1923.
    v. DEAN ECKERT, b. 19 Feb 1925, Springfield, Sarpy County, Nebraska; d. 1932, Springfield, Sarpy County, Nebraska.
    vi. HAROLD ECKERT, b. 27 May 1930, Springfield, Sarpy County, Nebraska.

1402. GLEN C.[9] MILKS *(ALVIN L.[8], BENJAMIN B.[7], JOHN[6] MILK, JONATHAN[5], JONATHAN[4], JOB[3], JOHN[2], JOHN[1])* was born 22 Dec 1891 in Springfield, Nebraska, and died 06 Dec 1950. He married MARTHA NICHOLSON 1921, daughter of DAVID NICHOLSON and SYLVIA STEPANEK. She was born 23 Nov 1900 in Springfield, Nebraska, and died 1967.

Children of GLEN MILKS and MARTHA NICHOLSON are:
2407. i. ALVIN HENRY "AL"[10] MILKS, SR., b. 12 Mar 1927, Springfield, Sarpy County, Nebraska; d. 16 Jan 2003,

Box Butte, Nebraska.
- ii. JOHN B. MILKS, b. 03 Jan 1929, Springfield, Sarpy County, Nebraska; m. MARILYN _____; b. Abt. 1930.
- iii. DARLENE MILKS, b. 04 Sep 1930, Springfield, Sarpy County, Nebraska; m. FRED GLESMANN; b. Abt. 1930.

2408. iv. GLEN C. MILKS, b. 08 Jun 1940, Springfield, Sarpy County, Nebraska.

1403. ANNA LILLIE[9] MILKS (*ALVIN L.[8], BENJAMIN B.[7], JOHN[6] MILK, JONATHAN[5], JONATHAN[4], JOB[3], JOHN[2], JOHN[1]*) was born 06 Jul 1893. She married EDWIN M. WHIPPLE. He was born 1890.

Children of ANNA MILKS and EDWIN WHIPPLE are:
2409. i. HARLOW[10] WHIPPLE, b. 05 Jul 1912, Little Valley, Cattaraugus County, NY; d. 19 May 1949.
2410. ii. CLARA ALMEDA WHIPPLE, b. 03 Feb 1915, New Albion, Cattaraugus County, New York.

1404. BESSIE IRENE[9] MILKS (*EUGENE BENJAMIN[8], BENJAMIN B.[7], JOHN[6] MILK, JONATHAN[5], JONATHAN[4], JOB[3], JOHN[2], JOHN[1]*) was born 1889 in Randolph, Cattaraugus County, New York. She married (1) PHIN SMITH Abt. 1904. He was born Abt. 1889. She married (2) EDWARD GEORGE HULBERT 03 Jun 1910 in Chautauqua County, New York, son of GEORGE HULBERT and ANNA MCGRATH. He was born 1889. She married (3) FRANK W. KUHANECK, JR. Abt. 1915 in Cattaraugus County, New York, son of FRANK KIYANECK and ELIZABETH _____. He was born Abt. 1889 in New York.

Children of BESSIE MILKS and PHIN SMITH are:
- i. EMMAGINE 'EMMIE'[10] SMITH, b. Abt. 1904, Cattaraugus County, New York; d. Bef. 14 Apr 2005; m. MISTTER COUDREY.
- ii. GEORGE EARL SMITH, b. 30 Jan 1906, Cattaraugus County, New York.

Children of BESSIE MILKS and EDWARD HULBERT are:
- iii. VIVIAN[10] HULBERT, b. Abt. 1911, Cattaraugus County, New York; d. Bef. 14 Apr 2005; m. MISTTER KOHUT.
- iv. CHESTER HULBERT, b. Abt. 1913, Cattaraugus County, New York.
- v. WILLIAM HULBERT, b. 05 Aug 1914, Cattaraugus County, New York.

Children of BESSIE MILKS and FRANK KUHANECK are:
- vi. WILLIAM[10] KUHANECK, b. 05 Jul 1915, Cattaraugus County, New York; d. 18 May 1993, Ravalli County, Montana; m. MAGNOLIA MAE MURRAY; b. 12 Apr 1897, Benton, Douglas County, Missouri; d. Apr 1974, Ravalli County, Montana.

2411. vii. ELIZABETH KUHANECK, b. 13 Jul 1917, Cattaraugus County, New York; d. Bef. 14 Apr 2005.
- viii. EDWARD KUHANECK, b. Abt. Oct 1918, Cattaraugus County, New York; d. Bef. 14 Apr 2005.
- ix. RUSSELL FRANK KUHANECK, b. 16 Apr 1922, Leon, Cattaraugus County, New York; d. Apr 1987, Ogden, Weber County, Utah.
- x. LILLIAN I. KUHANECK, b. 06 Sep 1925, Salamanca, Cattaraugus County, New York; d. 14 Apr 2005, Allegany, Cattaraugus County, New York; m. KENNETH P. WILLSEY, 15 Jan 1952; d. Jun 1985, Cattaraugus County, New York.

    OBITUARY
    Lillian I. Willsey
    Allegany: Lillian I. Willsey, formerly of Salamanca and a current resident of the Five Mile Road, Allegany died Thursday April 14, 2005 at her home.
    Born in Salamanca on September 6, 1925 she was a daughter of Frank and Bessie Milks Kuhaneck. On January 15, 1952 she married Kenneth P. Willsey who predeceased her in June of 1985.
    Mrs. Willsey was employed with Acme Electric for 24 years prior to her retirement. She was a member of the 60 plus club of Allegany and AARP, chapter 844. She enjoyed flowers and houseplants, decorating and traveling, especially bus trips.
    She is survived by several nieces and nephews including George J. Smith of AL, Shirley A. (Claude) Case of Killbuck, Rae L. (John) Earley, Marsha L. Mick of WV, Gail M. (Lyn) Hoard of CA,, Pamela K. (Larry) Sturdevant of Salamanca, George Kuhaneck, Gordon L. (Sylvia) Schultz, Jr. of Salamanca, Paula E. (Terry) Lacroix of Salamanca and Marsha (Tony) NIrton of VA and a very special friend Thomasina Washburn of Allegany.
    In addition to her husband she was predeceased by sisters Emogene Coudrey, Vivian Kohut and

Elizabeth Schultz; brothers George Smith, Chester Hulbert, William Kuhaneck, Edward Kuhaneck, Russell Kuhaneck and Lester Kuhaneck a nephew Miklas E. Kohut and nieces Yvonne Shongo and Margaret Brown.

Friends are invited to attend a funeral service on Monday April 18, 2005 at the Casey, Halwig & Hartle Funeral Home, 3128 West State Rd., Olean at 11:00 AM. Rev. Mark C. Schultz, great great nephew of Mrs. Willsey will officiate.

Burial will be in Allegany Cemetery, Allegany. Memorials may be made to Homecare and Hospice, 1225 West State St., Olean, NY or to a charity of the donor's choice. .

    xi. LESTER KUHANECK, d. Bef. 14 Apr 2005.

1405. ROSE^9 MILKS *(EUGENE BENJAMIN^8, BENJAMIN B.^{7}, JOHN^6 MILK, JONATHAN^5, JONATHAN^4, JOB^3, JOHN^2, JOHN^1)* was born 1893 in Ellington, Chautauqua County, New York. She married OSSIE D. LUCE 01 Oct 1908 in Cattaraugus, NY, by William Manning, son of EMERSON LUCE and ORA WAITE. He was born 1884 in Cattaraugus County, New York.

Children of ROSE MILKS and OSSIE LUCE are:
    i. FLORENCE^{10} LUCE, b. Abt. Mar 1917, Cattaraugus County, New York.
    ii. HELEN LUCE, b. Abt. 1921, Cattaraugus County, New York.
    iii. GERALD LUCE, b. Abt. Dec 1926, Cattaraugus County, New York.

1406. DAVID WESLEY^9 MILKS *(EDWARD R.^{8}, DAVID^7 MILK, JOHN^6, JONATHAN^5, JONATHAN^4, JOB^3, JOHN^2, JOHN^1)* was born 10 Jun 1881 in Red House, Cattaraugus County, New York, and died 06 Dec 1929 in Red House, Cattaraugus County, New York. He married ELLEN GERTRUDE EARL 14 Sep 1902 in Red House, Cattaraugus County, New York, daughter of JAMES EARL and ALLIE HOUGH. She was born 1885 in New York, and died 24 Aug 1963 in Friendship, Allegany County, New York.

Children of DAVID MILKS and ELLEN EARL are:
2412.   i. VERA VIOLA^{10} MILKS, b. 11 Oct 1903, Red House, Cattaraugus County, New York; d. 27 Sep 1997, Kennedy, Cattaraugus County, New York.
2413.   ii. HENRY WESLEY "HANK" MILKS, b. 13 Aug 1911, Red House, Cattaraugus County, New York; d. 26 Mar 1990, Olean, Cattaraugus County, New York.
2414.   iii. WILBUR L. MILKS, b. 07 Nov 1916, Red House, Cattaraugus County, New York; d. 24 Oct 1980, Bolivar, Allegany County, New York.
    iv. AUBREY R. MILKS, b. 03 Jul 1918, Red House, Cattaraugus County, New York; d. 11 May 1995, Salamanca, Cattaraugus, NY 14779 (never married).

1407. BERTHA MABEL^9 MILKS *(EDWARD R.^{8}, DAVID^7 MILK, JOHN^6, JONATHAN^5, JONATHAN^4, JOB^3, JOHN^2, JOHN^1)* was born 20 May 1882 in Red House, Cattaraugus County, New York, and died 10 Oct 1960 in Cuba, Allegany County, New York. She married ADELBERT KING Abt. 1914 in Not in Cattaraugus County Marriage records. He was born Abt. 1880, and died Bef. 10 Oct 1960.

Information on this family is from Helen (King) Leary, unless otherwise noted.

Children of BERTHA MILKS and ADELBERT KING are:
    i. ELVA J.^{10} KING, b. Abt. 1915; m. E. WILBUR SIMPSON; b. Abt. 1915.
    ii. HANFORD KING, b. Abt. 1917.
2415.   iii. THELMA LOUISE KING, b. 26 Jun 1919; d. 03 Jul 1991, Friendship, Allegany County, New York.
    iv. EUGENE "BUSTER" KING, b. Aft. 1919.
2416.   v. WILBUR "BUDDY" KING, b. 25 Nov 1925, Wirt, Allegany County, New York; d. 04 Jan 1992, Burlingame, San Mateo County, California.

1408. HOWARD HARDEN^9 HIXSON *(EVELINE LOUISE^8 MILKS, DAVID^7 MILK, JOHN^6, JONATHAN^5, JONATHAN^4, JOB^3, JOHN^2, JOHN^1)* was born 24 Apr 1874 in Valmont, Boulder County, Colorado, and died 05 Dec 1955 in Seattle, King County, Washington. He married VALLIE PEARL WHITE 1899, daughter of JOHN WHITE and NANCY MOORE. She was born Dec 1879 in Kansas, and died 06 Dec 1942 in Seattle, King County, Washington.

Children of HOWARD HIXSON and VALLIE WHITE are:
- i. CATHERINE[10] HIXSON, b. 01 Oct 1902, Denver, Colorado; d. Jan 1982, Seattle, King County, Washington; m. JOSEPH "FRENCHIE" LEMARB, 27 Mar 1937, Kitsap County, Washington; b. 11 Apr 1891, Montreal, Canada; d. Jan 1964, Seattle, King County, Washington.
- 2417. ii. HELEN ALICE HIXSON, b. 23 Oct 1903, Denver, Colorado; d. 17 Jun 1958, Bremerton, Kitsap County, Washington.
- iii. LUTHER N. HIXSON, b. 05 Aug 1906, Seattle, King County, Washington; d. 07 Mar 1975, Seattle, King County, Washington.
- 2418. iv. JOHN ROBERT HIXSON, b. 15 Feb 1925, Seattle, King County, Washington; d. 23 Oct 2010, Des Moines, King County, Washington.
- v. DOROTHY M. HIXSON, b. 20 Apr 1901, Denver, Colorado; d. 04 May 1901, Denver, Colorado.

1409. THOMAS EDSON 'TED'[9] HIXSON *(EVELINE LOUISE[8] MILKS, DAVID[7] MILK, JOHN[6], JONATHAN[5], JONATHAN[4], JOB[3], JOHN[2], JOHN[1])* was born 24 Dec 1875 in Valmont, Boulder County, Colorado, and died 03 May 1941 in Valmont, Boulder County, Colorado. He married DOLLIE ANN KING, daughter of JAMES KING and MARY _____. She was born 21 Nov 1877 in Colorado, and died 19 Jan 1964 in Valmont, Boulder County, Colorado.

Children of THOMAS HIXSON and DOLLIE KING are:
- 2419. i. CARLETON K.[10] HIXSON, b. 16 Apr 1905, Valmont, Boulder County, Colorado; d. May 1973, Caldwell, Canyon County, Idaho.
- ii. MABEL KING HIXSON, b. 19 Jun 1907, Valmont, Boulder County, Colorado; d. 06 Apr 1995, Fort Collins, Larimer County, Colorado. Never married.
- iii. MARY JANE HIXSON, b. 1911, Valmont, Boulder County, Colorado; d. 1977.
- iv. HELEN JOSEPHINE HIXSON, b. Apr 1917, Valmont, Boulder County, Colorado; d. 2005.

1410. MARY EMELINE[9] MILKS *(MANLEY DAVID[8], DAVID[7] MILK, JOHN[6], JONATHAN[5], JONATHAN[4], JOB[3], JOHN[2], JOHN[1])* was born 19 Sep 1881 in Conewango, Cattaraugus County, New York. She married EBER ALLEN 04 Jun 1908 in Conewango, Cattaraugus County, New York, son of GILBERT ALLEN and FRANCES HARTMANN. He was born 23 Jan 1887 in Gowanda, Cattaraugus County, New York.

Mary contributed records on her father's family.

Children of MARY MILKS and EBER ALLEN are:
- 2420. i. LAWRENCE G.[10] ALLEN, b. 08 Mar 1909, E. Randolph, NY; d. 01 Oct 1985, Gowanda, NY.
- 2421. ii. FLORENCE L. ALLEN, b. 03 Sep 1910.
- 2422. iii. GERTRUDE A. ALLEN, b. 19 Oct 1913.
- 2423. iv. RUBY ALLEN, b. 25 Dec 1916.

1411. MILFORD PENROSE[9] MILKS *(MANLEY DAVID[8], DAVID[7] MILK, JOHN[6], JONATHAN[5], JONATHAN[4], JOB[3], JOHN[2], JOHN[1])* was born 17 Jun 1888 in Cattaraugus County, New York, and died 04 Mar 1922 in Dallas, Texas. He married MAE ELSA KERNEY. She was born in Newfoundland, and died 26 Sep 1926 in Dallas, Texas.

Children of MILFORD MILKS and MAE KERNEY are:
- i. MILDRED I.[10] MILKS, b. 30 Sep 1909, East Randolph, Cattaraugus Co., NY; d. Bef. 22 Sep 2003; m. MARION R. MALONE; b. Abt. 1901, Texas.
- 2424. ii. FRANCES ALTHEA "BETTY" MILKS, b. 09 Mar 1914, East Randolph, Cattaraugus Co., NY; d. 29 Jun 2000, Dallas, Dallas, Texas.
- 2425. iii. MILFORD EDWARD MILKS, b. 23 Jan 1920, Cleveland, Ohio; d. 22 Sep 2003, Richardson, Dallas County, Texas.

1412. LOUIS ELMER[9] MILKS *(MANLEY DAVID[8], DAVID[7] MILK, JOHN[6], JONATHAN[5], JONATHAN[4], JOB[3], JOHN[2], JOHN[1])* was born 31 Dec 1896 in Jefferson County, Pennsylvania, and died 26 Mar 1974 in Westmoreland County, Pennsylvania. He married SAVILLA A. BOWMAN, daughter of HENRY BOWMAN and BERTHA _____. She was born 15 Jan 1903 in Jefferson County, Pennsylvania, and died 09 Feb 1988 in Westmoreland County, Pennsylvania.

Children of LOUIS MILKS and SAVILLA BOWMAN are:
- i. LOUIS ELMER[10] MILKS, JR., b. 03 Aug 1920, Westmoreland County, Pennsylvania; d. 14 Jul 1997, Westmoreland County, Pennsylvania; m. MARY M. _____; b. 05 Mar 1921; d. 14 Feb 2009, Westmoreland County, Pennsylvania.
- ii. MARION MILKS, b. Bet. 1924 - 1925, Westmoreland County, Pennsylvania.
- iii. FRANCES MILKS, b. Bet. 1927 - 1928, Westmoreland County, Pennsylvania.

1413. JOHN B. 'TINT'[9] CHAMPLIN *(THERESA MARY[8] CASE, DEBORAH[7] MILKS, JOHN[6] MILK, JONATHAN[5], JONATHAN[4], JOB[3], JOHN[2], JOHN[1])* was born 12 Aug 1866 in Little Valley, Cattaraugus County, New York, and died 1938 in Little Valley, Cattaraugus County, New York. He married (1) NELLIE POTTS DEGOLE. She was born Abt. 1866. He married (2) FRANCES HARTE. He married (3) EMMA BULLARD 1888 in Cattaraugus County, New York, daughter of ALLEN BULLARD and ELIZA GUTHRIE. She was born 27 Nov 1868 in Salamanca, Cattaraugus County, New York.

JOHN B. 'TINT' CHAMPLIN was associated with his father in the Cattaraugus Cutlery Co. and was its president for many years. He also was president of the Little Valley Board of Education.

Children of JOHN CHAMPLIN and EMMA BULLARD are:
- 2426. i. HAZEL R.[10] CHAMPLIN, b. 12 Jan 1889, Little Valley, Cattaraugus County, New York.
- 2427. ii. JOHN BROWN FRANCIS CHAMPLIN III, b. 01 May 1892, Little Valley, Cattaraugus County, New York.
- 2428. iii. PHILIP T. CHAMPLIN, b. 23 Apr 1899, Little Valley, Cattaraugus County, New York; d. Aug 1968, Little Valley, Cattaraugus County, New York.

1414. DEBORAH[9] CASE *(WILLIAM R.[8], DEBORAH[7] MILKS, JOHN[6] MILK, JONATHAN[5], JONATHAN[4], JOB[3], JOHN[2], JOHN[1])* was born Abt. 1870 in Furnas County, Nebraska, and died 26 May 1950 in Boulder, Colorado. She married HARVEY NIXON PLATTS. He was born Abt. 1870, and died 25 May 1947 in Boulder, Colorado.

Children of DEBORAH CASE and HARVEY PLATTS are:
- 2429. i. HARLOW CASE[10] PLATTS, b. 03 Mar 1893, Little Valley, Cattaraugus County, New York; d. 07 Mar 1983, Boulder, Colorado.
- 2430. ii. HARVEY REGINALD PLATTS, b. 23 Aug 1894; d. 01 Feb 1980, Boulder, Colorado.

1415. THERESA[9] CASE *(WILLIAM R.[8], DEBORAH[7] MILKS, JOHN[6] MILK, JONATHAN[5], JONATHAN[4], JOB[3], JOHN[2], JOHN[1])* was born Abt. 1875 in Furnas County, Nebraska, and died in Bradford, Pennsylvania. She married BERT CRANDELL, son of JAMES CRANDELL and MARY SIBLEY. He was born Abt. 1875 in Napoli, Cattaraugus County, New York, and died in Buffalo, New York.

Child of THERESA CASE and BERT CRANDELL is:
- 2431. i. RHEA[10] CRANDELL, b. Little Valley, Cattaraugus County, New York.

1416. ELLIOTT JEAN[9] CASE *(JEAN J.[8], DEBORAH[7] MILKS, JOHN[6] MILK, JONATHAN[5], JONATHAN[4], JOB[3], JOHN[2], JOHN[1])* was born 30 Mar 1876 in Furnas County, Nebraska, and died 08 Sep 1903 in Little Valley, Cattaraugus County, New York. He married MINNIE MAUD MILLER, daughter of WILLIAM MILLER and MARY CLARK. She was born Mar 1874 in Iowa.

Children of ELLIOTT CASE and MINNIE MILLER are:
- i. LEONE[10] CASE, b. Nov 1897, Furnas County, Nebraska; d. 1901, Little Valley, Cattaraugus County, New York.
- ii. THERESSA MAUD CASE, b. 14 Aug 1899, Furnas County, Nebraska; d. 01 Jun 1985, Little Valley, Cattaraugus County, New York; m. CHARLES EDWARD MORRIS, Bet. 1920 - 1930, Youngstown, Mahoning County, Ohio ??; b. 03 Jan 1891, Youngstown, Mahoning County, Ohio; d. 01 Nov 1942, Little Valley, Cattaraugus County, New York. No children.
- 2432. iii. E. EMERSON CASE, b. 18 May 1901, Little Valley, Cattaraugus County, New York.

1417. DEAN JOSEPH[9] CASE *(JEAN J.[8], DEBORAH[7] MILKS, JOHN[6] MILK, JONATHAN[5], JONATHAN[4], JOB[3], JOHN[2], JOHN[1])* was born 19 Sep 1883 in Napoli, Cattaraugus County, New York, and died 03 Apr 1951 in Ocean City, Maryland. He married (1) PEARL GLOVER, daughter of WILLIAM GLOVER and MINNIE SWAN. He married (2) CLOTHILDE HARPER SHANNON.

Children of DEAN CASE and PEARL GLOVER are:
i. WILMA JENNETTE^{10} CASE, b. 02 May 1907, Kane, Pennsylvania; d. Mar 1936; m. CORYDON CAMPBELL; b. Abt. 1907, Little Valley, Cattaraugus County, New York.
2433. ii. J. ELLIOTT CASE, b. 01 Sep 1918, Salamanca, Cattaraugus County, New York.

Child of DEAN CASE and CLOTHILDE SHANNON is:
2434. iii. CLARINE HARPER^{10} CASE, b. 15 Apr 1923, Little Valley, Cattaraugus County, New York.

1418. LINA^9 CASE *(JEAN J.^{8}, DEBORAH^7 MILKS, JOHN^6 MILK, JONATHAN^5, JONATHAN^4, JOB^3, JOHN^2, JOHN^1)* was born 21 Jul 1888 in Little Valley, Cattaraugus County, New York. She married ALSON JOHN CHAMPLIN, son of JOHN CHAMPLIN and CORA GLOVER. He was born 29 May 1882 in New Albion, Cattaraugus County, New York, and died 31 Jan 1935 in Little Valley, Cattaraugus County, New York.
Lina contributed records of the descendants of Deborah Milks Case.

Children of LINA CASE and ALSON CHAMPLIN are:
2435. i. ROBERT DEAN^{10} CHAMPLIN, b. 21 Feb 1922, East Randolph, Cattaraugus County, New York.
2436. ii. IDA MAY CHAMPLIN, b. 26 Jul 1921, Eldrid, Pennsylvania.

1419. ADDIE MAY^9 CASE *(JEAN J.^{8}, DEBORAH^7 MILKS, JOHN^6 MILK, JONATHAN^5, JONATHAN^4, JOB^3, JOHN^2, JOHN^1)* was born 09 Feb 1892 in Furnas County, Nebraska. She married HAROLD WILLIAM BURRELL, son of WILLIAM BURRELL and ALMEDA RIDEOUT. He was born 21 May 1890, and died 21 Jun 1950 in Ellicottville, Cattaraugus County, New York.

Children of ADDIE CASE and HAROLD BURRELL are:
2437. i. DEAN WILLIAM^{10} BURRELL, b. 22 Jan 1913, Little Valley, Cattaraugus County, New York.
2438. ii. HAROLD AINSWORTH BURRELL, b. 17 Sep 1915, Little Valley, Cattaraugus County, New York.
2439. iii. BETTY JUNE BURRELL, b. 04 Jun 1926, Little Valley, Cattaraugus County, New York.

1420. WALLACE E.^{9} BROWN *(EMMA E.^{8} CASE, DEBORAH^7 MILKS, JOHN^6 MILK, JONATHAN^5, JONATHAN^4, JOB^3, JOHN^2, JOHN^1)* was born Sep 1875 in Little Valley, Cattaraugus County, New York, and died 1924. He married MARY DAWSON. She was born Abt. 1875.

Child of WALLACE BROWN and MARY DAWSON is:
i. DANFORTH^{10} BROWN, b. Tidioute, Pennsylvania.

1421. ANNA^9 BROWN *(EMMA E.^{8} CASE, DEBORAH^7 MILKS, JOHN^6 MILK, JONATHAN^5, JONATHAN^4, JOB^3, JOHN^2, JOHN^1)* was born 1880 in Little Valley, Cattaraugus County, New York. She married FRANK HOUTE. He was born Abt. 1880.

Children of ANNA BROWN and FRANK HOUTE are:
i. MAXINE^{10} HOUTE, b. Little Valley, Cattaraugus County, New York.
ii. MARSHALL HOUTE, b. Little Valley, Cattaraugus County, New York.

1422. R. EMERSON^9 BROWN *(EMMA E.^{8} CASE, DEBORAH^7 MILKS, JOHN^6 MILK, JONATHAN^5, JONATHAN^4, JOB^3, JOHN^2, JOHN^1)* was born Feb 1883 in Little Valley, Cattaraugus County, New York, and died 1934 in Olean, Cattaraugus County, New York. He married ETHEL WYATT. She was born Abt. 1883.

Children of R. BROWN and ETHEL WYATT are:
2440. i. JANICE^{10} BROWN.
2441. ii. VIRGINIA BROWN.
2442. iii. BETTY BROWN.

1423. ETHEL E.^{9} BROWN *(EMMA E.^{8} CASE, DEBORAH^7 MILKS, JOHN^6 MILK, JONATHAN^5, JONATHAN^4, JOB^3, JOHN^2, JOHN^1)* was born 10 Nov 1887 in Little Valley, Cattaraugus County, New York. She married JOHN LLOYD, son of MATTHEW LLOYD and ELIZABETH CARDEN. He was born 07 Jun 1886 in Salamanca, Cattaraugus County, New York.

Children of ETHEL BROWN and JOHN LLOYD are:
- i. MARGARET[10] LLOYD, b. 25 Jul 1912, Little Valley, Cattaraugus County, New York.
- 2443. ii. EMILY LLOYD, b. 13 Mar 1916, Olean, Cattaraugus County, New York.
- 2444. iii. ROBERTA LLOYD, b. 21 Feb 1919, Olean, Cattaraugus County, New York.
- 2445. iv. NANCY LLOYD, b. 31 Oct 1923, Olean, Cattaraugus County, New York.

1424. MILLIE[9] BARNARD *(JESSIE[8] CASE, DEBORAH[7] MILKS, JOHN[6] MILK, JONATHAN[5], JONATHAN[4], JOB[3], JOHN[2], JOHN[1])* was born 1877 in Little Valley, Cattaraugus County, New York, and died 1899 in Little Valley, Cattaraugus County, New York. She married WILLIAM COTTER. He was born Abt. 1877.

Child of MILLIE BARNARD and WILLIAM COTTER is:
- i. EDWARD[10] COTTER, b. 1898, Little Valley, Cattaraugus County, New York; d. 1899, Little Valley, Cattaraugus County, New York.

1425. EMMA V.[9] CASE *(JOHN DEBORAH[8], DEBORAH[7] MILKS, JOHN[6] MILK, JONATHAN[5], JONATHAN[4], JOB[3], JOHN[2], JOHN[1])* was born Apr 1882 in Furnas County, Nebraska. She married JAMES ROE DUDLEY. He was born Abt. 1882 in Canisteo, New York, and died in Olean, Cattaraugus County, New York.

Children of EMMA CASE and JAMES DUDLEY are:
- 2446. i. RICHARD[10] DUDLEY, b. Little Valley, Cattaraugus County, New York.
- 2447. ii. DR. WILLIAM DUDLEY, b. Kane, Pennsylvania.
- iii. JAMES ROE DUDLEY, b. Olean, Cattaraugus County, New York; d. Bougainville Isle, South Pacific; m. JULIA RYAN; b. Portville, New York. No children.
- 2448. iv. DR. DANIEL CLINTON DUDLEY, b. Olean, Cattaraugus County, New York.

1426. JAY WYATT[9] CASE *(JOHN DEBORAH[8], DEBORAH[7] MILKS, JOHN[6] MILK, JONATHAN[5], JONATHAN[4], JOB[3], JOHN[2], JOHN[1])* was born 06 Oct 1885 in Little Valley, Cattaraugus County, New York, and died Mar 1968 in Tucson, Arizona. He married THEO WATERS 31 Dec 1907 in Salamanca Cattaraugus County, New York, daughter of RICHARD WATERS and INDIA COY. She was born Abt. 1885.

Children of JAY CASE and THEO WATERS are:
- i. INDIA[10] CASE, b. 1908, Little Valley, Cattaraugus County, New York.
- 2449. ii. RUSSELL CASE, b. 1912, Little Valley, Cattaraugus County, New York.
- 2450. iii. JANETT CASE, b. 1918, Kane, Pennsylvania.
- 2451. iv. HARRIETT JANE CASE, b. 1921, Bolivar, New York.

1427. CLIFTON CLINTON[9] CASE *(JOHN DEBORAH[8], DEBORAH[7] MILKS, JOHN[6] MILK, JONATHAN[5], JONATHAN[4], JOB[3], JOHN[2], JOHN[1])* was born 14 Dec 1888 in Little Valley, Cattaraugus County, New York, and died 05 Dec 1960. He married NELLIE BERG 19 Aug 1906 in Cattaraugus County, New York. She was born 22 Mar 1887 in New York, and died Dec 1967 in Olean, Cattaraugus County, New York.

Children of CLIFTON CASE and NELLIE BERG are:
- 2452. i. VIRGINIA N.[10] CASE, b. 23 Aug 1907, Little Valley, Cattaraugus County, New York; d. 04 Jan 1980, Orlando, Orange County, Florida.
- 2453. ii. JOHN CLIFTON CASE, b. 07 Jan 1909, Kane, Pennsylvania; d. 07 Nov 1976, Forest City, Seminole County, Florida.
- 2454. iii. GLADYS N. CASE, b. 18 Jul 1911, Little Valley, Cattaraugus County, New York; d. 31 May 1993, Olean, Cattaraugus County, New York.

1428. ARNOLD DANIEL[9] CASE *(JOHN DEBORAH[8], DEBORAH[7] MILKS, JOHN[6] MILK, JONATHAN[5], JONATHAN[4], JOB[3], JOHN[2], JOHN[1])* was born Oct 1889 in Little Valley, Cattaraugus County, New York and died 21 Jan. 1954. He married MARGARET WILLOVER Abt. 1922 in New York. She was born 09 Aug. 1904 in New York and died 19 Oct. 1989.

Children of ARNOLD CASE and MARGARET WILLOVER are:
- I ARNOLD DANIEL CASE, b. 1923; d. 1924

ii. WILSON RODGER[10] CASE, b. 30 Dec 1924, Olean, Cattaraugus County, New York; d. 26 Dec 1976, Lakeview, New York; m. (1) MARGERY _____; m. (2) BETTY LEARN; b. Abt. 1925; d. 1991, Lakeview, NY.
iii. NORMAN B. CASE, b. 02 Aug 1929, Olean, Cattaraugus County, NY; m. BARBARA A. ____; b. 16 Feb 1933.

1429. MINA M.[9] CASE *(JOHN DEBORAH[8], DEBORAH[7] MILKS, JOHN[6] MILK, JONATHAN[5], JONATHAN[4], JOB[3], JOHN[2], JOHN[1])* was born Nov 1892 in Furnas County, Nebraska, and died 1959 in Olean, Cattaraugus County, New York. She married EARL HENRY ZIMMERMAN, son of HENRY ZIMMERMAN and ELLEN GRUNDY. He was born 22 Jan 1893 in New York, and died Feb 1979 in Olean, Cattaraugus County, New York.

Child of MINA CASE and EARL ZIMMERMAN is:
2455. i. ROBERT H.[10] ZIMMERMAN, b. 03 Nov 1917, Olean, Cattaraugus County, New York; d. 06 Jun 2002, Naples, Collier County, Florida.

1430. JAMES ANDREW[9] CASE *(ANDREW J.[8], DEBORAH[7] MILKS, JOHN[6] MILK, JONATHAN[5], JONATHAN[4], JOB[3], JOHN[2], JOHN[1])* was born 06 Apr 1884 in Little Valley, Cattaraugus County, New York. He married AMY JOHANNA CARROLL, daughter of TIMOTHY CARROLL and MARGARET _____. She was born Abt. 1885 in Little Valley, Cattaraugus County, New York.

Children of JAMES CASE and AMY CARROLL are:
2456. i. JEROME CARROLL[10] CASE, b. 05 Feb 1908, Little Valley, Cattaraugus County, New York; d. 10 Jun 1960, Little Valley, Cattaraugus Co., NY.
2457. ii. GERALD C. CASE, b. 17 Feb 1911, Little Valley, Cattaraugus County, New York.
iii. ROGER LEO CASE, b. 14 Jul 1918, Little Valley, Cattaraugus County, New York; d. 25 Jul 1989, New Port Richey, Pasco County, Florida; m. (1) ELLEN M. _____; b. 1930; m. (2) KATHERINE ALICE MURPHY; b. Abt. 1918.
iv. MARGARET JANE CASE, b. 30 Mar 1920, Little Valley, Cattaraugus County, New York.

1431. LELA[9] CASE *(ANDREW J.[8], DEBORAH[7] MILKS, JOHN[6] MILK, JONATHAN[5], JONATHAN[4], JOB[3], JOHN[2], JOHN[1])* was born 31 Jul 1886 in Little Valley, Cattaraugus County, New York, and died in Salamanca, Cattaraugus County, New York. She married ALEXANDER WILLIAMS. He was born Abt. 1886.

Children of LELA CASE and ALEXANDER WILLIAMS are:
2458. i. JOSEPHINE[10] WILLIAMS.
2459. ii. JENNETTE WILLIAMS.
2460. iii. BONNIE WILLIAMS.

1432. ALLAN A.[9] CASE *(ANDREW J.[8], DEBORAH[7] MILKS, JOHN[6] MILK, JONATHAN[5], JONATHAN[4], JOB[3], JOHN[2], JOHN[1])* was born 18 Sep 1888 in Little Valley, Cattaraugus County, New York. He married MYRA RICHARDSON. She was born Abt. 1888.

Child of ALLAN CASE and MYRA RICHARDSON is:
2461. i. RICHARD[10] CASE.

1433. ETTIE ANN[9] MOSHER *(SUSAN J.[8] MILKS, GEORGE[7], JOHN[6] MILK, JONATHAN[5], JONATHAN[4], JOB[3], JOHN[2], JOHN[1])* was born 01 Nov 1867 in Leon, Cattaraugus County, New York, and died 06 May 1944. She married THOMAS ALFRED PLUNKETT. He was born May 1862, and died 1939.

Children of ETTIE MOSHER and THOMAS PLUNKETT are:
i. HAZEL[10] PLUNKETT.
ii. ELMA PLUNKETT.

1434. FREDERICK HERBERT[9] MOSHER *(SUSAN J.[8] MILKS, GEORGE[7], JOHN[6] MILK, JONATHAN[5], JONATHAN[4], JOB[3], JOHN[2], JOHN[1])* was born Jan 1870 in Leon, Cattaraugus County, New York, and died 09 May 1935 in Leon, Cattaraugus County, New York. He married (1) SARAH _____ 1889 in Leon, Cattaraugus County, New York. She was born Abt. 1870. He married (2) MINNIE E. DUNKLEMAN 1896 in New York. She was born May 1877 in New York, and died 07

Mar 1933 in Leon, Cattaraugus County, New York.

Child of FREDERICK MOSHER and MINNIE DUNKLEMAN is:
2462.   i. GEORGE W.[10] MOSHER, b. 07 May 1915, Cattaraugus County, New York; d. 04 Mar 2006, Corry, Erie County, Pennsylvania.

1435. SHERMAN ANDREW[9] MOSHER (*SUSAN J.[8] MILKS, GEORGE[7], JOHN[6] MILK, JONATHAN[5], JONATHAN[4], JOB[3], JOHN[2], JOHN[1]*) was born 22 May 1888 in New Albion, Cattaraugus County, New York, and died 01 Aug 1954 in Lake County, Ohio. He married MILDRED HARRIET HAIGHT, daughter of FRANCIS HAIGHT and LULU _____. She was born Feb 1893 in Perrysburg, Cattaraugus County, New York, and died 24 Jun 1978 in Painesville, Lake County, Ohio.

Children of SHERMAN MOSHER and MILDRED HAIGHT are:
   i. ELTON LORAIN[10] MOSHER, b. 16 Jul 1918, Buffalo, Erie County, New York; d. 14 Sep 1999, Rialto, San Bernardino County, California; m. LILA A. THOMAS, 10 Aug 1963, San Bernardino County, California; b. Abt. 1918.
   ii. RURH JEANETTE MOSHER, b. 08 Oct 1919, Buffalo, Erie County, New York; d. 20 Nov 1996, Painesville, Lake County, Ohio; m. JAMES E. TRUHE; b. 08 Oct 1913, New York; d. 22 Jan 1969, Painesville, Lake County, Ohio.

1436. GEORGE O.[9] RHOADES (*SARAH JANE[8] MILKS, GEORGE[7], JOHN[6] MILK, JONATHAN[5], JONATHAN[4], JOB[3], JOHN[2], JOHN[1]*) was born 19 Sep 1869 in Cattaraugus County, New York. He married ADDIE HUFF 1893, daughter of EDGAR HUFFF and EUNICE _____. She was born Abt. 1872 in Great Valley, Cattaraugus County, New York.

Addie's father Edgar lived with George & Addie after his wife died in 1906 and until he died in 1924.

Children of GEORGE RHOADES and ADDIE HUFF are:
   i.   BESSIE RHOADES[10] RHODES, b. 1894, Cattaraugus County, New York; d. 1896, Cattaraugus County, New York.
   ii. JESSAMINE A. RHOADES RHODES, b. 22 Feb 1903, Cattaraugus County, New York; d. Jul 1973, Dunkirk, Chautauqua County, New York. Never married.
   iii. MARGARET RHOADES RHODES, b. Abt. 1905.
   iv. GEORGIA RHOADES RHODES, b. 1910.

1437. FRANK A. RHOADES[9] RHODES (*SARAH JANE[8] MILKS, GEORGE[7], JOHN[6] MILK, JONATHAN[5], JONATHAN[4], JOB[3], JOHN[2], JOHN[1]*) was born Abt. 1872 in Cattaraugus County, New York. He married MARGARET MCGEE 1894 in Cattaraugus County, New York. She was born Abt. 1876 in Massachusetts.

Children of FRANK RHODES and MARGARET MCGEE are:
2463.   i. JOHN HADLEY RHOADES[10] RHODES, b. 20 Jan 1895, Great Valley, Cattaraugus County, New York.
2464.   ii. DONALD M. RHOADES RHODES, b. Abt. 1906, Cattaraugus County, New York.

1438. GRACE[9] RHOADES (*SARAH JANE[8] MILKS, GEORGE[7], JOHN[6] MILK, JONATHAN[5], JONATHAN[4], JOB[3], JOHN[2], JOHN[1]*) was born 08 May 1880 in Cattaraugus County, New York. She married FRED FRANK. He was born Abt. 1880.

Children of GRACE RHOADES and FRED FRANK are:
   i. ADA M.[10] FRANK, b. Mar 1900, Great Valley, Cattaraugus County, New York.
   ii. BEATRICE FRANK, b. Abt. 1903.

1439. CARRIE[9] RHOADES (*SARAH JANE[8] MILKS, GEORGE[7], JOHN[6] MILK, JONATHAN[5], JONATHAN[4], JOB[3], JOHN[2], JOHN[1]*) was born 29 Aug 1889 in Cattaraugus County, New York. She married ED CLARK. He was born Abt. 1889.

Children of CARRIE RHOADES and ED CLARK are:
2465.   i.   OTIS R.[10] CLARK, b. 14 Aug 1908, Great Valley, Cattaraugus County, New York; d. 30 Dec 2009, Springville, Erie County, New York.
2466.   ii. MILFORD L. CLARK, b. 18 May 1912, Great Valley, Cattaraugus County, New York; d. 28 May 2003.
        iii. GRACE L. CLARK, b. 28 Mar 1914, Great Valley, Cattaraugus County, New York; d. Jun 1982; m. JOHN

WOODWARD; b. 19 Feb 1899; d. Nov 1978.

1440. ELLA MARIE[9] MILKS *(GEORGE WILSON[8], GEORGE[7], JOHN[6] MILK, JONATHAN[5], JONATHAN[4], JOB[3], JOHN[2], JOHN[1])* was born 03 Nov 1896 in New Albion, Cattaraugus County, NY. She married CARL ALFRED HOLMES 26 Jul 1919 in New Albion, Cattaraugus County, New York, son of ALFRED HOLMES and MINNIE ROSENTHAL. He was born 20 Oct 1896 in Walden, New York.

Children of ELLA MILKS and CARL HOLMES are:
2467. i. MYRTLE ALICE[10] HOLMES, b. 08 Sep 1920, New Albion, Cattaraugus County, New York.
2468. ii. CARL ALFRED HOLMES, JR., b. 08 Oct 1925, Celeron, Chautauqua County, New York.
2469. iii. CORAL ELLEN HOLMES, b. 25 Apr 1929, Jamestown, Chautauqua County, New York.
iv. HAZEL JESSIE HOLMES, b. 15 Aug 1933, New Albion, Cattaraugus County, New York.

1441. HAROLD GEORGE[9] MILKS *(GEORGE WILSON[8], GEORGE[7], JOHN[6] MILK, JONATHAN[5], JONATHAN[4], JOB[3], JOHN[2], JOHN[1])* was born 23 Jan 1898 in New Albion, Cattaraugus County, NY, and died May 1968 in Little Valley, Cattaraugus County, New York. He married MILDRED ELLEN SAALFELD 23 Jun 1920 in Little Valley, Cattaraugus, NY, daughter of JOHN SAALFELD and MAMIE SWEENEY. She was born 02 Apr 1904 in New Albion, Cattaraugus County, NY, and died Nov 1987 in Little Valley, Cattaraugus County, New York.

Children of HAROLD MILKS and MILDRED SAALFELD are:
2470. i. JEAN BERTHA[10] MILKS, b. 22 Sep 1922, Salamanca, Cattaraugus County, New York; d. 18 Feb 2004, Olean, Cattaraugus County, New York.
ii. CORA ELEANOR MILKS, b. 05 Jul 1924, Cattaraugus County, New York; d. Bef. 18 Feb 2004; m. WILBUR ASKEY; b. Abt. 1924.
iii. HAROLD GEORGE MILKS, JR., b. 29 May 1928, Cattaraugus County, New York; d. 22 Apr 1939, Cattaraugus County, New York.
iv. DORIS MILDRED MILKS, b. 02 Mar 1931, Cattaraugus County, New York; d. Jun 1959, New York; m. MORRIS FIELD.
v. RAYMOND DEAN MILKS, b. 03 Mar 1933, New Albion, Cattaraugus County, New York; d. Oct 1974.
2471. vi. KATHRYN LOUISE MILKS, b. 15 Mar 1935, Cattaraugus County, New York.
vii. MARY LOU MARCIA MILKS, b. 15 Aug 1939, Cattaraugus County, New York; d. 15 Feb 1995, Texas ??; m. ROBERT CARROLL KOONCE; b. 13 Oct 1923; d. 24 Aug 2000, Angleton, Brazoria County, Texas.
viii. MARION MILKS, b. Cattaraugus County, New York; d. d.y..

1442. BLANCHE ELVIRA[9] MILKS *(HARVEY R. 'DADE'[8], GEORGE[7], JOHN[6] MILK, JONATHAN[5], JONATHAN[4], JOB[3], JOHN[2], JOHN[1])* was born 12 Feb 1880 in Napoli, Cattaraugus County, New York, and died Abt. 1954. She married (1) GUY EUGENE SIBLEY, son of AMENZO SIBLEY and ALZINA STRATTON. He was born 14 Feb 1879 in Napoli, Cattaraugus County, New York, and died 26 Jul 1911 in Napoli, Cattaraugus County, New York. She married (2) JAMES LESTER SHEARER 06 Aug 1917 in Cattaraugus County, New York, son of JAMES SHEARER and MARY DRACKSLEY. He was born 31 Mar 1890.

Blanche remarried to James Lester Shearer in 1917 and I have found no record of a divorce. It may have been a 'marriage of convenience' for some reason, because they are never shown living together in any of the census records. Starting with the 1920 census, James Lester is shown living with his parents/mother, but he is always shown as married.

Blanche is shown in the 1920 census as Blanche Shearer (married) along with her son Alan, as a housekeeper for Fred A. Fisher. in the 1930 census she is shown as Blanche Sibley, widow living with her parents. Harvey and Addie Milks.

Blanche contributed many records for Crofts book.

Child of BLANCHE MILKS and GUY SIBLEY is:
2472. i. ALAN L.[10] SIBLEY, b. 11 Jan 1902, Napoli, Cattaraugus County, New York.

1443. ARA LYNN[9] MILKS *(HARVEY R. 'DADE'[8], GEORGE[7], JOHN[6] MILK, JONATHAN[5], JONATHAN[4], JOB[3], JOHN[2], JOHN[1])* was born 16 Aug 1889 in Napoli, Cattaraugus Co, NY, and died 15 Jan 1956 in Little Valley, Cattaraugus County, NY. He married FLOSSIE V. OLMSTEAD 16 Aug 1910 in Little Valley, Cattaraugus, NY, daughter of ELMER OLMSTEAD and

EMMA BISHOP. She was born 26 Jun 1891 in Gowanda, Cattaraugus County, New York.

Child of ARA MILKS and FLOSSIE OLMSTEAD is:
2473.   i.   LYNN OLMSTEAD[10] MILKS, b. 30 Apr 1920, Napoli, Cattaraugus Co., NY; d. 20 Jan 2004, Cattaraugus County, New York.

1444. BERYL MAY[9] GARDNER (*LYDIA[8] MILKS, GEORGE[7], JOHN[6] MILK, JONATHAN[5], JONATHAN[4], JOB[3], JOHN[2], JOHN[1]*) was born Jun 1879 in New York, and died 25 Jun 1962 in Chautauqua County, New York. She married LUTHER LA DUE BLOOD Abt. 1905. He was born 13 Mar 1882 in New York, and died 21 Mar 1964 in Chautauqua County, New York.

Child of BERYL GARDNER and LUTHER BLOOD is:
         i.   CAROL[10] BLOOD, b. 1905, Pennsylvania; d. 1991.

1445. MARJORIE[9] MILKS (*FRANK W.[8], GEORGE[7], JOHN[6] MILK, JONATHAN[5], JONATHAN[4], JOB[3], JOHN[2], JOHN[1]*) was born 12 Dec 1889 in Napoli, Cattaraugus Co, NY, and died 03 Feb 1948. She married HARRY GLENN WATKINS 29 Sep 1909 in West Salamanca, New York, son of E. WATKINS and LILLIAN ROGERS. He was born 07 Mar 1887 in W. Salamanca, NY, and died in Jamestown, Chautauqua County, New York ??.

Children of MARJORIE MILKS and HARRY WATKINS are:
         i.   ESTHER M. "BOOPS"[10] WATKINS, b. 26 May 1911, Salamanca, Cattaraugus County, New York; d. 08 Apr 1990.
        ii.   CHARLES R. WATKINS, b. Abt. Jan 1916, Salamanca, Cattaraugus County, New York.
       iii.   GERTRUDE M. WATKINS, b. Abt. Nov 1918, Salamanca, Cattaraugus County, New York.

1446. BEULAH[9] MILKS (*FRANK W.[8], GEORGE[7], JOHN[6] MILK, JONATHAN[5], JONATHAN[4], JOB[3], JOHN[2], JOHN[1]*) was born 18 Jun 1893 in Napoli, Cattaraugus Co, NY. She married RAY M. NEWTON 23 Jun 1915 in Salamanca, Cattaraugus County, New York, by Harry C. Handz, son of A. NEWTON and MARY STROVER. He was born 1894 in Salamanca, NY.

Children of BEULAH MILKS and RAY NEWTON are:
         i.   RAE LOUISE[10] NEWTON, b. 06 Dec 1917, Salamanca, Cattaraugus County, New York.
2474.   ii.   VIRGINIA NEWTON, b. Abt. 1919, Salamanca, Cattaraugus County, New York.

1447. HARLAN PORTER[9] MILKS (*FRANK W.[8], GEORGE[7], JOHN[6] MILK, JONATHAN[5], JONATHAN[4], JOB[3], JOHN[2], JOHN[1]*) was born 08 Jan 1907 in Salamanca, Cattaraugus County, New York, and died 26 Apr 1971 in Guilderland, New York. He married EUNICE SLATER, daughter of HARRY SLATER and ELLA GRAVELLE. She was born 03 Aug 1915 in Hornell, New York, and died 12 Nov 2001 in Albany, New York.

OBITUARY
Albany, NY

Milks, Eunice Slater ALBANY -- Eunice Slater Milks, born in Hornell, NY, widow of Harlan Porter Milks, died Monday, November 12, 2001. Mrs. Milks has lived in Albany since 1951. She taught foreign languages and world studies at Philip Schuyler High School, 1962-1971, and volunteered for Albany Maritime Ministry, Seafarers' Center, 1983-2001, where she was the Director.

Survivors include three sons, Robert Milks of Nova Scotia, Michael Milks of Latham and Jonathan Milks of Guilderland; seven grandchildren, Bryn, Rebecca, Kirstin, Julia, Kurt, Katherine and Sabrina.

Memorial service at St. Paul's Lutheran Church, 10 Western Ave., Albany, across from the fire house, at 4:00 p.m. Sunday, November 18.

Donations may be sent to the Seafarers' Center in care of Rev. William G. Hempel, (518) 463-0571.

Children of HARLAN MILKS and EUNICE SLATER are:
2475.   i.   ROBERT WILLIAM[10] MILKS, b. 07 Mar 1949, Syracuse, Onondaga County, New York.
2476.   ii.   MICHAEL BRUCE MILKS, b. 01 Feb 1951, Syracuse, Onondaga County, New York.
2477.   iii.   JONATHAN DWIGHT MILKS, b. 10 Sep 1956, Albany, Albany County, New York.

1448. ELVA OLIVE^9 MILKS *(FRED^8, GEORGE^7, JOHN^6 MILK, JONATHAN^5, JONATHAN^4, JOB^3, JOHN^2, JOHN^1)* was born 27 Apr 1897 in Napoli, Cattaraugus Co, NY. She married LYLE T. UNDERWOOD 09 Apr 1917 in East Randolph, Cattaraugus County, New York, son of PERRY UNDERWOOD and MABEL MONROE. He was born 05 May 1896 in Napoli, Cattaraugus Co, NY, and died Aug 1970 in Tucson, Pima County, Arizona.

Children of ELVA MILKS and LYLE UNDERWOOD are:
2478.   i.   ELDENE OLIVE^{10} UNDERWOOD, b. 21 Aug 1922, Napoli, Cattaraugus County, New York.
2479.   ii.   JOYCE UNDERWOOD, b. 08 Feb 1928, Cattaraugus County, New York.

1449. AUDRA^9 MILKS *(ARCHIE B.^{8}, LUTHER P.^{7}, PRINCE WILLIAM^6, JONATHAN^5 MILK, JONATHAN^4, JOB^3, JOHN^2, JOHN^1)* was born 05 Dec 1888 in Napoli, Cattaraugus County, New York. She married (1) HENRY W. ALLEN 16 Aug 1909 in Limestone, Cattaraugus County, New York, son of FRANK ALLEN and ABBIE NICHOLS. He was born 26 Oct 1892 in Warsaw, New York. She married (2) FREDERICK J. RONAN Aft. 1910. He was born Abt. 1888.

Child of AUDRA MILKS and HENRY ALLEN is:
    i.   WILLIAM^{10} ALLEN, m. ERMA.

1450. MARK F.^{9} FREEMAN *(FRANCES ELLEN^8 MILKS, GILES^7, JOHN^6 MILK, JONATHAN^5, JONATHAN^4, JOB^3, JOHN^2, JOHN^1)* was born Mar 1875 in Salamanca, Cattaraugus County, New York. He married MAY J. _____ Abt. 1900. She was born 1883 in New York, and died Bet. 1920 - 1930 in Cattaraugus County, New York.

Children of MARK FREEMAN and MAY _____ are:
    i.   FLOSSIE^{10} FREEMAN, b. 1901, Cattaraugus County, New York.
    ii.   HAZEL FREEMAN, b. 1904, Cattaraugus County, New York.
    iii.   HOWARD F. FREEMAN, b. 04 Jun 1907, Cattaraugus County, New York; d. Feb 1977, Cattaraugus County, New York; m. MARY HELEN MAY BENSON, Bef. 1940; b. 23 Mar 1908, Canada ??; d. Aug 1978, Cattaraugus County, New York.
    iv.   VERN N. FREEMAN, b. 19 Jan 1911, Cattaraugus County, New York; d. Aug 1984, Salamanca, Cattaraugus County, New York.

1451. FRANK N.^{9} FREEMAN *(FRANCES ELLEN^8 MILKS, GILES^7, JOHN^6 MILK, JONATHAN^5, JONATHAN^4, JOB^3, JOHN^2, JOHN^1)* was born Jul 1879 in Salamanca, Cattaraugus County, New York. He married MARY E. _____. She was born Abt. 1879.

Children of FRANK FREEMAN and MARY _____ are:
    i.   ROBERT E.^{10} FREEMAN, b. 1906, Salamanca, Cattaraugus County, New York.
    ii.   LORRETTA C. FREEMAN, b. 1908, Salamanca, Cattaraugus County, New York.
    iii.   DONALD F. J. FREEMAN, b. 1911, Salamanca, Cattaraugus County, New York; d. 1977, Cattaraugus County, New York; m. KATHRYN _____; b. 1909, Pennsylvania.
    iv.   MARY FREEMAN, b. Abt. Jun 1917, Salamanca, Cattaraugus County, New York.
    v.   MARIAN FREEMAN, b. Abt. Jun 1917, Salamanca, Cattaraugus County, New York.
    vi.   BERNADETTE P. FREEMAN, b. 1921, Salamanca, Cattaraugus County, New York.

1452. CLARK BURNELL^9 MILKS *(JAMES^8, GILES^7, JOHN^6 MILK, JONATHAN^5, JONATHAN^4, JOB^3, JOHN^2, JOHN^1)* was born 29 Nov 1895 in Leon, Cattaraugus County, New York, and died 1962 in McKean County, Pennsylvania. He married ELIZABETH VIVIAN MOSHER 12 Jan 1925 in Cattaraugus County, New York, daughter of WILLIAM MOSHER and MATTIE LEMKE. She was born 1906 in New Albion, Cattaraugus County, New York, and died 1950.

Children of CLARK MILKS and ELIZABETH MOSHER are:
    i.   ELIZABETH LILLIAN^{10} MILKS, b. 24 Jul 1926, Cattaraugus County, New York.
2480.   ii.   ELROY L. MILKS, b. 21 Nov 1929, Eden, New York; d. 11 Jun 1975, Olean Hospital, Olean, NY.
2481.   iii.   ELEANOR G. MILKS, b. 21 Nov 1929, Eden, New York; d. 21 Aug 1999, Limestone, Cattaraugus County, New York.

1453. CLARENCE LELAND[9] MILKS *(JAMES[8], GILES[7], JOHN[6] MILK, JONATHAN[5], JONATHAN[4], JOB[3], JOHN[2], JOHN[1])* was born 09 Nov 1899 in Leon, Cattaraugus County, New York, and died Jan 1985 in Angola, Erie County, New York. He married LUCY MALINDA NILES 25 Nov 1920 in Cattaraugus, NY, daughter of MORTIMER NILES and ANNA MILKS. She was born 17 Aug 1900 in New Albion, Cattaraugus County, New York, and died Apr 1978 in Angola, Erie County, New York.

Children of CLARENCE MILKS and LUCY NILES are:
- i. HERBERT JAMES[10] MILKS, b. 18 Jul 1923, Cattaraugus County, New York; d. Feb 1976.
- 2482. ii. LLOYD C. MILKS, b. 30 Jan 1927, Eden, Erie County, New York.
- 2483. iii. DONALD E. MILKS, b. 28 Nov 1928, New York.
- iv. EMMETT L. MILKS, b. 13 Mar 1931, Eden, Erie County, New York; d. 03 Jul 2006, Buffalo, Erie County, New York; m. RUTH G. COOK; b. 12 Apr 1930, Allegany, Cattaraugus County, New York.

    OBITUARY - The Buffalo News (Buffalo, NY), July 4, 2006
    Emmett L. Milks, state trooper and veteran ; March 13, 1931 -- July 3, 2006
    Emmett L. Milks, of Perry, died Monday in Buffalo General Hospital after a brief illness. He was 75.
    Born in Eden, Mr. Milks graduated from Angola High School and served in the Army during the Korean War.
    He then worked as a New York State trooper for 22 years, retiring in 1976. He also worked as a manager for Brinks Co. in Rochester for 15 years.
    Mr. Milks also owned and operated Embers dairy bar in Perry for 17 years with his wife. He was justice for the town.
- v. EUNICE MILKS, b. Abt. 1933, Erie County, New York.
- vi. ALLAN R. MILKS, b. 06 Dec 1935, Erie County, New York; d. 09 Jan 1972, Angola, Erie County, New York; m. JERRIE E. _____; b. 12 Jul 1938; d. 11 Dec 2008, Angola, Erie County, New York.
- vii. MARJORIE MILKS, b. Abt. 1938, Erie County, New York.

1454. ARTHUR GLENN[9] MILKS *(ADELBERT[8], HIRAM[7], JOHN[6] MILK, JONATHAN[5], JONATHAN[4], JOB[3], JOHN[2], JOHN[1])* was born 18 Jul 1887 in Napoli, Cattaraugus County, New York, and died Jan 1966 in New York. He married MAUD ELSIE BULLOCK 25 Jun 1914 in Limestone, Cattaraugus County, New York, daughter of DELBERT BULLOCK and GRACE MORRISON. She was born 24 May 1894 in Gardean, Pennsylvania.

Athur's birth name was Hiram Glenn Milks (1892 & 1900 census). It appears that when he came of age he changed it to Arthur, which is what appears in all subsequent census records, and in his marriage record.

In 1945 Arthur Glenn and Maud advertised for two homeless war veterans to share their farm home and to take the place of their two sons who were World War II casualties. They received hundreds of letters from servicemen in response, and, subsequently, they received Tom Brenneman's "Good Neighbor Orchid" and much radio and press publicity. Maud trained as a nurse at Bradford Hospital, Bradford, Pa., where she met Arthur Glenn, convalescing at the time from injuries received in a railway braking accident. Maud was proprietor of a small pet shop in Cattaraugus; in 1946 the Governor of New York selected her to represent the state in the American Mothers Committee of the Golden Rule Foundation of New York City.

Children of ARTHUR MILKS and MAUD BULLOCK are:
- 2484. i. FERN LAJUNE[10] MILKS, b. 11 Mar 1918, Bradford, Pennsylvania; d. 27 Oct 2001, Salamanca, Cattaraugus County, New York.
- ii. STANLEY E. MILKS, b. 17 Jul 1919, Fredonia, Chautauqua County, New York; d. 19 Jul 1942, Cabanatuan Prison Camp near Manila, Philippines.
- iii. ROBERT G. MILKS, b. 17 Oct 1921, Bradford, Pennsylvania; d. 07 Sep 1944, Japanese Prison ship sunk off the Philippines in the South Pacific.
- 2485. iv. GRACE LOUISE MILKS, b. 30 Oct 1922, E. Randolph, Cattaraugus County, New York.
- 2486. v. GLORIA MILKS, b. 27 Sep 1927, Bradford, Pennsylvania; d. 11 Apr 1995, Cattaraugus County, New York.

1455. HAROLD E.[9] MILKS *(ADELBERT[8], HIRAM[7], JOHN[6] MILK, JONATHAN[5], JONATHAN[4], JOB[3], JOHN[2], JOHN[1])* was born 06 Jun 1891 in Randolph, Cattaraugus County, New York, and died Jul 1968 in Horseheads, Chemung County, New York. He married (1) HAZEL EUGENIA WHITMORE 05 Jul 1914 in Cattaraugus County, New York, daughter of EDSON WHITMORE and BERTHANDIA JAYNER. She was born 24 Oct 1894 in Coldspring, Cattaraugus County, New York, and died Apr 1966 in Binghamton, Broome County, New York. He married (2) PHOEBE JANE ROZELL 17 Jan 1919 in

Steuben County, New York, daughter of JAMES ROZELL and HARRIET WILCOX. She was born 05 Aug 1902 in New York, and died 12 Feb 1979 in Orlando, Orange County, Florida.

Children of HAROLD MILKS and PHOEBE ROZELL are:

2487.   i.   ARTHUR MANLEY[10] MILKS, b. 10 Sep 1920, Horseheads, Chemung County, New York.
2488.   ii. HAROLD E. MILKS, JR., b. 24 Jun 1928, Chemung County, New York.
        iii. EDGAR ROZELL MILKS, b. 02 Apr 1930, Chemung County, New York; d. 06 Jan 1986, Richmond County, Georgia; m. (1) VIVIAN ESTELLE GODWIN, 23 Jan 1953, White Oak Township, Jones County, North Carolina; b. Abt. 1934; m. (2) LINDA CAROLYN FOSTER PECKHAM, 15 Jul 1979, Orange County, Florida; b. 28 May 1943.
        iv. LOUELLA MILKS, b. 1932, Chemung County, New York.
             Studied in a Massachusetts Girl's College to be a missionary.

1456. GEORGE WASHINGTON[9] MILKS *(ADELBERT[8], HIRAM[7], JOHN[6] MILK, JONATHAN[5], JONATHAN[4], JOB[3], JOHN[2], JOHN[1])* was born 06 Apr 1894 in Napoli, Cattaraugus Co, NY, and died 25 Jul 1963 in Napoli, Cattaraugus Co, NY. He married MILDRED S. SIMPSON Abt. 1930 in Cattaraugus County, New York, daughter of PHILIP SIMPSON and MARY LOOP. She was born 28 Aug 1907 in Conewango, Cattaraugus County, New York, and died Jan 1984 in Randolph, Cattaraugus County, New York.

Children of GEORGE MILKS and MILDRED SIMPSON are:

        i.   CLAYTON G.[10] MILKS, b. 1938; d. 1942, East Randolph, Cattaraugus Co, NY (appendicitis).
2489.   ii. HOWARD SIMPSON MILKS, b. 07 Apr 1941.

1457. WILLIAM HENRY[9] MILKS *(ADELBERT[8], HIRAM[7], JOHN[6] MILK, JONATHAN[5], JONATHAN[4], JOB[3], JOHN[2], JOHN[1])* was born 18 Jul 1895 in Red House, Cattaraugus County, New York, and died 19 Dec 1986 in Hudson, Fremont County, Wyoming. He married (1) MAUDE MARY STEWARD Abt. 1918, daughter of WILLIAM STEWARD and LAURA _____. She was born 31 Aug 1894 in Osborne, Pipestone, Minnesota, and died 12 Mar 1991 in Hennepin County, Minnesota. He married (2) CORNELIA ELRIKA FRESEMAN 01 May 1929 in Glendive, Dawson County, Montana, daughter of CORNELIUS FRESEMAN and ALRIKA MINDERS. She was born 15 Nov 1905 in Scott, Franklin County, Iowa, and died 21 Mar 1991 in Glendive, Dawson County, Montana.

Ohio Soldiers in WWI, 1917-1918, Ohio Military Men, 1917-18 about William H. Milks
Name: William H. Milks, Serial Number: 954021, Race: W
Residence: Richfield, O., Enlistment Division: Regular Army, Enlistment Location: Columbus Barracks, O.
Enlistment Date: 15 Apr 1917
Birth Place: Reduced House, N. Y.
Birth Date / Age: 21 8/12 Years
   Assigns Comment: Co C 36 Infantry to 20 June 1917; Co L 36 Infantry to 7 July 1917; Machine Gun Company 36 Infantry to 19 Aug 1918; Machine Gun Company 73 Infantry to Discharge Private, first class 15 May 1918. Honorable discharge 30 Jan 1919.

DEATH NOTICE
   William Henry Milks
   William Henry Milks and Cornelia Elreka Freseman were married about 1928. William Henry MILKS and Cornelia Elreka Freseman had four daughters and a son, all living as of the source date. In April 1930, they lived in a rented home in School District 35 in Dawson County, Montana, where he was a laborer at odd jobs. Their first child, Arthur, had been born eight months earlier. Cornelia Elreka Freseman was born on 15 November 1905 in Iowa. Cornelia lists her parents as German born in the 1930 census, although her widowed father claimed Iowa as his birthplace in 1920 (although that might be a census-taker error). She died on 21 March 1991 in Hayden Lake, Kootenai Co., Idaho.

Children of WILLIAM MILKS and MAUDE STEWARD are:

2490.   i.   AUDREY LOUISE[10] MILKS, b. 19 Apr 1919, Minneapolis, Hennepin County, Minnesota; d. 14 Aug 2008, Hennepin County, Minnesota.
        ii. ELEANOR MARY MILKS, b. 24 Dec 1920, Minneapolis, Hennepin County, Minnesota; d. 17 Apr 2002, Robbinsdale, Hennepin County, Minnesota. Never married.

Children of WILLIAM MILKS and CORNELIA FRESEMAN are:

2491. iii. ARTHUR LYLE[10] MILKS, b. 25 Jul 1929, Dawson County, Montana.
  iv. CORNELIA A. MILKS, b. Abt. 1931, Dawson County, Montana.
  v. RICHARD MILKS, b. Abt. 1933, Dawson County, Montana.
2492. vi. RAYMOND AUGUST MILKS, b. 06 Feb 1934, Dawson County, Montana.
  vii. IRENE L. MILKS, b. Abt. 1935, Dawson County, Montana.
  viii. AUDREY MARIE MILKS, b. 12 Sep 1936, Dawson County, Montana; d. 21 Apr 2002, Beverly Hills, California; m. MICHAEL WAYNE PERRINE; b. 05 Dec 1923, Sage Creek Ranch, Judith Basin, Montana; d. 04 Nov 1970, Denton, Fergus County, Montana.

   OBITUARY - Billings Gazette (Billings, Montana) 6 Nov 1970
    Michael Perrine

   Denton - Michael Perrine, 46, died Wednesday while en-route to a Great Falls hospital.

   Requiem mass will be celebrated 10 am Saturday in St. Leo's Catholic Church. Rosary will be recited 8 pm Friday in the Cloyd Chapel. Burial will be in Calvary Cemetery with full military honors.

   He was born Dec 5, 1923, in Windham, a son of Mr. and Mrs. Wallace Perrine. He attended Stamford schools.

   On Feb 27, 1945, he married Delores M. Demars in Denton. They ranched near Coffee Creek in 1946 and later moved to Denton where he operated Mike's Repair Shop.

   He was a member of St. Anthony's Catholic Church, Denton Fire Department, Town Council, Lions and American Legion.

   Surviving are the widow, two sons, Gregory, Denton, and David, Billings; two daughters, Susan, Denton, and Audrey, Beverly Hills, Calif. three brothers, Russell, Norfolk, Va., Richard, Hobson and Scott, Clarkston, Wash.; five sisters, Mrs. Marjorie Stevens, Lewiston, Mrs. John Mohland and Mrs. Eugene Wolff, both of Billings, Mrs. Alfred Whitten, Hanford, Calif, and Mrs. William Morrison, Fort Leavenworth, Kan.; and a granddaughter.

  ix. ROSE M. MILKS, b. Abt. 1938, Dawson County, Montana.
  x. BETTY J. MILKS, b. Abt. Jul 1939, Dawson County, Montana.
  xi. INFANT MILKS, b. 1940, Dawson County, Montana; d. 10 Oct 1940, Dawson County, Montana.

1458. ELIZABETH 'LIZZY'[9] MILKS (*SIDNEY DAVID*[8], *HIRAM*[7], *JOHN*[6] *MILK, JONATHAN*[5], *JONATHAN*[4], *JOB*[3], *JOHN*[2], *JOHN*[1]) was born Jan 1888 in East Randolph, Cattaraugus County, New York, and died 15 Oct 1962 in Salina, Jefferson County, Iowa. She married EDWARD C. SCHILLERSTROM 13 Nov 1907 in Round Prairie, Jefferson Co, Iowa, son of JOSEPH SCHILLERSTROM and JOSIE EDMUND. He was born 24 May 1886 in Salina, Jefferson County, Iowa, and died 19 Jul 1934 in Salina, Jefferson County, Iowa.

OBITUARY -- Lockridge Times; Lockridge, Jefferson, Iowa; July 27, 1934
 Ed SCHILLERSTROM

Ed SCHILLERSTROM, aged 47, was found dying last Thursday evening about ten o'clock. His body was found in the garden of his home with a shot gun wound in his abdomen, and his throat slashed with a razor. He lived a few minutes, but was unable to make any statement.

Following an all night investigation by Sheriff Stansbery and Acting Coroner Tallman, assisted by a state agent, they issued a statement that the man had committed suicide. Relatives were not satisfied with this decision and requested further investigation, and on Saturday afternoon a coroner's inquest was held in Salina. The jury, composed of H.C. Pattison, Ted Garber and Fred Kann, with Acting Coroner Tallman and attorneys, held sessions in Fairfield Monday and Tuesday. After hearing witnesses the jury upheld the decision of suicide.

The deceased was a son of Joseph SCHILLERSTROM, the Salina merchant. His mother died in 1918. There is also one sister dead. Three sisters and three brothers survive as follows: Rev. Glen SCHILLERSTROM of Jacksonville, Ill., Curtis SCHILLERSTROM of Louisville, Ky., Mrs. Ralph JOHNSON of Fairfield, Townsend SCHILLERSTROM of Salina, Mrs. Paul PRINCE of Beckwith and Mrs. Pearl LINN of Lockridge.

Three children survive the father- Ralph and Joseph at home, and Mrs. Arlene JACOBS of Salina neighborhood.

Funeral services were held Sunday afternoon in Salina Presbyterian church, in charge of Rev. H.G. Ellsworth and Rev. H.W. Lundberg of Lockridge. The pall bearers, all cousins of the deceased were: Gus SCHILLERSTROM, Carl EDMUND, Amiel SANDELL, Charles SANDELL, Jelmer SANDELL and John LIBLIN. Burial was in the Salina cemetery.

[Ed. note: He was divorced from his wife, Elizabeth MILKS.]

Children of ELIZABETH MILKS and EDWARD SCHILLERSTROM are:
2493. i. RALPH CLIFFORD[10] SCHILLERSTROM, b. Abt. 1909; d. 03 May 1974, Fairfield, Iowa.
ii. ARLENE J. SCHILLERSTROM, b. 1912, Jefferson County, Iowa; d. 20 Jun 1998, Hawk Eye, Iowa; m. (1) RAYMOND JACOBS, 16 Jun 1929, Salina, Jefferson County, Iowa; b. Abt. 1910; m. (2) UNKNOWN MILKS, Aft. 1930.
iii. JOSEPH C. SCHILLERSTROM, b. Abt. 1915.

1459. WALTER BAUSMAN[9] MILKS *(SIDNEY DAVID[8], HIRAM[7], JOHN[6] MILK, JONATHAN[5], JONATHAN[4], JOB[3], JOHN[2], JOHN[1])* was born 12 Jan 1893 in Mt. Pleasant, Iowa, and died Apr 1964 in Iowa. He married ETTA BERTHA FOSTER 27 Dec 1913 in Henry County, Iowa, daughter of JAMES FOSTER and MARTHA STEVENSON. She was born 05 Oct 1889, and died 09 Nov 1962.

Children of WALTER MILKS and ETTA FOSTER are:
2494. i. GILBERT FOSTER 'GIB'[10] MILKS, b. 20 Jan 1915, Mt. Pleasant, Henry Co., Iowa; d. 03 Oct 1988, Iowa City, Henry Co., Iowa.
2495. ii. OPAL PAULINE MILKS, b. 04 Nov 1917, Mt. Pleasant, Henry Co., Iowa; d. 05 Oct 2003, Licking, Missouri.
2496. iii. CLIFFORD W. MILKS, b. 31 Dec 1920, Mt. Pleasant, Henry Co., Iowa; d. 11 Nov 1993, Salem, Henry County, Iowa.
2497. iv. KENNETH S. MILKS, b. 05 Jan 1922, Henry County, Iowa; d. 22 Oct 1981, Rock Island, Illinois.
2498. v. JAMES WARREN MILKS, b. 16 Mar 1924, Henry County, Iowa; d. 25 Dec 1993, Winfield, Henry County, Iowa.
2499. vi. MILDRED M. MILKS, b. 17 Apr 1927, Henry County, Iowa.
vii. DALE MILKS, b. Abt. 1930; d. d.y..

1460. IRENE BESSIE[9] MILKS *(WALLACE H.[8], HIRAM[7], JOHN[6] MILK, JONATHAN[5], JONATHAN[4], JOB[3], JOHN[2], JOHN[1])* was born 09 Sep 1888 in Napoli, Cattaraugus Co, NY. She married DR. RALPH P. KNIGHT 17 Jul 1920 in East Randolph, Cattaraugus County, New York, son of ARCHIBALD KNIGHT and JANE _____. He was born Bet. 1883 - 1884 in Machias, Cattaraugus County, New York.

Children of IRENE MILKS and RALPH KNIGHT are:
i. JANE[10] KNIGHT, b. 07 Feb 1924, Little Valley, Cattaraugus County, New York; m. ROBERT JAHNKE; b. Abt. 1924.
ii. WALLACE ARCHIBALD KNIGHT, b. 21 Jul 1926, Little Valley, Cattaraugus County, New York; d. 21 Dec 1979, Broward County, Florida.

1461. CLIFFORD PAUL[9] MILKS *(WALLACE H.[8], HIRAM[7], JOHN[6] MILK, JONATHAN[5], JONATHAN[4], JOB[3], JOHN[2], JOHN[1])* was born 26 May 1897 in Napoli, Cattaraugus Co, NY, and died 28 Mar 1969 in East Randolph, Cattaraugus, NY 14730. He married KATHRYN BUCHANAN 09 Jun 1928, daughter of JOHN BUCHANAN and MARY ROSSA. She was born 19 Oct 1903 in Wallkill, NY, and died 16 Apr 1997 in Palm Beach, Palm Beach, FL.

Children of CLIFFORD MILKS and KATHRYN BUCHANAN are:
2500. i. CLIFFORD PAUL[10] MILKS, JR., b. 30 Mar 1930, East Randolph, Cattaraugus Co, NY; d. 17 Feb 1997, Ellicottville, Cattaraugus Co, NY 14731.
ii. MARY KATHRYN MILKS, b. 13 Mar 1938, East Randolph, Cattaraugus Co, NY; m. MISTTER LENAHAN; b. Abt. 1938.

1462. HELEN D.[9] HAAS *(MARY B.[8] MILKS, HIRAM[7], JOHN[6] MILK, JONATHAN[5], JONATHAN[4], JOB[3], JOHN[2], JOHN[1])* was born 19 Nov 1904 in Napoli, Cattaraugus County, New York, and died 18 Apr 1998 in Ithaca, Tompkins County, New York. She married JAMES W. AVERY 30 Jun 1934, son of JAMES AVERY and LAVENCHIA WALKER. He was born 08 Dec 1893 in Vassar, Michigan, and died 1959.

Children of HELEN HAAS and JAMES AVERY are:
i. MARY BELL[10] AVERY, b. 28 Jul 1942.
ii. STANLEY JAMES AVERY, b. 13 Jun 1945; m. COLEEN ODONNELL; b. 05 Jul 1951.

1463. AUDRA^9 RHODES *(SIBYL^8 MILKS, HIRAM^7, JOHN^6 MILK, JONATHAN^5, JONATHAN^4, JOB^3, JOHN^2, JOHN^1)* was born 07 Apr 1900 in Conewango, Cattaraugus County, New York, and died 18 Aug 1999 in Melbourne, Brevard County, Florida. She married LEO EWING COVERT 03 Aug 1918, son of ASHER COVERT and MARGARET. He was born 23 Feb 1893 in Cold Spring, Cattaraugus County, New York, and died Feb 1969 in Fort Pierce, Saint Lucie County, Florida.

Children of AUDRA RHODES and LEO COVERT are:
2501.   i.   JEAN MARIE^{10} COVERT, b. Abt. Oct 1928, East Randolph, Cattaraugus County, New York.
2502.   ii. JAMES RHODES COVERT, b. 20 Jul 1931, East Randolph, Cattaraugus County, New York.

1464. RALPH E. 'DUSTY'^{9} RHODES *(SIBYL^8 MILKS, HIRAM^7, JOHN^6 MILK, JONATHAN^5, JONATHAN^4, JOB^3, JOHN^2, JOHN^1)* was born 26 Nov 1904 in Conewango, Cattaraugus County, New York, and died 02 Jun 2004 in Santa Barbara, California. He married RUTH WALLACE 19 Jun 1933, daughter of HENRY WALLACE and EMMA RICKARDS. She was born 17 Apr 1907 in Roscoe, Sullivan County, New York, and died 20 Jul 2004 in Santa Barbara, California.

OBITUARY

SANTA BARBARA, Calif. - *Ruth Wallace Rhodes, 97, died Tuesday (July 20, 2004) in Santa Barbara. She was born on April 17, 1907, in Roscoe, N.Y., the daughter of Henry Joshua and Emma Richards Wallace.*

She earned a bachelor of science degree in home economics in 1928 from Cornell University and pursued further education at the universities of Colorado at Boulder, Albany, Buffalo, Miami and Syracuse. She was inducted into the national honorary teacher's sorority, Delta Kappa Gamma. She was a history and home economics teacher at Bemus Point Central School, Jamestown High School and Southwestern Central School from 1931 until her retirement in 1962. She was a member of the Methodist Church of Bemus Point and was a bridge player at the Women's Club in Santa Barbara. During the Depression, when jobs were scarce, especially for women, she taught new owners of White Sewing Machines living in Chautauqua, Cattaraugus and Erie counties how to use their machines. She was active in sewing costumes for the Jamestown Little Theater and various Southwestern school musicals.

Ruth was first and foremost, a teacher. Truly a modern and educated woman for those early years, Ruth was someone to whom her students looked as a model of a professional woman. Inspired to travel, Ruth and her college roommate, with carefully saved money, traveled to the Middle East in 1930, climbed the Great Pyramid, and also saw King Tut's tomb and treasures before they were removed to the Cairo Museum. Ruth's love of travel took her all over the world with her husband, Ralph. Detailed journals of their experiences reflect her intense curiosity about history, current events, ancient cultures and people that continued throughout her life. She loved to recite poetry, had a wonderful sense of humor, and possessed a very practical and resilient personal philosophy that gave her strength and a healthy perspective about life.

Surviving are her children: Douglas Rhodes of Yardley, Pa., and Sondra Rice of Santa Barbara, with whom she made her home; four grandchildren: David Rice of London, England, William Rice of Hartford, Conn., Erica Rhodes Recker of Atlanta and Jennifer Rhodes Hern of Washington, D.C.; and four great-grandchildren.

She was preceded in death by her husband of 71 years, Ralph Rhodes, whom she married on June 19, 1933, and who died on June 2, 2004.

She will be buried in Cottage Cemetery, Cattaraugus County, New York.

Children of RALPH RHODES and RUTH WALLACE are:
2503.   i.   DOUGLAS WALLACE^{10} RHODES, b. 16 Oct 1938, Chautauqua County, New York.
2504.   ii. SONDRA LU RHODES, b. 02 Jun 1940, Chautauqua County, New York.

1465. KENNETH WALLACE^9 MILKS *(MANLEY KENNETH^8, HIRAM^7, JOHN^6 MILK, JONATHAN^5, JONATHAN^4, JOB^3, JOHN^2, JOHN^1)* was born 09 Dec 1907 in Frewsburg, Chautauqua County, New York, and died 25 Oct 1980 in Jamestown, Chautauqua Co, NY. He married (1) RUTH ADELINE HIRSCH Abt. 1926. She was born Bet. 1909 - 1910 in New York. He married (2) EDITH MURIEL CROSSLEY 16 Jun 1930 in Chautauqua County, New York, daughter of ROBERT CROSSLEY and EDITH GLEDHILL. She was born 18 Oct 1910 in Jamestown, Chautauqua County, New York, and died 23 Jul 1954. He married (3) BERNICE MOSHER 04 Nov 1955, daughter of WILLIAM MOSHER and NINA _____. She was born 14 Oct 1907 in Falconer, NY, and died 29 Mar 1992 in Jamestown, Chautauqua Co, NY.

Child of KENNETH MILKS and RUTH HIRSCH is:
2505.   i.   WALLACE BRUCE MILKS^{10} KURTZ, b. 09 Mar 1927, New York City.

Children of KENNETH MILKS and EDITH CROSSLEY are:

2506. ii. MARILYN JUNE[10] MILKS, b. 16 Jun 1931.
2507. iii. ROBERT DUANE MILKS, SR., b. 31 Oct 1934.
2508. iv. KENNETH WALLACE MILKS, JR., b. 08 Oct 1936, Queens, Long Island, New York; d. 17 Aug 2003, Jamison, Bucks County, Pennsylvania.

1466. JOHN HIRAM[9] MILKS *(MANLEY KENNETH[8], HIRAM[7], JOHN[6] MILK, JONATHAN[5], JONATHAN[4], JOB[3], JOHN[2], JOHN[1])* was born 25 Feb 1910 in Frewsburg, NY, and died 30 Jan 2004 in Cattaraugus Co., NY. He married ETHEL ELLEN FRANCIS 25 Oct 1930 in Jamestown, Chautauqua County, New York, daughter of FRANK FRANCES and ETHEL KEECH. She was born 18 Mar 1910 in Titusville, PA, and died 15 Mar 2006 in Dunkirk, Chautauqua Co., NY. John was an avid hunter and fisherman.

OBITUARY

Ethel Ellen Milks

3/17/2006 - A resident of Napoli for more than 60 years, she and her late husband owned and operated their Dairy Farm on Pigeon Valley Road for many years.

Ethel opened her home for farm vacations and holidays for over 10 years. For more than 25 years she was a caregiver in her home to clients from the Gowanda Psychiatric Hospital and later from the J.N. Adams Home in Perrysburg. In 1979 Ethel was awarded Caretaker of the Year. In addition, she worked in a greenhouse, making Christmas wreathes and pine roping. She cooked at the former Rock City Hotel in Little Valley, for Stan and Lillian Waite and also helped them with their food stand at the Cattaraugus County Fair.

Ethel was a current member of the Daughters of the American Revolution.

Surviving are a daughter, Marlene (James) Webster of Dunkirk, five sons, John E. (Norma) Milks of Hinsdale, Eugene M. (Clara) Milks and Sherwood Milks, both of Randolph, Charles (Priscilla) Milks of Little Valley, and Raymond (Sandra) Milks of Arcade, 34 grandchildren, 59 greatgrandchildren and numerous great-great-grandchildren.

Ethel was preceded in death by her husband, John H. Milks on Jan.30, 2004, whom she married Oct. 25, 1930 in Jamestown, a daughter, Martha Slater in 2002,

three brothers including her twin, Elmer, Charles and Sherwood Francis and a sister Charlotte "Pegî Custer.

Funeral services will be held at 1 p.m. Saturday, March 18, 2006 (her 96th birthday) in the Napoli United Methodist Church with the Rev. Mike Trenchard officiating. Burial will follow in the Little Valley Rural Cemetery.

The family will be received one hour prior in the church. Arrangements are entrusted to the VanRensselaer &Son Funeral Home, 14 Church Street, Randolph. Memorials may be sent to the Napoli United Methodist Church or to the Hospice of Chautauqua County, 4840 West Lake Road, Mayville, N.Y., 14757.

Children of JOHN MILKS and ETHEL FRANCIS are:

2509. i. JOHN EARL[10] MILKS, b. 16 Oct 1931, Jamestown, New York.
2510. ii. EUGENE MANLEY MILKS, b. 06 Jun 1934, Napoli, Cattaraugus County, New York.
2511. iii. MARTHA JOAN MILKS, b. 11 Jan 1937, Napoli, Cattaraugus County, New York; d. 24 Aug 2002, Dewittville, Chautauqua Co., NY.
2512. iv. CHARLES FRANK MILKS, b. 16 Jun 1939, Napoli, Cattaraugus County, New York.
2513. v. RAYMOND G. MILKS, b. 20 Apr 1941, Napoli, Cattaraugus County, New York.
       vi. MARLENE JUNE MILKS, b. 12 Jun 1944, Napoli, Cattaraugus County, New York; m. JAMES WEBSTER.
2514. vii. SHERWOOD CRAIG MILKS, b. 09 May 1948, Napoli, Cattaraugus County, New York.

1467. OLDICE HOMER ALTON[9] MILKS *(MANLEY KENNETH[8], HIRAM[7], JOHN[6] MILK, JONATHAN[5], JONATHAN[4], JOB[3], JOHN[2], JOHN[1])* was born 16 May 1912 in Frewsburg, Chautauqua County, New York, and died 07 Jul 2008 in Danville, Montour County, Pennsylvania. He married SIGNE ELIZABETH OLSON Abt. 1936. She was born 16 May 1916 in Jamestown, NY, and died Oct 1985 in Pipersville, Bucks County, Pennsylvania.

Children of OLDICE MILKS and SIGNE OLSON are:

2515. i. MARGARET ANN[10] MILKS, b. 04 Apr 1937, Willow Grove/Philadelphia, PA.
2516. ii. JAMES ALTON MILKS, b. 16 Jun 1938, Jamestown, NY.
2517. iii. WILLIAM ROGER MILKS, b. 09 Sep 1943, Philadelphia, PA.
2518. iv. DAVID ERIC MILKS, b. 23 Apr 1945, Philadelphia, PA.
2519. v. DOUGLAS RONALD MILKS, b. 10 Feb 1947, Philadelphia, PA.

1468. ROBERT LEE[9] MCELWAIN *(ANNIE J.[8] MILKS, MARTIN[7], JOHN[6] MILK, JONATHAN[5], JONATHAN[4], JOB[3], JOHN[2], JOHN[1])* was born 10 Apr 1879 in Conewango, Cattaraugus County, New York. He married MATTIE A. SHIELDS 23 Jan 1909 in Cattaraugus County, New York, daughter of PATRICK SHIELDS and MARY WILLY. She was born 1887.

Children of ROBERT MCELWAIN and MATTIE SHIELDS are:
      i. REX ROBERT[10] MCELWAIN, b. 1913, New York.
2520. ii. CLARENCE LEE MCELWAIN, b. 15 Feb 1915, New York; d. 03 May 1973, Steubenville, Jefferson County, Ohio.

1469. MARY ALICE[9] MCELWAIN *(ANNIE J.[8] MILKS, MARTIN[7], JOHN[6] MILK, JONATHAN[5], JONATHAN[4], JOB[3], JOHN[2], JOHN[1])* was born 02 Sep 1880 in Cattaraugus County, New York. She married WILLIAM H. FRAHM Abt. 1909, son of WILLIAM FRAHM and SOPHIA SCHUPENHAWER. He was born 05 Jan 1874 in Little Valley, Cattaraugus County, New York. Mary contributed many records on the descendants of Martin Milks.

Child of MARY MCELWAIN and WILLIAM FRAHM is:
2521. i. RAYMOND A.[10] FRAHM, b. 18 Apr 1910, Little Valley, Cattaraugus County, New York.

1470. ALBERT DOUGLAS[9] MCELWAIN *(ANNIE J.[8] MILKS, MARTIN[7], JOHN[6] MILK, JONATHAN[5], JONATHAN[4], JOB[3], JOHN[2], JOHN[1])* was born 12 Feb 1883 in Little Valley, Cattaraugus County, New York, and died Sep 1970 in Cattaraugus County, New York. He married BLANCH CLARINDA COOPER, daughter of CLINTON COOPER and ELLA MITCHELL. She was born 24 Jul 1894 in New York, and died 19 Mar 1991 in Cattaraugus County, New York.

Child of ALBERT MCELWAIN and BLANCH COOPER is:
      i. RALPH[10] MCELWAIN, b. Jan 1918, Conewango, Cattaraugus County, New York.

1471. BENJAMIN CLAYTON[9] MCELWAIN *(ANNIE J.[8] MILKS, MARTIN[7], JOHN[6] MILK, JONATHAN[5], JONATHAN[4], JOB[3], JOHN[2], JOHN[1])* was born 13 Jun 1885 in Conewango, Cattaraugus County, New York, and died 30 Dec 1966 in Randolph, Cattaraugus County, New York. He married BARBARA LAKE 1908 in Cattaraugus County, New York, daughter of FREMONT LAKE and ALLIE _____. She was born Oct 1885 in Randolph, Cattaraugus County, New York (adopted by Fremont and Allie).

Children of BENJAMIN MCELWAIN and BARBARA LAKE are:
      i. CLAIR J.[10] MCELWAIN, b. 04 Mar 1921, Randolph, Cattaraugus County, New York; d. 03 Jul 1986, Tiona, Warren County, Pennsylvania.
2522. ii. GRACE ELIZABETH MCELWAIN, b. 06 Aug 1912, Randolph Cemetery, Cattaraugus County, New York; d. 11 Nov 1985, Jamestown, Chautauqua County, New York.

1472. HARRIET J. 'HATTIE'[9] MCELWAIN *(ANNIE J.[8] MILKS, MARTIN[7], JOHN[6] MILK, JONATHAN[5], JONATHAN[4], JOB[3], JOHN[2], JOHN[1])* was born 13 Jun 1889 in Conewango, Cattaraugus County, New York. She married FRANK BURTON CARR 15 Jun 1915 in New York, son of AMOS CARR and MARY _____. He was born 05 May 1894 in Stockton, Chautauqua County, New York.

Children of HARRIET MCELWAIN and FRANK CARR are:
      i. MARIAN J.[10] CARR, b. 1916, Jamestown, Chautauqua County, New York.
2523. ii. PHILLIP BURTON CARR, b. 13 Dec 1917, Jamestown, Chautauqua County, New York; d. 17 Sep 1981, Alexandria, Fairfax County, Virginia.
     iii. BETTY M. CARR, b. 1921, Jamestown, Chautauqua County, New York.
     iv. FRANK BURTON CARR, JR., b. 12 Oct 1923, Pennsylvania; d. 12 Oct 2004, Roanoke, Roanoke County, Virginia; m. GENEVA P. _____; b. 1922.
        OBITUARY
        Frank B. Carr, Jr., of Roanoke, went to be with his Lord on his 81st birthday, October 12, 2004. During World War II, he served in the U.S. Army receiving numerous awards and medals including two Purple Hearts and a Bronze Star. He retired from General Electric after thirty years service. Mr. Carr attended Huntington Court United Methodist Church. Surviving are his wife of fifty-five years, Geneva P. Carr; a sister, Betty Miller of Washington, D.C.; sisters-in-law, Agnes Akers of Roanoke and Elaine Robinson

and husband, Dan of Huntington, W.Va.; brothers-in-law, Carl Combs of Roanoke and William Dulaney and wife....

1473. HESTER DOROTHY 'HETTIE'^{9} MCELWAIN *(ANNIE J.^{8} MILKS, MARTIN^7, JOHN^6 MILK, JONATHAN^5, JONATHAN^4, JOB^3, JOHN^2, JOHN^1)* was born 13 Jan 1892 in Conewango, Cattaraugus County, New York, and died Jan 1974 in Falconer, Chautauqua County, New York. She married HERMAN WILLIAM BEERS 01 Feb 1913 in New York, son of WILLIAM BEERS and CORNELIA LAWRENCE. He was born 16 Apr 1891 in Randolph, Cattaraugus County, New York, and died 1955 in Randolph, Cattaraugus County, New York.

Children of HESTER MCELWAIN and HERMAN BEERS are:
- i. ELEANOR D.^{10} BEERS, b. 1913, Randolph, Cattaraugus County, New York.
- ii. WILLIAM H. BEERS, b. Abt. Nov 1915, Randolph, Cattaraugus County, New York; m. LOIS J. _____; b. Abt. 1921, New York.
- 2524. iii. RICHARD D. BEERS, b. 16 Jan 1920, Ellington, Chautauqua County, New York; d. 20 Apr 1978, Falconer, Chautauqua County, New York.
- iv. EDWARD BEERS, b. 14 Jul 1931, Ellington, Chautauqua County, New York; d. 05 Sep 1990.

1474. GEORGE EARL^9 MCELWAIN *(ANNIE J.^{8} MILKS, MARTIN^7, JOHN^6 MILK, JONATHAN^5, JONATHAN^4, JOB^3, JOHN^2, JOHN^1)* was born 10 Jan 1893 in Conewango, Cattaraugus County, New York, and died Apr 1966 in Randolph, Cattaraugus County, New York. He married MILDRED G. HORTON 11 Nov 1916 in New York, daughter of ELMER HORTON and EMMA JONES. She was born 25 Dec 1900 in Mansfield, Cattaraugus County, New York, and died 18 Apr 1984 in WCA Hospital, Jamestown, Chautauqua County, New York.

Children of GEORGE MCELWAIN and MILDRED HORTON are:
- i. MILBURN E.^{10} MCELWAIN, b. Abt. Sep 1917, Cattaraugus County, New York; d. 1976.
- 2525. ii. REV. KENNETH EUGENE MCELWAIN, b. 13 Sep 1919, Cattaraugus County, New York; d. 15 Oct 1998, Robert Packer Hospital, Sayre, Pennsylvania.
- 2526. iii. MAXINE E. MCELWAIN, b. Abt. 1922, Cattaraugus County, New York.
- 2527. iv. LARRY D. MCELWAIN, b. 1937; d. Of Randolph, NY/Glasgow, KY.

1475. WILLIAM H.^{9} MCELWAIN, JR. *(ANNIE J.^{8} MILKS, MARTIN^7, JOHN^6 MILK, JONATHAN^5, JONATHAN^4, JOB^3, JOHN^2, JOHN^1)* was born 24 Jul 1895 in Napoli, Cattaraugus County, New York. He married ETTA M. _____. She was born Abt. 1903.

Children of WILLIAM MCELWAIN and ETTA _____ are:
- i. DORIS L.^{10} MCELWAIN, b. Abt. 1923, Randolph, Cattaraugus County, New York.
- ii. DONALD MCELWAIN, b. Abt. 1927, Randolph, Cattaraugus County, New York.
- iii. BETTY MCELWAIN, b. Abt. 1930, Randolph, Cattaraugus County, New York.
- iv. ROBERT MCELWAIN, b. Abt. 1933, South Dakota.

1476. PAUL OAKLEY^9 MCELWAIN *(ANNIE J.^{8} MILKS, MARTIN^7, JOHN^6 MILK, JONATHAN^5, JONATHAN^4, JOB^3, JOHN^2, JOHN^1)* was born 24 Sep 1899 in Randolph, Cattaraugus County, New York, and died Jun 1983 in Warsaw, Wyoming County, New York. He married MARGUERITE E. BAUER Abt. 1924, daughter of PAUL BAUER and OLIVE KITTLE. She was born 23 Jul 1907 in Sheldon, Wyoming County, New York, and died 30 Nov 1990.

Children of PAUL MCELWAIN and MARGUERITE BAUER are:
- i. PAULINE^{10} MCELWAIN, b. Abt. Jun 1925, Salamanca, Cattaraugus County, New York.
- ii. MARVIN MCELWAIN, b. Abt. Jun 1926, Salamanca, Cattaraugus County, New York.
- iii. HARLAN MCELWAIN, b. Abt. Jan 1929, Salamanca, Cattaraugus County, New York.
- iv. MARY MCELWAIN, b. 1932, Bradford, McKean County, Pennsylvania.
- v. FAYE MCELWAIN, b. 1934, Bradford, McKean County, Pennsylvania.

1477. WALTER^9 MCELWAIN *(ANNIE J.^{8} MILKS, MARTIN^7, JOHN^6 MILK, JONATHAN^5, JONATHAN^4, JOB^3, JOHN^2, JOHN^1)* was born Oct 1903 in Randolph, Cattaraugus County, New York, and died 26 Dec 1961 in Randolph, Cattaraugus County, New York. He married ISABEL HICKS. She was born Abt. 1905.

Child of WALTER MCELWAIN and ISABEL HICKS is:

      i.   ALBERTA M.[10] MCELWAIN, b. 13 Jul 1924, Randolph, Cattaraugus County, New York; d. Apr 1966; m. STANLEY EARL ANDREWS, 1943, Hillsborough County, Florida; b. 06 Sep 1922; d. 07 May 2005.

1478. ROSS JENNINGS[9] MILKS *(HARVEY C.[8], MARTIN[7], JOHN[6] MILK, JONATHAN[5], JONATHAN[4], JOB[3], JOHN[2], JOHN[1])* was born 25 Jul 1896 in Napoli, Cattaraugus County, New York, and died 15 Mar 1971 in Mccain, Hoke County, North Carolina. He married HILDA MILDRED GLOR, daughter of WALTER GOR and ROSETTA SPENCER. She was born 28 May 1901 in New York, and died 12 Sep 1974 in Charlotte, Mecklenburg County, North Carolina.

Children of ROSS MILKS and HILDA GLOR are:

2528.   i.   CAROL MAY[10] MILKS, b. 30 Oct 1929, Gowanda, Cattaraugus County, New York.
2529.   ii.   ADDIE JOYCE MILKS, b. 05 Jul 1931, Gowanda, Cattaraugus County, New York.

1479. HOWARD GEORGE[9] MILKS *(GEORGE B.[8], MARTIN[7], JOHN[6] MILK, JONATHAN[5], JONATHAN[4], JOB[3], JOHN[2], JOHN[1])* was born 18 Jun 1895 in Dunkirk, New York, and died Feb 1966 in Columbus, Franklin County, Ohio. He married (1) RUTH ANN CETTELL Bet. 1917 - 1918, daughter of CHARLES CETTELL and THERESA PHILLIPS. She was born 1901 in Perrysburg, Cattaraugus Co., NY ?? date. He married (2) GRETCHEN MARIE WOLSCHLEGER Abt. 1934, daughter of AUGUST WOLSCHLEGER and MARTHA MIX. She was born 15 Jul 1910 in Harbor Beach, Michigan. Ruth Ann was a ward of Harlan S. Quackenbush at the time of her marriage.

Child of HOWARD MILKS and RUTH CETTELL is:

2530.   i.   CHESTER HOWARD[10] MILKS, b. 18 Feb 1919, Dunkirk, New York; d. 30 Sep 1999, Poway, San Diego, Calif 92064.

Children of HOWARD MILKS and GRETCHEN WOLSCHLEGER are:

      ii.   DAVID LEE[10] MILKS, b. 20 Aug 1935, Columbus, Ohio; d. 10 Jun 2004, Columbus, Franklin County, Ohio; m. (1) JUDITH A. _____, Abt. 1960, Columbus, Ohio?; b. Abt. 1935; m. (2) BARBARA J. SEARCH, 01 Jan 1995, Franklin County, Ohio; b. 02 Aug 1949.
      iii.   DERIL VAN MILKS, b. 22 Sep 1943, Columbus, Ohio.
      iv.   DENNIS RAY MILKS, b. 10 Feb 1951, Columbus, Ohio.

1480. EARLE DONALD[9] MILKS *(GEORGE B.[8], MARTIN[7], JOHN[6] MILK, JONATHAN[5], JONATHAN[4], JOB[3], JOHN[2], JOHN[1])* was born 03 Feb 1900 in Dunkirk, New York, and died 13 Mar 1965 in Chautauqua, New York. He married CATHERINE RUMANE HAGADORN 04 Apr 1931 in Dunkirk, NY, daughter of SAM HAGADORN and CLARA ERB. She was born 30 Mar 1905 in Mt. Alton, Pennsylvania, and died 19 Mar 1990.

Children of EARLE MILKS and CATHERINE HAGADORN are:

      i.   FRED[10] MILKS, b. 04 Apr 1931, Where did this come from??.
      ii.   DONALD EARLE MILKS, b. 15 Jun 1932, Dunkirk, New York; m. ALICE BERGUSON, 30 Aug 1958, Elmira, NY; b. Abt. 1932, of Elmira, NY.
      iii.   DANIEL GEORGE MILKS, b. 08 Dec 1943, Jamestown, Chautauqua County, New York.

1481. WILLIAM MILKS[9] FOX *(ELIZABETH "LIZZIE"[8] MILKS, MARTIN[7], JOHN[6] MILK, JONATHAN[5], JONATHAN[4], JOB[3], JOHN[2], JOHN[1])* was born 08 Dec 1898 in Leon, Cattaraugus County, New York, and died Apr 1973 in Leon, Cattaraugus County, New York. He married ANNA M. _____ Abt. 1930 in Cattaraugus County, New York. She was born Abt. 1906.

Child of WILLIAM FOX and ANNA _____ is:

      i.   SHARON[10] FOX, b. 20 July 1935, Leon, Cattaraugus County, New York, d. 12 March 2012..

1482. EULA ALETHA[9] COMSTOCK *(ALMYRA "MYRA"[8] MILKS, MARTIN[7], JOHN[6] MILK, JONATHAN[5], JONATHAN[4], JOB[3], JOHN[2], JOHN[1])* was born 24 Oct 1891 in Cattaraugus County, New York. She married WILLARD ELWOOD BAILEY. He was born 03 Feb 1892 in Coldspring, Cattaraugus County, New York.

Children of EULA COMSTOCK and WILLARD BAILEY are:

2531. i. RITA A.[10] BAILEY, b. 24 Aug 1912, Salamanca, Cattaraugus County, New York; d. Jul 1982, Canisteo, Steuben County, New York.

2532. ii. ROWENA GERTRUDE BAILEY, b. 1915, Salamanca, Cattaraugus County, New York; d. 1959, Salamanca, Cattaraugus County, New York.

2533. iii. ROGERS ELMER BAILEY, b. 04 Oct 1918, Salamanca, Cattaraugus County, New York; d. 10 Jul 1991, Olean, Cattaraugus County, New York.

1483. CLAUDIA RUTH[9] COMSTOCK *(ALMYRA "MYRA"[8] MILKS, MARTIN[7], JOHN[6] MILK, JONATHAN[5], JONATHAN[4], JOB[3], JOHN[2], JOHN[1])* was born 09 May 1899 in Napoli, Cattaraugus County, New York, and died 13 Jun 1922 in Napoli, Cattaraugus County, New York (in Childbirth). She married JOHN CORCORAN 04 Aug 1920 in Cattaraugus, NY. He was born Abt. 1899, and died Abt. Jan 1922 in Napoli, Cattaraugus County, New York.

Child of CLAUDIA COMSTOCK and JOHN CORCORAN is:

i. BABY[10] CORCORAN, b. 13 Jun 1922, Napoli, Cattaraugus County, New York; d. 13 Jun 1922, Napoli, Cattaraugus County, New York (in Childbirth).

1484. ELLSWORTH M.[9] MILKS *(EMMET EARL[8], MARTIN[7], JOHN[6] MILK, JONATHAN[5], JONATHAN[4], JOB[3], JOHN[2], JOHN[1])* was born 04 Dec 1906 in Conewango, NY, and died May 1953 in Little Valley, Cattaraugus County, NY. He married AUTUMN EVA TIMME 21 Jul 1929 in Little Valley, Cattaraugus, NY, daughter of WILLIAM TIMME and NORA MILKS. She was born 08 Jul 1908 in Mansfield, Cattaraugus County, New York, and died 14 Jan 1992 in Olean, NY.

Children of ELLSWORTH MILKS and AUTUMN TIMME are:

i. ELLSWORTH ERVIN[10] MILKS, b. 26 May 1932, Salamanca, Cattaraugus County, New York; d. 03 Jul 2008, Olean, Cattaraugus County, New York.

OBITUARY

LITTLE VALLEY - E. Ervin Milks, 76, of Rock City Street passed away Thursday, July 3, 2008, at Olean General Hospital.

He was born May 26, 1932, in Salamanca, N.Y., the son of the late Ellsworth and Autumn (Timme) Milks.

Mr. Milks was a Korean War veteran, having served in the U.S. Army. He later was a teacher at Randolph Central School for 27 years.

He is survived by a sister, Diane Bergholtz of Bemus Point, two nephews: Martin Bergholtz of Olean and Gre-gory Bergholtz of Simsbury, Conn., and his caregivers, Christina Gassman and Terry Nichols.

Burial will be in the Little Valley Rural Cemetery.

Arrangements are under the direction of the Mentley Funeral Home Inc., 411 Rock City St., Little Valley.

Memorials may be made to the Little Valley Memorial Library.

2534. ii. DIANE FAY MILKS, b. 03 Oct 1941, Salamanca, Cattaraugus County, New York.

1485. CLIFTON LEE[9] MILKS *(HORACE 'LEE'[8], MARTIN[7], JOHN[6] MILK, JONATHAN[5], JONATHAN[4], JOB[3], JOHN[2], JOHN[1])* was born 06 Oct 1901 in Little Valley, Cattaraugus County, New York, and died May 1975 in Latrobe, Westmoreland County, Pennsylvania. He married (1) MARGARET B. _____. She was born 04 Dec 1910, and died 14 Mar 2002 in Latrobe, Westmoreland County, Pennsylvania. He married (2) EMILY ALICE BARNES 12 Nov 1930 in Salamanca, Cattaraugus County, New York. She was born 06 Jan 1912 in Wellsville, New York. He married (3) DOROTHY MCGURN Aft. 1932. She was born Abt. 1900.

Children of CLIFTON MILKS and EMILY BARNES are:

i. CLIFTON LEE[10] MILKS, JR., b. 09 Oct 1931, Salamanca, Cattaraugus County, New York; d. 17 Feb 1993, Tawas City, Iosco Co., Michigan; m. (1) ALICE _____, Jul 1953, Buffalo, New York; b. Abt. 1931; m. (2) ALICE A STDENIS, 26 Jul 1989, Clark County, Nevada; b. 15 Jun 1932.

ii. THELMA ANN MILKS, b. Feb 1933, Little Valley, New York; m. SAM MUSCAVELLA; b. Abt. 1930, Mt. Morris, NY.

1486. HAZEL G.^{9} MILKS *(HORACE 'LEE'^{8}, MARTIN^7, JOHN^6 MILK, JONATHAN^5, JONATHAN^4, JOB^3, JOHN^2, JOHN^1)* was born 07 Aug 1903 in Little Valley, Cattaraugus County, New York, and died Jun 1980 in Little Valley, Cattaraugus County, NY. She married FRED THEODORE CARLSON 03 Sep 1927 in Jamestown, New York, son of JOHN CARLSON and JENNIE VALONE. He was born 15 Oct 1900 in Randolph, New York, and died 12 Jul 1945 in Salamanca, Cattaraugus County, New York.

Children of HAZEL MILKS and FRED CARLSON are:
    i. JOYCE ANNE^{10} CARLSON, b. 27 Aug 1929, Little Valley, New York.
    ii. LAWRENCE HOBART CARLSON, b. 29 Jun 1931, Little Valley, New York.
    iii. SHIRLEY JEAN CARLSON, b. 06 Dec 1936, Little Valley, New York.

1487. MARGUERITE ARLENE^9 MILKS *(HORACE 'LEE'^{8}, MARTIN^7, JOHN^6 MILK, JONATHAN^5, JONATHAN^4, JOB^3, JOHN^2, JOHN^1)* was born 19 Sep 1906 in New York. She married (1) FRANKLIN J. CHAMBERLAIN Abt. 1927, son of WILLIAM CHAMBERLAIN and DELLA RHODES. He was born Abt. 1905. She married (2) LEE E. WHITCOMB Aft. 1930, son of EDWARD WHITCOMB and MARY SADLER. He was born 09 Feb 1895, and died Oct 1967.

Child of MARGUERITE MILKS and FRANKLIN CHAMBERLAIN is:
2535.   i. ROBERT F.^{10} CHAMBERLAIN, b. 09 Sep 1927, Salamanca, Cattaraugus County, New York.

Child of MARGUERITE MILKS and LEE WHITCOMB is:
2536.   ii. DIANE MARIE^{10} WHITCOMB, b. 14 Apr 1930, Little Valley, New York; d. 2005.

1488. KENNETH LEE^9 MILKS *(HORACE 'LEE'^{8}, MARTIN^7, JOHN^6 MILK, JONATHAN^5, JONATHAN^4, JOB^3, JOHN^2, JOHN^1)* was born 08 Jan 1913 in Little Valley, Cattaraugus County, New York, and died Apr 1976 in Cattaraugus County, New York. He married (1) MARJORIE MERLE SNYDER 12 Jan 1935 in Leon, Cattaraugus, NY, by Clyde C. Clark, JP. She was born 12 Feb 1918 in Pennsylvania, and died Abt. 1990 in Cattaraugus County, New York (traffic accident). He married (2) JOSEPHINE PHYLLIS SYPER Abt. 1946, daughter of ANDREW SYPER and FELIXIA _____. She was born 14 Nov 1913 in Pittsburgh, PA, and died 06 Apr 2003 in Bradenton, Florida.

Children of KENNETH MILKS and MARJORIE SNYDER are:
    i. JEAN LOUISE^{10} MILKS, b. 23 Jul 1936; m. CLYDE DONNELL, 1955; b. Abt. 1935.
2537.   ii. KENNETH ROBERT MILKS, b. 23 Apr 1937; d. 20 Aug 1994, Zebulon, NC.
    iii. RONNIE LEE MILKS.
2538.   iv. THOMAS (MILKS) FEE, b. 1941.

Child of KENNETH MILKS and JOSEPHINE SYPER is:
2539.   v. LESLIE S.^{10} MILKS, b. 30 Jun 1947, Erie, Pennsylvania.

1489. BYRON^9 HARRINGTON *(THOMAS A.^{8}, DAVID W.^{7}, DEBORAH^6 MILKS, JONATHAN^5 MILK, JONATHAN^4, JOB^3, JOHN^2, JOHN^1)* was born 1894 in Greenwich, Washington County, New York. He married IRENE KENYON. She was born Abt. 1897.

Child of BYRON HARRINGTON and IRENE KENYON is:
    i. DOROTHY^{10} HARRINGTON, b. 1920, Greenwich, Washington County, New York.

1490. MAUD^9 HARRINGTON *(MERRITT R.^{8}, DAVID W.^{7}, DEBORAH^6 MILKS, JONATHAN^5 MILK, JONATHAN^4, JOB^3, JOHN^2, JOHN^1)* was born 30 Aug 1888 in Greenwich, Washington County, New York. She married ALFRED SNELL. He was born Abt. 1888.

Child of MAUD HARRINGTON and ALFRED SNELL is:
    i. MARJORIE^{10} SNELL, b. 04 Jul 1918, Greenwich, Washington County, New York.

1491. FRED H.^{9} MILKS-HOWARD *(HENRY^8, LEONARD^7 MILKS, BENJAMIN^6, JONATHAN^5 MILK, JONATHAN^4, JOB^3, JOHN^2, JOHN^1)* was born 21 Jul 1865 in Dayton, Cattaraugus County, New York, and died 17 May 1926 in Leon, Cattaraugus County, New York. He married CORA A. SMITH 1888 in Cattaraugus County, New York. She was born 24 Jul 1868 in

Leon, Cattaraugus County, New York, and died 22 Jun 1930 in Leon, Cattaraugus County, New York.

Children of FRED MILKS-HOWARD and CORA SMITH are:
- i. NORMAN FREDERICK[10] MILKS-HOWARD, b. 02 May 1889, Leon, Cattaraugus County, New York; d. Feb 1976, Cherry Creek, Chautauqua County, New York; m. (1) ELSIE LAMPSON, 18 Oct 1912, Cattaraugus County, New York; b. 03 Dec 1895, Cattaraugus County, New York; d. 12 Mar 1943, Leon, Cattaraugus County, New York; m. (2) EDNA (PETERS) CRUMB, 16 Dec 1949; b. Abt. 1889; d. 26 Jul 1964. No children.
- 2540. ii. ADDIE HATTIE MILKS-HOWARD, b. 10 Aug 1891, Leon, Cattaraugus County, New York; d. 03 Jan 1994, Lake County, Ohio.
- iii. AMELIA M. MILKS-HOWARD, b. 07 May 1896, Leon, Cattaraugus County, New York; d. 13 Dec 1992, Fredonia, Chautauqua County, New York. Never married.

1492. HARRIET A. 'HATTIE'[9] MILKS-HOWARD *(HENRY[8], LEONARD[7] MILKS, BENJAMIN[6], JONATHAN[5] MILK, JONATHAN[4], JOB[3], JOHN[2], JOHN[1])* was born 10 May 1869 in Dayton, Cattaraugus County, New York, and died 12 Dec 1953 in Chester, Orange County, New York. She married WILLIAM FREDERICK PAYNE 1889. He was born 24 Jul 1863 in Conewango, Cattaraugus County, New York, and died Sep 1908 in Middletown, Orange County, New York.

Children of HARRIET MILKS-HOWARD and WILLIAM PAYNE are:
- 2541. i. FRANCES RUTH[10] PAYNE, b. Dec 1892, Sherman, Chautauqua County, New York; d. Mar 1984, Randolph, Cattaraugus County, New York.
- 2542. ii. EDITH M. PAYNE, b. 22 Nov 1897, Conewango, Cattaraugus County, New York; d. Sep 1972, Chester, Orange County, New York.

1493. JAMES HENRY 'JIMMY'[9] MILKS-HOWARD *(HENRY[8], LEONARD[7] MILKS, BENJAMIN[6], JONATHAN[5] MILK, JONATHAN[4], JOB[3], JOHN[2], JOHN[1])* was born 24 Jan 1875 in Dayton, Cattaraugus County, New York, and died 21 Apr 1955 in South Dayton, Cattaraugus County, New York. He married ANNA ELIZA GAVAGAN 1902 in Cattaraugus County, New York, daughter of JOHN GAVAGAN and KATIE _____. She was born 20 Aug 1876 in New York City, and died 21 Jun 1949 in South Dayton, Cattaraugus County, New York.

Children of JAMES MILKS-HOWARD and ANNA GAVAGAN are:
- i. FRANCIS[10] MILKS-HOWARD, b. 07 Aug 1903, Cattaraugus County, New York; d. Jul 1977, Cattaraugus County, New York.
- 2543. ii. JAMES HENRY MILKS-HOWARD, JR., b. 05 Nov 1904, Cattaraugus County, New York; d. 13 Apr 1964, Machias, Cattaraugus County, New York.
- iii. VIVIAN MILKS-HOWARD, b. 1907, Cattaraugus County, New York.
- iv. LOUIS MILKS-HOWARD, b. 1911, Cattaraugus County, New York.
- 2544. v. MYRON MILKS-HOWARD, b. 1913, Cattaraugus County, New York.
- vi. VIOLET MILKS-HOWARD, b. Feb 1915, Cattaraugus County, New York.
- vii. LILLIAN MILKS-HOWARD, b. Aug 1918, Cattaraugus County, New York.

1494. LEONARD GLENN[9] MILKS *(EDGAR[8], LEONARD[7], BENJAMIN[6], JONATHAN[5] MILK, JONATHAN[4], JOB[3], JOHN[2], JOHN[1])* was born 12 Mar 1877 in Cattaraugus County, New York, and died 20 May 1951 in Yankton County, South Dakota. He married (1) JENNIE PEARL NELLIS 1903 in Cattaraugus County, New York, daughter of OSCAR NELLIS and MAY RANDALL. She was born Bet. 1888 - 1889 in Iowa, and died 17 Oct 1918 in Ft. Pierce, South Dakota. He married (2) BERTHA MAY ROBBINS 25 Nov 1921 in Pierre, Hughes County, SD, daughter of Martin Harvey Robbins and Sophia Gehring. She was born 25 Jan 1894 in Minnesota, and died Dec 1982 in Centerville, Turner Co., SD.
Moved to South Dakota about 1902.

Children of LEONARD MILKS and JENNIE NELLIS are:
- 2545. i. LUELLA MABLE[10] MILKS, b. 15 Oct 1905, New Albion, New York; d. Jan 1971, King County, Washington.
- 2546. ii. GLENNIE ROSELLA MILKS, b. 29 Jul 1918, Ft. Pierce, South Dakota; d. 27 Sep 1996, Umatilla County, Oregon.

Child of LEONARD MILKS and BERTHA ROBBINS is:
    iii. BERTHA R.[10] MILKS, b. Abt. 1919, Minnesota (adopted).

1495. PORTIA EDNA[9] MILKS *(EDGAR[8], LEONARD[7], BENJAMIN[6], JONATHAN[5] MILK, JONATHAN[4], JOB[3], JOHN[2], JOHN[1])* was born 17 Aug 1888 in Franklinville, Cattaraugus County, New York, and died 25 Jul 1955 in Pittsburgh, Pennsylvania. She married (1) JAMES DANIEL DONOVAN 06 Jul 1907 in Tippecanoe, Indiana, son of WILLIAM DONOVAN and MARY RONAN. He was born 11 Oct 1880 in Bloomington, Indiana, and died 11 Oct 1919 in Pittsburgh, Pennsylvania. She married (2) JOHN MAHOLLINE 15 Mar 1922. He was born 16 Apr 1873 in Of Pittsburgh, PA, and died 30 Jun 1922 in Pittsburgh, Pennsylvania.

James and Portia also had two more sets of twins, all of whom died young.

Children of PORTIA MILKS and JAMES DONOVAN are:
    i. HELEN MARIE[10] DONOVAN, b. 28 Aug 1909; d. 07 Aug 1912.
    ii. EDNA FAYE DONOVAN, b. 01 Jun 1918, Pittsburgh, Pennsylvania; d. 15 Jan 1919, Pittsburgh, Pennsylvania.
    iii. JAMES LEROY DONOVAN, b. 01 Jun 1918, Pittsburgh, Pennsylvania; d. 24 May 1933, Pittsburgh, Pennsylvania.

Child of PORTIA MILKS and JOHN MAHOLLINE is:
2547.   iv. DONALD RAY[10] MAHOLLINE, b. 15 Apr 1923, Pittsburgh, Pennsylvania.

1496. MERVA ERDEN[9] MILKS *(EDGAR[8], LEONARD[7], BENJAMIN[6], JONATHAN[5] MILK, JONATHAN[4], JOB[3], JOHN[2], JOHN[1])* was born 03 Apr 1890 in Franklinville, Cattaraugus County, New York. She married (1) JOHN BROCK 20 Aug 1908 in Gowanda, Cattaraugus County, New York, by C. W. Thurber, son of JOHN BROCK and EMMA VALENTINE. He was born Apr 1882 in Lapeer, Michigan. She married (2) JAMES BERNARD TARDY 01 Oct 1925 in Wellsburg, West Virginia, son of PATRINELLA TARDY. He was born 24 Aug 1894 in Italy.

Children of MERVA MILKS and JOHN BROCK are:
2548.   i. PAUL ETHELBERT[10] BROCK, b. 12 Jun 1909, Oxford, Michigan; d. Dec 1978, Carson, Allegheny, Pennsylvania.
    ii. GERALD EDGAR BROCK, b. 31 Dec 1910, Gowanda, Cattaraugus County, New York; d. 23 Aug 1926, Pittsburgh, Pennsylvania.

Child of MERVA MILKS and JAMES TARDY is:
2549.   iii. MERVA ELLEN[10] TARDY, b. 01 May 1923, Pittsburgh, Pennsylvania.

1497. GRETCHEN IRENE[9] MILKS *(EDGAR[8], LEONARD[7], BENJAMIN[6], JONATHAN[5] MILK, JONATHAN[4], JOB[3], JOHN[2], JOHN[1])* was born 22 Dec 1891 in Gowanda, Cattaraugus County, New York, and died 22 Nov 1984 in Gowanda, NY. She married ISAAC ALLEN 03 Feb 1910 in Cattaraugus County, New York, son of MYRON ALLEN and HARRIET PATCH. He was born 16 Feb 1883 in Gowanda, Cattaraugus County, New York, and died Nov 1962 in Collins, Erie County, NY.

Children of GRETCHEN MILKS and ISAAC ALLEN are:
2550.   i. VERA IRENE[10] ALLEN, b. 11 Feb 1911, Collins, Erie County, New York.
2551.   ii. CHARLES LEROY ALLEN, b. 22 Sep 1916, Collins, Erie County, New York.
2552.   iii. RHEMA ARLENE ALLEN, b. 04 Mar 1920, Collins, Erie County, New York.
2553.   iv. SHERWIN EDGAR ALLEN, b. 11 Nov 1922, Collins, Erie County, New York.

1498. LEROY ETHELBERT[9] MILKS *(EDGAR[8], LEONARD[7], BENJAMIN[6], JONATHAN[5] MILK, JONATHAN[4], JOB[3], JOHN[2], JOHN[1])* was born 06 Nov 1894 in Collins, NY, and died 1960 in Collins, Erie County, New York. He married OROBELL OLLIE PINES 02 Oct 1915 in Chautauqua Co, NY, daughter of CHARLES PINES and ISABELL BREWER. She was born 21 Jun 1898 in Collins/Gowanda, NY, and died 09 Feb 1992 in Watertown, NY.

Children of LEROY MILKS and OROBELL PINES are:
2554.   i. MABEL INEZ[10] MILKS, b. 12 Sep 1915, Westfield, Chautauqua County, New York; d. 1979, Collins, Erie County, New York.

2555. ii. WARD RAYMOND MILKS, b. 28 Oct 1916, Lawton, New York; d. 03 Jul 1971, Gowanda, Cattaraugus Co., NY.

1499. FRED JAMES^9 MILKS *(FRANCIS JAMES 'FRANK'^{8}, LEONARD^7, BENJAMIN^6, JONATHAN^5 MILK, JONATHAN^4, JOB^3, JOHN^2, JOHN^1)* was born 31 Mar 1874 in Mansfield, Cattaraugus County, New York, and died 1953 in Cattaraugus County, New York. He married NELLIE I. BUTLER 1898 in Cattaraugus County, New York, daughter of HORACE BUTLER and MARY WIDRIG. She was born 23 Oct 1874 in Mansfield, Cattaraugus County, New York, and died 14 Jun 1934 in Salamanca, Cattaraugus County, New York.

Children of FRED MILKS and NELLIE BUTLER are:
2556. i. ELLA MAE^{10} MILKS, b. 27 May 1900, Franklinville, New York; d. 29 Dec 1992, Machias, Cattaraugus County, New York.
2557. ii. MAUDE MARIE MILKS, b. 10 Mar 1905, Machias, Cattaraugus County, New York; d. 01 Feb 1982, Machias, Cattaraugus County, New York.

1500. CHARLES H.^{9} MILKS *(FRANCIS JAMES 'FRANK'^{8}, LEONARD^7, BENJAMIN^6, JONATHAN^5 MILK, JONATHAN^4, JOB^3, JOHN^2, JOHN^1)* was born 23 May 1877 in Otto, Cattaraugus County, New York, and died 15 Apr 1943 in Ellicottville, Cattaraugus County, New York. He married LOUISE B. LOCKE 20 Dec 1899 in Cattaraugus County, New York, daughter of HARLAND LOCKE and ELLEN MARTIN. She was born 09 Aug 1879 in Machias, Cattaraugus County, New York, and died 1967 in Ellicottville, Cattaraugus County, New York.

Child of CHARLES MILKS and LOUISE LOCKE is:
2558. i. HARLAND F.^{10} MILKS, b. 23 Nov 1900, Ashford, Cattaraugus County, New York.

1501. FRANK W.^{9} MILKS *(FRANCIS JAMES 'FRANK'^{8}, LEONARD^7, BENJAMIN^6, JONATHAN^5 MILK, JONATHAN^4, JOB^3, JOHN^2, JOHN^1)* was born 12 Nov 1879 in New Albion, Cattaraugus County, NY, and died 15 Feb 1968 in Machias, Cattaraugus County, New York. He married LELA M. SMITH 09 Aug 1909 in East Ashford, New York, by John C. Irvine, daughter of JOHN SMITH and BERTHA BABCOCK. She was born 1892 in West Valley, Cattaraugus County, New York, and died 06 Oct 1978 in Springville, New York.

Children of FRANK MILKS and LELA SMITH are:
2559. i. LENORE E.^{10} MILKS, b. 07 Sep 1912; d. 1986, Olean, Cattaraugus County, New York.
       ii. VIRGINIA M. MILKS, b. 1914; d. 1914, Cattaraugus, NY.
       iii. MILLARD S. MILKS, b. 06 Apr 1916, Cattaraugus County, NY; d. 24 Apr 1974, Bath, Steuben County, NY.
2560. iv. LYNN L. MILKS, b. 17 Jul 1918, Machias, Cattaraugus Co., NY?; d. 04 Jul 1987, Amherst, Lorain Co., Ohio.
       v. CAROL JEAN MILKS, b. Bet. 1924 - 1925, Cattaraugus County, New York.
       vi. BERTHA L. MILKS, b. Sep 1926, Cattaraugus County, New York.
2561. vii. FRANK W. MILKS, JR., b. 20 Oct 1928, Cattaraugus County, New York.
       viii. JOHN CHARLES MILKS, b. 29 Jan 1931, Cattaraugus County, New York; d. 13 Mar 1931, Cattaraugus, NY.

1502. ROLAND^9 MILKS *(FRANCIS JAMES 'FRANK'^{8}, LEONARD^7, BENJAMIN^6, JONATHAN^5 MILK, JONATHAN^4, JOB^3, JOHN^2, JOHN^1)* was born 10 Jan 1883 in Leon, New York. He married DELLA DELONG 1915. She was born 04 Oct 1886 in Summit, Schoharie County, New York.

Children of ROLAND MILKS and DELLA DELONG are:
2562. i. LETA IRENE^{10} MILKS, b. 01 Jan 1917, Cobleskill, New York; d. 26 May 1997, Amsterdam, Montgomery County, New York.
2563. ii. EDITH M. MILKS, b. 23 Dec 1918, Cobleskill, New York; d. 09 Jan 2000, Albany, New York.
       iii. RUTH IRENE MILKS, b. 19 Feb 1921, Sharon Springs, Schoharie County, New York; d. 12 Oct 2009, Binghamton, Broome County, New York; m. JOEL W. ULLMAN, 21 Nov 1941, Gloversville, Fulton County, New York; b. 08 Oct 1920, Schoharie County, New York; d. 05 Nov 1977, Sharon Springs, Schoharie County, New York. No children.
             OBITUARY - Published in The Daily Gazette Co. on October 15, 2009
             Ruth M. Ullman, 88, formerly of Sharon Springs and more recently of Schenectady, died Monday, October 12, 2009 after a long illness.

Ruth was born February 19, 1921 in Sharon Springs. She was the third of five daughters of Roland and Della (DeLong) Milks. Ruth was raised in Sharon Springs and graduated from the Sharon Springs Central School in the Class of 1938. She loved sports of all kinds and played basketball during all four years of her high school years. She was also an avid and accomplished golfer through out her life.

On November 21, 1941 in Gloversville, NY she married Joel W. Ullman. He predeceased her on November 5, 1977. They lived in Sharon Springs for a number of years later moving to Schenectady.

Ruth worked in the Canajoharie National Bank for many years and thereafter for the Schenectady International Corporation where she was in charge of the employee's health care program for over 25 years. She was a member of the Sharon Springs United Methodist Church.

Ruth is survived by her sister, Mabel Chase (Jack) of Milford; her nephew, John A. Chase III (Debra) and their daughter, Mackenzie of Scottsdale, AZ; her nephew, Thomas Chase of Binghamton, NY; her nephew, James Spraker of Mechanicville, NY; her niece, Michelle Sharpe of Bristol, RI; as well as by a number of other nieces and nephews. She is also survived by her lifelong good friend, Mary Alpaugh, of Cobleskill, NY.

Ruth was predeceased by three of her sisters, Leta LaGuardia of Sidney, NY; Edith Spraker of Latham, NY and Alice Putnam of Clifton Park, NY.

Graveside services for Ruth will be held Saturday, October 17, 2009 in the Milford Cemetery, Milford, NY at 11 a.m. with the Rev. Rose Bellen pastor of the Westville United Methodist Church officiating. In lieu of flowers, the family suggests that those who so desire make donations in Ruth's memory to Catskill Area Hospice and Palliative Care, Inc., 1 Birchwood Drive, Oneonta, NY 13820. Arrangements are under the supervision of Tillapaugh Funeral Service, Cooperstown and Milford.

2564.   iv.   ALICE E. MILKS, b. 12 Jan 1923, Sharon Springs, New York; d. 20 Dec 1992, Clifton Park, Saratoga County, New York.

2565.   v.   MABEL R. MILKS, b. 09 Sep 1924, Sharon Springs, New York.

1503. JAY E.^{9} MILKS *(FRANCIS JAMES 'FRANK'^{8}, LEONARD^7, BENJAMIN^6, JONATHAN^5 MILK, JONATHAN^4, JOB^3, JOHN^2, JOHN^1)* was born 04 May 1885 in Leon, Cattaraugus County, New York, and died 1961 in Cattaraugus County, New York. He married ADA MAE LAW 04 Jul 1912 in Pavilion, Genesee County, New York, daughter of WILBUR LAW and EVA MABY. She was born 21 Jun 1887 in Portage, Livingston County, New York, and died 21 Feb 1954 in Cattaraugus County, New York.

Children of JAY MILKS and ADA LAW are:

2566.   i.   BEATRICE E.^{10} MILKS, b. 08 May 1913, Elton, Cattaraugus County, New York; d. Jun 1980, Delevan, Cattaraugus County, New York.

2567.   ii.   PAUL D. MILKS, b. 08 Aug 1915, Machias, Cattaraugus County, New York; d. 24 Feb 2009, Barker, Niagara County, New York.

2568.   iii.   JESSIE MARIE MILKS, b. 31 Oct 1922, Farmersville, Cattaraugus County, New York; d. 05 Jun 2005, East Aurora, Erie County, New York.

         iv.   EMERSON D. MILKS, b. 04 Sep 1924, Machias, Cattaraugus County, New York; m. JEAN ROSIN, 04 Jun 1949, Rochester, New York; b. 04 Sep 1924, Rochester, New York. No children.

2569.   v.   GLENNA DALE MILKS, b. 23 Apr 1927, Farmersville, Cattaraugus County, New York; d. 17 Dec 2009, Arcade, Wyoming County, New York.

1504. ROBERT^9 MILKS *(FRANCIS JAMES 'FRANK'^{8}, LEONARD^7, BENJAMIN^6, JONATHAN^5 MILK, JONATHAN^4, JOB^3, JOHN^2, JOHN^1)* was born 20 Sep 1886 in Conewango, Cattaraugus County, New York, and died 05 Jun 1970 in Covington, Miami County, Ohio. He married CARRIE LEMYRA PARKER 09 Jul 1925 in Franklinville, New York, daughter of WINFIELD PARKER and ELLA HOGG. She was born 14 Oct 1892 in Franklinville, Cattaraugus County, New York, and died 02 Mar 1983 in Newport News, Newport News County, Virginia.

Robert and Carrie contributed many family records.

Children of ROBERT MILKS and CARRIE PARKER are:

2570.   i.   MARION A.^{10} MILKS, b. 05 Dec 1926.

         ii.   ROBERT PARKER 'BOBBY' MILKS, b. 01 Dec 1929; d. 17 Jun 1942.

1505. EDWARD TRUMAN[9] JONES *(ELIZA JANE 'ALIDA[8] LOOP, CORDELIA[7] MILKS, BENJAMIN[6], JONATHAN[5] MILK, JONATHAN[4], JOB[3], JOHN[2], JOHN[1])* was born 15 Mar 1877 in Leon, Cattaraugus County, New York. He married (1) NANCY LUCINDA HENDERSON Abt. 1905 in Cattaraugus County, New York, daughter of SAMUEL HENDERSON and IDA MURRAY. She was born Oct 1887 in Pennsylvania, and died Bet. 1917 - 1920 in Cattaraugus County, New York. He married (2) NELLIE B. _____ Abt. 1928. She was born Abt. 1905 in New York.

Children of EDWARD JONES and NANCY HENDERSON are:
- i. ALICE ELIZABETH[10] JONES, b. Abt. Sep 1909, Great Valley, Cattaraugus County, New York.
- ii. LEROY S. JONES, b. Abt. 1912, Cattaraugus County, New York.
- iii. MARTHA M. JONES, b. Abt. 1915, Cattaraugus County, New York.
- iv. CLARA H. JONES, b. Abt. 1917, Cattaraugus County, New York.

Children of EDWARD JONES and NELLIE _____ are:
- v. CATHERINE AMA[10] JONES, b. Abt. Apr 1929, Salamanca, Cattaraugus County, New York.
- vi. HELEN J. JONES, b. Abt. 1931, Salamanca, Cattaraugus County, New York.
- vii. HAROLD D. JONES, b. Abt. 1934, Salamanca, Cattaraugus County, New York.

1506. GARRETT LANSING[9] MILKS *(GEORGE HENRY[8], GARRETT T.[7], BENJAMIN[6], JONATHAN[5] MILK, JONATHAN[4], JOB[3], JOHN[2], JOHN[1])* was born 30 Oct 1881 in Dayton, Cattaraugus County, New York, and died 10 Feb 1964 in Cattaraugus County, New York. He married JESSIE MAY KING 04 Jul 1911 in Cattaraugus, NY, daughter of LEONARD KING and ADELLA SMITH. She was born 1887 in Napoli, Cattaraugus Co, NY, and died 1947 in Cattaraugus County, New York.

Children of GARRETT MILKS and JESSIE KING are:
- 2571. i. LEONARD HOWARD[10] MILKS, b. 08 May 1913, Persia, Cattaraugus Co., NY; d. 12 May 1992, East Aurora, Erie County, New York.
- 2572. ii. HELEN IRENE MILKS, b. 02 Nov 1914, Persia, Cattaraugus Co., NY; d. 17 Jan 1998, Little Valley, Cattaraugus County, New York.
- iii. EDSON WARD MILKS, b. 07 Jun 1916, Persia, NY; d. 11 Jun 1992, Silver Creek, Chautauqua County, NY; m. VESTA ELLA DENNING, 04 Sep 1943; b. 03 Sep 1925, Caneadea, NY; d. 02 Dec 1998, Silver Creek, Chautauqua County, NY.
- iv. GORDON HENRY MILKS, b. 05 Jun 1918, Cattaraugus, NY; d. ??? Date.
- v. WALTER MILKS, b. 20 Jul 1920, Cattaraugus County, New York; d. 09 Nov 1924, Cattaraugus County, New York.
- vi. MARY ANNA MILKS, b. 28 Apr 1922, Dayton, Cattaraugus Co., NY; d. 17 Aug 1988, Napoli, Cattaraugus Co., NY; m. (1) WILLIAM CAMP, Abt. 1940; b. Abt. 1920, Of Allegany, PA; m. (2) HARRY BARNES, Aft. 1942; b. 1904; d. 1960, Napoli, Cattaraugus Co., NY; m. (3) CHARLES MIX, Aft. 1960.
- 2573. vii. GARRETT LANSING MILKS, JR., b. 24 Dec 1923, Leon, Cattaraugus Co., NY; d. 16 Feb 2011, Surprise, Sun City, Maricopa County, Arizona.
- 2574. viii. RICHARD WILLIAM MILKS, b. 28 Mar 1925, Leon, Cattaraugus Co., NY; d. 11 May 1979, South Napoli, Cattaraugus Co., NY.

1507. FREEMAN[9] MILKS *(GEORGE HENRY[8], GARRETT T.[7], BENJAMIN[6], JONATHAN[5] MILK, JONATHAN[4], JOB[3], JOHN[2], JOHN[1])* was born 07 Aug 1885 in Persia, Cattaraugus County, New York, and died 04 Aug 1955 in Madera, California. He married GOLDIE A. JOHNSON 07 Aug 1908 in Westfield, New York, by George L. MacClelland, Clergyman, daughter of ALBERT JOHNSON and HATTIE HAWKINS. She was born 25 Mar 1891 in Pennsylvania, and died 25 Nov 1978 in Madera, California.

Children of FREEMAN MILKS and GOLDIE JOHNSON are:
- i. ALICE C.[10] MILKS, b. Feb 1919, Jefferson County, Washington.
- 2575. ii. BERYL DORINE MILKS, b. 08 Jan 1922, Oregon; d. 01 Nov 2007, Pendleton, Umatilla, Oregon.

1508. FRANCES D.[9] MORGAN *(ALEDA[8] MILKS, GARRETT T.[7], BENJAMIN[6], JONATHAN[5] MILK, JONATHAN[4], JOB[3], JOHN[2], JOHN[1])* was born 18 Oct 1891 in Cattaraugus County, New York. She married FRANKLIN NAPOLEAN SINNING. He was born 16 Jan 1889 in Pennsylvania, and died 22 Nov 1961 in Los Angeles, California.

Children of FRANCES MORGAN and FRANKLIN SINNING are:
- i. MARIAN E.[10] SINNING, b. 1913, Titusville, Pennsylvania.
- ii. DOROTHY ALIDA SINNING, b. 21 Dec 1916, Titusville, Pennsylvania; d. 27 Jan 1987, Los Angeles, California; m. (1) ROBERT LELAND LEWIS, 08 Jul 1938, Los Angeles, California; b. 1917; m. (2) WILLIAM A. DEYOUNG, Abt. 1960; b. Abt. 1915. In 1940 Dorothy was 'married', but living with her parents, without her spouse, in Inglewood, California.
- iii. FRANK NAPOLEAN SINNING, JR., b. 03 Aug 1923, Titusville, Pennsylvania; d. 19 Apr 2005, San Diego, California.
- iv. ROBERT LOUIS SINNING, b. 16 Sep 1926, Los Angeles, California; d. 01 Apr 1973, Los Angeles, California.

1509. RAYMOND HERBERT[9] ROLFE *(HERBERT[8], GILBERT[7] MILKS, BENJAMIN[6], JONATHAN[5] MILK, JONATHAN[4], JOB[3], JOHN[2], JOHN[1])* was born 02 Apr 1888 in Persia, Cattaraugus County, New York, and died 26 Jul 1953 in Salamanca, Cattaraugus County, New York. He married HATTIE E. KING 01 Mar 1911 in Cattaraugus County, New York, daughter of LEONARD KING and UNKNOWN SMITH. She was born 25 Feb 1891 in Napoli, Cattaraugus County, New York, and died 18 Feb 1944 in Randolph, Cattaraugus County, New York.

Children of RAYMOND ROLFE and HATTIE KING are:
- i. IVA M.[10] ROLFE, b. 1912, Cattaraugus County, New York.
- ii. ERWIN B. ROLFE, b. Jun 1915, Cattaraugus County, New York; d. 1952.
- 2576. iii. ESTHER V. ROLFE, b. 1922, Napoli, Cattaraugus County, New York.
- iv. MILDRED ROLFE, b. 24 Dec 1924, Cattaraugus County, New York; d. 2002; m. MISTTER PASQUALE.
- 2577. v. CLIFFORD H. ROLFE, b. 19 Aug 1926, Cattaraugus County, New York; d. 13 May 1992.
- vi. WALTER C. ROLFE, b. 04 Feb 1928, Cattaraugus County, New York; d. 19 Jan 2000.
- vii. ROBERT ROLFE, b. 08 Jan 1929, Cattaraugus County, New York; d. 20 Dec 2007, Cattaraugus County, New York; m. PEGGY LOUISE BYRON; b. 29 Aug 1932, Cattaraugus County, New York; d. 01 Jul 2005, Cattaraugus County, New York.

1510. JOHN[9] CHARLESWORTH *(JOANNAH DAISY[8] MILKS, GARRETT T.[7], BENJAMIN[6], JONATHAN[5] MILK, JONATHAN[4], JOB[3], JOHN[2], JOHN[1])* was born 13 Dec 1903 in Persia, Cattaraugus County, New York, and died Feb 1970 in Little Valley, Cattaraugus County, New York. He married GEORGIA A. NEWTON (NORTON). She was born 14 Sep 1905, and died 27 Apr 1999 in Little Valley, Cattaraugus County, New York.

Children of JOHN CHARLESWORTH and GEORGIA (NORTON) are:
- i. HOWARD J.[10] CHARLESWORTH, b. 27 Mar 1926, Persia, Cattaraugus County, New York; m. ELSIE W. _____; b. 16 Jun 1931.
- ii. HAZEL CHARLESWORTH, b. 1931, Persia, Cattaraugus County, New York.
- iii. PHYLLIS CHARLESWORTH, b. 1933, Persia, Cattaraugus County, New York.
- iv. JANE CHARLESWORTH, b. 1937, Persia, Cattaraugus County, New York.
- 2578. v. JOHN ROGER CHARLESWORTH, b. 09 Jan 1942, Persia, Cattaraugus County, New York.

1511. ETHEL[9] ALLEN *(GILBERT WALLACE[8], JOANNA IRENE[7] MILKS, BENJAMIN[6], JONATHAN[5] MILK, JONATHAN[4], JOB[3], JOHN[2], JOHN[1])* was born Sep 1878 in Loyal, Clark County, Wisconsin, and died Bet. 1907 - 1910 in Loyal, Clark County, Wisconsin. She married WILLIAM JAMES WALSH 1898 in Loyal, Clark County, Wisconsin, son of PATRICK WALSH and MARGARET _____. He was born 01 Sep 1879 in Fairchild, Wisconsin.

Passport application in 1920 for the purpose of visiting Columbia, South America, Panama, and Venezuela as a surveyor in the timber industry.

Children of ETHEL ALLEN and WILLIAM WALSH are:
- i. GLADYS[10] WALSH, b. May 1899, Loyal, Clark County, Wisconsin.
- ii. DRUCILLA WALSH, b. Abt. 1902, Loyal, Clark County, Wisconsin.
- iii. WALLACE WALSH, b. Abt. 1904, Loyal, Clark County, Wisconsin.
- iv. ALLEN LAWRENCE WALSH, b. 05 Aug 1907, Loyal, Clark County, Wisconsin; d. 08 Nov 1949. Never married.
- v. ALICE FLORENCE WALSH, b. 05 Aug 1907, Loyal, Clark County, Wisconsin.

1512. LOIS^9 MILES *(ROSALIE 'ROSE'^{8} ALLEN, JOANNA IRENE^7 MILKS, BENJAMIN^6, JONATHAN^5 MILK, JONATHAN^4, JOB^3, JOHN^2, JOHN^1)* was born 25 Aug 1880 in Loyal, Clark County, Wisconsin, and died 25 Jul 1957 in Winona County, Minnesota. She married JOHN K. JENKS, son of GEORGE JENKS and MARIA MILLARD. He was born 1873, and died 18 Apr 1912 in Winona County, Minnesota.

Child of LOIS MILES and JOHN JENKS is:
  i. MILDRED MAY^{10} JENKS, b. 08 Nov 1903, Winona, Winona County, Minnesota; d. 22 Mar 1976, Winona County, Minnesota. Never married.

1513. WILLIAM WOODS^9 MILKS *(WILLIAM A.^{8}, LUTHER P.^{7}, PRINCE WILLIAM^6, JONATHAN^5 MILK, JONATHAN^4, JOB^3, JOHN^2, JOHN^1)* was born 23 Aug 1910 in East Randolph, Cattaraugus County, New York, and died 17 Oct 1968 in Bradford, McKean County, Pennsylvania. He married IRENE CHISHOLM 16 Jun 1937 in St. Bernard Church, Bradford, PA, daughter of ALONZO CHISHOLM and ANN GREEN. She was born 04 Dec 1904 in Pennsylvania, and died 08 May 1991 in Marin County, California.

Children of WILLIAM MILKS and IRENE CHISHOLM are:
2579. i. MARTHA ANN^{10} MILKS, b. 21 May 1939, Pennsylvania; d. 08 Jun 1996, Marin, California.
2580. ii. WILLIAM WOODS MILKS, JR., b. 16 Aug 1943.

1514. WINIFRED MAY^9 MILKS *(WILLIAM A.^{8}, LUTHER P.^{7}, PRINCE WILLIAM^6, JONATHAN^5 MILK, JONATHAN^4, JOB^3, JOHN^2, JOHN^1)* was born 18 Aug 1913 in East Randolph, Cattaraugus County, New York, and died 15 Apr 1991 in WCA Hospital, Jamestown, Chautauqua County, New York. She married HAROLD MURRAY WILLIAMS 24 Apr 1946, son of ERNEST WILLIAMS and HATTIE DAVIS. He was born 10 Nov 1909 in Ellington, Cattaraugus County, New York, and died 12 Jul 2004.

OBITUARY - April 24, 1991 - The Randolph Register
Winifred M. Williams, retired Randolph businesswoman, dies at seventy-seven.
Winifred M. Williams, 77, of Coldspring Road, R.D.2, Randolph, died at 9:31 am Monday, April 15, 1991, in WCA Hospital, Jamestown.
She was born Aug 18, 1913, in East Randolph, a daughter of William M. and Winifred Woods Milks.
Mrs. Williams was a member of St. Patrick's R.C. Church in Randolph and in Altar and Rosary Society. She was a member of the Randolph Fire Company Auxiliary and the Randolph Cemetery Association Auxiliary. Mrs. Williams was employed at Bigelow's Dept. Store and Gallagher's Drug Store in Randolph. She and her husband operated Williams Jewelry Store in Randolph until their retirement.
Surviving is her husband, Harold M. Williams, whom she married April 24, 1946; three daughters, Ann Harris of North Wales, Pa., Kay Jankowsky of New Hartford and Carol Johnson of Maitland, Fla; six grandchildren: Pamela Shenefiel of Arlington, Va., Caryn Kammann of Virginia Beach, Va., Christine Janowsky of Utica, Peter Johnson and Elizabeth Johnson, both of Maitland, Fla.; a sister, Ann Flood of Arlington, Tx.; three nieces, Martha Milks Connelly of Calif., Winifred Flood Bohall of Arizona, Mary Ann Flood Ricca of Texas; two nephews, John M. Flood of Randolph, William W. Milks of Hawaii; and several cousins in Kane, Pa.
She was preceded in death by a brother, William Milks.
Burial was in Randolph Cemetery.

Children of WINIFRED MILKS and HAROLD WILLIAMS are:
  i. ANN^{10} WILLIAMS, d. Of North Wales, Pa.; m. MISTTER HARRIS.
  ii. KAY WILLIAMS, d. Of New Hartford; m. MISTTER JANKOWSKY.
  iii. CAROL WILLIAMS, d. Of Maitland, Fla.; m. MISTTER JOHNSON.

1515. MARY ANN^9 MILKS *(WILLIAM A.^{8}, LUTHER P.^{7}, PRINCE WILLIAM^6, JONATHAN^5 MILK, JONATHAN^4, JOB^3, JOHN^2, JOHN^1)* was born 25 Sep 1915 in East Randolph, Cattaraugus County, New York, and died 23 Jun 2009 in Texas. She married ROSCOE 'JACK' FLOOD 1936 in Cattaraugus County, New York, son of JUDSON FLOOD and CORA _____. He was born 17 Oct 1913 in Randolph, New York.

OBITUARY - Published in Star-Telegram on 6/28/2009
Ann M. Flood, 93, passed away Tuesday, June 23, 2009.
Service: Ann Flood will be cremated and buried in East Randolph Cemetery, East Randolph, N.Y. A celebration of life party will be held in Arlington at a later date.

Memorials: In lieu of flowers, memorials may be given to Integra Care Hospice, 1305 Airport Fwy., Suite 401, Bedford, Texas 76021; Randolph Library, Jamestown St., Randolph, N.Y. 14772; or any charity of your choice.

Ann Milks Flood was born Sept. 25, 1915, in East Randolph, N.Y. She married Roscoe "Jack" Flood in 1936. She worked many years in Randolph Central School as a cashier and later retired in 1970 from the State Bank of Randolph. Ann moved to Arlington and once again entered the labor force and worked for a number of years for Tucker Manufacturing. She finally retired to pursue her many hobbies of crafts and bridge. Ann was a vendor at many local craft fairs for years. Ann's gifts to her many friends were her positive attitude and outging personality. She truly exemplified the slogan "When life gives you lemons, make lemonade." She was a member of St. Maria Goretti Catholic Church for many years.

The family gives a special thanks to Eden Terrace Assisted Living Center for their kind, professional and compassionate care given to our mother.

She was preceded in death by her parents; her husband, Jack Flood; brother, Bill; sister, Winifred; granddaughter, Ann Marie Ricca; and grandson, Matthew Crnkovich.

Survivors: Daughters, Winifred Bohall and husband, Curtiss, of Clarkdale, Ariz., and Mary Ann Ricca and husband, Paul, of Arlington; son, John Flood and wife, Vicki, of Little Elm; 10 grandchildren; many great-grandchildren; some great-great- grandchildren. She was known as "Texas Grandmother" to others in Arlington.

Burial: East Randolph Cemetery, East Randolph, Cattaraugus County, New York, USA

Children of MARY MILKS and ROSCOE FLOOD are:

2581. i. WINIFRED^{10} FLOOD, b. 04 Nov 1936; d. Of Clarkdale, Arizona.
2582. ii. JOHN MICHAEL FLOOD, b. 06 Jan 1938; d. Of Little Elm, Texas.
2583. iii. MARY ANN FLOOD, b. 15 Mar 1939; d. Of Arlington, Texas.

1516. CASSIE^9 LYON *(JAMES B.^{8}, MARY ELIZABETH^7 MILKS, PRINCE WILLIAM^6, JONATHAN^5 MILK, JONATHAN^4, JOB^3, JOHN^2, JOHN^1)* was born 24 Apr 1884 in Fairbank, Iowa, and died 02 Jun 1947 in Fairbank, Iowa. She married JAMES LEEHEY, son of MAURICE LEEHEY. He was born 1877, and died 1940 in Fairbank, Iowa.

Children of CASSIE LYON and JAMES LEEHEY are:

2584. i. VIOLA^{10} LEEHEY, b. 22 Feb 1906, Fairbank, Iowa; d. 21 Dec 1950, Waverly, Iowa ?.
2585. ii. HAROLD LEEHEY, b. 11 May 1908, Fairbank, Iowa.
      iii. AQUINAS LEEHEY, b. 04 Feb 1911, Fairbank, Iowa; d. unm..
2586. iv. ANITA LEEHEY, b. 09 Jan 1916, Fairbank, Iowa.
2587. v. EDWIN JOE LEEHEY, b. 01 Mar 1918, Fairbank, Iowa.
2588. vi. BERNICE LEEHEY, b. 09 Dec 1919, Fairbank, Iowa.

1517. JESSE J.^{9} LYON *(JAMES B.^{8}, MARY ELIZABETH^7 MILKS, PRINCE WILLIAM^6, JONATHAN^5 MILK, JONATHAN^4, JOB^3, JOHN^2, JOHN^1)* was born 17 Jan 1896 in Fairbank, Iowa, and died 06 Sep 1947 in Los Angeles, California. He married ELIZABETH FORTCH, daughter of HENRY FORTCH. She was born Abt. 1896.

Child of JESSE LYON and ELIZABETH FORTCH is:

      i. LORAIN J.^{10} LYON, b. 23 Apr 1926; m. VIOLA; b. Abt. 1926.

1518. ANN^9 LYON *(CHARLES H.^{8}, MARY ELIZABETH^7 MILKS, PRINCE WILLIAM^6, JONATHAN^5 MILK, JONATHAN^4, JOB^3, JOHN^2, JOHN^1)* She married CLEVE MATTHEWS.

Children of ANN LYON and CLEVE MATTHEWS are:

2589. i. HOWARD^{10} MATTHEWS, b. 04 Jul 1912.
      ii. EDWIN MATTHEWS.
      iii. DEE MATTHEWS, m. MISTTER MILLER.

1519. DELLA^9 LYON *(JESSE^8, MARY ELIZABETH^7 MILKS, PRINCE WILLIAM^6, JONATHAN^5 MILK, JONATHAN^4, JOB^3, JOHN^2, JOHN^1)* was born 06 Oct 1887 in Fairbank, Iowa, and died 09 Jul 1954 in Fairbank, Iowa. She married F. PATRICK MCCUNNIFF 16 Nov 1916 in Fairbank, Iowa, son of JOHN MCCUNNIFF and ELLEN MITCHELL. He was born 27 Jul 1887 in Fairbank, Iowa.

Children of DELLA LYON and F. MCCUNNIFF are:
2590.   i.   MARYELLEN[10] MCCUNNIFF, b. 31 Oct 1918, Farley, Iowa.
2591.   ii. MARJORIE MCCUNNIFF, b. 24 Aug 1921, Fairbank, Iowa.
2592.   iii. MARSHALL MCCUNNIFF, b. 18 Sep 1925, Fairbank, Iowa.

1520. HARRY NEAL[9] LYON *(JESSE[8], MARY ELIZABETH[7] MILKS, PRINCE WILLIAM[6], JONATHAN[5] MILK, JONATHAN[4], JOB[3], JOHN[2], JOHN[1])* was born 18 Nov 1890 in Fairbank, Iowa. He married OLIVE ANNETTE TREBON 26 Nov 1919. She was born Abt. 1890 in Of Monticello, Iowa, and died 21 Nov 1952.

Children of HARRY LYON and OLIVE TREBON are:
        i.   DONALD GORDON[10] LYON, b. 24 Sep 1922.
        ii. JOHN JOSEPH LYON, b. 13 Oct 1926.
2593.   iii. MARY ANN LYON, b. 23 Oct 1928.

1521. HAROLD[9] LYON *(JESSE[8], MARY ELIZABETH[7] MILKS, PRINCE WILLIAM[6], JONATHAN[5] MILK, JONATHAN[4], JOB[3], JOHN[2], JOHN[1])* was born Abt. 1901 in Fairbank, Iowa. He married CATHERINE WILSON. She was born Abt. 1901 in Of Independence, Iowa.

Children of HAROLD LYON and CATHERINE WILSON are:
2594.   i.   HOWARD[10] LYON, b. 1922.
        ii. DAVID LYON, b. 1929.

1522. WILMA[9] WALKER *(NORA R.[8] LYON, MARY ELIZABETH[7] MILKS, PRINCE WILLIAM[6], JONATHAN[5] MILK, JONATHAN[4], JOB[3], JOHN[2], JOHN[1])* She married MISTTER FOX.

Child of WILMA WALKER and MISTTER FOX is:
        i.   SON[10] FOX.

1523. HOWARD R.[9] LYON *(PRINCE ARTHUR "TIMOTHY"[8], MARY ELIZABETH[7] MILKS, PRINCE WILLIAM[6], JONATHAN[5] MILK, JONATHAN[4], JOB[3], JOHN[2], JOHN[1])* was born 07 Jul 1900 in Cattaraugus County, New York, and died Mar 1971 in Falconer, Chautauqua County, New York. He married DOROTHY G. _____ Abt. 1920. She was born 22 May 1897 in New York, and died Dec 1984 in Gerry, Chautauqua County, New York.

Children of HOWARD LYON and DOROTHY _____ are:
2595.   i.   HOWARD J.[10] LYON, b. 1920, Chautauqua County, New York; d. 1999, Chautauqua County, New York.
        ii. LAVERNE E. LYON, b. Abt. 1922, Chautauqua County, New York.
        iii. GRACE E. LYON, b. Abt. 1935, Chautauqua County, New York.

1524. DAISY[9] ALLEN *(MARY E.[8] BOTHWELL, CAROLINE P.[7] SEELEY, BATHSHEBA[6] MILKS, JONATHAN[5] MILK, JONATHAN[4], JOB[3], JOHN[2], JOHN[1])* was born 03 Mar 1884 in Harlan, Iowa. She married W. R. YOUNG. He was born Abt. 1884.

Child of DAISY ALLEN and W. YOUNG is:
        i.   SADIE ARLINE[10] YOUNG.

1525. CLARENCE LUKE[9] MILKS *(BUTLER WEBSTER[8], BENJAMIN FRANKLIN[7], LUKE[6] MILK, JONATHAN[5], JONATHAN[4], JOB[3], JOHN[2], JOHN[1])* was born 28 Mar 1886 in Fairbank, Iowa, and died Oct 1962 in New York. He married (1) ETHEL FRANCES RUNYON 10 May 1909, daughter of LAMONT RUNYON and HATTIE VAN DIKE. She was born 21 Sep 1891 in Brookfield, Missouri, and died 17 May 1924 in Butte County, South Dakota. He married (2) DORA PRENTICE 1927. She was born in Of Binghamton, NY. He married (3) ETHEL MAY SEARLES Aug 1930. She was born in Of Locke, NY. He married (4) LOUISA "RUTH" WILLIAMSON 24 Jun 1937 in Broome County, New York, daughter of HARVEY WILLIAMSON and ROSELTHA _____. She was born 13 Dec 1876 in Harford, Broome County, New York, and died Jan 1977 in Lisle, Broome County, New York.
    Clarence contributed many records for Croft's book.

Children of CLARENCE MILKS and ETHEL RUNYON are:

    i. HADASSA E.[10] MILKS, b. 25 Feb 1910, Moon Lake, Brown County, Nebraska; d. 23 Nov 1910, Moon Lake, Brown County, Nebraska.

    ii. GERALDINE L. MILKS, b. 16 Aug 1911, Ainsworth, Brown County, Nebraska; d. 01 Sep 1919, Minburn, Canada ?.

    iii. KENNETH C. MILKS, b. 14 Feb 1913, Ainsworth, Brown County, Nebraska; d. 02 Nov 1913, Brown County, Nebraska.

2596. iv. CLEO LATRA MILKS, b. 22 Oct 1914, Shining Bank, Alberta, Canada; d. 2006, Cortland County, New York.

2597. v. DORENE DORA MILKS, b. 20 May 1916, Shining Bank, Alberta, Canada; d. 31 Mar 2005, Auberndale, Polk County, Florida.

    vi. THEORA GRACE 'TEDDIE' MILKS, b. 29 Nov 1917, Minburn, Alberta, Canada; d. 03 Apr 1988, Washington DC; m. (1) BERNAL MCCONNELL, Abt. 1935; b. 15 Jan 1918, Cortland County, New York; d. 23 Dec 1989, Cortland, Cortland County, New York; m. (2) NICHOLAS MARBURY EFIMENCO, 19 Aug 1956, Cortland, New York; b. 13 Jun 1915, Cortland County, New York; d. 18 Nov 2008, Washington DC. No children.

        OBITUARY - December 18, 2008

        N. Marbury Efimenco, 93, of Foreign Service

        N. Marbury Efimenco, 93, a retired Foreign Service officer who served several tours of duty in India, died Nov. 18 at Suburban Hospital of kidney failure and complications from cancer.

        Before joining the Foreign Service in 1957, Dr. Efimenco taught courses in politics, foreign policy and government at the University of Minnesota, Lake Forest College near Chicago, Cornell University and the University of Michigan.

        As a scholar, he was particularly interested in the Middle East and at one point lived for several months in tents and mud huts in the Kurdish regions on the Iraq-Iran border.

        He told a University of Minnesota publication last year that, after his Middle Eastern adventure, "I just came to the point where I had had enough of lecturing on the abstract aspects of international relations. I decided that probably I should be out in the field, taking on the practical aspects. So I joined the Foreign Service."

        Originally assigned to Iran, he was sent at the last minute to Bombay (now Mumbai), India. Working as a cultural affairs officer, he arranged a tour that took jazz pianist Dave Brubeck and his combo into areas of India that were unfamiliar with jazz.

        His second foreign posting was to the U.S. Embassy in New Delhi, where his duties included speaking to Indian groups about U.S. foreign policy in Vietnam.

        Later, in Washington, he was assigned to recruit minorities into the Foreign Service. He retired in 1975.

        Nicholas Marbury Efimenco was born in Cortland, N.Y. He received an undergraduate degree with honors in 1937, a master's degree in 1940 and a doctorate in 1949, all in political science from the University of Minnesota.

        He established the N. Marbury Efimenco Graduate Fellowship in Political Science at his alma mater to assist students interested in international relations.

        A 30-year resident of the District, he was active in local politics as a volunteer. At the time of his death, he was writing a mystery novel.

        His wife, Theora Milks "Teddie" Efimenco, died in 1988.

        Survivors include two brothers.

        He had 2 published books:

            An Experiment With Civilization Dictatorship In Iran: The Case Of Mohammed Mossadegh by N. Marbury Efimenco; Thomas Y. Crowell Company (1963)

            World Political Geography by N. Marbury Efimenco(1957); Thomas Y Crowell

2598. vii. CONRAD WILSON MILKS, b. 01 Sep 1919, Minburn, Alberta, Canada.

2599. viii. PAULINE TISSIE MILKS, b. 29 Aug 1920, Sexmith, Alberta, Canada.

2600. ix. WARREN DEMPSEY MILKS, b. 05 Apr 1922, Iowa?\Ainsworth, Brown County, Nebraska; d. 07 Feb 2012, Bossier City, Bossier Parish, Louisiana.

    x. BLONDEL ALTHEA MILKS, b. 14 Oct 1923, Newell, South Dakota; d. 16 Jan 1924, Newell, South Dakota.

1526. GERTRUDE MAY[9] MILKS *(BUTLER WEBSTER[8], BENJAMIN FRANKLIN[7], LUKE[6] MILK, JONATHAN[5], JONATHAN[4], JOB[3], JOHN[2], JOHN[1])* was born 12 May 1889 in Pullman, Cherry County, Nebraska, and died 09 Mar 1968 in Norfolk,

Madison, Nebraska. She married (1) GEORGE W. OWENS Abt. 1908 in Pullman, Cherry, Nebraska, United States. He was born Abt. 1888 in Pullman, Cherry County, Nebraska. She married (2) HERMAN FREDERICK TEUPEL Abt. 1919 in South Dakota. He was born 18 Feb 1877 in Hamburg, Germany, and died 04 Jan 1956 in Lawrence County, South Dakota.

Gertrude and Fred Teupel probably were married in 1919, because in the 1920 census they are shown with no children, but their daughter, Gladys, was born 18 March 1920. Gertrude and Fred are shown together again in the 1925 New York state census, but in the 1930 census, Gertrude is living in Cortland County, New York, with their 2 youngest children, while Fred is living in Lawrence County, South Dakota with the first 5 children. Since the youngest child, Helen(1930 census)/Mabel(1940 census) was born early in 1929, Fred must have left for South Dakota in 1928 or 1929.

In the 1940 census for Kirk, Lawrence County, South Dakota, Fritz and Sam are living with their father, while Elmer, age 15 is in the Bethesda Children's Home in Pleasant, Lincoln County, South Dakota..

Children of GERTRUDE MILKS and GEORGE OWENS are:
- i. KENSER TIRE[10] OWENS, b. Abt. Dec 1909, Ainsworth, Nebraska.
- 2601. ii. ROYCE HUB OWENS, b. 24 Aug 1911, Ainsworth, Nebraska; d. 20 Aug 1984, Klamath Falls, Klamath, Oregon.
- iii. CLARABELLE OWENS, b. Abt. 1914, Canada
- iv. VENETTA MAY OWENS, b. 28 Aug 1916, Ainsworth, Nebraska, d. July 1975. Apparently, never married.

Children of GERTRUDE MILKS and HERMAN TEUPEL are:
- 2602. v. GLADYS JANET[10] TEUPEL, b. 18 Mar 1920, Lead, Lawrence County, South Dakota; d. 04 Apr 1972, Los Angeles, California.
- 2603. vi. FREDERICK 'FRITZ' TEUPEL, b. 08 May 1921, Lead, Lawrence County, South Dakota; d. 17 Sep 2000, Spearfish, Lawrence County, South Dakota.
- 2604. vii. SAMUEL 'SAMMY' TEUPEL, b. 08 Mar 1923, Kirk, South Dakota; d. 10 Jan 1996, Spearfish, Lawrence County, South Dakota.
- 2605. viii. PANZY CAROLINE TEUPEL, b. 08 Apr 1924, Lamatations, New York.
- 2606. ix. ELMER TEUPEL, b. 06 Apr 1926, Kirk, South Dakota; d. 10 Dec 1998, Wallace, Shoshone, Idaho.
- 2607. x. NELLIE MAY TEUPEL, b. 07 Mar 1928, Kirk, South Dakota.
- xi. MABLE JUNE TEUPEL, b. 23 Apr 1929, Kirk, South Dakota; m. MISTRE TRUELOVE.

1527. VERA ELAINE[9] MILKS (*BUTLER WEBSTER*[8], *BENJAMIN FRANKLIN*[7], *LUKE*[6] *MILK, JONATHAN*[5], *JONATHAN*[4], *JOB*[3], *JOHN*[2], *JOHN*[1]) was born 17 Apr 1892 in Pullman, Nebraska, and died 13 Feb 1984 in Scottsbluff, Nebraska. She married (1) WALTER LUTHER, son of HENRY LUTHER and ELIZABETH CLINE. He was born 18 Jul 1887 in Mason City, Nebraska, and died 27 Sep 1937 in Broken Bow, Nebraska. She married (2) LOUIS V. SLADEK. He was born in of Scottsbluff, Nebraska.

Children of VERA MILKS and WALTER LUTHER are:
- 2608. i. LINNIE ELAINE[10] LUTHER, b. 29 Nov 1913, Johnstown, Nebraska.
- 2609. ii. RUBY ARLENE LUTHER, b. 03 Jan 1916, Canada.
- iii. VALERIE WYONA LUTHER, b. 23 Apr 1918, Purdum, Nebraska; d. 24 Dec 1986; m. MELVIN UHLMER, 30 Nov 1936; b. 1914; d. 19 Mar 1937.
- 2610. iv. OMER LATEN LUTHER, b. 06 Jul 1920, Mason City, Nebraska; d. 02 Apr 1993, Portland, Multnomah County, Oregon.
- v. WALTER MARTIN LUTHER, b. 02 Feb 1923, Purdum, Nebraska; d. 30 Sep 1944, PELELIU ISLAND, PALAU ISLANDS, South Pacific.
  Tombstone inscription:
  KILLED IN ACTION AT PELELIU ISLAND, PALAU ISLANDS, E CO., 2ND BATT, 5TH MARINES
- 2611. vi. ELIZABETH JOYCE 'BETTY' LUTHER, b. 26 Mar 1926, Broken Bow, Nebraska.
- 2612. vii. TUTCIE DORIS LUTHER, b. 19 Jun 1928, Dunning, Nebraska.
- viii. DARRELL ARTHUR LUTHER, b. 20 Jun 1931; d. 20 Sep 1931.

1528. LILLIAN TRESSIE[9] MILKS *(BUTLER WEBSTER[8], BENJAMIN FRANKLIN[7], LUKE[6] MILK, JONATHAN[5], JONATHAN[4], JOB[3], JOHN[2], JOHN[1])* was born 27 Feb 1895 in Pullman, Nebraska, and died 20 Oct 1991 in Alachua County, Florida. She married FRANK LANMAN, son of RUBEN LANMAN and SARAH BROWER. He was born 15 Dec 1885 in Plainview, Nebraska, and died Jul 1970 in Norfolk, Madison County, Nebraska.

Children of LILLIAN MILKS and FRANK LANMAN are:
2613.   i. EZETTA LYDIA[10] LANMAN, b. 02 Sep 1914, Norfolk, Nebraska.
      ii. NATOMA ROSE LANMAN, b. 19 Aug 1916, Norfolk, Nebraska; d. 15 Jan 1996, Billings, Yellowstone County, Montana; m. HAROLD R. REMINGTON; b. 27 Jun 1914, North Dakota; d. 30 May 1990, Billings, Yellowstone County, Montana.
2614.   iii. VIVIAN LOVICE LANMAN, b. 26 Sep 1918, Newell, South Dakota; d. 08 May 2003, Eugene, Lane County, Oregon.
      iv. FRANK LAWRENCE LANMAN, b. 20 Feb 1923, Newell, South Dakota; d. 18 Jul 1983.
      v. LEA JOAN LANMAN, b. 13 Sep 1931, Norfolk, Nebraska.

1529. PERCIE L.[9] MILKS *(BUTLER WEBSTER[8], BENJAMIN FRANKLIN[7], LUKE[6] MILK, JONATHAN[5], JONATHAN[4], JOB[3], JOHN[2], JOHN[1])* was born 22 Jan 1898 in Nebraska, and died Sep 1983 in Cortland County, New York. She married JAY LAPP, son of FRED LAPP and MINNIE JOHNSONA. He was born 01 Aug 1888 in Michigan, and died Jun 1977 in Reno, Nevada.

Children of PERCIE MILKS and JAY LAPP are:
      i. CLIFFORD C.[10] LAPP, b. 26 May 1917, Shining Bank, Alberta, Canada; d. 30 Mar 2003, Galeville, Onondaga County, New York; m. HELENA A. O'DONNELL; b. 27 Jan 1922; d. 01 May 1997, Cortland, Cortland County, New York.
      ii. VERNA C. LAPP, b. 07 Jun 1919, Shining Bank, Alberta, Canada; d. 23 Nov 1941, Cortland County, New York.
      Never married.
      iii. LEROY GERALD LAPP, b. 30 May 1921, Edson, Canada; d. 19 Sep 2008, Scott, Cortland County, New York; m. HAZEL LOUISE MYERS, 24 Dec 1942, Washington, D.C.; b. 17 May 1923, Cortland County, New York.
         DEATH NOTICE - Published in the Cortland Standard on Monday, September 22, 2008.
         LeRoy "Roy" G. Lapp, 87, of Glen Haven Road, Scott, N.Y., died Friday, Sept. 19, 2008. Funeral services will be conducted at 11 a.m. Wednesday at the Wright-Beard Funeral Home, 9 Lincoln Ave., Cortland. Burial will follow in the Scott Union Cemetery. Calling hours will be Tuesday from 6 to 8 p.m. at the funeral home.

1530. MABEL[9] BACON *(LUCIUS[8], ZERUAH[7] MILKS, JONATHAN[6], JONATHAN[5] MILK, JONATHAN[4], JOB[3], JOHN[2], JOHN[1])* was born 04 Jul 1877 in Cattaraugus County, New York. She married FRANK E. BOARDMAN, son of ALPHONSO BOARDMAN and MARTHA. He was born Abt. 1875.

Child of MABEL BACON and FRANK BOARDMAN is:
2615.   i. MATTIE E.[10] BOARDMAN, b. 31 Oct 1894, Napoli, Cattaraugus County, New York.

1531. ANNA ZERUAH[9] BACON *(LUCIUS[8], ZERUAH[7] MILKS, JONATHAN[6], JONATHAN[5] MILK, JONATHAN[4], JOB[3], JOHN[2], JOHN[1])* was born 14 May 1885 in Leon, Cattaraugus County, New York. She married (1) LEE A. JOHNSON. He was born Abt. 1885. She married (2) WILLIAM BIGHAM, son of JAMES BIGHAM and EMMA. He was born 01 Aug 1898 in Buffalo, New York.

Children of ANNA BACON and LEE JOHNSON are:
2616.   i. HERMAN R.[10] JOHNSON, b. 27 Dec 1905, Leon, Cattaraugus County, New York.
2617.   ii. LELAND O. JOHNSON, b. 06 Aug 1909, Leon, Cattaraugus County, New York.

1532. MARY AMANDA[9] SATTERLEE *(GEORGE W.[8], MARY JANE[7] BENSON, SARAH[6] MILKS, JONATHAN[5] MILK, JONATHAN[4], JOB[3], JOHN[2], JOHN[1])* was born 08 May 1879 in Moline, Elk County, Kansas, and died Jun 1964 in Moline, Elk County, Kansas. She married HADLEY HALLECK MALONE 1892 in Kansas, son of JACOB MALONE and MARTHA SLOVER. He was born 27 Jan 1870 in Mercer County, Missouri, and died 12 Jan 1947 in Moline, Elk County, Kansas.

Children of MARY SATTERLEE and HADLEY MALONE are:

2618.   i.   HERBERT LEROY[10] MALONE, b. 21 Nov 1893, Moline, Elk County, Kansas; d. Nov 1968, Moline, Elk County, Kansas.

        ii.   LOIS E. MALONE, b. Abt. 1903, Kansas.

2619.   iii.   EVERETT CLINTON MALONE, b. 21 Sep 1906, Moline, Elk County, Kansas; d. 28 Apr 1990, Bartlesville, Washington County, Oklahoma.

1533. JOHN J.[9] ROBINSON (*MARY[8] WHITE, LYDIA[7] BENSON, SARAH[6] MILKS, JONATHAN[5] MILK, JONATHAN[4], JOB[3], JOHN[2], JOHN[1]*) was born 29 Jan 1870 in Illinois, and died 04 Feb 1961 in Chisago County, Minnesota. He married EMMA SCHWEPPE 1895 in Iowa. She was born 05 Apr 1877 in Wisconsin, and died 01 Jan 1971 in Chisago County, Minnesota.

Children of JOHN ROBINSON and EMMA SCHWEPPE are:

        i.   RAY WILLIAM[10] ROBINSON, b. 14 May 1896, Stratford, Hamilton County, Iowa; d. 02 Oct 1918, Winnebago County, Illinois.

           DEATH NOTICE - SOURCE: Chisago County Minnesota in the World War, Page 20, printed in 1920.

           Ray William Robinson was the son of John and Emma Robinson of Rush City, Mn. He was born May 14th, 1918 at Webster City, Iowa. On September 4th, 1918 he left Center City, MN for Camp Grant where he was assigned to the 5th Regiment. He died at Camp Grant on October 2nd, 1918 after a brief illness of pneumonia. His body was sent to Rush City, MN for burial and the funeral was held from the home of his parents. Full military honors were accorded the deceased by a detail of the National Guard from Fort Snelling.

        ii.   MAY C. ROBINSON, b. May 1899, Iowa.

        iii.   HAZEL B. ROBINSON, b. 1902, Minnesota.

        iv.   ADRIAN HOWARD ROBINSON, b. 22 Sep 1905, Martin County, Minnesota; d. 19 Jun 2000, Chisago County, Minnesota; m. EVELYN VICTORIA LARSEN, 03 Aug 1935, Hennepin County, Minnesota; b. 23 May 1907, Douglas County, Minnesota; d. 01 Nov 2007, Chisago County, Minnesota.

2620.   v.   KENNETH SAMUEL ROBINSON, b. 13 Aug 1908, Chisago County, Minnesota; d. 11 Apr 2001, Chisago County, Minnesota.

        vi.   MILTON FREDRICK ROBINSON, b. 14 Nov 1921, Chisago County, Minnesota; d. 25 Dec 1989, San Diego, California.

1534. CHARLES[9] JUNE (*SARAH[8] WHITE, LYDIA[7] BENSON, SARAH[6] MILKS, JONATHAN[5] MILK, JONATHAN[4], JOB[3], JOHN[2], JOHN[1]*) was born Sep 1882 in Kansas, and died 1948 in Kansas. He married GRACE G. NUNNEMAKER. She was born 1882, and died 1957 in Kansas.

Children of CHARLES JUNE and GRACE NUNNEMAKER are:

        i.   EVELYN E.[10] JUNE, b. Abt. 1907, Cowley County, Kansas.

2621.   ii.   CHARLES EVERETT JUNE, b. 28 Oct 1908, Cowley County, Kansas; d. 06 Jun 1990, Kansas.

        iii.   ETHEL M. JUNE, b. Abt. 1912, Cowley County, Kansas.

2622.   iv.   EARLE K. JUNE, b. 22 May 1914, Udall, Cowley County, Kansas; d. 06 Dec 2010.

1535. GLENN[9] JUNE (*SARAH[8] WHITE, LYDIA[7] BENSON, SARAH[6] MILKS, JONATHAN[5] MILK, JONATHAN[4], JOB[3], JOHN[2], JOHN[1]*) was born 26 Sep 1887 in Udall, Cowley County, Kansas, and died 04 May 1975 in Kansas. He married LAPERIA _____. She was born 20 Jan 1890 in Kansas, and died 06 Jan 1978 in Kansas.

Children of GLENN JUNE and LAPERIA _____ are:

        i.   NEVA S.[10] JUNE, b. May 1914, Gore, Sumner County, Kansas.

        ii.   MERLE PARKER JUNE, b. 1920, Gore, Sumner County, Kansas; d. 1942.

1536. HOWARD HENRY[9] JUNE (*SARAH[8] WHITE, LYDIA[7] BENSON, SARAH[6] MILKS, JONATHAN[5] MILK, JONATHAN[4], JOB[3], JOHN[2], JOHN[1]*) was born 17 Oct 1889 in Kansas, and died 07 Mar 1961 in Kansas. He married ORPHA PEARL PARKER, daughter of _____ PARKER and BLANCHE SHADE. She was born 01 Apr 1895 in Kansas, and died 19 Aug 1957 in Kansas.

Child of HOWARD JUNE and ORPHA PARKER is:
    i. LOUISE I.[10] JUNE, b. Abt. 1915, Gore, Sumner County, Kansas.

1537. PHILLIP TRAVIS[9] WHITE *(CHARLES[8], LYDIA[7] BENSON, SARAH[6] MILKS, JONATHAN[5] MILK, JONATHAN[4], JOB[3], JOHN[2], JOHN[1])* was born 12 Oct 1887 in Morris, Illinois, and died Aug 1964 in Washington. He married BEVERLY _____. She was born 03 Sep 1895, and died Aug 1971 in Canada. Philip and Beverly appear to have separated in 1940. They are living separately, but recorded as married.

Children of PHILLIP WHITE and BEVERLY _____ are:
    i. PHYLLIS[10] WHITE, b. Abt. 1922, Washington.
    ii. ROGER WHITE, b. Abt. 1924, Washington.
    iii. BERNARD WHITE, b. 1929, Washington.
    iv. JOYCE WHITE, b. Abt. 1934, Washington.
    v. DOUGLAS WHITE, b. Abt. 1938, Washington.

1538. EDWARD H.[9] PEACOCK *(LYDIA[8] WHITE, LYDIA[7] BENSON, SARAH[6] MILKS, JONATHAN[5] MILK, JONATHAN[4], JOB[3], JOHN[2], JOHN[1])* was born 11 Dec 1887 in Morris, Grundy County, Illinois. He married (1) MINNIE MAY REARDON. She was born Abt. 1890. He married (2) JESSIE FERGUSON. She was born Abt. 1890.

Child of EDWARD PEACOCK and JESSIE FERGUSON is:
    i. BLANCHE LUCILLE[10] PEACOCK, b. 16 Aug 1920.

1539. FLORENCE E.[9] PEACOCK *(LYDIA[8] WHITE, LYDIA[7] BENSON, SARAH[6] MILKS, JONATHAN[5] MILK, JONATHAN[4], JOB[3], JOHN[2], JOHN[1])* was born 11 Jul 1892 in Morris, Grundy County, Illinois. She married WILLIAM C. WHITE, son of WILLIAM WHITE and NANCIE TOPE. He was born 01 Sep 1887 in Gallipolis, Ohio, and died 1943.

Children of FLORENCE PEACOCK and WILLIAM WHITE are:
    i. KENNETH[10] WHITE, b. 11 Jul 1916; d. 1937, Unmarried.
    ii. MARGERY ELAINE WHITE, b. 13 Nov 1924; m. MISTTER BROWN; b. Abt. 1924.

1540. LESLIE[9] PEACOCK *(LYDIA[8] WHITE, LYDIA[7] BENSON, SARAH[6] MILKS, JONATHAN[5] MILK, JONATHAN[4], JOB[3], JOHN[2], JOHN[1])* was born 22 Aug 1901 in Morris, Grundy County, Illinois. He married FRIEDA KOLLMAN, daughter of HENRY KOLLMAN and MARGARET BRAUN. She was born 22 Feb 1902 in Morris, Grundy County, Illinois.

Child of LESLIE PEACOCK and FRIEDA KOLLMAN is:
    i. MARILYN LOUISE[10] PEACOCK, b. 15 Feb 1928, Morris, Grundy County, Illinois.

1541. MINNIE M.[9] WHITE *(WILLIAM J.[8], RUTH[7] BENSON, SARAH[6] MILKS, JONATHAN[5] MILK, JONATHAN[4], JOB[3], JOHN[2], JOHN[1])* was born 16 Jan 1880 in Grundy County, Illinois. She married (1) ALBERT HERMAN WALKER, son of ALBERT WALKER and EMMA LEAR. He was born 07 Jan 1879 in Morris, Grundy County, Illinois, and died 12 Nov 1937 in Morris, Grundy County, Illinois. She married (2) JAMES W. HERRON.

Children of MINNIE WHITE and ALBERT WALKER are:
2623. i. MILDRED[10] WALKER, b. 29 Apr 1901, Morris, Grundy County, Illinois.
2624. ii. HAZEL WALKER, b. 30 Mar 1903, Marengo, Iowa.

Child of MINNIE WHITE and JAMES HERRON is:
2625. iii. ARCHIE[10] HERRON, b. Coal City, Illinois.

1542. JAMES LAWRENCE[9] WHITE *(WILLIAM J.[8], RUTH[7] BENSON, SARAH[6] MILKS, JONATHAN[5] MILK, JONATHAN[4], JOB[3], JOHN[2], JOHN[1])* was born 14 May 1882 in Grundy County, Illinois. He married MARY HARRIS 26 Oct 1904, daughter of FRANK HARRIS and CARRIE PORTER. She was born 30 Mar 1881 in DeWitt, Nebraska.

Child of JAMES WHITE and MARY HARRIS is:
2626. i. EUGENE HARRIS[10] WHITE, b. 25 Feb 1906, Morris, Grundy County, Illinois.

1543. HORACE[9] SEVERNS *(CAROLINE[8] WHITE, RUTH[7] BENSON, SARAH[6] MILKS, JONATHAN[5] MILK, JONATHAN[4], JOB[3], JOHN[2], JOHN[1])* was born 14 Apr 1878 in Morris, Grundy County, Illinois. He married CODIE RYDER. She was born 27 Jun 1880 in Seneca, Illinois.

Children of HORACE SEVERNS and CODIE RYDER are:
2627. i. DELLA GRACE[10] SEVERNS, b. 26 Sep 1901, Seneca, Illinois.
2628. ii. LESTER SEVERNS, b. 28 Jul 1912, Grundy County, Illinois; d. 25 Dec 1937.

1544. JAMES LAWRENCE[9] PATTISON *(ALMIRA D.[8] WHITE, RUTH[7] BENSON, SARAH[6] MILKS, JONATHAN[5] MILK, JONATHAN[4], JOB[3], JOHN[2], JOHN[1])* was born 19 Feb 1890 in Morris, Grundy County, Illinois. He married LOUISE TELFER, daughter of JAMES TELFER and ALICE OHLENDORF. She was born Abt. 1890.

Children of JAMES PATTISON and LOUISE TELFER are:
    i. HELEN FLORENCE[10] PATTISON, b. 04 Apr 1915, Morris, Grundy County, Illinois; m. FRANK WERNESKI; b. Abt. 1915.
2629. ii. LOIS MARGARET PATTISON, b. 23 Jun 1918, Morris, Grundy County, Illinois.

1545. JAMES LAWRENCE[9] DEWEY *(SUSAN LINDSEY[8] WHITE, RUTH[7] BENSON, SARAH[6] MILKS, JONATHAN[5] MILK, JONATHAN[4], JOB[3], JOHN[2], JOHN[1])* was born 17 Feb 1892. He married EDITH EISINGER 29 Nov 1916. She was born 12 Dec 1888 in Gardner, Illinois.

Children of JAMES DEWEY and EDITH EISINGER are:
    i. MARION LAWRENCE[10] DEWEY, b. 11 Jul 1922.
    ii. SHIRLEY EDITH DEWEY, b. 31 Aug 1925.
    iii. EUGENE EISINGER DEWEY, b. 28 Mar 1927.

1546. FRED[9] DEWEY *(SUSAN LINDSEY[8] WHITE, RUTH[7] BENSON, SARAH[6] MILKS, JONATHAN[5] MILK, JONATHAN[4], JOB[3], JOHN[2], JOHN[1])* was born 21 May 1900. He married ELSIE TESAR 31 Dec 1927, daughter of FRANK TESAR and ANNA VILD. She was born 13 Jul 1905 in Coal City, Illinois.

Children of FRED DEWEY and ELSIE TESAR are:
2630. i. DELFRED ALAN[10] DEWEY, b. 06 May 1933, Chicago, Illinois.
    ii. BRUCE EVERETT DEWEY, b. 20 Feb 1938, Chicago, Illinois.
    iii. AVRIL SUZANNE DEWEY, b. 14 Aug 1942, Chicago, Illinois.

1547. AGNES[9] WHITE *(SAMUEL HOLDERMAN[8], RUTH[7] BENSON, SARAH[6] MILKS, JONATHAN[5] MILK, JONATHAN[4], JOB[3], JOHN[2], JOHN[1])* was born 16 Feb 1900 in Grundy County, Illinois. She married (1) MISTTER WILKINSON. He was born Abt. 1900. She married (2) THOMAS BROOKE. He was born Abt. 1900.

Child of AGNES WHITE and MISTTER WILKINSON is:
2631. i. ROBERT[10] WILKINSON.

Child of AGNES WHITE and THOMAS BROOKE is:
    ii. JANE[10] BROOKE.

1548. SAMUEL HOLDERMAN[9] WHITE, JR. *(SAMUEL HOLDERMAN[8], RUTH[7] BENSON, SARAH[6] MILKS, JONATHAN[5] MILK, JONATHAN[4], JOB[3], JOHN[2], JOHN[1])* was born 24 Jun 1904 in Grundy County, Illinois. He married IRENE DECKER. She was born Abt. 1904.

Children of SAMUEL WHITE and IRENE DECKER are:
    i. ROBERT SAMUEL[10] WHITE, b. 13 Jan 1938.
    ii. JAMES WHITE.

    iii. SUSAN WHITE.
    iv. BARBARA LEE WHITE, b. 09 Apr 1945; d. 29 Apr 1945.

1549. ORVILLE[9] WHITE *(GEORGE PERRY[8], RUTH[7] BENSON, SARAH[6] MILKS, JONATHAN[5] MILK, JONATHAN[4], JOB[3], JOHN[2], JOHN[1])* was born 09 Sep 1899 in Morris, Grundy County, Illinois. He married ANNA SISTECK. She was born Abt. 1900.

Children of ORVILLE WHITE and ANNA SISTECK are:
2632.   i. ELMER[10] WHITE, b. 09 Dec 1921.
    ii. GLEN ORVILLE WHITE.
    iii. NORMAN WHITE.

1550. BESSIE[9] WHITE *(GEORGE PERRY[8], RUTH[7] BENSON, SARAH[6] MILKS, JONATHAN[5] MILK, JONATHAN[4], JOB[3], JOHN[2], JOHN[1])* was born 28 Feb 1900 in Morris, Grundy County, Illinois. She married (1) LEO HOUGAS 1917. He was born Abt. 1900. She married (2) GEORGE WATSON Abt. 1925. He was born Abt. 1900.

Child of BESSIE WHITE and LEO HOUGAS is:
2633.   i. HARRIET[10] HOUGAS, b. 18 Oct 1918.

Children of BESSIE WHITE and GEORGE WATSON are:
    ii. BETHEL[10] WATSON, b. 18 Jan 1926, Evanston, Illinois.
    iii. WILLIAM WATSON, b. 06 Nov 1929, Evanston, Illinois.

1551. EVA ESTELLA[9] BARTLETT *(SARAH[8] MARSHALL, CAROLINE SARAH[7] BENSON, SARAH[6] MILKS, JONATHAN[5] MILK, JONATHAN[4], JOB[3], JOHN[2], JOHN[1])* was born 07 Nov 1885 in Coal City, Illinois, and died 10 Mar 1948 in Antigo, Langlade County, Wisconsin. She married MELVILLE THOMAS CANFIELD 21 Jun 1904 in Chicago, Cook, Illinois, son of THOMAS CANFIELD and ELLA PULVER. He was born 07 Mar 1880 in Minnesota, and died 17 Nov 1939 in Antigo, Langlade County, Wisconsin.

Children of EVA BARTLETT and MELVILLE CANFIELD are:
    i. HERBERT[10] CANFIELD, b. Abt. 1905, Antigo Cemetery, Langlade County, Wisconsin; d. Bef. 1910, Antigo, Langlade County, Wisconsin.
    ii. DOROTHY V. CANFIELD, b. 20 May 1907, Antigo, Langlade County, Wisconsin; d. Mar 1982, Eagle River, Vilas County, Wisconsin; m. EUGENE RICHMOND; b. 04 Sep 1912; d. 05 Aug 1991, Eagle River, Vilas County, Wisconsin.
    iii. MARJORIE V. CANFIELD, b. Abt. 1909, Antigo, Langlade County, Wisconsin; d. Abt. 1987; m. DONALD MOUNTZ GREEN; b. 06 Jul 1908; d. 18 Oct 1998, St. Lucie County, Florida.
    iv. MARION W. CANFIELD, b. Abt. 1912, Antigo, Langlade County, Wisconsin; d. Res. Antigo, Wis.; m. WILLIAM EDWARDS; d. Res. Antigo, Wis..
    v. BEVERLY B. CANFIELD, b. 20 Mar 1915, Antigo, Langlade County, Wisconsin; d. 29 Jul 2010, Cape Coral, Lee County, Florida; m. DANIEL DUVAL REED; b. 16 Nov 1913; d. 22 Feb 1993, Lee County, Florida.
    vi. JERRID L. CANFIELD, b. 27 Jul 1918, Antigo, Langlade County, Wisconsin; d. 29 Jun 1975, Wausau, Marathon County, Wisconsin. Jerrid was married 12 Jan 1948 (spouse unknown) and had six children, one of whom was Jerrid Scott Canfield b. 6 Feb 1952 in Wisconsin. Jerrid Scott Canfield m. 20 July 1991, Ruth Marie Onosko in Vilas County, Wisconsin.
    vii. MAUDE PHYLLIS CANFIELD, b. 03 Nov 1921, Antigo, Langlade County, Wisconsin; d. 25 Jul 1997, Langlade County, Wisconsin; m. EDWARD J. KEOHANE; d. 11 Oct 1987, Langlade County, Wisconsin.

1552. ALICE HESTER[9] BARTLETT *(SARAH[8] MARSHALL, CAROLINE SARAH[7] BENSON, SARAH[6] MILKS, JONATHAN[5] MILK, JONATHAN[4], JOB[3], JOHN[2], JOHN[1])* was born 31 Aug 1888 in Coal City, Illinois. She married CHARLES EDWARD FRALEY 08 May 1907, son of WILLIAM FRALEY and IDA BALSAL. He was born 05 Mar 1886 in Clearfield, Pennsylvania, and died 17 Jul 1940 in Morris, Grundy County, Illinois.

Children of ALICE BARTLETT and CHARLES FRALEY are:
2634.   i. FRANCES ALICE[10] FRALEY, b. 05 Nov 1908, Carbon Hill, Illinois.
2635.   ii. MELVIN CHARLES FRALEY, b. 16 Nov 1912, Carbon Hill, Illinois.

2636.	iii.	SHIRLEY ARLINE FRALEY, b. 19 Apr 1919, Morris, Grundy County, Illinois.
2637.	iv.	GLORIA MAXINE FRALEY, b. 23 Oct 1924, Morris, Grundy County, Illinois.
	v.	CATHERINE MAE FRALEY, b. 29 May 1926, Morris, Grundy County, Illinois.
2638.	vi.	MARY JANE FRALEY, b. 05 May 1932, Morris, Grundy County, Illinois.

1553. ETHEL DOVY^9 BARTLETT (SARAH^8 MARSHALL, CAROLINE SARAH^7 BENSON, SARAH^6 MILKS, JONATHAN^5 MILK, JONATHAN^4, JOB^3, JOHN^2, JOHN^1) was born 19 Nov 1897 in Grundy County, Illinois. She married ROBERT BENJAMIN DUDGEON 22 Jun 1915, son of ISRAEL DUDGEON and LENORA LEWIS. He was born 24 May 1894 in Morris, Grundy County, Illinois.

Child of ETHEL BARTLETT and ROBERT DUDGEON is:
  i. MAVIS JOYCE^{10} DUDGEON, b. 19 Feb 1930, Morris, Grundy County, Illinois; m. MELVIN MOYER; b. 10 Feb 1930, of Rochester, Wisconsin.

1554. FRANK CALVIN^9 ROSE (HESTER^8 MARSHALL, CAROLINE SARAH^7 BENSON, SARAH^6 MILKS, JONATHAN^5 MILK, JONATHAN^4, JOB^3, JOHN^2, JOHN^1) was born 16 Sep 1885 in Morris, Grundy County, Illinois, and died 09 Aug 1943 in Hamilton, Butler County, Ohio. He married (1) CARRIE ELIZABETH COBBLER Abt. 1902 in Grundy County, Illinois, daughter of JAMES COBBLER and MINNIE HARRISON. She was born 18 Sep 1886 in Morris, Grundy County, Illinois, and died 05 Oct 1919 in Hamilton, Butler County, Ohio. He married (2) SYLVIA AGNES BOCKMAN Aft. 1910, daughter of JOHN BOCKMAN and LINA HELLARD. She was born 22 Jul 1897 in Kentucky, and died 10 Nov 1922 in Hamilton, Butler County, Ohio. He married (3) MRYTLE _____ Aft. 1912.

Children of FRANK ROSE and CARRIE COBBLER are:
2639.	i.	CALVIN^{10} ROSE, b. Abt. 1903, Morris, Grundy County, Illinois.
2640.	ii.	CLARENCE S. ROSE, b. 27 Sep 1905, Morris, Grundy County, Illinois; d. 1963, Butler County, Ohio.
2641.	iii.	FRANKLIN E. ROSE, b. 24 Feb 1908, Morris, Grundy County, Illinois.
	iv.	NELLIE BELL ROSE, b. 06 Dec 1909, Hamilton, Butler County, Ohio; d. 01 Aug 1910, Hamilton, Butler County, Ohio.
	v.	FERN F. ROSE, b. 14 Dec 1911, Hamilton, Butler County, Ohio; d. 24 Aug 1997, Fairfield, Butler County, Ohio; m. MISTER MURPHY.
	vi.	RUSSELL HERBERT ROSE, b. 22 Oct 1913, Hamilton, Butler County, Ohio; d. 03 Jan 1916, Hamilton, Butler County, Ohio.
	vii.	ADELINE ROSE, b. Bet. 1914 - 1919, Hamilton, Butler County, Ohio.

1555. IDA MAY^9 ROSE (HESTER^8 MARSHALL, CAROLINE SARAH^7 BENSON, SARAH^6 MILKS, JONATHAN^5 MILK, JONATHAN^4, JOB^3, JOHN^2, JOHN^1) was born 21 Jan 1888 in Morris, Grundy County, Illinois. She married CLIFFORD LERETTE, son of JOSEPH LERETTE and CHARLOTTE. He was born 02 Feb 1882.

Children of IDA ROSE and CLIFFORD LERETTE are:
2642.	i.	ARDELLA GRACE^{10} LERETTE, b. 06 May 1904.
2643.	ii.	MELVIN LERETTE, b. 10 Feb 1906.
	iii.	FREDLIN LERETTE, b. 06 Apr 1912.
	iv.	DONALD LERETTE, b. 03 Aug 1916.
2644.	v.	LAVERNE LERETTE, b. 01 Jun 1918.
	vi.	ROBERT LERETTE, b. 26 Jul 1924.

1556. LELA HESTER^9 ROSE (HESTER^8 MARSHALL, CAROLINE SARAH^7 BENSON, SARAH^6 MILKS, JONATHAN^5 MILK, JONATHAN^4, JOB^3, JOHN^2, JOHN^1) was born 02 Sep 1892 in Morris, Grundy County, Illinois. She married (1) JAMES RISING. He was born Abt. 1890. She married (2) WALTER KOHLER 08 Sep 1910, son of WILLIAM KOHLER and FLORENCE DUBIN. He was born 14 Dec 1886 in Iowa, and died 17 Mar 1932 in Illinois.

Children of LELA ROSE and WALTER KOHLER are:
  i. WILBUR CLINTON^{10} KOHLER, b. 08 Nov 1911, Ottawa, Illinois.
  ii. FLORENCE ROSE KOHLER, b. 28 Nov 1914, Ottawa, Illinois; m. THOMAS; b. Abt. 1914.

1557. CAROLINE ADELINE[9] ROSE *(HESTER[8] MARSHALL, CAROLINE SARAH[7] BENSON, SARAH[6] MILKS, JONATHAN[5] MILK, JONATHAN[4], JOB[3], JOHN[2], JOHN[1])* was born 22 Mar 1895 in Morris, Grundy County, Illinois. She married EDWARD SINGER. He was born 07 Dec 1893 in Milwaukee, Wisconsin.

Child of CAROLINE ROSE and EDWARD SINGER is:
2645.   i.   HAROLD[10] SINGER, b. 14 Jun 1920.

1558. FERN AGNES[9] ROSE *(HESTER[8] MARSHALL, CAROLINE SARAH[7] BENSON, SARAH[6] MILKS, JONATHAN[5] MILK, JONATHAN[4], JOB[3], JOHN[2], JOHN[1])* was born 09 Mar 1898 in Morris, Grundy County, Illinois. She married WAYNE F. CARTER, son of MELVIN CARTER and ELLA GALLAGHER. He was born 29 Aug 1895 in Mazon, Illinois.

Child of FERN ROSE and WAYNE CARTER is:
    i.   EVELYN ROSE[10] CARTER, b. 08 Sep 1922; m. PERRY CLAUSS; b. 08 Jan 1925, Livingston County, Illinois.

1559. JEANETTE CATHERINE[9] MARSHALL *(GEORGE W.[8], CAROLINE SARAH[7] BENSON, SARAH[6] MILKS, JONATHAN[5] MILK, JONATHAN[4], JOB[3], JOHN[2], JOHN[1])* was born 10 Jul 1901. She married (1) TORVALD AARRESTAD. He was born 20 Mar 1896. She married (2) HENRY TATE. He was born Abt. 1900.

Child of JEANETTE MARSHALL and TORVALD AARRESTAD is:
    i.   PAUL TORVALD[10] AARRESTAD, b. 08 Jun 1918.

1560. LOUIS WINZENBURG[9] MARSHALL *(GEORGE W.[8], CAROLINE SARAH[7] BENSON, SARAH[6] MILKS, JONATHAN[5] MILK, JONATHAN[4], JOB[3], JOHN[2], JOHN[1])* was born 04 Apr 1917. He married (1) DOROTHEA _____. He married (2) MARY CARR 26 Jun 1943, daughter of CRAIG CARR and ELVA MCCLOUD. She was born 29 Jan 1919 in Kendall County, Illinois.

Children of LOUIS MARSHALL and MARY CARR are:
    i.   JAMES LOUIS[10] MARSHALL, b. 13 Apr 1944, Morris, Grundy County, Illinois.
    ii.   LEWIS ROBERT MARSHALL, b. 21 Feb 1946, Morris, Grundy County, Illinois.
    iii.   STEVEN WILLIAM MARSHALL, b. 16 Jul 1947, Morris, Grundy County, Illinois.
    iv.   MARY ELIZABETH MARSHALL, b. 15 Jan 1949, Morris, Grundy County, Illinois.

1561. CORA A.[9] BENSON *(BENJAMIN J.[8], ARVILLA[7], SARAH[6] MILKS, JONATHAN[5] MILK, JONATHAN[4], JOB[3], JOHN[2], JOHN[1])* was born 24 Jan 1896 in Grundy County, Illinois, and died Jan 1977 in Braceville, Grundy County, Illinois. She married ALPHONSE HERMAN, son of ALPHONSE HERMAN and PAULINE MORAN. He was born 02 Jan 1888 in Coal City, Illinois, and died Jun 1963 in Braceville, Grundy County, Illinois.

Ed. note:
Grace Croft listed, incorrectly, in her 2nd Edition, Francis J. Herman as a son of Alphonse and Cora Benson. Francis Joseph Herman was the son of another Alphonse Herman and his wife Mary Girot. He was born April 23, 1922 in Coal City, Grundy County and died Oct. 2, 2011 in Bradley, Kankakee County, Illinois. He married Joan Griggs in Morris, Grundy County on November 23, 1946 and they raised 5 children.

Children of CORA BENSON and ALPHONSE HERMAN are:
2646.   i.   EARL[10] HERMAN, b. 24 Dec 1916, Grundy County, Illinois; d. 19 Jun 2004, Illinois.
2647.   ii.   WILLIS HERMAN, b. 13 Dec 1918, Grundy County, Illinois; d. Jan 1977, Illinois.
    iii.   DALE W. HERMAN, b. 24 Nov 1921, Grundy County, Illinois; d. 26 Dec 1998, Grundy County, Illinois.
    iv.   DOROTHY ALBERTA HERMAN, b. 03 May 1925, Grundy County, Illinois.
    v.   ALICE JUANITA HERMAN, b. 03 Apr 1929, Grundy County, Illinois; m. ALVIN VANDERHYDEN.

1562. HERBERT[9] BENSON *(BENJAMIN J.[8], ARVILLA[7], SARAH[6] MILKS, JONATHAN[5] MILK, JONATHAN[4], JOB[3], JOHN[2], JOHN[1])* was born 24 Jul 1898 in Grundy County, Illinois. He married MYRTLE RYDER, daughter of JOHN RYDER and MARGARET DOYLE. She was born 16 Jul 1899 in Morris, Grundy County, Illinois.

Child of HERBERT BENSON and MYRTLE RYDER is:
    i.   ROBERT JOHN[10] BENSON, b. 13 Oct 1923, Joliet, Will County, Illinois; m. AVIS ANDERSON; b. Abt. 1923, Of Joliet, Illinois.

1563. MILDRED[9] BENSON *(BENJAMIN J.[8], ARVILLA[7], SARAH[6] MILKS, JONATHAN[5] MILK, JONATHAN[4], JOB[3], JOHN[2], JOHN[1])* was born 19 Sep 1900 in Grundy County, Illinois. She married WILLIAM ARTHUR STERRITT, son of JAMES STERRITT and SARAH PERRY. He was born 18 Jul 1898 in Morris, Grundy County, Illinois.

Children of MILDRED BENSON and WILLIAM STERRITT are:
    i. WILLIAM[10] STERRITT, b. 01 Apr 1925, Detroit, Michigan.
    ii. SHIRLEY ANN STERRITT, b. 04 Nov 1927, Detroit, Michigan.

1564. BERTHA[9] BENSON *(BENJAMIN J.[8], ARVILLA[7], SARAH[6] MILKS, JONATHAN[5] MILK, JONATHAN[4], JOB[3], JOHN[2], JOHN[1])* was born 09 Jan 1904 in Grundy County, Illinois. She married FRED MARTIN, son of FRED MARTIN and BERTHA BRIGHT. He was born 23 Oct 1903 in Morris, Grundy County, Illinois.

Child of BERTHA BENSON and FRED MARTIN is:
    i. ALLAN[10] MARTIN, b. 14 Feb 1931, Detroit, Michigan.

1565. RUSSELL[9] BENSON *(BENJAMIN J.[8], ARVILLA[7], SARAH[6] MILKS, JONATHAN[5] MILK, JONATHAN[4], JOB[3], JOHN[2], JOHN[1])* was born 26 May 1916 in Grundy County, Illinois, and died Nov 1983 in Morris, Grundy County, Illinois. He married MARION ELBERG 18 Oct 1942, daughter of PHILLIP ELBERG.

Child of RUSSELL BENSON and MARION ELBERG is:
    i. KENNETH RUSSELL[10] BENSON, b. 19 Jun 1944.

1566. VIOLET GERTRUDE[9] BENSON *(JOHN RIAL[8], JOHN MILKS[7], SARAH[6] MILKS, JONATHAN[5] MILK, JONATHAN[4], JOB[3], JOHN[2], JOHN[1])* was born 18 Apr 1913 in Grundy County, Illinois. She married LOWRY BUTTRY 28 Jun 1937, son of EDWARD BUTTRY and ROSA SOMMERS. He was born 09 Apr 1905 in Zelma, Missouri.

Children of VIOLET BENSON and LOWRY BUTTRY are:
    i. WANDA JUNE[10] BUTTRY, b. 05 Feb 1939, Morris, Grundy County, Illinois.
    ii. ALBERT LOWRY BUTTRY, b. 12 May 1940, Morris, Grundy County, Illinois.

1567. FLOYD ERNEST[9] BENSON *(JOHN RIAL[8], JOHN MILKS[7], SARAH[6] MILKS, JONATHAN[5] MILK, JONATHAN[4], JOB[3], JOHN[2], JOHN[1])* was born 14 Feb 1916 in Grundy County, Illinois. He married CHARLOTTE HALL, daughter of JOSEPH HALL and VIOLET JACKSON. She was born 23 Apr 1920.

Child of FLOYD BENSON and CHARLOTTE HALL is:
    i. CHERYLE ANN[10] BENSON, b. 16 Jul 1955, Sandwich, Illinois.

1568. QUENTEN EUGENE[9] BENSON *(JOHN RIAL[8], JOHN MILKS[7], SARAH[6] MILKS, JONATHAN[5] MILK, JONATHAN[4], JOB[3], JOHN[2], JOHN[1])* was born 20 Apr 1926 in Grundy County, Illinois. He married KATHRYN KOSINSKI 07 Oct 1951 in Joliet, Illinois, daughter of MICHAEL KOSINSKI. She was born Abt. 1926.

Child of QUENTEN BENSON and KATHRYN KOSINSKI is:
    i. KAREN SUE[10] BENSON, b. 28 Mar 1955, Joliet, Will County, Illinois.

1569. CORNELIUS WALLACE[9] HILDY *(GRACE MAE[8] BENSON, JOHN MILKS[7], SARAH[6] MILKS, JONATHAN[5] MILK, JONATHAN[4], JOB[3], JOHN[2], JOHN[1])* was born 21 Oct 1907 in Morris, Grundy County, Illinois. He married (1) GERDA EVA MAAS, daughter of OSCAR MAAS and ANNA NEUMANN. She was born 15 Jul 1906 in Danzig, Germany, and died 06 May 1944 in Pasadena, California. He married (2) JESSIE MARY OWENS, daughter of CLAUDE OWENS and ETHYL PERRY. She was born 25 Dec 1912 in Toronto, Canada. Wallace was a vice president of Brown Corp., an electronics company with offices in Sterling, Kansas and San Diego, California

Children of CORNELIUS HILDY and JESSIE OWENS are:
    i. KAREN JUDITH[10] HILDY, b. 22 Dec 1946, Long Beach, California.
    ii. KEITH OWENS HILDY, b. 14 Jan 1948, Long Beach, California.
    iii. KOREEN CHARLOTTE SUSANNE HILDY, b. 25 Apr 1949, Long Beach, California.

1570. GRACE OLIVIA ELSIE[9] HILDY *(GRACE MAE[8] BENSON, JOHN MILKS[7], SARAH[6] MILKS, JONATHAN[5] MILK, JONATHAN[4], JOB[3], JOHN[2], JOHN[1])* was born 24 Jan 1910 in Chicago, Illinois, and died 18 Mar 2006 in Provo, Utah County, Utah. She married (1) EVAN MARION CROFT 24 Jul 1935, son of JACOB CROFT and MARY ELIASON. He was born 06 May 1905 in Deseret, Utah, and died 30 Aug 1973 in Provo, Utah County, Utah. She married (2) WENDELL ABRAM CHRISTENSEN 20 Dec 1980 in Provo, Utah. He was born 10 Nov 1900 in Bloomington, Bear Lake County, Idaho, and died 02 Jul 1997 in Nephi, Juab County, Utah.

Grace Croft was the author, compiler and editor-in-chief of *History and Genealogy of the Milk-Milks Family*. as well as numerous other genealogies and books. One of the more notable books was "*With a Song in Her Heart*", a biography of Dr. Florence Jepperson Madsen. Grace was a member of the D.A.R. and American Guild of Organists.

Evan Marion Croft was a university professor, and author of Personality in Business and Life, as well as other texts.

Children of GRACE HILDY and EVAN CROFT are:
- i. FAYE LAVIEVE[10] CROFT, b. 29 Oct 1936, Provo, Utah County, Utah.
- ii. EVELYN MAE CROFT, b. 11 Aug 1940, Provo, Utah County, Utah.
- iii. OLIVIA RAE CROFT, b. 14 Jun 1944, Provo, Utah County, Utah.
- iv. MARCIA KAY CROFT, b. 27 Jul 1948, Provo, Utah County, Utah.
- v. PAMELA GAE CROFT, b. 26 Jul 1954, Provo, Utah County, Utah.

1571. ELMA MAE[9] WEBSTER *(MYRTLE OLIVIA[8] BENSON, JOHN MILKS[7], SARAH[6] MILKS, JONATHAN[5] MILK, JONATHAN[4], JOB[3], JOHN[2], JOHN[1])* was born 21 Jun 1917 in Morris, Grundy County, Illinois, and died 02 Feb 1998 in Morris, Grundy County, Illinois. She married ELMER THOMSON 15 Feb 1939, son of JAMES THOMSON and MARY MAGEE. He was born 06 Jan 1911 in Ransom, LaSalle County, Illinois, and died 14 Jun 1998 in Morris, Grundy County, Illinois.

Children of ELMA WEBSTER and ELMER THOMSON are:
- i. HAROLD JAMES[10] THOMSON, b. 15 Dec 1939, Ransom, Illinois; m. JOANNE _____; b. 23 Oct 1943.
- ii. PHYLLIS JEAN THOMSON, b. 21 Jul 1943, Ransom, Illinois; d. 03 Jul 1944, Ransom, Illinois.

1572. WAYNE EDMUND[9] WEBSTER *(MYRTLE OLIVIA[8] BENSON, JOHN MILKS[7], SARAH[6] MILKS, JONATHAN[5] MILK, JONATHAN[4], JOB[3], JOHN[2], JOHN[1])* was born 20 Apr 1919 in Morris, Grundy County, Illinois. He married MARY LOU THUNEMAN, daughter of DICK THUNEMAN. She was born Abt. 1920 in Long Beach, California.

Children of WAYNE WEBSTER and MARY THUNEMAN are:
- i. SHARON ANN[10] WEBSTER, b. 26 May 1949, Long Beach, California.
- ii. JANICE LEE WEBSTER, b. 14 May 1952, Long Beach, California.

1573. MARILYN EUNICE[9] WEBSTER *(MYRTLE OLIVIA[8] BENSON, JOHN MILKS[7], SARAH[6] MILKS, JONATHAN[5] MILK, JONATHAN[4], JOB[3], JOHN[2], JOHN[1])* was born 07 Dec 1923 in Morris, Grundy County, Illinois. She married MYRON A. ERICKSON 24 Jul 1943, son of CLARENCE ERICKSON and SARAH ANDERSON. He was born 23 Sep 1923 in Morris, Grundy County, Illinois.

Children of MARILYN WEBSTER and MYRON ERICKSON are:
- i. CURTIS ARNOLD[10] ERICKSON, b. 29 Jul 1947, Morris, Grundy County, Illinois.
- ii. BRIAN ERICKSON, b. 23 Dec 1948, Morris, Grundy County, Illinois.
- iii. CHRIS ALAN ERICKSON, b. 02 Jul 1951, Morris, Grundy County, Illinois.

1574. ROGER DANIEL[9] WEBSTER *(MYRTLE OLIVIA[8] BENSON, JOHN MILKS[7], SARAH[6] MILKS, JONATHAN[5] MILK, JONATHAN[4], JOB[3], JOHN[2], JOHN[1])* was born 16 Jul 1926 in Morris, Grundy County, Illinois, and died 30 Oct 1988 in Morris, Grundy County, Illinois. He married ANNA MAE OSMONSON 13 May 1950 in First Baptist Church Parsonage, Morris, Grundy County, Illinois, daughter of EARL OSMONSON and LOUISE MASSEY. She was born 07 Jul 1929 in Morris, Grundy County, Illinois, and died 11 Apr 2007 in Morris, Grundy County, Illinois.
OBITUARY - the Moriis Daily Herald (ILLINOIS), April 13, 2007 (Friday)
Anna Mae Webster
Mrs. Roger (Anna Mae) Webster, 77, of Morris, died peacefully Wednesday afternoon, April 11, 2007, at Morris Healthcare & Rehabilitation Center with her loving family by her bedside.
Born on July 7, 1929 in Morris, she was a daughter of Earl and Louise (Massey) Osmonson. She received her

education in Morris schools. On May 13, 1950, she married Roger D. Webster at the First Baptist Church Parsonage in Morris.

She enjoyed playing cards with the ladies at Elliott Manor, and spending time with her family, especially her grandchildren and great-grandchildren.

Mrs. Webster was a member of the First Baptist Church in Morris and the Morris Senior Citizens.

Survivors include two daughters, Carol (John) Adair, Morris, and Diane (Terry) Wakeman, Coal City; one son, David R. (Bonnie) Webster, Seneca; six grandchildren, James Adair, Morris, Debi (Todd) Schultz, Morris, Leslie (Michael) Meloun, Morris, Harold (Kris) Webster, Mazon, Brian (fiancée Brenda Cardenas) Webster, Coal City, Michelle Emmons, Coal City; seven great-grandchildren, Alex Adair, Olivia and Alyssa Schultz, Andrew Meloun, Jenna and Lauren Emmons, and Hannah Chesko; and several nieces and nephews.

She was preceded in death by her parents; her husband on Oct. 30, 1988; three sisters, Ruth Reagan, Donna Bell and Dorothy Osmonson; three brothers, Kenneth, Edward and Arthur Osmonson.

Funeral services will be at 10 a.m. Monday, April 16, at U.C. Davis & Sons Funeral Home, Ltd., 301 W. Washington St., Morris, with Rev. Rick Cunningham officiating.

Interment will be in Sample Cemetery.

Friends may call from 3 to 6 p.m. Sunday at the funeral home.

Pallbearers will be Dave Webster, Terry Wakeman, John Adair, James Adair, Harold Webster, Brian Webster and Todd Schultz.

Memorial gifts may be directed to the First Baptist Church Building Fund.

Children of ROGER WEBSTER and ANNA OSMONSON are:
2648.   i.   CAROL ANN^{10} WEBSTER, b. 08 Jul 1952, Morris, Grundy County, Illinois; d. Live Morris.
2649.   ii.   DAVID ROGER WEBSTER, b. 20 Jul 1954, Morris, Grundy County, Illinois; d. Live Seneca.
       iii.   DIANE S. WEBSTER, b. 07 Nov 1957, Morris, Grundy County, Illinois; d. Live Coal City; m. TERRY LEE WAKEMAN; b. 16 Feb 1955.

1575. JESSIE MARIA^9 RANNEY *(LUKE WINFIELD^8, NANCY MARIA^7 MILKS, LUKE^6 MILK, JONATHAN^5, JONATHAN^4, JOB^3, JOHN^2, JOHN^1)* was born 14 Apr 1889 in Waverly Bremer County, Iowa, and died 16 Mar 1943 in Coos Bay, Coos County, Oregon. She married HERBERT SELDON CLEVELAND 14 Jun 1906 in De Smet, Kingsbury, South Dakota, son of ALANSON CLEVELAND and ADELADE MCKINLEY. He was born 25 Jan 1881 in Humboldt County, Iowa, and died 30 Dec 1960 in Coos Bay, Coos County, Oregon.

Children of JESSIE RANNEY and HERBERT CLEVELAND are:
2650.   i.   ALICE MARIE^{10} CLEVELAND, b. 13 Mar 1907, DeSmet, Kingsbury County, South Dakota; d. 09 Feb 1976, North Bend, Coos County, Oregon.
2651.   ii.   ALANSON KILBOURNE CLEVELAND, b. 22 Jun 1909, Humboldt County, Iowa; d. 18 Oct 1999, Eugene, Lane County, Oregon.
       iii.   NINA GRACE CLEVELAND, b. 20 Nov 1912, Humboldt County, Iowa; d. 24 Jan 1913, Humboldt County, Iowa.
       iv.   BURTON LAUREL CLEVELAND, b. 19 Jun 1914, Humboldt County, Iowa; d. 06 Nov 1991, Coos Bay, Coos County, Oregon; m. VIOLET HELEN _____; b. 11 Apr 1915; d. 03 Sep 2007, Medford, Jackson County, Oregon.
       v.   LESTER WAYNE CLEVELAND, b. 17 Jan 1917, Havelock, Pocahontas County, Iowa; d. 09 Feb 1999, Klamath County, Oregon; m. HILDA IDA _____; b. 05 Apr 1922; d. 22 Jun 1995, Lane County, Oregon.
       vi.   JUANITA BETH CLEVELAND, b. 23 May 1919, Pocahontas, Iowa; d. 04 Nov 2006, Coos Bay, Coos County, Oregon.
       vii. LOLA EVELYN CLEVELAND, b. 16 Nov 1921, Pocahontas, Iowa; d. 26 May 1953, Coos Bay, Coos County, Oregon.
       viii. VIRGINIA RAE CLEVELAND, b. 17 Jan 1932, Calhoun County Iowa; d. 1932, Calhoun County Iowa.

1576. ELLA RACHEL^9 RANNEY *(LUKE WINFIELD^8, NANCY MARIA^7 MILKS, LUKE^6 MILK, JONATHAN^5, JONATHAN^4, JOB^3, JOHN^2, JOHN^1)* was born 09 May 1894 in of Havelock, Pocahontas County, Iowa (divorced), and died 14 Jun 1956 in Los Angeles, California. She married (1) GEORGE BRONSON 27 Nov 1912 in Humboldt, Humboldt County, Iowa, son of JESSE BRUNSON and MARTHA WEST. He was born 1889 in Kansas. She married (2) WALTER W HOFFERT 19 Jul 1920 in Lincoln County, South Dakota. He was born 1894 in Of Rolfe, Pocahontas County, Iowa (Bachelor).

Children of ELLA RANNEY and GEORGE BRONSON are:
- i. LYLE C.[10] BRONSON, b. Mar 1914, Iowa.
- 2652. ii. ERMA L. BRONSON-HOFFERT, b. Jun 1915, Iowa.

1577. WILLIAM FOSTER[9] RANNEY *(LUKE WINFIELD[8], NANCY MARIA[7] MILKS, LUKE[6] MILK, JONATHAN[5], JONATHAN[4], JOB[3], JOHN[2], JOHN[1])* was born 19 Mar 1896 in Pocahontas, Iowa, and died 25 Nov 1975 in Coos County, Oregon. He married CLARICE MAUD FOUTS Abt. 1923, daughter of GEORGE FOUTS and ANNIE _____. She was born 15 Apr 1900 in Iowa, and died 10 Jun 1992 in Coos County, Oregon.

Children of WILLIAM RANNEY and CLARICE FOUTS are:
- i. RUSSELL FOSTER[10] RANNEY, b. 09 Jun 1923, South Dakota; d. 15 Oct 2002, Coos County, Oregon.
- ii. CALVIN WINFIELD RANNEY, b. 22 Feb 1927, Minnesota; d. 27 Aug 1995, Lincoln County, Oregon; m. (1) PEGGY JEAN GILBERTSON, 18 Dec 1969, Reno, Nevada; b. Abt. 1927; m. (2) FLORENCE E. MARRS, 12 Feb 1978, Zephyr Cove, Nevada; b. 16 Feb 1927, DeKalb County, Illinois; d. 20 Mar 1994, Lincoln County, Oregon.
- iii. JOYCE RANNEY, b. Dec 1929, Pocahontas, Iowa.
- iv. AUDREY RANNEY, b. 03 Dec 1931, Pocahontas, Iowa; m. (1) LEROY DANIEL GLASS, Bet. 1945 - 1960, Oregon; b. 30 Oct 1926, Texas; d. 14 Aug 1992, Douglas County, Oregon; m. (2) KYLE N. MITCHELL, JR., 20 Aug 1994, Douglas County, Nevada; b. 27 Sep 1934.

1578. FRANKIE HELENE[9] RANNEY *(LUKE WINFIELD[8], NANCY MARIA[7] MILKS, LUKE[6] MILK, JONATHAN[5], JONATHAN[4], JOB[3], JOHN[2], JOHN[1])* was born 15 Jun 1902 in Beadle County, South Dakota, and died 22 Feb 1989 in Riverside, California. She married VERNE CHARLTON CALLON 15 Nov 1922 in Rolfe, Pocahontas County, Iowa, son of WILLIAM CALLON and MARTHA CHARLTON. He was born 15 May 1894 in Rolfe, Pocahontas County, Iowa, and died 26 Aug 1968 in California.

Child of FRANKIE RANNEY and VERNE CALLON is:
- i. LOIS MABEL[10] CALLON, b. 19 Apr 1923, Clinton,, Pocahontas County, Iowa; m. (1) STANISLAUS JOSEPH "STANLEY" DASCHLE, 1948, Los Angeles, California; b. 19 Apr 1924, Napoleon, Logan County, North Dakota; d. 20 Mar 2003, California; m. (2) JAMES W SMITH, 28 Jan 1971, Los Angeles, California.
  Lois graduated from U.S., World War II Cadet Nursing Corps on Sept 16, 1947 after 3 years of training at the California Hospital in Los Angeles.

1579. BLANCHE[9] RANNEY *(NATHAN AMES[8], NANCY MARIA[7] MILKS, LUKE[6] MILK, JONATHAN[5], JONATHAN[4], JOB[3], JOHN[2], JOHN[1])* was born 30 Aug 1887 in McLeod County, Minnesota. She married EDWARD BALDWIN. He was born 05 Oct 1882 in Mayville, Chautauqua County, New York.
Blanche was a writer of prose and poetry and many of her works have been published.

Children of BLANCHE RANNEY and EDWARD BALDWIN are:
- 2653. i. MARTIN COPP[10] BALDWIN, b. 07 Sep 1915, McVille, North Dakota; d. 26 Oct 2004, Scotts Valley, Santa Cruz County, California.
- 2654. ii. MARTHA BALDWIN, b. Abt. 1915, McVille, North Dakota.
- iii. RUTH BALDWIN, m. MISTTER DRAKE.

1580. RUSSELL RAY[9] RANNEY *(NATHAN AMES[8], NANCY MARIA[7] MILKS, LUKE[6] MILK, JONATHAN[5], JONATHAN[4], JOB[3], JOHN[2], JOHN[1])* was born 23 Feb 1892 in New Auburn, Minnesota, and died 01 Sep 1947 in Sheldon, North Dakota. He married LUCY MINNIE KOLD, daughter of C. A. D. KOLD. She was born 22 Mar 1895 in Illinois, and died 02 Sep 1974 in Hayward, Alameda County, California.

Child of RUSSELL RANNEY and LUCY KOLD is:
- i. MYRON NATHAN[10] RANNEY, b. 21 Nov 1922, North Dakota; d. 22 Sep 1988, San Mateo, California; m. JULIA A HUTCHINSON, 30 Jun 1975, San Mateo, California; b. Abt. 1926.

1581. LOLA VAUGHN[9] RANNEY *(NATHAN AMES[8], NANCY MARIA[7] MILKS, LUKE[6] MILK, JONATHAN[5], JONATHAN[4], JOB[3], JOHN[2], JOHN[1])* was born 04 Dec 1894 in New Auburn, Minnesota, and died 14 Feb 1984 in San Bernardino County, California. She married JAMES R. PUCKETT 1916. He was born 23 Nov 1892 in Hayes County, Texas, and died Jul 1967 in San Bernardino County, California.

Children of LOLA RANNEY and JAMES PUCKETT are:
- i. JEAN E.[10] PUCKETT, b. Abt. Sep 1918, North Dakota.
- ii. PATRICIA A. PUCKETT, b. Abt. 1922, Sunnyside, Snohomish County, Washington.
- 2655. iii. WILLIAM WILSON PUCKETT, b. 03 May 1928, Sunnyside, Snohomish County, Washington; d. 01 May 2006, Renton, King County, Washington.

1582. GOLDA RUTH[9] RANNEY *(HERMAN[8], NANCY MARIA[7] MILKS, LUKE[6] MILK, JONATHAN[5], JONATHAN[4], JOB[3], JOHN[2], JOHN[1])* was born 09 Apr 1888 in Maynard, Fayette County, Iowa, and died 18 Jul 1959 in Maynard, Fayette County, Iowa. She married J. L. FULLMER 01 Jan 1914 in Mackay, Idaho. He was born Abt. 1888.

Golda was a journalist and contributed many Ranney records.

Children of GOLDA RANNEY and J. FULLMER are:
- i. MILDRED MARY[10] FULLMER, b. Oct 1914, Maynard, Iowa; d. Oct 1914, Maynard, Iowa.
- 2656. ii. CLARENCE EDWARD FULLMER, b. 12 Aug 1915, Maynard, Iowa; d. 01 Jul 1990.

1583. LAURA PALMYRA[9] RANNEY *(HERMAN[8], NANCY MARIA[7] MILKS, LUKE[6] MILK, JONATHAN[5], JONATHAN[4], JOB[3], JOHN[2], JOHN[1])* was born 10 Sep 1896 in Maynard, Fayette County, Iowa, and died 05 Feb 1971 in Maynard, Fayette County, Iowa. She married HAROLD LEWIS ARTHUR 01 Mar 1917 in Maynard, Iowa. He was born 30 Jun 1894 in Clarion, Iowa, and died Sep 1966 in Maynard, Fayette County, Iowa.

Children of LAURA RANNEY and HAROLD ARTHUR are:
- 2657. i. ROBERT HAROLD[10] ARTHUR, b. 15 Dec 1917, Maynard, Iowa; d. 06 Aug 1944, France (WWII).
- 2658. ii. EARL P. ARTHUR, b. 24 May 1919, Maynard, Iowa; d. 15 Jan 1991, Prescott, Yavapai County, Arizona.
- iii. DOROTHY INEZ ARTHUR, b. 12 Dec 1921, Maynard, Iowa; m. RAY JOHNSON, Dec 1947; b. Abt. 1920.
- iv. WINIFRED ADEL ARTHUR, b. 12 Oct 1924, Maynard, Iowa; m. ERNEST L. 'ERNIE' SPANI, 1948, Butte, Montana; b. 26 Feb 1921; d. 05 Jul 1995, Missoula County, Montana.
- v. ELWYN JAMES ARTHUR, b. 15 May 1929, Maynard, Iowa; d. 22 Feb 1943, Maynard, Iowa.

1584. MILDRED MARY[9] RANNEY *(HERMAN[8], NANCY MARIA[7] MILKS, LUKE[6] MILK, JONATHAN[5], JONATHAN[4], JOB[3], JOHN[2], JOHN[1])* was born 25 Oct 1901 in Maynard, Fayette County, Iowa. She married (1) OLLEY WEAVER 11 Mar 1922. He was born Abt. 1900. She married (2) JAMES F. MASER 03 Aug 1935 in Oelwein, Iowa, son of WILLIAM MASER. He was born Abt. 1900.

Children of MILDRED RANNEY and OLLEY WEAVER are:
- 2659. i. LEE O.[10] WEAVER, b. 01 Nov 1922, Canyon City, Texas; d. Lived Norwalk, CA.
- 2660. ii. BRYCE O. WEAVER, b. 12 Jun 1928; d. Lived Oran, Iowa.
- 2661. iii. MARYLOU INEZ WEAVER, b. 09 Sep 1928.

1585. BURR T.[9] BARNES *(EVALINE SALOME[8] RANNEY, NANCY MARIA[7] MILKS, LUKE[6] MILK, JONATHAN[5], JONATHAN[4], JOB[3], JOHN[2], JOHN[1])* was born 16 Aug 1888 in Maynard, Iowa, and died 07 Feb 1970 in Fergus County, Montana. He married MAMIE NICHOLS 1913 in South Dakota. She was born Abt. 1896 in South Dakota.

Children of BURR BARNES and MAMIE NICHOLS are:
- i. EVELYN M.[10] BARNES, b. 1914, South Dakota.
- ii. NEVA G. BARNES, b. Mar 1916, South Dakota.
- 2662. iii. DELORNE G. BARNES, b. 24 Sep 1917, Valley County, Montana; d. 15 Apr 1993, Great Falls, Cascade County, Montana.
- iv. ORAN BURR BARNES, b. 24 Sep 1919, Valley County, Montana; d. 23 Aug 1995, Kent, King County, Washington; m. IRENE MYRTLE KJENSRUD, 13 Jul 1940, Wolf Point, Roosevelt County, Montana; b. 05 Mar 1921; d. 05 Feb 2006.

- v. AUDREY BARNES, b. 1921, Valley County, Montana.
- vi. LAUREL J. BARNES, b. 11 Sep 1922, Valley County, Montana; d. 25 May 1987, Custer, Valley County, Montana.
- vii. BETTY G. BARNES, b. 1930, Valley County, Montana.
- viii. MAXWELL BARNES, b. 1932, Valley County, Montana.
- ix. GAIL BARNES, b. 1934, Valley County, Montana.
- x. MARLENE BARNES, b. 1936, Valley County, Montana.

1586. ARDATH ARLOENE^9 RANNEY *(JUSTIN WARREN^8, NANCY MARIA^7 MILKS, LUKE^6 MILK, JONATHAN^5, JONATHAN^4, JOB^3, JOHN^2, JOHN^1)* was born 05 Jun 1913 in Alden, Hardin County, Iowa, and died 25 Feb 2001 in Maynard, Fayette County, Iowa. She married LOUIS HENRY GARNIER 27 Dec 1937 in Unionville, Missouri, son of HENRY GARNIER and ANNA SUESS. He was born 11 May 1910 in Fayette County, Iowa, and died 15 Jul 1998.

OBITUARY

Louis Henry Garnier was born May 11, 1910 on the family farm west of Maynard, the son of Henry John & Anna (Suess) Garnier. He graduated from the Maynard High School in 1927.

On December 27, 1937 he married Ardath Ranney at Unionville, Missouri. They then operated and lived on the family farm until Louis retired in 1975.

He was a member of the First Presbyterian Church in Maynard where he served as an elder. Louis served on the boards of the Fayette County Farm Bureau, FS Service Co., Harlan Co-op Creamery, County Extension Service and as a 4-H leader for Harlan Township.

Survivors include: Wife: Ardath Garnier of Maynard; 2 Sons & daughter-in-law: John Garnier of Maynard; Gary & Maryellen Garnier of Los Gatos, California; 3 Grandsons (Greg Garnier, Jeff Garnier, & Josh Garnier).

He was preceded in death by his parents, 2 sisters (Ethel Thompson of Portland, Oregon & Helen Garnier who died in infancy).

Burial: Long Grove Cemetery, Maynard, Fayette County, Iowa

Children of ARDATH RANNEY and LOUIS GARNIER are:
- 2663. i. JOHN L.^{10} GARNIER, b. 07 May 1940, Fayette County, Iowa; d. 20 Apr 1999.
- 2664. ii. GARY ELDON GARNIER, b. 18 Sep 1944, Fayette County, Iowa.

1587. KATHRYN BLANCHE^9 RANNEY *(JUSTIN WARREN^8, NANCY MARIA^7 MILKS, LUKE^6 MILK, JONATHAN^5, JONATHAN^4, JOB^3, JOHN^2, JOHN^1)* was born 24 Mar 1916 in Iowa, and died 15 Sep 2007 in Fayette County, Iowa. She married HUGO FICK 11 Apr 1941 in Hartley, O'Brien County, Iowa, son of WILLIAM FICK and AMELIA BRANDT. He was born 22 Apr 1916 in Hartley, O'Brien County, Iowa, and died 19 Aug 1998 in Oelwein, Fayette County, Iowa. On Kathryn's side of the tombstone is a representation of the medallion for the *"General Society of Mayflower Descendants"*

Children of KATHRYN RANNEY and HUGO FICK are:
- i. THOMAS^{10} FICK.
- ii. ROBERT FICK.

1588. JOSEPH WILLIAM^9 HANSON *(JENNIE^8 MILKS, BENJAMIN FRANKLIN^7, LUKE^6 MILK, JONATHAN^5, JONATHAN^4, JOB^3, JOHN^2, JOHN^1)* was born 27 Dec 1874 in Oelwein, Fayette County, Iowa, and died in Saco, Montana. He married MARY AUGUSTA HOGE. She died in Saco, Montana. Homesteaded in Saco, Montana in 1913

Children of JOSEPH HANSON and MARY HOGE are:
- i. RAYMOND OSCAR^{10} HANSON, b. 17 Jan 1908, Carrington, North Dakota; d. 16 Jan 1975, Missoula, Missoula County, Montana; m. EILEEN CREGO, 31 Aug 1937, Missoula, Missoula County, Montana; b. 1914, Montana; d. 04 Sep 1984.
- 2665. ii. VYDA MARGARET HANSON, b. 25 Mar 1909, Carrington, North Dakota; d. 24 Jun 1993, Deer Lodge County, Montana.
- iii. PAUL WILLIAM HANSON, b. 16 Apr 1912, Carrington, North Dakota; d. 14 Jul 1917, Saco, Montana.
- 2666. iv. BERTHA EDNA HANSON, b. 20 Jul 1913, Saco, Montana; d. 21 Apr 1974, Glasgow, Valley County, Montana.

1589. BENJAMIN JOHN 'BEN'[9] HIGGINS *(IDA LOUISE[8] MILKS, BENJAMIN FRANKLIN[7], LUKE[6] MILK, JONATHAN[5], JONATHAN[4], JOB[3], JOHN[2], JOHN[1])* was born 19 Feb 1886 in Lester, Black Hawk County, Iowa, and died Aug 1969 in Niobrara, Knox County, Nebraska. He married MARGARET MULLER, daughter of EUGENE MULLER and MARIE _____. She was born 13 Feb 1892 in Nebraska, and died Jan 1987 in Columbus, Platte County, Nebraska.

Children of BENJAMIN HIGGINS and MARGARET MULLER are:
- 2667. i. CLAYTON[10] HIGGINS, b. 10 Oct 1914, Lynch, Boyd County, Nebraska; d. 09 Jan 2006, Niobrara, Knox County, Nebraska.
- ii. GAIL WENDEL HIGGINS, b. 25 Oct 1918, Lynch, Boyd County, Nebraska; d. 15 Dec 1987, Tucson, Pima County, Arizona.
- 2668. iii. BERNARD HIGGINS, b. 24 Jun 1923, Nebraska; d. 19 Dec 1983, Arvada, Jefferson County, Colorado.

1590. BESSIE E.[9] HIGGINS *(IDA LOUISE[8] MILKS, BENJAMIN FRANKLIN[7], LUKE[6] MILK, JONATHAN[5], JONATHAN[4], JOB[3], JOHN[2], JOHN[1])* was born May 1890 in Iowa, and died 1966 in Lynch, Boyd County, Nebraska. She married FLOYD KAY FRANCE 1907 in Nebraska, son of HOSEA FRANCE and JUDA BROWN. He was born 24 Jun 1883 in Dorsey, Holt County, Nebraska, and died 17 Apr 1972 in Lynch, Boyd County, Nebraska.

Children of BESSIE HIGGINS and FLOYD FRANCE are:
- i. HAROLD F.[10] FRANCE, b. 18 Mar 1908, Scott, Holt County, Nebraska; d. 23 Nov 1986, Gering, Scotts Bluff County, Nebraska; m. FERN _____; b. 1917, Nebraska.
- 2669. ii. EVELYN GERALDINE FRANCE, b. 12 Oct 1911, Lynch, Boyd County, Nebraska; d. 07 Oct 2002, Lynch, Boyd County, Nebraska.
- iii. DOLORES I. FRANCE, b. Feb 1916, Nebraska; d. Bef. 07 Oct 2002.

1591. MABEL GRACE[9] HIGGINS *(IDA LOUISE[8] MILKS, BENJAMIN FRANKLIN[7], LUKE[6] MILK, JONATHAN[5], JONATHAN[4], JOB[3], JOHN[2], JOHN[1])* was born Oct 1891 in Nebraska, and died 1970 in Lynch, Boyd County, Nebraska. She married JOHN FREDRICK WIKE. He was born 03 Dec 1886 in Blair, Washington County, Nebraska, and died 06 Oct 1972 in Lynch, Boyd County, Nebraska.

Children of MABEL HIGGINS and JOHN WIKE are:
- i. VIVIAN G.[10] WIKE, b. Dec 1915, Lynch, Boyd County, Nebraska.
- ii. JACK LAVERN WIKE, b. 27 Jan 1922, Lynch, Boyd County, Nebraska; d. 01 Jul 1996, Roswell, Chaves County, New Mexico.
- iii. BETTY J. WIKE, b. 16 Apr 1927, Lynch, Boyd County, Nebraska (twin).
- iv. ROBERT DEAN WIKE, b. 16 Apr 1927, Lynch, Boyd County, Nebraska (twin).

1592. EDNA RUTH[9] HIGGINS *(IDA LOUISE[8] MILKS, BENJAMIN FRANKLIN[7], LUKE[6] MILK, JONATHAN[5], JONATHAN[4], JOB[3], JOHN[2], JOHN[1])* was born 18 Feb 1893 in Nebraska, and died 12 Nov 1979 in Rapid City, Pennington County, South Dakota. She married WILLIAM L. PINKERMAN 20 Dec 1910. He was born 15 Feb 1890 in Nebraska, and died 16 Aug 1978 in Rapid City, Pennington County, South Dakota.

Child of EDNA HIGGINS and WILLIAM PINKERMAN is:
- i. MAXINE V.[10] PINKERMAN, b. 1916; d. 1965; m. (1) WALTER ROBINSON, 19 Oct 1936, Pennington, Lawrence County, South Dakota; b. 1914; m. (2) MISTTER BLAKE, Aft. 1936.

1593. HAZEL LENNIE[9] HIGGINS *(IDA LOUISE[8] MILKS, BENJAMIN FRANKLIN[7], LUKE[6] MILK, JONATHAN[5], JONATHAN[4], JOB[3], JOHN[2], JOHN[1])* was born Mar 1898 in Nebraska. She married ELMER CHRISTENSEN 09 Oct 1919 in Gregory County, South Dakota, son of CHRIS CHRISTENSEN and MARY _____. He was born 26 Mar 1896 in Lynch, Boyd County, Nebraska, and died 25 Apr 1969 in Lynch, Boyd County, Nebraska.

Children of HAZEL HIGGINS and ELMER CHRISTENSEN are:
- i. JOYCE ELAINE[10] CHRISTENSEN, b. 05 Jul 1920, Nebraska; d. 06 May 2007, Lincoln, Lancaster County, Nebraska; m. JOHN A. 'JACK' REYNOLDS; b. 14 Jun 1918, Nebraska; d. 09 Mar 1989, Verdel, Knox County, Nebraska.
- ii. DONALD R. CHRISTENSEN, b. 01 Jun 1924, Nebraska; d. 29 Oct 1944.

2670.   iii. RICHARD LESLIE CHRISTENSEN, b. 30 Aug 1925, Monowi, Boyd County, Nebraska; d. 07 Apr 2011, O'Neil, Holt County, Nebraska.
         iv. ARLENE CHRISTENSEN, b. 1927, Nebraska; d. Bef. 07 Apr 2011; m. MISTTER COLLINS.

1594. GERTRUDE LILA[9] HIGGINS *(IDA LOUISE[8] MILKS, BENJAMIN FRANKLIN[7], LUKE[6] MILK, JONATHAN[5], JONATHAN[4], JOB[3], JOHN[2], JOHN[1])* was born Feb 1900 in Lynch, Boyd County, Nebraska. She married ALVIN L. SCOTT. He was born 1900 in Minnesota.

Child of GERTRUDE HIGGINS and ALVIN SCOTT is:
         i.   NORMA[10] SCOTT, b. Abt. Mar 1928, South Dakota.

1595. VERA ELLA[9] HIGGINS *(IDA LOUISE[8] MILKS, BENJAMIN FRANKLIN[7], LUKE[6] MILK, JONATHAN[5], JONATHAN[4], JOB[3], JOHN[2], JOHN[1])* was born 15 Mar 1903 in Lynch, Boyd County, Nebraska, and died 12 Apr 1995 in Nebraska. She married (1) WILLIAM THOMAS ALFORD 16 Jun 1925 in Yankton County, South Dakota. He was born 24 Feb 1894 in Monowi, Boyd County, Nebraska, and died Jul 1964 in Nebraska. She married (2) MISTTER KNIGHT Aft. 1940. He was born Abt. 1900.

Children of VERA HIGGINS and WILLIAM ALFORD are:
         i.   WILLIAM R.[10] ALFORD, b. 1926, Lynch, Boyd County, Nebraska.
2671.   ii. LORELLE EDWARD 'AL' ALFORD, b. 02 Jan 1928, Lynch, Boyd County, Nebraska; d. 19 Mar 2005, North Platte, Lincoln County, Nebraska.
         iii. DOUGLAS ALFORD, b. 1931, Lynch, Boyd County, Nebraska.

1596. MYRA O.[9] BOND *(NANCY MARIA[8] MILKS, BENJAMIN FRANKLIN[7], LUKE[6] MILK, JONATHAN[5], JONATHAN[4], JOB[3], JOHN[2], JOHN[1])* was born 22 Jan 1888 in Fairbank, Iowa. She married WILLIAM F. KRAFT 1908. He was born Abt. 1888.

Children of MYRA BOND and WILLIAM KRAFT are:
         i.   NYLMAH NEOLA[10] KRAFT, b. 18 Sep 1908, Fairbank, Iowa; d. 14 Dec 1920, Oelwein, Iowa.
2672.   ii. CLAIR OLNY KRAFT, b. 10 Jan 1913, Fairbank, Iowa; d. 08 Dec 1994, Oelwein, Fayette County, Iowa.
         iii. RUSSELL LORAINE KRAFT, b. 14 Oct 1918, Oelwein, Iowa; d. 27 Feb 1991, unmarried.
         iv. NORMA LOU KRAFT, b. 06 Aug 1926, Oelwein, Iowa; d. 16 Jul 1936, Oelwein, Iowa.

1597. HARRY ELWIN[9] BOND *(NANCY MARIA[8] MILKS, BENJAMIN FRANKLIN[7], LUKE[6] MILK, JONATHAN[5], JONATHAN[4], JOB[3], JOHN[2], JOHN[1])* was born 02 Mar 1890 in Lester Township, Black Hawk County, Iowa, and died Jan 1978 in Waterloo, Black Hawk County, Iowa. He married (1) ELIZABETH D. 'BESSIE' BISDORF 11 Nov 1912 in Waterloo, Black Hawk County, Iowa, daughter of JOHN BISDORF and MARGARET BUEHNER. She was born Apr 1898 in East Waterloo, Black Hawk County, Iowa. He married (2) ERMA _____. She was born 1918 in Iowa.

Children of HARRY BOND and ELIZABETH BISDORF are:
2673.   i.   DOROTHY LEILA[10] BOND, b. 04 Jul 1913, Black Hawk County, Iowa; d. 08 Sep 1969.
         ii. ILA BOND, b. Oct 1914, Black Hawk County, Iowa.
         iii. VERA BOND, b. Sep 1916, Black Hawk County, Iowa.
         iv. BESSIE ARLINE BOND, b. 27 Oct 1919, Black Hawk County, Iowa.
         v.   ELIZABETH JEAN BOND, b. 03 Apr 1923, Black Hawk County, Iowa.

1598. LUCY ORINDA[9] BOND *(NANCY MARIA[8] MILKS, BENJAMIN FRANKLIN[7], LUKE[6] MILK, JONATHAN[5], JONATHAN[4], JOB[3], JOHN[2], JOHN[1])* was born 04 Aug 1892 in Fairbank, Iowa, and died 07 Jun 1944. She married JESSE ABRAHAM PLATT 15 Dec 1909 in West Union, Fayette County, Iowa, son of LEW PLATT and EVA PUTNAM. He was born 21 Feb 1886, and died 24 May 1977 in Oelwein, Iowa.

Children of LUCY BOND and JESSE PLATT are:
         i.   VERA HAZEL[10] PLATT, b. 03 Oct 1910, Aurora, Buchanan County, Iowa; d. Bef. 1920, Aurora, Iowa.
         ii. VERNA HELEN PLATT, b. 03 Oct 1910, Aurora, Buchanan County, Iowa; d. Bef. 1920.
         iii. ARLENE RUTH PLATT, b. 14 Jan 1912, Aurora, Buchanan County, Iowa.

iv. VERNON LOUIS PLATT, b. 18 Nov 1913, Aurora, Buchanan County, Iowa; d. 27 Sep 1969, Cedar Rapids, Iowa; m. VELMA HELEN SCHAEFFER, 18 Jan 1943; b. 02 Jul 1917, Fayette, Iowa; d. 15 May 1993, Cedar Rapids, Iowa.

1599. OLIVE HAZEL[9] BOND *(NANCY MARIA[8] MILKS, BENJAMIN FRANKLIN[7], LUKE[6] MILK, JONATHAN[5], JONATHAN[4], JOB[3], JOHN[2], JOHN[1])* was born 13 Mar 1894 in Fairbank, Iowa, and died 15 Feb 1920 in Salt Lake City, Utah. She married MILES BURTON ERVIN 1910, son of THOMAS ERVIN and EMMA BELL. He was born 04 Aug 1891 in Red Willow County, Nebraska, and died 26 Dec 1949 in San Bernardino County, California.

Children of OLIVE BOND and MILES ERVIN are:
- i. BERTON LEROY[10] ERVIN, b. Mar 1913, Oelwein, Fayette County, Iowa.
- ii. VELVA H. ERVIN, b. May 1915, Oelwein, Fayette County, Iowa; d. Bet. 1915 - 1917, Oelwein, Fayette County, Iowa.
- iii. LAVERA M. ERVIN, b. Nov 1917, Oelwein, Fayette County, Iowa.

1600. CORA ELIZABETH[9] BOND *(NANCY MARIA[8] MILKS, BENJAMIN FRANKLIN[7], LUKE[6] MILK, JONATHAN[5], JONATHAN[4], JOB[3], JOHN[2], JOHN[1])* was born 17 May 1896 in Fairbank, Iowa, and died 1949 in Austin, Minnesota. She married FRANK WILLIAM SHERWOOD 1911. He was born Abt. 1896, and died 04 Jun 1949 in Austin, Mower County, Minnesota.

Children of CORA BOND and FRANK SHERWOOD are:
- 2674. i. HELEN IONE[10] SHERWOOD, b. 20 Apr 1912, Oelwein, Fayette County, Iowa; d. 10 Mar 2001, Waconia, Carver County, Minnesota.
- 2675. ii. CLEDA EVELYN SHERWOOD, b. 27 May 1919, Austin, Minn; d. Of Spring Park, MN.
- 2676. iii. DELORES JUNE SHERWOOD, b. 28 Jun 1923, Oelwein, Fayette County, Iowa; d. 21 Sep 2007, Minneapolis, Hennepin County, Minnesota.
- 2677. iv. JERRY FRANK SHERWOOD, b. 14 May 1934, Oelwein, Fayette County, Iowa; d. 11 Jan 1999, Mesa, Maricopa County, Arizona.

1601. LENORA[9] BOND *(NANCY MARIA[8] MILKS, BENJAMIN FRANKLIN[7], LUKE[6] MILK, JONATHAN[5], JONATHAN[4], JOB[3], JOHN[2], JOHN[1])* was born 06 May 1898 in Fairbank, Iowa. She married (1) GLENN PARKER. He was born Abt. 1898. She married (2) RAY RUSSELL.

Children of LENORA BOND and GLENN PARKER are:
- i. MARY K.[10] PARKER.
- ii. ROBERT PARKER.

1602. THOMAS BONNELL[9] BOND *(NANCY MARIA[8] MILKS, BENJAMIN FRANKLIN[7], LUKE[6] MILK, JONATHAN[5], JONATHAN[4], JOB[3], JOHN[2], JOHN[1])* was born 31 Mar 1904 in Fairbank, Iowa, and died 24 Apr 1993 in Independence, Buchanan County, Iowa. He married ALMA ELIZABETH HANSON 25 Dec 1926 in Webster County, Iowa. She was born 1901 in Iowa.

Children of THOMAS BOND and ALMA HANSON are:
- 2678. i. DONNA JEAN[10] BOND, b. 05 May 1928, Ainsworth, Nebraska; d. 29 Mar 2012, Waterloo, Iowa.
- ii. DOLORES M. BOND, b. Oct 1929, Iowa; m. CHARLES 'CHUCK' RUNYAN.
- iii. JOHN BOND, b. 1932; m. LAURA _____.
- iv. NANCY BOND, b. 1935; m. JOHN GAUL.
- v. ROBERT BOND, b. 1937.
- vi. RONALD BOND, b. Abt. 1940.

1603. DOROTHY MARGUERITE[9] BOND *(NANCY MARIA[8] MILKS, BENJAMIN FRANKLIN[7], LUKE[6] MILK, JONATHAN[5], JONATHAN[4], JOB[3], JOHN[2], JOHN[1])* was born 27 Jul 1906 in Lester Township, Blackhawk County, Iowa, and died 15 Nov 1986 in Corona, Riverside County, California. She married JOSEPH THEODORE BRUNEAU 06 Feb 1926 in Minneapolis, Minnesota, son of JOSEPH BRUNEAU and LEA BENOIT. He was born 28 Feb 1906 in Calumet, Michigan, and died 16 Dec 1985 in Corona, California.

Children of DOROTHY BOND and JOSEPH BRUNEAU are:

2679. i. JOHN JOSEPH[10] BRUNEAU, b. 17 Oct 1926, Minneapolis, Minnesota; d. 02 May 2002, Crosby, Crow Wing, Minnesota.
2680. ii. PAUL ARTHUR BRUNEAU, b. 28 Jun 1931, Minneapolis, Minnesota; d. 08 Jul 1984, Minneapolis, Minnesota.
2681. iii. NANCY LEE BRUNEAU, b. 06 Sep 1933, Minneapolis, Minnesota.

1604. IONE[9] VAN ETTEN *(RUTH ANN[8] MILKS, BENJAMIN FRANKLIN[7], LUKE[6] MILK, JONATHAN[5], JONATHAN[4], JOB[3], JOHN[2], JOHN[1])* was born 28 Nov 1896 in Iowa, and died 09 Apr 1977. She married JOHN FRED ENGLERT, son of LOUIS ENGLERT and MARY KLEIMAN. He was born 26 Jul 1892 in Oelwein, Fayette County, Iowa, and died 15 Dec 1977.

Child of IONE VAN ETTEN and JOHN ENGLERT is:

2682. i. FREDERICK J.[10] ENGLERT, b. 29 Jul 1918, Spirit Lake, Kootenai County, Idaho; d. 26 Feb 1972, Spokane, Spokane County, Washington.

1605. VERN LEO[9] MILKS *(THOMAS BENJAMIN[8], BENJAMIN FRANKLIN[7], LUKE[6] MILK, JONATHAN[5], JONATHAN[4], JOB[3], JOHN[2], JOHN[1])* was born 03 Nov 1895 in Black Hawk County, Iowa, and died 07 Aug 1969 in Buchanan Co., Iowa. He married EDNA BRADLEY, daughter of WILLIAM BRADLEY and ROSETTA _____. She was born 13 Feb 1896 in Black Hawk Co., Iowa, and died 26 Jun 1991 in Oelwein, Fayette County, Iowa.

Children of VERN MILKS and EDNA BRADLEY are:

2683. i. LLOYD VERN[10] MILKS, b. 05 Feb 1919, Glasgow, Montana; d. 27 Feb 1996, Oelwein, Fayette County, Iowa.
2684. ii. LYLE K. MILKS, b. 15 Nov 1921, Glasgow, Montana; d. 12 Nov 1993, Oelwein, Fayette County, Iowa.
2685. iii. DUANE LOREN MILKS, b. 29 Jun 1926, Fairbank, Bremer County, Iowa; d. 13 May 1994, Oelwein, Fayette County, Iowa.

1606. CHARLES WILLIAM[9] MILKS *(THOMAS BENJAMIN[8], BENJAMIN FRANKLIN[7], LUKE[6] MILK, JONATHAN[5], JONATHAN[4], JOB[3], JOHN[2], JOHN[1])* was born 05 Jan 1897 in Lester Township, Black Hawk County, Iowa, and died 24 Apr 1931 in Fairbank, Iowa. He married JESSIE ANGELINE MILLER 08 Sep 1915 in Independence, Buchanan County, Iowa, daughter of MARTIN MILLER and ELIZABETH BEARBOWER. She was born 23 Sep 1896 in Rowley, Buchanan County, Iowa, and died 22 Feb 1954 in Schoitz Memorial Hospital, .

OBITUARY - April 30, 1931, Bulletin Journal, Thursday, Fairbank news:

Charles W. Milk Dies:

Charles W. Milks was born Jan. 5, 1897, in Lester Township (Black Hawk Co, IA) and lived on the farm west of town most of the time. In 1915 he was married to Miss Jessie A. Miller, of Fairbank township. To this union were born eight children: Velma, Raburn, Zelma, Helen, Bennie, Wanda, Charles Jr, of whom Wilma preceded him in death. He also leaves his father and mother, Thomas and Lizzie Milks, of this place; two brothers, Vern and Russell, of this place, one sister, of Contentment, Montana. He also leaves many friends and relatives. He was baptized in the German Lutheran church of this place. He was a kind and loving husband and took great interest in his family and was well liked by all.

He passed away at his farm Friday evening at 6:30 p.m. at the evening meal.

The funeral services were held at the Methodist church in Fairbank Monday afternoon at 2 p.m. conducted by the pastor, Rev. Clarence Oelfke. Burial was in the Fairbank Cemetery.

OBITUARY - 23 Feb 1954

MRS. GEORGE M. TANN.

Funeral services will be at 2:30 j. m. Wednesday at O'Keefe & ibwne Funeral Home for Mrs. George M. Tann, -57, of Wyandotte t. in Maywood addition, who died at 10:20 a. m.. Monday at Schoitz Memorial hospital. Death was caused by a cerebral hemorrhage.

The Rev. William Crossley, pastor of St. Paul's Methodist Church, will officiate at the services.

Burial will be in Midwest Garden of Memories.

She was born Sept. 23, 1896, at Brandon, the daughter of Martin and Elizabeth Miller.

She was married Sept. 8, 1915, in Independence to Charles W. Milks who preceded her in death in 931.

She .was married to George M. Tann, Oct. 20, 1933, in Bloomington. Ill.

Surviving are her husband; five daughters, Mrs. Gust Fink. Fairbank; Mrs. Edward Tann, 412 longer St.; Mrs. Lyle D. Brown, Jesup; Miss Doris and Miss Darene, at home; three sons, Rayburn Milks, Rt. 3; Ben Milks, 1704 Sycamore St., and Charles W. Milks, 525 Evans Rd., Evansdale; a brother, Bert Miller, Independence; three sisters, Mrs. Joe Fraggert. Oran; Mrs. Harold Weber, Fairbank, and Mrs. Gladys Van Laningham, Independence; 26 grandchildren and one great grandchild

She was preceded ia death by two daughters and four grandchildren.

Children of CHARLES MILKS and JESSIE MILLER are:

2686.   i.   VELMA EULALIA[10] MILKS, b. 29 Mar 1916; d. 27 Feb 2003, Waterloo, Iowa.

2687.   ii.   RAYBURN LAVERN MILKS, b. 10 Apr 1918, Brandon, Buchanan Co., Iowa; d. Nov 1983, Waukon, Allamakee Co., Iowa.

           iii.   WILMA JUANITA MILKS, b. 25 Jul 1919; d. 18 Jun 1921.

2688.   iv.   ZELMA ARLENE MILKS, b. 25 Sep 1921, Fairbank, Iowa; d. 30 Nov 1989, Fairbank, Iowa.

2689.   v.   THELMA EILEEN 'TEENY' MILKS, b. 25 Oct 1922, Buchanan County, Iowa; d. 23 Dec 1983, Mercy Hospital, Oelwein, Iowa.

2690.   vi.   BENJAMIN FRANCIS 'BENNIE' MILKS, b. 11 Dec 1924, Lester Twp, Black Hawk County, Iowa.

2691.   vii.   NELMA WANDA MILKS, b. 21 May 1926; d. 18 May 1953.

2692.   viii.   CHARLES WILLIAM MILKS, JR., b. 25 Jun 1927; d. 25 Jan 2001, Waterloo, Black Hawk Co., Iowa.

1607. LEILA MARJORIE[9] MILKS *(THOMAS BENJAMIN[8], BENJAMIN FRANKLIN[7], LUKE[6] MILK, JONATHAN[5], JONATHAN[4], JOB[3], JOHN[2], JOHN[1])* was born 13 Jul 1907 in Black Hawk County, Iowa, and died 19 Dec 1997 in Malta, Phillips County, Montana. She married JEAN MICHEL 'MITCH' OXARART 15 Oct 1923 in Salt Lake City, Salt Lake County, Utah, son of NICOLAS OXARART and MARIE NAVARLATZ. He was born 11 Nov 1890 in France, and died 04 Aug 1965 in Malta, Phillips County, Montana.

Children of LEILA MILKS and JEAN OXARART are:

2693.   i.   MARY CATHERINE[10] OXARART, b. 24 Oct 1924, Havre, Montana; d. 29 May 2011, Cascade County, Montana.

2694.   ii.   JOHN MARTIN OXARART, b. 21 Nov 1925, Malta, Montana; d. 02 Nov 1996, Malta, Phillips County, Montana.

2695.   iii.   ALLAN MICHEL 'TWEET' OXARART, b. 28 Feb 1927, Tampico, Valley County, Montana; d. 19 Mar 2000, Great Falls, Cascade County, Montana.

2696.   iv.   FERN JOYCE OXARART, b. 14 Aug 1933, Malta, Montana; d. 1979, Malta, Phillips County, Montana.

1608. RUSSELL HAROLD[9] MILKS *(THOMAS BENJAMIN[8], BENJAMIN FRANKLIN[7], LUKE[6] MILK, JONATHAN[5], JONATHAN[4], JOB[3], JOHN[2], JOHN[1])* was born 27 Aug 1909 in Black Hawk County, Iowa, and died 08 May 1994 in Phillips, Phillips County, Montana. He married FLORENCE ARMSTRONG 14 Feb 1939 in Toole County, Montana, daughter of GEORGE ARMSTRONG and DELENA ROBERTORY. She was born 13 May 1920, and died Bef. 08 May 1994.

Children of RUSSELL MILKS and FLORENCE ARMSTRONG are:

           i.   EDITH ELAINE[10] MILKS, b. 09 Aug 1938, Malta, Phillips County, Montana.

2697.   ii.   BENNY LEE MILKS, b. 27 Jun 1940, Malta, Phillips County, Montana.

1609. CHARLOTTE JOHANNA 'LOTTIE'[9] MILKS *(THOMAS BENJAMIN[8], BENJAMIN FRANKLIN[7], LUKE[6] MILK, JONATHAN[5], JONATHAN[4], JOB[3], JOHN[2], JOHN[1])* was born 19 Feb 1927 in Fairbank, Bremer County, Iowa, and died 09 May 1984 in Waterloo, Black Hawk County, Iowa. She married (1) MR. WILLIAMS. He was born Abt. 1925. She married (2) ARNOLD C. MARSH 01 Sep 1956 in Wisconsin. He was born 22 Mar 1922, and died 16 May 1984.

Children of CHARLOTTE MILKS and MR. WILLIAMS are:

2698.   i.   LINDA CHRISTMAN[10] WILLIAMS, b. 23 Oct 1946, Waterloo, Black Hawk County, Iowa; d. 09 Sep 2007.

           ii.   REBECCA WILLIAMS, b. 17 May 1955, Germany.

Child of CHARLOTTE MILKS and ARNOLD MARSH is:

2699.   iii.   JEFF[10] MARSH.

1610. DONALD PAUL^9 MILKS *(THOMAS BENJAMIN^8, BENJAMIN FRANKLIN^7, LUKE^6 MILK, JONATHAN^5, JONATHAN^4, JOB^3, JOHN^2, JOHN^1)* was born 26 Mar 1928 in Iowa?, and died 27 Jun 2000 in Orlando, Orange Coutny, Florida. He married JIMMIE COOPER Mar 1962 in Hillsborough County, Florida, daughter of NOAH COOPER and GLADYS SHELFER. She was born 23 Oct 1923, and died 13 Sep 1985 in Orange County, Florida.

Children of DONALD MILKS and JIMMIE COOPER are:
2700. i. WILLIAM PAUL^{10} MILKS, b. 12 Jan 1966, Orlando, Orange County, Florida.
       ii. CHILDTWO MILKS.
       iii. CHILDTHREE MILKS, b. Donna (Milks) McCarthy?.

1611. VICTOR KENNETH^9 MILKS *(THOMAS BENJAMIN^8, BENJAMIN FRANKLIN^7, LUKE^6 MILK, JONATHAN^5, JONATHAN^4, JOB^3, JOHN^2, JOHN^1)* was born 30 Apr 1930 in Waterloo, Black Hawk County, Iowa, and died 21 Nov 2003 in Princeton, Bureau County, Illinois. He married JEAN LAGEST 25 Dec 1949.
OBITUARY - Bureau County Republican - Princeton, IL
  Victor Milks - BUREAU -- Victor K. Milks, 73, of Bureau died Friday, Nov. 21, 2003, at Colonial Hall Center in Princeton.
  Born April 30, 1930, in Waterloo, Iowa, to Tom B. and Minnie (Heinaman) Milks, he married Jean LaGest Dec. 25, 1949. They later divorced.
  He had attended Waterlook Schools and was a U.S. Army veteran, serving from 1946 to 1949. He had been employed in the heating and air conditioning field. He was a past governor of Moose Lodge 2102 in Bensonville and past commander of AMVETS of Bureau. He was a member of the American Legion, Masonic Lodge, Scottish Rite, 32nd Degree Shrine and Local 597 Pipefitters Union in Illinois.
  Survivors include one son, Paul (Julia) Milks of DePue; one daughter, Cindy Shipp of Bureau; one half brother, Bill Juergens; one sister, Irene Mixdorf of Waterloo, Iowa; six grandchildren; one great grandchild; one nephew, Jeff (Kim) Marsh of Waterloo, Iowa; and one niece, Linda (Terry) Gilmore of Waterloo, Iowa. He was preceded in death by his parents; one brother, Donald Milks; one half brother, Fred Juergens; and one sister, Scharlet Marsh.
  Graveside funeral services were held Monday in the Garden of Memories Cemetery, Waterloo, Iowa, with military rites provided by Becker-Chapman American Legion Post 138 and VFW Post 1623. The Garden View Chapel in Waterloo, Iowa, was in charge of arrangements.

Children of VICTOR MILKS and JEAN LAGEST are:
2701. i. PAUL V.^{10} MILKS, b. 22 Sep 1966.
       ii. CINDY MILKS, b. Of Bureau, Illinois; m. UNKNOWN SHIPP.

1612. DORA^9 KNIGHT *(MARY^8 GILMAN, URSULA^7 ROGERS, ISAAC^6, RHODA^5 CHASE, ABIGAIL^4 MILK, JOB^3, JOHN^2, JOHN^1)* was born 08 Aug 1880 in Palermo, Oswego County, New York. She married MILLARD CASS 06 Mar 1898 in New Haven, New York, son of MARTIN CASS and MINA MILLARD. He was born 30 Jun 1877, and died 05 Jan 1943 in Buffalo, New York.

Children of DORA KNIGHT and MILLARD CASS are:
2702. i. EARLE MILLARD^{10} CASS, b. 20 Jul 1901, Palermo, Oswego County, New York.
       ii. HAZEL CASS, b. 24 Sep 1906; m. ANTHONY LONGO, 30 Aug 1946; b. Abt. 1905.

1613. EDWIN AUGUSTUS^9 MILK *(JAMES MADISON^8, JAMES MADISON^7, JOHN^6, JOHN^5, JOHN^4, JOHN^3, JOHN^2, JOHN^1)* was born 15 Mar 1878 in Charleston, Massachusetts, and died 09 Dec 1947 in Beverly, Essex County, Massachusetts. He married MARY WATSON JOHNSTON 07 Oct 1903 in Boston, Massachusetts, daughter of WILLIAM JOHNSTON and MARGARET GORDON. She was born Abt. 1879 in Easton, Massachusetts.

Children of EDWIN MILK and MARY JOHNSTON are:
2703. i. JAMES HEMINGWAY^{10} MILK, b. 16 Jul 1904, Beverly, Massachusetts; d. 18 May 1980, Braintree, Norfolk, Mass..
2704. ii. EDWIN GORDON MILK, b. 05 Nov 1908, Beverly, Essex County, Massachusetts; d. 31 Mar 1996, Hyannis, Barnstable County, Massachusetts.

1614. HERBERT ATWOOD[9] MILK *(JOHN HENRY[8], JAMES MADISON[7], JOHN[6], JOHN[5], JOHN[4], JOHN[3], JOHN[2], JOHN[1])* was born 18 Jun 1897 in Boston, Massachusetts, and died 07 Jan 1987 in Norton, Bristol Co., Massachusetts. He married (1) MYRTLE L. KENNEDY Bet. 1910 - 1920 in Boston, Massachusetts?. She was born Abt. 1898 in Massachusetts. He married (2) KATHERINE E. _____ Bet. 1930 - 1940 in Massachusetts. She was born 10 Sep 1903 in Boston, Massachusetts, and died 14 Nov 1986 in Wareham, Plymouth County, Massachusetts.

Western Electric News, May 1918, p22 - "Boston sends this month a photograph of a former member of the bookkeeping department, Herbert A. Milk. He is now a Cadet at the School of Military Aeronautics at Princeton, University." [photo included in WE News]

The 1940 census lists Katherine as "An American citizen born abroad". Both parents were born in Massachusetts.

Child of HERBERT MILK and MYRTLE KENNEDY is:
- i. ROBERT LLEWELLYN[10] MILK, b. 06 Aug 1920, Lowell, Massachusetts; d. 22 Sep 1989, Pocasset, Barnstable, MA 02559; m. EDNA WENTWORTH MURPHY, 25 Dec 1947, Nashua, Hillsboro, New Hampshire; b. Abt. 1921, No. Alhambra, Calif..

INDEX for HEADS-OF-FAMILIES

GENERAL INDEX NOTES

1. This index is an index of HEADS-OF-FAMILIES, and not an all-name index. In other words, it is an index of heads-of-families who have known children, and it includes both spouses. If a person in a family never married, or married but did not have any known children, then their name will not be in the index. To locate those individuals in the book, you will have to look for a known parent or sibling in the index. There are close to 9,000 names in the current index, and the index would have grown to about 23,000 individuals if I had tried to include everyone. If I get the time to add the remaining names to the index, I will publish a new stand-alone index.

2. This index is presented in two sections, the first for MILK-MILKS surnames and variations, and the second for all other surnames.

3. I have included birth year dates, in most cases, but some of these are approximate dates and should not be taken as absolute. If anyone has definitive proof for a specific birthdate, I would be happy to add it to my data and include it in any future publication.

4. If a surname is shown in lower case (Milk, Brooks, Harness, etc.) as opposed to all upper case (MILK, BROOKS, HARNESS, etc.) that means that this is the married surname of that female, because her birth/maiden surname was not known.

NOTES FOR MILK-MILKS INDEX

1. The MILK-MILKS index includes surname variations of: MILKS, MILK, MILCKS, MYLKS, and MYLKES. Since MILKS has been the predominant spelling since the early 1800s, surnames in this index should be presumed to be MILKS, unless the all-caps surnames of MILK, MILCKS, MYLKS, or MYLKES follows the given name in the index. Often, there was conflicting spellings of the surname in the literature, and I have tried to show the most common or the latest spelling.

MILK-MILKS

Given Name	Birth Yr	Page
Abbie J.	1861	250
Abigail Letitia	1850	342
Abigail MILK	1730	12
Abigail MILK	1765	16
Abigail MILK	1790	41
Abram Lincoln	1860	182
Ada A.	1876	293
Ada H.	1886	369
Addie Hattie MILKS-HOWARD	1891	674
Addie Joyce	1931	672
Adelaide	1843	200
Adelbert	1854	242
Adeline Mildred	1909	375
Agnes E.	1902	399
Agnes Ida	1895	302
Agnes Irene (c1940)		510
Alan L.	1965	851
Alan Leroy	1959	820
Alanson	1810	57
Albert	1828	90
Albert Francis "Frank"	1900	313
Albert Thomas	1888	307
Alberta Genevieve	1920	622
Aleda	1860	249
Alex MILKS-COX	1888	220
Alexander B. MILK	1824	105
Alfred Warren	1883	357
Alice E.	1923	680
Alice Irene	1921	576
Alice M. Milks	1861	196
Alice MILK	1783	28
Allen Albert	1917	633
Allen Edgar	1856	203
Allen Henry	1917	578
Alma Celia	1916	408
Alma Celia	1916	637
Alma Elizabeth	1914	628
Almira	1842	76
Almira	1860	158
Almira	1896	309
Almyra	1872	245
Aloma MILK	1943	771
Alvan L.	1901	398
Alvin Henry, Jr.	1952	815
Alvin Henry, Sr.	1927	644
Alvin L.	1849	235
Alvin Lucius	1892	218
Ambrose	1823	74
Ambrose	1883	307
Amelia Ann Milks	1951	850
Amiee R. Milks	1950	674
Amos E.	1847	195
Amos Marsh	1802	84
Amy	1778	30
Amy Milks	1930	521
Andrew Hartman	1874	306
Andrew Hartman	1889	220
Andrew Lloyd	1906	511
Angela Lee	1979	871
Angele R.	1982	896
Angeline Milks	1813	85
Anik	1972	759
Ann Eliza MILK	1824	83
Ann Jane MILK	1845	172
Ann Margaret MILK	1954	770
Anna Ada	1869	167
Anna Bell	1871	408
Anna H.	1884	219
Anna Lillie	1893	411
Anna Louise	1916	585
Anna May	1883	365
Anna MILK	1861	202
Anna Sarah MILK	1854	182
Annah Milks	1798	38
Anne	1917	509
Annette Milks	1971	851
Annie J.	1860	243
Anthony	1859	163
Anthony James	1961	755
Anthony Ronald James	1934	515
Ara Lynn	1889	419
Archer B.	1867	251
Archie B.	1867	241
Ardys Lucille MILK	1920	467
Arlene Bessie	1921	403
Arlene E.	1915	296
Arlene Lois	1949	741

Name	Year	No.	Name	Year	No.
Arlyn Ray	1891	335	Bertha M.	1883	359
Arnold R.	1914	571	Bertha Mabel	1882	412
Arnold Richard	1907	375	Beryl Dorine	1922	683
Arthur Glenn	1887	422	Bessie Etta	1911	637
Arthur L. MILK	1905	552	Bessie Irene	1889	411
Arthur Lyle	1929	661	Beth Milks	1927	682
Arthur Lynn "Jack"	1927	537	Betsey Milk	1790	28
Arthur Manley	1920	660	Betsey MILK	1805	80
Arthur Rolland	1863	284	Betty C. Milks	1922	296
Atola Olive "Donna"	1914	387	Betty E.	1924	278
Audra	1888	421	Betty June	1933	383
Audrey Louise	1919	661	Betty Milks	1958	773
Audrey Margaret Grace	1932	516	Betty Ruth	1952	793
Augusta Frances MILK	1844	127	Beulah	1893	420
Barbara A. Milks	1957	820	Beverly Barbara	1929	521
Barbara Faye	1928	597	Beverly Rose Therese	1932	390
Barbara Helen MYLKS	1939	784	Beverly Susan	1953	759
Barbara Lynn	1970	755	Blanche	1885	408
Basil	1929	515	Blanche Elvira	1880	419
Bathsheba	1804	47	Blanche Luella	1892	301
Beatrice Catherine	1938	510	Bobby Jo	1964	885
Beatrice E.	1913	680	Brad Michael	1971	875
Benjamin	1794	42	Brenda MILK	1956	876
Benjamin	1799	39	Bret Brad		861
Benjamin	1800	46	Brian Allen	1962	826
Benjamin	1821	74	Brian Clement	1920	499
Benjamin B.	1816	110	Brian Lee MILK	1977	876
Benjamin B.	1828	63	Brittani	1986	910
Benjamin F. MILK	1842	172	Bryan	1965	797
Benjamin Francis	1914	707	Burton Henry	1879	397
Benjamin Franklin	1833	92	Burton Henry	1924	623
Benjamin Franklin	1835	122	Butler Webster	1862	263
Benjamin Franklin	1857	194	Butler Webster	1862	253
Benjamin J.	1853	156	Bythea	1914	511
Benjamin Kenneth	1971	830	Calvin Harry	1825	187
Benjamin L.	1851	148	Cara Lynn Milks	1932	575
Benjamin MILK	1750	19	Carl J.	1952	820
Benjamin MILK	1824	83	Carl John	1947	785
Benjamin MILK, Jr.	1780	35	Carl L.	1955	633
Benny Lee	1940	709	Carol Joseph	1890	403
Bernadette Catherine Grace Anne	1939	517	Carol Louise MILKS-HOWARD	1933	832
Bert	1874	241	Carol Marie	1945	471
Bert Abley	1890	353	Carol May	1929	672
Bert Leroy	1880	151	Carol Milks	1961	826
Bertha Gladys	1902	295	Carol Milks	1966	758

Name	Year	Page	Name	Year	Page
Carol Milks	1966	889	Charlotte Mary T.	1927	519
Caroline C.	1832	188	Charlotte Milks	1809	48
Carrie Ann	1974	872	Chester Howard	1919	672
Carrie M.	1892	378	Chloe B.	1872	394
Cary James MILK	1947	714	Chloe Milks	1845	236
Catheline	1925	521	Christa A.	1983	897
Catherine "Kate"	1846	160	Christian Nicole	1975	821
Catherine Lenore MYLKS	1917	574	Christina	1852	201
Catherine Lucretia "Kate"	1842	72	Christina Marie Milks	1978	829
Catherine MILK	1820	83	Christine	1821	70
Catherine Ann	1949	753	Christine	1965	756
Cecil G.	1907	777	Christine Renee Milks	1963	489
Charlene M. Milks	1956	598	Christopher John	1957	760
Charles	1835	75	Clara	1864	284
Charles	1819	105	Clara	1871	142
Charles Albert	1875	391	Clara	1879	357
Charles Arnold	1885	365	Clara L. Milks	1938	668
Charles Arnold	1925	584	Clara Louise	1915	316
Charles B.	1847	145	Clara Mahala	1875	213
Charles Barney	1839	200	Clara Rose	1918	522
Charles Chapple	1882	561	Clare Milks		753
Charles Corbett	1894	337	Clarence A.	1905	776
Charles Edward	1887	358	Clarence A. MILCKS	1906	385
Charles Everett	1873	352	Clarence Benjamin	1906	583
Charles Frank	1939	668	Clarence Benjamin	1925	790
Charles Frederick MYLKES	1882	289	Clarence G.	1854	343
Charles Frederick MYLKES	1954	829	Clarence Leland	1899	422
Charles G. MILK	1815	54	Clarence Leland	1899	639
Charles H. MILK	1845	174	Clarence Luke	1886	441
Charles H. MILK	1877	435	Clark Burnell	1895	421
Charles Harland	1930	835	Claudia E.	1865	244
Charles Hastings	1897	396	Clayton Frederick	1903	404
Charles Hector	1895	304	Clayton Frederick, Jr.	1926	635
Charles Jonathan	1828	99	Clayton Howard	1924	632
Charles L.	1915	577	Cleo Latra	1914	686
Charles Laurin	1951	807	Clifford Eugene	1947	824
Charles MILK	1814	78	Clifford Howard	1907	531
Charles Nelson	1866	216	Clifford Paul	1897	425
Charles Newman	1856	223	Clifford Paul, Jr.	1930	666
Charles Rolland	1815	69	Clifton Lee	1901	431
Charles William	1897	460	Clyde E.	1954	824
Charles William III	1949	850	Connie Lee	1942	743
Charles William, Jr.	1927	707	Conrad Wilson	1919	686
Charlotte H. "Lottie"	1841	143	Constance Louise	1947	741
Charlotte Johanna "Lottie"	1927	461	Cora Annabelle	1873	218

Name	Year	Page
Cora Diane	1887	410
Cordelia	1823	115
Corrine Milks	1888	284
Cynthia Ann	1948	809
Cynthia Blanche MILK	1887	267
Cynthia Jane MILK	1840	84
Cynthia MILK	1768	25
Cynthia MILK	1810	54
Cynthia MILK	1812	78
Cynthia MILK	1853	174
Daisey	1887	226
Daisy Ellen	1880	299
Dale Duane	1940	816
Daniel	1805	85
Daniel	1871	165
Daniel A.	1935	816
Daniel Benjamin	1875	212
Daniel Leroy	1946	838
Daniel Robert MILK	1848	714
Darla J. Milks	1964	823
Darlene Jean	1944	848
Darlene Milks		523
Darlene L.	1940	823
Darlene Prudence Milks	1948	793
Darrell Delbert MILK	1917	467
David	1786	38
David	1793	32
David	1812	67
David	1813	89
David	1825	63
David	1829	75
David	1861	164
David	1861	196
David	1883	409
David	1909	314
David A.	1960	889
David Allen	1946	719
David Ambrose	1891	312
David B.	1817	87
David Benjamin	1835	188
David Clayton	1952	809
David Eric	1945	669
David Estle, St.	1939	487
David Franklin	1838	102
David G.	1945	814
David Hartman	1883	216
David Lee	1942	608
David Lewis	1890	366
David MILK	1720	9
David MILK	1752	19
David MILK	1795	44
David MILK	1806	53
David MILK	1815	91
David MILK	1818	110
David MILK	1820	81
David Shepherd MYLKS	1838	199
David Tilden	1872	150
David Victor William	1892	307
David W.	1830	106
David W.	1848	223
David Wesley	1830	99
David Wesley	1881	412
Deah Marie MILKS-HOWARD	1928	831
Deborah	1798	46
Deborah	1819	111
Deborah	1836	117
Deborah L. Milks	1952	815
Deborah Lynne	1951	753
Deborah MILK	1802	79
Debra Ann	1956	489
Delbert Charles MILCKS	1908	385
Della Macie	1887	366
Delphine	1871	249
Delphine	1871	250
Dency M	1854	223
Dewain Elmer MILK	1934	554
Dewitt William	1878	133
Diana Marie Milks		889
Diane (c1955)		758
Diane Fay	1941	673
Diane Marie	1967	717
Dolores Milks	1930	598
Donald	1930	521
Donald E.	1928	659
Donald Edward	1919	534
Donald Frank	1932	575
Donald George MILK	1920	550
Donald Henry	1881	297
Donald Herbert	1921	634
Donald J.	1937	609

Name	Year	Page	Name	Year	Page
Donald Joseph	1954	611	Edward Howard	1933	760
Donald Leroy MILK	1916	467	Edward R.	1846	236
Donald Lester	1930	388	Edward Rosco	1976	871
Donald Lester	1959	610	Edwin A.	1895	369
Donald Paul	1928	462	Edwin Augusta MILK	1878	462
Donna M. Milks	1936	813	Edwin Charles, Sr.	1937	488
Dora Aleene	1914	382	Edwin Elmer	1882	151
Dorcas MILK	1741	14	Edwin Gordon MILK	1908	710
Doreen	1922	520	Edwin H.	1854	149
Doreen Kay	1959	826	Eileen Louise	1944	824
Dorene Dora	1916	686	Elizabeth MILK	1767	24
Dorene Sue	1955	745	Elaine M. Milks	1946	838
Doris Helen	1921	634	Elaine Ruth	1943	837
Doris Iona	1913	630	Elaine Ruth Milks	1920	672
Doris J.	1947	609	Elbert B.	1870	212
Doris Maxine	1929	503	Eleanor G.	1929	659
Dorothea Lilly	1906	495	Eleanor May	1914	614
Dorothy Elizabeth	1918	319	Eleanor MILK	1797	51
Dorothy Grace MILK	1905	546	Eleanor Milks	1801	32
Dorothy H.	1915	534	Eleanor R.	1847	235
Dorothy Lorraine	1919	382	Eleanor Sophia	1915	375
Dorothy Mae	1930	504	Elenore Mary	1876	218
Dorothy Maxine	1922	390	Eli S. MILK	1757	28
Dorothy Ruth	1913	570	Elizabeth	1870	244
Douglas	1938	609	Elizabeth	1888	424
Douglas Ronald	1947	669	Elizabeth	1905	275
Duane Leroy	1933	388	Elizabeth A. MILK	1849	174
Duane Loren	1926	705	Elizabeth Ann	1949	744
Duard Alvin	1884	410	Elizabeth Ann	1967	793
Duard Alvin, Jr.	1917	644	Elizabeth Ann "Betsy"	1845	147
Duncan William Hector	1862	165	Elizabeth Anne	1976	899
Earl Finan	1907	613	Elizabeth Cawley	1907	574
Earle Donald	1900	430	Elizabeth Milk	1753	18
Ebenezer	1827	68	Elizabeth MILK	1787	40
Edgar	1849	248	Elizabeth MILK	1853	225
Edgar	1861	226	Elizabeth Milks	1815	67
Edgar H.	1889	393	Elizabeth Milks	1835	63
Edgar Romain	1850	173	Elizabeth Milks	1928	679
Edith Elizabeth	1917	630	Elkanah	1776	30
Edith Elizabeth	1922	529	Elkanah B.	1816	69
Edith Frances MILK	1905	466	Ella	1863	197
Edith M.	1918	679	Ella Mae	1900	678
Edith S.	1907	633	Ella Mae MILK	1892	269
Edward D. MILK	1954	773	Ella Marie	1896	419
Edward H. MILK	1928	550	Ella MILK	1849	127

Name	Year	Page	Name	Year	Page
Ellard Anthony	1934	516	Eugene Manley	1934	668
Ellis Clyde	1890	360	Eugenia May	1953	794
Ellis David	1855	203	Eva	1859	227
Ellis David	1855	278	Eva	1903	295
Ellsworth M.	1905	431	Eva Arabella	1870	150
Ellsworth M.	1906	644	Eva Lionell	1915	585
Elmer F.	1849	236	Eveline Louise	1849	236
Elmer F.	1873	212	Everett W., Jr.	1950	471
Elmer William MYLKS	1908	374	Everett W., Sr.	1921	277
Elodie Marguerite	1893	306	Experience Milks	1787	32
Elroy L.	1929	658	Ezra	1781	36
Elsie	1919	627	Ezra	1818	90
Elsie Myrtle	1932	501	Ezra	1820	87
Elva Olive	1897	421	Ezra	1854	153
Elva Olive	1936	516	Fannie Milks	1830	76
Emaline	1850	152	Fanny	1879	351
Emaline Milks	1850	104	Faye Elizabeth MILK	1888	269
Emerson S.	1909	641	Fern Lajune	1918	659
Emily H.	1855	235	Fernella May	1927	602
Emma	1877	392	Flora A.	1877	352
Emma	1863	141	Flora Elizabeth	1918	634
Emma A.	1849	202	Florence	1886	309
Emmet Earl	1876	245	Florence Ann	1891	367
Era Eldie	1900	302	Florence Lucille	1911	386
Eric D.	1972	828	Floyd Edwin	1890	378
Erika Milks	1939	669	Floyd Leroy	1931	602
Erle Kenneth	1888	305	Floyd Wesley	1918	498
Erma Doris	1920	591	Ford Leroy	1928	500
Ernest Ambrose	1898	302	Frances	1917	628
Ernest Arnold	1928	586	Frances A.	1912	400
Ernest David	1923	383	Frances Althea "Betty"	1914	648
Ernest Ellis	1922	502	Frances Elizabeth	1910	614
Ernest L.	1856	201	Frances Ellen	1854	241
Ernest Oscar	1895	366	Frances Lavern	1852	149
Ernest Thurman	1912	584	Frances M. Milks	1956	807
Esther	1871	229	Francine Elaine	1958	796
Esther Ann "Hester"	1838	77	Francis Eli "Frank"	1868	133
Esther J.	1847	119	Francis James	1851	248
Esther J.	1908	275	Frank	1857	203
Esther Rosetta	1874	364	Frank	1887	219
Ethel	1882	393	Frank Albert	1863	229
Etta A.	1898	399	Frank Craycroft	1887	367
Etta Mae	1875	561	Frank E.	1947	633
Ettie Milks	1863	242	Frank Edwin	1859	228
Eugene Benjamin	1851	235	Frank Elmer	1923	403

Name	Year	Page	Name	Year	Page
Frank Lynn	1948	820	George Prince	1850	225
Frank W.	1856	241	George R.	1926	615
Frank W.	1879	435	George Richard	1871	213
Frank W., Jr.	1928	679	George Theodore MILCKS	1882	219
Frank Wheeler	1857	195	George Vernon	1941	622
Franklin Grant	1863	202	George Washington	1894	423
Franklin Horace	1877	357	George Washington MILK	1850	126
Fred	1860	241	George Wilson	1848	240
Fred A.	1873	228	Georgia America	1893	396
Fred A.	1878	322	Georgia Belle	1875	322
Fred H.	1865	432	Gerald A. C.	1927	512
Fred James	1874	435	Gerald A. MILK	1915	549
Frederick E.	1916	626	Gerald Dean MILKS-HOWARD	1925	831
Freeborn Garrettson	1797	33	Gerald Elmer	1919	512
Freeman	1785	32	Gerald Erwin	1924	502
Freeman	1885	437	Gerald K.	1923	576
Freeman B.	1864	210	Geraldine Abigail	1923	522
Garrett Lansing	1881	437	Geraldine Dianne	1943	505
Garrett Lansing III	1946	837	Geraldine Lee	1941	848
Garrett Lansing IV	1972	899	Gertrude E.	1900	373
Garrett Lansing, Jr.	1923	682	Gertrude May	1889	442
Garrett T.	1828	116	Gertrude Milk	1917	710
Garrison	1852	160	Gertrude P.	1879	395
Gary Lyle	1949	847	Gilbert	1838	117
Gaynell Milks	1918	790	Gilbert Foster	1915	663
Geneva	1911	624	Gilbert Lyle	1926	632
Genevieve H. MILK	1915	552	Giles	1827	76
Geoffrey G.	1979	827	Giles	1830	112
George	1822	71	Gladys Anna	1889	217
George	1823	111	Gladys I.	1896	403
George	1862	132	Glen Alan	1969	815
George Alfred	1895	401	Glen C.	1891	410
George Arnold	1895	353	Glen C.	1940	645
George B.	1867	244	Glenda Eileen	1961	716
George Clinton, Jr.	1910	633	Glenn Howard	1916	382
George Daniel	185	404	Glenna Dale	1927	680
George Earl	1899	316	Glennie Rosella	1918	675
George H. MILK	1850	181	Gloria	1927	660
George Henry	1854	249	Gloria J. Milks	1945	611
George Henry MILK	1847	172	Gloria Milks	1950	847
George Henry MYLKES	1875	288	Golda Eva	1917	585
George J.	1882	392	Gordon Joseph	1898	397
George Jerome	1841	72	Gordon Joseph	1939	622
George Jerome	1878	150	Gordon Wright MYLKS	1874	353
George MILK	1762	20	Gordon Wright MYLKS II	1904	573

Name	Year	Page	Name	Year	Page
Grace	1877	321	Hazel Turner	1888	293
Grace Aurelia	1877	344	Heather Lynn	1964	749
Grace Louise	1922	660	Hector Ernest	1901	316
Grace Milks	1928	660	Hector Mayne	1857	157
Grace O.	1911	577	Helen	1845	144
Gregory Joel	1977	802	Helen	1930	513
Gretchen Anne Milks	1974	900	Helen	1931	879
Gretchen Irene	1891	434	Helen	1941	517
Guy Stanley	1898	378	Helen Berta	1918	571
Gwendolyn Nora MILK	1927	553	Helen Bertie	1910	382
Gwynneth	1920	509	Helen E. MILKS-HOWARD	1929	831
Hannah Milks	1822	67	Helen Eldredge	1898	477
Harlan Porter	1907	420	Helen Elizabeth	1885	396
Harland F.	1900	678	Helen G.	1898	574
Harley Edward	1908	275	Helen Irene	1914	682
Harley Glen, Jr.	1963	716	Helen Isabelle MYLKS	1912	573
Harley Glenn, Sr.	1936	470	Helen L.	1834	77
Harley H.	1883	321	Helen Loretta	1911	632
Harmon William MYLKS	1836	199	Helen Margaret MILK	1912	546
Harold Clifford	1889	321	Henry	1862	168
Harold E.	1891	422	Henry Actor Gerald Hector	1905	310
Harold E., Jr.	1928	660	Henry Benjamin	1826	97
Harold F.	1913	614	Henry Benson	1844	235
Harold George	1898	419	Henry Edward	1878	364
Harold Keith	1908	535	Henry Edwin	1919	402
Harold Sherwood MILK	1906	466	Henry John	1880	407
Harold J.	1913	576	Henry Joseph	1862	228
Harriet	1827	123	Henry MIILS-HOWARD	1844	247
Harriet "Hattie"	1853	195	Henry MILK	1817	79
Harriet A. MILKS-HOWARD	1869	433	Henry W.	1914	584
Harriet B.	1884	293	Henry Wesley	1911	646
Harriet Louise	1848	222	Herbert	1889	309
Harriet Mariah	1823	58	Herbert Albert	1894	404
Harriet MILK	1839	125	Herbert Atwood MILK	1897	463
Harriett Emeline	1813	68	Herbert Gordon	1937	486
Harriett Melissa MYLKES	1878	289	Herbert Gordon MYLKS	1940	784
Harris	1809	91	Herbert Harry	1892	368
Harry J.	1869	210	Herbert James	1901	294
Harry Streator	1878	216	Herbert Joseph	1907	308
Harry W.	1920	589	Herbert William MYLKS	1938	598
Harvey C.	1863	244	Herbeta Milks	1928	473
Harvey R. "Dade"	1850	240	Herma Ann	1921	623
Hattie MYLKS	1868	355	Herman	1842	140
Hazel G.	1903	432	Herron Franklin	1939	794
Hazel Leona	1904	320	Hetty	1872	197

Name	Year	Page
Hilary		523
Hiram	1832	112
Homer P.	1877	282
Horace "Lee"	1878	245
Horace B.	1838	144
Horace Wayne	1904	612
Howard	1962	472
Howard Estle	1914	294
Howard George	1895	430
Howard Jay	1879	321
Howard L.	1962	821
Howard Ralph	1918	624
Howard Simpson	1941	660
Hubert Emanuel "Jack"	1912	294
Hugh Lincoln	1916	642
Humphrey	1879	218
Humphrey W.	1840	103
Ichabod	1810	67
Ida A.	1855	210
Ida Gwendole	1915	382
Ida Louise	1858	262
Ida Matilda	1867	160
Ila Jean	1926	503
Inez Irene	1908	381
Ira Charles	1904	375
Ira Charles, Jr.	1930	598
Ira Clayton	1920	587
Ira Eldie	1901	302
Ira Nelson	1847	101
Ira Richard	1920	503
Irene	1904	477
Irene Bessie	1888	425
Irene May	1924	498
Irma E.	1915	614
Irvin Leslie D.	1881	336
Isaac	1855	156
Isaac MILK	1815	79
Isabel MILK	1753	15
Ivah Lovina	1891	561
Ivan Edward "Joe"		523
Jack Arthur	1948	803
Jack K.	1922	576
Jaimee Lee	1985	861
James	1863	241
James Alton	1938	669
James B.	1913	567
James Burdette MILK	1937	769
James E.	1867	356
James Edward	1919	532
James F. MILK	1962	876
James Franklin	1845	101
James Hartman	1846	104
James Henry MILKS-HOWARD	1875	433
James Henry MILKS-HOWARD	1904	675
James Henry, Jr	1904	675
James I.	1936	599
James Madison	1831	123
James Madison MILK	1855	265
James MILK	1711	7
James MILK	1744	14
James Peter	1963	730
James Russell	1955	815
James Thomas	1888	311
James Thomas	1904	314
James Walker	1930	597
James Warren	1924	665
James William	1913	386
Jamie Ryan	1975	872
Jamithy	1979	888
Jane MILK	1739	13
Jane Ophelia	1833	58
Janet MILK	1815	81
Janette A.	1899	337
Janice Irene	1938	814
Janice Ann Milks	1953	488
Jason A. MILK	1978	876
Jay E.	1885	436
Jean	1928	813
Jean A. Milks	1936	736
Jean Bertha	1922	655
Jeanette Audrey MILKS-Howard	1934	832
Jeanette E.	1928	835
Jeanette Marie	1943	805
Jeannette Adelaide	1919	578
Jeffrey Alan	1968	875
Jeffrey D.	1955	847
Jemima	1812	109
Jennie	1857	262
Jennie	1880	395

Name	Year	No.	Name	Year	No.
Jennie E.	1876	408	John Harris "Harry"	1883	358
Jennie Minerva MILK	1855	127	John Henry MILK	1864	265
Jennie Ruth	1877	561	John Hiram	1910	427
Jerold Lee	1954	803	John Joseph	1934	389
Jerome	1854	209	John Leon	1951	763
Jerome Bonaparte	1857	228	John MILK	1630	1
Jerome Franklin	1879	365	John MILK	1732	13
Jesse	1858	202	John MILK	1765	23
Jesse David	1920	642	John MILK	1786	28
Jessica Marie Milk	1978	876	John MILK	1791	50
Jessie Edna	1865	210	John MILK	1793	45
Jessie Lynn	1954	839	John MILK, III	1708	6
Jessie M.	1907	625	John MILK, Jr.	1669	3
Jessie Marie	1922	680	John Oscar	1858	226
Jill Marie	1960	795	John Smith	1859	167
Joan C. Milks	1932	665	John Stanley "Jack"	1916	508
Joanna Irene	1834	116	John W.	1978	730
Joannah Daisy	1879	250	John W. MYLKS	1833	199
Job	1781	30	John Wesley	1843	173
Job MILK	1694	5	John Wesley	1917	536
Job MILK	1748	18	John William	1892	337
Job MILK	1763	16	John Worden	1948	486
Job MILK	1798	43	John, Jr.	1822	123
Job MILK, Jr	1725	9	Johnna Lee	1967	729
Jodi	1969	896	Jonathan	1821	68
John	1781	32	Jonathan B.	1830	102
John	1786	31	Jonathan B. "Tip"	1829	117
John	1790	26	Jonathan Dwight	1956	658
John	1813	63	Jonathan Elwood	1945	471
John	1815	109	Jonathan K. "Josh"	1948	719
John	1821	68	Jonathan MILK	1728	10
John	1824	74	Jonathan MILK	1751	18
John	1949	757	Jonathan MILK	1769	20
John A.	1878	334	Jonathan MILK	1774	34
John Austin	1889	311	Jonathan, Jr.	1789	31
John B. MILK	1831	176	Jonathan, Jr.	1806	48
John D.	1849	234	Joni Elizabeth	1955	747
John D.	1906	641	Jordan		896
John D., Jr.	1933	813	Joseph	1848	155
John Dallas	1915	389	Joseph Arnold Hector	1933	516
John Douglas	1946	786	Joseph Edward	1895	312
John Earl	1931	668	Joseph Edwin	1851	211
John Ebert	1920	512	Joseph Finley	1859	165
John Edward	1926	509	Joseph Gerald Cecil	1933	520
John Francis "Jack"	1943	611	Joseph Hiram	1892	366

Name	Year	Page
Joseph John Keith	1931	518
Joseph Lee	1941	794
Joseph Lee, Jr.	1967	885
Joseph Michael MILK	1965	903
Joseph Osborne	1886	304
Joseph Paul	1927	586
Joseph Richard	1933	523
Joseph S.	1972	889
Josephine C. Milks	1904	295
Joyce Ann Milks	1956	747
Joyce B.	1924	809
Joyce Edna	1944	505
Joyce Fern	1932	635
Juanita Ann	1941	805
Judith Ann	1946	824
Judith Lynn	1948	782
Judson David	1879	400
Judy Lee	1950	793
Julia Ann	1814	91
Julia Ann	1872	202
Julia Ann MILK	1829	84
Julia Frances	1857	203
Julia M.	1880	392
Julia Marion MILK	1901	546
Justin David	1934	816
Kallie Milks	1882	364
Karen E.	1952	489
Karen J. Milks	1941	609
Karen Milks	1950	803
Karla Jean	1956	826
Katherine E. Milk	1903	463
Kathleen Charlotte MILK	1921	554
Kathleen Edith	1907	316
Kathryn A. MILK	1917	549
Kathryn Louise	1935	656
Katie Milks		887
Katrina Genevieve	1973	730
Keith	1957	758
Keith Allen	1959	764
Kenneth L.	1956	839
Kenneth Lee	1913	432
Kenneth R.	1939	805
Kenneth Robert	1937	674
Kenneth S.	1921	665
Kenneth Wallace	1907	426
Kenneth Wallace, Jr.	1936	667
Kenneth Wallace, Jr.	1936	819
Kent	1959	823
Kevin W.	1968	797
Kristi	1979	888
Kristine D. Milks	1957	808
Kyle R. MILK	1967	876
Larry A.	1943	823
Larry James	1948	808
Laura	1894	310
Laura Ann	1817	57
Laura Jane	1824	70
Laura Milks	1880	562
Laura Milks	1962	822
Lawrence Erwin	1956	747
Lawrence R. MILK	1902	552
Leah Ethel	1889	305
Lee B.	1882	334
Legrande	1865	195
Lela Marjorie	1907	461
Lelia Belle	1868	324
Lemuel (c1765)		31
Lemuel MILK	1747	15
Lemuel MILK	1753	19
Lemuel MILK	1820	55
Lemuel MILK	1884	268
Lena	1875	321
Lena A. MILK	1862	185
Lena Almira	1884	304
Lena Amanda	1881	321
Lena Viola	1880	334
Lenore E.	1912	678
Leo Leroy	1887	359
Leonard	1820	115
Leonard	1844	152
Leonard Eugene MYLKS	1876	353
Leonard Glenn	1877	433
Leonard H.	1875	324
Leonard Howard	1913	681
Leroy Ethelbert	1894	434
Leroy Joseph	1913	577
Leroy St. Clair	1892	323
Leslie B.	1884	400
Leslie Osborne	1914	507
Leslie Roger	1910	473

Name	Year	No.	Name	Year	No.
Leslie Roger	1938	719	Louise Irene	1942	747
Leslie S.	1947	674	Lovina P.	1848	342
Lester Judson	1908	625	Lucille Josephine	1916	570
Lester L.	1902	337	Luella B.	1880	286
Lester Leonard	1943	836	Luella Evelyn	1917	385
Lester Raymond	1951	747	Luella Mable	1905	675
Lester Raymond "Guy"	1971	872	Luke MILK	1812	49
Leta Irene	1917	679	Luther P.	1831	117
Lettie M.	1891	394	Lydia	1853	240
Lettie Mae	1903	338	Lydia A.	1832	119
Levi Stephen	1825	82	Lydia Ann	1853	153
Lewis Eldie	1935	505	Lydia Jane MILK	1812	83
Lewis Ethil	1865	154	Lydia Milk	1750	19
Lewis Lyons	1863	209	Lydia Milk	1820	53
Lewis Terrel	1948	793	Lydia MILK	1845	173
Lillian Grace	1895	359	Lyle K.	1921	705
Lillian Joy	1949	744	Lyle N.	1900	358
Lillian Tressie	1895	443	Lynn L.	1918	679
Lillie Mae	1908	583	Lynn Olmstead	1920	657
Linda Fay Milks	1948	719	Mabel	1889	360
Linda Kay	1954	823	Mabel Inez	1915	677
Linda Lee	1954	754	Mabel M.	1890	368
Linda Lou	1952	745	Mabel Milks	1918	633
Llewellyn W. G. "Lou"	1932	512	Mabel R.	1924	680
Lloyd Albert	1901	381	Mabel Rose	1881	301
Lloyd Andrew	1941	752	Mable May	1910	583
Lloyd C.	1927	659	Madeleine	1944	523
Lloyd Elmer	1887	402	Malcolm Horace	1896	370
Lloyd Elmer	1919	630	Malcolm L. "Mack"	1924	592
Lloyd Elmer	1943	807	Malinda Martha	1898	309
Lloyd Vern	1919	705	Manley David	1852	236
Lois Ann Milks	1950	752	Manley H.	1857	226
Lois Ellen	1923	384	Manley Kenneth	1880	243
Lois L. Milks	1939	645	Manuel MYLKS	1843	199
Lois Milks	1836	106	Margaret	1929	808
Lola A.	1882	395	Marc	1976	889
Lonny G.	1966	895	Marcel	1944	524
Lorin Andrew	1951	489	Marcia Day MYLKES	1908	480
Lorin Charles	1913	296	Marcia Terry MILK	1983	877
Lorraine Alison		759	Margaret	1864	132
Lorraine Harriet MILCKS	1926	386	Margaret Ann	1934	521
Lottie Zella	1886	300	Margaret Ann	1937	669
Louis Elmer	1896	413	Margaret B. Milks	1910	431
Louisa Milks	1815	57	Margaret Euretta	1886	301
Louise Caroline MILK	1842	127	Margaret Jane	1966	755

Name	Year	Page
Margaret Joanne	1925	571
Margaret L.	1898	338
Margaret Marilyn	1932	504
Margaret May	1878	324
Margaret Milk	1795	28
Margaret Neoma	1916	388
Marge A.	1832	810
Margery	1914	588
Marguerite Arlene	1906	432
Maria	1818	68
Maria Eve Isabella Abigail	1893	312
Maria MILK	1770	34
Mariah E.	1828	58
Marian	1913	626
Marian Alice MILK	1870	185
Marian Elizabeth	1943	816
Marian F.	1916	588
Marian Isabella Lusk	1899	306
Marie Agnes	1917	532
Marie L.	1920	615
Marie Martha	1945	523
Marilyn June	1931	667
Marilyn Louise MILK	1923	468
Marion	1942	517
Marion A.	1926	681
Marion H. Milks	1835	176
Marion MILK	1935	773
Marion T. MILK	1924	550
Marjorie	1889	420
Marjorie	1934	593
Marjorie Ann	1927	878
Marjorie E.	1912	626
Marjorie Jane	1950	807
Mark Anthony	1953	840
Mark C.	1862	169
Mark James	1957	795
Marol Ann	1950	850
Marsha D. Milks	1945	666
Martella Milks	1879	284
Martha	1860	168
Martha Ann	1939	683
Martha Jane	1919	586
Martha Joan	1937	668
Martin	1835	113
Martin "Van"	1875	245
Marvel	1925	520
Marvin Elwood MILK	1915	466
Mary	1791	45
Mary	1861	112
Mary A.	1861	244
Mary Alice	1877	307
Mary Ann	1820	69
Mary Ann	1858	162
Mary Ann	1915	439
Mary Ann Majella	1954	754
Mary Arlene MILK	1916	549
Mary B.	1870	242
Mary B. Milks	1885	284
Mary Beatrice	1908	623
Mary Denzel	1905	381
Mary E. "Polly" MILK	1829	176
Mary E. "Polly" MILK	1861	201
Mary Elizabeth	1839	118
Mary Elizabeth	1918	390
Mary Elizabeth	1923	571
Mary Emeline	1881	413
Mary J.	1860	223
Mary Kathleen	1923	389
Mary Kathryn	1947	489
Mary Kiziah MILK	1869	173
Mary Louise	1953	598
Mary Louise Milks	1942	384
Mary M. MILK	1810	62
Mary MILK	1737	13
Mary Milk	1777	34
Mary MILK	1785	40
Mary Milks	1838	125
Mary Milks		212
Mary Myrtle Phyllis	1920	517
Mary S. "Mayme"	1883	352
Mary Sherwood MILK	1888	127
Mary V. MILK	1873	267
Matthew G.	1816	91
Matthew J.	1981	896
Matthew Mac Lean	1974	894
Maude Marie	1905	678
Maureen Milks	1945	794
Max Cleveland	1947	763
Max Leon	1914	536
Melanie Milks	1964	895

Name	Year	Page	Name	Year	Page
Melinda A.	1848	152	Nancy	1939	598
Melinda Em	1964	796	Nancy A. Milks	1934	797
Melissa	1832	75	Nancy Alice Theresa	1961	754
Melody Ann Milk	1947	714	Nancy Jane MYLKS	1938	784
Merle Douglas	1919	638	Nancy Lee	1945	847
Merrill V.	1880	213	Nancy Maria	1833	121
Merrill W.	1916	490	Nancy Maria	1865	263
Merritt Sidway	1840	101	Nancy Milks		752
Merritt Thomas "Putt"	1926	597	Nancy S.	1858	234
Merrl Thomas	1898	372	Neelin		523
Merva Erden	1890	434	Nellie Blanche	1903	381
Michael Bruce	1951	658	Nellie Caroline	1869	343
Michael Glenn	1953	608	Nellie Mae	1932	790
Michael Walter	1957	749	Nellie May	1883	337
Michelle M. Milks	1960	633	Nelma Wanda	1926	707
Michelle M. Milks	1972	472	Nelson Clarence	1879	213
Mildred	1884	369	Nelson Leslie	1884	301
Mildred B.	1912	576	Nelson Leslie III	1954	745
Mildred Evelyn	1926	592	Nelson Leslie, Jr.	1925	500
Mildred M.	1899	303	Neola Ina MYLKES	1910	480
Mildred M.	1927	665	Nettie	1865	241
Mildred Mae	1915	630	Nettie	1865	251
Mildred Marie	1922	572	Newton	1842	234
Milford Edward	1920	648	Nora Olive	1883	410
Milford Edward, Jr. "Butch"	1945	818	Norman Duane	1947	836
Milford Penrose	1888	413	Norman MYLKS	1914	574
Millie May	1876	150	Norris D.	1911	641
Mina Frances	1842	118	Norris D.	1911	683
Mina Marie	1913	602	Obed H. MILK	1837	125
Minnie	1873	321	Oldice Homer Alton	1912	427
Minnie Ann	1878	336	Olive Melvina	1923	500
Minnie C. Milks	1872	169	Opal Pauline	1917	664
Miriam Elizabeth MYLKS	1920	574	Ora Amelia "Amy"	1856	148
Miriam Harlene	1943	470	Orson L.	1891	403
Molly Kathryn	198	894	Orson Leroy	1871	229
Monterville	1833	106	Orval Robert	1912	624
Monteville Samuel	1888	402	Orville Joseph	1930	587
Moses	1820	71	Orville Walter	1913	495
Muriel Lydia Milks	1900	368	Oscar	1877	285
Myron	1913	675	Oscar Wyan	1883	299
Myron MILKS-HOWARD	1913	675	Owen Bernard	1902	310
Myrtle	1882	322	Owen Wade	1968	861
Myrtle A.	1874	408	Owen Willis	1941	737
Myrtle B.	1877	400	Pamela Lynn	1948	785
Myrtle Isobel	1904	405	Parna Rozella	1864	211

Name	Year	Page	Name	Year	Page
Parthena Ann	1844	188	Ralph P., Jr.	1926	624
Parthenia	1912	86	Ramona	1928	585
Patience	1809	86	Ramsey Wade	1973	887
Patience MILK	1753	16	Randall Joseph	1956	793
Patience Milk	1757	19	Randall Lyle	1964	821
Patience MILK	1773	40	Randy J.	1961	822
Patricia	1954	809	Rayburn Lavern	1918	705
Patricia Milks	1950	823	Raymond A., Jr.	1960	822
Patricia Milks		807	Raymond August	1934	662
Patricia Milks		815	Raymond Claude	1910	531
Patricia Rose	1963	802	Raymond Donald	1935	791
Patrick Albert Thomas	1848	161	Raymond G.	1941	668
Patrick Ambrose	1890	313	Raymond Mark	1962	753
Patrick Joseph	1963	755	Raymond Peter	1903	313
Paul D.	1915	680	Rebecca MILK	1759	20
Paul V.	1966	710	Reginald George MYLKES	1907	479
Pauline Milks	1951	814	Reginald Vincent	1927	513
Pauline Tissie	1920	686	Retha Ann	1947	471
Pearl	1881	183	Rhoda MILK	1750	15
Pearl Alma	1904	582	Richard	1820	73
Pearl Anne	1897	316	Richard A.	1944	808
Pearl Melissa	1871	216	Richard Alan	1952	763
Percie L.	1898	444	Richard Allen	1940	813
Perlina MILK	1808	80	Richard Ambrose	1857	153
Permilia MILK	1810	81	Richard Anthony	1905	313
Perry M.	1830	92	Richard Charles	1948	747
Peter	1837	76	Richard Dennis	1950	838
Peter	1854	162	Richard George MILK	1915	547
Peter Felix	1863	164	Richard Graves	1838	142
Phebe	1826	63	Richard Graves	1876	284
Phebe Milk	1753	18	Richard James	1908	373
Phillipe Milks		759	Richard Jerome	1920	390
Phoebe	1809	67	Richard Justin	1969	861
Phoebe Ann	1822	89	Richard Paul	1921	631
Phyllis MILK	1932	772	Richard Paul, Jr.	1949	807
Pollie Alpha	1854	211	Richard William	1925	682
Portia Edna	1888	434	Rick Allen	1951	850
Prince William	1802	47	Rick Eugene	1965	895
Priscilla Ann MILK	1917	548	Robert	1886	436
Priscilla Milks		668	Robert Bart	1907	295
Prudence	1807	86	Robert Dale MILK	1945	769
Prudence Milk	1800	44	Robert Duane, Jr.	1962	825
Rachel Esther Milks	1857	203	Robert Duane, Sr.	1934	667
Ralph Clinton	1922	512	Robert Dudley	1828	72
Ralph P.	1889	397	Robert Edwin, Sr.	1925	851

Name	Year	Num	Name	Year	Num
Robert Ernest	1926	530	Ruth	1859	196
Robert Franklin	1923	373	Ruth	1903	398
Robert Glenn	1934	384	Ruth Amanda	1947	471
Robert Hendricks MILK	1913	547	Ruth Ann	1840	192
Robert John	1950	754	Ruth Ann	1869	263
Robert Keith	1965	861	Ruth Ann Milks	1836	102
Robert Kenneth	1864	159	Ruth Kathryn	1892	353
Robert Lavern II	1961	730	Ruth Louise	1923	549
Robert Laverne	1941	487	Ruth Vivian MILK	1913	466
Robert Leroy	1923	631	S. Ruth Milks		473
Robert Leroy, Jr.	1953	808	Sally A.	1836	140
Robert Peter	1955	598	Sally Ann	1934	798
Robert S. MILK	1852	225	Samuel MILK	1799	34
Robert William	1949	658	Sandra	1943	817
Robert William MILK	1926	555	Sandra	1955	757
Roe Edwin	1883	562	Sandra A. MILK	1951	774
Roger Alan	1941	598	Sandra Yvonne	1946	782
Roger Dean	1947	823	Sara Milks		752
Roger Terry MILK	1948	769	Sarah	1812	48
Roger William	1949	838	Sarah Ann	1844	144
Roland	1883	435	Sarah Ann "Sally"	1803	85
Roland W. "Rod"	1926	810	Sarah Anna	1858	200
Rollin Charles	1904	374	Sarah Elizabeth	1868	149
Ronald D.	1960	820	Sarah Emma	1868	168
Ronald Herbert	1966	755	Sarah Ersula	1849	141
Ronald James	1921	577	Sarah Jane	1837	128
Ronald Owen	1947	763	Sarah Jane	1846	240
Rose	1893	412	Sarah Jane	1858	165
Rose	1964	822	Sarah MILK	1723	9
Rose Mary	1930	813	Sarah MILK	1749	17
Rose Milks	1830	97	Sarah MILK	1787	41
Rosemarie D. Milks	1953	808	Sarah Milks	1950	471
Rosemary	1921	532	Sarah S.	1824	72
Rosemary	1943	794	Sarah Sophronia	1858	223
Ross Elmer MYLKES	1916	480	Sarah W. Milks	1788	39
Ross Frederick MILK	1911	466	Scott Elliott	1962	893
Ross Jennings	1896	430	Scott Murl, Sr.	1955	827
Rowena R. "Tate"	1927	810	Shantel Marie	1970	730
Roxann Marie	1969	822	Sharlene S.	1967	611
Royal George MILK	1918	467	Sharon H. Milks	1948	669
Ruby C.	1883	246	Sharon K.	1949	609
Ruie Caroline	1885	402	Sharon Matilda Milks	1940	736
Russell Harold	1909	461	Sheila	1941	510
Russell J.	1951	815	Shelley	1961	759
Ruth	1775	32	Sheridan Ira	1876	364

Name	Year	Page	Name	Year	Page
Sherman George	1886	217	Thomas W.	1850	195
Sherry M.	1959	826	Thonon Wayne	1909	495
Sherwood Craig	1948	668	Thorah Hannah	1925	522
Shirley	1935	813	Tim G.	1970	900
Shirley Ann	1933	602	Timothy Alan	1965	825
Shirley Belle	1928	513	Tonja Ann	1964	893
Sibyl	1876	243	Trevor	1984	895
Sidney David	1858	242	Trowbridge MILK	1785	36
Silas E.	1841	200	Unknown	1948	795
Silas Edgar	1878	296	Ursula Milks		661
Silas W.	1786	39	Velma Eulalia	1916	705
Silas Wright MILK	1847	125	Velma Milks		409
Sophia Ann Milks	1822	48	Venetta Diane	1949	745
Stephanie Ann	1965	731	Vera	1891	305
Stephanie L. Milks	1977	827	Vera Althea MYLKES	1908	480
Stephanie M.	1980	875	Vera Elaine	1892	443
Stephen	1966	758	Vera V. Milks	1927	576
Stephen Albert	1940	488	Vera Viola	1903	645
Stephen Albert, Jr.	1967	731	Vern Leo	1895	460
Stephen Ernest	1953	746	Verna	1913	511
Stephen MILK	1804	80	Veronica MILK	1919	549
Steven Tracy	1963	893	Victor J.	1901	637
Stewart Lionel MILK	1929	553	Victor J., Jr.	1922	809
Sue	1952	815	Victor Kenneth	1930	462
Susan Elizabeth	1966	731	Vida Bernadette	1927	521
Susan J.	1844	239	Vincent S.	1814	57
Susanne Alvina	1954	489	Viola Reta	1924	521
Suzanne Marie Milks	1970	861	Violet L.	1905	473
Suzanne Milks	1948	836	Virgie M.	1891	159
Tamara Marie	1972	875	Virginia R. Milks	1941	667
Tammy Jo	1961	885	Virginia Rose	1919	385
Teresa A. MILK	1963	876	Wallace B.	1927	666
Teresa Denise	1959	762	Wallace Bruce MILKS KURTZ	1927	666
Teresa Lynn	1964	746	Wallace H.	1863	242
Teressa L.	1852	223	Wallace Joseph	1930	521
Terrel Daniel	1980	885	Walter Bausman	1893	425
Thaddeus Raymond "Ted"	1921	627	Walter H.	1886	358
Thelma Eileen "Teeny"	1922	706	Ward Raymond	1916	677
Thelma Irene	1912	489	Warren	1872	407
Theodore MILK	1924	555	Warren "Jack"	1850	201
Therman Franklin	1919	587	Warren Dempsey	1927	687
Thomas	1941	674	Warren Nelson	1916	575
Thomas Benjamin	1876	263	Warren W.	1922	296
Thomas MILKS FEE	1941	674	Warren Lee	1949	737
Thomas Patrick	1946	611	Washington G.	1836	107

Name	Year	Page	Name	Year	Page
Wayne E.	1949	806	William Willard W.	1909	295
Wayne Elias	1935	736	William Woods	1910	439
Wayne Richard	1947	732	William Woods	1943	684
Wayne Robert	1929	797	William Woods III	1970	840
Wendy Elaine	1952	753	Wilma R.	1918	615
Wesley Albert	1943	741	Winifred L.	1921	612
Wesley Jonathan "Doad"	1892	300	Winifred May	1913	439
Wilbur L..	1916	646	Winnifred J. L.	1911	511
Willard	1844	234	Winona	1912	623
William (c1950)		752	Wyan Wesley	1936	736
William A.	1872	252	Zadia Ella	1863	154
William Alexander Wilson	1889	307	Zadie Ann	1881	410
William Alonzo	1845	222	Zella L.	1875	119
William Ann	1950	488	Zelma Arlene	1921	705
William Asahel "Ace"	1888	304	Zerelda Peterson MYLKES	1904	479
William Claude	1886	367	Zeruah	1831	119
William Claude	1924	588			
William Claude III	1949	795			
William Clifton	1942	611			
William Edward	1874	391			
William Edwin MILK	1849	265			
William Fisher	1929	374			
William Frederick R. "Fred"	1894	316			
William H.	1878	213			
William Henry	1885	151			
William Henry	1895	423			
William James	1927	530			
William Jay	1918	532			
William Jewett MILK	1813	78			
William Jewett MILK	1842	171			
William Job	1892	220			
William John	1919	522			
William Joseph	1924	509			
William L. L.	1916	512			
William Leander	1852	343			
William Michael	1964	731			
William MILK	1783	25			
William MILK	1865	183			
William Patrick	1932	389			
William Paul	1966	710			
William Roger	1943	669			
William S.	1884	352			
William Thomas	1867	158			
William W. MILK	1807	53			
William Wesley	1897	367			

A

Surname	Given	Birth	Page
AARRESTAD	Torvald	1896	450
ABELL	Ethel Mae	1860	141
ABLEY	Maria E.	1860	196
ABRAMS	Calvin I.	1927	659
ACHESON	Joseph Robert Ross	1891	306
ACKERMAN	Marion	1915	648
ACKLER	Susan		838
ACKLEY	Emma	1857	247
ACKLEY	George Delos	1853	211
ACKLEY	Myrtle	1879	370
ADAIR	James Alex	1971	843
ADAIR	John	1939	695
ADAMS	Archie	1899	490
ADAMS	Archie	1899	491
ADAMS	Beverly Marion	1923	732
ADAMS	Clara		199
ADAMS	Clara		355
ADAMS	Edwin Simeon	1867	297
ADAMS	Ethel Leona	1914	691
ADAMS	Gilbert	1838	152
ADAMS	Gilbert Daniel	1892	490
ADAMS	Hattie Lenore	1895	490
ADAMS	Ida Luzina	1867	259
ADAMS	Joseph William	1872	288
ADAMS	Lawrence W.	1901	479
ADAMS	Lena C.	1876	210
ADAMS	Leroy	1904	491
ADAMS	Lovina	1810	107
ADAMS	Nancy W.		559
ADAMS	Robert Archie	1946	741
ADAMS	Roger Keating	1905	391
ADAMS	Saloma	1813	49
ADAMS	Stanley E.	1921	732
ADAMS	Tillman	1863	169
ADCOX	Virginia Clyde	1941	598
ADDY	Marlow	1905	579
ADEL	Mr.	1938	606
ADREON	Gary L.	1960	715
AFARION	Rebecca Elizabeth	1912	534
AGNEW	Betty G.	1923	594
AGNEW	Leslie W.	1920	594
AGNEW	Mr.		899
AGNEW	Ralph	1880	370
AINSWORTH	Ida May	1858	238
AKOM	Nancy Beth	1954	879
ALBERT	Eva	1874	285
			1
ALBERT	Nettie Ethel	1891	286
ALBRECHT	Louise D.	1866	228
ALBRIGHT	Jason Jeffery	1981	910
ALBRIGHT	Jon J.	1955	902
ALDRICH	Everett L.	1915	672
ALDRIDGE	Anna Mae	1869	286
ALEXANDER	William A.		203
ALFORD	James Allen	1922	571
ALFORD	Joan Elizabeth	1959	845
ALFORD	Lorelle Edward	1928	701
ALFORD	William Thomas	1894	458
ALFSON	Willard James	1916	690
ALGYA	Crystal Sue	1968	796
ALLARD	Arthur	1922	818
ALLEN	Aaron	1835	116
ALLEN	Albert Clinton	1917	636
ALLEN	Ann Marie	1820	64
ALLEN	Carol Jewell	1883	404
ALLEN	Charles Leroy	1916	676
ALLEN	Daniel W.	1849	252
ALLEN	Doris I.	1912	636
ALLEN	Eber	1887	413
ALLEN	Ethel	1878	438
ALLEN	Eunice	1786	28
ALLEN	Florence L.	1910	647
ALLEN	Frances	1915	473
ALLEN	Frances A.	1906	636
ALLEN	Gertrude A.	1913	648
ALLEN	Gilbert Wallace	1851	250
ALLEN	Helen L.	1907	636
ALLEN	Henry W.	1892	421
ALLEN	Humphrey B.	1809	62
ALLEN	Isaac	1883	434
ALLEN	Janet	1922	474
ALLEN	Lawrence G.	1909	647
ALLEN	Margaret H.	1824	91
ALLEN	Ralph F.	1883	406
ALLEN	Rhema Arlene	1920	676
ALLEN	Rosalie	1858	250
ALLEN	Ruby	1916	648
ALLEN	Sherwin Edgar	1922	677

ALLEN	Vera Irene	1911	676	ANDREWS	Sally	1801	67
ALLEN	William V.	1884	282	ANHALT	Alvin	1906	684
ALLIO	James N.	1862	393	ANSON	Charles	1880	318
ALLIO	James Newell	1937	799	ANTHONY	George	1865	253
ALLIO	James Raymond	1910	616	APPLETON	Jon Virgil	1964	888
Allio	Margaret D.	1945	799	APPLETON	Virgil L.	1940	805
ALLIO	Wilbur Lawrence	1933	799	ARBEITER	Henry J.	1947	829
ALLISON	Amanda Dawn	1984	905	ARGENBRIGHT	Arnie D.	1901	483
ALLISON	Michael Daryl	1957	856	ARMITAGE	Clinton	1926	761
ALLWOOD	Alice Marie	1943	836	ARMSTRONG	Curt Reynolds	1867	278
ALLWOOD	Doris	1946	837	ARMSTRONG	Florence	1920	461
ALLWOOD	Hazel	1947	837	ARMSTRONG	Frances		529
ALLWOOD	Leon Leroy	1905	682	ARMSTRONG	Hazel Lottridge	1896	472
ALTMAN	Cyrus	1850	279	ARNOLD	Avery A.	1917	843
ALTON	Phillip Carey	1957	854	ARNOLD	Edson	1894	690
AMELL	Francis Wilson	1917	676	ARNOLD	Eric		869
AMELOTTE	Cheryl A.	1957	839	ARNOLD	Henry F.	1910	718
AMES	Andrew	1864	364	ARNOLD	Lester F.	1899	492
AMES	Esther Mary	1901	582	ARNOLD	Lucinda H.	1951	611
AMES	Etta Macie	1906	582	ARNOLD	Mahala	1827	111
AMES	Minnie Pearl	1904	582	ARNOLD	Mr.		892
AMES	Roy F.	1887	301	ARNOLD	Polly Ann	1824	110
ANDERSON	Andrea L.	1967	893	ARNOLD	Robert R.	1938	812
ANDERSON	Anita L.	1964	893	ARNOLD	Steve C.	1967	895
ANDERSON	Charles	1843	204	ARNOLDT	Mr.		388
ANDERSON	Clarence Leonard	1896	320	ARRANCE	Paul B.	1908	643
ANDERSON	Clement Bailey		746	ARTHUR	Betty	1943	844
ANDERSON	Duane F.	1940	816	ARTHUR	Chad	1979	899
ANDERSON	Frank Howard	1870	361	ARTHUR	Earl P.	1919	697
ANDERSON	Howard Stone	1905	579	ARTHUR	Eileen Rae	1953	844
ANDERSON	James Elmer	1868	361	ARTHUR	Emma Dorothy	1910	474
ANDERSON	Jennifer Stokes	1945	738	Arthur	Florida V.	1951	845
ANDERSON	John A.	1840	72	ARTHUR	Harold Lewis	1894	455
ANDERSON	Mabel Harriet	1921	594	ARTHUR	Jerry Wayne	1952	845
ANDERSON	Ruth	1895	579	Arthur	Jo E.	1953	844
ANDERSON	Sarah	1837	131	Arthur	Rebecca Sue	1953	845
ANDERSON	Talina	1906	337	ARTHUR	Robert Harold	1917	697
ANDERST	Darlene Marilyn	1935	703	ARTHUR	Rodney E.	1957	845
ANDRES	Violet	1894	393	ARTHUR	Vernon H.	1950	844
ANDREW	Barbara	1918	818	ASHLEY	Cread	1927	790
ANDREW	Faith	1920	818	ASHLEY	Elsie	1885	322
ANDREW	James	1886	649	ASHELY	Nicole	1970	861
ANDREW	Shirley	1922	818	ASLIN	Florence Rose	1887	376
ANDREWS	Ephraim	1772	30	ATTENBERGER	Niles J.	1941	736
				ATWELL	Beverly Ann	1956	824

AUER	Edwin Rugby	1882	465
AUER	Edwin Rugby	1922	713
AUER	Martin S.	1918	713
AUGUSTINE	Walter	1917	623
AUSTIN	Billy Joe	1941	725
AUSTIN	Robert, III	1970	859
AUSTIN	William Brian	1970	857
AVERILL	James Kent	1904	391
AVERY	James W.	1893	425
AYCOCK	Gordon L	1948	850
AYCOCK	Robby	1970	903
AYERS	Kenneth Emory	1904	532
AYERS	Laurence L.	1908	533
Ayers	Minnie	1902	532
AYERS	Vernon	1880	322

B

BABCOCK	Darius	1820	95
BABCOCK	Ellen A.	1840	206
BABCOCK	Julia Catherine	1846	207
BACHMAN	Frederick	1903	477
BACHMAN	Frederick E.	1875	284
Bachman	Marie	1904	477
BACON	Anna Zeruah	1885	444
BACON	Lucius	1855	254
BACON	Mabel	1877	444
BACON	Peter	1830	119
BACON	Timothy		886
BAHR	Myrta May	1882	151
BAILEY	Beatrice	1906	616
BAILEY	Carolyn Lee	1947	486
BAILEY	Gettie	1901	618
BAILEY	Herman	1883	393
BAILEY	James	1930	674
BAILEY	James Robert	1952	829
BAILEY	Margaret M.	1921	616
BAILEY	Milton O.	1883	341
BAILEY	Oel	1854	223
BAILEY	Phebe	1815	71
BAILEY	Rita A.	1912	672
BAILEY	Rogers Elmer	1918	673
BAILEY	Rowena Gertrude	1915	672
Bailey	Wanda Aletha	1955	829
BAILEY	Willard Elwood	1892	430
BAINK	Helen K.	1890	356
BAINWAY	Francis	1801	67
BAINWAY	Mary Ida	1844	139
Baker	Bonnie C	1942	729
BAKER	Dorothea		796
BAKER	Edith	1892	359
BAKER	Frederick Harry	1935	729
BAKER	Harry	1912	486
BAKER	James C.	1942	729
BAKER	Jennie	1851	117
BAKER	Love G.	1806	29
BAKER	Mary	1780	35
BAKER	Mary	1859	253
BAKER	Roy E.	1909	699
BAKER	Sarah	1835	106

Surname	Given Name	Year	Page	Surname	Given Name	Year	Page
BAKER	Susanne K.	1964	860	BARLOW	John Clifford	1918	767
BAKER	Thomas C.	1841	133	BARNARD	Adonijah	1770	32
BALCOM	Alison W.		907	BARNARD	Adonijah, Jr.	1811	71
BALDWIN	Betty Lee	1922	576	BARNARD	Charles Fuller	1859	286
BALDWIN	Christopher Edw.	1948	753	BARNARD	George	1805	70
BALDWIN	Edward	1882	454	BARNARD	George	1833	147
BALDWIN	Jacob	1863	284	BARNARD	Harriet	1815	71
BALDWIN	Kate B.	1859	209	BARNARD	James	1855	238
BALDWIN	Martha	1915	697	BARNARD	Julia Fuller	1897	478
BALDWIN	Martin Copp	1915	696	BARNARD	Martin Miller	1834	147
BALDWIN	Mary Josephine	1880	397	BARNARD	Millie	1877	416
BALDWIN	Melvina H.	1838	175	BARNARD	Polly	1796	70
BALL	Bert Clarence	1883	293	BARNES	Asa Randall	1859	269
BALL	Beulah Ailleen	1898	710	BARNES	Burr T.	1888	455
BALL	Curtis Mack	1849	345	BARNES	Delorne G.	1917	698
BALL	Ira Eddie	1820	190	BARNES	Edith F. Emma	1875	165
BALL	Thomas W.	1920	646	BARNES	Edna Eunice	1907	479
BALL	Wealthy	1823	188	BARNES	Emily Alice	1912	431
BALL	Winifred	1880	563	BARNES	Gloria Mae	1930	623
BALLARD	Bradley	1964	888	Barnes	Inez Roseann	1926	698
BALLEW	Owen	1915	671	BARNES	Kim A.	1961	845
BALUCH	Ronald E. Stephen		874	BARNES	Laurel J.	1867	261
BANCROFT	Alfreda V.	1905	531	BARNES	Mr.	1847	119
BANCROFT	Gladys D.	1903	530	BARNES	Nettie		314
BANCROFT	John	1856	280	Barnes	Rochelle	1963	845
BANKS	Caroline	1876	538	BARNES	Thomas	1849	146
BANKS	Charles	1853	328	BARNETT	James O.	1923	702
BANKS	Marvin W.	1882	538	BARNEY	Paul James	1893	259
BANKS	Maryetta	1916	764	BARNHART	Carolee Irene	1925	595
BANKS	Myron James	1878	538	BARNHART	Eldred Wellington	1884	371
BANTIN	Susan Ann	1954	815	BARNHART	Kenneth Allen	1921	594
BARGY	Maxine	1937	621	BARNHART	Laurel Eldrene	1917	594
BARHYDT	Chauncey	1869	279	BARNUM	Carrie		277
BARKER	Charles	1827	109	BARNUM	Stephana Ostrum	1882	222
BARKER	Clyde	1912	569	BARRETT	Charles	1899	491
BARKER	Dale E.	1918	569	BARRY	Debbie Lynn		756
BARKER	Emma Janella	1868	232	BARRY	Diana Lynn	1954	755
BARKER	Esther	1903	569	BARRY	Harry M.	1871	538
BARKER	Ethel	1915	569	BARRY	Marguerite	1906	764
BARKER	Helen	1907	569	BARSE	Martha	1830	109
BARKER	Jay Thomas	1880	353	BARSOTTI	Arthur	1914	675
BARKER	Mabel	1878	352	BARTHEL	Leslie James	1950	821
BARKER	Sarah	1829	66	BARTLETT	Albert H.	1893	639
BARKER	Scott	1854	195	BARTLETT	Alice Hester	1888	448
BARKER	Viva	1905	569	BARTLETT	Ethel Dovy	1897	449

BARTLETT	Eva Estella	1885	448	BEACH	Richard	1917	766
BARTLETT	Kenneth Wayne	1961	802	BEACOM	Kim	1955	892
BARTLETT	William F.	1859	257	BEADLE	Euptra B. "Fay"	1890	273
BARTLOW	Alice Lillian	1919	372	BEAMISH	Angela	1970	861
BARTON	Eliz. Sherwood	1916	272	BEAR	Ethel Estella	1896	491
BARTON	Ella Gay	1896	291	BEARD	Mayme Bell	1869	171
BARTON	Ernest A.	1891	292	BEATTY	Bill	1923	652
BARTON	Goldie M.	1902	544	BEAVER	Melissa	1848	102
BARTON	Hubert Crampton	1887	127	BECKER	Beatrice	1922	475
BARTON	Hubert Crampton	1910	271	BECKER	Elizabeth	1855	328
BARTON	Mary "Nancy"	1785	27	BECKER	Fird	1889	764
BARTON	Mary Hathaway	1923	272	BECKER	Jennie	1851	117
BARTON	Minnie Belle	1915	485	BECKER	John C.	1896	539
BARTON	Nora	1941	470	BECKER	Paul J.	1921	765
BARTON	Preston Nichols	1913	272	BEDAU	Brent	1976	866
BARTON	Reta		516	BEECHER	Frederick Russell	1900	551
BARTON	Sherwood	1936	469	BEECHER	Viola	1927	772
BARTON	Thyrza Stevens	1921	272	BEECHER	Wenona	1929	772
BASHORE	Sandra Sue		751	BEEDING	Daniel L.	1981	910
BATER	Nora	1926	560	Beers	Ann Marie	1950	828
BATES	Asa	1793	41	BEERS	Cynthia J.	1951	829
Bates	Bessie C.	1877	208	BEERS	Herman William	1891	429
BATES	Charles Franklin	1871	208	BEERS	Mildred	1894	400
BATES	Charles W.	1830	97	BEERS	Richard D.	1920	670
BATES	Flora M.	1880	208	BEERS	Steven Douglas	1947	828
BATES	John A.	1819	95	BEETON	Louise	1903	213
Bates	Lisa		731	BEEVER	Melissa	1848	102
Bates	Lurinda F.	1821	95	BEHNKE	Edward Charles	1958	825
BATES	Mary Ann	1826	95	BELL	Chandra Darlene	1969	825
BATES	Matthew S.	1971	731	BELL	Jacob F.	1825	123
BATES	Morley James	1935	487	BELL	Priscilla	1971	750
BATES	Nelson L.	1827	97	BELL	Violet	1906	695
BATES	Roxcena	1815	95	BELLAND	Pearl Arlene	1918	498
BATTEY	Doris Emma	1910	580	BELLEROSE	Roger	1945	523
BAUER	Marguerite E.	1907	429	BELLINGER	Heather Lynn	1977	871
BAUGHMAN	Doris J.	1942	808	BELLINGER	Jo Ann		746
BAUMAN	Charles P.	1865	280	BELNAP	Cornelia L.	1839	172
BAUMAN	Donald H., Jr.	1939	786	BELNAPP	Naomi	1900	283
BAUSMAN	Lovina	1859	242	Belscher	Elizabeth	1940	799
BAXTER	Andrew E.	1980	717	BELSCHER	Gurney	1905	615
BAXTER	Michael J.	1948	795	BELSCHER	James H.	1935	799
BAXTER	Mr.	1915	697	BEMAN	John Leo	1897	398
BAYLEY	Dale		758	BEMIS	Asaph S.	1817	104
BAYNE	Mary	1860	199	BEMUS	Donna Louise	1895	320
BEACH	Ralph Wilson	1920	680	BEMUS	Elizabeth	1868	169

Surname	Given Name	Year	Page	Surname	Given Name	Year	Page
BEMUS	Erastus J.	1824	77	BENSON	Lydia	1833	119
Bemus	June	1895	320	BENSON	Marilyn E.	1923	604
BEMUS	Lloyd G.	1891	320	BENSON	Mary Jane	1831	119
BEMUS	Oscar E.	1863	169	BENSON	Mildred	1900	450
Bemus	Theresa	1901	320	BENSON	Myrtle Olivia	1894	259
BENDA	Geraldine Angela	1974	903	Benson	Phyllis E.	1929	603
BENDA	Terry Ludwig	1946	850	BENSON	Phyllis W.	1918	603
BENEDICT	Alice Hanning	1851	137	BENSON	Quenten Eugene	1926	451
BENEDICT	George William	1803	65	BENSON	Roy Edward	1891	258
BENEFIELD	C. D.		480	BENSON	Russell	1916	451
BENESH	Jerome Dale	1944	794	BENSON	Russell Leroy	1917	603
BENJAMIN	Ruby May	1918	532	BENSON	Ruth	1839	120
BENNETT	Audrey	1920	534	BENSON	Ruth	1918	603
BENNETT	Julia Evelyn	1877	299	BENSON	Ruth Anna	1898	379
BENNETT	Mary E.	1846	72	BENSON	Seneca	1810	48
BENOIT	Scott		893	BENSON	Sophronia	170	20
BENSON	Adelbert Theodore	1910	259	BENSON	Violet Gertrude	1913	451
BENSON	Arthur	1905	533	BENSON	Violet M.	1907	381
BENSON	Arvilla	1847	120	BENTLEY	Catherine J.	1839	142
BENSON	Benjamin J.	1870	258	BENTLEY	Deforest	1854	254
BENSON	Bertha	1904	451	BENTLEY	Hiram	1828	119
Benson	Betty		603	BERG	Nellie	1887	416
BENSON	Caroline Sarah	1843	120	BERGERON	Elizabeth	1947	658
BENSON	Clarence Eugene	1900	259	BERGHOLTZ	Gregory S. M.	1963	829
BENSON	Cora A.	1896	450	BERGHOLTZ	Robert William	1929	673
BENSON	Donald	1924	603	BERGQUIST	Mary Ann	1931	722
BENSON	Effie Adella	1904	259	BERKEY	Elmer I.	1945	609
BENSON	Emmet H.	1892	379	BERNARD	George J.	1887	619
BENSON	Ernest Clifford	1894	379	BERREA	Joan	1936	516
BENSON	Floyd Ernest	1916	451	BERTRAND	Yvon F.	1924	522
BENSON	Frank M.	1903	380	BEST	Marjorie J.	1929	835
BENSON	Fred Ernest	1907	259	BETHUNE	William John	1932	784
BENSON	George Martin	1868	216	BEYER	Andrea Sue	1966	906
BENSON	Gladys Irene	1900	380	BEYER	Arnold Raymond	1948	862
BENSON	Grace Mae	1885	258	BEYER	Gary J.	1948	862
BENSON	Harold G.	1905	380	BICK	Harry I.	1913	474
BENSON	Helen J.	1925	604	BIEDEKAPP	Amelia	1860	181
BENSON	Herbert	1898	450	BIEDEKAPP	Mary Catherine	1863	182
BENSON	Howard	1914	381	BIGGART	Francis James	1843	144
BENSON	Jack Owen	1921	603	BIGHAM	William	1898	444
BENSON	John Milks	1849	121	BILGER	Maurine	1928	607
BENSON	John Rial	1883	258	BINNING	Gary Allen	1960	762
BENSON	Keith M.		603	BIRNEY	John Francis	1865	169
BENSON	Keith M., Jr.	1945	797	BIRRELL	Jamesina	1910	295
BENSON	Leroy Ellis	1890	379	BISDORF	Elizabeth D.	1898	458

Surname	Given	Year	Page	Surname	Given	Year	Page
BISHOP	Bernice	1932	530	**BLOSSOM**	Elijah	1779	28
BISHOP	Edward Sidney	1892	316	**BLOSSOM**	Esther B.	1821	62
BISHOP	Hazel Margarite	1903	372	**BLOSSOM**	Frances Maria	1850	132
BISHOP	Lloyd	1921	530	**BLOSSOM**	Mary Ella	1879	275
BISHOP	Ralph A.	1901	546	**BLOSSOM**	Susan Miller	1887	275
BISHOP	Velma Irene	1911	641	**BLOSSOM**	William Elijah	1860	132
BISHOP	Velma Storey	1922	530	**BLOUGH**	Milan	1920	685
BITLER	Luther Elmer	1942	747	**BLUE**	Lillian I.	1900	490
BITLER	Sandra Lou Ann	1968	872	**BLUMENRADER**	Mr.		702
BITLER	Sherri Lynn	1963	871	**Bly**	Alison W.	1965	897
BITLER	William Luther	1965	871	**BLY**	Carl Thomas	1940	834
BIXBY	Albert Rufus		218	**BLY**	Scott Carl	1964	897
BJERKAAS	Robert Dale	1939	606	**BLY**	Steven C.	1963	897
BJORHEIM	Amy		902	**BLY**	Vernon Thomas	1903	678
BLACK	Lula Mae		655	**BOAM**	Harriet G.	1826	71
BLACK	Scott		796	**BOARDMAN**	Elizabeth Marna	1924	642
BLACK	Vincent	1922	594	**BOARDMAN**	Frank E.	1875	444
BLACKCHIEF	Darryl James	1979	910	**BOARDMAN**	Mattie E.	1894	690
BLACKMAN	Charles H.	1856	346	**BODEN**	Eleanor	1765	23
BLACKMAN	Mary	1864	365	**BOETHEL**	Cassandra K.	1969	894
BLAKE	Esther	1850	171	**BOGUE**	George McClelland		725
BLAKE	Henry	1841	171	**BOHALL**	Curtiss C.	1934	684
BLANCHARD	Earl Evans	1954	880	**BOHEM**	Irma	1921	627
BLANCHARD	Maria Elizabeth	1846	180	**BOILEAN**	Beatrice	1900	472
BLANCHFIELD	Mary M. Mildred	1893	311	**BOLDING**	Ernest E.	1910	583
BLANKENSHIP	Howard L.	1936	824	**BOLGER**	Alfred	1863	267
Blatter	Annie K. D.	1950	850	**BOLLINGER**	Delmar	1935	608
BLATTER	Elberta Jean	1948	850	**BOLLMAN**	Harry E.	1903	338
BLATTER	Ivan Wade	1923	707	**BOLTON**	Robert		543
BLATTER	Michael Wade	1947	850	**BOMAN**	Douglas	1970	872
BLATTER	Ruby Ann	1952	850	**BOMBARD**	Norma M.	1917	704
BLAYLOCK	Amanda Novella	1933	485	**BOMGAARS**	Mr.		877
BLAZER	Robert Owen	1924	592	**BOND**	Cora Elizabeth	1896	459
BLECHA	Larry	1954	889	**BOND**	Donna Jean	1928	703
BLECHA	Maurice	1930	810	**BOND**	Dorothy Leila	1913	702
BLISH	Jane	1800	36	**BOND**	Dorothy Marg.	1906	459
BLISS	David Carl	1947	749	**BOND**	Dwight		651
BLOOD	Charles	1847	129	**Bond**	Erma	1918	458
BLOOD	Luther La Due	1882	420	**BOND**	Frank Lawrence	1860	263
BLOOM	Barbara Joyce	1928	469	**BOND**	Harry Elwin	1890	458
BLOOM	Leslye E.	1956	719	**BOND**	Lenora	1898	459
BLOSSOM	Barnabas	1825	62	**BOND**	Lucy Orinda	1892	458
BLOSSOM	Benjamin B.	1811	61	**BOND**	Myra O.	1888	458
BLOSSOM	Clarissa	1815	61	**BOND**	Olive Hazel	1894	459
BLOSSOM	Eli Walter	1850	132	**BOND**	Rebecca	1975	906

Surname	Given	Year	Page	Surname	Given	Year	Page
BOND	Thomas Bonnell	1904	459	BOYER	James A., III	1966	886
BONGIARDINO	Tracey Ann	1967	876	BOYER	James Albert	1909	614
BONSOR	Hilda Mae	1900	581	BOYER	James Albert, Jr.	1934	798
BOOKMAN	Sylvia Agnes	1897	449	BOYER	Karen		886
BOOTH	Clause	1887	619	Boyer	Lisa Marie	1966	886
BOOTH	Margaret		518	BOYER	Marjorie	1921	531
BOOTY	Marjorie Marion	1930	509	BOYER	Thomas	1893	563
BORDELEAU	Christopher Lee	1976	899	BOYLE	John Nelson	1895	574
BORDEN	Russell Smith	1812	61	BOYLE	Martha Ann	1927	785
BORDMAN	Lillie Diana	1862	235	BRACEY	Susan Lynn	1952	725
BORG	Gladys Marie	1929	687	BRACY	Lucien	1878	325
BORN	Elizabeth Agnes	1890	258	BRADFORD	William Hamilton	1929	790
BOSSERDET	Susan Jane	1943	741	BRADLEY	Craig		528
BOSWELL	Amasa S.	1849	235	BRADLEY	Edna	1896	460
BOSWELL	Benjamin M.	1879	409	BRADLEY	Harold	1895	315
BOSWELL	Francis E.	1908	776	BRADLEY	Mary	1854	133
BOSWELL	Lydia A.	1860	235	Bradley	Mary		528
BOSWELL	Margaret M.	1915	776	BRADLEY	Melville		528
BOSWELL	William H.	1883	561	BRADLEY	Russell	1919	685
BOTHWELL	Caroline A	1851	253	Bradley	Unknown	1826	63
BOTHWELL	Charlotte Eliza	1858	280	BRADY	Beatrice E.	1901	637
BOTHWELL	Flora J.	1857	253	BRAKKE	Clara	1883	219
BOTHWELL	George B.	1824	137	BRAMAN	Clara	1870	172
BOTHWELL	George Grant	1867	254	BRAMMER	Nancy J.	1855	345
BOTHWELL	John Brady	1805	118	BRANSON	Betsy Ann	1935	632
BOTHWELL	John J.	1859	253	BRANSON	Billie Jo	1979	859
BOTHWELL	Lydia Zeruie	1865	253	BRANSON	Billy	1950	728
BOTHWELL	Lydia Zeruie	1865	263	BRANSON	Tabitha Dawn	1972	859
BOTHWELL	Mary E.	1849	252	BRANSON	Tina Denise	1975	859
BOTTING	Joan		528	BRAY	Constance Jeanette	1944	674
BOUCHER	Frances Laura	1860	158	BRAY	Nellie Jane	1872	215
BOUDREAU	Adeline Helen	1920	467	BRAYTON	Altha	1900	579
BOULA	Arthur Richard	1959	826	BRAYTON	Belva Marilyn	1934	787
BOURLAND	Mr.	1943	837	Brayton	Bevin Sue	1957	787
BOUSTEAD	Glen	1960	883	BRAYTON	Biship Elton	1905	580
BOWDEN	Edna May	1887	391	BRAYTON	Blaine William	1935	787
BOWDEN	Lillie Thurman	1888	397	BRAYTON	Dan L.	1907	580
BOWMAN	Bradley K.	1946	741	BRAYTON	Frank Ernest	1881	362
BOWMAN	Joseph B.	1820	62	BRAYTON	Helen L.	1896	580
BOWMAN	May E.	1882	296	BRAYTON	Linus	1841	205
BOWMAN	Melissa Maria	1970	867	BRAYTON	Mabel	1897	579
BOWMAN	Savilla A.	1903	413	BRAYTON	Robert Linus	1874	362
BOYENS	Andrea L.	1958	611	BRAYTON	Robert Vivian	1906	580
BOYER	Edna	1930	798	BRAYTON	William O.	1870	361
BOYER	Goldie Sadie	1890	394	BRAZEE	Floyd	1875	286

BRAZIE	Cecil Melvin	1930	771	HOFFERT			
BRAZIE	Charles Edmond	1873	335	BROOKE	Thomas	1900	447
BRAZIE	Charles Joseph		877	BROOKMAN	Eva	1907	636
BRAZIE	Clayton P.	1904	551	BROOKS	Ambrose Hensie	1855	208
Brazie	Dana		877	Brooks	Deborah S.	1958	889
BRAZIE	David Edward		877	BROOKS	Earl H.	1925	808
BRAZIE	Emmet A.	1886	336	BROOKS	Michael E.	1956	889
BRAZIE	Kenneth Charles	1912	551	BROOKS	Michael J.	1957	821
BRAZIE	Melvin	1851	182	BROOKS	Mr.		837
BRAZIE	Royal Melvin	1894	551	BROTH	Mary	1850	115
BRAZIE	Susan Mildred	1910	551	BROTT	Virginia B.	1911	358
BRAZIE	Timothy		877	BROULIK	William Donald	1928	686
BREAKEY	William O.	1891	319	BROW	Reynold James	1934	738
BRECKENRIDGE	Harriett H.	1820	65	BROWN	Anita May	1912	468
BREESE	Allie	1889	355	BROWN	Anna	1880	415
BRELAND	Melba	1921	788	BROWN	Benjamin W.	1881	563
BREWER	Hannah Mahala	1842	101	BROWN	Betty		651
BREWER	Lois Mae	1945	622	BROWN	Brenda	1944	728
BRIANS	Minnie M.	1909	583	BROWN	Clifford Ray	1885	269
BRICTSON	Charles	1940	782	BROWN	Clint W.	1913	485
BRIGGS	Henry	1900	625	BROWN	Daniel Lee	1963	869
BRIGGS	Lori J.	1952	658	BROWN	David Edward		746
BRIGGS	Mary Ella	1853	103	BROWN	Deane Marie	1938	486
BRIGGS	Mr.	1895	281	BROWN	Deanna Jean	1938	739
BRIGGS	Nancy	1930	762	BROWN	Dennis Lee	1950	849
BRIMMER	Evaline Lucinda	1825	63	BROWN	Edna Mary	1878	352
BRIMMER	Gladys I.	1907	302	BROWN	Ethel E.	1887	415
BROBST	Gertrude Faye	1897	372	BROWN	Francine Anne	1946	669
BROCK	Delores Elizabeth	1928	833	BROWN	Frank	1902	614
BROCK	John	1882	434	BROWN	Gene Lyle	1926	468
BROCK	Paul Ethelbert	1909	676	BROWN	Harold	1897	407
BROCK	Stuart Philip	1917	272	BROWN	Harriet P.		130
BROCK	William Gerald	1933	833	BROWN	Jane E.	1866	132
BROCKITT	Josephine	1884	398	BROWN	Janice		651
Brockitt	Margaret A.	1911	624	BROWN	John W.	1850	238
Brockitt	Nettie	1885	399	BROWN	Lyle Dale	1920	706
BROCKITT	Norman Alexander	1886	399	BROWN	Mary Ann	1827	94
BROCKITT	Orval E.	1917	624	BROWN	Mary Louise	1940	849
BROCKITT	Warren E.	1854	225	BROWN	Michele Rae	1967	901
BROCKITT	William	1887	399	BROWN	Minnie		537
BRODERICK	Mr.	1930	694	BROWN	Mr.		848
BROMLEY	Mr.	1935	469	BROWN	Mr.		901
BRONSON	George	1889	453	BROWN	Palmer	1824	59
BRONSON	William	1916	585	BROWN	R. Emerson	1883	415
BRONSON-	Erma L.	1915	696	BROWN	Robert Laurelle	1929	469

BROWN	Sarah	1720	7	BUCKLEY	John		339
BROWN	Sarah A.	1881	358	BUFFINGTON	Phene A.	1852	248
BROWN	Sylvia Kathryn	1929	686	BULFINCH	George H.	1859	348
BROWN	Virginia		651	BULFINCH	Ruth E.	1897	565
BROWN	Wallace E.	1875	415	BULL	Archie John	1884	393
BROWN-BOYER	Edna	1930	798	BULL	Clifford James	1908	615
BROWNE	Merton T.	1920	761	BULL	Douglas J.	1963	887
BROWNE	Susannah	1735	13	BULL	Esther	1770	29
BROWNELL	Albert R.	1865	278	Bull	Faith	1938	799
BROWNELL	Alice C.	1847	131	BULL	Isaac	1746	17
BROWNELL	Amy Shepherd	1814	53	BULL	James	1851	222
BROWNELL	Amy Shepherd	1814	59	BULL	Richard E.	1936	799
BROWNELL	Benjamin	1760	16	BULL	Richard E., II	1961	887
BROWNELL	David Milk	1789	26	BULLARD	Emma	1868	414
BROWNELL	Ezra Plummer	1819	64	BULLIS	Mr.	1845	160
BROWNELL	George	1746	15	BULLOCK	Maud Elsie	1894	422
BROWNELL	George Milk	1787	26	BUMGARNER	Cecil James, Jr.	1929	792
BROWNELL	Holder White	1800	29	BUMGARNER	Christopher David	1970	860
BROWNELL	Jirah	1786	29	BUMP	Genie Hazel	1892	293
Brownell	Mary H.	1866	278	BUMPUS	William		263
BROWNELL	Phebe	1758	16	BUNK	Lucinda J.	1954	889
BROWNELL	Stephen A.	1844	136	BURBECK	Edward	1741	13
BROWNING	Charles Russell	1973	885	BURCH	Otis	1917	584
BROWNLEE	Jemina	1847	160	BURCHARD	Beatrice A. E.	1877	212
BROWNLEE	Woodrow W.		789	BURCHARD	Edith Sophia	1864	212
BRUBAKER	Patricia Mary	1931	503	BURCHARD	Grace Anna	1869	211
BRUNDAGE	Albert	1903	567	BURCHARD	Joseph Clark	1833	99
BRUNDAGE	Ruth Ann	1929	782	BURCHARD	Mara Eleanor	1862	211
Bruneau	Deboorah A.	1951	846	BURCO	Darwin Paul	1929	847
BRUNEAU	John Joseph	1926	704	BURCO	Kim Bryan	1956	900
BRUNEAU	Joseph Theodore	1906	459	BURCO	Ms.	1960	900
BRUNEAU	Michael Lawrence	1951	846	BURDICK	Myrtle D.	1890	561
BRUNEAU	Nancy Lee	1933	704	BURGESS	Priscilla		559
BRUNEAU	Neil Paul	1953	847	BURKE	Mary Frances	1863	163
BRUNEAU	Paul Arthur	1931	704	BURKHART	Ross	1910	689
BRUNETTE	Adeline	1924	512	BURKHART	Ross Allan	1942	842
BRUNNER	Pearl Elizabeth	1903	363	BURKWELL	Bertha	1917	653
BRYANT	Leona Ruth	1924	620	BURLESON	Charles F.	1939	625
BRYANT	Mr.	1940	470	BURLESON	Theodore C.	1902	400
BUCHANAN	Kathryn	1903	425	BURNETT	Ellis R.	1927	764
BUCK	Margaret		601	BURNETT	Leroy	1885	539
BUCKINGHAM	Anthony	1944	807	BURNETT	Sylvia Evelyn	1917	466
Buckingham	Bonnie C.	1968	889	BURNS	Viola		515
BUCKINGHAM	Harvey	1966	889	BURR	Edith E.	1876	252
BUCKLEY	Ethelyn Maria		557	BURR	James Harvey	1869	409

BURR	Louisa N.	1907	642
BURR	Odessa P.	1909	643
BURRELL	Betty June	1926	651
BURRELL	Dean William	1913	650
BURRELL	Harold Ainsworth	1915	651
BURRELL	Harold William	1890	415
BURT	John	1850	206
BURTON	Albert A.	1840	192
BURTON	Kimberly G.	1968	821
BUSH	Aaron F.	1856	200
BUSH	Arthur Blaine	1884	356
BUSH	Chester A.	1887	356
BUSH	Dorothy K.	1895	356
Bush	Gertrude	1889	356
BUSH	Helen K.	1913	574
Bush	Margaret V.	1885	356
BUSH	Paul		557
BUSSEY	Craig Patrick	1965	730
BUTLER	Bruce Byron	1936	854
BUTLER	Chauncey		543
BUTLER	Diane Isabel	1937	854
BUTLER	Edgar	1866	186
BUTLER	Elizabeth	1890	342
BUTLER	Ernest J.	1909	720
BUTLER	Gerald Ernest	1934	854
BUTLER	Harriet S.	1828	187
BUTLER	Kenneth Leo	1918	588
Butler	Lois	1935	854
BUTLER	Maria	1845	184
BUTLER	Maria Julia	1900	342
Butler	Nancy	1937	854
BUTLER	Nellie I.	1874	435
BUTTON	Deiadamia	1802	50
BUTTRY	Lowry	1905	451
BUZZELL	Inez	1926	624
BYERS	Matthew	1963	860

C

CADLIN	Louise Catherine	1861	343
CAGWIN	Alice V.	1846	129
CAGWIN	Eunice Adelaide	1843	128
CAGWIN	Orville Dean	1811	58
CAINE	Jane Angela	1951	754
CALDWELL	Edna	1879	213
CALDWELL	Sarah A.	1850	101
CALKINS	James		908
CALKINS	Ordelia Eva	1857	225
CALLAN	Deloris	1922	720
CALLISON	Gail		882
CALLISON	Gordon Douglas	1918	780
CALLISON	James J.	1865	347
Callison	Karen		882
CALLISON	Karen L.	1942	882
CALLISON	Oscar Lovelace	1893	564
CALLISON	Randy		882
CALLON	Verne Charlton	1894	454
CALSBEEK	Shirley	1914	381
CALVIN	Mary Armenia	1867	348
CAMERON	Luella	1850	248
CAMERON	Marjorie Louise	1926	555
CAMERON	William R.	1920	586
CAMMER	Marshall John	1919	549
CAMPBELL	Betty Jane	1926	721
CAMPBELL	George Dewey	1899	319
CAMPBELL	George Nelson	1838	168
CAMPBELL	Hugh Donald	1918	517
CAMPBELL	James		529
Campbell	Mabel B.	1904	319
CAMPBELL	Margaret	1953	757
CAMPBELL	Mildred L.	1896	319
CAMPBELL	Susan	1948	757
CAMPBELL	Wayne A.	1892	319
CAMPOLI	Dolores K.	1933	667
CANARY	Irene M.	1884	320
CANFIELD	Melville Thomas	1880	448
CANFIELD	Paul David		760
CANNON	Harold A.	1896	582
CANTRELL	Beverly L	1938	824
CANTRELL	Glen	1910	664
CANTWELL	Albert V.	1878	370
CANTWELL	Esther	1912	593

CANTWELL	Vaughn E.	1908	593	CASE	Clifton Clinton	1888	416
CAPLES	Mary	1798	64	CASE	Dean Joseph	1883	414
CAPPS	Joyce Elaine	1941	725	CASE	Deborah	1870	414
CAPRAUM	Vern		819	CASE	Donna Joan	1935	667
CAPWELL	Allen B.	1835	118	CASE	Donna Joan	1935	819
CARE	John Lorraine	1922	595	CASE	Donna Marie	1964	888
CARLSON	Fred Theodore	1900	432	CASE	Douglas Alan	1965	888
CARMICHAEL	Carrie Ellen	1962	900	CASE	E. Emerson	1901	650
CARMICHAEL	John Eldon		901	CASE	Edith Abbott	1871	270
CARMICHAEL	Michelle Lynn		901	CASE	Elliot Jean	1876	414
CARMICHAEL	Russell Dean	1944	848	CASE	Emma E.	1855	238
CARNEGIE	Annie	1875	258	CASE	Emma V.	1882	416
CARNELL	Joyce Sheila	1924	508	CASE	Ernest Lee	1942	805
CARPENTER	Bessie Rose	1935	615	CASE	Frances	1888	150
CARPENTER	Catherine Erma	1916	646	CASE	Frederick	1857	407
CARPENTER	Donna G.	1955	897	CASE	Gerald C.	1911	653
CARPENTER	Pamela Beth	1954	739	CASE	Gladys N.	1911	653
CARR	Frank Burton	1894	428	CASE	Guy L.	1900	506
CARR	Mary	1919	450	CASE	Harriett Jane	1921	652
CARR	Phillip Burton	1917	670	CASE	J. Elliott	1918	650
CARR	Violet	1894	393	CASE	James Andrew	1884	417
CARROLL	Amy Johanna	1885	417	CASE	Janett	1918	652
CARROLL	J. C.	1932	530	CASE	Janine Suzanne	1968	889
CARROLL	John Flood	1932	596	CASE	Jay Wyatt	1885	416
CARRUTHERS	Dorothy	1907	465	CASE	Jean J.	1853	238
CARTER	Allen John	1939	669	CASE	Jerome Carroll	1908	653
CARTER	Catherine Ann	1965	827	CASE	Jesse Worden	1823	233
CARTER	Irene		692	CASE	Jessie	1856	238
CARTER	James Harding	1970	909	CASE	Job Russell	1821	111
CARTER	John H.	1967	909	CASE	John Clifton	1909	653
CARTER	Lora Ella	1853	255	CASE	John Deborah	1858	239
CARTER	Mary	1830	117	Case	Julia	1847	237
CARTER	Michael Layne	1971	858	CASE	Karen D.	1954	820
Carter	Michelle		909	CASE	Lela	1886	417
Carter	Rita Susan	1968	909	CASE	Lina	1888	415
CARTER	Wayne F.	1895	450	CASE	Lori Ann	1962	888
CARTER	William Dan	1947	884	CASE	Maggie Olivia	1877	297
CASANOVA	Juanita Ann	1973	906	Case	Margaret	1847	237
CASE	Addie May	1892	415	CASE	Martha	1836	112
CASE	Aileen		815	CASE	Mina M.	1892	417
CASE	Allan A.	1888	417	Case	Ms.		888
CASE	Andrew J.	1862	239	CASE	Myrtle C.	1879	239
CASE	Anna Virginia	1844	237	Case	Rebecca	1965	888
CASE	Arnold D.	1889	416	CASE	Richard		654
CASE	Clarine Harper	1923	650	CASE	Russell	1912	652

CASE	Theresa	1875	414	CHANEY	Delbert C.	1917	675
CASE	Theresa Mary	1845	237	CHANEY	Earl Lee	1937	833
CASE	Virginia N.	1907	653	CHANEY	Richard	1899	478
CASE	William Harding	1845	152	CHAPEL	Penny M.	1962	742
CASE	William R.	1847	237	CHAPMAN	Abraham W.	1849	342
CASEY	Anthony Gordon	1964	855	Chapman	Alma	1878	560
CASEY	Arthur Lee	1925	723	CHAPMAN	Augusta Elizabeth	1880	561
CASLER	Muriel	1906	642	CHAPMAN	Charles Aaron	1883	396
CASPER	Bert	1878	332	CHAPMAN	Clarence H.	1872	560
CASS	Ada Ball	1931	851	CHAPMAN	Frank	1848	342
CASS	Earle Millard	1901	710	CHAPMAN	Frank Edward	1920	620
CASS	Millard	1877	462	CHAPMAN	Fred E.	1874	560
CASSELS	Audrey Emily	1926	530	CHAPMAN	Gertrude M.	1909	775
CASTANGUAY	Cecile	1932	512	CHAPMAN	Grace Mae	1910	620
CASTEN	Emily	1830	109	CHAPMAN	Ivah Dorothy	1888	560
CASTNER	Temma	1866	269	CHAPMAN	Jessie	1910	694
CATHER	Agnes	1926	775	CHAPMAN	Laura	1841	200
CAUNITZ	Patricia		558	CHAPMAN	Leona A.	1884	561
CAUSEY	William	1944	734	CHAPMAN	Pauline Mabel	1908	619
CAVE	Lance H.	1950	809	CHAPPELL	Paula J.	1948	806
CAVE	Leo Quentin	1926	635	CHARLES	Elna R.	1861	201
Cave	Shirley M.	1948	809	CHARLES	Ida L.	1857	202
CAVNER	Robert	1861	232	CHARLESWORTH	John	1875	250
CAWLEY	William C.	1832	200	CHARLESWORTH	John	1903	438
CAYWOOD	James W. "Charles"	1910	483	CHARLESWORTH	John Roger	1942	683
CENTER	Byron	1860	202	Charlesworth	Mary L.	1945	683
CETTELL	Ruth Ann	1901	430	Chase	Abbie W.	1869	284
CHAFFEE	Charlotte Lucile	1918	578	CHASE	Alzina Bianca	1830	122
CHALIFOUR	Deedee		756	CHASE	Amy	1747	17
CHAMBERLAIN	Barbara		768	CHASE	Charles	1920	655
CHAMBERLAIN	Franklin J.	1905	432	CHASE	David	1752	17
CHAMBERLAIN	Robert F.	1927	673	Chase	Debra S.	1950	835
CHAMPION	Anne M.	1979	870	CHASE	Desire	1760	23
CHAMPION	Hattie L. (TRUAX)	1860	145	CHASE	Dorcas	1775	23
CHAMPLIN	Alson John	1882	415	CHASE	Floyd Milks	1899	369
CHAMPLIN	Hazel R.	1889	649	CHASE	Ford G.	1877	332
CHAMPLIN	Ida May	1921	650	CHASE	George Hiram	1843	143
CHAMPLIN	John B.	1866	414	CHASE	John	1774	23
CHAMPLIN	John Brown Francis	1841	237	CHASE	John A. H., III	1950	835
CHAMPLIN	John Brown Francis	1892	649	CHASE	John H.	1922	680
CHAMPLIN	Judith Emma	1928	818	CHASE	Julia Agnes	1847	145
CHAMPLIN	Philip T.	1899	649	CHASE	Justus	1762	22
CHAMPLIN	Philip T., Jr.	1921	818	CHASE	Lemuel	1765	22
CHAMPLIN	Robert Dean	1922	650	CHASE	Martha Scovil	1878	284
CHAMPLIN	Theresa Kay	1922	819	CHASE	Marvin		882

CHASE	Mary Sargent	1872	221	CLARK	Addie		204	
CHASE	May Mabel	1895	368	Clark	Cathleen Lynn	1960	742	
CHASE	Nathan	1723	12	CLARK	Charlotte M.	1850	197	
CHASE	Nathan, Jr.	1768	22	CLARK	Doris Belle	1926	762	
CHASE	Orrin	1802	50	CLARK	Ed	1889	418	
CHASE	Rhoda	1767	22	CLARK	Gertrude		527	
CHASE	Roy	1904	369	CLARK	Hollis T.	1896	534	
CHASE	Seth	1722	9	CLARK	Hyrum Don Carlos	1856	273	
CHASE	William Baker	1862	210	CLARK	James W.	1954	742	
CHASE	William G.	1869	284	CLARK	Jimmy Lee	1934	608	
CHATELAIN	Clyde L.	1905	776	CLARK	John N.	1865	285	
CHATELAIN	George	1881	561	CLARK	John S.	1828	176	
CHATLAIN	John Kenneth	1915	767	CLARK	John W.	1837	188	
CHESSHIRE	Edna Fay	1895	319	CLARK	Makenzie Lynn		908	
CHEVALIER	Ethel E.	1921	732	CLARK	Milford L.	1912	655	
CHICHESTER	Keith Allen		867	CLARK	Otis R.	1908	655	
CHICK	Juliet Gossett	1918	547	CLARK	Richard Augustus	1896	478	
CHICKERING	Frank Edward	1881	286	CLARK	Richard Wagstaff	1929	721	
CHILTON	Hubert Leon	1902	585	CLARK	William Joseph	1925	498	
CHISHOLM	Irene	1904	439	CLARKE	Glen		756	
CHISM	Virginia Ruth	1933	587	CLARY	Bradley Grayson	1950	853	
CHOQUETTE	Gilbert	1894	309	CLARY	Mary Ellen	1895	216	
CHRIST	Elizabeth	1822	53	CLAYTON	Mr.		295	
CHRISTENSEN	Elmer	1896	457	CLEAVER	Harrell	1911	557	
CHRISTENSEN	Richard Leslie	1925	700	CLEMA	Carl	1918	390	
CHRISTENSEN	Wendell Abram	1900	452	CLEMENS-COCAGNE	Carol A.	1943	808	
CHRISTIAN	Adlebert Lincoln	1867	394	CLERDUX	Rachelle	1972	756	
CHRISTIAN	David Darius	1895	619	CLEVELAND	Alanson Kilbourne	1909	696	
CHRISTIAN	Dora E.	1891	618	CLEVELAND	Alice Marie	1907	696	
CHRISTIAN	Frank A.	1893	618	CLEVELAND	Herbert Seldon	1881	453	
CHRISTIAN	Paul James	1924	801	CLIFTON	Patricia M.	1955	805	
CHRISTIE	Helen Catherine	1900	305	CLOSE	Ella	1890	283	
CHRISTINE	Carrie Lee	1925	383	CLOUS	Albert Anthony	1883	301	
CHRISTY	Thomas	1765	24	CLOUS	Arthur John	1945	749	
CHUGG	John	1866	167	CLOUS	Lea Ann	1972	872	
CHURCH	Mary J.	1865	233	CLOUSE	Joseph	1895	302	
CHURCH	Ruby Lillian	1906	565	COATS	Betty J.	1925	577	
CHURCHILL	Richard Russell	1936	802	COBBLER	Carrie Elizabeth	1886	449	
CHURCHILL	Rosamond		271	COBBLER	William	1853	120	
CINCO	Brittney Lynnea	1986	907	COCAGNE	Carol A.	1943	808	
CLAIRMONT	Thomas Alden	1923	602	COCHRANE	Mabel R.	1889	305	
CLAPPER	Harry	1920	766	CODDING	Sarah A.	1843	125	
CLAPPER	Leta	1917	766	COE	Anita Lynn	1961	857	
CLAPPER	Timothy	1890	541	COE	Beverly Ann	1961	856	
CLARK	Achsa	1862	241	COE	Brenda Gayle	1969	857	

COE	Chelsea Nicole	1987	905	COMSTOCK	Francelia G.	1862	249
COE	Doris Marion	1920	762	COMSTOCK	Fred Spencer	1861	244
COE	Gregory Eugene	1963	857	COMSTOCK	Melissa	1799	65
COE	Joshua Blaine	1982	905	CONLEY	Eustace H.	1884	169
COE	Patricia Gail	1965	856	CONNELLY	Mr.	1939	683
COE	Peggy Bernice	1940	725	CONNOLLY	Donald Phillippi	1950	755
COE	Tammy Lynn	1963	856	CONNOLLY	Karrie-Anne	1974	874
COE	Thomas Edward	1916	484	CONNOLLY	Patrick Ian	1977	874
COE	Thomas Eugene	1938	725	CONRAD	George Edward	1838	127
COE	William Albert	1937	724	CONRAD	Georgia May	1890	353
COLE	Almeda	1890	290	CONROE	Mr.		543
COLE	Anna		290	CONROY	Steve Allan	1953	505
COLE	Elida Mae	1919	560	COOGAN	Lillian Theresa	1900	313
COLE	Elijah	1787	41	COOK	David C.	1912	545
COLE	Ella Genevieve	1912	696	COOK	David Caleb	1850	180
COLE	Esther Marie	1913	560	COOK	David Charles	1881	334
COLE	Eva	1858	199	COOK	Ezra Asher	1841	180
COLE	Floyd Addison	1877	270	COOK	Ezra Sprague	1811	81
COLE	George E.	1867	327	COOK	Flora Beach	1878	331
COLE	Hannah Amanda	1854	326	COOK	Frances	1910	545
COLE	Irene	1906	469	COOK	Jonathan Blanchard	1881	333
COLE	Joel Sebastian	1853	325	COOK	Louise Desire	1839	179
COLE	Minnie Bell	1883	537	COOK	Lulu G.	1898	492
COLE	Nellie	1856	167	COOK	Mary Amelia	1844	180
COLE	Orien	1923	766	COOK	Nathaniel Ezra	1836	179
COLE	Sebastian	1825	175	COOK	Olive	1864	328
COLE	Sela Earl	1926	560	COOK	Warren W.	1840	171
COLE	Sela Leander	1891	342	COOKE	Albert	1833	170
COLLESEL	Doris	1913	385	COOLEY	Helen M.	1838	126
COLLIER	Raymond Fred	1903	338	COOLEY	Homer W.	1869	292
COLLINS	Clara Marie	1880	222	COOLEY	Mary Eliza	1836	126
COLLINS	Jason Lee	1974	906	COOLEY	Samuel Wilbur	1807	54
COLLINS	Mark Michael	1971	906	COOLIDGE	Ann	1883	362
COLLINS	Melissa	1973	858	COOPER	Blanch Clarinda	1894	428
COLLINS	Phillip		865	COOPER	Carlos	1964	893
COLLINS	Robert Lee	1949	862	COOPER	Cleo	1910	690
COLLINS	Roger Phillip	1951	727	COOPER	Harold	1908	593
COLLINS	Scott Allen	1976	906	COOPER	Jimmie	1923	462
COLVIN	Bert	1873	362	COOPER	Norma M.	1917	704
COLVIN	Mark	1840	207	COOPER	Sue A.	1944	812
COMSTOCK	Carrie Esther	1872	241	COOVER	James Lloyd, Jr.	1971	901
COMSTOCK	Chloe	1805	53	COOVER	James Lloyd, Sr.	1944	848
COMSTOCK	Claudia Ruth	1899	431	COOVER	Mr.		900
COMSTOCK	Elmer Owen	1864	245	COOVER	Ms.		901
COMSTOCK	Eula Aletha	1891	430	CORBETT	Jerusha	1825	74

Surname	Given Name	Year	No.	Surname	Given Name	Year	No.
CORBITT	Margaret Malinda	1823	73	CRANDELL	Rhea	1897	649
CORBY	Patrick John	1965	827	CRANS	Mary Caroline		221
CORCORAN	John	1899	431	CRANSTON	Albert B.	1885	480
CORDELL	Victor J.	1942	605	CRAPO	Peter	1788	41
CORNEL	Emmet Wilbert	1895	318	CRASPER	Ida	1858	331
CORNISH	Mildred M.	1913	591	CRAWFORD	Gary Lavar	1938	734
COSENZA	Charles	1925	520	CRAWFORD	Winnie Jo	1929	738
COSENZA	James		520	CREELEY	Harold Ephraim	1905	619
COTTER	William	1877	416	CREGGER	Dollie Mae	1940	726
COUNTS	Ann		728	CREGGER	Earl Martin	1925	484
COURTER	Helen	1900	406	CRILL	Lucille	1907	615
COVEDILL	Clarence H.	1876	408	CRIPPEN	Cora	1869	286
COVEDILL	Etta P.	1899	640	CRIPPEN	Eugene	1844	146
COVEDILL	Everett Frederick	1933	812	CRIPPEN	Grace	1876	286
COVEDILL	Frederick C.	1911	640	CRIPPEN	John A.	1849	147
COVEDILL	Leo D.	1913	640	CRIPPEN	Wellington Elijah	1818	70
Covedill	Marcella	1933	812	CRIPPIN	John R.	1880	285
COVEDILL	Pearl D.	1908	640	CRIPPIN	John Sidney	1842	144
COVEDILL	Rita Jean	1946	813	CRIPPIN	John Sidney	1903	477
COVEDILL	Robert C.	1918	640	CRIPPIN	Margaret	1865	285
COVERT	James Rhodes	1931	666	CRIPPIN	Mary L.	1866	285
COVERT	Jean Marie	1928	666	CRIPS	Ethel		542
COVERT	Leo Ewing	1893	426	CRITTENDEN	Michael		869
COX	Alex MILKS	1888	220	CRNKOVITCH	Mr.	1935	684
COX	Anderson Bruce	1861	129	CROFT	Evan Marion	1905	452
COX	Ernest W.	1940	844	CRONK	Elizabeth Ann	1984	910
COX	George		253	CRONKHITE	Elsie	1899	301
COYLE	Cletus Ebehart	1930	782	CRONKHITE	Elsie	1899	303
COYLE	David Dean	1963	883	CROSBIE	Edward Archibald	1909	522
COYLE	Steven Joseph	1954	883	CROSBIE	Gloria Jean	1951	758
CRABTREE	Tessa	1975	873	CROSBIE	Heather June	1935	758
CRAIG	Archibald	1859	160	CROSBIE	Richard Alexander	1953	759
CRAIG	Leona Marjorie	1930	510	CROSSLEY	Edith Muriel	1910	426
CRAIG	Verna		524	CROUSE	Charles H.	1915	617
CRAMER	George F., Jr.	1915	272	CROUSE	Dennis George	1939	800
CRAMER	Mary Ann	1929	735	CROUSE	George	1860	223
CRAMER	Thomas L.	1917	382	CROUSE	George	1912	617
CRANCH	John Eliot	1922	715	CROUSE	Henry John	1943	800
CRANCH	Jonathan	1963	854	CROUSE	John C., Jr.	1929	617
CRANCH	Judith Lisa	1961	854	CROUSE	John Charles	1882	394
Cranch	Nancy		854	CROUSE	Katherine T.	1923	617
CRANDALL	Alice Ovella	1860	223	Crouse	Kathleen E.	1917	618
CRANDALL	Arthur E.	1867	292	CROUSE	Mary	1913	617
CRANDALL	Homer Gregory	1905	486	Crouse	Mary A.	1942	800
CRANDELL	Bert	1875	414	CROUSE	Michael J., Sr.	1970	887

Crouse	Patricia L.	1945	800
CROUSE	Raymond	1882	394
CROUSE	Raymond John, Jr.	1903	618
Crouse	Theresa	1908	618
Crouse	Tonya M.		887
CROW	Jane	1867	215
CROWLEY	John S.	1967	731
CROY	Clayton Wilson	1943	863
CROY	Clayton Wilson, Jr.	1977	907
CROZIER	Dorothy	1940	488
CRYER	Ray	1899	691
CUDDY	Patsy	1934	723
CULLEN	Greg		758
CULLEN	Orville Joseph Gerald	1923	519
CULLEN	Patrick James	1890	312
CULLEN	Wilbert James	1914	518
CULLINGS	Clara F.	1868	215
CULLINGS	Clifford Russell	1886	377
CULLINGS	Ebenezer	1832	102
CULLINGS	James Ebenezer	1858	214
CULLINGS	Nellie E.	1888	377
CUMMINGS	Donald Raymond	1917	801
CUMMINGS	Donald Raymond	1945	887
CUMMINGS	Mary L.	1907	470
CUMMINGS	Mary Louise		807
CUMMINS	James	1914	588
CUMMINS	James Bruce	1919	646
CUNNINGHAM	Frank I.	1879	351
CUNNINGHAM	Isabelle	1903	567
CUNNINGHAM	Margaret E.	1901	567
CURRIE	J. Thomas	1893	626
CURTIS	Elton	1877	212
CURTIS	George	1867	142
CURTIS	Martha E.	1891	490
CURTIS	Minnie M.	1888	283
CURTIS	Raymond	1898	283
CURTIS	Rexford	1902	283
CUTHBERTSON	Agnes	1866	159

D

DACEY	Catherine	1859	162
DAELLENBACH	Willard Dean	1947	850
DAGGETT	Harry Albert	1877	582
DAGGETT	Harry Leon	1921	789
DAGGETT	Juanita Delphine	1919	789
DAGGETT	Linda Jean	1947	884
DAHL	Alfred L.	1922	507
Dahl	Betty J.	1928	507
DAHL	John Alfred	1900	303
DAICEY	Barberah	1868	164
DAILY	Mary	1844	200
DALE	Barbara Ellen Dale	1972	885
DALE	Lewis	1899	545
DALE	Norman David	1978	885
DALE	Robert H.	1948	793
DALEY	Mary Arlene	1922	614
DALY	Robert	1927	765
DALY	Shannon		899
DALZAL	Wendy	1971	869
D'AMBROSIO	Louis John	1970	908
DAMRON	Leon	1939	725
DAMRON	Sharon Kay	1961	857
DAMRON	Steven Leon	1969	857
DANES	Elizabeth	1782	44
DANGEL	Arthur	1910	603
DANGEL	Robert Allen	1952	797
Dangel	Roxanna M.	1955	797
DANIELS	Lucius A.	1847	174
DANN	Charles C.	1914	475
DANN	Elmer J.	1887	283
DANN	Elmer J., Jr.	1912	475
DANN	Leone	1907	283
Dann	Martha		475
DARDER	Daniel Ray	1950	771
Darder	Deborah		771
Darder	Kim		771
DARDER	Michael R.	1956	771
DARDER	Rhonda Marie	1947	771
DARDER	Ronald	1924	550
DARLING	Alton Burchard	1893	371
DARLING	Ann Phyllis	1933	596
Darling	Barbara A.	1939	596
DARLING	Bradley Ross	1934	596

DARLING	Dawn Audrey	1924	595	DAVIS	Gertrude Estelle	1874	563
DARLING	Denis Alton	1927	596	DAVIS	Jean		528
DARLING	Edgar Allen	1862	212	DAVIS	John Quincy	1847	344
DARLING	Edgar Dale	1905	372	DAVIS	Mary	1790	26
DARLING	Esmarie	1897	370	DAVIS	Mary Kathryn	1917	587
DARLING	Esmarie	1897	371	DAVIS	Nancy Marie	1831	62
DARLING	Grace Irene	1892	371	DAVIS	Sarah	1841	75
DARLING	Jean Ellen	1937	596	DAVOL	Abigail	1694	5
DARLING	Jessie Lucille	1899	372	DAVOL	Fallie TRIPP	1797	26
DARLING	June Amy	1922	595	DAVOL	Zilpha	1797	26
DARLING	Kenneth Clark	1903	372	DAWES	Laurie		889
Darling	Phyllis A.	1943	596	DAWSON	Alyce	1927	713
DARLING	Robert		477	DAWSON	Mary	1875	415
DARLING	Winifred Marguerite	1901	372	DAY	Clarendon	1842	118
DARROHN	Maurice D.	1919	651	DAYTON	Eldred	1899	546
DAUB	Ann	1906	553	DAYTON	Harvey	1903	546
DAULEY	Ford	1904	542	DAYTON	Hilton	1916	546
DAULEY	Helen	1902	542	DAYTON	Howard	1897	545
DAULEY	John	1891	542	DAYTON	Irving	1878	334
Dauley	Margaret	1891	542	DAYTON	Mildred	1899	545
DAULEY	Marvin	1861	329	DAYTON	Mildred	1918	768
DAULEY	Nellie	1900	540	DEAN	Arthur Lewis	1900	363
DAULEY	Nellie	1900	542	DEAN	Burt		741
DAVENPORT	Elizabeth	1916	764	DEAN	Darren Dennis	1969	908
DAVENPORT	Julius	1885	537	DEAN	Dennis Edward	1947	879
DAVEY	Charles Rollins	1884	281	DEAN	Edna Ruth	1924	767
DAVID	Mr.		763	DEAN	Grace Maria	1889	133
DAVIDSON	Alice	1915	482	DEAN	Gus L.	1875	208
DAVIDSON	Fayette James	1870	289	DEAN	Katrina L	1974	867
DAVIDSON	George Washington	1892	481	DEAN	Laura E.	1892	300
DAVIDSON	Harriet	1899	481	DEAN	Mr.		354
DAVIDSON	Helen V.	1908	481	DEBOER	Ella Mabel	1908	378
DAVIDSON	Henry	1900	481	DEBORD	Frank	1905	482
DAVIDSON	Hjalmar		527	DEBOY	Diane E.	1941	625
DAVIDSON	Joseph W.	1893	480	DEBRACCIO	Naomi	1924	765
DAVIDSON	Margaret	1922	723	DEBUSK	Travis	1978	859
DAVIDSON	Maria	1903	481	DECARLO	Thomas George	1933	798
DAVIDSON	Susie Louise	1906	484	DECHOW	Lorraine Alice	1932	811
DAVIDSON	Vincent N.	1912	601	DECHOW	Richard Earl	1907	637
DAVIDSON	William Monte	1913	482	DECKER	Cylinda	1838	184
DAVIS	Alba Z.	1870	563	DECKER	Gertrude Helen	1917	682
DAVIS	Avis L.	1925	589	DECKER	Irene	1904	447
DAVIS	Cora May	1865	210	DECKER	Margery Morse	1835	191
DAVIS	Flora	1913	612	DEERING	James	1766	24
DAVIS	George Rex	1788	64	DEERING	Linda	1953	861

DEERING	Mary	1742	14		DEWEY	Charles H.	1856	251
DEERING	Nathaniel	1739	14		DEWEY	Delfred Alan	1933	692
DEFILIPPO	James Henry	1951	794		DEWEY	Fred	1900	447
DEGOLE	Nellie Potts	1866	414		DEWEY	James Lawrence	1892	447
DEGRAAF	Angela K.	1958	865		DEWEY	Marcella Elmira	1914	720
DEGRAAF	Dana M.	1959	865		DEWEY	Mark Byron	1883	477
DEGRAAF	Edgar J., Jr.	1937	739		DEYO	Jessie	1871	339
DEGRAAF	Edward Charles	1962	865		DIAL	Harold Henry, Jr.	1951	824
DEGRAAF	Michael E.	1961	865		DIAL	Kelly	1972	896
DEGRAAF	Michelle Marie	1969	866		DIAL	Tony	1975	896
DEISINGER	Richard Joseph	1964	755		DIAMANT	Jo-Anne Elizabeth	1960	883
DELANCEY	Clarence H.	1903	530		DIAMANT	Nicholas E.	1936	784
DELANCEY	James Elton	1883	318		DIBBLE	Adeline	1833	177
DELANCEY	Lee R.	1906	531		DIBBLE	Ann Eliza	1808	80
DELONG	Della	1886	435		DIBBLE	Benjamin	1838	178
DEMCHAK	Yvonne A.	1956	829		DIBBLE	Bethiar	1877	331
DENNIS	Kim C.	1954	746		DIBBLE	Caleb	1801	80
DENNIS	Raymond Emerson	1958	890		Dibble	Caroline	1836	178
DENNIS	Rosa	1879	298		DIBBLE	Cora	1872	331
DENNY	Cary J.	1874	542		DIBBLE	Etta	1879	332
DENNY	Cornelius	1849	330		DIBBLE	Harlan	1886	332
DENNY	Corwin C.	1900	540		DIBBLE	Isaac	1836	178
DENNY	Doris P.	1930	765		DIBBLE	James Patrick	1830	177
DENNY	Marian Eunice	1926	765		DIBBLE	Jennifer	1882	332
DENTZ	Mary Elizabeth	1966	821		DIBBLE	Lloyd L.	1909	331
DEPINO	Mr.		489		DIBBLE	Margaret	1909	543
DERMONT	William	1910	647		DIBBLE	Marion G.	1847	178
DEROCHA	Dawn Michelle	1970	908		DIBBLE	Mary	1884	332
DEROME	Ray	1918	692		DIBBLE	May A.	1888	331
DERUDDER	Ruth	1958	760		DIBBLE	Perlina	1825	177
DESELMA	Alta Mae	1879	273		DIBBLE	Polly Margaret	1827	177
DESELMA	John Bernard	1844	128		DIBBLE	Robie	1874	331
DETOUR	Margaret	1910	491		DIBBLE	Sarah Elizabeth	1865	330
DEUEL	Jonathan	1753	16		DIBBLE	Sarah Emeline	1844	178
DEUEL	Katie Rosilla	1884	274		DICKENS	William	1840	152
DEUEL	Lewis	1782	27		DICKERSON	Emma I.	1910	474
DEUEL	Lewis	1851	131		DICKEY	John W.	1916	590
DEUEL	Lillys	1785	28		DICKINSON	Cynthia	1833	205
DEUEL	Minerva Adeline	1843	131		DICKINSON	Frances	1835	205
DEUEL	William Henry	1811	60		DIEDERICHS	John	1934	802
DEVINASPRE	Sara Lopez		903		DIEDIKER	Cliff	1919	384
DEVINE	Genevieve R.	1921	382		DIETLEY	Hazel S.	1892	356
DEVOE	Laura	1856	235		DIETLEY	Mary E.	1900	357
DEWEY	Arthur Amos	1865	256		DIETLEY	Philip W.	1861	201
DEWEY	Byron Nellis	1912	720		DIETLEY	Philip W.	1897	357

DIETLEY	Phyllis A.		575	**DOYLE**	Elizabeth F.	1910	676
DIETLEY	Richard William	1922	575	**DOYLE**	Margaret	1827	123
DIETLEY	Uras. A.	1894	357	**DOYLE**	Rosanna	1834	123
DIETZ	Ruth Arlene	1928	707	**DRAKE**	Myrtle E.	1896	320
DIGENNARO	Christine L.	1965	878	**DRAPEAU**	Eugene Joseph	1918	766
DINWIDDIE	Mr.		543	**DRAPER**	Christine Kay	1953	862
DIPLEY	Olive E.	1862	153	**DRAPER**	Clifton		526
DITTUS	Klaus	1940	817	**DRAPER**	Edward		525
DITTUS	Rhonda	1964	893	**DRAPER**	Keith		526
DITTUS	Stacy Ellen	1967	894	**DRAPER**	Kenneth		526
DITTY	Janice Harvey	1940	816	**DRAPER**	Lorna		527
DIXON	Mildred	1900	357	**DRAPER**	Marjorie		527
DIXON	Tony Martin	1953	856	**DRAPER**	Myrtle		526
DIXON	Winnie Jo	1929	738	**DRAPER**	Shirley		527
DOANE	Shirley Scott	1938	724	**DRAPER**	Sybil		526
DOCHTERMANN	Grace	1890	341	**DRAPER**	Viola		525
DOCKERY	Grace	1893	258	**DRAPER**	William	1890	315
DODD	Leona	1912	381	**DREAVER**	Dustin		887
DODGE	Charles Greely	1918	779	**DREAVER**	Jeffrey S.	1957	801
DODGE	James Foster	1955	880	**DREW**	Benjamin	1887	246
DODGE	Joyce Ann	1958	880	**DREW**	Caroline A.	1837	106
DODGE	Nancy Auralee	1950	880	**DREW**	Levi	1734	13
DODSON	Gregg J.	1955	745	**DREW**	Loretta	1910	641
DOERR	Delores	1933	833	**DRONE**	Alaine E.	1953	740
DOING	Julia Ann	1841	176	**DRONE**	Carole Marie	1955	740
DOLAN	Elissa	1905	374	**DRONE**	Charlotte Angeline	1927	497
DOMEK	Susan Marie	1959	795	**DRONE**	Edward Arthur	1926	497
DONALD	Jean Marie	1915	557	**DRONE**	Edward Darwin	1871	300
DONATHAN	Daniel Damien	1961	746	**DROWN**	Ida Amanda	1866	228
DONOVAN	James Daniel	1880	434	**DRUMMOND**	Theresa M.	1827	90
DOOLITTLE	Jaime	1949	897	**DUBEY**	Gayle Ann	1953	863
DOTY	Priscilla Helen	1938	845	**DUBOIS**	Marie Clara	1918	779
DOTY	Robert Monier	1919	702	**DUBOIS**	Maurice	1930	715
DOTY	Robert Monier, Jr.	1940	845	**DUDGEON**	Robert Benjamin	1894	449
DOTY	Susan Marie	1957	846	**DUDLEY**	Alvin Lyle	1935	751
DOUGHERTY	Carlene Amelia	1885	358	Dudley	Blanche		652
DOUGHERTY	Edward A.	1916	585	**DUDLEY**	Daniel Clinton		652
DOUGHERTY	Lillian	1902	378	**DUDLEY**	Delores Louise	1937	751
DOUGHTY	Brenda May	1941	805	**DUDLEY**	Garry Grant	1945	752
DOUGLAS	Emeline	1805	104	**DUDLEY**	Grant	1914	506
DOUGLAS	Lulu	1890	339	**DUDLEY**	James Rose	1882	416
DOWE	Hector H.	1891	305	Dudley	Linda Jean	1950	752
DOWE	Mary Louise	1885	304	**DUDLEY**	Richard		652
DOWNING	Donald	1942	792	**DUDLEY**	Rodney Bruce	1948	752
DOXTATER	Jack	1870	202	**DUDLEY**	William		652

DUFF	Gary Allen, Sr.	1960	742		**DUTTON**	Walter Albert	1911	677
DUFF	Kenneth Wesley, Sr.	1959	742		**DYE**	Jonathan W.	1847	285
DUFF	Sandra Kay	1953	742		**DYE**	Judith	1922	800
DUFF	Vernon Leroy	1930	498		**DYER**	George Alfred	1880	333
DUFF	Yolanda Ann	1951	742		**DYER**	John Lewis	1917	545
DUFFY	Agnes	1890	220		**DYER**	Lewis	1848	179
DUFLOTH	Emil	1912	699		**DYER**	Mary	1883	333
DUFRANCE	Linda Louise	1949	669		**DYER**	Phebe	1837	179
DUHAMEL	Denise	1940	784		**DYER**	Will Richard	1924	589
DUKE	Robert P.	1965	717		**DYER**	Winthrop	1808	80
DUMAS	Adeline	1895	303					
DUMOND	Paul H.	1932	773					
DUNAWAY	Stefanie		870			**E**		
DUNBAR	Malissa	1824	71					
DUNCAN	Delores Irene	1928	468		**EARING**	Julia	1974	710
DUNCAN	Isaac S.	1874	215		**EARL**	Ellen Gertrude	1885	412
DUNCAN	Kenneth	1910	377		**EARLE**	Cora	1854	240
DUNHAM	Augusta Samantha		558		**EARLE**	Mary Elizabeth	1842	113
DUNHAM	Bertha		339		**EARLE**	Sophia	1837	112
DUNHAM	Carolyn	1961	775		**EARLY**	Catherine	1952	625
DUNHAM	Charles	1856	185		**EASTMAN**	Archie B.	1875	344
DUNHAM	Charles C.		558		**EASTMAN**	Hattie	1861	344
DUNHAM	Clarence E.	1884	340		**EASTON**	Ean Orillee	1926	780
DUNHAM	Corydon Bushnell	1890	341		**EASTWOOD**	George R.	1870	272
DUNHAM	Hommell E.		558		**EBERHARD**	William Alan	1951	749
DUNHAM	Jerry, II		906		**EBERHARDT**	Ruth	1917	566
DUNHAM	Julia	1888	341		**ECKERT**	James Worthy	1885	410
Dunham	Marjorie A.	1937	558		**ECKLER**	Earlene Etta	1923	707
DUNHAM	Sharon	1954	868		**EDDY**	Loulie B.	1868	242
DUNHAM	Ward James	1880	340		**EDDY**	Theresa	1879	407
DUNHAM	Ward James, Jr.	1929	558		**EDMUNDS**	Menzo	1858	223
DUNKLE	Mable May	1888	402		**EDWARDS**	Alvin Charles	1895	568
DUNKLEMAN	Minnie E.	1877	418		**EDWARDS**	Claire Grace	1955	867
DUNLAP	Donald M.	1917	529		**EDWARDS**	George W.		130
DUNLAP	Donna	1946	759		Edwards	June	1920	783
DUNLAP	Roberta	1957	759		**EDWARDS**	Kathryn Grace	1918	783
DUNLOP	Larry W.	1951	744		**EDWARDS**	Valerie Ruth	1953	867
DUNN	Annie	1711	7		**EDWARDS**	William	1897	499
DUNN	Rosielean	1873	335		**EDWARDS**	William Brandt	1920	783
DUNWIDDIE	Roger		784		**EDWARDS**	Winfred Nelson	1921	742
DURHAM	Emmett	1915	685		**EGELER**	Evelyn M.	1908	492
DURLAND	Doris		897		**EISELE**	Albert E.	1915	589
DURLAND	Ira E.	1920	830		**EISELE**	Dorothy	1914	589
DUTTON	Eric Joel	1936	834		**EISELE**	Edward A.	1890	368
Dutton	Karen J.	1939	834		**EISELE**	Evelyn J.	1923	590

EISELE	Jack		795		EMLICK	David		751
EISELE	Marjorie M.	1919	590		ENDRES	Christine Lynn	1952	862
Eisele	Merilee		795		ENDRES	David Allen	1951	862
EISINGER	Edith	1888	447		ENDRES	Frank J., Jr.	1928	737
EITUTIS	Laura I.	1966	821		ENDRES	Mary Regina	1948	862
ELAM	Evelyne	1909	535		ENDRES	Melissa Jean	1973	906
ELAM	Warden John	1906	466		ENDRES	Michael	1950	862
ELANSIVICH	Mary	1915	491		ENGELBERTSON	Elmer		748
ELBERG	Marion		451		ENGELMANN	Larry Daniel	1941	846
ELDREDGE	Frank Augustus	1863	269		Engelmann	Margo M.		846
ELDRIDGE	Lena	1872	361		ENGELMANN	Michael Stanley	1952	846
ELDRIDGE	Saloma	1760	17		ENGELMANN	Stanley Daniel	1923	702
ELLETT	Steve	1959	898		ENGER	Jack Henry	1929	733
ELLIDGE	Bertie V.	1881	216		ENGER	Joel Thomas	1953	861
ELLIOT	Timothy	1924	278		ENGER	Ole		297
ELLIOTT	Delbert Earl	1900	381		ENGER	William Henry	1898	491
ELLIOTT	George Warren	1830	126		ENGLERT	Frederick J.	1918	704
ELLIOTT	Henry Franklin	1831	128		ENGLERT	John Fred	1892	460
ELLIOTT	Lloyd Otto	1925	607		ENGLISH	Albert	1863	246
ELLIOTT	Patricia Louise	1928	607		ENGLISH	Margaret	1777	20
ELLIS	Blanche	1899	217		ENSTAD	Florence I.	1913	696
ELLIS	Ethel Irving	1899	649		EPPERSON	Mary J.	1909	385
ELLIS	Eva C.	1892	397		EPTON	John E.	1867	150
ELLIS	Jane Hill	1915	650		ERB	Paul	1960	865
ELLSWORTH	Emma Louise	1923	470		EREAUX	Mike		851
ELLSWORTH	Leslie Karen	1958	829		ERICKSON	Mr.		385
ELLSWORTH	Rudolph Tapken	1905	275		ERVIN	Miles Burton	1891	459
ELWOOD	James O.	1939	798		ERWAY	Juli Kay	1961	865
ELWOOD	James O.		886		ERWIN	Eva	1886	314
Elwood	Joann		886		ESKURI	Ethel	1906	295
ELWOOD	Kathleen M.	1967	886		ESOLEN	Raymond	1910	553
ELYEA	Jennie	1859	256		ESTES	Cora F.	1914	694
EMANS	Betty Jean	1924	735		ESTES	Thomas Luke	1865	197
EMANS	Charles J., Jr.	1926	735		ESTUS	Edgar A.	1919	624
EMANS	Charles William	1902	495		ESTUS	Edgar Albert	1947	805
EMANS	Dennis Paul	1949	861		Estus	Jean C.	1924	625
EMANS	Diana Lynn	1944	736		ESTUS	Kenneth R.	1947	805
EMANS	Gerald Everett	1932	736		ESTUS	Ross F.	1897	399
EMANS	Sharleen Marie	1950	861		ESTUS	Ross F., Jr.	1923	625
EMANS	Walter Wayne	1928	735		ETHERINGTON	Alice Mae	1936	388
EMERICK	James Perry	1875	324		ETSEL	Emma	1875	252
EMERSON	Harold Garnet	1950	753		EVANS	Mr.		501
EMERSON	Harold Garnet Scott	1968	872		EVANS	Harriet	1793	36
EMERSON	Shawn Reginald John	1969	873		EVANS	Howard Leroy	1933	746
EMERSON	Sonnie Roger Gerald	1971	873		EVANS	Rita	1952	809

EVANS	Terry	1941	736	FANCHER	Miles Elbridge	1878	393
EVENCE	Laura A.	1792	31	FANCHER	Orien	1903	541
EVEREST	Laura A.	1792	31	FANCHER	Perlina	1861	329
EVERETT	Martha	1917	549	FANCHER	Robert Morris	1898	538
EVERS	Jane	1923	820	Fancher	Ruby		539
EVERSON	Edna	1920	628	FANCHER	Sanford	1906	541
EVERSON	Harvey L.	1888	401	FANCHER	Stephen	1890	539
EVERSON	Harvey L., Jr.	1920	629	FANCHER	Viola	1885	539
EVERSON	Myrlee Loreen	1941	845	FANCHER	William Albro	1823	177
EVERSON	Patricia	1946	807	FARLEY	Floyd C.	1927	832
EYE	Lucile	1923	695	FARLEY	Susan		897
EZELL	Elsie	1934	774	FARMER	Wesley	1920	676
				FARNHAM	Marshall Allen	1918	655
				FARNSWORTH	Sarah E.	1860	251
				FARNUM	Leon	1904	477

F

				FARNUM	Robert Leon	1926	721
FAHLMAN	Katherine	1910	777	FARRAR	Gordon Maxwell	1923	604
FAHRENKROG	Roy C.	1917	585	FARRAR	Maxwell Rundel	1897	379
FAILOR	Guy Frederick	1885	324	FARRAR	Muriel Jean	1926	604
FAIR	William G.	1916	570	FARRAR	Shirley R.	1930	604
FAIRCLOTH	Mr.		902	FARRELL	Laura	1894	307
FALCETTI	Roberta Jo		722	FARRELL	Mike	1964	717
FALLON	Edna	1910	377	FARRINGTON	Mary	1818	106
FANCHER	Adeline	1853	328	FARRINGTON	Sarah Ann	1824	115
FANCHER	Albro William	1902	540	FARRIS	Forrest Edward	1916	601
FANCHER	Arkel	1900	541	FARRIS	Gladys May	1917	601
FANCHER	Bertha J.	1884	537	FARRIS	Walter Henderson	1888	377
FANCHER	Byron	1897	540	FAST	Mr.		867
FANCHER	Byron	1897	542	FATTA	Mary		558
FANCHER	Caleb	1859	329	FAWKES	Dinah	1909	466
FANCHER	Dora Belle	1900	616	FAY	Winifred C.	1895	403
FANCHER	Ernest Caleb	1887	539	FAYE	Lola		843
FANCHER	Ethel	1890	541	FEATHERSTONE	Margaret		558
FANCHER	Eunice	1900	540	FEE	Thomas MILKS	1941	674
FANCHER	Fannie Esther	1869	329	FELT	Sarah E.	1860	251
FANCHER	Florence E.	1905	540	FENNELSON	Belle		254
FANCHER	Gertrude Marion	1908	616	FENTON	Frances	1861	233
FANCHER	Gordon	1891	539	FERCHEN	Russell N.	1953	598
FANCHER	Helen M.	1924	766	FERGUSON	Essie	1890	446
FANCHER	Hiram J.	1857	328	FERGUSON	Hollie	1982	907
FANCHER	James Russell	1866	329	FERGUSON	James Harvey	1875	350
FANCHER	Lester	1924	765	FERRILL	William	1811	94
FANCHER	Mabel	1896	539	FERRIS	Adeline	1856	104
FANCHER	Margery	1927	765	FERRIS	Clara	1864	204
FANCHER	Marvin R.	1851	328	FETZER	Luella E.	1923	800

FETZER	Samuel Morgan	1882	618	FISH	Franklin R.	1927	553
FIALA	Ralph J.	1930	596	FISH	Hazel V.	1894	323
FICK	Hugo	1916	456	FISH	Kathryn A.	1950	838
FIEBELKORN	Clair H.	1924	812	FISHER	Florence	1908	375
FIEBELKORN	Herman	1902	640	FISHER	Frank J.	1877	213
FIEBELKORN	James B.	1955	892	FISHER	Jessie Bedford	1902	375
FIEBELKORN	Mark H.	1958	892	FISHER	Lena Evelyn	1918	689
Fiebelkorn	Ruth L.	1928	812	FISHER	Pearl Serilla	1888	247
Fiebelkorn	Tamara L.	1962	892	FISK	Linda Jessica	1945	471
FIEDORCZYK	Casimira Anne	1914	466	FITZE	Bernard Baker	1922	778
FIELDS	Sally	1788	30	FIUMERA	Charles	1925	772
FINCH	Caroline L.	1835	91	FLAGG	Lena A.	1886	243
FINCH	Florence E.	1918	547	FLAGLER	Floy	1876	360
FINDLEY	Allan		524	FLAHERTY	Donald	1920	278
FINDLEY	Annie Azelda	1893	315	FLECKENSTEIN	Joyce	1940	834
FINDLEY	Beryl		524	FLECKINGER	Kenneth Gerald	1965	872
FINDLEY	Clara "Jennie"	1897	315	FLEMING	George		514
FINDLEY	Clifton		529	FLEMING	Theresa	1891	309
FINDLEY	Edna		525	FLETCHER	Donald Edward	1923	595
FINDLEY	Ellen		525	FLETCHER	Mildred	1927	631
FINDLEY	Elmer		525	FLIPOWICZ	Mr.		894
FINDLEY	Eric		524	FLOOD	John Michael	1938	684
FINDLEY	Ernest		525	FLOOD	Mary Ann	1939	684
FINDLEY	Evelyn		524	Flood	Patricia	1941	684
FINDLEY	Florence May	1890	315	FLOOD	Roscoe Jack	1913	439
FINDLEY	Fred Balmer	1887	314	Flood	Vicki A.	1950	684
FINDLEY	George David	1886	314	FLOOD	Winifred	1936	684
FINDLEY	Gerald		524	FOGG	Deborah	1834	90
FINDLEY	Hazel		524	FOIT	William	1930	598
FINDLEY	Joseph Hector	1898	315	FOLLANSBEE	Conrad Gordon	1901	480
FINDLEY	Keith		525	FOLLANSBEE	Conrad Gordon	1926	722
FINDLEY	Leonard		525	FOLLANSBEE	John Nathan	1936	722
Findley	Lynn		525	FOLLETT	Miriam Ellen	1925	713
Findley	Mary		525	FONDA	Emma	1896	220
FINDLEY	Sadie Lula	1895	315	FONDOTS	John George	1953	826
FINDLEY	Samuel	1855	165	FOOTE	Austin	1880	541
FINE	Martha Elizabeth	1888	366	FOOTE	Myrtle Anna	1910	643
FINGER	Lillian R.		720	FOOTE	Nellie	1923	766
FINK	Charlene Wilma	1935	848	FOOTE	Olma	1918	766
FINK	David Paul	1965	826	FOOTE	Winthrop	1921	766
FINK	Gustave A.	1903	705	FORBES	Iva	1891	229
FINK	Shirley Mae	1933	847	FORD	Gertrude L.	1884	350
FINK	Wayne Paul	1937	848	FORNESS	Heather Dawn	1977	910
FISCHER	Dorothy	1903	657	FORNESS	Roger Renee	1955	890
FISH	Amy	1729	9	FORSYTHE	Eleanor Mary	1920	513

Surname	Given Name	Year	Page	Surname	Given Name	Year	Page
FORT	J. Warren	1834	131	FRANCIS	Ethel Ellen	1910	427
FORT	Louis	1813	61	FRANCIS	Frank Wilson	1899	533
FORTCH	Elizabeth	1896	440	FRANCIS	George Charles	1929	762
FORTON	Selina E.	1883	168	FRANCIS	Maria	1831	205
FORTUNATO	Joseph Anthony	1915	549	FRANCIS	Mary Emily	1904	534
FOSLIEN	Donald Leland	1930	704	FRANCIS	Mary Virginia	1932	762
FOSLIEN	Steven Wayne	1954	847	FRANCIS	Oralla	1895	533
FOSTER	Aaron Blaine	1976	887	FRANCIS	Percy G.	1897	533
FOSTER	Elizabeth		895	FRANCIS	Robert Merle	1920	534
FOSTER	Etta Bertha	1889	425	FRANCIS	Ruth Satira	1928	761
Foster	Francine L.	1946	800	FRANCIS	Stanley Edward	1927	762
FOSTER	Harry C.	1870	289	FRANCISCO	Octavia Lavinia	1874	560
FOSTER	Harvey	1912	617	FRANK	Fred	1880	418
FOSTER	Lutie E.	1875	362	FRANK	Peter M.	1881	363
FOSTER	Merrill Turner	1908	702	FRANK	Susan M.	1910	582
FOSTER	Paul	1935	800	FRANKE	Cynthia	1957	714
FOURNIER	Mr.	1960	888	FRANKE	Sidney S.	1919	465
FOUTS	Clarice Maud	1900	454	FRANKLIN	Martha A.	1920	403
FOWLER	Anna	1860	338	FRANZ	Amy Regina	1901	371
FOWLER	Myrtis Mae		499	FRARY	Addie Leona	1860	240
FOX	Addie Mary	1847	237	FREAR	Edward Hughson	1875	321
Fox	Anna M.	1906	430	FREDERICKSON	Herbert	1923	560
FOX	Cora Elizabeth	1869	347	FREDLEY	John Joseph	1927	833
FOX	Jane	1858	254	FREEMAN	Frank N.	1872	301
FOX	Lydia	1854	234	FREEMAN	Frank N.	1879	421
FOX	Mr.		441	FREEMAN	George Wellington	1885	370
FOX	Rex L.	1911	628	FREEMAN	Gertrude Irene	1900	499
FOX	William J.	1868	244	FREEMAN	Halycone Calista	1914	594
FOX	William Milks	1898	430	FREEMAN	Joanna	1825	110
FRAHM	David Shaw	1948	828	FREEMAN	Laurie A.	1962	822
FRAHM	Raymond A.	1910	670	FREEMAN	Malcolm Nelson	1853	241
Frahm	Susan S.	1950	828	FREEMAN	Mark F.	1875	421
FRAHM	William H.	1874	428	Freeman	Mary E.	1879	421
FRAIZER	Dorothy	1935	537	Freeman	May J.	1883	421
FRALEY	Charles Edward	1886	448	FREIDENSTINE	Viola	1907	546
FRALEY	Frances Alice	1908	693	FREILICH	Robin Dee	1957	863
FRALEY	Gloria Maxine	1924	693	FRENCH	Joyce Mable		499
FRALEY	Mary Jane	1932	694	FRENCH	Lillian		499
FRALEY	Melvin Charles	1912	693	FRENTZ	Alta J.	1909	659
FRALEY	Shirley Arline	1919	693	FRENTZ	Claude Emmory	1900	638
FRANCE	Evelyn Geraldine	1911	700	FRENTZ	Theo R.	1942	812
FRANCE	Floyd Kay	1883	457	FRENZ	Joyce A.	1923	650
FRANCIS	Albert Jem	1868	322	FRESEMAN	Cornelia Elrika	1905	423
FRANCIS	Albert Lawrence	1902	534	FREUND	Edgar Matthew	1933	787
FRANCIS	Albert Lawrence, Jr.	1928	762	FREUND	George R., Jr.		884

FRIEDMANN	Louisa Elizabeth	1874	263	FULLMER	Clarence Edward	1915	697
FRIELINK	Helen Elizabeth	1924	503	Fullmer	Evelyn	1957	899
FRIMAN	Carolyn	1943	606	FULLMER	J. L.	1888	455
FRIMAN	Doris	1934	605	FULLMER	Larry Edward	1940	844
FRIMAN	Dorothy J.	1923	605	FULLMER	Larry Edward, Jr.	1962	899
FRIMAN	Eldo Omer	1901	380	FUNK	Betty Jean	1949	727
FRIMAN	Eleanor J.	1938	606	FUREIGH	Barbara Ellen Dale	1972	885
FRIMAN	Genette	1940	606	FUREIGH	Chris M.	1950	793
FRIMAN	Geraldine	1925	605	FURFARO	Robert Peter	1926	833
FRIMAN	Kenneth J.	1924	605	FURGINSON	Margaret Ann	1934	738
FRIMAN	Margaret E.	1938	606	FURSETT	Herbert Anton	1890	565
FRITSCH	Elsie A.	1898	320				
FRITZ	Anna Margaret	1927	531				
FRONK	Antonia William	1890	281		**G**		
FRONK	Antony	1862	138				
FRONK	David	1899	281	GABEL	Gerald	1913	648
Fronk	Jessie P.	1906	281	GABEL	Josephine Lucille	1926	634
Fronk	Mae		281	GAFFNEY	Alice G.	1926	629
FROST	Kathy	1951	748	GAGE	Paul	1904	544
FRY	Hazel M.	1896	370	GAINES	Euclide Dewayne, Sr.	1949	878
FRYE	Elizabeth	1927	485	GAINES	Joseph	1928	775
FRYE	Fada Marie	1948	726	GAISER	Milton	1918	658
FRYE	Frank	1922	484	GALLAGHER	John M.	1948	841
FRYE	Jerry Franklin	1953	728	GALLINEAU	George Newton	1912	612
FRYE	Kathy Virginia	1951	727	GAMPP	Abraham	1849	211
FRYE	Kristi Michelle	1970	859	GAMPP	Genevieve Alice	1894	370
FRYE	Melanie Suzanne	1980	860	GAMPP	George Elmer	1898	370
FRYE	Roger Lee	1951	728	GAMPP	George Elmer	1898	371
FRYE	Ronald Eugene	1949	727	GAMPP	Gertrude	1896	371
FRYE	Stuart Montgomery	1924	485	GAMPP	Isaac	1853	211
FRYE	Timothy Allen	1960	727	GAMPP	Mamie D. Christine	1889	370
FRYE	Timothy Allen	1960	855	GANGER	Betty Jean	1946	744
FRYE	Treva Joyce	1954	727	GANGER	Marie Elaine	1949	744
FULLBRIGHT	Patrick John	1961	885	GANGER	Susan Yvonne	1947	744
FULLER	Cyrus Hewitt	1833	117	GANGER	Willard Jay	1944	744
FULLER	Donald A.	1909	626	GANGER	William Edward	1925	500
FULLER	Donald A., Jr.	1932	806	GARBER	Mr.		869
FULLER	Jane Sophia	1835	147	GARDNER	Austin S.	1850	240
FULLER	Lemira	1847	83	GARDNER	Beryl May	1879	420
FULLER	Linda Jean	1949	824	GARDNER	Everett C., Jr.	1944	813
Fuller	Mary J.	1932	806	GARDNER	Johnny	1965	859
FULLER	Olive	1835	109	GARDNER	Scott E.	1966	892
FULLER	S. Jackson	1861	250	GARDNER	Victor	1927	773
FULLER	Sharon		850	GARDNER	William Allan	1869	222
Fullmer	Bonnie Lee	1944	844	GARFIELD	Solomon Bird	1863	563

GARNER	Gary Eldon	1944	698	**GERWITZ**	Dorothy	1920	834
GARNER	John L.	1940	698	**GESLER**	Molly Ann	1929	833
GARNER	Rebecca Ann	1953	622	**GETMAN**	George Arnold	1899	581
GARNIER	Louise Henry	1910	456	**GETMAN**	George Arnold, Jr.	1921	788
GARRETSON	Ernest Nelson	1884	302	**GETMAN**	George Mason	1866	363
GARRETSON	Gloria Pauline	1954	746	**GETMAN**	Mattibell	1890	581
GARRETSON	Luanne Sylvia	1955	746	**GETTYS**	Mildred	1915	571
GARRETSON	Richard Charles	1924	501	**GETZ**	Magdalene T.	1885	394
GARRETT	Rebecca L.	1954	801	**GHASTIN**	Beverly R.	1925	501
GARSIDE	Martha Ann	1847	176	**GHASTIN**	David Paul	1934	741
GARY	Carol Ann	1957	749	**GHOCA**	Georgia	1880	361
GARY	Irving G.	1930	504	**GIBBS**	Bette Price	1919	469
GARY	Sheila Marie	1951	749	**GIBBS**	Elsie Faith	1914	777
GARZA	Joe	1958	865	**GIBBS**	Flosscelia June	1916	777
GAST	Mary A.	1870	244	**GIBBS**	Grace Louise	1924	778
GATCHEL	Joseph B.	1818	136	**GIBBS**	Maurice Allison	1883	562
GATES	Elton L.	1882	406	**GIBSON**	Elwin	1910	511
GAULT	Vira	1878	334	**GIBSON**	Helen E.	1918	512
GAULT	William	1844	181	**GIBSON**	Laurie	1946	598
GAUTHIER	Chantal M. Francoise	1977	874	**GIBSON**	Maude	1883	245
GAUTHIER	Claire	1977	874	**GIERTZ**	Vernon Leroy	1918	467
GAUTHIER	Helen	1942	741	**GIERTZ-PORTER**	Marla Vernele	1948	714
GAUTHIER	Joseph Roland	1920	509	**GIFFORD**	Alden	1831	60
GAUTHIER	Larry Orville	1945	752	**GIFFORD**	Alden M.	1814	59
GAUTHIER	Marie G. Isabelle	1974	874	**GIFFORD**	Clara F.		130
GAUTHIER	Orville	1914	507	**GIFFORD**	David M.	1820	59
GAVAGAN	Anna Eliza	1876	433	**GIFFORD**	Deborah M.	1847	130
GAY	Gloria Jane	1930	760	**GIFFORD**	Eliza		131
GAYLORD	Xenia S.	1887	363	**GIFFORD**	George Washington	1830	60
GEARHISER	John Richard	1933	383	**GIFFORD**	Gideon D.		130
GEER	Alice Marjorie	1896	337	**GIFFORD**	Gustavus A.	1844	60
GEER	David A.	1866	290	**GIFFORD**	Harriet S.	1824	59
GEER	Susan Lee	1900	483	Gifford	Hattie E.	1857	130
GEIGER	Charles W.	1942	763	**GIFFORD**	Ida Emme	1864	131
GEMPELER	Walter Christ	1895	368	**GIFFORD**	John	1747	15
GENCO	Joseph Salvatore	1975	898	**GIFFORD**	John	1800	27
GENCO	Salvatore Henry	1937	837	**GIFFORD**	John A.	1826	59
GENCO	Sandra Elaine	1964	898	**GIFFORD**	Ladette George	1857	130
Genenbacher	Cheryl L.	1958	609	**GIFFORD**	Mary Earle	1818	59
GENENBACHER	Clarence Joseph	1918	386	**GIFFORD**	Minnie Electra	1865	131
GENENBACHER	Steven Dale	1957	609	**GIFFORD**	Squire	1795	27
GEPHART	Eileen L.	1919	468	**GIFFORD**	Stephen C.	1836	130
GERMOND	Eva B.	1861	132	**GILBERT**	Albert	1896	291
GERNATT	Martha Ruth	1927	831	**GILBERT**	Carrie Myrtle	1884	290
GEROW	John Wesley	1919	530	**GILBERT**	Daphne Helen	1930	485

Surname	Given	Year	Page	Surname	Given	Year	Page
Gilbert	Debbie		856	GLOW	Irene Mae	1920	642
GILBERT	Elizabeth Lucille	1934	724	GLUESING	Ms.		849
GILBERT	Emmett Ray	1879	290	GLYNN	Mary A.	1917	480
GILBERT	Emory Henry	1879	290	GOCHENCOUR	Mary Alice Jo	1923	778
GILBERT	Fred	1891	291	GODDARD	Alice Jean	1931	515
GILBERT	Hattie	1897	292	GODDARD	Mary Ann	1851	126
GILBERT	Henry Dunkley	1910	484	GOEWY	Pieter	1765	34
GILBERT	Henry T.	1847	148	GOFF	Lloyd		856
Gilbert	Ingrid C.	1937	724	GOFORTH	Dwight Davis	1972	858
GILBERT	Jimmy	1961	856	GOLDEN	Kathleen Jean	1964	857
GILBERT	Jimmy Estel	1938	724	GOLDEN	Roger Neil	1948	763
GILBERT	Kathy	1958	856	GOLDEN	W. E.	1917	385
GILBERT	Kenneth Wayne	1947	727	GOLTZ	Elsa	1908	678
GILBERT	Kimberly Ann	1966	859	GOODE	Harold		650
GILBERT	Margaret S.	1862	265	GOODFELLOW	Gladys	1900	539
GILBERT	Mary	1889	291	GOODRUM	Sallie		364
GILBERT	Maryland Virginia	1924	484	GOODWIN	Eva Maud	1866	327
GILBERT	Maude	1882	290	GORDON	Charles Albert	1925	743
GILBERT	Ora Juanita	1920	484	GORDON	Charles Albert, Jr.	1947	867
GILBERT	Phyllis Diane	1952	728	GORDON	Dollena Ann	1935	743
GILBERT	Ralph Junior	1927	485	GORDON	Edith I.	1930	743
GILBERT	Rebecca	1886	291	GORDON	Maxine I.	1928	743
Gilbert	Susan	1940	724	GORDON	Ronald John	1949	868
GILBERT	Valerie Denise	1977	859	GORDON	Thomas E.	1899	583
GILCHRIST	Robert A.	1920	718	GORDON	William Roy	1884	499
GILES	Phebe	1807	34	GOSSELIN	Ms.		660
GILL	Charles E.	1888	406	GOTHAM	Deborah Freeman	1811	27
GILL	Wanita L.	1927	664	GOULD	Charlotte Elizabeth	1907	581
GILLETT	Laura Leonora	1847	92	GOULD	Doris Anna	1912	581
GILLETTE	David B.	1799	86	GOULD	Frank Arnold	1871	363
GILLOW	Monica		877	GOULD	Jay Carroll	1881	398
GILLOW	Paul		771	GOULD	Laura Louise	1909	581
GILMAN	Daniel	1810	122	GOULD	Miriam L.	1901	710
GILMAN	Mary	1840	264	GOULD	Royal Frank	1914	581
GILMORE	Terry Donavon	1944	709	GOULD	Royal Asa	1846	208
GITCHO	Boris	1918	695	GOURLEY	Augusta Margaret	1891	321
GITNER	Helen Olga	1951	754	GRAHAM	David Ernest	1917	509
GIVANT	Mr.		900	GRAHAM	Thelma		526
GLASCO	Deborah		855	GRAM	Kirsten	1939	779
GLASGOW	Cali		885	GRAMMER	Marie A.	1917	271
GLEASON	Dorothy Irene	1928	687	GRANDON	Blanche M.	1890	399
GLENN	Alfred	1866	285	GRANSBURY	Lillian	1912	551
GLENN	David Francis	1967	908	GRANT	George F.	1920	474
GLESSNER	Janet Lee	1937	848	GRANT	Mariah	1845	179
GLOR	Hilda Mildred	1901	430	GRASMUK	Elizabeth	1901	342

GRASSMEYER	Inez	1901	375		**GROSS**	Shirley	1935	729
GRAVELINE	Paul N.	1917	521		**GROVERMAN**	Kay	1920	535
GRAVES	Roger Dale, Jr.	1979	905		**GUBA**	Peter	1953	877
GRAVES	Sylvia	1792	31		**GUERRA**	Mauro	1914	548
GRAY	Donald Paul, Jr.	1953	839		**GUEST**	Mr.		757
GRAY	Mary Eveline	1888	355		**GUETABA**	Bernard Koudjo	1974	874
GRAY	Ms.		900		**GuGGENBERGER**	Phiilomena Barbara	1920	677
GREEN	Bessie Fannie	1880	228		**GUION**	Charles F.	1837	127
GREEN	Clarence E.	1940	836		**GUION**	Elizabeth Ives	1875	271
GREEN	Dale Richard	1930	709		**GUION**	Frances A	1866	270
GREEN	Herbert L.	1919	646		**GURNSEY**	Constance Ruth	1934	751
GREEN	Jane	1825	61		**GUTH**	Thekla J.	1855	325
GREEN	Paula Kay	1950	752		**GUZIK**	Michele Lynn	1972	716
GREEN	Rebecca		836					
GREEN	Sibyl E.	1868	356					
GREEN	Velma I.	1925	728					
GREENE	Mildred		525					

H

GREENER	Una	1896	320		**HAAS**	Helen D.	1904	425
GREER	Gerald Gardner	1901	644		**HAAS**	Stanley E.	1876	242
GREER	Gerald Parks	1927	815		**HABEL**	Clifford	1925	772
Greer	Pamela L.		815		**HACKETT**	Mr.		835
GREGG	Richard L., Sr.	1929	681		**HADLEY**	Niles W.	1943	812
GREGORIUS	Esther	1910	559		**HADLEY**	Raymond		891
GREGORY	Mary Louise	1901	477		**HAEDRICK**	Robin	1962	826
GRIEN	Minnie	1898	490		**HAFFEN**	Donna Marie	1956	879
GRIFFIN	DeWitt	1836	185		**HAGADORN**	Catherine Rumane	1905	430
GRIFFIN	Dewitt Clinton	1882	339		**HAGAN**	Sharon Rae	1951	611
GRIFFIN	Dewitt James	1914	557		**HAGEN**	June Juanita	1923	620
GRIFFIN	Donald V.	1907	557		**HAGERDON**	Bessie	1885	393
GRIFFIN	Matthew Sharpe	1886	340		**HAGGERTY**	Ella T.	1885	321
GRIFFIN	Roxanne		893		**HAGLIN**	Tore	1914	816
GRIFFIN	Viola Catherine	1916	557		**HAGMAN**	Heidi Louise	1965	855
GRIFFIN	Warner George	1920	557		**HAHN**	Andrew A.	1960	878
GRIFFIN	Warner Miller	1889	340		**HAHN**	David L.	1958	877
GRIFFITHS	Shirley A.	1930	733		**HAHN**	Eugene F.	1928	772
GRIMM	John H.	1855	253		**HAHN**	Jane		878
GRIMSSLEY	Eva Mae	1934	708		**HAHN**	Pamela Jean	1955	877
GRINNEL	Dorcas C.	1804	39		**HAHN**	Susan	1953	877
GRISWOLD	John J.	1845	145		**HAIGHT**	Donald Clayton	1920	554
GRISWOLD	Laura A.	1850	146		**HAIGHT**	Donna Kathleen	1950	774
GRISWOLD	Lyman	1816	69		**HAIGHT**	John C.	1946	773
GRISWOLD	Mary	1818	69		Haight	Lois H.	1948	773
GRISWOLD	Wickham H.	1876	286		**HAIGHT**	Melanie	1957	774
GROSHONG	Joanne L.	1940	791		**HAIGHT**	Mildred Harriet	1893	418
GROSS	Ruth Jean	1937	661		**HALL**	Benny Lee	1934	743

HALL	Brenda Lee		769	HANNAH	Nellie Marie	1916	490
HALL	Charlotte	1920	451	HANSEN	Lester F.	1921	605
HALL	Edgar Harold	1889	305	HANSON	Alma Elizabeth	1901	459
HALL	Elizabeth	1858	125	HANSON	Bertha Edna	1913	699
HALL	Hamlyn Robert	1928	509	HANSON	Harold Hartvig	1911	601
HALL	J. B.		130	HANSON	Joseph	1827	262
HALL	Mildred	1913	625	HANSON	Joseph William	1874	456
HALL	Mr.	1927	790	HANSON	Vyda Margaret	1909	699
HALL	Penny Marie	1952	868	HARD	Norman		505
HALL	Sarah	1769	14	HARD	Paul Joseph	1970	750
HALLENBECK	Alvero L.	1919	764	HARDEN	Margaret	1900	541
HALLENBECK	Bert	1870	229	HARDER	Mary Gertrude	1929	820
HALLENBECK	Hazel	1895	405	HARDING	Edward Snyder	1854	327
HALLENBECK	Laura	1959	658	HARDY	Lediah	1887	402
HALLETT	Alfred William	1899	372	HARIG	Robert L.	1930	504
HALLOCK	Harriet A.	1855	250	HARKNESS	Olney	1909	616
HALLOCK	Kate		147	HARMEL	Erick F.	1910	696
HALLORAN	Paul		768	Harness	Cynthia E.	1956	793
HALSTEAD	Margaret E.	1863	153	HARNESS	David Lionel	1954	793
HALSTEAD	Margaret E.	1863	166	HARNESS	Donald Eugene	1933	792
HAMANN	Leila Clara	1919	495	HARNESS	Elizabeth Ann	1935	792
HAMILTON	Eliza	1830	92	HARNESS	Kenneth Carl	1913	585
HAMILTON	Katherine	1910	479	Harness	Maecelle B.	1940	792
HAMILTON	Leroy James, Sr.	1930	813	HARNESS	Patricia Louise	1942	792
HAMILTON	Ruth	1910	647	HARPER	Bessie	1904	481
HAMLEY	David L.	1964	896	HARRINGTON	Allen	1843	114
HAMLEY	Leonard H., Jr.	1936	829	HARRINGTON	Benjamin	1833	114
Hamley	Margaret A.	1962	896	HARRINGTON	Byron	1894	432
HAMLIN	David William	1959	825	HARRINGTON	Cynthia	1862	246
HAMLIN	Walter A.	1928	667	HARRINGTON	David W.	1834	114
HAMM	Alice C.	1908	374	HARRINGTON	Dora	1862	246
HAMMERLY	Ralph	1921	597	HARRINGTON	Edward	1874	247
HAMMOND	David		654	Harrington	Ellen	1830	113
HAMMOND	James	1910	386	HARRINGTON	George	1865	247
HAMMOND	Priscilla	1815	59	HARRINGTON	Hannah	1837	114
HAMPEL	Anthony H.	1892	582	HARRINGTON	Howard	1860	246
HAND	Violet	1900	465	HARRINGTON	Job	1821	113
HANHIMAKI	James Jari	1962	754	HARRINGTON	John J.	1849	115
HANICHEN	Christopher		909	HARRINGTON	Leroy	1923	693
HANICHEN	James M.	1925	786	HARRINGTON	Lewis	1871	247
HANICHEN	Joy		884	HARRINGTON	Lucy	1865	246
HANICHEN	Michael Eric	1953	884	HARRINGTON	Mary Matilda	1848	114
HANKS	Charles A.	1930	808	HARRINGTON	Maud	1888	432
HANKS	Percy	1895	633	HARRINGTON	Merritt R.	1863	247
HANNAH	Bethel	1918	584	HARRINGTON	Richard, Jr.	1796	45

HARRINGTON	Richard, Jr.	1796	48	HAYNES	Heather Lynn	1970	883
HARRINGTON	Ruth	1824	114	HAYNES	Joyce Ava	1938	470
HARRINGTON	Thomas A.	1858	247	HAYNES	Robert Elroy	1939	784
HARRINGTON	William	1872	247	HAYNES	Terry Ann	1966	883
HARRIS	Clarissa May	1871	354	HAYNES	Whitney Mae	1964	883
HARRIS	Jack	1920	686	HEALEY	Catherine	1861	104
HARRIS	Mary	1881	446	HEATH	Ernest W.	1869	218
HARRIS	Shirley	1949	727	HEATH	Esther		277
HARSH	Nathan Reid	1975	869	HECHINGER	Sarah Clementine	1879	364
HART	Bernice	1894	649	HEDGES	Delton Leroy	1923	743
HART	Joy K.	1956	863	HEGLER	Louise	1900	491
HARTE	Frances		414	HEILMAN	Charles	1930	607
HARTFORD	Benjamin B.	1829	124	HEIMBACK	Sandra L.	1948	795
HARTLOFF	Gordon Stanley	1903	581	HEINEMAN	Beverly Ann	1927	705
HARTLOFF	Walter Sheldon	1903	581	HEINEMANN	Minnie	1897	263
HARTSOCK	George	1851	326	HEINLY	Clarence Oliver	1890	580
HARVEY	Charles S.	1843	139	HEISE	Phil		853
HARVEY	Hattie E.	1875	281	Helsley	Helen	1923	780
HARVEY	Jan		793	HELSLEY	Leslie		881
HARVEY	Velma	1930	642	HELSLEY	Lester Bailey	1896	562
HASKINS	Margaret Maria	1820	105	HELSLEY	Wayne	1923	780
HASKINS	Theresa L.		154	HEMENWAY	Dwight L.	1844	180
HASSE	Jeremy Douglas	1976	872	HEMENWAY	Edwin H.	1837	179
HASTINGS	Mr.	1868	349	Hemingway	Araminta	1855	142
HASTY	Jerry Noel	1938	824	Hemingway	Clara	1845	142
HASWELL	Julia Ann	1808	65	HEMINGWAY	Joseph R.	1842	142
HATHAWAY	Mary	1779	25	HEMINGWAY	Joseph Russell	1813	68
HAVENDER	Claude Sylvester	1895	302	Hemingway	Mary A.	1853	142
HAVENER	Eva Leona	1917	501	HEMINGWAY	William	1852	142
HAVERCROFT	Alice Ethelyn	1875	168	HEMMENWAY	Henry C.	1830	123
HAWKINS	Addie		204	HEMPFIELD	Elizabeth	1670	3
HAWKINS	Dale	1950	728	HENDERSON	Brian	1961	859
HAWKINS	Frank G.	1866	207	HENDERSON	Carl B.	1910	489
HAWKINS	George B.	1861	170	HENDERSON	Nancy Lucinda	1887	437
HAWKINS	Richard Elon	1933	811	HENDGES	Beverly Jean	1947	868
HAWLEY	Edna Anna	1905	313	HENDGES	Delton Leroy	1949	868
HAY	Alice	1912	636	HENDLEY	Christopher		515
HAY	Clarence C.	1916	637	HENDRICKS	Edith Viola	1912	662
HAYDEN	Chris	1977	859	HENDRICKS	Martha Priscilla	1886	334
HAYDEN	Pearline		854	HENLY	Lillian	1901	323
HAYDON	May		355	HENNESS	Harry V.	1879	542
HAYES	Barbara Anna	1949	879	HENNESS	Josephine Mary	1916	767
HAYES	Claude G.	1900	764	HENNESS	Peter J.	1854	330
HAYES	Cynthia R.		742	HENNESS	Rosalee	1913	766
HAYNES	Anne	1890	358	HENRY	Edward	1920	818

HENRY	Virginia Lee	1926	687	**HILL**	Charles	1870	202
HEOFT	Helen	1924	783	**HILL**	Cleo A.	1954	868
HERBST	Florence May	1894	403	**HILL**	Eunice	1931	816
HERDMAN	James	1859	185	**HILL**	Mary	1843	72
HERDMAN	Mary	1858	338	**HILL**	Mary E.	1833	99
HERMAN	Alphonse	1888	450	**HILL**	Nora Jean	1928	704
HERMAN	Earl	1916	695	**HILL**	Orrin E.	1895	645
HERMAN	Willis	1918	695	**HILL**	Patsy Lou	1927	673
HERR	Viola Maxine	1927	688	**HILL**	Peter	1966	793
HERRICK	Diana	1832	66	**HILL**	Stanley D.	1932	743
HERRICK	Gertrude	1870	241	**HILL**	Stanley D., Jr.	1952	868
HERRON	Archie		692	**HILL**	Vivian Viola	1922	816
HERRON	James W.		446	**HILLESTAD**	Ingrid	1920	390
HERSHEY	Lewis Blaine. II	1957	864	**HILLIARD**	Betty		784
HERSTEAD	Louis J.	1928	690	**HILLIARD**	Clara	1855	198
HESS	Dale Stanley	1943	786	**HILLIARD**	Daniel Mareno	1846	197
HEUGH	Herbert John	1947	754	**HILLIARD**	Dean		572
HEUGH	Jennifer Lisle	1977	873	**HILLIARD**	Ebenezer B.	1817	89
HEUGH	Jodi Lynn	1980	873	**HILLIARD**	Ethel	1889	355
HEUGH	John Hall Weir	1926	513	**HILLIARD**	Ezra Milks	1849	197
HEUGH	Nancy Jean	1948	754	**HILLIARD**	Frank	1879	354
HEYBECK	George J.	1855	201	**HILLIARD**	Grace		354
HEYN	Jennifer Louise	1979	866	**HILLIARD**	Hazen I.	1898	293
HICE	Jerome	1845	72	**HILLIARD**	Isaac N.	1865	150
HICKS	Isabel	1905	429	**HILLIARD**	Lonson Darius	1849	197
HICKS	Laura	1846	147	**HILLIARD**	Lorenzo Merrill	1870	354
HICKS	Mary A.	1853	225	Hilliard	Mary Elizabeth	1923	572
HIGBY	Ellen E.	1850	259	**HILLIARD**	Maud		354
HIGBY	Sherill	1831	140	**HILLIARD**	Myrtle	1887	151
HIGGINS	Benjamin John	1886	457	Hilliard	Nellie	1902	293
HIGGINS	Bernard	1923	699	Hilliard	Rena	1850	197
HIGGINS	Bessie E.	1890	457	**HILLIARD**	Samuel David	1860	149
HIGGINS	Clayton	1914	699	**HILLIARD**	Shirl	1908	572
Higgins	Dorothy Lucille	1926	700	**HILLIARD**	Sumner Hale	1858	199
HIGGINS	Edna Ruth	1893	457	**HILLIARD**	Trella	1884	354
Higgins	Ella Mae	1920	699	**HILLIARD**	Violet Irene	1915	486
HIGGINS	Gertrude Lila	1900	458	**HILLIARD**	William Ezra	1885	293
HIGGINS	Hazel Lennie	1898	457	**HILLIKER**	Mary E.	1902	283
HIGGINS	John S.	1860	262	**HILLMAN**	Lucy	1852	114
HIGGINS	Mabel Grace	1891	457	**HILSINGER**	Louisa	1852	178
HIGGINS	Vera Ella	1903	458	**HILTS**	Jay	1935	854
HILDY	Charles Edward	1880	258	**HINES**	Robert O.	1938	803
HILDY	Cornelius Wallace	1907	451	**HINGSTON**	Genevieve Clark	1880	222
HILDY	Grace Olivia Elsie	1910	452	**HINMAN**	Christine L.	1959	801
HILL	Carl		652	**HINMAN**	James Duane	1934	814

HINSCH	Mark Charles	1955	846	**HOLMES**	Carl Alfred	1896	419
HINTZ	Emma	1890	406	**HOLMES**	Carl Alfred, Jr.	1925	655
HIRSCH	Ruth Adeline	1909	426	**HOLMES**	Christopher C.	1874	309
HIXSON	Carleton K.	1905	647	**HOLMES**	Cora Ellen	1929	655
HIXSON	Helen Alice	1903	646	**HOLMES**	Hilliary		515
Hixson	Hilda	1907	647	**HOLMES**	Lillian	1915	514
HIXSON	Howard Harden	1874	412	**HOLMES**	Mary		515
HIXSON	John Robert	1925	647	**HOLMES**	Mary Morna		515
HIXSON	Luther N.	1843	236	**HOLMES**	Myrtle Alice	1920	655
HIXSON	Thomas Edson	1875	413	**HOLMES**	Phebe J.	1957	821
HOAG	Anna	1832	97	**HOLMES**	Roma	1910	514
HOAG	Isaac	1784	28	**HOLMES**	Sullivan G.	1862	265
HOAG	Jacob	1825	61	**HOLT**	Orol Evelyn	1917	389
HOAG	Jane	1815	61	**HOMEL**	Nellie Bly		340
HOAG	Julia E.	1813	61	**HOOKER**	Florence E.	1852	205
HOBBS	Alexander Stephen		759	**HOOLIHAN**	Alma Minnie	1900	551
HODGINS	Asa F.	1878	169	**HOOLIHAN**	Clarence	1871	336
HODGINS	Ethel Maude	1874	169	**HOOPER**	Bruce	1979	907
HODGINS	Roland Deo	1896	320	**HOOPER**	Katharine T.	1851	279
HODGINS	William	1839	76	**HOOPER**	Lawrence S.		807
HODGINS	William Rugless	1869	168	**HOOVER**	Hedric	1918	587
HODSON	Fred Walter	1899	373	**HOOVER**	Minnie		480
HODSON	Mary Lou	1933	597	**HOPKIN**	Eleanor Louisa	1910	324
HODSON	Russell Blake	1930	597	**HOPKINS**	Mr.	1860	215
HOEFT	Mr.	1905	569	**HOPP**	Allen	1910	676
HOEGER	Enno August	1894	696	**HOPP**	Amy L.	1972	889
HOEHNE	Norman Paul	1948	863	**HOPP**	Berdena Irene	1928	833
HOFFERT	Erma L.	1915	696	**HOPPER**	Nelson, II	1913	567
HOFFERT	Walter W.	1894	453	Horan	Aileen	1951	761
HOFFMAN	Kathryn Rose	1917	673	**HORAN**	Daniel	1951	761
HOFFMAN	Mary Elizabeth	1870	183	**HORAN**	Jane Bernadette	1906	310
HOGE	Mary Augusta		456	**HORAN**	Robert James	1920	532
HOGEN	Philip N.	1944	840	**HORGAN**	William G.	1947	763
HOGENCAMP	Charles L.	1956	774	**HORROCKS**	Elizabeth	1871	139
HOGENSON	Marguerite	1904	542	**HORTON**	Amy	1765	22
HOLDERMAN	Samuel	1866	256	**HORTON**	Marie J.	1924	633
HOLDREDGE	Olive	1869	244	**HORTON**	Mildred G.	1900	429
HOLLAND	Donna Inez	1928	537	**HORTON**	Robert L.	1937	837
HOLLAND	Henry Bright	1912	630	**HOSMER**	Margaret G.	1918	646
HOLLAND	Mary Nellie	1910	511	**HOUGAS**	Harriet	1918	693
HOLLAND	Vincent		525	**HOUGAS**	Leo	1900	448
HOLLENBECK	Linda M.	1947	763	**HOUGH**	Florence	1905	776
HOLLY	Forest	1909	653	**HOUGH**	Hannah	1854	230
HOLLY	Gwendolyn		819	**HOUGH**	John	1875	561
HOLMES	Abel S.	1818	122	**HOUGH**	Leonard A.	1885	472

HOUGHTON	Curtis		790
HOUR	Cora E.	1866	169
HOUSE	Harold Campbell	1922	830
HOUSE	Harry Ferdinand	1890	674
HOUSE	Harry Frederick	1919	830
HOUSMAN	Sherman Willis	1916	572
HOUTE	Frank	1880	415
HOVER	Lillian	1900	539
HOVEY	Donald Eugene	1929	772
HOWARD	Amanda	1821	115
Howard	Ella	1872	360
HOWARD	Fred H. MILKS	1865	432
HOWARD	Guy L.	1895	578
HOWARD	Harry W.	1872	360
HOWARD	Henry MILKS	1844	247
HOWARD	James A.	1841	203
HOWARD	James Henry MILKS	1875	433
HOWARD	James Henry, Jr	1904	675
HOWARD	Mary Ann	1836	116
HOWARD	Myron	1913	673
HOWE	Marion	1898	341
HOWE	Mary Hannah	1907	633
HOWIE	Thomas	1925	521
HOWLAND	Charles S.	1922	475
HOWLAND	Clifton	1918	768
HOWLAND	Elias Pollock	1847	141
HOWLAND	Elizabeth	1820	59
HOWLAND	Elsie L.	1929	475
HOWLAND	Ethel Mae	1931	475
HOWLAND	Hazel E.	1925	475
HOWLAND	Lizzie	1883	282
HOWLAND	Milton E.	1913	474
HOWLAND	Seth Adam	1885	283
HOWLAND	Vera	1920	474
HOWLISON	Oleta Isabelle	1920	624
HOXIE	Robert J.	1961	846
HOYT	Barthena	1831	91
HUBBARD	Emily	1834	233
HUBBARD	Homer J.	1906	568
HUBBARD	Manley M.	1810	109
HUCKLE	Patricia Ann	1932	851
HUCKLEBERRY	Zenda M.	1938	586
HUDSON	Linley Moses	1886	297
HUFF	Addie	1872	418
HUGGINS	Ollie	1850	184
HUGHES	Edward Charles	1908	323
HUGHES	Frances Marian	1932	596
HUGHES	Francis J., Jr.	1944	743
HUGHES	Ida Belle	1900	551
HUGHES	Jacob Watson	1885	381
HUGHES	John C., Jr.	1914	614
HUGHES	Lois Kathryn	1929	596
HUGHES	Lorraine C.	1941	798
HUGHES	Nadine	1921	818
HUGHES	Thomas Gerard	1902	372
HUGHS	Herbert Warren	1898	552
HULBERT	Edward George	1889	411
HUME	Betty	1924	693
HUNT	Bernadette	1930	735
HUNT	Dorothy	1905	568
HUNT	Edna Sarah Marie	1911	495
HUNT	Franklin B.	1874	352
HUNT	George Russell	1892	465
HUNT	George Russell	1953	853
HUNT	George Russell, Jr.	1923	713
HUNT	Juanita Joyce	1932	498
HUNT	Marvel Lillian	1901	568
HUNT	Mary Louise	1956	853
HUNT	Sadie F.	1913	300
Hunt	Trish		853
HUNTER	Doris	1915	651
HUNTINGTON	James R.	1922	768
HUTCHESON	Emma	1865	215
HUTCHINSON	Elizabeth Guion	1901	469
HUTCHINSON	Harold Feld	1879	271
HUTCHINSON	Robert		899
HUTTON	Martha Ann	1826	95
HUTTON	Myrtle	1907	483
HUTTON	Samuel J.	1872	290
HUTZ	Robert P.	1919	590
HYATT	Charlotte	1902	283
HYDE	Allan		527
HYLAND	Raymond Scott	1926	831

I, J

IFLAND	Jane	1932	588
ILIFF	Chauncy Emory	1875	298
ILIFF	Wesley	1837	153
ILSLEY	Almira		24
INGRAM	Annah	1805	43
INMAN	Sarah	1803	32
IRELAND	Martha	1785	38
IRISH	Donald Scott	1971	866
IRONS	Anna		247
IRVING	John Christie	1864	355
IRVING	Marguerite Lucille	1910	374
IRWIN	Alice	1860	280
IRWIN	James	1830	137
IRWIN	Kay		524
IRWIN	Libbie	1851	279
IRWIN	Willis	1857	279
IVERSON	Elizabeth	1872	195
JACKSON	Jamee	1977	907
JACKSON	John Morgan	1919	789
JACKSON	Lillian	1906	472
JACKSON	Mary Ann	1847	199
JACKSON	William K.	1954	740
JACOB	Shanda Marie	1974	908
JACOBS	James C., II	1932	716
JACOBS	James C., Jr.	1896	469
Jacobs	Nancy C.	1936	716
JACOBS	Wilber	1913	788
JACOBSON	Eldor Burton	1926	602
JACOBSON	Olive	1880	354
JAGEACKS	Mary Ann	1934	621
JAMES	Alice M.	1860	129
JAMES	Betty Bee Pearl	1929	833
JAMES	Dennis Kelly	1949	897
JAMES	Donald Claude	1898	675
JAMES	Ernest Kelly	1926	833
JAMES	Gertrude C.	1846	279
JAMES	Thomas	1810	136
JANSEN	Clarence Robert		559
JANSEN	Evelyn		558
JANSEN	John Dunham		558
JANSEN	Ruth		559
JANSEN	Thomas		341
JANSEN	William D.		559
JEFFERSON	Betty Rae	1928	689
JEMISON	FITZHUGH	1898	405
JEMISON	Joan	1927	635
JENKINS	Orie George	1907	544
JENKS	John K.	1873	439
JENNEY	Elizabeth B.	1846	130
JIMERSON	Edward Dean	1894	405
JOHNS	Vivien Violet	1911	294
JOHNSON	Alec	1856	331
JOHNSON	Chalmer C.	1915	501
JOHNSON	Charles Ray	1958	715
JOHNSON	Corey		854
JOHNSON	Daniel Leigh	1946	809
JOHNSON	Devon	1922	497
JOHNSON	Devon Jeffrey	1949	740
JOHNSON	Elsie Elvena	1903	302
JOHNSON	Fern Maurice	1913	493
JOHNSON	Genevieve Frances	1922	543
JOHNSON	George		843
JOHNSON	Goldie A.	1891	437
JOHNSON	Gregory Scott	1962	856
JOHNSON	Harold E.		537
JOHNSON	Herman R.	1905	690
JOHNSON	Isabelle	1928	555
JOHNSON	Jack Duane	1937	746
JOHNSON	Kimberly A.	1960	820
JOHNSON	Krista Elaine		864
JOHNSON	Laverne D.		896
JOHNSON	Lee A.	1885	444
JOHNSON	Leland O.	1909	690
JOHNSON	Mabel Luella	1906	691
JOHNSON	Marie	1875	257
JOHNSON	Marion Eleanor	1918	578
JOHNSON	Marsha L.	1961	715
JOHNSON	Melvin	1918	693
JOHNSON	Mr.		468
JOHNSON	Mr.		900
JOHNSON	Orol Evelyn	1917	389
JOHNSON	Patricia	1916	590
JOHNSON	Pearl	1894	365
JOHNSON	Ralph L.	1939	828
JOHNSON	Robert		878
JOHNSON	Sarah M.	1885	357
JOHNSON	Stanley H.	1912	590
JOHNSON	T. Edward	1883	369

JOHNSON	Teressa Elaine	1951	741
JOHNSON	Timothy Edward	1964	741
JOHNSON	Tina Louise	1965	888
JOHNSON	William		603
JOHNSON	William Joel	1840	176
JOHNSTON	Mary Watson	1879	462
JOHNSTON	Sharon		903
JOINER	Edward L.	1926	666
JOLLY	William	1760	23
JONES	Althera	1857	231
JONES	David Samuel	1834	249
JONES	Edward Truman	1877	437
JONES	Frank K.	1865	131
JONES	John Rasten	1874	364
JONES	Londa Jean	1945	842
JONES	Lydia Alice	1895	303
JONES	Martha Elizabeth	1880	364
JONES	Mary Frances	1960	723
JONES	Maryellen E.	1947	698
JONES	Mildred	1897	545
JONES	Mr.		894
JONES	Muriel Maxine	1921	719
Jones	Nellie B.	1905	437
JONES	Rick		742
JONES	Rowena Helen	1901	366
JONES	Tiney	1901	364
JORDAN	Charles E.	1916	555
JORDAN	Sarah	1837	193
JORDON	Barbara		272
JORDON	Lydia		272
Joslin	Dannielle	1962	875
JOSLIN	Vernon L., Jr.	1958	875
JOYCE	Gerald Robert	1939	516
JOYCE	Patrick Gerald Robert	1971	756
JUDD	Lissa R.	1954	719
JUDD	Rachael	1844	181
JUDD	Redmond	1815	81
JUETT	Martin William	1919	594
JUMP	Bethier	1831	178
JUNE	Charles	1882	445
JUNE	Charles Everett	1908	691
JUNE	Earle K.	1914	691
June	Geneva W.	1912	691
JUNE	Glenn	1887	445
JUNE	Howard Henry	1889	445
June	Laperia	1890	445
JUNE	William	1850	255
JUNGBLUT	William	1923	389
JURS	Helen	1905	690

K

Kahut	Carol J.	1938	765
KAHUT	Matthew J.	1905	540
KAHUT	Peter Matthew	1935	765
KAMMIRE	Donald		654
KANE	Lou Ann	1956	847
KANE	Mary C.	1856	251
KARNES	Frank Andrew	1942	610
KASSIAN	Wilma L.	1941	662
KAUFFMANN	Gene Vernon	1946	749
KEALEY	William Edward	1892	563
KEATING	Jeanne A	1958	658
KEECH	Pauline Fern	1936	500
KEHR	Anna Carrie	1874	363
KEITH	Clara M.	1918	670
KEITH	Danny Thurman		885
KEITH	Laurie A.	1963	892
Keith	Mr.		813
KELLEY	Wilma	1920	640
KELLOCK	Jennie	1865	279
KELLOGG	Alice	1866	265
KELLOGG	Benjamin F.	1871	288
KELLOGG	Bertha May	1879	288
KELLOGG	Eva Louise	1869	287
KELLOGG	Florilla	1855	343
KELLOGG	George Henry	1861	287
KELLOGG	Ira	1835	147
KELLOGG	James Monroe	1863	287
KELLOGG	Margaret	1844	57
KELLOGG	Matilda Melissa	1870	287
KELLOGG	Stella	1911	478
KELLY	Augustus	1839	125
KELLY	Basil Wilber	1940	751
KELLY	Elnora M.	1931	737
KELLY	Evelyn Jean	1938	750
KELLY	Florence	1907	557

KELLY	Fredric Douglas	1943	751	**KESTNER**	Larry Allen	1956	855
KELLY	Helen	1920	512	**KESTNER**	Theresa Gail	1959	856
KELLY	Katherine Elizabeth	1863	267	**KEYES**	Grace Audrey	1905	304
KELLY	Kristina J.	1983	896	**KEYES**	Sarah J.	1839	60
KELLY	Verna Dee	1941	751	**KHURT**	Marcella	1920	390
KELLY	Vernal Earl	1914	506	**KIBBE**	Eva	1863	348
KELLY	Victoria Elaine	1946	751	**KIDDER**	Alice	1885	214
KELLY	William F.	1865	280	**KIESTER**	Annie	1880	353
KELSEY	Catherine	1851	131	**KIGHT**	Mr.		757
KELSO	Teresa	1920	594	**Kilburn**	Karen Ann	1956	820
KEMP	Allan		848	**KILBURN**	Marshal G.	1926	660
KEMP	Debra L.	1957	902	**KILBURN**	Marshal G., Jr.	1953	820
KEMP	Denise A.	1958	901	**KILBY**	Dorothy Irene	1926	639
KEMP	Mary	1963	902	**KILBY**	Florence Leola	1906	638
KEMP	Samuel John	1952	746	**KILBY**	James Montell	1880	408
KEMPER	Adolph H.	1880	377	**KILE**	Adam	1820	72
KEMPER	Ardys Marion	1914	601	**KILE**	Chester Pierce	1853	148
KEMPER	Carlos E	1911	600	**KILE**	Hazel Violet	1887	292
KEMPER	Evelyn	1912	600	**KILLINGSTAD**	Edward O.	1914	573
KEMPER	Kathryn Elizabeth	1919	601	**KILMARTIN**	Joan L.	1935	519
KENNEDY	Kenneth	1950	749	**KIMBALL**	Cora E.	1871	292
KENNEDY	Myrtle L.	1898	463	**KIMBALL**	Dighton William	1846	149
KENNEY	Robert	1851	253	**KIMBALL**	Edward L.	1928	720
KENNY	Julia	1868	161	**KIMBALL**	Minnie M.	1873	292
KENNY	Rose Helen	1882	282	**KIMBALL**	Robert Homer	1877	293
KENT	Henry Clarence	1930	762	**KIMBERLIN**	Dewayne Judson	1970	858
KENT	Ian Trevor	1963	883	**KINCADE**	Franklin P.	1890	356
KENYON	Carrie	1852	179	**KINCADE**	Mary Jane	1920	575
KENYON	Emma	1855	179	**KING**	Adelbert	1880	412
KENYON	Irene	1897	432	**KING**	Billi Jo		610
KENYON	Maria	1842	116	**KING**	David Allen	1970	894
KENYON	Mr.	1842	118	**KING**	Dollie Ann	1877	413
KEPPLE	Mary	1798	64	**KING**	Donald W.	1930	501
KERCHER	Martha C.	1915	473	**KING**	Ella	1906	541
KERKENDORF	Iva		654	**KING**	Hattie E.	1891	438
KERL	Christopher	1820	79	**KING**	Helen May	1951	817
KERN	Charles M.	1970	875	**KING**	Jessie May	1887	437
KERNEY	Mae Elsa		413	**KING**	Lori	1970	869
KERNS	John J.	1921	651	**KING**	Lucien Minor	1882	290
KERR	Frances Lois	1880	334	**KING**	Steve A.	1950	839
KESSLER	Chester Lee	1892	269	**KING**	Thelma Louise	1919	646
KESSLER	Robert Noble	1918	469	**KING**	Wilbur	1925	646
KESSLER	Ruth Ann	1920	469	**KINGSTON**	Clara Belle	1906	573
KESTNER	Edward Eugene	1952	855	**KINNEE**	David Bryan	1955	745
KESTNER	John William	1924	724	**KINNEE**	David Bryan, Jr.	1978	871

KINNEE	Deanna Marie	1980	871	**KNIGHT**	Mr.	1900	458
KINNEE	Shawn Lynn	1975	870	**KNIGHT**	Ralph P.	1884	425
KINNICUTT	Emeline L.	1826	110	**KNOCHE**	Elaine	1933	597
KINNICUTT	Leander W.	1822	112	**KNOOP**	Mark Kevin	1954	823
KIPP	Mary Ann	1815	57	**KNUTSON**	Kenneth	1925	604
KIR	Hazel	1919	567	**KOBUSKIE**	John Charles	1947	470
KIRBY	Sarah	1786	29	**KOBUSSEN**	Mr.		902
KIRK	Bertha	1868	186	**KOCH**	Frank Jacob	1905	570
KIRK	Laura June	1972	710	**KOEBEL**	Donna		685
KIRKE	Angelo	1860	338	**KOGIN**	Don	1914	571
KIRKE	Celestie Marie	1928	775	**KOGLER**	Dorothy Joyce	1933	713
KIRKE	John Judson	1943	878	**KOHART**	Cheryl		794
KIRKE	Judson	1832	183	**KOHLER**	Walter	1886	449
KIRKE	Judson Fabian 'Jay'	1888	556	**KOLD**	Lucy Minnie	1895	454
KIRKE	Medard Paul Sidler	1916	774	**KOLLMAN**	Frieda	1902	446
KIRKE	Van Rensselaer	1858	338	**KORSBECK**	Elizabeth Jane	1928	708
Kirke	Virginia C.	1944	878	**KOSH**	Patricia	1941	722
KIRKPATRICK	Philip	1920	575	**KOSINSKI**	Kathryn	1926	451
KIRKWOOD	Debra Susan	1954	737	**KOSKI**	Christa	1990	895
KIRT	Stanley Joseph	1951	868	**KOSKI**	Troy A.	1967	822
KITCHNER	Jeanette E.	1967	876	**KOTLER**	Mark Bryan	1947	740
KITTREDGE	Marion L.	1924	817	**KOVACH**	Andrew Joseph	1954	746
KLEINER	Eugene Killian	1876	186	**KOZLOWSKI**	Barbara	1952	805
KLEINER	Eugene Wesley	1912	342	**KRAENZLEIN**	Harold O.	1929	504
Kleiner	Margorie	1913	342	**KRAFT**	Clair Olny	1913	701
KLEVIN	Astrid Greta	1943	879	**KRAFT**	William F.	1888	458
KLINGLER	Marion	1896	649	**KRAKOW**	Sophia A.	1879	213
KLITZ	Virginia B.	1911	358	**KRAMER**	Magdaline C.	1888	357
KLOTZ	Joseph H., Jr.	1952	770	**KRATOCHVIL**	Mr.		688
KNAPP	Frank F.	1859	129	**KREINBUNG**	Kenneth	1910	624
KNAPP	George L.	1881	301	**KREISER**	Carl Albin	1929	504
KNAPP	Harriet E.	1853	129	**KREISER**	David Francis	1955	749
KNAPP	John Fremont	1856	129	**KREISER**	Janet Marie	1952	749
KNAPP	Laura Louise	1897	337	Kreiser	Judy		749
KNAPP	Raymond Siam	1901	595	**KREISER**	Karen Louise	1953	749
KNAPP	Solomon S., Jr.	1829	58	**KROHN**	Robert Merriel		866
KNAPP	Verna	1908	684	**KRUCZ**	Stephanie	1970	873
KNAPPEN	Mary	1912	590	**KRUGER**	Sharon L.	1950	821
KNIGHT	Carol		751	**KUHANECK**	Elizabeth	1917	645
KNIGHT	Charles S.	1879	355	**KUHANECK**	Frank W., Jr.	1889	411
KNIGHT	Dora	1880	462	**KUHANECK**	Harold W.	1923	813
KNIGHT	Dorothy	1934	659	**KUIPER**	Marianne	1948	785
KNIGHT	George		198	**KURTZ**	Kenneth Bruce	1955	825
KNIGHT	Henry	1840	264	**KURTZ**	Richard Allen	1951	825
KNIGHT	Leslie		757	**KURTZ**	Susan Elizabeth	1958	825

KURTZ	Wallace Bruce MILKS	1927	666		**LANDON**	Bertha J.	1867	327
KURTZHALS	Quentin Lloyd	1957	897		**LANDRY**	Deborah Elsie	1953	881
KURTZHALS	Rudolph W.	1923	830		**LANE**	Aurora Michelly Lyn		900
KUSCHEL	Agnes Florence	1911	633		**LANE**	Richard		848
KYLE	James		309		**LANGESS**	June		635
KYLE	Lola		514		**LANGLOIS**	Marie Jeanne	1875	165
					LANMAN	Ezetta Lydia	1914	690
					LANMAN	Frank	1885	444
					LANMAN	Vivian Joyce	1918	690
					LANNEN	Rachel Jo	1977	870

L

LABELLE	Victoria	1915	518		**LANNI**	Nicola Joseph	1946	864
LACHARITY	Catherine	1865	164		**LAPP**	Jay Wyatt	1888	444
LACHARITY	Mary J.	1924	519		**LARABY**	Olive L.	1867	154
LACKI	Carl John	1960	740		**LARCOM**	Wendy Jo	1968	869
LADOUCEUR	Monique	1937	523		**LARCOM**	William Edward	1966	869
LADOW	Hannible	1855	235		**LARCOM**	William Thomas	1945	744
LAFLEUR	Erica Scott	1979	730		**LARDI**	Stella Edith	1910	259
LAGESSE	Joan	1936	715		**LARDIE**	Anna Lou	1928	500
LAGEST	Jean	1931	462		**LARDIE**	Anna Marie	1953	863
LAGUARDIA	Enrico D.	1915	679		**LARDIE**	Catherine Marie	1976	907
LAIDIG	Timothy Harlan	1957	902		**LARDIE**	Chanel Denise	1979	907
LAKE	Barbara	1885	428		**Lardie**	Katie	1986	907
LAKIN	Florence Elizabeth	1881	365		**LARDIE**	Myrtle E.	1882	239
LAKINGS	Elva Blanche	1894	379		**LARDIE**	Robert Alan	1951	863
LAMB	Merritt Norton	1853	253		**LARDIE**	Robert Allen	1928	738
LAMB	Sherri		608		**LARDIE**	Russell Alan	1978	907
LAMBERT	Mary	1910	496		**LARDIE**	Sandra Kay	1950	863
LAMBERT	Ruth	1942	609		**LARDIE**	Shawn Thomas	1975	907
LAMBKIN	Lulu B.	1888	297		**LARDIE**	Sierra Topaz	1985	908
LAMIE	Charles William	1947	727		**LAROE**	Amy	1920	830
LAMIE	Kara Shea	1975	858		**LAROE**	Stewart	1891	675
LAMIE	Kimberley Shannon	1973	858		**LARREAU**	Goldie	1912	377
LAMIE	Kristin Suzanne	1970	858		**LARSON**	Edna	1914	552
LAMOUREUX	Donald Joseph	1923	718		**LARSON**	Emma Viola	1886	169
LAMOUREUX	Florence L.	1920	718		**LARSON**	Karl Edwin	1914	788
LAMOUREUX	Joseph Sylvio, Jr.	1933	719		**LARUE**	Nellie Elsie	1881	150
LAMOUREUX	Jospeh Sylvio, Sr.	1899	473		**LASLEY**	Virginia Jewel	1921	788
LAMPHEAR	Louis Knapp	1912	575		**LATHBERY**	Belle	1876	360
LAMPSON	Archie D.	1894	674		**LATHEM**	Gwendolyn Theresa	1905	313
LAMPSON	Ruth Millicent	1925	830		**LAUGHLIN**	Christopher Scott	1963	906
LANCASTER	Charles	1919	560		**LAUGHTON**	Richard William	1940	531
LANCE	Frances B..	1889	319		**LAUTNER**	Duane Stephen	1947	862
LANCE	Jennie Rai	1885	317		**LAVALLA**	Melvina Lovina	1814	26
LAND	Elwood William	1907	375		**LAVAN**	Hazel Jane	1915	616
LANDINI	Ralph J.	1940	803		**LAVELLE**	Catherine Rose	1889	311

LAW	Ada Mae	1887	436	LEOHR	Kris		910
LAWLESS	George Ronald	1953	899	LEONARD	Cecile		314
LAWLOR	Lawrence		515	LEONARD	Christine Elizabeth	1975	908
LAWRENCE	Anna May	1914	545	LEONARD	Sean Leslie	1974	871
LAWRENCE	Leslie Leeann	1980	885	LERETTE	Ardella Grace	1904	695
LAWRENCE	Orinda	1839	122	LERETTE	Clifford	1882	449
LAWRENCE	Reva Pearl	1935	799	LERETTE	Laverne	1918	695
LAWTON	Rebeccah	1726	9	LERETTE	Melvin	1906	695
LAY	Joseph Coleman	1881	274	LETHERER	Roy Christopher	1892	293
Lazell	Dorothy	1940	799	LETTS	Ethel Caroline	1899	369
LAZELL	Stanley J., Jr.	1934	799	LEURS	Emil A.	1888	377
LAZELL	Stanley J., Sr.	1932	614	Leurs	Helen	1908	600
LEAF	Bessie May	1893	358	LEURS	Leroy J.	1908	600
LEARNED	Almira C.	1846	173	LEWIS	Arthur L.	1885	267
LEARY	David Allen	1970	894	LEWIS	Caroline	1847	174
LEARY	Donald Robert	1950	817	LEWIS	Harriett M.	1876	212
LEBECK	Claude R.	1880	208	LEWIS	Jane Margaret	1922	465
LECHNER	Robert Walter	1922	605	LILE	Glen Kurt	1952	745
LEDERER	David C.	1950	763	LILE	Jason Curt	1972	870
LEDERER	Julius David	1913	535	LILE	Kimberly Marie	1984	870
LEDERER	Linda	1949	763	LILE	Tamela Lynn	1975	870
Lederer	Margaret Rose	1956	763	LILLETHUN	Jeannine	1931	601
LEDERER	Susan Jean	1946	763	LINCICUM	Beulah	1922	783
LEE	Eliza J.	1853	204	LINCICUM	Dorothy	1930	783
LEE	Ernest Dean	1878	392	LINCICUM	Marjorie	1923	783
LEE	Glen Selmer	1907	386	LINCICUM	Mr.	1900	569
LEE	Jessie Beth	1913	590	LINCICUM	Velma	1926	783
LEE	John Lawrence	1934	609	LINCOLN	Jeanine Marie	1975	906
LEE	Marvin	1895	368	LINCOLN	Mina	1864	169
LEE	Orrie	1892	565	Linderleaf	Barbara		733
LEE	Mr.		901	LINDERLEAF	Kenneth Max	1933	733
LEEHEY	Anita	1916	684	LINDERLEAF	Kenneth R.	1905	493
LEEHEY	Bernice	1919	685	LINDERLEAF	Lois Elaine	1938	734
LEEHEY	Edwin Joe	1918	685	LINDSEY	Benny Boone		836
LEEHEY	Harold	1908	684	LINDSEY	Hugh	1939	723
LEEHEY	James	1877	440	LINDSEY	Justin Arthur		898
LEEHEY	Viola	1906	684	LINDSEY	Mary Elizabeth	1910	474
LEFEBVRE	Stephane	1971	874	LINK	Florence	1920	616
LEFLER	Ruby P.	1921	644	LINK	Leola	1936	709
LEGG	Maxine	1920	701	LITCHFIELD	Keith Leroy	1942	863
LEIDY	Effie	1866	210	LITTLE	Matilda	1846	101
LEISINGER	Barbara	1949	658	LITTLE	Robert	1930	879
LEMAY	Robert Arthur		756	LITTLEFIELD	David H.	1924	714
LENZ	Lauretta	1920	788	LITTLEFIELD	Ida Adele	1860	221
LENZ	Margaret		652	LIVINGSTON	Joseph Ira	1950	748

LIVINGSTON	Joseph J.	1921	503	LOTTRIDGE	Isaac Bull	1798	65
LIVINGSTON	Kathleen Irene	1945	748	LOTTRIDGE	Janie Esther	1833	137
LIVINGSTON	Linda Sue	1951	748	LOTTRIDGE	John B.	1800	65
LIVIO	Calegro Carlos	1905	546	LOTTRIDGE	Maria	1806	65
LLOYD	Emily	1894	312	LOTTRIDGE	Mary Ellen	1825	136
LLOYD	Emily	1916	651	LOTTRIDGE	Mordecai	1802	65
LLOYD	John	1886	415	LOTTRIDGE	Robert	1773	29
LLOYD	Nancy	1923	652	LOTTRIDGE	Robert, Jr.	1808	65
LLOYD	Roberta	1919	651	LOTTRIDGE	Stephen Smith	1873	279
LOCKE	Dale M.	1906	486	LOTTRIDGE	Thomas	1795	64
LOCKE	Earl L.	1885	292	LOUCKS	Tom		894
LOCKE	Louise E.	1879	435	LOVE	Maud	1878	221
LOCKE	Robert Milton	1929	728	LOVELACE	Calvin S.	1832	192
LOCKWOOD	Laurence J.	1908	642	LOVELACE	Charles Ford	1914	566
LOCKWOOD	Mary	1830	108	Lovelace	Darlene Louise	1931	781
LOCKWOOD	Mary Eunice	1927	714	LOVELACE	David Leslie	1955	883
LOCWOOD	Harold Rollin	1889	465	Lovelace	Edith	1911	566
LOFTIS	William Randall		905	LOVELACE	Elizabeth Ruth	1843	193
LOHMES	Harry L.		575	LOVELACE	Ethelyn	1872	348
LONG	Penny Jo	1956	488	LOVELACE	George Nelson	1860	348
LONGLEY	Eleanor	1827	124	LOVELACE	Harrison	1839	193
LONGLY	Josiah Nottage	1896	51	LOVELACE	Harry Eugene	1906	565
LONSDALE	Mildred Susan	1903	316	LOVELACE	Hattie B.	1865	347
LOOP	Asahel	1822	115	LOVELACE	Jefferson	1837	193
LOOP	Eliza Jane	1848	249	LOVELACE	Jeremiah	1807	86
LOPEZ	Sergio David	1974	894	LOVELACE	Joe Nelson	1916	566
LORE	Mary Alice	1851	194	Lovelace	Lanita Marie	1961	883
LORENZEN	Drucilla Marie	1960	891	LOVELACE	Lila M.	1901	565
LOSEE	Albert Robert	1880	282	LOVELACE	Marcia M.	1894	565
LOSEE	Lawrence Kenny	1910	474	Lovelace	Martha Jane	1835	192
LOSEE	Robert Lawrence	1910	474	LOVELACE	Mildred Vivian	1919	781
LOSEE	Thelma Irene	1913	474	LOVELACE	Nelson R.	1846	194
LOSEE	William Guy	1884	282	LOVELACE	Orrin Eugene	1886	564
LOSEE	William L>	1842	141	LOVELACE	Oscar Roy	1880	350
LOTTRIDGE	Alvin Durham	1835	136	LOVELACE	Richard E.	1930	781
LOTTRIDGE	Amy	1793	64	LOVELACE	Ross Craig	1909	566
LOTTRIDGE	Arthur Clifford	1862	278	LOVELACE	Sarah Florence	1896	565
LOTTRIDGE	Charles	1829	137	LOVELACE	Stewart Anson	1866	348
LOTTRIDGE	Delia	1812	66	LOWN	Jerry Lynn	1946	744
LOTTRIDGE	Eliza	1810	66	LOWN	Kimberly Sue	1968	869
LOTTRIDGE	Emma Loduska	1860	203	LOWN	Sherri Lee	1970	869
LOTTRIDGE	Emma Loduska	1860	278	LOWN	Tony Lynn	1967	869
LOTTRIDGE	Esther	1831	137	LUCAS	Corlan B.	1818	59
LOTTRIDGE	Etta	1867	278	LUCAS	Elizabeth	1826	59
LOTTRIDGE	Frances Caroline	1821	136	LUCAS	Lydia B.		130

LUCAS	Sean James	1986	909	
LUCE	Ossie D.	1884	412	
LUISIER	James Brian	1951	489	
LUNDGREN	Irene		380	
LUNDQUIST	Douglas T.	1956	875	
LUPER	Charles E.	1946	733	
Luper	Dina Lee	1951	733	
LUPER	Ernest		299	
LUPER	Irvin Ezra	1912	493	
LUPER	Minetta	1913	493	
LUSK	Deborah	1827	74	
Luther	Dorothy Louise	1920	689	
LUTHER	Linnie Elaine	1913	689	
LUTHER	Omer Laten	1920	689	
LUTHER	Ruby Arlene	1916	689	
LUTHER	Tutcie Doris	1928	689	
LUTHER	Walter	1887	443	
LYDELL	Grace B.	1893	297	
LYDELL	Mr.	1900	568	
LYNCH	Allene L.	1917	589	
LYNCH	Robin	1965	717	
LYNNE	Dorothy	1908	580	
LYNNE	Percy A.	1880	362	
LYNOTT	Martin	1839	162	
LYON	Ann		440	
LYON	Cassie	1884	440	
LYON	Charles H.	1860	251	
LYON	Della	1887	440	
Lyon	Dorothy G.	1897	441	
LYON	Fred Morris	1873	344	
LYON	Gregory William	1951	734	
LYON	Harold	1901	441	
LYON	Harry Neal	1890	441	
LYON	Howard	1922	686	
LYON	Howard J.	1920	686	
LYON	Howard R.	1900	441	
LYON	James B.	1858	251	
LYON	James M.	1834	118	
Lyon	Jean M.	1920	686	
LYON	Jesse	1862	252	
LYON	Jesse J.	1896	440	
LYON	Mary Ann	1928	686	
LYON	Mary Elizabeth	1856	251	
LYON	Mr.		896	
LYON	Nora R.	1867	252	
LYON	Prince Arthur	1874	252	
LYONS	Helen	1915	693	
LYONS	Richard	1861	246	
LYTLE	Ella Mae	1882	167	
LYTLE	Frederick H.	1941	751	

M

MAAS	Gerda Eva	1906	451
MAC LEAN	Mary Kathryn	1945	818
MACALOLODY	Teresa Elaine		877
MACATINAING	Cecillia Cernandez	1951	825
MACCLURE	Elizabeth Ardis	1923	556
MACCLURE	Raymond	1903	338
MACDONALD	Charles Gordon	1917	574
MACDONALD	Roderick	1940	784
MACDONALD	Vicki Lynn	1963	884
MACDOUGH	Mr.	1950	742
MACE	Tracey D.		253
MACHSON	Neneen	1898	538
MACKEY	Frances Emily	1897	542
MACOMBER	Sophia	1795	27
MAHOLLINE	Donald Ray	1923	676
MAHOLLINE	John	1873	434
MAHONEY	Ellen F.	1852	265
MAIDEN	Cindy Jane		855
MAKELY	Hazel Eliza	1886	341
MALENSHEK	Ann	1920	590
MALENSHEK	William J.	1913	590
MALEY	Emma Reta	1917	507
MALLERY	Barbara		721
MALONE	Everett Clinton	1906	690
MALONE	Hadley Halleck	1870	444
MALONE	Herbert Leroy	1893	690
MALONE	Latricia	1954	899
MALONE	Marvin Loren	1929	843
MALSOM	Sheila Marie	1952	821
MANAHAN	Jessie	1873	229
MANCHESTER	Leland	1905	764
MANCHESTER	Ralph		558
MANDEVILLE	Charles	1919	567
MANDEVILLE	Esther Lucile	1913	567
MANDEVILLE	Ralph C.	1883	352

MANG	Adam	1872	303	MARTIN	Jennie	1867	186
MANN	Emma May	1878	133	MARTIN	Lawrence Wallace		138
MANNING	Gladys	1906	533	MARTIN	Loretta		721
MANNING	Gladys	1907	558	MARTIN	Minnie Marian	1869	202
MANNING	Iris Daniel	1850	172	MARTINELLO	Michael Heugh	1974	873
MANNING	Leland Brown	1880	322	MARTINELLO	Nancy Theresa	1981	873
MANNING	Pearl Ethel	1879	322	MARTINELLO	Vincent	1948	754
MANQUEN	Flora	1913	612	MARTINSON	Vera		380
MANRO	Charles Henry	1871	270	MARVIN	Jane	1711	6
MANRO	Elizabeth Cooley	1860	269	MASER	James F.	1900	455
MANRO	Fred Jonathan	1863	269	MASON	Gary	1951	880
MANRO	Jennie Bell	1866	269	MASON	Heather Auralee	1980	909
MANRO	Jonathan Squire	1821	126	MASON	Marjorie		524
MANSCHEAFFER	Laura	1928	767	MASON	Paul	1946	861
MANSON	Sarah	1880	409	MASSEY	Olan Ray	1914	648
MANVILLE	Janice Louise	1951	868	MASTERS	Charles S.	1841	100
MANWARREN	Allen Potter	1886	359	MATHIS	Earl G.	1920	628
MAPES	Idiel		23	MATOON	James Ward	1915	645
MARHOEPER	Ruth	1916	546	MATSON	Mildred Ann	1926	467
MARION	Carolyn	1945	807	MATSUOKA	Kenny Sueo		880
MARNE	Dorothy	1930	605	Matthews	Bernice	1920	685
MAROHL	Todd William	1962	796	MATTHEWS	Cleve		440
MARSALISI	Marie A.		489	MATTHEWS	Darlene Joyce	1934	487
MARSH	Arnold C.	1922	461	MATTHEWS	Elmer Lewis	1896	295
MARSH	Dana S.	1877	344	MATTHEWS	Howard	1912	685
MARSH	Debbie		811	MATTHEWS	Mr.	1935	860
MARSH	Dorothea Louise	1898	562	MAUCH	Mary A.	1894	478
MARSH	Jeff		709	MAURER	Gertrude Mary	1908	486
Marsh	Kim		709	MAXON	Newell	1928	768
MARSH	Ruth	1782	36	MAXWELL	Diantha	1792	26
MARSHAL	George W.	1869	257	MAXWELL	Viola	1908	384
MARSHAL	Hester	1867	257	MAY	Elda Irene	1919	553
MARSHAL	Sarah	1864	257	MAY	John D.	1892	337
Marshall	Dorothea		450	MAY	Philip	1927	521
MARSHALL	H. Grant	1910	507	MAYHEW	Carl		815
MARSHALL	Jeanette Catherine	1901	450	MAYHEW	Mary Ida	1887	307
MARSHALL	Louis Winzenburg	1917	450	MAYNARD	Evelyn L.	1921	626
MARSHALL	William	1836	120	MAZERA	Sue	1904	534
MARSTON	Walter M.	1934	848	MCABOY	Clara	1880	282
MARTIN	Augustus	1839	84	MCALINDEN	Mary Ann	1826	74
MARTIN	Charles Briggs	1872	187	MCALLISTER	Guy	1900	579
MARTIN	Earl Augustus	1907	342	MCALLISTER	Sarah Jane	1837	75
MARTIN	Eileen L.	1919	468	MCAULEY	Norman Henry	1908	317
MARTIN	Esther Anna	1837	192	MCCAFFREY	Victoria Lynn	1956	742
MARTIN	Fred	1903	451	MCCARTHY	Dolores Rita	1932	719

MCCLELLAN	John W.	1942	505	MCEDWARD	Pennie	1963	880
MCCLELLAN	Richard B.	1974	867	MCEDWARD	Perry Allen	1926	780
MCCLELLAND	Hattie	1893	295	MCEDWARD	Robert Jenkins	1931	780
MCCLELLAND	John	1866	150	MCELREE	Mary Ruth	1926	705
MCCLUNE	Phoebe Emily	1895	365	MCELWAIN	Albert Douglas	1883	428
MCCOLLUM	Ida May	1871	287	MCELWAIN	Benjamin Clayton	1885	428
MCCONNELL	Linda	1987	905	McElwain	Beverly A.	1919	671
MCCORDY	Ruth		652	MCELWAIN	Clarence Lee	1915	670
MCCORMACK	John M.	1886	369	McElwain	Diane J.	1952	829
MCCORMICK	Addie H.	1909	591	McElwain	Donna M.	1947	671
MCCORMICK	Frederick Michael	1929	591	McElwain	Etta M.	1903	429
MCCORMICK	Jedd	1913	591	MCELWAIN	George Earl	1893	429
McCormick	Shirley A.	1929	591	MCELWAIN	Grace Elizabeth	1912	670
MCCRAITH	Sally Florence	1940	813	MCELWAIN	Harriet J.	1889	428
MCCREADIE	Ruth	1911	373	MCELWAIN	Hester Dorothy	1892	429
MCCRIMMON	Jerry W.		489	McElwain	Judith J. K.	1954	829
MCCUNNIFF	F. Patrick	1887	440	MCELWAIN	Kenneth Eugene	1919	671
MCCUNNIFF	Marjorie	1921	685	MCELWAIN	Larry D.	1937	671
MCCUNNIFF	Marshall	1925	685	MCELWAIN	Mary Alice	1880	428
MCCUNNIFF	Maryellen	1918	685	MCELWAIN	Maxine E.	1922	671
McDaneils	Theresa J.	1950	808	MCELWAIN	Paul Oakley	1899	429
MCDANIELS	Charles Melvin	1913	634	MCELWAIN	Raymond Dean	1937	828
MCDANIELS	Donald Melvin	1939	808	MCELWAIN	Robert Lee	1879	428
MCDONALD	Sadie	1878	229	MCELWAIN	Sharon L.	1941	829
MCDOUGAL	Michael James	1977	870	MCELWAIN	Sherman	1952	829
MCDOWELL	Melinda L.	1952	763	MCELWAIN	Steven Eugene	1950	829
MCDOWELL	Tamera Lynn	1968	865	MCELWAIN	Walter	1903	429
MCEDWARD	Bruce Michael	1944	879	MCELWAIN	William H.	1858	243
MCEDWARD	Donald Angus	1952	879	MCELWAIN	William H.	1895	429
MCEDWARD	Donald Angus, Jr.	1979	909	MCELWAINE	Charles G.	1869	409
MCEDWARD	Donald David	1896	562	MCELWEE	William A.	1942	771
MCEDWARD	Donald George	1945	879	MCFARLAND	Joseph Forgus	1920	686
MCEDWARD	Donald Gordon	1920	779	MCFARLANE	Slim		525
MCEDWARD	Donna Norma	1948	879	MCGEE	Evelyn	1927	512
MCEDWARD	Foster Albra	1921	779	MCGEE	Margaret	1876	418
MCEDWARD	Holly Ann	1959	881	MCGEE	Mary Louise	1874	169
MCEDWARD	Jackie Grace	1961	880	MCGOVERN	William	1920	650
MCEDWARD	James Alden	1958	881	MCGREGOR	Don	1925	607
MCEDWARD	James Angus	1918	778	MCGREGOR	Mamie	1871	216
MCEDWARD	James Davidson	1867	344	MCGREGOR	Marjorie	1895	564
MCEDWARD	Jennifer Susan	1948	879	MCGUIRE	Sheila	1968	872
MCEDWARD	Jill Diane	1954	880	MCHALE	Mary M.	1840	60
MCEDWARD	Karen Leigh	1958	880	MCINTIRE	Clara B.	1878	563
MCEDWARD	Larry Robert	1955	881	MCINTOSH	June E.	1924	592
MCEDWARD	Norma Auralee	1923	779	MCINTYRE	Dorothy Ann	1945	738

MCINTYRE	Julia	1890	541	MCNULTY	Richard Edward David	1952	755
MCKANABE	Marie	1869	164	MCNULTY	Sharan Elizabeth	1954	755
MCKAY	Evelyn	1924	638	MCNULTY	Tracey Ellen	1983	874
MCKIE	Sarah L.	1829	68	MCPHERSON	Alphonse		514
MCKINLEY	Allison James	1915	532	MCREYNOLDS	Deanna R.	1945	700
MCKINLEY	Judith Marie	1943	760	MCWETHY	Helen Maxine	1926	732
MCKINLEY	Marsha Ann	1941	760	MCWHORTER	Alice Belle	1859	194
MCKINLEY	Virginia Ellen	1947	760	MEACHAM	Albert	1910	670
MCKINNEY	Mabel	1911	646	MEACHAM	Jeanette Augusta	1856	223
MCKINNON	Angus		515	MEACHAM	Shirley M.	1942	828
MCKINSTRY	Jennifer A.	1978	722	MEAD	Earl	1882	342
MCKISICK	Joe Robert	1930	607	MEAD	Esther	1921	766
McKnight	Anna P.	1894	324	MEAD	Grover E.	1888	541
McKnight	Clarice	1895	323	MEAD	Harry	1918	766
MCKNIGHT	Edna Myrtle	1894	323	MEAD	Kenneth Earl	1909	559
MCKNIGHT	Eunice Constance	1898	323	MEAD	Lorissa	1883	541
MCKNIGHT	George	1900	324	MEAD	Spencer	1860	329
MCKNIGHT	George S.	1862	347	MEALEY	Calvin	1904	632
MCKNIGHT	James Buford	1872	173	MEDINA	Marta Kathryn	1966	755
MCKNIGHT	James Ian	1897	323	MEEKER	Ira Donald	1887	560
MCKNIGHT	Mary Amanda	1858	346	MEEKS	Tammy Rene		898
MCKRELL	Sarah	1924	557	MEIGHEN	Thomas John	1930	390
MCLAGGAN	Betty	1926	801	MEISSNER	Thelma	1936	600
MCLAGGAN	Jay Bliss	1889	619	MELCHER	Freeda	1905	511
MCMAHON	Mr.	1940	606	MENGE	Herbert	1898	582
MCMAHON	Tom		893	MENGE	Virginia Lee	1926	788
MCMANUS	John Bernard	1927	782	MENGES	Dorothy M.	1921	680
MCMILLAN	Alfred	1893	315	MERCHANT	Edna E.	1877	409
MCMILLAN	Chesley		527	MERCHANT	Frank E.	1854	234
MCMILLAN	Dorothy		528	MERCHANT	Ora V.	1879	409
MCMILLAN	Elmer		528	MERCHANT	Pearl M.	1888	409
MCMILLAN	Enid		527	MEREDITH	Clayton L.	1902	699
MCMILLAN	Hartley		528	MERKLE	Josiah Christian	1892	320
MCMILLAN	Janice	1926	584	MEROW	Helen	1903	650
MCMILLAN	Leslie		527	MERRIFIELD	Ira	1888	305
MCMILLEN	Jerry		505	MERRIMAN	Adelaide Lucy	1928	513
MCMURRAY	Betty Lou	1931	597	MERSELES	Ann Elizabeth	1940	722
MCNAMARA	Patricia VonDracek	1940	842	MESKA	Barbara A.	1935	602
MCNEIL	Agnes	1873	306	MESSENGER	Ira E.	1907	775
MCNEIL	Esther	1886	332	METZGER	George Alfred	1876	322
MCNIFF	Vera	1905	374	MEYER	Donna B.	1919	697
MCNULTY	Barbara Christine	1961	756	MEYERS	Edna	1886	537
MCNULTY	Barry Richard David	1974	874	MEYERS	Franklin Jay	1902	543
MCNULTY	David Robert, Jr.	1930	516	MEYERS	Hiram	1827	177
MCNULTY	Gordon Anthony	1959	756	MEYERS	John		537

MEYERS	Reuben	1850	328	MILLIAS	Laura A.	1904	544
MIAENHULDER	Elizabeth	1885	340	MILLIAS	Neva	1928	768
MICHELLE	Donna	1936	816	MILLIAS	Otho Jeremiah	1895	544
MICKLE	Edward	1900	542	MILLIAS	Phebe G.	1907	544
MICKLE	Harrison	1862	332	MILLIAS	Ruth	1923	768
MICKLE	Pearl	1885	543	MILLIAS	William Eugene	1864	332
MIDDAUGH	Martha H.	1845	171	MILLIAS	Winthrop L.	1859	332
MIDDLETON	George Ernest	1892	356	MILLIKEN	Albert Darling	1870	267
MIKULAY	Velma Johana	1925	502	MILLIKEN	Arnold White	1899	465
MILER	Wayne Gary	1914	601	MILLS	Rhonda Rae	1955	825
MILES	Ada	1864	242	MILLS	Sally	1950	807
MILES	Arthur	1850	250	MILLSON	Sarah E.	1867	278
MILES	Lois	1880	439	MILMINE	Cheryl	1950	740
MILES	Ruth Agnes	1897	313	MILNOT	Casimira Anne	1914	466
MILLEON	Alvin	1920	661	MINER	Charles		692
MILLEON	Angeline Louise	1954	821	MINZIE	Edna E.	1881	357
MILLEON	James Alexander	1950	821	MISENER	George		798
MILLER	Ada Gay	1882	339	MISER	Robert Frank	1911	570
MILLER	Adah	1881	333	Mishler	Barbara A.	1935	845
MILLER	Alida	1800	46	MISHLER	Garry Herbert	1932	845
MILLER	Betty Gray	1934	799	MISHLER	Harland Herbert	1909	702
MILLER	Cecil C.	1904	511	MITCH	Bernadine Wilma	1901	619
MILLER	Charles M.	1865	363	MITCHELL	Edith Raye	1927	790
MILLER	Charles M.	1914	582	MITCHELL	George R.	1905	582
MILLER	Connie	1960	863	MITCHELL	Georgia Alma	1926	790
MILLER	Elizabeth	1883	307	MITCHELL	Jean	1923	596
MILLER	Grace E.	1893	369	MITCHELL	Molly Therese	1960	610
MILLER	Helen E.	1845	172	MITCHELL	Rueben James	1888	303
MILLER	Irvin Leroy	1929	851	MITCHELL	Thelma Jean	1929	790
MILLER	J. P.	1857	253	MIX	Katherine Kathleen	1897	340
MILLER	Jessie Angeline	1896	460	MOBLEY	Evelyn B.	1941	719
MILLER	John	1877	307	MOBLEY	Michelle		855
MILLER	Luella M.	1920	569	MOCK	Joshua	1986	895
MILLER	Mary	1900	378	MODER	George	1874	405
MILLER	Minnie Maud	1874	239	MOELLER	Delbert L.	1941	823
MILLER	Minnie Maud	1874	414	MOHRMAN	Walter L.	1926	848
MILLER	Ruth Ellen	1937	388	Moline	Anita L.	1955	797
MILLER	Sarah N.	1837	68	MOLINE	Brent A.	1956	797
MILLIAS	Alice	1930	768	MOLINE	Stanley Burton	1923	604
Millias	Burnesina D.	1862	332	MOLLACH	Francis Leslie	1933	769
MILLIAS	Donald	1925	768	MOLLACH	Jennifer M.	1959	875
MILLIAS	Helen F.	1921	768	MOLLACH	Martha M.	1964	875
MILLIAS	Jennie B.	1862	332	MONETTE	Joan	1939	722
MILLIAS	Joel Sebastian	1836	179	MONROE	Aura	1860	215
MILLIAS	Joel Sebastian	1898	544	MONROE	Fred S.	1870	408

MONROE	Harold S.	1928	761	MOORE	Polly	1806	42
MONROE	John S.	1897	640	MOORE	Sarah E.	1799	33
MONTAGUE	Charles O.	1877	273	MOORE	Sarah E.	1799	66
MONTAZARI	Abol Hassan L.	1951	793	Moore	Seraph	1876	138
MONTGOMERY	James Michael	1959	856	MOORE	Steve	1960	888
MONTGOMERY	Jeffrey	1969	883	MOORE	Stuart Eugene	1961	858
MONTIETH	Ellen	1850	166	Moore	Susan	1810	66
MONTVILLE	Albert E.	1900	567	MOORE	Susan Karen	1969	869
MOOERS	Arthur Beard	1892	320	MORDEN	Carl Eugene	1941	785
MOOERS	Cynthia	1843	171	MORDEN	Catherine Elizabeth	1947	785
MOOERS	Esther	1845	171	MORDEN	Garnet Cotter	1916	574
MOOERS	Frank C.	1874	320	MORDEN	Lynn		884
MOOERS	Henry	1807	78	MORGAN	Frances D.	1891	437
MOOERS	Henry Clay	1849	171	MORGAN	George W.	1899	399
MOOERS	Mary	1836	170	MORGAN	Louie H.	1854	249
MOORE	Addison	1831	205	MORGAN	Michael Dean	1961	857
MOORE	Betsey	1842	205	MORGAN	Mr.	1905	506
MOORE	Charles D.	1872	361	MORGAN	Pamela Denise	1964	858
MOORE	Clara Diana	1863	138	MORGAN	Preston Reno	1940	726
MOORE	Daniel L.	1801	94	MORGAN	Sylvia	1928	646
MOORE	David	1819	66	MORRELL	Martha Julia	1898	366
MOORE	Dorothy E.	1895	281	MORRIS	Anna Alfredine	1851	214
MOORE	Dudley	1747	17	MORRIS	Cyrus	1824	101
MOORE	Dudley	1773	29	MORRIS	Frank	1907	653
MOORE	Edith	1911	280	MORRIS	Kenneth William	1910	403
MOORE	Eldridge		579	MORRIS	Marie C.	1896	397
Moore	Elizabeth	1900	281	MORRIS	Mary Etta	1860	214
MOORE	Emily	1844	205	MORRIS	Shirley Pamela Eville	1942	784
MOORE	Eva Elizabeth	1899	281	MORRIS	Webster Cyrus	1873	214
MOORE	Franklin	1861	138	MORRIS	William W.	1900	381
MOORE	Freeman	1905	723	MORRIS	William W.	1924	607
MOORE	George R.	1903	481	MORRISEY	Mary	1950	740
MOORE	H. Pauline	1911	580	MORRISON	Michael Stanley	1949	862
MOORE	Harold Raymond	1891	281	MORSE	Cullen Bryant	1961	880
MOORE	Harriet	1810	53	Morse	Ethel	1912	543
MOORE	Irene Burgholtz		653	MORSE	Harry B.	1905	543
MOORE	Joshua Ryan	1986	905	MORSE	John A.	1879	331
MOORE	Leonard	1918	818	MORTHY	Dianna	1971	873
MOORE	Lester J.	1855	138	MORTIMER	Frank Raymond	1905	574
MOORE	Lois	1897	649	MORTON	Shirley Athelme	1920	779
MOORE	Lora Elizabeth	1887	539	MOSES	Della Lottridge	1872	280
MOORE	Maria Frances	1847	206	MOSES	Thomas Lanier	1849	138
MOORE	Massena	1833	205	MOSHER	Alfred Paddock	1827	239
MOORE	Parley Eugene	1897	281	MOSHER	Anna	1886	405
MOORE	Parley Parker	1865	139	MOSHER	Bernice	1907	426

MOSHER	Donald George	1936	819	MURPHY	Margaret M.	1963	900
MOSHER	Elizabeth Vivian	1906	421	MURRAY	Catherine	1903	546
MOSHER	Emily L.	1842	63	MURRAY	Ronald Buchan	1911	573
MOSHER	Ettie Ann	1867	417	MURRAY	Stacy Ellen	1975	871
MOSHER	Frank	1866	232	MUTH	Joan E.	1964	749
MOSHER	Frederick Herbert	1870	417	MYERS	Amelia Myria	1871	187
MOSHER	Geroge W.	1915	654	MYERS	David Wesley		836
MOSHER	Irving Henry	1896	406	MYERS	Emma P.	1863	329
MOSHER	Leland	1899	406	MYERS	Florence	1903	541
MOSHER	Raymond	1888	406	MYERS	Genevieve	1902	540
Mosher	Sarah	1870	417	MYERS	John Weldon	1923	681
MOSHER	Sherman Andrew	1888	418	MYERS	Susan	1950	836
MOSIER	Ruth	1765	22	Mykel	Bonnie	1940	806
MOSS	Elizabeth Alberta	1907	342	MYKEL	Scott J.	1941	806
MOULTON	Mary	1774	29	MYKEL	Walter Scott	1905	625
MOUSSEAU	Connie		518	Mylkes	Patricia		722
MOZDY	Julie Lynn	1985	886	MYRICK	Evelyn		553
MUDGE	Julia Ann	1803	70				
MUELLER	Craig		910				
MUELLER	Edward B.		897				

N, O, P, Q

Mueller	Lynn		910
MULCAHEY	Anne Elizabeth Ellen	1908	310
MULCAHEY	Catherine Theresa	1899	309

NAIL	Nellie Mildred	1903	583
NAKANISHI	Marie	1945	684
NASH	Robert Charles	1923	732

MULFORD	Edwin Hastings	1855	221	NASON	Durward	1917	615
MULLER	Margaret	1892	457	NASON	Flora Angeline	1922	777
MULLIGAN	Anna Audrey		507	NASON	Winfred Earl	1886	562
MULLIGAN	Edith Clarissa	1910	507	NATHAN	Brent	1979	873
MULLIGAN	Joseph Frederick Allan	1884	304	NAYLOR	Frederick W.		687
MULLIGAN	Lois		528	NAYLOR	Grace Mary	1918	717
MULLIGAN	Mary	1892	220	NAZAREK	Kim	1955	879
MULLIGAN	Rita		526	NEAGUS	Edward C.	1845	130
MULLIN	Joyce Marie	1936	692	NEAL	Ernest	1928	698
MULLIN	Sandra	1945	668	NEAL	Mary	1862	252
MULLINS	Alisha Marie	1982	905	NEELY	Celeste A.	1959	847
MULLINS	Everette Lynn	1959	857	NEER	Lucinda	1830	81
MULNIX	Audrey	1925	572	NEER	Sally Ann	1826	81
MULVAGH	Robert Charles	1897	316	NEGUS	Arthur	1883	376
MUMEY	Maurice Elwood	1914	732	NEGUS	Clarence W.	1886	376
MUNN	Donald Burton	1909	576	NEGUS	Harvey Myrl	1891	376
MUNN	Marlea Genna	1932	786	NEGUS	Lendal Dean	1887	376
MUNSON	Bill	1928	607	Negus	Octavia	1884	376
MUNSON	Margaret Archibald	1920	474	NEGUS	Thomas Rae	1851	214
MURAT	Margaret	1852	180	NEGUS	Wayne A.	1907	599
MURPHY	Ada	1875	285	NEIL	Cynthia	1961	755
MURPHY	Gregory	1965	883				

NEILLY	Anna May	1916	590	NEWTON	Georgia A.	1905	438
NEILLY	Grace	1918	590	NEWTON	Ray M.	1894	420
NEILLY	Roy	1895	368	NEWTON	Vera	1920	522
NEILLY	William Alexander	1920	590	NEWTON	Virginia	1919	657
NEIMEIER	Hazel	1905	380	NICHOLS	Chester W.	1905	357
NEISH	Robert H.		555	NICHOLS	Maggie	1888	298
NELLIS	Edward	1863	284	NICHOLS	Mamie	1896	455
NELLIS	Jennie Pearl	1889	433	NICHOLSON	Martha	1900	410
NELLIS	Laney C.	1842	144	NICKERSHER	William		652
NELLIS	Marcia Belle	1885	477	NIELSEN	Natasha		909
NELSON	Carrie	1967	886	NIELSON	Ruth C.	1897	281
NELSON	Cynthia Ann	1956	847	NIEMAN	Zana Ione	1891	407
NELSON	George	1896	407	NIFFENEGGER	Shelley Lynne	1965	895
NELSON	Harold		690	NILES	Eva May	1899	639
NELSON	Nicholas	1942	795	NILES	Herbert Albert	1905	639
NELSON	Thelma	1912	593	NILES	Lucy Malinda	1900	422
NEMEC	Michael W.		744	NILES	Lucy Malinda	1900	639
NESSLAND	Dreng Ole	1901	699	NILES	Mortimer A.	1847	408
NETHERY	James Edward	1922	788	NILES	William Mortimer	1902	639
NEU	Marsha Joanne	1955	825	NITZEL	Milton B.	1913	493
NEUMAN	Helen	1909	552	NIVISON	Muriel	1916	567
NEWELL	Clifton Lee	1943	734	NIXON	Ted		897
NEWHALL	George William	1898	565	NOBLE	Manley Howard	1891	478
NEWLAND	George Glen	1890	295	NOLAN	John		749
NEWMAN	Donna Jean	1948	838	NOLAN	Thomas		832
NEWMAN	Dorothy	1911	614	NOLPH	Sarah Jane	1918	650
NEWMAN	John	1877	392	NOLTE	Ethel	1920	695
NEWMAN	Thomas C., Jr.	1915	534	NORLANDER	William	1906	545
NEWMAN	Warren James	1921	594	NORMAN	Rebecca A.	1983	885
NEWMAN	Wesley	1908	483	NORTHRUP	Grace B.	1888	352
NEWMARCH	Andrew Thompson	1855	166	NORTON	Georgia A.	1905	438
NEWMARCH	Arthur E.	1891	319	NOSWORTHY	Jeremy	1985	861
NEWMARCH	Cora	1884	318	NOWAKOWSKI	Michael	1959	716
NEWMARCH	David	1857	166	NOWALK	John	1946	471
NEWMARCH	Earl Roy	1886	318	NOWALK	Tammy	1967	717
NEWMARCH	Ernest Lee	1888	319	NOWOCIEN	Joseph	1930	813
NEWMARCH	Floyd Lee	1922	531	NULL	Ashley Renee	1989	905
NEWMARCH	Howard B.	1862	167	NULL	Curtis W.	1949	854
NEWMARCH	Isaac James	1854	166	NULL	James Otis	1914	723
NEWMARCH	James	1822	75	NUNN	David		873
NEWMARCH	James John	1880	317	NUNNEMAKER	Grace G.	1882	445
NEWMARCH	Laura Viena	1880	318	NUTTER	Evaline Fannie	1871	290
NEWMARCH	Mary Ellen	1875	317	NUTTER	Timothy Wayne	1978	859
NEWMARCH	Melissa Sarah Ellen	1878	317	OAKES	Amelia	1854	236
NEWMARCH	William C.	1859	167	OAKES	Fidelia	1860	236

OAKES	Kenneth L.	1942	812	**OUELETTE**	Joseph	1950	758
OAKES	Lloyd	1938	811	**OVERLY**	Paul	1919	385
OAKES	Lyle Frank	1916	637	**OVERTON**	Robert		526
OAKES	Mabel E.	1945	812	**OWEN**	Mr.		510
OAKFIELD	Dewey M.	1897	295	**OWENS**	George W.	1888	443
OAKLEY	Carrie A.	1876	542	**OWENS**	Jessie Mary	1912	451
OATLEY	Todd M.	1967	886	**OWENS**	Melvin Lavern	1920	707
OBERN	Esther Elizabeth	1835	113	**OWENS**	Royce Hub	1911	687
O'BRIEN	Edward	1889	355	**OXARART**	Allan Michel	1927	708
O'BRIEN	Florence Elizabeth	1881	265	**OXARART**	Fern Joyce	1933	709
OCKERHAUSEN	Nina	1897	367	**OXARART**	Jean Michel	1890	461
OCKERT	Rose Marie	1925	494	**OXARART**	John Martin	1923	708
O'DANIEL	Betty	1910	531	**OXARART**	Mary Catherine	1924	707
OHL	Lenora		902	**OXARART**	Nancy		851
OHL	Leonard Dale		849	**OXARART**	Patti		850
OHL	Leonard Dale, Jr.		902	**OXARART**	Vicki		850
O'KANE	John J.	1907	650	**OXLEY**	Belle	1876	360
OLEZEWSKI	Henrietta	1923	502	**PACK**	Ella O.	1863	233
OLIVER	B.	1908	275	**PACKARD**	Charlotte Angeline	18744	261
OLIVER	Lottie	1860	246	**PAGE**	Arthur F.	1900	776
OLMAN	Hazel Marie	1908	493	**PAGE**	Leon C.	1912	776
OLMAN	John	1875	298	**PAGE**	Richard		651
OLMAN	Mabel R.	1900	492	**PAGE**	William C.	1877	561
OLMSTEAD	Esther	1912	692	**PALMER**	Charlotte Virginia	1858	325
OLMSTEAD	Flossie V.	1891	420	**PALMER**	Ethel M.	1918	536
OLNEY	Alice Aurora	1846	188	**PALMER**	Florence	1862	156
OLSEN	Kathy	1961	877	**PALMER**	Frederick W.	1947	782
OLSON	Darrell		850	**PALMER**	Millard	1927	765
OLSON	Earl	1919	693	**PALMER**	Sarah M.	1828	76
OLSON	Erik		853	**PANICO**	Olga M.	1907	378
OLSON	Helge Martin	1887	323	**PANZEER**	Ernest	1877	364
OLSON	Jeannette Merle	1919	535	**PAPE**	Carrie L.	1908	612
OLSON	Lynn Helge	1917	535	**PAPE**	Wilbur	1917	385
OLSON	Ms.	1945	763	**PAPPE**	Beatricee M.	1900	294
OLSON	Signe Elizabeth	1916	427	**PAPPIN**	Muriel Mary Eliza	1889	307
OMAN	Elizabeth G.	1819	69	**PAQUETTE**	Gilles	1966	755
ONAN	Cora M.	1882	322	**PARADIS**	France		756
OPHEIM	Alfred Ira	1908	386	**PARKER**	Carrie Lemyra	1892	436
OPLIGER	Linda Marie	1948	744	**PARKER**	Glenn	1898	459
ORALLS	Dale R.	1959	876	**PARKER**	Joseph	1908	489
O'ROURKE	Angus J.	1921	519	**PARKER**	Laura M.	1935	798
OSBORNE	Harold E.	1900	649	**PARKER**	Mary Virginia		652
O'SHEA	Jenny N.	1939	523	**PARKER**	Mr.		874
OSMONSON	Anna Mae	1929	452	**PARKER**	Orpha Pearl	1895	445
OTTIS	Maurice	1923	650	**PARKER**	Thuresa A.	1894	294

PARKER	Willie Ann	1935	816	PEAKE	Jeane J.	1926	555
PARKS	Edmond R.	1877	410	PEAKE	Maurice K.	1893	338
PARKS	Helen I.	1902	644	PEAKE	Zelda	1924	551
PARNET	Geiseltraud	1946	723	PECHETTE	Denise		487
PARR	Tami K.	1967	815	PECK	Flora Grace	1876	362
PARSONS	Larry		856	PECK	Rita Jane	1922	532
PARSONS	Mr.		383	PEEBLES	Lois Elizabeth	1918	536
PARSONS	Nicole Lynn	1980	871	PELHAM	Florence Mary	1897	340
PATERSON	Penelope Jane	1940	784	PELTZ	Hattie Paulina	1866	166
PATRICK	Clarence William	1869	286	PENFIELD	Agnes	1880	362
PATRICK	Daniel H.	1969	867	PENFIELD	Charles E.	1883	362
PATRICK	Sidney H.l	1885	482	PENFIELD	Charles T.	1840	206
PATRIDGE	Carrie Dell	1872	363	PENIX	Lucy	1912	584
PATRIDGE	Susan May	1879	363	PENTON	Harry Sackett, Jr.	1904	582
PATRIDGE	Worth Mason	1848	208	PENTON	Robert Louis	1920	788
PATTERSON	Alma Mary Catherine	1934	515	PERELLA	Herman	1880	321
PATTERSON	Audrey M.	1916	577	PEREZ	Stella	1933	609
PATTERSON	Lulu	1890	341	PERHALL	Delia Alice	1920	506
PATTISON	Bartin V.	1854	256	PERHALL	John	1869	303
PATTISON	James Lawrence	1890	447	PERHALL	Katie	1873	297
PATTISON	Lois Margaret	1918	692	PERHALL	Lettie Irene	1907	506
PATTON	Esther	1928	878	PERHALL	Mary Ella	1903	506
PAUL	Barbara		803	PERKINS	Alfred	1897	579
PAUL	Edward E.	1909	600	PERKINS	Edith I.	1909	776
PAUL	Viola Janet	1935	603	PERKINS	Mabel E.	1902	776
PAULSON	Elinor	1909	600	PERKINS	Marlene		881
PAULSON	Lorrain C.	1907	381	PERKINS	Nellie Maud	1868	287
PAYNE	Clarissa	1848	117	PERKINS	Thornton C.	1918	835
PAYNE	Cora A.	1865	260	PERKINS	Wendy Kay	1967	909
PAYNE	Edith M.	1897	675	PERRIN	Ernest E.	1910	375
PAYNE	Frances Ruth	1892	674	PERRON	Jean	1935	516
PAYNE	Francis Maynard	1923	767	PERRON	Paul		756
PAYNE	Margaret Louisa	1912	372	PERRY	George	1830	139
PAYNE	William Frederick	1863	433	PERRY	Jonathan	1804	67
PEACOCK	Edward H.	1887	446	Perry	Mary J.	1843	139
PEACOCK	Florence E.	1892	446	PERRY	Vera Gladys	1894	562
PEACOCK	Leslie	1901	446	PERSONS	Addison	1853	186
PEACOCK	Robert W.	1856	256	PERSONS	Addison Frederick	1912	559
PEAK	Barbara Lou	1934	608	PERSONS	Alfred Otis	1886	341
PEAK	Kenneth	1909	382	PERSONS	Frances Elizabeth	1913	559
PEAKE	Calla A.	1869	334	PERSONS	Olive May	1883	341
PEAKE	Carolyn M.	1920	555	PERSONS	Ray Eugene	1890	341
PEAKE	Elizabeth	1923	555	PETE	Josie	1896	150
PEAKE	Francis	1915	549	PETEMAN	Jeanette	1867	148
PEAKE	Grace	1922	550	PETERS	Mary	1860	226

PETERSEN	Alvia Helen	1923	604	**PIERCE**	Dema Emily	1914	401
PETERSEN	Laura Louise	1956	881	**PIERCE**	Herbert Douglas	1863	209
PETERSON	Lucia Day	1875	288	**PIERCE**	Howard Arnold	1886	364
PETERSON	Patrick	1864	168	**PIERCE**	Inez Eulela	1910	466
PETIT	Lucy F.	1857	407	**PIERCE**	Ivan W.	1915	733
PETITT	Hester May	1945	388	**PIERCE**	Laura A.	1850	208
PETTEY	Ernest F.	1887	275	**PIERCE**	Laura Sarah	1884	363
PETTIE	Jerrine	1912	575	**PIERCE**	Susan Maria	1845	208
PETTIE	Thomas Frank	1879	357	**PIKER**	Joseph Earl	1921	785
PETTIT	Donald Lloyd	1931	601	**PILLER**	Rachel Erin	1981	866
PETTIT	Frank Burr	1862	215	**PILLER**	Rudolf	1950	741
PETTIT	Fred Silas	1865	215	**PILLER**	Sarah Kate	1976	866
PETTIT	Harold George	1905	378	**PILLER**	Seth Joseph	1977	866
PETTIT	Harry Lloyd	1900	378	**PILLER**	Zachariah Crayton	1979	866
PETTIT	Lavonne Edna	1924	705	**PILOTE**	Horace	1944	523
PETTIT	Mamie Estella	1894	377	**PINDAR**	Arthur Dewitt	1925	767
PETTIT	Mary Ettola	1859	215	**PINDAR**	Carol Denise	1969	855
PETTIT	Pearl Rhea	1889	377	**PINDAR**	Duane Wilday	1923	767
PETTIT	Silas Burr	1835	102	**PINDAR**	Frances Xavier, Jr.	1943	724
PETTIT	Vera Ann	1929	601	**PINDAR**	Leon Daniel	1902	543
PETTIT	Will D.	1867	215	**PINDAR**	Roger Elliot	1928	767
PFAFF	Jason		888	**PINE**	Ellen Marie	1851	248
PFEIL	Robert C.	1931	835	**PINES**	Orogell Ollie	1898	434
PFISTHNER	Ethel Mae	1904	302	**PINGLETON**	Helen	1900	406
PFISTHNER	Gilbert James	1923	502	**PINKERMAN**	William L.	1890	457
PFUND	Agnes	1895	369	**PINKERTON**	Betty Jane	1925	700
PFUND	Mr.	1915	569	**PINKNEY**	Barbara Jean	1940	813
PHILBRICK	Elizabeth	1811	47	**PINKSTON**	Minor Pate	1897	564
PHILLIPS	Alfred		689	**PINKVOSS**	Henry	1918	783
PHILLIPS	Anna	1816	109	**PIPER**	Ellowene	1892	379
PHILLIPS	Bernard		768	**PIPER**	Henry C.	1891	378
PHILLIPS	Helen Ilene	1925	682	**PIPER**	Patricia A.	1971	885
PHILLIPS	Phoebe L.	1859	209	**PITCHER**	Grace	1886	332
PHILLIPS	Polly	1825	87	**PITTS**	Mary Lucy	1922	705
PHILLIPS	Thaddeus S.	1850	240	**PIZON**	Dorothy A.	1944	621
PHIPPS	Robert	1955	877	**PLACE**	Elizabeth M.	1854	195
PICKERILL	Delores Ann	1931	607	**PLANK**	Julia		184
PICKERILL	Denzel Maxine	1926	607	**PLARK**	Mary J.	1865	233
PICKERILL	Donald Ray	1928	607	**PLATT**	Jane A.	1831	55
PICKERILL	Earl	1896	381	**PLATT**	Jesse Abraham	1886	458
PICKERILL	Grace Lorraine	1935	608	**PLATTS**	Harlow Case	1893	649
PICKERILL	Jeanette Ellen	1932	607	**PLATTS**	Harvey Nixon	1870	414
PIERCE	Arnold D.	1816	97	**PLATTS**	Harvey Nixon	1925	819
PIERCE	Bonnie	1952	825	**PLATTS**	Harvey Reginald	1894	649
PIERCE	Clement Winfield	1883	491	**Platts**	Johanna	1926	819

PLETCHER	Ameila Jane	1833	176	POTTS	Victor Morrell	1912	732
PLOUGH	Melvina	1852	234	POULIN	Kevin		757
PLUMMER	Douglas Arthur	1960	822	POUTAIN	Sarah Nicole	1983	872
PLUNKETT	Thomas Alfred	1862	417	POWELL	Catherine O.	1918	637
PLYMALE	Hannah E.	1856	209	POWELL	Donald	1912	636
POEHL	Amelia M.	1874	165	POWELL	Jonathan	1876	406
POLOK	Merlin		902	POWELL	Walter Stanley	1912	777
POOLE	Georgianna	1843	103	PRATT	Anna Viola	1893	404
POOLE	Harold		315	PRATT	Ceciia J.	1869	226
POOLE	John		528	PRATT	Delbert E.	1908	580
POOLE	Laura		529	PRATT	Virginia Ellen	1924	670
POORE	James	1875	291	PREISENDORFER	Jack G.	1919	627
POPE	Teresa	1972	802	PREMO	Mary Jane	1942	737
POPPERT	Searl R.	1910	565	PRENTICE	Dora		441
PORTELANCE	Fernande	1910	314	PRENTICE	Harry Edwin	1888	275
PORTER	Alma	1834	131	PRESCOTT	Amy Lauson	1886	472
PORTER	Ann Eliza	1862	273	PRESCOTT	Charles Lyman	1821	136
PORTER	Annabelle	1904	552	PRESCOTT	Harry Lauson	1852	279
PORTER	Annie Margaret	1929	789	PRICE	Barbara Loveland	1928	720
PORTER	Marla Vernele	1948	714	PRICE	Boyce Edward	1910	382
PORTER	Maureen	1963	898	PRICE	Curly	1960	714
PORTER	Orson Merritt	1869	274	PRICE	John B.	1866	168
PORTER	Robert Johnson	1915	467	PRICE	Marvin	1899	546
PORTER	Thomas J.	1938	882	PRICE	Nancy Lee	1950	714
PORTER	Valeria	1899	470	PRICE	Robert Evan	1952	747
POSEY	Rita Y.	1968	825	PRICE	Vincent Herbert	1891	477
POSSINGER	Denise	1972	826	PRICE	Vincent Herbert, Jr.	1922	720
POST	Norma J.	1936	668	PRICE	Warren Eldredge	1918	719
POSTON	McClellan	1860	280	PRIEST	Robert H.	1949	741
POTEET	Franklin R.	1913	602	PRINCE	Samantha	1798	44
POTTER	Elizabeth S.	1825	108	PRITCHARD	Merlen John	1917	660
POTTER	Helen M.	1881	212	PROFFITT	Dollie Elizabeth	1899	291
POTTER	Holder White	1841	125	PROFIT	Catherine S.	1967	895
POTTER	Josephine Margaret	1873	166	PROLUX	Lloyd		758
POTTER	Joshua	1799	53	PROPER	Catherine E.	1830	177
Potter	Linda	1879	232	PROPER	Ethel Jane	1895	539
POTTER	Orlando Warren	1910	478	PROSSER	Adelia	1812	94
POTTER	Silas	1818	108	PROSSER	Barney	1785	40
POTTER	William	1810	107	PROSSER	Elmina M.	1851	206
POTTER	William	1857	232	PROSSER	James Lemuel	1809	94
POTTLE	Robert Austin	1881	366	PROSSER	Jane	1815	94
POTTS	Morrell	1890	490	PROSSER	Joshua	1782	40
POTTS	Patricia Ann	1932	860	PROSSER	Maria Lydia	1807	94
POTTS	Ramona Lenora	1914	732	PRUST	Marvin	1918	590
POTTS	Sharon Kay	1936	860	Puckett	Eleanora Emma	1939	697

PUCKETT	James R.	1892	455			**R**		
PUCKETT	Nanine	1954	728					
PUCKETT	William Wilson	1928	697	RABER	Fern L.	1879	325	
PUFFER	Louisa	1836	140	RABER	Irwin E.	1857	174	
PUGH	John C.	1848	137	RACALLA	Florence Victoria	1917	577	
PULLIN	Marjorie Helen	1900	357	RACINE	Marie Louise	1888	359	
PURDY	Alfred	1810	115	RADFORD	John Edward	1929	767	
PURVIS	Andrew J.	1922	585	RADTKE	Tarylyn R.	1972	872	
PURVIS	Frederick Dennis	1944	785	RAE	Everett		528	
PUTNAM	Roger Lester	1922	680	RAINER	Reamer Clyde	1907	583	
PYNE	Wayne	1895	692	RAIPORT	John	1915	648	
QUAILE	Louise		502	RAKAN	Rudy I.	1959	749	
QUICK	Jamie	1980	876	RAMSEY	Lila Mae	1913	732	
QUIMBY	Leola May	1906	580	RAMSEY	Suzanne	1924	588	
QUINES	Donald	1906	616	RANCICH	Christ August	1895	646	
QUINN	Theresa Jane	1859	161	RANCICH	Christina		894	
				RANCICH	George Christopher	1925	817	
				RANCICH	Georgia		894	
				Rancich	Geraldine Anne	1943	817	
				RANCICH	Joseph		894	
				RANCICH	Robert Howard	1952	817	
				RANCICH	Thenne		894	
				RAND	Matthew Dearborn	1964	880	
				RANER	Ema Catherine	1922	698	
				RANES	Marcilla Arnitus	1955	863	
				RANNELLS	Anna King	1867	280	
				RANNELLS	Helena Dorr	1861	280	
				RANNELLS	Pauline Wolf	1868	280	
				RANNELS	David V.	1840	137	
				RANNEY	Alfred Herrick	1858	260	
				RANNEY	Ardath Arloene	1913	456	
				RANNEY	Blanche	1887	454	
				Ranney	Cassie	1858	260	
				RANNEY	Evaline Salome	1867	261	
				RANNEY	Frankie Helene	1902	454	
				RANNEY	Golda Ruth	1888	455	
				RANNEY	Herman	1863	260	
				RANNEY	Jessie Maria	1889	453	
				RANNEY	Julius Caesar	1829	121	
				RANNEY	Justin Warren	1870	261	
				RANNEY	Kathryn Blanche	1916	456	
				RANNEY	Laura Palmyra	1896	455	
				RANNEY	Lola Vaughn	1894	455	
				RANNEY	Luke Winfield	1850	259	
				RANNEY	Mildred Mary	1901	455	

RANNEY	Nathan James	1853	260	REYNOLDS	David D.	1956	819
RANNEY	Russell Ray	1892	454	REYNOLDS	Duane G.	1931	656
RANNEY	William Foster	1896	454	REYNOLDS	Gary Michael		826
RAUSCH	Scott Ryan	1954	489	Reynolds	Mary H.	1956	820
RAVER	Charles	1900	342	Reynolds	Mattie Jean	1937	791
RAY	Michelle		877	REYNOLDS	Mr.		583
RAYMOND	Anna	1868	349	REYNOLDS	Richard	1949	745
RAYMOND	Harriet	1842	193	REYNOLDS	Ronald E.	1933	791
RAYMOND	Helen	1918	565	RHINES	Sondra J.	1940	698
RAYMOND	Howard	1867	349	RHOADES	Carrie	1889	418
RAYMOND	Jeremiah L.	1864	349	Rhoades	Clara N.	1896	654
Raymond	Laura M.	1882	349	RHOADES	Donald M.	1906	654
RAYMOND	Lewis L.	1871	349	Rhoades	Elizabeth	1910	654
RAYMOND	Marie	1898	566	RHOADES	Frank A.	1872	418
Raymond	Nellie M.	1876	349	RHOADES	George O.	1869	418
RAYMOND	Seth	1835	193	RHOADES	Grace	1880	418
REARDON	Minnie May	1890	446	RHOADES	John Hadley	1895	654
REDINGTON	John	1818	68	RHOADES	Otis Dimmock	1840	240
REDINGTON	Willard Dennis	1856	141	RHODES	Audra	1900	426
REED	Gladys I.	1929	658	RHODES	Charis Beth	1980	909
REED	Grace E.	1891	479	Rhodes	Daphne M.	1937	666
REED	Ira Asa J.	1844	237	RHODES	Douglas Wallace	1938	666
REED	Margaret	1879	218	RHODES	Edward	1878	243
REED	Mitchell Delphus	1958	845	RHODES	Ervin Charles	1951	890
REED	Nora	1888	377	RHODES	Ralph E.	1904	426
REED	Robert J.	1896	582	RHODES	Sondra Lu	1940	666
REED	Sarah M.	1812	61	RHORSON	Magdaline A.	1900	361
REEDER	John Lewis	1859	185	RHYNHART	Donald		881
REEDER	Paul Asbury	1903	340	RIBERA	Joseph Spagnoletti	1906	594
REESE	Matilda	1870	284	RICCA	Paul J.	1939	684
REEVE	Belle Burdeta	1902	567	RICCI-KIRKWOOD	Debra Susan	1954	737
REEVE	Emily Isbelle	1894	566	RICE	David M.	1934	666
REEVE	George Hues	1858	351	RICE	Ellis William	1899	678
REEVE	Myrtle Melissa	1898	566	RICE	Mabel Josephine	1878	344
REEVES	Clinton E.	1872	409	RICE	Stephen		875
REEVES	Lloyd Vinton, Sr.	1899	642	RICE	Theron E.	1840	188
REIGLE	Pearl	1925	570	RICE	William Burdell	1865	344
REIMNK	Dona June	1964	741	RICH	Charles Adrian		556
REINCKE	Orpha Lucille	1929	497	RICH	Cora	1870	250
REINER	Mabel Darlene	1944	822	RICH	Mary Louise	1920	631
REINHUBER	Marie	1904	551	RICHARDS	Paul Randall	1975	910
REISNER	Derek Shawn	1967	903	RICHARDSON	Dorothy Jane	1937	724
REMINGTON	Patricia J.	1925	657	RICHARDSON	Kenneth B.	1944	840
RENNER	Steven B.	1950	842	RICHARDSON	Lee M.	1918	483
RENNIE	Willis	1934	521	RICHARDSON	Myra	1888	417

Surname	Given Name	Year	Page	Surname	Given Name	Year	Page
RICHARDSON	Paula J.	1933	816	**ROBERTS**	Sarah Clementine	1879	364
RICHARDSON	William Smith	1910	581	**ROBERTSON**	June	1921	530
RICHERT	Henry Francis	1903	466	**ROBINETT**	Haddy Manila	1896	353
RICHMOND	Herbert A.	1939	808	**ROBINSON**	Adelle	1874	270
RICHMOND	Margaret Elizabeth	1869	212	**ROBINSON**	Elmer Alvin	1914	591
RICHMOND	Vance Robert	1916	634	**ROBINSON**	Eula Mae	1898	482
RICHTER	Nelson	1906	406	**ROBINSON**	Hubert R.	1893	482
RICKARD	Blanche	1885	336	**ROBINSON**	James	1901	482
RICKER	Ronald James	1951	754	**ROBINSON**	James Edwyn	1947	795
RICKOW	Mr.		689	**ROBINSON**	Janice Evelyn	1943	795
Rider	Janet B.	1935	722	**ROBINSON**	John	1833	255
RIDER	Paul L.	1905	479	**ROBINSON**	John Dixon	1841	127
RIDER	Reginald C.	1928	722	**ROBINSON**	John J.	1870	445
RIDLON	Polly Pettee	1923	718	**ROBINSON**	Jordan	1983	886
Riedel	Ayne Kay	1951	839	**ROBINSON**	Kenneth Samuel	1908	691
RIEDEL	Bill E.		839	**ROBINSON**	Laamma	1863	209
RIEDEL	Dale L.	1920	683	Robinson	Mary	1892	482
RIEGEL	Richard Ernest	1917	577	**ROBINSON**	Mary Alice		273
RILEY	Claude A.	1905	558	**ROBINSON**	Melissa Virginia	1871	289
RILEY	Edith Rebecca	1883	298	**ROBINSON**	Mercy	1819	107
RILEY	Elsie A.	1904	492	**ROBINSON**	William	1837	148
RILEY	Florence		297	**ROBINSON**	William, Jr.	1873	290
RILEY	George C.	1926	775	**ROBLEE**	Essie A.	1900	619
RILEY	George Ogden	1881	340	**ROBSON**	Arthur G.	1864	321
RILEY	James	1845	152	**ROCHA**	John		756
RILEY	Jessie Inez	1899	490	**ROCHA**	Linda Lee		787
RILEY	Jessie Inez	1899	491	**ROCKWELL**	Carlton W.	1930	475
RILEY	Lottie J.	1890	491	**ROCKWELL**	Frances	1901	396
RILEY	Mary Jane	1845	152	**ROCKWELL**	Harold C.	1906	653
RILEY	Melvin M.	1901	492	**ROCKWOOD**	Charles D	1846	279
RILEY	William J.	1869	297	**RODGERS**	Dorothy Irene	1928	687
RILEY	William Leroy	1895	492	Rodman	Adeline	1830	174
RIPLEY	Mabel	1864	132	Rodman	Ama May	1866	327
RIPLEY	Rosemary J.	1924	660	**RODMAN**	Asa Benjamin	1832	174
RIPPLE	Angela	1974	906	Rodman	Asinath	1834	175
RISING	James	1890	449	**RODMAN**	Cecile	1863	327
ROBBINS	Bertha May	184	433	**RODMAN**	David E.	1841	176
ROBBINS	Lorenzo	1836	92	**RODMAN**	Ezra Cook	1836	175
ROBE	Rowena	1926	792	**RODMAN**	Frances Marie	1855	327
ROBERTS	Amelia Minerva	1881	221	**RODMAN**	Grant A.	1867	327
ROBERTS	Clarinda		97	Rodman	Hannah	1827	174
ROBERTS	Dorothy	1914	582	**RODMAN**	Harry E.	1873	327
ROBERTS	Fred Alvin		280	**RODMAN**	John Culver	1802	79
ROBERTS	Lydia	1898	336	**RODMAN**	Levi Gallop	1832	175
ROBERTS	Roberta Kathleen	1944	505	**RODMAN**	Mary	1827	175

Rodman	Mary Jane	1830	174		ROSE	Clarence S.	1905	694
Rodman	Mary Josephine	1840	175		ROSE	Fern Agnes	1898	450
Rodman	Maude B.	1871	327		ROSE	Frank Calvin	1885	449
RODMAN	Melissa Jane	1838	175		ROSE	Franklin E.	1908	694
RODMAN	Menzo W.	1853	325		ROSE	Ida May	1888	449
RODMAN	Permelia Elizabeth	1844	176		Rose	Irene	1909	694
RODMAN	William Henry	1830	175		ROSE	Juliana Ann	1825	194
ROGERS	Delia Honora	1886	282		ROSE	Lela Hester	1892	449
ROGERS	Isaac	1759	22		ROSE	Lori		899
ROGERS	Isaac, Jr.	1869	50		ROSE	Pamela K.	1962	760
Rogers	Rachel	1785	50		ROSE	Ronald	1937	843
ROGERS	Ray R.	1915	585		ROSE	Solomon M.	1860	257
ROGERS	Ursula	1810	122		ROSENBARK	Sarah	1838	92
ROGUSTA	Sue Lynn	1962	865		ROSENBERGER	David	1960	826
ROLEN	Jill	1980	905		ROSENTHAL	Bonnie Sharon	1946	610
ROLFE	Clifford H.	1926	683		ROSENTHAL	Dudley Norman	1906	387
ROLFE	Edna G.	1909	533		ROSENTHAL	Marlene K.	1943	610
ROLFE	Esther V.	1922	641		ROSINE	Marjorie Edith	1910	340
ROLFE	Esther V.	1922	683		ROSS	Harriet J.	1857	224
ROLFE	Herbert	1867	249		ROSS	Hazel M.	1946	824
ROLFE	Herbert	1867	250		ROTHBARTH	Lauretta	1900	678
ROLFE	Janice L.	1958	839		ROUND	Sarah	1827	87
ROLFE	Linda L.	1954	839		ROUSE	Jill D.	1947	805
ROLFE	Raymond Herbert	1888	438		ROWAN	John	1965	893
ROLMAN	Bessie	1902	367		ROWAN	Lillie E.	1966	750
ROMESBURG	Robert Chester	1923	777		ROWE	Lucy Hamilton	1878	355
ROMSEK	Anna Elizabeth	1913	294		ROWE	William Dowe	1843	158
RONAN	Frederick J.	188	421		ROWLAND	Claude Anderson	1896	678
ROOD	Ella M.	1883	400		ROWLEY	Henry		91
ROOD	George B.	1862	227		ROWSE	Leslie Elliott	1924	786
Rood	Ida	1890	401		ROY	Gordon	1914	511
ROOD	Mamie	1874	228		ROZELL	Phoebe Jane	1902	422
ROOD	May	1893	401		RUBIN	Aaron James	1973	870
ROOD	William	1891	401		RUBY	Edith R.	1927	667
ROOST	Dorothy	1916	695		RUGG	Emma Mary	1858	173
ROOT	Dale Everett		740		RUGG	Fennell	1906	636
ROSA	Esther Taylor	1901	472		RULE	Phyllis Constance	1936	835
ROSA	Francis Yates	1906	472		RULE	William Rycroft	1913	680
ROSA	Gertrude Banker	1869	279		RUNDELL	Elizabeth C.	1836	83
ROSA	Richard	1819	137		RUNYAN	Eula Marie	1933	843
ROSA	Richard III	1899	472		RUNYON	Avis	1924	277
ROSA	Richard, Jr.	1863	279		RUNYON	Ethel Frances	1891	441
ROSA	Robert James	1914	473		RURY	Jasmine	1981	909
ROSE	Calvin	1903	694		RUSCH	Chester	1916	590
ROSE	Caroline Adeline	1895	449		RUSH	Vivian	1927	624

RUSHNELL	Maud Ethel	1885	289
RUSK	Kenneth	1938	606
RUSK	Sally	1959	797
RUSS	Scott Richard	1968	731
RUSSELL	Elva Alberta	1925	801
RUSSELL	Lloyd	1920	616
RUSSELL	Louis L.	1915	617
RUSSELL	Nona I.	1895	218
RUSSELL	Rachel	1842	87
RUSSELL	Ray		459
RUSSELL	Unknown	1795	42
RUSSELL	Virginia M.	1922	571
RUTLEDGE	Josephine E.	1850	195
RUTZ	John F.	1878	337
RUTZ	John L.	1903	553
RUTZ	Lettie L.	1901	553
RUTZ	Louisa	1881	336
RYAN	Alice A.	1940	798
RYAN	Helen Elizabeth	1925	534
RYAN	Joy Ann	1947	747
RYAN	Thomas	1906	614
RYAN	Thurlo	1915	388
RYBERG	Paul	1925	475
RYBERG	Paul, III	1947	719
Ryberg	Robin L.	1957	719
RYBERG	Virgil	1929	475
RYCHEL	Leo Carlton	1902	576
RYDER	Codie	1880	447
RYDER	Myrtle	1899	450
RYDER	Vincent	1963	884
RYKER	Otto. O.	1902	296

S

SAALFIELD	Mildred Ellen	1904	419
SABOURIN	Marilyn Lou	1930	737
SAGE	Alice J.	1859	149
SALA	Alice Lydia M.	1911	366
SALLY	Elizabeth Margaret	1864	156
SAMMONS	Cecil L.	1921	663
SAMPSON	Reiley W.	1859	327
SAMUELSON	Edward B.	1929	655
SANDEE	Donald Alan	1947	744
SANDEE	Donald Alan, Jr.	1979	870
SANDEE	Rick Alan	1968	869
SANDEE	Timothy Don	1971	870
SANDEFUR	Hazel	1901	480
SANDERS	Adella Loretta	1875	150
SANDERS	Elizabeth Susan	1820	93
SANDERSON	Brian Charles	1962	866
SANDY	Earl D., Jr.	1908	636
SANFORD	Harry Otis	1871	288
SANFORD	Harry Whitmore	1893	479
SANFORD	Thomas Patrick	1964	900
SAROWATZ	Albert	1907	468
SAROWATZ	Fay Amelia	1934	715
SAROWATZ	Jacob Ray*	1931	715
SASENBURY	Louisa	1855	140
SATTERLEE	Alice J.	1861	208
SATTERLEE	David B.	1847	207
Satterlee	Dehlia A.	1856	207
SATTERLEE	George W.	1852	255
SATTERLEE	Juliette	1830	97
SATTERLEE	Mary Amanda	1879	444
SATTERLEE	Maryette	1830	97
SATTERLEE	Oel D.	1833	206
SATTERLEE	Orrin	1827	119
SATTERLEE	Sarah L.	1850	207
SATTERLEE	Zina	1824	95
SATTERLEE	Zina E.	1885	363
SAUERBRE	Mr.		900
SAUERBRE	Steffanie Ann	1969	900
SAUERBREI	Walter H.	1945	847
SAUNDERS	Maggie	1888	298
SAVAGE	Vivian Eileen	1927	742
SAVAGE	William	1909	591
SAWADE	Aaron		888

SAWYER	Mina	1864	169		SCOLLY	Mary	1670	3
SAXTON	William Samuel	1868	317		SCOTT	Alvin L.	1900	458
SAYERS	Alexander	1852	154		SCOTT	Anna	1890	538
SAYERS	Bernice	1893	303		SCOTT	Florence Gertrude	1891	304
SAYERS	Bruce Alvin	1890	303		SCOTT	Lena Jane	1935	505
SAYERS	Emeretta June	1916	507		SCOTT	Mr.	1954	839
SAYERS	Emma Louise	1916	506		SCOTT	Nora	1872	288
SAYERS	Myrtle Orinda	1883	303		SCOTT	Sheryl Ann	1950	748
SAYERS	Walter Paul	1895	303		SEAMANS	Douglas V.	1946	807
SAYLOR	Larilyn Ann	1969	893		SEAMONS	Gerald	1910	280
SCALISE	Yolanda A.	1931	810		SEARLE	Muriel	1907	546
SCARLINO	Jeanette	1962	893		SEARLES	Ethel May		441
SCHAEFFER	Elizabeth Louise	1889	340		SEARS	Ellen Jane	1838	136
SCHAMBERS	Mary	1855	222		SEAVEY	David	1922	474
SCHANCE	Doris	1927	644		SEAVEY	Gene Wesley	1931	610
SCHAUER	Shirley M.		657		SEDAR	Helen Anna	1924	718
SCHELMANN	Mr.		902		SEEGMILLER	Adam	1867	317
SCHERFF	Brad		857		SEEHUSEN	Larry D.	1938	845
SCHERI	Richard		909		SEELEY	Caroline P.	1829	118
SCHILLERSTROM	Edward C.	1886	424		SEELEY	Horace Gibbs	1804	47
SCHILLERSTROM	Ralph Clifford	1909	662		SEELYE	Adelbert R., Jr.	1940	759
SCHILLERSTROM	Robert G.	1946	822		SEES	Henry Otto	1912	578
SCHMIDT	Emma B. (SCHULTZ)	1892	151		SEHL	Ronald Dwight		750
SCHMIDT	Julie	1976	866		SEIBERT	Jean E.	1928	666
SCHMITZ	Delia	1883	392		SEIFFERT	Dorothy Marie	1919	743
SCHNEIDER	Lenora Louise	1926	682		SEK	Irene	1925	831
SCHNELL	John P.	1931	593		SELBY	Howard	1902	585
SCHONE	Jeanette Ellen	1913	613		SELBY	Joseph Wesley	1926	792
SCHRADER	Viola	1914	640		Sell	Barbara Jean	1955	786
SCHRECKINGAST	Hila	1895	401		SELL	Earl Emil	1908	577
SCHROEDER	Anna E.	1892	564		SELL	Robert E.	1941	786
SCHUCKER	Dorothy	1912	575		SELLERS	Anthony D.	1974	730
SCHULER	Paul E.	1897	492		SEMPLE	Lucetta J.	1830	106
SCHULTZ	Gordon L.	1920	645		SENADENOS	Theodore Samuel	1929	596
SCHULTZ	Gordon L., Jr.	1947	816		SENEAR	Florence M.	1910	655
Schultz	Sylvia	1947	816		SEVERNS	Della Grace	1901	692
SCHUSTER	Joseph	1943	868		SEVERNS	George Edward	1852	256
SCHUTTE	Michael Karl	1953	742		SEVERNS	Horace	1878	447
SCHWARTZ	Steve	1969	866		SEVERNS	Lester	1912	692
SCHWEPPE	Emma	1877	445		SEWELL	Alfonso	1834	103
SCISSONS	Bonnie		756		SHACKLEFORD	Craig	1964	906
SCISSONS	Danny		517		SHAFER	Marvin	1910	382
SCISSONS	John	1971	757		SHAFFER	Agnes	1925	607
SCOFFIN	Brad J.	1966	865		SHAFFER	John	1859	196
SCOFIELD	Samuel E.	1906	574		SHAFFER	Mark	1873	197

SHAFFER	Rachael Olivia	1863	121	SHEPPARD	Luther Ray	1912	484
SHANER	Olive	1902	776	SHERIDAN	Edward		510
SHANK	Linda Sue	1960	764	SHERMAN	George		524
SHANK	Paula	1944	849	SHERMAN	Rodney Lynn		893
SHANKLE	Arey T.	1950	734	SHERMAN	Waldo A.	1879	275
SHANNON	Clothillde Harper		414	SHERMAN	Wendell B.	1907	470
SHARPE	Revillo	1823	83	SHERMAN	Wilson R.	1902	470
SHARPE	Viola	1856	185	SHERO	Olive	1888	364
SHARRA	William	1923	590	Sherwood	Camille	1959	846
SHAW	Bebia Ann	1954	840	SHERWOOD	Cleda Evelyn	1919	702
SHAW	Catherine Laurel	1883	355	Sherwood	Constance Kathleen	1968	846
SHAW	Charles Leroy	1912	620	SHERWOOD	Delores June	1923	702
SHAW	Elizabeth	1910	670	SHERWOOD	Frank William	1896	459
SHAW	Lyra		525	SHERWOOD	Gregory Dean	1962	846
SHAW	Rowena	1798	25	SHERWOOD	Helen Ione	1912	702
SHAW	Winifred	1879	245	SHERWOOD	Jerry Frank	1934	703
SHAWE	Norman Lee	1936	728	SHERWOOD	Luanne	1959	846
SHAWE	Tammy	1966	860	SHERWOOD	May Elizabeth	1866	55
SHEA	Victoria Mary	1887	335	SHERWOOD	Steven Frank	1957	846
SHEARER	James Lester	1890	419	SHIELDS	Madeline		645
SHEARER	Jane	1922	809	SHIELDS	Mattie A.	1887	428
SHEARS	William	1860	280	SHIELDS	Mr.	1954	839
SHEDD	Florence	1887	409	SHILLINGS	Jasper Leonard		790
SHEDD	Mary Justina	1855	265	SHIMON	Cynthia Garnette	1954	731
SHEETS	Thomas	1959	826	SHIRER	Robert Lewis	1920	469
SHEFFIELD	George Glover	1914	659	SHOCK	Hallie	1860	255
SHEFFIELD	Rosa Etta	1907	397	SHORE	David Mark, Sr.	1965	860
Sheldon	Anna	1926	782	SHORT	Otto R.	1877	293
SHELDON	Clarence John	1894	566	SHULINGBARGER	Charles		127
SHELDON	Clinton Clarence	1916	781	SHUMAR	George Dean	1982	870
SHELDON	Elizabeth Ann	1931	782	SHUMWAY	Mable G.	1878	349
SHELDON	Etta	1865	233	SHUPIERY	Ronald	1934	751
SHELDON	George Wendell	1917	781	SIBLEY	Alan L.	1902	657
SHELDON	Grant		557	SIBLEY	Dora F.	1866	236
SHELDON	John		775	SIBLEY	Guy Alan	1923	820
SHELDON	Lyle Donald	1924	781	SIBLEY	Guy Eugene	1879	419
SHELDON	Merl Dean	1926	782	SIBLEY	Ray Duane	1928	820
SHELDON	Winifred	1887	314	SIDEBOTHAM	Elizabeth	1810	57
SHEPHERD	William Giles	1831	176	SIDLER	Anita	1890	556
SHEPLEY	Orin	1915	572	SIDWAY	Clarence Spaulding	1877	222
SHEPPARD	Bessie	1901	650	SIDWAY	Dorothy	1896	390
SHEPPARD	Betty Jean	1949	725	SIDWAY	Edith	1872	222
SHEPPARD	Bobby Wayne	1950	725	SIDWAY	Edith	1913	391
SHEPPARD	Linda C.	1955	719	Sidway	Frances M.	1900	391
SHEPPARD	Linda Carol	1947	725	SIDWAY	Frank St. John	1869	221

SIDWAY	Franklin	1834	105	**SISSON**	Mary L.	1845	136
SIDWAY	Franklin	1900	391	**SISTECK**	Anna	1900	448
SIDWAY	George	1805	104	**SIVEK**	William James	1931	860
SIDWAY	Gilbert Douglas		221	**SKALA**	Kristi L.	1970	815
SIDWAY	Harold Spaulding	1868	221	**SKEFFINGTON**	Paul Francis		760
Sidway	Hazel	1897	390	**SKINNER**	Katherine L.	1881	360
SIDWAY	James	1759	20	**SKIZEWSKI**	Richard, Jr.		880
SIDWAY	James	1898	390	**SKOKOS**	George		510
Sidway	Jane	1904	390	**SKRYPER**	John Robert	1968	855
SIDWAY	Jonathan	1784	44	**SKUTT**	Claude	1882	301
SIDWAY	Jonathan	1832	105	**SLADEK**	Louis V.		443
SIDWAY	Kate Baldwin	1861	221	**SLATER**	Clifford	1916	684
SIDWAY	Katherine R.	1827	104	**SLATER**	Eunice	1915	420
SIDWAY	Kenneth L.	1891	390	**SLATER**	John C., Jr.	1933	668
Sidway	Lois H.	1929	612	**SLATER**	Linda Lee	1949	861
SIDWAY	Margaret St. John	1907	391	**SLIGHTS**	Edward Ellis	1894	533
SIDWAY	Martha Roberts	1908	391	**SLIGHTS**	Helen Jane	1920	761
SIDWAY	Peter	1929	612	**SLIGHTS**	Mary Ellen	1924	761
SIDWAY	Ralph Huntington	1884	222	**SLOAN**	Addie Ellen	1863	211
SIDWAY	William	1782	44	**SLOAN**	Michael Lee		862
SIDWAY	William Henry	1860	221	**SLOCUM**	Ina E.	1910	398
SILVAS	Javier Luis	1979	750	**SMEAL**	Leonard		782
SILVAS	Mr.		505	**SMEDLEY**	Helen Louise	1949	732
SILVERNAIL	Goldie	1886	538	**SMITH**	Ananias		120
SILVERS	Mr.	1848	152	**SMITH**	April Victoria	1954	864
SILVERY	Minnie	1900	283	**SMITH**	Betsey	1768	22
SIMCICK	Robert	1928	818	**SMITH**	Betty Lou	1926	603
SIMMONDS	Edith	1855	225	**SMITH**	Carl	1927	878
SIMMONS	Etta Ann	1871	226	**SMITH**	Carole	1941	632
SIMMONS	Gertrude	1915	679	**SMITH**	Charles Lawrence	1899	481
SIMMS	Mr.		296	**SMITH**	Charles Leslie	1868	343
SIMON	Lillian Grace	1964	716	**SMITH**	Charles Porter	1929	739
SIMONE	Teresa Ann	1959	745	**SMITH**	Cora A.	1868	432
SIMONS	Frederick A.	1914	672	**SMITH**	Cora B.	1868	361
SIMONS	Rose M.		106	**SMITH**	Derue Colvin	1918	788
SIMPSON	Augustus		559	**SMITH**	Dianna	1961	727
SIMPSON	Evelyn Devee	1920	697	**SMITH**	Dianna	1961	855
SIMPSON	Lou		525	**SMITH**	Ebert S.	1884	217
SIMPSON	Mildred S.	1907	423	**SMITH**	Elizabeth	1838	76
SINGER	Edward	1893	449	**SMITH**	Elma		528
SINGER	Harold	1920	695	**SMITH**	Eloise Cecil	1897	376
SINNING	Franklin Napolean	1889	437	**SMITH**	Emerson	1914	511
SISSON	Anna	1860	233	**SMITH**	Etta E.	1892	319
SISSON	Laura Shipe	1910	531	**SMITH**	Flossie Glenn	1886	324
SISSON	Mary	1747	15	**SMITH**	George	1879	334

SMITH	George Walter	1907	546	**SMITH**	Sarah Matilda	1858	171
SMITH	Geraldine	1928	698	**SMITH**	Savina	1811	67
SMITH	Grace	1932	618	**SMITH**	Sophronia	1841	146
SMITH	Gwendolyn L.	1936	599	**SMITH**	Warren	1924	766
SMITH	Harold	1934	723	**SMITH**	William	1856	250
SMITH	Harold Larkin	1908	384	**SMITH**	William Garrett	1930	501
SMITh	Ida	1857	407	**SMOTHERMAN**	John M.	1871	365
SMITH	James Lyle	1944	714	**SMOTHERMAN**	Verona Bethel	1905	585
SMITH	Jean		527	**SMYTHE**	James R.	1845	173
SMITH	John Laverne	1945	901	**SNELL**	Alfred	1888	432
SMITH	John W., Jr.	1929	672	**SNELL**	Alice B.	1835	114
SMITH	Katherine	1936	768	**SNELL**	Robert Leroy	1927	831
SMITH	Kevin McDonald	1966	855	**SNYDAM**	Abigail	1757	17
SMITH	Lawrence		760	**SNYDER**	Amanda	1840	107
SMITH	Lela M.	1892	435	**SNYDER**	Carl L.	1901	553
SMITH	Leslie	1906	623	**SNYDER**	Charles	1922	819
SMITH	Lewis	1812	83	**SNYDER**	Donald Eljin	1921	762
SMITH	Louis A.	1862	210	**SNYDER**	Josiah	1840	152
SMITH	Lydia Jane	1841	184	**SNYDER**	Joyce	1927	773
SMITH	Lyle William	1920	468	**SNYDER**	Marjorie Merle	1918	432
SMITH	Mabel C.	1899	219	**SNYDER**	Melissa M.	1842	247
SMITH	Malcolm Darling	1922	596	**SNYDER**	Mr.	1924	783
SMITH	Mary Alice	1874	157	**SNYDER**	Pamela Virginia	1945	867
SMITH	Mary Louise	1907	482	**SNYDER**	Russell W.	1921	800
SMITH	Mary Sue	1923	723	**SNYDER**	Sally Ann	1934	668
SMITH	Mildred May	1898	318	**SNYDER**	Virginia B.	1916	624
SMITH	Milton Ray	1904	546	**SOMMERS**	Irene E.	1888	367
SMITH	Miss	1785	36	**SONNANSTINE**	Ruth	1915	576
SMITH	Mitchel	1839	117	**SONNDEREGGER**	Jacob J.	1953	868
SMITH	Mr.	1885	226	**SOOTER**	Sylvia Evelyn	1917	466
SMITH	Mr.		130	**SOULE**	Valeria Alice	1920	594
SMITH	Nannie Bell		482	**SOULLE**	Henry Ward	1892	370
SMITH	Nathaniel	1897	371	**SOUSLEY**	James D.	1928	601
SMITH	Opal Lenore	1892	562	**SOWERS**	Walter		532
SMITH	Otis	1875	321	**SPADE**	William M.	1922	571
SMITH	Owen Andrew	1973	730	**SPARR**	Ernest Paul	1926	791
SMITH	Pamela	1830	60	**SPARR**	Guy Soliday	1886	583
SMITH	Paul	1902	543	**SPARR**	Helen Wilene	1924	791
SMITH	Phillip Charles	1956	864	**SPAULDING**	Charlotte	1843	105
SMITH	Phin	1889	411	**SPAULDING**	Edith	1865	195
SMITH	Phoebe	1857	201	**SPAULDING**	Virgil	1876	332
SMITH	Ron S.	1950	841	**SPEARS**	Mr.	1890	359
Smith	Sandy		714	**SPECIAL**	Robert	1926	555
SMITH	Sarah	1855	148	**SPEENBURG**	Charles	1847	184
SMITH	Sarah Helen	1897	368	**SPEENBURG**	Delmar	1871	339

SPELTS	Ralph Chester	1905	700	STEEP	Clyde	1904	695
SPENCE	Charles		507	STEEP	Lois Jane	1924	843
SPENCE	Genevieve M.	1907	653	STEFF	Donald	1925	800
SPENCER	Brett	1969	717	STEFFENHAGEN	Dale	1924	809
SPENCER	Dorothy Pearl	1921	581	STEIN	Marie	1929	701
SPERRY	Elizabeth BARNES	1825	68	STEINHOFF	Mr.	1920	783
SPETA	Dale Henry	1953	892	STEPANEK	Gertrude	1880	235
SPETA	Helen O.	1919	646	STEPHENS	Clarissa	1824	190
SPETA	Joseph	1921	816	STEPHENS	Clarissa B.	1868	347
SPINK	William Lewis		867	STEPHENS	Crystal Anna	1978	874
SPINNING	Alpheus	1795	70	STEPHENS	Elizabeth Effie	1858	351
SPOON	Ethel M.	1917	654	STEPHENS	Ezra Milks	1831	191
SPOON	Shari Anne	1942	487	STEPHENS	Ezra Parker	1862	346
SPRAKER	Clayton E.	1912	679	STEPHENS	George W.	1792	86
SPRINGER	Emma	1867	247	STEPHENS	Gerald Edgar		756
SPRINGER	Harriet A.	1879	247	STEPHENS	Harrie Ellis	1866	347
SQUIRES	Garry	1958	841	STEPHENS	Irma V.	1890	563
ST. ALBIN	David John	1973	873	STEPHENS	James Parker	1833	192
ST. AUBIN	Raymond W.	1953	754	STEPHENS	Laura	1856	346
ST. JOHN	Parnell	1801	44	STEPHENS	Leander Milks	1824	194
ST. LOUIS	Mr.		759	STEPHENS	Mary Olive	1899	564
STABLER	Lura Beatrice	1883	268	STEPHENS	Polly	1804	84
STACKHOUSE	Kendal		875	STEPHENS	Reuben Doty	1799	85
STADNIKA	Lorie		891	STEPHENS	Ruby	1894	563
STAIR	Roberta Kathleen	1944	505	STEPHENS	Susan E.	1847	344
STAMPHTON	Nellie Celia	1894	319	STEPHENS	Sylvester Reese	1822	188
STANHOPE	Cecil		527	STEPHENSON	Archibald M.	1844	128
STANHOPE	Clarence		525	STEPHENSON	Barbara M.	1928	607
STANKEY	Fred		640	STEPHENSON	Kathy	1963	755
Stanley	Blanche	1905	625	STEPHENSON	Ura Mae	1872	272
STANLEY	Donald	1934	782	STERRITT	William Arthur	1898	450
STANLEY	George	1898	625	STEVENS	Alice Clair	1929	791
STANLEY	John	1916	508	STEVENS	Angela M.	1980	896
STANLEY	Mildred M.	1903	625	STEVENS	Benjamin Henry	1910	686
STANLEY	Pauline M.	1916	568	STEVENS	Doris Venetta	1931	500
STANLEY	Sylvester	1872	400	STEVENS	Raymond Wilber	1900	628
STANTON	Judy		877	STEVENS	Stevan I.	1900	391
STANTON	Theresa Ruth		771	STEWARD	Maude Mary	1894	423
STARBUCK	Maud M.	1900	578	STEWART	Beverly Ann	1956	824
STARCEVICH	Mr.		896	STEWART	Caroline M.	1886	378
STEAD	Janet	1928	530	STEWART	Joyce	1954	795
STEARN	Minerva	1836	179	STEWART	Nathaniel M.	1895	403
STEEL	Virginia		608	STICKFORT	Viola I.	1918	697
STEELE	Joseph Clarke	1894	566	STIDHAM	Ronnie Edwin	1960	857
STEELE	Sylvester	1887	360	STILES	Janice Elaine	1959	809

STILLWELL	Jerry Martin	1939	723	**SUNDBERG**	Ethel F.	1925	647
STIMPSON	Wayne	1927	823	**SURBER**	Mary Ann	1940	727
STINGLEY	Ms.		901	**SURBER**	Scottie	1982	905
STINSON	Dorrine J.	1950	821	**SWAIN**	Lucinda	1828	79
STITES	Erma		496	**SWAINSTON**	Minerva A.	1858	153
STLOUIS	Kristin	1981	874	**SWART**	Joyce	1920	766
STOCKMAN	Margaret I.	1902	470	**SWARTHOUT**	Muriel	1934	554
STOLL	Patricia Marie	1928	739	**SWARTZ**	Christina Joy	1967	908
STOLL	Phyllis Elaine	1932	739	**SWARTZ**	John Harold	1944	879
STOLL	Victor William	1901	496	**SWEATON**	Jeremy Albert	1971	857
STONE	Ada	1870	361	**SWEEK**	Jack Orlan	1923	778
STONE	Emory I.	1864	131	**SWEET**	Helen		671
STONEWALL	Effie V.	1899	568	**SWEETINGHAM**	Ronald William	1945	879
STONEWALL	Frank	1865	352	**SWENSEN**	Gail A.	1958	746
STONEWALL	Harry A.	1910	568	**SWICK**	Mary May	1919	296
STONEWALL	Ralph C.	1901	568	**SWIFT**	Amy Louisa	1890	465
STONIER	Edward	1924	521	**SWIFT**	Dorothy	1925	878
STOOPS	Mr.	1925	790	**SWIFT**	George Henry	1853	267
STOREY	Martha	1840	152	**SWIFT**	Harriet Hardy	1888	465
STORY	Laura	1870	560	**SWIFT**	Herald	1905	776
STOTTS	Grace Emeline	1893	376	**SWIFT**	Herald John	1928	878
STOVER	Carl	1914	777	**SWIFT**	Mary Eunice	1893	465
STOVER	John Wesley	1846	202	**SWIFT**	Robert Lynn	1904	465
STRATTI	Rosa Maria Larnia	1947	769	**SYMONS**	Mary Elizabeth	1940	662
STREATOR	Mary Melvina	1848	102	**SYPER**	Josephine Phyllis	1913	432
STREMPHA	Viola	1912	617	**SZYMANSKI**	Bertha	1923	635
STROH	Catherine A.	1858	328				
STRONG	Franklin E.	1844	174				
STRUCK	James C.	1956	892				
STRUEVER	William	1950	864				
STRUNK	John Richard	1944	753				
STRUVER	Clara M.	1918	386				
STUART	Maybelle Clara	1884	362				
STUART	Mildred A.	1889	370				
STUART	Ward H.	1866	211				
STUBBS	Clyda Marie	1928	534				
STUDD	Doris	1914	640				
STUFT	Carol	1937	674				
STURGIS	Elizabeth	191	545				
STURGIS	Julia Evalyn	1877	299				
SULLY	Elodie Marguerite	1914	510				
SULLY	John Alfred	1892	306				
SUMMERS	Almira C.	1821	79				
SUMMERS	Elizabeth	1827	79				
SUMPTER	Bert	1969	859				

T, U, V

TABER	Emily	1898	315
TACL	Mr.	1930	783
TALEB	Mr.		821
TALLMAN	Janice Cole	1931	715
TALLMAN	Keith	1906	469
TANN	Bonnie		848
TANN	Edward	1916	705
TANN	Gary Elmer	1946	849
Tann	Patricia	1946	849
TANN	Sharon Elizabeth	1940	848
TANN	Stanley Edwin	1942	849
TANN	Teri Ann	1967	902
TANN	Traci J.	1969	902
TANNER	Elizabeth	1871	213
TANNER	Lina	1847	237
TANNER	Mary Ann	1846	72
TAPPEN	Leon		505
TAPPEN	Timothy James	1960	750
TARDY	James Bernard	1894	434
TARDY	Merva Ellen	1923	676
TARR	Ruth "Bessie"	1892	219
TARULA	Ruben S.	1961	611
TATE	Henry	1900	450
TATE	Isolene L.	1879	241
TATRO	James R.	1931	848
TAUNT	Caroline Baldwin	1835	105
TAWES	Mr.		894
TAYLOR	Annie Mae	1918	685
TAYLOR	Edward		364
TAYLOR	Gary	1965	906
TAYLOR	Julia G.	1865	138
TAYLOR	Mark D.	1948	862
TAYLOR	Mary E.	1873	214
TAYLOR	Mr.	1899	281
TAYLOR	Ramona	1922	677
TEASDALE	Cathryne	1851	138
TEASDALE	Thomas C.	1808	66
TEDFORD	John		128
TELFER	Louise	1890	447
TEMPLE	Eliza	1855	254
TEN BROECK	Louie	1869	332
TEN EYCK	Mary Catherine	1925	597
TERHUNE	David A.	1928	621
TERHUNE	Diane L.	1960	801
Terhune	Dixie L.	1939	621
TERHUNE	Eugene L.	1956	801
Terhune	Geraldine T.	1915	620
TERHUNE	Glen M.	1926	621
TERHUNE	Joseph R.	1934	621
TERHUNE	Joseph R., Jr.	1958	801
TERHUNE	Leo D.	1920	620
TERHUNE	Leo George	1891	396
TERHUNE	Michael	1971	801
Terhune	Patti		801
TERHUNE	Richard T.	1937	621
TERHUNE	William A.	1912	620
TESAR	Elsie	1905	447
TEUPEL	Carolyn Mae	1945	840
TEUPEL	Debbie L.	1955	842
TEUPEL	Donyell	1987	899
TEUPEL	Elmer	1926	689
TEUPEL	Evelyn Janet	1947	841
TEUPEL	Frederick	1921	687
TEUPEL	Gladys Janet	1920	687
TEUPEL	Herman Frederick	1877	443
TEUPEL	John E.	1962	840
TEUPEL	Marilyn J.	1946	840
TEUPEL	Merle L.	1959	842
TEUPEL	Nellie May	1928	689
TEUPEL	Panzy Caroline	1924	688
TEUPEL	Samuel	1923	688
THAYER	Mr.	1875	218
THIBAUDEAU	Bernard		515
THIBAUDEAU	Bernice		515
THIBAUDEAU	Henry C.	1891	310
THOMA	Adaline Rhuamy	1852	236
THOMAS	Birdeen F.	1913	566
THOMAS	Dorothy Ann	1910	692
THOMAS	Edwin H.	1914	589
THOMAS	Gertrude	1876	393
THOMAS	Harry	1840	101
THOMAS	Joseph	1842	223
THOMAS	Kyle	1974	910
THOMAS	Mary	1817	78
THOMAS	Philip Winston	1943	807
THOMAS	Reba Sue		799
THOME	Anna	1935	802
THOME	Beatrice	1931	802

THOME	Elizabeth Joyce	1942	803	TOLBERT	Cathy Pamela	1953	728
THOME	Francis J.	1906	623	TOLBERT	Charles King	1943	723
THOME	John F.	1936	802	TOLBERT	Charlotte Verda Lee	1969	855
Thome	Marie	1938	802	TOLBERT	Claudine	1930	723
THOME	Mary J.	1937	803	TOLBERT	Howard Dunkley	1909	483
THOMES	Evelyn E.	1924	665	TOLBERT	King	1882	291
THOMPSON	Clarence Henry	1896	466	TOLBERT	Michael	1974	859
THOMPSON	Dora Lee	1950	879	TOLBERT	Pearl Edith	1920	483
THOMPSON	Gordon L.	1869	361	TOLBERT	Shirley Jean	1941	723
THOMPSON	Helen Louise	1922	503	TOLBERT	Teresa Jayne	1961	858
THOMPSON	Jean	1924	786	TOLMAN	Maggie Belle	1877	274
THOMPSON	Marilyn	1926	503	TOMLINSON	Joseph	1910	510
THOMPSON	Mary Jane	1857	203	TOMPKINS	Crystal	1982	717
THOMPSON	Patricia Ann	1922	543	TOMPKINS	Katrina	1964	717
THOMPSON	Robert George	1891	579	TOMPKINS	Keith D.	1939	471
THOMPSON	Sally	1903	546	TOMPKINS	Michelle May	1969	717
THOMSON	Elmer	1911	452	TOMPKINS	Timothy D.	1965	717
THORNTON	Natalie Marie	1968	869	TOOMBS	Ms.		901
THORNTON	Ray S.	1946	744	TOWN	William		244
THORPE	Anthony R.	1965	906	TOWNSEND	Robert Harold	1936	510
THORSON	Pamela Pauline	1953	880	TRAVIS	Hallie	1860	255
THUNEMAN	Mary Lou	1920	452	TREBON	Olive Annette	1890	441
THURSTON	Florence A.	1941	769	TRICHEL	Tiffany Michelle	1976	898
THURSTON	Mary	1753	20	TRIESTRAM	Cheryl Ann	1958	863
TIBBETS	William Burnham	1891	323	TROCKS	Harriett	1875	298
TIBBITS	Mamie	1889	391	TROMBLEY	Daniel Michael	1945	489
TILLER	Danny Levi	1960	858	TRONSON	Albert	1897	359
TILLET	Josephine E.	1910	776	Tronson	Maribeth	1947	786
TILSTRA	Luanne	1956	864	TRONSON	Mr.		884
TIMME	Autumn Eva	1908	431	TRONSON	Patricia Kay	1944	786
TIMME	Autumn Eva	1908	644	TRONSON	Robert R.	1947	786
TIMME	William Ernest	1887	410	TRONSON	Ronald Leroy	1916	578
TIMMS	Margaret		523	TRONSON	Ross Michael	1998	884
TIMPSON	Bathia	1836	199	TRONSON	Ruth Lorraine	1945	786
TINGLE	Leigh E.	1886	409	Trout	Donna	1940	608
TINGUE	Frank Lee	1917	643	TROUT	Leland Duane	1940	608
TIPPING	Jack	1919	657	TROUT	Leland Roy	1913	382
TISDALE	Andrew	1962	796	TROWBRIDGE	Mercy	1726	10
Tisdale	Erica L.	1967	796	TROWBRIDGE	Sally A.	1969	750
TISDALE	Mr.	1938	597	TRUESDALE	Emma Gertrude	1871	361
TOBIN	Raymond	1900	567	TRUESDALE	Lena	1878	362
TODD	Harold	1915	689	TRUESDALE	Marvin	1840	205
TODD	Oscar H.		558	TRUESDELL	Don Meredith	1924	735
TOINTON	William James	1913	781	TRUESDELL	Jay	1880	339
TOLBERT	Carol Lee	1946	724	TRUMBLE	Gary Lavern	1950	748

TUBBS	Harvey	1820	114	Van Ostran	Carrie		865
TUCKER	Herbert Henry, Jr.	1942	890	VAN OSTRAN	Bert Leslie	1952	739
TUCKER	Jami Leigh	1981	910	VAN OSTRAN	Charles Edwin, IV	1955	864
TUCKER	Lee R.	1934	724	VAN OSTRAN	Douglas Edward	1966	865
TUCKER	Nathaniel David	1984	910	VAN OSTRAN	Charles Elda	1935	739
TUCKER	Vashit H.	1900	303	VAN OSTRAN	Doris Elaine	1938	739
TUCKER	Wilma Ethel	1918	713	VAN OSTRAN	Ruth Marie	1954	740
TURNER	Debra K.	1952	747	VAN VALKENBURGH	Aaron Jacob	1874	338
TURNER	Harriet E.	1830	99	VAN VALKENBURGH	Adelaide		557
TURNER	Laura Ann	1833	72	VAN VALKENBURGH	Alvaretta		339
Tuttle	Donna J.	1953	897	VAN VALKENBURGH	Benjamin	1845	184
TUTTLE	Mr.		831	VAN VALKENBURGH	Carrie	1863	186
TUTTLE	Silas	1814	71	VAN VALKENBURGH	Charles W.	1887	341
TUTTLE	William R.	1952	897	VAN VALKENBURGH	Christchana	1836	183
TWISS	Alice Louise	1931	780	VAN VALKENBURGH	Cyrus Wilbur	1878	338
TYLER	Edwin Albert	1891	403	VAN VALKENBURGH	Dayton		339
TYLER	James E.	1822	70	VAN VALKENBURGH	Eleanor Mae	1922	559
TYLER	Vivian Agnes	1934	621	VAN VALKENBURGH	Ella	1871	186
UGGENTI	Leigh Anne		873	VAN VALKENBURGH	Evelyn		557
ULMER	Robert	1927	810	VAN VALKENBURGH	George A.	1889	339
UNDERHILL	Rith	1911	653	VAN VALKENBURGH	George Angelo	1838	184
UNDERWOOD	Chris		840	VAN VALKENBURGH	George Arlington	1910	556
UNDERWOOD	Eldene Olive	1922	658	VAN VALKENBURGH	Glenn M.	1901	342
UNDERWOOD	Joyce	1928	658	VAN VALKENBURGH	Isaac J.	1839	184
UNDERWOOD	Lyle T.	1896	421	VAN VALKENBURGH	James	1867	186
UTTER	Joseph	1885	219	VAN VALKENBURGH	James Gilbert	1813	83
UTTER	Katherine	1912	386	VAN VALKENBURGH	James Gilbert	1813	84
UTYRO	Darren William	1970	716	VAN VALKENBURGH	Jane	1861	185
UTYRO	Walter	1941	471	VAN VALKENBURGH	Lodema	1847	184
VAHEY	Mary Loretta	1924	586	VAN VALKENBURGH	Lydia	1883	339
VALENTINE	John K.	1950	774	VAN VALKENBURGH	Minnie	1880	338
VAN ALSTINE	Cornelius D.	1862	170	VAN VALKENBURGH	Nina L.	1873	338
VAN BUREN	Arthur	1870	331	Van Valkenburgh	Patrice	1911	556
VAN BUREN	Mr.		543	VAN VALKENBURGH	Pearl	1884	340
VAN CAMPEN	John	1915	651	VAN VALKENBURGH	Romaine W.	1860	185
VAN DEUSEN	Clayton	1910	551	VAN VALKENBURGH	Samantha	1859	185
VAN DEUSEN	Ethel	1926	772	VAN VALKENBURGH	Wesley	1848	184
VAN EPPS	Grace	1850	197	VAN VORIS	Andrew	1858	331
VAN ETTEN	Charles Frederick	1918	616	VAN VORIS	Catherine	1854	330
VAN ETTEN	Fred Luther	1888	394	VAN VORIS	Emma	1856	331
VAN ETTEN	Ione	1896	460	VAN VORIS	Hannah Elizabeth	1850	330
VAN ETTEN	James	1862	263	VAN VORRIS	Joseph	1823	177
VAN NORMAN	Lena	1858	247	VAN WIE	Elizabeth	1841	145
VAN OSDOL	Johnnie M.	1918	774	VANASSE	Cora	1900	313
Van Ostran	Carmen		864	VANCE	James E.	1925	833

VANCE	Lee	1910	545
VANCE	Theresa L.	1955	787
VANDEMHEMMEL	Debra Marie	1962	610
VANDYKE	Jack Garrett	1938	848
VANHORN	George		839
VANVORIS	Virginia	1921	765
VARGO	Richard E.	1940	798
VAUGHN	Ella Jane	1863	260
VAUGHN	Elva	1883	333
VENABLE	Luther Wayne	1951	727
VERDON	Lisa		757
VERDON	Mr.		517
VEREL	Eugene	1931	597
VIAU	Murielle	1945	524
VILLALON	Jazzmine Edward	1992	908
VILLALON	Marcial Reynaga	1976	871
VIMMERSTADT	Peter		654
VIRTUE	Mr.	1925	783
VODVARKA	Robert J.	1945	785
VOLK	Charles Carl	1902	405
VOLK	Clara Minnie	1895	404
VOLK	Kanneth Charles	1925	635
VON BONBECQUE	Louisa	1841	125
VON BORRIES	Emily	1927	631
VOORHEES	Pamela Jo	1964	742
VORHIES	Karen Kay	1951	823
VOSE	Lena Mabel	1884	321
VOUGHT	Warren J.	1931	596
VREDENBURGH	Clarence		557
VROLYK	Mildred Ann	1926	467

W, X, Y, Z

WACKER	Hedwig A. Adelaide	1888	360
WADDINGTON	Kevin	1980	873
WADE	Fred	1890	371
WADE	William Henry	1903	583
WAGNER	Valeria	1920	486
WAITE	Albert	1857	233
WAITE	Angelina	1849	203
WAITE	Anna	1792	45
WAITE	Bathsheba	1811	107
WAITE	Benjamin	1829	109
WAITE	Butler R.	1830	109
WAITE	Clara	1857	232
Waite	Clara R.	1859	232
WAITE	David	1814	107
WAITE	Ettie E.	1867	245
WAITE	Florence E.	1897	407
WAITE	Franklin	1856	232
WAITE	Fred	1863	233
WAITE	George B.	1859	233
WAITE	George C.	1825	108
WAITE	Gladys	1905	406
WAITE	Horace	1850	232
WAITE	Isaac	1786	45
WAITE	Isaac, Jr.	1821	92
WAITE	Isaac, Jr.	1821	108
WAITE	Jane	1827	109
WAITE	Jonathan	1819	108
WAITE	Jonathan	1845	231
WAITE	Lucy J.	1868	233
Waite	Mariah	1836	107
WAITE	Martin	1809	107
WAITE	Martin B.	1841	230
WAITE	Mary Ann	1816	108
WAITE	Mertie Mae	1883	406
WAITE	Nettie M.	1888	406
Waite	Oscar	1861	232
Waite	Phebe	1841	230
WAITE	Rosa E.	1874	405
WAITE	William A.	1861	233
WAKEFIELD	Gladys E.	1887	341
WALBURG	Doris Jane	1930	598
WALBURG	Richard A.	1898	375
WALDRON	Nathan Napolean	1859	330

WALKER	Ada	1900	533	WARREN	Walter Wallace	1925	588
WALKER	Albert Herman	1879	446	WARTHAN	Merle Maxine	1920	648
WALKER	Alvin Ray	1896	470	WASHBORN	Charles Arthur	1907	636
WALKER	Elfrieda Rae	1958	842	WATERFIELD	Lorraine	1928	762
WALKER	Elizabeth Hardy	1942	807	WATERMAN	Elizabeth	1913	475
WALKER	Ellis Arthur	1940	610	WATERMAN	Mary	1778	30
WALKER	Hal Hammer	1918	630	WATERMAN	Robert James	1927	680
WALKER	Harrison G.	1888	478	WATERS	Barber	1859	246
WALKER	Hazel	1903	692	WATERS	Elizabeth	1801	50
WALKER	Jacqueline Eulis	1927	467	WATERS	Grace	1876	252
WALKER	Mildred	1901	691	WATERS	Theo	1885	416
WALKER	Port		252	WATKINS	Carrie	1856	240
WALKER	Wilma		441	WATKINS	Harry Glenn	1887	420
WALLACE	Ruth	1907	426	WATKINS	Mr.	1844	237
WALLEY	Clyde Gerald	1886	402	WATSON	Clark W.	1898	472
WALSH	Daisy Irene	1905	291	WATSON	Elva L.	1896	407
WALSH	Nelson	1901	693	WATSON	Frances	1930	374
WALSH	Rena	1907	639	WATSON	George	1865	233
WALSH	Verda Mae	1911	483	WATSON	George	1900	448
WALSH	William James	1879	438	WATSON	Jean Esther	1922	718
WALTER	Abijah Eugene	1869	292	WATSON	Jennie Armina	1886	299
WALTERS	Martha Elizabeth	1907	533	WAYMAN	Tobias	1877	331
WALTERS	Sophia Bailey	1895	316	WAYMAN	Virginia	1926	543
WALTON	James Oscar	1914	630	WEATHERFORD	Bonnie	1958	825
WALTON	Margaret Elizabeth	1918	632	WEAVER	Bryce O.	1928	698
WARBURTON	Claude D.	1931	599	WEAVER	Gertrude	1927	764
WARBURTON	Fred	1899	376	WEAVER	John M.	1920	559
WARBURTON	Galen Ray	1955	796	WEAVER	Lee O.	1922	698
WARBURTON	James		796	WEAVER	Mary Enid	1925	403
WARBURTON	Mark A.	1955	796	WEAVER	Marylou Inez	1928	698
WARBURTON	Robert Lee	1929	599	WEAVER	Nancy Elizabeth	1959	846
WARBURTON	Shannon		796	WEAVER	Olley	1900	455
WARBURTON	Walter R.	1933	600	WEBB	Bill		850
WARBURTON	Walter William	1856	214	WEBB	Helen L.	1916	573
WARD	Charles	1860	280	WEBB	Homer De Wayne	1882	354
WARD	Gladys M.	1904	338	WEBB	Leona Grace	1904	369
WARD	Melvin D.	1871	183	Webb	Louise	1915	572
WARDELL	Donna Mae	1919	603	WEBB	Wayne J.	1907	572
WARN	Arlene		617	WEBBER	James William	1883	333
WARNER	Augusta		146	WEBBER	Mabel Louise	1906	545
WARNER	Grace M.	1909	544	WEBER	Howard	1907	636
WARNER	Nancy Carol	1955	864	Webster	Bonnie	1958	696
WARREN	Florence Wanda	1926	589	WEBSTER	Carol Ann	1952	695
WARREN	Gary David	1951	734	WEBSTER	David Roger	1954	696
WARREN	Walter	1900	367	WEBSTER	Elma Mae	1917	452

WEBSTER	Emma	1860	279	**WESTON**	Sarah	1630	1
WEBSTER	George L.	1873	395	**WEYMOUTH**	Erwin	1925	475
WEBSTER	Harold Forest	1891	259	**WHALEY**	Fred N.	1861	270
WEBSTER	Roger Daniel	1926	452	**WHALEY**	Sarah	1810	65
WEBSTER	Wayne Edmund	1919	452	**WHALEY**	Sophronia	1854	207
WEEKS	Blanche	1897	479	**WHEADON**	Frederick W.	1937	722
WEEKS	Edwin L.	1856	129	**WHEATON**	John		480
WEEKS	George Clarence	1891	478	**WHEATON**	Maria	1809	54
WEEKS	Harriet E.	1895	478	**WHEELER**	Iola	1866	329
Weeks	Hazel	1901	478	**WHEELER**	Pauline	1930	767
WEEKS	Howard W.	1888	273	**WHIPP**	Bonnie L.	1949	868
WEEKS	James Goodman	1853	287	**WHIPPLE**	Annette Adelia	1846	204
WEEKS	John H.	1830	58	**WHIPPLE**	Arelia A.	1819	90
WEEKS	Stella R.	1892	478	**WHIPPLE**	Clara Almeda	1915	645
WEEKS	William James	1894	478	**WHIPPLE**	Edwin M.	1890	411
WEILER	Erma	1908	375	**WHIPPLE**	Erle Inman	1876	361
WEISKOPF	Louis	1928	739	**WHIPPLE**	Ford Ghoca	1904	579
WEISS	Leroy		692	**WHIPPLE**	Harlow	1912	645
WEK	Lawrence		604	**WHIPPLE**	Ira	1819	94
WELLEN	Margaret	1834	87	**WHIPPLE**	Ira Frank	1849	205
WELLER	Edna T.	1869	265	**Whipple**	Margaret M.	1907	579
WELLER	Robert Harold	1975	907	**WHIRLEY**	Maureen	1963	898
WELLMAN	Mr.	1920	783	**WHITCAER**	Mr.	1842	118
WELLS	Alice Lucile	1919	780	**WHITCOMB**	Diane Marie	1930	674
WELLS	Brandy	1978	857	**WHITCOMB**	Ina	1875	245
WELLS	Eula Maria	1912	690	**WHITCOMB**	Lee E.	1895	432
WELLS	Todd	1983	876	**WHITCOMB**	Maude Mae	1889	410
WELLS	Velma	1930	642	**WHITCOMB**	Virginia E.	1917	655
WELSH	Dorothy May	1908	398	**WHITE**	Agnes	1900	447
WELTY	Fay F.		354	**WHITE**	Almira D.	1863	256
WELTY	Jack	1924	572	**WHITE**	Alvin Wesley	1920	522
WELTY	Marda	1916	572	**WHITE**	Amelia	1811	89
WENGLIKOWSKI	Steven	1956	871	**WHITE**	Bessie	1900	448
WERB	Diane Elizabeth	1974	728	**WHITE**	Caroline	1858	256
WERKHEISER	Chad A.	1978	875	**WHITE**	Charles	1855	255
WERLE	Harold P.	1951	821	**WHITE**	Deborah	1804	53
WERY	Ernest J.	1893	301	**WHITE**	Donald James	1917	782
Wesley	Christina Marie	1974	860	**WHITE**	Eileen		515
WESLEY	Floyd Clinton	1968	860	**WHITE**	Elizabeth Brownell	1871	267
WEST	Edwin L.	1847	132	**WHITE**	Elmer	1921	693
WEST	Lucille	1911	568	**WHITE**	Eugene Harris	1906	692
WEST	Martha Conger	1916	575	**WHITE**	George Milk	1837	125
WEST	Miss	1830	109	**WHITE**	George Perry	1874	257
WEST	William		513	**WHITE**	Harold B., Jr	1919	272
WESTEGARD	Leslie		604	**WHITE**	Holder, Jr.	1768	25

WHITE	Holder, Jr.	1812	53	WILDAY	Charles George	1897	542
WHITE	Holder, Jr.	1812	59	WILDAY	Elsa Elizabeth	1933	767
WHITE	James Lawrence	1882	446	WILDAY	Emma	1849	178
WHITE	Lawrence James	1814	120	WILDAY	George	1851	178
WHITE	Lillian	1902	378	WILDAY	Grace Marie	1899	543
WHITE	Lydia	1867	256	WILDAY	Howard Marion	1922	543
WHITE	Mary	1852	255	WILDAY	Marion Caleb	1875	331
WHITE	Minnie M.	1880	446	WILDAY	Marjorie Alice	1927	767
White	Norma	1906	692	WILDAY	Olive	1926	767
WHITE	Orville	1899	448	WILDAY	Ruth Emeline	1902	543
WHITE	Samuel Holderman, Jr.	1904	447	WILES	Mary V.	1922	653
WHITE	Sarah	1854	255	WILHELM	David		899
WHITE	Steve		524	WILHELMI	Robert John	1952	844
WHITE	Steven		524	WILKINS	Abraham	1810	57
WHITE	Susan Lindsey	1864	256	WILKINS	Abram	1855	253
WHITE	Vallie Pearl	1879	412	WILKINS	Frances Almeda	1845	128
WHITE	William	1822	119	WILKINS	Harriet M.	1850	128
WHITE	William	1887	565	WILKINS	Oliver Perry	1864	324
WHITE	William C.	1887	446	WILKINSON	Emma		247
WHITE	William J.	1855	256	WILKINSON	Margaret	1864	247
WHITEHEAD	Edna L.	1927	488	WILKINSON	Martin Charles		760
WHITEMAN	Donna Jean	1950	862	WILKINSON	Mr.	1900	447
WHITEN	Dorothy		559	WILKINSON	Robert		651
WHITENACK	Ilene	1910	670	WILKINSON	Robert		693
WHITING	Eliza Avery	1819	60	WILKINSON	Sharel Lynn	1955	759
WHITMORE	Hazel Eugenia	1894	422	WILKINSON	Tare L.	1974	828
WHITNEY	Laamma	1863	209	WILKS	Barbara Ellyn	1951	864
WHITNEY	Laurel Mae	1941	784	WILKS	Harry Thomas	1925	739
WHITNEY	Susan M.	1889	399	WILKS	Nancy Jane	1953	864
WHITNEY	Thomas King	1916	574	WILKSON	Marilyn	1948	752
WHITTACAR	Maria		775	WILLARD	George E.	1903	375
WHITTAKER	Alice M.	1851	224	Willett	Arlene F.	1940	800
WIBBENS	Henrietta	1898	379	WILLETT	Clara Chase	1925	800
WICK	Richard	1917	549	WILLETT	David Allen	1935	800
WIDEMAN	Claude Elmer	1890	353	WILLETT	Edna	1919	676
WIDEMAN	Elizabeth Eleanor	1917	570	WILLETT	Henry Lloyd	1902	616
WIDEMAN	John Frank	1922	570	WILLETT	Henry Lloyd, Jr.	1921	800
WIESE	Oliver F.	1913	559	WILLGANSZ	Edna May	1881	213
WIGTON	Kari		721	WILLIAMS	Alexander	1886	417
WIKE	John Frederick	1886	457	WILLIAMS	Bonnie		654
WILBER	Grace	1917	843	WILLIAMS	Caroline M.	1898	619
WILCOX	Lewis T., III	1928	802	WILLIAMS	Catherine	1874	170
WILCOX	Lisle	1909	308	WILLIAMS	Dorothy May	1904	259
WILCOX	Lucy	1847	234	WILLIAMS	Edith M.	1902	619
WILCOX	Margaret W.	1914	639	WILLIAMS	Eva M.	1898	640

WILLIAMS	Francis	1838	77	**WILSON**	Wenda M.	1951	734
WILLIAMS	Gwendolyn	1929	469	**WILTSE**	Michael A.	1957	796
WILLIAMS	Harold Murray	1909	439	**WINDELER**	Ruth Johnston		509
WILLIAMS	Harry Andrew	1875	395	**WINGO**	Amy		853
WILLIAMS	Harry J.	1872	169	**WINGO**	Dawn		853
WILLIAMS	Hattie B.	1863	228	**WINGO**	Harold		853
WILLIAMS	Helen E.	1872	170	**WINGO**	Mr.	1948	714
WILLIAMS	Jane	1826	108	Wingo	Rochelle		853
WILLIAMS	Jennette		654	**WINIARSKI**	Josephine	1927	625
WILLIAMS	Josephine		654	**WINSHIP**	Lee	1927	658
WILLIAMS	Laurence	1920	834	**WINSON**	Albert Vinson	1866	395
WILLIAMS	Leola May	1906	580	**WINSOR**	Legurn Adelbert	1899	619
WILLIAMS	Linda Christman	1946	709	**WINTERS**	Harriet		184
WILLIAMS	Marvin F.	1922	834	**WINZENBURG**	Angie	1870	257
WILLIAMS	Mary Ann	1839	117	**WINZENBURG**	Kate	1871	256
WILLIAMS	Mary Louise Grace	1903	316	**WIRTANEN**	Wain John		480
WILLIAMS	Merton L.	1899	678	**WISEMAN**	Robert M.	1908	473
WILLIAMS	Mr.	1925	461	**WISEMAN**	Robert Milks	1937	719
Williams	Ruth B.	1937	834	**WITKOP**	Richard Derk	1894	493
WILLIAMSON	Charles Reed	1928	672	**WITMER**	Mary C.	1850	193
WILLIAMSON	Judy	1941	785	**WITT**	Bertha M.	1878	240
WILLIAMSON	Louisa Ruth	1876	441	**WITT**	Eva Myrl	1897	690
WILLIAMSON	Ramona Ethel	1931	704	**WOLCOTT**	Glenn Gordon	1953	759
WILLOVER	Margaret	1904	416	**WOLD**	Mr.		699
WILLS	Evelyn	1917	259	**WOLF**	Andrew	1810	66
WILLS	Florence E.	1865	129	**WOLF**	Lydia M.	1840	137
WILSON	Benjamin E.	1868	299	**WOLF**	Sarah Maria	1836	137
WILSON	Beverly	1942	734	**WOLFE**	A. Gordon	1917	777
WILSON	Carol Ann	1944	734	**WOLFE**	George Douglas	1921	765
WILSON	Catherine	1901	441	**WOLFE**	Jay Carroll	1886	405
WILSON	Dean Parks	1923	703	**WOLFE**	Louisa L.	1887	151
WILSON	Franklin J.	1850	201	**WOLFE**	Orrin	1920	685
WILSON	George B. "Pete"	1923	494	**WOLFE**	Rosie B. L.	1864	227
WILSON	Harriet Ann	1857	197	**WOLFF**	Herman Albert	1895	566
WILSON	Helen Elizabeth	1899	473	**WOLFF**	Janice Lou	1940	782
WILSON	Janet		751	**WOLFF**	Lois Jean	1929	782
WILSON	Johnny	1971	859	**WOLINSKI**	Frances P.		808
WILSON	Joseph Arthur	1892	472	**WOLK**	Douglas J.	1956	774
WILSON	Joseph Arthur, Jr.	1917	717	**WOLSCHLEGER**	Gretchen Marie	1910	430
WILSON	Kay Ellen	1952	734	Wood	Brenda J.	1955	809
WILSON	Linda S.	1958	803	**WOOD**	Charles H.	1872	119
WILSON	Marian	1930	521	**WOOD**	Flora Isabell	1866	229
WILSON	Mr.		901	**WOOD**	Kate L.	1876	279
WILSON	Sterling Armstrong	1926	718	**WOOD**	Kenneth R., Jr.	1953	809
WILSON	Walter Gordon	1873	281	**WOOD**	Mayte G.	1868	278

WOOD	Robert H.	1931	635	**WRIGHT**	Mr.		671
WOOD	Robin L.	1961	887	**WRIGHT**	Nathan Frank	1956	891
WOODMAN	Eugene C.	1869	537	**WRIGHT**	Rebecca Dawn	1953	890
WOODRUFF	Charles	1840	101	**WRIGHT**	Ross W.	1915	571
WOODRUFF	Julia Evalyn	1884	275	**WUETHRICH**	Mr.	1905	569
WOODRUFF	Lucian John	1859	132	**WYATT**	Adeline	1861	239
WOODRUFF	Ora N.	1877	167	**WYATT**	Ethel	1883	415
WOODS	Cynthia	1950	795	**WYATT**	Sabra Ann	1968	870
WOODS	Keith	1925	878	**WYATT**	Sarah Jane	1865	239
WOODS	Steve	1950	749	**WYLIE**	J. E.	1907	623
WOODS	Winifred	1878	251	**WYMER**	Dale Martin	1961	891
WOODSMALL	Denzell Leroy	1923	665	**YAREMCHUK**	Kenneth Peter		759
WOODSMALL	Glen W.	1978	896	**YATES**	Carolina Francetta	1806	65
WOODSMALL	Glen Wayne	1950	825	**YATES**	Roy J.	1945	609
WOODS-ROBINSON	Jordan	1983	886	**YEARWOOD**	Jeff	1966	717
WOODWARD	Mary Lou Jo	1920	672	**YEDNICK**	Mary		294
WOODWORTH	Gerald Sylvester	1913	622	**YINGLING**	RUSSELL J.	1913	506
WOODWORTH	Jennette Mae	1939	802	**YORKER**	Mary E.	1839	137
WOODY	Jack F.	1924	791	**YORKS**	Christopher	1982	907
WOOLEY	Ernest	1913	493	**YORKS**	Daisy Edwina	1907	496
WOOLMAN	Barton G.	1873	360	**YORKS**	Elda Surrell	1883	300
WOOLMAN	Evan L.	1886	361	**YORKS**	Gerald Albert Russell	1906	496
WOOLMAN	George Martin	1847	204	**YORKS**	Geraldine	1928	737
WOOLMAN	George W.	1810	93	**YORKS**	Joann Virginia	1932	738
WOOLMAN	Heman	1784	40	**YORKS**	Marie Maxine	1917	496
WOOLMAN	Lemuel	1808	93	**YORKS**	Marshall	1942	738
WOOLMAN	Nelson Joseph	1859	204	**YORKS**	Mitchell Wayne	1954	862
Woolman	Sally	1821	93	**YORKS**	Nancy Lynn	1951	862
WOOLMAN	Urban Victor	1879	360	**YORKS**	Robert Gerald	1934	738
Woolman	Vera W.	1895	361	**YORKS**	Steven Robert	1955	863
WORRELL	George Ingram, III	1979	871	**YORKS**	Wilfred Louis	1931	737
WORSTER	Norton	1907	546	**YORKS**	William Thomas	1964	863
WRIGHT	Alverna Ruth	1923	676	**YOUNG**	Ella J.		132
WRIGHT	Annie Louisa	1856	155	**YOUNG**	Florence		526
WRIGHT	Beth Ellen	1955	890	**YOUNG**	Harper		527
WRIGHT	Clayton R.	1901	492	**YOUNG**	Leah	1962	893
WRIGHT	Crystal Marie	1978	910	**YOUNG**	Minnie Marie	1909	583
WRIGHT	Emily Helen	1849	199	**YOUNG**	Mirl		526
WRIGHT	Fay Lorraine	1962	891	**YOUNG**	Mr.	1955	746
WRIGHT	Frank Nathan. Jr.	1931	811	**ZAHRA**	Michael Paul	1956	883
WRIGHT	Laura Jane	1919	788	**ZALSMAN**	Elsie Alberta	1902	358
WRIGHT	Lillian	1931	683	**ZARBO**	David P.	1968	886
WRIGHT	Loretta Ellen	1918	788	**ZAWOYSKY**	Charlene Marie	1956	531
WRIGHT	Losey Leo	1891	581	**ZAWOYSKY**	Michael	1909	319
WRIGHT	Mary Helen	1859	155	**ZEHRENDT**	Otto	1863	218

ZELLER	Kathryn Marie	1912	275
ZETH	Mary L.	1963	827
ZICKERT	Mr.		699
ZIELENIEWSKI	Walter	1935	758
ZIMMER	Catherine	1852	178
ZIMMER	Leslie		857
ZIMMERMAN	Earl Henry	1893	417
ZIMMERMAN	Robert H.	1917	653
ZIMMERMAN	Ronald L.	1932	501
ZISSLER	Florence	1892	320

www.ingramcontent.com/pod-product-compliance
Lightning Source LLC
Chambersburg PA
CBHW081206170426
43198CB00018B/2872